African American National Biography

African American National Biography

SECOND EDITION

HENRY LOUIS GATES JR.

EVELYN BROOKS HIGGINBOTHAM

Editors in Chief

VOLUME 10: RULEY, ELLIS – SYLVESTER

OXFORD
UNIVERSITY PRESS

OXFORD
UNIVERSITY PRESS

Oxford University Press is a department of the University of Oxford.
It furthers the University's objective of excellence in research, scholarship,
and education by publishing worldwide.

Oxford   New York
Auckland   Cape Town   Dar es Salaam   Hong Kong   Karachi
Kuala Lumpur   Madrid   Melbourne   Mexico City   Nairobi
New Delhi   Shanghai   Taipei   Toronto

With offices in
Argentina   Austria   Brazil   Chile   Czech Republic   France   Greece
Guatemala   Hungary   Italy   Japan   Poland   Portugal   Singapore
South Korea   Switzerland   Thailand   Turkey   Ukraine   Vietnam

Oxford is a registered trademark of Oxford University Press in the UK and certain other countries.

Published in the United States of America by
Oxford University Press
198 Madison Avenue, New York, NY 10016

Library of Congress Cataloging-in-Publication Data
African American national biography / editors in chief Henry Louis Gates Jr., Evelyn Brooks Higginbotham. – 2nd ed.
p. cm.
Includes bibliographical references and index.
ISBN 978-0-19-999036-8 (volume 1; hdbk.); ISBN 978-0-19-999037-5 (volume 2; hdbk.); ISBN 978-0-19-999038-2 (volume 3; hdbk.);
ISBN 978-0-19-999039-9 (volume 4; hdbk.); ISBN 978-0-19-999040-5 (volume 5; hdbk.); ISBN 978-0-19-999041-2 (volume 6; hdbk.);
ISBN 978-0-19-999042-9 (volume 7; hdbk.); ISBN 978-0-19-999043-6 (volume 8; hdbk.); ISBN 978-0-19-999044-3 (volume 9; hdbk.);
ISBN 978-0-19-999045-0 (volume 10; hdbk.); ISBN 978-0-19-999046-7 (volume 11; hdbk.); ISBN 978-0-19-999047-4 (volume 12;
hdbk.); ISBN 978-0-19-992077-8 (12-volume set; hdbk.)
1. African Americans – Biography – Encyclopedias.   2. African Americans – History – Encyclopedias.
I. Gates, Henry Louis.   II. Higginbotham, Evelyn Brooks, 1945-
E185.96.A4466 2012
920'.009296073 – dc23
[B]
2011043281

1 3 5 7 9 8 6 4 2
Printed in the United States of America
on acid-free paper

African American National Biography

R CONTINUED

Ruley, Ellis (3 Dec. 1882–16 Jan. 1959), artist, was born to Joshua Ruley and Eudora Robinson in Norwich, Connecticut. Ruley's father found refuge in the North after escaping from slavery as a stowaway on a coal ship leaving Wilmington, Delaware. Ruley, the eldest of five boys, ended his schooling in the third grade and followed his father into work at coalyards and construction sites. He continued to work as a laborer into his adulthood. From a brief marriage that ended in 1925 with Ida Bee, he had one daughter, Marion.

In 1929 a lumber truck hit Ruley and a coworker as they drove from a construction site, and he suffered serious head injuries. He received $25,000 in a court-ordered insurance settlement as compensation in 1932. The unexpected change of circumstance allowed Ruley a few extravagances: brass beds, a new phonograph, and a sporty new green Chevrolet that his family would dub "the Green Hornet." Yet for the most part Ruley—then fifty years old—continued to live with a degree of prudence and modesty. In the midst of the Great Depression, he secured a stable homestead for himself and his extended family, buying three wooded acres with a century-old house at 20 Hammond Avenue. With his own labor, he cleared the land, built ponds and stone walkways, raised a garden, and renovated the house. Though he possessed a small fortune for the times, Ruley continued to work, hauling rocks as a mason's tender for various Norwich building contractors.

Ruley's new life flouted social conventions of early twentieth-century Norwich. In 1933 he stepped across taboos against interracial sex and marriage and wed Wilhelmina Fox, a white woman of German descent (and his brother's ex-wife) in 1933. Ruley wasn't hindered from buying a home in the traditionally all-white Laurel Hill neighborhood, nor inhibited from moving there with his white wife and his daughter Marion's new family. Over time the neighbors' expressed their disapproval of his nonconformist family, often taunting and harassing his black grandchildren who were growing up in the house.

Perhaps as a continuation of his do-it-yourself renovation, in about 1939 Ruley began to paint decorations onto the screens covering his windows. Apparently, no window in the house was left without a painted scene, which incorporated exotic landscape and animal elements. Since the house sat on a high point of the neighborhood, many of the windows would have had remarkable views against which Ruley's imaginary creations would have been seen.

From these painted decorations, Ruley soon turned to easel paintings. He did not use specialized or professional media. He employed the kind of common house paints he might have used to restore his home. As a surface for the painting, he sometimes used cardboard from old cartons or storage containers. All his existing works are on either paper-based posterboard or on masonite, a wood-based material that might have been familiar to Ruley from its use in construction.

Ruley's paintings incorporate familiar elements drawn from his surroundings, imaginatively transformed into vignettes that amalgamate the real and fantastic, the local and the exotic. Norwich landmarks, animals, and foliage find their way into his compositions, as do references to commercial sources, including *Life* and *National Geographic* magazines. American pop cover girl models are imagined in alluring paradises, where they cavort with tropical animals. In *Adam and Eve* local fauna frolic around the biblical couple. Ruley may have painted himself into some depictions—imagining himself a beloved lion, or a MGM Hollywood star surrounded by an adoring Polynesian harem.

Ruley's works, while fantastic, often express the progressive values he lived by, such as living respectfully with nature. In one particularly poignant painting, a cow tenderly suckles small deer, perhaps an allegorical tribute to his interracial family. While his real life transgressed social norms in remarkable ways, Ruley confronted significant real world strife. Darker depictions may hint at his troubles, suggesting vulnerability and confrontation—stealthy hunters, battling creatures, and both man and beast chased, captured, or attacked.

Though he worked without recognition for nearly all of his life, Ruley expressed great pride in his artistry. Many works are embossed with a custom-made stamp, "Ellis W. Ruley." In the 1950s he retired from his job to commit himself fully to painting. Around the same time he sought out an instructor, Joseph Gaultieri, at the Norwich Free Academy art school, to get his opinion of his work. Gualtieri was impressed: "there were all of these paintings everywhere and I was struck not only by the quality of the work ... but also by the quantity. Here was a person very committed to his art. He was not some Sunday painter" (Fitzpatrick). Although Gualtieri tried, he could not find a gallery to represent Ruley's work in New York. But in 1952, as director of the Slater Museum on the academy campus, he arranged the only museum exhibition of his work during Ruley's lifetime. Subsequently, without professional representation, Ruley settled for selling his paintings at local fairs and restaurants.

In 1959 Ruley's dead body was found on the road close to his home, lying frozen and with blood from a head wound staining the ground. The coroner speculated that Ruley had stumbled, gashed his head, and died from exposure in the winter night. But his family and others in the black community suspected a more sinister cause. For decades afterward Ruley's art remained known to only a few, and his mysterious death went unremarked. This changed dramatically in 1993, with "Discovering Ellis Ruley," a national touring exhibit of all (about sixty) of his known paintings. The show catalog included one collector's investigation into Ruley's life and death, revealing a history of racism in Norwich and exploring hypotheses about

his death. Above all, the exhibition confirmed Ruley as an important figure in American folk art. Paintings that Ruley had happily sold for fifteen dollars were commanding tens of thousands of dollars. His untutored yet magical works are part of tradition-steeped collections at the Wadsworth Athenaeum in nearby Hartford and the Slater Museum in his hometown.

FURTHER READING

Cotter, Holland. "A Moralist's Landscapes with a Hint of Danger," *New York Times*, 5 Apr. 1996.

Driskell, David C. *The Other Side of Color: African American Art in the Collection of Camille O. and William H. Cosby, Jr.* (2001).

Fitzpatrick, Jackie. "The Long-Lost Art of Ellis Ruley," *New York Times*, 21 Apr. 1996.

Smith, Glenn Robert, with Robert Kenner. *Discovering Ellis Ruley: The Story of an American Outsider Artist* (1993).

Obituary: "Elderly Norwich Man Found Dead in Road," *Norwich Connecticut Bulletin-Record*, 17 Jan. 1959.

TODD PALMER

Run. *See* Reverend Run.

Runnels, Peleg (?–Oct. 1832), Revolutionary War soldier, was a slave in Rhode Island prior to the war. Details of Runnels's early life, including information as to his place of origin, whether in the American colonies or Africa, are unknown, as is his occupation. Perhaps Peleg Runnels worked on one of Rhode Island's many plantations, but the state's slaves also worked in a wide variety of other trades. Because Rhode Island was the center of the slave trade in New England, slaves in the state were often trained in more skilled occupations, working as stone masons, coopers, carpenters, or even as mariners and fishermen. Whatever tasks Peleg Runnels may have been forced to undertake while enslaved, he would soon learn a new set of skills, those of a soldier and free man.

Four years after the American Revolution began Rhode Island was in serious difficulties; the state's economy, maritime and slave based, was wrecked by the British Navy blockade and the capture of Newport, its capital city. Additionally, a large percentage of the colony's men were already soldiers for the Continental Army and efforts to raise further troops to meet its quota were largely unsuccessful. In December 1777 General James Varnum, a delegate to the Continental Congress, wrote to Washington stating that "a battalion of Negroes can easily be raised" from the state's slave population

(Greene, 149). Washington supported Varnum's proposal, and efforts were soon underway to raise a black regiment. While there was opposition to this unusual idea, a law was passed in Rhode Island in February 1778 authorizing the enlistment of slaves, persuaded by the argument that "the wisest, the freest, and bravest Nations [in times of emergency have] liberated their slaves and enlisted them as soldiers to fight in defense of their Country" (Greene, 152). Consequently, examination boards were set up to evaluate potential recruits; a slave owner, if he agreed to his slave's enlistment, might receive for the most valuable slave 120 pounds, or less depending on a slave's value and fitness to serve as a soldier. Once a slave was enlisted, he was obligated to serve for the entire war, the only Continental Army regiment so enlisted, and was guaranteed that in return "Liberty is given to every effective slave to enter the service during the war; and upon passing muster, he is absolutely made free, and entitled to all the wages, bounties, and encouragements given to Congress by any soldier" (Greene, 156).

The number of men that enlisted in the black 1st Rhode Island Regiment, and their names, may never fully be known due to a lack of records; the historian Lorenzo Greene estimates the number at about 250 men. Among the enlistees were Richard Cozzens, a fifer born in Africa and Cato Greene, the slave of Governor William Greene. As might be expected, the opposition of those involved in the slave trade in the state soon prevailed, and in May 1778 a law halting the enlistments of slaves was passed that took effect on 10 June 1778. However, this did not mean that blacks could no longer serve in the regiment; a number of free blacks enlisted after this time, including Reuben Roberts, a resident of Newmarket, New Hampshire, who had previously served in the Continental Army for that state and for Massachusetts before seeking duty in the 1st Rhode Island in 1779. As for Peleg Runnels, he likely joined the regiment prior to June 1778, later stating that he "was placed by his master … under Colonel Christopher Greene, on condition that if he would serve two years he should then have his freedom" (Knoblock, 294).

Organized under the command of Colonel Christopher Greene, an experienced and well-respected officer, and Lieutenant Colonel Jeremiah Olney, the men of the 1st Rhode Island Regiment performed capably and valiantly through the American Revolution from 1778 until its disbandment at Saratoga, New York, in 1783. Fittingly, the regiment would gain renown in its first months of operation during the Battle of Rhode Island on 29 August 1778. Here, the men of the 1st Rhode Island Regiment were stationed in the brigade of General Sullivan. Their task was to support the withdrawal of American troops to the mainland, occasioned by the fact that French naval support for the planned recapture of Rhode Island had evaporated, as well as the imminent arrival of British troop reinforcements. British General Robert Pigot, with several battle-tested Hessian regiments under his command, hotly pursued the Americans in hopes of bagging Sullivan's army. Dug in at Butts' Hill, the Americans made a stand and, despite three "furious assaults," the British were repulsed and forced to retreat. Among the heroes of the day were the former slaves of the 1st Rhode Island Regiment, praised for their "desperate valor" in repelling the British assaults (Boatner, 792).

The success of the 1st Rhode Island Regiment was such that General Washington denied Governor Greene's request to keep the regiment in the state for its defense, instead sending them to more urgent duty in New York. After Colonel Greene's death in an engagement with Tory forces at Croton River in 1781, the men were commanded by Olney until their service ended. At its disbandment on 13 June 1783, the men of the regiment were praised in Olney's farewell speech for their "unexampled fortitude and patience through all the toils and dangers," and he also noted "their valor and good conduct displayed on every occasion when called on to face the enemy in the field" (Greene, 171).

Upon their return to Rhode Island, the former slaves now resumed a new life as freemen. Some would experience legal difficulties with unscrupulous master's that tried to re-enslave them, and most had to fight for the back pay that was due them. Peleg Runnels would soon leave Rhode Island behind, moving first to Massachusetts, and then to New Hampshire. His military pension records indicate that Runnels first lived in Salem, Massachusetts, where he was married to Martha Hall, date unknown, in the Baptist church of Elder Trefford. Soon thereafter, the couple moved to New Hampshire, living first in Somersworth, and subsequently in Rochester. After 1805, the Runnels' moved northward to Alton, where they would spend the remainder of their years. Unfortunately, little is known of the details of the Runnels' life in New Hampshire as free blacks, though Peleg likely earned his living as a farmer or laborer. The couple had seven children, only two of whom are known by name; James, the eldest, and Peleg Jr. Runnels would apply for a military pension for his Revolutionary War service in 1818, but was denied due to a lack of proof of service. When he reapplied in 1824, his claim for a pension was allowed. Five years after her husband's death in1832, Martha Runnels was granted a widow's pension in the amount of $80 annually.

The service of men such as Peleg Runnels in the 1st Rhode Island Regiment was truly remarkable, yet the legacy of this regiment, through no fault of the men themselves, is a complicated and contradictory one; though organized in a time of dire need, and only with slaves allowed to do so by their masters, the fact that these men were freed forever in return for their service was a noble endeavor. However, the concept of blacks serving together in one regiment was not the norm for the American army in the Revolution; blacks from other northern colonies, men such as LONDON DAILEY and OLIVER CROMWELL, served alongside their fellow white soldiers without difficulty and with equal pay and enlistment terms. Indeed, it may be argued that the formation of the 1st Rhode Island Regiment, albeit unintended, became the model for the American army in future conflicts from the Civil War until the Korean War, where black soldiers serving in segregated regiments led by white officers would be official policy.

FURTHER READING

Boatner, Mark M., III. *Encyclopedia of the American Revolution* (1994).

Greene, Lorenzo J. "Some Observations on the Black Regiment of Rhode Island in the American Revolution," in *Journal of Negro History* 32 (Apr. 1952).

Knoblock, Glenn A. *Strong and Brave Fellows; New Hampshire's Black Soldiers and Sailors in the American Revolution, 1775–1784* (2003).

GLENN ALLEN KNOBLOCK

RuPaul (17 Nov. 1960–), drag performer, singer, songwriter, and actor, was born RuPaul Andre Charles in San Diego, California, the only son of four children to Ernestine "Toni" Fontenette (a registrar) and Irving Andrew Charles (an electrician). RuPaul was close to his sisters Renae, Renatta, and Rosalind, and to his mother, particularly after his parents' bitter 1967 divorce. Shortly afterward, RuPaul moved in with Renatta and her husband in El Cajon, California, and then moved with them to Atlanta in the summer of 1976. While there, RuPaul worked with his brother-in-law as a used car salesman, but also attended the Northside School of the Performing Arts. RuPaul's experiences as a drama major at Northside, as well as his exposure to the liberating and bohemian climate in Atlanta, fueled his desire to succeed as a performing artist. RuPaul

RuPaul holds his RuPaul dolls at the launch party and gallery opening for the RuPaul Doll Photo Exhibit held at the Arcadia Gallery, 4 August 2005 in New York. The doll was designed by Jason Wu and photographed by Mike Ruiz. (AP Images.)

experienced his first drag queen performance in Atlanta in 1978, seeing Crystal Labajia performing a DONNA SUMMERS song. He eventually saw many other black drag queens around Atlanta, including Charlie Brown. RuPaul tested a number of drag styles over the course of his career and occasionally performed as a man. However, his sassy, friendly persona (as opposed to the "bitchy" drag queen persona that was more popular during this time) found early inspiration in these southern black queens.

RuPaul's first performance opportunity arose through a local public access cable show called *The American Music Show*, which featured a troupe of comedians and music performers in a talk show/ sketch comedy format. RuPaul felt a connection to the irreverent content and performance approaches he saw on the show. In 1981 he and two of his girlfriends made their debut performance there as RuPaul and the U-Hauls on the show, wearing costumes he designed and sewed. They performed Junior Walker's "Shotgun" and were a hit. They toured Atlanta as the opening act for the Now Explosion, another act that came-out of the *American Music Show*'s cast, and performed at New York's famous Pyramid Club. In 1983 two Northside students, Robert Warren (bass) and Todd Butler (guitar), asked RuPaul to front a band called Wee Wee Pole. Wee Wee Pole featuring RuPaul and the U-Hauls made it big on the new wave/punk club scene in Atlanta and gave RuPaul the opportunity to further hone his singing and songwriting skills. RuPaul capitalized on his rising star in Atlanta musical circles through DIY (Do It Yourself) strategies of self-promotion and, later, acting. He pasted Xerox posters of himself all over the city—to telephone poles, in phone booths, on walls—that advertised his appearances or that featured phrases like, "RuPaul Is Hot." He also created a Xeroxed, stapled pastiche of an autobiography called "If You Love Me, Give It to Me" that he sold in clubs for $2. He followed this with other titles; "Your Guide to Health, Beauty and Nigger Love" and "New York is a Big Fat Greasy Ho" were popular in Atlanta's underground club circles for their irreverent views on sexuality, race, and the "scene."

In 1984 RuPaul initiated his film career in *Trilogy of Terror*, shot on his brother-in-law's home video camera by John Witherspoon (LaHoma Van Zant). This film was followed by *Terror 2* and *Terror 3D*, in which RuPaul and costars Lady Bunny and Floyd portrayed girls who are haunted, first by an unseen but malevolent force, and then an evil murderer. In 1986 RuPaul rejoined director Witherspoon for the *Starrbooty* trilogy, a series of takeoffs on the blaxploitation films of the 1960s and 1970s in which RuPaul played Starrbooty, an ex-model turned crime-fighting undercover agent. The movies became cult classics and served as the early groundwork for his later film success.

During the late 1980s RuPaul moved back and forth between New York and Atlanta. In New York, he performed as a go-go dancer and emcee at the Pyramid, Sauvage, and other nightclubs, and made important connections with influential underground and club figures such as Suzanne Bartsch and Larry Tee. In 1985 he returned to Atlanta and recorded his first album, *RuPaul: Sex Freak*, for Funtone Records. But by 1990 his personality and his self-transformation from a "punk" drag or "genderfuck" style to a sexier "black hooker" approach garnered him enough attention to stay in New York. That year, he was voted "Queen of Manhattan," the highest honor in the city's nightlife, by Djs, party promoters and other influential figures in the city's club scene. The year as high-profile club and party promoter was tiring to RuPaul and he refocused on his career in 1991, writing material for and focusing on promoting his demo. He also adjusted his performance style and began developing his "glamazon" supermodel-of-the-world persona. His timing was a key element of his success; the supermodel phenomenon was gaining more and more media attention. Tommy Boy Records, a label better known for its roster of hip-hop artists, signed him and by the next year, the single "Supermodel" was released, catapulting RuPaul to international stardom. The song peaked at only number forty-five on the *Billboard* Hot 100, but became a gay and dance anthem.

Many successes followed that dance hit. In 1994 RuPaul recorded a remake of "Don't Go Breaking My Heart" with Elton John and had a role in SPIKE LEE's *Crooklyn*, followed by roles in the films *The Brady Bunch Movie* and *To Wong Foo, Thanks for Everything! Julie Newmar* as well as an appearance on the *Arsenio Hall Show*. In 1995 RuPaul made history as the first face and spokesperson of M.A.C. (Makeup Art Cosmetics, a Canadian company founded in 1985). Subsequent spokespeople have included Lil Kim, Boy George, and Diana Ross. Through his contract with the company (now owned by Estee Lauder), he raised over $22 million dollars for the M.A.C. AIDS fund. RuPaul released his second album, *Foxy Lady*, in 1996 and remade the disco classic and gay anthem "It's Rainin' Men" with Martha Walsh (who first recorded the song in 1982 as a member of the Weather Girls). The cable music network VH1 created *The RuPaul Show* that same year, on which he interviewed artists such as Mary J. Blige, Nirvana, and, in a bold move, the gay porn directors Chi Chi LaRue and Tom Chase. Finally, as a fitting transition into a new millennium, RuPaul attended the unveiling of his likeness at Madame Tussaud's Wax Museum in New York during the week of his fortieth birthday.

In addition to releasing two more albums, RuPaul continued to perform and to serve as a fund-raiser and awareness raiser for people with HIV/AIDS and as a spokesperson for gay rights into the 2000s. The positive message he brought to performances uplifted audiences the world over.

In 2007 RuPaul appeared in a fourth movie in the *Starrbooty* series. She said of that film, "The goal was to make an exploitation film that was part Russ Meyer, John Waters and *The Naked Gun*, and we succeeded." (http://www.starrbooty.com/about. html). RuPaul also starred in and hosted two popular television reality shows for the Logo channel between 2009 and 2012: *RuPaul's Drag Race*, which sought to find "America's next drag superstar," and a spinoff, *RuPaul's Drag U*, in which women are given drag makeovers to find their "inner diva." *RuPaul's Drag Race*, which is also shown on Vh1, won the

2010 GLAAD Media Award for Outstanding Reality Program and the 2010 NewNowNext award for "Best New Indulgence." RuPaul also released several music albums after 2007, including *Glamazon* (2011).

FURTHER READING

RuPaul. *Lettin It All Hang Out: An Autobiography* (1996).

Cohen, Scott. *Yakety Yak: The Midnight Confessions and Revelations of Thirty-Seven Rock Stars and Legends* (1994).

Larkin, Colin, ed. *The Encyclopedia of Popular Music* (2006).

MONICA HAIRSTON

Rush, Bobby L. (23 Nov 1946–), Democratic politician, was born in Albany, Georgia, one of eight children of Jimmy Lee Rush and Cora Lee. Rush's parents separated and his mother moved the family to the North side of Chicago, Illinois. In 1963, at the age of seventeen, Rush dropped out of Marshall High School in Marshall, Illinois, and enlisted in the U.S. Army. He served until 1968.

The 1960s were a pivotal time in Rush's life. All around him, there was increased awareness about discrimination and inequality. Rush became a student of social justice and an activist in the civil rights movement. As an army serviceman stationed in Chicago's Jackson Park, Rush joined the Student Nonviolent Coordinating Committee (SNCC). SNCC leader STOKELY CARMICHAEL encouraged Rush and Bob Brown to start an Illinois chapter of the Black Panther Party for Self Defense (BPP). Rush would oblige and serve as Defense Minister; his title was later changed to state coordinator. He became a close associate of BPP leader FRED HAMPTON. In 1968 Rush was honorably discharged from the Army. The following year, he had his first child, Huey Malik Rich, with his girlfriend, Saundra Rich. Rush named his son in honor of legendary Black Panther leader HUEY NEWTON.

A year into their BPP activities in Illinois, local leaders Fred Hampton and Mark Clark were killed in a police raid. The killings traumatized Rush and made him fear for his own life. The police also raided Rush's home and issued a warrant for his arrest. Working with JESSE L. JACKSON SR. through his Operation Breadbasket initiative, Rush was able to work with black police officers and lawyers to arrange a safe way to turn himself in. Charges against him were eventually dropped.

In the aftermath of the killings, Rush enrolled at Roosevelt University and earned a B.A. in 1974. He continued his studies, pursuing a master's degree at the University of Illinois, Circle campus. To earn an income, Rush worked in various jobs as an insurance agent, a teaching assistant, and an associate dean of Daniel Hale Williams University in Chicago. During this time he also launched an unsuccessful campaign to unseat city council alderman William Barnett.

In 1983, witnessing HAROLD WASHINGTON's successful bid for Chicago mayor, Rush decided to again run for public office. This time he launched a successful bid for city council, becoming alderman for the second ward. Rush became a vocal advocate for his predominately black constituency, serving for nearly a decade. In 1992 Rush was elected to Congress representing the 1st Congressional District, which comprised Chicago's South and West sides.

In 1994 Rush completed an M.A. in Political Science at University of Illinois at Chicago. He saw education as a way to gain the skills necessary to better serve his district. Although his militant background alienated some white constituents, Rush was overwhelmingly popular. He garnered respect for his effectiveness as a legislator, advocating for social justice, improved health care, and neighborhood development, among other issues.

In 1998 Rush obtained an M.A. in theological studies from McCormick Seminary in Chicago. During this time, his frustrations with the progress of local government grew. He launched a challenge against the political stalwart Mayor Richard Daley for his office. Rush used the election to highlight some of the shortcomings he saw in the Daley administration, particularly in relationship to the black community. Daley's win was decisive, with Rush unable to gain votes outside of blacks and his district; however, Rush was committed to serving in public office, choosing to stay in Congress.

Shortly after the election, in October 1999 Rush's twenty-nine-year-old son, Huey Rich, was murdered during an attempted robbery in Chicago. This was a challenging period for Rush who also had to contemplate how to run a reelection campaign in 2000. He directed his energy toward addressing street violence and making that a central theme of his campaign. He faced his toughest campaign to date against a field led by State Senator BARACK OBAMA. Many black leaders and his community rallied behind Rush. He eventually won the 2000 election with more than 65 percent of the vote, besting his closest opponent, Obama, nearly 2-to-1.

With a renewed sense of purpose, Rush became a strong voice against violence, holding numerous anti-crime rallies and summits across the city. Rush also began broadening his advocacy, becoming a vocal critic of the Sudanese government over human rights abuses. In 2004 he was arrested for protesting at the Sudanese Embassy in Washington, D.C.

Rush continued to expand his political influence, becoming involved in numerous committees and attracting investment to his district. He and his wife, Carolyn Thomas, opened the Bobby L. Rush Community Technology Center in Englewood, Illinois. With interests in improving access to technology, Rush joined the Republican Joe Barton in authoring a bill that would allow competition between telephone and cable companies. The bill was controversial, and critics accused Rush of having too close a relationship with big business. Despite controversy, his support never waned. When Barack Obama, by then the US Senator from Illinois, announced his intention to run for the presidency in 2008, Rush endorsed him, despite their previous rivalry and Rush's long-time support for Obama's main rival, Senator Hilary Clinton (D-NY). Clinton, in the Democratic Primary and—to a much greater extent—Republican John McCain in the general election, repeated Rush's criticism of Obama that he was an out-of-touch Harvard elitist, but both did so with considerably less success than Rush in the 2000 Congressional race. With the exception of 1994, when he lost his seat with 76 percent of the vote, Rush was re-elected to Congress with more than 80 percent of the 1st Congressional District's votes between 1993 and 2010. In 2011 Congressional redistricting changed the boundaries of Rush's district to add more suburban and white voters, but Rush retained his seat in 2012, winning more than 70 percent of the votes.

FURTHER READING

Black Enterprise (Nov. 1995): 28.

Newsweek (29 Nov. 1999): 52.

Chicago Defender (3 Jan. 2000): 4.

MICHAELJULIUS IDANI

Rush, Gertrude Elzora Durden (5 Aug. 1880?–5 Sept. 1962), attorney, was born in Navasota, Texas, the daughter of Frank and Sarah E. Reinhardt Durden. Her birth year is chronicled in some sources as 1880 and in others as 1883 (and erroneously listed as 1909 in yet others). She completed high school in Parsons, Kansas, and received a degree from Quincy (Illinois) Business College (reportedly in 1906, although *Who's Who in Colored America* listed 1919 as her graduating year). She moved to Des Moines, Iowa, in 1907, where she married James B. Rush on 23 December of that year. She subsequently obtained a B.A. at Des Moines College in 1914 and prepared for the Iowa bar exam by reading law with her husband, a successful criminal trial attorney;

she also took some courses at Drake University Law School in Des Moines. Her husband passed away prior to the completion of her studies.

When she was admitted to the Iowa bar on 3 October 1918, Gertrude Rush became the first African American woman licensed to practice law in Iowa, and the only one to do so until 1953. She was also a member of the Illinois bar, and her practice included offices in Des Moines, Buxton (Iowa), and Chicago. She was the first African American woman in the United States to pass the examination in code law, the first to head a state bar organization (becoming president of the Iowa Colored Bar Association in 1921), and as of 1933 was one of two female African American attorneys admitted to argue before the U.S. Supreme Court.

Throughout her life, Rush was an extraordinarily active leader of and participant in civic, religious, and professional organizations, as well as a seasoned world traveler. Of these, the most influential has been the National Bar Association (NBA), which she co-founded in August 1925 with fellow African American attorneys George H. Woodson, S. Joe Brown, James B. Morris, and Charles B. Howard. Each of them had been rejected by the American Bar Association, which maintained a "whites only" policy at the time of their applications. Initially named the National Negro Bar Association, with fifteen lawyers in attendance at its inaugural meeting, the NBA's membership had grown to over 20,000 by the 2000s, with over eighty chapters established across the United States. The NBA's yearly awards banquet is named after Rush, and its Iowa chapter has cosponsored an annual Gertrude Rush Award with the Iowa Organization of Women Attorneys since 2003. The first recipient of the award was Willie Stevenson Glanton, the second African American woman admitted to the Iowa bar and the first elected to the Iowa legislature. Under the aegis of the NBA, there is also a national Gertrude E. Rush Distinguished Service Award, and it is considered one of the association's highest honors; in its first year, 1982, the honorees were SADIE TANNER MOSSELL ALEXANDER, GWENDOLYN BROOKS, Arthur D. Shores, and Edward B. Toles.

Rush was also a president of the Iowa State Federation of Colored Women's Clubs (1911–1915), and a chairman of the National Association of Colored Women's Department of Law and Legislation (1924), as well as of its Mother's Department. She also served on the board of the Des Moines Health Center and as secretary of the Des Moines Comfort Station Commission, and participated in the Parliamentary Law and Culture Club of Des Moines and the first MARY CHURCH

TERRELL Club, a private African American women's club. She founded both the Charity League (an influential welfare agency) and the Protection Home for Women and Girls (1917), and she was a charter member of the Des Moines Playground Association and the Blue Triangle YWCA branch, and a past chair of her church's board of trustees. She was affiliated with the Republican Party and named a national honorary member of Delta Sigma Theta, the first African American sorority established west of the Mississippi River.

The daughter of a minister, Rush was a member of Corinthian Baptist Church and attended the Nineteenth Annual Session of the Woman's Convention of the National Baptist Convention (1919) as a delegate, speaking in favor of women's suffrage as a means of improving social and professional conditions. Rush would later chair the Citizenship Department and serve as the attorney for the Woman's Auxiliary from 1926 into the 1950s. She was outspoken about morals, denouncing flappers and other women she considered to be lacking in self-respect in articles such as "Forces Contributing to the Delinquency of Our Girls" (*National Association* [of Colored Women] *Notes*, July 1924).

Rush was also respected for her endeavors in the creative sphere. The information available about her songwriting endeavors is sketchy and unreliable, but she apparently focused primarily on religious themes. Her published compositions may have included "If You But Knew," "Uncrowned Heroines," "Black Girl's Burden," and "Shadowed Love." She scripted a number of pageants as well, including *Building the American Flag* (1927), *Links in the American Union* (1927), and *True Framers of the American Constitution* (1928).

Forced into partial retirement after suffering a stroke in 1958, Rush shared a house with her brother Albert O. Durden during her final years. She was considered the second-oldest practicing lawyer in Iowa at the time of her death, which was caused by another stroke. Her posthumous honors included monuments at the Des Moines Public Library and St. Paul African Methodist Episcopal (AME) Church of Des Moines, and being named to the Iowa Women's Hall of Fame (1994).

FURTHER READING

Bergmann, Leola Nelson. *The Negro in Iowa* (1948; rpt. 1969).

Fleming, G. James, and Christian E. Burckel. *Who's Who in Colored America* (1950).

Silag, Bill, ed. *Outside In: African American History in Iowa, 1838–2000* (2001).

Obituary: *Iowa Bystander*, 13 Sept. 1962.

PEG DUTHIE

Rush, Otis (29 Apr. 1934–), blues singer and guitarist, was born in Philadelphia, Mississippi, to O. C. Rush and Julia Boyd, farmers. One of seven children, Otis dabbled in guitar and sang occasionally in church. He moved to Chicago in 1948 to live with his sister and worked various jobs until smitten by the blues of MUDDY WATERS. Rush recognized his life's calling and practiced incessantly on a cheap electric guitar and amplifier, learning much from blues records. Though the constant ruckus was vexing to family and neighbors alike, it provided the opening for his professional career. When a featured act canceled at the last minute, the owner of the Alibi nightclub remembered the constant sounds coming from an upstairs apartment nearby. He went over and fetched the young Otis to fill in. Rush began appearing steadily at the Alibi, formed his own band, and was soon playing other clubs.

The young bluesman became a leading exponent of the West Side sound developed in the mid-1950s. Though Rush has subsequently pointed out that he lived and forged his sound on Chicago's South Side, the West Side label has remained. An amalgamation of the electric Delta stylings of Muddy Waters and HOWLIN' WOLF and the more urbane style proffered by B. B. KING, the West Side sound combined the toughness of Chicago blues with an emphasis on minor-chord voicings and sympathetic horn support, resulting in a powerful, mournful sound.

WILLIE DIXON, the entrepreneurial songwriter, producer, and bass player, heard the fresh sounds of Otis Rush and recognized an opportunity that he could exploit separately from the dominant Chess Records where he worked. He brought Rush over to Eli Toscano's newly formed Cobra Records on the West Side of Chicago and proceeded to record a string of powerful songs whose intensity and plaintiveness remain unsurpassed.

Dixon put a crack studio band together around Otis that contained, among others, such notables as IKE TURNER on guitar, Little Walter on harmonica, Lafayette Leake on piano, Jackie Brenston on saxophone, Fred Below on drums, and of course Dixon himself on bass. Most Chicago blues of the 1950s featured an upfront harmonica sound, and although the two finest purveyors of this style, LITTLE WALTER JACOBS and SHAKEY (WALTER)

HORTON, were present on several tracks, they did not figure prominently in this new sound.

The saxophones helped lend the brooding intensity to these tracks. Unlike B. B. King's horn sections, there were no trumpets to brighten the sound. The moody saxes combined with the minor keys to set up Rush's all-important voice. His was a voice that sounded much older than his twenty-two years, a voice that fairly quaked and quivered with an emotion that reaches out and pierces the listener. No less an authority than Muddy Waters gave his approval by claiming that there were no blues deeper than Rush's.

Starting with the Dixon composition "I Can't Quit You Baby," which became a national rhythm and blues hit, Rush recorded "Double Trouble," "All Your Love (I Miss Loving)," "Keep Loving Me Baby," and others that have become blues classics and have been covered by artists such as Led Zeppelin, Eric Clapton, and Paul Butterfield. Otis Rush was the first of a triumvirate of urban blues artists to record for Cobra or its affiliates. MAGIC SAM and BUDDY GUY both sang and played electric guitar with great emotion, with Sam, like Rush, also drawing on the minor keys to great effect.

Unfortunately Rush's auspicious beginning served as a peak for years to come. Rush married his second wife, Kathy Guyton, and they had four children. (There is no record of his first marriage.) Hampered by ineffectual support from the record company and by personal problems, Rush floated in limbo for a number of years. After Cobra folded and following a brief association with Chess Records, which yielded the powerful "So Many Roads, So Many Trains," Rush was tied up with Duke Records for five years with very little to show for it, though his classic "Homework," cut during this time, was later recorded by Fleetwood Mac and the J. Geils Band. A short-lived relationship with Vanguard Records was marred by personal and technical complications. After years of toiling with a top-notch band in the 1960s, Rush recorded *Mourning in the Morning* (1969) for Cotillion, an Atlantic Records subsidiary. This record, co-produced by the guitarist Michael Bloomfield and the singer-songwriter Nick Gravenites, was regarded by critics as heavy-handed and did not show off Rush's brilliance.

Rush was managed at this time by Albert Grossman, who boasted clients such as Bob Dylan, Janis Joplin, Paul Butterfield, and Peter, Paul, and Mary. Grossman got Rush signed to a Capitol Records deal in 1971, which resulted in the recording of one album, *Right Place, Wrong Time.* Co-produced by Nick Gravenites and Rush, the record captured the shining brilliance and intensity of Rush's vocal and guitar mastery. Inexplicably, the record languished unreleased until Bullfrog, a small independent label, put it out in 1976. Capitol did not exercise its options for any future recordings.

In the 1970s and 1980s Rush's music had been issued on various compilations, and some live sets had been released. Rush gave up playing at various periods and became bitter about his treatment by the music industry over the years. During the 1990s, however, his old friend Buddy Guy got Rush a record deal with Silvertone Records, and the Grammy-nominated *Ain't Enough Coming In* (1994) was released to critical acclaim. Rush's career was reinvigorated, and he began to play frequently at blues festivals and various upscale venues. In 1999 he won a Grammy Award for *Any Place I'm Going* (1998) on the House of Blues label.

Rush may be mercurial and uneven in performance, but he possesses two gifts—his voice and his guitar prowess—that outweigh these shortcomings. His vocal delivery, with its sweeping emotion and striking falsetto, is reminiscent of the finest gospel singers. Like fellow left-handed guitar legend ALBERT KING, Otis Rush played a right-handed guitar upside down. With the high strings on top, it is possible to bend notes further, lending a strong emotional quality to his playing that matches his voice and lyrics. When he was at the height of his powers, Otis Rush's blues were as good as it gets.

FURTHER READING
Humphrey, Mark. "Bright Lights, Big City: Urban Blues," in *Nothing but the Blues*, ed. Lawrence Cohn (1993).
Palmer, Robert. "The Guitar Is a 2nd Voice for the Blues," *New York Times*, 27 Apr. 1982.
Provencher, Norman. "Otis Rush Set the Blues Standard Almost a Half-century Ago," *Ottawa Citizen*, 22 July 2002.
Rowe, Mike. *Chicago Blues* (1984).
Sharp, Steven. "Bad Luck Hasn't Stilled the Voice of Bluesman Otis Rush," *Milwaukee Journal Sentinel*, 30 Apr. 1998.
Shurman, Dick. Liner notes to *Right Place, Wrong Time* (1971).

DISCOGRAPHY
Groaning the Blues: Original Cobra Recordings 1956–58 (Flyright 594).

MARK STEVEN MAULUCCI

Rushen, Patrice Louise (30 Sept. 1954–), pianist, singer, composer, and producer, nicknamed "Baby Fingers," was born in Los Angeles to Ruth L. and Allen Roy Rushen; Allen Rushen was a computer analyst. Her preschool teacher first recognized her musical talent and Rushen began studying classical piano formally at the age of five. In her teens she began playing jazz and started composing and arranging while in high school. While attending Locke High School in Los Angeles, she played in a jazz group, Msingi, an outgrowth of a high-school jazz workshop. The combo won the All-Star High School Competition at the 1972 Monterey Jazz Festival.

In that same year Rushen entered the University of Southern California, graduating in 1976 with a bachelor's degree in music education and piano performance. In her early twenties she worked with the trombonist and composer Melba Liston, the singer ABBEY LINCOLN, and the pop group the Sylvers. As a sophomore she recorded with Jean-Luc Ponty. During her college years she signed with Profile records, where she released *Prelusion*, her first jazz album as a leader (1974). She recorded two more albums, *Before the Dawn* (1975) and *Shout it Out* (1976), before leaving the label. During these years she also worked as a session player, recording with jazz notables Bennie Maupin, the trumpeter Donald Byrd, and the saxophonists STANLEY TURRENTINE and SONNY ROLLINS in the late 1970s. In 1977 she played piano and keyboards with Lee Ritenour's group.

Signing with Elektra-Asylum Records, Rushen changed styles, venturing into pop, rhythm-and-blues, funk, and singing. With its blend of jazz-soul, her eponymous *Patrice* (1977) and the 1978 single "Hang It Up" marked her new direction as a rhythm-and-blues artist. The albums *Posh* (1979) and *Pizzazz* (1980) firmly established her as an artist in this genre. Her 1982 album, *Straight from the Heart*, brought critical success and yielded three hit singles, one of which, "Forgot Me Nots," entered the Top 40. Her next release, *Now* (1984), saw Rushen moving into more dance-oriented popular music, especially the successful single, "Feel So Reel," a song heavily based on synthesizer and programmed drum machine rhythms. Rushen left Elektra-Asylum and signed with Arista, releasing *Watch Out* in 1986. The title song received the ASCAP Songwriter's Award.

Although some critics panned her blend of popular music styles and jazz, Rushen nonetheless continued to find success in both the pop and jazz fields. She appeared in 1980 with her own jazz-funk band at the New York nightclub the Bottom Line. In 1982 she joined Ernie Watts and Ndugu Chancler in a group called the Meeting. In August she appeared at the Long Island Jazz Festival and at the Kool Jazz Festival the following year. She returned to the popular music charts with "Feels So Real (Won't Let Go)," which reached #3 in 1984, and "Watch Out," which reached #9 in 1987. In January 1986 she married Marc St. Louis, a concert tour manager.

For the remainder of the 1980s, Rushen continued to bridge jazz and pop, joining a group led by Carlos Santana and WAYNE SHORTER in 1988. The following year she formed a duo with drummer Ndugu Chancler, 1+One. Rushen toured Europe in 1988 and in 1989 she toured Japan. After that tour, Rushen returned to the Bottom Line, performing with Terri Lyne Carrington. Her 1990 release was aptly titled *The Meeting*, which featured Ernie Watts (saxophone), Alphonoso Johnson (bass), and Ndugu Chancler (drums), and reaffirmed Rushen's blend of jazz and funk.

During the 1990s Rushen limited her live performances. With the exception of a 1991 tour of Japan and a 1995 tour of Europe, she rarely ventured outside the Los Angeles area, instead increasing both her session work and her work as a composer, arranger, and producer for film and television. Her first foray into film music composition had been in 1987, when she composed music (with Udi Harpaz) for the Robert Townsend film *Hollywood Shuffle*. In 1990 she returned to film music, composing the original score for Sandra Bernhard's feature film *Without You I'm Nothing*. She also composed music for *Waiting to Exhale* (1995) and *Men in Black* (1997). Her television credits included the *Steve Harvey Show* (1996), *The Women of Brewster Place* (1989), and *Robert Townsend and His Partners in Crime* (1991). Rushen also amassed a distinguished list of credits as a musical director for television awards shows. She became the first female musical director of the NAACP Image Awards in 1989, a role she continued to fill into the 2000s, and the first African American female musical director for the Emmy Awards (1991, 1992). She was also musical director of Comic Relief V in 1992, and of the Grammy Awards for three years in the mid-2000s.

As pianist and composer Rushen recorded more than a dozen albums as a leader. As a sideman she recorded with jazz notables as varied as KENNY BURRELL, Kevin Eubanks, HERBIE HANCOCK, Ramsey Lewis, Dianne Reeves, JOSHUA REDMAN, GROVER WASHINGTON JR., and LIONEL HAMPTON. She recorded with or produced for pop musicians such as STEVIE WONDER, PRINCE, Chaka Khan, and MICHAEL JACKSON. She also ventured into classical music, serving as Artist-in-Residence with the Detroit Symphony in 2000–2001. Her symphonic works included *Of Dreams and Other Possibilities* (2002) and *Mine Eyes Have Seen the Glory* (2001), commissioned by the Detroit Symphony Civic Orchestra to commemorate MARTIN LUTHER KING JR.

FURTHER READING
Dines, Kaylyn Kendall. "Forget Her Not: Patrice Rushen," *Vibe* 10 (Nov. 2002).
Lyons, Len. "Profile: Patrice Rushen," *Down Beat* 43 (29 Jan. 1976).
Nemko, Frankie. "Patrice Rushen's Hat Trick," *Jazz Times* 21 (Sept. 1991).
Pitts, Leonard, Jr. "Patrice Rushen: Diminutive Drawbacks," *Musician* 73 (1984).

GAYLE MURCHISON

Jimmy Rushing, blues vocalist and composer, 1936. (AP Images.)

Rushing, Jimmy (26 Aug. 1903–8 June 1972), singer and composer, was born James Andrew Rushing in Oklahoma City, the son of musical parents who ran a family luncheonette business. In addition to his mother and brother, who were singers, his father played trumpet well enough to be in the Oklahoma City Knights of Pythias Marching Band. A relative, Wesley Manning, resident pianist in a "gaming house," taught young Jimmy the basics of piano playing. The youngster even managed to pick up enough violin technique to claim that instrument as well. In fact, he first thought of singing more as a hobby than as a profession. After finishing Douglas High School in Oklahoma City in 1921, Rushing attended Wilberforce University in southwestern Ohio for two years, where he participated in the school's outstanding choral program. In addition to his native intelligence and sophistication, he was a thoughtful and trained musician, one of the few professional band or cabaret singers of his era who could read music fluently.

Rushing was blessed with a remarkably accurate ear and a uniquely focused voice, a sound that could cut through a tangled band texture yet still project a pathos ideally suited for the blues. His vocal range was exceptionally wide (two octaves), and within that baritone-plus-tenor territory he exercised precise control. For this reason alone it is a pity that what one hears in many of his recorded performances, especially with bands, is limited to the high end of his tenor range. (For instance the 1938 recording with the COUNT BASIE band of "Sent for You Yesterday" winds through a narrow band of only about six notes.)

While only twenty, Rushing was singing professionally in California (on occasion to the accompaniment of JELLY ROLL MORTON), at the Jump Steady Club and at the Quality Club on Los Angeles's legendary South Central Avenue. But he returned

to his hometown in 1925 to help his family run the luncheonette service for over a year. His next professional engagement was a tour with the Billy King Review, followed by brief stints with the traveling bands of JAY McSHANN and ANDY KIRK.

The bassist WALTER PAGE led the band for the King show. Rushing's association with him led to appearances for two years with the Blue Devils band, also led by Page. It was during this tenure that he first met and played with the pianist Basie who would play a dominant role in his career. When Basie and Page abandoned the Blue Devils to join the BENNIE MOTEN band in Kansas City in 1929, Rushing went with them. He recalled frequently how the Moten band provided a new and exciting musical experience for him because of its unique rhythmic vitality, a quality he described as sounding "like a train a-comin.'" His affiliation with that ensemble lasted until just after Moten's death in 1935. (Buster Moten kept the band working for a brief time following his brother's sudden death.) The big turn toward success in Rushing's career began when he joined the new Basie Band in Kansas City. Consisting of no more than seven to eight pieces when it began its inaugural run at the Reno Club in 1935, the Basie group so prospered during its first two years that Basie could add personnel to bring the band into conformity with the norm that was developing in the country. A recording session for the band in 1937 ("One O'Clock Jump") lists thirteen players, including Basie. Rushing was featured singer with Basie until 1948 and even after that appeared frequently with the band as a guest singer until 1950, and sporadically even into the 1960s. He was one of the few real blues artists who occupied a headliner-vocalist role in the band world of the 1930s and 1940s, most organizations opting for straight ballad and/or "novelty" singers of a more pop-commercial persuasion. Rushing had begun his own professional life singing music of more pop-ballad orientation. He nonetheless claimed his first and greatest influences to have been BESSIE SMITH and MAMIE SMITH, dating back to their appearance at a theater in Oklahoma City in 1923.

Rushing's identity is dominated by his long association with the Basie Band, although after 1950 he enjoyed the success of an established solo entertainer. For two years he fronted, as singer, his own small band in the Savoy Ballroom in Harlem. Following that he made solo appearances throughout the United States and Canada, sometimes accompanying himself, at other times accompanied by a pianist or small instrumental group. European tours presented a new and especially lucrative performance source for American jazz artists following World War II, and Rushing made three. He first toured as a solo act, then as featured singer with the Benny Goodman band for the Brussels World's Fair in 1958, and as featured singer with a band led by the trumpeter BUCK CLAYTON in 1959.

Rushing was a popular participant at the jazz festivals in this country—mostly summer outdoor affairs that took root during the late 1950s—until ill health forced him into virtual retirement during the final year of his life. His later tours with groups covered a broad array of jazz styles. They included one with Harry James, another with the Benny Goodman Sextet, and in 1964 a tour to Japan and Australia with Eddie Condon. Back in New York in 1965 he filled an extended contract at the Half-Note, returning there during the early 1970s on a permanent weekends-only schedule, this capped by one brief string of performances in Toronto during early 1971. He died in New York, never having married.

This ebullient rotund figure, an original Mr. Five-by-Five, was one of the great blues singers of the first half of this century. With such artists as Bessie Smith, JOE WILLIAMS, Jack Teagarden, BILLIE HOLIDAY, and later RAY CHARLES, he brought that genre into the mainstream of jazz, to become a national commodity cutting across the race lines that had confined it until the Great Depression.

FURTHER READING
Schuller, Gunther. *The Swing Era* (1989).
Williams, Martin. *Jazz Heritage* (1985).
This entry is taken from the *American National Biography* and is published here with the permission of the American Council of Learned Societies.

WILLIAM THOMSON

Russel, Chloe (c. 1785–after 1833), fortune-teller and author, does not appear in public records until 1820, at which time she is listed in the federal census, and nothing definitive is known about her parentage or childhood. A purportedly autobiographical text that introduces one extant copy of Russel's *The Complete Fortune Teller and Dream Book* claims that she was born in 1745 in the "Fuller nation" three hundred miles southwest of Sierre Leone, taken into slavery, and sold to Virginia planter George Russel after experiencing the horrors of the Middle Passage. In Virginia, the narrative asserts, after great torment, she gained the power of divination and then great fame as a seer, was freed, and raised money to free other slaves.

Though the veracity of this narrative is doubtful for several reasons—for example, the birthplace it gives is in the Atlantic Ocean—it is clear that the title-page attribution of *The Complete Fortune Teller* to a "Chloe Russel, a Woman of Colour in the State of Massachusetts, commonly termed the Old Witch or Black Interpreter" nonetheless invoked both a collection of fanciful stereotypes and a historical personage. The historical Chloe Russel, found in Boston censuses, directories, and property records and almost always marked as "black," was probably born after the American Revolution. She may have married around 1800, as the 1820 census shows her living with three children, two girls and a boy, who seem to have been born between 1800 and 1814. No male of her age group or older appears; city directory listings expand on this absence and mark her as a widow. By 1830 only a teenage boy appears in her household. Unfortunately neither the 1820 census nor the 1830 census lists names other than those of heads of households.

Boston directories include Russel between 1821 and 1833. In all entries her address locates her in Boston's black community, most often on Belknap Street. Her occupation shifts from washerwoman (1821–1825) to cook (1829–1833), though some directories do not list any such information. No record of her birth, marriage, husband, children, or death has yet been found. Indeed were it not for this handful of listings in the public record, Russel would be counted among the mass of members of Boston's black community who struggled for an existence only slightly above the level of basic sustenance.

But beyond her work in the occupations of laundress and cook—which were among the few jobs open to free African Americans—Russel apparently owned some property, told fortunes, and gained at least local notice. Sometime in the early nineteenth century, the Boston printer Tom Hazard published *The Complete Fortune Teller and Dream Book.* In 1824 Abel Brown, a printer in Exeter, New Hampshire, who had Boston connections, reprinted the book under his imprint; in 1827 he included the text—perhaps actual remainders from his first printing—in a larger bound miscellany that seems to have been called *The Amusing Budget* and that included other texts ranging from *The Comical Sayings of Paddy from Cork* to *More Light on Masonry.* Unfortunately the composition history of *The Complete Fortune Teller*—including how much of it Russel actually wrote—is not known, but all of the editions boldly proclaim Russel as the text's author.

The text of the Brown editions of *The Complete Fortune Teller* consists of six sections: directions for young women on finding husbands; directions for young men on finding wives; an extended dream dictionary, which lists objects (from angels and bees to teeth and water) and explains each object's significance in dreams; instructions for reading palms; instructions for reading moles; and a chart that readers are to prick—probably with eyes closed—with a guide to the prophecies each pinprick portends.

As such the text is exceedingly similar to a range of dream books and fortune-telling guides that circulated in the early United States (and even plagiarizes from some), including several that called attention to their authors' exoticism (most often authors' vaguely Middle Eastern backgrounds). It seems to have been-this linkage of the other and mysticism that allowed Russel—and a group of other black and mixed-race individuals in the North—to enter the field that the historian Peter Benes calls "cunning people" (p. 127).

If Russel's authorship—in part or whole—could be authenticated, *The Complete Fortune Teller* would have to be recognized as one of the first texts published by an African American woman in the United States. Even as a text that simply invokes a real black fortune-teller of the early nineteenth century, the chapbook and Russel's proximity to the richly active black community of the time (the Paul family, DAVID WALKER, and MARIA STEWART, for instance) call on historians to reconsider and diversify their sense of how African Americans came to and used texts.

FURTHER READING
Extant copies of *The Complete Fortune Teller* are owned by the Library Company of Philadelphia, Illinois Wesleyan University, the Boston Athenaeum, and the American Antiquarian Society.

Benes, Peter. "Fortunetellers, Wise-Men, and Magical Healers in New England, 1644–1850," in *Wonders of the Invisible World, 1600–1800*, ed. Peter Benes (1995).

Cromwell, Adelaide M. "The Black Presence in the West End of Boston" in *Courage and Conscience: Black and White Abolitionists in Boston*, ed. Donald M. Jacobs (1993).

Gardner, Eric, ed. "*The Complete Fortune Teller and Dream Book*: An Antebellum Text 'By Chloe Russel, a Woman of Colour,'" *New England Quarterly* 78.2 (June 2005).

ERIC GARDNER

Russell, Bill (12 Feb. 1934–), basketball player and coach, was born William Fenton Russell in Monroe, Louisiana, the son of Charles and Katie Russell, both laborers. Mister Charlie, as his two sons called him, worked in a paper-bag factory, while his wife worked odd jobs on a stopgap basis. She took jobs as a maid in white households only when money was especially scarce or when she particularly wished to spoil Bill, whom she openly considered her favorite child. Both Mister Charlie and Russell's paternal grandfather, usually called simply "the Old Man," set a high bar for their male progeny in Monroe. Before his ninth birthday, Russell had witnessed his father ward off an armed white man with only a tire iron and his grandfather punch a mule to its knees with just one blow.

In 1943, unable to tolerate the pressures of Jim Crow any longer, Mister Charlie left for Detroit, Michigan, and then for Oakland, California, to work as a laborer and save up enough money to send for his family. Bill, his brother Charlie, and their mother, Katie, joined him in California later that same year. Oakland afforded the Russells slightly better opportunities; Mister Charlie launched a successful trucking business, and the family began saving money. But when Russell was twelve his mother died, and Mister Charlie had to abandon his business to take a foundry job closer to his sons.

Frustrated by their teachers' skeptical opinions of their intellectual capacities, the Russell boys immersed themselves in athletics—Charlie, two years older than Bill, was much more successful early on. While Charlie's basketball prowess got him into Oakland Tech high school, Bill drifted through Hoover Junior High, where he was cut from football and basketball teams, and finally landed at nearby

Bill Russell, center for the University of San Francisco basketball team, shows how he scores baskets on 23 February 1956. (AP Images.)

McClymonds High. Discouraged after being cut from the varsity basketball team as a sophomore, Russell was accepted by the jayvee coach George Powles for his squad. With only fifteen jerseys for sixteen youths, Russell and a teammate alternated games as the fifteenth player. By his senior year Russell had grown to six feet nine inches but did not distinguish himself until his final game, scoring a career high of fourteen points. A University of San Francisco (USF) alumnus was informally scouting Russell's opponent but signed Russell instead. It was the young center's only scholarship offer. Before attending USF, Russell played for a few months on a California high school all-star team that toured the Pacific Northwest and British Columbia. Russell's skills grew significantly, as did his body, and he entered his freshman year at his full height of six feet ten inches.

Led by Russell at center and K. C. Jones (also a future Celtic) at guard, the San Francisco Dons won fifty-five straight games, including national championships in 1955 and 1956. Russell was also a world-class high jumper for the track-and-field team but

characteristically credited his success in that event more to what he called "the psych" than to any exceptional athletic ability. As he put it, "There wasn't a guy I jumped against I couldn't beat if I had the chance to talk to him beforehand" (Wolff, 138). Between his junior and senior years Russell was delighted to witness an NCAA rule change that sportswriters dubbed the "Russell rule." Since an offensive player can stand in the foul lane for no longer than three seconds, officials widened the lane from six feet to twelve feet, hoping to push Russell, who by this time could redirect his teammates' shots at will, farther from the basket. But since Russell himself placed more emphasis on defense, he relished the advantage he gained from defending a more spread-out offense; he could now roam the less crowded paint with ease and block a greater number of shots, each block a potential two-point advantage for the Dons.

After graduation, Russell played on the U.S. Olympic team in the 1956 Melbourne Games. By no means naive, he was still tremendously affected by the political and economic corruption that permeated the event. Russell later wrote in *Go Up for Glory* that the Olympics "has to be the greatest bit of sugar-'n-spice-in-the-mouth-and-bourbon-in-the-belly-carney-type-conning since Barnum and Bailey" (56). After beating the Russians in the gold-medal game 89–55, Russell flew back to Oakland, married his college sweetheart, Rose Swisher, and joined the Boston Celtics in midseason.

The Celtics' coach, Red Auerbach, had orchestrated a dramatic trade with the team's strongest rival, St. Louis, in order to sign Russell—which they did for $19,500, making him the highest-paid NBA rookie. Averaging 14.7 points and 19.6 rebounds per game, Russell infused the Celtics with a newfound defensive rigor, helping them beat St. Louis in 1957 for their first world championship. The next year Russell sprained his ankle early in the finals, and the Celtics lost to St. Louis. Then, from 1959 to 1966, the Celtics won eight consecutive NBA championships, a feat that has never even been approached by a professional team in any other American sport. Russell earned league MVP honors in 1958, 1961, 1962, 1963, and 1965 as well as an All-Star game MVP award in 1963. Besides his formidable scoring threat and Herculean rebounding—rivaled only by his legendary foe, WILT CHAMBERLAIN—Russell's forte was the blocked shot, for which he routinely deployed the same "psych" he had developed as a college high jumper and player. (Unfortunately, statistics were not kept for the blocked shot during Russell's career.)

Russell also distinguished himself as an outspoken human rights figure. (Like MALCOLM X, he vehemently preferred the phrase "human rights" over "civil rights.") Already a notorious opponent of unwritten NBA quotas, he held integrated basketball camps in the South after the assassination of MEDGAR EVERS, and he visited Africa in 1959 as a liaison of the U.S. Department of State to teach children basketball. He was so impressed with the ongoing project of Liberia that he invested in a rubber plantation that significantly bolstered the country's economy. Back home a few years later, he met with MUHAMMAD ALI to discuss Ali's refusal to answer the U.S. draft, and he proclaimed afterward his belief in the boxer's sincerity: "I'm not worried about Muhammad Ali. What I'm worried about is the rest of us" (*Sports Illustrated*, 19 June 1967). In 1964 Russell declared in the *Saturday Evening Post* that celebrity black athletes, no matter their fame or wealth, have a responsibility to "the total condition of the Negro." In 1966 he demonstrated his commitment to that philosophy by writing a blistering autobiography, *Go Up for Glory*, in which he interprets his life primarily through challenges related to race, rather than sports.

Early in his career Russell became known for vomiting before every game; privately, during the last couple of seasons of the Celtics' championship run, he came to depend on high doses of sleeping pills to calm his nerves. The vomiting embodied the tension in his life between an intense competitiveness and a high-strung vulnerability, all of which contributed to a nervous breakdown in 1965. Nonetheless, upon Auerbach's retirement the next year, Russell was named player-coach for the 1967 campaign, thereby becoming the first African American coach of an integrated team in a major professional sports league. The next season the Celtics lost to Chamberlain's Philadelphia 76ers, but before retiring in 1969 Russell would lead the Celtics to two more consecutive championships, quipping late in his career, "Now I just throw up for the playoffs" (Wolff, 138).

His last year as a player-coach was also the last year of his marriage to Rose, with whom he had three children, William "Buddha" Felton Jr., Jacob, and Karen Kenyatta. In 1974 Russell was elected to the Basketball Hall of Fame despite his personal objections to the hall's treatment of minority players as well as his aversion to the vacuity of celebrity honors. At this time Russell was still an NBA coach for the fledgling Seattle Supersonics; following a four-year record of 162–166, he backed away from the game and married Didi Anstett in 1977. A decade later Russell gave coaching another try, this time with the Sacramento Kings—but after a 17–41 start he stepped down before season's end.

Russell wrote two more books: a supplemental autobiography in 1979, *Second Wind: The Memoirs of an Opinionated Man* (with Taylor Branch), and *Russell Rules: Eleven Lessons on Leadership from the Twentieth Century's Greatest Winner* (2002). Whatever the mixed results of his latter-day coaching efforts, Russell holds the distinction of being the "winningest" competitor in any major U.S. sport in any era. Between 1955 and 1969 Russell tallied two NCAA championships, an Olympic gold medal, and eleven NBA world championships. Popularly regarded as a consummate team player, Russell still totaled seven MVP awards during that run. In 2011 President BARACK OBAMA awarded Russell the Presidential Medal of Freedom, one of the nation's two highest civilian awards.

FURTHER READING

Russell, Bill. *Russell Rules: Eleven Lessons on Leadership from the Twentieth Century's Greatest Winner* (2002).

Russell, Bill, with Taylor Branch. *Second Wind: The Memoirs of an Opinionated Man* (1979).

Russell, Bill, with William McSweeny. *Go Up for Glory* (1966).

Shapiro, Miles. *Bill Russell* (1991).

Wolff, Alexander. *100 Years of Hoops* (1991).

DAVID F. SMYDRA JR.

Russell, Clayton (1910–1981), minister and political activist, was born in Los Angeles, California. The names of his parents are unknown. Primarily educated in Los Angeles–area schools, Russell also studied theology in Copenhagen, Denmark, in the early 1930s at the nation's International College. Russell later remarked that his experiences studying abroad profoundly influenced his thinking about the plight of fellow African Americans in the United States. Foremost among his overseas memories was a visit to Weimar Germany, where the Los Angeles cleric witnessed firsthand the rise of Adolph Hitler's Nationalist Socialist (Nazi) Party and its racist ideology.

In 1936 Russell took over the pastorate of Los Angeles's People's Independent Church. This church, which had emanated in 1915 from the black community's more conservative and powerful First African Methodist Episcopal (AME) Church, became known for its outreach programs for poor and disenfranchised blacks. Within a year into Russell's tenure, the People's Independent Church had become the most popular church in Los Angeles's black community. Spurred on by Russell's charisma and exceptional organizational skills, parishioners of the People's Independent Church confronted the problems of the Great Depression with unusual zeal. Under his direction the church set up a medical outreach service for the poor, a free employment service, a staffed youth center, a college scholarship program, and a homeless shelter for neglected young men.

With the outbreak of World War II Russell expanded his efforts to galvanize and organize the city's black community, with particular emphasis on getting the community behind the Allied war effort. Using his popular radio show—he was the first African American in Los Angeles to have his own radio program—as a bully pulpit Russell organized the Negro Victory Committee, whose dual purpose was to defeat fascism abroad and racism at home. To those ends Russell led several large-scale protests against defense industry companies that continued to refuse to hire blacks despite their desperate need for defense workers. So successful were these protests that they caught the attention and open political support of both President Franklin Roosevelt and California governor Culbert Olsen.

After helping to open Los Angeles's massive defense industries to previously neglected minority groups, in 1944 Russell led another successful protest campaign that culminated in black and Latino men being allowed to work as streetcar conductors for the city's large urban railway system.

While continuing to work on opening up jobs for minorities, Russell labored tirelessly to desegregate the city's schools. A strong proponent of education, he feverishly worked to convince local school board authorities that the city's continued practice of educational segregation was both un-American and harmful to all concerned. Within the black community Russell vocally encouraged the study of science and mathematics.

Another of Russell's lifetime goals was to make the black community as self-sufficient as possible. To that end he planned and created the nation's first black-owned cooperative market system. Opened on 11 April 1942 the Negro Victory Market played an important role in aiding black war workers and their families. Although it closed when World War II ended, the Negro Victory Market served as testament to the strong will and organizational skills of Russell and his followers.

Following the war Russell continued his work to forward the cause of civil rights. In addition, in 1953 he founded the Church of Divine Guidance. Although his death was not highly publicized outside the black community of Los Angeles, his legacy of black self-sufficiency, the opening of defense jobs for women and minorities, and the desegregation of the nation's largest school system remain a living testament to those who believe that one individual can make a difference.

FURTHER READING

Anderson, E. Frederick. *The Development of Leadership and Organization Building in the Black Community of Los Angeles, 1900 through World War 2* (1982).

Verge, Arthur C. *Paradise Transformed: Los Angeles during the Second World War* (1993).

This entry is taken from the *American National Biography* and is published here with the permission of the American Council of Learned Societies.

ARTHUR C. VERGE

Russell, George Allen (23 June 1923–27 July 2009), percussionist, pianist, and composer, was born in Cincinnati, Ohio, and nurtured in the care of foster parents. He first became interested in jazz on hearing FATE MARABLE on a riverboat. He was also impressed by JIMMY MUNDY, an arranger for the Benny Goodman Orchestra. At age fifteen Russell was earning a living playing drums. By seventeen he was a member of the Wilberforce University band, where he shared the stage with ERNIE WILKINS, the saxophonist who was later COUNT BASIE's arranger.

Three years later, after recovering from tuberculosis, Russell took a step toward maturity as a musician when he became part of Benny Carter's orchestra, where he contributed "Big World," his first composition. After serving a period of apprenticeship in Chicago in the employ of the pianist EARL "FATHA" HINES along with some cabarets, Russell decided he needed to be in New York. In 1945, when bebop was in its nascent stages, he met the alto saxophone innovator CHARLIE PARKER, who offered him a drumming job. Again, however, major illness struck, taking Russell out of circulation for almost a year and a half.

This time, though, Russell spent the sixteen months it took him to recuperate in a Bronx, New York, hospital formulating the principles of what would become identified as his Lydian theory of tonal organization, based on a mode or scale from F to F on the white keys of a piano. Upon leaving the hospital, Russell enhanced his reputation with the pathbreaking jazz and Afro-Cuban blend composition "Cubana Be, Cubana Bop," performed with the DIZZY GILLESPIE orchestra, featuring the *conguero* extraordinaire and Cuban virtuoso CHANO POZO, in a memorable 1947 Carnegie Hall concert. The two-part suite, co-written by Gillespie and Russell and consisting of the highly rhythmic brassy scores "Cubana Be" and "Cubana Bop," was recorded on 22 December 1947. Along with Pozo, the suite boasted JOHN LEWIS on piano, the bebop standard-bearer KENNY CLARKE on drums, and stellar brass and reed section work. With his addition to the Gillespie book, Russell helped create a modern classic.

Russell subsequently concentrated on the Lydian concept that began to appear in such recordings as *Ezz-thetic* and dominated his writing and sound designs in the 1950s and 1960s. He had assimilated such contemporary trendsetters as THELONIOUS MONK and devised a musical workshop concept reminiscent of yet wholly distinct from that of CHARLES MINGUS, with whom some of his work and approaches bear comparison. Yet it is also true that much about Russell was unique, making it difficult to find parallels between him and other modern composers. As a writer, arranger, and soloist, Russell carved an individual path in African American musical tradition.

Russell's exceptional intellect was showcased in 1953 with the publication of *The Lydian Concept of Tonal Organization*, which laid the groundwork of his compositional outlook. The effect of the appearance of this text, together with Russell's own experimentation in recording and live performance, was extremely significant and far-reaching. Ultimately it not only led to his own influential work as a leader, writer, orchestrator, and performer but also helped broaden the vocabulary of both mainstream and avant-garde composition and interpretation. There is a direct line, for example, between Russell's Lydian concept and the modal approaches adopted by MILES DAVIS in 1959 in *Kind of Blue* and JOHN COLTRANE (also part of that Davis recording) in his key role as a leader, beginning with *My Favorite Things* in 1961.

By 1958 Russell stepped back to capture the excitement of "Manhattan," as *New York, New York* opens with a staccato, staggered duet by the drummer Charlie Persip and the rhythmic recitative of the eloquent elocutionist Jon Hendricks ("Think you can lick it / get to the wicket / buy you a ticket / go"). It then morphs into a lush and luxuriant horn fanfare, out of which Coltrane's tenor saxophone erupts in lavishly lyrical phrases flowing from the chords and melody of this Tin Pan Alley ditty with such sonorous suggestiveness that a listener might think it was crafted for this occasion. *New York, New York* is a time capsule preserving the vibrancy of 1958–1959 in amber.

In 1960 Russell released *Jazz in the Space Age*, which marked a further exploration of the Lydian concept. The album highlights the pianists Bill Evans and Paul Bley, the trombonists Dave Baker and Frank Rehak, and the trumpeter Ernie Royal. Russell himself took turns on percussion, using tuned drums on "The Lydiot" and "Chromatic Universe," working beside Don Lamond, and ceding the trap chair to Persip for "Waltz from Outer Space" and "Dimension."

In September 1964 Russell's artistic trajectory took a dramatic turn when he was invited to the Berlin Jazz Festival. He found audiences there so receptive that he decided to settle down in Europe and relocated to Stockholm. A year later he produced an ambitious sextet album recorded live at Stuttgart's Beethoven Hall that included DON CHERRY and Bertil Loewgren on trumpet, Ray Pitts on tenor saxophone, Brian Trentham on trombone, ALBERT "TOOTIE" HEATH on drums, Cameron Brown on bass, and Russell, the leader, on piano. On this two-disc set, one taken from the concert, a second recorded in the studio, Russell explores the Lydian mode in six different contexts. Three are Lydian variations on classic works of the bebop canon, Parker's "Confirmation," Monk's tender ballad "Round Midnight," and MILT JACKSON's "Bag's Groove."

From this point onward Russell joined the ranks of African American expatriate artists in Europe, and his subsequent works were not easily accessed in the United States. He recorded his *Othello Ballet Suite* in Radio, Sweden, on 3–4 November 1967 and his Electronic Organ Sonata No. 1 in Oslo, Norway, on 1 October 1968, but these recordings did not appear in the United States until 1970, when Bob Thiele's independent Flying Dutchman label released them. Two years later Flying Dutchman released a 1969 concert recorded at Oslo's Sonja Henie/Niels Onstad Center for the Arts under the title *Electronic Sonata for Souls Loved by Nature*. That same year Russell received a Guggenheim Fellowship.

Russell remained one of the most imaginative innovators of the last half of the twentieth century. More than two dozen of his compositions have been recorded, performed in a variety of styles by such major players as MAX ROACH, Art Farmer, Gerry Mulligan, Lee Konitz, Miles Davis, and Gil Evans. Russell's Living Time Orchestra and his other endeavors, including the orchestra's *Eightieth Birthday Concert* double CD, recorded live on tour in 2003, made him one of the singular voices in African American improvisational music.

Russell died in Boston from Alzheimer's-related complications.

FURTHER READING

Feather, Leonard. Liner Notes, *New York, New York, and Jazz in the Space Age* (1973).

Harrison, Max. "George Russell," in *Jazz on Record: A Critical Guide to the First Fifty Years, 1917–1967*, eds. Albert McCarthy, Alun Morgan, Paul Oliver, and Max Harrison (1968).

Obituary: *New York Times*, 29 July 2009.

DISCOGRAPHY

Modern Jazz Concert (Columbia WL 12, 1957).

Jazz Workshop (RCA, 1962).

Othello Ballet Suite, Electronic Sonata No. 2 (Flying Dutchman FDS 122, 1970).

Electronic Sonata for Souls Loved by Nature (Flying Dutchman FD10124, 1971).

George Russell Sextet at Beethoven Hall (MCA Records MC25125, 1973).

New York, New York, and Jazz in the Space Age (MCA Records MCA2-4017, 1973).

Ezz-thetics (Fantasy, 1983).

DAVID H. ANTHONY III

Russell, James Solomon (20 Dec. 1857–28 Mar. 1935), educator and priest, was born on the Hendrick Estate in Mecklenburg County near Palmer Springs, Virginia. His father, Solomon, and his mother, Araminta (maiden name unknown), both lived as slaves on adjoining properties with the North Carolina state line between them. With the ambiguity of slave status following Abraham Lincoln's Emancipation Proclamation in 1863, the largely illiterate black people were left wondering how they might survive. After sharecropping during and following the war, in 1868 Solomon rented a nearby plot with his brother as partner. They raised a good crop of corn and eighty dollars worth of tobacco. Then the brothers' barn burned and the Russells, with son James, ten years old, were again destitute. In spite of their poverty Araminta insisted that her son learn to read, and even in the absence of public schools for blacks, James's fortunes improved.

A plantation overseer, Thomas Wade, allowed James to ride behind him on his rounds and to ask questions. An elderly woman with only a second-grade education also coached him in reading and writing for fifty cents per month. In 1870 the white lay missionaries John E. P. Wright and Mack Duggar started a Sunday school for black children, and in the same year a private school for blacks was opened by Armisted Miller. By 1873 young Russell had established himself as an excellent student and at sixteen was superintendent of the Wright-Duggar Sunday School. The state of Virginia opened a school for blacks that Russell attended when busy with farm work. He went on to board at the Hampton Institute for a year, but was prevented by family obligations from returning in 1875. He received a teaching certificate from Brunswick County, and after teaching two years near his home, he returned to Hampton for another year.

At this point a benefactor entered his life. Patti Hicks Buford, the wife of a prominent lawyer in the county, was just beginning what would become her life's work—a school for black children and later a hospital for black patients (the first one in Virginia, according to her obituary in a 1901 Richmond paper). Russell so captivated her that in due course she gave him fifty dollars and told him to visit the Episcopal bishop, Francis M. Whittle, to discuss furthering his education. Because the Diocese of Virginia had never had a black postulant and the seminary at Alexandria was not to desegregate for nearly another hundred years, Whittle's solution was to form the Bishop Payne Divinity School, an all-black institution in Petersburg, with Russell as its first matriculant.

Russell developed a fast friendship with the Reverend Giles Buckner Cooke, rector of St. Stephen's parish in Petersburg, principal of its school for black students, and a former major on the staff of Robert E. Lee. This extraordinary man tutored him during what would normally have been his college and seminary years. Russell became well known as a speaker. In 1882, the year that he was ordained a deacon in the Protestant Episcopal Church, he made such a moving appeal at the diocesan convention for missionary work among blacks that he was voted a horse, saddle, bridle, and three hundred dollars. Thereafter, "Ida" was the all-purpose animal who delivered him to his missions, hauled bricks for campus construction, and later pulled the water wagon at Saint Paul's School.

Also in 1882 Russell married Virginia Morgan, an accomplished organist and graduate of Cooke's St. Stephen's School. Together they started a church and Sunday school in Lawrenceville, Virginia, and opened one mission after another in surrounding towns; she taught when she was not caring for their five children.

With his lofty title, the archdeacon for colored work for southern Virginia, and his dignified humility, Russell was able to coexist with the white half of the population. In 1888 he opened Saint Paul's Normal and Industrial School in Lawrenceville, which in 1969 became a four-year college. He held the title of principal until 1929, when he was succeeded by his son James Alvin Russell. Russell's business acumen was remarkable. He bought the first electric generator in the community and soon was selling electricity to neighboring businesses. He acquired an ice machine; henceforth, when the Southern Railway's passenger trains stopped at nearby Emporia, they loaded one-hundred-pound ice blocks from the school's wagon. His reputation for reliability was such that when he bought the school's first piece of land, 3.1 acres for one thousand dollars, he was not required to pay down any cash. All that was required was a promissory note cosigned by Virginia Russell. The next year he bought "the Hill," which became the center of the campus. In 1921 Russell sold enough timber to cover the entire cumulative cost of the land. He continued buying and trading land until, at the time of his death, the college owned 1,600 acres, many of these purchased with the disapprobation of Bishop Whittle, who felt that land speculation was inappropriate for an Episcopal priest.

In 1904 Russell borrowed the idea of an annual farmer's conference, originally conceived by BOOKER T. WASHINGTON, his friend and contemporary at Hampton Institute. In two years, attendance at the conference had grown to two thousand. Experts were brought in to urge the planting of food as well as cash crops. Russell lost no opportunity to preach his philosophy—own land, keep out of debt, add rooms to your house, pay your poll tax, and vote. All of these concepts were anathema to many whites. Saint Paul's became the biggest business in Brunswick County. Practically all surgery for blacks in the area was performed in the school's infirmary. Ninety percent of the black teachers in the county were Saint Paul's graduates.

During Russell's active career of over a half century, the Episcopal Church's principal medium of evangelistic communication was a little magazine called the *Spirit of Missions*. Russell's reports in it were powerful appeals. He began making regular trips to New York, Boston, and Philadelphia, Pennsylvania. He attracted the interest of well-known individuals—Francis L. Stetson, George Foster Peabody, J. Pierpont Morgan, and Charles Lewis Tiffany. Before World War I he had become the best-known black priest in the Episcopal Church. When the Diocese of Arkansas was seeking a suffragan bishop for work among blacks, Russell was elected by the House of Bishops, but he declined. When North Carolina offered the same opportunity, he declined once more. Had he accepted he would have been the first black bishop in the Episcopal Church in the United States, but Russell was convinced that he had found in his school the place in which he could be of greatest use to God and humanity. Three thousand people attended his funeral, including three dozen vested clergy. His great magnetism, force, energy, judgment, and dedication carried him to remarkable success. He died in Lawrenceville and was buried near the campus of the school he founded.

Russell's charity and compassion, combined with astute business acumen, won him such admiration among whites and blacks that the churches, businesses, and schools of the area remained at peace at a time when crosses were burned in many other parts of the South.

FURTHER READING

Most of the material about Russell can be found in Lawrenceville, Virginia, where he spent his adult life after 1882. The Saint Paul's College Library has the best collection of his letters and papers.

Russell, James Solomon. *Adventure in Faith* (posthumous ed., 1936).

Chitty, Arthur Ben. *Miracle Worker of Southside Virginia* (1982).

Obituary: *New York Times*, 29 Mar. 1935.

This entry is taken from the *American National Biography* and is published here with the permission of the American Council of Learned Societies.

ARTHUR BEN CHITTY

Russell, Luis Carl (6 Aug. 1902–11 Dec. 1963), jazz bandleader, arranger, and pianist, was born in Careening Cay in Bocas Del Toro Province, Panama, the son of Felix Alexander Russell, a pianist and music teacher who taught him several instruments. In 1917 he played piano accompanying silent films and the next year moved to Colon, where he played in the Casino Club with a small dance band. Nothing is known of Russell's mother except that in 1919 she and her daughter accompanied him to New Orleans after he had won three thousand dollars in a lottery. Once settled he studied jazz piano with Steve Lewis and in the fall of 1921 worked at the Cadillac Club in Arnold De Pass's band, where he first met the clarinetist ALBERT NICHOLAS. In 1923 he played with Nicholas's six-piece jazz band at Tom Anderson's Cabaret, and when the clarinetist left for Chicago in May 1924 to replace BUSTER BAILEY in KING OLIVER's Creole Jazz Band, Russell was given temporary leadership of the group. Later in the year, after Nicholas had returned, he too went north to work with Doc Cook's Orchestra at the Dreamland Ballroom, but by 1925 he was reunited with Nicholas in King Oliver's newly formed Dixie Syncopators at the Plantation Café.

A sideman on all of the Dixie Syncopators' recordings between March 1926 and April 1927, Russell debuted as a leader at the beginning of this period when he took his Hot Six, with the cornetist GEORGE MITCHELL and some Oliver sidemen, including Nicholas, the trombonist KID ORY, and the tenor saxman BARNEY BIGARD, into the Vocalion studios to record two numbers in definitive New Orleans "hot dance" style. This coupling was followed in November 1926 by four titles on the Okeh label under the name of Luis Russell's Heebie Jeebie Stompers, another six-piece group drawn from Oliver's working band, this time including the cornetist Bob Shoffner, the trombonist Preston Jackson, and reedmen Darnell Howard and Bigard. In March 1927, after the Plantation was bombed in a gang war, Russell went with Oliver on a tour through Milwaukee, Detroit, St. Louis, and New York, where in May the band played two weeks at the Savoy Ballroom. When Oliver ran out of bookings the men dispersed, with Russell leaving in September 1927 to join drummer George Howe's band at the Nest Club. The next month Howe was fired by the management for repeatedly falling asleep on the bandstand, and Russell was appointed leader, a position he maintained through the following year.

After Howe's dismissal Russell brought in the New Orleans drummer PAUL BARBARIN and replaced the trumpeter and trombonist, respectively, with Louis Metcalf, a LOUIS ARMSTRONG devotee, and J. C. HIGGINBOTHAM, who was then playing in the lusty, broad-toned manner of KID ORY. By the end of the summer of 1929 Russell had added Nicholas and the bassist POPS FOSTER and replaced Metcalf with RED ALLEN, an even better Armstrong-influenced New Orleanian. Unlike any other northern-based orchestra of the time, the Russell band now had five New Orleans musicians in its ranks, as well as the brilliant solo talents he already had in Higginbotham and the alto saxophonist Charlie Holmes, himself a disciple of SIDNEY BECHET. With a personnel so deeply immersed in New Orleans–style polyphony, blues timbre, and rhythm, Russell had a band that was truly one of a kind.

In 1929 and 1930 the group played at a number of New York venues, including the Savoy Ballroom, the Saratoga Club, and Connie's Inn, as well as touring theaters as a backup band for Louis Armstrong. During this period Russell's orchestra also recorded fourteen titles that remain definitive examples of early big-band jazz. They also recorded, in whole or in part, under the names of Armstrong, Allen, and Higginbotham, and as accompanists to the blues singers VICTORIA SPIVEY and Addie "Sweet Pease" Spivey. Between 1931 and 1934 the Russell band continued to tour, while also playing residencies at Connie's Inn, the Arcadia Ballroom, and the Empire Ballroom, where the cornetist REX STEWART briefly joined the band as featured soloist. The records of 1934 indicate a total abandonment of the 1929–1930 New Orleans–based orchestral style, with its emphasis on polyphonic ensembles and loosely swinging rhythm, and instead display an attempt to come closer to the more heavily arranged patterns of other contemporary dance bands. Russell encouraged the tenor saxman Bingie Madison to contribute his own arrangements to the band's library, and these rather tricky and virtuosic charts reflect the more mechanical but highly popular styles of the Casa Loma and JIMMIE LUNCEFORD orchestras, a far cry from the free and jubilant swing of only a few years before. In effect this was a move toward the commercialism that would characterize the band's playing for the remainder of its days.

In September 1935 Armstrong's manager, Joe Glaser, decided that Russell's band would be the ideal setting for his star trumpeter and singer, who had recently returned from a long European tour and was ready to front a permanent band of his own. On 1 October, with little rehearsal time, Armstrong and Russell opened at Connie's Inn, and from that time through early 1943 the Russell band, once on a level with McKinney's Cotton Pickers and the orchestras of FLETCHER HENDERSON and DUKE ELLINGTON, functioned as a mere backdrop to Armstrong. The records of the early period indicate a drastic change in the Russell sound, as Armstrong had an inexplicable liking for the syrupy saxophones and clipped-brass-section phrasing of Guy Lombardo and no doubt asked Russell to follow that example. Additionally, because he was so confident of his ability to capture and maintain his audiences' attention all by himself, Armstrong seemingly expressed little interest in such niceties of orchestral performance as uniform intonation and sectional precision. Russell's and Madison's arrangements were designed to showcase Armstrong's solos and vocals, and it was undoubtedly Glaser, as much as Armstrong, who dictated this musical policy. But, as leader, Armstrong ultimately must be held responsible for the shoddiness of the band's performance standards at this time. Presumably, Russell and Madison did the best they could under existing stylistic restrictions and with the popular and novelty song material they were obliged to arrange, but because of the pedestrian nature of their work the records of this period are valued not for the band's contributions but for Armstrong's brilliance as a performer. However, the band does begin to rise to the occasion by May 1936, when it recorded "Swing That Music," with Foster's prominent bass and effective riffing by the horn sections, and "Mahogany Hall Stomp" in a competent version that nevertheless demands comparison with the far superior Armstrong/Russell collaboration on the same number from March 1929.

By 1935 only a handful of the original Russell bandsmen were still present, but in the summer of 1937 Allen, Higginbotham, and Nicholas returned, and in late 1938 Barbarin was replaced by SID CATLETT, one of the finest of all swing drummers, whose subtle but strong propulsion added a valuable rhythmic impact that was lacking in the more rigid playing of his predecessor. However, even by mid-1937 the band was performing up to standard, and the arrangements were beginning to reflect the influence of Fletcher Henderson. According to Nicholas, who solos to advantage on the spirited "I've Got a Heart Full of Rhythm," the band played even better in person than it did on record, which by this time was already quite an improvement over what it had been doing in 1935. Recording dates in 1939 and 1940 indicate that the band was being allowed more liberties than before, and there are a number of excellent performances that survive, such as the sessions that produced remakes of some of Armstrong's late 1920s classics.

However, after his departure from Armstrong, in 1944 Russell formed another totally different orchestra that opened at the Savoy and in 1945 and 1946 recorded several commercial sessions for the Manor and Apollo labels that bear no stylistic relation to his previous work. He divided his time between touring and appearing at New York–based theaters and ballrooms, but unfortunately the band had no major soloists, and its arrangements possessed neither distinction nor originality. With little prospect for continued work for his band, in 1948 Russell retired from full-time music and opened a candy and stationery store in Brooklyn, at the same time leading small bands for occasional jobs, managing the Town Hill nightclub, and teaching piano and organ. During the 1950s he married the concert singer Carline Ray. Russell's last years were spent teaching, and he also worked as a chauffeur for the president of Yeshiva University. He died in New York City.

In the words of Gunther Schuller, Russell "was a gifted composer and a constantly explorative arranger," but Albert McCarthy believes that "compared with the McKinney or Henderson bands, Russell's offered little in the way of innovatory scoring." McCarthy quite rightly points out that the main virtues of the original band lay not in its arrangements but in its swinging rhythm section and its inspired, inventive soloists. If the arrangements that Russell churned out for Armstrong in the 1930s and for his own band in the mid-1940s constituted the only evidence of his writing extant, then estimations of his talent would not be so different. But, to his credit, early in his career he wisely sensed his limitations as a pianist and rarely took solos. What little we do hear of him reflects a stiff and awkward touch and a decidedly un-swinging sense of time. Russell was at his best when writing for his own orchestra in a style shaped by his musical experiences in the 1920s in New Orleans and Chicago, but by the time the swing era was in full gear he had already passed his prime. He should more properly be remembered for his accomplishments in 1929–1930 than for his subsequent activities with Armstrong and beyond.

FURTHER READING

Allen, Walter C., and Brian Rust. *King Oliver* (1987).
Foster, Pops. *The Autobiography of Pops Foster: New Orleans Jazzman* (1971).
McCarthy, Albert. *Big Band Jazz* (1974).
Schuller, Gunther. *The Swing Era* (1989).

DISCOGRAPHY

Bruyninckx, Walter. *Swing Discography, 1920–1988* (12 vols., 1989).

Rust, Brian. *Jazz Records, 1897–1942* (1982).

This entry is taken from the *American National Biography* and is published here with the permission of the American Council of Learned Societies.

JACK SOHMER

Russell, Nipsey (15 Sept. 1918–2 Oct. 2005), stand-up comic, actor, singer, and emcee, was born Julius Russell in Atlanta, Georgia. Nicknamed "Nipsey" by his mother, Russell exhibited talent early. At age three he was dancing locally with the Ragamuffins of Rhythm tap dance team. At six he was the singing and dancing emcee of a children's entertainment troupe, and by nine or ten he was inspired by another black performer, Jack Wiggins, a dancing comedian who told jokes between dance numbers and whom Russell had seen perform.

Growing up, Russell was also a keen student of language and showed an interest in a wide variety of literature, including Homer, John Keats, and Paul Laurence Dunbar. As a teenager he used that facility with language. He attended BOOKER T. WASHINGTON High School in Atlanta and then the University of Cincinnati. His education was interrupted by a four-year stint in the U.S. Army, where he served as a medical field officer during World War II, one of the few African American men to achieve the rank of captain in what was then a segregated army. When his tour of duty was over, he returned to the University of Cincinnati and graduated with a B.A. in English in 1946. Originally intending to be an English teacher, he was ineluctably drawn to show business.

Russell's television debut came in 1950 with an appearance on *The Show Goes On*, starring Robert Q. Lewis, a talent showcase that jumpstarted his career and led to his many performances on the chitlin' circuit, the group of small clubs that existed in the southern and northeastern United States where African American entertainers were welcomed and celebrated during segregation. As a result of this exposure, Russell often performed his comedy routine at venues like the legendary Apollo Theater in Harlem and frequently served as an emcee there. He was also a disc jockey on the New York City radio station in the early 1950s. As his reputation grew, he became a sought-after entertainer at Catskills resorts and performed regularly at various Harlem venues, including Small's Paradise and the Club Baby Grand. His humor drew whites and blacks alike, especially to the Baby Grand, where he earned the nickname "Harlem's Son of Fun." In 1957, an appearance on the *Ed Sullivan Show* gained him a larger audience. Two years later and as a result of his appearance at a Carnegie Hall benefit for MARTIN LUTHER KING JR., Russell was invited to appear on *The Tonight Show*, by then-host Jack Paar. His burgeoning career also brought him a record deal with the Borderline label, which resulted in the release of several comedy albums.

In 1961 Russell was cast in the sitcom *Car 54, Where Are You?* The series ran for three seasons, and in 1964 Russell moved on to *Missing Links*, where he became the first black performer to serve as a regular panelist on a network game show. His stint on this program earned him the moniker "the Poet Laureate of Comedy" because of his quick, poetic improvisations. His poetry—and comedy—focused on universal subjects, such as taxes, children, and in-laws. This approach was purposeful in part because Russell did not wish to be viewed as a black comic. Indeed in a 1993 interview with the *Los Angeles Times*, he commented, "The comedians who came along in my era, came as ourselves, not as comedy characters which had been true of Lincoln Perry as STEPIN FETCHIT and EDDIE ANDERSON as Rochester [on *The Jack Benny Show*]" (7 Feb. 1993, 83).

Russell distinguished himself in all of his television appearances as the debonair poet, nattily dressed in a conservative suit and tie, wearing a porkpie hat. Throughout his career, he remained committed to his brand of comedy, even as other comics such as RICHARD PRYOR and DICK GREGORY presented rawer or more political material. Even though many of his jokes had a satirical edge, especially during the height of the civil rights movement, he was sometimes accused of being a sellout.

In spite of this criticism, Russell saw continued success. In 1965 he became cohost of *The Les Crane Show*, a talk show. He continued his appearances on *The Ed Sullivan Show* and in the late 1960s and early 1970s made guest appearances on a number of variety shows, including *Rowan and Martin's Laugh-In*, *The Jackie Gleason Show*, and *The Dean Martin Show*. In 1971 Russell became a featured panelist on *To Tell the Truth*, which paved the way for his work two years later on *The Match Game*. During the same period he was also a frequent guest on *The Tonight Show* hosted by Johnny Carson, and over the next decade and a half continued his game show appearances on programs such as *The Hollywood Squares* and *The $25,000 Pyramid*.

Russell's frequent appearances on game shows and variety shows did not preclude his work on the stage. He was a fixture on the nightclub circuit, making regular appearances in Reno, Lake Tahoe, Las Vegas, and Atlantic City. During this time he also starred in touring company productions of the Broadway musicals *Hello, Dolly!* and *A Funny Thing Happened on the Way to the Forum*. At the end of the decade Russell was lauded for his performance as the Tin Man in the 1978 film version of the Broadway musical *The Wiz*.

In 1983 Russell hosted *Juvenile Jury* on the Black Entertainment Television (BET) network. In 1984 he had a minor role in the movie *Dream One*, and a year later he appeared in another film, *Wildcats*. He hosted the short-lived game show *Your Number's Up* in 1985 and thus became the first African American to ever host a game show.

When game shows became unfashionable in the 1990s, Russell thrived on the nightclub circuit. He also returned to film in 1993 with an appearance in Mario Van Peebles's revisionist western *Posse*. In that same year he was a featured performer in the documentary *Mo' Funny: Black Comedy in America*. In the last years of his life, he was a frequent guest on *Late Night with Conan O'Brien*, *The Chris Rock Show*, and *The Hollywood Squares*.

Russell, who never married, died after a bout with stomach cancer. He is remembered as a pioneering figure in television history because of his sophisticated mien, his ready wit, and his mainstream appeal.

FURTHER READING
Holley, Joe. "Rhyming Funny Man Nipsey Russell Dies," *Washington Post* (4 Oct. 2005).
King, Susan. "Nipsey Russell, Comic Laureate," *Los Angeles Times* (7 Feb. 1993).
Watkins, Mel. "Nipsey Russell, A Comic With a Gift for Verse, Dies at 80" *New York Times* (4 Oct. 2005).

ELEANOR D. BRANCH

Russwurm, John Brown (1 Oct. 1799–9 June 1851), journalist and first nonwhite governor of Maryland in Liberia Colony, West Africa, was born in Port Antonio, Jamaica, the son of John Russwurm, a white American merchant, and an unidentified Jamaican black woman. As a boy known only as John Brown, Russwurm was sent to Canada for an education by his father. After his father's settlement in Maine and marriage in 1813 to a white New England widow with children, he entered the new family at his stepmother's insistence. John Brown thereupon assumed his father's surname and remained with his stepmother even after the senior Russwurm's

death in 1815. His schooling continued at home and, later, at preparatory institutes such as the North Yarmouth Academy in Maine. He made a short, unhappy visit to Jamaica and returned to Portland, Maine, to begin collegiate study. Thrown on his own after just one year because of his sponsor's inability to continue support, young Russwurm took a succession of brief teaching jobs at African free schools in Philadelphia, New York, and Boston.

Russwurm entered Bowdoin College in Brunswick, Maine, in September 1824 and soon evinced an interest in books by joining the Athenean Society, a campus literary group. He graduated two years later with a B.A. Asked to give a commencement oration, he titled his speech "The Condition and Prospects of Hayti." He claimed that Haitians, having overthrown French rule, exemplified the truth that "it is the irresistible course of events that all men, who have been deprived of their liberty, shall recover this previous portion of their indefeasible inheritance." That a young man partially of African descent had graduated from college, the second or third nonwhite to do so in the United States, and had spoken so eloquently of freedom garnered attention from several newspapers and journals, which published extracts of his remarks. Bowdoin College awarded Russwurm an honorary master of arts degree in 1829.

As a college student Russwurm entertained the idea of emigrating to Haiti, but, diploma in hand, he went to New York City and, with SAMUEL CORNISH, a Presbyterian minister, began publishing *Freedom's Journal*, the first black newspaper in the United States. The editors declared in the inaugural issue, on 16 March 1827, that they wanted to disseminate useful knowledge of every kind among an estimated five hundred thousand free persons of color, to bring about their moral, religious, civil, and literary improvement, and, most important of all, to plead their cause, including their civil rights, to the public. They emphasized the value of education and self-help. Although they vowed that the journal would not become the advocate of any partial views either in politics or in religion, it spoke clearly for the abolition of slavery in the United States and opposed the budding movement to colonize freed blacks in Africa. Weekly issues carried a variety of material: poetry, letters of explorers and others in Africa, information on the status of slaves in slaveholding states, legislation pending or passed in states that affected blacks, notices of job openings, and personal news such as marriages and obituaries. Advertisements for adult education classes appeared frequently, and Russwurm even appealed for subscribers to attend an evening school in lower New York where he taught reading, writing, arithmetic, English grammar, and geography. Agents in twelve states as well as in Canada, Haiti, and England sold subscriptions, but total circulation figures can only be guessed as several hundred copies. Six months after the newspaper's beginning, Cornish resigned as an editor, ostensibly in order to return to the ministry and to promote free black schools, but more likely because he disagreed with Russwurm's new views on African colonization.

Russwurm was becoming convinced that blacks could not achieve equality with whites in the United States and that emigration to Africa was their best hope. In one of his last editorials, he wrote that "the universal emancipation so ardently desired by us & by all our friends, can never take place, unless some door is opened whereby the emancipated may be removed as fast as they drop their galling chains, to some other land besides the free states." The final issue of the journal appeared on 28 March 1829, whereupon, two months later, Cornish resumed its editorship under a new title, *The Rights of All*. His vigorous denunciation of the colonization movement in fact represented the majority view among slaves and free blacks.

That fall Russwurm sailed for Monrovia, capital of the colony of Liberia, which had been established in 1822 by the American Colonization Society, a national group that favored the voluntary repatriation of blacks to Africa as a solution to accelerating racial problems. He assumed editorship of the foundering, government-controlled *Liberia Herald* in 1830, became the official government printer by virtue of his appointment as colonial secretary, undertook the supervision of public education, and engaged in trade. In 1833 he married Sarah E. McGill, daughter of George R. McGill, a Baltimorean who had emigrated to Liberia six years earlier and was then acting colonial agent for the society. The couple had five children, including an adopted son. Russwurm's tenure in the public affairs of Liberia was characterized by controversy over freedom of the press and his close links with unpopular colonial officials. The colonists wanted the *Herald* to be independently run, which it could not be, they believed, if the editor were a government employee. Russwurm was removed from his editorship and from other posts in 1835.

Of equal importance historically to his role in pioneering the American black press is Russwurm's fifteen-year career as the governor of Maryland in Liberia, a colony founded in 1834 at Cape Palmas, two hundred miles south of Monrovia, by the Maryland State Colonization Society. This organization was originally a state auxiliary of the American Colonization Society, but its leaders, disappointed by the disparate views among supporters from northern and southern states, by the slow pace of emigration, and by poor management in Monrovia, created a settlement of their own to which primarily freed Maryland blacks would emigrate. It was heavily subsidized by annual grants from the Maryland legislature. The first two governors of the colony, both whites, were overcome by ill health during their brief stays on the West African coast. The society's board of managers in Baltimore therefore concluded that it must appoint a nonwhite who was already acclimated to Africa and familiar with the governance of a settlement and who not only could survive but also develop in the colonists a sense of autonomy and an expectation of self-government.

Russwurm received his appointment in September 1836 and, proceeding immediately to Cape Palmas, found a small town called Harper, a few outlying farms, a mission of the American Board of Commissioners for Foreign Missions, and a population of about two hundred immigrants. Over the next ten years, the governor created a currency system, improved business procedures, and adopted a legal code. He attempted to smooth relations with neighboring African groups but, having mixed success, enlarged the militia and encouraged the American African Squadron, whose goal was the suppression of the slave trade, to visit along the coast as a display of support. He worked to stimulate agriculture, both by encouraging the colonists on their own farms and by the enlargement of the public farm on which he planted a nursery and experimented with various crops. He oversaw numerous public improvements and the addition of territory to the colony.

Russwurm's judicious application of the colony's constitution and ordinances, political preeminence over the often fractious settlers, and ability to govern well with decreasing supervision of the board in Baltimore coincided with a mounting demand among the colonists in the late 1840s that Maryland in Liberia either be granted independence or that it seek annexation to the newly created Republic of Liberia. The governor himself seems not to have taken a stand, possibly because of his disappointment with the current generation of colonists, whom he characterized as still too unenlightened to accomplish much. Furthermore, he was in poor health and suffered from ulcerations on his foot, which may have been related to gout. In spite of these factors and the sudden death of his adopted son, Russwurm continued to direct the colony, and even on the day of his own death, he attended to a portion of his official duties before succumbing to multiple ailments at the government house in Cape Palmas.

The citizens lauded Russwurm as statesman, philanthropist, and Christian. They named an island off Cape Palmas and a township after him. Back in Baltimore, members of the board recalled his visit to the United States in 1848, when he not only exhibited an excellent and courteous bearing but confirmed that he was an educated and accomplished gentleman. They spoke of his faithful service and how he had vindicated their belief in "the perfect fitness of his race for the most important political positions in Africa." They ordered the construction of a marble obelisk with suitable inscriptions over his grave at Cape Palmas. The board's high estimate was reinforced by his stepmother in a laudatory letter in which she characterized him as a literary man whose family and library were to him the world. By the time of Russwurm's death, the settlement numbered nearly a thousand inhabitants and owned a strip of coastline stretching northward more than a hundred miles.

Russwurm sometimes likened himself to Moses, leader of the Israelites, in trying to push his people ahead; indeed, under his administration a colony of former American slaves achieved a large degree of self-government. He proved capable of handling difficulties with settlers, with adjacent Africans, and with white missionaries. His physical and executive perseverance gave the settlement the benefit of stability until it could consider viable alternatives to its dependent relationship with the Maryland State Colonization Society. The survival of the colony, now known as Maryland County in the Republic of Liberia, is attributable principally to the success of Russwurm's governorship.

FURTHER READING
Bowdoin College in Brunswick, Maine, holds about nine hundred items, many of them of a secondary nature, in its special collections and also has copies of Russwurm material from the Tennessee State Library and Archives, Nashville. Smaller collections can be found at the Maryland Historical Society, in the American Colonization Society Papers at the Library of Congress, in the African Squadron Papers at the National Archives, and in the American Board of Commissioners for Foreign Missions Papers at Houghton Library, Harvard College.
Campbell, Penelope. *Maryland in Africa, the Maryland State Colonization Society, 1831–1857* (1971).
Hutton, Frankie. *The Early Black Press in America, 1827 to 1860* (1993).

This entry is taken from the *American National Biography* and is published here with the permission of the American Council of Learned Societies.
PENELOPE CAMPBELL

Rustin, Bayard Taylor (17 Mar. 1912–24 Aug. 1987), civil rights organizer and political activist, was born in West Chester, Pennsylvania, the son of Archie Hopkins and Florence "Cissy" Rustin. Hopkins abandoned his sixteen-year-old lover before their child was born, and it was not until Bayard was eleven that he discovered that Cissy was his mother, not his sister, and that his "parents" Janifer Rustin, a caterer, and Julia Rustin, a nurse, were, in fact, his grandparents. Throughout his life, Bayard Rustin referred to Janifer as "papa" and Julia as "mama" and enjoyed a more comfortable family life than his complicated origins might suggest.

Rustin attended the public schools of West Chester and displayed a precocious talent for dissent. In grade school he resisted teachers who tried to make him write with his right hand, and in high school he refused to compete in a state track meet unless he and a fellow black student could stay in the same hotel as their white teammates. In both cases he won. The teenage Rustin was less successful in his attempts to desegregate West Chester's movie theater, however, resulting in the first of nearly thirty arrests for civil disobedience. On graduating from high school in 1932, Rustin attended Wilberforce University in Ohio, though he spent barely a year there before being dismissed, either for refusing to join the ROTC or for falling in love with the son of the university's president. He then returned to West Chester to study at Cheyney State Teachers College and appeared as a tenor soloist on several radio shows in Philadelphia. He also became active in the Society of Friends, a move that pleased his grandmother, who had been raised in the society and remained a Quaker in spirit, even though she had joined the African Methodist Episcopal (AME) Church. After Cheyney State dismissed him in 1937 for an indiscretion that he later alluded to as "naughty," Rustin left for Manhattan (Anderson, 38). There he attended a few classes at the City College of New York but divided most of his time between social activism—serving as an organizer for the Young Communist League (YCL) in Harlem—and music. In 1939 he sang in the chorus of JOHN HENRY, an all-black musical starring PAUL ROBESON, and performed with the blues singer LEAD BELLY and the folk-song revivalist JOSH WHITE at the Café Society Downtown, an integrated nightclub in Greenwich Village. Although he sang at demonstrations—and in jails—throughout his career, Rustin increasingly focused on social and political organizing.

In 1941 he began working with the labor leader A. PHILIP RANDOLPH, who mentored Rustin on the tactics and strategies required of mass political organizing and persuaded him to abandon communism in favor of democratic socialism. Randolph also introduced Rustin to the writings of Mohandas K. Gandhi, the pacifist leader of the Indian resistance to British rule, and to A. J. Muste, who adhered to the Gandhian principle of achieving social change through nonviolent direct action and who led the Fellowship of Reconciliation (FOR), a pacifist organization. In 1942, after Muste appointed him the FOR's youth secretary, Rustin traveled throughout the nation in the hope of recruiting a cadre of pacifists and raising awareness of the plight of Japanese Americans placed in internment camps. Given the vast public sympathy for the war effort once Japan attacked Pearl Harbor in December 1941, that proved to be no mean task and often a dangerous one. In 1944 federal authorities imprisoned Rustin for refusing to appear before his military draft board.

On release from prison in 1947 Rustin joined the Congress on Racial Equality (CORE) in its Journey of Reconciliation, an attempt to end segregation in interstate travel by sitting in the front seats of buses designated by law and custom for whites only. The unwillingness of southern whites to countenance such a change became clear in Chapel Hill, North Carolina, when Rustin was dragged from the front of a Trailways bus by police and sentenced to thirty days on a chain gang. The failure of CORE's campaign did not shake Rustin's belief that nonviolent direct action could help destroy Jim Crow, however, and in the early 1950s he embarked on a series of lectures and workshops promoting civil disobedience in the United States, Europe, South Africa, and Ghana. Many in the international peace movement viewed Rustin as an inspirational speaker and expert tactician and expected that he might replace the aging Muste as head of the FOR.

Instead, in 1953, the FOR board demanded Rustin's resignation after his arrest in Los Angeles on a morals charge, the euphemism of the day

Bayard Rustin, civil rights leader, in his Park Avenue South office, New York City, April 1969. (AP Images.)

for performing homosexual acts in public. Rustin agreed to leave the organization immediately, reflecting both his inner conflict about his sexual orientation at that time and the prevailing homophobic mood of 1950s America. Even though he was unwilling to abandon his sexual preference, he agreed with Muste that his homosexuality was wrong and that his actions had diminished the FOR's moral standing.

Although the arrest chilled his friendship with Muste, Rustin's other mentor, A. Philip Randolph, stood by him, sending Rustin to Alabama in December 1955 to advise MARTIN LUTHER KING JR., the leader of the Montgomery bus boycott. Rustin counseled King on the theories and practicalities of nonviolent direct action and helped transform the young minister's narrowly defined boycott into a fully formed Gandhian mass movement. King later wrote of the Montgomery protest that "Christ furnished the spirit while Gandhi furnished the method" (quoted in Anderson, 188). He might have added that Rustin furnished the essential tactical knowledge, based on a lifetime of practicing nonviolent resistance. Along with ELLA BAKER, Rustin also founded In Friendship, a New York–based group, to raise northern awareness of, and money for, the Southern Christian Leadership Conference (SCLC), a regional civil rights body led by King, which Rustin had helped organize in 1957.

In March 1960 Rustin headed the Committee to Defend Martin Luther King, after the state of Alabama indicted the SCLC leader on trumped-up charges of tax evasion and perjury. Three months later, however, the congressman ADAM CLAYTON POWELL JR. threatened to announce publicly—and mendaciously—that King and Rustin were lovers; Powell was furious that Rustin had planned a demonstration at that summer's Democratic National Convention without consulting him. Even though he knew the charges were false, Rustin resigned as King's special assistant, to prevent a scandal he feared would jeopardize the movement at a critical juncture. Rustin later commented that King's refusal to support him or even to ask him personally to resign was "the only time Martin really pissed me off" (quoted in Levine, 121).

Exiled from the main leadership of the civil rights struggle, Rustin worked from 1961 to 1962 with the World Peace Brigade, an organization dedicated to the nonviolent overthrow of colonial rule in Africa. He returned a year later to an American civil rights struggle in which the Student Nonviolent Coordinating Committee (SNCC) had joined the SCLC and CORE in supporting nonviolent direct action to challenge segregation. Randolph, King, and Rustin believed that only a mass demonstration could build on those protests and persuade Congress to pass meaningful civil rights legislation, and Randolph insisted that his deputy should organize that mass protest. Building on a lifetime of working with civil rights, labor, and peace activists across the nation, Rustin orchestrated a broad, multicultural coalition of support for the March on Washington in August 1963. Most of the 250,000 marchers and the millions watching on television that day would remember King's "I have a dream" speech, but the overall success of the demonstration owed as much to Rustin's meticulous attention to detail as to King's stirring rhetoric.

The March on Washington served as a springboard for the 1964 Civil Rights Act and the 1965 Voting Rights Act, but it also marked the high point of unity in the civil rights movement. While younger members of SNCC and CORE began to embrace Black Power, Rustin argued that blacks, poor whites, and other disenfranchised Americans could win social justice only through the same broad-based coalitions that had ended segregation. His equivocal stance on the Vietnam War provoked even more fury from former allies like JULIAN BOND of SNCC, who believed that Rustin had sold his soul to President Lyndon Johnson and the Democratic Party. The reality was somewhat more complex. Rustin certainly wanted influence in the Democratic Party, and he feared that opposing Johnson's policies in Vietnam would jeopardize the president's domestic War on Poverty. But Rustin's support for a gradual, negotiated withdrawal of U.S. troops also reflected an evolution in his thinking about war and peace. He had begun to question his absolute pacifism after World War II, in part because of guilt about being a conscientious objector in a war that had resulted in the Holocaust. Like many former communists, he also despised the Soviet Union's repressive domestic and foreign policies and feared that a victory for the Vietcong would destroy any vestiges of democracy in South Vietnam.

Rustin's influence on international politics and the civil rights agenda waned in the 1970s and 1980s. He earned praise for his work to aid Haitian and Southeast Asian refugees, but was criticized for supporting increased U.S. economic and military aid to Israel, and for comparing the Palestine Liberation Organization to the Ku Klux Klan. On domestic matters Rustin gave qualified support to the affirmative action programs favored by most African Americans, but he continued to favor policies that would radically redistribute wealth to the poor of all races.

In his final decade Rustin became more open about his homosexuality, but he did not take an active role in the growing gay rights movement. He died in New York City in August 1987 after being hospitalized for a burst appendix and then suffering a heart attack in the hospital. He was survived by his partner of twelve years, Walter Naegle. Rustin's most enduring legacy is his stewardship of the 1963 March on Washington, a demonstration that reflected his own dream of a grand multiracial coalition working peacefully for social and economic justice.

FURTHER READING

Bayard Rustin's papers are housed at the A. Philip Randolph Institute in New York City and are also available on microfilm from the University Publications of America.

Rustin, Bayard. *Down the Line: The Collected Writings of Bayard Rustin* (1971).

Rustin, Bayard. *Strategies for Freedom: The Changing Patterns of Black Protest* (1976).

Anderson, Jervis. *Bayard Rustin: Troubles I've Seen* (1997).

D'Emilio, John. *Lost Prophet: The Life and Times of Bayard Rustin* (2003).

Levine, Daniel. *Bayard Rustin and the Civil Rights Movement* (2000).

Obituaries: *New York Times*, 25 Aug. 1987; *Jet* (7 Sept. 1987); *New Republic* (28 Sept. 1987).

STEVEN J. NIVEN

Ruth, William Chester (1882–1971), inventor of agricultural and other machinery, was born on his parents' farm in Ercildoun, Pennsylvania. His father, Samuel Ruth (1850–1937), was born a slave on the plantation of Robert Frederick Ruth in Beauford District, Saint Peter's Parish, South Carolina. Samuel Ruth came north after being swept up by the Fifty-fourth Massachusetts Infantry as a thirteen-year-old and subsequently served as a water boy and then as a personal servant to First Sergeant Stephen A. Swails, later an important figure in the South during Reconstruction. In 1865 Samuel traveled north with two army friends from the Fifty-fourth and the same year married Maria "Louisa" Pinn, the sister of one of his friends and the daughter of the Baptist minister, attorney, and war veteran Robert Andrew Pinn. The young newlyweds followed other Fifty-fourth veterans to settle in the Pennsylvania Quaker area near the town of Chatham. Following inspiration from Church of Christ revival meetings, the Ruths proselytized in the nearby town of Ercildoun, where local Quakers in 1868 allowed them to use their Abolition Hall for indoor services for the African American congregation that the Ruths had gathered.

William Chester Ruth was the ninth of twelve children born to the Ruths between 1870 and 1895 (two died in infancy). During this period his parents acquired enough money by working—threshing, leather tanning, and local domestic work—to acquire first a small and then a larger farm. In 1894 the Ruths conveyed land from their farm on which to build a small meetinghouse, the Church of Christ, Ercildoun, where Samuel Ruth served as preacher. Their children, including "Chester," as he was known in the family, helped to hand-carry the stones for the foundation.

As a boy Chester Ruth displayed a special aptitude for mechanical problem solving. Though bright, he often came in conflict with his father for taking apart toys and experimenting with devices around the farm. He needed to understand how mechanical things worked, and he took the most direct route to this knowledge, usually by disassembling any mechanical objects at hand. Time and again young Ruth found himself struggling to reassemble gadgets before his father could encounter the useless disassembled pieces, though he sometimes did not succeed. Samuel punished his son on a number of occasions for not keeping his curiosity in check.

An event characteristic of Ruth's boyhood development was his attempt to modify a bicycle pump for use as a wagon jack, and the pump was then ejected by the pressure of the wagon and struck him on the head. As he matured, however, Ruth's innate mechanical interests and determination prevailed. In 1894, at the age of twelve, he began to learn blacksmith skills. Acquainted with the rigors of labor on his parents' farm, in 1923 he opened his own blacksmith shop near the town of Gap, in neighboring Lancaster County. Ruth's skills as a farrier and general blacksmith were in demand among Lancaster County's Pennsylvania German Amish and Mennonite farmers. Teaching himself machinist's skills, he began to attack some of the difficulties of mechanized harvesting.

As the son of a thresherman and metalsmith to a farm community, Ruth focused particularly on the difficulty of feeding straw from the steam-engine-driven thresher into the bale press. Starting in the mid-1920s he designed a device with whirling tines, seated upon a turntable, that could be installed atop a bale press. He applied for a patent, which he was granted in 1928 on his perfected design of the "Ruth Feeder." It was the first, and ultimately the most profitable, of several patents he received in the 1920s and early 1930s. It enabled him to hire several assistants, expand his blacksmith shop into a machine shop (still extant) for building and installing baler feeders, and parlay his lifelong mechanical skills into a successful business.

Ruth's egalitarian principals kept him working side by side in overalls and shirtsleeves with the assistants in his shop, though demand for his feeder sometimes took him to other parts of the country. During the decades from the Great Depression to post–World War II, Ruth carried on a highly successful business by manufacturing various agricultural machines. In 1950 *Ebony* magazine featured him in the article "Inventor Businessman." He also proved heir to his father's spiritual leadership in the small Church of Christ meetinghouse in Ercildoun. In 1914, at the age of thirty-two, he began to preach to the small congregation in Ercildoun, founded by his father and mother. Working in Gap and continuing to live in Ercildoun, Ruth still led that congregation in his seventieth year. In 1971 he died at age eighty-eight when he was struck by an automobile near his shop.

FURTHER READING

Blatt, Martin H., Thomas J. Brown, and Donald Yacovone, eds. *Hope and Glory: Essays on the Legacy of the Fifty-fourth Massachusetts Regiment* (2001).

"Inventor Businessman," *Ebony* (Oct. 1950).

Williams, Ida Jones. *Great-Grandmother Leah's Legacy* (2000).

BRUCE D. BOMBERGER

Saar, Alison (5 Feb. 1956–), sculptor and multimedia artist, was born in Los Angeles to Betye and Richard Saar. Alison Saar's education and early artistic exploration were influenced by her richly multicultural background; her mother's ancestry included European, Native American, and African American heritage, while her father was of German and Scottish origin. One of three daughters, Alison Saar was raised in Laurel Canyon, where her parents encouraged her artistic development by taking her to area museums and to noninstitutional works of art, such as Simon Rodia's Watts Towers in south Los Angeles and Grandma Prisbrey's Bottle Village in Simi Valley. BETYE SAAR was an active artist who exposed her daughters to printmaking and collage processes, as well as to her belief in the spiritual power of objects. Her father, a conservator and artist, introduced Alison to the composition and aesthetics of the non-Western art he handled through his work.

After high school, Saar attended Scripps College in Claremont, California, where she studied African and Caribbean art with the artist and art historian SAMELLA LEWIS. She wrote her senior thesis on African American folk art in the southern United States and graduated in 1978 with a bachelor of arts degree. She continued her education at the Otis College of Art and Design in Los Angeles, earning a master of fine arts degree in studio art in 1981. Formal education grounded Saar in the artistic traditions of Africa, Haiti, the Caribbean, and Mexico. These years also allowed her to develop further a creative affinity with the influences of her childhood: African American folk art and the spiritual power of found and ritual objects.

Saar moved to New York in 1982 and held an artist's residency at the Studio Museum in Harlem in 1983. Her largely figurative sculptures are made of wood, metal, glass, paint, and a variety of found objects. Both male and female figures are usually clothed and often include small hinged doors that open to reveal the inside of a head, heart, or abdomen and the secrets contained therein. Saar also began using recycled ceiling tiles as metal skin for her figures, finding resonance between the decorative patterns and scarification. New York City's social issues of the 1980s, among them poverty and homelessness, are interpreted in Saar's work of this decade, alongside her continuing engagement with race and individual subjectivity.

The 1988 installation *Love Potion No. 9* demonstrates many of Saar's artistic concerns during this era. The focal point of the installation is the large, standing figure of a woman. Entitled *Love Zombie: A Potent Hex That Robs 'Em of All Sense*, the woman is carved from wood and covered with sheets of tin and copper. She is barefoot, wearing a red dress, and her skin has the green patina of aged metal. With one hand she gestures to her breast, which is hinged to her body and open. Behind the breast is a hole, and the woman's chest cavity houses a mysterious wrapped object that is punctured by nails.

Though her voluptuous body and the mysteries it contains beckon the viewer, *Love Zombie* deflects any possibility that the viewer might understand her internal experiences. Her eyes are directed upward, but missing pupils suggest that her thoughts and gaze are focused internally. Her ears are plated over with metal; she can hear only her own thoughts. Both the figure and the wrapped object in her chest allude to *minkisi*, power figures made by the Kongo people of central Africa. The title refers to New Orleans's African and Afro-Caribbean culture and the commercialization of Vodun. It is the obsessive power of love that has acted like a hex and rendered the woman a zombie: her eyes are unseeing, while metal hardens her skin and covers her ears, effectively robbing her of all sense. Finally, the figure is about breasts as internal, private, and capable of holding secrets rather than as external, public, sexualized objects.

In the 1990s Saar moved toward the near-exclusive representation of women, and often of nonwhite female nudes. Hair became an increasingly important metaphor, often mediating between the objects and expectations of daily life and the dream life of the subject. In the middle and late 1990s she created a series of sculptures that addressed the overlapping spheres of work and social convention. *Ho* (1995), *Pitch* (1995), *Sledgehammer Mama* (1996), and *Clean Sweep* (1997) all fuse a nonwhite, nude woman's body with a tool of hard or domestic labor—the hoe, the pitchfork, the sledgehammer, the broom—to comment on women's strength and endurance. These qualities, Saar pointed out, are often conflated, associating functional and objectifying notions with the female body in a patriarchal social system.

In the late 1990s Saar also began her *Skillet* series, an ongoing project in which the faces of black women were painted on the backs of used, cast-iron skillets. Made of found and recycled objects, the *Skillet* series comments on the invisibility of the black, female domestic worker by associating her portrait with both the tools of her profession and her metaphorically powerful—yet unacknowledged—role in the white household.

In 1995 Saar returned to Laurel Canyon, where she lived with her husband and two children. She had married Tom Leeser in 1985. In addition to working from her home studio and teaching international art to elementary schoolchildren, Saar maintained an active exhibition schedule. She said that being a mother made the female figure more central in her work; such focus is evident in her later work, such as *Afro-di(e)ty*.

In this installation, created for the J. Paul Getty Museum in Los Angeles in 2000, the central sculpture is a large female nude, inspired by Yemaya, the Yoruba goddess of the sea, and the Getty's marble statue *Lansdowne Herakles* (c. 125 CE). There is a mirror embedded in the woman's stomach, and she holds another mirror and a towel in her hands as she stands in a small, metal tub of water. Surrounded by piles of salt and basins of water, the figure references multiple African cultural traditions and religious practices.

Saar created the piece in response to the lack of female figures in the Getty's collection, and she endowed *Afro-di(e)ty's* figure with the male nude's powerful pose in the *Lansdowne Herakles*. With the title *Afro-di(e)ty*, Saar puns on the name of the Greek goddess Aphrodite, an often-represented subject of idealized beauty in Western art. In Saar's postmodern vision, beauty and strength are visualized in an African form and through the symbols of African diasporic cultures.

Saar's oeuvre demonstrates a sustained engagement with the bodies and psyches of nonwhite subjects. The tension between physical exterior and psychological interior serves as muse, while Saar's sculptures negotiate dreams and desires within a social reality that is often overdetermined by political histories of slavery, colonialism, and racism: "I think of all my sculptures as self-portraits, although they never look like me. They are all invented figures. But … they are all, in some way, about being left out, about being outsiders" (Lyons, 49).

Her work, however, is also about bringing outsiders in—into the gallery and into the viewer's imaginative landscape.

FURTHER READING

Lyons, Lisa. *Departures: 11 Artists at the Getty* (2000).
Roberts, Mary Nooter, and Alison Saar. *Body Politics: The Female Image in Luba Art and the Sculpture of Alison Saar* (2000).

REBECCA PEABODY

Saar, Betye (30 July 1926–), artist and educator, was born Betye Irene Brown in Pasadena, California, to Beatrice (maiden name unknown), a seamstress who enjoyed quilting, and Jefferson Brown, a salesman who liked to sketch and write. Jefferson Brown died from kidney problems when Saar was six years old, and Betye and her brother and sister lived with her mother's great-aunt and great-uncle until her mother remarried a man named Emmett six years later. After the second marriage, Beatrice had two more children, a boy and a girl. Saar spent summers with her grandmother in Watts, where she saw Simon Rodia's *Watts Towers*, a vernacular example of assemblage consisting of eight tall conical spirals. Built from steel rods, covered in concrete, and encrusted with found objects like bottle caps, glass, broken tiles, and shells, the *Watts Towers* seemed like "fairy-tale castles" (Isenberg, *State of the Arts*, 23) to Saar and became an important early influence on the artist. As a child, Saar enjoyed drawing and working with crafts, puppetry, and clay, and she often played in her grandmother's garden and at the beach, digging up small beads, shells, and stones that she saved in her collection. Saar received her B.A. in design from the University of California, Los Angeles in 1949, and in 1952 she married another artist, Richard Saar. The couple had three daughters—Lezley and ALISON SAAR (who became artists) and Tracye. Like many female artists during the 1950s and 1960s, Saar worked at home while she raised her children. She turned her kitchen into a printmaking studio and also worked as a designer and jewelry maker. In 1956 she began graduate work in education and printmaking at the University of Southern California and the California State universities at Long Beach and Northridge. In 1968 Saar and her husband divorced. That year she saw an exhibition of the American surrealist Joseph Cornell; his boxes made of found objects appeared like intimate, mysterious worlds and gave her the idea to use boxes to create art.

By this time Saar had already used windows as the armature for numerous prints and drawings, such as *Sorcerer's Window* (1966) and *Black Girl's Window* (1969), the latter an autobiographical work depicting a young black girl peering through and pressed up against a closed window. Into the various panes Saar incorporated objects like tarot cards, zodiac signs, and fetishes that suggest an interest in mysticism and spirituality. Like many African American artists at this time, Saar began thinking more deeply about her personal connection to African history and religion, and some of her works, such as *Nine Mojo Secrets* (1971) and *Spirit Catcher* (1976–1977), suggest this fascination. On a trip to Chicago, Saar visited the Field Museum and made sketches based on works in its collection of Oceanic, Egyptian, and African art.

In the late 1960s and early 1970s, against the backdrop of the civil rights movement, the black power movement, and the burgeoning women's art movement, Saar began collecting popular racist images that stereotyped African Americans. In her words, "I felt these images were important as documentation of how whites have historically perceived African Americans and how we have been portrayed as caricatures, as objects, as less-than-human. ... I began to recycle and transform Sambos, Toms, and Mammies in my assemblages" (Michael Rosenfeld Gallery, 3).

In 1972 Saar created what has become her most famous work, *The Liberation of Aunt Jemima*, which transformed a demeaning collectable Mammy figurine into a powerful, confrontational revolutionary, part feminist and part black power icon. The work not only suggests her allegiance to Cornell but also demonstrates her understanding of contemporary art movements like pop. Against the background of the box are serial repetitions of Aunt Jemima as she appeared on the General Mills pancake boxes. Instead of a grid of apolitical Campell's soup cans, such as the ones Andy Warhol produced, Saar appropriated an image circulated in the mass media that reinforces stereotypes about African American women. Using a deconstructive strategy, Saar adopted these racist images and deployed them in a new context as a way to critique them.

During the 1970s Saar also created a series of nostalgic assemblages using turn-of-the-century photographs and pieces of personal clothing and jewelry. Saar found photographs of unknown African Americans in secondhand stores, flea markets, and yard sales and combined them with various objects to construct stories about anonymous people overlooked by history. One work, *Record for Hattie* (1976), however, is biographical and represents her beloved great-aunt through the use of personal memorabilia, including a pearl necklace, a hand mirror, a small cross, a dried rose, a pincushion, a baby picture, and a childhood autograph book. Using objects Saar acquired after Hattie's death in 1974, at age ninety-eight, *Record for Hattie* relies on associative play that allows the viewer to move from detail to detail to conjure a sense of who this woman once was.

During the 1970s, in addition to galleries, Saar began to exhibit in museums more frequently, garnering increasing critical acclaim. In 1973 she had a solo exhibition at the California State University, and in 1975 the Whitney Museum of American Art in New York City hosted a one-person show of Saar's work. At a time when artists in the Art Workers' Coalition and other related groups were protesting the scarcity of women and minorities in the Whitney's permanent collection and special exhibitions, this retrospective demonstrated the importance of Saar's work. Additional shows followed in 1976 in Hartford, Connecticut, at the Wadsworth Atheneum, in 1977 at the San Francisco

Museum of Modern Art, and in 1980 at the Studio Museum of Harlem in New York.

Like many artists during the 1980s, Saar began to build on the environmental implications of assemblage, extending her works into large-scale installations that often filled entire rooms. In 1987 she worked as artist-in-residence at the Massachusetts Institute of Technology. There she exhibited her newest altar-like work, *Mojotech*, a piece that investigates the interrelationships between science and magic through a horizontal series of altars that gives the impression of a miniature city rising into a mist filled with small objects, or mojos.

During the 1990s Saar returned to political art in response to what she saw as a troublesome resurgence of racism. In 1998 she received a traveling exhibition, her first solo show at the Michael Rosenfeld Gallery in New York, titled *Workers+Warriors, the Return of Aunt Jemima*. In this new series dealing with African American women's roles as domestic workers, Saar used antique washboards, creating pieces such as *Dubl-Duty-I'se Back Wid a Vengeance* (1997) and *Call to Arms* (1997) that resuscitate the stereotypical Mammy imagery that Saar first appropriated in the early 1970s. While working on this series, Saar began to gather tin signs, postcards, advertisements, household objects, and other commercial materials containing racist imagery from flea markets in New York. Reconfiguring these objects in new ways, she created a series that was shown in 2000 at her second exhibition at the Michael Rosenfeld Gallery, *Betye Saar: In Service: A Version of Survival*. The works in this show emphasized the roles, such as butlers, cooks, shoe-shine boys, entertainers, and porters, that African Americans played in the service industry during Reconstruction and after emancipation from slavery. In 2002 Saar presented her third show at the Rosenfeld Gallery, *Betye Saar: Colored: Consider the Rainbow*. In this series she investigated the ways in which African Americans have judged one another based on the color of their skin, dating back to slave-plantation culture. In celebration of her eightieth birthday, in 2006 the Pennsylvania Academy of the Fine Arts in Philadelphia organized a traveling retrospective titled *Betye Saar: Extending the Frozen Moment*. In the same year, the Rosenfeld Gallery exhibited *Migrations/Transformations*, Saar's reflection on ancestral narratives. Saar aimed to portray ancient life in Africa, the African diaspora, and the transition from slavery to freedom by integrating previous themes of her work.

Saar has often been lauded for her work and especially for integrating into it many issues of concern to feminists and African Americans. Among her numerous awards, she has received five honorary doctorates, honors from the National Endowment for the Arts and the John Simon Guggenheim Memorial Foundation, and a fellowship from the J. Paul Getty Fund for the Visual Arts. Over the course of her career she has participated in more than fifty solo exhibitions and many group exhibitions. Her work is represented in more than thirty major museum collections throughout the United States.

FURTHER READING

Saar, Betye. *Extending the Frozen Moment* (2005).

Isenberg, Barbara. *State of the Arts: California Artists Talk about Their Work* (2000).

Michael Rosenfeld Gallery. *Betye Saar: Workers+Warriors, the Return of Aunt Jemima* (1998).

Nemser, Cindy. *Art Talk: Conversations with 15 Women Artists* (1995).

Wright Gallery, University of California, Los Angeles. *Secrets, Dialogues, Revelations: The Art of Betye and Alison Saar* (1990).

LISA D. FREIMAN

Saddler, Joseph. *See* Grandmaster Flash (Joseph Saddler).

Said, Umar ibn (c. 1770–1863), Islamic slave and autobiographer, was African born and also known as Omar, Uncle Moro, and Moreau. The son of moderately wealthy parents in Futa Toro (northeastern Senegal), whom he honored in several of his American writings, he may have been related, at some remove, to some of the other Fulbe or Fulani caught up in the Atlantic slave trade, such as Job Ben Solomon, IBRAHIMA ABD AL-RAHMAN, BILALI, SALIH BILALI, and Charno (a literate Fula enslaved in South Carolina). All were steadfast adherents to Islam. According to Said's own statements, he was educated for some twenty years by Fulani instructors, became a teacher himself, and while in Futa Toro closely followed the tenets of his religion. He never mentioned having a wife or children.

Said did write that an unidentified African army he belonged to was defeated by an infidel, non-Muslim enemy. It is likely that he was captured in one of the battles that Imam Abd al-Qadir lost to the non-Muslim Bambarras in eastern Senegal in 1807. He was sent to the Atlantic coast probably via the Gambia River, and sold to Christians. He survived a six-week passage across what he called the "great sea" and arrived in Charleston, South Carolina, just before the end of the international slave trade in 1808. In Charleston, Said was purchased by a fair owner who soon died and then was sold to a cruel and unreligious man from whom he fled. A month's wanderings brought him to Fayetteville, North Carolina, where he was jailed. Somehow Said avoided being sold and returned to Charleston. His frail appearance, spiritual manners, attempts to pray, and Arabic writing attracted the attention of two local citizens, John and James Owen. The latter purchased Said and treated him respectfully, even tenderly, for the remainder of his days. He was allowed, perhaps encouraged, to maintain his inoffensive Muslim ways and—according to two known ambrotype portraits—his West African Muslim dress. It can be assumed that he also adhered to his dietary codes. In an introductory note to one of Said's earliest writings, Owen revealed that people read an English translation of the Koran to Said and that he had expressed some interest in reading the Christian Bible. Several sources stated that Said enjoyed accompanying his white purchaser to Presbyterian meetings in Fayetteville and Wilmington; in 1821 his name was entered in the records of both churches.

Many inquisitive visitors met Said and attempted to discover his geographical origins and literacy, and his status as a Muslim or a possible Christian convert after witnessing his visibly heartfelt prayers, spirituality, and obvious intelligence. Although a few recognized that he was African and that his literacy was gained there, most could not accept the idea of African literacy and concluded that he must have been a Moor or an Arab somehow lost in Africa. His Christian interviewers wanted him to convert and became convinced that he had when they heard him recite the Lord's Prayer and talk of Jesus of Nazareth as the Messiah. Whether he was quoted fully or accurately cannot be known, but they were undoubtedly unaware that Jesus was respected as a prophet by all Muslims. The Koran, however, would not have referred to him as the son of God—a blasphemous notion to Muslims. Beyond what hopeful whites heard, however, are Said's extant writings. His 1819 manuscript, with its quotations from the Koran (Surah, 67) and hadith in Arabic and sections probably in Pullo, his own language, does not offer even a hint of conversion. Rather, it asserts his faith and some hope that his purchaser might be a good Muslim and maintains that Allah alone can claim sovereignty over human beings.

After 1821, however, when Said received a Bible in Arabic, he pleased ministers with his transcriptions of two biblical excerpts, the Lord's Prayer and the Twenty-third Psalm, in Arabic. Neither offers evidence of a conversion to Christianity nor includes statements that would be disagreeable to a Muslim. The earliest known copy of the Lord's Prayer (with an 1828 date on the reverse) is preceded by "This is how you pray, you" (Austin, 1997, 137, fig. 25). Further, all but one extant version of these two texts is surrounded by conventional Muslim formulae. A second copy is preceded by an invocation of Allah and his Prophet Muhammad and followed by Said's often repeated prayer for his mother's peace. An 1855 copy of the Twenty-third Psalm is also preceded by the same invocation—revealing, as a later translator declared, "a little weakness for Mohammed" (Austin, 1997, 144). Another version of the psalm followed the ritual "All good is from Allah, and no other" (Austin, 1997, 144, Fig. 32). Yet another invocation is extended by a line translated as "You recognize as a servant and son [of God?] Jesus" (Austin, 1997, 144, fig. 33).

Two other manuscripts were labeled by unknown hands as Christian prayers but are actually lists of Owen family members. Finally, from an inventory of some Said manuscripts, one item dated 1857 is called the "Lord's Prayer" but is actually Surah 110, one of the last chapters recorded in the Koran. It asks for Allah's help and forgiveness. Said's last minister, Mathew Grier, believed that Said had converted, but perhaps he actually hedged when he wrote, "by all outward signs, [Omar seemed to be a] sincere believer in Jesus Christ" (Austin, 1997, 135).

In 1834 or 1835 Said sent an autobiographical manuscript dated 1831 to Lamine Kebe, whom he had been told was then in New York City. This "Life" was accompanied by letters from Said that a contemporary translator read as an attempt to convert Kebe to Christianity. None of the originals of these letters nor Kebe's responses have been found. Yet Ralph R. Gurley, secretary of the American Colonizationist Society, and several ministers decided both men had become converts. Kebe, however, returned to Africa in 1835 a faithful Muslim. Before he left the United States, Kebe gave Said's manuscript to his own amanuensis, the ethnologist Theodore Dwight Jr., who had it translated and partially published in 1864. The original manuscript remained lost until 1995.

Said's 1831 "Life" begins with the Fatiha, the first chapter of the Koran, followed by the long Surah 67 (found also in Umar's 1819 MS). The chapter asserts the necessity of right thinking about the power, creation, and true prophet of God—and recognizing that power over all creation. It names neither Jesus nor Muhammad. Conventional apologies for his weak writing skills follow, then Said turns to the task at hand. As all Muslims do, he proceeds with the Bismillah: "In the name of Allah or God, ..." Said relates some information about his teachers and activities in Africa, his capture, ocean passage, slavery, and near redemption by James Owen: "What food they eat they give me to eat" (Austin, 1997, 152).

He went on to say that in Africa he had enjoyed reading the Koran, in America he had liked hearing an English version, and he now enjoys reading the "gospel of God, our Lord, and Saviour, and King ... who regulates all our circumstances, our health and wealth, and who bestows his mercies willingly, not by constraint" (Austin, 1997, 152). The references to Jesus are formulaic Christian while Said's description of the deity is formulaic Muslim. While such a statement might appear to reinforce assumptions about his conversion, Said's description of the deity is more Muslim or Koranic than Christian. After a line break, he declares that in Africa he had properly followed the obligatory Muslim Five Pillars and adds notes about his African family and his adopted Americans.

Said then writes the Fatiha and the Lord's Prayer before concluding with two paragraphs praising Owen's goodness to him. Indeed, according to all reports, Owen's family treated Said very well and required little from him. He seems to have died a natural death.

While legitimate questions remain over the nature of Said's religiosity, the preponderance of the evidence clearly points toward Said's continued adherence to his Muslim faith. More important, however, is what the continuing controversy over his faith says about nineteenth and twenty-first century Americans.

FURTHER READING

Alryyes, Ala. "'And in a Christian Language, They Sold Me': Messages Concealed in a Slave's Arabic Language Autobiographical Narrative," in *American Babel: Literatures of the United States from Abnaki to Zuni*, ed. Marc Shell (2002).

Austin, Allan D. *African Muslims in Antebellum America: A Sourcebook* (1984).

Austin, Allan D. *African Muslims in Antebellum America: Transatlantic Stories and Spiritual Struggles* (1997).

"Autobiography of Omar ibn Said, Slave in North Carolina, 1831," *American Historical Review* 30 (July 1925).

Hunwick, John, "'I Wish to be Seen in Our Land Called Afrika': Umar B. Sayyid's Appeal to be Released from Slavery (1819)," *Journal of Arabic and Islamic Studies* 5 (2003).

ALLAN D. AUSTIN

Salem, Peter (c. 1750–16 Aug. 1816), slave, patriot, and soldier, was born in Framingham, Massachusetts. Jeremiah Belknap owned Salem for the first twenty-five years of Salem's life. Before the outbreak of hostilities between the American colonies and Great Britain, Belknap sold Salem to Major Lawson Buckminster. The War of Independence offered African Americans an opportunity to exploit several roads to freedom. Some hoped to escape to British lines, while others simply ran off into the interior of the colonies to form alliances with Native Americans. Still others, such as Salem, used the War of Independence to obtain freedom. At the beginning of the war, Salem negotiated his own freedom in return for service in the Continental army.

During the first stages of the war, Salem served under the command of Captain Simon Edgell at Concord in April 1775. After this engagement Salem enlisted in Colonel Thomas Nixon's Fifth Massachusetts Regiment. In addition to his duties as a soldier, Salem also served as Colonel Nixon's body servant. On 17 June 1775 Nixon's regiment fought the British at Bunker Hill. During this battle Salem probably fired the shot that killed the British major John Pitcairn. Shortly after this engagement, in July 1775, George Washington banned African Americans from military service. Washington reversed this order after Virginia's Loyalist governor Lord Dunmore encouraged slaves owned by patriots to flee their masters and join the British forces. Some regiments from the New England states included both black and Native American men. Salem reenlisted in early 1776 and fought at the battles of Saratoga (1777) and Stony Point (1779). He continued his service until the conclusion of the war. In each of these engagements Salem acquitted himself well.

After the war Salem returned to Framingham and married Katy Benson in 1783. Salem remained in Framingham to try his hand at various occupations before moving to a small cabin near the town of Leicester, Massachusetts. There he worked in his garden and attempted to grow vegetables and herbs. Small-scale agricultural production did not provide him with subsistence, so he also earned a livelihood by making baskets, chairs, and canes. Despite his difficult financial situation, Salem was a popular figure in the town because of his military service. In his old age he returned to Framingham, where the local poorhouse cared for him until his death.

FURTHER READING

Documents relating to Salem are in the Massachusetts State Archives, and the Framingham Historical Society has important local histories that touch on his life.

Berlin, Ira, and Ronald Hoffman, eds. *Slavery and Freedom in the Age of the American Revolution* (1983).

Quarles, Benjamin. *The Negro in the American Revolution* (1961; rpt. 1973).

Temple, J. H. *History of Framingham, Massachusetts, Early Known as Danforth's Farms, 1640–1880* (1887).

HARVEY AMANI WHITFIELD

Salih Bilali (c. 1765–c. 1855), Muslim plantation manager on St. Simons Island, Georgia, was called Tom by his master. His history, including details from his earlier life in Africa, was published by America's first student of African—including Arabic—languages, the Georgia linguist William Brown Hodgson. Hodgson prevailed upon Salih Bilali's second master, the prominent James H. Couper, to write him a personal letter about Salih Bilali in 1838. Six years later, disappointed that the master would not grant him a personal interview with Salih Bilali, Hodgson published the letter under the title *Notes on Northern Africa, The Sahara and Soudan* (1844).

In the letter Couper summarized what Salih Bilali had told him about his African life and homeland of Massina (later Mali), then contested by the powerful Bambaras, a branch of Manding people, and his immigrant Fulbe—there called Fulani. Massina was agriculturally valuable as it lay in the productive Niger delta not far from famed Jenne, one thousand miles east of his future American friend BILALI's village of Timbo. His descriptions of Massina precede the area's becoming a Fula Muslim nation. They also precede the intrusion of any Europeans before the Scottish explorer Mungo Park famously reached the Niger in 1796. Salih

Bilali was vividly impressed by his homeland's commerce, of seeing "forty boat convoys" on the river. Salih Bilali remembered that these carried traders of salt, cotton and cotton cloths, guns, rice and other grains, gourds, okra, tomatoes, figs, indigo, horses and other animals, and kola nuts. They also traded slaves, but Salih Bilali left this item off his list.

Salih Bilali was only fourteen or fifteen when he was kidnapped by Bambarans from near his prosperous family and home and was marched at least five hundred miles to the coastal port of Anomabu, in what is now Ghana. Obviously observant, he described some of the local people on his way: their religion or lack of it, houses, mosques, manners, farming pursuits, clothes, hair, and languages. By then he had become used to hardships over which he had no control, but he could not have anticipated his upcoming sea voyage and New World slavery.

In America, Couper described Salih Bilali as being tall, thin, small-featured, with lips and nose less protruding and flat "than is usual with the negro race." A few paragraphs earlier, Couper noted that his hair was "brownish black" and "woolly." Couper's letter concluded with a list of Salih Bilali's mostly Fula (Fulfulde or Pular) words and numbers.

But these biographical details, so unusually extended from a slaveholder, were preceded by even more unusual appreciations. The letter begins with Couper's assertion that there were at least a dozen "negroes" on the plantation who spoke Fula. He does not say they were also Muslims, though this is likely, as later slave reminiscences make clear. He then launches into his encomium on "Tom, whose African name was Sali-bul Ali." He praises his "industry, intelligence, and honesty," which advanced him from laborer status in 1816 to "head driver" (a position he maintained until 1846). He headed "a gang of about four hundred and fifty negroes, which number, he has shown himself fully competent to manage with advantage. I have several times left him for months, in charge of the plantation, without an overseer; and on each occasion, he has conducted the place to my entire satisfaction."

Continuing, Couper waxed eloquent: "He has quickness of apprehension, strong powers of combination and calculation, a sound judgment, a singularly tenacious memory, and what is more rare in a slave, the faculty of forethought. He possesses great veracity and honesty. He is a strict Mahometan; abstains from spirituous liquors, and keeps the various fasts." Omitting Salih Bilali's religion, Couper was identifying traits he admired in any man, including managing with advantage—presumably toward efficiency and profit.

The early age at which Salih Bilali was taken away explains why, as Couper wrote, he was able to read but not write Arabic. It does not tell what the presumably powerful African influences were that made him the ardent Muslim and leader that he was recognized as being in Georgia. In a personal letter to his grandchildren, Couper's son, James Maxwell Couper, called Salih Bilali "the most religious man that he had ever known." Further, he reported that on his deathbed the man proclaimed: "Allah is God and Mohammed his prophet" the fundamental Muslim belief (copy of letter from Mary J. Thiesen, another descendant, 1981).

The memory of Salih Bilali has been overshadowed by that of his longtime Georgia neighbor and friend, BILALI. Much has been written about the latter's impressive adherence to his native religion, his Arabic manuscript, and his descendants' remembrances of his heritage on Sapelo Island. Perhaps Salih Bilali's name offers a clue reflecting a rigorous African training that may have been continued under Bilali. Their shared name reflects the popularity in West Africa of the story of the Prophet Muhammad's first *muezzin*, or singer of the call to prayer, a freed black African slave and the second man to become a believer or servant of Allah named Bilali.

Some southeastern seaboard travelers had heard, vaguely, about Salih Bilali, but even in 1829, when the Florida slave trader Zephaniah Kingsley first referred to him he seems to have been confused with Bilali. Kingsley conflated the two plantation managers as remarkable Muslim saviors of their island slave charges in 1815 and 1824. In those latter days of the War of 1812, around two hundred slaves ran off from St. Simons Island with the British. While other plantations lost hundreds of slaves, Salih Bilali and Bilali saved all theirs by forcing them into buildings made of tabby—lime, cement, and oyster shells, similar to buildings in West Africa—capable of withstanding hurricane winds. By 1830, Salih Bilali's first purchaser, John Couper, had increased his holdings and slaves on and near St. Simons from a handful purchased in the Bahamas after 1800 to more than one hundred. John Couper's son, James Hamilton Couper, soon enlarged the family's holdings even further.

The elder Couper's Cannon's Point plantation and the younger Couper's Hopeton plantation, familiar sites to Salih Bilali, would be visited and admired by some of the well-known travelers who visited Bilali's Sapelo Island plantation. These included Aaron Burr in 1804; the Royal Navy's Basil Hall and his wife, Margaret Hall, both writers, in 1828; John D. Legare, the editor of the *Southern Agriculturist*, in 1833; Fanny Kemble Butler, the British actress and wife of a nearby slaveholder, in the mid-1830s; the British geologist and slave apologist Charles Lyell, who included relatively confused notes on slave drivers after meeting "Tom" and lesser taskmasters in 1842; the Swedish novelist Fredrika Bremer in 1851; and the British courtier Amelia Murray in 1855. A letter from Couper to Hodgson claimed that Salih Bilali had fallen into "a second childhood" in 1857—the last year of available information. Despite the declared interest of these writers in the slaves, or because of James Couper's reluctance to let visitors meet with them personally, nothing more was written about Salih Bilali by contemporaries besides Lyell's short note on slave drivers generally.

In the late 1930s interviewers of former slaves on St. Simons Island heard about Salih Bilali's Muslim ways, of a son named Bilali, and about other Muslims, especially women (as was true on Sapelo Island), who strove to pray at least three times a day facing the east and reciting Arabic formulas. St. Simons's black islanders have been increasingly pushed out to make room for the ever-growing crowds of vacationers, and so the islanders' proud, accomplished, ancestor, Salih Bilali, and his religion have almost been forgotten and left unstudied by both antebellum Georgia island histories and by modern black Muslim movements.

FURTHER READING

Austin, Allan D. *African Muslims in Antebellum America: A Sourcebook* (1984).

Austin, Allan D. *African Muslims in Antebellum America: Transatlantic Stories and Spiritual Struggles* (1997).

Bagwell, James. *Rice Gold: James Hamilton Couper and Plantation Life on the Georgia Coast* (2000).

Bailey, Cornelia, with Christena Bledsoe. *God, Dr. Buzzard, and the Bolito Man: A Saltwater Geechee Talks About Life on Sapelo Island* (2000).

Ferguson, T. Reed. *The John Couper Family at Cannon's Point* (1994).

Hodgson, William Brown. *Notes on Northern Africa, the Sahara, and the Soudan* (1844).

Savannah Unit of the Georgia Writers' Project of the Works Projects Administration. *Drums and*

Shadows: Survival Studies among the Georgia Coastal Negroes, 1940 (1986).

Wilks, Ivor. "Salih Bilali of Massina," in *Africa Remembered: Narratives by West Africans from the Era of the Slave Trade*, ed. Philip D. Curtin (1967).

ALLAN D. AUSTIN

Sampson (?–?), coastal pilot during the American Revolution, was operating in South Carolina waters when the war began in 1775. Sampson was such a skilled mariner that he was among a group of blacks, possibly slaves, utilized by the British navy—whether by force or of their own volition is not known—to help guide the frigates Syren, Sphinx, and Actaeon up the channel during the British assault on Charleston on 28 June 1776. Sampson in particular was known for his valuable knowledge of local waters, so much so that when the firing began, he was sent below decks to safety. Whether by deception, as a result of a British miscalculation, or because Sampson was sent below decks is unknown, but all three ships ran aground on the Middle Ground shoals. Two of the ships made it off the shoals but had to withdraw for repairs. The Actaeon was not so fortunate; rendered immobile, it was set on fire and abandoned the next day. The grounding of these ships saved the day for the American forces and resulted in a bitter defeat for the British. Unfortunately, nothing else of Sampson is known, including his ultimate fate.

Sampson's service during the American Revolution is representative of the experiences of many blacks on the British side during the war and may have occurred under several different scenarios. It has often been stated that Sampson was a slave; if so, he may have been owned by a Loyalist master living in or around Charleston, South Carolina, who hired him out to the British. If this was the case, Sampson may have been among those Loyalists evacuated by the British navy. However, it is equally possible that Sampson may have been a runaway from a "rebel" slave owner who offered his services to the British. Such runaways frequently joined the British cause, as it was the prevailing attitude among slaves early in the war that blacks would be freed by British officers in return for their service. A flight to the British by such men as COLONEL TYE and possibly Sampson, though a calculated risk, often offered a greater possibility for personal freedom than those lofty words in the Declaration of Independence that, it was soon realized, were never meant for them. If Sampson was a runaway slave who offered his services willingly to the British, it is possible he remained with the British navy as a laborer or servant after the defeat. One intriguing possibility is that Sampson arrived back in South Carolina when the British finally captured Charleston in May 1780, perhaps given a second chance to guide British warships through local waters.

One final bit of intrigue may be speculated upon regarding Sampson's service. Was he, instead, a true patriot who, forcibly impressed into British service, gained a measure of revenge by helping to lead British ships astray in the heat of battle? The answer to this question and others regarding the nature of Sampson's loyalties will always remain a mystery.

FURTHER READING

Kaplan, Sidney, and Emma Nogrady Kaplan. *The Black Presence in the Era of the American Revolution* (1989).

Quarles, Benjamin. *The Negro in the American Revolution* (1961).

GLENN ALLEN KNOBLOCK

Sampson, Edith Spurlock (13 Oct. 1901–8 Oct. 1979), attorney and jurist, was born in Pittsburgh, Pennsylvania, one of eight children of Louis Spurlock and Elizabeth A. McGruder. Her father managed a cleaning and dyeing business. Her mother worked from home as a weaver and retail merchant of buckram hat frame switches. Her parents eventually saved enough money to buy a home, which was unusual for urban African Americans in the early twentieth century. Although the Spurlocks were poor, they never lacked food and were always clean and neatly dressed. Everyone, including Spurlock's brothers and sisters, worked to contribute to the household income. During grade school Edith had to quit school and work full-time to help support her family. When finances permitted, she eventually resumed her studies and graduated from Peabody High School.

Spurlock was always a high academic achiever. When she graduated from high school, her Sunday school teacher helped her get a job with Associated Charities, a New York social work organization. Her new employer arranged for her to attend the New York School of Social Work. While Spurlock was enrolled in his criminology course, Professor George W. Kirchwey of Columbia University Law School, noticed her sharp intellect and realized her potential. Kirchwey suggested that she leave social work to study law. However, Spurlock maintained her original plan and earned a degree in social work.

In 1922 Spurlock married Rufus Sampson, a Tuskegee Institute field agent, and moved to Chicago, where she worked for the Illinois Children's Home and Aid Society. Her work included placing abused and neglected children into foster care and arranging adoptions. While in Chicago, Edith Sampson again encountered Kirchwey, who reiterated his belief that she should study law. This time Sampson relented and enrolled in Chicago's John Marshall Law School. She took evening classes and continued to work full time as a social worker. She excelled in her coursework and ranked number one among ninety-five students in a jurisprudence course. For this Sampson received special commendation from the dean.

Sampson graduated from Loyola University Law School in 1925, becoming the first black woman as well as the first woman of any ethnicity to receive a law degree from Loyola. She immediately took the Illinois bar exam but did not pass. She later said that failing the exam was for the best because it forced her to focus and work harder. Also in 1925 Sampson began work in the Juvenile Court of Cook County, Illinois. Sampson retook and passed the bar in 1927. That same year she opened a solo law office on Chicago's South Side, specializing in criminal law and domestic relations. Many of her clients were poor African Americans. In 1930 Sampson was appointed a Cook County probation officer and referee, and she served in this post until 1940. During this time she and her husband divorced, but Sampson continued to use his name professionally.

In 1934 Sampson achieved a career milestone when she was admitted to practice before the U.S. Supreme Court. Later that same year she married the attorney Joseph E. Clayton. They worked together as law partners until his death in 1957. Sampson's success continued, and in 1938 she was honored as a member of the National Association of Women Lawyers. Sampson and fellow attorney Georgia Jones Ellis were the first African Americans to join that group's Chicago chapter.

Sampson was appointed assistant state's attorney for Cook County in 1947. Two years later, while chairing the executive committee of the National Council of Negro Women, she was invited to participate in America's Town Meeting of the Air, a live international radio broadcast. The participants, U.S. cultural, civic, labor, and welfare advocates, debated with peer leaders from other countries about various political and social questions pertaining to the United States and democracy. Sampson addressed civil rights questions from citizens of Pakistan, India, and the Soviet Union. Many of the questions were about the status of African Americans in the United States. Sampson acknowledged that there were problems for African Americans, but she defended the concept of democracy for the opportunities it offered all U.S. citizens. She often noted that despite racism, African Americans had the freedom to change their lives. Sampson used herself as an example of a black person from a poor family who was able to get an education and become a U.S. delegate. Sampson addressed each question with dignity. She was so effective in her answer delivery that when the town hall delegation concluded successfully in 1950, the World Town Hall Seminar was created as a permanent organization, and Sampson was elected as its president.

Sampson's work caught the attention of President Harry S. Truman, and he appointed her as an alternate delegate for the 1952 session of the United Nations General Assembly. She was the first African American woman named as an official American representative to the United Nations (UN). In her UN position she served on the Social Humanitarian and Cultural Committee and worked on land reform and prisoner reparations. National media outlets began to take notice of Sampson, and she was interviewed for articles in many popular periodicals, including *Time*, the *Christian Science Monitor*, and the *New York Times*.

Sampson became increasingly involved in international relations. During the 1950s she was a spokesperson for the State Department, visiting countries in South America, Europe, and the Middle East. By 1961 she had been appointed to the U.S. Commission on the North Atlantic Treaty Organization (NATO).

Sampson's work as a legal representative also grew. In 1962 she became an associate judge for the Chicago Municipal Court. She heard cases for divorce, child custody, and other domestic disputes. In 1966 she was elected an associate judge for the Circuit Court of Cook County, remaining on the bench until she retired in 1978.

Despite her career advances and education success, Sampson often experienced racial prejudice. However, she refused to allow base prejudices to deter her from her goals. She believed that hard work, perseverance, and a positive outlook were the formula for success, and her life work was a testament to her belief. Sampson died on 8 October 1979.

FURTHER READING

Cartwright, Marguerite. "The United Nations and the U.S. Negro," *Negro History Bulletin* 18 (Mar. 1955).

Davis, Marianna W., ed. *Contributions of Black Women to America* (1982).

Kramer, Dale. "America's Newest Diplomat," *New Republic* (22 Jan. 1951).

Potter, Joan. *African American Firsts: Famous, Little-Known, and Unsung Triumphs of Blacks in America* (reprint ed. 2002).

ANGELA BLACK

Sampson, John Patterson (13 Aug. 1837–?), lawyer, minister, teacher, writer, and editor, was born free of African and Scottish descent in Wilmington, North Carolina. He was educated in the public school system of Cambridge, Massachusetts, and then went on to Comer's College in Boston, graduating in 1856.

After graduation, Sampson moved to Jamaica, Long Island, to begin his career teaching in its public school system. By 1862 he had moved to Cincinnati, Ohio, and started the newspaper, *The Colored Citizen*, the only black newspaper in the North established during the Civil War. Sampson edited the newspaper along with JOSEPH C. CORBIN, Charles W. Bell, H. F. Leonard, and Reverend George Williams. Even by its title, one can surmise that the newspaper spoke out for and about African Americans as a citizenry. The paper lived up to its title with pronouncements such as, "considering what the nation owes the negro, what it has promised him, and remember the lesson of the war, it is evident there is no course for us to tread, either safe, just, or honorable, except to guarantee to him at once every political right enjoyed by every citizen."

After the war Sampson and many other black leaders in North Carolina, mainly educated blacks who were free before the Civil War and black immigrants from the North, arranged mass meetings that culminated in the first Freedman's Convention at City Hall, North Carolina, on 20 September 1865. On 23 September 1865 the *Wilmington Herald* identified the convention as "one of the largest gatherings of the kind ever before in council in this city," and reported that Sampson served as keynote speaker. His speech focused on the right of blacks to universal suffrage. Historically, free black men had the right to vote as late as 1835 in North Carolina. With this precedent set years before the war, the Freedmen's Convention had firmer ground upon which to base its suffrage demands. Blacks

in North Carolina must vote if emancipation is to have any real significance, Sampson and his fellow convention delegates claimed. But this demand for universal suffrage was not just significant to blacks in North Carolina. So soon after the Civil War, North Carolina was still rethinking its relationship to a reunited nation, and Sampson wanted his audience at the convention to understand that universal suffrage would give black North Carolinians a more decisive role in the future of their state and of their nation. The large population of blacks in North Carolina and intense organizing created a strong political constituency. Universal suffrage was necessary to making sure that they played a direct, integral role in their state. Of course, it would be hard to divorce these more immediate and local interests from an ideal of universal suffrage nationally, which would further guarantee their freedom to participate fully in politics.

Sampson's address was impressive and the *Wilmington Herald* published the speech in its entirety. In one passage Sampson answers the question, "Why do we want suffrage?":

I will tell you why we want it: we want it because it is our RIGHT, first of all. No class of men can, without insulting their own nature, be content with any deprivation of their rights. We want it again as a means of educating our race. ... I want the elective franchise, as a colored man, because ours is a peculiar government, based upon a peculiar idea, and that idea is universal suffrage.

He also turned to the many evidences of black participation in the state but does so by the persuasive rhetorical move of accepting a common challenge to black enfranchisement, only to undermine that challenge:

It is said that we are ignorant; I admit it; but if we know enough to be hung, we know enough to vote. If we know enough to pay taxes to support the government, we know enough to vote. Taxation and representation go together. If we know enough to shoulder a musket and fight for the flag—fight for the government—we know enough to vote (*Wilmington Herald*, 23 Sept. 1865).

As these passages suggest, Sampson made great use of an American tradition that granted other citizens suffrage and the recent efforts of blacks in the war and the common operation of the state. Sampson actually admits, then, that the old "dodges" used to avoid discussion of universal suffrage and the prejudicial arguments against it have little place in this newly forming republic, full of the promise that comes with an expanded constituency that will contribute to debating and deciding public matters.

At the convention Sampson was appointed assessor and clerk to the superintendent of Freedman Schools at Wilmington, North Carolina. In 1868 Sampson graduated from the National Law University and was admitted to the District of Columbia bar. From the 1870s into the 1880s Sampson served in many public positions. He served as clerk to the school superintendent of the Freedmen's Bureau in Wilmington in 1869; he served as assessor and as treasurer in New Hanover County in 1870; and as an alderman in 1874. He also worked periodically as a clerk in the Treasury Department in Washington, D.C. for fifteen years. He then served as president of the Frederick Douglass Hospital and Training School in Philadelphia, Pennsylvania, in the 1880s. This hospital and school was intended to train black women to become nurses, especially since they were often barred attendance at other training schools in the area. He also became a lecturer at Hampton School (later Hampton University).

In 1882, Sampson entered ministry with the African Methodist Episcopal church. To further equip himself for this lifelong pursuit he studied Theology at the Western Theological Seminary, an evangelical seminary associated with the Reform church in Allegheny, Pennsylvania. It did not take long for Sampson to become well known in African Methodist Episcopal circles, because his activities were often publicized, especially in the *Christian Recorder*, his denomination's official news organ. He served as a senior or associated minister for churches in the Philadelphia area and New Jersey. He also gave many memorable speeches at special church occasions. He lectured on topics as diverse as the importance of education to phrenology to "The Progress of Reconstruction" (an address given in 1868).

But Sampson also drew from his experience with *The Colored Citizen* and wrote often in the *Christian Recorder* concerning issues of black politics and political organizing. For instance, Sampson was a strong opponent of the Democratic Party. In Sampson's view, this party "brought on a bloody conflict against the loyal people by its sympathy with the Southern leaders, costing the nation five hundred thousand lives, and $5,000,000,000." The party urged "disorder and mob violence against lawful authority; it cripples every industry, defies the executive government in its efforts to maintain the public peace." With these factors in mind, one can understand why Sampson felt led to militate against this party for the sake of mainlining some "public peace." But this did not mean that he was totally devoted to the Republican Party, although he felt that, for the time being, that party would better represent the interests of black folk until suffrage could be attained. His main concerns were with black political organizing, finding political allies to aid black people in becoming more self-sufficient, and in avoiding political alignments that would reverse what they had already accomplished. Indeed, this is an important lesson and has not lost its relevance some one hundred and thirty-two years since its first publication.

Sampson married Mary A. Cole in 1880. As late as 1916, he was still serving as an AME pastor in Morristown, New Jersey. His date of death and location of his grave are unknown.

FURTHER READING

Christian Recorder. African American Newspapers: Nineteenth Century Database.

Foner, Eric. *Freedom's Lawmakers: A Directory of Black Officeholders during Reconstruction* (1993).

Nowaczyk, Elaine Joan. "The North Carolina Negro in Politics, 1865–1876." Ph.D. diss., University of North Carolina at Chapel Hill (1957).

Penn, Garland I. *The Afro-American Press, and Its Editors* (1891).

"The African-American Experience in Ohio, 1850–1920." http://dbs.ohiohistory.org/africanam/nwspaper/citizen.cfm.

Wright, Richard Robert. *Centennial Encyclopaedia of the African Methodist Episcopal Church* (1916).

JAMES EDWARD FORD III

Sanchez, Sonia (9 Sept. 1934–), poet, playwright, activist, and educator, was born Wilsonia Benita Driver in Birmingham, Alabama, the daughter of Wilson L. Driver, a jazz drummer and teacher, and Lena Jones, who died in childbirth when Wilsonia was a year old. Sanchez was raised by her paternal grandmother until she was six. After her grandmother's death, Sonia, as her family called her, was moved from relative to relative and developed a stutter. She began to hide in her aunt's bathroom at night to write poetry as a way to overcome the stutter and to make sense of her grandmother's death. When Sonia was nine, she and her older sister Patricia moved with their father and his third wife to Harlem; her half-brother Wilson remained with relatives in the South. Sonia continued to write poetry and attended Hunter College, graduating with a degree in political science in 1955. She then studied poetry with Louise Bogan at New York University. Bogan encouraged Sonia to publish her work and to hone her craft in traditional poetic forms. Sonia married Albert Sanchez, a Puerto Rican poet, in the late 1950s, and they had a daughter. She began publishing as Sonia Sanchez in the 1960s, during which she was a major force in the black arts movement. Sanchez, her second husband, ETHERIDGE KNIGHT, and their fellow poets Don L. Lee (Haki Madhubuti) and NIKKI GIOVANNI wrote and performed as the Broadside Quartet, which developed Sanchez's experimental style of poetic street talk, expressed through lowercase letters, slashes, minimal punctuation, unusual spellings, and abbreviations. She recalled using curse words to get the attention of bar patrons at her first poetry reading in a Harlem bar with Madhubuti and AMIRI BARAKA (LeRoi Jones). She credited MALCOLM X's truth-telling and oratorical skills with inspiring black arts writers to use language as a force for change. Sanchez and Knight had twin sons.

Sanchez published her first two collections of poetry in quick succession: *Home Coming* (1969), an impassioned expression of black identity, and *We a BaddDDD People* (1970), an overtly militant collection containing "assassin poems" as well as a conscious exploration of jazz musical forms in language. In addition to performing her own poetry, Sanchez had several plays produced and published during the black arts movement, notably *The Bronx Is Next* (1968) and *Sister Son/ji* (1969). In the 1970s her poetry focused less on militant themes and more on personal relationships, though her work deepened in its exploration of black female identity. In *Love Poems* (1973) Sanchez challenged her poetic voice with the seemingly restrictive forms of haiku, tanka, and sonnet. She wrote a spiritual autobiography in poetic form, *A Blues Book for Blue Black Magical Women* (1974), inspired in part by her membership in the Nation of Islam from 1972 to 1975, which she left largely because of her belief that the organization repressed women. Her marriage to Knight ended during this period, and in 1978 she published old and new works with a focus on an evolving African American female sensibility in *I've Been a Woman: New and Selected Poems.*

Sanchez's work, whether political or personal, is inherently revolutionary in its vision and in its experimentation with form. She recalls her aunt Pauline being forcibly ejected from a bus after refusing to comply with segregation laws, and

her sensibility is shaped by both the South of her childhood and the street rhythms of Harlem. Her travels to China inspired her to embrace haiku, which she employs with a distinctly African American voice:

did ya ever cry
Black man, did ya ever cry
til you knocked all over? (*Shake Loose My Skin*, 12)

Haiku becomes a three-line jazz refrain in a distilled expression of erotic energy:

if i had known, if
i had known you, i would have
left my love at home. (*Shake Loose My Skin*, 16)

Sanchez's awards and honors included several honorary doctorates as well as the American Book Award for *Homegirls and Handgrenades* (1984). In this collection Sanchez combined poetry and lyrical prose pieces to reflect on love, drug addiction, violence, and hope in a pastiche many critics compared to JEAN TOOMER's *Cane*. Her later works lost none of the urgency of her 1960s protest poetry while evincing a more mature, rounded vision of the world, a product no doubt of her extensive travels lecturing and reading her poetry. From the beginning Sanchez wrote poetry to major black figures, such as MALCOLM X, MARTIN LUTHER KING JR., and FANNIE LOU HAMER, and her later poems celebrated the young rap artists TUPAC SHAKUR and CHUCK D. of Public Enemy. Danny Simmons, the executive producer of HBO's *Def Poetry*, called Sanchez "the spiritual mother" of contemporary hip-hop.

Sanchez's work as an educator was also revolutionary, starting with her cofounding of the first black studies program in the United States at San Francisco State College in the late 1960s, which prompted surveillance by the FBI. In the 1970s she held teaching positions at various institutions, including Amherst College and Rutgers University. In 1977 she began teaching literature and women's studies at Temple University, where she became the Laura Carnell Chair in English. Throughout her years at Temple she regularly visited Philadelphia city schools to work with students of all ages on creating their own poetry, leaving rhyming dictionaries behind for future poets and rappers. She retired from Temple in 1999 but continued to tour extensively, and in January 2005 she began a teaching residency at Columbia University.

Sanchez continued to write and produce plays, including *Black Cats Back and Uneasy Landings*

(1995). She also published several children's books, including *It's a New Day: Poems for Young Brothas and Sistuhs* (1971), *The Adventures of Fat Head, Small Head, and Square Head* (1973), and *A Sound Investment and Other Stories* (1979). A longtime Philadelphia resident, she responded to the 1985 police slaughter of the black radicals of MOVE (authorized by Mayor W. WILSON GOODE) and the decimation of an entire city block in her poem "Elegy: For MOVE and Philadelphia." She chronicled the painful loss of her brother Wilson to AIDS in the NAACP Image Award–winning *Does Your House Have Lions?* (1997), in which she also explored her troubled relationship with their father, determined to love and accept the man "come to collapse the past" (*Shake Loose My Skin*, 120). Other poetry collections include *Wounded in the House of a Friend* (1995), *Like the Singing Coming off the Drums: Love Poems* (1998), and *Shake Loose My Skin: New and Selected Poems* (1999). In 2001 she was awarded the Robert Frost Medal. Sanchez also released a spoken-word CD in 2004 titled *Full Moon of Sonia*, with jazz, blues, gospel, and hip-hop backings for her poetry.

Truly a "people's poet," Sanchez remained committed to reaching out and giving voice to the voiceless and vulnerable. Critical interest in her work is increasing, as evidenced by a June 2001 symposium Poetry and Politics: Sonia Sanchez's Works in Tours, France, and the journal *BMa: The Sonia Sanchez Literary Review*, published twice yearly since 1994. Her writing and her activism update the ideals and vision of the black arts movement for contemporary audiences.

FURTHER READING

Baker, Houston A., Jr. "Our Lady: Sonia Sanchez and the Writing of a Black Renaissance," in *Reading Black, Reading Feminist*, ed. Henry Louis Gates Jr. (1990).

Jennings, Regina B. "The Blue/Black Poetics of Sonia Sanchez," in *Language and Literature in the African American Imagination*, ed. Carol Aisha Blackshire-Belay (1992).

Joyce, Joyce A. *Ijala: Sonia Sanchez and the African Poetic Tradition* (1994).

Lee, Felicia R. "A 'Spiritual Mother' of Spoken Word for a Hip-Hop Generation," *New York Times*, 29 Jan. 2005.

Reich, David. "'As Poets, as Activists': An Interview with Sonia Sanchez," *World* (May–June 1999).

ALICE KNOX EATON

Sanders, Barry David (16 July 1968–), Hall of Fame running back for the Detroit Lions of the National Football League (NFL), was born in Wichita, Kansas, the seventh of eleven children of William Sanders, a carpenter and roofer, and Shirley Ann Sanders, a nurse. By his own account, he benefited from attentive and supportive parenting and a disciplined family life that included regular Sunday attendance at Paradise Baptist Church.

Growing up in the northeast quadrant of Wichita, Sanders displayed athletic talent from an early age. He frequently accompanied his older brother Byron to neighborhood pickup football games and competed successfully against older boys. Disregarding his father's admonition that he was too young and too small, Sanders began to play organized youth football at age nine. Sanders sensed early on that his destiny lay on the gridiron. Looking back on his childhood decades later in his Hall of Fame induction speech, he said, "I think football chose me. When I first came into contact with the game … [i]t wasn't that I wanted to play, I had to play."

As he played in the youth leagues, Sanders became immersed in team sport culture and enjoyed competing regardless of whether he played a starring role. Entering Wichita North High School as a freshman in the fall of 1982, Sanders—whose mature height would be five feet eight inches—was smaller than most of the other football players. He played on the junior varsity team in his sophomore year, not as a running back but in the defensive backfield, as well returning kickoffs and punts. The following year, Sanders joined the varsity squad under Bob Shepler, a local coaching legend nearing retirement. Sanders still did not carry the ball on offense, but when Coach Dale Burkholder was hired as Shepler's successor one year later, Sanders's future career began to take shape. With Sanders still playing cornerback at the beginning of his senior year, Burkholder took notice of his speed and quickness and moved him to running back in the fourth week of the season. Sanders responded with 1,417 rushing yards, a 10.2 yard-per-carry average, and seventeen rushing touchdowns, earning him Kansas All-State honors but few scholarship offers because of his small size. He accepted a scholarship from Oklahoma State University and entered in the fall of 1986, majoring in business administration.

Ever the team player, Sanders never complained about having to wait for a starring role on the Oklahoma State football team. He watched and waited for two years as future NFL Hall of Famer

Barry Sanders catches a pass during training drills at Saginaw Valley State University in Saginaw, Mich., on 21 July 1997. (AP Images.)

Thurman Thomas carried the ball and then moved into the starting tailback role for his junior year in the fall of 1988. Sanders's days of laboring in obscurity ended quickly as he raced through opposing defenses, racking up a National Collegiate Athletic Association single-season record of 2,628 yards, scoring thirty-nine touchdowns, and averaging more than 200 rushing yards per game. At season's end Sanders outpolled quarterbacks Troy Aikman and Rodney Peete (a future Detroit Lions teammate) for the Heisman Trophy, becoming the first Oklahoma State player ever to win the coveted award; he would also be selected to the College Football Hall of Fame fifteen years later. Following his junior year, Sanders elected to capitalize on his success by entering the NFL draft, in which the Detroit Lions took him as the third selection in the first round.

Sanders's impact on the NFL was immediate. As a rookie in 1989 he rushed for 1,470 yards, scored fourteen touchdowns, and was recognized as NFL Rookie of the Year. Despite his lack of height and his unimposing weight of two hundred pounds, Sanders had deceptive strength and exceptional speed in footraces, the ability to change direction

in the blink of an eye, and explosive quickness that allowed him to embarrass the league's best defenders every Sunday. Sanders's 1989 season was the start of a remarkable ten-year period highlighted by uniform weekly excellence, 1,000 or more rushing yards each season, avoidance of serious injuries, and universal respect for his abilities and character throughout the league. Even with his astonishing success, which included one season with over 2,000 rushing yards, a Most Valuable Player award, and a prodigious 15,269 career rushing yards (third on the all-time NFL rushing list), Sanders's self-effacing personality remained intact. Unfailingly polite, he spoke little to the press, was rarely heard to complain, and passed up opportunities to promote his own accomplishments. On one occasion, informed by teammates near the end of a season's final game that he was a few yards short of the NFL rushing yardage title, Sanders declined to reenter the game and capture the crown.

With Sanders in the backfield, the Lions were a threat to score on every offensive play, but the team's deepest excursion into the playoffs during the Sanders era was an appearance in the 1991 National Football Conference championship game, a loss to the Washington Redskins. The Lions' overall record from 1989 to 1999 was a mediocre 78–82, with five postseason berths and only one playoff victory. Following a poor 1998 season with just five victories and a winter marked by infrequent communication with his team, the thirty-one-year-old Sanders—still at the peak of his skills—stunned the football world on 28 July 1999 with a brief newspaper release announcing his retirement from football. The sudden announcement on the eve of training camp, with no press conference, no meeting with teammates, no substantive explanation for his departure, and a trip to England to avoid the media, caused dismay and some resentment among Lions management, players, and fans. The *New York Times* called Sanders's abrupt retirement "one of the great mysteries of professional sports" (2001). Sanders's father stated that his son had become "sick of losing" (*New York Times*, 1999, http://www.nytimes.com/1999/07/29/sports/pro-football-sanders-puts-it-in-writing-he-s-gone.html). Despite persistent rumors over the next several years that Sanders would return to the Lions, he neither did so nor hinted at doing so. He was elected to the Pro Football Hall of Fame in 2004, his first year of eligibility. Following his retirement from football Sanders managed a number of business interests and traveled widely.

On 11 November 2000, Barry Sanders married Detroit television journalist Lauren Campbell, with whom he had three children. Sanders also had an older son, Barry James Sanders, from a previous relationship.

FURTHER READING

Sanders, Barry, with Mark E. McCormick, *Barry Sanders* (2003).
Transcript of Barry Sanders' Pro Football Hall of Fame induction speech, http://www.profootballhof.com/enshrinement/release.aspx?release_id=1259.

DAVID BORSVOLD

Sanders, Deion Luwynn (9 Aug. 1967–), professional football and baseball player, was born in Fort Myers, Florida, the only child of Buck Sanders and Connie Knight. Until Sanders was six, he lived with his mother and father, who were not married. His father moved less then a year later because of a drug problem. His mother worked long hours as a janitor at both the hospital and the local school to make sure she could afford luxuries for her son, such as sports equipment. Sanders excelled in all of his athletic undertakings.

At the age of eight, he was exposed to organized football through a Pop Warner program. Over three years the only game his team lost was the one he missed. Sanders was virtually unstoppable due to his incredible speed. While the genes for speed may have come from his father, whose fleet feet were legendary, Sanders attributed his speed to a fear of graveyards. He passed several cemeteries on his nightly walk home, and would wait for a car to pass and then sprint behind it so he could use its lights to assuage his fears.

Throughout his junior high years, Sanders excelled in basketball, baseball, and football with flashy style. He entered Fort Myers High School expecting to continue as a standout. After being slated as the junior varsity backup quarterback his sophomore year, he transferred to North Fort Myers High School. There by his junior year he was playing varsity basketball, football, and track. His enormous talent not only attracted attention from top college football programs but also from the Kansas City Royals, who drafted him to play professional baseball at the end of his junior year. Sanders, a childhood Royals fan, was tempted to accept this offer, which included a $75,000 signing bonus. Ironically it was advice from the Royals manager Dick Hauser that Sanders says

"gave [him] the confidence" to turn down this offer and attend college (Sanders, 36). Hauser told Sanders that if he was good enough to get drafted out of high school, then he would be good enough to get drafted out of college, and college would give him a chance to find out how good he was at football.

After turning down the Royals, Sanders was inundated with offers to play football at top collegiate programs. Although he was excited and intrigued by large out-of-state colleges, he decided to attend Florida State University (FSU) so his mother would be able to attend his games. He also liked FSU because he would be able to play both baseball and football. When football started, he began to play cornerback, taking up this position because it gave him a chance to start as a freshman. When he entered college he also decided to stop using profanity and broke himself of this habit by paying everyone he swore at five dollars.

Sanders played baseball and football and ran track during his freshman and sophomore years. Dedicated and hardworking in all three sports, he was superbly conditioned and once ran two track events in his baseball uniform between games of a doubleheader. This frenetic schedule started to affect his grades, and Sanders decided to only play football his sophomore year. Nevertheless, he was drafted by the New York Yankees. The Yankees gave him such a large signing bonus that he decided to play professional baseball during the college football off-season. As a result he lost his scholarship status and played his final seasons as a walk-on.

On the football field, Sanders was part of one of the greatest secondaries in college football history alongside the future National Football League (NFL) players Leroy Butler and Martin Mayhew. When he concluded his college career, Sanders had intercepted the second most passes in school history (fourteen), had become the school's leading punt returner, and had played in three bowl games. He was honored as a third team All-American in 1986 and a first team All-American in 1987 and 1988 and was the Jim Thorpe Award winner in 1988. In recognition of these accomplishments, his number 2 jersey was retired in 1995.

During his senior year, drawing national attention as both a college football star and a professional baseball player, Sanders became concerned about the low salaries that marquee cornerbacks were receiving in the NFL. As a result he decided that he needed to create an on-field persona that, when combined with his play, would enable him to earn a larger salary. In creating this image he resurrected his high school nickname "Prime Time" and started to dress flashily and make flamboyant comments to the media.

Sanders was taken by the Atlanta Falcons as the fifth selection in the NFL draft. He made history his rookie year by hitting a home run for the New York Yankees and returning an interception for a touchdown in the same week. The next season he signed with the Atlanta Braves and began playing baseball and football in the same city. He continued playing for the Braves through the 1993 season, which included an appearance in the World Series. In 1994 he left the Falcons and signed with the San Francisco Forty-niners, who won the Super Bowl. This appearance made him the only person to have played in both the World Series and the Super Bowl. He signed with the Dallas Cowboys the next season and won a second Super Bowl. He retired in 2001 and worked briefly as a television commentator. He returned for the 2005 and 2006 NFL seasons with the Baltimore Ravens before retiring permanently.

Over his nine years in baseball, Sanders was a .261 hitter. His best season was 1992, when he hit .304 and stole 26 bases in 97 games. During his football career he started at cornerback and wide receiver and returned kicks. Over his fourteen seasons in the NFL, he intercepted 53 passes, caught 60 passes, returned 155 kickoffs, and scored 22 touchdowns. He set the NFL record for defensive and return touchdowns with nineteen. After retiring, Sanders worked for a variety of networks as a sports commentator. In 2011, Sanders was inducted into the Pro Football Hall of Fame in Canton, Ohio.

FURTHER READING

Sanders, Deion, with Jim Nelson Black. *Power, Money, and Sex: How Success Almost Ruined My Life* (1998).

JACOB ANDREW FREEDMAN

Sanders, Frank Cook (9 Mar. 1931–), Coast Guard veteran and agent in the Federal Bureau of Alcohol, Tobacco, and Firearms, was born in Charleston, South Carolina, the son of Thomas, an auto mechanic, and Zerline (Cook) Sanders, a schoolteacher. Following World War II, Sanders and two friends joined the military. He joined the Naval Reserve in 1947 as a seaman, and in 1948 joined the Coast Guard. While he did not want to be a steward, he was told that there were no vacancies in the service for seamen so instead he had no choice but to enlist in the rating traditionally held by blacks in both the Navy and Coast Guard that of

steward. Sanders later recalled that "I bought that idea … and naively accepted the assurance that a rate change could be made in boot camp. This, of course, proved not to be true," and Sanders completed his training as a steward's mate. Despite the fact that just the year before President Harry Truman had desegregated the American military by issuing Executive Order 9981, actual enlistment practices took far longer to change and the segregated Steward's Branch was still the predominant assignment for new black recruits in America's sea services.

Upon completing boot camp, Sanders served in the Miami area in the Seventh Coast Guard District and Miami Air Station until assigned to the Cadet Mess at the Coast Guard Academy in New London, Connecticut. While stationed here, Frank saw his first sea duty on the USCGC *Eagle*, a sailing ship used for cadet training. At this duty station Sanders discussed the possibility of attending the academy, but "the interest level was not high and these discussions did not proceed." However, he did begin "a campaign of regularly submitting requests for yeoman-storekeeper training" and was finally selected in 1950. Later that same year he became a yeoman third class, leaving behind his steward's rating much like the author ALEX HALEY had done the prior year.

Following this promotion, Frank Sanders served in Puerto Rico and was "adopted" by his white executive officer, Lieutenant Commander John Natwig. Given a full range of autonomy based on his excellent performance, Sanders soon developed an interest in becoming a federal narcotics agent based on his friendship with a Puerto Rican agent. Realizing that he could gain experience in the Coast Guard's Intelligence Branch that might lead to his ultimate goal, Frank soon began submitting applications for the intelligence training program. It is also in Puerto Rico that Sanders met and married his future wife, Leticia Morales, of San Juan. Married from 1953 to 1988, the two would have four children, Carmen Maria, Frank III, Carlos, and Howard.

For years Frank Sanders's requests to join the intelligence branch were ignored. However he continued his studies at various duty stations to improve his chances for selection, in addition to performing sea duty on the cutters *Pandora* (1955) and *Westwind* (1959–1960). Finally in 1962 Sanders caught a break when he learned that his old executive officer, Captain John Natwig, was now chief of Enlisted Personnel and his former *Westwind* executive officer Captain Fred Hancock was chief of Enlisted Personnel Training; within two weeks of contacting his old bosses, Sanders was selected for intelligence training and in December 1962 became the Coast Guard's first African American intelligence agent. Subsequently posted to San Francisco, Sanders encountered heavy prejudice while working there, but did have several agents, including Jack Slaughter and Albert McClelland who respected him for his abilities without regard to race. During his time in Coast Guard intelligence, Sanders gained valuable investigative experience and established excellent relations with local, federal, and state law enforcement agents and performed in dignitary protection details for President Lyndon Johnson. By 1967 Sander's intelligence tour was coming to end and he asked for an extension but was denied. In 1968 Frank Sanders retired from the Coast Guard as chief yeoman after twenty years service.

Despite the fact that Sanders was no longer in the military, he fully believed that his "success in becoming an intelligence agent gave [him] an opportunity," and he pursued it to the fullest. On 8 January 1968 he became a customs port investigator in San Francisco and worked a variety of undercover details resulting in seizures of jewelry, narcotics, and other valuables. However opportunity called just months later when the enforcement branch of the Alcohol and Tobacco Tax Division's Western Region was in need of agents; on 30 June 1968 Frank Sanders was sworn in as the first African American agent ever hired by the agency (later the Alcohol, Tobacco, and Firearms Agency [ATF]) west of the Mississippi River.

Frank Sanders would work for the ATF for nearly twenty years until his retirement on 30 January 1998. Just as with his early days in the Coast Guard, discrimination was rampant in the ATF and Sanders was not always a welcome presence. While such treatment would lessen over the years, the late 1960s and early 1970s were a trying time for African Americans trying to advance in predominantly white federal law enforcement agencies at the same time that black militancy groups such as HUEY NEWTON's Black Panthers and Donald DeFreeze's Symbionese Liberation Army (SLA) were at the peak of their illegal activities. However, Frank Sanders's outstanding investigative skills could not be ignored; his work ran the gamut from seizing liquor stills in the hills of California to conspiracy cases involving militant groups as a member of an Organized Crime Strike Force Group, as well as international service as a deputy sky marshal on Pan Am flights from New York to Europe during an intense period of Middle East hijackings in 1970. All the cases Sanders brought before a court resulted in at least one guilty charge for the defendant, a true demonstration of his thorough competence as a Coast Guard and ATF agent. Through it all, despite leading the fight in an antidiscrimination class-action lawsuit against the ATF, Sanders amassed a truly amazing record. One of the highlights of his ATF career came in 1983 when Sanders administered the oath of office as a special agent in the ATF to Howard Sanders, his youngest son. Frank and Howard Sanders were the first ever father-son African American agents in the ATF, and likely the first in any federal law enforcement agency. In 1993 Frank Sanders achieved yet another first, becoming the first African American special investigator for the California Department of Toxic Substances Control, a position he held for nearly four years.

In retirement, though occasionally performing work as a private investigator, Frank Cook Sanders moved to Stockton, California where he was active in a number of black law enforcement and military associations.

FURTHER READING
This article is based on the author's interview with
     Frank Sanders on 9 March 2007 and on private
     records and documents provided by Sanders.
                                   GLENN ALLEN KNOBLOCK

Sanders, Hayes Edward "Big Ed" (24 Mar. 1930–12 Dec. 1954), Olympic champion boxer, was born in the Watts neighborhood of Los Angeles, California, to Hays Sanders, a municipal garbage worker, and Eva Sanders, a homemaker. Sanders, the oldest male child of the family, was mature and physically strong, even at an early age. He and his friends exercised vigorously as children, collecting coffee cans and then filling them with cement and connecting them to steel bars to make weight sets. As Sanders grew during his teen years, he continued working on his strength and speed, becoming a star athlete in football (he played wide receiver) and track and field (specializing in the four-hundred-meter run) at Jordan High School in Watts.

After high school, Sanders attended a nearby junior college in Compton, California. At Compton Junior College, he continued to excel in football as both a wide receiver and end. With the urging of a local coach, he also took up boxing. In 1950, at the

National Junior College Boxing Championships in Ogden, Utah, the six-foot four-inch, 220-pound Sanders attracted the attention of not only the boxing coach of Idaho State University, Dubby Holt, but also ISU's football coach, Babe Caccia: "He had a good left hand, and for the big man that he was, he was a real orthodox, skilled boxer," Holt later recalled. Ultimately, Sanders earned an athletic scholarship to Idaho State University in Pocatello, Idaho, where he would box and play football.

Sanders flourished academically, socially, and athletically at the nearly all-white Idaho State. He was an All-State football player; with his rare combination of speed, size, and power, Sanders was versatile enough to play several different positions, although he excelled as a wide receiver. This versatility was also reflected in Sanders's participation in track and field, where he competed in the ten-event decathlon, under the coaching of Ken Carpenter, a former Olympian. In his first collegiate boxing match, Sanders knocked out the Pacific Coast Heavyweight Champion. Sanders went on to set a record at Idaho State by never losing a bout in a collegiate dual meet. His brother Don joined him on Idaho State's boxing team in 1951. While at Idaho State, Sanders fell in love with Pocatellan Mary LaRue, a secretary in Idaho State's athletic department. The two were married in 1952.

In 1951, before he could graduate from college, Sanders was drafted by the U.S. Army to fight in the Korean War. A short time later, he was convinced to join the navy by his boxing coaches. In the navy, Sanders was probably a cook, although it is also possible he was trained to some degree as a diver. However, Sanders spent most of his time in the service as a member of the famed U.S. Navy Boxing Team (then recognized as the finest of all the military boxing teams); his membership on the team protected him from being given the menial tasks generally reserved for African American sailors.

Sanders would score a string of major boxing victories, including his defeat of the navy's heavyweight champion, Kirby Seals, in San Diego. He also won both the Los Angeles and Chicago Golden Gloves tournaments. He subsequently toured Europe, sending letters home in which he described kissing the Blarney Stone in Ireland and walking the streets of Paris. During his European tour, he won the Golden Gloves tournament in Berlin, Germany, further enhancing his reputation as a dominant heavyweight. Upon his return to the United States, Sanders began training for the Olympics at naval facilities in Maryland.

Previously no more than a pipe dream, the Olympics were suddenly within Sanders's grasp. But the trials loomed as a major test, as more experienced boxers from around the country vied for the few coveted team spots. In the Midwest Regional in Omaha, Nebraska, Sanders was defeated by U.S. Army Corporal Lloyd Willis, but Sanders still advanced to the finals because of his prior victory over the navy champion Seals. Sanders and Willis would meet again in a much-anticipated match in Kansas City, Missouri, that would decide the last spot on the U.S. boxing team. Suffering from a broken hand, Sanders still knocked out Willis, felling him with his patented left hook in only one minute.

Ironically, the 1952 Summer Olympics in Helsinki turned out to be hardly a challenge for Sanders. Sanders knocked out the Swiss fighter Hans Jost in the first round, defeated the Italian Giacomo DiSegni, and knocked out South African Andries Nieman in the second round of the semifinal bout. At that point, the only man who stood between Sanders and a gold medal was the future heavyweight champion Ingemar Johansson, a Swede.

The fight for the gold medal between Sanders and Johansson would become boxing legend. Johansson entered the ring with confidence, but became noticeably fearful when Sanders disrobed. With his excellent physique and good looks, Sanders often drew gasps of admiration from European crowds when he removed his robe. He was medium-brown with close-cropped hair, an open and engaging smile, large and well-defined shoulder and arm muscles, a tightly muscled stomach, and thin but strong legs. During the first round, Johansson avoided Sanders by circling along the edges of the ring. The crowd, growing impatient, called for Johansson to fight. However, in the second round, Johansson continued the same timid strategy. Finally, still refusing to fight, in the third minute of the second round Johansson was disqualified by the referee. Now the subject of the crowd's ire, Johansson was ushered from the ring by policemen and was subsequently denied the silver medal (he would be awarded this silver medal thirty years later).

The first African American Olympic heavyweight champion and the first American to win a gold medal in that weight class since 1904, Sanders returned to the United States a national hero. The combination of his tenacious fighting style, self-assurance, and humble demeanor attracted constant media attention. The city of Los Angeles named a day in his honor, and he was inundated with requests for his attendance at athletic, social, and religious events.

As a member of the U.S. Navy, Sanders was prevented from boxing professionally; but after the Olympics, Sanders's amateur status became complicated by his stardom and the need to provide for his wife and young son, Russell, who was born in 1953 and who would later play basketball for Washington State. Sanders left the navy two years after winning the gold medal, although he continued to box in the amateur ranks while lawyers and commissions dealt with his desire to turn professional. It was during this time period that Sanders fought the future heavyweight champion Charles "Sonny" Liston. Liston won the fight, though witnesses at the fight accused Liston of clutching Sanders illegally. Sanders ended his amateur career with a record of forty-three wins and only four losses.

Sanders applications for professional status were ultimately approved and he fought eight professional fights within nine months. Although considered by most people to be a top contender for the championship belt held by Rocky Marciano, he lost two of those fights in close decisions. On Saturday, 12 December 1954, Sanders fought his last bout against Willie James, New England's heavyweight champion, at the Boston Garden. Sanders, who had complained previously of headaches and shoulder cramping, appeared uncharacteristically listless to some observers. Even so, James and Sanders traded heavy blows for ten rounds. In the eleventh round, looking tired to James, Sanders was knocked down by a simple punch combination that normally would not have affected him. This time he fell unconscious to the canvas, lying on his side and breathing laboriously. Carried from the ring on a stretcher, he never regained consciousness. Sanders died after a long surgery to relieve hemorrhaging in the brain. Doctors and boxing officials disagreed on the cause of Sanders's death, but most expressed the view that he had probably suffered a prior injury that was aggravated in the James fight.

The death of Big Ed Sanders was a great loss to the boxing world, where his calm and sunny demeanor made him a standout in a sport so often diminished by unsavory characters. In many ways, Sanders is a forgotten man in boxing history. After his death and the ascendancy of other fighters such as SONNY LISTON and Ingemar Johannson (who Sanders beat), he became something of a footnote—a fighter who everyone expected would be the world heavyweight champion but who died in his prime before he could achieve lasting significance. In later years, he became known primarily for his victory over Johannson. His fighting style combined speed and power, but his strength and the power of his punches were his dominate qualities. He had a vicious left hook and a wicked right uppercut. Sanders's critics have said he was a dilettante athlete, someone who boxed well but who also did too many other things that kept him from achieving his full potential as a boxer. He was also criticized for being too nice because he did not try to hurt his opponents. An intelligent, thoughtful man and athlete, Sanders kept a personal journal for years in which he reflected on his daily experiences. He was laid to rest in Santa Monica, California, where his service in the navy was honored with a twenty-one-gun military salute.

JUSTIN SANDERS

Sanders, Mingo (c. 1857–23 Aug. 1929), soldier whose dishonorable discharge became a rallying point for opponents of President Teddy Roosevelt, was born in Marion, South Carolina. Little is known about his parents or early life, but he may have worked as a cotton hand before enlisting in the army on 16 May 1881.

Like many African American men of his time, Sanders benefited from an 1866 Act of Congress, which authorized two cavalry and four infantry regiments within the Regular Army to "be composed of colored men," giving blacks a permanent place within the Armed Forces of the United States. The Twenty-fifth Infantry division was stationed in Louisiana and Texas for over a decade before it was transferred to Fort Randall in the Department of Dakota and later to Fort Missoula (Montana) in May 1888. In 1896 Lieutenant James A. Moss, commander of the Twenty-fifth Infantry, organized a bicycle corps at Fort Missoula to explore the military potential of the newly invented bicycle. After several short journeys and the success of an eight-hundred-mile bicycle excursion to Yellowstone Park, Moss decided to take the Twenty-fifth Infantry soldiers on a round-trip bicycle expedition from Fort Missoula to St. Louis, Missouri.

On the journey to St. Louis, Lt. Moss's First Sergeant was a man named Mingo Sanders. Sanders, partially blind from an explosion, was the oldest and most experienced member of the bicycle corps at age thirty-nine. He had already served in the Army for sixteen years and was well respected by his commanding officers. While Lt. Moss was responsible for logistics, Sanders ensured that

The 25th Infantry Bicycle Corps, en route to St. Louis, Missouri, in 1897. (Archives and Special Collections, Mansfield Library, The University of Montana-Missoula.)

Moss's plans were carried out and that the morale of the corps remained high. On 14 June 1897, the bicycle corps set out on their nineteen-hundred-mile journey. The conditions of the roads, if roads existed at all, were poor at best and the troops were often wet, exhausted, and short of rations during their forty-one-day ordeal. Despite the hardships, the corps arrived in St. Louis on 24 July 1897 and performed bicycle drills for a crowd of ten thousand people. Despite Moss's intention to return by bicycle, the Army ordered the regiment back to Montana by rail, and the Twenty-fifth Infantry's commission in Missoula ended in 1898 at the outbreak of the Spanish-American War.

Black regiments were some of the first called to fight and constituted almost 25 percent of the U.S. force in Cuba. Sanders and the Twenty-fifth Infantry assisted in the victory of the U.S. Army at San Juan Hill on 1 July 1898—a victory that later helped launch Theodore Roosevelt's political career. At one point in the battle Roosevelt summoned Sanders and requested that his troops surrender some of their rations to help feed the weary "Rough Riders," who were credited with the victory.

Sanders distinguished himself in Cuba when he helped capture the Spanish-held fort of El Viso near El Caney. Eight years later, Sanders was noted for bravery in the Philippines when he captured an enemy sergeant and rescued five prisoners—a deed for which he received an honorable mention.

By 1906 Sanders had a distinguished twenty-six-year military record and was stationed with the Twenty-fifth Infantry at Fort Brown, near Brownsville, Texas. He was a veteran of several wars, had the commendations of his superiors, and was just over a year away from retirement and collecting his pension. On the night of 13 August 1906, however, shots were fired in Brownsville, killing a white bartender and wounding a police officer. Immediately, blame was cast on the black soldiers at Fort Brown, though the white commanders of the Twenty-fifth Infantry insisted that all soldiers were in their barracks at the time of the shooting.

Despite inconclusive evidence against them, 167 soldiers were summarily judged without trial and dishonorably discharged by President Roosevelt. For Sanders and the other soldiers, the discharge without honor meant the loss of their pensions with no possibility of reenlistment in the military.

Many rose in defense of Sanders's distinguished military career. The *Cleveland Gazette* wrote that Sanders "has the respect and esteem of every officer in his regiment, and now, in his old age, blind of an eye, and within a few months of … a pension, he is cast out 'without honor' from the service he loves and the flag he fought for, to make a struggle in civil life for his bread and butter. The old soldier divided the bread of his company with the hungry Rough Riders at El Caney, upon the request of him whose order now drives him out to beg" (*Cleveland Gazette*, 1 Dec. 1906).

Distinguished military officers also defended Sanders. Brig. Gen. Andrew S. Burt testified that "there was no better First Sergeant in the army; that his [Sanders's] veracity was beyond question, and that he could be depended upon under all circumstances" (*New York Times*, 12 Feb. 1907). Sanders himself made the following statement before the Senate Committee on Military Affairs on 11 February 1907: "I'm a poor man. I've served my country honest and faithful. I offered my life to be destroyed for the Government, my body to be buried in the earth, and cattle to eat grass off the substance of my blood, and now I am to be cast on the world as a condemned man. Can't you do something for me?" (*New York Times*, 12 Feb. 1907).

Not until 1972 did Congress do something for Mingo Sanders.

By the early twentieth century, the number of black voters in some northern communities was high enough to help sway an election for the party that could garner their support. Republican leaders to that point had taken the black vote for granted because African Americans tended to loyally support the party of Lincoln. But the controversy of Roosevelt's action against the Twenty-fifth Infantry heralded a shift in black consciousness toward a more active protest tradition, which was first endorsed by the Niagara Movement, led by W. E. B. DuBois, and later adopted by the newly formed National Association for the Advancement of Colored People (NAACP). Mingo Sanders's outstanding military record and disgraceful discharge from military service made him the perfect political tool for opponents of Roosevelt.

President William Howard Taft used Sanders's victimhood to attempt to win black votes. In 1912 he appointed Sanders to positions in the Washington Navy Yard and then in the Interior Department. Sanders and his story were exhibited at anti-Roosevelt campaign rallies, a role Sanders initially declined but after presidential appointments could not refuse. While the battle between Taft and Roosevelt (running as a third-party candidate) bitterly split the Republican Party in the 1912 election, DuBois and the NAACP mobilized an estimated 100,000 black voters to support Woodrow Wilson, for the first time abandoning the Republican Party. It was an important moment in African American political history because many black voters realized that they could barter their vote to protect their interests. In the 1908 election DuBois explicitly mentioned Brownsville as his reason for voting Democrat: "You can do as you please—you are free, sane and twenty-one," he stated. "If between two parties who stand on identically the same platform you can prefer the party who perpetrated Brownsville, well and good! But I shall vote for [William Jennings] Bryan!" (Indianapolis *Freeman*, 18 July 1908). Although Bryan lost in 1908, this growing assertion of black political independence continued and was one factor in the election of Wilson as the twenty-eighth President of the United States in 1912.

Following the election, however, Sanders disappeared from the public arena. Sanders, with his wife Luella, settled in Washington, D.C., became a member of the Masonic Lodge, and died in 1929 during the amputation of a gangrenous, diabetic foot. He was buried at Arlington Cemetery.

In 1972 Congress reopened Sanders's case and found that he was wrongly accused in the Brownsville affair. Sanders and the other soldiers of the Twenty-fifth Infantry were granted an honorable discharge and $25,000 each in restitution. Unfortunately, only one survivor of Brownsville, Dorsie Willis, was alive to receive it.

FURTHER READING

In addition to the articles listed below, information on Mingo Sanders may be gleaned from the *New York Times*, 12 February 1907, 5; and 4 Aug. 1912, 3.

"Mingo Sanders, Out Now, Fed Roosevelt's Men; The Colonel, Now President, Applied to Him Before Santiago. Seeks Right to Re-Enlist Did His Duty at Brownsville, but Was Discharged with the Others—Fine Record in 25 Years' Service." *New York Times*, 22 Dec. 1906, 1.

"Mingo Sanders Centre of Fight on Roosevelt; Republican Senators to Rally Around Negro

ex-Sergeant. Playing for Negro Voters Foraker and
Others Using This Issue in an Attempt to Control
Their Party in 1908." *New York Times*, 25 Dec. 1906, 1.

"Mingo Sanders to Aid Taft; Discharged Soldier Will
Be Used to Win Ohio Negro Vote." *New York Times*,
14 May 1912, 2.

"A Brownsville Statement; Roosevelt Will Explain Why
He Cannot Take Sanders Back." *New York Times*,
25 Oct. 1908, 1.

Schubert, Irene, and Frank N. Schubert. *On the Trail of
the Buffalo Soldier II: New and Revised Biographies
of African Americans in the U.S. Army 1866–1917*
(2004).

SARA BRUYA

Sanders, Pharoah (13 Oct. 1940–), tenor saxophonist, composer, arranger, and painter, was born
Farrell Sanders in Little Rock, Arkansas. The names
of his parents, who were both music teachers, are
unknown. "[I was] the only child in a musical family," Sanders recalled in a 1994 interview, "my whole
family could sing." He loved music, but he also
thought that he would like to become an abstract
painter. Because his family had no money to give
him art lessons, he made the practical decision to
stay with music. For one thing he was surrounded
by teachers. His family, church, and neighborhood
were brimming over with musicians.

For $17.50 Sanders bought a metal clarinet
from a member of his family's Baptist church,
and every Sunday he paid twenty cents until the
debt was paid off, playing in rhythm-and-blues
gigs to earn the money. Since music continued
to be profitable, he stayed with it. "I didn't often
see the musicians I wanted to hear," he recalled;
they did not often come to his part of his state.
But he had easy access to the music that black
Americans were listening to on recordings—the
clarinetists SIDNEY BECHET, Benny Goodman,
Tommy Dorsey, Pete Fountain, Lawrence Welk,
and later on Artie Shaw and the alto saxophonist CHARLIE PARKER. Later Pharoah, who changed
his name early in his career, would smile about his
first jazz influences—so many, though not all, of
them white. He became famous for his work later
in life with the reeds virtuoso and composer JOHN
COLTRANE, but just as important earlier were the
blues guitarists—men who taught young Pharoah
to play the blues by ear in every key. Sanders also
played with the pianist Art Porter, with whom he
grew up, and he was invited to play sax for shows
with B. B. KING and Bobby Blue Bland when they
passed through town.

Well-known black musicians did not often play
in Arkansas, either, but Sanders fell in love with the
recordings of such African American geniuses as
the deaf tenor and multireed player James Moody,
who became his most important early influence.
All through high school Sanders heard Moody on
recordings in a drive-in restaurant near Sanders's
house. "It had music blasting day and night. I heard
it all the time. As a teenager I was hip; I'd wear my
little dark glasses and order a soda pop and smoke
a cigarette. And I played a James Moody recording over and over. He played alto on a song 'Hard
to Get.'" Secondary but still powerful influences
were COUNT BASIE, especially his version of "April
in Paris," DUKE ELLINGTON, and the trumpeter
CLIFFORD BROWN.

Sanders did not fall in love with jazz per se; he fell
in love with the spirituality of music and the sound
of the saxophone. He did not remain a Baptist, but
he remained a believer in religion. "I try to tell the
truth through my music," he said about his career.
"I'm trying to tell the truth through my music, and
I'm trying to convey that kind of honesty, whether
it's jazz or what. It's whatever you want it to be. I'd
feel that whatever experience you get from it is the
most honest way to look at it."

After finishing high school in 1959, Sanders
went to live in California with his uncle to study
art at Oakland Junior College, a small community
school with low tuition. He still felt very attracted
to art—oils and other media—and tried to set his
own standards for abstract work—"to put colors
where I thought people would like them." But he
kept moving more toward music. His uncle offered
to sign for him to buy a five-hundred-dollar saxophone, and Sanders took the challenge to pay it off.
Playing music also helped him pay his rent when
he moved out of his uncle's house.

Sanders became friends with older musicians in
the San Francisco Bay area who encouraged him
to buy a tuxedo and learn all the ballads and standards. And they exposed him to Charlie Parker,
Clifford Brown, and THELONIOUS MONK, instruct-
ing him to work on chords, to play piano, and to
voice the chords as a help for improvisation. "You
should learn a different arpeggio every day to keep
from playing the same thing all the time. To keep
on searching, you should try different ways and patterns and create your own way of doing it," Sanders
reminisced about these lessons from older players;
"I'm still learning about the chords."

In 1962, when he didn't have the money to
pay his rent, Sanders hitchhiked to New York.

He arrived around Thanksgiving Day and lived on the street, sleeping inside the doors of apartment houses, in basements, or in the subway—any place that he could lie down on his coat. He spent his days in Washington Square Park, where he noticed a sign saying that there was a place to get paid five dollars for giving blood. So he did that, and with his first fifteen cents he bought himself a slice of pizza, then candy and butternuts (white walnuts)—junk food. When the money was gone, he sold more blood. Sanders spent most of his time in Greenwich Village and found a job as a cook at a club on MacDougal Street called the Playhouse, where SUN RA and his orchestra played. The job paid him nothing, but it kept him out of the cold weather, and he ate for free.

When the owner of a club called the Speakeasy told Sanders that he would pay thirty-five dollars for a group to work four nights a week, a saxophonist called C Sharp helped Sanders get the group together. Joining them were the drummer BILLY HIGGINS, the pianist John Hicks, and the bassist HENRY GRIMES. Sanders paid all the money to the other members, keeping nothing for himself. His reward came in the person of John Coltrane, whom Sanders had met in California. Coltrane was playing in New York and was out on the town for a night to hear Sanders play. Sanders and Coltrane remained in touch, sometimes spending their afternoons searching the city for the mouthpiece of their dreams. Sanders was hired to play for a few more jobs in New York. The little additional income from these gigs brought him a regular diet of pizza and wheat germ. "When I got hungry, I'd take some wheat germ. I was living off wheat germ."

By 1965 Sanders and Coltrane began working together at the Jazz Workshop in San Francisco and on tour. One tour involved eighteen concerts in Japan and resulted in the album *Kulu Se Mama* (1965) on the Impulse label, which led to other recordings. Especially notable was *Ascension* (1965). Critics were stunned by the intense screaming on that album. They called Sanders's work amelodic and frenzied. He became wary of critics and concentrated on his own sound and his own way. He loved John Coltrane's sound: "Mostly it was John Coltrane's sound that I loved, and his phrasing, and his whole concentration and direction and the way he built his solos, playing on the chords."

Coltrane died in 1967, and Sanders tried to keep working along the lines that Coltrane had set up. Sanders led his own group, which produced his well-loved song "The Creator Has a Master Plan," with vocals and words supplied by Leon Thomas. Max Gordon, who owned the famous Village Vanguard jazz club, invited Sanders to play there, and Sanders also played at Slug's, on the Lower East Side.

Sanders tolerated any criticisms that arose. Critics have said that he has not gone far enough beyond what he did with Coltrane. Sanders might agree that he has not done enough, but has said simply, "I really like to express myself, to get the point across, until I get tired or until I wear out everybody that's listening—if I'm allowed to do that." Like Coltrane's, Sanders's music is intensely spiritual, and shows the influence of the music he listened to for inspiration: harp music, meditation tapes, piano music, Tibetan bowls (round metal bowls rubbed with a piece of wood to produce musical tones), and a large prayer horn blown for religious purposes on top of a mountain. It is, in short, always searching.

FURTHER READING

Blum, J. *Cadence* 15 (July 1989).

Blum, J. "Interview," *Musician* (Dec. 1982).

Blum, J. "Tribute to John Coltrane," *Saxophone Journal* 13 (May–June 1989).

Bogdanov, Vladimir. *All Music Guide to Jazz*, 4th ed. (2002).

Gourse, Leslie. *The Golden Age of Jazz in Paris and Other Stories about Jazz* (2000).

LESLIE GOURSE

Sanderson, Jeremiah Burke (10 Aug. 1821–19 Aug. 1875), abolitionist and African Methodist Episcopal (AME) minister, was born in Bristol, Rhode Island, or in New Bedford, Massachusetts, to Daniel and Sarah Burke Sanderson, a racially mixed couple. As a young boy he attended integrated schools in New Bedford. He moved to California in 1854, residing variously in San Francisco, Sacramento, and Stockton. He was employed as a barber and minister of the AME Church, and he was by avocation a chronicler of the abolitionist and equal rights movements. He was active as an abolitionist and an agitator for equal rights, especially equal access to public schools for black students.

While still a young man in the early 1840s, Sanderson, as an agent of the *Liberator*, William Lloyd Garrison's newspaper, joined local abolitionist societies, lectured widely against slavery, and quickly established himself as an antislavery leader in New Bedford. He lived briefly with FREDERICK DOUGLASS, he reported on speeches and events, and served as a source of information for WILLIAM COOPER NELL, who became the authoritative historian of early African American life during the mid-nineteenth century. Though the provenance of his own education is unclear, Sanderson's literary style in his sermons indicates familiarity with the giants of English and American literature as well as with the Bible.

In the late 1840s Sanderson began agitating for better education for black children in Massachusetts. In 1848 he married, but in 1854 he moved to California in search of economic opportunity. He left his wife, Catherine, and four small children behind for about six years, under the watch of area relatives, and sent back whatever spare money he had earned.

During his first few years in northern California, he drifted from town to town and worked at a variety of jobs, but failed to earn enough to return to New Bedford or bring his family to the West Coast. Great fortune eluded him, but Sanderson quickly became a leader in the cause of black education. The first schools for black children in San Francisco and Sacramento were charity schools, and in the 1850s separate public schools were founded for black students. The various California black state conventions, at which Sanderson served as one of the secretaries, began meeting and calling for equal rights in 1855. The 1856 convention demanded black access to public schools, but also endorsed charity schools as a temporary measure. In 1859 he took over San Francisco's first school for black students, a position he held until at least 1865.

Eventually, however, he became a leading force in the AME church, particularly in Stockton, where he served beginning in about 1868 and where he ran a school for black children. Sanderson apparently was forced out of his position as principal of his San Francisco school after the city hired a white female teacher and refused to allow him to supervise a white person. Although his church in Stockton had only eleven members, its church building was valued at $5,000 and it had a parsonage, a Sunday school with thirty-six students and three teachers, and a library with one hundred volumes. He had just taken over a new church in Oakland in 1874 when, according the *Christian Recorder* (9 Sept. 1875), Sanderson was killed by a streetcar as he was crossing or walking on the railroad tracks.

His wife, Catherine, outlived him. His children were Mary, Florence, Kate, Sarah, Jeremiah, and Abraham, and there were possibly some offspring who died in early life. His daughter Mary Sanderson Grassen became the first black public school teacher in Oakland.

FURTHER READING
Brown, William Wells. *The Black Man: His Antecedents, His Genius, and His Achievements* (1863).
Lapp, Rudolph M. "Jeremiah B. Sanderson: Early California Negro Leader," *Journal of Negro History* 53 (Oct. 1968): 321–333.
McFeeley, William S. *Frederick Douglass* (1991).
Ripley, C. Peter, et al., eds. *The Black Abolitionist Papers: Volume III, The United States, 1830–1846* (1991).

JOHN SAILLANT

Sandfield, Richard (16 June 1938–), ventriloquist known best as the human member of the duo Richard and Willie, was born in Memphis, Tennessee, to Richard Sandfield Sr. and Janie Massey. Sandfield Jr. lived in Memphis until he was seventeen years old, when he joined the U.S. Air Force. He served in a medical unit as a clerk typist. At the age of twenty, Sandfield was discharged from the Air Force in Los Angeles, California. Unwilling to return to the racist atmosphere and lack of economic opportunities he had known in Tennessee, he chose to stay in Los Angeles.

His early years in Los Angeles were tough. He arrived there with only two pairs of pants and $100, which he used to rent a room in the area of the city known as Skid Row. Sandfield recalled that he ate only a can of soup a day until he obtained a job. He found work for a couple of years at the post office as a mail carrier before managing a night club called C-Go Go. The club began to sponsor talent shows and Sandfield went on stage between acts and told jokes. In addition, he filled in for acts that did not show up. In essence, he became a stand-up comedian, who was influenced by white comics such as the Three Stooges, Edgar Bergen, and Paul Winchell. In 1966 he purchased a set of hand puppets to entertain his two children, who began telling folks in the neighborhood that their daddy had purchased hand puppets for them. Soon other children became interested in coming over the Sandfields' house to be entertained with the hand puppets. After seeing how much enjoyment the children were having and the laughter, Sandfield came up with the idea that this would be a great night club act. Sandfield believed if puppetry could work such an effect on children, it could also work on adults of all ages. At the age of twenty-eight, he purchased his first dummy, a Charlie McCarthy dummy for $15 from a toy store in Los Angeles. Because the dummy came only in white, Sandfield painted him black. Sandfield did his first show the same year at a night club, making $7 an hour. At the time he considered ventriloquism just a hobby. About six months later Sandfield purchased a professional ventriloquist dummy and performed at the Dootone Center in Los Angeles on the bill with singer Bobby Blue Bland. Sandfield performed his first major show in front of five thousand people at the Hollywood Palladium. There his first embarrassing moment happened. After walking off the stage, he fell into the audience. Some members in the audience helped Sandfield back onto the stage and he continued performing. Dootsie Williams, a record producer, saw the act of Richard and Willie at the Dootone Center in 1968 and signed Sandfield to a four-year contract. From 1969 to 1971 Richard and Willie produced five comedy albums. Sandfield was still performing on the Chitlin' Circuit at this time. In July 1968 Sandfield performed with Willie at a benefit show and dance that was sponsored by Les Femmes Moindaines Social-Charity Club. The proceeds for this event went to the Southern Christian Leadership Council. In 1969 Laugh Records signed the comedy team of Richard and Willie, which produced seven comedy albums from 1972 to 1980. In July 1971 Sandfield performed at the Carter Barron Amphitheatre with Roberta Flack on a show called Black Music 71. In September 1971 Richard and Willie appeared on a television show by KNBC called "We've Only Just Begun." The show was a series of ethnic specials with a musical variety program that was introducing young talent from the African American community. While working with Laugh Records, John Levy, an owning manager who managed entertainers, helped Sandfield move from the Chitlin' Circuit to the mainstream comedy circuit. Under John Levy, Richard and Willie performed at the Apollo Theatre. While performing at the Apollo Theatre, a local KNBC television producer in New York suggested that Sandfield audition for a television show. He won the audition and hosted a show called "What's Happening," out of New York City. Sandfield went on to perform on "The Nancy Wilson Show," "Merv Griffin," and "The Steve Allen Show." In addition, Sandfield hosted "The Richard & Willie Show" for nine episodes. The show was a local children's program that was produced on WNBC in New York City. Comedian Robin Harris did opening acts for Richard and Willie before he became a popular stand up act. In March 1970 Richard and Willie performed on "The Rosey Grier Show" and was a guest along with Ann Miller and Frank Ponti. In November 1972 Sandfield performed at The Comedy Store, where he received great reviews from *Variety Magazine*. During April 1973, Sandfield performed at The Apollo Theater in New York on the same bill with Nancy Wilson, Billy Paul, and the Persuaders. On 3 August 1974 Sandfield performed as special guest on "The Nancy Wilson Show"; guests included Cliff Arquette, the Pointer Sisters, and actress Pat Finley. In 1988 Sandfield worked his ventriloquist act as a support to the O'Jays in Santa Clara, California. Sandfield performed until 1992, when he decided to retire from performing. Despite his retirement, Richard Sandfield's comedy albums have become collector's items and are often hard to find. Every now and then, collectors can find an album or two on eBay.

FURTHER READING

Littleton, Darryl. *Black Comedians on Black Comedy: How African Americans Taught Us to Laugh* (2006).

Murray, Ken. "Richard Sandfield: He's No Dummy," *Right On*, Jan. 1975.

CHARLIE T. TOMLINSON

Sandifer, Jawn Ardin (6 June 1914–1 Sept. 2006), civil rights lawyer and New York state jurist, was born in Greensboro, North Carolina, the sixth of nine children of Netti and Charles Sandifer. His father died when Sandifer was four, and Nettie raised all the kids with some help from her oldest child, Herbert, a hotel baker. In Greensboro, he was known as "John" but he thought that name was too common so he changed the spelling to *Jawn* while at Johnson C. Smith University. Growing up within a short walk from North Carolina A&T State University, Sandifer wanted out of Greensboro after finishing in the first class to graduate from Dudley High School in the early 1930s. He was disillusioned with the racial discrimination he faced regularly in his boyhood in Greensboro. A caddy master from one of the country clubs stood outside the black school Sandifer attended and urged students to skip school to carry bags for well-to-do white men. Sandifer stood up for himself and refused him every time, thereby earning the nickname "schoolboy" from the caddy master. This was his first initiation to golf, a sport that he loved and played his whole life.

Sandifer graduated from Johnson C. Smith University in Charlotte in 1935. While studying at

Howard University, where he eventually received his law degree in 1938, Sandifer was influenced by his professors who emphasized training in civil rights. The professors left such an impression on him that he was later prompted to state, "The passion of my times was to overturn the segregation laws in the South and later the de facto segregation in the North" (*New York Times*, 7 Sept. 2006).

Sandifer served in the criminal investigation unit of the Army Air Corps during World War II (1939–1945). He then moved to New York in the mid-1950s and joined the legal staff of the NAACP. Sandifer was one of two staff lawyers for the association who successfully argued the *Henderson v. United States* case before the U.S. Supreme Court in 1950. Abolishing segregated railroad cars on interstate trains, this ruling set an important precedent for the 1954 landmark *Brown v. Board of Education*, in which the Supreme Court overturned school segregation. In its 8-0 decision, the court noted, "The denial of dining service to any such passenger subject him to a prohibited disadvantage. The right to be free from unreasonable discriminations belongs to each particular person" (*New York Times*, 7 Sept. 2006). Sandifer pointed out the extent of humiliation that his client Elmer W. Henderson had faced in the 1995 *New York Times* interview, "Even if a black person bought in New York a first-class ticket on a train that included dining privileges, once that train left Washington and went south, he or she could not eat in the dining car. You could walk in, every seat could be empty and there was no room for you. At best, they'd put you behind a curtain." This pathbreaking case was a major accomplishment, one of which Sandifer was justly proud.

Mayor Robert F. Wagner appointed Sandifer to the New York Civil Court in 1964; thus began Sandifer's judicial career. In 1968 he was elected to the New York State Supreme Court, where he served on the bench until 1992. Sandifer was one of the nationally appointed officers of Alpha Gamma Lambda Chapter of which he was also a life member. He was a former board director of Hope Day Nursery & Windham Children's Services and member of the resource committee, for the New York Board of Education. He coauthored *Minorities: U.S.A.* and was the general editor for *The Afro-American in United States History*.

Sandifer lamented that, "after *Brown v. Board of Education* was handed down in 1954, we thought the battle was over. We were wrong" (*New York Times*, 7 Sept. 2006). He said that as a judge he was most proud of his ruling in a case involving the New York Sanitation Department, which secured a place for women to be hired in that department. In 1986 a number of women scored higher than most men on the civil service test used as a criterion for hiring sanitation workers. To protect the gender-typed occupation, the New York sanitation workers' union sued to bar these women from being hired, contending that such work was a "man's job" and the women were not strong enough to do it. Sandifer, who always fought discrimination, posited, "That position might have been valid 20 years ago when workers were lifting heavy cans from basements. But by this time the law required owners to bag garbage and put it out on the sidewalk. You don't have to be Hercules. I threw out the suit" (*New York Times*, 7 Sept. 2006). As a result women were hired by the city to handle garbage for the first time.

Sandifer died at the age of ninety-two in Sarasota, Florida. He was survived by his second wife, Elsa Kruger Sandifer, whom he married in 2005, adopted son Floyd Sandifer, and a granddaughter. His first wife, Laura Sandifer, died in 1993. Reflecting on his life and career in 2007, Sandifer remarked, "If I have a legacy, it's that I opened minds as doors," a motto that he lived by as he "dreamed of a world where no ugly heads of discrimination would raise heads" (*New York Times*, 7 Sept. 2006).

FURTHER READING
Some of the information for this entry was gathered through personal communications with Elsa Kruger Sandifer in March 2007.
Jakes, Thomas, Sr., and Jennifer York. *Who's Who among African Americans* (1998–1999).
Obituary: *New York Times*, 7 Sept. 2006.

MOU CHAKRABORTY

Sands, Diana (23 Aug. 1934–21 Sept. 1973), actress, was born Diana Patricia Sands in the Bronx, New York, the daughter of Rudolph Thomas Sands, a carpenter, and Shirley Walker, a milliner. Sands spent her childhood in suburban Elmsford, New York, but returned to Manhattan to attend the High School for the Performing Arts. She graduated in 1952 and made her acting debut as a bar girl in the film *Caribbean Gold* (1952). Sands soon discovered that few paying jobs were offered to black actresses, and the roles that did exist were degrading or one-dimensional. Rather than submit to a career of maid and mammy parts, Sands worked days as a

Diana Sands as Adelaide Smith in *Tiger, Tiger* on 29 Jan. 1963. (Library of Congress/Photographed by Carl Van Vechten.)

keypunch operator for Con Edison and acted on the off-Broadway stage, extending her dramatic range with traditionally white roles in *An Evening with Will Shakespeare* (1953), *The World of Sholom Aleichem* (1953), and *Major Barbara* (1954).

Sands joined the Pantomime Art Theatre in 1955. By 1956 she was working fairly regularly off Broadway, in *The Man with the Golden Arm* (1956), *A Land beyond the River* (1957), and *The Egg and I* (1958), and in the films *Four Boys and A Gun* (1957) and *The Garment Jungle* (1957). In 1959 Sands made her Broadway debut as the idealistic student Beneatha Younger in LORRAINE HANSBERRY's *A Raisin in the Sun* (1959). Her performance in the play won her the Outer Circle Critics' Award for best supporting actress and the Variety Critics' Award for most promising young actress, and when the film version was released in 1961, she added an International Artist Award to her collection.

Sands returned to off Broadway for the revues *Another Evening with Harry Stoones* (1961) and *Brecht on Brecht* (1962). Her performance in *Tiger Tiger Burning Bright* (1962) brought her a Theater World Award, and her performance in *Living Premise* (1963) won an Obie (Off-Broadway Theater Award). She began to pick up good television parts as well. She was nominated for an Emmy Award for her work in the series *East Side, West Side* (1963) and the next year won the award for the special *Beyond the Blues* (1964).

Sands filmed the slight *Ensign Pulver* (1964) before being cast in JAMES BALDWIN's explosive *Blues for Mister Charlie* (1964). The play, which *Time* magazine described as telling "every white man how much every Negro hates him" (5 June 1964), cast Sands as a woman whose lover had been killed by a white man. Her climactic monologue was termed "an unparalleled tour de force" by the *New York Times* (10 May 1964), and she was nominated for a Tony Award as best supporting actress. The same year, 1964, she married Lucien Happersberger, James Baldwin's manager. The couple was divorced in 1967 and had no children.

Sands was next cast opposite Alan Alda in the romantic comedy *The Owl and the Pussycat* (1965), in a part originally written for a white actress. The color-blind casting was controversial in some quarters (the *New York Times* critic Martin Gottfried continued to complain about it five years later), but most audiences found the pairing pleasant and unremarkable. A critic for *Ebony* magazine wrote that the show proved "how attractive and natural interracial casting can seem when it is handled casually." The show was a hit, with rave reviews for both actors and a Tony nomination for best actress for Sands. "This is the first Broadway show in which I was cast as a person rather than a racial type," she said at the time. "I love it."

When Sands finished the London production of *The Owl and the Pussycat*, she spent a year playing in repertory around the United States. In an eleven-month period during 1967 she performed in *Macbeth* at Spelman College in Atlanta, in *Caesar and Cleopatra* at Theater Atlanta in Georgia, in *Antony and Cleopatra* at Macarthur Park in Los Angeles, and in *Phaedra* at the Theatre of the Living Arts in Philadelphia, Pennsylvania. She capped the year of classics with *Saint Joan* at Lincoln Center in New York. Her Joan of Arc was widely praised, and the *New York Times* critic Clive Barnes noted that "the fact that she is colored adds a quite fortuitous yet theatrically not irrelevant forcefulness to her rebellion and subsequent persecution" (5 Jan. 1968).

Though Sands enjoyed playing the classics, she resented that she had had to prove her abilities in regional theater. "Most white actresses who have been received as I have been received on Broadway and television would not have to go into repertory; they wouldn't have time," she told *Look* magazine. "I had no choice but to go to repertory if I wanted to do roles that offer me some kind of challenge, besides racial roles." She continued to speak out against the lack of "uptown" black roles and to push for color-blind casting for other black actors. "It has to become the rule, not the exception," she told Mel Gussow. "If it only works for me, that means I'm the freak. I don't want to be somebody's token" (*New York Times*, 31 Dec. 1967).

Sands found a strong role in Hal Ashby's film *The Landlord* (1970) as the slum dweller who has an affair (and a child) with Beau Bridges's fair-haired title character. The *New York Times* deemed the satiric film a "brilliant piece of cinema craftsmanship" and called Sands "as fine an actress as we have with us today, filling the screen with a warmth that haunts and sorrow that manages again and again to induce chills" (30 Sept. 1973).

Despite the good notices, an award from the Black Academy of Arts and Letters, and a recurring role in the popular television series *Julia*, Sands worked less than she wished, often taking roles in regional theater and summer stock. After filming the forgettable *Doctors' Wives* (1971), she opened the Diana Sands Sitting Service, a forty-employee child-care agency. Not long after, she and actor/director OSSIE DAVIS cofounded Third World Cinema, a film production company dedicated to showcasing black artists and experiences. Sands appeared in *Georgia, Georgia* (1972), *Willie Dynamite* (1973), and *Honeybaby, Honeybaby* (1974) for Third World and was scheduled in 1973 to star with JAMES EARL JONES in *Claudine*, the love story of a welfare mother and a sanitation worker. However, shortly before filming began in July, Sands was diagnosed with cancer. Two months later she died in New York City.

Sands is remembered for her talent and for her contribution to integration and acceptance of blacks in theater and on film. Ossie Davis wrote, "The stage was not only good to Diana, it was good for Diana. ... Out there she became what America is not yet prepared to let black women be within their private lives: invulnerable, inviolate,

invincible!" Sands's final project, *Claudine*, released in 1974 with DIAHANN CARROLL in the lead, finally presented what Sands often said was missing in American cinema: a black female as a real woman and romantic lead.

FURTHER READING
"Diana Sands: Notes on a Broadway Pussycat," *Look* (9 Feb. 1965).
"The Passion of Diana Sands," *Look* (9 Jan. 1968).
Reyes, Delia. Article on Sands in *Black Women in America: An Historical Encyclopedia*, ed. Darlene Clark Hine (1993).
Obituary: *New York Times*, 23 Sept. 1973.
This entry is taken from the *American National Biography* and is published here with the permission of the American Council of Learned Societies.

DIANA MOORE

Sands, Sarah (1842–?), sailor and sojourner, was born near Rochester, New York. Little is known of her lineage, but she is believed to have been the daughter of a John Sands, and a descendant of Virginia slaves. Her father, who may have been a fugitive slave, was in Rochester by 1841, and the family moved westward to Buffalo around 1848, where John Sands found work first as a laborer and then as a cook on a Lake Erie steamer. Among African Americans the family name "Sands" most often comes from the white Sands (variously spelled "Sandys") family: Sir Edwin Sandys and George Sandys (also pronounced "Sandz") were involved in the Jamestown settlement; others of that surname can be found in the northern colonies as well.

Sarah Sands grew up in the neighborhood of the Vine Street African Methodist Episcopal (AME) Church, not far from what would much later be the site of Buffalo's central library. Living in residential clusters, interspersed among white New England migrants and German immigrants, the small black community was anchored around the AME Church and the Michigan Street Baptist Church. Both churches were known to shelter fugitive slaves, host political and cultural meetings, and nurture mutual aid and civic associations. Sands attended the one public school open to blacks, Public School No. 9, known as the "Vine Street Colored School," located across the street from the AME Church. Although her classmates included the children of community leaders, many parents boycotted the school, reflecting a larger division of opinion over the best strategy for achieving shared goals. Nothing is known about Sarah's mother, and the 1855 state census lists Sarah as a twelve-year-old servant of a white family originally from Rochester, with none of her relatives in the vicinity.

Making a living became even more difficult for blacks in Buffalo in the 1850s, as the influx of Irish fleeing the Great Famine provoked job competition and social conflicts between these two groups that periodically erupted into violence, as happened in the Civil War conscription riots in New York City in 1863. It was in that year that Sarah Sands left Buffalo, telling friends that she was off to secure a position as a cook on an ocean vessel. She joined the crew of the *Carlotta*, a small bark out of Baltimore, Maryland. She appears on the ship's manifest as Sarah Butler, stewardess, having apparently married black crewmember John Butler (Bark *Carlotta*, Shipping & Crew Lists, U.S. National Archives, Pacific Branch). Ports of call took the *Carlotta* to South and Central America, Australia, Liverpool, San Francisco, and then to south China, where Sands was left behind in a sailor's hospital. In the British colony of Hong Kong she was provided small sums by the colonial magistrate's court and urged to go elsewhere, unwanted and unneeded given the abundance of local cheap labor.

Not especially numerous in the region before World War I, African American sojourners were typically sailors and stewardesses who had stayed on to make new lives in different ports, finding employment in boarding houses, taverns, and related services directed to sailors of color.

By 1866 Sands was the recognized wife of Stanley Bennett, whom she had met in Shanghai. An African American former sailor, he had joined the foreign mercenary force known as the Ever Victorious Army, made famous by helping the Qing Dynasty to quash the Taiping Rebellion. Shanghai, a foreign enclave run by and for merchants, was inhospitable to the couple, and Stanley Bennett's income came largely through capitalizing upon his status as a privileged foreigner exempt from Chinese laws. He was repeatedly brought before U.S. State Department consular courts, and in 1867 was shipped out among the crew of a vessel headed for San Francisco.

Anxious to be rid of Sands as well, the U.S. Consul at Amoy provided her with a ticket on a coastal steamer to Hong Kong, where she said she had friends. Arriving there in the spring of 1867 she again affiliated with an African American

male, another former sailor. Over the next few years she was in and out of Victoria Gaol, the local prison, on charges ranging from disorderly conduct to vagrancy, with the local U.S. consulate refusing to intercede on her behalf or to provide her passage home. A downward spiral took her into late October of 1874, when she "became insane" during a stint in the jail. Editorials and letters in local English-language papers, expressing both annoyance and pity, describe symptoms that suggest manic depression, as her "terrible cries and shouts" could be heard over several blocks, punctuated by loud talking and laughing, each cycle ending with "an awful and desperate yell, as of utter desolation and despair" (*Hong Kong Daily Press*, 27 October 1874). Colonial officials had resisted pressures from London to construct a "lunatic asylum," believing that the total absence of decent facilities made friends, distant relatives, and foreign governments more inclined to rescue the afflicted. In early January 1875 Sands was transferred to the Old Civil Hospital, which had become "Old" the previous September when a typhoon of unprecedented destruction took off its roof. She was put in the care of a married European couple, with periodic visits from the colonial surgeon.

A formal request to the U.S. government for her repatriation was accompanied by an affidavit from one of the jail employees, Alfred Taylor, who had been her classmate at the Vine Street School before going off to sea in the mid-1850s. The State Department's inquiry to the Buffalo mayor brought confirmation of the essential details, with former neighbors readily recalling both Sands and Taylor. Yet, because Sands had "abandoned the sea" years earlier, she did not qualify for seaman's relief, and until the 1960s the federal government lacked legal authority to pay for the return of "distressed" nationals, whatever their race.

In April 1877, with the new colonial governor's arrival imminent, British officials asked the U.S. consul to order the captain of a Pacific Mail steamer to transport Sands to San Francisco. Consul David Bailey declined, but said that he would not interfere in arrangements made by the British themselves. Sands's ultimate fate remains unknown, as there is no subsequent mention of her in surviving British colonial or U.S. records, and San Francisco passenger manifests for this era were destroyed by fire and earthquake. A free woman of color, Sands was one of a handful of African American sojourners in late nineteenth-century coastal China, exiles of a kind, home neither there nor in their native country.

FURTHER READING

Bolster, W. Jeffrey. *Black Jacks: African American Seamen in the Age of Sail* (1997).

Horton, James O. *Free People of Color: Inside the African American Community* (1993).

Scully, Eileen P. *The Map Song of Sarah Sands* (forthcoming).

EILEEN SCULLY

Sanford, Isabel (29 Aug. 1917–9 July 2004), actress, was born Eloise Gwendolyn Sanford in Harlem, New York, to James Edward Sanford, a chauffeur, and Josephine Perry, a house cleaner. She was her parents' seventh child and the only one to survive infancy. Sanford's parents separated when she was three, and when she was of school age, she began attending P.S. 81, an all-girl school. She showed her acting prowess there in many productions, often playing male roles because of her deep, husky voice. She attended both Evander Childs and Textile High Schools and continued to act and take drama classes. She occasionally appeared at the Apollo Theater on amateur nights, gaining valuable experience and winning over the notoriously difficult crowds. She could not, however, win the support of her deeply religious mother, who disapproved of acting.

In the 1930s Sanford began her professional career with the Star Players (later the American Negro Theatre). In 1946 she made her theatrical debut in *On Strivers' Row*, playing the role of Sophie. In future productions she worked alongside classmates SIDNEY POITIER and HARRY BELAFONTE. Sanford then found work as a secretary and devoted her evenings to New York City YWCA drama projects, performing with CICELY TYSON among others. Although her career kept her busy, Sanford met and married William Edward Richmond (Sonny), a housepainter from North Carolina, and gave birth to three children. The union was not a happy one, and the couple separated. Sanford never remarried.

With children to support, Sanford worked as a keypuncher for the New York City Welfare Department. For a while, she even juggled four jobs—two office and two acting ones—to provide for her family and keep her acting dream alive. She landed roles in a few off-Broadway productions, *Shakespeare in Harlem* and *The Egg and I*, but she was persuaded that a move to California might further her career. In 1960 she and her children traveled to Los Angeles by bus.

Sanford got her first break in California in 1962 when she was offered the role of Tallulah Bankhead's maid in a tour of *Here Today*. Although it was a fine acting opportunity, this tour was not altogether positive. Sanford faced several instances of discrimination: she was refused service in a restaurant and was not allowed the same sleeping accommodations as the white actors in the company.

After the tour, Sanford longed for film work, but discovered it was virtually impossible to find any because she did not have a Screen Actors Guild card. She persevered, finding work in stage productions of *Purlie Victorious* and *The Blacks*. In 1965 she was given a role in JAMES BALDWIN's *The Amen Corner*, a production that made it all the way to Broadway. Her strong performance caught the attention of Hollywood insiders, and she won the role of Tillie, the feisty housekeeper, in Stanley Kramer's film *Guess Who's Coming to Dinner* (1967).

Her portrayal in this film drew critical praise, paving the way for appearances on several popular television shows, including *Bewitched* (1968), *The Mod Squad* (1968), and a semiregular spot on the *Carol Burnett Show* (1967–1969). The turning point in her career, however, came in 1971 when she was cast as Louise Jefferson, Archie Bunker's neighbor, on the hit show *All in the Family*. In 1975 Sanford continued her role as Louise (Weezy) in *The Jeffersons*, a spin-off in which she, husband George, and son Lionel found themselves "movin' on up" (according to the show's theme song) to New York City's tony Upper East Side, all made possible by George's success in the dry cleaning business. Sanford's practical Louise was a perfect foil to the blustery George, played by the inimitable SHERMAN HEMSLEY. This popular series showcased Sanford's screen charisma and excellent comedic timing, earning her NCAA Image awards in 1975 and 1978, and Emmy nominations from 1979 to 1985. In 1981 she received the Emmy for Outstanding Lead Actress in a Comedy Series, making her the first African American woman to win this award. At the awards ceremony Sanford, who had not anticipated winning, was at a backstage buffet table when her name was called. She walked up to the podium, still munching cheese, and told the appreciative audience: "I've waited so long, all my humility is gone" (Thomas, 80).

After *The Jeffersons* ended its eleven-year run in 1985, Sanford's career slowed, but she returned to television two years later in a short-lived syndicated sitcom, *Hollywood Hotel*. She followed up this disappointment with stage appearances in *The Subject Was Roses* (1988), *La Cage aux Folles* (1991), and film roles in *Original Gangstas* (1996) and *Click Three Times* (1999). Throughout the 1990s she was a frequent guest star on television, appearing in *The Fresh Prince of Bel-Air* (1995–1996), *Roseanne* (1995), and *The Parkers* (2001). She even lent her distinctive voice to an episode of *The Simpsons* (2004). Later she reteamed with Hemsley to make commercials for Old Navy, AT&T, and Denny's restaurants.

When Sanford was not working, she enjoyed reading, responding to fan mail, and relaxing at her beach house. She also continued her charity work, but this interest in philanthropy was nothing new. In the early 1970s she had been one of the founding members of the Kwanza Foundation, an organization that provides gifts for children at Christmas, and in 1984 she was named the celebrity Mother of the Year for her work on behalf of the March of Dimes.

In late 2003 Sanford had preventive surgery on a neck artery, and her health began to decline. She was sufficiently healthy in January 2004 to appear before more than 300 family, friends, and well-wishers, to receive yet another honor: a star on the Hollywood Walk of Fame. On 4 July that same year Sanford became ill and was admitted to Cedars-Sinai Medical Center in Los Angeles, where she died of natural causes at the age of eighty-six. Sanford is buried in Forest Lawn Memorial Park (Hollywood Hills) in Los Angeles, California.

FURTHER READING

Smith-Shomade, Beretta. *Shaded Lives: African-American Women and Television* (2002).

Thomas, Bob. "Isabel Sanford: Movin' On Up." *Good Housekeeping* (June 1982).

Thorsen, Connie. "Isabel Sanford," in *Scribner Encyclopedia of American Lives: 2003–2005* (2006).

Obituary: *New York Times*, 13 July 2004.

LARRY SEAN KINDER

Santamaría, Mongo Ramón (7 Apr. 1917–1 Feb. 2003), percussionist, arranger, and composer, was born Ramón Santamaría Rodríguez in the poor Afro-Cuban neighborhood of Jesús María in Havana, Cuba. The grandson of a Congolese slave, Santamaría was the son of Ramón Santamaría Gimenez, a construction worker, and Felicia Rodríguez Bazan, a coffee and cigarette vendor.

Mongo Ramón Santamaría plays the conga drums at the Super Jazz Concert at the Apollo Theater in New York on 10 Dec. 1988. (AP Images.)

He was raised by his mother, grandmother, and cousins, and his upbringing was unexceptional for an Afro-Cuban child of the time. He was surrounded by religious and secular music, especially the African ritual drums and dances that seduced him from an early age and set the course of his personal and professional life. Although the exact circumstances are unclear, during his childhood he earned the nickname Mongo, from the Mali word meaning "chief of the tribe." When he grew older he was introduced to the Afro-Cuban syncretic religion Santeria and became a devout adherent. At age seventeen Santamaría quit school to work as a mailman by day and as a percussionist by night. He began his career playing the bongos but quickly switched to the larger congas for which he became best known. He developed a solid reputation in Cuba in the 1940s based on performances in the musical spectacles at the Tropicana, the Sans Souci, and the Montmartre. Nevertheless by the end of the decade, after brief stints in Mexico City and Manhattan and frustrated with the economic and artistic limitations imposed upon him by the openly racist society, Santamaría resolved to leave Cuba and seek his fortune elsewhere.

In 1950 Santamaría legally immigrated to the United States, finding work in the nightclubs of New York. His timing was perfect: the mambo craze was reaching a frenzied peak under the direction of the Cuban pianist and bandleader Damaso Pérez Prado, with whom Santamaría toured and recorded, and the singer and maraca player Frank Grillo, better known by his nickname "MACHITO." The atmosphere was thick with musical experimentation fueled by hybrids of Latin rhythms and jazz harmonies, most famously realized in the "Cu-Bop" collaborations of the 1940s between the trumpeter DIZZY GILLESPIE, the saxophonist CHARLIE PARKER, and the Afro-Cuban conga player CHANO POZO. Such work also laid the foundation for the rise of the Puerto Rican vibraphonist and timbale player Tito Puente, who hired Santamaría to play congas for his band in 1951. Santamaría performed with Puente throughout much of the 1950s and made six records with the bandleader before leaving to join Cal Tjader in 1958.

While Santamaría was performing with Puente and Tjader, he also recorded under his own name. He began in 1955 with the legendary *Changó*, named after the Yoruba god of thunder, lightning, drums, and dance. A collection of Afro-Cuban liturgical and secular music, the recording holds the distinction of being the first of its kind made in the United States. Its release introduced previously unknown rhythms to North American jazz and Latin music fans, and it remains a classic. He followed up the success with the stylistically similar *Yambú* in 1958 and the jazzier *Mongo* in 1959. The latter is especially notable for Santamaría's composition "Afro Blue," which quickly became a standard and has been recorded nearly thirty times, most famously by the saxophonist JOHN COLTRANE. A 1960 visit to Havana resulted in two more records, *Our Man in Havana* and *Bembé*, quite probably the last recordings made in Cuba by a North American record company before the trade embargo.

In 1961 Santamaría formed the ensemble La Sabrosa. While the group initially seemed an attempt to take advantage of the "pachanga" dance craze among New York Latin teens, it quickly evolved into an outfit for harmonic and rhythmic explorations of Latin jazz. Short-lived but prolific, La Sabrosa made five records in less than two years. Within months of the dissolution of La Sabrosa, Santamaría formed another Latin jazz group under his own name featuring the 21-year-old piano virtuoso Armando "Chick" Corea. When Corea was unable to make a performance, another

rising legend of jazz piano, the twenty-two-year-old HERBIE HANCOCK, was called to fill in. During a break between sets, Hancock played an original blues for Santamaría. The percussionist was immediately taken with the tune and its possibilities. He sat down behind his congas and began to play an Afro-Cuban groove to complement Hancock's piano. Within moments the entire ensemble had returned to the bandstand to play for the first time what was to become the composition with which Santamaría would always be inextricably identified: "Watermelon Man."

The song and subsequent record *Watermelon Man!* proved crossover gold for Santamaría, opening doors to cities and venues that were outside of the usual jazz circuit. It also led to interest from larger record companies with distribution outside of the limited jazz market. After fulfilling his contractual obligation to Riverside Records, Santamaría signed with Columbia Records. As the popularity of Latin jazz waned over the course of his tenure with Columbia, Santamaría modified his style, incorporating rhythm and blues elements into his Latin jazz sound. The result kept him commercially and creatively viable, and eight of the ten records he made for Columbia between 1965 and 1969 broke the *Billboard* Top 200. The successes continued with Atlantic Records, for which he recorded until 1973. The popularity of his musical hybrids, contemporary with the black power movement, led Afro-Cuban hand percussion to become a standard part of 1970s rhythm and blues; this, in turn, contributed to a rise in the number of African American percussionists in the United States.

Santamaría finished out the decade with Fania Records, a label associated with the burgeoning salsa style. While the relationship was uneasy—Santamaría publicly denounced the term "salsa" as nothing more than a politically correct name for Cuban music—it resulted in Santamaría's first Grammy Award for the album *Dawn (Amanecer)*. While Santamaría switched labels often throughout the 1980s and 1990s, his music was of a consistently high quality. He continued to push the limits of Afro-Cuban music and Latin jazz, mentoring young musicians and working with famous old friends until his retirement from public performance in 1999. His legacy is twofold: he introduced Afro-Cuban secular and religious music to the world outside of Cuba, and in doing so he pushed and redefined the parameters of jazz and popular music.

FURTHER READING

Gerard, Charley. *Music from Cuba: Mongo Santamaría, Chocolate Armenteros, and Cuban Musicians in the United States* (2001).

Roberts, John Storm. *The Latin Tinge: The Impact of Latin American Music on the United States* (1979; 2d ed., 1999).

Sweeney, Philip. *The Rough Guide to Cuban Music: The History, the Artists, the Best CDs* (2001).

ROBERT NASATIR

Santop, Louis (17 Jan. 1890–6 Jan. 1942), Negro League baseball player, was born Louis Santop Loftin in Tyler, Texas, to parents whose names remain unknown. Nothing else is known about Santop's family or personal life.

Santop began his professional career in 1909 when he played for the all-black baseball teams the Fort Worth Wonders and the Oklahoma Monarchs; he then played through the 1910 season with the Philadelphia Giants, where he was primarily a catcher. Like many of the era's players he played for many teams. Most Negro League teams lacked organization and stable finances. Player contracts were nonexistent or ignored; it was common for players to jump from team to team, seeking better money, better playing conditions, or simply the chance to play every day. Teams in large Midwest and East Coast cities attracted the best players because they had the most resources, had the largest fan base, and, through leasing arrangements with major league clubs, played in the better stadiums. Except for a brief stint playing for the Chicago American Giants, Santop spent his career playing for various East Coast teams, including the New York Lincoln Giants, the Brooklyn Royal Giants, and the New York Lincoln Stars. His best years were before World War I, when he played for the New York Lincoln Giants and Lincoln Stars. He caught two of that era's best pitchers, SMOKEY JOE WILLIAMS and "CANNONBALL" DICK REDDING, and hit for averages of .470, .422, .429, and .455 for the years 1911, 1912, 1913, and 1914 respectively.

Santop was one of the marquee players in Negro League baseball. At six feet, four inches and two hundred and forty pounds, this right-handed throwing, left-handed hitting catcher could hit for power and average. During his seventeen-year career he compiled a .406 batting average, making him one of the most prolific hitters in history. His hitting power earned him the nickname "Big Bertha," after the enormous World War I German artillery gun, because he used a large, heavy bat and could hit prodigious home runs. His tape-measure homers, including one hit in 1912 that measured more than five hundred feet, were all the more impressive because he played in the dead-ball era when the ball, by the nature of its construction, was softer and did not travel as far when hit as baseballs used today.

Santop was also a showman who entertained the fans with animated play and impressive feats of baseball skill. It is reported that he could stand behind home plate and throw the ball over the centerfield fence. Fans marveled at his pregame warm-up in which he would position himself behind home plate in his catcher's crouch and fire the ball around the infield for fifteen minutes with deadly accuracy. Stories tell of him calling his home runs, sometimes after a dare from a fan. Because of success at calling his shots in the way Babe Ruth did, he was called "the black Babe Ruth."

After a two-year tour in the navy during World War I, Santop finished his professional career with the Hilldale Daisies in Darby, Pennsylvania, where he became one of the league's biggest draws and earned what at the time was the enormous sum of five hundred dollars a month. Santop played for the Hilldale club during its three pennant-winning years of 1923, 1924, and 1925. Despite hitting .333 in the 1924 Negro World Series against the Kansas City Monarchs, Santop's fielding miscue proved to be the beginning of the end of his career. In the fateful game Hilldale held a slim 2–1 lead in the bottom of the ninth inning. The Monarchs had the bases loaded but were down to their last out. The batter, Frank Duncan, hit an easy pop foul behind the plate, but Santop muffed the catch, and on the next pitch Duncan drove in two runners to win the game. Besides the embarrassment, Santop suffered the public humiliation of a severe chewing out by his manager Frank Warfield. The next season Hilldale brought in a new catcher, BIZ MACKEY, and Santop's role was reduced, primarily to pinch-hitting. He was released during the 1926 season.

His career ended in relative obscurity as a player and manager of his own semipro team, the Santop Bronchos, on which he played from 1927 until 1931. When his playing days ended he became a radio broadcaster for the Philadelphia station WELK. His final years were spent tending bar in Philadelphia. Santop developed severe arthritis and other illnesses and eventually died in a Philadelphia naval hospital.

Because professional baseball was segregated until 1946, one of the great questions about black ballplayers of Santop's era was how good they were compared to major leaguers. The general consensus among those who played in the Negro Leagues was that the level of play was roughly equal to triple-A ball, the uppermost minor league in professional baseball. Most Negro League teams had a few outstanding players but lacked a deep pitching staff and did not field star players at every position. However, sometimes enough quality black players got together to form a team that was the equal of any major league club. In 1917 the Hilldale club recruited Santop to play in a three-game exhibition series against the Philadelphia Athletics. Santop collected six hits against two of the Athletics' best pitchers, and Hilldale won two of three games. In a 1920 postseason exhibition game against a group of major league all-stars that included Babe Ruth, Santop collected three hits while the Babe went 0-4. Over his career, records show that Santop compiled a .296 batting average in fourteen exhibition games against major-league pitching.

FURTHER READING

Peterson, Robert. *Only the Ball Was White: A History of Legendary Black Players and All-Black Professional Teams* (1970).

Riley, James A. *The Biographical Encyclopedia of the Negro Baseball Leagues* (1994).

DOUGLAS FLEMING ROOSA

Sapphire (4 Aug. 1950–), poet, performance artist, and novelist, was born Ramona Lofton at Fort Ord military base near Monterey, California, one of four children. Sapphire and her family lived on and off army bases in California and Texas for the first twelve years of her life. She suffered sexual abuse from her father as early as age three. When Sapphire was thirteen, her father retired from the army and moved to Europe. Following her parents' separation, Sapphire and her siblings moved with their mother to South Philadelphia, her mother's hometown. Soon after their move her mother abandoned the family, and Sapphire moved back to California with her siblings, to Los Angeles.

At age twenty-one Sapphire hitchhiked to San Francisco, where she attempted to reconstruct her life after bearing the burden of being guardian to her two siblings. In 1973 she enrolled in San Francisco City College as a premed student. Despite excellent grades, she soon lost interest in medicine and transferred to a private college in California, where she studied dance and other performance arts. She began keeping a journal while living in the Tenderloin district of San Francisco. Influenced by NTOZAKE SHANGE's experimentation with choreography and poetry, Sapphire began to perform her own poetry on the stage and in nightclubs in the late 1970s. She also read the poetry of Don L. Lee (Haki R. Madhubuti), SONIA SANCHEZ, and JAYNE CORTEZ.

A follower of the new age movement, she legally changed her name from Ramona to Sapphire. During this time she decided to pursue a career in dance. Sapphire left California and moved to New York City, where she made ends meet working as a stripper. In 1977 Sapphire had her first publication in *Azalea: A Magazine by and for Third World Lesbians.* Later that year Sapphire co-created NAPS, the first known black lesbian performing group in the United States, with Aida Mansuer and Irare Sabasu.

In 1983 Sapphire earned a bachelor of fine arts degree from the Davis Center for the Performing Arts. In the same year, her mother died, and her brother, then homeless, was killed in a public park. She moved to Harlem that year and in addition to her writing and performing began to teach reading and writing to teenagers and adults in Harlem and the Bronx. In the course of this work she encountered firsthand accounts of students who had been sexually abused by their parents, many of whom were pregnant before their teens. Her primary literary influence during this period was ALICE WALKER's *The Third Life of Grange Copeland.* This novel's treatment of physical battery of women by men informed much of Sapphire's later work.

Sapphire published her first book of poetry, *Meditations on the Rainbow*, in 1987. The collection captures Sapphire's spirit as a black lesbian, feminist, and survivor of abuse. *Meditations* comprises seven "colorful" poems: "yellow," "red," "black," "lavender," "green," "blue," and "white." Each color reflects the poet's perception of how color relates to the world around her. For example, the section "blue," a metaphor for the blues, offers a melancholy reflection on a black American nightmare of rape, racism, stolen music, and stolen dreams. Similarly, "lavender" describes the trials of lesbians and gays ostracized by a society that would prefer for them to hide their homosexuality.

In 1990, when Sapphire staged her last major performance, a fifty-minute choreopoem titled

"Are You Ready to Rock?," her business manager challenged her for what she considered her one deficiency as a writer: that she had never published a novel. This same year, Sapphire celebrated her fortieth birthday, marked by what she described as a midlife crisis. Sapphire recalled that, compared to her mentors like Shange, who was a prolific author by age 39, she recognized in herself a lack of confidence and sustained commitment to any one project, which stifled her pursuits as a writer.

Committing herself to becoming a writer, in 1993 Sapphire earned an MFA in modern dance from Brooklyn College, where she worked under the tutelage of the poet Allen Ginsberg. His use of abrasive language and controversial themes influenced Sapphire's poetry.

In 1994 Sapphire published *American Dreams*, a collection of poetry and prose that collectively represents the American dream deferred. The title poem, "American Dreams," explores themes of racism among blacks, murder, and global warfare. Short prose narratives, such as "Reflections from Glass Breaking" and the transcribed "Are You Ready to Rock?" employ a child's voice to relate the experiences of young rape victims.

In 1996 Sapphire published her first novel, *Push*, the story of Claireece Precious Jones, a black, illiterate, sixteen-year-old HIV-positive mother of two, struggling to find her place in a society that constantly fails her. Precious fights to overcome the pain of a father who is also the father of her two children, and a mother who physically abuses her because she faults Precious for taking her husband. Like Sapphire, who began writing in a journal in her early twenties, Precious finds a sense of freedom from a world of pain when she enrolls in a literacy class, learns to read, and begins keeping a journal. The novel concludes with a series of poems by Precious and three short personal narratives by her classmates, who also were raped and molested. These narratives reinforce the fact that Precious's story represents the voices of many, including Sapphire and the students she had taught in Harlem and the Bronx. The book received renewed attention in 2009, when the film adaptation *Precious: Based on the Novel Push, by Sapphire*, was released. The widely acclaimed film, directed by Lee Daniels, earned multiple awards (including an Academy Award for the actress Mo'Nique) and brought the book and its intense subject matter to the attention of a wider audience.

Sapphire has described her writing as witnessing and testimony. She has identified herself as a black person and a woman who has changed from heterosexual to lesbian to bisexual. Through her writing, Sapphire has sought to counter the idea that racism is the only challenge affecting people's ability to live happy, peaceful lives. As a feminist, she has remained dedicated to eradicating the oppression of all women.

FURTHER READING

Bell-Scott, Patricia. "Sapphire: The Artist As Witness," in *Flat-footed Truths: Telling Black Women's Lives* (1998).

Jewell, Terri L. "Sapphire," in *Contemporary Lesbian Writers of the United States: A Bio-Biographical Critical Sourcebook*, ed. Sandra Pollack and Denise D. Knight (1993).

Walters, Tracey. "Sapphire," *Contemporary African American Novelists: A Bio-Bibliographical Critical Sourcebook*, ed. Emmanuel S. Nelson (1999).

ONDRA KROUSE DISMUKES

Sargent, Ruppert Leon (6 Jan. 1938–15 Mar. 1967), Vietnam War soldier and Medal of Honor recipient, was born in Hampton, Virginia. Little is known about his early life, except that his mother was an adherent to the Jehovah's Witness faith. Ruppert Sargent was likely a follower of his mother's beliefs through his teenage years, and as a young adult married a woman who also practiced the faith. Sargent later attended the Hampton Institute and Virginia State College at Petersburg (now Virginia State University), where he was a cadet in the ROTC (Reserve Officer Training Corps) "Warrior" Battalion. Sargent's positive experiences with the ROTC while at Virginia State College likely led him to seek a career in the military, for on 8 January 1959 he enlisted in the U.S. Army, despite the religious objections of his mother and wife.

During Ruppert Sargent's first six years in the army, he served as an enlisted man; while little is known about his specific activities, there is little doubt that he demonstrated not only the skills of an accomplished soldier, but also that he showed great leadership potential. In 1965 Sargent was selected to attend Officer Training School, and on 15 October 1965 he was commissioned a lieutenant. His rise to officer status was not only an outstanding personal achievement, but it was also an indicator of just how far the army had progressed when it came to career opportunities for African Americans serving in the military. While some black officers were commissioned in previous wars, including JOHN FOX, VERNON BAKER, and CHARLES THOMAS in World War II, career opportunities for these men were extremely limited due to the racial attitudes then prevailing. However, it was during the Korean War that segregation in the army was finally ended, and by the time of the Vietnam War many outstanding black officers, men like Sargent, RILEY PITTS, JOHN WARREN, and CHARLES ROGERS, could be found in positions of leadership. While the army still had its inequities during the Vietnam War era, including a disproportionately large amount of black draftees compared to whites (and a correspondingly smaller number of granted deferments), the old ideas that African American soldiers were inferior and could not provide the needed leadership on the field of battle were put to rest once and for all.

Following his promotion to first lieutenant, Ruppert Sargent was assigned to Company B, 4th Battalion, 9th Infantry Regiment, 25th Infantry Division. He was subsequently assigned for service in Vietnam, beginning his tour of duty there on 30 September 1966. On 15 March 1967 Lieutenant Sargent was leading his platoon in Hau Nghia Province, investigating reports of a Vietcong meeting house and weapons cache. While working to flush enemy soldiers from a booby-trapped tunnel, Sargent's platoon sergeant killed one combatant, but while Sargent and several soldiers were approaching the tunnel entrance, a second Vietcong soldier threw two hand grenades in the midst of the platoon. Sargent fired on the soldier, and then quickly, without any regard for his own safety, threw himself on the two live grenades. When the grenades subsequently exploded, Sargent had saved the lives of two of his men, who were but lightly wounded, but at the expense of his own life. Mortally wounded by the grenade blasts, Ruppert Sargent soon expired.

Ruppert Sargent was buried in the Hampton National Cemetery in his hometown of Hampton, Virginia, but his heroism was not forgotten; he was soon recommended for the Medal of Honor, which award was approved in July 1968. The medal was subsequently scheduled to be presented to his wife by President Lyndon Johnson later that year, but complications arose when Mary Jo Sargent refused to accept the award, as it was in conflict with the Jehovah's Witness belief that allegiance should be professed to God alone, not to any other power or organized government. Ruppert Sargent's mother supported her daughter-in-law's decision, leaving the army in a quandary. Finally, in early 1969, Sargent's family agreed to accept the award in a private ceremony. On 7 March 1969 the Medal of Honor was presented to Mrs. Ruppert Sargent at her home by General Donley Bolton. Sargent's Medal of Honor award was unique not only because of these unusual circumstances, but also because it had to be approved by two U.S. presidents. Originally approved under the administration of Lyndon Johnson, Ruppert Sargent's Medal of Honor had to again be approved in early 1969 under the administration of newly elected President Richard Nixon. Despite the delay, Ruppert Sargent was the first African American officer to earn the Medal of Honor, and one of twenty black recipients overall, during the Vietnam War. He is honored in his hometown of Hampton, Virginia, where the city's administration building bears his name.

FURTHER READING
Hanna, Charles W. *African American Recipients of the Medal of Honor* (2002).
"VSU Pays Tribute to a 'True American Hero.'" *Virginia State University Magazine* 6, no. 1 (Summer 2006): 15.

GLENN ALLEN KNOBLOCK

Sash, Moses (1755–?), soldier and rebellion participant, was born in Stoughton, Massachusetts, the son of Moses Sash and Sarah Colley, free blacks who were listed as "molatoes" in the church record of their marriage. Moses Sash the younger served in the American Revolution, enlisting on 17 August 1777 in Colonel Ruggles Woodbridge's regiment and serving until 29 November 1777. His unit saw action at the battle of Saratoga. On 17 April 1781 Sash reenlisted for a term of three years as part of the quota of men assigned to the town of Cummington, Massachusetts. He was a private in the Seventh Regiment of Lieutenant Colonel John Brooks, serving mostly in the area of West Point, New York.

Sash played a significant role in the western Massachusetts uprising of 1786 and early 1787 led by Captain Daniel Shays over matters of debt, taxation, and the feeling of western Massachusetts farmers that their needs were subordinated to those of Boston. Other African American participants in Shays's rebellion included Tobias Green of Plainfield, Massachusetts, and Aaron Carter and Peter Green of Colrain, Massachusetts. Sash was indicted twice for his participation in Shays's rebellion. Both indictments were issued on 9 April 1787 from the grand jury at Northampton, county seat of Hampshire County in western Massachusetts, and are preserved in a group of thirty-three indictments. In this group Sash is the only person indicted twice and the only African American.

The first indictment, identifying Sash as a "Negro Man and a laborer," includes a number of charges generally related to participation in the rebellion. On the back are written the words, "A Captain and one of Shaises Council." It is the only indictment in the group so marked. The meaning of this phrase is unclear. Sash did not hold the military rank of captain in either the Revolutionary army or the Massachusetts militia, although Shays's forces did sometimes create their own officers. The meaning of "Shaises Council" is not specific. Sash is not recorded as being a member of the Committee of Seventeen established in Worcester, Massachusetts, in the fall of 1786 to organize Hampshire militia forces. It is possible that as an officer Sash participated in councils of war with Shays and other commanders of the insurgent forces. Whatever Sash's participation in councils, his identification as a council member also served to justify the indictment. Those who served on the rebels' war council in the period following 20 January 1787 were specifically excluded from the indemnity resolved by the General Court of Massachusetts on 10 March. This resolve offered participants in the rebellion indemnity on taking an oath of allegiance.

That Sash was still participating in the rebellion in late January is clear from the second indictment, which is much more specific than the first one, and charges Sash with having stolen two guns worth five pounds on 30 January in South Hadley. This would indicate that Sash remained with the rebel forces following their failure to take the federal arsenal at Springfield on 20 January and their subsequent retreat through Chicopee and South Hadley before their final defeat at Petersham on 3 February. Presumably Sash was foraging for guns for the rebels.

Although Sash could have faced the death penalty—two men were hanged for their participation in the rebellion—there was a popular reaction in Massachusetts against harsh punishment of the rebels. John Hancock, elected governor in May, dropped actions against all those still under indictment, presumably including Sash.

Sash returned to Worthington, where he was the only black head of household listed in the 1790 census of the Worthington district of Hampshire County. His household was listed as containing four members. By 1820 he lived in Connecticut with his wife's family, supporting himself as a day laborer. In that year he wrote to Worthington asking for support. Nothing else is known about his marriage, family life, or death.

FURTHER READING

Kaplan, Sidney. "A Negro Veteran in Shays' Rebellion," *Journal of Negro History* 33 (1948).

WILLIAM E. BURNS

Sasser, Clarence Eugene (12 Sept. 1947–), soldier and Medal of Honor recipient, was born in Rosharon, Texas. The second eldest of seven children, Sasser grew up on the farm, his parents making a living growing crops and raising livestock on twenty-five acres of land. Military service in the Sasser family was nothing new; Clarence's father, Will, had served as truck driver in the army during World War II. When he was still a youth, Sasser's parents divorced and he was subsequently brought up by his mom and his stepfather, Jerome Brown. After graduating from Marshall High School in Angleton, Texas, in 1965, Sasser enrolled at the University of Houston and hoped to become a doctor. However, Sasser could only attend part-time because he had to work to pay for his tuition. He subsequently had to give up his college deferment and was drafted into the army on 15 June 1967 for a term of two years. Though Clarence Sasser never gained a medical degree, in a combat career lasting less than five months he not only put his army-trained medical skills to extraordinary use, but also earned our nation's highest award for valor in the process.

Clarence Sasser entered the service at Houston, Texas, and was subsequently trained as a combat medic. His first three months of training and service were spent stateside, including basic training at Fort Polk, Texas, and medic training at Fort Sam Houston in San Antonio. In late September 1967 he was sent to Vietnam, serving as part of the Headquarters Company, 3rd Battalion, 60th Infantry Regiment, 9th Infantry Division in the Mekong Delta area. Specialist 5th Class Sasser's tour of duty in Vietnam lasted less than four months. During the Vietnam War, from 1960 to 1975, about 200,000 African Americans served in the entire military as both enlisted men and officers. Not only was this the first war since the American Revolution in which black soldiers fought entirely in units that were nonsegregated for the duration of the conflict, but their overall contribution in Vietnam was significant in terms of both numbers and their meritorious actions. Indeed, one of the many controversies of the Vietnam War was the perception that it was largely, as the Medal of Honor historian Charles Hanna states, "a rich man's war but a poor man's fight, with blacks doing a disproportionate share of the fighting" (145). This disparity is amply demonstrated by the fact that educational deferments during the war were granted in disproportionately higher numbers to white men as opposed to African Americans. Despite these incongruities, black soldiers in Vietnam, men like Sasser, WEBSTER ANDERSON, DONALD LONG, and WILLIAM BRYANT, performed at high levels, with twenty of them earning the Medal of Honor.

During his first months in Vietnam, Clarence Sasser experienced little combat action, but this would change. On 10 January 1968 Sasser was serving as a medic with Company A of the 3rd Battalion during a reconnaissance in force mission being conducted in Dinh Tuong Province on the Mekong River Delta. As he later recalled, "We were going to have an easy time of it that day. At least that is what we thought" (Smith, 323). However, when the nearly two dozen helicopters of the force were approaching the landing zone, Vietcong forces responded with automatic rifle and rocket fire, shooting down the lead helicopter. The other helicopters quickly landed to offer protection and aid to the crew and soldiers in the downed craft, but in the first few minutes after landing over thirty men were wounded or killed. Clarence Sasser, the only medic in the unit to survive that day, made it out of his helicopter and immediately sought to aid his wounded comrades amid bursts of enemy gunfire. While picking up a wounded man and dragging him to cover, Sasser was hit in the shoulder by shrapnel from an exploding enemy rocket, but continued to aid the wounded when he was hit yet again, this time by machine-gun fire in both legs, and knocked down. He subsequently used his arms to crawl through the mud for a hundred yards to aid a wounded soldier, and though in severe pain and suffering from great blood loss, continued his duties as a medic. When he saw a group of soldiers close to him huddled together and paralyzed to inaction by the heavy gunfire, Sasser encouraged them to keep fighting and to seek shelter behind a nearby dike so that they could fire on the enemy from a more secure position; after they did just that, Sasser subsequently treated some of their wounded. Of his actions on that eventful day, Sasser would later state that "guys were dropping like flies, and

now they're hollering 'Medic! Medic! Doc! Doc!' All that kind of stuff....The first guy I got to was badly hurt. He had been shot through the chest.... After I bandaged him, I told him to try and keep his head above water...that's all you can do, and go on to the next one. Bullets were flying, mortars were coming in" (Smith, 324–325).

Eventually, American forces cleared out the Vietcong and were able to evacuate the area the following morning; though twenty-four men were killed and fifty-nine wounded in the battle, the casualties would certainly have been greater were it not for the actions of Specialist 5th Class Clarence Sasser.

Sasser was subsequently sent to Japan for medical treatment and would not regain the use of his legs for several months. It was during his recovery here that he was told that he had been awarded the Medal of Honor, making him one of just fifteen combat medics who would earn the decoration during the Vietnam War, and one of two African American medics so honored, the first being LAWRENCE JOEL. Sasser received the Medal of Honor from President Richard Nixon during a White House ceremony on 7 March 1969. After fulfilling his military duty, Clarence Sasser returned to college and earned a degree in chemistry at Texas A&M University, after which he worked at an oil refinery for a time before gaining a position with the U.S. Department of Veterans Affairs in 1977.

In 2011, Sasser held the distinction of being the only living African American Medal of Honor recipient; though he still found the memories of that fateful day when he earned the medal painful, he made occasional appearances at schools and military bases. In 1971 he married his wife Ethel Morant, with whom he had three sons, Ross, Benjamin, and Billy. The couple eventually built their own home in Rosharon in 1986, but Ethel was killed in a car crash in 1996.

FURTHER READING

Collier, Peter. *Medal of Honor: Portraits of Valor beyond the Call of Duty* (2003).

Hanna, Charles W. *African American Recipients of the Medal of Honor* (2002).

Smith, Larry. *Beyond Glory: Medal of Honor Heroes in Their Own Words* (2003).

GLENN ALLEN KNOBLOCK

Satcher, David (2 Mar. 1941–), physician, scholar, and U.S. surgeon general, was born in Anniston, Alabama, the son of Anna and Wilmer Satcher, a foundry worker. Although neither parent had completed elementary school, they instilled in Satcher a high regard for scholarly accomplishment and perseverance amid segregation. A childhood bout with whooping cough and pneumonia began his long and fruitful interest in medical research and health, particularly with regard to the health of minority and disadvantaged groups. He often recalled that his own difficulty in getting health care and gaining access to hospitals as well as his experience of "people dying at home" led him into medicine "with the view that I wanted to be like the physician who came out to the farm to see me, and I wanted to make a difference for people who didn't have access to care" (*NewsHour: A NewsHour with Jim Lehrer Transcript*, 21 Jan. 2002).

Satcher attended segregated public schools in Alabama. Despite the use of secondhand schoolbooks in these separate and unequal facilities, the teachers and administrators took a real interest in the students, and Satcher was pushed toward excellence in the classroom by a few of his teachers. In high school he won an American Legion essay contest with the assistance of his English teacher. Observing his excellence in chemistry, another teacher, taking Satcher under his wing, took him to visit the historically black Morehouse College in Atlanta, Georgia. Upon graduation from high school Satcher entered Morehouse, where he excelled in academics, as a member of the track-and-field team, and in the school's choir.

After Satcher graduated from Morehouse in 1963 with a B.A. in science, he entered Case Western Reserve University in Cleveland, Ohio, where he received his M.D. and also a Ph.D. in cytogenetics, a branch of genetic research that studies the structure of chromosomes, in 1970. It was as a student in the 1960s that Satcher began to work as an advocate for the training of black physicians and for better health care for disadvantaged and minority groups. As a student, he spearheaded efforts at Case Western to increase African American enrollment in the medical program. In 1970 he began a two-year residency at the Strong Memorial Hospital at the University of Rochester in New York, followed by a position in South Central Los Angeles at the Charles R. Drew Postgraduate Medical School and Martin Luther King Jr. Hospital, a facility opened in the Watts community after the 1965 riots.

During the 1970s Satcher directed an innovative sickle-cell anemia treatment program at King-Drew Hospital for six years and served for two years as a faculty member at the UCLA School of Medicine and Public Health. Working between UCLA and King-Drew, he created a joint program where medical students could broaden their training and where physicians would become more involved in the care of residents in the Watts neighborhood. By 1977 Satcher had risen to the post of interim dean of the Drew Medical School. In 1979 he left California, returning to his alma mater, where he served as professor at the Morehouse School of Medicine and as chair of the department of community medicine until 1982.

During this time of professional growth and advancement, Satcher and his wife, Nola Richardson, also reared four children. By this time he was widely respected for his administrative ability and for his activism and research in community health. In 1982 he became president of Meharry College in Nashville, Tennessee, where he remained until 1993, when he was asked to lead the Centers for Disease Control and Prevention (CDC). As director of national CDC programs, Satcher focused on taming the rising threat of breast cancer in the United States and on upgrading prevention and screening programs for breast and cervical cancer, which under his tenure at the CDC were extended from eighteen to fifty states. He also directed considerable attention to the issues of childhood immunization and infectious diseases.

In 1998 President Bill Clinton nominated Satcher to become the sixteenth surgeon general of the United States. As was the case with one of his predecessors, JOYCELYN ELDERS, Satcher's appointment to the post of surgeon general was not without controversy. Conservatives attempted to block his nomination, citing his views on sex education as a means of improving health, his support of AIDS research in the developing world, his support for needle-exchange programs in the fight against AIDS in the United States, and his opposition to the U.S. Congress's efforts to enact a ban on so-called partial-birth abortions. Despite this criticism, Satcher's appointment was confirmed by a Senate vote of 63 to 35.

After his confirmation Satcher also served as assistant secretary for health, making him only the second person in history to hold both positions simultaneously. As surgeon general, Satcher served as administrator and chief spokesperson for the Public Health Sevice Commissioned Corps and as the principal adviser to the president on public health issues affecting the nation, providing national leadership and guidance for developing public health strategies. As assistant secretary for health, Satcher conducted broad assessments designed to anticipate future public health problems and coordinated population-based, minority health, and women's health initiatives.

Preventing suicide, improving mental health, reducing cigarette smoking, stemming the tide of youth violence, preventing and treating obesity, and improving sex education were among the many central issues that defined Satcher's term as surgeon general. He also continued the community health activism that had been the backbone of his professional career. Among Satcher's major accomplishments was a report from his office on suicide and mental health, drawing public and professional attention to particular hidden aspects of these problems. Satcher placed the issue of suicide among teenagers on a national platform and led the development of prevention programs targeting youths. On the topic of sex and sexuality, Satcher insisted that the nation had condoned a kind of "conspiracy of silence," and he worked to promote public discussion on sex education and health. His June 2001 report on sex education, *Call to Action to Promote Sexual Health and Responsible Sexual Behavior*, proved to be controversial, eliciting disapproval from conservatives. Satcher, however, remained steadfast in his determination to push this agenda.

After Satcher's term as surgeon general ended in 2002, he served as visiting senior fellow at the Henry J. Kaiser Family Foundation in Washington, D.C., and then returned to the Morehouse School of Medicine to direct the newly established National Center for Primary Care. This center focused attention on the health disparities among minorities, disadvantaged groups, and vulnerable populations and their lack of access to health care, issues of critical concern for Satcher.

During his distinguished career, Satcher received numerous awards and honorary degrees. He was a Robert Wood Johnson Clinical Scholar and Macy Faculty Fellow and received honors from the National Medical Association, American Medical Association, American College of Physicians, American Academy of Family Physicians, American Academy for the Advancement of Science, and *Ebony* magazine. In 2000 his contributions to the study of mental health and illness earned him the Didi Hirsch Erasing Stigma Mental Health Leadership Award and the National Association of Mental Illness Distinguished Service Award. He also received the Bennie Trailblazer Award (named for the Morehouse president BENJAMIN E.

MAYS) and the Jimmy and Rosalynn Carter Award for Humanitarian Contributions to the Health of Humankind from the National Foundation for Infectious Diseases. In 1997 Satcher received the New York Academy of Medicine Lifetime Achievement Award. Satcher also became a member of the Omega Psi Phi Fraternity Inc.

FURTHER READING

Edmunds, M., and C. Fulwood. "Strategic Communications in Oral Health: Influencing Public and Professional Opinions and Actions," *Ambul Pediatrics* 2, Suppl. (Mar. 2002).

Kleinman, D. V. "2001 Public Service Award: David Satcher, M.D., Ph.D.," *Journal of Public Health Dent* 61, no. 4 (Fall 2001).

Lewis, Jolie. "A New Season for David Satcher," *Case Western Reserve University Magazine* (Fall, 2002).

McBeth, A. "Community Care Partnership: Planning with the Community," *Semin Nurse Management* 8, no. 2 (June 2000).

KEITH WAILOO
RICHARD M. MIZELLE JR.

Sauldsberry, Woody (11 July 1935–3 Sept. 2007), basketball player, was born Woodrow Sauldsberry Jr. in Winnsboro, Louisiana. His father, Woodrow Sauldsberry Sr., was a laborer who worked in foundries and shipyards and performed odd jobs, such as janitorial and lawn work. His wife, whose name is not known, worked in a sweatshop making clothes. The family moved to the Los Angeles suburb of Compton in 1937, in search of a better life than they could have in the Jim Crow, pre–civil rights South. Sauldsberry's basketball career began in Los Angeles when he joined a team in the eighth grade. He had never really played basketball, but his tall, lanky frame attracted the attention of Compton Union High School basketball coach Ken Fagan. By the time he was in eleventh grade Sauldsberry was the star of a team that went 32-0 in his junior year and eventually built the streak to fifty-three straight wins.

Fagan envisioned his young star in a UCLA jersey, and another L.A.-area school, Pepperdine University, offered Sauldsberry a scholarship. But a scout for historically black Texas Southern University, Al Tabor, spotted Sauldsberry and recruited him for the Houston college for coach Ed Adams. The 6'7" forward left Texas Southern in 1956, without graduating, to join the Harlem Globetrotters main team.

During his time in college, Sauldsberry got his girlfriend back in Los Angeles (name withheld by request) pregnant. The couple married in November 1954, and their daughter, Debra Irene, was born the following March. In addition to Debra Irene, he had a son, Woody III, with his second wife in 1958. Sauldsberry's two marriages were both short-lived, and for years afterward he saw little of his two children.

Life as a Globetrotter gave Sauldsberry and his teammates a chance to see the world. During his time on the team they visited more than eighty countries and played more than five hundred games. Growing up, Sauldsberry had watched the Trotters from afar and had admired their skill and showmanship. But he soon realized that being a Globetrotter meant playing minstrel to mostly white audiences who would tolerate watching a black team beat a squad of white stooges as long as everyone enjoyed a good laugh. It didn't take long for the showbiz side of the game to wear on Sauldsberry and the team's other serious players.

After two years, Sauldsberry left the Trotters and went on to the NBA Philadelphia Warriors. By the end of the 1957–1958 season, Sauldsberry had established himself as a force on the court. His inside game was aggressive, but he could also rain down a long jumper from the corner. He was named the league's Rookie of the Year—the second African American to win the award, after MAURICE STOKES in 1956. In his sophomore season he was tapped to play in the NBA All-Star game, scoring fourteen points and pulling down a pair of rebounds in eighteen minutes on the court. Over the course of his seven-year NBA career, he averaged 10.7 points and 7.8 rebounds per game.

Sauldsberry left the Warriors in 1960 amid a contract dispute, but he continued to establish himself as one of the league's top players. In 1961, playing for the St. Louis (later Atlanta) Hawks, he was named the outstanding player of the Western Division playoffs. There is some irony to Sauldsberry, one of the league's more outspoken African American players at the time, playing for the Hawks. This was the franchise that traded the draft rights to BILL RUSSELL to the Boston Celtics in 1956 rather than add a black man to the all-white Hawks squad.

Sauldsberry had met Russell a few years earlier, when he was still a Globetrotter and Russell was starring at the University of San Francisco. He steered Russell clear of the Globetrotters and told him to go pro. But despite their fame and accomplishments, Sauldsberry, Russell, and their black contemporaries often found themselves at odds with the racial politics of the time. In October 1961 Russell's Celtics paired up with the Sauldsberry's Hawks for an exhibition road trip through the heart of Dixie. Satch Sanders, a teammate of Russell's that year, and fellow Celtic Sam Jones, both black, had been denied service at a coffee shop in a hotel in Lexington, Kentucky, the final stop on the tour. A similar incident had occurred at a restaurant in Marian, Indiana, two days earlier. When the black players returned to the coffee shop to address the matter, the managers told them that since they were ballplayers the rules could be waived and they could be served. The seven black players on the teams—the Celtics' Russell, Sanders, SAM JONES (1933–), K.-C. JONES, and Al Butler, and the Hawks' Sauldsberry and Cleo Hill—chose instead to leave the tour without playing the Lexington game. It went on anyway, with St. Louis easily beating shorthanded Boston.

The incident struck a chord with several white Celtics. Frank Ramsey, who played college basketball in Lexington, was upset enough to organize some hometown friends, who wired personal apologies to the Hawks. But there was no such remorse expressed in St. Louis. Sauldsberry was sent to the Chicago Packers, an expansion team that after two moves and five name changes eventually became the Washington Wizards. Sauldsberry played the 1961–1962 season for Chicago, but in the middle of the next season St. Louis lured him back to beef up for the playoffs. Sauldsberry was a top-notch defensive player who the Hawks believed would help them neutralize the Lakers' electrifying ELGIN BAYLOR. He played part of another year and retired for the first time.

By 1965 Sauldsberry was well out of the NBA, working as a sales rep for Trans World Airlines, but Russell hadn't forgotten him. In 1965 the Boston star convinced Celtics coach Red Auerbach to add Sauldsberry to the roster for the coming season. He played sparingly, spending much of the season injured, but when the 1965–1966 Celtics won the NBA title, their eighth straight, he got his only championship ring. After that, he retired for good.

In 2001 Sauldsberry was inducted into the Black Legends of Professional Basketball Foundation Hall of Fame. He died in Baltimore, Maryland, at the age of 72.

JAMES MICHAEL BRODIE

Saunders, Prince (?–Feb. 1839), author and colonizationist, was born in either Lebanon, Connecticut, or Thetford, Vermont, the son of Cuff Saunders and Phyllis Saunders (maiden name unknown). Although the exact date of Prince Saunders's birth remains unknown, he was baptized on 25 July 1784 in Lebanon and received his early schooling in Thetford. He taught at a black school in Colchester, Connecticut, and later studied at Moor's Charity School at Dartmouth College in 1807 and 1808. President John Wheelock of Dartmouth recommended Saunders as instructor at Boston's African School in late 1808. By 1811 Saunders was secretary of the African Masonic Society and had founded the Belles Lettres Society, a literary group. He also taught at the African Baptist Church in Boston, founded by THOMAS PAUL. He was engaged to a daughter of emigrationist and sea Captain PAUL CUFFE. Although the engagement ended for unknown reasons, his acquaintance with Cuffe undoubtedly awakened Saunders to Pan-Africanism and the black colonization movement.

In 1815 Saunders and Thomas Paul traveled to London as delegates to the Masonic Lodge of Africans. Saunders met with many influential British figures, including abolitionist leaders William Wilberforce and Thomas Clarkson. As a result of these meetings, Saunders focused his interest on Haiti, the first black republic in the Western Hemisphere. He shared the British abolitionists' desire to anglicize Haiti. In 1816 he made his first visit to Haiti, where King Henri Christophe greeted him enthusiastically. Saunders introduced the concept of vaccination by vaccinating Christophe's children, and he introduced the Lancastrian system of education. Adopted by many schools in the United States, including the African Free Schools, the system used student monitors to assist teachers and emphasized learning by rote. Saunders then returned to England, where he published his first work, *Haytian Papers* (1816), a collection of Haitian civic laws governing agriculture, commerce, the police, and politics. In December 1816 he traveled again to Haiti. Christophe accused him of publishing *Haytian Papers* without permission and dismissed him as an adviser. Saunders was allowed, however, to continue his work in schools and medicine until 1818, when he sailed to Boston. There he published a second edition of his book.

Living in Philadelphia in 1818, Saunders served as a lay reader for ABSALOM JONES's St. Thomas's African Episcopal Church. He joined the Pennsylvania Abolition Society and promoted colonization to the Caribbean, especially Haiti.

Although it had been supported earlier by black leaders, by 1818 colonization had become intensely unpopular among blacks. JAMES FORTEN and RICHARD ALLEN both denounced colonization as a trick of the newly organized American Colonization Society. Generally, African American and white abolitionists regarded the society as an organization seeking to protect slavery and counteract antislavery. Saunders persisted in his views, however, publishing in 1818 two pamphlets: *An Address Delivered … before the Pennsylvania Augustine Society for Education of People of Color* and *A Memoir Presented to the American Convention for Promoting the Abolition of Slavery.*

Saunders settled in Haiti in 1820. He took with him letters from Philadelphia alleging the desire of thousands of free blacks to emigrate to Haiti. Saunders convinced Christophe to supply a ship and twenty-five thousand dollars to initiate colonization. As the agreement neared completion, however, a coup displaced Christophe, who then committed suicide. Saunders was left penniless and friendless. Newly installed President John Pierre Boyer received Saunders politely but refused to guarantee support for the former ally of Christophe. Despite Boyer's expressed desire to promote greater democracy in Haiti, Saunders became disillusioned and feared that Boyer's approach (he abolished the universal education established by Christophe) would cause the downfall of black Haiti. Convinced of Boyer's inability to rule effectively, he lobbied the British and Russian governments to intervene to replace Boyer.

Saunders's disaffection with Haiti's government did not lessen his zeal for emigration to Haiti. It is doubtful that he played a key role in Haitian politics, although a claim has been made that he was Boyer's attorney general. There is no evidence to support this claim in Haitian records, however. Saunders lived in Haiti until his death in Port-au-Prince.

Saunders sustained his position on colonization—initially sparked by the Pan-Africanism of Paul Cuffe and the Sierra Leone settlers in the late eighteenth century—despite its unpopularity among blacks in the United States after 1817. Though his efforts to create a Pan-African nationalism, of which his involvement with Haitian politics was an exceptional example, became politically unpopular, he should be recognized for his remarkable abilities as an educator, abolitionist, writer, and public speaker.

FURTHER READING

Griggs, Earl Leslie, and Thomas Clarkson, eds. *Henri Christophe and Thomas Clarkson: A Correspondence* (1952; repr. 1968).

White, Arthur D. "Prince Saunders: An Instance of Social Mobility among Antebellum New England Blacks." *Journal of Negro History* 55 (1975): 526–535.

This entry is taken from the *American National Biography* and is published here with the permission of the American Council of Learned Societies.

GRAHAM RUSSELL HODGES

Saunders, Raymond (1934–), artist and educator, was born Raymond Jennings Saunders and raised in Pittsburgh, Pennsylvania. He attended Schenley High School and the Carnegie Institute of Technology, where talented high school students could pursue the arts six days a week and exhibit their work in a prestigious venue. Saunders later said,

> "From a young age I was going to school six days a week and loving it. You were welcomed to do all kinds of things. I had no conception that those opportunities weren't available to everybody. When I got to the outside world, I found a lot of pain. But my teachers told me, 'If you ever think about stopping making art, come talk to us.' So that support followed me" (Chase).

In 1953 Saunders received a National Scholastic Scholarship. His academic achievements and the strong support of his teachers gave him the lifelong desire to teach and inspire young art students. After leaving Carnegie in 1953 he enrolled at the Pennsylvania Academy of the Fine Arts in Philadelphia, the oldest art school in the country. There he received foundation training in painting and drawing, working from classical and historical models.

As a counterpoint to studio classes, Saunders attended lectures at the Barnes Foundation in Merion, Pennsylvania (one of the world's largest collections of impressionist art), where the study of art was based not on historical precedent but rather through the eyes and method of the idiosyncratic collector Dr. Albert Barnes and his disciples. Rounding out his academic roster, Saunders attended classes at the University of Pennsylvania, finishing up at all three schools by 1957. Saunders garnered several prizes during his college years, including the Pennsylvania Academy's Cresson European Traveling Scholarship (1956) and the University of Pennsylvania's first prize in oil painting (1957).

After serving in the U.S. Army at Fort Ord, California, from 1957 to 1959, Saunders returned to the Carnegie Institute of Technology and received a bachelor of fine arts degree in 1960. Crisscrossing the country one more time, he earned a master of fine arts degree in 1961 at the California College of Arts and Crafts (CCAC), Oakland, where he settled after his graduation.

Saunders continued to attend art schools during the period in which abstract expressionism attained prominence in the United States, particularly in New York. Abstract expressionism was characterized by a lively painterly surface, improvisational gesture, monumental canvases, and the lack of reference to real objects. Though Saunders had been studying art in the regional art centers of Philadelphia, Pittsburgh, and Oakland, he could not have remained immune to the force and radicalism of abstract expressionism. He embraced the movement's respect for the unique vision of the individual artist, as well as its insistence on the authority of that artist. His paintings combined uninhibited gestures and personal memory with a love for traditional, visual illusionism, nineteenth-century landscapes, and still lifes.

Often featuring black figures embedded in organized fields of textured, vibrant color, Saunders's early work showed an affinity with that of the modernist artists ROMARE BEARDEN and CHARLES ALSTON at mid-century. Shortly after graduation from CCAC, Saunders began exhibiting in group shows in San Francisco and Oakland; henceforth he was considered a San Francisco Bay Area artist.

The 1960s and 1970s saw increasing organization among black artists, who advocated for inclusion in mainstream institutional exhibitions and for recognition by critics and art historians. The Black Emergency Cultural Coalition (1969–1971) in New York was one of the groups formed to achieve these ends. In the same era other black artists lobbied for the formation of separate, black cultural institutions and the advancement of a black and pan-African creative aesthetic. The ensuing debates between these positions prompted Saunders to write a pamphlet entitled *Black Is a Color* (1967) in which he denounced the practice of using art as a political tool or a showcase for insecurity. "Racial hang-ups are extraneous to art… can't we get clear of these degrading limitations, and recognize the wider reality of art, where color is the means and not the end?" (Powell, 125).

Given that Saunders did not consider his work to be "black art," it is ironic that East Coast museum curators organizing such exhibitions sought to include his paintings. He was selected for the exhibitions *Portrayal of the Negro in American Painting* at the New School of Social Research in New York City (1966) and *Afro-American Artists, 1800–1969* at the Philadelphia Museum of Art in 1969. Two years later he was included in the groundbreaking show *Contemporary Black American Art* at the Whitney Museum.

Black figures played a role in Saunders's work into the early 1970s. But they lost their figural authority as the artist scrawled messages across them with paint or chalk, cropped off body parts, and affixed bits of paper ephemera to the canvas. Saunders's graffiti and bold color strokes predated those of the avant-garde artist JEAN-MICHEL BASQUIAT by a decade.

Around 1970 Saunders moved into the realm of abstract assemblages and torn mixed-media collages. Like the pop artists Robert Rauschenberg and Jasper Johns, he used both impersonal objects from popular culture and those with personal significance to construct visual tableaux layered with enigmatic meaning. Like jazz, Saunders's compositions were often in a state of flux as he added ephemera from his frequent travels and removed sections at will. Multicultural in spirit, his work included Asian and Mexican imagery that was incorporated into his ever-present black backgrounds and hearts shapes. His designs for printed work included the poster for the 1984 Los Angeles Olympics and the broadside for David Mamet's play *Dr. Faustus* (2004).

Saunders succeeded in his goal to have universal appeal; after the 1960s his art was shown in galleries and museums on every continent. Among his numerous recognitions were the Prix de Rome (1964), a Guggenheim Fellowship (1976), National Endowment for the Arts fellowships (1977, 1984), and the Southeastern Center for Contemporary Art award (1989). His work is featured in many public collections, including the Pennsylvania Academy of the Fine Arts, the Museum of Modern Art, the Walker Art Center, and the San Francisco Museum of Modern Art.

In 1968 Saunders accepted a faculty position at California State University, Hayward, where he taught for almost two decades. He stated, "I came for a job at Hayward, hoping to find a 'blue collar' mixed situation. I hoped to help kids who never had access to art to discover what they could do" (Chase). In 1987 Saunders became professor of painting and drawing at the California College of the Arts in Oakland, his alma mater.

FURTHER READING
Chase, Hank. "Raymond Saunders Comes Full Circle," *American Visions* (Dec. 1999).
Gibson, Ann, Steve Cannon, Frank Bowling, and Thomas McEvilley. *The Search for Freedom: African American Abstract Painting 1945–1975* (1991).
Patton, Sharon F. *African-American Art* (1998).
Powell, Richard J. *Black Art and Culture in the Twentieth Century* (1997).
Wright, Beryl. *The Appropriate Object* (1989).

CYNTHIA HAVESON VELORIC

Savage, Augusta (29 Feb. 1892–26 Mar. 1962) sculptor, educator, and advocate for black artists, was born Augusta Christine Fells in Green Cove Springs, Florida, the seventh of fourteen children of Edward Fells, a laborer and Methodist minister, and Cornelia Murphy. As a child, Savage routinely skipped school, preferring to model small figurines at local clay pits, much to the consternation of her religious father, who, as she recalled in a 1935 interview, "almost whipped the art out of me" (Bearden, 168). At age fifteen, Augusta married John T. Moore, and a year later a daughter, Irene Connie Moore, was born; John Moore died several years later. In 1915 the Fells family moved to West Palm Beach, where Savage taught clay modeling at her high school. She later spent a year at Tallahassee Normal School (now Florida A&M). At some point after 1915 she married a carpenter named James Savage. The couple had no children and divorced in the early 1920s.

Encouraged by sales of her small sculptures at local events, Savage left her daughter in the care of her parents and moved to New York City in 1921. With the help of the sculptor Solon Borglum, she was granted admission to Cooper Union, a tuition-free art school, where she completed the four-year program in only three years. Savage augmented her studies with self-directed reading in African art at the Harlem branch of the New York Public Library. When the librarian Sadie Peterson (later SADIE DELANEY) persuaded the library to commission a bust of W. E. B. DuBois, Savage's life as a working artist began. Several commissions followed, including a bust of MARCUS GARVEY, who sat for the young artist on Sunday mornings in her Harlem apartment. It was through Garvey that Savage met her third husband, Robert L. Poston. The couple married in October 1923; five months later, however, she was again widowed. In 1922 Savage applied to a summer art school program for American women at the palace of Fontainebleau outside Paris. The seven white American artists who constituted the selection committee, however, yielded to complaints from two Alabama women who refused to travel with a "colored girl" and rejected her application. When Savage exposed the committee's racism, becoming the first black artist to challenge the white art establishment openly, the story was reported in both the African American and the white press. Making her case directly to the public, Savage reasoned: "Democracy is a strange thing. My brother was good enough to be accepted in one of the regiments that saw service in France during the war, but it seems his sister is not good enough to be a guest of the country for which he fought" (*New York World*, 20 May 1923). Despite her protestations, the committee's decision was not reversed, and while Savage's outspoken position brought her respect as a civil rights leader, she also won a reputation within the art world as a troublemaker. "No one knows how many times she was excluded from exhibits, galleries, and museums because of this confrontation," speculated ROMARE BEARDEN (170).

Economic limitations denied Savage a second opportunity to study abroad when, in 1925, through the efforts of W. E. B. DuBois, the Italian-American Society offered her a scholarship to the Royal Academy of Fine Arts in Rome. Savage, who was working at menial jobs to support herself and her parents, was forced to turn down the scholarship when she was unable to raise enough money for living expenses. Her economic and familial burden increased—by 1928 she had eight relatives living in her three-room apartment—and Savage remained in Harlem, studying when she could and exhibiting wherever possible.

A lifesize bronze bust of an adolescent boy, *Gamin* (1929), revived Savage's dream of studying abroad. The sculpture, which *Opportunity* magazine put on its first cover in June 1929, delighted audiences and helped Savage secure two consecutive Julius Rosenwald Fund fellowships for study in Paris. While in Paris, she studied at the Académie de la Grand Chaumière and with the award-winning sculptors Felix Benneteau-Desgrois and Charles Despiau. She exhibited at the key Parisian salons and enjoyed the company of an expatriate social circle that included CLAUDE McKAY, HENRY OSSAWA TANNER, COUNTÉE CULLEN, and ELIZABETH PROPHET.

Upon her return to New York in 1932 Savage exhibited at the Anderson Galleries, the Argent Gallery, and the Harmon Foundation and received commissions for busts of JAMES WELDON JOHNSON, W. C. HANDY, and others. But by 1932 much had changed. The Depression was taking its toll on institutions and innovations that had flourished in Harlem in the previous decade. Private funding for the arts was drying up, and by 1933 even the Harmon Foundation had suspended giving monetary awards. Savage recognized the effect of these shifts on her own endeavors and on the artistic community more generally. Convinced that her work might not be economically viable, she focused on generating her own creative opportunities, on teaching, and on supporting other African American artists.

Savage had long been unhappy with exhibition and patronage systems that gave white bureaucrats power over opportunities extended to African American artists, and after the Fontainebleau controversy, she had the skills to confront institutional racism and garner public support. Through the establishment of a series of influential art institutions and exhibitions, Savage became an aggressive spokesperson for nurturing black talent, for bringing art into the community, and for including black artists in mainstream arenas. In 1932 she opened the Savage School of Arts, which became the largest program of free art classes in New York. A demanding and devoted teacher, Savage was a powerful influence on her students, who included JACOB LAWRENCE, Norman Lewis, WILLIAM ARTIS, and ERNEST CRICHLOW. The psychologist KENNETH B. CLARK, also a former Savage student, recounts her unique and open approach: "Once I was doing this nude and was having trouble with the breasts. … Augusta came along and said, 'Kenneth, you're having trouble with that breast.' I said, 'Yes I am.' And she simply opened her blouse and showed me her breast" (Bearden, 173).

Harlem's leading intellectuals often met at Savage's studio, and in 1933 she and AARON DOUGLAS cofounded the Vanguard, a salon-style group that met weekly to discuss progressive causes and cultural issues. Two years later Savage and CHARLES ALSTON established the Harlem Artists Guild, which lobbied for funding for African American artists. In 1936 Savage was appointed an assistant supervisor for the Federal

Arts Project (FAP), a division of the Works Progress Administration (WPA), employing thousands of artists. Savage convinced WPA administrators of the existence of nearly two hundred active African American artists and demanded that they be given assignments and supervisory positions through WPA programs. Within a year she became the first director of the Harlem Community Art Center, the FAP's most successful community center. More than three thousand students and ten thousand visitors were drawn to the Center during its first year. Under Savage's direction, an interracial staff of artists, including Douglas, Alston, WILLIAM H. JOHNSON, PALMER HAYDEN, and SELMA BURKE, taught workshops in a variety of mediums.

Savage took a break from administration in 1938, after she received a commission to create a monumental statue reflecting "the American Negro's contribution to music, especially to song" for the 1939 New York World's Fair. One of only four women given a commission and one of only two black artists represented at the fair, she produced a harp-shaped sixteen-foot sculpture of a stylized African American choir supported by a monumental arm. Even though the sculpture, inspired by James Weldon Johnson and JOHN ROSAMOND JOHNSON's song "Lift Every Voice and Sing," was one of the fair's most popular and most publicized attractions, it was destroyed at the close of the fair when Savage was unable to pay for the piece to be cast.

Savage had intended to return to the Harlem Community Art Center, but her opponents at the WPA effectively pushed her out, and she officially resigned in April 1939. "In the end Savage was left a famous but poor, unemployed black artist," lamented Bearden (177). At age forty-seven, never having received a one-woman show or a museum exhibition, Savage organized a retrospective of her work at Argent Galleries. Frustrated by poor reviews, she returned to arts administration and in June 1939 opened the Salon of Contemporary Negro Art in Harlem, the nation's first gallery devoted to the exhibition and sale of work by African American artists. Although more than five hundred people came to see the work of such artists as RICHMOND BARTHÉ, BEAUFORD DELANEY, JAMES LESESNE WELLS, LOÏS MAILOU JONES, and META WARRICK FULLER, poor sales and lack of resources forced the gallery to close a few months after its opening. The next year Savage attempted to jump start her sculptural career with a nine-city tour of her work to conclude at the American Negro Exposition in Chicago in July 1940. But while the popular response to her work was positive, she sold very few pieces, and when she could not cover the shipping costs to New York, many of her works were abandoned or destroyed.

Savage continued to teach but increasingly isolated herself from her contemporaries. In the early 1940s she moved to an old chicken farm in Saugerties, New York, where she remained until 1961, when failing health necessitated a move to her daughter's house in the Bronx. Augusta Savage died of cancer in 1962. Unfortunately, few of her sculptures remain; for a 1988 exhibition at the Schomburg Center, only nineteen small pieces could be located.

FURTHER READING

Bearden, Romare, and Harry Henderson. *A History of African-American Artists: From 1792 to the Present* (1993).

King-Hammond, Leslie, Tritobia Hayes Benjamin, and the Afro-American Historical and Cultural Museum. *Three Generations of African American Women Sculptors* (1996).

Schomburg Center for Research in Black Culture. *Augusta Savage and the Art Schools of Harlem* (1988).

LISA E. RIVO

Savage, Augustus "Gus" (30 Oct. 1925–), politician, was born in Detroit, Michigan, to Thomas Frederick and Molly Wilder. Information about his parents and early life is scarce. When he was five his family relocated to the South Side of Chicago, where Savage attended Wendell Phillips High School, graduating in 1943. He joined the army and served in World War II in a segregated unit. Upon his return to the United States in 1946 he attended Chicago's Roosevelt University. Savage graduated from Roosevelt in 1951 with a Bachelor of Arts in philosophy. He elected to pursue a life dedicated to civil rights, perhaps influenced by his experience in the military, where the poor treatment of African American recruits was epidemic. He worked as a journalist around Chicago for a number of years, eventually founding, operating, or editing a number of small, community newspapers and publications, including the *Westside Booster* (1958–1960), the *Bulletin* (1963–1964), and the *America Negro* magazine (1954). In 1946 he married Eunice King. The couple had two children. Meanwhile, Savage and his work came to national attention following the 1955 murder of EMMETT TILL when Savage published the now-famous photograph of Till's brutalized body, helping to train national attention and outrage on the case.

Savage was active in local Chicago politics too, both through the voice of his various publications and through his attempts to secure elective office. In 1968 and 1970 he was defeated by better funded and better known candidates in primary contests for a seat in the U.S. House of Representatives. In 1980, however, Morgan Murphy retired from Illinois' Second Congressional District, and Savage decided to run for the open seat in the largely African American district. This time he was successful, in large part because of his (self-appointed) reputation as the bane of local machine politics. Despite the district's demographics, Savage was its first African American representative. His campaign tactics, however, sometimes created controversy. Savage delivered a speech in 1990 in which he identified by name a number of his opponent's Jewish campaign contributors. Reacting to the subsequent criticism, he expressed the opinion that racism was the exclusive province of whites. It was not the last time that Savage would use accusations of racism as a shield against his own often dubious (if not criminal) behavior.

During his tenure of office in the House, Savage proved himself an outspoken advocate of civil rights and the rights of the poor. He was a harsh critic of the fiscal and military agenda of President Ronald Reagan's administration—for example, he opposed much of the president's agenda in the Caribbean and Central and Latin American, including the 1983 invasion of Grenada. He was an also an outspoken critic of the South African apartheid regime and advocated greater U.S. attention to and assistance for Africa, more generally. His frequent criticism of the government's close relationship with Israel made him a controversial figure at a time when few politicians were willing to publicly give voice to the Palestinian perspective. In 1981 Eunice King died of lung cancer. From 1989 to 1993 Savage served as chair on the House Public Works and Transportation Subcommittee on Economic Development.

In 1989 Savage was accused of sexually assaulting a Peace Corps worker during a visit to Zaire (the Democratic Republic of Congo). To the astonishment of many observers, a subsequent investigation by a House committee found that Savage had,

in fact, behaved inappropriately but refused to take further action after Savage penned a letter of apology to the volunteer. For his part, Savage denied ever writing a letter of apology and criticized what he described as his unfair treatment by the "racist press." He also described the Peace Corps volunteer as "a traitor to the black movement" (*Chicago Sun-Times*, 21 July 1989).

His reputation now battered, Savage faced an uncertain future. In 1992 he faced his long-time political rival MEL REYNOLDS in a primary contest. Savage again suggested that his opponent's campaign was part of a Jewish plot to unseat him. During the campaign Reynolds was shot at by unknown assailants. Reynolds blamed the event on Savage, who in turn accused Reynolds of attempting to create sympathy and votes by stage-managing the entire incident. On primary election day, Savage went down to a hard defeat, losing by nearly 26 percentage points. Not helping Savage's cause was the fact that the district had been recently redrawn to include a greater number of suburban voters. Savage's sometimes rocky relationship with his urban constituency was diluted even further. In 2009 he continued to reside in Washington, D.C., and has not again sought elective office.

Gus Savage served as an outspoken critic of certain conservative public policies that he characterized—correctly—as being tilted against the working poor and the underclass, for example, the lending policies of mortgage carriers that seriously disadvantaged, denied outright, or took advantage of minority applicants. Likewise, his dedication to paying heed to the problems of the African continent presaged what would be a movement among later officeholders to do the same. However, his reliance on anti-Semitic tactics and his predictable deployment of racism as a defense against his own confessed misdeeds render him more an oddity among national African American politicians than an example of an independent political actor achieving success against entrenched interests.

FURTHER READING

Freedman, Eric. *African Americans in Congress: A Documentary History* (2008).

"Racism, To Gus Savage," *New York Times*, 4 Apr. 1990. [The piece is an unsigned editorial.]

Rasky, Susan F. "Congressman in Sex Case Bitterly Attacks Critics," 2 Feb. 1990, *New York Times*, A15.

JASON PHILIP MILLER

Savage, Howard Thornton (28 Aug. 1920–6 Oct. 1992), attorney, was born in Pittsburgh, Pennsylvania, the son of Howard S. Savage, an ironworker and teacher, and Mary Thornton. Early on the family moved to Chicago, Illinois, where Savage's mother died when Savage was only five. He and his brother were then sent to Talladega, Alabama. He attended Drewry Practice High School, the only high school in the county where black students could earn a traditional rather than a vocational degree. After graduating from high school as class valedictorian, Savage received a full four-year scholarship to Talladega College by winning an achievement contest that ran in thirteen states.

Savage graduated from Talladega in 1942 with highest honors and a degree in political science. From there he won another competitive scholarship to attend a law school of his choice. The scholarship covered only half of his school costs. To earn additional money, Savage worked as a waiter in a whites-only country club, but he left that for a lower-paying but more palatable job as a shipfitter in Chester, Pennsylvania. He fell from the ship and sustained life-threatening injuries. After his recovery, he chose to enroll at the University of Chicago Law School because he knew people in Chicago with whom he could live to save expenses. Again showing the intellectual rigor that would be the hallmark of his career, he finished the three-year program in just over two years and graduated second in his class. He began practicing law in Illinois in 1946.

Despite his stellar record, Savage was not offered a job at the white-owned law firms in Chicago and was refused both a handshake and entrance to the American Bar Association upon graduation. He started a career that would make history at a desk in the hallway of the largest black-owned law firm in Chicago, Braden, Hall, Barnes, and Moss. In 1947 he married Ruth Williams, whom he had known since childhood. The couple had four children.

With the civil rights movement beginning to take shape in the early 1950s, Savage, now a lawyer with some seasoning, was poised to play his part. During this period he won the first of what would be a string of precedent-setting cases that gave individuals legal protections that subsequently became taken for granted. In 1954 he successfully argued that testimony from a person found as a result of an illegal search was inadmissible in court (*People v. Albea*), in 1957 he successfully argued that defense attorneys were entitled to police records and reports against their clients (*People v. Moses*), also in 1957 he successfully argued that the right of an individual to remain in a public establishment to demand service took precedence over the right of the establishment's owner to force that individual to leave (*People v. Corney*), and in 1977 he successfully argued that forcing defendants to divulge information they had withheld from police violated both the defendants' right to privacy and their right against self-incrimination (*People v. White*). He handled hundreds of cases involving free speech and obscenity laws from 1962 through 1979. He felt that in the most important of these cases he convinced the court that the seizure of books by police during a search that exceeded the scope of the search warrant was illegal and that book seizures had to be limited to the purpose of gathering a copy for evidence rather than suppressing its sale until a hearing on the book's status could be held (*People v. Kimmel*).

It was during this time that Savage established his own law firm, Savage, Frazin, and Spencer, in Chicago. Perhaps drawing on his experiences of exclusion while he was a student at the University of Chicago and being denied access to the white-owned law firms, his was one of the first law firms to be integrated by race and gender. As Savage's reputation grew, he became the obvious choice in 1970 for the appointment as Illinois assistant special prosecutor to try the state's attorney Edward Hanrahan for conspiracy and obstruction of justice in the killing of the Black Panthers Mark Clark and FRED HAMPTON. Though Savage failed to win a conviction, Hanrahan's reputation was tarnished, and he lost his bid for reelection. Throughout his career Savage continued to fight for police, governmental, and judicial accountability. He was widely known for his dramatic courtroom style and his success in prosecuting high-profile murder and death penalty cases.

Savage was known as a "lawyer's lawyer." He argued cases in Illinois courts, in federal courts, and in front of the U.S. Supreme Court. He received the Edward Wright Award in 1970 for his legal contributions to the state of Illinois. In 1976 he became the second black attorney in history to be inducted into the exclusive American College of Trial Lawyers (the first was THURGOOD MARSHALL). In 1985 Savage became the first person in state history to be appointed associate judge of the Circuit Court of Cook County, Criminal Courts Division, by a unanimous vote of the sitting judges, a position Savage held until his death. Six months after his death, Savage was honored by his peers, who named a courtroom in the Criminal Courts Building in Chicago after him—the first associate justice of the Circuit Court of Cook County given such an honor.

JANET MARIE SAVAGE

Savage, John Anthony (18 Sept. 1856–1 Jan. 1933), minister and educator, described as an "unassuming gentleman of much natural ability" (Richings, 178), was born into slavery to Frances and William Savage of Henderson, Louisiana. John and his parents were manumitted shortly before the outbreak of the Civil War, possibly through the efforts of his father to purchase the family, and began an arduous journey to Liberia searching for a better future. Savage received his elementary education in Sierra Leone. When malaria claimed the lives of both his parents, he returned to the United States with a group of orphaned youths, accompanied by Presbyterian missionaries, aboard the ship *Thomas Pope*. They arrived in New York City on 12 June 1872. In 1873, with financial assistance from the Presbyterian Synod, he entered Lincoln University in Chester County, Pennsylvania, and in 1879 earned an B.A. degree. He married Melvina Baldwin in 1879, and the couple would have four children.

In 1882 Savage earned a bachelor's degree in sacred theology and a master of arts from Lincoln University and was also ordained a Presbyterian minister. The same year, the Presbyterian Church bestowed the honorary title of Doctor of Divinity upon him. He soon traveled south and was successful in building several Presbyterian churches in North Carolina, including the Shiloh Church in Kinston, circa 1885. From Kinston he moved to New Bern and in 1892 became the principal of Albion Academy in Franklinton, a school founded in 1878 by Moses A. Hopkins, who left his post to become minister to the Republic of Liberia. Albion was financed by the Presbyterian Board of Missions for Freedmen and also supported by the First Presbyterian Church of Albion, New York. In the school's early years, most of the teachers came from Northern schools and colleges, but most of their students were drawn from Franklinton and other towns in the Carolinas (although other students had come from other parts of the United States and even some foreign countries). The academy trained its students to become teachers, but many went on to careers in law, medicine, and business. Savage was credited with building

the academy's faculty to sixteen teachers and a student body of over three hundred. By traveling around the state speaking with other ministers and educators he recruited both students and additional faculty. When North Carolina began to accredit high schools, Savage worked hard to earn the highest rating. He remained president for forty years; under his leadership the school thrived, becoming one of the outstanding schools and cultural centers for African American youth in the state. He enhanced the campus by building dormitories, a dining hall, and a classroom building, and included Mt. Pleasant Presbyterian Church as part of the religious program for the institution.

Savage had a fruitful ministry and was much beloved as a pastor and church builder. In 1895 he built St. Paul's Presbyterian Church in Louisburg, North Carolina, and rebuilt the church in 1915 after it was damaged by a fire. This church remains the only Presbyterian Church in Louisburg.

In 1896 his first wife died in childbirth. Fourteen years later, in 1910, he married Mary Dover of Wilmington, Delaware. No children were born of this union.

Savage also belonged to the national staff of the Board of National Missions of the Presbyterian Church in the USA, served as a clerk of the Cape Fear Presbytery and of the Catawba Synod, and filled the pews at both Mt. Pleasant and St. Paul's Presbyterian Church. He died suddenly on New Year's Day 1933, shortly after entertaining visitors in his role as president of Albion Academy. With the opening of free public high schools for African American youth in the state, Albion's student enrollment and financial aid declined. Savage's former home on the campus fell into disrepair, as did other structures on the campus. Albion became a public high school in 1933 and merged with the B.F. Person school on another site in 1957.

FURTHER READING

Anderson, James D. *The Education of Blacks in the South, 1860–1935* (1988)

Hawkins, Carrie Savage, *A Brief History of Albion Academy 1879–1933* (Paper).

Hill, M. Dora. *Historical Highlights of Saint Paul's Presbyterian Church* (1980).

Richings, G. F. *Evidences of Progress Among Colored People* (1902).

Obituary: *Franklinton News*, 5 Jan. 1933.

DIANE SAVAGE MCLAUGHLIN

Savary, Charles Joseph (c. 1755–22 Jan. 1830), military officer, was born into an influential family of free persons of African descent in the city of Saint-Marc in the French colony of Saint-Domingue (later Haiti). He married the Saint-Marc native Marie Charlotte Lajoie, and the couple had at least two sons, Belton and Bertile Savary. The family fled their native land during the Haitian Revolution and eventually emigrated to New Orleans in a massive Saint-Domingue refugee movement in 1809 and 1810 that nearly doubled the size of the city.

Charles Joseph Savary's life spanned the American, French, and Haitian revolutions, and because of the tumultuous age in which he lived the facts related to his history are scarce, fragmentary, and sometimes contradictory. Part of the problem also stems from circumstances that forced Savary to conceal his identity. In Saint-Domingue's repressive three-caste society and in slave regimes throughout the Americas, free men of color like the republican insurgent Savary posed a dangerous threat. After 1809 and his emigration to Louisiana, however, Savary's activities are better documented. In New Orleans his open and long-standing alliances with French Jacobin exiles of the most radical stamp, as well as the esteem with which he was held by his fellow émigrés (both black and white), attest to the important role that he played in the momentous events of the revolutionary era.

Savary was alleged to be the brother of Vincent Ogé, a free man of color whose ill-fated 1790 revolt against the French colony's white planter regime signaled the onset of the Haitian Revolution. His surname also appears on a listing of Saint-Domingue soldiers who volunteered for military service in the American Revolution (1775–1783). The French colonial contingent of more than five hundred soldiers of African descent played a key role in 1779 in ousting the British from Savannah, Georgia. The volunteer force included André Rigaud, Henri Christophe, Alexandre Pétion, and other young men like Savary who were destined for leadership in the Haitian Revolution.

During the French Revolution (1789–1799) Savary enlisted in the revolutionary government's republican army in Saint-Domingue and advanced to the rank of lieutenant colonel. When in 1791 the French Republic extended voting rights to the colony's freemen of African descent born of free parents, it appears that the residents of Saint-Marc elected him mayor of the city. During the Haitian Revolution (1791–1804), however, invading British forces overthrew Savary's faction and forced him into flight after he refused to surrender the city.

Apparently captured and imprisoned by the Spanish, Savary was released in 1796 in Cap Français (later Cap Haitien) where he barely escaped arrest by Toussaint L'Ouverture in the revolution's fratricidal strife. Though black revolutionaries had won their demands for racial equality and slavery's abolition by the time that Savary arrived in Cap Français, factional tensions mounted as L'Ouverture consolidated his power. In 1799 civil war erupted, and L'Ouverture's victory over André Rigaud's republican army forced seven hundred of Rigaud's best soldiers into exile in Cuba. Savary and the garrison he commanded in Saint-Domingue were likely among the exiles.

When the Spanish government expelled Saint-Domingue refugees from Cuba in 1809, more than ten thousand white, free black, and slave exiles sought asylum in New Orleans. Despite the territorial governor C. C. Claiborne's insistence on strict adherence to an 1807 law that barred the entry of free black adult males, Savary and hundreds of freemen of color entered Louisiana. They found safe haven in Louisiana's Attakapas region, an area linked geographically to Barataria, a coastal settlement near the mouth of the Mississippi River. In Barataria Savary mingled with the French Jacobin corsairs Louis Aury and Renato Belouche and with the white privateers Jean and Pierre Lafitte, all of whom were refugees, like Savary, of the Haitian Revolution.

In 1813 Savary boldly announced his presence when he offered to put a force of five hundred Saint-Domingue freemen of color in the service of Mexican revolutionaries under the command of General Jean-Joseph Humbert. Like Savary, Humbert had served in Saint-Domingue's French republican army. Humbert was, however, distrusted by Napoleon Bonaparte for his republican extremism, and in 1802 he was relieved of his Saint-Domingue command for consorting with subversive elements. In Louisiana, when the 1813 expedition to assist the republican army in Mexico failed, Savary, Humbert, and their supporters rallied to the defense of the United States in the War of 1812.

In 1814 free black leaders representing Savary's Saint-Domingue soldiers and the native-born veterans of Louisiana's colonial militia met with Governor Claiborne. As the likelihood of a British invasion mounted, they assured Claiborne of their loyalty and offered to raise a force of six hundred men. The opposition of white New Orleanians not withstanding, General Andrew Jackson directed the recruitment of free black soldiers. In October Jackson issued an appeal in which he addressed the men as "brave fellow Citizens," "sons of freedom," and "adopted Children" of Louisiana (Bassett, vol. 2, 58). Jackson's glowing invitation and his assurance that the men would receive the same compensation in pay and land as white soldiers encouraged the men to anticipate equal citizenship in the new democratic republic.

When Jackson arrived in New Orleans on 2 December, he mustered the existing battalion of 350 free black soldiers into the U.S. Army and called for the organization of a second battalion. Savary immediately raised a second battalion of approximately 250 soldiers from among the veteran troops that he had commanded in Saint-Domingue. Jackson inducted the men into the army. Aware of Savary's considerable influence and his reputation as "a man of great courage" (Marigny, 74), Jackson personally elevated him to the rank of second major of the volunteer battalion. The former French officer and veteran of the Haitian Revolution became the first African American in the United States to achieve that military rank.

Savary and the two battalions of six hundred men-at-arms distinguished themselves in the Battle of New Orleans. Their presence in a U.S. force of only three thousand soldiers proved decisive. After the victory Jackson wrote that "Captain Savary continued to merit the highest praise" (McConnell, 91). In the last significant skirmish Savary and a detachment of his men had volunteered to clear the field of a detail of British sharpshooters. They succeeded in their mission though suffered heavy casualties. Savary's son, Sergeant Belton Savary, was gravely wounded in the fighting and died two days later.

In the immediate afterglow of victory the Louisiana legislature praised the two battalions of Afro-Creoles and singled out "the brave Savary" who had organized a battalion of men and taken the field "to face the enemy a few hours after its formation" (Everett, 397–398). Within weeks of the battle, however, tensions flared when Savary and his unit were ordered to a remote outpost on Chef Menteur Pass to repair a fortification. Offended by the command, Savary instructed his commanding officer, Major Louis Daquin, to tell the general that his men "would always be willing to sacrifice their lives in combat in defense of their country as had been demonstrated but preferred death to the performance of work of laborers." Daquin relayed Savary's message with an apology: "I am very sorry, *mon Général*, for being unable upon this occasion to carry out the wishes of the government" (Jackson Papers, 15 Feb. 1815).

Jackson noted the "mutiny and desertion from Chef Menteur" and the refusal of Savary's corps "to march out of the city agreeable to my order" (Bassett, vol. 2, 183). He refrained, however, from taking action. Instead, when Savary, Humbert, and representatives of Mexico's revolutionary government resumed plans to assist republican insurgents in Mexico, Jackson authorized them to create a new military unit. Savary and thirty-one members of his former battalion joined the newly created fighting force. They identified with the independence movement in Mexico. Indeed, like their counterparts in Spanish America and their native Haiti, they supported democratic change throughout the hemisphere.

In 1816, when news of support from President Alexandre Pétion of the Republic of Haiti and the French Jacobin privateer Louis Aury reached New Orleans, the Mexican Republic's ambassador to the United States, José Manuel de Herrera, dispatched Savary to Haiti. In Les Cayes Aury agreed to support the revolutionary cause by attacking Mexico's royalist ports.

Savary returned to New Orleans with Aury and his veteran crew of Haitian sailors aboard the privateer's flagship. Together with Herrera and Humbert they proposed to attack Tampico after rendezvousing at Galveston. Savary, commanding a contingent of forty free black soldiers, accompanied Herrera to the island, where the ambassador took possession of Galveston in the name of the Republic of Mexico. Early in 1817, however, repeated setbacks forced the men to abandon the expedition.

Savary returned to New Orleans, and in 1819 the state legislature awarded him one of the highest pensions granted to any of the veterans of the Battle of New Orleans. Still, he undoubtedly felt a profound sense of disillusionment at the emergence of an increasingly harsh slave regime that negated the nation's founding ideals and relegated all persons of African descent to a separate and inferior caste.

With Savary's death in 1830, the Louisiana legislature provided that his pension be awarded to his widow, Marie Charlotte Lajoie. She was survived by her son Bertile Savary when she died in 1844 at the age of seventy-two. Such was Savary's stature at the time of the Civil War that when freemen of color organized a Native Guard Regiment in 1861, the Catholic Church praised them as the "worthy grandsons of the noble Savary" (Bell, 237). Not surprisingly, one of the regimental companies designated itself the Savary Guard in honor of its celebrated military hero. Today he should be remembered for his heroism in the French and Haitian revolutions and for being an unyielding champion of revolutionary republicanism and a celebrated veteran of the Battle of New Orleans during the War of 1812.

FURTHER READING

Bassett, John S., ed. *Correspondence of Andrew Jackson*, 6 vols. (1926–1933).

Bell, Caryn Cossé. *Revolution, Romanticism, and the Afro-Creole Protest Tradition, 1718–1868* (1997).

Everett, Donald E. "Emigres and Militiamen: Free Persons of Color in New Orleans, 1803–1815," *Journal of Negro History* 38 (Oct. 1953).

Gayarré, Charles. *History of Louisiana*, 4 vols. (1903).

Jackson, Andrew. Papers. Library of Congress, Washington, D.C.

Marigny, Bernard. "Reflections on the Campaign of General Andrew Jackson in Louisiana in 1814 and 15," *Louisiana Historical Quarterly* 6 (Jan. 1923).

McConnell, Roland C. *Negro Troops of Antebellum Louisiana: A History of the Battalion of Free Men of Color* (1968).

CARYN COSSÉ BELL

Sayers, Gale (30 May 1943–), football player, was born in Wichita, Kansas, one of three children of Roger Winfield Sayers, a car polisher and mechanic for Goodyear Tire and Rubber Company, and Bernice Ross. In 1951 the family moved to Omaha, Nebraska, where Roger Sayers's brother lived. But financial difficulties forced the family to move within the city nine times in eight years. By the time Gale entered high school, his parents were suffering from depression and alcohol abuse, and the family lived in poverty. Because they often had no coal for their furnace, Gale and his two brothers would turn on the kitchen's gas oven for nighttime heat, which often caused them to wake up feeling sick. Despite such adversity, Sayers thrived while in Omaha because the city gave him opportunities to compete in sports. At the Howard Kennedy grade school, Sayers led his teams to city titles in baseball, football, and basketball, and also excelled in track and field. He then enrolled at Central High School. During his freshman year, Sayers led the football team to its first intercity championship in twenty-three years. By his junior year, he was a

Gale Sayers of the University of Kansas paces the sidelines in front of the Kansas bench during the Big Eight Conference game against Missouri on 26 November 1973. (AP Images.)

sensation, leading the intercity league in scoring and attracting the attention of seventy-five colleges and universities. At the end of his senior season, however, Sayers got what he called "my first recognition of what being a black man could mean" (Sayers, 107). The *Omaha World Herald* newspaper had always selected a high school athlete of the year in Nebraska. Sayers was a high school All-American, had won three gold medals at the state track meet, and had set a state record in the broad jump. Yet he was bypassed for the award, which was given to a white athlete who Sayers felt lacked his accomplishments.

Sayers chose to attend the University of Kansas in 1961, but struggled academically during his freshman year, often cheating on tests that he felt he could not otherwise pass. He flunked an English class and his grade-point average was low enough for him to be put on academic probation. He had to attend summer school in order to maintain his eligibility. Following his freshman year, Sayers stopped cutting class, and became more serious about his schoolwork, eventually earning a 3.0 grade-point average. Although he left school ten credit hours short of earning his degree, the years were key to his development. During the summer following his freshman year, Sayers married his high school sweetheart, Linda McNeil, with whom he would have three children before their 1971 divorce. During his college football career, Sayers was twice an All-American. He set a Big Eight career rushing record with 2,675 yards and held the NCAA record for the longest run from scrimmage (ninety-nine yards against Nebraska in 1963). He also starred in track and field, competing in the high hurdles and 100-yard dash. He also set a school long-jump record of 24 feet and 10½ inches.

After his senior season at Kansas, Sayers was drafted by the Chicago Bears of the National Football League (NFL) and in 1965 began one of the most electrifying careers in football history. In his fifth game he scored four touchdowns. Two months later he scored six touchdowns in a game, tying the NFL record. That season, he scored twenty-two total touchdowns, setting an NFL record. He was the league's Rookie of the Year. The next season he won the NFL rushing title. The year after that he was selected the Most Valuable Player of the All-Star Game. After just three seasons in the NFL, Gale Sayers was voted by sportswriters the starting halfback of the NFL's First 50 Years All-Star Team. He was an awe-inspiring runner whose ability to slip tacklers and execute sharp cuts left observers and opponents stupefied. Midway through the 1968 season, however, Sayers suffered a knee injury. Despite the injury's seriousness, he was able to rehabilitate himself enough to return the next year and again win the league rushing title. He was also awarded the George Halas Award given to the most courageous player in professional football. At the awards presentation, he dedicated his prize to his best friend Brian Piccolo. Piccolo and Sayers had been roommates since 1967, and it was Piccolo who was Sayers's most important support during the rehabilitation of his knee. By the time Sayers had returned to action, however, doctors had discovered a malignant tumor in Piccolo's chest. Despite his valiant fight, cancer claimed Piccolo in June 1970. During that season, Sayers again injured his knee. Although he underwent a serious rehabilitation program, it was unsuccessful, and Sayers retired after playing only four games over his final two seasons. In 1977 Sayers became the youngest man to be voted into the NFL Hall of Fame, despite playing professionally for only five full seasons. In these five seasons, however, Sayers was masterful. He led the league in rushing twice and finished in the top five every year, making the Pro Bowl

four times. In total, he gained about 5,000 yards on approximately 500 carries for the Bears, and an additional 1,300 yards receiving. In addition to being a top-flight running back, Sayers was also a superb special teams player who still holds the all-time career best mark for kickoff return average at 30.6 yards.

Life after football was good to Gale Sayers. He had started writing his autobiography during his fourth professional season, and the section about his relationship with Piccolo was excerpted by *Look*, one of the biggest-selling weekly magazines in the country. A producer felt that the story would make a good movie and in November 1971 the made-for-television *Brian's Song* became the highest-rated TV movie ever. Sayers's 1970 autobiography, *I Am Third*, ended up selling over 100,000 copies in hardcover and millions more in paperback. During the first few years following his career, Sayers worked as a stockbroker for Paine Webber and hosted a talk show on a Chicago radio station. In 1973 he became assistant athletic director at the University of Kansas. He also remarried that year, to Ardythe Bullard. During his four years at Kansas he returned to class to earn his bachelor's degree in physical education. He would later add a master's degree in educational administration. In 1976 Sayers became athletic director at Southern Illinois University, becoming the first African American to fill such a post at a major university. He stayed at the school for five years before starting Sayers Computer Source, a Chicago-based computer supply company. It was a major success. By 2000 the company did $330,000,000 in revenues and employed 350 people at its ten nationwide locations. Sayers and his wife lived in Chicago and were active in local political, community, and philanthropic activities.

FURTHER READING

Sayers, Gale, with Al Silverman. *I Am Third* (1971; rpt. 2001).

Ashe, Arthur. *A Hard Road to Glory: A History of the African-American Athlete in Football* (1993).

Ross, Charles. *Outside the Lines: African Americans and the Integration of the National Football League* (2000).

MICHAEL EZRA

Sayles Belton, Sharon (13 May 1951–), politician and civil rights activist, was born Sharon Sayles in St. Paul, Minnesota, to William Wellford "Bill" Sayles Jr., a neighborhood activist, mechanic, and car salesman, and Pearl Marian Sayles. A nationally recognized expert on public safety, neighborhood livability, and economic development, she was the first African American and first female mayor of Minneapolis.

Sayles Belton graduated in 1973 from Macalester College, where she studied biology and sociology. In 1989 she participated in the Senior Executives in State and Local Government Program in the John F. Kennedy School of Government at Harvard University. After graduating from Macalester, Sayles Belton worked as a parole officer at the Minnesota Department of Corrections, working primarily with sexual assault victims. In 1983 she became associate director at the Minnesota Program for Victims of Sexual Assault. As the assistant director, she worked to build twenty-six centers to assist rape victims statewide and helped to establish the Harriet Tubman Shelter, one of the first shelters in the United States for abused women. Sayles Belton was elected as a member of the Minneapolis City Council, representing the 8th Ward in 1983 and became Minneapolis City Council president in 1990.

In 1993 she announced her candidacy for mayor of Minneapolis, running on a platform focusing on education, anticrime measures, city growth, and city unity. Unlike her opponent, John Derus (also a member of the Democratic-Farmer-Labor Party), who used polls, debates, and televised advertisements, Sayles Belton used grassroots strategies to garner the support of voters—using phone banks, making public appearances, and campaigning door-to-door. The election results revealed that Sayles Belton had received 58 percent of the votes, in a city that had a 78 percent white population at the time. As a result of her grassroots approach, 8,500 new voters registered at the polls, and most of them voted for her. Taking office in January 1994, she served two terms as mayor of Minneapolis, from 1 January 1994 to 31 December 2001. She was reelected in 1997, defeating the Republican candidate Barbara Carlson. However, in the 2001 election, Sayles Belton lost her party's endorsement and popularity among the more affluent. She lost the primary, defeated by fellow Democratic-Farmer-Labor (DFL) candidate Raymond Thomas "R.T." Rybak.

When Sayles Belton took office, she knew she had a difficult job ahead of her because of a high and increasing crime rate in the city. In order to rectify this situation, resources were allocated to public safety from other departments to adopt a computerized strategy used to send officers to high crime areas, a strategy later adopted by the New York City Police Department. By 1998, under police chief Robert Olson, the rate of serious crime in the city had dropped 16 percent. This success rate was beneficial to Sayles Belton's efforts to attract business investment in downtown. Among the new businesses attracted to the city's Nicollet Mall were a Target retail store, the U.S. Bancorp Center, and the American Express Business Center. She also established the Block E entertainment and shopping redevelopment, which serves as an important link in Minneapolis's skyway system, connecting the Target Center (an arena sponsored by the Target Corporation, home to the NBA's Minnesota Timberwolves and the WNBA's Minnesota Lynx) to the Minneapolis City Center. Also credited to her list of accomplishments as mayor, Sayles Belton improved the city's utilities billing system, improved water treatment processes, and addressed flooding issues in various neighborhoods. By the end of the decade, the city of Minneapolis experienced an increase in property values and population. She also worked to stabilize neighborhoods in the midst of racial tensions. After her tenure as mayor, Sayles Belton became a senior fellow at the Roy Wilkins Center for Human Relations and Social Justice at the University of Minnesota's Hubert H. Humphrey Institute of Public Affairs. At the Center, she was responsible for working on antiracial initiatives.

She has also served as the director of community relations and corporate philanthropy for the GMAC Residential Finance Corporation, headquartered in Minneapolis. During her tenure at GMAC, Sharon Sayles Belton was beneficial in pioneering a nonprofit organization called the Homeownership Preservation Foundation, which offered a national hotline and free counseling to assist individuals in preserving their home ownership. She also oversaw a national financial education program to help consumers learn how to make responsible financial decisions. In 2010 she joined Thomson Reuters, a newsgathering organization specializing in business reporting, as vice president of Community Relations and Government Affairs. Based out of the company's Eagan, Minnesota, office, Sayles Belton has been responsible for managing the company's relationship with the government and developing strategies for its legal research division.

Sayles Belton's areas of expertise include public policy development, community development, neighborhood revitalization, family and children's issues, police-community relations, racial inequality, antiracism programs, women's issues, and youth development. Her numerous accolades for such work include: recipient of the 1990 Leadership Award, Minnesota Minority Lawyers Association; 1992 Distinguished Citizen Award, Macalester College; 1994 Public Citizen of the Year Award, National Association of Social Workers—Minnesota Chapter; 1994 Distinguished Achievement Award, University of Minnesota College of Education; 1994 Susan B. Anthony Award, Minnesota Center for Woman in Government—Hamline University; 1997 Rosa Parks Award, American Association for Affirmative Action; and 1998 Gertrude E. Rush Distinguished Service Award, National Bar Association.

Sayles Belton is married to Steven Belton, a trial attorney. They have three children—Kilayna (from Sayles Belton's previous relationship), Jordan, and Coleman.

FURTHER READING

Lesinski, J. "Belton, Sharon Sayles 1951–."
Contemporary Black Biography (1998).

Lupkin, M. "The Mayor's Mission." *Multifamily Executive Magazine*, n.a. (2010).

Olson, D. (2001). "The political legacy of Sharon Sayles Belton." *Minnesota Public Radio*.

"Sayles Belton Presents Party Platform." *Minneapolis Star-Tribune*, 16 Aug. 2000.

"Thomson Reuters Names Sharon Sayles Belton VP of Community Relations and Government Affairs for Its Legal Business." *Minnesota Business Magazine*. Retrieved from http://www.minnesotabusiness.com/article/thomson-reuters-names-sharon-sayles-belton-vp-community-relations-and-government-affairs-its.

CRYSTAL L. JOSEPH

Scales, Jesse (12 Aug. 1875–Nov. 1950), a public health nurse, was born Jesse Sleet in Stratford, Ontario. She was the seventh of nine children born to Benjamin and Betsy Sleet. Little is known about the Sleet family except that members were always concerned about her health. Her parents pampered her throughout her childhood and teen years because she was frail and was plagued with frequent illnesses. Despite her ill health, however, she managed to complete her education in the Ontario public school system. She always expressed a desire to become a nurse, according to family members— likely a result of her constant childhood illnesses. After graduation from secondary school she was admitted to Chicago's Provident Hospital Training School for Nurses. Provident Hospital's main purpose was to provide a dignified, reputable, and lucrative occupation for women of color.

When Sleet began her nurse's training program, Provident had been open for only two years. She completed her nursing program in 1895, and because of the high quality of the Provident program she was eligible to sit for the state registration examination in several states. No record exists concerning the amount of time she remained in Chicago or if she practiced nursing there. She did travel to Washington, DC, and in 1897 completed a six-month graduate nursing course taught by Dr. DANIEL HALE WILLIAMS at Freedmen's Hospital. Nurses at the end of the nineteenth century had few employment opportunities, and this was especially true for black nurses. Working as a private duty nurse in a patient's home or as a floor nurse in hospitals that admitted black people were the only avenues open to black graduate nurses, and competition for available positions was fierce. Sleet moved to New Jersey and was employed as a private duty nurse in the resort town of Lakewood from 1897 to 1899. Although friends discouraged her, Sleet went to New York City in 1899 to become a district (visiting) nurse.

Blacks were losing their lives to tuberculosis—a preventable, curable disease—at extremely high rates. Women from all other nationalities were employed as district nurses in New York City. Black nurses had tried and failed to find work in this public health area; nevertheless, Sleet interviewed for positions at agencies with reputations for interviewing African Americans. There was initial interest in her, but whenever she shared her desire to work in public health she was informed that there were no positions available. The irony was that this was a time when most working nurses had not graduated from a formal program as Sleet had. She was discriminated against because of her color. Finally in October 1890 the Charity Organization Society hired Sleet for two months, on an experimental basis, as a district nurse who would go into the black community and persuade residents to accept treatment for tuberculosis.

Although she accepted the position with reservations because she knew that the Tuberculosis Committee did not want her, Sleet was determined to make the experiment work. She was so successful in working with African Americans and impacting their health in a positive way that the Charity Organization Society hired her permanently.

Her work was recognized in the first issue of the *American Journal of Nursing* (July 1901) as the news item "A Successful Experiment." In addition to the direct nursing care she gave to patients, Sleet conducted nursing research. She completed a six-week study about residents and the social and health conditions that contributed to the high rate of tuberculosis in the black community of a targeted area in Manhattan. Her article "Tuberculosis among Negroes: A Report to the Committee on the Prevention of Tuberculosis" was published in the *Third Annual Report of the Committee on the Prevention of Tuberculosis of the Charity Organization Society of the City of New York 1904–1905* (1905). She remained employed by the charity agency from 1900 to 1909, providing nursing care for hundreds of people and encouraging them to seek further medical care as needed.

Sleet married John R. Scales in 1909 and resigned her position with the Charity Organization Society after training her successor, Cecile Batey Anderson, another black nurse graduate, who was from the Lincoln School for Nurses in the Bronx. John and Jessie Scales had one daughter, Edna. No other information exists about Sleet's professional life after her marriage, and very little is known about her private life. She died in November 1950 after a lengthy illness that kept her bedridden for fifteen years. Although large numbers of African American professional nurses did not find positions open to them in public health until the 1930s, the pioneering work of Jesse Sleet Scales blazed a pathway for their clinical practice.

FURTHER READING

Carnegie, M. Elizabeth. *The Path We Tread: Blacks in Nursing 1854–1990* (1991).

Mosley, Marie. "Jesse Sleet Scales: First Black Public Health Nurse," *ABFN Journal* (Mar.–Apr. 1994).

ADELE BEVERLY

Scarborough, John Clarence, Sr. (17 June 187?–30 Jan. 1972), businessman, philanthropist, and civic political leader, was born in Kinston in eastern North Carolina, the son of the former slave Fannie Harrison. Information about his father is not known. Following the Civil War, Kinston, located on the Neuse River, emerged as a mercantile and industrial center, and the town witnessed a continuing influx of business-minded African Americans. Many of Kinston's new households were headed by former slaves who moved to town from the rural countryside seeking employment.

In addition to working as laborers, cooks, house servants, laundry women, and nannies, Kinston's newly freed blacks also worked as builders, horse grooms, draymen, brick masons, hotel waiters, distillers, barbers, roofers, woodcutters, basket makers, and gardeners.

By 1872 a stable African American community was established that included the former slave Wiley Lowery, who operated a general store, one of several African American businesses along South Queen Street. At an early age Scarborough worked in Lowery's grocery business as an errand boy, and eventually he became a clerk. Two schools for former slaves were established in Kinston by northern whites immediately following the Civil War, one of which Scarborough may have attended. The first permanent school for African Americans was established in 1888. Scarborough's education is evidenced by his clerking status in the Lowery store.

Scarborough continued to work at the store until Lowery's death. He then was hired by the former slave and Kinston merchant John Crooms Hargett, who owned a general merchandise, grocery, and funeral supply business (coffins, shrouds, veils, etc.). Hargett was so impressed with the young man's intelligence and work ethic that he encouraged him to attend Kittrell College in Kittrell, North Carolina, a school founded by the African Methodist Episcopal (AME) Church in 1886. Scarborough and Hargett may have been members of Kinston's Saint James African Methodist Episcopal Church. Scarborough worked to support himself while he was a student.

Upon Scarborough's return to Kinston, Hargett helped him obtain a U.S. rural mail route and even supplied the horse and carriage required for the position. In 1888 Hargett expanded his funeral accessory business and, with Scarborough as his partner, established Scarborough and Hargett's Funeral Service. White morticians generally did not conduct funerals for African Americans with dignity and respect, but Scarborough and Hargett Funeral Service quickly gained a reputation for providing a dignified funeral service for all its customers.

In 1901 Scarborough married Hargett's eldest daughter Daisy Elizabeth Hargett. In 1906 Scarborough graduated from the Renouard Training School for Embalmers in New York, the school's first African American graduate. He also became the first licensed African American funeral director and embalmer in North Carolina. Daisy had a respiratory condition that prompted Scarborough in 1906 to consider relocating to the mountain town of Asheville, North Carolina, to improve her health. However, Alex Moore, an agent with the North Carolina Mutual Life Insurance Company in Durham, encouraged Scarborough to move to that town instead. Scarborough and his wife moved to Durham in 1907.

In 1907 Durham had a progressive and educated African American business and social community. The founding of the North Carolina Mutual Life Insurance Company in 1898 by AARON McDUFFIE MOORE (1864–1923), JOHN MERRICK (1859–1921), and CHARLES CLINTON SPAULDING (1874–1952) created business and cultural endeavors supported by the tobacco town's rising African American middle class. Scarborough was soon in the forefront of Durham's African American business, political, and social affairs. The Scarboroughs became members of Saint Joseph's AME Church. The couple's two children were born into a life of privilege, and their parents stressed the value of hard work, the importance of family, and the principle of service to the community. In 1914 the family moved into their two-story colonial revival house fronted by double front porches and four monumental Doric columns that remains one of the most carefully detailed residences in Durham. "Scarborough House" on fashionable Fayetteville Street reflects the rise of Durham's urban middle class in the city's renowned business and residential section of Hayti.

Daisy's death in 1924 inspired Scarborough to purchase the buildings and property of Hayti's Lincoln Hospital in 1925, which he donated to the Black Ministers' Alliance for a senior citizens and orphans home. The property later expanded into the Daisy E. Scarborough Nursery School, which now provides child care that has enabled thousands of women to work and pursue their educations. Scarborough also established the Daisy E. Scarborough Foundation to assist financially in the care of young children. In 1926 Scarborough married Clydie Quinn Fullwood, who would direct the nursery school for well over fifty years. Their daughter and Scarborough's two older children witnessed the business, social, educational, and political achievements of their parents, who were committed to helping the less fortunate and to the fight for civil rights. Although never formally adopted, Ronald Scarborough was reared by the Scarborough family and was employed at Scarborough and Hargett Memorial Chapel and Gardens for over fifty years. Scarborough's son and older daughter also worked most of their adult lives in their father's business.

In 1908 Scarborough became a charter board member of black Durham's Mechanics and Farmers Bank, and in 1928 he founded the Colored Undertakers and Embalmers Association (now the Funeral Directors and Morticians Association of North Carolina). He organized the One O'Clock Luncheon Club of the Durham Business and Professional Club; was a charter member of Doric Lodge number 28 Free and Accepted Masons. In 1935 he was a founding member of the Durham Committee on Negro Affairs (now the Durham Committee on African American Affairs). Beginning in 1941 Scarborough served as a board member of Hayti's Stanford L. Warren Branch Library and was a member Omega Psi Phi Fraternity, Incorporated (Beta Phi Chapter). In 1947 he became the first African American to run for the Durham City Council; he was also a director of the Bankers Fire Insurance Company and president of the Southern Fidelity Mutual Insurance Company. In the late 1940s he donated land on Fayetteville Street for a Girl Scout campsite later named for Daisy Scarborough, and he served as steward, trustee, and chairman of Boy Scout Troop 105 of Saint Joseph's AME Church. Scarborough remained actively involved in community affairs until his death in Durham. His grandchildren and great-grandchildren continued to operate the family business into the early twenty-first century.

FURTHER READING

Weare, Walter B. *Black Business in the New South: A Social History of the North Carolina Mutual Life Insurance Company* (1993).

ALICE ELEY JONES

Scarborough, William Sanders (16 Feb. 1852–9 Sept. 1926), educator, author, editor, and first professional African American classical scholar, was born in Macon, Georgia, the only survivor of three children of Jeremiah Scarborough, a railroad employee, and Frances Gwynn, a slave. His enslaved mother was permitted by her owner, Colonel William de Graffenreid, to live with her emancipated husband. Jeremiah Scarborough was given funds to migrate to the North by his emancipator, who left $3,000 in trust for him should he decide to move to the North. Not wanting to leave his enslaved wife and son, he chose to remain in Macon. According to the Bibb County, Georgia, census of 1870, he had accumulated $3,500 in real property and $300 in personal property.

The Scarboroughs were literate and encouraged their son's academic development. They provided a variety of learning experiences for him; they apprenticed him to a shoemaker and carpenter for practical training and financed music lessons. William Scarborough began studying reading, arithmetic, grammar, and geography at age six. Since it was illegal to provide education for slaves, he received his lessons secretly from white and free black neighbors. Precocious, by the age of ten he was secretary to an adult organization in Macon, providing reading and writing services for the members who were enslaved or illiterate. To prevent physical punishment of slaves who left their owners' property without written permission, Scarborough forged passes for them.

In 1867 Scarborough enrolled at Macon's Lewis High School, forerunner of the Ballard Normal School sponsored by the American Missionary Association. Completing the high school program in 1869, he entered Atlanta University. After two years he registered at Oberlin College, where he did manual labor to supplement the tuition supplied by his parents. In 1875 he graduated with honors with a bachelor of arts degree in the classics. Scarborough was then hired to teach Latin, Greek, and mathematics at Lewis High School. A short while later he returned to Oberlin to study in the Department of Theology, concentrating on Greek and Hebrew. Armed with a master's degree, in 1878 he became principal of South Carolina's Payne Institute (now Allen University) and served also as professor of New Testament Greek and literature. Scarborough spent the majority of his career and made his greatest scholarly contributions at Wilberforce University, an institution sponsored by the African Methodist Episcopal (AME) Church. In 1891, Bishop Daniel Payne hired him to teach Greek and Latin. Later Scarborough taught Slavic languages and a variety of others, including Sanskrit. He organized the library and assisted with the editing of a Wilberforce publication, the *Author's Review and Scrapbook*. Named Wilberforce's vice president in 1897, he was elevated to the presidency in 1908.

In 1881 Scarborough published a textbook, *First Lessons in Greek*. Acclaimed by numerous scholars, including those from Howard University, Yale University, and the University of Wisconsin, it was the first such book written and published by an African American. A paper Scarborough presented at Cornell University was in such high demand by academicians that it was subsequently published and sold. In 1892 he lectured on the writings of Plato at the University of Virginia, at a time when African Americans could only enter the campus as laborers and servants. He was the third African American member of the American Philological Association and contributed numerous scholarly articles to its journal. He regularly contributed articles to the *Cleveland Gazette* and the Hampton University publication the *Southern Workman*. He served as editor of the AME Church's *Christian Recorder* from 1892 until his death. Many of his articles advocated for classical education for African Americans, and he editorialized against the unfair treatment accorded to returning African American World War I soldiers. Scarborough certainly had felt the sting of racial prejudice. In 1909 the management of Baltimore's Belvidere Hotel objected to his participation in the American Philological Association's annual meeting, where he was scheduled to present a paper. Since the hotel threatened to file a breach of contract suit if the organization canceled its meeting, Scarborough was asked not to attend. His paper was read by a white man.

The first African American member of the Modern Language Association, Scarborough assisted in writing the Oxford English Dictionary. Additionally he held membership in the American Social Science Association and the American Spelling Reform Association. He was invited to join the exclusive American Negro Academy, whose purpose was to promote scholarship. Among its members were W. E. B. DuBois, the Episcopal clergyman ALEXANDER CRUMMELL, the poet PAUL LAURENCE DUNBAR, and the bibliophile ARTHUR SCHOMBURG.

Although he outwardly opposed BOOKER T. WASHINGTON's belief that the majority of African Americans should train their hands rather than their minds, Scarborough nevertheless viewed Washington as a "much needed leader" (Scarborough). His resistance to Wilberforce's plan to increase industrial arts courses led to a brief interruption of his teaching career there. While he favored a form of education to which most African Americans were not exposed, Scarborough actively participated in efforts to improve conditions for all members of his race. He was a member of the National Negro Committee, one of the local organizations from which the NAACP evolved. As president of the Afro-American League of Ohio, he was instrumental in successfully challenging school segregation, and he fought against discrimination in railroad cars coming from the South. He was active in Republican Party politics and in the AME Church, representing his church at the Ecumenical Methodist Conference in London in 1901.

In 1881 Scarborough married Sarah C. Bierce, a white divorcée who taught at Oberlin and served as principal of the Normal Department of Wilberforce. The couple had no children. Scarborough remained president at Wilberforce until his retirement in 1920. Subsequently he conducted studies of African American farms for the U.S. Department of Agriculture. Scarborough died at his Wilberforce home, and his body lay in state at the school. HALLIE Q. BROWN, the civil and women's rights activist, read poems, and the eulogy was delivered by the AME bishop REVERDY RANSOM. At a time when African Americans suffered some of the worst repression in the nation's history, Scarborough's accomplishments refuted the belief that blacks were incapable of intellectual excellence. He inspired countless students to expand their academic horizons.

FURTHER READING

Scarborough, William S. *The Autobiography of William Sanders Scarborough: An American Journey from Slavery to Scholarship*, ed. with an introduction by Michele Valerie Ronnick (2005).

Franklin, John Hope. *Race and History, Selected Essays* (1938-1988).

Woodford, John. "A Classical Scholar's Odyssey from Slavery to Academic Renown." *The University Record*, University of Michigan, 24 February 2003.

Wright, Richard R. *The Encyclopaedia of the African Methodist Episcopal Church*, 2d ed. (1947).

DONNA TYLER HOLLIE

Schmoke, Kurt (1 Dec. 1949–), lawyer, mayor, and law school dean, was born Kurt Lidell Schmoke in Baltimore, Maryland, the son of Murray A. Schmoke Sr., a civilian chemist in the U.S. Army, and Irene Bennett Reid, a social worker. Schmoke had two half siblings, a sister, Karla Reid Young, and a brother, Murray A. Schmoke Jr., who died tragically in a traffic accident in South Africa in 1994. Coming of age in the Deep South during the Jim Crow era, Schmoke's parents experienced the viciousness of racism firsthand. Their pursuit and successful completion of college degrees at that time exhibited to their son that, with steadfast faith, courage, and self-assurance, opportunity and success would be plentiful to him.

Schmoke received his early education in Baltimore's public school system. A beneficiary of the landmark *Brown v. Board of Education* (1954) Supreme Court decision, Schmoke attended the integrated Baltimore City College High School. There he not only earned good grades but also starred as a varsity quarterback for the school's football team. During his senior year he became the first African American ever elected as the high school's student body president. He graduated from Baltimore City College High School in 1967.

That fall Schmoke entered Yale University. Perhaps one of his most enduring legacies as a student at Yale came as a result of his working with university officials to establish a day care center for the children of the university's custodial workers. Named the Calvin Hill Day Care Center after the former Yale football star Calvin Hill, it became a center of educational outreach and children's learning in the New Haven, Connecticut community.

In the spring of 1970 the Black Panther Party chairman BOBBY SEALE and eight other Black Panthers went on trial in New Haven for the murder of the former Black Panther Alex Rackley. Yale students led a mass demonstration that descended on New Haven and the Yale campus to protest the perceived unfairness of the trial. Students saw the trial as an effort to discredit the prominent leadership of the Black Panther Party, particularly Seale, and questioned if he would receive a fair trial. When members of the university's faculty and administration met to form a response to the protests, they requested to meet with Schmoke, then in his junior year, so he could articulate the students' position. Schmoke told the gathered faculty and administrators:

> Many of the students in the group [that had gathered outside the meeting] are committed to a cause, but there are a great number of students on campus who are confused and many who are frightened. They don't know what to think. You are our teachers. You are the people we respect. We look to you for guidance and moral leadership. On behalf of my fellow students, I beg you to give it to us (Zengerle, 21).

According to Bruce Fellman in an article written for the November 2000 *Yale Alumni* magazine, "the professors were primed for angry and abusive rhetoric" but, were "overcome by the filial courtesy and the implacable challenge of [Schmoke's] words." Schmoke's measured words helped Yale avoid what could have been a chaotic turn of events and earned him, the secretary of the class of 1971 and leader of the Black Student Alliance, the respect of the university's faculty, administration, and trustees.

Named a Rhodes scholar after graduating from Yale in 1971 with a B.A. degree in history, Schmoke studied social anthropology for two years at Oxford University. Upon his return from England, he enrolled in Harvard Law School and graduated with a law degree in 1976. While in law school, he married Patricia Locks, an ophthalmologist. They had two children.

After passing the Maryland bar, in 1976, Schmoke joined the Baltimore law firm of Piper and Marbury as one of its first black associates. He served for a short while, 1977–1978, on the White House domestic policy staff during the Jimmy Carter administration. Schmoke soon left Washington in 1978, preferring to focus his attention on Baltimore and electoral politics. In 1978 he served as U.S. attorney in Baltimore, and in 1982 he won his first elected office, becoming Baltimore's state attorney. He held this position for four years.

In 1987 Schmoke became the first elected black mayor of Baltimore. Despite a majority African American population, Baltimore had taken longer than many of its urban counterparts to elect a black mayor, in large part because of the popularity of Schmoke's predecessor, William Donald Schaefer. Schaefer had served as mayor of Baltimore from 1972 to 1987, and over the course of his fifteen-year tenure, he had helped redevelop and transform the city. With the development of the Inner Harbor, and a major push to draw hotels, restaurants, and shops to the downtown area, Baltimore emerged as a major tourist center. Although he applauded Schaefer for his civic improvements, Schmoke pointed out during his campaign that many had not benefited from the city's resurgence. Upon taking office, Schmoke used tactics considered unconventional and controversial to address the city's soaring crime rate and the poor performance of its public schools. He called for the decriminalization of some illegal drugs, such as heroin, marijuana, and cocaine, and during his tenure hired a Nation of Islam security force to police a Baltimore housing project. He was reelected in 1991 and again in 1995. During his three terms as mayor, Schmoke built upon some of the successes of his predecessor, pumping more than $1 billion dollars into Baltimore's downtown area. Baltimore became one of only six cities to be awarded federal grants that created Empowerment Zones, a program that provided incentives for businesses to locate in economically depressed areas of the inner city. New sports arenas were built, a new football team, the Baltimore Ravens, was acquired, and Schmoke promoted a reading program aimed at curbing adult illiteracy.

By the end of his third term in 1998, however, neither his success nor his popularity could mask the fact that much of Baltimore remained plagued by urban decay. He chose not to seek a fourth term as mayor. According to a 24 September 1999 article written in the *Afro-American Red Star*, "Three police commissioners gone and five school superintendents through the revolving door on North Ave. and Schmoke has only failing schools and record murder rates to show for his tenure in office. And relatedly, despite six months of media and state attention, the courts are still not working properly and the jails are full of offenders who shouldn't be there. Kurt Schmoke may not have created these problems, but certainly did little, in the end, to fix them."

After leaving office as mayor of Baltimore in 1999, Schmoke became a partner in the law firm of Wilmer, Cutler, and Pickering. He left the law firm in 2002, and in 2003 became the dean of the Howard University Law School. Under his leadership, Howard University School of Law developed a comprehensive clinical legal education program focusing on the provision of fair housing opportunity to all citizens. This new clinical program was funded initially by a $1,000,000 grant from the U.S. Department of Housing and Urban Development as part of its Historically Black Colleges and Universities Education Outreach Initiative. Howard Law's Fair Housing Clinical Program was a model for replication at any law school in the country.

FURTHER READING

Biles, Robert. "Black Mayors: A Historical Assessment," *Journal of Negro History* 77, no. 3 (Summer 1992).

Fellman, Bruce. "Power Persuader," *Yale Alumni Magazine*, Nov. 2000. Available at www.yalealumnimazazine.com/issues/00_11/schmoke.html.

"The Search for Former Glory: Howard University School of Law Has a New Dean," *Journal of Blacks in Higher Education* 38 (Winter 2002–2003).

Zengerle, Jason. "Up in Schmoke: Why Biracial Politics Failed in Baltimore," *New Republic* (10 Aug. 1998).

JESSICA CHRISTINA HARRIS

Schomburg, Arthur Alfonso (24 Jan. 1874–10 June 1938), historian, bibliophile, and curator, was born Arturo Alfonso Schomburg in San Juan, Puerto Rico, the son of Mary Joseph, an unwed midwife

Arthur Alfonso Schomburg's personal library formed the core of the New York Public Library's Schomburg Center for Research in Black Culture. (Library of Congress.)

or laundress who had been born free in 1837 on St. Croix, Virgin Islands. His father's name is unknown, though Schomburg recorded that he was born in 1839, the son of a German émigré merchant.

Details of Schomburg's education are also sparse. He may have attended the College of St. Thomas, a secondary school, but there is no documentation. Schomburg knew French, and his writings in Spanish are both grammatically correct and eloquent. His lack of formal education ate away at him all his life, and it was surely one of the spurs to his untiring search for information and his efforts to make the results widely known. As a child he belonged to a club of young people who studied history, and also learned about Puerto Rican history and nationalism from the island's cigar makers. Schomburg moved to New York City on 17 April 1891. He lived among tobacco workers and participated in their meetings, fund-raising, and publication activities. The Cuban and Puerto Rican

independence movements of that time inspired his youthful activism and scholarly bent, and the Cuban Revolutionary Party's newspaper, *Patria*, published his first article, a description of Las Dos Antillas, a political club he had cofounded earlier that year. Still a teenager, Schomburg worked as an elevator operator, bellhop, printer, and porter, and also taught Spanish in the night school where he learned English. Schomburg, an exceptionally social and fraternal man, joined a Masonic lodge, El Sol de Cuba No. 38, founded by Cuban and Puerto Rican exiles in 1881. English-speaking blacks were encouraged to join, and Schomburg translated the proceedings into English. He began acquiring and organizing the lodge's papers, books, correspondence, and photographs, and was elected master in 1911. The lodge, by then mostly black, changed its name to PRINCE HALL, after the first black Mason in the United States.

This name change was emblematic of Schomburg's realization that his future was in America. The Spanish-American War of 1898, which put Cuba, Puerto Rico, and the Philippines under the control of the United States, effectively ended the revolutionary efforts of the exiles. Family ties also strengthened Schomburg's commitment to his adopted land. In 1895 he married Elizabeth Hatcher, an African American from Staunton, Virginia, but she died in 1900 having borne three children. His second marriage, to Elizabeth Morrow Taylor of Williamsburg, North Carolina, lasted from 1902 until 1909, when she died, leaving two children. Visits to his five children, who were being raised by maternal relatives, exposed the New Yorker to the full-blown racism of the Jim Crow South.

Schomburg worked as a clerk and messenger for Pryor, Mellis, and Harris, a law firm, from 1901 to 1906. On 1 February 1906 he took a job with the Bankers Trust Company on Wall Street, where he remained for twenty-three years. He rose from messenger to supervisor of the bank's foreign mailing section, where his knowledge of French and Spanish, his exceptional memory, and his attention to detail were valuable qualities.

But Schomburg's real work was not on Wall Street; it was wherever he found others equally impassioned to prove that black people did indeed have an international history of accomplishment that stretched past slavery days to Africa. In April 1911 Schomburg was one of five founders of the Negro Society for Historical Research. The society aimed "to show that the Negro race has a history that antedates that of the proud Anglo-Saxon race"; they planned "to collect useful historical data relating to the Negro race, books written by or about Negroes, rare pictures of prominent men and women ... letters ... African curios of native manufacture" (Sinnette, 43). It acquired members in Europe, the Americas, the Caribbean, and Africa, including the vice president of Liberia, James Dossen, EDWARD BLYDEN of Sierra Leone, and Mojola Agbebe of Nigeria—which must have gratified Schomburg, a Pan-Africanist.

Schomburg, activist and expansive in outlook, generously made available to those in his wide network his private library, acquired with a limited budget. He had already begun to carry out the society's mission of collecting historical documents. At about this time he married his third wife. By 1916 their household was filled with three young children and Schomburg's growing library.

The American Negro Academy, founded in Washington, D.C., in 1897 and limited to forty members, elected Schomburg to membership in 1914. Schomburg became the academy's fifth president (1920–1929). The group held annual conventions, encouraged publication of scholarly works, and urged members to acquire books and manuscripts by and about people of African descent. At the 1915 convention, Schomburg's paper, "The Economic Contribution by the Negro to America," brought to the academy's attention the theme that had always engaged him: that people of African origin, wherever they were in the world, had made significant but unrecognized contributions in all fields to white society. Schomburg's research, writings, and talks about Haitians and blacks of European, Central, and South American birth broadened the perspective of the academy's members.

In 1918 Schomburg was elected grand secretary of the Prince Hall Grand Lodge of the State of New York, a position that required frequent travel and attention to many organizational activities, including planning a new temple. He was still able to mount a weeklong exhibition at the Carleton Street YMCA in Brooklyn. On view were rare books, manuscripts, engravings, paintings, and sculpture, as well as African art. Only one earlier exhibition, in New York in 1909, had displayed African art as art, not as ethnographic curiosities.

By 1925 Schomburg had formed a library of nearly 4,000 books and pamphlets and about 1,000 manuscripts and prints, which he wished to make widely available to inspire Negro youth. With a grant of $10,000 from the Carnegie Corporation in 1926, the New York Public Library purchased the collection and housed it in its 135th Street Library. Among its rarest items were BENJAMIN BANNEKER's almanacs (1792–1796) and manuscripts by PAUL LAURENCE DUNBAR and Toussaint-Louverture.

The library also became a gathering place for the writers and artists of the Harlem Renaissance. Schomburg's most influential essay, "The Negro Digs Up His Past," appeared in one of the preeminent texts of that movement, ALAIN LOCKE's *The New Negro* (1925), and was often reprinted. His essay called for rigorous historical research, not "a pathetically over-corrective, ridiculously over-laudatory ... apologetics turned into biography." Though he urged that "history must restore what slavery took away," half a century passed before his collection was recognized as a treasure house and received funding for renovation and new construction.

After the sale of his collection, Schomburg began to spend more time at the 135th Street Library. When he retired from Bankers Trust at the end of 1929, he planned to devote his time to research and to travel to Spain again. Even before his retirement, however, CHARLES S. JOHNSON, chairman of the social science department of Fisk University in Nashville, Tennessee, invited him to build Fisk's Negro Collection. From November 1930 until the end of 1931 Schomburg was the curator of that collection, acquiring 4,524 books out of a total of 4,630. The Fisk librarian Louis Shores wrote that Schomburg's "bibliographic memory was spectacular." Schomburg returned to New York in 1932 to accept his final position as curator in charge of his own collection, serving until his death six years later.

Money was short because of the Great Depression, but Schomburg managed to add outstanding items to the New York collection, including the long-sought *Ad Catholicum* of Juan Latino (1573) and a folio of engravings by PATRICK HENRY REASON, a nineteenth-century black artist. The marble-and-bronze sculpture of IRA ALDRIDGE as Othello, which often serves as the graphic symbol of the Schomburg Center, was bought in 1934, with assistance from a fellow bibliophile, Arthur B. Spingarn. Donations from authors, artists, and Schomburg's many friends further enriched the collection, as did purchases paid for by Schomburg himself.

The acquisition of Schomburg's collection by the New York Public Library vindicated his forty-year search for the evidence of black history. He was gratified that it would be freely available to all.

A teenage immigrant without influential family, formal education, or ample funds, consigned to a segregated world, he nevertheless amassed a collection of inestimable value. Schomburg was "a man who built his own monument," said one eulogist. From his core of five thousand items, the Schomburg Center for Research in Black Culture would grow to five million items and become the world's most important repository in the field. Schomburg's name is also commemorated in a street in San Juan, Puerto Rico, an elementary school in the Bronx, and a housing complex in Harlem.

FURTHER READING

A large collection of Schomburg's papers is at the Schomburg Center for Research in Black Culture of the New York Public Library, along with extensive clipping files about him.

Gubert, Betty Kaplan, and Richard Newman. *Nine Decades of Scholarship: A Bibliography of the Writings 1892–1983 of the Staff of the Schomburg Center for Research in Black Culture* (1986).

Sinnette, Elinor Des Verney. *Arthur Alfonso Schomburg: Black Bibliophile and Collector* (1989).

Obituary: *New York Times*, 11 June 1983.

This entry is taken from the *American National Biography* and is published here with the permission of the American Council of Learned Societies.

BETTY KAPLAN GUBERT

Schuyler, George Samuel (25 Feb. 1895–31 Aug. 1977) journalist, was born in Providence, Rhode Island, to George Francis Schuyler and Eliza Jane Fischer, both cooks. He was raised in Syracuse, New York, and often remarked that his family had never lived in the South and had never been slaves. That did not mean that they had not suffered discrimination, however, for as Schuyler wrote in his 1966 autobiography: "A black person learns very early that his color is a disadvantage in a world of white folks. This being an unalterable circumstance, one also learns to make the best of it" (Schuyler, 1).

For Schuyler, that early exposure to racism came on his first day at school, when he registered three firsts: he was called "nigger," fought the Italian American boy who used the slur, and received a bloody nose for his pains. After that experience, his mother told him to always fight back when called names, and she also taught him about the achievements of FREDERICK DOUGLASS, HARRIET TUBMAN, and other great African Americans. From then on, Schuyler later recalled, he never felt inferior to whites, even though he saw no person of color in any position of authority until he was fourteen and witnessed black soldiers on exercise in Syracuse.

Perhaps because of the childhood school incident and because he saw few prospects for young black men in his hometown, Schuyler left school at seventeen and joined the army. He served for seven years in the Twenty-fifth U.S. Infantry, a predominantly black regiment famed for its Buffalo Soldiers, who had been recruited for "pacification" campaigns against Indians in the post–Civil War American West. Stationed at first in Seattle, Washington, Schuyler found the Pacific Northwest to be little different from upstate New York in terms of racial discrimination. Schuyler's next posting, in Hawaii, proved much more congenial to him, in part because of the camaraderie among African American recruits and the seemingly endless opportunities in Honolulu for "rum and roistering" (Schuyler, 71). But he also loved the breathtaking landscape of Hawaii and initially planned to stay in Honolulu at the end of his service in 1915.

Finding few opportunities in civilian life, he reenlisted in his former regiment and began his first efforts at journalism, writing satirical pieces for the *Service*, a weekly magazine for soldiers in Hawaii. When the United States entered World War I, he received a commission and, according to his autobiography, served at Camp Dix, New Jersey, and Camp Meade, Maryland. Schuyler's memoir does not mention, however, that he went AWOL for three months in 1918 after he had visited Philadelphia, Pennsylvania, in uniform and was denied service by a Greek bootblack. He later surrendered to military authorities in San Diego and was sentenced to five years in prison on Governors Island in New York; in his autobiography, he claims to have worked at that prison as a clerk.

After serving only nine months in jail, Schuyler was released for good behavior and worked a series of low-paying laboring jobs in Syracuse, where he joined the Socialist Party in 1921. He then moved to New York, where he drew upon his experiences in a Bowery flophouse in "Hobohemia," a satirical essay that he wrote in 1923 for the *Messenger*, a socialist newspaper founded by A. PHILIP RANDOLPH. That same year, Schuyler joined the *Messenger*'s editorial staff and wrote a monthly column, "Shafts and Darts: A Page of Calumny and Satire," which aimed to "slur, lampoon, damn, and occasionally praise anybody or anything in the known universe" (Peplow, 22). Although he also targeted white hypocrisy and racism, Schuyler most effectively skewered what he saw as the cant and hypocrisy of African American leaders, notably MARCUS GARVEY.

As he no doubt intended, Schuyler's satirical barbs provoked outrage among his targets, especially his fellow African American intellectuals. In "The Negro-Art Hokum," which appeared in the *Nation* in 1926, Schuyler declared that there is no distinct, unified African American aesthetic separate from an American aesthetic. More controversially, he summarized that view by stating that "the Aframerican is merely a lampblacked Anglo-Saxon" (Leak, 14). The essay provoked a bitter response among Harlem Renaissance artists—notably LANGSTON HUGHES—who were at that time exalting the unique achievements of black American culture. Schuyler's combative essays proved good copy, however, and by the late 1920s he was the most widely read black journalist in America. In addition to a regular opinion column in the *Pittsburgh Courier*, his essays appeared in national publications such as the *American Mercury*, a periodical founded by the gadfly journalist H. L. Mencken, who greatly influenced Schuyler's iconoclastic style. Schuyler's prodigious journalistic output coincided with his marriage in 1928 to Josephine Cogdell, a white Texas heiress, artist, and former model. The union produced a daughter, PHILIPPA DUKE SCHUYLER, a child prodigy who, at the age of thirteen, performed her own composition, "Manhattan Nocturne," with the New York Philharmonic.

The 1930s marked the peak of Schuyler's influence as a cultural critic. *Black No More* (1931), the first black science fiction novel, reversed traditional American race roles by means of a whitening agent that made Americans of African descent a shade lighter than whites of European descent. In the process, Schuyler lampoons W. E. B. DuBois as Dr. Shakespeare Agamemnon Beard—a portrayal DuBois greatly enjoyed—and introduces a black nationalist character, Santop Licorice, a thinly veiled Garvey, who was less forgiving of Schuyler's acerbic wit. DuBois joined Garvey, however, in criticizing *Slaves Today* (1931). This satire was drawn from Schuyler's experiences in Liberia in the early 1930s, when he had written a series of articles—published in the *Courier* and syndicated to several other newspapers—criticizing the African republic for its corrupt government and toleration of slavery.

Despite his frequent criticisms of Garvey, Schuyler wrote two black nationalist pulp science fiction serials under the pseudonym of Samuel I. Brooks for the *Pittsburgh Courier* in the late 1930s. Schuyler's adoption of a nationalist alter ego and his criticisms of "Brooks's" serials as "hokum and hack work" appear paradoxical. The literary scholar HENRY LOUIS GATES JR. suggests, however, that Schuyler/Brooks purposely adopted the dual role in an intellectual playing out of DuBois's metaphor of black double-consciousness.

Around the same time, Schuyler's political philosophy also changed; George Schuyler, radical and socialist, metamorphosed into George Schuyler, reactionary and conservative. One factor may have been what Schuyler saw as the exploitation of the SCOTTSBORO BOYS' case by the Communist Party in the late 1930s, but the bulk of his writings before the McCarthy era place him firmly on the progressive left. Indeed, from 1934 to 1944 he served as business manager of the NAACP and worked closely with his protégé, ELLA BAKER, in promoting workers' and consumers' cooperatives. Both before and during World War II, Schuyler used his columns in the *Pittsburgh Courier* to attack the hypocrisy of blacks fighting against fascism abroad while suffering Jim Crow at home.

After World War II, Schuyler's conservatism became unambiguous. His anticommunism and opposition to the Soviet Union may not have been unique among black intellectuals at that time, but his strident defense of Senator Joseph McCarthy certainly was. Likewise, most African Americans would have agreed with Schuyler's contention in "The Negro Question without Propaganda" (1950) that lynching had declined since 1900, but few, especially in the South, could take seriously his claim that force was rarely used to keep blacks from the polls. Indeed, as the civil rights movement made impressive legal and political victories in the 1950s and 1960s, Schuyler moved farther and farther to the right, not only criticizing MALCOLM X as a latter-day Garvey, but also attacking MARTIN LUTHER KING JR. as a communist stooge. When black newspapers refused to publish his essay discrediting King's 1964 Nobel Prize, Schuyler published the piece in the rabidly conservative *Manchester (N.H.) Union Leader*. In the 1960s and 1970s Schuyler also contributed several articles to *American Opinion*, the journal of the John Birch Society, an organization so profoundly right wing that it regarded President Dwight Eisenhower as a communist sympathizer.

Schuyler died in relative obscurity in New York City. Most commentators noted his political journey from left to right, but the historian JOHN HENRIK CLARKE was probably more accurate in noting Schuyler's consistency as a rebel. Clark recalled that he "used to tell people that George got up in the morning, waited to see which way the world was turning, then struck out in the opposite direction" (*New York Times*, 7 Sept. 1977).

FURTHER READING

Schuyler's papers are housed at the Schomburg Center for Research in Black Culture of the New York Public Library.

Schuyler, George S. *Black and Conservative* (1966).

Gates, Henry Louis, Jr. "A Fragmented Man: George Schuyler and the Claims of Race," *New York Times Book Review*, 20 Sept. 1992.

Leak, Jeffery B. *Rac[e]ing to the Right: Selected Essays of George Schuyler* (2001).

Peplow, Michael W. *George S. Schuyler* (1980).

Obituary: *New York Times*, 7 Sept. 1977.

STEVEN J. NIVEN

Schuyler, Philippa Duke (2 Aug. 1931–9 May 1967), pianist, composer, writer, and journalist, was born to Josephine Codgell, a blue-eyed blonde beauty from a wealthy white Texas family, and GEORGE SCHUYLER, a prominent black journalist. In 1927, while in New York, Codgell went to meet George Schuyler, the black editor of a modest left-wing publication, *Messenger*, which had published her poetry and prose since 1923. They were immediately smitten with each other, and despite the social taboo of their union they quietly married on 6 January 1928. Codgell believed that the way to solve America's racial intolerance was through interracial marriages and biracial offspring. Schuyler proved herself a child prodigy. She began to crawl at one month, sat up at four months, spoke at one year, and could read and write by the age of three. She began playing the piano when she was four years old, and was just five when she composed her first piece and gave her first performance at the YMCA on West 135th Street. In 1937, by invitation of the director Mother Stevens, she began attending the prestigious Pius X School of Liturgical Music at the College of the Sacred Heart in Harlem. In 1938 she also spent afternoons at Durlich and Emerson, a school for the gifted sponsored by New York University. Throughout her childhood Schuyler received numerous awards for her performances and her original compositions. She composed music as if telling a tale, and her compositions

Philippa Duke Schuyler, concert pianist, photographed in 1959. (Library of Congress.)

reflected a capacity for musical complexity far beyond her young age. In 1939 *Look* magazine dubbed her the "Shirley Temple of American Negroes." She received numerous awards during the 1939 World's Fair in New York, including her own day; 19 June 1940 was proclaimed Philippa Duke Schuyler Day. Schuyler was featured in four issues of *Time*, in 1935, 1936, 1940, and 1946. The 1946 *Time* proclaimed her the brightest young composer in the United States. Joseph Mitchell profiled her in the *New Yorker* on 31 August 1940. She appeared often in *Ebony*, *Sepia*, *Newsweek*, *Seventeen*, *Time*, and many newspapers throughout the 1940s. In 1942, at age eleven, she was the youngest member to be inducted into the National Association for American Composers and Conductors.

In 1950 Schuyler began her extensive and extraordinary travels around the world. For the next four years she performed in almost every country in South and Central America and many Caribbean islands. She kept a grueling performance schedule, many times arriving only hours before she was scheduled to perform. Her remarkable talent and intellect afforded her success and opportunities that were normally unavailable to black women, and she inspired many black girls and boys to play piano and follow their dreams. She was an important and visible model of black success in spite of widespread racism. Yet Schuyler spent her life trying to overcome a persistent sense of placelessness, a feeling of disconnection and isolation from people. The racism she experienced in the United States and her status as a "half-caste" consigned her to neither the white nor the black world, and she struggled to fit in. She had a contentious and manipulative relationship with her mother, who acted as her manager and exerted control over all aspects of her life. Schuyler roamed the world, performing tirelessly, seeking the acceptance that eluded her. She wrote extensively in journals throughout her life, and she was particularly observant of different cultural attitudes toward race in the countries she visited. In Central and South America she experienced for the first time an acceptance that did not disparage her blackness. There she enjoyed rank, respect, and privilege.

Schuyler visited Europe for the first time in 1953 when she was twenty-two and again experienced a public acceptance that buoyed her spirits and fostered a lifelong love of Europe. On that first trip she performed a grueling schedule: twenty concerts over seven weeks in Sweden, Denmark, Norway, Finland, Holland, and Belgium.

In 1955, when she was twenty-four, Schuyler went to the African continent for the first time. Her visit to Egypt inspired her to publish her first book, a quasi-autobiographical account of her experience, *Adventures in Black and White* (1960). In 1957 she began a four-month tour to Africa and Europe. It would be her first time in West Africa, and in four weeks she performed in eight countries. But it was during her second trip to West Africa, in 1960, to the Katanga province of Congo, that her career took a new direction: she witnessed the Congo revolution for independence. There were no reporters there at the time, so Schuyler began sending news dispatches to her publisher in New York. In 1962 she published her second book, *Who Killed the Congo*, which sought to illuminate the West's misconceptions about the Congo as a dangerous and lawless place. Schuyler had evolved into a devout Catholic, finding in Catholicism a gentle relief from the persistent feelings of loneliness and isolation. Her experiences in Africa were the inspiration for her third book, *Jungle Saints: Africa's Heroic Missionaries* (1963), an examination of the work of Catholic missionaries in Africa.

In September 1966 Schuyler was invited to perform at the National Conservatory of Music in Vietnam. She performed throughout Vietnam, but she did so as an aside to her now more prominent role as foreign correspondent, and she reported regularly to the *Manchester Union Leader*. Schuyler dressed as a local Vietnamese and wore a long-haired wig, a disguise that allowed her entry into areas other reporters could not enter. Her skill at slipping under the CIA radar so she could send firsthand reports back to the States made her a target of constant CIA surveillance throughout her time in Vietnam. Schuyler authored her third book, *Good Men Die* (1969), about the war and made a second trip to Vietnam in 1967 to continue her wartime coverage. During the siege of Hue, she helped evacuate seventy children and nuns from the St. Joan of Arc orphanage to Da Nang. While evacuating boys from the Binh Linh school by helicopter, the craft went down, killing Schuyler and the small child she held in her lap. She never finished her second book on Vietnam, *Dau Tranh* (*Struggle*).

FURTHER READING

Elwood-Akers, Virginia. *Women War Correspondents in the Vietnam War, 1961–1975* (1988).

Talalay, Katheryn. *Composition in Black and White: The Life of Philippa Schuyler* (1995).

DEBBIE CLARE OLSON

Scobell, John (–), the name bequeathed to history and literature of a trusted agent of the Pinkerton intelligence network during the Civil War. According to Allan Pinkerton's own memoirs, this agent was born into slavery on the Mississippi plantation of James MacFarland Scobell, and taken by his then-master, a soldier in the 2nd Mississippi infantry regiment, to Manassas Junction, Virginia.

The 2nd Mississippi was assigned to the third brigade, Army of Northern Virginia. However, none of the rosters that have been compiled, listing the officers and enlisted men serving in the 2nd Mississippi, include a James McFarland Scobell. Nor do census records from Mississippi in 1860, 1850, or 1840. In fact, there is no such person in any roster of any unit of the confederate army. There was a W. J. S. Scobell, originally from New Orleans, who published a newspaper for the confederate settlement in British Honduras after the war. We have only Pinkerton's word for the entire account; all other published work relies, ultimately, on Pinkerton.

Pinkerton had, on the one hand, every reason to disguise the identity and origin of his agents. The names may have been a proper cover story. During the time Pinkerton ran the Army Secret Service, he was known at General George B. McClellan's headquarters as Major E. J. Allen. On the other hand, he was given to exaggeration. During 1861–1862, Pinkerton cost McClellan any chance he had to capture the confederate capital, Richmond, by informing him that confederate General Joseph Johnston had 100,000 to 120,000 troops, when in fact he bad barely 50,000, half McClellan's force. When Robert E. Lee took command six weeks later, Pinkerton assured his commander the confederate forces had swelled to 180,000. After the war, Pinkerton wrote to boost his own public image, often at the expense of sober truth.

According to the account Pinkerton related, Scobell reported that General P. G. T. Beauregard wanted soldiers to do their own work, and didn't want slaves eating up army rations; he ordered that all slaves of private soldiers should be sent home. Scobell and his wife were provided papers declaring them free, and John Scobell immediately sought the lines of the federal army, while his wife obtained work as a cook in Richmond. Brought for questioning to Pinkerton, Scobell made a good impression and was enrolled as an operative.

There is independent corroboration for the existence, and execution by the confederate military, of another Pinkerton agent, Timothy Webster, whose wife, Charlotte, was granted a pension 1 March 1869. Accounts of Webster's work are at times closely intertwined with that of John Scobell, who was dispatched to his first field assignment in company with Webster, probably in the fall of 1861. They traveled together as far as Leonardstown, Virginia, then separated. Webster went to a hotel kept by a bitter secessionist named Miller.

Webster picked up that a Dr. Gurley, staying in the neighborhood, had visited Miller for help getting to Richmond. Gurley had resigned an officer's commission in the U.S. Army to join with the confederacy, and had dispatches from Southern sympathizers for the confederate war department. Webster found Scobell still in the area, and arranged for him to rob Gurley of his dispatches at the first opportunity. Scobell later communicated to Webster that he had arranged with "an intelligent and loyal colored man" who was leaving for Washington the next morning. Wanting to see the man first, Webster was introduced by Scobell to the secret meeting place of a Loyal League lodge, with the passwords "Friends of Uncle Abe" and "Light and Liberty."

There were such leagues and lodges—whether they had such convenient snug meeting places and dramatic passwords, or whether this was a Pinkerton embellishment, may never be known. Scobell, according to Pinkerton, continued a reconnaissance mission through Dumfries, Accoquan, Manassas, and Centreville, observing military units, numbers of men and horses, and size and strength of artillery batteries, while also making sketches of fortifications and trenches. He then returned to the Potomac and Washington by way of Leesburg. His cover roles included selling food through the camps, laboring on earthworks, cooking, and singing his vast repertoire of "Negro" and Scottish songs.

Scobell was next assigned as a resident operative in Richmond, where his cover would be serving as a groom to a woman going by the name of Hattie or Carrie Lawton, who may have been born Angie Warren in Chemung, New York. She was a Pinkerton agent already established in the Confederate capital, and wife of a U.S. Army major, referenced by Pinkerton as "Hugh Lawton." During a period when "Mrs. Lawton" had to get reports directly to her husband, because the opposing armies were moving too quickly to wait for reports to go through Washington, it was Scobell, with a tip from a stable boy, who first identified a Confederate counteragent at their meeting point, allowing for a dramatic escape to federal lines. Hattie Lawton was, according to some accounts, later sent to Richmond again, posing as Timothy Webster's sister, when he was arrested and eventually executed. She may also have pretended to be his wife. Lawton was released in a prisoner exchange in January 1863.

When McClellan was removed from command in November 1862, replaced in rapid succession by generals Ambrose Burnside and Joseph Hooker, Pinkerton was out of a job in army intelligence. There is no record from other sources of "John Scobell's" later service, or life after the war ended. The stories of John Scobell's work, however much they have been embroidered with drama, give a rare insight into the work of intelligence agents of African descent whose reports were known among United States Army officers as "black dispatches."

FURTHER READING
Foster, Allen G. "John Scobell: Union Spy in Civil War." *Ebony*, 19, no. 2 (Dec. 1963): 135–145.

Pinkerton, Allan. *The Spy of the Rebellion* (1883).

CHARLES ROSENBERG

Scott, Alberta Virginia (1875–2 Sept. 1902), the first African American graduate of Radcliffe College (now part of Harvard University), was born near Richmond, Virginia, the daughter of Smith A. Scott and Fanny Bunch Scott. Very little is known about her childhood. When she was six years old, her family moved to Cambridge, Massachusetts, where they lived in several locations in the "lower Port," a long-established black neighborhood near the present day location of M.I.T. in Kendall Square, now replaced by office buildings. Her father was a boiler tender and stationary engineer. Although her parents were not wealthy, they worked very hard to give their daughter a good education and a promising future. According to some sources, Cambridge people spoke of her parents with considerable admiration.

Scott graduated with distinction from the Cambridge Latin School in 1894 and entered Radcliffe College, where she studied mostly the classics. For the first three years she took courses in Greek, Latin, English, and German and alternated courses in French, history, and philosophy, as well a half course in geology, obtaining very good grades. During her last year, she focused only on two particular subjects: Greek and philosophy. She was a member of the Idler and German clubs at Radcliffe. While attending college, because Radcliffe had no dormitories at that time, Scott lived for the first two years with an African American family at 20 Parker Street in Cambridge. In her junior year she was at 7 Dickinson Street and in her final year she lived at home at 28 Union Street; both of these locations were situated in nearby Somerville, Massachusetts.

In an article published in the *Boston Globe* on 23 June 1898 celebrating Scott's graduation from college, she is described as a girl of a studious disposition and most welcome among her college associates. Her classmates spoke of Scott with great admiration and one of them, probably interviewed by the chronicler of the newspaper, expressed this feeling for her: "The friendship which Miss Scott cultivated with us during our four years at Radcliffe will be as long as life will last and I believe this is the honest sentiment of every member of the class" (*Boston Globe*, 23 June 1998). It is said that even outside of college Cambridge people accorded Scott the highest respect, and the fact that she attended college was a source of great pride, especially to her neighbors. Both Alberta and her father were also active members of their religious community and attended the Union Baptist Church on Main Street, where Mr. Scott was a deacon. She taught Sunday school there under the guidance of her friend, Charlotte Hawkins Brown, who refused to attend Radcliffe a few years after Scott had entered the college.

Scott was the first African American woman trained entirely in the schools of Massachusetts to be graduated from one of its colleges in 1898. There had been only three known black women to be graduated from a women's college in Massachusetts, two from Wellesley and one from Smith, but they came from places outside of Massachusetts. After the Civil War, Cambridge's African American population had grown quickly, rising from 371 in 1865 to 921 in 1875 and 3,500 in 1910. The population was supported by a sympathetic abolitionist community that provided jobs as well as sponsorship and training for the newcomers. Scott graduated from Radcliffe College soon after a few black men had attended Harvard University. The first among them had been RICHARD T. GREENER, who graduated in 1870, whereas W. E. B DuBois graduated with honors in 1890 and became the first African American to receive a Ph.D. from Harvard in 1895.

When Scott finished college in 1898 she decided that it was her duty to teach African American children. Although many friends had promised to help her obtain a good position in the North, she planned to leave Massachusetts for the South. At first she taught in an Indianapolis High School. In 1900 BOOKER T. WASHINGTON recruited her to teach at the Tuskegee Institute. A few sources state that, during that time, she stayed at Washington's house. After a year in Alabama, she felt sick and returned to her family in Cambridge. She died at 37 Hubbard Street, her parents' last home in North Cambridge, on 30 August 1902. Her dear friend CHARLOTTE HAWKINS BROWN sang at her funeral, which was conducted by the reverend Jesse Harrell of the Union Baptist Church. She was buried in the Cambridge cemetery, like her father a few years later. On 2 September 1902 the *Boston Guardian* published her obituary, entitled "Died in Life's Bloom. Miss Alberta Scott, the Young Radcliffe Girl, Passes Away after a Lingering Illness," in which are given the names of relatives and friends who attended her funeral.

Cambridge is home to one of the oldest African American communities in the nation and particularly during the last decades of the nineteenth century many black lives enriched its history. William Edward Burghardt DuBois, the founder of the National Association for the Advancement of Colored People, was largely educated in Cambridge and his classmate CLEMENT GARNETT MORGAN was a local politician who joined DuBois and Cantabrigian Emery T. Morris to found the Niagara Movement in 1905. MARIA BALDWIN, who was appointed headmaster of the Cambridge's Agassiz Grammar School in 1889, attended Cambridge public schools. Charlotte Hawkins Brown and PAULINE HOPKINS, among a few other African American women, were also eminent Cantabrigians who deservedly obtained national prominence. Scott's promising future and career as a teacher were tragically cut short by her premature death.

FURTHER READING

African American Heritage Trail. Cambridge, Massachusetts (2000).

"Radcliffe's Colored Graduate," *Boston Globe*, 23 June 1898.

Sollors, Werner, Caldwell Titcomb, and Thomas A. Underwood. *Blacks at Harvard: A Documentary History of African-American Experience at. Harvard and Radcliffe* (1993).

Obituary: "Died in Life's Bloom. Miss Alberta Scott, the Young Radcliffe Girl, Passes Away after a Lingering Illness." *Boston Guardian*, 2 September 1902.

ANNA RUSSO

Scott, Daisy Levester (24 Oct. 1897–20 Aug. 1946), cartoonist, was born in Blevins, Arkansas, the first daughter of Julia Miller, a homemaker, and Lemuel Dixon, a preacher. A few years later, her parents separated and Julia Miller moved to St. Louis. After living for a short time with her maternal grandmother, Daisy was sent to live with her grandmother's sister-in-law, Josephine Hurst and her husband, Peter, in Little Rock, Arkansas. When she was nineteen years old, Daisy met Jack Scott, a former middleweight boxer, and they were married on 2 May 1917. The couple moved from Little Rock to Tulsa, Oklahoma, where they lived in Greenwood, the city's African American section. The 1920 census listed Daisy as a cartoonist and her husband as a janitor. They had twelve children: Judith, Juanita, Julius, Eloise, Panchita, Sidney, Pauline, Guy, Altamese, Jonetta, Benjamin, and Toussaint.

Scott worked as a cartoonist for the *Tulsa Star*, edited by A. J. SMITHERMAN. Her cartoons reflected the key political themes of African American intellectuals in the Progressive era: the threat of lynching, riots, and the burdens that race hatred placed on the African American community (such as the costs of racial violence and segregation)— particularly African American women—and African Americans' patriotism. For instance, one Scott cartoon depicted an African American man carrying a hammer, headed to work, while radicals at the side plotted anarchy. Scott was an important part of a rich intellectual community in Tulsa prior to the infamous 1921 Tulsa riot. Other members of that community included MARY JONES PARRISH, J.B. STRADFORD, B. C. FRANKLIN, and activists such as O. B. Mann, who had been influenced by W. E. B. DuBois's *The Crisis* and Smitherman's *Tulsa Star*. On the evening of 31 May 1921 Mann led a band of African American World War I veterans—including Jack Scott—to the Tulsa courthouse to protect Dick Rowland from a threatened lynching. It was said of Mann that after the riot, he "came back from the war with France with exaggerated notions about equality and thinking he can whip the world" (Brophy, 33). Scott's cartoons illustrated Mann's attitude: a pride in the community and a desire to protect against violence.

Scott survived the Tulsa riot, although the 1930 U.S. Census did not list an occupation for her. Like many other people in Greenwood, the riot dramatically altered Scott's life. She and her husband even lived in a tent while they built a new house in Greenwood. Moreover, the riot destroyed the *Tulsa Star*, so Scott no longer had a publication outlet for her work. So far as we can tell, she did not work as a cartoonist after the riot. Jack had a boxing ring in their backyard, where he taught boxing. In the depths of the Great Depression, the couple won a case in the Oklahoma Supreme Court against a white person, to whom they allegedly owed a debt: *Scott v. Marshall* (1933). It is a reminder that in rare instances African Americans could get a modicum of justice in the Oklahoma courts. Scott lived in Tulsa until her death in 1946 of a cerebral hemorrhage; funeral services took place on 20 August 1946 at St. Monica's Catholic Church in Tulsa.

FURTHER READING

Brophy, Alfred L. *Reconstructing the Dreamland: The Tulsa Riot of 1921* (2002).

Ellsworth, Scott. *Death in a Promised Land: The Tulsa Race Riot of 1921* (1982).

Final Report of the Oklahoma Commission to Study the Tulsa Race Riot of 1921 (2001).

ALFRED L. BROPHY

Scott, Dred (c. 1800–17 Sept. 1858), slave and plaintiff in the 1857 landmark U.S. Supreme Court case *Dred Scott v. John F. A. Sanford*, was born of unknown parentage in Southampton County, Virginia, the property of plantation owner Peter Blow. After brief sojourns in Huntsville and Florence, Alabama, in 1830 the Blow family settled in St. Louis where, strapped for funds, Blow sold Scott to Dr. John Emerson. In 1833 Emerson's career as an army surgeon took him, among other places, to Illinois and to what was then a part of Wisconsin Territory (now Minnesota). Scott accompanied him into these areas, one a free state and one a territory that had been declared free by the Northwest Ordinance of 1787 and the Missouri Compromise of 1820. In 1836 or 1837, while at Fort Snelling in Wisconsin Territory, Scott married Harriet Robinson, whose master, Major Lawrence Taliaferro, transferred her ownership to Emerson. Dred and HARRIET SCOTT subsequently had two daughters. Posted in 1840 to the Seminole War in Florida, Emerson left his wife, Eliza Irene Sanford Emerson, and the slaves in St. Louis. Emerson returned the following year but died shortly thereafter. The exact whereabouts of the Scotts for the next few years are uncertain, except that they were hired out to various people in St. Louis, a frequent experience for city-dwelling slaves. They seem also to have reestablished close relations with the Blow family, Dred's former owners.

On 6 April 1846 Dred and Harriet Scott sued Irene Emerson for freedom. *Dred Scott v. Irene Emerson* was filed in a Missouri state court under Missouri state law. (Two separate litigations were pursued. Since both entailed the same law and evidence, only Dred's advanced to conclusion; Harriet's suit was held in abeyance, under agreement that the determination in her husband's case would apply to hers.) Contrary to later widespread rumor, no political motivation attached to the institution of this suit; only when it reached the Missouri Supreme Court did it acquire the political overtones that made it so famous later. The suit was brought for one reason only: to secure freedom for Dred Scott and his family. Evidence suggests that Scott learned of his right to freedom from the white abolitionist lawyer Francis Butter Murdoch, recently moved to St. Louis from Alton, Illinois, where he had prosecuted criminal offenders in the Elijah P. Lovejoy riots and murders. Another possible instigator was the Reverend John R. Anderson, a former slave who was pastor of the Second African Baptist Church in St. Louis to which Harriet Scott

Dred Scott, in a wood engraving that appeared in *Century Magazine*, 1887. (Library of Congress.)

belonged. Murdoch posted the necessary bonds and filed the legal papers that actually instituted the suit. Shortly thereafter, however, he moved to California.

Based on Missouri law and precedents, Scott's case for freedom seemed incontrovertible. Earlier Missouri Supreme Court decisions had emancipated a number of slaves whose travels had taken them to free states or territories. Indeed, one of those cases was strikingly similar to Scott's; that slave had also accompanied an army officer to the same military posts in Illinois and Wisconsin Territory as Dred Scott had done. Perhaps that explains why members of the Blow family so readily backed the slave's case when Murdoch left St. Louis. Indeed, even as the litigation dragged on beyond what had promised to be a very quick solution, they continued to provide necessary legal and financial support.

Unanticipated developments converted an open-and-shut freedom suit into a cause célèbre. In the trial on 30 June 1847, the court rejected one piece of vital evidence on a legal technicality—that it was hearsay evidence and therefore not admissible—and the slave's freedom had to await a second trial when that evidence could be properly introduced. It took almost three years, until 12 January 1850, before that trial took place, a delay caused by events over which none of the litigants had any control. With the earlier legal technicality corrected, the court unhesitatingly declared Dred Scott to be free.

But during the delay, money earned by the slaves had been held custodially by the local sheriff, to turn over to either the estate of the late John Emerson (which really meant to Irene Emerson, according to her husband's will) or the freed slaves, depending upon the outcome of the suit. Though not a large sum, those accrued wages made ownership of the slaves more worthwhile in 1850 than it had been in 1847. Meanwhile, Irene Emerson had left St. Louis to marry Dr. Calvin Clifford Chaffee, a Massachusetts abolitionist, who was unaware of the litigation involving his wife. She left her St. Louis affairs in the hands of her businessman-brother, John F. A. Sanford, who had earlier been named executor of Dr. Emerson's estate. In Irene Emerson's name, then, and hoping to secure the accumulated Scott family wages, Sanford's attorneys appealed the freedom decision to the Missouri Supreme Court. But also during the delay, slavery had become a national issue of voluble divisiveness. In a singularly partisan 2 to 1 decision, which overturned long-standing "once free always free" judicial precedent—that once a slave resided in free territory with the knowledge and even tacit consent of the master, he or she became free by virtue of that residence and did not lose that freedom merely upon returning to a slave state—the Missouri Supreme Court on 22 March 1852 blatantly endorsed proslavery tenets, reversed the lower court, and remanded Dred Scott to slavery (*Dred Scott v. Irene Emerson*, 15 Missouri 576).

To clarify the "once free always free" doctrine based on freedom secured under the Northwest Ordinance of 1787 and the Missouri Compromise of 1820, friends of Scott instituted a new case in the federal courts, *Dred Scott v. John F. A. Sanford*. (Court records erroneously misspelled the name as "Sandford.") Though often in St. Louis, Sanford was a legal resident of New York. Scott as a citizen of Missouri suing Sanford thereby created a "diversity" case—that is, a citizen of one state suing a citizen of another state—which could litigate in the federal courts. But it also created a new issue when Sanford's attorneys claimed that Scott was not a citizen because he was "a negro of African descent" and therefore lacked the right to sue in the federal

courts. Rather than deal with the matter on those jurisdictional grounds, the court found for Sanford, and the case was appealed to the Supreme Court of the United States.

There, nationally known legal figures argued the case: Montgomery Blair and George T. Curtis for Scott, and Reverdy Johnson and Henry S. Geyer for Sanford. The suit was argued twice, in February 1856 and in December 1856. Up to then virtually unknown, the case now aroused nationwide publicity and deep partisan interest. At first the Court exercised judicial restraint and thought cautiously to avoid controversial slavery matters. Prodded by the pro-southern chief justice Roger B. Taney and the associate justices James M. Wayne and Peter V. Daniel, and by the antislavery associate justices John McLean and Benjamin R. Curtis, the Court decided to deal with those explosive issues.

The famous—or infamous—decision, which remanded Dred Scott to slavery, was pronounced on 6 March 1857 by Chief Justice Taney. Each of the concurring and dissenting justices rendered a separate opinion (*Dred Scott v. John F. A. Sanford*, 19 Howard 393). Extreme proslavery and extreme antislavery views were expressed. According to Taney's "Opinion of the Court," blacks were not considered citizens of the United States. Slaves were property protected by the Constitution, and any law prohibiting slavery in the territories (e.g., the Missouri Compromise) was unconstitutional. Regardless of prior free or slave condition, the status of a person entering into a slave state depended on the law of that state.

The decision triggered violent reaction in an already tense sectional-ridden atmosphere. Fearing that it pushed American law close to legalizing slavery throughout the entire country, antislavery forces mounted unprecedented assaults on the decision and on the majority members of the Court. Proslavery forces responded with equal fervor to defend their cause. The tragic result was to split a divided country even more and push it closer to civil war.

As to the slaves themselves, they remained in St. Louis throughout all this litigation, working at various jobs. Legally, however, they had become the property of Dr. Chaffee, Irene Emerson's second husband. Incredibly, though, he did not become aware of that consequence until just a week or two before the decision was announced, and his attorneys informed him that he could do nothing about that ownership until the litigation was concluded. Shortly after the Supreme Court announced its decision, the embarrassed Chaffee transferred his ownership to Taylor Blow in St. Louis—since by Missouri law a slave could be emancipated there only by a citizen of that state. Accordingly, on 27 May 1857 Blow executed the necessary documents to free the slaves. Scott lived only a year and a half longer, working most of that time as a porter in Barnum's Hotel in St. Louis. There he died of tuberculosis. His remains are interred in St. Louis.

FURTHER READING

Ehrlich, Walter. *They Have No Rights: Dred Scott's Struggle for Freedom* (1979).

Fehrenbacher, Don E. *The Dred Scott Case: Its Significance in American Law and Politics* (1978).

Finkelman, Paul. *An Imperfect Union* (1981).

Hyman, Harold M., and William M. Wiecek. *Equal Justice under Law: Constitutional Development, 1835–1875* (1982).

This entry is taken from the *American National Biography* and is published here with the permission of the American Council of Learned Societies.

WALTER EHRLICH

Scott, Emmett Jay (13 Feb. 1873–12 Dec. 1957), educator and publicist, was born in Houston, Texas, the son of Horace Lacy Scott, a civil servant, and Emma Kyle. Scott attended Wiley College in Marshall, Texas, for three years but left college in 1890 for a career in journalism. Starting as a janitor and messenger for a white daily newspaper, the *Houston Post*, he worked his way up to reporter. In 1894 he became associate editor of a new black newspaper in Houston, the *Texas Freeman*. Soon he was named editor and built this newspaper into a leading voice in black journalism in its region. Initially, he tied his fortune to the state's preeminent black politician, NORRIS CUNEY, and was his secretary for a while.

When Cuney retired, Scott turned to BOOKER T. WASHINGTON, the founder of the Tuskegee Institute in Alabama. Scott greatly admired Washington, praising his 1895 "Atlanta Compromise" speech. Two years later he invited Washington to speak in Houston. Scott handled the publicity and promotion so well that Washington hired him as his private secretary. When Scott moved to Tuskegee on 10 September 1897, he brought with him his wife, Eleonora Juanita Baker, the daughter of a newspaper editor. They had been married in April 1897 and eventually had five children.

From 1897 until Washington's death in November 1915, Scott was his closest adviser and friend. The two worked together so smoothly that determining which man authored a particular letter can be a challenge. As his top aide, Scott ran Tuskegee when Washington was away. Washington acknowledged that Scott made "himself invaluable not only to me personally, but to the institution" (Washington, *The Story of My Life and Work* [1901]). Scott developed and operated the "Tuskegee Machine," an elaborate apparatus by which Booker T. Washington controlled, influenced, and manipulated African American leaders, press, and institutions. He also worked closely with Washington in founding the National Negro Business League in 1900. Washington was president of the league, but Scott, as secretary from 1900 to 1922, actually ran it. The two coauthored *Tuskegee and Its People* (1905).

Scott served on the three-man American Commission to Liberia in 1909, the report of which led to an American protectorate over Liberia. In 1912 Tuskegee Institute's board made Scott the secretary of the school. When Washington died in 1915, Scott was a leading candidate to succeed him, but ROBERT RUSSA MOTON of Hampton was chosen instead. Scott remained as secretary. He and Lyman Beecher Stowe coauthored a highly laudatory biography, titled *Booker T. Washington*, published in 1916. That year, Scott and others in the Tuskegean camp reconciled with Washington's rival and National Association for the Advancement of Colored People (NAACP) founder W. E. B. DuBois, at the Amenia Conference on Long Island, New York.

The entrance of the United States into World War I gave Scott a chance to leave Tuskegee and end any rivalry with Moton. He became special assistant to the secretary of war and was in charge of affairs relating to African Americans. While in this post he wrote *Scott's Official History of the American Negro in the World War* (1919). He also wrote *Negro Migration during the War* (1920), under the auspices of the Carnegie Endowment for International Peace. Scott stayed in Washington after the war, becoming a top administrator at Howard University. From 1919 to 1932 he was the university's secretary-treasurer and business manager. He was the top black official until Howard's first black president, MORDECAI JOHNSON, was appointed in 1926. The two clashed, and Scott was relegated to the position of secretary of the university but remained at Howard until he retired in 1938.

Meanwhile, he was active in business and politics. Among his business ventures in the African American community were banking, insurance, and real estate. In politics he was a staunch Republican. He served on an advisory committee for the 1924 Republican National Convention, specializing in black affairs, and he was the assistant publicity director of the Republican National Committee from 1939 to 1942. In 1941 Scott went to work at the Sun Shipbuilding Company of Chester, Pennsylvania, at the request of the Republican Party. The company president, John Pew, was a major funder of the party. Pew's company was nonunion. With Scott's help the company established Yard No. 4, staffed by African Americans supervised by Scott. When the war ended in 1945, Scott's yard was dismantled, and Scott retired to Washington. From time to time, he did public relations work. He died in Washington, D.C.

FURTHER READING

Scott's personal papers are in the Morris A. Soper Library of Morgan State University, Baltimore. His letters and other materials are also found among the Booker T. Washington Papers in the Library of Congress.

Harlan, Louis. *Booker T. Washington: The Making of a Black Leader, 1856–1901* (1972).

Harlan, Louis. *Booker T. Washington: The Wizard of Tuskegee, 1901–1915* (1983).

Logan, Rayford W. *Howard University* (1969).

Meier, August. *Negro Thought in America, 1880–1915* (1963).

Obituaries: *Atlanta Daily World* and *Washington Post*, 13 Dec. 1957; *Washington Afro-American* and *New York Times*, 14 Dec. 1957; *Afro-American* (national edition), 21 Dec. 1957.

This entry is taken from the *American National Biography* and is published here with the permission of the American Council of Learned Societies.

EDGAR ALLAN TOPPIN

Scott, Harriet Robinson (c. 1818–17 June 1876), litigant, slave, and laundress, was born probably in Virginia to enslaved parents about whom nothing is known. By the 1830s, she had become the slave of Lawrence Taliaferro, an Indian agent and a major in the U.S. Army. When Taliaferro, a Virginian who had transplanted to Pennsylvania, was stationed at Fort Snelling, Minnesota, he brought Harriet with him. There she met DRED SCOTT soon after his master, Dr. John Emerson, was also posted at Fort

Snelling. Though such weddings were exceedingly rare, Taliaferro, also a justice of the peace, performed a formal marriage ceremony between Scott and Robinson in 1836 or 1837. After the marriage, Harriet Scott was either given or, more likely, sold to Emerson.

Emerson hired the Scotts out to various officers at Fort Snelling before he married Irene Sanford on 6 February 1838. After a brief period at the Jefferson Barracks in St. Louis, Emerson was transferred to Louisiana's Fort Jessup. The Scotts accompanied him to both postings, but another transfer brought them back to Fort Snelling in October 1838. It was during this period that the Scotts' daughter Eliza was born—reportedly onboard the ship taking the Scotts to Fort Snelling. When Emerson was transferred again—this time to Florida—his wife and the Scotts settled in St. Louis on the estate of Irene Sanford Emerson's father. A second daughter, Lizzie, as well as two sons who died in infancy, were born during this period, and evidence shows that both Dred Scott (as a porter/valet) and Harriet Scott (as a laundress/domestic) were hired out in the St. Louis area. When Emerson died of consumption on 29 December 1843, the Scotts' title passed to Irene Emerson. Dred Scott reportedly attempted to purchase himself and his family but found his mistress unwilling.

For reasons that are still unclear, both Harriet and Dred Scott filed individual suits for their freedom on 6 April 1846; both cited their extended time in free territory as the central grounds. Recent scholars have argued, based on the circumstances surrounding most St. Louis freedom suits, that Harriet Scott may actually have instigated the action, perhaps with the aid of her minister, John R. Anderson. She may have acted, like other slave women who filed such suits, to obtain freedom for her daughters. Regardless, the Scotts had by this time built a number of connections among St. Louis's black communities—ties that would likely have led them to the attorney Francis Butter Murdoch, who was the most active representative of slaves suing for freedom in St. Louis in the 1840s. Murdoch, though, worked with the Scotts only briefly, as did their second attorney, C. D. Drake. When the Scotts' third attorney, Samuel Bay, took the case to trial in June of 1847 before Judge Alexander Hamilton, the Scotts initially lost—but Bay filed a motion for a new trial based on a technicality. That new trial, held in January of 1850 with the Scotts now represented by Alexander Field and David Hall, resulted in a victory for the Scotts. For the moment, they were technically free. Like many of the slaves who filed freedom suits, though, the Scotts had been hired out through the sheriff's office for much of the time since they had filed papers—with the understanding that they would receive their wages if they won, and their owner would receive the wages if they lost. Perhaps because of this and perhaps simply because of the value of the Scotts, Irene Emerson immediately appealed to the Missouri Supreme Court, but, by an agreement of all parties made on 12 February 1850, only Dred Scott's case went forward, with the understanding that Harriet's fate would follow her husband's. Ironically, contemporary legal scholars suggest that Harriet actually had stronger grounds for her freedom suit because, in addition to the time in Minnesota she shared with her husband, she also had an extended residence with Taliaferro in Pennsylvania.

In a surprising reversal of several years of precedent, on 22 March 1852, in a 2 to 1 verdict, the Missouri Supreme Court ruled against Scott. At this point Irene Emerson, now the wife of Calvin Chaffee (soon to be a Massachusetts congressman elected on an antislavery platform), seems to have transferred ownership of the Scotts to her brother John F. A. Sanford, who was named as the defendant when the Scotts' friends (especially the Blow family, who had been early owners of Dred Scott) and new attorney Roswell Field moved the case to the U.S. federal court system in November of 1853. The Scotts lost again, but Field appealed to the U.S. Supreme Court at the end of 1854. Now fully based on Dred's case alone, the Scotts' fate rested with the pro-southern and pro-slavery Court headed by Chief Justice Roger Taney, who heard the case (argued by friends of Field who had Washington connections Montgomery Blair and George T. Curtis) in 1856 and issued its infamous 7 to 2 ruling against Dred Scott on 6 March 1857. However, Chaffee, who played no part in the trial but whose politics would be open to question by Massachusetts voters when he came up for reelection, seems to have decided to free the Scotts. He thus transferred ownership to Taylor Blow, who emancipated Dred, Harriet, and their two daughters under a Missouri law that allowed a resident of the state to emancipate his slaves.

Dred Scott obtained a job as a porter at St. Louis's Barnum Hotel soon after—though he was, in essence, there as a curiosity for hotel guests. The Scotts took a small house off of Carr Street, and Harriet continued to work as a laundress. Dred Scott died 17 September 1858, and most of the few accounts that mention Harriet at all suggest that she died soon after. Recent scholars, though, have found evidence that she continued to work as a laundress until at least 1870 and lived in St. Louis with her daughter Lizzie, who married Wilson Madison and had two sons, Harry and John Alexander. Harriet Scott died at their home. Although she is not as well known as her husband—in large part because of the heavily gendered decision to allow his suit alone to proceed—Harriet Scott was a key figure in the nineteenth-century struggle for basic human rights for African Americans.

FURTHER READING

Douglass, Katherine. "Harriet Robinson Scott," in *In Her Place: A Guide to St. Louis Women's History*, ed. Katharine T. Corbett (1999).

Kaufman, Kenneth C. *Dred Scott's Advocate: A Biography of Roswell M. Field* (1996).

VanderVelde, Lea, and Sandhya Sumramanian. "Mrs. Dred Scott," *Yale Law Journal* 106 no. 4 (Jan. 1997).

ERIC GARDNER

Scott, Hazel Dorothy (11 June 1920–2 Oct. 1981), jazz pianist and singer, was born in Port of Spain, Trinidad, the daughter of R. Thomas Scott, an English professor, and Alma Long, a musician. The Scott family (Hazel, her parents, and her maternal grandmother) moved to the United States in 1924, settling in Harlem. A child prodigy, Hazel was reading by age three. By age four she was using both hands at the piano (playing by ear), and by age five she was improvising. Her first piano instructor was her mother. At age eight she was heard by the Juilliard School of Music professor Paul Wagner, who explained that although she was too young to enter Juilliard formally, he would accept her as his pupil.

She made her debut at age thirteen, advertised as "Little Miss Hazel Scott, Child Wonder Pianist." The recital program announcement added, "Mrs. Alma Long Scott Presents ..." In addition to being a piano teacher, her mother was a professional alto and tenor saxophonist who organized her own women's orchestra, American Creolians, now that she was sole breadwinner following Hazel's father's death. In her early teens Hazel played piano in her mother's group and doubled on trumpet, an instrument she soon abandoned.

Hazel Scott, a pianist whose repertoire ranged from Bach to boogie-woogie, on her arrival at Paddington Station, London, 4 September 1951. (AP Images.)

Scott's first professional appearance was in 1935, when she performed with COUNT BASIE and his orchestra at the Roseland Ballroom. Of the experience, she said, "It scared me to death. I had three footprints on my back—those of LESTER YOUNG, JO JONES and Basie." According to all reports, the performance was a memorable one. Scott made her Broadway debut in 1938, appearing in the show *Sing Out the News*. The showstopper was the tune "Franklin D. Roosevelt Jones," as played by Hazel Scott, age eighteen. So successful was her performance that it consistently garnered rave reviews and her salary was increased to one hundred dollars a week. Also during her eighteenth year, Scott organized her own short-lived band. She early mastered the classics but found it difficult to avoid altering the original score. In December 1940 she played Franz Liszt's *Second Hungarian Rhapsody* at Carnegie Hall. During the performance Scott began "swinging it." And as she often recalled, "The 'long hair' audience loved it." From that day forward, the distinguishing feature of her piano performances was quasi-jazz renditions of classical pieces. She played both jazz and classical music in concert, swung the classics, and mixed styles. As reported

in *Time*, "Where others murder the classics, Hazel Scott merely commits arson. ... She seems coolly determined to play legitimately, and, for a brief while, triumphs. But gradually it becomes apparent that evil forces are struggling within her for expression. ... The reverse is also true: Into 'Tea for Two' may creep a few bars of Debussy's *Clair de Lune*" (5 Oct. 1942, 88, 90).

Scott made her recording debut in 1939, on a date arranged by the jazz journalist, critic, and encyclopedist Leonard Feather. Publicized as "The Sextet of the Rhythm Club of London," the group was a racially mixed band that included three blacks of West Indian descent. In 1939 Scott was hired for a three-week fill-in engagement at the newly opened Cafe Society, Downtown, a Greenwich Village nightclub. When owner Barney Josephson (who loved pianists) heard her, he offered her "a job for life." She was so successful that when Josephson opened a new Cafe Society, Uptown (at East Fifty-eighth Street), the star would be Hazel Scott.

There were occasional forays into other prosperous clubs, including Boston's Ritz-Carlton Hotel Roof and the New York City Paramount. Also in 1939 she did two performances at the New York World's Fair. The Hazel Scott/Cafe Society association, formed in 1939, lasted until 1943. Another side trip was to perform in the vaudeville-type show *Priorities of 1942* on Broadway. Of her piano performance, Brooks Atkinson wrote, "She was the most incandescent personality of anyone in the show. ... There is not a dull spot in her number."

Between 1943 and 1945 Hazel appeared in five movies: *Something to Shout About*, *I Dood It*, *The Heat's On*, *Broadway Rhythm*, and *Rhapsody in Blue*. She shocked Hollywood by going on strike during the filming of *The Heat's On* because "black women extras weren't dressed properly." Filming was halted and was not resumed until the costumes were changed. She was permitted to appear in *Rhapsody in Blue* (her final film) simply because she was already under contract. In 1943 she received the Page One Award from the Newspaper Guild of New York. (In 1978 Scott was inducted into the Black Filmmakers Hall of Fame in celebration of Fifty Years of Black Music Achievement in Film.) By the late 1940s, all of Scott's performance contracts included a clause stating that she would not perform before segregated audiences.

Much has been written about Scott's marriage to the flamboyant congressman and minister ADAM CLAYTON POWELL JR. Always attracted to artists and the social elite, Powell frequented those places where such persons mingled. In addition, Scott had appeared frequently at various political rallies in New York City, including many for Powell as Harlem's congressional candidate. Soon the two were dining out, most often at "21" and the Stork Club. Powell was the first black elected to the New York City Council in 1941, and in 1944 he was elected to the U.S. House of Representatives, an office he was returned to in each subsequent election until 1970. Throughout his political career he maintained his position as pastor (inherited from his father in 1937) of Abyssinian Baptist Church in Harlem, one of the country's largest black congregations. Scott and Powell were married in August 1945 at Bethel African Methodist Episcopal Church in Stamford, Connecticut, shortly following a divorce from his first wife. Jazz impresario Barney Josephson hosted a reception in Manhattan at Cafe Society, where a host of celebrities were in attendance. The couple had one child.

In early October 1945 newspapers across the country carried the story, "Constitution Hall Ban on Hazel Scott." The Daughters of the American Revolution (owners of Constitution Hall) refused a concert permit to Scott. Though the ban stood, Powell asked President Harry S. Truman to intervene. Shortly following this incident, Scott was scheduled to appear at the National Press Club's annual dinner honoring the president. But she canceled the engagement, citing as her reasons that several members of the seven-member executive committee had protested her appearance and that black journalists were being discriminated against.

Her marriage failing, Scott moved to Paris in 1957 with the intention of remaining for three weeks; their divorce became final in late 1960. Three months later, in 1961, she married a Swiss Italian, Ezio Bedin; this marriage was short-lived. Scott remained in Paris for ten years.

On her return to the United States, she spent three years on the West Coast, appearing in the television productions "The Bold Ones," "The Doctors," "Julia," and CBS's "Playhouse 90." Returning to New York City in 1970, she formed the Hazel Scott Trio (with changing personnel). Her last performance was at Kippy's, less than two months before her death in New York City.

FURTHER READING

Haygood, Will. *King of the Cats: The Life and Times of Adam Clayton Powell, Jr.* (1993).

Taylor, Arthur. *Notes and Tones: Musician-to-Musician Interviews* (1977).

Obituary: *Washington Post*, 4 Oct. 1981.

This entry is taken from the *American National Biography* and is published here with the permission of the American Council of Learned Societies.

ANTOINETTE HANDY

Scott, James Sylvester (c. Feb. 1885–30 Aug. 1938), ragtime composer, pianist, and bandleader, was born in Neosho, Missouri, the second of six children. His parents, James Scott, a laborer originally from North Carolina, and Molly Thomas Scott, from Texas, had moved to Missouri around 1880. Around 1901 the family moved to Carthage, where Scott completed his education at the all-black Lincoln School. Initially playing piano by ear, he received his first formal lessons from a Neosho teacher and saloon keeper named John Coleman; these were supplemented with lessons in Carthage from a local teacher Emma Jones. For the most part, however, Scott was musically self-taught. By his late teens, Scott showed himself to be a precociously gifted pianist, possessing perfect pitch and a strong technique. He was also composing; his first rag, "The Fascinator," was published in 1903 by Dumars, a local music store. The store's owner, Charlie Dumars, was the director of the Carthage Light Guard Band, and he supported Scott's career in various ways, publishing his first three rags, performing his music, providing lyrics for his songs—and, most importantly, providing steady employment for him in the store. Scott was employed initially in menial roles, but later he worked as a demonstration pianist and "song plugger."

Around 1904 Scott found long-term employment from a second source, Lakeside Amusement Park, in Webb City, a few miles from Carthage. There he provided piano accompaniment for silent movies, performed on the steam calliope, and put on dances for the black community. Scott worked there for at least fifteen years. At the same time, he was musically active in the community in other ways. He frequently performed for local political, educational, and cultural events and was a tireless organizer. Between 1904 and 1906, for example, he set up and directed both a sixteen-piece black marching band and a male chorus of twenty-five voices.

In 1906 Scott married Nora Johnson, a concert singer from Springfield, Missouri. The marriage, which was childless, seems to have been a stable one and lasted until Noras's death in about

1930. The year 1906 also marked the start of Scott's most important long-term professional relationship. He came to the attention of John Stark, the St. Louis music publisher known for his championing of ragtime, especially the work of SCOTT JOPLIN. Stark published Scott's "Frogs Legs Rag" and was to become the most important promoter of his music, publishing twenty-nine of his thirty-eight works, the last in 1922. "Frogs Legs Rag" was Scott's first mature work and also one of his most successful, both musically and commercially. Scott's early rags published by Dumars, while clearly the work of a competent composer, lack an original voice, being strongly influenced by Joplin and other contemporaneous ragtime composers. While "Frogs Leg Rag" is also clearly Joplinesque (its first two sections, for example, showing a clear allegiance to Joplin's "Maple Leaf Rag"), it is nevertheless a highly individual work. It displays important stylistic features that Scott was to make his own, including the frequent use of call and response patterns, the building of entire sections from short figures, a strongly melodic bass line, and—binding these traits into a coherent whole—a deep, heartfelt lyricism.

These characteristics are further integrated in the rag "Grace and Beauty," which Stark published in 1909 and which became Scott's best-known rag. Its expanded use of chromatic harmony (especially in its first section), enhanced use of piano texture, innate lyricism, and excellence of overall design (each of its four sections carefully balancing the others) make this one of the most successful of all ragtime compositions.

From 1909 to the beginning of the 1920s, Scott's life was relatively stable. He was a well-known, widely respected, hardworking musician in the Carthage community. He produced a long series of compositions over this period, mainly rags, most of which were published by Stark. Scott's compositional style was relatively consistent throughout his mature rags, although it seemed they became on average ever more densely scored, a reflection of his prowess on the piano. Always unusually technically demanding by the standards of published ragtime, his work became increasingly iconoclastic throughout the 1910s.

Scott refused to compromise on the question of genre. Ragtime, increasingly unfashionable in the 1910s, became supplanted first by new dance styles like the foxtrot and then, decisively, by jazz after 1917. Scott, however, made no attempt to adapt to the new genres, the only exceptions being a 1920 song titled "The Shimmie Shake" (words by Cleota Wilson), which celebrated a popular dance of the era, and three unpublished blues arrangements. Instead, he continued to produce a steady stream of ragtime, his last work published in 1922, by which time the genre was essentially obsolete (it seems possible that he continued to compose rags after this time, although if he did, nothing has survived). In the early 1920s Scott relocated with his wife to Kansas City, Kansas, where he quickly acquired a reputation as one of the most reliable and able black pianists in the city. Between 1922 and 1930 he played for vaudeville shows and accompanied silent movies in three theaters: the relatively small Panama (c. 1922–1924), then the larger Lincoln (1924–1926), and finally the Eblon (1926–1930). In addition to the piano, he also played organ when the Eblon replaced the house band with a new pipe organ in 1928. With the coming of the Depression and the rapid decline of vaudeville and silent movies, Scott's main sources of employment dried up. Little is known of his activities in the 1930s, except that he taught music privately and organized an eight-piece band for special occasions. He remained in Kansas City but moved frequently, ending up in the home of his cousin Ruth Callahan. He died of kidney failure and hardening of the arteries.

During his lifetime, Scott's reputation remained largely local. Although many of his works were recorded on piano roll, almost nothing appeared on phonograph, and sheet music sales were modest except perhaps for "Frogs Leg Rag" and one or two other works. His reputation as a major writer of ragtime was therefore almost entirely posthumous, initially as a result first of Blesh and Janis's book *They All Played Ragtime* in the 1950s and then solidified during the ragtime revival of the 1970s. Nowadays he is generally regarded, along with Joseph Lamb, as second only to Joplin in terms of sheer quality. His work is usually placed under the label "classic ragtime," a category devised by John Stark to describe the style of Scott, Joplin, Lamb, and others. And while the validity of this term has been challenged, the combination of refined elegance, balance, and sophisticated understatement found in Scott's rags, combined with their enduring quality, makes his music ideally suited for this description.

FURTHER READING

Scott, James, Scott DeVeaux, and William Howard Kenney III. *The Music of James Scott* (1993).

Blesh, Rudi, and Harriet Janis. *They All Played Ragtime* (1971).

DeVeaux, Scott. "James Scott," in *International Dictionary of Black Composers*, ed. Samuel A. Floyd Jr. (1999).

Jasen, David A., and Trebor J. Tichenor. *Rags and Ragtime: A Musical History* (1978).

PETER MUIR

Scott, John Henry (30 Dec. 1901–22 June 1980), minister and human rights activist, was born in Transylvania, Louisiana, the second of four children of Lucy Conn, a homemaker, and John Henry Scott Sr., a farmer. After his parents divorced when he was three, Scott went to live with his father's parents, Harriet Sides Scott and Charley Scott, a farmer and former Union soldier. Scott received his grammar school education at the local church school and irregularly attended the high school operated by the Baptist Association in the nearby town of Lake Providence. Scott passed the teacher's examination after the eighth grade, but instead of teaching he decided to become a trapper, fur trader, and farmer with his grandfather. Income from trapping and his grandfather's monthly soldier's pension gave Scott a degree of economic and social independence uncommon in a community where many former slaves resided. Scott returned to school as an adult, eventually earning his bachelor's degree in theology in 1953 from the United Theological Seminary in Monroe, Louisiana.

In 1937 Scott became an ordained minister and in 1939 led his first effort to unite his community. The land that comprised Transylvania was to be sold to poor farmers under one of President Franklin Roosevelt's New Deal programs. Approximately 250 black families in Scott's community were ordered to move because black farmers were not allowed to purchase land under the program. While others thought it futile to fight a federal program, Scott did not. He helped organize and became the president of Transylvania's first NAACP branch, and through the NAACP's national media campaign, protest letters flooded President Roosevelt's office. Although the families were evicted, the national attention on Transylvania led to the inclusion of black farmers in the land purchase program. THURGOOD MARSHALL, as special counsel to the NAACP, came to north Louisiana to ensure that homes and schools were built according to the negotiated agreement for the new all-black settlements.

After the land in Transylvania was sold, Scott moved to Lake Providence, where in 1942 he met and married Alease Truly. They had eight children. In the 1940s Scott increased his involvement in the NAACP and was appointed to the executive committee of the Louisiana State Conference of NAACP Branches, which made decisions on projects throughout the state. He also became interested in voting rights. Although Scott's East Carroll Parish was predominantly black, no blacks had been allowed on the voter registration rolls since 1922, and none had actually voted since 1879, when black officials had been removed from office at gunpoint. When Scott, who was not yet a pastor, was taken to task by other ministers for "upsetting white folks by talking about voting," the community in 1946 did the unprecedented, electing Scott president of the local Baptist Association, a position traditionally held only by pastors. The following year, in 1947, Scott became pastor of the North Star Baptist Church, where he remained for twenty-five years.

Scott first attempted to register to vote in 1946 but was told by the registrar that an applicant had to be identified by two existing registered voters, a requirement Scott found impossible to meet. After years of trying to meet this requirement, Scott in 1951 decided to file suit against the registrar of voters through the NAACP. After years of legal maneuvering, the suit was dismissed by Judge Ben Dawkins in 1954. In 1956, when Louisiana placed a statewide injunction against the NAACP, Scott was the first north Louisiana NAACP leader identified by the press. He was subsequently brought before a grand jury for soliciting funds for the NAACP, but there was insufficient evidence.

In 1960 in New Orleans, Scott appeared as the lead witness at the U.S. Commission on Civil Rights hearings on voting rights abuses, representing one of the four remaining parishes with no black registered voters. Three of the four were the predominantly black northeast parishes bordering Mississippi. Scott had written to the commission in Washington, D.C., asking to be allowed to testify on their behalf. After a full economic boycott against commission witnesses from East Carroll, Scott convinced the Justice Department to file suit against the state. *The United States v. Cecil Manning of East Carroll Parish and the State of Louisiana* was filed in April 1961 by Attorney General Robert Kennedy. The U.S. District Court for the Western District of Louisiana ruled in May 1962 that there had been a pattern of racial discrimination and that the requirement for blacks to be identified by two registered voters made blacks dependent on the white community for permission to register. This ruling should have ended eighty-four years of disenfranchisement of black voters; however, the registrar of voters resigned rather than comply with the ruling. Scott and twenty-five others were issued voter registration cards in federal court under Section 601, a special provision of the Civil Rights Act of 1960 that allowed disenfranchised voters an opportunity to register through the courts if they could not register locally.

On the night of 22 August 1962, after testifying in the contempt hearing for the registrar of voters, Scott was shot in his car as he traveled home with his wife and four children. No one was ever arrested for the crime. For four years Scott suffered attempts on his life along with threatening phone calls, cross burnings, and articles designed to damage his reputation. Scott faced the question shared by many leaders in the 1960s—should he abandon the struggle because of the danger to his family? His family's encouragement coupled with his sense of dedication and faith in God compelled him to continue.

Scott, a thin, soft-spoken, small-town preacher, dedicated his life to resolving rural community issues, working with the state and local NAACP for more than thirty years. His fearlessness and unshakable determination garnered him significant respect from people in positions of power. He communicated directly with the people who could provide solutions, successfully addressing critical issues of his day—land ownership, voting, police brutality, and legal misconduct. Scott died in Lake Providence.

FURTHER READING

Scott's papers are in the Archives and Manuscript Department, Earl K. Long Library, University of New Orleans, New Orleans, Louisiana.

Scott, John H., with Cleo Scott Brown. *Witness to the Truth: My Struggle for Human Rights in Louisiana* (2003).

Fairclough, Adam. *Race & Democracy: The Civil Rights Struggle in Louisiana, 1915–1972* (1995).

Hearings before the United States Commission on Civil Rights. Hearings held in New Orleans, Louisiana, September 27, 1960, September 28, 1960, May 5, 1961, May 6, 1961 (1961).

CLEO SCOTT BROWN

Scott, Joyce J. (1948–), an artist active in a variety of mediums, was born to Charles and Elizabeth Talford Scott (a steel worker and a fiber artist/domestic care provider). Joyce Scott is descended from three generations of artists. Elizabeth Talford Scott is renowned for her quilts, which she extensively exhibited during the late twentieth century. From an early age, Scott was encouraged by her parents to make and study art. In 1970 she graduated from the Maryland Institute College of Art, Baltimore, with a bachelor of fine arts degree in art education. In 1971 she gained her master of fine arts degree from the Instituto Allende, San Miguel Allende, Guanajuato, Mexico.

From 1974 to 1976 Scott continued her education with a residence at the Haystack Mountain School of Crafts in Deer Isle, Maine, where she studied Yoruba weaving techniques with the Nigerian artists Twins Seven Seven and his wife, Nike Seven Seven. In the late 1970s and early 1980s, Scott spent time at the Rochester Institute of Technology, where she learned about surface design technology. In 1992 Scott was the artist-in-residence at the Pilchuck Glass School, Seattle, where she experimented with large glass sculptural forms. Between 1981 and 2007 she had more than thirty-five solo exhibits, and her work was included in many group exhibitions. In 2000 the Baltimore Museum of Art and the Maryland Institute College of Art presented a major retrospective of Scott's work: *Joyce Scott: Kickin' It with the Old Masters*. The accompanying exhibit catalog includes an extensive list of Scott's awards, residencies, exhibitions, commissions, selected performances, and curated exhibitions.

Scott's art defies categorization. It addresses a range of challenging social issues using an array of media including book art, fashion, jewelry, quilt making, performance, printmaking, sculpture, and multimedia. She draws inspiration for her art from a range of cultures, including African, Latino, Native American, and American. Art historian Keith Morrison, in his exhibition *Joyce J. Scott: Kickin' It with the Old Masters* catalog essay, eloquently describes Scott's eclectic style:

> The thread that runs through her work is the sprit of craft, which she explores as a source of late twentieth century imagery. She weaves together what is traditionally considered fine art with techniques of craft to create images whose purpose is as much for contemplation as utility: jewelry pieces that function both as decorative ornament and sculptural narrative; quilts layered with symbolic meaning which could also serve as houseware; costumes for her original performance pieces, which could function for street wear as well as for artistic statement.

Scott was especially well known for her works using beads—a material that recalls the long history

SCOTT, R. C. 109

of art and craft in Africa and the Americas. However, she used the beads for more than their cultural connotations; she used them in new ways, taking advantage of their material character, creating bright, textured sculptures that are visually dependent on the patterning of the hard, small, glass balls. These pieces include *What You Mean Jungle Music?* (1991), *Rodney King's Head Squashed like a Watermelon* (1991), and *Buddha Gives Basketball to the Ghetto* (1991). Robert Silberman, a University of Minnesota professor, describes these works in a 1999 article for *American Craft*: "There can be something cartoon- or doll-like about Joyce's bead figures, but that only lends them poignancy and power, since it establishes an immediate tension between apparently simple, childlike charm and the weight of the issues addressed."

Scott's mastery of different artistic techniques enables her to vary the scale of her work. Her beaded pieces are defined by the small scale of this media and require the viewer to step up and intimately confront uncomfortable subject matter. For example, *Catch a Nigger by His Toe* (1987), a literal and distressing piece that measures eight by ten by fourteen inches, references and criticizes the racism of the twentieth-century child's counting rhyme "Eeny Meeny Miny Mo."

Scott's facility with a variety of materials allowed her to create large-scale works as well, compelling the viewer to step into or on top of her constructed, frequently uncomfortable environments. She made a number of installation pieces. One of the largest is *Believe I've Been Sanctified* (1991), a piece set among monumental neoclassical pillars, all that remains of an edifice originally built for a Confederate veterans' reunion in Charleston, South Carolina. Scott used Chinese bead curtains and branches to turn the pillars into shrouded trees. Below, a pile of colorful logs spills out around the base of the pillars; from the center of the ring of columns a figure ornamented with textiles, wire, and beads rises suspended in midair. Of this piece Scott said in the Baltimore exhibit, *Joyce J. Scott: Kickin' It with the Old Masters*:

For me, those enormous white columns symbolized both the antebellum South and lynching trees. I decided to turn the columns into enormous trees by covering them with beads to make them weeping willows, to represent tears. At the base I added 500 logs, as a funeral pyre. Then I thought, 'If you've got a fire, it's got to be burning something, maybe like a lynched figure, or a person dying, which represents the end of slavery and the beginning of a new era, reconstruction.'

Though Scott traveled around the world and drew inspiration from these international sources, she was an American artist confronting uniquely American problems and highlighting her country's shortcomings. Her art had much to offer, requiring viewers to think about the painful parts of our national past and present. In a 1994 interview with Curtia James printed in *Sources: Multicultural Influences on Contemporary African American Artists*, Scott responded to a question about the most fascinating place she had ever been:

America. It really is. I've been all around America. You can travel around and be in a desert, and then be the mountains, and then be in a tropical area. There's a smashing of lies, of stereotypes. Because I'll be in the mountains, and there's a Black person in the mountains. And I'll be in a tropical desert and there he is. So what it has taught me is that not only are we everywhere, but we're suitable for all kinds of living. By that I mean we're absolutely that intelligent. We're absolutely that fabulous that we can live everywhere and do everything.

FURTHER READING

Baltimore Museum of Art and the Maryland Institute College of Art. *Joyce J. Scott: Kickin' It with the Old Masters* (1999).

Bloemink, Barbara J., ed. *Re/Righting History: Counternarratives by Contemporary African-American Artists* (1999).

Silberman, Robert. "Scott+Scott," *American Craft* 58 (Dec. 1998/Jan. 1999).

University of Maryland Art Gallery. *Sources: Multicultural Influences on Contemporary African American Sculptors* (1994).

ANNE KINGERY

Scott, Kody. *See* Shakur, Sanyika (Kody Scott).

Scott, R. C. (1 May 1888–1 Nov. 1957), undertaker and insurance executive, was born Robert Crafton Scott in Richmond, Virginia, to Alpheus Scott, a skilled, self-employed shoemaker, and homemaker Angela Wilson Scott. When a teacher asked seven-year-old Robert Scott what he wanted to be when he grew up, he surprised the class by saying that he wanted to be an undertaker. Undertakers represented one of the most lucrative, highly respected, and socially significant professions in the African American community, rivaled perhaps by the ministry. Undertakers' essential role in the burial rite reflected the critical cultural and spiritual importance blacks placed on the transition to the afterlife. The class was likely surprised at young Scott's choice because, despite advances in mortuary science necessitated by the Civil War, at the turn of the twentieth century undertaking remained a gruesome mix of science, ritual, and mystery.

In 1897 Scott's mother died, and his father sent his sister Cleopatra to a Catholic boarding school in the North while Scott stayed on with his father. Alpheus, concerned about the company his young son was keeping, feared his son might end up laboring away his youth in low-paying, dangerous factory work with a bleak future and little social status. In 1900 Alpheus decided to train Scott to take over his business and teach him the cobbler's trade. However, the ambitious young Scott clashed with his father about almost every aspect of the business. Scott wanted his father to institute more modern, progressive business methods and up-to-date technology. In 1905, as the shoemaking trade declined in the first decade of the twentieth century, Alpheus diversified and started a small undertaking operation. He may have acquiesced to his son's enthusiasm for the venture, but it is more likely that Alpheus responded to the coveted status undertakers enjoyed in the community. The undertaking business proved impervious to depressions, market fluctuations, and industrialization that often crippled, destroyed, or rendered other businesses anachronistic. More important, the retreat of white patronage from black businesses beginning after Reconstruction only strengthened some black business sectors, especially insurance and undertaking.

Undertaking became even more financially lucrative as financing for funerals became more sophisticated in the centuries after the first secret burial societies that slaves imported from Africa. During the eighteenth and nineteenth century, churches, mutual benefit societies, fraternal orders, and even doctors offered low cost burial policies. People paid a few cents a month to ensure that they would receive a respectful burial after they died. In the late 1800s, when insurance became more formalized, burial maintained its importance in the black community, and the interconnections between black cultural and business institutions endured. For example, in Richmond the Grand United Order of True Reformers took the significant step from fraternity to formal entrepreneurship in 1881, starting the first incorporated black bank in the United States. It also organized related enterprises, including an insurance company, department store, undertaking establishment, hotel, and newspaper. The growth of formal insurance companies, coupled with the continuance of small burial policies, allowed undertakers to provide more elaborate, expensive services, expand their funeral parlors, purchase cemeteries, and vertically integrate a number of related stages in the burial process from coffin manufacturing to funeral shrouds.

Even though Alpheus agreed to go into the undertaking business, he did not agree to listen to his son's newfangled ideas. Alpheus refused when the younger Scott asked if they could be equal partners. Alpheus fully expected to leave his business to his son after his death, but his traditional, highly conservative attitude about business suffocated the ambitious Scott. In 1906 Scott became one of the youngest men in the state to get an embalming license. Embalming science had improved the care and preservation of the body after death, but it was expensive and unpopular, especially among blacks who disliked the way many embalmers disfigured the body to introduce the embalming chemicals. In the early 1900s undertakers relied on the popular but unreliable "freezing method," which involved placing blocks of ice around the body until the funeral showing. Unfortunately, practitioners could not guarantee the condition of the body and the threat of disease remained a persistent problem. However, an ambitious Scott believed embalming represented the future of the funeral business.

Scott married Janie Epps in 1910, and they had one daughter Grayce. In the same year Scott convinced John Lewis, who ran a seafood business and owned a number of horses and carriages, to enter into a partnership with him. Virtually all undertakers also ran livery service as a sideline (or even as their primary) business. However, Lewis was never particularly interested in the undertaking business and, like Alpheus, did not share Scott's ambition or enthusiasm for modernizing the funeral industry. The partnership lasted only two years, but Scott had spent that time creating a reputation for himself and promoting the advantages of embalming. He not only stressed its reliability and hygiene but also stressed it as a forward-looking, progressive process that dovetailed with the growing emphasis on middle-class respectability and professionalism within African American society. When he went into business on his own in 1912, his business blossomed. He determined that he would be a trailblazer in the industry.

He built a large funeral parlor with the largest stable in the city and with well-appointed rooms that he rented out for fraternal meetings and social functions. He used embalming exclusively and was the first to switch to a completely motorized fleet of hearses and ambulances for transporting the bodies and traveling cars for the funeral procession. Though an incredibly expensive and risky move, it paid off handsomely. Scott stepped up the level of competition among undertakers and emerged on top. In the 1920s and 1930s Scott noted the declining influence of fraternal orders and believed that direct marketing to consumers assured the future prosperity of his business. As other businesses fell to the Great Depression, Scott spent over $50,000 to remodel his funeral home. He remained a pioneer: he was the first to open "branches"—satellite funeral chapels nested within predominately African American neighborhoods. The move increased his name recognition and provided unparalleled convenience for consumers. The embalming and preparation services remained centralized at his headquarters, but the arrangements and funeral services occurred at the neighborhood chapels.

He built his reputation and invaluable relationships through service to the community. Scott's influence on the African American funeral industry extended beyond Richmond. He joined over twenty fraternal orders and cultivated relationships with churches, local social organizations, and national organizations, which he saw as important networking and referral opportunities. For example, he was a lifetime member of the NAACP. Scott was also instrumental in the growth of the National Negro Funeral Directors Association, an affiliate of the National Negro Business League until 1924 when it became the Independent National Funeral Directors Association. In the 1950s it merged with another organization to become the National Negro Funeral Directors and Morticians Association. Scott served on the board of the St. Luke Penny Savings Bank for several years. During the Depression, he provided baskets of food to needy families throughout Richmond. Five cars were required to deliver all of the baskets.

His professional relationships helped him beyond the funeral business. When the National Benefit Life Insurance Company fell into receivership in 1932, Scott used his connections with black professionals and the community as well as with white civic and professional leaders to reorganize the company and save the investments of tens of thousands of policyholders. National Benefit, the largest African American–owned insurance company in the United States at the start of the Depression, with over $40 million worth of policies in force, extended itself too rapidly and severely undermined its own stability in its attempt to save Standard Life Insurance Company, another well-known African American insurance company. Scott and a number of black business owners and professionals in Richmond solicited the support of over 95 percent of National Benefit's policyholders. Scott's personal relationship with Judge Julien M. Gunn influenced Gunn to place the company and its $3.7 million in assets under the direction of Scott, the African American businessman S. W. Robinson Jr., and three whites: Judge Leon M. Bazile, attorney W. H. Cardwell, and insurance expert John H. Dinneen Jr. They reorganized the company as the Virginia Mutual Benefit Life Insurance in 1933, making it the first insurance company to operate with an interracial board. Scott eventually served as chairman of the board.

Scott incorporated his funeral business in 1936. Scott divorced Janie in 1944, and he married Mattie Olivia Cumber the same year. Scott and Mattie had one son, Robert Jr. Unlike his own father, Scott encouraged his children in their business pursuits. Grayce ran a florist shop opened by her father, which he placed under her sole ownership in 1948. Also, Mattie apprenticed under her husband and helped him manage his headquarters and four neighborhood chapels. Scott's sound, conservative financial management and willingness to stay ahead of the industry curve contributed to his company's survival into the twenty-first century.

FURTHER READING

Boyd, Robert L. "Funeral and Mortuary Enterprises," in *Encyclopedia of African-American Business History*, ed. Juliet E. K. Walker (1999).

Plater, Michael A. *African American Entrepreneurship in Richmond, 1890–1940: The Story of R. C. Scott* (1996).

Stuart, M. S. *An Economic Detour: A History of Insurance in the Lives of American Negroes* (1940).

SHENNETTE GARRETT

Scott, Robert Cortez "Bobby" (30 Apr. 1947–), lawyer, congressman, and influential force in the Virginia Democratic Party, was born in Washington, D.C., the son of Charles Waldo Scott, a medical practitioner, and Mae Hamlin, a teacher whose father was from the Philippines. Charles Waldo

Scott, at the time of his son's birth, was attending medical school at Howard University, and the Scott family relocated to Newport News, Virginia, in 1949, when Robert was two years old. He attended Huntington High School in Newport News and subsequently Groton School (Massachusetts) and Harvard University, from which he graduated in 1969 with a bachelor of arts degree. In 1973 he received his J.D. from the Boston College School of Law. From 1970 to 1974 he served in the U.S. Army Reserve and from 1974 to 1976 in the National Guard.

Gaining admission to the Virginia bar (Newport News Old Dominion Bar Association), Scott set up a legal practice in Newport News, where from 1973 to 1991 he specialized in civil rights cases. He also established himself as a community activist through his work in the NAACP; he was elected president of the Newport News branch of the NAACP in 1974. In 1978 he campaigned successfully as a Democrat for a seat in the Virginia House of Delegates (the lower chamber of that state's legislature). In 1980 he was vice chair of the Virginia Democratic Black Caucus. After six years (three terms) as a delegate, he was elected in 1983 to the Virginia state senate.

Scott served as state senator for nearly ten years before winning election to the U.S. House of Representatives from Virginia's Third Congressional District in his second attempt at a congressional seat. In 1984 Scott tried unsuccessfully to unseat the incumbent, the white conservative Republican Herbert Harvell Bateman, in the First Congressional District. Court-ordered redistricting later relocated Scott's residency to the Third Congressional District, which was predominantly black. With the Reverend JESSE JACKSON campaigning on his behalf, Scott received nearly 80 percent of the votes cast on 3 November 1992 to become the first African American in Virginia to win election to the House of Representatives in more than a century. Before Scott's victory, the Reconstruction statesman and president of Virginia Normal and Agricultural Institute (later Virginia State University) JOHN MERCER LANGSTON, from Louisa County, Virginia, had served from 1889 to 1891. Congressman Scott was reelected six times. In 2004 he won 69 percent of the vote to defeat his black Republican challenger, the former state delegate Winsome E. Sears, who had also opposed him in 1996.

While serving in the Virginia state legislature, Scott was instrumental in securing the passage of the Neighborhood Assistance Act, aimed at encouraging private businesses to contribute to socially focused programs in return for tax incentives; creating the Governor's Employment and Training Council; and raising the state minimum wage. In the House of Representatives, Scott was the highest-ranking Democrat on the Subcommittee on Crime, Terrorism, and Homeland Security of the Committee on the Judiciary and the third highest-ranking member on the Subcommittee on the Constitution. He held positions on the Committee on Education and the Workforce and the Committee on the Judiciary and served on the Subcommittees on Education Reform, Twenty-first Century Competitiveness, and Antitrust Reform. He served briefly on the House Budget Committee (2002–2004).

In Congress Scott championed or sponsored such legislation as the Death in Custody Act of 2000, requiring full disclosure of circumstances surrounding the death of any person during the process of arrest and while held in custody, and the Individuals with Disabilities Education Act (IDEA). In 1999 he voted in support of intervention in Kosovo. In 2001 he opposed the Patriot Act as well as suggestions for a successor bill to the Patriot Act and in October 2002 voted against retroactively authorizing the George W. Bush administration's deployment of troops in Iraq. In June 2005 Scott joined the Out of Iraq Congressional Caucus. His political stance in Congress encompassed consistent support for abolishing the death penalty, the TRIO Programs (federal educational opportunity programs aimed at assisting students from low-income backgrounds) and community health centers, the Mortgage Revenue Bond Program, the Low-Income Energy Assistance Program, pro-choice abortion measures, civil rights, education for disabled youths and children, juvenile delinquency prevention, gun control, juvenile and adult criminal rehabilitation, consumer safety, and the separation of church and state. He voted against the House impeachment of President Bill Clinton on all four charges and unsuccessfully against the Bankruptcy Reform Act of 2005, which sought to place greater restrictions on the qualifications for filing for bankruptcy.

Scott also held membership in Alpha Phi Alpha and Sigma Pi Phi fraternities, the Peninsula Association to Combat Sickle Cell Anemia, the Boy Scouts of America, the Peninsula Chamber of Commerce, and the March of Dimes Board of Directors. He was president of the Peninsula Legal Aid Center from 1976 to 1981 and president of the

Peninsula Bar Association from 1974 to 1978, and he was a member of the Virginia delegation at the Democratic National Conventions of 2000 and 2004.

FURTHER READING

"Robert C. Scott," *Congressional Quarterly Weekly Report* 51 supplement (16 Jan. 1993): 141.

Tate, Katherine. *Black Faces in the Mirror: African Americans and Their Representatives in the U.S. Congress* (2003).

United States House of Representatives. Biography of Robert C. Scott. Available at http://www.house.gov/scott/bio.print.htm.

RAYMOND PIERRE HYLTON

Scott, Shirley (14 Mar. 1934–10 Mar. 2002), jazz organist and pianist, was born in Philadelphia, Pennsylvania, the youngest of the four children of Willie Scott and Eliza. She attended Elverson Elementary School and graduated from Philadelphia High School for Girls, where she played trumpet and piano. Her family had musical roots in the community; her father ran a private jazz club in the basement of the family home, and her older brother T. L. Scott played the saxophone. At the age of six Shirley played piano in her father's club. Scott began her formal musical studies on piano at the Germantown Settlement House and later studied at the Ornstein School of Music. She literally ran away with a touring band to play piano when she was a senior in high school. Her mother followed and brought her home a week later. Scott was active as a pianist on the thriving Philadelphia club scene in the mid-1950s, often performing with the young JOHN COLTRANE.

Scott was inspired to play the organ after hearing a record by the former LOUIS JORDAN organist Jackie Davis during her senior year in high school. Scott switched from piano to organ in 1955, when a club owner needed her to fill in one night. This was the year that the Hammond Company had introduced its B-3 model, which became the popular jazz instrument of the period. Scott was known for her swinging, signature sound and style almost from the beginning of her career. The Hammond B-3 organ jazz groups of the 1950s and 1960s were known for their hard-swinging soul jazz repertoire. Scott, however, had a graceful and lyrical touch along with a deep feeling for blues and gospel. She was also known for her approach to accompaniment. "She knew how to complement a soloist. She was one of the few organists who could maintain a serious swing pulse on the keyboard while pumping out bass lines on the foot pedals," said Mickey Roker, Scott's drummer for many years (*Philadelphia Inquirer*, 12 Mar. 2002). Working in a trio that also included tenor saxophone and drums, Scott's unique style in her use of the bass pedals on the organ elevated her into the top level of jazz organ players. Her major influences on the organ were COUNT BASIE and Jimmy Smith.

Tenor saxophonist EDDIE "LOCKJAW" DAVIS, known for his work with the Count Basie Orchestra, came through Philadelphia in 1956 and offered Scott a job with his band. Her first recording was with Davis for King Records in 1956. They worked extensively together, eventually recording seventeen albums and releasing the hugely popular series of recordings called *The Eddie Davis Cookbook* for Prestige Records during the late 1950s. These included the 1958 hit "In the Kitchen." They also released several singles with Scott on organ and Count Basie on piano. The group had an extended engagement at Count Basie's Club on 7th Avenue at 132nd Street in Harlem, New York, in 1959. Scott's work with Davis lasted until 1960 and established her as a major jazz artist. She appeared at the Apollo Theater in New York City, the Uptown Theater in Philadelphia, and the Howard Theater in Washington, D.C., plus clubs in black neighborhoods across the country.

In 1958 Scott made her debut as a leader for Prestige Records with the album *Great Scott!* featuring George Duvivier on bass and Arthur Edgehill on drums. She recorded twenty-three albums for Prestige between 1958 and 1964, ten for Impulse between 1963 and 1968, three for Atlantic from 1968 to 1970, and three for Cadet from 1971 to 1973. In 1960 she married tenor saxophonist STANLEY TURRENTINE, with whom she performed and recorded from 1961 to 1971. They had three daughters: Nicole, Pamela, and Lisa. For the recordings on Turrentine's albums, Scott used pseudonyms like Little Miss Cott, for contractual reasons. Many of these recordings include original compositions by Scott. She also recorded with saxophonists Oliver Nelson, HAROLD VICK, JIMMY FORREST, George Coleman, and DEXTER GORDON and had long associations with trombonist Al Grey and drummers Roker, BILLY HIGGINS, and Bobby Durham. In 1964 she recorded the album *Queen of the Organ*, which became her title from that date forward.

In 1974 Scott produced and recorded the album *One for Me*, which she considered her finest work to date. During the 1980s she returned to playing piano in a trio featuring Arthur Harper on bass and Roker on drums. In the 1980s Scott returned to school and earned B.A. and M.A. degrees in music from Cheyney University of Pennsylvania (the oldest of the "historically black colleges and universities" in the United States). In 1991 she was appointed assistant professor of music at Cheyney, where she taught jazz history, piano, and theory. The Cheyney University Shirley Scott Scholarship is awarded annually to students majoring in music or participating in the musical arts (choir or band). In 1992 Scott served as musical director of BILL COSBY's television game show *You Bet Your Life*, which had a live band onstage. She was the recipient of the Mid-Atlantic Arts Foundation Legacy Jazz Award, two National Endowment for the Arts fellowships, and numerous other honors and awards.

Scott's health began to fail when she developed primary pulmonary hypertension after taking the now-banned diet drug fen-phen. In 2000 she was awarded a settlement from a lawsuit against American Home Products, manufacturers of the drug, and the doctor who prescribed it. She succumbed to the illness in Philadelphia in 2002. Analysis of Scott's career as "Queen of the Organ" has often focused on her enormous talent as a performer, recording artist, composer, and educator.

FURTHER READING

Enstice, Wayne, and Janis Stockhouse. *Jazzwomen: Conversations with Twenty-One Musicians* (2004).

Kernfeld, Barry. *New Grove Dictionary of Jazz*, 2nd ed. (2002).

Obituary: *Philadelphia Inquirer*, 12 Mar. 2002.

MAXINE GORDON

Scott, Stan (2 July 1933–4 Apr 1992), journalist, politician, and businessman, was born Stanley Southall Scott in Bolivar, Tennessee, the grandson of black publishing icon WILLIAM ALEXANDER SCOTT II, founder of the *Atlanta Daily World*—the first black daily newspaper in America. Upon his parents' divorce, Scott moved to Atlanta to live with his grandparents and was trained in the family business. After graduating from the all-black David T. Howard Junior High in 1951, Scott enrolled in the journalism program at the University of Kansas, only to have his education cut short by a two-year military deployment to Korea. When he returned, Scott enrolled in Lincoln University in Missouri, graduating with a degree in journalism in 1959. Additionally, to pay for his education Scott had worked as a streetcar driver in Illinois and a dining car waiter in Utah. These experiences were transformative for Scott, giving him deep insight into American racial inequalities and teaching him how to interact with complicated personalities.

After graduation, Scott became the editor and general manager of the *Memphis World*. The newspaper was part of the Scott family publishing empire, which included over thirty black-operated periodicals across the country. The rise and success of the Scott newspaper empire was notable given the turbulent and oftentimes violent nature of the Jim Crow South. However, the Scott family resisted societal constraints by fighting for a two-party political system and using their newspapers as a beacon for all African Americans. In 1961, Scott was reassigned to the *Atlanta Daily World* where he served as a general news reporter, editorial writer and copy editor. Reporting on a vast array of critical events, Scott covered the freedom rides, meetings, speeches, marches, and boycotts that defined the civil rights movement. Upon his return to Atlanta, Scott also married Bettye Lovejoy, a schoolteacher, on 23 December 1962. They were the parents of three children—Susan, Stanley Jr., and Kenneth (Scott's son from a previous relationship).

Hoping to branch out to national coverage, Scott left the *Atlanta Daily World* in 1964, and quickly found work as the first black general assignment reporter at United Press International–New York City division. Scott exclusively covered a number of civil rights events, including the meetings of the Organization of Afro-American Unity, and thus was the sole reporter to witness the assassination of black militant activist MALCOLM X on February 21, 1965 at the Audubon Ballroom. And while his detailed firsthand coverage of the tragedy garnered him a Pulitzer Prize nomination, Scott left United Press International in 1966 for a job as assistant director of public relations for the National Association for the Advancement of Colored People (NAACP).

At the NAACP, Scott worked closely with VERNON JORDAN, who would later become the executive director of the National Urban League in 1972. The two men worked together on a number of federal civil rights issues, including African American voting rights. Undoubtedly, executive director ROY WILKINS was grooming Scott for a national leadership position, taking into account Scott's family history, deep commitment to civil rights issues, and rising national prominence. However, a restless Scott left the NAACP after only ten months. He was persuaded to leave after receiving a groundbreaking job offer from the Westinghouse Broadcasting Corporation to be their first black radio newsman, reporting from WINS in New York City, the twenty-four-hour news station. Scott stayed with Westinghouse several years, building a comfortable lifestyle in suburban New York, until Herb Klein, chief of communications for the Nixon White House, approached Scott about adopting a career in government. Initially reluctant, Scott soon accepted Klein's offer and joined the White House staff as assistant to the chief of communications in 1971. Scott said that as an African American committed to change, it was his responsibility to accept a role in government, noting "we hear a lot of rhetoric about what's wrong with the government. If the opportunity comes along, we have an obligation to right some of the wrongs."

As Klein's assistant, Scott served as a liaison to minority media, addressing the questions and concerns of representatives from newspapers, television stations, and radio. Working closely with Robert Brown, President Richard Nixon's assistant on minority affairs, Scott generated White House initiatives geared toward the African American population. After only a year as Klein's assistant, Nixon appointed Scott as Brown's successor, naming him special assistant to the President on Minority Affairs. With this appointment, Scott became the highest-ranking black man in the White House, a job that was made all the more difficult by the fact that most black Americans did not approve of Nixon. However, Scott was aggressive in his presidential support, maintaining that the civil rights behavior of the 1960s needed to evolve during the 1970s—African Americans needed to create change by taking government positions, pursuing national unity, and creating effective solutions to societal woes. Scott also lashed out at black leaders who disparaged the Republican Party, arguing that such behavior did not benefit the two-party political system, and that in order for black Americans to be taken seriously, they needed to engage in dialogue across party lines. He continually influenced the Nixon administration and the country by fighting for equal employment, welfare reform, job training, and voting initiatives. Under Scott's collaborative efforts, federal civil rights funding rose from $1.1 billion in 1970 to $3.2 billion in 1974, while finances for federal civil rights enforcement rose from $75 million in 1969 to $521 million in 1974.

Scott continued in his role throughout the Ford administration, working with the president to secure a series of White House meetings for black leaders in order to discuss the problems of black America in the 1970s. He left the White House in 1975 to become an administrator for the Agency of International Development, where he concentrated on providing solutions for problems unique to newly independent nations. Leaving the public sector for the private industry, Scott returned to his communications roots, joining Philip Morris, Inc. in 1977 where he quickly became Vice President of Corporate Affairs. Scott relocated to New Orleans in 1988 and purchased Crescent Distributing of New Orleans, a distributor for the Miller Brewing Company; he owned and operated the business until his death from cancer at age fifty-nine in April 1992.

FURTHER READING

DuBose, Carolyn P. "Stan Scott: The President's Special Assistant," *Contact* (Summer 1973).
Kotlowski, Dean J. *Nixon's Civil Rights: Politics Principle, and Policy* (2001).
Murphy, Reg. "A Black Man in Nixon's White House," *The Atlanta Constitution* (19 Aug. 1972).
Obituary: *New York Times*, 7 Apr. 1992.

LEAH M. WRIGHT

Scott, Wendell (25 Aug. 1921–23 Dec. 1990), race-car driver, was born Wendell Oliver Scott in the Crooktown section of Danville, Virginia, the first of two children of William Scott, a mechanic, and his wife, Martha, who each had one daughter from previous marriages. Before Scott entered the first grade, William took a mechanical job in Pittsburgh and moved the whole family to Pennsylvania. After a few years they relocated to Louisville, Kentucky, to live with Martha's aunt. (This side of the family was related to MUHAMMAD ALI, making Scott a distant cousin of the famed boxer.) Meanwhile, Martha's mother, who owned Scott's Grocery back in Danville, took ill. Martha moved the family back to Virginia so that she could run the store, where Scott worked while he went to school.

At the age of eighteen Scott began driving for a local taxicab company and, four years later, joined the army. He served as a mechanic and a paratrooper in the 101st Airborne and returned to Danville after his discharge in 1945. Scott proceeded to run moonshine from illegal rural stills to

Wendell Scott, the first African American to win a race in NASCAR's top series. (AP Images.)

the Danville Fairgrounds Speedway with a specially outfitted truck that he later claimed could "do 95 [mph] in second gear, and 118 in high" (Wilkinson). He would then remain at the fairgrounds to watch the stock car races held there on short-distance dirt tracks.

During one run in 1948, however, Scott swerved to avoid pedestrians and crashed. He sustained no major injuries but was cited by the police and received three years' parole. In 1950 the Danville racing promoter Martin Roberts asked the police if they knew of any fast black drivers in the county. They named Scott, who at the time had opened and was successfully managing Scott Garage. Scott bought a used race car, and though he was denied entry to many races, he eventually debuted at the Danville Fairgrounds as the first black racer in a Dixie Circuit event. The Dixie Circuit operated throughout Virginia and North Carolina but was not recognized by the National Association for Stock Car Auto Racing (NASCAR). Scott won more than eighty Dixie Circuit contests in less than four years. He then graduated to the Modified Division of NASCAR, whose entrants were permitted to alter their vehicles in ways that were generally not allowed on the top-flight Grand National Series (now called the Winston Cup Series). This aspect of the Modified Division was crucial to Scott's success, as his skin color blocked him from securing a sponsor who could supply him with a competitive car. Thus, Scott used his own mechanical skills to outfit his number 34 car in ways that more than compensated for this handicap. His friend and competitor Earl Brooks remembered that Scott often used a set of baby scales to perform the same measurements

of engine parts for which other racing teams employed highly calibrated equipment.

Scott persevered on the Dixie and Modified circuits despite numerous incidents in which racing organizers prohibited him from competing by citing specious regulations that they invented especially for him, such as the presence of too many paint chips on his car. And since stock car races were primarily held in the segregated South, most crowds would cheer when Scott's competitors attempted to force his car off the track. But Scott's mild-mannered patience, combined with his abilities in the garage and on the track, garnered him more than forty Modified racing victories as well as the 1959 Virginia State Championship.

In 1961 NASCAR finally deemed Scott's accomplishments worthy to qualify him for Grand National competition, and he debuted at the Spartanburg Fairgrounds in South Carolina. Five times that year he finished in the top ten, earning $3,240. Scott doubled his success the following year, tallying eleven top ten finishes and $7,000 in winnings. The Grand National Series operated on a point system that considered a driver's starting positions, laps completed, average speeds, and finishing positions—and Scott's point totals increased steadily from thirty-second place in 1961 to sixth in 1966. In 1964 he set the Grand National record for a last-place starter; he began the World 600 in Charlotte in fortieth place and finished in ninth. Scott's most successful year overall came in 1969, when he won $47,451 and placed ninth in the point standings.

The only Grand National victory of Scott's career came on 1 December 1963 in Jacksonville, Florida, yet even this occasion was marked by yet another outright display of racism. On the Jacksonville Speedway's half-mile track, Scott lapped Buck Baker twice, traveling 101 miles by the time Baker, in second place, completed the requisite one hundred. But the race organizers awarded Baker the checkered flag, the trophy, and photo ops in the winner's circle with the white beauty queen. Once the crowd left, organizers apologized to Scott and presented him with the $1,150 winner's check and a block of wood to serve as his trophy.

With his consistent racing success Scott was eventually approached—twice—to receive sponsorship, but both deals quickly soured. In 1964 the Ford executive Lee Iacocca provided Scott with a race car, albeit a used one. And even though it was the most advanced car Scott had ever had, he still saw fit to redesign the frame more to his liking. Ford, however, supplied Scott with engine parts that, as Earl Brooks characterized them, did not fully meet NASCAR specifications. Apparently thinking that Scott would not know the difference, Ford had attempted to outfit him with a car that gave him a decided, though illegal, edge in competition. Scott insisted that the car must adhere to NASCAR rules, and the sponsorship subsequently dissolved. In 1971 a white promoter promised Scott a top-quality race car for an event at the Charlotte Motor Speedway but reneged under pressure from other racing executives.

Scott was involved in only two multiple-car pileups during his career. The first was a thirty-seven-car accident at the Daytona Speedway in 1960, in which he was not seriously injured. In the second, an eighteen-car pileup at Talladega, Alabama, in 1973, Scott suffered fractures in his pelvis, ribs, and leg, as well as a gash in his arm that required seventy stitches. The incident forced him into retirement, though Scott occasionally raced again. He settled in Danville once again and continued managing Scott Garage.

By the end of his twelve-year NASCAR career, Scott had earned a total of $188,000, racing in 506 events. In 1977 his life and career were the inspiration for the RICHARD PRYOR movie *Greased Lightning*, for which Scott served as technical adviser. He was not impressed with the stuntmen employed for the driving scenes and received scant payment for his work.

Wendell Scott received numerous awards and has been inducted into several halls of fame, including the National Black Athletic Hall of Fame in 1977, the International Motorsports Hall of Fame in 1999, and the Black Sports and Entertainment Hall of Fame in 2003. Until the early 1970s Scott was the only black driver on the Grand National Series, and by the end of his career there were only two others. Scott died from complications resulting from spinal cancer in December of 1990. The General Assembly of Virginia officially mourned Scott's death with a resolution on 16 January 1991, and on the anniversary of his death in 1997, Danville renamed his hometown street Wendell Scott Drive. He was survived by seven children, including four sons who often served as his pit crew.

FURTHER READING

Daniel, Pete. *Lost Revolutions: The South in the 1950s* (2000).

Golenbock, Peter. *American Zoom: Stock Car Racing—from the Dirt Tracks to Daytona* (1993).

Wilkinson, Sylvia. *Dirt Tracks to Glory: The Early Days of Stock Car Racing as Told by the Participants* (1983).

Obituary: *New York Times*, 25 Dec. 1990.

DAVID F. SMYDRA JR.

Scott, William Alexander, II (29 Sept. 1902–7 Feb. 1934), newspaper publisher, was born in Edwards, Mississippi, the son of the Reverend William Alexander Scott Sr., a Christian Church minister and owner of a printing shop that produced church publications, and Emeline Southall, a typesetter who printed her husband's publications. Scott learned printing from his mother. At Jackson College in Mississippi (1920–1922) and at Morehouse College in Atlanta (1923–1925), he studied business and mathematics. He helped publish the Morehouse yearbook, was a quarterback on the football team, and with his older brother Aurelius became a champion debater. He left college without graduating.

After a year of teaching at Swift College in Knoxville, Tennessee, Scott began his business career in sales, advertising, and publishing. In 1927 in Jacksonville, Florida, he teamed with Aurelius to sell advertising for and to publish the *Jacksonville Negro Business Directory*, the first business listing to meet the needs of merchants catering to African Americans who migrated in the 1920s from farms to cities. In 1928 he published a similar directory for Atlanta's African American businesses, printing it with equipment bought with a loan from an African American bank. Scott planned to print a directory for Augusta when an Atlanta business executive persuaded him to publish a weekly newspaper. He decided that a newspaper could succeed financially if he made advertising rather than circulation his primary revenue source. Although Scott's banker warned him that there were not enough advertisers, Scott persisted, securing a loan with only his name.

The only African American weekly in Atlanta, the *Independent*, was in decline, largely because its policies were linked to partisan politics. Scott was determined that his *Atlanta World* would be nonpartisan. From his first run (fewer than two thousand copies) on 3 August 1928 Scott was sensitive to his market. He specialized in news about African American religious, social, and educational activities, items that were systematically neglected by Atlanta's three white-owned dailies. The *World*'s news pages also contained national news of importance to African Americans. The newspaper's logo carried the words "Dixie's Standard Race Journal."

As Scott expanded his local advertising base and attracted national advertising, he followed the lead of successful big-city papers, sponsoring promotions. He also offered advertisers free illustrations and layout and copy services. He sold the paper to white merchants, advertising the *World* as the way to reach Atlanta's "90,000 Negroes."

National advertising grew as Scott converted the paper from a weekly to a three-times-a-week paper and finally to a daily, and he built a syndicate consisting of three family-owned and dozens of affiliated weeklies and semi-weeklies. By 1930 he was publishing the *Atlanta World* twice a week and owned two other semi-weeklies, the *Birmingham World* and the *Memphis World*. Despite the onset of the Depression, Scott, led on by what his family called his "dead reckoning," spent most of 1930 traveling and selling his plan to link African American newspapers across the South.

On 1 January 1931 Scott launched his Scott Newspaper Syndicate, the first such independent venture by an African American newspaper publisher. He created a financial base that enriched him and supported the expansion of the African American press. Under cooperative agreements, members shared advertising revenue. The *World* kept income from national advertising in its national edition, which was shipped by train and inserted in the local weeklies or semi-weeklies. The local publishers kept revenue from local advertising and from local circulation sales. The syndicate's members also exchanged articles and news items.

Scott next aimed to make the *Atlanta World* into a daily. As a step toward that, in 1931 he hired as managing editor a Chicago journalist, Frank Marshall Davis, who helped him publish all three *World*s three times a week. From this time on Scott focused entirely on the business operation, delegating content to Davis and the printing of local and national editions to his younger brother Cornelius. On 14 March 1932 Scott unveiled a six-day daily; six weeks later he added the Saturday paper. Although the newspaper remained nonpartisan, Davis's editorials (usually written without Scott's knowledge) became a voice for criminal justice and civil rights. His first editorial criticized the state for "legal lynching" because it sentenced a disproportionate number of African Americans to the electric chair.

Scott's four marriages and his aggressive personality made him a target of controversy and may have contributed to his murder. Scott's first marriage in 1922 was to Lucile McAllister, daughter of a minister; they had two sons before they divorced in 1929. That same year Scott wed Mildred Jones of South Carolina, from whom he was separated within months. In 1932 Scott wed Ella Ramsay of Atlanta, a marriage that lasted about a year. On 21 October 1933 he secretly married Agnes Maddox, an Atlanta librarian, fueling rumors that he had not been divorced properly from his third wife. In January 1934 Scott was shot from behind at night as he parked his car in his garage. He survived surgery but developed peritonitis and died eight days after the shooting. On his deathbed he reportedly named a suspect, his fourth wife's brother, who was exonerated after an inquest. No one was ever tried for Scott's murder.

The first African American publisher of a chain of newspapers and the first African American since the Civil War to publish a daily newspaper, Scott overcame innumerable odds. At his funeral his banker observed, "To break down the barriers is the problem of every young Negro" (*Atlanta Daily World*, 11 Feb. 1934). At his death the *World* employed fifty full-time employees, including Cornelius Scott, who remained as the publisher into the 1990s. The syndicate grew to include fifty minority-owned newspapers, including a Cherokee tribal weekly in Oklahoma. As the only African American daily in the United States for twenty-four years, the *World* helped launch the careers of a generation of promising young black journalists. In 1976 *Jet* magazine named Scott one of the nation's top two hundred African Americans during the two hundred years of American independence. In 1988 he was elected to the Howard University Hall of Fame for African American journalists, and in 1996 he was inducted into the Georgia Newspaper Hall of Fame.

FURTHER READING

Tidwell, John Edgar, ed. *Frank Marshall Davis: Livin' the Blues: Memoirs of a Black Journalist and Poet* (1992).

Obituaries: *Atlanta Constitution*, 8 Feb. 1934; *Atlanta Daily World*, 12 Feb. 1934.

This entry is taken from the *American National Biography* and is published here with the permission of the American Council of Learned Societies.

LEONARD RAY TEEL

Scott-Heron, Gil (1 Apr. 1949–27 May 2011), poet, singer, songwriter, was born in Chicago, Illinois, to Bobbie Scott, a librarian, and GILES "GIL" HERON, a professional soccer player. Scott-Heron was an adult when he met his father, a member both of Glasgow's Celtic Football Club and the Canadian Air Force. When his parents divorced, Scott-Heron moved to Jackson, Tennessee, to live with his grandmother. Chosen as one of three black children set to integrate an elementary school in Jackson, Scott-Heron endured brutal racism. Displeased, his grandmother sent him to join his mother in New York, where he enrolled in a school in the Bronx. He began playing the piano and writing mysteries at an early age. While attending DeWitt Clinton High School, he won a scholarship to the Ethical Culture Fieldston School, a private academy in the Riverdale section of the Bronx.

Inspired by LANGSTON HUGHES, Scott-Heron, like Hughes, chose to attend Lincoln University, one of the nation's oldest black colleges. While living in Chester County, Pennsylvania, he worked various jobs to support himself. An English major, he played on the basketball team and met visiting writers such as ISHMAEL REED and LARRY NEAL. Scott-Heron met Brian Jackson, a fellow student, and each realized they shared a common interest in music and social activism. The two began collaborating on music (Jackson was a musician and songwriter). Performing on college campuses in the Philadelphia area, Scott-Heron and Jackson longed to take their political message to the masses.

In 1968 Scott-Heron won Lincoln University's Langston Hughes Creative Writing Award. Two years later, he published his first novel, *The Vulture*, and a collection of poetry and photographs he titled *Small Talk at 125th & Lenox*. He transformed the latter into his debut album, a mixture of spoken word poetry and jazz music, released in 1970 on Flying Dutchman records. Produced by the veteran music industry insider Bob Thiele, *Small Talk at 125th & Lenox* included one of Scott-Heron's earliest versions of the often-cited "The Revolution Will Not Be Televised," a satire of the media's depiction of social unrest coupled with American's obsession with television. Scott-Heron earned a master's degree in Creative Writing at Johns Hopkins University in Baltimore, Maryland. From 1972 to 1976, he taught creative writing at Federal City College in Washington, D.C. He left his post after deciding that his music career interfered with the quality of his teaching.

Scott-Heron left Flying Dutchman after recording two more albums, *Pieces of a Man* (1971) and *Free Will* (1972), both with Jackson. He published his second novel, *The Nigger Factory*, in 1972. Like his first novel, *The Nigger Factory* was a crime story. Loosely based on his experiences as an organizer of a strike while attending Lincoln, the novel critiqued 1960s America. Issues and themes, such as American hypocrisy, injustice, social unrest, inequity, poverty, and substance abuse made up the novel's landscape. These themes were echoed in his music.

In 1974 Strata East released his next album, *Winter in America*. In 1975 he and Jackson became the first artists to sign with Clive Davis at Arista Records. Scott-Heron and Jackson, who played piano, keyboard, and flute, formed the Midnight Band. The group debuted on Scott-Heron's *The First Minute of a New Day*. Jackson and the Midnight Band remained with Scott-Heron until each decided in 1978 to work on solo albums. Scott-Heron's first single, "Angel Dust," arguably represented his greatest solo success, climbing to #15 on the 1978 R&B charts.

In 1975 Scott-Heron formed a band called Amnesia Express. The group defined its music as bluesology, a mixture of jazz and the blues. From 1975 until 1985 he and Amnesia Express released eleven records with Arista, including *The First Minute of a New Day* (1975) and *From South Africa to South Carolina* (1975), which was twenty-ninth on the 1975 R&B charts.

Scott-Heron married actress Brenda Louise Sykes in the late 1970s, and the couple had a daughter, Gia Louise, who was featured on the cover of *Real Eyes* (1980). The marriage ended in divorce. In 1982 Robert Mugge produced and directed a documentary featuring Scott-Heron's music and political views, *Black Wax*. Mugge shot the film during Scott-Heron's performance at the Wax Museum Nightclub in Washington, D.C.

After Arista severed ties with Scott-Heron, the singer stopped recording albums, arguing that he suffered from a hereditary illness he referred to as "scoliotic condition." However, he continued to tour around the world and collaborated with MILES DAVIS on "Let Me See Your I.D.," a part of *Sun City*, an antiapartheid album released in 1985 that included a number of popular recording artists. In 1994 he released *Spirits*, his first album since 1984, for TVT Records. Jackson, his former partner, worked as a writer and producer on the album.

Scott-Heron started his own record label, Rumal-Gia, an imprint of TVT Records. It reissued a CD that contained material from several earlier albums, including *The Best of Gil Scott Heron* and *It's Your World*. Most of *It's Your World* was originally recorded with the Midnight Band and Jackson live in Boston during the Bicentennial. It included memorable singles such as "Home Is Where the Hatred Is" and "The Bottle," an antidrinking ballad. In 2000 Scott-Heron was a guest performer on Jackson's first solo album, *Gotta Play*. In November 2000 Scott-Heron was arrested after police saw him purchase cocaine in Harlem, New York. The courts sentenced the fifty-two year old to up to three years in prison for refusing to seek help for drug addiction. He went to jail in November 2001. In a 2008 interview with *New York Magazine*, Scott-Heron revealed that he had been HIV-positive for a number of years.

Heineken USA and the American Society of Composers, Authors and Publishers (ASCAP) presented Scott-Heron with the Heineken Ampt/ASCAP Recognition Award in 2003. Scott-Heron was an acclaimed jazz musician and social activist who was credited with being one of the founding artists of rap music. Like traditional rap music, Scott-Heron's song lyrics about politics and social injustices were delivered naturally via spoken word.

Scott-Heron died in Manhattan at the age of 62, just after returning home from a European tour.

FURTHER READING

Massa, Suzanne Hotte. "Gil Scott-Heron," in *Contemporary African American Novelists: A Bio-Bibliographical Critical Sourcebook*, ed. Emmanuel S. Nelson (1999).
Woodson, Jon. "Gil Scott-Heron," in *Dictionary of Literary Biography: Afro-American Poets since 1955*, eds. Thadious M. Davis and Trudier Harris (1985).
Obituary: *Washington Post*, 29 May 2011.

KAAVONIA HINTON

Scottsboro Boys Olen Montgomery (1914–?), Clarence Norris (12 July 1912–23 Jan. 1989), Haywood Patterson (1913–24 Aug. 1952), Ozie Powell (1915–?), Willie Roberson (4 July 1916–c. 1959), Charlie Weems (1911–?), Eugene Williams (1918–?), Andrew "Andy" Wright, (1912–?), and Leroy "Roy" Wright (1918–1959), became an international cause célèbre after they were accused of raping two white women on a Southern Railroad freight train traveling on 25 March 1931 through northern Alabama en route to Memphis, Tennessee. Like many Depression-era Americans, the nine young men and the two women had been riding the rails in search of work. Shortly after their train crossed into Alabama, a white male hobo stepped on the hand of Haywood Patterson, who had been hanging on to one of the freight carriages. A scuffle ensued in which Patterson and his friends forced the white hobo and his colleagues off the train, after which the whites reported the assault to a stationmaster, who in turn informed the sheriff of Jackson County, Alabama. The sheriff deputized a posse of heavily armed white men, who stopped the train at the small town of Paint Rock and rounded up every black male on the train. The nine youths were then tied together, loaded on a truck, and driven to jail in Scottsboro, the Jackson County seat.

When the prisoners arrived at the jail, they found that the two women, Ruby Bates and Victoria Price, had told the authorities that twelve African Americans armed with pistols and knives had raped them. Price later identified six of the nine jailed teenagers as her assailants, prompting a prison guard to declare—though he provided no evidence—that the three others must have raped Bates. A presumption of the black youths' guilt led hundreds of angry whites to surround the jail in the hope of lynching the accused, but their plans were thwarted when the governor of Alabama ordered the National Guard to protect the Scottsboro jail. However, the state of Alabama showed less interest in the defendants' broader procedural rights, assigning them two ineffective attorneys—one drunk and the other elderly—who defended their clients with little skill and even less enthusiasm. The lawyers failed to probe inconsistencies in the women's testimony, including a physician's report that contradicted Price's claim of a brutal gang rape. They also ignored the fact that Willie Roberson, suffering from syphilis, could barely walk and certainly could not jump from one railroad car to another as claimed; his condition—which had left him with sores on his genitals—would also have made intercourse extremely painful. The defense was also compromised when Roy Wright, Haywood Patterson, and Clarence Norris testified that they had seen some of the others rape the two women, though it later emerged that these accusations had been coerced by prison guards. Roy Wright told a *New York Times* reporter in 1933 that the guards "whipped me and it seemed like they was going to kill me. All the time they kept saying, 'Now will you tell?' and finally it seemed like I couldn't stand no more and I said yes. Then I went back into the courtroom and they put me up on the chair in front of the judge and began asking a lot of questions, and I said I had seen Charlie Weems

Scottsboro Boys. Left to right are Deputy Sheriff Charles McComb, attorney Samuel Leibowitz, and the defendants Roy Wright, Olen Montgomery, Ozie Powell, Willie Roberson, Eugene Williams, Charlie Weems, and Andy Wright. The youths, along with Clarence Norris and Haywood Patterson, were charged with an attack on two white women on 25 March 1931. (AP Images.)

and Clarence Norris with the white girls" (quoted in Goodman, 97).

After a trial lasting only three days, the all-white, all-male jury found the teenagers guilty and recommended that eight of them be sentenced to death in the electric chair on 10 July 1931. The prosecution had requested that Roy Wright, who was only twelve or thirteen, should receive a life sentence, but because seven of the jurors held out for the death penalty for him, too, the judge declared a mistrial in his case.

The Scottsboro Boys were hardly the first black victims of injustice in southern courts, but their youth and the paucity of evidence against them provoked an immediate uproar. Four of the teenagers were from Chattanooga, Tennessee, and had been traveling to Memphis in search of work hauling logs on the Mississippi. Roy Wright and his nineteen-year-old brother, Andy, had been raised by their mother, Ada, after their father died when Andy was twelve. His father's death had forced Andy, who had shown promise in grade school, to find work as a truck driver, though at the time of his arrest he was unemployed. Roy worked in a grocery store. Eugene Williams, thirteen years old, had been a dishwasher in a Chattanooga cafe. Haywood Patterson was the fourth of nine surviving children born to sharecroppers in Elberton, Georgia. In March 1931 he was eighteen and had spent the previous four years riding the rails of the South and Midwest in search of work. Patterson could barely read and write, having left school after the third grade, but he "knew the train schedules, when the freights left and where they arrived [and] could light a butt in the wind on top of a moving boxcar" (quoted in Goodman, 93).

The five other Scottsboro defendants did not know the four Chattanooga teenagers before boarding the train to Memphis; they also did not all know each other. At nineteen or twenty, Charles Weems was the oldest of the nine youths arrested. His mother had died when he was only four, and six of his seven siblings had also died. Clarence Norris was the second of eleven children born to a former slave and his wife in Warm Springs, Georgia. He had attended school up to the second grade, and at age seven he joined his sharecropping parents in the cotton fields, where he did "everything a grown man could do ... or my daddy would whup me good" (Norris, 28). By the time he was a teenager, beatings from his father had become more frequent, and Norris left home, working a series of laboring jobs before seeking his luck on the rails.

Ozie Powell had also been born in rural Georgia and, like Norris, could barely read and write. Sixteen at the time of his arrest, he had been living in Atlanta for three years, working in sawmills and lumber camps. Seventeen-year-old Olen Montgomery was from Monroe, Georgia, and had attended school through the fifth grade. His vision was extremely poor because of cataracts, and he was traveling to Memphis to buy new glasses when he was arrested. Montgomery, like Powell, had not participated in the fight on the freight train. Nor had Willie Roberson, who was born in Columbus, Georgia. His father abandoned the family a few weeks after Willie's birth, and his mother died two years later, leaving him in the care of his grandmother until she, too, died around 1930. At the time of his arrest, Roberson, who was illiterate and had a severe speech defect, was traveling to Memphis to get treatment for syphilis and gonorrhea. These diseases had left him crippled, but his cane, like Olen Montgomery's glasses, was confiscated after his arrest.

The nation's leading civil rights organization, the NAACP, might have been expected to take on the Scottsboro Boys' case, but its executive secretary, WALTER WHITE, was initially reluctant to get involved in a controversial rape case in the Deep South. The American Communist Party had no such qualms and quickly convinced the Scottsboro Boys and their parents that their best hope of overturning their convictions lay with its legal arm, the International Labor Defense (ILD). When the U.S. Supreme Court overturned the boys' convictions in *Powell v. Alabama* (1932) and ordered a retrial in March 1933, the ILD's Joseph Brodsky and the famed criminal attorney Samuel Leibowitz—who was not a Communist—took up their case.

The Communist Party's involvement in the case helped dramatize the Scottsboro case throughout the nation. On May Day of 1931, demonstrations by 300,000 workers in more than 100 American cities demanded the Scottsboro Boys' release. In addition to communist and socialist agitation, a wide range of black and white church leaders, liberal politicians, including New York City's mayor, Fiorello LaGuardia, and thousands of ordinary men and women voiced their criticism of the Alabama courts. Although W. E. B. DuBois was suspicious of the ILD's and the Communists' motives in supporting the Scottsboro Boys, most African Americans agreed with the Oklahoma journalist ROSCOE DUNJEE, who asked: "What does it matter whether God, the devil, or Communists save those helpless black boys?" (quoted in Goodman, 69). Both COUNTÉE CULLEN and LANGSTON HUGHES wrote poems demanding justice for the Scottsboro Boys.

International support for the Scottsboro Boys was perhaps even more dramatic. A series of European demonstrations, at which Roy and Andy Wright's mother, Ada, was a prominent speaker, also began that summer. More than 150,000 people attended one rally in Berlin in 1932, while other, occasionally violent, protests were staged in Geneva, Paris, and Glasgow. Thousands of Canadian, African, South American, and Chinese supporters of the Scottsboro Boys also sent petitions and letters to the governor of Alabama and to the White House, demanding the boys' release.

International pressure was one thing, but getting justice for black men accused of raping white women in Alabama was quite another. While they waited for a retrial, the Scottsboro Boys remained on death row in appalling conditions; from their cells they could hear the screams of inmates being electrocuted. In all, Clarence Norris recalled, he saw fifteen men walk through the notorious green door to the death chamber. Only one of them was white.

In the first retrial, which involved only Haywood Patterson, Leibowitz exposed the weaknesses of the prosecution's original case. He called the physician who had treated Price and Bates to testify that he had found no bleeding or vaginal damage. A white male witness also testified that he and another white man had had sexual intercourse with Price and Bates on the evening before the two women boarded the train at Huntsville, Alabama, which, Leibowitz argued, explained the nonmotile semen found inside the women's vaginas. Most dramatically, Ruby Bates now testified that there had been no rapes and that she and Price had concocted the original charges out of a fear that they would be arrested for vagrancy. Regardless of that evidence, the jury again found Patterson guilty—after deliberating for only five minutes—and again sentenced him to death. However, the presiding judge, James Horton, agreed with Leibowitz that the evidence indicated Patterson's and the other boys' innocence and ordered a retrial.

That retrial in November 1933 proved even more farcical than the first trial. The presiding judge, William Callahan, all but instructed the jury to convict Patterson. They did so. Patterson later recalled that the judge could not get him to the chair fast enough. He added: "When Callahan sentenced me to death for the third time, I noticed he left out the Lord. He didn't even want the Lord to have any mercy on me" (Patterson, 50). One week later Clarence Norris was also convicted and sentenced to death.

Throughout 1934 the ILD petitioned the Alabama courts for a retrial and publicized the inhumane conditions and the physical and mental abuse the Scottsboro Boys received in jail. The Alabama authorities denied those petitions, but in January 1935 the U.S. Supreme Court allowed a review of the convictions of Norris and Patterson. That April, in what proved to be a landmark case, *Norris v. Alabama*, the Supreme Court reversed both convictions on the ground that African Americans had been excluded from the pool of jurors selected to try the case. In the long term the ruling can be seen as one of the first steps in a series of Supreme Court decisions assuring blacks equal protection rights, leading to the 1954 *Brown v. Board of Education* decision that declared racial segregation unconstitutional. In the short term *Norris v. Alabama* required only that African Americans be included in the pool of potential jurors; it did not guarantee equal black representation on actual juries. This became readily apparent in November 1935, when an Alabama grand jury, with only one black member, issued new indictments that again charged the nine Scottsboro defendants with rape.

The indictments prompted the ILD to make common cause with other civil rights groups, including the NAACP, in a broad-based Scottsboro Defense Committee (SDC) for the next trial in January 1936. Patterson was again convicted—again by an all-white jury—and sentenced to seventy-five years in prison. The following day, however, when Norris, Roy Wright, and Powell were being driven back to Birmingham jail, they got into an argument with their escorts, Sheriff Sandlin and his deputy. The deputy struck Powell about the head; Powell responded by slashing the deputy's throat with a knife that he had concealed. Sheriff Sandlin then shot Powell in the head at close range. The doctors who removed the bullet from his brain gave him a 50 percent chance of surviving; Powell did survive, but he suffered from severe brain damage for the rest of his life.

That incident and a series of appeals by the SDC delayed the trials of the other prisoners until the summer of 1937. Clarence Norris was again found guilty and again received the death sentence, though the governor of Alabama later commuted that sentence to life imprisonment. Andy Wright and Charlie Weems were also found guilty and received prison sentences of ninety-nine and seventy-five years, respectively. Ozie Powell, the only Scottsboro Boy to plead guilty—to a lesser charge of assault—was sentenced to twenty years. The SDC reached a compromise with the Alabama authorities to drop all charges against Roy Wright and Eugene Williams, the youngest of the Scottsboro Boys, and against Olen Montgomery and Willie Roberson, who had not been in the boxcar when the alleged rape took place.

Upon their release, Wright, Williams, Montgomery, and Roberson traveled to New York, where they were mobbed by crowds and appeared briefly in a vaudeville show at Harlem's famed Apollo Theater. Williams and Montgomery had both dreamed of music careers while in prison, and the latter had even composed a song, "Lonesome Jailhouse Blues," but neither found lasting success as musicians. Williams left to live with relatives in St. Louis, Missouri, apparently with plans to attend Western Baptist Seminary, and was not heard of again. Along with Roy Wright, Montgomery embarked on a publicity tour to raise funds for the release of the remaining Scottsboro Boys and spent the next few years traveling between New York, Atlanta, and Detroit in search of work. A heavy drinker, Montgomery was arrested several times for public disorder and probably returned to Georgia in 1960.

Roy Wright at first adapted well to his newfound freedom. Sponsored by the entertainer BILL "BOJANGLES" ROBINSON, he enrolled in a vocational school and later served in the army, married, and then joined the merchant marine. While on leave from the army in 1959, however, he shot and killed his wife, believing that she had been unfaithful, and then committed suicide. Willie Roberson remained in New York City, settling in Brooklyn, where he found regular employment, though he was arrested once—wrongfully, he claimed—for disorderly conduct. He died sometime around 1959, following an asthma attack.

The release of four of the boys signaled the end of one part of the Scottsboro saga. By the late 1930s American and international opinion had begun to focus on the impending world war, and even the black press devoted less attention to the case. The SDC and the ILD persisted in their efforts to gain the release of the five others, but the Alabama authorities proved equally determined that their sentences should stand. Andy Wright, Weems, and Norris were assigned to a new prison, Kilby, where they worked twelve-hour shifts at a cotton mill and were beaten systematically by their guards. On one occasion a guard stabbed Weems, though he had intended to stab Wright. Norris had a finger severed in a work accident and received several whippings and beatings.

In August 1943 Weems was paroled and found a job in an Atlanta laundry. Little is known about him after that, other than that he married and that his eyesight continued to suffer from a tear-gas attack by prison guards, who had found him reading a communist publication in his cell. Wright and Norris were paroled in early 1944 on the condition that they labor at a lumberyard near Montgomery, Alabama. Forced to share a single bed in a tiny room, their living and working conditions were worse than at Kilby. They were nonetheless free to marry—Norris to Dora Lee of Montgomery and Wright to Ruby Belle of Mobile, Alabama. Both men left Montgomery in violation of their paroles in late 1944 but later returned to serve more time at Kilby prison.

Ozie Powell served his sentence at Atmore farm, a penitentiary that, like Parchman in Mississippi and Angola in Louisiana, was notorious for its brutal and inhumane treatment of prisoners. Little is known about Powell's experiences there, other than that he was beaten and that he continued to suffer from depression and paralysis on his right side, a consequence of the gunshot wounds he had suffered at the hands of Sheriff Sandlin. He was released from Atmore in 1946 and returned to Georgia.

Much more is known about Haywood Patterson's time at Atmore because of his memoir, *Scottsboro Boy* (1950). In February 1941 a guard paid one of Patterson's friends a few dollars to kill him; he stabbed Patterson twenty times and punctured a lung, but the Scottsboro Boy survived. The certainty of violence and the uncertainty of when it might occur made Patterson keep faith only in himself and in the knife that was his constant companion. Like other men who survived Atmore, Patterson became a sexual predator; by giving a brutal beating to a "young wolf" who had made advances on his "gal-boy," he gave warning to his fellow prisoners that nobody would "make a girl" out of him.

After an escape attempt in 1943, the authorities sent Patterson to work in the cotton mill at Kilby prison. At first the violent reputation he had earned at Atmore served him well. The guards left him alone to run what he called his "store," selling cigarettes and other goods to fellow prisoners. He was not immune to unofficial beatings and official whippings from the guards, however, and he endured several spells in solitary confinement. In July 1948, believing that he would never be released, Patterson decided to "parole himself" by escaping from the Kilby farm, where he was working at the time, to his sister's home in Detroit, Michigan. There, at age thirty-six, he drank his first beer, but his freedom was short-lived.

He took a series of laboring jobs and began working on his autobiography with the writer Earl Conrad. Two weeks after the release of *Scottsboro Boy* in June 1950, the FBI arrested him in Detroit for escaping from Kilby; he was released on bail, and the governor of Michigan refused to extradite him to Alabama to serve his sentence. In December 1950 Patterson was charged with murder after he stabbed and killed a man in a barroom fight. Patterson claimed that he had acted in self-defense, but he was convicted in September 1951 of manslaughter and sentenced to six to fifteen years in the Michigan State penitentiary. He died in prison of cancer less than a year later.

In June 1950, nineteen years after being arrested in Paint Rock, Andy Wright was the last of the Scottsboro Boys to be released, and he moved to Connecticut. Like Montgomery, Powell, Weems, and Williams, it is not known when—or if—Andy Wright died. The failure of historians, journalists, and documentary filmmakers since the 1960s to find them suggests that, if they lived, they probably chose obscurity rather than having to relive the trauma of their years in prison and on death row.

That Clarence Norris titled his own memoir *The Last of the Scottsboro Boys* (1979) suggests that he believed the others had died. This autobiography detailed Norris's life after breaking parole in 1946. He moved first to his sister's home in Cleveland,

Ohio, where he found a job shoveling coal in a furnace room and spent some of his first wages at a brothel. There he slept with a white woman to discover why the Alabama authorities had been enraged by even the idea of interracial sex. He discovered, however, that when it came to sex, there "ain't no difference" between white and black women (Norris, 208). He married again, worked a series of laboring jobs interspersed with bouts of unemployment, and moved to New York in 1953. There he was arrested several times, once for stabbing his girlfriend.

By 1960 Norris had settled down with Melba Sanders, his third wife, with whom he had two children, Adele and Deborah. He moved to Brooklyn, found a permanent job that he liked, as a vacuum sweeper in a warehouse, and in the early 1970s began working with the NAACP to get his parole violation expunged. After a lengthy battle, the state of Alabama eventually relented, and in October 1976 Governor George Wallace granted Norris an official pardon. Norris was later diagnosed with Alzheimer's disease and died in January 1989. None of the Scottsboro Boys or their families has ever received compensation for their wrongful arrests and imprisonment.

Some historians have depicted the campaign to-free the Scottsboro Boys as a harbinger of the post–World War II civil rights movement that challenged and finally ended legal segregation and second-class citizenship for African Americans. Others have viewed the case as one of the first modern global campaigns for human rights, a forerunner of efforts to win the release of political prisoners from Andrei Sakharov to Nelson Mandela. Both assessments are true, but the Scottsboro Boys knew instinctively that the *reasons* for their imprisonment and inhumane treatment were brutally simple. As Olen Montgomery told a Tuskegee psychiatrist in 1937, "I'm just being held here because I'm a Nigger. That's why I'm in jail; not nothing I've done" (Goodman, 275).

FURTHER READING

Carter, Dan T. *Scottsboro* (1969, rev. ed., 1979).

Goodman, James. *Stories of Scottsboro* (1994).

Miller, James A., et al. "Mother Ada Wright and the International Campaign to Free the Scottsboro Boys, 1931–1934," *American Historical Review* (Apr. 2001).

Norris, Clarence. *The Last of the Scottsboro Boys* (1979).

Patterson, Haywood. *Scottsboro Boy* (1950).

STEVEN J. NIVEN

Scurlock, Addison M. (19 June 1883–16 Dec. 1964), photographer, was born in Fayetteville, North Carolina, to George Clay Scurlock, a politician. In 1900, when Addison was seventeen, George Scurlock moved his family to Washington, D.C., where he worked for the U.S. Treasury Department and studied law. In Washington Addison became interested in photography. He started working for Moses P. Rice, a white photographer who owned a studio on Pennsylvania Avenue.

In 1904 Scurlock left Rice to open his own studio, which he operated out of his parents' house. Most of his early work focused on photographing African American students at universities and high schools, not only in Washington but also in the Deep South. Early in his career he became the official photographer for Howard University. He held this position until his death.

Scurlock married Mamie Estelle Fearing in 1907. They had four children: Addison Jr., Robert S., George H., and Walter. Walter died at the age of two, and Addison Jr. died at the age of seventeen.

In 1907 Scurlock won a gold medal for his photography at the Jamestown Exposition, a world's fair celebrating the three hundredth anniversary of the founding of Jamestown. After operating for seven years out of his parents' house, in 1911 he opened the Scurlock Studio at 900 U Street, N.W. Although his early clientele consisted primarily of the African Americans who lived in the neighborhood near the studio, Scurlock's reputation grew. Despite discrimination in Washington, Scurlock photographed white as well as black Washingtonians, and he was frequently called upon to record the visits of prominent African Americans who traveled to the capital. He even photographed President Calvin Coolidge, an event that raised the Secret Service's concern, not because of Scurlock's race but because he physically repositioned Coolidge during the shoot.

The operation of the Scurlock Studio was a family affair. His wife, Mamie, was the manager, allowing Scurlock to focus on photography. He not only took the photographs but also used darkroom techniques that allowed him to retouch the photographs as he developed them. The historian Jane Freundel Levey described the "Scurlock look" as "a very high technical quality in which light plays evenly and attractively across the features of the subjects. ... Perhaps the most distinctive hallmark of the Scurlock photograph is the dignity, the uplifting quality of demeanor of every person, captured by photographers who saw clearly each subject as above the ordinary" (Levey, 44). Scurlock's surviving sons, Robert and George, inherited their father's love of photography; both were involved with the studio, Robert increasingly so after his World War II military service.

Though Scurlock photographed a variety of subjects and events, portraiture was his passion. When his sons entered the business, Scurlock turned over the non portraiture work to them. He treated his subjects, famous or ordinary, with the same sense of professionalism and respect, and he was able to make them look their best through his use of lighting, darkroom techniques, and retouching ability.

Scurlock is best remembered for his portraits of famous African Americans. He took exquisite photographs of BOOKER T. WASHINGTON, W. E. B. DuBois, PAUL LAURENCE DUNBAR, MARY McLEOD BETHUNE, MARY CHURCH TERRELL, and prominent whites such as First Lady Mamie Eisenhower. One of his more famous photographs is of MARIAN ANDERSON, the opera singer, on the steps of the Lincoln Memorial in 1939. Because the Daughters of the American Revolution protested her invitation to sing at Constitution Hall, Anderson sang on the steps of the Lincoln Memorial to an audience of more than seventy-five thousand people. The historian CARTER G. WOODSON commissioned Scurlock to photograph prominent African American leaders so that those portraits could be distributed to schools. Scurlock and his sons also took photographs for African American newspapers. Robert Scurlock said, "In the 1930s and '40s, there were few sources for black news. We filled the gap. We covered things just like the Associated Press" (Sullivan, 94). Beginning in the early 1930s Addison also produced newsreels about African American activities for the Lichtman Theatres, which catered to African American audiences.

In 1948 Robert and George used the skills learned from their father to open the Capital School of Photography. Although it closed in 1952, they had several students who went on to become photographers with prominent newspapers. Among their students was Jacqueline Bouvier, who met her future husband, then the senator John F. Kennedy, during an assignment. After the school closed, Robert opened his own shop, experimenting in the use of color photography.

Robert bought Scurlock Studios shortly before his father's death in 1964. It was not until 1976 that Addison Scurlock's work was exhibited in a one-artist show at the Corcoran Gallery of Art in Washington, D.C. After Robert's death in 1994, his father's portfolio became part of the Smithsonian Museum of American History.

Addison Scurlock recorded the lives of many prominent African Americans, while passing on a legacy of photography that influenced not only his sons but also other African American and white photographers. Some of Scurlock's photographs came to national attention with the issuing of the Black Heritage series of stamps. In 1996 the nineteenth stamp in the series was a reproduction of Scurlock's photograph of the marine biologist ERNEST EVERETT JUST. This stamp was the first reprint of a photograph rather than a drawing. Another Scurlock photograph, of the entrepreneur MADAM C. J. WALKER, became the twenty-first stamp in the series in 1998.

FURTHER READING

The Scurlock collection, including photographs by both Addison Scurlock and his sons, is in the Smithsonian Institution National Museum of American History's archives.

Haberstitch, David. "The Scurlock 90-Year Project: Black Washington in Black America," *Exposure* 32.1 (1999): 64–73.

Levey, Jane Freundel. "The Scurlock Studio," *Washington History* 1 (Spring, 1989).

Sullivan, George. *Black Artists in Photography, 1840–1940* (1996).

Willis, Deborah. *Reflections in Black: A History of Black Photographers, 1840 to the Present* (2000).

TODD M. BRENNEMAN

Scurlock, George Hardison (19 Aug. 1919–10 Aug. 2005), photographer and entrepreneur, was born in the Freedmen's Hospital in Washington, D.C., the son of ADDISON SCURLOCK, a successful photographer and the proprietor of Scurlock Studios, and Mamie Estelle Fearing, the receptionist and business manager of Scurlock Studios. George and his three siblings grew up in Washington, not far from their father's studio, which was founded in 1911. As young men, George and his brother Robert Scurlock apprenticed with their father and developed into accomplished photographers, later taking over the family business, which they operated for more than four decades. Scurlock Studios became one of the nation's most successful black businesses. George attended Garrison Elementary and Garnett-Patterson Junior High School. All of the Scurlock children attended Dunbar High School, considered one of the top black schools in the country. Robert graduated in 1933, and Addison, who was named for his father, graduated in 1932, having served as president of the school's camera club. George, who managed the basketball team and was a member of the school's cadet team graduated in 1936. Although they had little experience working in their father's lab up to this point, all of the sons had aspirations to be photographers like their father. After high school, they attended Howard University. Both George and Robert were involved in social activities at the university while completing their studies, Robert in economics and George in business. They belonged to the Beta chapter of Alpha Phi Alpha fraternity and participated in the ROTC program. Robert graduated from Howard in 1937 and then went directly into his father's studio, where he concentrated on photo journalism and stock photography. George earned his B.S. in business administration in 1941 before joining the family business. Addison died of scarlet fever in his sophomore year.

Under the elder Scurlock's guidance, Scurlock Studies flourished as a portrait studio and as the official photographer for numerous black-owned businesses, organizations, and schools, including Howard University, their biggest client. Both George and Robert inherited their father's artistry, attention to detail, and skill in creating "the Scurlock look," which encompassed black beauty and pride. During the war years, while Robert left to serve with the 301st Fighter Squadron in Italy, George handled most of the commercial photography work at the studio. George had completed the ROTC training program while he was at Howard but failed to pass the physical examination. When George joined the business, he covered commencements, programs, and reunions at most of the schools, while his father handled studio work, particularly graduation portraits.

When Robert returned from the war, he took advantage of the GI Bill and bought a building, opening the Capitol School of Photography in 1948. George taught evening courses while continuing to work in his father's studio during the day. The school ceased operating after only four years, but it graduated some of the top African American photographers, among them Maurice Sorrell and Elsworth Davis. Each of the Scurlocks excelled in their own area of the photographic business. Addison Scurlock Sr. was a master of many aspects of fine photography but particularly portraiture and lighting, whereas George was known for his skills in retouching and tinting, and Robert introduced color photography to the business. In 1952 Robert opened the first color photography lab in Washington and taught color photography and processing to George, who also sold cars part time to supplement his income. Addison Scurlock Sr. retired in 1963 and sold the business to his sons, who reincorporated it into two divisions under the name Custom Craft Studios. The Scurlock Studio division continued to handle photography assignments, and the Custom Craft division covered the lab work of processing and printing. George left the business to become a full-time sales associate for a Chrysler Plymouth dealership, where he also excelled and was named to the Chrysler National Sales Honor Society. Robert died in 1994. George retired in 1996 and died in 2005. Throughout its existence of more than eighty years, Scurlock Studios recorded a vibrant local African American community and captured internally, nationally, and locally known figures and events. Among the many subjects photographed by George Scurlock are THURGOOD MARSHALL and the former mayor of Washington, D.C., Walter Washington. His most notable work is the photographic coverage of Senator John F. Kennedy on the campus of Howard University during his 1960 campaign for the presidency, the most requested series of images from the studio's operations.

FURTHER READING

The Scurlock Collection, containing business records, negatives, equipment, and more than 250,000 images is in the Archives Center of the Smithsonian Institution National Museum of American History.

Smithsonian National Museum of American History. "Portraits of a City: The Scurlock Photographic Studio's Legacy to Washington, DC," http://americanhistory.si.edu/archives/scurlock/index.html.

Willis, Deborah, and Jane Lusaka, eds. *Visual Journal: Harlem and D.C. in the Thirties and Forties* (1996).

Obituary: Holley, Joe. "George H. Scurlock Dies at 85: Photographer to Black Society," *Washington Post,* 16 Aug. 2005.

DONNA M. WELLS

Seale, Bobby (22 Oct. 1936–), cofounder of the Black Panther Party, was born Robert George Seale in Dallas, Texas. His mother, Thelma (maiden name unknown), raised Bobby, as well as his brother, sister, and cousin, while his father, George Seale, worked as a carpenter throughout Texas. Seale recalled that his father was often absent, and, when home, would often beat him. During World War II, after moving throughout Texas, the family moved

Bobby Seale in New Haven, Conn., on 28 May 1971, after being freed after serving 21 months in prison. (AP Images.)

to Oakland, California, where George Seale opened his own store.

Seale enlisted in the air force as a sheet metal mechanic at age eighteen and was stationed in South Dakota. After almost four years, he was dishonorably discharged following a dispute with a colonel, in part because he owed money to a relative of the officer. After returning to Oakland, Seale worked as an aircraft mechanic, a draftsman, and as a comedian and jazz drummer. In 1960, after spending eighteen months in Los Angeles, he enrolled in Merritt College in West Oakland and supported himself by working for a government antipoverty program. Though his original interest was in engineering, Seale soon immersed himself in studying black history. He also married Artie, his nineteen-year-old girlfriend, with whom he had a son, Malik; they separated several years

later as Seale became more involved in civil rights organizing. At Merritt he joined the black nationalist Afro-American Association, where he met his fellow student HUEY NEWTON. They soon became dissatisfied with the organization's emphasis on "cultural nationalism" and developed an interest in establishing a more radical nationalist agenda influenced by the black Martiniquean intellectual Frantz Fanon, author of *Wretched of the Earth*. Like Fanon, Seale and Newton envisaged a nationalism that not only promoted black unity but also highlighted the struggle against racial oppression and economic inequality. With this new perspective, Newton and Seale helped found the Soul Student Advisory Council, which organized a protest on campus against the military conscription of blacks.

Both admired the uncompromising attitude and militancy of MALCOLM X, whom Seale had heard speak in Oakland, and Malcolm's assassination in 1965 spurred them to continue organizing to defend the rights of black people. In early 1966 Newton, a law student, decided to observe the police in order to publicize their violations of the rights of blacks. Seale and Newton developed a distinctive uniform of leather jackets and black berets. More significantly, inspired by the dissident North Carolina NAACP leader ROBERT F. WILLIAMS, the author of *Negroes with Guns* (1962), they began carrying guns for self-defense. (According to California law at the time, carrying loaded weapons was legal so long as they were not concealed.)

In the spring of 1966 police arrested Seale and Newton in Berkeley for fighting the police at an antiwar rally; after pleading no contest, they were each sentenced to a year of probation. In October they formed the Black Panther Party in Oakland, which they named after the symbol of the Lowndes County Freedom Organization, which had been organized by civil rights activists in Alabama. The Panthers' initial ten-point program focused on the oppression of black people in the urban North, particularly problems of unemployment, poor housing, police brutality, and bad schools. The first point read: "We want freedom. We want power to determine the destiny of our black community." The tenth point began, "We want land, bread, housing, education, clothing, justice, and peace." Adapting Fanon's perspective to American conditions, the early Panthers placed a heavy emphasis on organizing poor blacks, the "lumpen proletariat" or the "brothers on the block," as they were known in Panther parlance. Within three years the Panthers grew into a national organization, with offices in the Midwest and Northeast as well as California. They soon developed an eclectic ideology, mixing black nationalism with socialism, and drawing not only from Fanon, but also from Cuban, Vietnamese, and Chinese socialist revolutionaries.

Almost as soon as the Panthers had become a national force, there was a concerted effort by local and federal authorities, led by COINTELPRO (the FBI's counterintelligence program), to infiltrate and weaken the group. COINTELPRO's tactics were so successful that, by the end of the decade, most Panther leaders were either dead, in jail, or in exile. In May 1967 Sacramento police arrested Seale, along with thirty other Panthers, for having protested— arms in hand—a bill that would have prohibited carrying loaded weapons. In October Newton was arrested on murder charges. Six months later, in April 1968, after a shoot-out with police left the

Panther BOBBY HUTTON dead, Panther Minister of Information ELDRIDGE CLEAVER was arrested and, by the end of the year, went into exile. In January 1969 an FBI-aggravated feud between the Panthers and a rival "cultural nationalist" organization led by MAULANA KARENGA resulted in the death of two Panthers in a gun battle on the UCLA campus. In December 1969 the Chicago Panther leaders FRED HAMPTON and Mark Clark were killed by the police.

Seale did not escape this campaign of repression. In 1968 he was among eight leftists (including the white radicals Tom Hayden, Abbie Hoffman, and Jerry Rubin) who were arrested for protesting at the Democratic National Convention in Chicago. Ironically, Seale was not involved in the planning of the protests, but had merely substituted for Cleaver. After having his case separated from the other defendants', and after he had spent two years behind bars, the authorities ultimately dropped the charges against Seale. The case was most memorable, however, for the remarkable treatment of Seale during the trial. Prior to trial, Seale's attorney was hospitalized; instead of granting a delay in the case, the judge insisted that the trial go ahead, but refused Seale the right to defend himself. When Seale insisted on his right to cross-examine witnesses, the judge had him bound and chained to his chair. For many, Seale's treatment illustrated the deep-rooted racism of the American justice system. While on trial in Chicago, Seale was also indicted for the 1969 killing of a former Panther, Alex Rackley, in New Haven, Connecticut. Rackley, the prosecution argued, had been suspected of being a police informer by the Panthers. Seale, along with thirteen other Panthers, was arrested. On the basis of testimony of a Panther rumored to be an informer himself, the prosecution claimed that Seale, who had been in New Haven as part of a lecture tour, had ordered local Panthers to torture and kill Rackley. Convinced that this was part of the government's campaign to destroy the Panthers, many students at nearby Yale University protested the trial by calling the university's first student strike. Even Yale's president declared that it was impossible for black militants like Seale to receive a fair trial amid the racist, antiradical hysteria created by the police and the prosecution. On 1 May 1970 some twelve thousand people protested Seale's trial and the court's refusal to grant him bail. After a six-month-long trial in 1970–1971, three of the "New Haven Nine" were convicted, but Seale and his codefendant ERICKA HUGGINS, whose connections to Rackley's death were tenuous at best, were released after the jury returned a hung verdict and the judge ruled that a fair trial was impossible.

The government's relentless repression of the Panthers aggravated tensions within the organization. Newton and Seale sought to strengthen the Panthers by launching community initiatives, such as its famous free-breakfast program. They also sought allies among white liberal intellectuals. Cleaver, in exile in Algeria, emphasized traditional, revolutionary Panther rhetoric, and the party began to split. In 1973 Seale ran for mayor of Oakland and came in second among nine candidates.

Seale soon drifted out of politics, however, and left the Black Panther Party in 1974. He married the former Panther Leslie M. Johnson, with whom he had a son and a daughter, and he maintained his interest in helping the black community, though no longer as a radical activist. During the mid-1980s he worked with Youth Employment Strategies in Philadelphia, Pennsylvania, encouraging young people to work and to continue their education. In 1988 he wrote a cookbook, *Barbeque'n with Bobby Seale*, and he has also marketed his own barbecue sauce. He lectures widely, both on the history of the Panthers and on his theory of social change, which he termed "polylectic reality" and "cooperational humanism."

FURTHER READING

Freed, Donald. *Agony in New Haven: The Trial of Bobby Seale, Ericka Huggins, and the Black Panther Party* (1973).

Seale, Bobby. *Seize the Time: The Story of the Black Panther Party* (1970).

Seale, Bobby. *A Lonely Rage: The Autobiography of Bobby Seale* (1978).

JACOB ZUMOFF

Seals, Frank Son (13 Aug. 1942–20 Dec. 2004), guitarist, songwriter, and singer, was born in Osceola, Arkansas (near Memphis, Tennessee), the last of thirteen children, to Jim Seals and a mother about whom little is known. His father, known as "Old Man Son," played drums, guitar, piano, and trombone, and toured with the Rabbit Foot Minstrels (which featured such famous performers as BESSIE SMITH and MA RAINEY). Seals's mother played keyboards and sang. The elder Seals owned a roadhouse called the Dipsy Doodle. The family lived in the rear of the building, and it was there that Seals learned to play and write music. His first instrument was the piano, but he later shifted to drums and then to the guitar. The Dipsy Doodle hosted some

of the most noted blues performers of the period, including ALBERT KING, SONNY BOY WILLIAMSON, Kansas City Red, and ROBERT NIGHTHAWK. When Seals entered his teens, he began playing full time with the professional musicians at his father's club. In his first group, Son Seals and the Upsetters, formed in 1959, he played a Sears Silvertone guitar that his father had purchased for him. Seals toured the Arkansas region with the group. He also went on the road as a drummer with King and EARL HOOKER's Roadmasters. When at home Seals played as a backup guitarist or drummer at his father's roadhouse. At eighteen, he started his own band in Little Rock, Arkansas.

In 1971 his father died. Seals, who was twenty-nine, moved to Chicago. He joined the famous blues scene in the Windy City. He played with BUDDY GUY, HOUND DOG TAYLOR, and JUNIOR WELLS. When Taylor left his regular show at the Expressway Lounge, Seals took his place. His first major record deal came in 1973 when he recorded for Alligator Records. Alligator released his first album that year, *The Son Seals Blues Band*. In 1977 the company released his second album, *Midnight Son*. It featured a photograph of his childhood guitar on the cover. Both albums brought him worldwide critical acclaim. Seals built on his popularity by touring widely both in the United States and in Europe. As his blues-based style evolved into one that emphasized jazz, Seals lost some of his early fans. But his 1991 album *Living in the Danger Zone* reconnected with his old blues fan base. Beginning in the late 1970s, Seals became a popular headliner for blues festivals throughout the United States and world. In addition, he recorded nine albums for Alligator and two for Telarc. He also played as a sideman on nearly one hundred albums for other artists.

Seals credited his father and King for influencing his guitar style. His father taught him the basics. Seals also recalled playing with King after hours at his father's roadhouse. Because King played his guitar left-handed and upside down, Seals did not attempt to duplicate his fingering, but rather listened to and appreciated his sound and styling. Guitarist FREDDIE KING was another one of Seals's favorite players, and he also listened intently to the records of the COUNT BASIE Orchestra, an influence evident in the number of horns and the style of the horn charts that predominated on several of Seals's albums.

Health concerns became a constant issue as Seals got older. Diabetes and its various complications affected his physical stamina beginning in the 1970s. By the 1990s his condition had worsened. Yet despite being hospitalized several times, he continued to play without informing the press of his failing health. During one of Seals's marriages, in 1997, he received national attention when his wife shot him in the jaw during an argument. Doctors reconstructed his jaw, Seals divorced his wife, and he continued to play guitar and sing. In 1999 his diabetes forced doctors to amputate his left leg, but again he persisted in performing, though he did now limit his shows to the Chicago area. Fans could find Seals every weekend in various venues on the north side of the city. His last performance was a rare trip to California in October, two months before he died.

Seals's stylistic influence in the world of rhythm-and-blues was wide. Members of the band Phish listened to Seals when they were young, later recorded one of his early tunes, and even performed with him in a series of concerts. Seals also appeared with B. B. KING and Johnny Winters on various concert tours, including regular tours in Europe. President Bill Clinton, a fellow native of Arkansas, was a Seals fan and invited him to the White House to perform for official functions. Seals inspired admiration for his live performances and his raw-edged guitar solos. He was a major draw in the Chicago blues district until the last year of his life when he could no longer perform due to complications from diabetes. Seals had fourteen children from his marriages and various relationships.

During his career, Seals received the 1985, 1987, and 2001 W. C. HANDY Awards, an honor named for the "Father of the Blues" recognized as the equivalent of the Grammy Awards for blues music. He also was nominated for a Grammy in 1981 for the album *Blues Deluxe*.

FURTHER READING

Danchin, Sebastian. *American Made Music Series: Earl Hooker, Blues Master* (2001).

Davis, Francis. *The History of the Blues* (2003).

Emery, Mike. "Son Seals: Dues-Paying Bluesman Perseveres," *Blues Access* 45 (Spring 2001).

Obituaries: *Chicago Sun-Times* and *New York Times*, 22 Dec. 2004.

PAMELA LEE GRAY

Seals, Willie Brown (22 Nov. 1910–19 Apr. 1995), minister, musician, and photographer, was born in Bayou Rapides, Louisiana, to Irene Lair and Giuseppe "Joe" Nasello. Nasello, who immigrated to the United States from his native Sicily in 1901, owned a dry goods store in Alexandria, Louisiana, that Willie remembered visiting with his mother from time to time. However, Joe Nasello had another family, and given the mores of the time, "Papa" Joe never acknowledged the two children he fathered with Irene. (A daughter, Alice, was born in 1912.) Although Joe Nasello lived until 1958, it appears that father and son never met face to face nor openly acknowledged their relationship. Seals talked freely yet sparingly of his paternity, and he jokingly noted to his children that he was an "Italian."

According to Willie, "Seals" was a made-up name that he took from Lucille Ceil, a favorite grade school teacher. Initially he spelled his name Seal and later added the "s" because he believed it sounded better.

Seals and Alice grew up in the Louisiana cities of Alexandria and Lake Charles. He attended schools in both cities, but given the low value placed on education for black children, and perhaps the needs of his single mother, he dropped out of school after the sixth grade. Yet he was an inquisitive and intelligent child and pursued knowledge throughout his life. He perfected his reading skills by reading the newspapers used to wallpaper the shanty home that he shared with his mother and sister. As a result he was often able to read materials that his older classmates found too difficult to read. In later years he applied the same diligence to mastering the tenets in his chosen fields of ministry, music, and photography.

At an early age Seals demonstrated musical ability and was allowed to take piano lessons with a local teacher. He quickly became an adept musician who mastered classical pieces as well as gospel and spirituals. In his early twenties Willie was asked to be the choral director, pianist, and organist for several area churches in Alexandria. He also gave music lessons in his home or in those of his pupils throughout his life.

Seals and Nettie Mae Patterson, a childhood sweetheart, were married in 1931. They had four children. Two years later, at age twenty-three, Seals professed a calling to the ministry. Though his formal ordination did not occur until 1954, the ministry was a lifelong avocation. He served as pastor at several churches in the Alexandria area, and later in Buffalo and Niagara Falls, New York. In a 1981 interview that appeared in the *Buffalo Criterion*, an African American newspaper, Seals acknowledged that he had planned to pursue a musical career. "I felt that I had greater success in music, but I had a greater conviction for the ministry," he said. Asked if he had any regrets, Seals replied, "I later discovered that I received just as much—if not more—pleasure from the ministry as I did as a pianist" (*Buffalo Criterion*, 7 Apr. 1981).

After ten years of marriage, Seals and Nettie Mae divorced, and in an unusual ruling for the time, Seals was awarded custody of their children. In 1943 he married Clara Ellis, and they had a daughter in 1944. From 1943 until 1947 the Sealses lived in Alexandria, where, in addition to teaching piano in his home, acting as choral director and pianist for several churches, and pastoring his own church, Seals maintained a full-time job at an auto parts store.

In 1947 the Sealses relocated to Buffalo, where his sister, Alice, and their mother had moved in 1943. Although Irene Lair died in 1946, the children made Buffalo their home, and the families shared a four-room, cold-water flat at 266 Broadway. The Sealses and Alice, her husband John Jones, and their daughter Dorothy were members of Buffalo's growing post–World War II black population. In that era many southern blacks moved north in search of greater opportunity in an exodus known as the second Great Migration. Between 1940 and 1950 Buffalo's black population swelled from eighteen thousand to 36,745; by 1960 it had almost doubled from the 1950 total. Seals found work at the Chevrolet plant on River Road in Tonawanda and remained employed there for more than twenty-five years. The Sealses also had four sons during their years in Buffalo.

The Sealses joined the St. John Baptist Church, only a block away their home. At the request of the church's young people, he started a choir, the Bells of St. John, in 1948. At various times he also served as the assistant and associate pastor of the church, as well as the Bible study and Sunday school teacher.

Seals's ministry extended outside of the St. John congregation. In 1956 he assumed the pastorate of the Cold Spring Baptist Church on Glenwood and Verplanck streets. He remained there until the early 1960s, leading the congregation in retiring its mortgage debt and significantly increasing its membership. From 1981 to 1982 he was interim pastor of the New Hope Baptist Church in Niagara Falls, as well as of the New Hope Baptist Church in Buffalo. He was invited to numerous churches as a guest preacher and Bible study teacher. After his retirement he visited and ministered to sick and shut-in members of the congregations. In an April 1981 *Buffalo Criterion* article he shared his philosophy on the attributes of a good ministerial leader: the dedicated minister "is a good teacher and organizer. He should be committed to his calling and responsibilities God has placed on him."

The Reverend Seals's ministerial calling and musical skills began in Louisiana, but his interest in photography grew after his move to Buffalo. He learned to take photos, process and develop the negatives, and print the pictures. He was particularly skilled in lighting and composition. Before color photography was available, he hand painted black-and-white pictures with oil paints. He spent countless hours at his desk with a paint palette, tubes of oils, Q-tips, and cotton swabs and painstakingly detailed eyes, hair, cheeks, and jewelry. In later years he added special effects photography, such as double exposure and unusual backgrounds, to his repertoire.

Seals practiced for nearly fifty years, building a hobby into a professional business that he named Seals Ebony Studio. He documented the history of several generations of African Americans in the western New York area, from births to deaths to marriages and other celebrations, to changes in the life of a community over time. After his death in 1995 his children discovered thousands of carefully preserved, documented negatives representing a half century of photographic records; an extraordinary, intact collection portraying an African American community seen through the lens of an African American.

FURTHER READING

Nevergold, Barbara A. Seals. "Fantastic Color and Special Effects: The Seals Ebony Studio," *Western New York Heritage Magazine* (Spring 2002).

BARBARA A. SEALS NEVERGOLD

Sealy, Lloyd (4 Jan. 1917–4 Jan. 1985), police officer, was born Lloyd George Sealy in New York City, the second of three brothers to Henry Sealy, an apartment building custodian, and Lilian Augustus clarke. Lloyd Sealy's parents, both natives of Barbados, named him for Britain's prime minister during World War I, David Lloyd George. Lloyd Sealy grew up in Brooklyn. At Thomas Jefferson High School he was one of only a dozen blacks, but he served as chief justice of the students' arbitration court and in his senior year was elected president of the school's student organization. "On Lloyd you can always depend. Thru thick and thin he is your friend," read his high school yearbook.

After high school Sealy worked for several years as a railroad clerk and in the General Accounting Office in Washington, D.C. In 1942 he joined the New York Police Department (NYPD), which was only nominally integrated at the time. He began his career as a patrolman, walking the beat in the Bedford-Stuyvesant section of Brooklyn. While working full-time he earned his bachelor's degree in sociology from Brooklyn College in 1946. A year later he joined the NYPD's Youth Division, where he was promoted to sergeant. But further promotions came slowly. Not until 1959 was he made a lieutenant, seven years after he received his law degree from Brooklyn Law School. In 1963 he rose to captain, only the third black officer in the history of the NYPD to reach that rank.

On 18 July 1964 violence and disorder erupted in Harlem after a white, off-duty NYPD officer in plainclothes shot and killed a black teenager allegedly armed with a knife. The incident followed years of tension between residents and the NYPD over issues of police brutality and corruption as well as police neglect of black neighborhoods. Two days later a rally to protest the suspected murder of three civil rights workers in Mississippi, JAMES CHANEY, Andrew Goodman, and Michael Schwerner (the three had been missing since 21 June, and their bodies were found on 4 August), turned into a march on the Twenty-eighth Precinct, where officers and demonstrators clashed. For the next week street rallies in Manhattan and Brooklyn escalated into violent confrontations as police battled protesters hurling bricks and bottles. Arson and looting followed, with scores of injuries and one reported death. In the coming years similar riots occurred in Watts, Newark, and Detroit. But it was in Harlem, in the symbolic and historic heart of black America, that a new dynamic in the racial politics of the nation truly began.

In the aftermath of the civil unrest in New York in July 1964, which came to be known as the Harlem riots, Sealy became the first black officer to command a police precinct in Harlem. In August 1964 Sealy took charge of the Twenty-eighth Precinct in the center of Harlem. The *Amsterdam News*, New York's major African American newspaper, welcomed his appointment but noted that it came only after the civil unrest and community pressure. Sealy nevertheless made his presence felt quickly. A tall, slender man who kept fit by swimming and relaxed by listening to jazz and classical music, Sealy became a fixture in Harlem, striding the streets in full uniform at all hours, speaking to anyone and everyone. "I try to explain to the Negro groups the role of the policeman and why he's here," he stated, "[and I] try to show the police that this is a community of decent people with the same values and same standards as any other community, people who resent strongly any implication that they don't have these values" (*New York Times*, 15 Aug. 1964).

For the next eighteen months Sealy helped keep the peace in Harlem. Despite taunts of "Uncle Tom" from younger blacks, he promoted better police-community relations by insisting that officers treat residents with respect and follow proper procedures. "Remember," he would tell the officers under his command, "lock 'em up, don't beat 'em up" (*New York Times*, 4 Sept. 1969). Sealy also met regularly with the Harlem Unity Council, where Black Nationalists, Black Muslims, the Urban League, and small-business owners gathered to ask questions and demand action. "It gets rough," he admitted. "If you're a cop, you take a lot of hell, but it's better than having it explode in the streets" (*New York Journal-American*, 29 Aug. 1965). Under Sealy's watch the streets remained quiet even during the Watts riot in Los Angeles in August 1965.

In February 1966 Sealy was appointed assistant chief inspector, the highest rank ever attained by a black officer in the NYPD. In September of that year he achieved another first when he assumed command of Brooklyn North, which included the neighborhoods of Brownsville, downtown Brooklyn, East New York, and Bedford-Stuyvesant, where racial strife was rampant. For the next three years, while civil unrest roiled virtually every other major city in the United States, Sealy and Mayor John Lindsay frequently walked the streets, defusing tensions before they exploded. The work was difficult and dangerous. It also left Sealy exposed to pressure from every side, which he handled with patience and forbearance. On a hot night in July 1967, for instance, seventy uniformed policemen with nightsticks prepared to confront a large group of black youths. Although violence seemed imminent, Sealy kept the peace by ordering the officers to remain calm and by keeping his composure despite provocations from the crowd that included, "Take off your black mask and show us your white face" (*New York Times*, 5 Jan. 1985).

In September 1969, after he was bypassed for promotion to chief inspector, Sealy resigned from the NYPD and joined the faculty at John Jay College, where he taught in the law and political science department. An avid reader and dedicated teacher, he delighted in the opportunity to shape young minds. He was also a productive scholar who worked tirelessly to promote his vision of police work. In *The Community and the Police—Conflict or Cooperation?* (1974) Sealy and his co-author Joseph Fink wrote, "Police who continue to see themselves solely as law enforcers will remain at a distance from communities that are evolving a concept of the police that is grounded in community service" (193).

Sealy was a devoted husband and father. Prior to joining the NYPD in 1942, he married Elsie Harris; together they had four children, Margaret, James, Daisy, and Diane. In 1953 Elsie Sealy died of heart failure. In that same year Lloyd Sealy married Estelle Smith, a corrections officer who liked to observe, "Lloyd is in the business of catching wrong-doers. My line is rehabilitating them" (*New York Herald Tribune*, 15 Aug. 1964). Sealy's stepson, Estelle Smith's son Irving, later became a patrolman with the Metropolitan Transit Authority and died in 1980 while trying to stop an armed robbery.

In January 1985 Sealy suffered a heart attack at John Jay College and died on his sixty-eighth birthday. To the end he was committed to serving his students, school, and community. And he remained an inspiration to those who followed in his path. "To black officers in particular he was an inspiring model of what a top-notch policeman can be," said the police commissioner Benjamin Ward, the first black officer to head the NYPD, who added that Sealy was "tremendously valuable to this department" (*New York Times*, 5 Jan. 1985).

FURTHER READING

Sealy's papers are housed in the Lloyd G. Sealy Library at John Jay College in New York City.

Lardner, James, and Thomas Repetto. *NYPD: A City and Its Police* (2001).

Obituary: *New York Times*, 5 Jan. 1985.

MICHAEL W. FLAMM

Seaton, Willie Mae (14 July 1916–), restaurant owner and chef, was born Willie Mae Johnson in Hinds County, Mississippi, outside of Crystal Springs, the only child of Zella Moncure and Oscar Johnson, farmers. Seaton grew up immersed in a rich southern tradition of hand-me-down, unwritten recipes and culinary techniques. She described her southern upbringing in an interview with Carol Wilkinson for the *Observer Food Monthly* in 2006. "I'm a country girl," she said. "We used to raise a little cotton, corn, peanut, potatoes and all kinds of vegetables. We'd get it out and fix it up good and then peddle it in Jackson, the state capital. I learnt to cook in my mother's kitchen and I've been cooking all my life. We had a stove kitchen with a warm-up on top and those old iron pots" (Wilkinson).

At the young age of seventeen, she married L. S. Seaton, a Mississippi sharecropper, and by 1937 the couple had four small children. In 1940, leaving the children in the temporary care of relatives, the Seatons moved south to New Orleans, hoping to better their economic condition. L.S. found work in the shipyards during the day, and he soon began to drive a cab in the evenings. Willie Mae worked at a dry cleaner's business. She attended beautician's school and eventually opened up her own beauty shop. She also sometimes drove the cab during the day, while her husband worked at the shipyards.

Seaton opened her first bar on Treme Street in the heart of the Treme Faubourg District, an area especially important to the African American community. It is one of the oldest neighborhoods in New Orleans, and early in the city's history it was the main quarter for free people of color. It includes the Congo Square—originally known as the Place de Negroes—where slaves were allowed to transact business and purchase their freedom. Slaves also gathered there on Sundays to dance and socialize.

Seaton's bar was at first known simply as Willie Mae's. It was launched as a small bar but quickly gained popularity among shipyard workers. "Scotch House" was added to the original moniker after Seaton won neighborhood acclaim for her trademark cocktail of milk and Johnny Walker Black whiskey. It was a drink she concocted before she procured a beer license; she was initially restricted by a license to trade liquor only.

Sometime around 1957 Seaton moved her establishment to the corner of St. Anne and Tonti Streets across from a lot where the Phillis Wheatley Elementary School would eventually be built. This "double shotgun" house became not only the residential home for Seaton and her family but also housed a beauty shop, barber's chairs, the small bar, and a thirty-seat Creole–soul food restaurant. Scotch House customers smelled the food that Willie Mae cooked for her family and begged her to make some for them as well. The restaurant evolved from there, and by 1972 Seaton had converted the beauty salon in the front of her double shotgun home into a seven-table restaurant.

The restaurant grew in both stature and size. Despite its humble beginnings, its reputation became unimpeachable. Seaton was proud of the fact that she was never visited by the police—unless they were paying guests. Seaton also told the *Observer*: "I've never had problems with the board of health and I've never been held up or had to call the police, which they say is remarkable. If the youngsters get loud in here all I have to do is step in and look. One look does it! I don't have to say nothing" (Wilkinson). This is especially impressive considering that the Scotch House was located only blocks from the Lafitte, which was one of the city's most notorious high-crime areas.

Both Seaton and her restaurant, often referred to as simply Willie Mae's, became local legends. Seaton's fried chicken, red beans and rice, and smothered pork chops drew crowds from the neighborhood and business people from nearby downtown. "We kept business," Seaton said. "We had lawyers and judges, black and white. FATS DOMINO and all the big shots came through here. … I can't keep them out of my kitchen, they have to come and speak to me. They're like family to me" (Wilkinson). Seaton has even received praises from New Orleans mayor C. Ray Nagin, a frequent midday diner. "I can assure you that she does, in fact, cook the best fried chicken in America" (Price).

From 1957 through 2005 Seaton kept a demanding schedule, opening at 11:30 A.M. and not closing until around 5:00 P.M. To prepare for the opening, Seaton rose at 5:00 A.M. each day. As demanding as this schedule was, she had no plans to retire or slow down. In her interview with Wilkinson in the *Observer*, Seaton said: "God makes the plans for when I stop cooking. I work so much. I'm a workaholic. I never get tired" (Wilkinson).

Food critics eventually discovered Willie Mae's and brought fame to the restaurant. In the spring of 2005 Seaton won the prestigious James Beard Foundation Restaurant Award, the restaurant world's equivalent of an Oscar. Her Scotch House was also honored with the James Beard Foundation America's Classics Award, which recognizes restaurants that are revered by their communities.

On 29 August 2005 Hurricane Katrina struck, severely affecting both Seaton's life and her restaurant. Hurricane Katrina was one of the costliest (both monetarily and emotionally) and deadliest hurricanes in U.S. history. The hurricane and its aftermath were particularly devastating to the Treme District of New Orleans. The Scotch House was almost completely destroyed. The storm and ensuing floodwater left only a hulk of an old stove, a few gallons of unopened vegetable oil, and a shrine to Jesus.

After spending several weeks in September 2005 at motels in Louisiana and Texas, Seaton booked her own flight back to New Orleans and took a cab into the city to check on her business. Flooded with four feet of water, the building was ruined. Seaton had little savings and no insurance, so at first it seemed doubtful Willie Mae's would reopen. However, volunteers from New Orleans and across the country stepped to the forefront. The Heritage Conservation Network, a preservation group based in Colorado, raised funds to restore and refurbish the 1890s structure. In addition the Southern Foodways Alliance, based at the University of Mississippi, put out a call for helpers. Over one hundred volunteers answered the call to clean out Willie Mae's. Once work started, the workers discovered that the house had serious termite damage and that part of the building was not built to code. Clifton James, principal owner of the architectural and engineering firm Clifton C. James and Associates, donated free professional services to help to rebuild Willie Mae's Scotch House better than before. This volunteer effort was captured in the thirty-minute documentary *Scotch and Milk: Saving Willie Mae's Restaurant* (2007), which was later renamed *Above the Line: Saving Willie Mae's Scotch House*, directed by Joe York of the University of Mississippi Center for Documentary Projects and shown at the Oxford Filmfest.

In May 2007 the Scotch House joined the other members of the New Orleans restaurant community in collectively accepting the James Beard Foundation Humanitarian of the Year Award. The award was given in part because city restaurant owners had banded together to feed the police and aid workers after Hurricane Katrina and also in recognition of how the restaurants used southern cooking to regenerate the city. In mid-2007 Seaton's efforts to reopen were thwarted by the costs of expensive upgrades needed for old-line neighborhood spots, such as the Scotch House, to meet modern health code standards, but by late 2007 the restaurant was open, operated by Seaton's great-granddaughter.

FURTHER READING
Levine, Ed. "New Orleans: 'Food Is What We're All About,'" *BusinessWeek* (27 Mar. 2000).
Price, Todd A. "Food News," *Gambit Weekly* (17 May 2005).

Severson, Kim. "Can New Orleans Save the Soul of Its Food?" *New York Times* (11 Jan. 2006).

Wilkinson, Carol. *Observer Food Monthly* (28 May 2006).

YVONNE L. HUGHES

Seay, Richard (Dick) (30 Nov. 1904–6 Apr. 1981), Negro League baseball player and soldier, was born in West New York, New Jersey. Seay's family was the only black family in the community, and Seay was accidentally marked as white on his birth certificate. He worked as a batboy with local New York baseball clubs and quit high school after one year to pursue a career in the game.

In 1924 he broke into Negro League baseball with the Philadelphia Giants. He would play only one season there before signing in 1925 with both the Pennsylvania Red Caps of New York and the Brooklyn Royal Giants. Both were lower-echelon Negro League teams, and neither played full seasons. In 1926 Seay signed with the Baltimore Black Sox of the Eastern Colored League, which competed for the Negro League World Series. Seay and the team struggled in 1926. He played shortstop, hitting .160, and the Black Sox finished the season with twenty-three wins and thirty-six losses. The next year he returned to the Brooklyn Royal Giants, but continued to struggle at the plate. He was released in 1928 by the club because of his erratic throwing arm.

That same year, Seay signed on with "CHAPPIE JOHNSON's All-Stars." Chappie Johnson was a catcher in the Negro Leagues at the turn of the century but was better known for his coaching. He converted Seay into a second baseman, a position in which Seay would thrive. Before the 1928 season ended, the Brooklyn Royal Giants resigned him. As a second baseman, Seay turned his career around. His release from the Royal Giants, and his subsequent position change, ignited his baseball career.

Seay played with the Brooklyn Royal Giants until 1931 and did not consistently hit much higher than .200. Those statistics, however, belie Seay's offensive production. He handled the bat exceedingly well, was an excellent bunter, and was adept at executing hit-and-runs. It was in the field, however, that Seay made his greatest contribution. He was one of the best second basemen in the Negro Leagues at turning a double play, and his acrobatic fielding made him a crowd favorite. Like many Negro League players, Seay played winter ball in Latin America. In Puerto Rico, he became a national hero because of his strong play as well as his behavior off the field. Seay neither used profane language nor drank much.

Seay, earning only $175 a month, left the Royal Giants in 1931 because of penny-pinching management. The second baseman signed on again with the Baltimore Black Sox and enjoyed two of his best offensive years, batting over .300 in both 1932 and 1933. In 1934 Seay played for the Philadelphia Stars. The team won the Negro League Championship that year, and Seay was named to his first All-Star team. The following year, Seay moved to the Pittsburgh Crawfords. He played second base for the club in both the 1935 and 1936 seasons. The Crawfords won the Negro League Championship in both.

In 1937 Seay played second base for the Newark Eagles. The Eagles infield was dubbed "the million dollar infield" and was regarded as one of the finest infields ever assembled in Negro League baseball. Seay played for the Eagles until halfway through the 1940 season when he moved to the New York Black Yankees. In 1940 and 1941 Seay was selected as an All-Star.

In 1943 Seay was inducted into the military. After his discharge, he rejoined the Black Yankees before retiring in 1947 at the age of forty-three and with over twenty years of experience in the Negro Leagues. SATCHEL PAIGE, the Negro League pitcher and Major League Baseball Hall of Fame inductee, would later declare Seay as the greatest second baseman in the history of the Negro Leagues.

Seay died in his home in Jersey City, New Jersey, at the age of seventy-five.

FURTHER READING

Holway, John B. *The Complete Book of Baseball's Negro Leagues* (2001).

Riley, James A. *The Biographical Encyclopedia of the Negro Baseball Leagues* (1994).

LOU MANZO

Sebastian, Simon Powell (10 June 1879–24 June 1937), organist, stenographer, college professor, physician, and hospital founder, was born in St. John, Antigua, British West Indies, the son of John Sebastian and Sara Elizabeth Roberts. He studied at Antigua's Mico College, a normal school established for blacks by Lady Mico Trust, where he studied a rigorous curriculum that included English, Latin, Greek, mathematics, science, astronomy, history, and geography. Sebastian, like many of the students at Mico College, viewed his normal training as preparation for a career other than teaching.

In 1901 Sebastian immigrated to the United States. After arriving in Philadelphia, he obtained employment as a stenographer and an organist. A year later he moved to Greensboro, North Carolina, to work at the Agricultural and Mechanical College (later North Carolina A&T State University). Sebastian, who was broadly educated in the Caribbean, taught English, geography, foreign languages, and mathematics and was also assistant to President James Benson Dudley.

In 1907 Sebastian applied to Leonard Medical School of Shaw University in Raleigh, North Carolina. Shaw University, the oldest historically black college in the South, was largely responsible for educating black professionals around the beginning of the twentieth century, especially in law, medicine, and pharmacy. In 1908 Sebastian left his faculty position at A&M College to pursue a medical degree full time. At Leonard he took a four-year curriculum during a time when the state's white medical schools offered a less rigorous two-year program. During the first and second years of study, Sebastian studied chemistry, anatomy, physiology, bacteriology, pathology, pharmacology, toxicology, minor surgery, physical diagnosis, and hygiene and practice. In 1912 Sebastian graduated from Leonard Medical School with an M.D. and became the first intern at St. Agnes Hospital in Raleigh. St. Agnes Hospital was located on the campus of St. Augustine's College, a historically black college in Raleigh supported by the Episcopalian Church. After completing a short internship, Sebastian returned to A&M College to become the campus physician, a position he held for the next twenty-five years. He also established a private practice as a physician and general surgeon in Greensboro on East Market Street, a thriving area for black business owners during this time. On 27 December 1915 Sebastian married Martha Josephine Oxford, a librarian at the Carnegie Negro Library on the campus of Bennett College for Women. They had two children.

Sebastian and fellow Greensboro physicians Charles Constantine Stewart and John Walter Vincent Cordice recognized the need to establish a hospital for the city's African American residents. All three of the doctors had immigrated to the United States from the British West Indies around the beginning of the century with the hope of obtaining a medical education. Stewart, a native of Jamaica, and Cordice, a native of St. Vincent, both received their medical training at Howard University Medical School, the nation's oldest medical school for African Americans. Both Stewart and Vincent graduated from Howard in 1911, but it was not until 1912 that they moved to Greensboro to join Sebastian. They found only six beds available to African American patients at the predominantly white St. Leo's Hospital. In 1918 Sebastian, Stewart, and Cordice addressed this disparity by founding Trinity Hospital on East Market Street. The facility provided a critical service to Greensboro's African American citizens, but it was much too small to adequately address the wide spectrum of health issues faced by its constituents. In 1918 Sebastian also joined the U.S. Public Health Service, and he remained a member until 1923.

Sebastian, Stewart, and Cordice realized the need for a larger, more expansive facility. In 1923 the trio formed the Greensboro Negro Hospital Association along with fifty-eight other concerned citizens. Shortly thereafter the association launched a campaign to raise $100,000 to build a new hospital. The group appealed to Mary Lynn Richardson, whose husband Lunsford Richardson had founded Vick Chemical Company. Richardson and her son, H. Smith Richardson, awarded the group $50,000 toward the new hospital. Other benefactors included Estelle Sternberger, who donated $10,000 for the X-ray and operating rooms, and C. D. Benbow Jr. and A. L Brooks, who donated five acres of land valued at $10,000 for the site of the proposed building.

On 18 May 1927 the Greensboro Negro Hospital opened on the corner of Benbow Road and East Washington Street with sixty beds. Sebastian was named superintendent, medical director, and resident physician of the hospital. He built a large, Gothic Tudor–style home across the street from the hospital so he could be nearby. Prior to the opening of the hospital, as many as half of the African American women in Greensboro received no prenatal or postpartum care. On average the hospital served four thousand patients annually. Under Sebastian's leadership, the hospital was fully accredited by the American Medical Association and the American College of Physicians.

The hospital served as an important training facility for Greensboro's African American health professionals for many years. In 1929 the Greensboro Negro Hospital established a nurses training school. Geneva S. Collins, a graduate of St. Agnes Hospital and Nurses Training School in Raleigh, served as the director, and Sebastian was the school's resident physician. The school graduated 152 nurses from its inception in 1930 until its closing in 1954. In 1954 five of Greensboro's six black doctors had completed their internships and residencies at L. Richardson Hospital, one of the few facilities in the country where medical interns took a fifth course in medicine and surgery.

Sebastian held memberships in a number of professional organizations, including the National Medical Association and the local affiliate, the Old North State Medical, Dental, and Pharmaceutical Association. The National Medical Association, a professional organization for African American physicians, dentists, and pharmacists, was founded in 1895, when only white medical professionals were eligible for membership in the American Medical Association. Sebastian was also active in such civic organizations as the Elks and the Masons.

On 24 June 1937 Sebastian was killed accidentally when his car was struck by a fire engine in front of his home. In 1953 the trustees of North Carolina A&T State University voted unanimously to name the campus infirmary in honor of his many contributions to medicine, the city of Greensboro, and the campus community.

FURTHER READING

Durham, Diana K. "Leonard Medical School: The Making of African American Physicians," *Carolina Peacemaker*, 16 Feb. 2006.

Elkins, W. O. "The History of L. Richardson Memorial Hospital, Greensboro, N.C.," *Journal of the National Medical Association* 30, no. 4 (1969).

Phillips, Robert L. *History of the Hospitals in Greensboro, N.C.: Including the Sanitariums, Infirmaries, and Institutes* (1996).

Thompson, Thelma B. *The Jamaican Teachers' Colleges: Resources from and for a Country, The Journal of Negro Education* 56, no. 3 (1987).

DIANA KRISTINE DURHAM

Sebree, Charles (16 Nov. 1914–27 Sept. 1985), painter, dancer, playwright, and set designer, was born in White City, Kentucky, to parents whose names and occupations are unknown. John Robinson, a coal miner uncle with an interest in drawing and painting, encouraged young Sebree's artistic talents. "Robinson tutored Charles in drawing by having him sketch pictures with a stick in the soil and taught him how to make little figures of men out of mud and twigs" (Marshall, 3). In 1924, when Sebree was ten years old, he and his mother joined the flood of African Americans

moving north in the Great Migration. They settled in Chicago, where the preadolescent Sebree soon launched himself into the city's thriving cultural scene.

An elementary school teacher jumpstarted Sebree's career when she showed his artwork to members of the University of Chicago's Renaissance Society. The group was impressed enough with the fourteen-year-old's work to pay Sebree $25 and put his drawing *Seated Boy* on the cover of their magazine. But Sebree was living alone, struggling to support himself, although he was still intent on pursuing his artistic goals. In 1932 he graduated from high school and began to study at the School of the Art Institute of Chicago and the Chicago School of Design.

During the 1930s Sebree befriended intellectuals of local, national, and international importance. In 1933 he met KATHERINE MARY DUNHAM, an innovator in modern American dance. Sebree designed sets and costumes for Dunham's dance company and eventually became one of the dancers. He also designed costumes and worked at the South Side Community Art Center (SSCAC) with Dunham's husband, John Pratt. The SSCAC, located in Chicago's historically black South Side neighborhood, included a talented roster of African American artists who took classes and exhibited in its space during the 1930s. Under the tutelage of some of the most successful black artists in Chicago, Sebree created paintings done in pastel shades of egg tempura paint. Already present in his work were the images of harlequins, clowns, and wide-eyed figures that interested him throughout his career. In 1935 Sebree held his first solo show at the Randolph Galleries in Chicago.

From 1936 to 1938 Sebree worked for a Depression-era public art program at the Works Progress Administration, which brought him into contact with many of Chicago's leading white artists. Friends soon introduced Sebree to novelist and playwright Thornton Wilder, who supported Sebree emotionally and financially by writing him encouraging letters and paying him a small stipend.

ALAIN LOCKE, a Howard University professor and one of the primary thinkers behind the Harlem Renaissance, met Sebree in the late 1930s. Sebree was one of the youngest artists to receive mention in Locke's 1940 book, *The Negro in Art*. Locke proved to be an invaluable friend, arranging for Sebree to illustrate *The Lost Zoo*, a children's book written by poet COUNTÉE CULLEN in 1940. Despite these friendships and his burgeoning success as an artist, Sebree lived an itinerant lifestyle for much of the 1930s, struggling with financial and emotional problems.

If the Great Depression, with its attendant economic woes and progressive public art projects, shaped Sebree's early life, America's entry into World War II ushered in the next phase of his career. In 1942 the U.S. military drafted Sebree and sent him to a segregated naval training base, Camp Robert Smalls, in northern Illinois. Living as part of a segregated group pushed Sebree to explicitly address race in his art as he never had before. Also stationed at Camp Smalls was Owen Dodson, a poet and playwright who became Sebree's lifelong friend. Together they wrote and produced plays designed to raise the morale of the camp's enlisted men. The best known of these, *Ballad of* DORIE MILLER, told the story of a black sailor who acted heroically during Japan's attack on Pearl Harbor on 7 December 1941. The play appeared in February of 1943. Sebree responded to Miller's story again at the end of 1943 when he painted *Boys Without Penises*. The three boys in the painting have been said to represent Sebree, Dodson, and Miller (Finch, 20).

After leaving the U.S. Navy under rather nebulous circumstances, Sebree resumed his place on the art circuit. From the 1940s onward Sebree felt a deep distrust for gallery owners. He felt that gallery owners who bought his work outright made large profits by then reselling his work for much higher prices than they paid him and thus began organizing the sale of his art from his own home. Some of his collectors were also his close friends. For a man whose life was crowded with people, activities, and ideas, Sebree remained circumspect about his personal life. Scholars have stated that Sebree was gay, but the extent to which his sexual orientation shaped some of his closest male friendships has not been determined.

During the 1950s Sebree designed sets for more plays written by Dodson and befriended a young TONI MORRISON, then a student at Howard University. In 1954 he wrote a play, *Mrs. Patterson*, which opened on Broadway one year later with EARTHA MAE KITT in the lead role. Soon thereafter Sebree made Washington, D.C., his permanent home. Although he saw moderate successes throughout his life in many fields, Sebree also regularly encountered financial difficulties. Asked late in life why his paintings became noticeably smaller midway through his career, Sebree replied, "I didn't have a studio. I painted in the kitchen, and my

paintings had to conform to the space available. I also needed to be able to collect my things quickly and move if I wasn't able to come up with the rent" (Shine, 8).

As Sebree entered the 1960s, his lifestyle slowed down and his temper cooled. Still passionate about his art, Sebree continued painting up until his death from cancer in 1985 in Washington, D.C. A dynamic man whose interests ranged from painting to writing to set design to dance, Sebree could count some of the twentieth century's leading African American artists among his friends and artistic collaborators.

FURTHER READING

Finch, Tony. "Charles Sebree's *Boys without Penises*: a hermetic self-portrait?" *International Review of African American Art* (2002).

Marshall, Melvin, and Blake Kimbrough. "Above and Beyond Category: The Life and Art of Charles Sebree," *International Review of African American Art* (2002).

Obituary: *Washington Post*, 7 Oct. 1985.

ANGELA R. SIDMAN

Sedric, Gene (17 June 1907–3 Apr. 1963), jazz tenor saxophonist and clarinetist, was born Eugene P. (or Hall) Sedric in St. Louis, Missouri, the son of Paul Sedric, a ragtime pianist. Nothing is known of his mother. Sedric, who began playing clarinet around age ten, joined Charlie Creath's band at the Alamac Hotel in St. Louis in early 1922, and later worked on the riverboats and at other locations with the bands of FATE MARABLE, Dewey Jackson, and Ed Allen. A job playing in the traveling burlesque show *Black and White Revue* took him in late 1923 to New York City, where he freelanced until joining SAM WOODING's Orchestra at the Club Alabam.

In May 1925 he sailed to Europe with Wooding as a member of the *Chocolate Kiddies* revue, which opened on 25 May at the Admiralspalast in Berlin. Besides Sedric, the eleven-piece band included the trumpeter Tommy Ladnier, the trombonist Herb Flemming, and the multireedman Garvin Bushell. In addition to the band the show boasted more than thirty singers and dancers from the worlds of vaudeville, musical comedy, and cabaret, including the future stars ADELAIDE HALL and EDITH GOODALL WILSON. After leaving Berlin, *Chocolate Kiddies* appeared in Hamburg, Stockholm, Copenhagen, Zurich, Barcelona, Paris, Nice, and in Moscow and Leningrad for more than two months between March and May 1926.

So popular was the band that in virtually every country it visited the troupe was asked to stage command performances before royalty and heads of state. After leaving Russia the show concluded its tour in Danzig, but Wooding's band remained intact and moved on to play concerts and residencies in Turkey, Egypt, Romania, Hungary, and other neighboring countries. In the spring of 1927 the orchestra sailed from France to Argentina for a brief South American tour before returning to New York that summer, the most widely traveled jazz-oriented orchestra in the world. Among the offers the band received in New York was one from the new Cotton Club, but because the men preferred to return to Europe, where they were treated like celebrities, Wooding turned down the December opening, which then went to the fledgling DUKE ELLINGTON Orchestra.

Sedric stayed with Wooding during the intervening period and returned to Europe in June 1928 with a band that now included DOC CHEATHAM and Ladnier on trumpets, the trombonist Al Wynn, the clarinetist Jerry Blake, and the pianist Freddie Johnson. For three years the Wooding men toured Germany, France, Scandinavia, Italy, Spain, Romania, and Turkey before finally disbanding in Belgium in the fall of 1931. After he returned to the United States Sedric continued to work with Wooding from the summer of 1932 on. He also played for a short while with both LUIS RUSSELL and FLETCHER HENDERSON before joining FATS WALLER in 1934 as a regular member of his touring and recording band. Although he remained in that capacity until 1942, during November 1937 and the winter of 1938–1939, when Waller went on solo tours, Sedric also worked with Mezz Mezzrow's Disciples of Swing and the DON REDMAN Orchestra.

In late 1942 Waller decided to concentrate exclusively on solo appearances, which contributed to Sedric's formation of his own small group in March 1943, which played at clubs in New York, Chicago, New Jersey, Boston, and Detroit. In late 1944, after recovering from an illness, he joined the Phil Moore Four for a short time and then, in late 1945, toured with the HAZEL DOROTHY SCOTT show. Sedric left Scott in the summer of 1946 and formed another band that played relatively long engagements in New York. Starting in 1950 Sedric played clarinet frequently at the Friday night all-star jazz concerts at Stuyvesant Casino and Central Plaza, and in the spring of 1951 he joined Bobby Hackett's sextet for a residency at Lou Terrasi's.

After a stint in Jimmy McPartland's band Sedric returned to France in February 1953 to tour with Mezzrow. In August 1953 he again appeared at Central Plaza, this time with the film actor and trombonist Conrad Janis, in whose band he remained on and off until late 1961, at which time he became too ill to continue playing. He died in New York's Goldwater Memorial Home.

Primarily because of his extended absences from New York during the mid- and late-1920s and the scarcity of new American jazz records overseas, Sedric's style on clarinet and saxophone remained rooted in the syncopations of his most formative years. Thus, although smoothly played in the conventional dance band manner, his saxophone solos on the Wooding records from 1925 through 1929, as recorded in Berlin, Barcelona, and Paris, scarcely compare with the contemporaneous work of COLEMAN HAWKINS or PRINCE ROBINSON in the United States. Wooding wanted his orchestra to combine the best elements of Paul Whiteman and Fletcher Henderson; that is, to have the versatility to play symphonic overtures, classically arranged "American" themes, and novelty popular songs, yet also to be able to incorporate the rhythmic vitality and improvising skills of the best African American hot dance music. To be sure, some of Wooding's arrangements come close to the mark of the best early big band jazz, but the majority is of the sort that most bands played to satisfy the tastes of polite society. From 1934 on Sedric participated in scores of recording sessions, most with Waller, but also several with Alex Hill, Redman, JAMES P. JOHNSON, Pat Flowers, Cliff Jackson, McPartland, Janis, Louis Metcalf, and others. In 1953, as a member of Mezzrow's band in Paris, he recorded in concert with BUCK CLAYTON and Big Chief Moore. He last appeared on record in 1961 on sessions by Dick Wellstood and ELMER SNOWDEN.

There is no doubt that Sedric enjoyed a far better lifestyle playing in Europe during the twenties than did many of his colleagues back home. But from a strictly musical point of view, he paid a price for it. Because of Wooding's commercial obligations, little time was devoted to hot jazz, either in the form of swinging arrangements or creative solo improvisation. Similarly, in his eight years with Waller, Sedric merely served as a backdrop for the ebullient singer and pianist. Although he soloed on almost all of Waller's many recordings from 1934 to 1942, his efforts rarely rose above the ordinary. By the same token, when he started concentrating on clarinet during the Dixieland revival of the fifties, he was at a clear disadvantage in comparison with other clarinetists who had been playing pure jazz for decades. Pee Wee Russell, EDMOND BLAINEY HALL, ALBERT NICHOLAS, and OMER SIMEON were unquestionably the preferred artists in this milieu, and Sedric had to resort to vaudevillian mugging and purposefully contrived tricks to attract the public's attention. In sum, Sedric was a reliable journeyman rather than a significant jazz stylist, one whose abilities as a showman often obscured to the public his limited gifts for creative expression.

FURTHER READING

Deffaa, Chip. *Voices of the Jazz Age* (1992).
Kirkeby, Ed. *Ain't Misbehavin': The Story of Fats Waller* (1966).
McCarthy, Albert. *Big Band Jazz* (1974).
Wright, Laurie. *Fats in Fact* (1992).
This entry is taken from the *American National Biography* and is published here with the permission of the American Council of Learned Societies.

JACK SOHMER

Séjour, Victor (2 June 1817–c. 21 Sept. 1874), playwright, was born in New Orleans, Louisiana, the son of Juan François Louis Victor Séjour Marcou, owner of a small business, and Eloisa Philippe Ferrand. His father was a black native of the West Indies, and his mother a Creole from New Orleans. Séjour attended an academy in New Orleans for the children of free men of color. As a young man he was an active member of the Artisans, a middle-class Creole society. In 1836 Séjour was sent to Paris to finish his studies. In that same year his short story "Le Mulâtre" was published in *La Revue des Colonies* (Paris). Another early literary success was a poem, "Le Retour de Napoléon," first published in Paris (Dauvain et Fontaine, 1841), then in New Orleans (H. Lauve et Compagnie, 1845).

Séjour made his playwriting debut at the Théâtre-Français on 23 July 1844 with *Dégarias*. The central character of the play—set in fifteenth-century Spain—is a persecuted Jew who must hide his identity because he married a Christian woman. This was followed by *La Chute de Séjan*, which opened at the same theater on 21 August 1849. During this time Séjour became involved in Paris literary circles that included Emile Augier, Alexandre Dumas, and Jules Janin. Like certain other Louisiana blacks, he found he could live a life in Paris relatively free of the racial prejudice

that would have hounded him in the United States.

Using Shakespeare and Victor Hugo as models, Séjour spent most of his career writing serious plays—some in verse and some in prose—that varied in genre from vast historical dramas to musical melodramas. After his initial successes at the Théâtre-Français, the bulk of his earlier plays was produced at the Porte-Sainte-Martin: *Richard III* (1852), *Les Noces Vénitiennes* (1855), *Le Fils de la Nuit* (1856), *Le Paletot Brun* (1858), *La Tireuse de Cartes* (1859), and *Les Volontaires de 1814* (1862). Like most of Séjour's plays these often revolve around relationships that are strained by religious, ethnic, or political differences. Two were produced at the Odéon—*André Gérard* (1857) and *Les Grands Vassaux* (1859). *L'Argent du Diable*, a collaboration with Jaime [Adolphe] fils, opened in 1854 at the Théâtre des Variétés. At the Théâtre Impérial du Cirque, Séjour saw two of his major spectacles mounted: *Les Massacres de la Syrie* (1860) and *La Prise de Pekin* (c. 1860).

Séjour's later plays were produced at the "Boulevard Theatres"—the Ambigu-Comique and the Gaité. The first produced *Le Martyr du Coeur* (1858), a collaboration with Jules Brésil; *Compère Guillery* (1860); *Les Mystères du Temple* (1862); and *Les Fils de Charles-Quint* (1864). At the Gaité, *Les Aventuriers* (1860) and *Le Marquis Caporal* (1864) were produced, as were two collaborations with Théodore Barrière—*Les Enfants de la Louve* (1865) and *La Madone des Roses* (1868). At the time of Séjour's death *Le Vampire* (1874) had been accepted for production at one of the two Boulevard theaters. No matter what the subject matter, the theme of tolerance was always important to Séjour.

Scholars have debated Séjour's importance during his lifetime. At least one contemporary critic, Théophile Gautier, was fond of him; another, L. Félix Savard, felt that his work—violent, unrealistic, and overwritten—exerted a "détestable influence" on the theater of his time (*Chronique Littéraire* 2 [1862]). Séjour's dramatization of the Mortara Case (in which a young Jewish girl had been kidnapped and brought up as a Christian)—*La Tireuse de Cartes*—sparked an ongoing controversy as to the political and religious (but not the ethnic) nature of the playwright. Séjour's reply was that he was a Christian who despised intolerance and a man of "sentiment" not of politics.

Several of Séjour's plays were translated and occasionally produced in other countries during the nineteenth century: *Les Noces Vénitiennes* became *The Outlaw of the Adriatic* (London), *André*

Gérard was published in Portuguese (Lisbon), and *Le Martyr du Coeur* in Turkish (Constantinople). *La Tireuse de Cartes* was published in Lisbon as *A Mulher Que Deita Cartes* and in Rotterdam as *De Kaartlegster*. *Richard III* was translated into Spanish and produced at the Teatro del Principe in Madrid just months after its Paris opening; two different Spanish versions were published shortly afterward. The play was also produced and published in New Orleans in the original French. Also in New Orleans, *Le Paletot Brun* was produced six months after its run in Paris. In the twentieth century the play was translated twice into English: once for publication (1970), and once for a New York production at Circle in the Square (1972).

Jean-François-Constant Mocquard (also known as Moquart)—playwright, Napoleon III's private secretary, and friend to Séjour—arranged for Séjour to write a trio of plays in honor of the monarch. He also wrote *André Gérard* for the great Romantic actor, Fréderick Lemaître. After the play's initial success at the Odéon in 1857, Lemaître revived the title role at the Gaité in 1861.

Séjour died in Paris of tuberculosis; he was working on *Cromwell* at the time. Almost twenty years later the critic Francisque Sarcey was still making references to him in reviews of other plays—as the representative of a style of melodramatic playwriting that the critic abhorred. Minor playwright or not, he was still a reference point for the French audience many years after his death.

Séjour's plays are best remembered for their themes of social protest, especially his concern with anti-Semitism. As well as being one of several playwrights of color in nineteenth-century Paris, such as Dumas, Séjour has come to be considered part of the growing canon of African American playwrights.

FURTHER READING

All of Séjour's plays and contemporary reviews are in Paris at the Bibliothèque Nationale.

Daley, T. A. "Victor Séjour," *Phylon: The Atlanta University Review of Race and Culture* 4 (1943).

O'Neil, Charles E. *Séjour: Parisan Playwright from Louisiana* (1996).

Peterson, Bernard L., Jr. *Early Black American Playwrights and Dramatic Writers* (1990).

This entry is taken from the *American National Biography* and is published here with the permission of the American Council of Learned Societies.

NADINE D. PEDERSON

Selby, Joe (7 Jan. 1893–5 Sept. 1960), deckhand, scow man, sailor, and marine artist, was born in Mobile, Alabama, the son of Nelson Selby and Margaret Hicks, occupations unknown. Nothing more is known of Selby's family, and little is known about his youth. By 1905, as a child of twelve, he was employed as a deckhand working the ships in Mobile Bay—schooners from ports around the Gulf of Mexico and the Caribbean. One day his leg was mangled in a snapped towline and had to be amputated. In spite of the loss he managed to engage successfully in various manual and unskilled jobs and earn a precarious living.

Selby spent some of his early working years in Baltimore, Maryland, as a scow man for the Atlantic Transport Line. Even with a peg leg he could climb a rope ladder as deftly as anyone without his disability. Nor did the work of scow man suppress his innate artistic sensibilities. He collected the discarded cardboard backing of paper pads on which tug captains recorded their daily activities and found that they served as canvas for his maritime-theme watercolors. He also discovered that his drawings would sell. His earliest known ship portrait was of the Atlantic Transport tug *Esther Phillips* (now privately owned), dated 1919. He painted portraits of ships for the Baltimore-Carolina Line and a portrait of the Merchant and Miners Line's *Berkshire* (Chesapeake Bay Maritime Museum). A portrait of *T. W. Bush* (manifesting a so-called bugeye rig, peculiar to Chesapeake Bay) is also owned by the Chesapeake Bay Maritime Museum. A painting of the 1925 steamship *Esther Weems* (Maryland Historical Society) probably marks his last commission from the Baltimore area and his subsequent move to Miami. One 1939 commission of a gaff-rigged schooner yacht inscribed on the back "T. W. Campbell Richmond Buick Company, Richmond, Virginia" suggests an interim if temporary stay in Virginia or thereabouts.

Miami had considerable appeal to both yachtsmen and Selby. It was a growing fine-weather resort, real estate was booming, particularly in 1925, and prohibition laws were not diligently enforced. Thus it provided Selby with a robust market for his talents. By the late 1920s he specialized in painting portraits of luxurious cabin cruisers and sailing yachts.

There is no direct evidence to suggest that any particular artist inspired Selby or that he had any artistic training. His artistic career, however, was similar to those of many who had come before him.

The art of the so-called pier-head painter is a long-standing worldwide phenomenon. Many thousands of ship's portraits survive in maritime museums and private collections. The practice is first attested in the Netherlands in the eighteenth century and thrived everywhere into the twentieth. Ship portraitists occupied the docks at each of the world's major port cities soliciting and obtaining commissions. There was the Roux family in Marseilles, the DeSimones in Naples, and Henry Mohrmann (1857–1913) in Antwerp. There were many in Liverpool, in the Baltic ports, and in Sydney, Rangoon, and Macao. New York and Boston had many more. Antonio Jacobsen (1849–1921), for example, working in Hoboken, New Jersey, was the most prolific of all, painting more than three thousand vessels.

In Mobile one could have seen classic ship paintings by Edward Arnold (1824–1866), James Guy Evans (active 1850), or Renfroe D. Willcox (active 1900). In Baltimore there were the primitive works of Otto Muhlenfeld (1871–1907). By coincidence Selby's work as a scow man echoed the similar employment of Evans, once a sailor in the U.S. Navy, and of Muhlenfeld, once a laborer on his father's tug. In Miami there had never been a ship portrait painter. The venue was Selby's to exploit.

Throughout his forty-year career, Selby's unique style never changed, nor is it derivative of the work of those who had gone before him. Rather than hearken back in time, it evokes the streamlined, art deco look often seen in the *Motor Boating*, *Rudder*, and *Yachting* magazines of the early twentieth century. Selby's style reflects his subject matter, the cabin cruiser that flourished as the predominant choice of leisure yachtsmen after World War I. The steam yacht had first appeared in the 1850s, had reached two hundred feet in length, required very expensive maintenance, and needed large operating crews. The less extravagant cabin cruiser with its internal combustion engine first appeared before World War I. It was much smaller, designed to be more efficient, and in many cases could be operated by one person. Whereas only those of very substantial means could own a steam yacht, the cabin cruiser, though still a luxury, was more affordable and was available to a far greater number of people. It became the staple subject of Selby's art. Neither the cabin cruiser's style nor Selby's changed significantly over the years. Even his signature remained the same, with a unique flourish that has confused some. The initial "S"

is embellished and is sometimes read as "Sh" or "C," so there are those who may think they own a painting by "Shelby" or "Celby."

There are few examples of Selby's art dating from the World War II years. There is, atypically, a 1943 portrait of a 711 subchaser (privately owned). The obvious dangers to shipping along the Atlantic coast during those years must certainly have discouraged leisure boat travel to Florida. What else Selby did during the war, obviously ineligible for service, is unknown. Since it was customary for him to date his work, it is evident that he painted continuously from 1919 to 1959. The painting of the cabin cruiser *Banshee* (privately owned), dated 1959, may have been his last.

Selby lived many years in public housing at NW 66th Street in Miami until a measure of prosperity allowed him to build a modest brick house at 22 Court Street, his last home. He never married and evidently had no local relatives. He gave regularly to a local orphanage, and those who remembered him described him as a gentle man, intelligent, and well spoken.

Selby was always the sailor and took to the sea periodically. When yachting season ended and reduced the number of painting opportunities, necessity dictated that Selby take work aboard ship. He crewed on trips to Jamaica and the Cayman Islands and would chat about his visits there. He told of having crewed aboard the 1887 steamer *Tarpon*, out of Mobile, Alabama, which was lost in a 1937 hurricane. Some thirty seamen were lost. Though no crew list survives, among those saved was one "Negro cook's helper." The Mobile Museum of History has a photo of Selby's *Tarpon* sketch, though the whereabouts of the sketch itself is unknown.

When a yachtsman came ashore at Pier 4 City Docks, Selby would ask, "Would you like me to paint your boat?" The exchange would often continue something like this:

"My boat doesn't need painting."
"No, I would like to paint a picture of your boat."
"When?"
"Right now!"

A price would be negotiated, usually around twenty-five dollars in the early years and seventy-five later on. Selby would come aboard, take measurements, return to the dock, sit on a fish rack under a shade tree near the old fire station and paint the ship's portrait. Satisfaction was guaranteed. One client recalled that the finished portrait had shown the yacht at rest. When the client said that he preferred a view at sea, Selby took back the otherwise finished work and added the foam and spray of a windswept sea. Another client recalled that his portrait depicted a port-side view and told Selby that he preferred the starboard. Selby obliged by doing another version without additional charge. Yet another client recalled sharing gin and tonics with him. Within hours after a deal had been struck, Selby would present his painting with confident self-satisfaction and collect his modest commission. He had neither gallery nor agent.

Selby's clientele included such notables as Alfred P. Sloan and Charles Kettering of General Motors, the Morgans, the Rockefellers, and the DuPonts. A portrait of T. Colman DuPont's cabin cruiser *Tech* (privately owned) survives together with a note of thanks to Captain Billsborough from President Calvin Coolidge.

There is no evidence of the effect that Selby's race had on his career. Without education—and there is no record that he received any—it followed that he would earn his way as a laborer. But his talent allowed him to enter and thrive in a world that no other black had ever entered. Selby created steadily, save for his last seventy-one days spent at the Jackson Memorial Hospital in Miami, where he died practically penniless.

FURTHER READING

Peluso, A. J., Jr. "'I Would Like to Paint a Picture of Your Boat': Joe Selby," *Maine Antique Digest* (Apr. 1991).

Potts, Erwin. "'Old Joe,' Nautical Artist, Dead at 69," *Miami Herald* (5 Sept. 1960).

Ruckert, Norman G. *Historic Center: Baltimore's Industrial Heartland ... and Its People* (1978).

"Speaking of People: Bayside Painter," *Ebony* (July 1957).

Obituary: *Miami Times*, 10 Sept. 1960.

A. J. PELUSO JR.

Selika (Marie Smith Williams) (c. 1849–19 May 1937), singer, was probably born Marie Smith in Mississippi—most sources say Natchez—and may have been born into slavery. Little is known of her youth, and nothing is known of her parentage. The historian EILEEN SOUTHERN suggested that Selika's family moved to Cincinnati, Ohio, where her vocal talent attracted the patronage of a wealthy white family, who apparently paid for singing lessons.

At some point in the early 1870s Selika moved to San Francisco. There she studied with Giovanna Bianchi, an opera singer who, along with her husband,

Eugene, gave private lessons. Selika made her debut in 1876, and the San Francisco composer Frederick G. Carnes wrote a piece titled "Selika: Grand Vocal Waltz of Magic" specifically for her a year later. The publication of this piece in 1877 suggests that she had already assumed the name under which she became famous. She apparently took the name from the character Selika in *L'Africaine*, Giacomo Meyerbeer's 1865 opera of a fictive love triangle among the Portuguese explorer Vasco da Gama, a noblewoman named Ines, and Selika, queen of Madagascar.

That Carnes dedicated his piece to Selika Williams indicates that by 1877 Selika had married Sampson Williams, a singer she met in Chicago. The couple had no children. Selika and her husband, who performed under the name Signor Velosko and was sometimes referred to as the "Hawaiian tenor," both studied with Antonio Farini in Chicago before moving east for further training.

Selika appeared at the Philadelphia Academy of Music, accompanied by Thomas Beckett, on 21 November 1878 and apparently sang portions of the opera that featured her namesake character. She opened in New York City's Steinway Hall in early May 1879. The 8 May 1879 *New York Times* reported that, while weakly accompanied, her "performance was generally credible" and she had "a voice of considerable power and musical quality." Selika, the *Times* concluded, "has every reason to expect to excel" in "the art of singing." In addition to this praise, the *Times* noted that she had secured the endorsement of the Strakosch brothers, one of whom, Maurice, was well known as the manager and early teacher of his sister-in-law, the diva Adelina Patti. Selika gave a second concert at Steinway later that month. At some point during this period she performed at the White House for President Rutherford B. Hayes.

In 1882 Selika and her husband began a European tour that stretched until 1885 and included stops from Great Britain to Russia. In October 1883 Selika gave a command performance for Queen Victoria at St. James Hall; this performance, as well as some American press coverage, enabled a successful touring schedule in the United States, the West Indies, and Europe between 1885 and the early 1890s. In addition to her tremendous vocal power, she became especially noted for technique and garnered the nickname "Queen of Staccato." She worked actively to encourage this reputation—and, more largely, her representation as a coloratura—by emphasizing vocal ornamentation (trills, runs, and the like) and regularly included E. W. Mulder's "Polka Staccato" in performances.

When in the United States and not touring, Selika and her husband lived in Cleveland. Even there Selika was in demand, and she seems to have graced a number of local events in the late 1880s, including the 1888 Centennial Jubilee of Freedom in Columbus, where she shared a bill with the young elocutionist HALLIE Q. BROWN. Some sources also suggest that, as a matter of racial pride, she had few performances in venues that excluded African Americans.

The 1890s saw what may have been two crowning moments of Selika's career, though both were marred by American racism. She performed at the 1893 Chicago World's Fair, but the performance was overshadowed by the debate on the "White City" and the racism both implicitly and explicitly expressed there. On 12 October 1896 she sang at Carnegie Hall alongside her fellow black divas SISSIERETTA JONES and FLORA BATSON. While the audience gushed with praise, the performance was also a reminder of the ways racial discrimination put the three together when none were allowed to sing a full-length opera in the city.

Such limits became more apparent as Selika aged. While Jones managed to create an uneasy balance—touring nationally well into the twentieth century with a company that featured not only her singing but also some minstrel-like elements—Selika and her husband seem to have moved away from extended touring. When Sampson Williams died in 1911, Selika settled for good in New York City. There she taught at the young Martin-Smith Music School, which had been founded by the violinist David I. Martin and the pianist Elise Smith to offer training to young black musicians; instruction was given largely by black teachers and retired performers. Selika's last major performance seems to have been in 1919 at a concert in New York given in her honor; still, as late as 1930 she listed her occupation in the federal census of Manhattan as "concert singer." She was active in teaching until her death.

Limited by her period's overarching racism, Selika nonetheless became world renowned for her talent and skill. In later years she actively shared what she had learned with a new generation of black performers.

FURTHER READING

The sheet music for Carnes's composition "Selika" and a circular for the Centennial Jubilee are in the Library of Congress.

"Black Prima Donnas of the Nineteenth Century," *Black Perspectives in Music* 7 (Spring 1979).

Hitchcock, H. Wiley, and Stanley Sadie, eds. "Selika," in *New Grove Dictionary of American Music* (1986).

New York Times, 8 May 1879.

New York Times, 25 May 1879.

"Selika and the Color Line." *Cleveland Gazette*, 20 Oct. 1888.

Southern, Eileen. *The Music of Black Americans: A History*, 2d ed. (1983).

ERIC GARDNER

Sellers, Cleveland L., Jr. (8 Nov. 1944–), civil rights leader and educator, was born and grew up in Denmark, South Carolina, the son of Cleveland Louis Sellers Sr., a part-time farmer and small businessman, and Pauline Taggart, a dietician and English teacher. Young Sellers grew up in a middle-class family and attended a segregated elementary school and Voorhees High School, the town's only high school for black youth, on the nearby campus of historically black Voorhees College. Although his father grew up in poverty, he revered BOOKER T. WASHINGTON and would begin his day before 5 A.M. and work into the evening to provide a financial cushion and a comfortable family life. In his autobiography, *The River of No Return*, Cleveland Jr. recalls as a ten year old seeing photographs and articles about the 1955 lynching of fourteen-year-old EMMET TILL in Mississippi. Nothing affected Sellers more, and it set the direction his life would follow.

By 1960, television brought into his home the powerful images of military enforcement of court-ordered school desegregation in Little Rock, Arkansas, and the bus boycott in Montgomery, Alabama, that launched the civil rights of DR. MARTIN LUTHER KING JR. For young Sellers as a fifteen year old completing his Eagle Scout requirements, watching TV news reports in the student lounge at Voorhees College of student sit-ins at lunch counters in Greensboro, North Carolina, created a burning desire to join in direct action protests.

He soon participated with a group of Voorhees College students in planning the first protest ever in Denmark, only two weeks after the Greensboro sit-ins. Although only college students marched the almost three miles from the campus to the lunch counter at the town's only drugstore, Sellers informed his mother of his role. Students were arrested but then released without charges after the town's adult black population began to mobilize in their support.

When Sellers at sixteen years old became the president of a new National Association for the

Cleveland Sellers, right, of Denmark, South Carolina, prepares to enter a car for a trip to Atlanta jail on 27 April 1968 after receiving a five-year prison sentence for refusing induction into the Army. (AP Images.)

Advancement of Colored People Youth Chapter that planned a downtown rally with a speaker from Atlanta, his father confronted him angrily and insisted he stay home. Sellers decided to go away to college, settling on urban Howard University. He soon developed a close friendship with fellow student Stokely Carmichael, who shared his passion about racial justice. They became early members of the new Student Nonviolent Coordinating Committee (SNCC).

At nineteen years old in 1964, Sellers and Carmichael joined a request for support from GLORIA RICHARDSON, leader of a protest movement in Cambridge, Maryland. There, Sellers first encountered nausea gas released by a National Guardsman using a converted flame thrower to expel the gas and chasing the sickened students for several blocks. The nausea gas made his throat and stomach feel like he had swallowed a mouthful of burning acid, and he was briefly jailed.

Mississippi Freedom Summer followed later that year. There, Sellers and Carmichael first helped train white and black, male and female volunteers to cope with fear and sometimes with fearful parents. Weeks later, Sellers found himself searching after midnight with black sharecroppers on back country roads for three missing civil rights workers—whites Andrew Goodman and Michael Schwerner and black Mississippian JAMES CHANEY, whose beaten bodies were found buried in an earthen dam.

It was an unforgettable summer of horror—a thousand arrests, thirty-five churches burned, and at least six people killed. Sellers once got arrested and another time raced at 105 miles an hour for thirty miles to escape twenty chasing carloads of threatening whites.

He also worked that summer in organizing the Mississippi Freedom Democratic Party and joined them at the Democratic National Convention. In challenging the state's regular Mississippi delegates before the Credentials Committee, they gained nationally televised attention of the discrimination and deprivation of black Mississippians. Their failure to get seated as the official state delegation, however, led Sellers and others to refocus their struggle as one not of civil rights, but of liberation. He returned to Mississippi with increased responsibilities, moving at the age of twenty into SNCC's leadership ranks. He helped coordinate a challenge in January against the seating of all five Democratic congressmen from Mississippi. The outcome surprised him, with the challenge getting almost 40 percent support from 271 House members. Sellers was elected to a major position as SNCC Program Director, working under Chairman JOHN LEWIS.

Meanwhile, SNCC earlier had begun organizing voter registration efforts in Selma, Alabama. Sellers joined that effort as a logistical coordinator in March 1965, two months after Dr. King announced that he and his Southern Christian Leadership Conference would lead a voter registration effort there. The Selma to Montgomery march that followed led directly to the 1965 Voting Rights Act.

During the summer of 1966, Sellers joined Carmichael, FLOYD McKISSICK (Congress of Racial Equality), and Dr. King in the "Mississippi Meredith March against Fear in Mississippi" that JAMES MEREDITH, who desegregated the University of Mississippi in 1962, had initiated before being shot and wounded. As Carmichael launched the slogan of "Black Power," Sellers found an opportunity to engage Dr. King in long conversations ranging from the Vietnam War to black power and the Freedom Movement's changing tactics. They developed a personal relationship and friendship.

As the SNCC began to disintegrate, Sellers turned his attention to black power, education, and identity, and he recognized a need for the black community to learn their history and culture as an affirmation of their heritage. He returned in 1967 to South Carolina, aware of student activism at South Carolina State College in Orangeburg, his mother's alma mater twenty miles from Denmark. There and at the five other historically black colleges and now-integrated University of South Carolina, he focused on the idea of "Black Awareness" and opposition to the war in Vietnam.

Meanwhile, long-simmering complaints in Orangeburg with the county seat town's only bowling alley's refusal more than three years after the 1964 Civil Rights Act to admit black patrons boiled over in February 1968. Although Sellers had shown no interest in the issue, he learned at an antiwar coffee house forty miles away in Columbia that violence had broken out at the bowling alley between law enforcement officers and protesting students and returned to Orangeburg to see what was happening. Roughly two dozen students were beaten, including several females held by one officer and clubbed by another. Angry students returned to campus almost five blocks away and broke windows in parked cars and some businesses.

Two nights later, as tension escalated, highway patrolmen ordered onto the edge of the campus opened a barrage of buckshot-loaded riot guns and other weapons after one officer fired what he intended as warning shots in the air to a wave of unarmed students approaching to watch firemen hose down a bonfire. Sellers, who stayed on the campus because highway patrolmen and a National Guard armored personnel carrier were stationed in front of his nearby house, was among the twenty-eight injured by gunfire, most of them shot from the side or rear as they attempted to retreat. Three others were killed, one with seven gunshot wounds.

Nine highway patrolmen charged with imposing summary punishment without due process of law were subsequently acquitted in federal court. Sellers, arrested after treatment of his wound, was charged with seven criminal violations, driven to the state's maximum security prison, and placed in a cell on Death Row. After being released on bond, he was restricted from going into the vicinity of Orangeburg. He was aboard a flight to Washington, D.C., when he learned of the assassination of Dr. King, his friend.

Two weeks later, he was jailed for the entire summer, in several federal prisons, for refusing to step forward when his name was called out of turn for draft into the Army. Sellers challenged the Selective Service in South Carolina, where only one of the state's forty-six counties had a black board member. Although a federal district judge ordered a lengthy prison sentence, Chief Judge Elbert P. Tuttle of the Fifth Circuit Court of Appeals, a retired Army Reserve major general, enjoined it, a move affirmed by Supreme Court Justice Hugo Black.

In January 1969, Sellers accepted an offer to teach a spring semester course on black ideology in the black studies program at Cornell University. He enrolled that fall in the graduate program at the Harvard University School of Education, receiving a master's degree in 1970.

That fall he was finally tried on the Orangeburg charges. All charges related to the night of the shooting were dropped or dismissed, but the judge ruled he could be tried for "riot" for activities two nights earlier at the bowling alley. Although the Orangeburg police chief testified he had observed Sellers closely and saw him commit no crime, an

FBI agent said he observed him going from group to group, and they appeared more agitated after he moved on. The jury found him guilty. The judge sentenced him to a year in prison.

While on appeal, Sellers was allowed to leave the state, then meeting future wife Gwendolyn Williamson. They married before his imprisonment, which ended five months early for good behavior. They have three adult children.

They lived twenty years in Greensboro, North Carolina, where Sellers held jobs at North Carolina A&T University, the city of Greensboro, and the City Housing Authority. He received a Ph.D. in education administration in 1987 from the University of North Carolina, Greensboro.

After his father's death in 1990, Sellers and his family returned to Denmark, where he managed family-owned rental property, engaged in civil activity, and worked on becoming emotionally whole. Although he received an appointment to the State Board of Education, he was unable to obtain a teaching position in the state until after receiving a pardon from the state Probation, Pardon, and Parole Board in 1993.

He received a temporary appointment that fall at the University of South Carolina, where he became a popular faculty member and director of a program in African American studies that received accolades. In 2006, he formally received his Eagle Scout award after the Boy Scouts of America certified paperwork previously missing from its records. Attendees at the ceremony included Chief Justice Jean Toal of the State Supreme Court, who, as a young white woman, had participated in Mississippi Freedom Summer in 1964. Also in 2006, the youngest Sellers child, twenty-one-year-old Bakari, was elected to the state House of Representatives, becoming the youngest state legislator in the nation.

In 2008, Cleveland Sellers became president of Voorhees College.

FURTHER READING

Cleveland Sellers' papers are housed at Avery Research Center for African American Life and History, College of Charleston, Charleston, SC.

Bass, Jack, and Jack Nelson. *The Orangeburg Massacre*, revised edition (2002).

Sellers, Cleveland, with Robert Terrell. *The River of No Return: The Autobiography of a Black Militant and the Life and Death of SNCC* (1973; with afterword by Cleveland Sellers, 1990).

JACK BASS

Selmon, Lee Roy (20 Oct. 1954–4 Sept. 2011), Hall-of-Fame football player, was born in Eufaula, Oklahoma, the youngest of nine children of Lucious and Jessie Solomon, both agricultural workers. Growing up in a large farming family, Lee Roy learned at an early age the value of teamwork. This was especially important as the family could not afford a tractor, and the boys had to do all the heavy work on the family's forty-acre farm. Selmon played his first football game in the eighth grade, though he initially did not like the sport. He played high school football at Eufala High School with his brothers Lucious and Dewey and excelled academically. All three brothers were elected to the National Honor Society, and Lee Roy graduated in 1972. Although he was heavily recruited by a number of colleges, Selmon enrolled at the University of Oklahoma, following his brother Lucious and joining his brother Dewey. A big man at six feet two inches and 256 pounds, Selmon became a standout defensive lineman for the Sooners. He and his brothers were all starters on the team in 1973—a year Selmon considered the best in his entire football career—and helped build Oklahoma into a national powerhouse. The three brothers were National Collegiate Athletic Association All-Americans that year, the first time siblings had ever been named All-American during the same year—a popular bumper sticker in Oklahoma read "Thank You Mrs. Selmon." During Selmon's time at Oklahoma, the team's overall record was 43–2–1 and never ranked lower than third nationally. In 1975 Selmon earned All-American honors, the Rotary Lombardi Award for best college lineman or linebacker, and the Outland Trophy for the best college lineman. His 1976 team beat Michigan in the Orange Bowl for the national championship, and Selmon earned Academic All–Big East Conference honors. He graduated in 1977 with a bachelor's degree in special education.

In the 1976 National Football League (NFL) draft, the Tampa Bay Buccaneers, an expansion franchise, made Selmon the first overall pick, and soon Selmon was the cornerstone of the team. The Buccaneers named him their starting right defensive tackle, playing alongside his brother Dewey who was drafted in the second round. Selmon also played end and linebacker at times, as his coaches tried to take advantage of his versatility, speed, and agility. Although Selmon quickly developed into a dominant defensive player, the Buccaneers lost their first twenty-six games and won only seven games in his first three seasons (1976–1978). Selmon also experienced the first injuries of his career and required knee surgery at the end of the 1976 and 1978 seasons. The one highlight from this period of his life came off the field, when he married Claybra Fields, a nurse practitioner, on 18 June 1977; they would have three children.

In 1979 the Buccaneers developed into a play-off-caliber team. Led by Selmon, a strong defensive effort in the final game of the season led the Buccaneers to a 3–0 victory over the Kansas City Chiefs. On 29 December 1979 Tampa Bay played its first playoff game in franchise history, which was against the Philadelphia Eagles. In one of the most memorable games of his career, Selmon recalled the electric atmosphere in the stadium, which made up for years of losing seasons (O'Donnell, 68). He had two quarterback sacks and helped the defense hold the Eagles' rushing attack to only fifty yards as Tampa Bay won 24–17. For his efforts in achieving the team's first winning season, Selmon won both the Associated Press and *Sporting News* Defensive Player-of-the-Year awards in 1979. Over the next five seasons, Selmon continued to be a dominant defensive player and played in six consecutive Pro Bowls (1979–1984), including winning the Most Valuable Player award for the 1981 Pro Bowl game. He was also a four-time winner of the Defensive Lineman-of-the-Year award given by the NFL Players Association.

During the off-season, Selmon worked for the First National Bank of Miami and was also active in the community, working with the Special Olympics and serving as the chairman of the United Negro College Fund Sports Committee. A back injury forced Selmon to miss the 1985 season, and he would retire in 1986. For his career, Selmon compiled 78.5 sacks, 742 tackles, 28.5 forced fumbles, and 10 fumble recoveries. In 1995 he was inducted into the Pro Football Hall of Fame, where his brother Dewey gave the introduction speech; he had become the first player from the University of Oklahoma to be chosen for the Hall of Fame. In 1993 Selmon became the associate athletic director at the University of South Florida (USF). He managed the external affairs of the athletic department, such as marketing and corporate sponsorships. In July 2000 Selmon took over as chairman of the Florida State Fair, replacing New York Yankees owner and Tampa Bay businessman George Steinbrenner. In May 2001 he became director of Intercollegiate Athletics (AD) at USF, where he could keep a close eye on his son Lee

Roy Jr., a starting tackle for the USF football team. Selmon resigned as AD on 26 February 2004, citing health reasons. A short time later, he was named president of the USF Foundation Partnership for Athletics and entered a partnership with the Outback Steakhouse chain to establish restaurants that served cuisine inspired by his mother Jessie, such as her Kitchen Sink Gumbo; the establishments were also slated to feature memorabilia from his Oklahoma boyhood days and his Hall-of-Fame football career. Selmon died in Tampa at the age of 56, two days after suffering a stroke.

FURTHER READING

Aeseng, Nathan. *Football's Punishing Pass Rushers* (1984).
O'Donnell, Chuck. "Lee Roy Selmon," *Football Digest* (October 2002).
Pierson, Don. *Lee Roy Selmon: Giant From Oklahoma* (1982).

MICHAEL C. MILLER

Sengstacke, Robert Abbott (29 May 1943–), photographer, was born in Chicago, Illinois, the son of newspaper publishing pioneer, John H. Sengstacke, and Myrtle Elizabeth Picou, a publishing executive. His namesake uncle, ROBERT SENGSTACKE ABBOTT, was the founder of the historic *Chicago Defender* newspaper, which commenced publishing in 1905. His elementary school years were spent at the University of Chicago Lab School, Manument boarding school in Pennsylvania, and Howalton day school in Chicago. He attended Hyde Park High School but graduated from Central YMCA High School (1962). He studied for three and a half years at Bethune Cookman College in Florida and then returned to Chicago to begin his career without taking a degree.

From the young age of fourteen, Sengstacke honed in on the visual arts as his calling in life. As a child, he studied drawing and painting. By the age of sixteen, he had graduated to photography. Not only did he work as a freelance photojournalist for the youth section of his family's newspaper but he also opened a photo studio in their basement and quickly made it a success.

Pursuing an inclination to "learn by doing," he studied his trade through the 1950s and 1960s with senior black photographers who were trailblazers of their time. These included Bob Black, the first African American photographer employed by the *Chicago Sun-Times* newspaper in 1968; fashion photographer Lemont McLemore; and Billy

Abernathy, author of *In Our Terribleness* (1970), a photographic account of African American life on Chicago's South Side. In the decade from 1970 to 1980, Sengstacke served as an artist-in-residence at Fisk University, photojournalist for the *Los Angeles Sentinel*, editor and head of photography for the *Chicago Defender* newspaper, and general manager and publisher of the Memphis *Tri-State Defender* (another property in the Sengstacke newspaper group). He also undertook major assignments for companies and media, including work for the Kodak film company, AT&T, and the once popular *Phil Donahue* network television show. His photographs appeared in the *New York Times*, *Chicago Tribune*, and *Houston Post* newspapers, as well as *Ebony*, *Jet*, *Essence*, and *Life* magazines.

Relationships in the newspaper business were a great asset to Sengstacke. They put him up front with news events and newsmakers during some turbulent moments in American history. He was on the road with Reverend Dr. MARTIN LUTHER KING JR., documenting his work not only in Chicago but also throughout the South during the 1960s. In 1987 the *New York Times* deemed Sengstacke "one of the most significant photographers of the Civil Rights generation" (www.uwm.edu/Dept/dac/blog/archive/2006_04_01_archive.html).

Besides his work with King, his strikingly artistic black-and-white photography also recorded iconic subjects such as boxing champion MUHAMMAD ALI, poet GWENDOLYN BROOKS, MALCOLM X, and poet and writer AMIRI BARAKA. *Spiritual Grace* and *Savior's Day*, two of his most popular works, were included in the *We Shall Overcome: Photographs from the American Civil Rights Era* traveling exhibition mounted by the Smithsonian Institution from 1998 to 2004. As noted in the exhibition catalog, the photos came from the personal collections of seven of "America's most thoughtful and gifted photographers" and reflected "both the power and the beauty of the photographic medium when used as a tool for social change."

Social change was something Sengstacke ardently supported, defining himself as a "visual historian" with "a desire to counter the negative images of African Americans in the American press." His vision was enhanced by extensive travels in the Middle East, North Africa, Central and South America, and the Caribbean. In the 1960s, he was the first non-Muslim staff photographer for *Muhammad Speaks*, the national newspaper of the Nation of Islam. His work, including evocative photos of Dr. Martin Luther King Jr., Malcolm X,

ELIJAH MUHAMMAD, and Muhammad Ali, appears in most of the black arts movement anthologies produced during the 1960s and 1970s. Two of his most popular photos: *Martin Luther King: Dream* and *Spiritual Grace* were commercially marketed as posters.

Exhibitions of his photographs were mounted by many prestigious institutions, including the DuSable Museum of African American History, the Museum of Science of Industry, the University of Illinois at Chicago, Spelman College, the University of Illinois at Urbana, the University of Minnesota, the Statue of Liberty, the Schomburg Center for Research in Black Culture in New York, and the Chicago Public Library. His work was also represented in many private collections, including those of former U.S. President William Jefferson Clinton, actor Robert Guillaume, late comedian REDD FOXX, Stanford University, the Chrysler Museum, and esteemed African Art Collector Paul Jones. The Schomburg Center has an archive of fifty of his photographs related to King and twenty depicting scenes from the Nation of Islam.

Cinematography was added to his long list of credits in 1969 when he was invited to establish a program in photography and cinematography at Fisk University in Nashville, Tennessee. His patron was DAVID C. DRISKELL, the chairman of the institution's art department at the time. Sengstacke succeeded in creating and nurturing a world-class program that provided a training ground for black filmmakers who produced prizewinning films. Alumni of the program include John W. Simmons, professor of cinematography at UCLA, and producer and director Charles O'Bannon Jr.

In 1970, Sengstacke formed his own video production company, Sengstacke Media Productions, to produce minidocumentaries. In association with Charles O'Bannon, Jr., Sengstacke produced over fifty documentaries, including *Portraits of Black Chicago* (2007), which tells the stories of people and places deeply rooted in Chicago black history. The one-hour production delves into the lives of poet and playwright OSCAR BROWN JR., his daughter, Maggie Brown, the Association for the Advancement of Creative Musicians, the Art Ensemble of Chicago, WVON (Chicago's first black-owned and programmed radio station), and Muldrow Pharmacy (the oldest black-owned drugstore in Chicago). Also featured was the African Festival of the Arts, which is the largest annual African festival in the United States. The film was a feature of the *Fountainhead XXII Black International Cinema* festival in Berlin, Germany (2007).

FURTHER READING
Willis, Deborah. *Black Photographers Bear Witness: 100 Years of Social Protest.* Exhibition Guide, Williams College Museum of Art (1989).
Willis, Deborah. *Reflections in Black: A History of Black Photographers 1840 to the Present* (2002).

SHARON LESLIE MORGAN

Senna, Danzy (13 Sept. 1970–), writer, was born in Boston, Massachusetts, one of three children of Carl Senna, a black writer, journalist, and activist, and Fanny Howe, a white poet and novelist. Howe's mother, Mary Manning, an Irish-born actress and playwright, acted for the Abbey Theatre in Dublin before she moved to the United States. Senna commented in an interview with Susan Comninos published in June 2004 and entitled "Coat of Many Colors" that she was the descendant of two opposed family trees. In the interview Senna revealed that her mother's father belonged to the Dewolfe family, slave traders in the Northeast of the United States. A descendent of Josiah Quincy, the congressman, judge, and mayor of Boston, he was born into white privilege and became a civil rights activist and a distinguished law professor at Harvard University. On the other hand, as Danzy Senna suggested in "Passing and the Problematic of Multiracial Pride" published in *Black Renaissance* (Fall/Winter 1998), her father's racial and social background was quite different. He was a black man of mixed African American and Mexican heritage. His black mother had moved from Louisiana to Boston, where she was a schoolteacher and piano player. Furthermore, according to the introduction of Fanny Howe's novel *The Wedding Dress: Meditations on Word and Life* (2003), Carl Senna's father was a Mexican boxer who was deported from the United States under the so-called wetback laws, aimed at stemming the immigration of Mexicans into the country, of the 1950s.

Senna was raised in Roxbury, a predominantly black section of Boston, in the 1970s. At that time the city was experiencing political and social turmoil and racial tensions. Racial politics played an important role in her early life. Her parents were deeply influenced by the civil rights movement and were also involved in the black power movement that was at its peak when Danzy was a child. Senna's parents believed in ending racial discrimination

and taught their daughter that she was black, despite her light complexion. It was a way of increasing her sense of personal identity and helping to shield her from the racism in 1970s Boston. (She commented that, in 1975, people could not claim their hybridity in Boston; they had to be either white or black.) The political and economic influence of black activists led to a proposal to integrate the public schools through the Massachusetts Racial Imbalance Act of 1965. A federal decision ordering the busing of black children from Roxbury to white South Boston led to riots and the failure of school busing. In *Half and Half*, Senna explained that as a biracial girl she did not have a lot of options because of the racial tensions that plagued the city. Throughout the city's racial turmoil, Senna wrote to escape the problems of everyday life.

Senna's racial experience had a powerful influence on her future career as a writer and on the formation of her racial identity. Along with her older sister, she did not have an easy time in the black community. She attended the Roxbury public schools and the late Elma Lewis's arts programs, where—as a student in an Afrocentric school—she was discriminated against because of her white looks. In her *Black Renaissance* autobiographical article, she explained that her sister, who was darker-skinned than she, would attempt to protect her from the racial slurs of the other children. At school she was not allowed to perform in the annual Christmas show, even though her school preached the Kwanzaa value of community. For Senna, this event revealed "the hypocrisy of black nationalism" (77).

In 1974 Danzy Senna's parents divorced, and one year later she moved with her mother to Connecticut. In 1978, however, they both returned to Boston. In 1992 Senna received her bachelor's degree in American studies with honors from Stanford University, and in 1996 she obtained a MFA in creative writing from the University of California at Irvine.

From 1992 until 1994 Senna was a researcher and reporter at *Newsweek*, and from 1996 until 1997 she was the contributing editor of *The American Benefactor* in New York City. During the same year, she was a McDowell Colony fellow and received the Stephen Crane First Fiction Award for her debut novel *Caucasia* (1998) that became the Los Angeles Times Best Book of the Year. In 2002 she was the recipient of the Whiting Writer's Award, given every year since 1985 to emerging writers of exceptional promise.

In her fiction Senna wrote about the experience of being mistaken for white in American society and about racial prejudice. She also composed essays on race, identity, and gender in a number of literary magazines and newspapers such as *Self*, *Glamour*, the *Village Voice Literary Supplement*, *O*, *Utne Reader*, and the *Nation*. In addition she contributed essays to books such as *To Be Real: Telling the Truth and Changing the Face of Feminism*, edited by Rebecca Walker (1995). Her short stories and essays were anthologized in *Half and Half: Writers on Growing Up Biracial and Bicultural* (1998), and *Giant Steps: A New Generation of African American Writers* (2000). She appeared on several television shows, including *Makers of Race* that aired on PBS in 2003. In 2004 she was a fellow at the New York Public Library's Cullman Center for Scholars and Writers and taught creative writing at the Holy Cross College in Worcester, Massachusetts. That same year she published a novel, *Symptomatic*, a thriller about two biracial women passing for white. Senna was married to the author Percival Everett.

FURTHER READING

Senna, Danzy. "Passing and the Problematic of Multiracial Pride," *Black Renaissance* 2.1 (Fall/Winter, 1998).

Comninos, Susan. "Coat of Many Colors," www.nextbook.org (June 2004).

Howe, Fanny. *The Wedding Dress: Meditations on Word and Life* (2003).

GINETTE CURRY

Sermon, Isaac (26 May 1918–26 Sept. 1982), World War II soldier and Silver Star Medal recipient, was born in Waynesville, Georgia, the son of James and Mary Sermon. His father worked as a naval stores laborer, while his mother was a homemaker, taking care of their children, including sons Earnest, Ivory, Jim, Theodore, Elwood, and William, and daughters Ora and Essie. As was common with many African American youths in the south at this time, Isaac Sermon attended elementary school for only several years before going to work to help support his family at the age of ten. Years later, Sermon was working as a truck driver for a furniture store in Jacksonville, Florida, for eight months prior to joining the army in 1941.

Isaac Sermon was inducted into the U.S. Army on 11 August 1941 at Fort Benning, Georgia; while he joined via the Selective Service system, it is uncertain whether he was drafted, or volunteered through this system. Either way, the Selective Service was Sermon's only option for joining the army at this time, as white recruiting personnel in local communities nearly always rejected African American volunteers. After undergoing initial recruit training, Private Sermon's early duty station and the unit to which he was assigned is unknown. He likely served in a quartermaster company, a transportation unit, or some other service related group as these were the types of noncombat units to which most African American soldiers were assigned during World War II. However, Isaac Sermon would soon be one of the exceptions to this type of service; when the 93rd Infantry Division was activated in May 1942 he was almost certainly one of its first soldiers.

The 93rd, as well as the 92nd Infantry Division, were segregated units composed of black enlisted men and junior officers, commanded by white senior officers. They were the only such combat units in the army, and their men saw the greatest fighting during the war among black soldiers. The men that served in these units, soldiers like Isaac Sermon, JOHN FOX, and LEONARD DOWDEN, were important to the army's efforts during the war on a practical level by providing additional manpower at a critical time late in the war. However, their greater importance lies in the heroic actions of some of their individual soldiers and what this represented for the advancement opportunities for their fellow black soldiers in the future. During the war, many of the old racial stereotypes still prevailed among top army brass, namely that black soldiers were inferior to their white counterparts. Because of these attitudes, African American soldiers, greatly aided by black civic groups, had to fight just to be allowed to serve in a combat role, rather than just service units. Finally, by 1944 the army relented and allowed the 92nd and 93rd Infantry divisions to serve in a combat role. Though these segregated units would receive a fair amount of unwarranted criticism for their performance under fire, men like Isaac Sermon quickly proved that black soldiers *could* serve both competently and, in many cases, with distinguished valor.

The 93rd Division—which included among its components the 24th and 25th Infantry regiments, which were lineal descendants of the first black regiments formed by the army after the Civil War—began its training at Fort Huachuca, Arizona, in 1942 and subsequently trained in Louisiana and California between 1942 and January 1944. Isaac

Sermon rose to rank of private first class and, as a member of the 25th Infantry Regiment, received training as a rifleman, learning to use a rifle, pistol, hand grenades, and the Browning Automatic Rifle (BAR), as well as becoming skilled in operating a mortar and light machine gun. Finally, when advance units of the 93rd were sent into combat in the Pacific in early 1944, Isaac Sermon was among them, departing the United States for Guadalcanal on 23 January 1944. Here, the unit gained further combat training, and in April 1944 the 93rd Division was sent to Bougainville to take part in their first fighting action of the war. Within less than a week, on 8 April, PFC Isaac Sermon was on patrol with his company when it was ambushed by Japanese soldiers and he was wounded in the neck. Despite this, Sermon "went into position with his BAR and returned fire, killing three of the enemy. After his ammunition was exhausted, he started crawling to his patrol and was shot three more times while doing so. When the patrol moved out of the area at a fast pace, Private Sermon determinedly maintained his place in the column for over 600 yards before he dropped from exhaustion and loss of blood and had to be carried in. By his devotion to duty, stamina and courage, Private Sermon enabled his patrol to reorganize, break through the ambush, and return to our lines safely after accomplishing its mission" (General Orders No. 131, HQ XIV Corps, Silver Star Citation). For his valorous actions, Isaac Sermon was subsequently awarded the Silver Star Medal on 31 October 1944, one of only seven men in the 93rd Division to earn this award or a higher-level combat decoration while serving in the Pacific.

Following this action, after recovering from his wounds, Isaac Sermon continued his overseas combat service as a scout and rifleman, earning the Combat Infantryman Badge on 20 September 1944. He subsequently returned stateside in January 1945 and received his honorable discharge from the army on 17 May 1945 at Fort Sam Houston, Texas. He returned to his home in Brunswick, Georgia, and his wife Esther and stepson Edward. The couple would later have one daughter, Lorene. Sermon remained in Brunswick for the remainder of his life and was a longtime employee at the Brunswick Pulp and Paper Company. A modest man, Isaac Sermon seldom discussed his wartime activities with his family; his daughter would later recall that he briefly talked about how difficult it was to kill a man. Isaac Sermon was buried at the Masonic Cemetery in his hometown of Waynesville, Georgia.

FURTHER READING

The author gratefully acknowledges the help of Lorene Cross, the daughter of Isaac Sermon, in the preparation of this article. She provided copies of Sermon's service records, including the Silver Star Citation quoted earlier.

Converse, Elliot V., Daniel K. Gibran, John A. Cash, Robert K. Griffith, and Richard H. Kohn. *The Exclusion of Black Soldiers from the Medal of Honor in World War II* (2008).

GLENN ALLEN KNOBLOCK

Sessions, Lucy Stanton Day (1831–1910), teacher, missionary, writer, and abolitionist, was born Lucy Stanton in Cleveland, Ohio, the daughter of Samuel and Margaret Stanton. In Cleveland, Lucy's father owned a barbershop business with his partner John Brown. Samuel Stanton died when Lucy was two years old, and Brown became Lucy's stepfather, helping Margaret raise Lucy along with the four children from their marriage.

John and Margaret Brown and their household played a significant role in the Underground Railroad, housing many runaway slaves until they could escape to Canada. In addition John Brown funded and constructed a school for black children, providing his children and many others with educational opportunities.

In 1850 Sessions became the first woman of African American descent to graduate from a four-year college program. She studied literature at Oberlin College and became a teacher. Oberlin's literary program for ladies did not require women to take Greek, Latin, or advanced math, but all other requirements were the equivalent of a B.A. One of her roommates was Sarah Kinsey, the first African woman to attend college in the United States; however, Kinsey returned to Africa as a missionary without obtaining a degree. MARY JANE PATTERSON, who also graduated from Oberlin, became the first African American woman to obtain a B.A. in 1862.

At Oberlin, Sessions was involved in the Lady's Literary Society, serving as president in 1850. She also revamped the society's mission, which revived the organization's popularity after its decline in 1847, when Lucy Stone, the women's rights advocate, graduated. Sessions resolved that the society would foster its members' writing, speaking, and debating abilities.

During Oberlin's graduation ceremony, Sessions exhibited her oratory and writing talents when she delivered "A Plea for the Oppressed," a speech against slavery that was so moving that the *Oberlin*

Evangelist published it in December 1850. In the speech Sessions asked the audience, "Ye that advocate the great principles of Temperance, Peace, and Moral Reform will you not raise your voice in behalf of these stricken ones!—will you not plead the cause of the Slave?" (Lawson and Merrill, 203). After her address, an official from the school proclaimed to the audience that Sessions's speech exemplified the college's sound investment in admitting black students. The audience, although asked not to applaud during the ceremony, enthusiastically clapped after this affirmation.

After graduation Sessions taught school in Columbus, Ohio, and married WILLIAM HOWARD DAY, an antislavery advocate who made contributions in writing, speaking, and printing endeavors and who also graduated from Oberlin (1847). While living in Cleveland, Ohio (1852–1854), the couple endured the deaths of their first two infant children. In 1854 Sessions wrote a short story on two slaves who escaped to Canada that was published in the *Aliened American*, a newspaper her husband edited. Although FRANCES ELLEN WATKINS HARPER was "previously recognized as the first black woman writer," Sessions's short story was published before Harper's work (Lawson and Merrill, 197).

Sessions and her husband moved to Canada in 1856 to join a new black community named Buxton. Two years later Sessions gave birth to a girl. In 1859 William Day traveled to England for a fund-raising campaign. Sessions and her husband apparently separated after his departure. While Day wanted a divorce, Sessions did not grant him one. She was a faithful Christian and apparently did not want to break her marital vows.

Toward the end of the Civil War, Sessions applied to teach in the South with the American Missionary Association (AMA). However, the AMA did not accept her application, not because of race but because of her marital status. In 1864, when she applied, Sessions was supporting her daughter in Cleveland by working as a seamstress. The AMA at that time accepted only women who were married, widowed, or single, seeing any other status as immoral. Since Sessions's marital status was not her fault, she was deeply "aggrieved" by the AMA's rejection of her application (Lawson and Merrill, 200).

However, in 1866 Sessions moved to Georgia to teach, sponsored by the Cleveland Freedman's Association. As far back as her childhood Sessions had possessed a desire to teach in the South. In her thirties and forties this dream became a reality as she had the opportunity to teach in at least three southern states. After teaching in Georgia, she moved with her daughter to Mississippi, where in 1872 she consented to divorce Day, thirteen years after their initial separation. In 1878 she married Levi Sessions, whom she met in Mississippi; the couple lived in Mississippi, Tennessee, and finally California. They were among the first blacks to live in Los Angeles, where at the time only a few thousand African Americans resided.

Throughout her life Sessions was actively involved in educational, social, and religious organizations that supported the development of the African American race. In 1996 the Early Settlers Association of the Western Reserve inaugurated Sessions as a member of the Cleveland Hall of Fame. One of the first black women to attend college and the first to graduate with a four-year degree, she inspired and encouraged many people to gain a solid education and elevate the African American race before, during, and after the Civil War. Her life and accomplishments served as an affirmative answer to anyone who questioned the capabilities of the African American woman in the nineteenth century.

FURTHER READING

Documents about Sessions are in the Oberlin College archives. http://www.oberlin.edu/archive/

Lawson, Ellen NicKenzie, with Marlene D. Merrill, comps. *The Three Sarahs: Documents of Antebellum Black College Women* (1984).

"New Cleveland Hall of Fame Member," *Around the Square* (Oberlin College, Jan. 1997).

ALLISON KELLAR

Settle, Josiah Thomas (30 Sept. 1850–16 Aug. 1915), attorney and politician, was born somewhere in the Cumberland Mountains of Tennessee in the eastern part of the state as his parents moved from North Carolina to Mississippi. His father, Josiah, a member of the popular Settle family of Rockingham, North Carolina, was a wealthy planter. He owned Nancy Graves, Josiah's mother. However, unlike many white men in his position, he became devoted to Nancy and their eight children. After living in Mississippi for a few years, Settle's father eventually manumitted Nancy and their children and moved them to Hamilton, Ohio, in March 1856, since Mississippi law forbade newly emancipated blacks from residing in the state. The family settled in Hamilton, and he eventually married Graves in 1858, after his Northern neighbors protested his common-law relationship. He spent the summers with his family in Ohio, but lived in Mississippi the rest of the year on his plantation.

Young Josiah pursued his early education in Hamilton until he turned sixteen. In 1868 his parents sent him to Oberlin College, where he matriculated as a freshman. Josiah not only excelled in academics but also became known for his athletic prowess on the college baseball team. He transferred to Howard University his second year and graduated with his bachelor's degree from the school in 1872, a member of its inaugural graduating class. Next, Settle enrolled in Howard's law school where he studied under the capable JOHN MERCER LANGSTON, a noted statesman, orator, and scholar. Langston had been a leading black abolitionist, former member of the U.S. House of Representatives from Virginia, and was an attorney and Dean of Howard's law school. In 1875, after three years of study, Settle graduated with a degree in law.

Shortly after completing his studies, Settle married the highly refined Theresa T. Vogelsang of Annapolis, Maryland, in May of 1875. Unfortunately, she died in 1888. However, on 20 March 1890, Settle married the former Fannie A. McCollough of Memphis, Tennessee. At the time of their marriage, Fannie headed the music department at LeMoyne Normal Institute in Memphis. Observers regarded her as a "vocalist of unusual ability, and for years was the leading musical artist of the city of Memphis" (Hamilton, 485). The couple had two sons, Josiah T. Settle Jr. and Francis McCollough Settle.

Settle had a varied and distinguished career. After being admitted to the Bar in Washington, D.C., he moved to Sardis, Mississippi, to practice law in March 1875. He took the state's legal examination in Vicksburg, Mississippi, and was admitted to the Mississippi Bar that same year. According to one source, "he had hardly put his feet on Mississippi soil before he was unanimously nominated by the Republican Party for the exalted position of District Attorney of the Twelfth Judicial District of Mississippi" (Hamilton, 478). However, due to an anti-Republican tide in the state he was defeated. That defeat did not end Settle's political career. In 1876 he served as a member of the Mississippi Republican Convention, which sent delegates to the national convention in Cincinnati, Ohio. He also became a delegate and elector for the state-at-large on the Hayes and Wheeler ticket at that convention. Members of the Mississippi delegation even

chose him to second the nomination of Stewart L. Woodford of New York, for the office of vice president of the United States, which he did during the meeting, giving what one observer called "a telling speech." The substance of his speech is unknown. Four years later, in 1880, Settle served as a presidential elector on the Garfield and Arthur ticket.

Perhaps the pinnacle of Settle's political career came in 1883 when Republicans and Democrats in Mississippi made a fusion ticket for state offices. Settle vigorously opposed this effort and ran as an independent for the state legislature. He canvassed his district and proved to be a remarkable elocutionist. As a student at Oberlin officials chose him as one of eight speakers to represent his class of around fifty. When he graduated from Howard's law school, he orated once again on behalf of his class. One of Settle's contemporaries praised his speaking abilities: "He is such a master of elocution, and displays such fluency, and indeed brilliancy, that he invariably captivated those who listened to him" (Kletzing and Crogman, 523). Indeed, one of Settle's greatest assets was his abilities as an orator and they paid off in his bid for state office. Ultimately, Settle won the election by more than 1,200 votes over his nearest opponent. He served in the Mississippi legislature, representing Panola County with distinction and was "regarded as one of the ablest men in the House" (Simmons, 543). In fact, when his term ended, his colleagues gave him a gold-beaded cane as a token of the esteem in which he was held.

At the end of his term in 1885, Settle decided to leave elected political office and after meeting Tennessee's Bar requirements, Settle and his family relocated to Memphis where he planned to practice law full time. However, about two months after the Memphis move, he received an appointment as assistant attorney general of the criminal court of Shelby County. Settle did exceptional work as assistant attorney general. Judge Addison H. Douglas commented on Josiah's outstanding performance, saying: "His uniform attention to official business, his manly courtesy and amiability won for him the esteem and respect of the bench, the bar and litigants, and went very far to break down the existing prejudice against his color in the profession" (Hamilton, 481). After his term ended in 1887 Settle practiced law full time. Although he had not been in Memphis very long, his reputation led to patronage from an unusually high number of clients, especially for a black lawyer at the time. A contemporary of his in Memphis called him "one of the leaders of the Memphis bar," and said "there are few advocates at the bar that have a more lucrative practice than he." In addition to practicing law in several states, "the crowning glory of his professional career" was "being admitted to practice before the highest tribunal of justice in the land" (Hamilton, 482–483). Indeed, on 20 April 1903, Settle was admitted to practice before the U.S. Supreme Court. Settle's African American peers held him in such high regard they elected him as the first president of the National Negro Bar Association in 1909.

Not only did Settle have a lucrative legal practice but he also held considerable real estate in Memphis, which added to his financial success. Moreover, he served as attorney and director of the Solvent Savings Bank and Trust Company in Memphis starting in 1906. Characteristic of members of the black elite, Settle and his family lived in a large, two-story Victorian home located at 421 South Orleans Street in Memphis. And even by a conservative estimate, Settle's total property holdings were valued anywhere between $50,000 and $60,000 by 1911.

Though Settle never ran for office again, he remained active in Republican politics while in Tennessee. In 1888 he became a member of the Republican State Executive Committee and served in that capacity for sixteen years. Settle also became a delegate to the Republican National Convention held in Minneapolis, Minnesota, in 1892. In 1900 he was elected a delegate-at-large, and in 1896 and 1904 state Republicans chose him to serve as an alternate delegate from the state-at-large. Settle lived a remarkable life, and he serves as an example of what some African Americans could accomplish under the oppressive circumstances in the Jim Crow South.

FURTHER READING

Hamilton, Green P. *Beacon Lights of the Race* (1911).

Kletzing, H. F., and William H. Crogman. *Progress of a Race or The Remarkable Advancement of the Afro-American Negro* (1900).

Simmons, William J. *Men of Mark; Eminent; Progressive and Rising* (1887).

Smith, John C. *Emancipation: The Making of the Black Lawyer 1844–1944* (1993).

Obituary: *Washington Bee*, 21 Aug. 1915.

DAVID H. JACKSON JR.

Seymour, Lloyd Garrison (16 Apr. 1831–4 Sept. 1908), civil war soldier, was born in Lebanon, Connecticut. His parents are unknown; however, it was noted that his maternal grandmother was a Native American from the Pequot tribe and lived in Bozrah, Connecticut. He is listed as a mulatto according to the 1880 Federal Census. In his civilian life, Seymour worked as a coachman, a gardener, a waiter at a hotel, and a janitor. He was a sergeant in the Civil War, a political activist, and an estate owner.

On 22 November 1854, Thanksgiving Day, Lloyd G. Seymour, age twenty-three, married Nancy P. Williams at the Talcott Street Congregational Church. According to an 1880 Federal Census, Nancy was also mulatto. Nancy's father "lived in the family of Roger Williams of Rhode Island" ("Golden Wedding"). Her grandfather, Dudley Hays, was a soldier in the American Revolution and at the Seymour golden wedding anniversary celebration he was given a posthumous honor. Together, Lloyd and Nancy Seymour had three sons: Lloyd E., Alonzo M., and Frederick W. Seymour.

In December 1863 Seymour signed up with the Union Army and on 8 March 1864 enlisted in Company E of the Twenty-ninth Regiment. The Twenty-ninth was the first black regiment from Connecticut. Over one thousand African Americans joined and most survived the war. Although it was formed in Hartford in 1863, the regiment was not supplied with Springfield rifles until spring of the following year; blacks were not permitted to carry firearms while they were still in Connecticut under the pretext that African Americans who were descended from slaves were not allowed the rights of a white citizen, including the right to bear arms (Carter, 4). The colonel heading up the regiment was seasoned white officer William B. Wooster.

Seymour joined the Twenty-ninth as a first sergeant right around the time they were restationed as part of the Ninth Corps in Hilton Head, South Carolina. Here, the members of the Twenty-ninth trained with their new weapons for four months and then went on to Bermuda Beach, Virginia. The Twenty-ninth helped in the attack on Fort Harrison on 28 September 1864 and aided William G. Birney's Brigade of David B. Birney's Division of the Tenth Corps in defending against the subsequent counterattack from the Confederate army. After losing members of their regiment, the Twenty-ninth was publicly recognized by General Hawley and General Birney.

Following the battle of Fort Harrison, the Twenty-ninth and its parent brigade fought more battles, sustaining minor losses overall—by the Civil War's end, the Twenty-ninth had 159 wounded and 1 captured and had only lost 29 soldiers in combat, with a total death count of 228. In the beginning of March 1865, the Twenty-ninth was once again stationed in Fort Harrison, where they were able to see first hand the Union march on Richmond, Virginia. Unfortunately, Seymour did not see the final taking of the city because he had contracted chronic malaria and had been discharged on disability.

The members of the Twenty-ninth regiment were treated unjustly compared with members of the other white regiments. Racism was prominent in the army, and equipment for black soldiers was often scarce. Despite this unequal treatment, Lloyd Seymour felt very supportive of the unit and its mission.

Upon arriving back in Hartford, Connecticut, Seymour did not forget his time in the Twenty-ninth regiment. He came back to his home state having had an important experience in a unit for persons of color, and he decided to write a letter to the Republican governor of Connecticut, William A. Buckingham. This letter petitioned the governor to establish an African American company of the Connecticut National Guard. Governor Buckingham elected to honor the veteran sergeant's wishes and made Seymour captain of the new Company C of the Fifth Battalion Connecticut National Guard. Around Hartford Connecticut, this company was affectionately called the Twenty-ninth Union Guard because it was made up of many men who had served in the Twenty-ninth regiment.

Seymour later joined a fraternal group of Civil War Union veterans, the Robert O. Taylor Post of the Grand Army of the Republic (GAR). The Connecticut department of the GAR was started on 11 April 1861. The GAR posts all over the country were integral in presidential elections, and for a period of forty years from 1868 to 1908 Republican candidates needed the support of the GAR to take the nomination.

In addition to founding the first black company of the state's National Guard, Lloyd Garrison Seymour was a steadfast Republican. Seymour participated actively during the 1884 election. He supported James G. Blaine and John Alexander Logan for the Republican nomination. He organized the black Blaine and Logan Club in the Republican headquarters in Hartford. Seventy-two African Americans signed up for the organization and then went on to elect Seymour as president. In the end, however, Blaine and Logan lost both the state

of Connecticut and the greater electoral vote as Grover Cleveland and Thomas Hendricks took the White House.

In 1880 Seymour ended his career in the military. Toward the end of his life, he worked as a janitor at South Baptist Church and Grand Army Hall and by his last few years he had stopped working altogether because of his declining health.

At 9 o'clock on 4 September 1908, at Number 1 Atlantic Street, Hartford, Connecticut, Captain Lloyd G. Seymour died in his sleep. He was seventy-seven years old and had been suffering from months of paralysis, most likely caused by his worsening chronic malaria.

A census from 1870 shows that Seymour's real estate was valued at $6,000 and that his personal estate was worth $500. A 1900 census indicates that he owned the house on Atlantic Street and that it was under mortgage. A Hartford Courant article detailing Lloyd Seymour's will and testament reported that his entire estate, along with his personal effects, was to be left to his wife Nancy. In addition, a codicil to his will was made in early 1908 so that his son, Lloyd E. Seymour, would inherit $500. He was recognized in his obituary as "one of the best known old veterans in Hartford" (quoted in Mustered Out).

FURTHER READING

Carter, Gregg. *Guns In American Society An Encyclopedia*, Two Vol. Set (2002).

"Golden Wedding Thanksgiving Day," *Hartford Courant* (22 Nov. 1904).

"Mahoney Will Probated: Seymour Will Has a Codicil for Son's Benefit," *Hartford Courant* (17 Sept. 1908).

ProQuest Historical Newspapers, *Hartford Courant* (1764–1984).

Obituary: *Hartford Courant*, 5 Sept. 1908.

SØREN HENRY HOUGH

Seymour, William Joseph (2 May 1870–28 Sept. 1922), religious leader and preacher, was born William Joseph Seymour in Centerville, Louisiana, to Simon Seymour and Phyllis Salabarr, former slaves. His father was a Union Civil War veteran who had enlisted in October 1863 as part of the Ninety-third U.S. Colored Troops. In 1866 he met Phyllis Salabarr and they were married on 27 July 1867. On 4 September 1870 Simon and Phyllis Seymour brought William to the Catholic Church of the Assumption in Franklin, Louisiana, to be christened as William Joseph by Father M. Harniss. In 1883 Simon Seymour purchased a four-acre farm abutting Bayou Teche Parish, but he died in 1890, forcing William and his two brothers to take jobs throughout the parish to help support the family. Seymour's mother attempted to draw a pension from her husband's Civil War service, but payments did not begin until 1893. As a result of the family's financial burdens, Seymour's mother was forced to sell half of the farm.

Seymour migrated to find employment, arriving in Indiana sometime around 1890, where he joined the Simpson Chapel Methodist Episcopal Church and experienced a life-altering conversion. He shifted his priorities, changing his public life and employment goals from secular-driven choices to sacred ones. He ceased looking for work as a bartender and conformed his dress to the Holiness attire of the day. The Holiness believers were known for their drab clothing and abstinence from certain foods and entertainment that they perceived to be sinful. In 1901, while in Cincinnati, Ohio, Seymour experienced sanctification, an experience characteristic of the Holiness movement, in which a believer claims to have been "sanctified" when he or she senses that their proximity to Christ has grown closer. Seymour's sanctification occurred while he was attending a service at the Church of God. During this process, he embraced the premillennial fervor of the Holiness movement, which stipulates that before the second coming of Jesus Christ the Christian church will experience an outpouring of the Holy Spirit, similar to that experienced by the Apostles as recounted in the book of Acts, chapter two, known as the Day of Pentecost. On that day believers will be granted the gifts of the Holy Spirit and become empowered to preach salvation.

Seymour was attracted to the egalitarian nature of the Holiness Church, which openly embraced blacks, the poor, and other marginalized people. Spiritually awakened, Seymour experienced a bout of smallpox that blinded him in one eye, but convinced him that the Lord called him to minister to open spiritually blinded eyes. In 1902 Seymour left Cincinnati and resurfaced in 1905 in Houston, Texas. Some accounts claim that Seymour left Ohio for Texas in search of siblings who had been sold away during slavery, while others assert that he was led by divine inspiration to fulfill his ministerial calling. He located some family members and in the process encountered Lucy Farrow, the pastor of a Holiness church. Born a slave in Virginia, Lucy Farrow had been driven west through various slave auctions and search for employment. Farrow befriended Seymour and introduced him to Charles

Fox Parham, a Holiness teacher who had become interested in speaking in tongues (glossolalia) as a manifestation of the Holy Spirit. This aspect of Christianity, Seymour came to believe, would be restored to the church in the last days before the return of Jesus.

In 1905 Charles Parham moved Bethel Bible College to Houston, and Seymour attended. Because Texas law at this time forbid blacks from attending school with whites, Seymour listened to lectures from the hallway through an open door and was not allowed to seek the gift of speaking in tongues at the altar. It is unclear how much overt racism Seymour experienced within the Holiness movement itself, or whether Parham upheld stringent segregationist beliefs. Still, Seymour attended and embraced this aspect of Christianity, although he did not experience the gift of speaking in tongues. He began to preach in local Holiness churches, including Farrow's congregation, and to spread the doctrine of the baptism of the Holy Spirit through speaking in tongues.

In Houston Seymour encountered another black female pastor, Neely Terry of Los Angeles, California. When Terry returned to California she requested that Seymour come to the West Coast to preach the Holiness doctrine. Seymour experienced a sense of urgency in his preaching mission and believed that his purposes would be fulfilled in Los Angeles. On 22 February 1906, Seymour preached his first sermon in Los Angeles at a Holiness church organized by Julia Hutchins, a Holiness minister. His service charged the believers to embrace a multiracial congregation of Holiness believers who ardently sought the Lord for the baptism of the Holy Spirit. When Hutchins heard about the Holy Spirit baptism, she rejected that aspect of Seymour's teaching; this doctrinal division would remain a point of contention between Holiness and Pentecostal believers. However, Hutchins and Seymour were able to agree that there are other aspects of the Holy Spirit that should be evident in the life of a believer.

Afterward Seymour preached his twofold Holiness message of unity and tongues at the house of Mr. and Mrs. Richard Asberry at 214 Bonnie Brae Avenue. On 9 April 1906, while preaching his unique doctrine, the congregation experienced an outpouring of the Holy Spirit, and all began speaking in tongues, except Seymour. For the next three days people flooded the house seeking the experience, and on 12 April 1906 Seymour finally spoke in tongues. As the news spread and a crowd gathered, the porch collapsed, forcing Seymour to find another location to hold services. He decided on 312 Azusa Street, a former African Methodist Episcopal (AME) church building. From there the twentieth-century Pentecostal movement was born. People of all races and ages attended Azusa Street services. Prayer was held twenty-four hours a day, seven days a week, and at its zenith from 1906 to 1909, the Apostolic Faith Mission, as the church came to be known, attracted thousands. Unlike the vast majority of Christian churches of the day, services held there were interracial and promoted the leadership of both men and women. For Seymour and many others, such diversity embodied their vision of reconciliation that characterized God's plan for humanity. Many outside observers disagreed. People came to gawk at the proceedings from miles away, and local newspapers reported mockingly on the strange proceedings and race mixing. When Charles Parham visited the Apostolic Faith Mission, he was shocked at the style of interracial and intergender worship, and spoke publicly against Seymour's revival.

On 13 May 1908 Seymour married Jennie Evans Moore, an African American who had attended services at the Asberrys' house. The union disturbed several white women of the congregation who thought they would be his choice for a wife. In protest, one of them, Clara Lum, left Apostolic Faith Mission with the Apostolic Faith newspaper and mailing list of fifty thousand subscribers. In 1911 William H. Durham, a white preacher, attempted to co-opt the Apostolic Faith Mission pastorate while Seymour was away traveling. When Seymour returned, he had to change the locks to thwart Durham's efforts. In 1913 a doctrinal dispute within Pentecostalism divided Trinitarians and Apostolic believers (who were separated by their beliefs in the proper nature of baptism and speaking in tongues, among other doctrinal differences). The congregation dwindled. In 1915 Seymour published *The Doctrines and Disciplines of the Azusa Street Apostolic Faith Mission*, calling for an interracial, black-led, Spirit-filled church (that is, a church in which the Holy Spirit is allowed to control the services). Although this publication did not have the effect he hoped, he continued to preach Holiness-Pentecostalism.

By the time Seymour died in 1922 of a heart attack, his Apostolic Faith Mission had dwindled to a small remnant of the original congregation. Nevertheless, Seymour is remembered as the African American cofounder of the American Pentecostal movement. Indeed, Seymour's Apostolic Faith Mission was the origin from which numerous future Pentecostal church leaders came and had their initial Holy Spirit baptism. Domestic denominations such as Church of God in Christ, Assemblies of God, and international ministries throughout Africa, Asia, Latin America, Europe, and the Caribbean trace their roots to the revival-*cum*-church located on 312 Azusa Street, Los Angeles, California.

FURTHER READING

Bartleman, Frank. *Azusa Street: An Eyewitness Account* (1980).

Burkett, Randall K., and Richard Newman, eds. *Black Apostles: Afro-American Clergy Confront the Twentieth Century* (1978).

Clemmons, Ithiel C. *Bishop C. H. Mason and the Roots of the Church of God in Christ* (1996).

Cox, Harvey. *Fire from Heaven: The Rise of Pentecostal Spirituality and the Reshaping of Religion in the Twenty-first Century* (1995).

DuPree, Sherry Sherrod. *Biographical Dictionary of African-American Holiness-Pentecostals, 1880–1990* (1989).

DuPree, Sherry Sherrod, ed. *African American Holiness Pentecostal Movement: An Annotated Bibliography* (1996).

Martin, Larry. *The Life and Ministry of William J. Seymour* (1999).

Payne, Wardell J., ed. *Directory of African American Religious Bodies: A Compendium by the Howard University School of Divinity* (1991).

Sanders, Cheryl J. *Saints in Exile: The Holiness-Pentecostal Experience in African American Religion and Culture* (1996).

Synan, Vinson. *Aspects of Pentecostal-Charismatic Origins* (1975).

IDA E. JONES

Shabazz, El-Hajj Malik El-. *See* Malcolm X.

Shabazz, Hajj Bahiyah "Betty" (28 May 1936–23 June 1997), activist, was born Betty Dean Sanders in Pinehurst, Georgia (though she later claimed Detroit, Michigan), to Shelman "Juju" Sandlin, a Philadelphia steelworker, and Ollie Mae Sanders, who conceived her out of wedlock as a teenager. Rumors of maternal neglect (Sandlin was an absent father) landed Betty in Detroit, Michigan, with her devout Catholic foster parents Helen Lowe, a grammar school teacher, and Lorenzo Don Malloy

Hajj Bahiyah (Betty) Shabazz at her husband's graveside at Ferncliff Cemetery in Hartsdale, N.Y. on 27 February 1965. (AP Images.)

a shoemaker and proprietor. She was their only child.

Growing up with the Malloys, young Betty witnessed Helen Malloy's activism in social uplift causes through a Detroit affiliate of the National Housewives League, the National Council of Negro Women, and the then-militant National Association for the Advancement of Colored People. Betty participated in the Detroit League's youth program, where she competed in debutant contests, studied "Negro history," and affiliated with the well-regarded Del Sprites social club. Long before she encountered "Brother Malcolm" and the Nation of Islam (NOI) and its brand of black nationalism, Betty Sanders had a full dose of militant black religion, self-help, race consciousness, quasi-nationalism, and middle class black women's social activism. In 1952 Betty Sanders returned to the South and attended Tuskegee Institute, majoring in education and then nursing. In 1953 Betty was recommended to the faculty of Brooklyn State College School of Nursing, a Tuskegee affiliate, in New York, where she graduated with a B.A. degree in Nursing in 1956. Shortly after arriving in New York, Betty Sanders was "fished" by

a nurse friend, to use NOI terminology for proselytizing, who belonged to the Harlem "Temple Number 7" of ELIJAH MUHAMMAD's Lost-Found Nation of Islam in the West. Politically the Harlem temple was second only to Muhammad's Chicago headquarters, due in large part to its dynamic ex-con turned minister, MALCOLM X. Despite its unfamiliar theological claims concerning race and the duplicity of racial Christianity (dismissed as the "white man's religion") the NOI appealed to many of the communitarian values with which Betty Sanders had been familiar since her youth in Detroit and at Tuskegee. Sanders remained set on a career in nursing until 1956, when she at last heard and submitted to Malcolm X's jeremiad against naked white supremacy. Betty Sanders was now "Sister Betty X." In the short interval between Sister Betty's submission to Allah-God and her marriage to Malcolm X, she focused her energies in helping the Nation's women's auxiliary—known as the Muslim Girls in Training and General Civilization Classes—teaching hygiene, health, and many of the issues that she learned as a young woman in the Housewives League.

On 14 January 1958 Sister Betty and Malcolm X were married. Despite tremendous demands on his time, travel, and energy during their seven-year marriage, the couple had six daughters. Malcolm X was not well known outside of the NOI when he and Sister Betty married. This quickly changed in July 1959, when the newsman Mike Wallace and the black journalist LOUIS EMANUEL LOMAX produced a five-part exposé on the Nation of Islam for a local television station in New York called "The Hate that Hate Produced." The FBI had already opened a file on Malcolm X in March 1953 after he joined the NOI, but hostilities intensified as his exposure increased. Federal postal police and New York Police Department officers shot into the home on 14 May 1958 after they were turned away from entering. Upon their return with a warrant, officers arrested several adults in the home, including a pregnant "Mrs. Malcolm X," whom they threatened to push down a flight of stairs. Sister Betty X understood then that her role as partner of an increasingly notorious Muslim minister posed serious dangers for her and her family.

Malcolm's duties within the NOI took him away from home for extended periods and during his absence, Sister Betty was expected to assume management of the household and other family duties. Her most persistent disagreement with her husband was over her desire to work outside the home in a career or as a teacher of the young women in the NOI. Whereas Sister Betty held Malcolm X in high esteem for his commitments to the liberation of African Americans, she was not a passive woman. After the birth of each of her first three children Sister Betty X left her husband for brief periods, apparently over disagreements regarding a woman's proper role. Yet Malcolm also loved and respected his wife. According to ALEX HALEY, Malcolm X insisted: "[Betty is] the only woman I ever even thought about loving. And she's one of the very few women—four women—whom I have ever trusted." She was the model of a "good Muslim mother and wife," whom he claimed to trust "75 percent."

In July 1960 when Betty was pregnant with Qubilah, the family moved to a new home in the East Elmhurst section of Queens, New York. They had a third daughter, Ilyasah. In March 1964 Malcolm X announced that he was leaving the NOI and that he was creating two organizations, one religious, the other political. The Muslim Mosque Incorporated was to service the spiritual needs of the community, while the Organization of Afro American Unity (OAAU) focused on domestic race relations and international politics. He left the United States for nearly five months in 1964 meeting with heads of states throughout Africa and the Middle East. After he completed a Hajj to Mecca, Malcolm X took the Muslim name El Hajj Malik El Shabazz. Tensions intensified between Malcolm X and the NOI, and in June 1964, the family was formally evicted from its Elmhurst Queens home by a civil court judge. The family was given seven months to leave by 31 January 1965. When the family of Malcolm X remained after appealing the ruling, the house was destroyed in a firebombing on 13 February 1965.

On Sunday, 21 February 1965, pregnant with twins, Betty Shabazz, was tending to three of their four daughters who were present at the front row of Manhattan's Audubon Ballroom where Malcolm X was giving his fifth address to the OAAU and planned to outline his organization's charter. After a thunderous welcome by an audience of more than 400 people, and a commotion which Malcolm attempted to quell before sixteen bullets struck him, Betty shouted "they are killing my husband!" Malcolm X, her husband and the most prominent advocate of black nationalism, Pan-Africanism, and human rights among his contemporaries in the country, was dead at thirty-nine by multiple gunshot wounds. Of the thousands of telegrams that came from the heads of state of several nations, one of the first to reach her was from his political rival and admirer MARTIN LUTHER KING JR., who expressed his sadness over the shocking and tragic assassination. Her husband's death, however, was welcomed by as many as mourned it. Indeed, for the next fifteen years few aside from students and young nationalists celebrated Malcolm X and his work.

Overwhelmed by her family's predicament, Betty Shabazz went on her own Hajj to Mecca (Malcolm had gone in 1964), partly to brace her sanity, partly to walk in the footsteps of her slain hero and husband El Hajj Malik El Shabazz and in the footsteps of Hajar (Hagar of the Bible), the Egyptian concubine of Abraham, a woman who similarly found herself a mother, lost, and in the desert at the behest of death. The trip gave Betty Shabazz the strength to rebuild her shattered life and the life of her family. There, she took the name "Bahiyah," which in Arabic means fittingly "beautiful and radiant" one.

Betty Shabazz and her daughters eventually moved to the Mount Vernon suburb of New York

City and lived on the proceeds of the *Autobiography* and support from friends and admirers of her husband, including Juanita Poitier, then wife of the famed actor SIDNEY POITIER, PERCY ELLIS SUTTON, and the actors OSSIE DAVIS (who eulogized Malcolm X) and RUBY DEE, his wife. Over the next decade Betty Shabazz dedicated herself to her daughters, community service, and her education. She supported the young militants who touted and celebrated "black power" in her husband's name, even when she found some of Malcolm's supporters immature and recklessly committed to violence. Initially she supported the widespread unlicensed vending of her husband's name, recorded speeches, and image among the poor and working class elements with whom he mostly identified. As a curator of her husband's legacy and in the interest of her family, however, Betty Shabazz initiated lawsuits against unscrupulous vendors and acted as a consultant on the first major film about her husband's life (*Malcolm X: His Own Story as it Happened* directed by Arnold Perl and released by Warner Bros.) in 1972, a film that went on to receive an Oscar nomination for best documentary film. She also selectively gave access to journalists and scholars who became increasingly enamored with Malcolm X's ongoing popular appeal. When historian JOHN HENRIK CLARKE assembled an impressive list of contributors to the book *Malcolm X the Man and His Times* (1969), Shabazz wrote an article titled "Malcolm X as a Husband and a Father."

In the early 1970s Betty Shabazz also returned to school at Jersey City State College, from which she took a bachelor's degree in public health administration and later a master's degree in early childhood education. In 1975 she earned a Ph.D. from the University of Massachusetts, Amherst. Her dissertation was titled "The Organization of African Unity (Organisation de L' Unite Africaine): Its Role in Education," an examination of the Pan African organization that inspired her husband to create the OAAU in 1964. In addition to working in several capacities in Westchester County, Shabazz took on teaching and administrative positions at Medgar Evers College in New York City, where she worked for the next two decades. When local activists in Brooklyn and later Harlem campaigned to have major thoroughfares named after Malcolm X, especially Harlem's famous Lenox Avenue, she was deeply moved and participated along with MUHAMMAD ALI, the tennis great ARTHUR ASHE, and many others in 1983. At a rally held at the Adam Clayton Powell State Building on 125th Street,

Dr. Shabazz insisted it was important to symbolically "bring back my husband." With the production of a Harlem play titled *When the Chickens Came Home to Roost* (1981), the emergence of NOI leader LOUIS ABDUL FARRAKHAN in national politics in 1983, and SPIKE LEE's 1992 *Malcolm X* film, a renewed interest in Malcolm X, especially among young people in the 1980s and 1990s, motivated Shabazz to convey his deep sense of spirituality and religiosity. She felt Malcolm X's religious life was downplayed in Lee's film and that the NOI inaccurately depicted him as being more "political" than religious. The controversy surrounding Malcolm X's assassination, in which Farrakhan was deeply implicated, continued to haunt Farrakhan and the NOI at the very time in the early 1990s when its popularity was resurgent. Tensions came to a head in 1994 when Shabazz publicly accused Farrakhan of having a larger part in her husband's murder than he previously admitted. When an FBI informant and childhood friend of her second child Qubilah sought to orchestrate an assassination attempt on Farrakhan, Shabazz assembled the force of her friends, associates, husband's admirers, and even Farrakhan to thwart the serious charges facing her daughter. Shabazz walked triumphantly to the podium at the October 1995 "Million Man March/Day of Absence" event organized by the NOI and local, grassroots organizations committed largely to her husband's early political philosophy. She had come full circle, all at once confronting her husband's enemies and admirers urging them, without once mentioning Farrakhan or Malcolm X, to seek "self determination," and to tend to family and community. Dr. Betty "Bahiyah" Shabazz died tragically in a fire set by her twelve-year-old grandson Malcolm Shabazz in June 1997 but only after she had risen as a symbol of survival, strength, and endurance in her own right. Her remains rest along with Malcolm's in Westchester County, New York, completing an often turbulent but historically important journey that began as an orphaned girl in Georgia.

FURTHER READING

Collins, Rodnell P., and A. Peter Bailey. *Seventh Child: A Family Memoir of Malcolm X* (1998).

DeCaro, Louis A, Jr. *On the Side of My People: A Religious Life of Malcolm X* (1996).

Malcolm X, with Alex Haley. *The Autobiography of Malcolm X* (1964).

Natambu, Kofi. *The Life and Work of Malcolm X* (2002).

Rickford, Russell J. *Betty Shabazz: A Remarkable Story of Survival and Faith Before and After Malcolm X* (2003).

Shabazz, Ilyasah, with Kim McLarin. *Growing Up "X"* (2002).

JAMES LANCE TAYLOR

Shadd, Abraham Doras (2 Mar. 1801–11 Feb. 1882), abolitionist and community activist, was born in Mill Creek Hundred, Delaware, the tenth child of free blacks Jeremiah Schad, a butcher and shoemaker, and his first wife, Amelia. After Shadd's mother died, his father married another woman named Amelia, an astute businesswoman who reportedly emigrated to America from Santo Domingo. Abraham's grandfather was Hans Schad, a German Hessian soldier whom the British recruited to bolster their troops during the Seven Years' War. Hans married Elizabeth Jackson, a free black woman in whose house he'd recuperated from war wounds, in January 1756. They had two sons, Hans II and Jeremiah, Abraham's father, and eventually settled near Wilmington, Delaware. By the early 1800s the family name, Schad, was Anglicized to Shad and then to Shadd.

Abraham grew up in Wilmington's small, prosperous free black community. He likely did not obtain a formal education because he was fifteen years old by the time the school organized by the African School Society began operating. His letters and speeches indicate that he and his siblings did receive some instruction, however, possibly at a school founded in 1798 by the Delaware Abolitionist Society that offered classes in reading, writing, and arithmetic once a week. His father died when Abraham was eighteen years old, leaving him not only a trade (he had taught Abraham the shoemaking trade) but also a social legacy that enabled Abraham to quickly establish himself in the community. About five years after his father's death he acquired property and operated a successful shoemaking shop. After achieving financial security Shadd married Harriet Parnell on 6 February 1824, and they eventually had thirteen children, one of whom was MARY ANN SHADD CARY. By 1830 his shoemaking business had become so successful that he apprenticed two cordwainers, artisans who handcrafted fitted leather shoes. Shadd not only taught the young men his trade but he also provided clothing and tools, and gave them access to education.

Shadd went on to become a significant figure in the abolition movement, offering his home as a station on the Underground Railroad for fugitive slaves. The development of the American Colonization Society (ACS) compelled Shadd to become more involved in community uplift efforts. In 1816 the Presbyterian minister Robert Finley founded the American Colonization Society to provide government-sponsored relocation of free blacks to Africa because he believed they would never experience freedom and equality in the United States. While some colonizationists were concerned about the welfare of African Americans, others sought to strengthen slavery by ridding the country of free blacks. In 1830 Shadd represented Delaware at a national convention in Philadelphia, Pennsylvania, organized by free blacks to develop ways to improve their communities. Shadd joined delegates from six states in laying the groundwork for the establishment of the National Convention for the Improvement of Free People of Color, supporting emigration to Canada and opposing the American Colonization Society's goal of colonizing Africa. Shadd's participation in the colored conventions during the 1830s enabled him to take on increasingly visible leadership roles. In June 1831 he represented Delaware at the First Annual Convention of Colored People in Philadelphia and delegates elected him vice president of the convention. He also served on a committee that encouraged delegates to assemble annually to address community needs; to develop a fund to support the conventions; to promote education, temperance, and economy; and to resist colonization efforts. Shadd believed the ACS should have provided education rather than emigration to assist blacks in obtaining equality.

By early July 1831 the Union Colonization of Wilmington began to recruit free blacks to emigrate to Liberia. Wilmington's black community quickly challenged this development at a meeting on 12 July 1831 organized by Rev. Peter Spencer at the African Union Church, where Shadd and three others addressed the crowd. Shadd helped draft a declaration for publication in the *Liberator* that disavowed colonization, opposed all organizations that sought to remove blacks from America, and claimed citizenship rights for black Americans. The Shadd home soon became an important meeting place for Wilmington's abolitionist movement. Meanwhile Shadd's responsibilities continued to increase on the national scale, for at the 1832 Colored Convention in Philadelphia, delegates appointed him to several committees, and he participated in the continuing debate about emigration to Canada.

As Shadd's involvement in community uplift grew, so too did his dissatisfaction with living conditions in Delaware, a slave state. In 1833 he and his wife, Harriet, relocated their family to West Chester, Pennsylvania, a free state where they had greater access to educational opportunities for their children and could be closer to the active abolition community in Philadelphia. The move also enabled them to continue their work with the Underground Railroad, for one of the main northern routes ran near their home. The ledger that Shadd kept during this time indicates that he distributed shoes to slaves, conferred with Quaker abolitionists, and solicited money for the Quaker school that his children attended. He gained more prominence in the Colored Convention movement after he settled in Pennsylvania. Delegates elected him president of the third national meeting in 1833. He oversaw a convention where the conversation shifted from colonization and emigration to local concerns such as the development of temperance societies. In his presidential address Shadd emphasized his support of the convention's position of "improvement, but without emigration, except it be voluntary," his sympathy for enslaved blacks, his belief in education, and his desire to create manual labor schools.

In 1833 Shadd also became involved in national organizations that emphasized the Garrisonian concept of the brotherhood of all men, particularly the American Anti-Slavery Society that William Lloyd Garrison created. At the first meeting from the 4th to 6th of December 1833 sixty-three delegates ratified a Declaration of Sentiments and named a six-member board of managers, one of whom was Abraham Shadd. He attended the 1834 and 1835 meetings and worked on a committee that considered how free blacks could support Garrison's *Liberator* and other antislavery newspapers. He exhibited his personal commitment to the papers by becoming an agent for the *Liberator*, *National Reformer*, *Colored American*, and *Emancipator*. Shadd furthered his commitment to national organizations in 1835 by affiliating himself with the American Moral Reform Society, whose members pledged to "practice and sustain the general principles of Moral Reform as advocated in our country, especially those of Education, Temperance, Economy, and Universal Liberty." Shadd attended the society's first meeting, but it is not known how active he was in subsequent meetings over the next four years.

While Shadd contributed to the growth of national organizations, he diligently worked to establish a comfortable life for his family and to organize uplift efforts in his community. Public records show that he started paying taxes in Pennsylvania in 1833, and he rented a house for six years while he managed his shoemaking business. In 1839 he and his wife purchased a small farm and continued to acquire adjoining land over the next fifteen years until his family owned property valued at more than two thousand dollars. Living in a free state did not protect the Shadds from racist practices, however. In 1848 Shadd attended the first State Convention of the Colored Freemen of Pennsylvania in Pittsburgh, during which delegates focused on how to regain voting rights the state legislature had prohibited in 1833. Delegates appointed Shadd to the twenty-member committee tasked with implementing their plans, particularly to promote paying taxes and pursuing education, and to support and create black newspapers. In December 1848 Shadd attended the Convention of the Board of Managers of Pennsylvania in Harrisburg, where delegates continued to discuss suffrage rights for black citizens. Shadd helped write an *Appeal to the Voters of the Commonwealth of Pennsylvania*, beseeching white voters to petition the state legislature to reinstate voting rights for blacks, and *An Appeal to the Colored Citizens of Pennsylvania* that encouraged free blacks to sue the government for their rights. Despite free blacks' efforts to uplift the black community locally and nationally, whites continued to undermine black citizenship rights. After the passage of the Fugitive Slave Act of 1850 Shadd began seriously to consider emigration to Canada for his family. In 1851 he attended the North American Convention on emigration in Toronto. Mary Ann Shadd, his eldest child, had already moved to Canada West (later Ontario). Shortly after the convention Shadd visited Canada to explore relocation options. In 1852 he purchased a farm in Raleigh Township, Kent County, Canada West, and he and his wife moved to Canada with several members of their extended family and residents of their West Chester community.

Shadd remained active in public life in his new home, particularly in the areas of education, politics, and abolition. He established and financially supported a school on his property, and he helped set up S.S. #13 Raleigh, a school in the Elgin Settlement. In 1859 Raleigh residents elected Shadd to the town council, making him the first elected black official in Canada West. He continued to assist fugitive slaves, and when renowned abolitionists visited the settlement he often entertained them in his home. He served on the board of commissioners of the National Emigration Convention that offered limited support to Martin Delaney's settlement and missionary plans for West Africa. Shadd was also a popular lecturer whom residents frequently asked to speak for emancipation celebrations and other public functions. After the Civil War many of Shadd's children and friends returned to the United States; however, he chose to remain in Canada. One of his final major activities was to help establish St. John's Black Freemasonry Lodge in Chatham in 1866. Shadd died of diabetes at the age of eighty.

FURTHER READING

The Buxton National Historic Site & Museum in Buxton, North Carolina, houses Shadd family records, including portions of Shadd's journal and records of his activities in Canada.

Bell, Howard Holman, ed. *Minutes of the Proceedings of the National Negro Conventions, 1830–1864* (1969).

Foner, Phillip S., and George E. Walker, eds. *Proceedings of the Black State Conventions, 1840–1865, Vol. 1. New York, Pennsylvania, Indiana, Michigan, Ohio* (1979).

Litwack, Leon, and August Meir, eds. *Black Leaders of the Nineteenth Century* (1988).

Rhodes, Jane. *Mary Ann Shadd Cary: The Black Press and Protest in the Nineteenth Century* (1998).

Ripley, C. Peter, et al., eds. *The Black Abolitionist Papers, Vol. III. The United States, 1830–1846* (1985).

RHONDDA ROBINSON THOMAS

Shadd Cary, Mary Ann Camberton. *See* Cary, Mary Ann Camberton Shadd.

Shadd, Furman Jeremiah (24 Oct. 1852–24 June 1908), physician and educator, was born in Washington, D.C., the son of Absalom Shadd, a prosperous restaurateur, and Eliza Brockett. About 1855 Absalom Shadd sold his business and, following his brother ABRAHAM DORAS SHADD's example, relocated his family to Chatham, Ontario, where he took up farming. Following Absalom's untimely death, the family returned to the United States.

In August 1867 Shadd began a thirty-eight-year affiliation as student, educator, and administrator with Howard University and its associated institutions. He first enrolled in the preparatory course at the model school administered by the university. Graduating from the model school, he became one of Howard's first university students. He earned his B.S. in 1875, followed by his M.S. in 1878 and his M.D. in 1881. He was selected valedictorian of both his undergraduate and his medical convocations.

While pursuing his own education, Shadd served from 1874 through 1878 as a tutor of mathematics at Howard University's normal school, then as assistant principal in 1878 and as principal from 1879 until 1881, when he completed his medical studies. In 1882 he married Alice Parke; they had three children.

CHARLES BURLEIGH PURVIS, surgeon in chief of Freedmen's Hospital in Washington, D.C., offered Shadd the position of assistant surgeon and resident physician in October 1881. Freedmen's Hospital had been established in 1863 to serve African American civilians and soldiers during the American Civil War. When the medical department at Howard University was established in 1868, Freedmen's became the teaching facility for the university. Shadd was the third African American to receive a faculty appointment in the university's medical department, an appointment that he held until 1895. For a period of time he was also responsible for the dispensary and clinic at the hospital.

Shadd's tenure at Howard University's medical department was a lengthy one, both as an educator and as secretary-treasurer for the medical department, dental college, and pharmaceutical college. From 1885 through 1908 he taught primarily materia medica and therapeutics, but he also lectured on such subjects as clinical gynecology, pharmacology, and medical jurisprudence. In 1891 he was made a full professor. As an African American physician, Shadd in 1891 joined the ranks of Purvis, ALEXANDER THOMAS AUGUSTA, and Alpheus Tucker, who had all previously attempted to join the local chapter of the American Medical Association only to have their petitions denied solely on the basis of their race. When the opportunity presented itself, Shadd continued his quest for knowledge. In 1893 he consulted with Rudolph Virchow, a renowned German pathologist who was visiting Washington, D.C., at the time. While traveling through Europe in 1906, Shadd met with another specialist, Robert Koch, a famed bacteriologist.

In the community Shadd served from 1890 to 1896 on the board of trustees for the District of Columbia public schools, sixth division, where he was noted for his advocacy of industrial training and egalitarian education. He participated in the first sessions of the American Conference of Education held in Washington, D.C., in 1890 and became chairman of what was perceived as a radical organization, the District of Columbia branch of the Afro-American Council, which was dedicated to increasing the educational, moral, and political ranking of African Americans.

Outside of education Shadd was a trustee with the Fifteenth Street Presbyterian Church, a member of the Bethel Literary and Historical Association, a patron of the Samuel Coleridge Taylor Choral Society, and chairman of the Citizen's Committee of the New Building Campaign of the African American branch of the Young Men's Christian Association. Cognizant of the value of money and the need to save, Shadd was the founder and director of the Industrial Building and Savings Company. He died in Washington, D.C.

FURTHER READING

Lamb, Daniel Smith. "Furman Jeremiah Shadd, A.M., M.D.," in *Howard University Medical Department, Washington, D.C.: A Historical, Biographical, and Statistical Souvenir* (1900; rpt. 1971).

Robinson, Henry S. "Medical History: Furman Jeremiah Shadd, M.D., 1852–1908," *Journal of the National Medical Association* 72, no. 2 (1980).

This entry is taken from the *American National Biography* and is published here with the permission of the American Council of Learned Societies.

DALYCE NEWBY

Shakur, Assata (16 July 1947–), nationalist, activist, author, poet, and member of the Black Panther Party (BPP) and Black Liberation Army (BLA), was born Joanne Deborah Bryon in New York, New York, the oldest of two children, daughter of an accountant for the federal government and Doris Johnson, an elementary school teacher. Little is known about her father. Bryon was convicted on several felony charges in 1977 in connection to the 1973 murders of New Jersey state trooper Werner Foerster and activist Zayd Malik Shakur. In 1979 she escaped from prison and fled to Cuba, where she lived with political asylum beginning in 1984.

Bryon spent the early part of her life with her mother, aunt, grandmother, and grandfather in the Bricktown area of Jamaica, New York. When she was three years old, her family moved to Wilmington, North Carolina. By the time she was eight years old, her family sent her back to Jamaica, New York, to be with her mother and stepfather. In elementary school, she was a smart, proud, and outgoing, student who was always ready to fight to earn her respect. As a teenager, she dropped out of high school and began running away from home. She tried to make it on her own by working all kinds of unusual jobs. For a short time she stayed with a family of professional thieves and found herself working in a bar hustling drinks at the age of thirteen.

Thanks to her aunt, Bryon turned her life around, and eventually earned her GED after dropping out of school permanently at the age of sixteen. In the late 1960s, she attended Manhattan Community College and City College of New York. She became immediately attracted to the school's expanding black studies program. In 1967 she married Louis Chesimard and then divorced three years later in 1970. She then began attending civil rights meetings and becoming involved in numerous political activities. At that time, she began to dress in a way that reflected her African roots. Upon this new awakening, she adopted a Muslim name. Joanne Deborah Bryon Chesimard became Assata Shakur. In 1970 Shakur joined the BPP and was designated to provide assistance to the black community through a breakfast and medical program. However, she soon became frustrated with the lack of unity within the BPP, and came to the conclusion that it was too weak and botched at drawing its members together in unity. Instead, she became more attracted to the radical style of the BLA, which advocated taking up arms to liberate African Americans and achieve black self-determination.

Shakur's involvement with the BLA made her a target of the Federal Bureau of Investigation (FBI) counterintelligence program (COINTELPRO). During that time this program executed the attacks and defamation of black groups such as the BPP and the Student Nonviolent Coordinating Committee. The program's first target was Dr. MARTIN LUTHER KING JR., along with thousands of other civil rights activists. From 1972 to 1977, Shakur had numerous run-ins with police and the courts of both New Jersey and New York. Shakur was indicted ten times on criminal charges tied to seven criminal cases. Among these was an armed robbery case stemming from a robbery at the Hilton Hotel in New York City, but this charge was dismissed. Shakur was later acquitted on a charge of a bank robbery in Queens. Following that, she had a hung jury in a bank robbery case in the Bronx. She was tried and acquitted in the kidnapping of a drug dealer and was also charged but dismissed for killing a drug dealer. Charges that held her responsible for an ambush and attempted murder of a police officer were also dismissed. The case that would land her in prison was the murder of the state trooper on the New Jersey Turnpike.

On 2 May 1973 Shakur along with black panther members Sundiata Acoli and Zayd Malik Shakur were stopped by state troopers James Harper and Werner Foerster on the New Jersey Turnpike for driving with a broken taillight. Somehow during the incident, shots were exchanged, resulting in the deaths of Zayd Shakur and Trooper Foerster and the wounding of Assata Shakur and Trooper Harper. Acoli then drove off with Shakur and the body of Zayd Shakur. Shakur was apprehended several miles down the road, and Acoli was arrested the following day. The pair were originally scheduled to be tried together in 1974, but Shakur was granted a separate trial because she was pregnant. Acoli was convicted, but Shakur's trial ended in a mistrial. During the trial medical evidence proved that Shakur would have been unable to fire a weapon after sustaining a gunshot wound to her upper right arm. In addition forensic evidence showed no fingerprints by Shakur on any weapon nor any gunpowder residue on her fingers. Despite these testimonies in March 1977, Shakur was eventually charged and convicted of being an accomplice to the murders of both Trooper Foerster and Zayd Shakur, possession of weapons, assault, and the attempted murder of Trooper Harper. She was sentenced to life plus an additional thirty-three years.

Early on in her incarceration, Shakur was moved around quite often. At first, Shakur was sent to New Jersey State Reception and Correction center in Yardville, Middlesex County, New Jersey. She was and then later moved to solitary confinement in Rikers Island Correctional Institute for Women in New York City. Kakuya Shakur, Shakur's only child, was born while she was incarcerated. In 1978 Shakur was transferred two more times to Alderson Federal Prison Camp in Alderson, West Virginia, and then to Clinton Correctional Facility for Women in New Jersey. The next year, on 2 November in 1979, Shakur escaped Clinton Correctional Facility for Women. Those charged with aiding in her escape were her brother, Mutulu Shakur, Marilyn Bucks, and Silvia Baraldini. After living as a fugitive for several years, wanted by the FBI, Shakur fled to Cuba in 1984 where she gained political asylum.

In 1985 after enduring so much pain, Shakur experienced some long overdue joy when she was able to come together with Kakuya. In 1987 Shakur published *Assata: An Autobiography*. Shakur also wrote numerous poems and articles. In 1997 after talks with Cuban president Fidel Castro, Carl Williams, superintendent of the New Jersey State Police, wrote a letter petitioning the Pope John Paul II to raise the issue of Shakur's extradition.

In 1998 the U.S. Congress passed a resolution (House Concurrent Resolution 254) asking Cuba to return Joanne Deborah Bryon Chesimard. In the same year there were reports that the U.S. State Department had offered to lift the Cuban embargo if they agreed to return Shakur. As of 2005 the FBI recognized her as a "domestic terrorist" with a $1 million bounty on her head.

FURTHER READING
Shakur, Assata. *Assata: An Autobiography* (1987).

WILLIAM E. BANKSTON

Shakur, Sanyika (Kody Scott) (Nov. 1963–), author, former gang member, was born Kody Scott in south central Los Angeles, the fifth of six children of Birdie M. Scott and the only one fathered by professional football player Dick Bass. Shakur was the godson of musician RAY CHARLES. He was a formative member of the Crip gang from the age of eleven. He joined his set (chapter) of the Crips, the Eight-Tray Gangsters, in June 1975.

The Eight-Tray Gangsters organized in 1974, but the Crip gang to which they belonged began in the wake of the 1965 Watts rebellion. The riots in Watts exposed police brutality and aggravated racial tensions in south central Los Angeles. Between 1968 and 1969 Raymond Washington founded the Crips at Fremont High School in Watts and persuaded STANLEY "TOOKIE" WILLIAMS and "Godfather" Jimel Barnes from Washington High School in Los Angeles to follow. Barnes affirmed that the name Crip is a contraction of *crib* and the acronym *RIP* and is meant to symbolize the lifelong commitment expected of its members.

The Crips reacted to their violent environment in kind and adopted the group-based militancy of familiar organizations, such as the Black Panther Party, but these new street gangs reduced the targets of their disaffection to other local youth. In response to the intimidation tactics of the Crips, rival youths in south central Los Angeles formed an oppositional gang and took the name Bloods, a term that black American soldiers serving during the Vietnam conflict used in reference to one another. The rivalry between Crips and Bloods proliferated in both space and intensity while Shakur was an active Crip, and sporadic truces in the late 1980s and the 1990s did little to stop a transnational spread of Crip-Blood affiliation, imitation, and violence that continued into the twenty-first century.

However, Shakur described the violence of intergang warfare—clashes between neighboring sets of the same gang—as ultimately more vicious. Between 1974 and 1975 a series of altercations between several Crip sets sparked the Crip wars that determined the majority of Shakur's gang-banging (gang activity, including murdering members of rival gangs or sets). Between 1978 and 1983 Shakur was in and out of various penal institutions for youth in Los Angeles, where he continued his gangbanging by beating or murdering inmates affiliated with rival gangs or sets. In 1983 Shakur claimed he achieved original gangster status (commonly abbreviated to OG, it is a title of distinction for meritorious service to the gang, the equivalent of "untouchable" or "made man" in Mafia verbiage). Ironically, Shakur was introduced to Islam in the same year by the Youth Training School's Muslim leader Muhammad Abdullah. Though Shakur was not initially receptive to religion, Islam had a significant impact, from developing his literacy skills to instilling a political consciousness. Abdullah furnished him with the writings of MALCOLM X, GEORGE JACKSON, and FRED HAMPTON, all of which resonated deeply with the similarly young, militant, and imprisoned Shakur and informed his reconsideration of the causes and effects of urban street gangs.

After his parole in 1984, Shakur was arrested on weapons charges and convicted as an adult for the first time. While in Soledad Prison in 1985, he became involved with the Consolidated Crip Organization (CCO), a group of Crip OGs and members determined to diffuse the violence between Crip sets. But the failure of the CCO to make a coordinated effort toward ending inter-Crip violence, let alone achieve a palpable truce between Crips and Bloods, led to Shakur's disillusionment. By 1987 Shakur focused his militancy on political endeavors and espoused the New Afrikan Independence movement while renouncing his Crip affiliation. It was in this period that he adopted his Kiswahili name and dedicated his energy to black nationalism.

Shakur was paroled in November 1988. In 1990 he married Tamu Naima, mother of his three children. But an assault charge in 1991 was weighed against his previous felonies, and Shakur was given a seven-year prison sentence. During that term he wrote *Monster: The Autobiography of an L.A. Gang Member* (1993), a detailed account of street gang activity in south central Los Angeles from his induction into the Crips in 1975 through the riots in 1992. Shakur's book became immensely popular with those already engaged in urban counterculture. But *Monster* was also prominent in postsecondary curricula. It was on course reading lists in several disciplines, including history, sociology, and psychology, from Georgetown University to Washington State University to the University of Texas at El Paso to the University of Manitoba (Canada).

Monster chronicles Shakur's transformation from atheist gang member to Muslim black nationalist, from notorious participant in to staunch critic of gang violence. More importantly, Shakur criticized the conditions precipitating street gangs in urban America. The testimony of an authentic source linking systemic inequality, especially in economics and education, to the proliferation of street gangs was a welcome addition to the debate. And Shakur's popularity ensured that *Monster* reached a wider audience than other contemporary writings on the issue and made his contribution a significant one.

After parole in 1995, Shakur continued his work with the New Afrikan Independence movement, which joined the New Afrikan Liberation Front the same year. He conducted interviews for *Vibe* magazine, gave a taped lecture for the University of Massachusetts, and authored various articles, including "Flowing in File: The George Jackson Phenomenon." Like Shakur, Jackson was a young prisoner who developed a strong political consciousness in jail. Jackson joined the Black Panther Party and founded the Black Guerilla Family while inside Soledad prison in California. His letters from prison were published in the book *Soledad Brother* and strongly influenced Shakur's writing. Through these media, Shakur projected his belief that systemic racial inequalities maintained the socioeconomic divide to which he attributed the propensity for black youth to join street gangs.

At the close of the 1990s and into the new millennium, Shakur was repeatedly imprisoned for parole violations, and both in and out of prison his political writing and public speaking engagements gave way to his concentration on television and movie scripts and features in SNOOP DOGGY DOGG's hip-hop compilation album *Dogg Pound Mix* (2005). Shakur's political militancy dissipated as he embraced his ghetto celebrity image (an urban black who emerges from a poor neighborhood to achieve wealth and fame, often through cultural vehicles like athletics, music, or entertainment). In this new context Shakur reemphasized his gangbanger background over his religious and political development, and the potency of his anti-gang violence message waned accordingly.

FURTHER READING

Shakur, Sanyika. *Monster: The Autobiography of an L.A. Gang Member* (1993).

Bing, Léon. *Do or Die* (1991).

Hayden, Tom. *Street Wars: Gangs and the Future of Violence* (2004).

Jah, Yusuf, and Sister Shah'Keyah. *Uprising: Crips and Bloods Tell the Story of America's Youth in the Crossfire* (1995).

Phillips, Susan A. *Wallbangin': Graffiti and Gangs in L.A.* (1999).

ANDREW SMITH

Shakur, Tupac Amaru (16 June 1971–13 Sept. 1996), rapper, was born Lesane Parish Crooks in New York City to Afeni Shakur (born Alice Faye Williams), a black panther, and Billy Garland, who had very little contact with his son. Tupac was named after the last Inca chief, Tupac Amaru—Tupac meaning "he who shines" and Amaru meaning "large serpent," often translated as "shining serpent"; Shakur is Arabic for "thankful to God." Raised by their mother, with some help from their stepfather, Jeral Wayne Williams (also known as Mutulu Shakur), Tupac and his sister, Sekyiwa, had to learn to cope with their mother's drug addiction, abandonment by their father, and scrutiny from law enforcement. The family was often destitute and moved numerous times throughout Tupac's childhood.

Although Shakur's family life was often in disarray, his mother encouraged him to develop his interests in the arts, and he continued his creative arts education even as he moved from school to school. He spent much of his childhood in New York, where he joined the 127th Street Ensemble Theater group in Harlem and performed at the Apollo Theater in 1984, where he debuted as Travis in LORRAINE HANSBERRY's *A Raisin in the Sun*. His family later moved to Baltimore, Maryland, where he attended the High School for Performing Arts and focused on acting and dance. He moved to Marin County, California, in 1988 and attended the Tamalpais School for the Performing Arts. He did not graduate from high school, but earned his GED after dropping out to become a dancer and rapper.

Shakur began writing rap and poetry as a teenager. His book of poetry, later published by his mother under the title *The Rose That Grew from Concrete* (1997), provides early evidence of his skill with language, especially to represent the angst, sense of betrayal, and regrets of an adolescent black male overwhelmed by the effects of poverty, longing, and abandonment. Many of the poems, while immature, are political in content and critique the criminal justice system, the U.S. government, and the treatment of the Black Panther Party. When Shakur entered the hip-hop scene in earnest in 1991, he did so as a young black man with an artistic background, a trenchant political and social viewpoint, and a score to settle with the world.

After participating in several musical groups in the San Francisco Bay Area, Shakur joined the Digital Underground as a tour dancer and then as a rapper. In late 1991 he released his first solo album, *2pacalypse Now*, which sold more than a half million copies, and created one of the most socially critical songs and videos of the 1990s. "Brenda's Got a Baby" is critical of black culture as well as of the police and the U.S. government, and it framed Shakur's public persona for years to come. In this song he was exploring the problems of teenage pregnancy and child neglect at a time when pregnancy and birth rates were alarmingly high for African American girls. He describes the devastation in detail and challenges families and communities to act as well as to care.

2pacalypse Now became infamous when it was cited in the defense plea of Ronald Howard, a young man in Houston, Texas, who had murdered a state trooper, allegedly after listening to Shakur's recording of "Souljah's Song," which depicts a young man harassed by the police to the point that he retaliates. Howard's attorneys argued that the recording was the cause of the shooting. As a result of the publicity from this case, Shakur was denounced by Vice President Dan Quayle and by various black political leaders. The depiction of the police-hating hip-hop artist fit perfectly with popular notions of the West Coast "gangsta" style of rap that glorifies gang violence and depicts women in unabashedly sexist terms. To compound his gangsta image, Shakur starred in Ernest Dickerson's 1992 film *Juice*, in which he portrayed Bishop, who expresses his identity and manhood through violence.

The early 1990s also resulted in several disputes between Shakur and the police. In late 1991 Shakur filed a $10 million lawsuit against the Oakland police for alleged brutality following an arrest for jaywalking. In 1992 he was implicated in the fatal shooting of a six-year-old child in Marin City, a shooting he said haunted him for the rest of his life. By the end of that year the image of Shakur as the typical gangsta rapper was indelibly stamped on the popular imagination, although the socially conscious aspects of his work were hardly mentioned at all. The public attention paid to Shakur's troubles with the law and the lack of attention paid to his political criticism and messages of empowerment frustrated him as well as his fans. In fact, the representation of Shakur as a menace without a critical view of society or "the game" may have fueled his followers' commitment. They savored debate about his problems, beliefs, artistic ability, politics, actions, and antics. His fan base grew stronger in the face of mounting criticism of his actions.

During 1993 Shakur's success was offset by legal problems. His release *Strictly 4 My N.I.G.G.A.Z.* quickly went gold with the party anthem "I Get Around" and the tribute to black women "Keep Ya Head Up," in which he talks not only about strength and survival but about healing as well. It was perhaps at this time that the split between the public image of Shakur and his fans' notion of him as a complex analyst of social ills and truths began to emerge in earnest. For instance, while he could be misogynistic on one recording, on another he might represent a feminist and class-oriented perspective. In 1993, he costarred with Janet Jackson in the JOHN SINGLETON film *Poetic Justice*. That same year, after moving to Atlanta, he was arrested on several charges, including shooting two off-duty police officers, though he was later acquitted.

Accused of sexual assault and weapons charges in November 1993, Shakur was found guilty of sexual abuse and ordered to serve four and a half years in New York's Rikers Island penitentiary. Death Row Records CEO Suge Knight posted $1.4 million bond to release Shakur, who immediately flew to Los Angeles and signed with Death Row. While out on bail before sentencing, Shakur was shot five times as he entered a recording studio in New York. This shooting fueled a long-standing feud between East Coast and West Coast artists about respect, airplay, and record promotion. Shakur publicly accused the rapper the NOTORIOUS B.I.G. (also known as Biggie Smalls or Christopher Wallace) and B.I.G.'s friend and producer Puff Daddy (SEAN COMBS, also known as P-Diddy) of being implicated in his attempted murder. Several confrontations between Shakur and B.I.G. and their crews followed. In response Shakur released the single "Hit 'Em Up," an angry, profanity-laced, and caustically insulting rant against those whom he perceived to be his enemies. Shakur recovered from his wounds and produced *Me against the World*, which was released in 1995 while he was in prison in New York's Rikers Island Penitentiary. This album, which includes the song "Dear Momma," a tribute to black mothers and a public apology to and declaration of love for his own mother, sold more than 2 million copies. In March 1996, paroled from jail, Shakur released the first hip-hop double CD, *All Eyez on Me*, which sold more than 3 million copies.

On 7 September 1996, after leaving the MIKE TYSON–Bruce Seldon fight in Las Vegas, Shakur was shot four times while riding in a car driven by Suge Knight. He died six days later, only twenty-six years old. In many respects, Shakur's death initiated a deeper discussion of both social and political problems among youth, many of whom consider him a hero and martyr. On 5 November 1996, two months after his death, his album *The Don Killuminati: Seven Day Theory* was released posthumously under the pseudonym Makaveli. This was followed by a major release in November 1997 of *RU Still Down? [Remember Me]*, a double CD of previously unreleased tracks on Amaru Records, a label established by Shakur's mother. A year later *2Pac's Greatest Hits*, a double CD, was released by Death Row/Interscope/Amaru Records. These releases fueled speculation that Shakur was still alive. In 2001 *Forbes* magazine listed him as "one of the top grossing celebrities no longer alive" with the 2001 album *Until the End of Time*, which reportedly sold 2.7 million copies and earned an estimated $7 million.

Many were concerned that the violence of rap, exemplified in Shakur's death, would be emulated by youth. Instead, young people heard lyrics of empowerment, responsibility, and self-love. Shakur's final video, "I Ain't Mad at Ya," was one of many songs that predicted his violent death while pointing out injustice and arguing for redemption. He claimed that his concept of the "thug life," a phrase he had tattooed on his chest and that he explained as an acronym for "The Hate U Give Little Infants Fucks Everybody," led to hundreds of ministries organized around hip-hop and what they referred to as thugology—the saving of the spiritual self and community by dealing with the realities of youth. It also became the organizing force around self-empowerment programs and after-school programs. Shakur starred in six movies, released four albums, and earned two Grammy nominations. Since his death there have been at least four posthumous albums and numerous books, videos, and tributes. Shakur struggled through words and performance and through his outward show of love, outrage, hate, and confusion to find a moral center in his life. Despite all that he endured, his loudest message may have been that even through conflict, one should keep trying. The

2003 release of the documentary and soundtrack *Resurrection* not only implies a resolution with many of his foes, but also includes a statement of his purpose: "to reach the kid who believes it hopeless." As he assures his fans in "Keep Ya Head Up," "While the rich kids is drivin' Benz / I'm still tryin' to hold on to my survivin' friends / And it's crazy, it seems it'll never let up, but please / you got to keep your head up." Shakur's five-year solo recording career included many hits that his fans considered prophetic, insightful, socially conscious, and at times violent. By the time of his death he was considered one of the most influential, talented, and controversial hip-hop artists and entertainers of his time. While his music, his life, and his death articulate many of the problems of race and class in the United States, it remains to be seen how his fans will translate their understanding of Shakur into action in their own lives.

FURTHER READING

Batsfield, Darren Keith. *Back in the Day: My Life and Times with Tupac Shakur* (2002).

Brooks, Darren. *Maximum 2Pac: The Unauthorised Biography of 2Pac* (2003).

Datcher, Michael, Kwame Alexander, and Mutulu Shakur. *Tough Love: The Life and Death of Tupac Shakur, Cultural Criticisms and Familial Observations* (1997).

Dyson, Michael Eric. *Holler If You Hear Me: Searching for Tupac Shakur* (2001).

Frokos, Helen. *Tupac Shakur (They Died Too Young)* (2000).

Jones, Quincy, and the Editors of *Vibe* Magazine. *Tupac Amaru Shakur, 1971–1996* (1997).

MARCYLIENA MORGAN

Shange, Ntozake (18 Oct. 1948–), poet, playwright, novelist, and performer, was born Paulette Williams in Trenton, New Jersey, the eldest of four children of Paul T. Williams, a surgeon, and Eloise Owens, a psychiatric social worker. Paul Williams played African drums for a time with a band, and the Williams home was always filled with music and often with prominent musicians such as DIZZY GILLESPIE, MILES DAVIS, and CHUCK BERRY. Both of Shange's parents exposed her to a wide range of African American cultural forms, from literature to opera and ballet, and she later recalled childhood visits from W. E. B. DuBois, PAUL ROBESON, and other African American luminaries. Shange's family moved to St. Louis, Missouri, when she was eight, and the positive expression of African American

Ntozake Shange, playwright and actress, in New York City in July 1976. (AP Images.)

culture in her home environment was thrown into stark contrast at school, where she experienced cruel racism as one of few black students. Though Shange's family returned to New Jersey when she was thirteen, her difficult experience with school integration left an indelible mark and provided the source material for her autobiographical novel *Betsey Brown* (1985).

Shange began writing as a child and excelled academically. At age eighteen she married a law student, but the marriage ended in divorce. Following the divorce she attempted suicide, the first of several attempts. Despite these emotional setbacks she completed her studies at Barnard College, earning a B.A. in American studies (with honors) in 1970. In 1971 she took a Zulu name, Ntozake, meaning "she who comes with her own things," and Shange, meaning "who walks like a lion." In 1973 she earned a master's degree in American studies from the University of Southern California. During this period she immersed herself in African American literature and began writing and performing her own poetry.

In 1972 Shange moved to Northern California to teach at Sonoma State College and later at the University of California Extension. During this period Shange created and performed in a series of interrelated "choreopoems" with the theater company that she cofounded, For Colored Girls Who Have Considered Suicide. These performances became the play for which she is best known: *for colored girls who have considered suicide / when the rainbow is enuf*. Shange moved to New York City in 1975 where *for colored girls* received a series of professional productions. The play, the first by a black woman author to run on Broadway since LORRAINE HANSBERRY's groundbreaking *A Raisin in the Sun* opened in 1959, was nominated for Tony, Grammy, and Emmy awards and won the 1977 Obie for Best Original Play; *for colored girls* quickly became a perennial theater staple, regularly performed throughout the country in a variety of professional and nonprofessional venues. Although she received mostly positive reviews for her depiction of seven women telling stories of love and betrayal, rape and survival, Shange was also criticized for what some alleged was the play's lack of positive male characters and for its unconventional pastiche structure.

Though she found instant celebrity an "isolating, alienating experience" (Betsko and Koenig, 376), Shange continued to perform and lecture around the country, as well as continuing to write. She published a novella, *Sassafrass*, in 1977 and a collection of poetry, *Nappy Edges*, in 1978, followed by the novels *Sassafras, Cypress, and Indigo* (1982) and *Betsey Brown* (1985). Her plays *Spell #7* and *A Photograph: Lovers-in-Motion* were produced in a number of regional theaters and at the New York Shakespeare Festival in 1979, and in 1980 her adaptation of Bertolt Brecht's *Mother Courage*, featuring an African American family during the Civil War, won her another Obie Award. Shange married the jazz musician and painter David Murray in 1977. The couple had a daughter, Savannah, before separating.

Shange's writing challenged the traditional boundaries of genre, as evidenced by her creation of the new form the choreopoem, which combined poetry, music, and dance. Her written and performative work combined poetry and performance, fiction and essay. In her use of lowercase letters, slashes, phonetic spelling, and unconventional line spacing, Shange's experimental use of language built on the oral tradition of African American culture as well as on the work of her fellow African American innovators JUNE JORDAN, NIKKI GIOVANNI, and AMIRI BARAKA (Leroi Jones), all of whom influenced later rap and spoken-word poets. In *See No Evil: Prefaces, Essays, and Accounts, 1976–1983* (1984) Shange explained, "i can't count the number of times i have viscerally wanted to attack deform n maim the language i waz taught to hate myself in" (21). In a 1987 interview Shange described her work as distinctly female, describing the plot of her fiction as "not going forward. It undulates, I hope. And I hope it has more to do with the flow of rivers and streams and tides and lakes, because I relate to life more completely in that way and it feels more real to me" (Lyons, 691).

Shange continued to write prolifically in several genres, to nearly unanimously positive reviews, often collaborating with other artists. She provided a poetic introduction to Robert Mapplethorpe's *Black Book* (1986), a collection of photographs of black men. In 1996 she created the play *Nomathemba* with the South African musicians Ladysmith Black Mambazo. In 2004 she contributed the poetry to accompany a collection of photographs for *The Sweet Breath of Life: A Poetic Narrative of the African-American Family*, edited by the photographer Frank Stewart, and also produced a volume of poetry for young people, *Ellington Was Not a Street*, with paintings by Kadir Nelson, about the giants of African American culture, many of whom she met as a child. She produced several volumes of poetry, many of which she adapted for the stage; a novel, *Liliane: Resurrection of the Daughter* (1994); a cookbook with accompanying essays, *If I Can Cook / You Know God Can* (1998); and a new collection of poetry, *Lavender Lizards and Lilac Landmines: Layla's Dream* (2003). Her influence can also be felt through the continued popularity of the poetry slam, a performance style that she helped establish with the Nuyorican poets.

Shange's determination to push the boundaries of language secured her steady employment as a writer, performer, and academic, but it also kept her from achieving consistent mainstream recognition for new work. Despite her steady outflow in multiple genres, Shange is still best known for the early success and continued production of *for colored girls*. A committed teacher and scholar, who taught at the University of Florida both in the theater and performing arts and in the women's and gender studies departments, Shange articulated an aesthetic for black women artists that defies traditional parameters. As she explained in 1998, "We have to be careful that the way we devise feminist scholarship is done in a way that is as threatening as feminism is. We have to question all the rules. Every single rule that can contribute to our misunderstanding of ourselves has got to be questioned" (Bobo, 199). Like other black women writers, Shange explained, "I started writing because there's an absence of things I was familiar with or that I dreamed about. One of my senses of anger is related to this vacancy—a yearning I had as a teenager" (Lyons, 690). Committed to a continued articulation of the experience of oppression in language largely overlooked by the mainstream, Shange's characters speak in a language all their own; as her character lou puts it in *Spell #7* (1982):

> crackers are born with the right to be
> alive/i'm making ours up right here
> in yr face/ & we gonna be
> colored and love it

FURTHER READING

Betsko, Kathleen, and Rachel Koenig, eds. *Interviews with Contemporary Women Playwrights* (1987).

Bobo, Jacqueline, ed. *Black Women Film and Video Artists* (1998).

Lyons, Brenda. "Interview with Ntozake Shange," *Massachusetts Review* (Winter, 1987).

ALICE KNOX EATON

Shankle, James and Winnie Brush Shankle

(c. 1811–1887) and (c. 1814–c. 1883), farmers, entrepreneurs, and community founders, were born into slavery, James in Kentucky and Winnie in Tennessee. According to family tradition, both were sold as children and sent to work on the Isaac Rollins plantation in Wayne County, Mississippi. Jim, as he was called, labored in the cotton fields, while Winnie worked as a house slave and became her young master's mistress. Winnie, a "mulatto" according to the 1880 census, bore her master three children.

When Winnie's master, in around 1834–1835, learned that she and Jim had "jumped over the broom" in a slave wedding ceremony, he, in a fit of jealousy and revenge, sent Winnie and their three children to the auction block and sold them to a slave owner from Texas. In an interview, Elzie D. Odom, a descendant of the Shankles and former mayor of Arlington, Texas, said that Jim heard from the slaves who accompanied Winnie and her three children to the slave auction that they had been "sold to Texas" (Odom). Knowing full well that runaway slaves could be severely whipped

or even killed, Jim nevertheless determined to search for Winnie and her children. "Jim headed west with only the clothes he wore" (Odom). He never dared to walk along established roads or to reveal his presence in daylight. The young runaway traveled only by night, resting during the day and concealing himself in all manner of places. Sometimes he could only cover himself with leaves and brush in a wooded area. Other times he was lucky enough to find shelter in a slave shanty or in the barn of a plantation house, where other slaves hid him while he rested for the long journey that began anew at each nightfall. Occasionally Jim's benefactors had a little food to share; otherwise he ate only what he gathered and what small game or fish he caught. He searched for Winnie for months. He swam the Mississippi River and the Sabine River at night and sneaked onto plantations, inquiring of the slaves about Winnie and her three children. Winnie was reportedly strikingly beautiful, and her children appeared white. Because of Winnie's beauty and the fact that she traveled with what appeared to be three white children, they were noticed as they journeyed to Texas, and Jim learned of their travel route from several plantations and farms. He reached Texas after months of weary travel.

The slave grapevine had progressed ahead of Jim, and many slaves in East Texas had learned of his quest to find Winnie. Still, it was a miracle that he found Winnie one early morning on her new owner's plantation as she fetched water at a nearby spring. "Late one evening she heard a muffled whisper" (Odom) emanating from the willows surrounding the spring. Jim stepped out of the trees torn and tattered, thin and exhausted, but triumphant. Love, luck, perseverance, and determination had overcome every obstacle that Jim faced on his long journey. For a few days Winnie sneaked food to Jim, and then she gathered her courage to confide in her new master, a kind man and a Methodist minister. Winnie and Jim found sympathy from her new owner, who negotiated to buy Jim from his Mississippi master. The minister later freed the couple, performed a religious wedding ceremony for the devoted pair, and granted a small house to the grateful family. Winnie and Jim had six more children.

After the Civil War, Jim bought a league of land, 4,428.4 acres, which included part of their former master's land and the spring where he and Winnie found each other. The Shankles farmed cotton and cleared much of their land of the pine and oak trees that grew in abundance in the rich East Texas soil and milled it into lumber in the small lumber mill they built. There Jim and Winnie established the all-black community of Shankleville. At one time it was a bustling community of churches, schools, stores, and farms, and for a short time it even included a college, McBride College, founded by Stephen McBride, another former slave who partnered with Jim Shankle in several business enterprises.

During Shankleville's most prosperous period, from 1866 to 1909 when the college closed its doors, the population numbered over two thousand, not counting the inhabitants residing in the countryside surrounding the community who worked, attended school, shopped, and worshipped there. The community, though small, still existed in the early twenty-first century. A few of the churches still stood, and the Shankleville Cemetery holds the remains of a Jim and Winnie. A large, hand-made tombstone is carved with their names and the names of the nine children they raised. The bottom of the monument reads, "Remembered for what they did."

FURTHER READING

Frazier, E. Franklin. *The Free Negro Family* (1932).
Gutman, Herbert G. *The Black Family in Slavery and Freedom: 1750–1925* (1976).
Heglar, Charles J. *Rethinking the Slave Narrative: Slave Marriage and the Narratives of Henry Bibb and William and Ellen Craft* (2001).
Odom, Elzie D. Interview with author, 11 November 2003.
Ramos, Ralph. *Rocking Texas' Cradle* (1974).

LINDA J. FRAZIER

Shanks, Lela Knox (16 Sept. 1927–), activist, journalist, and teacher, was born Lela Knox in Oklahoma City, Oklahoma, to Lila Griggs Knox and William Medford Knox and grew up fifteen miles from Oklahoma City in the all-black town of Green Pastures. She graduated from Lincoln University in Jefferson City, Missouri, in 1949 with a bachelor's degree in journalism. In 1946, at age nineteen, she met Hughes Hannibal Shanks, a disabled World War II veteran; they married on 26 November 1947 and had four children.

Soon after their marriage Hughes enrolled in law school. The Shanks wanted to help African Americans, but they also wanted a "normal and happy life" (author interview). Lela Shanks found the latter goal impossible to achieve because

"everywhere we turned there was a racial barrier up." Shanks noticed that enforcement of racial separation seemed especially stringent when it came to acquiring education for their children.

After Hughes graduated from law school in 1951, the family moved to Denver, Colorado, where Shanks became a civil rights activist.

Throughout the 1960s she worked with community groups and with the Congress of Racial Equality (CORE). Her entry into the movement began after her first grader was assigned to an overcrowded segregated classroom in Denver. Her daughter was allowed to attend school for only a half day so that two separate daily sessions could be conducted for black and poor children. Shanks despaired because under this system African American children received half the instruction afforded white children in the same district. Shanks observed that there was ample room for additional students at a nearby neighborhood school, but it catered only to whites. Despite the Supreme Court ruling in *Brown v. Board of Education* three years earlier, the Shanks found their local school board unwilling to comply with desegregation laws. Shanks sought help from the local Urban League and the local NAACP. Both agencies told her that they could offer her no help. Shanks then started a petition drive to improve the physical size of the school building so the children could attend all-day sessions. Although the school did eventually add portable classrooms, Shanks had already begun teaching her children supplementary lessons at home.

In May 1961 the Shanks family moved to Kansas City, Kansas. When the Shankses arrived, they learned that their neighborhood school was segregated. Leaders of the North West District Citizens Committee approached the Shankses for help. They had been told that Hughes Shanks had a law degree and that the couple owned a typewriter. Shanks recalled, "They came over to our home and told us about their movement." The neighborhood children had all attended Hawthorne School, which was populated by equal numbers of African American and white students. The Kansas City School District suddenly redrew its boundary lines, re-creating a segregated, white-only population for a newly built school and Hawthorne as a school for black children. Whites on Shanks's block were given transfers to the white campus.

Shanks attempted to enroll her children in the white school, Bryant Elementary, but they were denied entry. She and her husband joined other local activists in filing suit against the Kansas City

School Board. While the case, *Randolph v. Kansas City, Kansas School Board*, was pending Shanks opened a school for neighborhood children in her home. In 1963 Shanks was visited at home by agents from the Federal Bureau of Investigation, who claimed that she was being investigated for the possible commission of a federal crime. Shanks's "crime" was her participation in a peaceful protest at the federal building in Kansas City. While Shanks was confronting harassment from the bureau, city officials threatened to declare Shanks and her husband unfit parents because of her public activism and Shanks and her husband were arrested for truancy.

Hughes Shanks did not like to speak in public but was an excellent strategist, a gift that benefited further from his legal training. He believed his wife had a right under the Constitution to publicly state her views, and he provided legal support for her and other movement activists. Lela Shanks felt comfortable speaking in public and often did so while her husband stayed with the children. At times she and other CORE chapter members made press statements. For the remainder of the 1960s Shanks's involvement in the movement deepened. She participated in sit-ins, swim-ins, and other demonstrations. In 1963 Shanks ran unsuccessfully for a seat on the Kansas City School Board and for the Kansas state legislature. Her activism notwithstanding, she also focused on being a mother. For most of the years her children were growing up, Shanks worked at home. Prior to this period she wrote for the *Chicago Defender*, the *St. Louis News*, and the *St. Louis Argus*.

The Shanks family eventually relocated to Lincoln, Nebraska, where Shanks continued to write. She also began to lecture publicly on African American history, multiculturalism, and human rights. She became well known in Lincoln intellectual circles as one who refused to pretend that the effects of segregation had ended with the integration of the public schools. "Prejudice is really a matter of tradition," she once said, "and discrimination is hard to eradicate because it became a part of the culture." Shanks received an honorary degree in Humane Letters from Nebraska Wesleyan University in 1998. She spent fourteen years caring for Hughes, who was stricken with Alzheimer's disease, and subsequently wrote *Your Name Is Hughes Hannibal Shanks: A Caregiver's Guide to Alzheimer's* (1996). As a committed civic leader, Shanks served on the boards of the University of Nebraska YWCA, Child Guidance, and the Nebraska Panel of American Women. She participated in the University of Nebraska's Training Teachers of Teachers Project, aimed at providing cultural-sensitivity training for classroom teachers, and which provided the model for the nation for integrating multicultural education into public schools. With her children grown, Shanks devoted increasing amounts of time to public speaking. In 2000 she was identified by the *Lincoln Journal Star* as one of the top one hundred people who had shaped Nebraska's history in the twentieth century.

Shanks continued to fight for racial justice throughout the first years of the new millennium. "The older I get, the more I realize that it's all connected. Racism and sexism … I believe that I have a responsibility as a human being to write and speak what I think is the truth." Shanks believed that for the country to change people must first change internally. "America is in its infancy when it comes to the concept and practice of racial equality and … we have barely begun to scratch the surface." Many exterior changes had been made, such as the voting rights act and other legislation, but Shanks argued that the majority of changes still had to be made within people's hearts.

Shanks continuously agitated for social justice. In 2006 she demonstrated outside of the federal building in Lincoln, Nebraska, in support of bringing American troops home from Iraq. She also gave testimony before the Nebraska state legislature's Judiciary Committee on a constitutional amendment in support of an American Civil Liberties Union lawsuit that would limit sections of the Patriot Act. Although the resolution did not pass, thirty-seven cities passed ordinances limiting or condemning the Patriot Act. Shanks continued to write social commentary for newspapers, addressing wide-ranging issues, including human rights, elitism, classism, multiculturalism, racism, and world peace.

FURTHER READING
All quotes in this article are taken from the author's interview with the Shanks on 22 July 2006. The Lela Knox Shanks Family Papers are housed in the home of Lela Shanks in Lincoln, Nebraska.
Shanks, Lela Knox. "It Will Take Full Acknowledgement to Have Full Healing," *Nebraska Humanities* (Spring 1994).
Shanks, Lela Knox. *Your Name Is Hughes Hannibal Shanks: A Caregiver's Guide to Alzheimer's* (1996, rev. ed. 1999, 2005).

TEKLA ALI JOHNSON

Sharpton, Al (3 Oct. 1954–), minister, activist,-and U.S. presidential candidate, was born Alfred Charles Sharpton Jr. in Brooklyn, New York, the younger of two children of Alfred Charles Sharpton Sr., a contractor, and Ada Richards Sharpton, a seamstress. His father and mother had migrated to Brooklyn from Florida and Alabama, respectively. Their son, Al, became steeped at an early age in the culture of the Pentecostal Church, gaining recognition as a "wonder boy preacher." He was ordained at the age of ten by his pastor, Bishop Frederick Douglass Washington, the charismatic founder of the Sharpton family's church, the Washington Temple Church of God in Christ.

Sharpton's first residence was in the working-class neighborhood of East New York in Brooklyn, but while he was still young his family moved to the nearby black middle-class community of Hollis, Queens. His idyllic childhood was dealt a devastating blow when his father left the household and moved in with another woman; the trauma was aggravated by the fact that the other woman was Ada Sharpton's daughter from a previous marriage—Sharpton's half sister, Tina. Ada and her two children, Al Jr. and Cheryl, fell into dire economic straits. Unable to pay the bills, they lived for a time without electricity or heat and eventually went on welfare, finding a succession of apartments in the Crown Heights and East Flatbush neighborhoods of Brooklyn.

In the coming years Sharpton would associate with a series of mentors, who would set the pattern for his personal, religious, and political development. The boy preacher became increasingly enchanted by a flashy minister on the other side of the East River, in Harlem. The Reverend ADAM CLAYTON POWELL JR. was the pastor of the Abyssinian Baptist Church and a U.S. congressman. One of Powell's notable traits was that he was "particularly irritating to whites," Sharpton later noted. Young Sharpton spent hours with the brash, cigar-chomping minister, consciously trying to imitate Powell's fearless panache and his suave and savvy manner.

While he was a student at Samuel J. Tilden High School in Brooklyn, Sharpton immersed himself in student government and the debating team. Michael Klein asserted in his biography of Sharpton, *The Man behind the Sound Bite*, that when many black and white students were becoming radicals, Sharpton took debating positions against the Maoists and black panther sympathizers. In high school Sharpton was introduced to the strategy of the economic boycott when he was appointed in 1969 as youth director of the Brooklyn office of Operation Breadbasket, an organization that was led by the Reverend JESSE JACKSON, Sharpton's mentor who later became his rival. Affiliated with the Southern Christian Leadership Conference (SCLC), Operation Breadbasket targeted businesses believed to be discriminating against blacks and then boycotted those companies until they agreed to adopt procedures to promote sensitivity and increase diversity within their organizations. Some critics equated this tactic with extortion, but both Sharpton and Jackson had seen the effectiveness of boycotts during the civil rights movement and found its use (and even threatened use) to be powerful options in their overall political strategy. When Jackson left Operation Breadbasket in 1971, Sharpton also resigned to start his own organization, the Brooklyn-based National Youth Movement.

As leader of the National Youth Movement, Sharpton would become a major figure in New York City, organizing boycotts and leading protests against police brutality in the 1980s. Glib in the language of the streets, he was able to draw large numbers of young people to his demonstrations. His advance to fame, and to controversy, was also linked with the personality of JAMES BROWN, the so-called Godfather of Soul, whom Sharpton met in 1973. Brown wore his hair in the "conked" or straightened style that some blacks, as the Afro came into fashion, considered a sign of racial self-loathing. As a tribute to Brown's influence, Sharpton began wearing his own hair in the same fashion, which made him easily recognizable among black activists and also made him the butt of unkind jokes.

In 1975 Sharpton dropped out of Brooklyn College after two years of study to begin promoting Brown's concerts, which is how he met Kathy Jordan, a backup singer for Brown whom he married in 1983; they had two children. In 1974, while Sharpton was arranging a performance for Brown in Zaire, Africa—during the "Rumble in the Jungle," a boxing match between MUHAMMAD ALI and GEORGE FOREMAN—Sharpton began dealing with the boxing promoter DON KING. Because of King's alleged connections to organized crime, FBI agents also turned their attention to Sharpton. In the early 1980s they approached him and threatened to prosecute him if he did not become an informant.

Sharpton later acknowledged turning over information about suspected drug dealers, but he denied spying on black radicals. But the New York City newspaper *Newsday* published a series of stories in 1988 showing that Sharpton helped the FBI try to locate a black revolutionary, Joanne Chesimard (also known as ASSATA SHAKUR), who was wanted in the killing of a New Jersey state trooper. Through most of the 1980s, these dealings with the FBI were unknown to Sharpton's fellow activists. His notoriety as a militant civil rights leader crested after the December 1986 death of Michael Griffith, a young black man killed in the predominantly white section of Howard Beach in Queens. Teaming up with two black lawyers, Alton Maddox and C. Vernon Mason, Sharpton led protest marches and demanded the appointment of a special prosecutor. A special prosecutor was named, and in December 1987 a jury convicted three white youths from Howard Beach of manslaughter. It was considered a vindication of his street protests. Law enforcement officials would later indict Sharpton and the National Youth Movement with a variety of tax and financial charges for which Sharpton was acquitted on all counts.

In November 1987 a black teenager named Tawana Brawley said that she had been sexually assaulted by white men in Wappingers Falls, New York. Sharpton, Maddox, and Mason began their fateful involvement in the case as advisers to the girl and her family. Sharpton and the other advisers continued to maintain that Brawley had been raped, even after the state attorney general and newspaper investigative reports had concluded the allegations were a "hoax." Witness testimony and physical evidence showed that Brawley and her mother fabricated the tale of abduction and assault because she feared punishment from her stepfather for staying out all night. In 2001 Sharpton paid sixty-five thousand dollars in damages, following a jury's determination that he had defamed Steven A. Pagones, a white attorney whom Sharpton had accused of involvement in the sexual attack and who was exonerated by a special grand jury in 1988.

Sharpton's reputation was severely damaged in January of 1988, when *Newsday* published its first articles on Sharpton's ties to the FBI. The disclosures divided the black activist community, and many radicals refused to participate in protests with Sharpton, fearing that he was spying on them. Sharpton claimed that the articles were part of a plot to have him assassinated. One of the most verbally agile figures to set foot on the public stage in New York, Sharpton rebounded from that crisis, as he did from many others.

In the early years of the 1990s Sharpton went through a personal and spiritual transformation that changed the course of his political career. During a 12 January 1991 demonstration in the Bensonhurst section of Brooklyn—where the black teenager Yusuf Hawkins had been murdered the previous year by a gang of whites—Sharpton was stabbed in the chest by a white man. While recovering in the hospital, Sharpton began to reassess and redirect his energies, and he became a more traditional politician, soon casting his eye on elective office. His shift to establishment politics was eased on 2 July 1990, when a jury acquitted him of all sixty-seven counts of fraud, which had been brought by the state attorney general Robert Abrams. Abrams had accused Sharpton of stealing about a quarter of a million dollars from the National Youth Movement.

In 1992 Sharpton ran in the Democratic primary race for U.S. Senate. While he did not win the election, he garnered two-thirds of the black vote and established himself as a credible power broker. He made a similarly strong challenge in a 1994 U.S. Senate race and set the stage for a run in 1997 for the mayoralty of New York City. All the while, Sharpton maintained his image as the city's leading voice of protest against police brutality. Yet Sharpton's growing popularity in the black community sent chills through much of the city's white population, resulting in a white political backlash that contributed to the 1993 reelection defeat of the city's first black mayor, DAVID DINKINS. Reacting to the February 1999 killing of Amadou Diallo—an unarmed African immigrant shot in a hail of forty-one bullets fired by four white policemen—Sharpton put together one of the most effective civil disobedience campaigns in modern city history. He persuaded hundreds of politicians, actors, labor leaders, and others to join him in getting arrested at protests outside police headquarters in Manhattan.

He also increasingly began to appeal to the Latino community, traveling, for example, to the Puerto Rican island of Vieques to protest U.S. bombing exercises there. On 23 May 2001 he was sentenced to three months in jail for that act of civil disobedience. He served the time at a federal detention center in Brooklyn. In 2003 Sharpton filed papers as a candidate for the U.S. presidency. His candidacy drew the support of the leading black intellectual CORNEL WEST, who agreed to serve as an adviser. Sharpton's quick wit, refreshing candor, and populist appeal distinguished him among a crowded field of

Democratic contenders—even though his chances of winning the Democratic nomination were known to be slight. Sharpton was nonetheless clearly hoping to emerge as a spokesman for black America, a role that had been played during the 1980s and early 1990s by his onetime mentor, Jesse Jackson.

In 2007 Sharpton was shocked when it was discovered that his great grandfather's family had been enslaved by relatives of the segregationist senator Strom Thurmond. This news brought a mixture of emotions to bear on Sharpton, yet he recognized that, primarily, it is "America's shame is that I am the heir of those who were property to the Thurmond family."

Sharpton sat out the 2008 Democratic Party presidential primary, and initially was quite critical of the eventual nominee, Senator BARACK OBAMA (D-IL), claiming that he did not represent the views of the African American community and that his candidacy had been generated by white interests. Obama's support of the conservative former Democrat Joe Lieberman in the 2006 Connecticut Senate race particularly irked Sharpton who supported the official Democratic candidate. But nor did Sharpton endorse Senator Hillary Clinton (D-NY) who enjoyed the support of many black Congressional and community leaders, especially in New York. Without formally endorsing Obama, Sharpton gradually made clear his backing for him. By 2011, when talk show host TAVIS SMILEY and public intellectual CORNEL WEST were openly critical of the Obama administration's economic and foreign policies, Sharpton emerged as one of Obama's most passionate defenders. In September 2011 Sharpton began hosting his own talk show on the MSNBC network, PoliticsNation.

FURTHER READING

Sharpton, Al. "My Link to Strom Thurmond," *Los Angeles Times*, 1 Mar. 2007.

Sharpton, Al, and Anthony Walton. *Go and Tell Pharaoh: The Autobiography of the Reverend Al Sharpton* (1996).

Sharpton, Al, and Karen Hunter. *Al on America* (2002).

Klein, Michael. *The Man behind the Sound Bite* (1991)

Mandery, Evan J. *The Campaign: Rudy Giuliani, Ruth Messinger, Al Sharpton, and the Race to Be Mayor of New York City* (1999).

RON HOWELL

Shavers, Charlie (3 Aug. 1917–8 July 1971), jazz trumpeter, arranger, and composer, was born Charles James Shavers in New York City. His parents' names are unknown, but his father ran a barbershop underneath the Savoy Ballroom in Harlem. Shavers recounted that the family was poor but not destitute. His father, also an amateur musician, played banjo and trumpet, and from his grammar school years onward Shavers played piano, banjo, guitar, and string bass before settling on the trumpet.

Shavers became devoted to music while in high school. In the trumpeter Carl "Bama" Warwick, who lived at Shavers's home and went to school with him, Shavers had a companion with whom he could practice. "I always think of him as my real brother," Shavers told the writer Sinclair Traill. The two trumpeters played in lesser-known bands and joined Laurie Simmons in New York when Shavers was only fifteen. They then moved on to the Hardy Brothers band in Washington—Shavers had presumably dropped out of high school by this point—and then to Frankie Fairfax's band in Philadelphia, Pennsylvania, in 1936. Fairfax's trumpet section also included DIZZY GILLESPIE, whose early style was shaped when he and Shavers worked together imitating ROY ELDRIDGE's recorded solos. The brotherly partnership of Shavers and Warwick continued with work in Tiny Bradshaw's big band, which they joined in Baltimore in 1936, and in LUCKY MILLINDER's big band from early 1937 onward.

In November 1937 Shavers left both Warwick and big bands to replace the trumpeter FRANKIE NEWTON in string bassist JOHN KIRBY's sextet at the Onyx Club on Fifty-second Street in New York. Working with the singer MAXINE SULLIVAN, Kirby's unusually quiet instrumental swing sextet was popular in its day. The group had come into existence on the strength of Sullivan's swing-era adaptation of the Scotch-Irish ballad "Loch Lomond," but in large part the group owed its character to Shavers, who now both soloed and wrote for it. Shavers composed "Rehearsin' for a Nervous Breakdown" and the hit song "Undecided," preserved at Kirby's first recording session in October 1938. He arranged "Anitra's Dance," recorded in 1939, and wrote politely jazzed-up arrangements of classical themes. Pianist Billy Kyle and Shavers were the sextet's finest soloists. In this capacity Shavers occasionally played open trumpet, as heard on "Royal Garden Blues" (also recorded in 1939), but his normal procedure was to use a trumpet mute to muffle both volume and tone quality.

Kirby's sextet held a long engagement at the Onyx, in the course of which it became the first African American band to have its own sponsored network radio show, *Flow Gently, Sweet Rhythm*. Engagements followed at the Famous Door in New York and at the Pump Room of the Hotel Ambassador East in Chicago. From 1942 to 1944, when Shavers finally quit, the band gradually disintegrated: Kirby and Sullivan's marriage broke up; drummer O'Neill Spencer became terminally ill, and he died in 1944; and reed players BUSTER BAILEY and RUSSELL PROCOPE were drafted. In later decades Kirby's band faded from importance, its music seeming excessively cute and of little historical consequence, but late in life Shavers named the sextet as his favorite by far of all the bands in which he had played.

Independent of Kirby, Shavers contributed to historic sessions, recording "Melancholy" (Jan. 1938) with the clarinetist JOHNNY DODDS, "Them There Eyes" (July 1939) with the singer BILLIE HOLIDAY, and "I'm Coming, Virginia" (Sept. 1941), "Texas Moaner" (Sept. 1941), and "Mood Indigo" (Oct. 1941) with the clarinetist and soprano saxophonist SIDNEY BECHET. In 1943 Shavers worked on the staff of CBS radio as a member of Raymond Scott's orchestra, while doubling with Kirby and, by one account, also making his first guest appearances with the trombonist Tommy Dorsey's big band. In 1944, his final year with Kirby, Shavers played in Benny Goodman's big band and recorded the ballad "Stardust" under his own name.

Shavers joined Dorsey in February 1945, and until the leader's death in 1956 they toured regularly, at one point performing for two months in Rio de Janeiro, Brazil. In marked contrast to Kirby's sextet, Dorsey's band featured the trumpeter's exhibitionist upper-register playing—heard, for example, on numerous performances of "Well, Git It!" Apart from Dorsey, Shavers participated in Kirby's unsuccessful attempt to revive the sextet in 1946, and the following year Shavers recorded another celebrated version of "Stardust" at a concert in Pasadena, California, with vibraphonist LIONEL HAMPTON's Just Jazz All Stars. In 1950 Shavers co-led a sextet with drummer Louie Bellson and vibraphonist Terry Gibbs. As a member of Jazz at the Philharmonic, Shavers also recorded solos in "What Is This Thing Called Love?" and "Funky Blues" at a concert in July 1952. He toured with this aggregation, visiting Europe and, in 1953, Japan. He was a member of Benny Goodman's small group in Chicago in 1954. Shavers's other notable recordings from these years include the pianist and comedian Steve Allen's album *Jazz for Tonight* (1955) and,

under the name of the All Stars, the album *Session at Riverside* (1956).

From 1956 into the 1960s Shavers led bands and worked with tenor saxophonist COLEMAN HAWKINS, clarinetist Buster Bailey, and other swing-era jazz celebrities at the Metropole nightclub in New York. In 1959 he recorded tenor saxophonist Hal Singer's album *Blue Stompin'*. At some point during this period he also performed at the Embers nightclub in New York. By 1964 Shavers had returned to Dorsey's big band, now a memorial group under the direction of tenor saxophonist Sam Donahue. After performances in England in 1964, international tours continued from 1965 into 1966 under the leadership of the singer Frank Sinatra Jr., Shavers returned to Europe as a soloist in 1969 and 1970. At the Half-Note in New York in May 1971 Shavers gave his last performance as a guest with the J. P. J. Quartet, which comprised tenor saxophonist BUDD JOHNSON, pianist Dill Jones, bassist Bill Pemberton, and drummer Oliver Jackson. Shavers died in New York City of throat cancer. He was survived by his widow, Blanche; her maiden name and details of the marriage are unknown.

In both his writing for Kirby and his decades of recordings as a trumpeter, Shavers often lacked taste, his music suffering from ideas that might be considered pretentious, technical, bombastic, schmaltzy, corny, or squealing. Two tracks from a Jazz at the Philharmonic concert in Tokyo in November 1953—the swing tune "Cottontail," in which he engages in a showy solo contest with trumpeter Roy Eldridge, and the ballad "Embraceable You"—are typical representatives of these failings. Nevertheless, at his intermittent and unpredictable best—in his composition "Undecided," in lovely versions of "Stardust," in a bluesy, emotional, sprightly solo in "The Man I Love" from the Just Jazz group (but without Hampton), and in a lyrical solo and ensemble lead that blossoms from delicacy into forthrightness at the end of Allen's "Limehouse Blues"—Shavers must be reckoned among the leading swing musicians.

FURTHER READING

Bryce, Owen. "Charlie Shavers: An Appreciation," *Jazz Journal International* 32 (Nov. 1979): 16–17.

Chilton, John. *Who's Who of Jazz: Storyville to Swing Street*, 4th ed. (1985).

Schuller, Gunther. *The Swing Era: The Development of Jazz, 1930–1945* (1989).

Shaw, Arnold. *The Street That Never Slept* (1971; rpt. as *52nd Street: The Street of Jazz* [1977]).

Obituary: *New York Times*, 9 July 1971.
This entry is taken from the *American National Biography* and is published here with the permission of the American Council of Learned Societies.

BARRY KERNFELD

Shaw, Bernard (22 May 1940–), network television news reporter and news anchor, was born in Chicago, Illinois, to Edgar Shaw, a New York Central Railroad employee and housepainter, and Camilla Murphy Shaw, a domestic worker. His childhood idol was the CBS News legend Edward R. Murrow. He graduated in January 1959 from Dunbar Vocational High School in Chicago, where he served as president not only of the Dunbar student council but also of the citywide High School Student Council Presidents Association. While serving in the U.S. Marine Corps from 1959 to 1963 in Oahu, Hawaii, Shaw met the CBS News anchor Walter Cronkite, who was in Hawaii filming a documentary on World War II. Shaw called Cronkite's hotel thirty-four times before Cronkite finally agreed to see him, and their meeting led to a lifelong friendship.

In 1964 Shaw entered the University of Illinois at Chicago as a world history major while continuing to work in news. The following year he joined the staff of WNUS, Chicago's first all-news radio station, as a reporter. Hired as a writer at Chicago's WFLD-TV in 1965, Shaw became news anchor and education reporter the next year for WIND Radio, owned by the Westinghouse Broadcasting Company. In 1968 he was promoted to White House reporter and transferred to Washington, D.C. Shaw left the University of Illinois in his junior year, stating later, "I didn't have time to graduate—the promotion to Washington was critical advancement." In 1971 Shaw was hired by CBS News, where he enjoyed collegial relationships with Cronkite and commentator Eric Sevareid, whom Shaw described as "a philosophical compass for me."

In 1974 Shaw married Linda Marie Allston of Darlington, South Carolina, with whom he had a son, Amar Edgar, and a daughter, Anil Louise.

After six years with CBS, Shaw was hired by ABC News as its Latin American bureau chief and correspondent (1977–1979) and Capitol Hill correspondent (1979–1980). He traveled to Iran in fall 1979 to cover the takeover of the U.S. Embassy in Tehran, where the staff was held hostage for 444 days. The following year Shaw was approached by the fledgling Cable News Network (CNN), which was not yet on the air, to become its principal Washington anchor. ABC News president Roone Arledge advised Shaw that this would be an unwise career move, but Shaw, seeing CNN as "the last frontier in network television news," disagreed. He signed with CNN and in June 1980 coanchored with Don Farmer and Chris Curle the first live hour of the new network.

On 30 March 1981 Shaw and CNN made history by beating the "Big Three" television networks to a breaking story: Shaw was on the air four minutes before ABC, CBS, and NBC with news of the assassination attempt on President Ronald Reagan. Shaw, however, refused to repeat unconfirmed reports that Reagan's press secretary, James Brady, had been killed; Brady had, in fact, been badly wounded. Shaw averted embarrassment for CNN, as ABC, CBS, and NBC broadcast Brady obituaries, which they were then forced to retract.

In October 1987, the reputations of both Shaw and CNN were solidified with viewers when the White House invited him to join the Big Three network news anchors—Peter Jennings, Dan Rather, and Tom Brokaw—for a pre–Reagan/Gorbachev summit interview with Reagan.

In May 1989 Shaw traveled to Beijing to cover the first summit in forty-one years between China and the Soviet Union. Chinese students, agitating for economic and political freedoms in outlying cities, and joined by many in the professional classes, took their pro-democracy demonstrations into Tiananmen Square, where they grew into a million-person revolt. Shaw anchored CNN's continuous live coverage from Tiananmen Square until the moment that the Chinese government blindfolded the world by shutting down the network's satellite link to the globe in advance of the army's bloody suppression of the revolt.

In January 1991 Shaw was posted to Baghdad on the eve of the first U.S. war with Iraq. Arriving at the invitation of the Iraqi government to follow up his October 1990 interview with Saddam Hussein, Shaw was soon called upon to report live and around the clock as coalition bombs began to fall with the onset of Operation Desert Storm on 16 January. Shaw's courage in the midst of extreme danger and his superior coverage of the Gulf War brought him fame and recognition and helped to further bolster CNN's standing as a major news outlet. Other important stories Shaw covered at CNN included the first Reagan/Gorbachev summit in Geneva in 1985, the bombing of the Murrah

Federal Building in Oklahoma City in 1995, and the impeachment proceedings against President Bill Clinton in 1998.

Apart from his regular anchoring of *The International Hour* and *Your World Today*, Shaw anchored *Inside Politics* and covered all facets of national political campaigns. A seminal moment of Shaw's broadcasting career occurred in 1988 while moderating a presidential debate between then-Vice President George H. W. Bush and Massachusetts Governor Michael Dukakis. Seeking a candid response from Dukakis, Shaw opened with a blunt question that addressed a major issue in the campaign: "Governor, if [your wife] Kitty Dukakis were raped and murdered, would you favor an irrevocable death penalty for the killer?" Dukakis's unemotional response to Shaw's question was a defining moment in the campaign, which ended in a landslide victory for Bush. While Shaw was both criticized and praised for phrasing the death penalty question in that manner, he maintained that it was the answer, not the question, that mattered.

Departing from CNN in February 2001 in what he called "stepping back" rather than "retiring," Shaw, at age sixty, brought to an end the most significant part of a career that had taken him to forty-six countries and brought him many professional honors, including the Eduard Rhein Foundation's Cultural Journalistic Award in 1991 (he was the first non-German recipient), six cable ACE awards (1988, 1990, 1991, 1993, 1994, and 1996), the George Foster Peabody Award in 1990, and the 2001 Edward R. Murrow Lifetime Achievement Award.

Among Shaw's other awards were honorary degrees from Francis Marion College, Northeastern University, and the University of Illinois; induction into several journalism halls of fame; three Emmy awards (1989, 1992, and 1996); the National Association of Black Journalists' Journalist of the Year (1989); the Alfred I. DuPont–Columbia University Silver Baton Award; the Pioneer in Broadcasting Award from the National Association of Blacks in Broadcasting (2001); and the David Brinkley and Walter Cronkite awards for Journalism Excellence (1991 and 1994, respectively).

Shaw was a member of Sigma Delta Chi, the Society of Professional Journalists. His alma mater, the University of Illinois, created the Bernard Shaw Endowed Scholarship Fund to assist promising students. Shaw himself contributed more than $300,000 to the endowment.

FURTHER READING
Whittemore, Hank. *CNN—The Inside Story* (1990).
Wiener, Robert. *Live from Baghdad: Gathering News at Ground Zero* (1992).

DAVID BORSVOLD

Shaw, Earl D. (26 Nov. 1937–), a pioneer in experimental laser physics, professor and chair of the Department of Physics and Astronomy at Rutgers University, was born in his grandparents' house in Clarksdale, Mississippi, where he attended a three-room school at Hopson Plantation. His parents, both sharecroppers, married early, separated, and divorced. He was three years old when he last saw his father, who was later killed in a shootout with police in Chicago, at the age of twenty-six. Shaw's mother remarried in 1942.

Hopson Plantation, established in 1852, was a 3,500-acre operation, with four distinct "Places" where tenant farmers lived, each place having its own barns. Around 1935, just before Shaw was born, the Hopson family began switching over from manual human labor and mules to a mechanized operation with tractors. A crew of mechanical engineers from International Harvester in Chicago worked every fall at the Hopson Plantation, perfecting the automated cotton picker, introduced in 1944. Shaw's mother and stepfather moved to Chicago in 1948; Shaw remained in Mississippi, in a foster home for two years, making such high scores on academic tests that he skipped from sixth to eighth grade. Rejoining his mother in Chicago, he was accepted into Crane Technical High School at the age of twelve, graduating in 1954.

Shaw earned a bachelor's degree in physics from the University of Illinois in 1960, married a woman named Erin, had twin boys, and moved to Hanover, New Hampshire, to work as a lab technician for the Army Corps of Engineers. The Shaws' third son, Alan, was born in Hanover in 1963. (Continuing in his father's footsteps, Alan D. Shaw obtained a Ph.D. in computer science from Massachusetts Institute of Technology in 1995.)

Shaw returned to school full-time with a scholarship in physics, completing a master's degree from Dartmouth College in 1964 with a thesis, "Optical and Thermal Transformation of V-centers in Potassium Chloride." After enrolling in the University of California at Berkeley, Shaw earned a Ph.D. in physics in 1969, writing his dissertation on "Nuclear Relaxation in Ferromagnetic Cobalt." At Berkeley he had also been elected president of the Black Students Union. His marriage ended in divorce in 1966; in 1969 he married a counselor for students resisting the military draft.

Shaw began work in 1970 at Bell Laboratories, in Murray Hill, New Jersey, where he and Chandra K. N. Patel developed the Raman spin-flip laser, for which they shared a patent. The spin-flip laser was based on the 1928 discovery by C. V. Raman that whenever a beam of light hits any substance, some photons in the beam gain or lose energy from the collision. The resulting beam has a different wavelength from the original beam. Capturing and amplifying this second beam produces a new laser beam that can be adjusted by placing a semiconductor in a magnetic field, and varying the field—a process known as spin-flip tuning. As a result, the frequency of the beam can be augmented within a range of a few micrometers (millionths of a meter), and the emitted wavelength can be adjusted in a manner as convenient as adjusting a dimmer switch.

Patel and Shaw published an early paper on the process in 1971, in *Physical Reviews B*. Tunable lasers particularly improved use of the technology for examining biological specimens: certain frequencies of laser light were known to destroy a cell wall, but Shaw and Patel's device could be adjusted to a lower frequency, which would not. It also proved useful in air pollution analysis.

While his association with Bell Labs continued for nearly twenty years, in 1972 Shaw held the position of assistant professor of physics and astronomy at the University of Rochester, which garnered a National Science Foundation grant of $69,700 to support Shaw's continued research on the spin-flip laser (*Optical Spectra*, Aug. 1972, 12). Shaw developed applications for air pollution studies, astrophysics, and spectroscopy.

In July 1985, Shaw patented a free-electron amplifier device with an electromagnetic radiation delay element. Building on his previous work with the spin-flip laser, the free-electron device has been the focus of his subsequent research. In 1988, Shaw left Bell Laboratories to accept an appointment as professor of physics at Rutgers University's Newark, New Jersey, campus. There, in addition to teaching, he continued research on the far-infrared free electron laser, which beams electrons through a magnetic field to generate infrared radiation.

His own description of his later research included the following note: "I have been developing infrared lasers and recently moved a far-infrared free electron laser to the Newark Campus. The laser that will be operational by the end of 1995 generates short tuneable far-infrared light pulses that will permit the analog of pulsed magnetic resonance techniques for the first time in this optical wavelength regime. I intend to study the time dependence of the vibrational motion of DNA and other biological molecules with the ultimate aim of enhancing biochemical activity with far-infrared radiation" (Rutgers Dept. of Physics and Astronomy, Earl D. Shaw—professional activities,http://www.physics.rutgers.edu/people/pdps/Shaw.html).

Named in 1996 as chair of the Rutgers-Newark campus Department of Physics and Astronomy, in 1999–2000 Shaw developed a comprehensive program in astronomy for undergraduate students at Rutgers, working through a partnership between the Newark campus of Rutgers and the New Jersey Institute of Technology. To facilitate accurate astronomical observations within an urban setting—an area affected by extensive light pollution throughout the night—the project acquired special imaging equipment for the campus's Meade 299 KX telescope.

Shaw arranged for Rutgers to host the annual conference of the National Society of Black Physicists in 1994; in 2000 at the society's twenty-fourth annual meeting he presented a paper on free electron lasers, and the development at that time of "third generation synchrotrons." Shaw served on the planning committee for the Liberty Science Center in Jersey City, designed to draw inner-city youth into scientific fields. "Science has done so much for me," he observed. "It's the social and economic vehicle that sprang me out of nothing." If he could be credited with inspiring four or five black students who obtained Ph.D.'s he added, "It would be as good as winning the Nobel Prize" (Russell, 316).

Shaw retired from Rutgers in 2004, continuing to live in Harding Township, Morris County, New Jersey. A few years later, Dr. John Madey, director of the Free Electron Laboratory at Duke University, observed that "What Earl has done is bring a light source into existence to provide answers to pretty specific questions relating to the way electrons in semiconductors work, and the way atoms and molecules in biology absorb and give off energy and how they move. There is no equivalent system like it anywhere in the world" (Russell, 306).

FURTHER READING

Russell, Dick, and Alvin F. Poussaint. "The Laser Physicist and the Computer Wizard: Earl and Alan Shaw," *Black Genius: Inspirational Portraits of America's Black Leaders* (2009).

Schlager, Neil, and Josh Lauer. *Science and Its Times: Understanding the Social Significance of Scientific Discovery* (2000).

Van Sertima, Ivan. *Blacks in Science: Ancient and Modern* (1983).

CHARLES ROSENBERG

Shaw, Herman (18 May 1902–3 Dec. 1999), farmer, mill worker, and the spokesman for the survivors of the Tuskegee Syphilis Study at the formal federal apology at the White House on 16 May 1997, was born in Tallassee, Alabama, the second of four children of Frank Shaw, a farmer. After his mother's death, Shaw's father moved the family to Plano, Texas, in search of a better life. Shaw excelled in his studies at the local segregated grammar schools, remembering always his lessons on the ancient world. When the farmland in Texas proved unyielding, Shaw returned to Tallassee and farming. The depression years proved difficult on the land, and Shaw was hired as the first black man to run a cord machine in a nearby textile mill. He would stay at the mill for forty-four years, while continuing to grow cotton, corn, and collard greens that were prized by his neighbors. He married Fannie Mae Greathouse and continued to emphasize the importance of education. They had two children, Herman Jr. and Mary Mullins, and an especially close relationship to a nephew Johnny Frank Shaw.

Government health officials recruited Shaw into the Tuskegee Syphilis Study in the 1930s when he was tested for his "bad blood," a commonly used phrase to denote syphilis. As with the other 399 subjects and 201 controls in the study, he was deceived into thinking he was being treated rather than simply observed by medical personnel as the study continued until 1972. In the late 1940s, he learned that the government had set up rapid treatment centers in Birmingham to cure those with early syphilis. Shaw went to Birmingham, but was turned away, assuming later that this was done because he was in the study as his name was on a list. It may have been, however, because he was in the late stage of the disease. Others in the study did manage to get treated in Birmingham. Regardless of why he was turned away, Shaw's testimony about this experience, given before a Senate hearing and repeated many times in the media, became a hallmark of the study's deception. It was fictionalized in the play and film about the study *Miss Evers' Boys* (HBO 1997), although Shaw was critical of parts of the way the story was recast in this version. He always thought the men should have been what

he labeled "guinea hogs," not "guinea pigs," because of the enormity of what was done to them.

Shaw joined in the lawsuit organized by attorney FRED D. GRAY to sue the government over the study. He remained close to Gray, was interviewed many times for films and newspaper stories, and became the spokesman for the survivors. In 1997 he spoke in the East Room of the White House at the formal federal apology ceremony and introduced President Bill Clinton. The picture of the two of them embracing was on the front page of the *New York Times* the next day. Shaw emphasized the need for a permanent memorial in Tuskegee and the requirement to make sure "the kind of tragedy that happened to us in the Tuskegee Study" would never be repeated. He lived to see the beginnings of the Tuskegee Human and Civil Rights Multicultural Center as that memorial. He was a member of the New Adka Baptist Church and is buried in Reeltown, Alabama.

FURTHER READING

Gray, Fred D. *The Tuskegee Syphilis Study* (1998).

Reverby, Susan M., ed. *Tuskegee's Truths: Rethinking the Tuskegee Syphilis Study* (2000).

SUSAN M. REVERBY

Shaw, Nate (Ned Cobb) (1885–1973), farmer and sharecroppers union activist, was born Ned Cobb in rural east-central Alabama. Shaw was one of six children of former slaves Hayes and Liza Culver Shaw. Ned Cobb is best known under the pseudonym Nate Shaw, because of the magnificent oral autobiography Shaw shared with Theodore Rosengarten. The book, *All God's Dangers: the Life of Nate Shaw* (1974), was perhaps the best single source for the consciousness and politics of the millions of illiterate black women and men who struggled in the decades after Emancipation to create a life in freedom. The fictionalized names of people and places in *All God's Dangers* are the best guide to this rich story.

Nate Shaw's father, Hayes, put Nate to work at farming tasks while he was a still a young boy. Shaw's mother Liza died when he was nine years old, and although he resented his father's exploitation of his labor, he embraced his fate as a farmer in the black belt. He worked dutifully for the family under his father's direction, mastered the skills for mixed farming with cotton as the market crop, and he planned for a future living off the land.

In 1906 Shaw came of age and married Hannah Ramsey, nicknamed "Sweet," the literate daughter from a small landholding family. Shaw shared his sense of himself at the time, saying "I was a poor young colored man but I had the strength of a man who comes to know himself" (Rosengarten, 82). Nine children were born to the couple.

Shaw learned how disadvantageous sharecropping was from his experience from 1907 to 1910. After four years of hard farm labor, he felt that "what little I did get I had to work like the devil to get it" (108). Shaw was ambitious, and felt exploited and disrespected under the sharecropping regime, so he decided to become a cash renter. A renting farmer needed to own a plow animal: either a mule or a horse. Shaw spent $100 in 1910 for his first mule, Lu. In 1911 Shaw moved his young family in a wagon pulled by Lu onto a twenty-two-acre farm he had rented, leaving sharecropping behind. That first year as a renter, Shaw observed, "I commenced making a heavier crop … handlin' my own affairs. Paid cash rent and made a profit from my farmin': I come up from the bottom then" (118).

The Shaw family began to live a life of landed independence, lacking only freehold land ownership. Shaw and Hannah worked out their philosophy of life. Shaw and his sons would work in the fields. In the off-season, Shaw would haul lumber and obtain other cash jobs. He caned furniture and also fish baskets used for African-style river fishing. Hannah would look after the children and handle many of the household duties, but she would never work in the field or take in the laundry of whites. Shaw laid aside a portion of the cotton crop for Hannah: he harvested and ginned the cotton, then delivered the cash to her.

The Shaw children were born at home but with a physician in attendance: most rural people, both blacks and whites, used midwives in early-twentieth-century Alabama. The Shaw children went to school, after which the girls worked in the house and the boys on the farm. Shaw intended that his family would live like free people. He remembered with some anger his father's exploitative philosophy of family life and seems to have consciously chosen the opposite direction.

By the 1920s, although still farming with mules, Shaw bought first one car, and then another, leaving the older one for his sons to drive. In other parts of the world this would have been called "the peasant's dream," though the Shaws would never have used this term.

The success of the Shaw family was noticed, with some envy, in the 1920s. Some complained that Shaw had too much meat for his smokehouse.

Others noted that a black farmer did not need two cars. Some of this jealousy was expressed by blacks but more often from whites. The petty jealousies and conflicts of Jim Crow rural life sometimes irritated Shaw, but he rose above it. He prospered during what amounted to an agricultural depression in the South after the end of World War I. The Great Depression, however, would be far crueler to Shaw and his neighbors. During this crisis Shaw's character was tested in the most profound way and he both stood firm and changed fundamentally.

Shaw had attempted to buy a piece of land under a program promoted by the Hoover administration, and a white farm broker named Watson decided to involve himself in this particular business transaction. He would have swindled Shaw into mortgaging everything he owned against the land in question if wife Hannah, who was literate, had not been present at the bank with Shaw. The entire southern economy was collapsing, with cotton down to five cents a pound; white men in the system attempted to survive by trying to steal assets held by blacks.

The Sharecroppers Union (SCU), derivative of the Communist Party at or near the height of its strength, intervened on behalf of black farmers. The SCU's original strategy was to organize and push for local demands by blacks, in preparation for revolutionary struggle to create a "Blackbelt Republic" in confederation with a socialist United States. These were revolutionary times and with white planters increasingly employing Fascist tactics, black renters and sharecroppers turned toward Communism. The historical model for the resolution of injustice in the South, apparent in the 1930s, was revolutionary violence like that of the Civil War, not gradualist reforms.

Lester Watson, one of Shaw's most rapacious landlords, had a friend going around the county announcing that Watson was going to take everything that black renters Shaw and Virgil Jones owned in the fall settlement: livestock, tools, everything. In hopes of protecting their livelihoods, Shaw and Jones joined the SCU. Within weeks of Shaw's joining the SCU, Watson got a writ for seizure of Virgil Jones's working stock and sent sheriff's deputies to serve the writ. Shaw's SCU local called the members to come stand together with Jones. Shaw arrived armed with a revolver.

Shaw understood that for his class of farmers, the loss of stock meant, at best, a return to sharecropper status; at worst, it meant unemployment and starvation. Shaw believed that the only defense was a united, militant one. Soon, he found himself engaged in a shootout with the deputies, who retreated in a rout after shooting Shaw with buckshot. Shaw was taken to Tuskegee where his wound was treated; he was also pledged to secrecy and sent back to his home county. He was ultimately captured along with other members of the SCU. While some members and nonmembers were murdered before trial, Shaw, fortunately, was not known to have been armed and was put on trial for simply being present. Even with an International Labor Defense lawyer to champion his case, Nate Shaw, at age forty-seven, was sentenced to twelve to fifteen years in the Alabama state penitentiary.

In jail, prior to his trial, Shaw experienced a full-fledged conversion to Christianity. He saw no conflict between the SCU, revolutionary unity, and Christian piety. Shaw noted that "in Beauford— God spoke to my dyin soul … surely that helped me through prison." Shaw had an ILD lawyer but he knew he had no civil rights. His trial lasted one day and within five months he was at the Alabama State prison farm.

He was released from prison in 1945, a fifty-nine year old mule farmer in the age of tractors and mechanized farming. He worked hard to reconstitute his family. His son Vernon continued to farm as did Shaw for a while. Then, as Shaw aged, he rented out land, sold his housewares as antiques, and ruminated on his long, complicated life. Finally, in 1969 a researcher from the North, Theodore Rosengarten, found Shaw and urged him to reminisce about his life. Shaw's life story tells much about black life in the heartland and the rural South, when much of it was still dominated by the memory and social structures of slavery. Nate Shaw shared the courage and political commitment that millions of rural folk have used to reshape the nineteenth and twentieth centuries.

FURTHER READING

Kelley, Robin D. G. *Hammer and Hoe: Alabama Communists During the Great Depression* (1990).

Rosengarten, Theodore. *All God's Dangers: The Life of Nate Shaw* (1974).

HAROLD S. FORSYTHE

Shaw, Patricia Walker (26 June 1939–30 June 1985), business executive and social worker, was born Lily Patricia Walker in Little Rock, Arkansas, the daughter of Harriet Ish and Antonio Maceo Walker Sr.,

an actuary. Both of her parents descended from middle-class families. Her mother, from Little Rock, Arkansas, was the daughter of George Washington Stanley Ish, a physician, whose father, Jefferson Garfield Ish, was a teacher. Shaw's father was the son of Lelia O'Neal Walker, cofounder of the Mississippi Boulevard Christian Church and daughter of the former slaves George and Pat Hill Walker of Tillman, Mississippi. Antonio Walker's father was Joseph Edison Walker, a medical school graduate, 1923 founder of the Universal Life Insurance Company in Memphis, Tennessee, and 1946 cofounder of the Tri-State Bank. Antonio Walker succeeded his father as president of Universal Life Insurance Company in 1952. In 1958 Joseph Edison Walker was murdered, and Antonio succeeded his father as president of Tri-State Bank, instantly becoming the leader of two of the most prominent and successful black businesses in the United States. It is in these footsteps that Shaw would eventually stand.

The eldest of three children, Shaw was raised in a middle-class Memphis, Tennessee, neighborhood, and education was a Walker family priority. She attended Hamilton Elementary School in Memphis and in 1956 graduated from Oakwood High Boarding School in Poughkeepsie, New York. In 1961 She graduated cum laude from Fisk University in Nashville, Tennessee, with a bachelor of arts degree in business administration. After graduation, she worked as an underwriting clerk at the Memphis company founded by her grandfather, Universal Life Insurance Company. Shaw's first stint at her family's company was short. While at Fisk University, she met Harold R. Shaw, whom she married on 17 June 1961. Later that year the couple moved to Chicago, where Patricia Shaw enrolled in the University of Chicago Graduate School to pursue her studies in business administration. She took a day job with the Illinois Department of Public Aid as a social worker. Shaw only remained in Chicago for about a year before she moved to Nashville, where in 1962 she enrolled at Tennessee State University and earned a teacher's certificate. She returned to her social work roots, however, when she and her husband moved to her childhood town of Memphis. She enrolled in the Memphis branch of the University of Tennessee Graduate School of Social Work and worked in Memphis as a social worker.

In 1966 Shaw left her social work career behind and once again joined Universal Life. Initially she worked as a keypunch operator and familiarized herself with the operations of the company. Later she moved to the data processing department and was promoted to a chief clerk position in 1967. She eventually became department supervisor and rose through the company's ranks and other departments, including a supervisory position in accounting. Shaw was promoted to assistant vice president in 1971 and vice president and associate controller in 1974. She entered the upper-management tier in 1980 with a promotion to senior vice president and assistant secretary. In 1981 she was promoted to executive vice president. Shaw spent seventeen years rising through the ranks at Universal. In 1983 her father decided to retire. Subsequently the Universal Life Insurance Company Board of Directors held an election to fill his position and elected Shaw as president and chief executive officer, making her Universal's first female president. It also positioned her nationally as one of the few women in the country holding highest management positions.

Although her father retired as president, he continued to work at the company as chairman of the board and chairman of the finance and investment committee and held a controlling amount of company stock. Shaw assumed responsibility for daily operations of the company, focusing on marketing with the goal of expanding Universal's customer base by utilizing resources she herself set in place during her rise through the company.

Shaw also was committed to service and support of minorities and the community at large. She held various positions with associations and organizations nationally and in the Memphis area. She served as a member of the Federal Reserve Bank of Memphis and then chaired its board of directors. She was a commissioner and vice president of the board of the Memphis Light, Gas, and Water Division, a commissioner of the Tennessee State Commission of Minority Economic Development, and a commissioner of the Memphis and Shelby County Jobs Advisory Council. She was a member of the Memphis Economic Club, the Memphis Development and Plough Community Foundations, Graduate Leadership Memphis, the Lemoyne-Owen College Advisory Council, Operation PUSH, the YWCA, the Panel of American Women, the Links, and Delta Sigma Theta Sorority. Shaw was the first woman president of the National Insurance Association, a national syndicate of black-owned insurance companies in the United States.

As a result of Shaw's philanthropic involvement, she was the recipient of numerous honors and awards. The Memphis chapter of the National Coalition of 100 Black Women offers an annual college scholarship in her name. The Memphis Light, Gas, and Water Division honored Shaw by naming two facilities for her, the Patricia Walker Shaw Pumping-Station/Water Treatment Plant and the Patricia Walker Shaw Water Treatment Plant Expansion. She was named Business Person of the Year by Memphis's National Business League and was honored by *Dollars and Sense* magazine and Delta Sigma Theta Sorority as one of America's top business professionals. *Ebony* magazine presented Shaw with an American Black Achievement Award, Coca Cola and Dr. Pepper Bottling Company of Memphis named her an outstanding leader, and Operation PUSH selected her for their par Excellence Award.

An accomplished business person, Shaw touched many lives. Unfortunately, her life ended shortly after she reached the height of her success. Two years after taking the helm at Universal Life Insurance Company, Shaw died after a long but courageous battle with cancer.

FURTHER READING

Ingham, John M., and Feldman, Lynne. *African-American Business Leaders* (1993).

Smith, Jessie Carney. "Patricia Walker Shaw (1939–1985)." *Notable Black American Women, Book II* (1996).

NANCY T. ROBINSON

Shaw, Thomas (c. 1846–23 June 1895), Buffalo Soldier and Medal of Honor recipient, was born enslaved in Covington, Kentucky. When he ran away from his owner, Mary Shaw, at the age of twenty, toward the end of the Civil War, she subsequently applied for compensation but was denied. Thomas Shaw, meanwhile, soon joined the Union Army, enlisting in the 119th U.S. Colored Troop (USCT) at Camp Nelson, Kentucky. This unit, one of many African American infantry units formed during the war after 1863, was organized in the first months of 1865 and performed garrison duty in its home state and took part in no major battles. While nothing is known of Shaw's specific activities during this time as a young soldier, it is clear that he enjoyed a soldier's life and was proficient at his duties. When the 119th USCT was mustered out of service on 27 April 1866, it would not be long until Shaw continued his military career.

In September 1866, Thomas Shaw joined the U.S. Army at Covington, Kentucky. Subsequently assigned to the 9th Cavalry Regiment, he was one of the army's first professional soldiers of color, along with such men as EMANUEL STANCE and THOMAS BOYNE, many of whom were also veterans of the Civil War. Indeed, black troops had performed so well during that war that afterward Congress authorized the formation of six permanent African American units (soon reduced to four) in the regular army. These units, the 9th and 10th cavalry regiments, as well as the 24th and 25th infantry, were segregated in nature, manned by black enlisted personnel and junior officers, but commanded by white senior officers. These regiments were soon deployed in the west and were most notably employed in protecting frontier settlements from attacks by Native Americans and became known as "Buffalo Soldiers." The skill, daring, and bravery of these black soldiers like Shaw, WILLIAM MCBRYAR, and ISAAC PAYNE—was recognized by fellow soldiers and foe alike, and would soon gain them the nickname "Buffalo Soldiers."

Serving in Company K of the 9th Cavalry, Thomas Shaw quietly gained a reputation as a good soldier and served with his regiment out west in such far flung posts as Fort Griffin, Texas, Fort Leavenworth, Kansas, Fort Robinson, Nebraska, and Fort McRae, New Mexico. Though details of Shaw's individual career are largely unknown, his history of service is one and the same as that of the celebrated 9th Cavalry Regiment, about which much has been written. However, it is known that by 1876 Thomas Shaw, who was fair-skinned and five feet, eight inches in height, was described as having an excellent character and was also acknowledged as a skilled marksman, perhaps the best in his company. His command and leadership skills are evidenced by the fact that he rose to the rank of corporal by 1871, and a few years later he was promoted to the rank of sergeant, a noncommissioned officer position—quite a change for a man who had once been enslaved. A photograph of Shaw shows that he wore a large bushy beard and had a commanding presence. In the summer of 1881 he would need all of his leadership and fighting qualities when he took part in what was surely the most difficult battle of his military career.

The years of 1880–1881 were difficult ones for the Buffalo Soldiers in the New Mexico Territory; tasked with subduing the highly skilled warriors of the Apache nation, led by their great chiefs Victorio and Nana, all four of the army's black regiments were heavily involved in the Apache War. When Victorio was finally killed by Mexican troops in

Thomas Shaw, Medal of Honor recipient, c. 1900. (Library of Congress/Daniel Murray Collection.)

October 1880 after being forced to cross the border by the Buffalo Soldiers of the 10th Cavalry, Nana continued to lead the Apache warriors and renewed their raids into southern New Mexico in the summer of 1881. On 5 August Captain Charles Parker and his troopers of the 9th Cavalry's K Company were dispatched from Fort Wingate to Carrizo Canyon to intercept Nana and his warriors; among the men in the company was Sergeant George Jordan, who was awarded the Medal of Honor the year before in a fight against Victorio, and Sergeant Thomas Shaw, who was acting first sergeant and the lead noncommissioned officer during the mission. On 12 August the men of K Company finally met up with Nana near the canyon and a brisk fight ensued; Jordan commanded the right flank, while Shaw rode with Captain Parker. The Apaches soon retreated into the canyon to make their stand, forcing the black troopers to dismount. Though they were confronted by a force at least double their own, the men of K Company held their ground for nearly two hours. Thomas Shaw, being the sharpshooter of the company, held the point position with several men and continually turned back the Apache assaults, while Jordan skillfully prevented Nana's warriors from turning their flank and surrounding them. In the end, the Apaches escaped, but only because Captain Parker and his men had to tend to their wounded and had lost nearly half of their horses. The two sergeants of K Company were recognized for their heroism, and eventually Shaw was awarded the Medal of Honor in December 1890.

Following this action, Sergeant Shaw continued his career with the 9th Cavalry for another thirteen years. In 1889, even before he received the Medal of Honor, Shaw was honored by being chosen to serve as part of the honor guard for the body of the 9th Cavalry's first commander, Lt. Col. Edward Hatch, accompanying the remains from Fort Robinson, Nebraska to his final resting place at Fort Leavenworth. On Memorial Day 1892 Shaw was probably also one of the five Buffalo Soldiers who laid a wreath on the grave of Captain Charles Parker at Arlington National Cemetery. Having served in the 9th Cavalry since 1866, Shaw knew both of his white commanders well. Shaw retired from the army in 1894 after nearly twenty-nine years of service to his country, subsequently residing in Virginia after having served in his final post at nearby Fort Myer. The men of the 9th Cavalry were transferred to this quiet post as a reward for their years of hard frontier service. Sadly, Thomas Shaw would not live the life of a civilian for long; likely worn out by his years of arduous service, he died less than a year later and was interred at Arlington National Cemetery where a Medal of Honor gravestone marks his final resting place.

FURTHER READING

Hanna, Charles W. *African American Recipients of the Medal of Honor* (2002).

Kenner, Charles L. *Buffalo Soldiers and Officers of the Ninth Cavalry* (1999).

Schubert, Frank N. *Black Valor: Buffalo Soldiers and the Medal of Honor, 1870-1898* (1997).

GLENN ALLEN KNOBLOCK

Shaw, Woody (24 Dec. 1944–9 May 1989), jazz trumpeter, was born Woody Herman Shaw Jr. in Laurinburg, North Carolina, the son of Woody Shaw Sr. and Rosalie Pegues, factory workers. The family had settled in Newark, New Jersey, when Woody Jr.'s mother returned to the South to give birth to him. She brought the two-month-old Shaw back to Newark, where he was raised. Named after both his father and the bandleader Woody Herman, Shaw's childhood was steeped in music; he later recalled childhood nights of listening to his father's gospel group, the Diamond Jubilee Singers, rehearsing in their home.

After taking up single-valve bugle in the Junior Elks and Junior Masons Drum and Bugle Corps, Shaw switched to trumpet in June 1956 and studied with Jerry Zierling (or Ziering—published accounts are conflicting) at Cleveland Junior High School. By this time he was already suffering from a hereditary disease that caused night blindness (retinitis pigmentosa), a considerable handicap for someone whose profession brought him regularly into the murky world of nightclubs. At about age fourteen he was caught for vandalism—evidently his poor vision impeded his escape—but in lieu of traditional punishment a sympathetic security guard brought him into the Newark YMCA big band under the rigorously disciplined leadership of Lavozier Lamar, whose young musicians included saxophonist WAYNE SHORTER.

Shaw had been an outstanding student who skipped directly from seventh to ninth grade, but to his parents' dismay he lost interest in school. Devoted instead to music, he dropped out of Newark's Arts High School before finishing. In 1963, after many local professional jobs and jam sessions, he joined the band of the percussionist Willie Bobo, which included the pianist Chick Corea and the tenor saxophonist Joe Farrell. While with Bobo, Shaw also performed alongside vibraphonist Bobby Hutcherson as a member of the band of the wind player ERIC DOLPHY for rehearsals in New York, performances in Pittsburgh, and the recording of Dolphy's album *Iron Man*. The next year Dolphy invited Shaw to Paris, but shortly before Shaw's departure Dolphy died. Shaw decided to make the trip nonetheless, and he found steady work with the saxophonist Nathan Davis and such veteran expatriate American musicians as BUD POWELL, KENNY CLARKE, Johnny Griffin, and Art Taylor. Shaw performed in Paris, Berlin, and London with a group that included the organist Larry Young.

Shaw returned to the United States in May 1965 and the following month joined HORACE SILVER's quintet, with which he recorded the albums *The Cape Verdean Blues* (1965) and *The Jody Grind* (1966). Silver's formidable tenor saxophonist JOE HENDERSON was replaced by Shaw's friend Tyrone Washington in 1966, and according to Shaw, he and Washington preferred melodic improvisations that sometimes used phrases of free jazz playing. These solos carried the band in a stylistic direction that the leader disliked, and consequently Silver split the group up.

Shaw also recorded two sessions with Young (*In the Beginning* and *Unity*, as a leader and as a sideman, late in 1965), and he made albums with Corea (*Tones for Jones Bones*, 1966), with the alto saxophonist JACKIE MCLEAN (including *Demon's Dance*, 1967), and with MCCOY TYNER (*Expansions*, 1968). From about 1968 to 1970 Shaw worked with Tyner as a member of a group that the members jokingly called the starvation band, because during this golden age of rock the great pianist Tyner could scarcely find work in jazz. In 1968 Shaw also began to work occasionally with the drummer MAX ROACH, appearing with him at a festival in Iran. But by 1969, when Shaw recorded with the pianist ANDREW HILL, Shaw had become a heroin addict, and Roach let him go. Shaw then worked temporarily as a studio musician and in pit orchestras for Broadway musicals.

In 1970 Shaw formed a quintet with Joe Henderson and recorded the album *Blackstone Legacy* as a leader. He toured with the drummer ART BLAKEY's Jazz Messengers (1971–1972) before settling in San Francisco. Shaw played on Blakey's albums *Anthenagin* and *Buhaina*, which were recorded in Berkeley in March 1973, while working with the drummer at the Keystone Korner in San Francisco. Shaw briefly led a group with Hutcherson that performed at the Montreux Jazz Festival in Switzerland in July. Details of Shaw's first marriage are unknown, but in a 1978 interview he mentioned in passing that the marriage had disintegrated during these years.

In December 1974 a new contract brought Shaw to New York to record the first of several albums for the Muse label, *The Moontrane*, with the trombonist Steve Turré, pianist Onaje Allan Gumbs, and drummer Victor Lewis. By this point Shaw's drug problems were under control, and he had begun teaching at jazz clinics, an activity that he continued into the mid-1980s. As a jazz educator he was concerned with upholding the hard-bop tradition in the face of popular jazz-rock and jazz-soul styles that he felt to be musically shallow, and he was concerned with trying to bring young African American musicians into jazz.

Shaw returned to San Francisco from February to July 1975 and then moved to New York City to join the LOUIS HAYES–Junior Cook Quintet, which after tenor saxophonist Cook's departure became the Woody Shaw–Louis Hayes Quintet. Cook was soon replaced by Rene McLean and then by expatriate tenor saxophonist DEXTER GORDON. Gordon adopted the band for his acclaimed homecoming from Paris performances late in 1976, which marked the beginning of the revival of the bop style in the United States.

Shaw, however, began to feel hemmed in by this style, and from mid-1977 onward he worked as the sole leader of small groups that were still oriented toward bop but that also incorporated the comparatively static accompanimental patterns of modal jazz and some of the harmonic and expressive freedom of free jazz. In 1977 he also made his furthest venture into free jazz on several tracks of his album *The Iron Men*, recorded by ad hoc small groups featuring the saxophonists ANTHONY BRAXTON and ARTHUR BLYTHE, the pianist MUHAL RICHARD ABRAMS, and the bassist Cecil McBee. Also in 1977 Shaw's manager Maxine Gregg secured a Columbia recording contract, a consequence of Shaw's well-publicized work with Gordon and of the support and encouragement of MILES DAVIS. Shaw and Gregg married, probably that same year; they had one child. Among Shaw's regular sidemen during this period were the saxophonist Carter Jefferson, Gumbs, the bassist Stafford James, and Lewis—all heard on Shaw's albums *Rosewood* (1977), featuring Shaw's big band, and *Stepping Stones* (1978), presenting the quintet live at the Village Vanguard in New York's Greenwich Village. From 1980 to 1983 Shaw's quintet included Turré, the pianists Larry Willis or Mulgrew Miller, James, and the drummer Tony Reedus. Their albums include *United* (1981) and *Master of the Art* (1982); *Master of the Art* was recorded live at the Jazz Forum in New York with the vibraphonist Hutcherson added to the quintet after a six-week European tour.

Unfortunately Shaw's personal life plunged from great promise to tragedy as he became overwhelmed by artistic dissatisfaction, the pressures of leadership, and the effort to achieve financial stability through his recordings for Columbia. As his dependency on drugs increased, he began to have trouble keeping his sidemen. Instead he toured and recorded with groups of constantly changing personnel. And yet the effect on his music was not at all obvious. Not only *Setting Standards* (1983), but even albums as late as *Solid* (1986) and *Imagination* (1987) find Shaw playing consistently well and offering no clues of his ongoing personal crises. His sight was deteriorating, and he was suffering from

AIDS, contracted from injecting narcotics with a contaminated syringe. Finally he began to lose his teeth, and by 1989 he could no longer play. On 27 February 1989 he fell down the stairs of a Brooklyn subway station, rolled in front of a train, and lost his left arm. He spent his last months in Bellevue Hospital in New York City. Published reports attribute his death variously to kidney disease, pneumonia, and a heart attack.

Like many brass players of his era, Shaw doubled on flugelhorn (particularly during the mid- to late-1970s on record), but his trumpet sound was so inherently deep and rich that he scarcely needed the flugelhorn to achieve the fuller sound that other trumpeters were seeking from this instrument. Indeed at those sessions on which his choice of instrument is not differentiated track by track in the album liner notes, it is not always clear which instrument he is playing. On Gordon's album *Homecoming* (1976) Shaw may be playing the flugelhorn in the ballad "'Round Midnight," since his tone seems even broader than usual. From 1977 to 1978 Shaw sometimes recorded on cornet rather than on trumpet, but with the same characteristic timbral breadth and warmth; the cornet may be heard in "The Jitterbug Waltz" from *The Iron Men* and on *Stepping Stones*.

Shaw's beautiful sound was matched by his brilliant technical control of the trumpet. He could improvise rapid, precise, subtle melodies in the tradition of CLIFFORD BROWN's trumpeting, while also slotting in dissonant phrases or an impassioned brassy shout. Early in his career Shaw was often mistaken on recordings for another of Brown's disciples, Freddie Hubbard, who had taken an identical stylistic path. Later their paths diverged, however. Although Shaw never stooped to Hubbard's penchant for crassly commercial jazz, badly done—for which the always outspoken Shaw criticized Hubbard repeatedly in published interviews—he never achieved the brilliant originality and conceptual perfection of Hubbard's finest work.

FURTHER READING

Shaw, Woody. "My Approach to the Trumpet and to Jazz," *Crescendo International* 15 (Mar. 1977): 14–15.
Baraka, Amiri, and Amina Baraka. *The Music: Reflections on Jazz and Blues* (1987).
Shaw, Arnold Jay. "Woody Shaw," *Down Beat* (24 Apr. 1975), 34–35.
Obituary: *New York Times*, 12 May 1989.

This entry is taken from the *American National Biography* and is published here with the permission of the American Council of Learned Societies.

BARRY KERNFELD

Shell, Art, Jr. (26 Nov. 1946–   ), professional football player and coach, was born in Charleston, South Carolina, to Arthur Shell, a paper mill employee, and Gertrude Shell. Growing up in the Daniel Jenkins housing project in Charleston, Shell learned early in his adolescent years the value of family and community. After losing his mother, who at the age of thirty-five suffered cardiac failure, Shell, only fifteen at the time and the oldest of five children, became responsible for the upbringing and rearing of his siblings. The family's strict Southern Baptist roots and place within the segregated African American community guided and influenced the behavior of Shell and his siblings, while the residents of Daniel Jenkins provided a secure and nurturing environment for the motherless children.

While attending the segregated Bond-Wilson High School in North Charleston, the quiet and contemplative Shell came into his own through his participation in sports, standing out in both basketball and football. Under the guidance and training of coaches James Fields and Eugene Graves, Shell developed into a star player and was offered a football scholarship to Maryland State College (later University of Maryland-Eastern Shore) in 1964. At MSC, Shell would learn football and valuable life lessons from head football coach Roosevelt Gilliam, who took the 6-foot, 4-inch, 250-pound athlete and groomed him into a man. Shell played both offense and defense for the Fighting Hawks, excelling and starting at offensive tackle in his junior and senior years. Shell also played center on the MSC basketball team, where his style of play, a combination of power and grace, was compared to that of the National Basketball Association (NBA) star CHARLES BARKLEY. From 1965 to 1968 Shell was honored as an All-Central Intercollegiate Athletic Association player, earning All-American recognition from the *Pittsburgh Carrier*, as well as *Ebony* magazine from 1966 to 1967. In 1967 Shell, a senior at MSC, was selected to the Little All-America football team, which honored athletes from small colleges and universities.

In 1968, after four years at MSC, Shell graduated with a B.S. in industrial arts. In that same year during the 1968 AFL-NFL draft, the 6-foot, 5-inch, 285-pound Shell became a third round pick for the

American Football League's (AFL) Oakland Raiders. Playing on special teams in relative silence, Shell took the starting job as left tackle at the start of the 1970 season and never looked back. Big, athletic, and intelligent, Shell's quiet demeanor and shadowy presence was complimented by that of tremendous Raider left guard, the fierce and competitive leader EUGENE UPSHAW. In drafting Shell, the Raiders would solidify their success in the 1970s, as well as forge one of the NFL's most productive tandems in the history of the league. Shell and Upshaw cleared the way for Raider running backs and were the so-called body guards for quarterbacks Kenny Stabler and Jim Plunkett. Known for his attention to detail, Shell studied film of every opponent he played against, keeping notes about what to expect and how to react to certain defensive schemes. In 1976, during Super Bowl XI, Shell demonstrated his brilliant command of the game by denying Minnesota Viking All-Pro defensive end Jim Marshall a tackle or a sack in the Raiders decisive 32–14 victory. After a fifteen-year career in which he played in 207 games, twenty-three postseason games, was on two Super Bowl Championship teams, was selected to eight pro-bowls, was named All-Pro in 1973, 1974, 1976, and 1977, and was All-AFC six-times, Shell retired in 1982.

Upon retirement in 1982 Shell became a scout for the Raiders, and a year later he would take over as the offensive-line coach. As a player, Shell had always demonstrated his superior knowledge of the game through his preparation and recognition of the details. It was this ability that former Raiders head coach John Madden observed in Shell that made him believe that the formidable Shell could one day be a successful coach. As a coach in the NFL, he could teach this kind of awareness as a source to achieving an almost flawless performance. Under the direction of head coach Tom Flores and assistants such as Shell, the Raiders (later in Los Angeles) would win another NFL Championship in 1984, defeating the Washington Redskins 38–9 in Super Bowl XVIII. For six seasons (1983–1988), Shell remained an assistant under Flores. In 1988 the former offensive coordinator of the Denver Broncos, Mike Shanahan, took over as head coach of the Raiders, retaining Shell as offensive line coach. However, after a lackluster 1988 season and a 1–3 start to the 1989 campaign, Shanahan was fired by majority partner Al Davis and replaced by Shell on 3 October 1989.

Historically significant, Shell's hiring represented the first time in the NFL's modern era that an African American was named head coach. Prior to Shell, FREDERICK "FRITZ" POLLARD, of Brown University fame, coached the Hammond, Indiana Pros from 1923 to 1925. Immediately, Shell gained the respect of his players, primarily due to his success with the Raider organization for twenty-two years as both a player and a coach. In 1989 Shell's team produced an 8–8 record after winning seven of twelve games.

In 1989 Shell's outstanding career as a player would be punctuated by his induction into professional football's Hall of Fame in Canton, Ohio. In that same year Arthur Shell Sr. would die of complications associated with diabetes.

In 1990, with a healthy team that featured Marcus Allen and BO JACKSON in the backfield, the Raiders reached the playoffs amassing a 12–4 record, only to lose to the Buffalo Bills 51–3 in the 1990 AFC championship game. After coaching four more seasons with the Raiders, compiling a 56–41 record as a head coach, Shell was replaced by Mike White. In 1995 Shell joined the Kansas City Chiefs as offensive line coach, leaving after to two seasons to join head coach Dan Reeves and the Atlanta Falcons. In 2001 Shell resigned from the Falcons, taking a position with the NFL head office as the senior vice president of Football Operations & Development. In 2006 Shell returned to the Oakland Raiders organization as the team's new head coach. Unfortunately, Shell's second stint would be short-lived. After recording a 2–14 season, the worst in team history, and coming under constant criticism of the players, Shell was fired in January 2006. Shell and his wife Janice had two sons, Arthur III and Christopher.

FURTHER READING
Anderson, David. "The Silver and Black Head Coach," *New York Times*, 5 Oct. 1989.
Janfosky, Michael. "Shell is First Black Coach in N.F.L. Since 20's," *New York Times*, 4 Oct. 1989.
Jones, Jason. "Agent Denies Raider 'offer': Art Shell's future with team has yet to be revealed," *The Sacramento Bee*, 27 Jan. 2007.
Porter, David L. *African American Sports Greats* (1995).
Wagaman, Michael. *The Unofficial Oakland Raiders Book of Lists* (2002).

PELLOM MCDANIELS III

Shelton, Lee. *See* Stagolee.

Shepard, James Edward (3 Nov. 1875–6 Oct. 1947), educator and college founder, was born in Raleigh, North Carolina, the eldest of twelve children of

Hattie Whitted and Augustus Shepard, a prominent Baptist minister. He attended local primary schools and graduated in 1894 with a pharmacy degree from Shaw University in Raleigh. In 1895 he married Annie Day Robinson, the granddaughter of THOMAS DAY, a well-known antebellum cabinetmaker. The couple had two daughters, Annie Day and Marjorie Augusta.

After college Shepard practiced pharmacy for several years and quickly established himself among North Carolina's leading black entrepreneurs. In 1898 he became one of the first seven investors in the North Carolina Mutual Life Insurance Company in Durham, which eventually became the largest black-owned business in the South. He also helped incorporate another Durham institution, the Mechanics and Farmers Bank, in 1907. While making these entrepreneurial inroads, Shepard kept one foot in the world of politics. An active member of the Republican Party, he held two political appointments at the turn of the century: a clerkship in the Recorder of Deeds Office in Washington, D.C., from 1898 to 1899, and Raleigh's deputy collector for the Internal Revenue Service from 1899 to 1905.

In the wake of black disfranchisement in North Carolina in 1900, Shepard recognized that future political appointments were unlikely. When his Internal Revenue Service appointment expired, he turned his attention to matters of religious service and social uplift. From 1905 to 1909 he served as field superintendent for the International Sunday School Association and was the only African American to address the World Sunday School Convention in Rome in 1907.

During the early years of Jim Crow, Shepard urged southern blacks to focus on moral and educational development rather than political agitation. His accommodationist approach proved amenable to local Democratic elites and allowed Shepard to build a broad network of white southern patrons. At the same time, he did not abandon his interest in politics and maintained close ties with national leaders in the Republican Party.

Shepard drew upon his local and national connections in raising money for the National Religious Training School and Chautauqua for the Colored Race, which he opened in Durham in 1910. The school initially held short institutes for ministers and offered a selection of liberal arts, home economics, and commercial courses. Shepard's early promotional pamphlets for his school hewed to white-approved precepts for black education by promising to combine academic and industrial training and to instill in his students a solid work ethic. Such carefully crafted appeals won him endorsements from local and national white leaders, including Theodore Roosevelt. Shepard's growing ambitions for his school, however, soon outstripped its budget. The institution ran into such severe debt in 1915 that he was forced to put it up for auction. The school survived this crisis when the wife of the philanthropist Russell Sage purchased it for Shepard, who then reopened it as the National Training School and began training future teachers as well as preachers. In the late 1910s Shepard developed his school along collegiate lines and expanded its offerings in the liberal arts.

Again facing mounting debts in the early 1920s, Shepard engaged in talks with state officials about the possibilities for the incorporation of his school as a public institution. The state, which needed an increased supply of black teachers, agreed to assume Shepard's debt on the condition that he discontinue all college work except that required to operate a normal school. Shepard agreed to this plan; when the fall semester opened in 1923, the National Training School had become the Durham State Normal School.

Despite his agreement with state officials, Shepard never fully accepted the idea of limiting his school to a teacher-training curriculum. In 1925 he hired a lawyer to author and find legislative sponsorship for a bill allowing for the creation of a liberal arts college at Durham State Normal School. Shepard himself went before a legislative committee and offered an impassioned plea for his plan. The North Carolina General Assembly granted his request, acknowledging both Shepard's enduring political talents and the white South's growing desire to curb black migration and contain the more assertive "New Negro" of the 1920s. In February 1925 the Durham State Normal School became the North Carolina College for Negroes, the first publicly supported liberal arts college for blacks in the nation. Shepard faced enormous challenges during the school's first decade, including a devastating fire in 1925 and the tight state budgets of the Depression years. Nonetheless, through a combination of private donations and state and federal aid, he quickly expanded North Carolina College for-Negroes, which in 1938 won an "A" rating from the Southern Association of Colleges and Secondary Schools.

In addition to his college presidency, Shepard held numerous other positions of leadership in

North Carolina. In the 1920s he served as president of the state's black teachers association and as Grand Master of the PRINCE HALL Free and Accepted Masons. By the early 1930s Shepard's civic leadership had become more explicitly political. In 1935 he became one of the founding members of the Durham Committee on Negro Affairs, a coalition that sought to increase local black political power. He took that goal on the air in the 1940s with statewide radio addresses that urged black citizens to register to vote.

In mobilizing black communities, however, Shepard consistently avoided political strategies and organizations that met with strong southern white disapproval. He disassociated himself from the growing NAACP membership in the South and frustrated that association's efforts to organize educational equalization lawsuits. In 1930 he opposed the NAACP's campaign to block the Supreme Court nomination of Judge John J. Parker, a native North Carolinian who had used race-baiting tactics in past campaigns. He also opposed—and helped derail—the NAACP's 1933 sponsorship of Thomas Raymond Hocutt, a graduate of the North Carolina College for Negroes who attempted to integrate the pharmacy school at the University of North Carolina at Chapel Hill. Throughout the early 1930s Shepard discouraged members of the black teachers association from waging a salary equalization suit against the state. And in the late 1930s he refused to support the future civil rights activist and Durham native PAULI MURRAY, when she, like Hocutt, sought admission to the state's flagship white university.

Some black critics charged that Shepard's antagonism toward the NAACP amounted to self-serving attempts at institutional preservation and expansion. Not long after the University of North Carolina denied admission to Pauli Murray, state legislators voted to add graduate work at the North Carolina College for Negroes. The school began offering master's degrees in 1939, opened a law school in 1940, and established a school of library science in 1941. As the NAACP, nationally and locally, pushed for racial integration within higher education, Shepard called for the development of his school into a full-fledged university.

Shepard did not live to see his school attain university status or to witness the civil rights movement that fundamentally changed the course of educational development in the South. After suffering a stroke in 1947, he died in Durham at the age of seventy-one. Less than two years after his death,

a group of students from North Carolina College for Negroes picketed the state capitol, protesting conditions at their unaccredited law school. Their demonstration helped pave the way for the 1951 integration of the law school at the University of North Carolina at Chapel Hill, the first major victory in the desegregation of higher education in the state.

Shortly after his death, a local white newspaper columnist commented that Shepard "was regarded by many legislators [as] the best politician ever to come before them" (*Greensboro Daily News*, 31 Dec. 1948). Toward the end of his life, Shepard's deferential style of politics earned him the admiration of white southerners, even as it distanced him from a new, more radical generation of blacks in the emerging civil rights movement. Nevertheless, his pragmatic interracial bargaining helped create a school (renamed North Carolina Central University in 1969) that stands as an enduring testament to his role in black institution building in the Jim Crow South.

FURTHER READING

There is a small collection of Shepard's speeches and related clippings at the James E. Shepard Memorial Library, North Carolina Central University, Durham, North Carolina.

Gershenhorn, Jerry. "*Hocutt v. Wilson* and Race Relations in Durham, North Carolina, during the 1930s," *North Carolina Historical Review* 78 (July 2001).

Murray, Pauli. *Song in a Weary Throat: An American Pilgrimage* (1987).

Weare, Walter B. *Black Business in the New South: A Social History of the North Carolina Mutual Life Insurance Company* (1973).

Obituaries: *New York Times* and *News & Observer* (Raleigh, N.C.), 7 Oct. 1947.

SARAH C. THUESEN

Shepp, Archie Vernon (24 May 1937–), saxophonist, playwright, and educator, was born in Fort Lauderdale, Florida, and grew up in Philadelphia, Pennsylvania. He studied clarinet in his youth but switched to alto saxophone at about the age of fifteen; as a teenager he played in local rhythm-and-blues bands and also apprenticed with Cal Massey, who had earlier influenced JOHN COLTRANE. Shepp graduated from Goddard College with a B.A. in dramatic literature in 1959 and moved to New York City in search of theater work, playing alto saxophone in dance bands to earn money.

Influenced by Coltrane, Shepp switched to tenor sax and immediately began to make a name for himself. Coltrane's emphasis on the African American spiritual values of jazz certainly shaped his approach to the music, but by Shepp's own account it was his playing with CECIL TAYLOR, from 1960 to 1962, that truly transformed him musically. Shepp co-led a quartet with trumpeter Bill Dixon from 1962 to 1963, recording one album, and from 1963 to 1964 he was a member of the avant-garde New York Contemporary Five, a group informed by the music of ORNETTE COLEMAN and including Coleman's trumpeter, DON CHERRY. Shepp recorded two albums and toured Europe with the New York Contemporary Five.

Shepp soon emerged as a leader in his own right, recording a series of critically acclaimed albums for Impulse! Records in the middle and late 1960s. *Four for Trane* (1964), dedicated to his mentor, features trombonist Roswell Rudd, John Tchicai on reeds, Reggie Workman on bass, and Charles Moffett on drums. The album reflects Shepp's emotional debt to Coltrane and includes a gorgeous version of "Naima," as well as his own raw, passionate playing in his own composition, "Rufus." *Fire Music* (1965) contains a ravishing version of DUKE ELLINGTON's "Prelude to a Kiss" and a dedication to MALCOLM X, "Malcolm, Malcolm, Semper Malcolm."

On This Night (1966) marks a significant step forward. It contains varied ensembles from trios to sextets, drawn from Bobby Hutcherson on vibes, HENRY GRIMES and David Izenzon on bass, RASHIED ALI, Joe Chambers, and J. C. Moses on drums, and ED BLACKWELL on percussion. Shepp showcases his deep romanticism in a version of Ellington's "In a Sentimental Mood," while the title piece, with vocals by Christine Spencer, is dedicated to W. E. B. DuBois and is one of Shepp's most successful political statements, a call for fundamental social change accompanied by Shepp's own powerful, shouting tenor playing.

Live in San Francisco is an even more impressive quintet; from early 1966 it is a typically stylistically eclectic Shepp performance. The albums *Three for a Quarter* (1966) and *The Magic of Juju* (1967) are more overtly African influenced and include five percussionists. *Mama Too Tight* (1967), an octet that includes Rudd, Charlie Haden on bass, and Beaver Harris on drums, is a somewhat quieter ensemble with a strong Ellington influence and with Shepp himself more in the background. For the most part, these early recordings are rooted in collective improvisation and an exploration of atonality, with Shepp playing passionate, intense solos.

From the mid-1960s on, Shepp often incorporated poetry and African percussion into his performances. The tunes are often explicit political statements; though the singing is not always completely convincing, the music is a powerful mixture of tradition and experimentalism. Indeed, Shepp's exploration of the jazz tradition, in the form of marches, ballads, and slow blues, is as impressive as his free playing. His tone became fuller, with a wide vibrato, and the influences of SONNY ROLLINS and particularly the emotionalism of BEN WEBSTER is increasingly apparent.

The Way Ahead from 1969 is a fine expression of this more mature style. The most adventurous sideman was trombonist Grachan Moncur III, but the session also had Ron Carter on bass, Walter Davis on piano, and Beaver Harris (also a free player) or boppish ROY HAYNES on drums. The music was a mix of blues and gospel with a strong rhythm-and-blues base. In 1972 Shepp recorded *Attica Blues*. Inspired (or incited) by the tragic prison riot in Upstate New York, the album is graced with Ellingtonian swing but filled with mournful blues, funk, and avant-garde playing. *The Cry of My People* (1972) continues this approach, with a richly varied mixture of gospel singers, big bands, quartets, sextets, and chamber orchestras.

Shepp recorded extensively during the 1970s and 1980s, continuing to mine a more traditional jazz vein than the one he explored in the 1960s. The best of these records include a pair of live recordings from the Montreaux Festival and Arista/Freedom (1975); two duets with pianist Horace Parlan—*Goin' Home* (1977) and *Trouble in Mind* (1980)—both for Steeplechase Records, deeply emotive explorations of gospel and blues tunes; and two albums of duets with drummer MAX ROACH for HatArt records (1979). Shepp also recorded a tribute to CHARLIE PARKER for Steeplechase (*Lookin' at Bird*, 1980), as well as a second tribute to Coltrane (*Ballads for Trane*) for Denon Records in 1977.

Shepp recorded little during the 1990s, experiencing problems with his intonation. But he returned with a strong effort in 1999's *Conversations*, a tribute to the late bassist Fred Hopkins with Khalil el-Zabar on bass and Malachi Favors on drums. In 2000 he recorded one of his strongest albums in years, *Live in New York*, a reunion with Rudd, Moncur, Workman, and drummer Andrew Cyrille. Shepp's playing is emotive and powerful, the style slightly more restrained than his 1960s work with these veterans of the avant-garde.

Shepp remained true to the jazz tradition in his refusal to fall easily into categories, a powerful, emotional player rooted in the blues who embraced both the musical experimentalism and racial radicalism of the 1960s. His organic mixture of jazz, blues, and political statement was perhaps the most successful such effort of the decade. Shepp also maintained a lifelong involvement in the theater, penning, for instance, a successful 1967 play, *Junebug Graduates Tonight!* From 1969 to 1974 he was a member of the black studies department at the State University of New York at Buffalo, and in 1974 he was appointed to the faculty at the University of Massachusetts at Amherst. In 1995 he was awarded the New England Foundation for the Arts Achievement in Music Award. But Shepp's greatest achievement is a style and sound that bridges decades of jazz, from Duke Ellington and Ben Webster to John Coltrane and beyond.

FURTHER READING

Baker, David. *The Black Composer Speaks* (1978).

Cadence 5 (Mar. 1979) and 15 (Aug. 1989).

Down Beat 41 (1974), 45 (1978), and 49 (Apr. 1982).

Hardin, Christopher L. *Black Professional Musicians in Higher Education* (1987).

Weinstein, Norman C. *A Night in Tunisia* (1992).

RONALD P. DUFOUR

Sheppard, Lucy Gantt (21 Feb. 1867–27 May 1955), teacher, missionary, and social worker, was born Lucy Gantt in Tuscaloosa, Alabama, the daughter and only child of a mixed-race former slave, Eliza Gantt. Her father, who may have been white, played no role in her upbringing. As a young child Lucy attended school between cotton seasons. At the age of eleven she gained admission to Talladega College, a school for blacks run by the Missionary Association of the Congregational Church. Eliza Gantt worked as a domestic servant to pay her daughter's tuition for the nine years that Lucy spent at Talladega.

During her last several years at Talladega, Gantt taught in one-room rural schools during the summer months. She took voice lessons at Talladega and toured for a year with FREDERICK J. LOUDIN's Jubilee Singers. In 1886 she secured employment as a teacher in Grayton, Alabama, where she lived and taught in a one-room log cabin. The following year she found a position in Birmingham. In the summer of 1887 Gantt met WILLIAM HENRY SHEPPARD,

at the time a student at a Presbyterian seminary in Tuscaloosa. Gantt and Sheppard became engaged, but Sheppard had applied for missionary service in the Congo and intended to delay the marriage until after his initial years of service.

William Sheppard returned from the Congo in 1893, and the couple married on 21 February 1894. Along with several other African American recruits, the Sheppards sailed for the Congo via London and traveled up the river to the American Presbyterian Congo Mission's station at Luebo. Lucy Sheppard had become pregnant shortly after the wedding and gave birth prematurely to the couple's first child, Miriam, in late 1894. The child died after several weeks.

Lucy Sheppard quickly learned the native language and contributed to the first published Tshiluba dictionary. She opened the mission's first school, staffed by several other black Presbyterian women. By 1897 there were forty-five children studying at the school. She devoted herself to "civilizing" the mission's children by introducing them to Western clothing, teaching them domestic skills, and talking to them about her Christian faith. Sheppard contributed to Sunday worship services and evangelistic meetings by singing hymns in both English and native languages. She also served as the mission's nurse, providing care to both African children and her missionary colleagues.

By 1898 Sheppard had lost a second daughter, Lucille, in infancy and had given birth to a third, Wilhelmina. In light of the deaths of her first two children and the growing political instability in the region, Sheppard returned to the United States while William founded a new mission station at Ibanche. While on furlough Sheppard stayed with the family of William's sister and published a volume of forty-six hymns that she had translated into Tshiluba.

In 1900 Sheppard left Wilhelmina with William's sister in Staunton, Virginia, and returned to the Congo, where she joined William at the new Ibanche mission station. She decorated a new home, learned a new language, and opened another new school. She also organized a sewing class and a women's group. Within a year she gave birth to William Lapsley Sheppard, called "Maxamalinge" or "Max" in honor of a Kuba prince whom the Sheppards had befriended. Within several years the school attracted more than one hundred children, whom Sheppard taught reading, Christianity, and Negro spirituals. She also established a home for orphaned girls in Ibanche. The mission station flourished, as evidenced by a growing number of converts and the construction of progressively larger churches.

In 1904 the Sheppards returned together on a furlough trip to the United States. In addition to reuniting their children, the Sheppards traveled widely to churches across the United States, chiefly visiting Presbyterian churches in the South but also traveling to Chicago and Princeton, New Jersey. William lectured on their African experiences, and Lucy sang hymns in several languages.

In 1906 the couple again left Wilhelmina with William's sister and returned to the mission field. During their absence the relationship between the various Congolese peoples and the Belgian colonial administration had grown increasingly violent. William wrote an article detailing the ways that the Belgian officials and rubber companies had reduced the native people into slavery. The leading rubber concern sued William, who was acquitted of libel in 1909.

Shortly after her husband's acquittal the Sheppards decided to return to the United States permanently. Although the official reason for their departure was concern for William's health, several of their white colleagues had gathered evidence that William had engaged in a series of affairs with Congolese women. One of those relationships resulted in the birth of a son. William initially admitted to one indiscretion during Lucy's furlough but later confessed to repeated infidelity.

The Sheppards moved to Staunton, Virginia, where Lucy joined William in teaching a Sunday school class. In 1912 William accepted a pastorate at Grace Presbyterian Church in Louisville, Kentucky. Lucy taught Sunday school, directed the church choir, and formed a junior choir that accompanied her when she gave talks on her missionary experiences in local churches. In 1918 Lucy Sheppard worked for the federal government's Interdepartmental Social Hygiene Service as a social worker among Louisville's African American population. Her job involved policing the morals of young black women: she visited dance halls and the homes of young women in an effort to "keep young girls off the streets at night." In 1919 she accepted a similar position with the Family Service Organization of Louisville as a "Negro case worker."

William died in 1927, but Lucy Sheppard remained active at Grace Presbyterian Church. She resigned her position with the Family Service Organization in 1935 because of declining health. She continued to serve on the board of the Colored Red Cross Hospital and the Colored Advisory Board of the Family Service Organization. Lucy Sheppard died in Louisville in 1955. Although the fame that she and her husband briefly enjoyed in the early 1900s had long since faded, Sheppard's accomplishments were manifold: teaching in rural Alabama, pioneering missionary work in the Congo, and philanthropic and civic service in Jim Crow Louisville.

FURTHER READING

Kellersberger, Julia Lake. *Lucy Gantt Sheppard: Shepherdess of His Sheep on Two Continents* (1937).

Phipps, William E. *William Sheppard: Congo's African American Livingstone* (2002)

JOHN G. TURNER

Sheppard, Samuella "Ella" (4 Feb. 1851–9 June 1914), singer, pianist, arranger, teacher, writer, and assistant director of the original Fisk Jubilee Singers, was born in Nashville, Tennessee, to slave parents Simon Sheppard, a liveryman, and Sarah Hannah Sheppard, a domestic servant.

On 22 December 1871, ten African American students from Fisk University in Nashville—all but two former slaves—stood before the large, wealthy white congregation of Plymouth Church in Brooklyn and forever transformed American music. On a mission to raise money for their destitute school—formed by the American Missionary Association in 1866 to train black teachers—the Jubilee Singers had struggled across the eastern United States performing choral arrangements of slave spirituals to small and largely uncomprehending white audiences. On the verge of defeat, the group was invited to sing at Plymouth Church by its pastor, Henry Ward Beecher, the most influential religious figure in America. Beecher and his congregation were transfixed. "I never saw a cultivated Brooklyn assemblage so moved and melted under the magnetism of music before," wrote one witness.

Beecher's subsequent endorsement transformed the tour from defeat bordering on tragedy to triumph. The soprano Maggie Porter later recalled, "Every church wanted the Jubilee Singers to sing for them. ... From that time on we had success" (Ward, 154). Within months, this small group of young African Americans was known throughout the United States. A triumphant performance at Patrick Gilmore's gargantuan musical extravaganza the World Peace Jubilee, in Boston in 1872, catapulted them to genuine star status.

The group that became known as the Fisk Jubilee Singers began as the school's choir, singing conventional choral music arrangements. The choir's director, George White, was deeply moved by the sacred songs he heard Fisk students singing among themselves and encouraged his most promising student and assistant, Ella Sheppard, to transcribe them. At first Sheppard resisted. "The slave songs were never used by us then in public. They were associated with slavery and the dark past and represented the things to be forgotten," she later recalled (Ward, 110). White persisted and, finally convinced by his enthusiasm, Sheppard agreed. She and White then arranged them for the choir.

Ella Sheppard sang soprano with the Jubilee Singer and was the group's pianist. She also was White's more-than-capable assistant, and at times—often at moments of crisis—she was the ensemble's director. Along with White, she guided an enthusiastic but inexperienced band of impoverished students, against all odds, to international fame. In the process she played a pivotal role in introducing the world to African American spirituals.

Sheppard, whose ancestors were Native American, African, and European, was born a slave in Nashville, Tennessee, in 1851. Her mother, Sarah, was head nurse and housekeeper in the household of planter Benjamin Harper Sheppard. Her father, Simon, who was the half brother of Benjamin Sheppard, was a liveryman. Simon Sheppard had been permitted to hire himself out, and he saved $1,800 to purchase his own freedom. Simon tried to buy Sarah's freedom, but her mistress refused to part with her. He was allowed, however, to purchase Ella's freedom in 1854.

At first Ella lived with Simon and his wife Cornelia in Nashville, where Simon owned a livery stable. In 1860 the family moved to the safer and comparatively more hospitable Cincinnati, Ohio. Ella was musically talented and began studying music with a German woman when she was thirteen. Although the family struggled financially, Simon purchased an old piano for his daughter, on which she practiced incessantly.

Simon died of cholera in 1865, and fourteen-year-old Ella, forced to find work, took a series of short-lived jobs around Cincinnati. She came to the attention of a photographer, J. P. BALL, who was impressed by her talent and offered to pay for her musical education. Sheppard was accepted by a prominent voice teacher, Madame Caroline Revé,

but only under the condition that she not reveal the teacher's name. Ella also was required to enter through a back door, receiving her lessons at night in a back room. After twelve lessons Ball ran into financial trouble and withdrew his patronage.

Still only fourteen years old, Sheppard landed a position as a teacher at a black subscription school in Gallatin, Tennessee. It was a courageous move for such a young woman: black schools were frequently attacked by white arsonists, and teachers were often harassed, threatened, and sometimes beaten. Fortunately for Ella, her school was not targeted. She nonetheless lasted for only one term, forced to leave because most students could not afford the tuition and she was unable to support herself.

Sheppard returned to Nashville and enrolled at the newly formed Fisk, where she initially made a living by sewing and giving music lessons. She soon came to the attention of George White, who was the school's treasurer as well as its choir director. White immediately envisioned a source of income for the financially beleaguered school in Sheppard's talent: "If she has the right sort of stuff, I shall hope to raise money by a concert or two after a while," he wrote in a letter (Ward, 73). Sheppard was soon hired as an assistant music teacher, which made her the first black teacher at Fisk.

Encouraged by the success of several local concerts given by the Fisk University choir, White organized a special group of the best singers. With Sheppard on piano, he rigorously rehearsed them until they were a finely honed choral ensemble. On 5 October 1871 the group, which was so ill-equipped that none of the members even had winter coats, set out to tour Ohio to raise money for the school. The tour quickly ran into trouble, both financially and as the result of the prejudice that barred the students from hotels and restaurants in town after town. Sheppard's quiet determination and skill as a choir director played a key role in holding the troupe together and keeping the singers focused on their goal. With White serving as advance man, traveling ahead of the rest to book halls and arrange accommodations, it fell to Sheppard to run rehearsals, conduct performances, and help manage day-to-day activities. Even when White was present for the performances he did not appear on stage, leaving instead it to Sheppard to conduct the group.

Subsequent to the pivotal performances at Plymouth Church and the World Peace Jubilee, the Jubilee Singers began a successful tour of England

and Scotland in April 1873. They performed for Queen Victoria on 7 May. In February 1874, while still on tour, White's wife died of typhoid fever. White, himself in poor health and shattered by the death of his wife, became bedridden. Sheppard took over fully as director for much of the rest of the tour.

In January 1875, the Jubilee Singers began a third tour. In May the troupe again headed abroad and spent more than two years touring England and Continental Europe. A professional choir director, Theodore Seward, had been hired, but his health gave in under the rigors of touring. White and Sheppard again took control of the group's musical affairs while White's brother-in-law, Erastus Cravath, handled the business end. Cravath badly mismanaged the group, prompting several singers to threaten to leave. "Miss Sheppard will go next and then the Jubilee Singers work … will be at an end," White complained in a letter (Ward, 341). As it turned out, it was White who resigned, and Sheppard was given leadership of the group.

Over the course of seven years, the Jubilee Singers made three extended tours on behalf of Fisk. They raised $150,000 for the school, an enormous sum at the time. Fisk declined to sponsor a fourth tour, so Jubilee member FREDERICK LOUDIN recruited White, who in turn recruited Sheppard, to lead a private troupe made up of some of the Jubilees. The group toured the North and parts of the Upper South from September 1879 until May 1882.

In December 1882 Sheppard married George Washington Moore, a minister. The Moores moved to Oberlin, Ohio, and later to Washington, D.C. George Moore was the minister of a prominent Washington church, taught in the theology department of Howard University, and in 1885 was appointed the first black trustee of Fisk. The Moores were active in the temperance movement and were credited with reviving a blighted Washington neighborhood by shutting down thirteen saloons. While in Washington, Ella befriended FREDERICK DOUGLASS.

In 1892 George Moore took a senior position with the American Missionary Association, and the family, now including a son and a daughter, returned to Nashville. Shortly after returning to Nashville, Ella had another son. She subsequently became president of the Tennessee's Women's Missionary Union and a writer, publishing numerous articles about the early days of the Jubilee Singers and the plight of women in slavery. She continued to train Fisk's student choirs and was a mentor to its members. She gave her last performance in 1913, singing "Swing Low, Sweet Chariot" in Nashville's Ryman Auditorium at the close of a Jubilee concert. Ella Sheppard Moore died in 1914 from sepsis resulting from a burst appendix.

FURTHER READING

Pike, Gustavus D. *Jubilee Singers, and Their Campaign for Twenty Thousand Dollars* (1873).

Trotter, James. *Music and Some Highly Musical People: Containing brief chapters on: A Description of Music, the Music of Nature, a Glance at the History of Music, the Power, Beauty, and Uses of Music. Following which are given sketches of the lives of remarkable musicians of the colored race. With portraits, and an appendix containing copies of music composed by colored men* (1878).

Ward, Andrew. *Dark Midnight When I Rise: The Story of the Fisk Jubilee Singers* (2001).

DAVID K. BRADFORD

Sheppard, William Henry (8 or 28 Mar. 1865– 25 Nov. 1927), missionary, explorer, and human rights advocate, was born in Waynesboro, Virginia, the son of William H. Sheppard, a barbershop owner, and Sarah Francis "Fannie" Martin, a bath maid at a local spa, who had been born free. Because of his mother's free status, William, born just weeks before the end of the Civil War, was never classified as a slave, but his father may have been. Compared with most blacks in postbellum Virginia, the Sheppards lived in relative comfort, though William began full-time employment at eleven, first as a stable boy and then as a waiter. In 1881 Sheppard enrolled at the night school run by BOOKER T. WASHINGTON at Hampton Institute, Virginia, and financed his education by working on the institute's farm and in its bakery. He also helped found a mission school for poor blacks nearby and wrote in his autobiography, "I felt from that afternoon that my future work was to carry the gospel to the poor, destitute, and forgotten people" (Kennedy, 11).

To achieve that goal, Sheppard studied for the ministry at Tuscaloosa Theological Institute (now Stillman College) in Alabama in the mid-1880s and was assigned by the southern Presbyterian Church to congregations in Montgomery, Alabama, and Atlanta, Georgia. Disliking his urban pastorates, he lobbied the Presbyterian Foreign Mission Board for two years to send him to Africa, but the board refused to do so until 1890, when it recruited a white Alabamian minister, Samuel Lapsley, to join him in founding a mission to the Congo. Leaving his fiancée, Lucy Gantt, behind, Sheppard sailed with Lapsley from New York to London in February 1890. Before leaving for the Congo, Lapsley met with and received assistance for the mission from King Leopold II of Belgium, a man recognized by his fellow European monarchs as "Protector of the Congo." In truth, Leopold's governance of the Congo more closely resembled a protection racket, benefiting the Europeans who invested in his rubber plantations, mines, and railroads, but at a tragic cost to millions of native Congolese, driven out of their homes and beaten, tortured, and enslaved in brutal labor camps.

Sheppard and Lapsley were, however, unaware of the ongoing genocide when their ship anchored at Sharks Point on the Congo River delta in May 1890. The two men then embarked on an arduous twelve-hundred-mile journey through territory rarely traversed by outsiders, braving storms, treacherous, crocodile-filled rivers, and exposure to malaria and other diseases. Sheppard proved adept at navigating the unknown terrain and establishing an easy rapport with locals, which was greatly enhanced when he shot two hippopotami to save a village of Bateke people who were near starvation. The Bateke repaid their debt to the man they called Mundele Ndom, "the black white man," by rescuing him from attack by a crocodile. Booker T. Washington would have been proud of Sheppard's entrepreneurial skills—and frugality—as he cajoled, haggled, and bartered in several villages to find the porters and supplies needed for the final stage of the missionaries' journey, first by canoe and then by steamship, through the perilous Kasai River basin.

On 18 April 1891 Sheppard and Lapsley finally arrived at Luebo in the Kasai District, where they established the American Presbyterian Congo Mission among the Kete, a moderately prosperous farming people. After the dangers of the previous year, Sheppard marveled at the beauty of the Upper Kasai's palm tree-filled landscape and gloried at the clear night skies that "shine nowhere so brightly and beautifully as in 'Darkest Africa'" (Kennedy, 64). Even though the men established a small farm and built several huts and rudimentary roads, they failed in their primary task of converting the Kete to Christianity.

When Lapsley died from blackwater fever in 1892, Sheppard assumed sole charge at Luebo and immediately planned a new mission, this time to the Kuba people, who lived in uncharted lands deep within the Kasai interior. After mastering the Kuba language

and navigating the byzantine pathways of the Kasai outback, he arrived at a village on the edge of the Kuba kingdom, only to be apprehended by a prince, N'toinzide, who threatened to put the entire village on trial for entertaining a foreigner. Sheppard expected to be put to death, but he was instead brought to N'toinzide's father, King Kot aMweeky, who declared the missionary to be the spiritual reincarnation of Bope Mekabe, an ancient king of the Kuba. Sheppard remained at the king's palace for several months, observing the orderly, prosperous, and technologically advanced culture of the Kuba and collecting fine pottery, intricate tapestries, and ceremonial wood carvings, among other artifacts, that he would later donate to the Hampton Institute. Although Sheppard found much to admire in Kuba society, he deplored the practice of poisoning suspected witches and the ritual killing of enemy captives in funeral sacrifices. Hoping eventually to discourage such traditions, he persuaded Kot aMweeky to grant him nine acres of land upon which to build a mission. On receiving that grant, Sheppard left for London in 1893, where his exploits among the Kuba had earned him comparisons to the famed Scottish missionary and explorer David Livingstone and membership in the Royal Geographic Society.

Traveling back to America, Sheppard married Lucy Gantt in Jacksonville, Florida, in February 1894 and returned with her to the Congo three months later. There she had three daughters, Miriam and Lucille, who died as infants, and Wilhelmina, who survived the malarial Congo for five months before being taken home to Virginia to be raised by an aunt. In 1901 LUCY GANTT SHEPPARD had a son, William Lapsley Maxamalinge, shortened to Max, who was named after her husband's first partner at Luebo and a Kuba prince. Sheppard also had a relationship with a Kuba woman, who bore him a son, Shepete, in 1900.

From 1894 to 1896 Sheppard's mission at Luebo was staffed entirely by African Americans, until the Presbyterian leadership in America insisted on assigning a white missionary, William Morrison, to oversee them. Morrison shared Sheppard's goal of establishing a mission among the Kuba but was even more concerned about exposing the mounting evidence of atrocities perpetrated by the Belgian colonial regime. In 1899 Morrison dispatched Sheppard to report on an alleged massacre of Kuba villagers by native Zappo-Zap forces armed with European weaponry. Posing as a Belgian official, Sheppard took photographs of piles of dead bodies and dying people and persuaded the Zappo-Zap leader to admit that they had killed more than eighty villagers for refusing to pay their Belgian overlords a "tax" of rubber, food, and slaves. In addition to the charred, dismembered bodies—a scene reminiscent of a southern lynching—Sheppard made the grisly discovery of a pile of eighty-one right hands. Even though the Belgian courts assigned blame to the Zappo-Zaps alone, Sheppard's report provoked a flurry of international protests against the Congo regime and prompted Mark Twain to publish a damning satire of Belgian colonialism, "King Leopold's Soliloquy."

In the main, however, Sheppard was less vocal than Morrison or Twain in condemning Belgian atrocities, at least as long as he remained in the Congo and needed the colonial regime's support for a planned new mission. That accommodationist stance did not, however, prevent the Belgian state rubber company from attempting to sue him in 1908 for slander; Sheppard had published an article criticizing the company's forced labor practices and their destruction of Kuba traditions and culture. The Belgian authorities ultimately dismissed the charges, but the trial helped focus global attention on atrocities in the Congo and made Sheppard one of the first internationally recognized human rights advocates.

Sheppard's moment of fame was short-lived, however. He returned to the United States in 1910, after the Presbyterian Foreign Missions Board expelled him for several counts of adultery, charges that he admitted. Not wishing to tarnish the reputation of a bona fide hero—or the reputation of the church itself—the Missions Board kept the charges secret but placed Sheppard on probation, forcing the minister and his family to scrape together a living in Staunton, Virginia. In 1912 the church relented and hired Sheppard as a pastor in Louisville, Kentucky, where he died after a stroke in 1927. Although he lived his final years in relative obscurity, more than a thousand people attended his funeral, a testament to Sheppard's enduring appeal.

At the turn of the twentieth century, no other black missionary enjoyed a greater international reputation than William Sheppard. Sheppard's condemnation of Belgian atrocities and his public lectures on the treasures of the Kuba also provided a necessary antidote to prevailing Victorian notions that contrasted civilized Europe with the uncultured savagery of "darkest Africa."

FURTHER READING

There are two main collections of Sheppard materials and manuscripts: the Presbyterian Historical

Society, Montreat, North Carolina, and the Hampton University Archives, Hampton, Virginia.

Sheppard, William H. *Presbyterian Pioneers in Congo* (1917).

Kennedy, Pagan. *Black Livingstone: A True Tale of Adventure in the Nineteenth-Century Congo* (2002).

STEVEN J. NIVEN

Sherrod, Charles (2 Jan. 1937–), civil rights activist, was born to the fourteen-year-old Martha Walker and the unemployed Raymond Sherrod. The eldest of six children, he was raised in Petersburg, Virginia, by his mother and his devoutly Baptist grandmother. As a child, Sherrod sang in the Mount Olivet Baptist Church choir and was known to preach to his fellow students. He also worked to support his family, developing a strong will that drove him to study religion at Virginia Union University while still providing for his family. He received his B.A. in 1958, followed by a B.D. in 1961. In February 1961 Sherrod joined his first official civil rights protest with the Student Nonviolent Coordinating Committee (SNCC) in Richmond, Virginia. After joining a sit-in at segregated department stores, Sherrod was arrested and jailed. He adopted the "jail, no bail" tactic that was enthusiastically embraced by other SNCC activists.

After being appointed SNCC's first field secretary, Sherrod conducted nonviolence workshops alongside MARION BARRY in SNCC's McComb, Mississippi, office before moving to Albany, Georgia, in October 1961. He and Cordell Reagon coordinated SNCC activities in the region, having noted that students at Albany State College took no part in the sit-in movement that had swept the South during the previous year. Sherrod led SNCC's Southwest Georgia Project, encouraging local youths to practice nonviolence while challenging racial discrimination, helping adults to register to vote, and holding workshops on the movement. Within a month, local students had initiated a sit-in at the local bus station. This action sparked a wave of protest in Albany, laying the foundations for the movement that invited MARTIN LUTHER KING JR. to the city in December 1961. The first SNCC leader to integrate a project as a matter of policy, Sherrod led a team of eleven SNCC workers, five of whom were white. While this was in part due to Sherrod's commitment to integration, it also revealed his cynicism: he firmly believed that violence towards the white workers would arouse antisegregationist sentiment in the country and probably spur the Justice Department to action. He was also aware of the power of the liberal press and was not averse to tipping off reporters about potential flashpoints. His distrust of federal law enforcers was demonstrated on 29 February 1962, when he participated in a sit-in at Attorney General Robert Kennedy's office to protest Kennedy's failure to act upon the arrest of three SNCC workers on criminal anarchy charges in Baton Rouge, Louisiana.

Although dispirited by the collapse of the Albany movement in 1963, Sherrod remained active in SNCC through 1964 and fully supported the Mississippi Freedom Democratic Party's refusal to accept two seats-at-large at the 1964 Democratic National Convention. The Democratic Party's refusal to seat the whole MFDP delegation was proof to Sherrod that the civil rights movement had not addressed the real problem of power: "[W]e are a country of racists with a racist heritage, a racist economy, a racist language, a racist religion, a racist philosophy of living, and we need a naked confrontation with ourselves," he wrote in response (Carson, 128). At SNCC's Waveland retreat the following November he urged SNCC to widen its campaign to challenge poverty as well as racism. By this time, Sherrod had left Georgia to study at Union Theological Seminary (where he received a master's degree in sacred theology in 1967) and he remained in SNCC until 1966, whereupon he founded the Southwest Georgia Independent Voters Project to replace the Southwest Georgia Project. His resignation from SNCC was prompted by the unanimous rejection of his plan to invite northern white students to work in southwest Georgia by the increasingly nationalist-oriented Central Committee.

After SNCC's demise, Sherrod remained in Georgia. In line with his growing conviction that economics was at the heart of racial inequality, Sherrod started working more closely with the New Communities Corporation in 1969, a cooperative farming project that had been established to address economic inequality in the region and that he led until 1985. For seventeen years, New Communities held 6,000 acres of land in an attempt to develop a land base for southwest Georgia farmers and a food delivery service that would link rural and urban communities in the area. Sherrod hoped that this would become a larger project to develop trade links with the developing world, but drought and USDA interference led to New Communities' collapse. Between 1976 and 1990 he served on the Albany City Commission. He ran unsuccessfully in the 1992 Democratic State Senate primary and in the 1996 State Senate election. These failures were arguably due to Sherrod's refusal to accept large campaign donations from wealthy individuals and his reliance on a volunteer staff. They reveal that, while Sherrod's campaign to register Georgia's rural African American population was a success, his broader attack on poverty and economic inequality faced a more implacable foe. Beginning in 1994 he worked as prison chaplain at Georgia State Prison in Homerville.

Sherrod was one of the civil rights movement's most committed and able activists. The Southwest Georgia Project was one of SNCC's most important testing grounds for its community organization approaches and was one of the few civil rights initiatives to move into the rural South. By the early 1960s it was becoming clear that the region's cities were in the early stages of desegregation. Yet the rule of federal law rarely extended into the more remote areas of the South. Sherrod, like BOB MOSES in Mississippi, was one of the few activists to recognize that the rural population needed more encouragement, more protection, and more bravery if it was to end Jim Crow. Sherrod realized that direct action would be less effective in such areas, and so focused on community organizing and on educating and encouraging local individuals to consider themselves as political beings. For him, this work was not only focused on the vote but also on engaging in a "psychological battle for the minds of the enslaved" (Tuck, 162). Rather than retiring from agitation in the 1970s Sherrod, like many SNCC activists, continued to fight against oppression at the local level, encouraging people to make their own decisions and take control of their lives, continuing to work according to the template that he set out in the 1960s. His life illustrates that the civil rights struggle might have disappeared from the front pages, but its ideals continued to inform the lives of many of its participants even while its more ambitious aims remained unfulfilled.

FURTHER READING

Carson, Clayborne. *In Struggle: SNCC and the Black Awakening of the 1960s* (1981).

Tuck, Stephen G. N. *Beyond Atlanta: The Struggle for Racial Equality in Georgia, 1940–1980* (2001).

JOE STREET

Sherrod, Shirley Miller (20 Nov. 1947–), a civil rights activist, dedicated civil servant, and distinguished advocate for rural farmers, known for her candid accounts of her own struggles with the way

Shirley Sherrod speaks to student members at the National Association of Black Journalists Convention in San Diego, California on 29 July 2010, less than two weeks after she was ousted from her job at the United States Department of Agriculture. (AP Images.)

racism infuses American culture, was born Shirley Miller in Baker County, Georgia, to Hosea and Grace Miller. As a child she picked cucumbers, cotton, and peanuts, coming home from school and going directly to work in the fields. She was the oldest child, with four sisters, and one brother who was born two months after their father died. The family lived in an area called Hawkins Town, made up of several related families who owned their own farms, and a few landless agricultural laborers who, Sherrod recalled "were also like family," some of whom continued years later to attend family reunions. Everyone pitched in to help with each other's harvests (Melissa Walker, *Southern Farmers and Their Stories: Memory and Meaning in Oral History*, 2006, 202).

In 1965, when she was a senior in high school, her father, who also served as a Baptist church deacon, was fatally shot in the back over a livestock dispute. The farmer who shot him was not indicted, a common event in Georgia when the grand jury and the accused were all people who thought of themselves as "white," and the deceased was not. Sherrod had

intended to get as far away from agriculture as she could, and to get out of the South, but she made a commitment after her father's death not to leave. "I was making a commitment to black people, and to black people only," she recalled years later, "but God will show you things and he'll put things in your path," such as "The first time I was faced with having to help a white farmer save his farm."

Instead of going to college in a northern state, she enrolled at Fort Valley State College, then transferred to Albany State College (later University), where she earned a bachelor's degree in sociology. Joining the Student Nonviolent Coordinating Committee (SNCC), she participated in efforts to register African Americans to vote. She saw her future husband, CHARLES SHERROD, a twenty-two-year-old veteran of sit-ins in Richmond, Virginia, and McComb County, Mississippi, pushed down the court house stairs by the sheriff. He had been sent to Albany by SNCC in 1961, as field secretary and director for southwest Georgia. The Sherrods resigned from SNCC in 1969, after STOKELY CARMICHAEL demanded that all civil rights workers identified as "white" leave the organization—a policy the Sherrods disagreed with.

Sherrod and her husband were among the founders in 1969 of New Communities, Inc., which acquired six thousand acres of land in Lee County, Georgia, establishing a farming cooperative that grew and marketed soybeans, corn, cotton, and fruit. Voter registration campaigns in rural Georgia, particularly Baker, Lee, and Terrell counties, had shown that while SNCC could resist violence, no adult supporting a family economically dependent on "white" employers would register to vote when threatened with losing their job. The nonprofit cooperative was intended to form an economic and land-ownership base freeing African Americans in southwest Georgia to speak freely and participate fully in politics. The Democratic governor Lester Maddox blocked federal Office of Economic Opportunity development funds for New Communities from entering the state.

Sherrod also served as the Georgia director for the Land Assistance Fund of the Federation of Southern Cooperatives, which by 1974 had set up over 130 cooperatives across the South, owned and controlled by thirty thousand previously impoverished families; New Communities was the largest (*Ebony*, Oct. 1974, 100). Among those who came for assistance were Roger and Eloise Spooner; Roger Spooner later said, "I tell you what, I never was treated no better than Shirley." Sherrod, however, in her own mind, saw that this farmer was "white," and years later recited to the NAACP's twentieth annual Freedom Fund banquet how she had to struggle with her own sense of race and racial history, in order to advocate for the Spooners as she would for anyone of her own color.

In 1984 New Communities dissolved in the face of $1.5 million in debt, with Prudential Life Insurance Co. initiating foreclosure (*Jet*, 28 May 1984, 24). This triggered a lawsuit against the Department of Agriculture over refusal, from 1981 to 1985, to provide irrigation loans or allow New Communities to restructure existing loans. With successive secretaries of agriculture named as defendant, the case was partially settled as *Pigford v. Vilsack* in 2009, acknowledging racial discrimination by the department, and awarding New Communities $13 million for loss of land and income (www.pigfordmonitor.org).

Sherrod entered the Rural Development Leadership Network in 1985, received a master's degree in community development from Antioch University through RDLN in 1989, and the same year received the network's Harold Gaines Award. She published her research in *The "Multi-Purpose" Farm Cooperative as an Approach to Saving the Black Farm,* and served on the board of RDLN until she resigned to accept a position with the Department of Agriculture. On 25 July 2009, Sherrod was appointed Georgia State director for the United States Department of Agriculture's Rural Development program, by U.S. Secretary of Agriculture Tom Vilsack.

Sherrod's life and work became a matter of momentary high-profile controversy the following year, when the web blogger and Tea Party activist Andrew Breitbart took remarks she made out of context, to score political points against the administration of President BARACK OBAMA. Breitbart, a well-known and controversial conservative activist and owner of the biggovernment.com Internet blog, posted a brief video clip taken from a speech Sherrod had given, as keynote speaker at the Georgia state National Association for the Advancement of Colored People (NAACP) 20th Annual Freedom Fund Banquet, 27 March 2010.

Sherrod had candidly related her thoughts about "the first time I was faced with helping a white farmer save his farm" when working with the Federation of Southern Cooperatives. She recalled "struggling with the fact that so many black people had lost their farmland" and now she was "faced with having to help this white farmer save his land." She continued to explain how the county board had prevented the farmer from filing Section 12 bankruptcy, and the "white lawyer" she referred him to had done virtually nothing for him, ultimately telling him, in Sherrod's presence, "why don't you just let the farm go," and she had to step in.

Allegations that Sherrod had discriminated against a "white" farmer because of his race were cut off in full cry when the farmer concerned, Roger Spooner, told Cable News Network (CNN) "No way in the world" is she a racist. "They don't know what they're talking about." His wife, Eloise Spooner, said "She's a good friend. She helped save our farm, getting in there and doing all she could to help us. They have not treated her right. She's the one I give credit for helping us save our farm." As the Spooners recalled, they had suffered a lot of dry weather, had to run the irrigation a lot, and even when they made a good crop, they wouldn't get a good price. They too recalled that "After the lawyer in Albany did us like he did," Sherrod had been the one who stepped in and organized the assistance they needed.

Exactly who in the Obama administration said what to whom has never been fully determined. Events suggested to many that some White House or Agriculture Department staff reacted hypersensitively to the potential for negative publicity and pressed for Sherrod to resign before the allegations could be thoroughly investigated. Agriculture Secretary Tom Vilsack, who effusively praised Sherrod when he appointed her, publicly took full responsibility for Sherrod's resignation. Sherrod told *CBS News* that someone from the White House "called me twice" on 19 July. "The last time they asked me to pull over the side of the road and submit my resignation on my Blackberry, and that's what I did" (Condon).

The NAACP released a statement on 20 July supporting the Agriculture Department's decision—although the full context of Sherrod's remarks was a presentation at a videotaped NAACP function. NAACP president Benjamin Jealous said, "According to her remarks, she mistreated a white farmer in need of assistance because of his race." Late the next day Jealous announced, "we were snookered by Fox News and Tea Party Activist Andrew Breitbart." While Sherrod told CNN that she "Would've appreciated having the NAACP at least contact me," before issuing a statement, in a letter to NAACP members the following month, Sherrod wrote "the last thing I want to see happen is my situation weaken support for the NAACP" (*Washington Times,* 17 Aug. 2010).

Fox News host Bill O'Reilly, who had publicized the initial allegations, said on the air the following Wednesday, "I owe Ms. Sherrod an apology for not doing my homework, for not putting her remarks in the proper context" (*Los Angeles Times,* 21 July 2010). The same day, White House press secretary Robert Gibbs said, "A disservice was done, for which we apologize" (*Los Angeles Times,* 22 July 2010); "One of the great lessons we will take away from this is to ask all the questions first." Vilsack offered her a new job with the department's Office of Advocacy and Outreach, but she declined.

FURTHER READING

Boswell, Angela, and Judith N. McArthur. *Women Shaping the South: Creating and Confronting Change* (2006).

Condon, Stephanie. "Shirley Sherrod: White House Forced My Resignation." *CBS News,* 20 July, 2010. http://www.cbsnews.com/ 8301-503544_162-20011099-503544. html?tag=contentMain; contentBody.

Davidson, Osha Gray. *Broken Heartland: The Rise of America's Rural Ghetto* (1996).

CHARLES ROSENBERG

Shines, Johnny (26 Apr. 1915–20 Apr. 1992), blues singer and guitarist, was born John Ned Shines in Frayser, Tennessee, the son of John Shines Sr., a farmer. The name of his mother is not recorded. Though born just outside Memphis, Shines was raised in Arkansas and labored briefly as a sharecropper in the early 1930s near Hughes. His mother taught him how to play guitar, and he began performing in juke joints and at weekend fish fries.

Around 1934, two years after he is believed to have first married, Shines was introduced to the blues prodigy ROBERT JOHNSON in the Helena area by a pianist known as M&O (after the Mobile and Ohio Railroad). Awed by Johnson's talents, Shines would recount decades later, "The things he was doing was things I'd never heard nobody else do" (Palmer, 118).

Like restless nomads Shines and Johnson wound up roving together throughout the Delta, hitching rides and hopping freight trains to play at house parties, bars, and work camps. In 1937 Shines and Johnson ventured to Canada and even performed gospel music on *The Elder Moten Hour,* a popular religious radio broadcast in the Detroit area. Upon returning home, Shines moved to Memphis. Johnson resumed his wandering and womanizing, and was allegedly given a fatal serving of strychnine-laced whiskey by a vengeful husband in rural Mississippi in 1938.

In Memphis, Shines played in nightclubs and at Church's Park (now W. C. Handy Park), and accompanied Baby Boy Warren and other musicians on stage throughout the region. In 1941 Shines relocated to Chicago, where he initially played for tips on Maxwell Street. He later formed a trio and performed part-time as a musician as he worked by day in construction. Shines first recorded in 1946 for Okeh, but the recordings were not released until years later. He recorded for Chess (1950) and J.O.B. (1952), but failed to sell sufficiently well due to the rising popularity of electric blues. The former Rolling Stones bassist Bill Wyman insists, "Shines' material did not click with the record buyers, though there was no real rhyme or reason for that, because he cut some really good songs. In particular, 'Brutal Hearted Woman' deserved to do well" (Wyman, 353). By 1958 Shines was disheartened and sold his guitar in disgust.

Redemption came in 1965, when Shines recorded tracks for Vanguard Records' monumental *Chicago: The Blues Today!* (1966). Shines's appearance on this celebrated project and his subsequent touring with the Chicago All Stars renewed interest in his music. He would later perform on university campuses and in music festivals, including the Newport Jazz Festival (1976).

Shines married his third wife, Hattie Tucker, on 25 November 1965. They had one daughter.

Additionally Shines helped raise some ten grandchildren after Rosetta Frazier Owens, his daughter from a previous marriage, died giving birth to her eleventh child. Shines moved his family in 1969 to Holt, Alabama, near Tuscaloosa, where they resided on Eleventh Street (now Johnny Shines Street). In Holt, Shines worked as an upholsterer and continued performing. Frustrated because youngsters, particularly African Americans, often lacked interest in blues music, Shines strived to educate children about the genre's significance in America's musical heritage.

A stroke in 1980 rendered Shines void of dexterity in his fingers. He resorted to playing slide guitar. *Hangin' On* (Rounder), a project he recorded with Johnson's stepson, Robert Lockwood Jr., was nominated for a Grammy Award in 1980. *Back to the Country* (Blind Pig), a collaboration with Snooky Pryor, was released in 1991. The record won a coveted W. C. Handy Award.

Though his record sales were only marginal, Shines thrilled nostalgic blues devotees by perpetuating the Johnson legacy throughout his career, perhaps to the detriment of his own artistic identity. Frequently asked to recount his adventures with Johnson or attempt to mimic the mysterious, hard-living singer's inimitable guitar playing, Shines dutifully obliged by retelling his stories to scholars and journalists and delighting fans with a repertoire of Johnson-penned songs such as "I Believe I'll Dust My Broom," "Ramblin' on My Mind," and "Sweet Home Chicago." Shines even appeared and played in the documentary, *The Search for Robert Johnson* (1992).

Shines died at the DCH Medical Center in Tuscaloosa following the amputation of his left leg due to complications from diabetes. In 1992, he was inducted into the Blues Foundation's Hall of Fame. And, in 2010, Holt held its first Johnny Shines Blues Festival, an event for which Shines's daughter, the blues performer Carroline Shines, had lobbied for years.

FURTHER READING

Harris, Sheldon. *Blues Who's Who: A Biographical Dictionary of Blues Singers* (1979).

Palmer, Robert. *Deep Blues* (1981).

Wyman, Bill. *Bill Wyman's Blues Odyssey: A Journey to Music's Heart and Soul* (2001).

Obituary: *Jet*, 11 May 1992.

GREG FREEMAN

Shinhoster, Earl (5 July 1950–11 June 2000), civil rights activist, was born Earl Theodore Shinhoster in Savannah, Georgia, the fourth child of Willie Shinhoster, a foundry worker, and Nadine Pullen, a custodian and licensed beautician. Earl was influenced by his grandfather, Ezekiel Shinhoster, who founded the first National Association for the Advancement of Colored People (NAACP) branch in rural Pulaski County, Georgia, in the 1940s. At the age of thirteen, Earl became an active member of the NAACP Youth Council, where he was mentored by W. W. LAW during the height of the civil rights movement.

Shinhoster graduated from S. M. Tompkins High School in 1968 and earned a B.A. in Political Science from Morehouse College in 1972. He attended the Cleveland State University College of Law. There he continued to volunteer with the NAACP, but illness forced him to leave Cleveland before completing law school. Upon returning to Georgia, Shinhoster reaffiliated himself with the NAACP where Bobby Hill, the first black state representative from Savannah to the General Assembly since Reconstruction, noticed his work. When the state legislature accepted Hill's proposal to initiate an office for minority consumers, Hill recommended Shinhoster, and Governor George Busbee appointed Shinhoster as director of the Office of Human Affairs. On 30 August 1975 Shinhoster married Ruby Dallas of Atlanta, Georgia, and they had one son, Michael Omar Shinhoster.

Shinhoster left his position with the State of Georgia to become the NAACP's Southeast regional director in 1978. He was the youngest regional director in the organization's history, and his region, Region V, included the states where the most notable civil rights battles occurred: Georgia, Alabama, the Carolinas, Florida, Mississippi, and Tennessee. Shinhoster was instrumental in attacking national and international issues, such as police brutality and the race riots in Miami, the Haitian refugee crisis, the tension between the black and Jewish communities, and the anti-apartheid struggle. He represented the NAACP in conferences throughout Africa, Europe, and the Caribbean.

In 1994 Shinhoster was promoted to national field director of the NAACP. As the third highest-ranking official, he oversaw the work of eighteen hundred branches and coordinated an NAACP delegation to conduct voter education and mobilization training for South Africa's African National Congress. Later in 1994 Shinhoster became the interim (and in 1995 acting) executive director and CEO of the NAACP, which had a $4 million deficit, a loss of corporate donations, and a severe membership decline. By the time a new CEO was named in 1996, Shinhoster had reduced more than $1 million of the debt, and the membership had grown from six hundred thousand to nearly 1 million.

Shinhoster left the NAACP in 1996 but returned in 1999 as director of voter empowerment to register four million new voters for the 2000 presidential election. During his departure from the NAACP, Shinhoster worked in Africa and the United States. From 1996 to 1997 he served as field director in Ghana, West Africa, for the National Democratic Institute for International Affairs. He also consulted with the Ghana and Burkina Faso Olympic Committees in preparation for the Centennial Olympic Games in Atlanta. From 1997 to 1998 he acted as the interim director of Voting Rights Programs for the Southern Regional Council. He once again returned to Georgia, where he worked as the coordinator of voter education for the state until his return to the NAACP. His international work continued as the U.S. coordinator for the African Renaissance Festival in the province of KwaZulu Natal, South Africa. Months before the 2000 election, Shinhoster was killed in a car accident in Macon County, Alabama, while escorting the first lady of Liberia. He left behind a legacy of social and civil service.

FURTHER READING

Shinhoster's speeches, correspondence, and other papers are in the NAACP regional office in Atlanta and the Ralph Mark Gilbert Civil Rights Museum in Savannah, Georgia.

Charles, Bettina. "Earl Shinhoster: A Committed CEO," *Crisis,* July 1995.

Obituary: *Washington Post,* 12 June 2000.

ADRIENNE CARTHON

Shipp, E. R. (1955–), journalist and columnist, was born in Conyers, Georgia, a small town in the state's north-central region. She was the oldest of six children. Little information appears to be available about her early life, except that her family was quite poor, lacking running water and plumbing in the family home. She attended schools in and around Conyers and was a good student with a flair for language and defending her opinions and ideas. When she was still in high school, she found work at a local newspaper. Despite this interest in writing, her family expected her to take a job in a local factory.

After graduating high school, though, Shipp matriculated to Georgia State University, from which in 1976 she took a B.A. in journalism. She then relocated to New York, where she enrolled at Columbia University, from which she took a master's in 1979 and a law degree a year later. In 1994 she earned her M.A. degree in history from the same institution. In 1980 she got a job at the *New York Times,* first as a stringer and later as an editor. From that position, Shipp wrote about affirmative action (of which she was somewhat skeptical, though generally supportive), the problems of poverty, crime, and government corruption, and, famously, the O. J. SIMPSON murder trial.

In 1990 she coauthored *Outrage: The Story behind the Tawana Brawley Hoax* with five of her *Times* colleagues. Brawley was a young African American from New York who in 1987 had accused six white men of raping her. The story soon began to draw national attention and generate controversy. The African American community largely united behind Brawley, whereas polls showed that many whites soon began to doubt the truthfulness of her claims. A subsequent grand jury determined that Brawley's claims to having been abducted and sexually assaulted had no basis in fact. Shipp's book came to the same conclusion, and much of it involves an examination of the relationship of the black community with law enforcement and the criminal justice system.

In 1993 Shipp quit the *Times.* She returned to Columbia University and began to study toward a Ph.D. in History. In 1994 she began penning a weekly column for the *Daily News,* and authored much of her most famous and widely read opinion writing. Among her more talked about work was her writing about the murder trial of the former professional football star O. J. Simpson, who had been accused of the 1994 murder of his ex-wife and her friend in Los Angeles. The trial—which dragged on for nine months—revealed a sharp division between blacks and whites; polls consistently showed blacks to be far more likely to believe that Simpson was the victim of either police negligence or a conspiracy.

E.R. Shipp, left, of the *New York Daily News,* receives her Pulitzer Prize award from George Rupp, president of Columbia University, during the presentation ceremony at Columbia in New York Monday, 20 May 1996. (AP Images.)

For her part, Shipp believed Simpson to be guilty and wrote scathingly of the circus-like atmosphere of the trial and the antics of Simpson's high-profile lawyer JOHNNIE COCHRAN. In 1996 she was awarded the Pulitzer Prize for Commentary. The prize jury noted her "penetrating columns on race, welfare and other social issues." Since that time, she has continued to work in the news business, occasionally appearing on the cable news station MSNBC. Meanwhile, in 2011 she was teaching classes at Columbia University, where she was professor.

FURTHER READING

Belford, Barbara. *Brilliant Bylines: A Biographical Anthology of Notable Newspaperwomen in America* (1986).

JASON PHILIP MILLER

Shippen, John (5 Dec. 1879–16 July 1968), golfer, was born John Matthew Shippen Jr., in Washington, D.C., one of nine children of John Matthew Shippen Sr. and Eliza (Spotswood) Shippen. In 1888, Shippen's father, a Presbyterian minister, accepted a mission to the Shinnecock Indian Reservation near Southampton, Long Island. Two years after the Shippens arrived, a group of wealthy New Yorkers established the Shinnecock Hills Golf Club, one of the first modern golf courses in the United States, and Shippen earned money helping to clear the land. After completion of the eighteen-hole course in 1895, the local professional, a Scotsman named Willie Dunn, employed local youths to caddy for the club's members. Among his hires were Shippen and his friend Oscar Bunn, a member of the Shinnecock tribe. In their spare time, Shippen and Bunn practiced the game under Dunn's tutelage, and the two youths proved to be quick learners.

In 1896 the United States Golf Association (USGA) scheduled its annual U.S. Amateur and U.S. Open championships for the newly completed Shinnecock Hills course. Several club members encouraged the two young caddies to enter the Open tournament to test their skills against the best professionals in the country. A few days before the Open, however, a group of the mostly Scottish and English professionals confronted USGA President Theodore Havemeyer and demanded the withdrawal of the two nonwhite competitors. Havemeyer, who was also a co-owner of the American Sugar Refining Company, brusquely dismissed the protest and reportedly told the striking pros that the event would proceed even if Shippen and Bunn "were the only two who played" (St. Laurent, 17). The pros hastily dropped their objections and none skipped the tournament.

The sixteen-year-old Shippen shocked the sporting community by shooting a first-round 78 to tie for the lead after the first day of the thirty-six-hole event. Over the last eighteen holes he remained in contention until he carded an eleven on the thirteenth hole to drop him off the leader board. He recovered to finish in a tie for fifth place and won ten dollars in prize money, making him the first American-born golfer to earn money in a professional event. Bunn completed the tournament but finished near the bottom of the standings.

Shippen's performance won him numerous accolades and allowed him to earn a living at the game he loved. The following summer the new Maidstone Country Club on Long Island hired him to be the club professional and teach the game to its members. He worked at Maidstone until 1899 when he accepted a similar job at Aronimink County Club in suburban Philadelphia. That same year the U.S. Open returned to the Mid-Atlantic for the first time since 1896, and Shippen entered the event hosted by the Baltimore County Club. Even though the tournament took place in a Jim Crow state, the USGA followed Havemeyer's precedent and readily accepted Shippen's registration. He played all four rounds without incident in Baltimore, and though he finished a disappointing twenty-fourth, he was undoubtedly one of the last African Americans to play at a southern country club until the 1960s.

After the Open he finished the summer at Aronimink and then worked for one season at both Spring Lake Country Club in New Jersey and Brooklyn's Marine and Field Golf Club. He played the U.S. Open in Chicago in 1900 (tying for twenty-fifth), and two years later he again surprised the golfing establishment with a fifth-place finish at the Open, eleven strokes off the lead. He took home eighty dollars and won praise as one of the best native-born golfers in the country.

In 1898, Shippen had married Effie Walker, a Shinnecock Indian, but she died after a year of marriage. Two years later he wed another Shinnecock woman, Maude Elliot Lee, and the couple would have six children.

After 1902 he returned to Maidstone as the club professional, but he inexplicably stopped entering professional tournaments. For the next decade he toiled anonymously at the Long Island club and faded from the national scene. In 1913, his last year at Maidstone, he briefly reappeared at the U.S. Open, finishing in a tie for forty-first place. Shippen left Maidstone in 1913 and for two years worked as a private instructor for such clients as the steel magnate Henry Clay Frick and the future U.S. senator from New Jersey, Joseph S. Freylinghausen. In about 1916 he returned to Shinnecock Hills as the head groundskeeper for two years before taking a similar job at the nearby National Links of America. He soon moved on to Washington, D.C., where he worked for the Department of Public Grounds. Shippen soon tired of his civil service job, however. In 1921 he designed the National Capital Country Club in Laurel, Maryland, one of the country's first African American country clubs, and he became the professional there. After about four years, the Shady Rest Country Club in Scotch Plains, New Jersey, another pioneering all-black organization, hired Shippen, and he found a niche there as a jack-of-all-trades, working as the club pro, maintaining the course as head groundskeeper, and repairing clubs. He settled down at Shady Rest and remained the club pro for thirty-five years.

Shippen retired in 1960 and his health soon deteriorated. He died in Newark, New Jersey, and was interred at the Rosedale Cemetery in Linden, New Jersey. In the 1990s, renewed interest in his life caused relatives and Scotch Plains residents to found the John Shippen Memorial Foundation. The Foundation holds an annual golf tournament to fund a minority scholarship program, and, in 1993, it erected a new headstone on Shippen's grave to detail his pioneering accomplishments.

FURTHER READING

Dawkins, Marvin P. and Graham C. Kinloch. *African American Golfers during the Jim Crow Era* (2000).

St. Laurent, Philip. "The Negro in World History: John Shippen," *Tuesday Magazine* (Apr. 1969).

Sinnette, Calvin H. *Forbidden Fairways: African Americans and the Game of Golf* (1998).

Strafaci, Frank. "Forgotten Pioneer Professional," *Golfing* (Mar. 1957).

GREGORY BOND

Shirley, Aaron (3 Jan. 1933–), a doctor and civil rights activist, was born in Gluckstadt, Mississippi, to Charlie Shirley, a brickmaker and housewright, and Eddie McDill, a nurse's aide. Shirley's father died when Aaron was only eighteen months old, leaving his mother to rear him, two older brothers, and five sisters. One brother died of congenital heart failure at age nine, another brother died during his teen years, and one sister died of sickle-cell anemia before finishing college. Eddie Shirley was a determined woman with sufficient business savvy to make a decent living for her family by selling several of the houses that her husband had built before he died. To make ends meet, she rented parts of another house, the largest her husband had built, to black teachers who came to Jackson to earn their teaching certification, something they could obtain no where else in Mississippi. She ran a disciplined household, even though she worked constantly. At one point she worked as a nurse's aide to a group of black doctors in town, leaving Shirley (at two years old) in the care of his brother Arlington.

Shirley was exceptionally bright, with an affinity for math and science, and he was already capable of reading by the time he got to Sallie Reynolds Elementary School in 1939. His oldest sister, also named Eddie, was a registered nurse, and she both encouraged and made decisions about his education. Shirley really wanted to study electrical engineering, but there were no scholarships available in that field and so he instead chose medicine. He was expected to do well, and he did not disappoint. At Lanier High School in Jackson, his teachers were dedicated and talented; but with few resources, science lessons were often improvised. Shirley remembered learning about heat conduction by watching his teacher heat an iron skillet and use dry and wet cloths to lift it.

During the Korean War many of Aaron Shirley's schoolmates wanted to join the military. Shirley himself entertained notions of becoming a black paratrooper until his mother put an end to his plans. She had different goals for Shirley, and she was pleased when he graduated as a class officer from Lanier in 1951. In the fall he enrolled at Tougaloo College in Mississippi. In his first year he met an upperclassman named Ollye Brown from Mound Bayou, near his home in Jackson. Brown was an accelerated student who graduated early, and after the two married, Shirley continued with his premedical studies while his new wife worked. He graduated cum laude in premedicine in 1955 and enrolled at Meharry Medical School in Nashville, Tennessee. Shirley found the rigorous academics at Meharry particularly tough in his first year, and he realized that he had to relearn much of what he had been taught in college. In addition, he was competing against students from more prosperous backgrounds and stronger schools, especially in the sciences, from all over the country. It was during his last year at Tougaloo that he and Ollye had their first child, a boy. Three years later their second son was born.

Shirley graduated from Meharry in 1959, and because of a stipulation in his scholarship he was required to do a one-year rotation as an intern, rather than do further study to specialize in any particular field. The scholarship required that he return to Mississippi. Vicksburg was one city open to him, and it was near his mother and sister, so he moved his family there. Jim Crow laws were extraordinarily strong in Vicksburg, and no black doctor had ever applied for hospital privileges there. Shirley caused quite a stir when he submitted his application, which was denied. Rather than give up, however, he appealed the decision all the way to the U.S. Department of Justice. He eventually got hospital privileges, but only after he was accepted into a residency program and officials realized that he would be leaving. His wife worked in the school system, and one upshot of Shirley's appeals was that she was made superintendent of schools in Vicksburg. Shirley still planned on getting pediatric training, but because of these activities he put off leaving until 1965.

Shirley completed his residency in Jackson at the University of Mississippi Medical Center in 1967 as the first black resident. By this time he had seen so much poverty and misery in Jackson and the surrounding counties that he felt obligated to stay and make a difference, especially for the children. As the chief resident, he had as his patients children from all over the state. So rather than accept an offer to attend Johns Hopkins Medical School in Maryland for his master's degree in public health, he opened a private practice in Jackson and became a consultant on health services to the American Academy of Pediatricians. He was the sole black pediatrician in Mississippi. He expanded his activities to include work with Head Start as well, and in 1970 he set out to establish the Jackson-Hinds Comprehensive Health Center.

Again he was met with fierce resistance from the state of Mississippi, whose decisions could be overruled only by the federal government under an exception written into the Great Society programs. Mississippi refused to grant any funds to him for the health center. On appeal and in an extreme political move, a young director of the Office of Economic Opportunity, Donald Rumsfeld, overruled Governor John Bell Williams. These events were unfolding at the same time that the massacres at Kent State and Jackson State were taking place. Rumsfeld came to Mississippi to show the government's concern with the incidents, and with Shirley as his guide, he visited the families of the dead Jackson State students. But Mississippi was not going to give up easily on refusing Shirley's request for funding the health center. The state attempted to get around Rumsfeld's override by implying that in the health center's charter documents a deal had been struck between Rumsfeld and Shirley, ensuring funding for the center if Shirley would assist Rumsfeld in making sure that no riots followed the student shootings. This effort to thwart the center also failed.

The Jackson-Hinds Comprehensive Health Center was initially housed in a church Sunday school; the clinic operated during the week in the classrooms that were cleaned and returned for church uses every Friday. In rural Hinds County, Shirley and his staff used an old bus that was gutted and outfitted with the bare essentials for seeing patients. The infant mortality rate was a staggering sixty per thousand live births for black children, compared to thirty per thousand for whites, all mainly because of disparities in adequate health care and nutrition. But the state continued its fight against the clinic.

In 1993 Shirley was awarded a MacArthur Fellowship. In 1994 he became member of President Bill Clinton's Health Care Initiatives panel, chaired by Hillary Clinton. In 1995 he became a member of the board at Tougaloo College. Jackson State University endowed the Aaron Shirley chair at its school of public health, and in 2004 its college of public service was renamed the Aaron Shirley College of Public Service. In 2005 the University of Mississippi endowed a chair at its medical center as the Aaron Shirley chair for the study of health disparities.

FURTHER READING

Dryfoos, Joy. *Full-Service Schools: A Revolution in Health and Social Services for Children, Youth, and Families* (1998).

LUTHER BROWN JR.

Shirley, George Irving (18 Apr. 1934–), opera singer and college professor, was born in Indianapolis, Indiana, and grew up in Detroit, Michigan, where his family moved when he was six years old. His mother, Daisy Bell Shirley, was born in Fort Smith, Arkansas, and died at ninety years of age. She sang in the church choir as a soprano and recited poetry. His father, Irving Ewing Shirley, was born in Summer Shade, Kentucky, and died at one hundred years of age. He was an untrained musician who played guitar, fiddle, piano, and sang bass. An insurance salesman, he remained professionally active in insurance until age ninety.

The younger Shirley, encouraged by his musically inclined parents, began singing in church at the age of six. As a teenager, while playing the baritone horn in a community band, he decided upon a career in music. Shirley graduated from Detroit's Wayne State University in 1955 with a B.S. in music education. He began teaching choral music at the high school level in the Detroit public schools during his last semester before graduation. He became the first African American appointed to teach high school music in that school system.

Shirley's public school career was short lived, however. After only a year and a half of teaching, he was drafted into the U.S. Army. He entered basic training a week after being married, still unhappy at being drafted. During his army service, however, Shirley began serious voice study. Though he was aware of the U.S. Army Chorus, Shirley did not audition for the group because he felt that his race and lack of vocal experience would hinder his acceptance. As a regular foot soldier, he instead successfully tried out for a place in the band. Transferred to Fort Leonard Wood, Missouri, Shirley found the band experience boring and unrewarding. At that point, he and two colleagues took a weekend pass to Washington, D.C., to audition for the army chorus. Following a successful audition, as well as some behind-the-scenes maneuvering on his behalf by the conductor, Captain Samuel Loboda, Shirley was accepted and

George Irving Shirley on 10 Dec. 1961. (Library of Congress/ Photographed by Car Van Vechten.)

became the organization's first African American member. Coincidentally, the U.S. Army Chorus was organized in 1955. In that momentous year, Shirley graduated from college, MARIAN ANDERSON made her historic Metropolitan Opera debut, becoming the institution's first African American soloist, and the Montgomery Bus Boycott began.

One of his fellow choristers was John Gillas who was studying voice privately in Washington, D.C., with Themy Georgi. Gillas was relentless about Shirley accompanying him to a voice lesson. He finally agreed to go just to stop his fellow chorister from pestering him. Shirley sang for Themy, who advised him that after one year of study he would be ready for a career.

Shirley had planned to return to Detroit and resume his teaching career. With the support of his wife, he changed his mind, stayed in the army for another year (his encounter with Themy happened as his two-year enlistment was concluding) so that he could have an income to support his family (he now had a daughter), and studied voice. Other

teachers with whom Shirley studied and coached included Amos Ebersole, Edward Boatner, and Cornelius Reid. It was his experience as an army chorister that changed the direction of his career, ultimately serving as a prelude to his becoming the first African American tenor and the second African American man to sing major roles at the Metropolitan Opera and his becoming an internationally acclaimed performer, teacher, lecturer, and adjudicator.

Following his discharge from the military in 1959, Shirley made his operatic debut as Eisenstein in Strauss's *Die Fledermaus* with the Turnau Opera Players. From there he went to the major companies and festivals in the world. In addition to the Metropolitan, he also sang at the Royal Opera (Covent Garden, London); Deutsche Oper (Berlin); Teatro Colon (Buenos Aires); Netherlands Opera (Amsterdam); L'Opera (Monte Carlo); New York City Opera; Scottish Opera (Glasgow); Chicago Lyric Opera; San Francisco Opera; Washington Opera; Michigan Opera Theater; Glyndebourne Festival; Santa Fe Opera; Bregenz Festival and Glimerglass. From Eisenstein in Strauss's *Die Fledemaus*, he went on to perform many of the major operatic tenor roles in the repertoire from Monteverdi; to Stravinsky: Elvino (*Sonnambula*); Alwa (*Lulu*); Don Jose (*Carmen*); Riccardo (*Anna Bolena*); Nemorine (*Eliser*); Edgardo (*Lucia*); Sportin' Life (*Porgy and Bess*); Des Grieux (*Manon*); Eumente (*Il Ritorno D'ulisse in Patria*); Ferrando (*Cosi fan tutte*); Don Ottavio (*Don Giovanni*); Tamino (*Zauberflöte*); Rodolfo (*Boheme*); Pickerton (*Butterfly*); Des Grieux (*Manon Lescant*); Cavaradoss (*Tosca*); Almaviva (*Barbiere di Siviglia*); Bacchus (*Ariadne auf Naxos*); Appolo (*Daphne*); Ein Sänger (*Rosenkavalier*); Herodes (*Salome*); Tom Rakewell (*Rake's Progress*); Fenton (*Falstaff*); Ducadi Mantova (*Rigoletto*); Gabfriele (*Simon Boccaneger*); Alfredo (*Traviata*); Erik (*Fliegender Holländer*); David (*Meistersinger*); Loge (*Rheingold*); and the title roles in *Pelleas et Melisande, Idomeneo,* and *Oedipus Rex*.

Recitals and concert performances with some of the world's most renowned conductors and accompanists (Solti, Klemperer, Stravinsky, Ormandy, von Karajan, Colin Davis, Bohm, Ozawa, Haitink, Boult, Leinsdorf, Boulez, DePreist, Krips, Cleva, Lewis, Dorati, Goldovsky, Pritchard, Bernstein, Maazel, Rudel, Bolcom, Brice, Isepp, Katz, Sanders, Wadsworth, and Wustman) also were a part of his offerings. The civil rights movement was not born to bring democracy into the performing arts, but as the twentieth century's major sociopolitical phenomenon, the civil rights movement created positive ripple effects of opportunity for African American singers. Before the civil rights movement, hearing and seeing African American singers in performances of concert works with orchestra that required multiple soloists alongside Caucasian singers was as remote as African American singers being cast with Caucasian singers in opera. African American singers performed those concert works with orchestra that required only one soloist. The recital format for African American singers was the most accessible performance medium. The political, psychological, and sociological fallout from the civil rights movement gave Shirley's career as a concert and operatic artist major impetus, and his success was a source of motivation for other African American singers, particularly men.

In 1980 Shirley returned to teaching, first at the University of Maryland, and then beginning in 1987 at the University of Michigan as a professor of voice.

FURTHER READING

Cheatham, Wallace McClain. "Black Male Singers at the Metropolitan Opera," *Black Perspective in Music* 16 (Spring 1988).

Cheatham, Wallace McClain. *Dialogues On Opera and The African American Experience* (1997).

Gray, John. *Blacks In Classical Music* (1988).

Southern, Eileen. *Biographical Dictionary of Afro-American and African Musicians* (1962).

WALLACE MCCLAIN CHEATHAM

Shirley, Ollye Levervia Brown (10 Jan. 1934–), civil rights activist and educator, was born near Mound Bayou, in Bolivar County, Mississippi, the oldest of three children, and the only girl, born to Wilbert Simmons and Walter Gee Brown.

Mound Bayou is an independent black community founded by former slaves in 1887. Shirley's parents both taught at the local one-room school, and she then attended Mound Bayou High School. In a 1999 oral history, Shirley remembered that her parents, who owned their property, would feed poor white children who were waiting for a school bus. But Shirley and her siblings had to walk to school because only white children were allow to ride the bus, which would sideswipe them as they walked, and the white passengers would throw things out of the window at them.

Shirley moved briefly to Chicago with her parents and then lived with her grandparents in Oklahoma before returning to Mississippi in 1949 to attend Tougaloo College, a historically black liberal arts college in Jackson. She majored in English, receiving her B.A. in 1953. At Tougaloo, Ollye Brown met and married Aaron Shirley on 2 June 1953. They moved to Nashville, Tennessee, where Aaron Shirley attended Meharry Medical College. They had four children.

After they moved to Vicksburg, Mississippi, Ollye Shirley began to teach elementary and junior high school. She had been promised a teaching job in Jackson, but because she had worked with Dr. Theodore Roosevelt Mason (T. R. M.) HOWARD, a well-known civil rights figure, the job offer was withdrawn, and she was told she would never work in Jackson. She later served on the Jackson School Board (1978 to 1993), and when she was president (1988 to 1993), honored Howard with a plaque.

Shirley discovered that black teachers were paid less than the white teachers, and that black schools had fewer books and desks, and larger classes, than white schools. As a black woman, she was not allowed in either the Vicksburg library, or the library in nearby Jackson. She covered her classroom windows with Sunday newspaper comic pages because the white superintendent would not purchase blinds. She protested to the federal government when the superintendent used money meant for black schools to purchase supplies and equipment for white schools, then passed the old things to the black schools. She succeeded in having the money held up in Washington.

In 1964 Shirley and her husband began the *Vicksburg Citizens' Appeal*, because white newspapers were not reporting civil rights issues. They had it printed in New Orleans, Louisiana, when they could not get it printed in Mississippi. Shirley began to attend National Association for the Advancement of Colored People (NAACP) meetings, though teachers were forbidden to do so, as it was deemed a subversive organization. She insisted on being addressed as Mrs. Aaron Shirley, because she felt it was demeaning to be addressed by her first name. And she demanded that department stores bill her, not her husband, when she shopped, a radical idea for a woman in the 1960s.

The Shirleys held civil rights meetings at home in Vicksburg, despite threats of violence. If her husband had to make medical calls at night, they would go with their children in the car and take along a gun for protection. Shirley participated in voter registration drives in Vicksburg in the early

1960s, and organized a march protesting Governor John Bell Williams's veto of a Head Start grant in 1968. The family traveled to Atlantic City in 1964 for the historic Mississippi Freedom Democratic Party challenge to the all-white Mississippi delegation to the Democratic Convention.

In 1969 Shirley was one of the first three to integrate Mississippi College, and earned a master's degree in guidance and counseling. In 1978 she received her Ed.S. at Jackson State University, and in 1988, completed a Ph.D. in education from the University of Mississippi. Her dissertation was entitled "The impact of Multicultural Education on the Self-Concept, Racial Attitude, and Student Achievement of Black and White Fifth and Sixth Graders."

Shirley brought the Children's Television Workshop (producer of *Sesame Street*) to Mississippi, and worked with The Links, a national leadership organization of black women. She also chaired the Education Office of the Mississippi NAACP. Shirley was president of the Board of Directors at the First American Bank, the only minority owned bank in Mississippi in 1994.

In 2010 Dr. Shirley was appointed to the Civil Rights Education Commission for the state of Mississippi to design a K-12 teaching curriculum on civil rights, and was director of the New Focus Program in Jackson, a public school dropout prevention program. She was coordinator of the Quantum Opportunities Program, an afterschool educational program for high school students, and cofounded Visions 2000 Plus, which offers students help with test preparation.

Shirley was always a spirited fighter for her individual rights, as well as the rights of her community. In the first decade of the twenty-first century, she continued to work on state and local education projects to keep children in school, and to keep the legacy of the civil rights movement alive.

FURTHER READING

Dr. Shirley was interviewed in 1999 for the Civil Rights Documentation Project of the University of Southern Mississippi, L. Zenobia Coleman Library, Tougaloo College, Tougaloo, M.S. (http://www.usm.edu/crdp/html/transcripts/manuscript-shirley_ollye-brown.shtml); by Bonnie Lefkowitz for *Community Health Centers: A Movement and the People Who Made It Happen* (2007), and by Human Rights Watch in 2007 about corporal punishment in United States public schools.

Thompson, John E. *The Black Press in Mississippi, 1865–1985* (1993).

JANE BRODSKY FITZPATRICK

Shockley, Ann Allen (21 June 1927–), journalist, librarian, bibliographer, and fiction writer, was born in Louisville, Kentucky, to Henry Allen and Bessie Lucas Allen, social workers. Her mother, in fact, was the first African American social worker in Louisville. Shockley's aspirations to be a writer began at Madison Junior High School when a teacher encouraged her in her work; she later became editor of the school newspaper.

Shockley left Louisville in 1944 for Nashville, Tennessee, to attend Fisk University, where she wrote for and served as the fiction editor for the *Fisk University Herald*. When she returned to Louisville for the summer after her freshman year, she wrote a column titled "Teen Talk" for the *Louisville Defender*. Upon graduating from Fisk in 1948, Shockley moved to Maryland, where she convinced the white editor of the *Federalsburg Times* to include a column called "Ebony Topics," in which she covered issues of interest to the black community such as the activities of the local NAACP, church matters, and Negro History Week events. Shockley's budding political activism was apparent in several of these columns as she criticized the South's attempts to resist equality in education and spoke out for the rights of women.

In 1953 Shockley married William Leslie Shockley, a schoolteacher in Seaford, Delaware. They had two children, William Leslie Jr. and Tamara Ann. The couple later divorced. She continued to pursue her career in journalism after marrying, writing another column focused on black interests in the *Bridgeville News*. The column was discontinued after three years when the editor was pressured by "local bigots" to stop her from speaking out on racial and political issues (Dandridge, 1987, xv).

Shockley completed her Master's of Library Science at Case Western University in 1959. That same year, she completed a monograph titled *A History of Public Library Services to Negroes in the South: 1900–1955*, which was the first of an impressive body of work on African American librarianship and bibliography. During the years that she worked as a librarian, cultivating the collections at Delaware State College (1959–1960) and the University of Maryland, Eastern Shore Branch (1960–1969), Shockley continued to write. Her articles explored the history of black librarians and the need for more of them; the damaging effects of racist children's literature; and how libraries could build their collections of works by African American writers and publish them in key library journals, including *College and Research Libraries* and *College Library Notes*. In 1969 she returned to Fisk University to work in its library, becoming the associate librarian for special collections and the university archivist. She published *A Handbook for the Administration of Special Black Collections* in 1970 and co-authored *Living Black American Authors: A Biographical Directory* in 1973.

Shockley's interest in fiction had been keen since she was a child, and she had short stories published as early as 1945 in the *Louisville Defender* and in the *Afro-American, Pittsburgh Courier, Fisk University Herald*, and numerous other newspapers and periodicals from the 1940s through the 1960s. The subjects of these early stories ranged from a preacher who used deception to gain his meals (which gently indicated what would later become a much more pointed criticism of the church in her writings) to send-ups of academic life, issues of masculinity and sexism in the black community, and the stinging racism faced by African Americans at the time.

The publication of the novel *Loving Her* in 1974, however, marked the first of the works for which Shockley became most well known, exploring a formerly taboo subject, particularly in African American literature: black lesbianism and lesbian life. While she had written two novels with a lesbian theme, one in 1950 and one in 1960, *Loving Her* was the first to find a publisher. The novel explores the experiences of an African American woman who enters into a loving, compassionate relationship with a white woman after leaving her ne'er-do-well husband. Although *Loving Her* met with many negative reviews from critics for literary weaknesses (Dandridge, 1987, 26–27), it was immensely popular at gay and lesbian bookstores around the country. The novel was followed by a short story collection, *The Black and White of It* (1980), which explored such plots as a professor-student lesbian relationship, a famous concert singer who remains closeted because of fears for her career, and the rejection an interracial lesbian couple confronts when attending the black woman's family reunion. In many of these stories Shockley accurately depicted the lives of black lesbian women attempting to survive during the pre-Stonewall era and the triple discrimination they faced as women, African Americans, and lesbians.

Shockley continued to explore black lesbian characters and culture in what became perhaps her most famous book, *Say Jesus and Come to Me* (1982), which recounted the adventures of the Reverend Myrtle Black, a charismatic preacher who seduces the women in her congregations/audiences, settling for momentary pleasures, until she meets the weary blues singer Travis Lee, who is in the midst of discovering her own sexual and spiritual identities. Their love story is set against the backdrop of Nashville, Tennessee, and the political storms brewing in the city at that time. The novel is daring in its depiction of the black church and offers a biting critique of the homophobia within it. At the same time, Shockley continues to assert the importance of the erotic and to depict black lesbian sexual identity. Like most of her fiction, the novel was criticized for stereotypical characters, occasional clumsy plotting, and sections of needless description. During this time she also published early works of black lesbian criticism, among them "The Black Lesbian in American Literature: An Overview" (1979) and "Black Lesbian Biography: Lifting the Veil" (1982).

In 1988 Shockley returned to bibliographic work with the publication the seminal anthology *Afro-American Women Writers 1746–1933: An Anthology and Critical Guide*. This book in many ways was the culmination of much of the work she had been involved with over the years as a librarian and archivist. The anthology includes not only the work of well-known writers such as IDA B. WELLS BARNETT and FRANCES E. W. HARPER but also more obscure ones such as HENRIETTA CORDELIA RAY, a New England poet of the nineteenth century, and VICTORIA EARLE MATTHEWS, a prolific New York City journalist at the turn of the twentieth century.

Shockley published several short stories in the late 1980s and early 1990s, including "The World of Rosie Polk" in *Black American Literature Forum* (1987) and "Soon There Will Be None" in *African American Review* (1994). She retired from the Fisk University Library in 1998 after nearly thirty years of service. In 2005, at age eighty, she published her third novel, *Celebrating Hotchclaw*, through A&M Books, a small press founded in 1995 by Muriel Crawford and Anyda Marchant, life partners who had earlier gained recognition as the founders of the prominent lesbian publishing company Naiad Press. The novel is set on the campus of a struggling historically black college in a fictional Tennessee town; as the college celebrates its centennial, the inner workings and secrets of the college and its faculty are exposed. Shockley herself said of it: "This could well be the first novel of its kind to focus on the internal aspects of black academia and the first to address cross-dressing in black American fiction. Issues of homophobia, class and race are explored" (http://prideindex.com/ncms/content/view/34/52).

FURTHER READING

Dandridge, Rita B. *Ann Allen Shockley: An Annotated Primary and Secondary Bibliography* (1987).

Dandridge, Rita B. "Ann Allen Shockley," in *The Oxford Companion to African American Literature*, ed. William L. Andrews, Frances Smith Foster, and Trudier Harris (1997).

Davidson, Adenike Marie. "Ann Allen Shockley (1927–)," in *Contemporary African American Novelists: A Bio-Bibliographical Critical Sourcebook*, ed. Emmanuel Nelson (1999).

Houston, Helen R. "Ann Allen Shockley," in *Afro-American Fiction Writers after 1955, Dictionary of Literary Biography* 33, ed. Thadious M. Davis and Trudier Harris (1984).

CHRISTINA G. BUCHER

Shorey, William T. (1859–April 1919), whaling master, was born in Barbados, the eldest of eight children of a Scottish sugar planter named Shorey, and an African Caribbean woman, Rosa Frazier, whom the younger Shorey's biographers have invariably described as a "beautiful creole lady" (Tompkins, 75). Some biographical sources incorrectly suggest that William was born either in Provincetown, Massachusetts, or in India. Although he was born free twenty-five years after slavery was abolished in the British West Indies, Shorey's prospects as a black man in Barbados were limited. He apprenticed for a while as a plumber on the island, but sometime in the mid-1870s, when he was still a teenager, Shorey found work as a cabin boy on a ship headed to Boston, Massachusetts. The English captain of the vessel quickly took to the eager, quick-witted, and adventurous lad and began to teach him navigation.

Upon arriving in New England, Shorey determined that he would seek a life at sea, continuing his education in navigation and seamanship under Captain Whipple (or Whiffer) A. Leach of Provincetown, on Cape Cod. That Shorey chose a hazardous life aboard a whaling vessel was probably not simply a coincidence. Many other African Americans had been prominent in the whaling industry and in the ports of New Bedford and Provincetown, notably LEWIS TEMPLE, the inventor of an innovative harpoon, the Temple Iron,

in the 1840s. Although the great age of American whaling described by Herman Melville, among others, passed in the 1850s, the industry still enjoyed a reputation for meritocracy. Unlike on other vessels, an ambitious, young man, even an ambitious young man of color, could still expect to rise through the ranks on a whaler, that is, if he managed to survive the typically arduous and highly dangerous journeys into the Arctic that were made by the New England whaling fleet. Shorey very nearly did not. In 1876 he completed his maiden voyage as a "green hand" on a whaler out of Provincetown with relative ease, rising to the position of boat steerer, but on another journey shortly after, he almost died when a sperm whale he was pursuing attacked his boat. Shorey was saved when his crewmates succeeded in firing a bomb into the whale.

Shorey's rise through the ranks was impressive. By 1880, still aged only twenty-one, he was appointed as third mate on the *Emma F. Herriman*, a fairly large whaler, which set off from Boston that November and took Shorey around the globe over the next three years. The *Herriman* crossed the North and South Atlantic oceans, stopped on the west coast of Africa (where Shorey's maternal ancestors had probably been born), rounded the Cape of Good Hope in southern Africa, and sailed into the Indian Ocean. Another lengthy journey brought the vessel to Australia, where it passed through the Tasman Sea, traversed the wide southern Pacific, rounded Cape Horn, and made calls at several South American ports, including Panama, before ending at San Francisco, California, in late 1883. By the end of his voyage, Shorey had been promoted to first officer. He undoubtedly owed his rapid rise through the ranks to his skills as a whaler, though the changing demographics of the industry after the Civil War was also a factor. By that time, native-born white seamen were finding better-paying work in the rapidly industrializing North, so more than two-thirds of whaling crews were foreign-born, many of them people of color from the Caribbean, Cape Verde, and even the South Pacific. While this reflected the low pay, harsh conditions, and extreme danger of life on a whaler, it also provided opportunities for ambitious sailors such as Shorey.

The destination of San Francisco and the timing of his arrival proved fortuitous for Shorey. By then, the more temperate waters of the Pacific Northwest had replaced New England as the new center of the American whaling industry. The typical voyages of

West Coast whalers were also considerably shorter than the New England ships, usually lasting less than a year. In 1886, Shorey was promoted to full command of the *Herriman*, making him the only black captain of a whaling vessel in the Pacific fleet. The position must have been a daunting one for a man still in his mid-twenties, for as one whaling historian has noted, a whaling master had to act as "physician, surgeon, lawyer, diplomat, financial entrepreneur, taskmaster, judge, and peacemaker" in charge of a racially and ethnically diverse crew (Tompkins, 79).

Shortly before becoming master of the *Herriman*, Shorey married Julia Shelton, the daughter of a prominent San Francisco minister and one of the leading black families in California. For their honeymoon, the couple traveled to Hawaii on the *Herriman*, and Shorey also brought his daughter Victoria on several whaling trips. Several of these proved hazardous, though his family was not on board Shorey's next vessel, the *Alexander*, when it sunk in an ice pack off the Bering Sea in 1891. Captain Shorey managed to rescue all of his crew members. Shorey's skills as a captain and as a businessman soon assured him a new charge, the *Andrew Hicks*, which he commanded for eight voyages between 1892 and 1902. On a typical journey he returned from the Sea of Japan with as much as five thousand pounds of whalebone and nearly six hundred barrels of whale and sperm oil. During the mid-1890s Shorey also sailed on the *Gay Head*, a famous San Francisco whaler, to Hawaii, taking his wife and daughter Zenobia with him. On this voyage, however, Zenobia fell ill and died shortly after returning to San Francisco.

Shorey's final voyages were aboard a Maine-built whaler, the *John and Winthrop*, which he commanded between 1903 and 1908. In one of his final tours to the Okhotsk Sea between Siberia and Japan, he successfully and safely steered his vessel through two major typhoons that lasted several days. The crewmen of the *John and Winthrop* later credited the "coolness and clever seamanship" of their commander for preventing a near-certain shipwreck. Although he retired from whaling in 1908, Shorey continued to work as a police officer for the Pacific Coast Steamship Company. He also remained active in fraternal affairs in Oakland, California, and served on the board of a home for the aged in the same city. Revered in the California press as the "Black Ahab," after the captain of the whaler in *Moby Dick*, Shorey enjoyed a life that was as dramatic as the main protagonist in Melville's novel, and was, in fact, a much more successful whaler than the tormented, fictional Captain Ahab, who died aboard his vessel. Shorey died peacefully at his home in Oakland in 1919.

FURTHER READING

Beasley, Delilah L. *The Negro Trail Blazers of California* (1919).

Tompkins, E. Berkeley. "Black Ahab: William T. Shorey, Whaling Master," *California Historical Quarterly*, LI (Spring 1972).

Obituary: *San Francisco Newspaper Union*, April 1919.

STEVEN J. NIVEN

Short, Bobby (15 Sept. 1924–21 Mar. 2005), cabaret singer and pianist, was born Robert Waltrip Short in Danville, Illinois, the ninth of ten children of Rodman Jacob Short, a civil servant, and Myrtle Render. Although he was born into poverty, four-year-old Bobby had a few piano lessons, but he essentially taught himself on the household instrument. Before age ten, Short was playing the piano for money in nearby roadhouses. Soon afterward he began to perform sophisticated ballads at private parties while wearing white tails in the manner of CAB CALLOWAY. During the Depression, Short's father, who had become a coal miner out of necessity, died in an accident. In 1936 eleven-year-old Bobby was spotted by booking agents, who offered him ice cream and candy to go on the road. With his mother's blessing, he traveled to Chicago. Marketed as "the Miniature King of Swing," he sang and played the piano in vaudeville theaters, cocktail lounges, and bars. After finishing grade school in Danville, Short played shows in Cleveland and Toledo and went to New York City at age thirteen to star in nightclubs and at the Apollo Theater.

Short returned to Danville in 1938 to attend high school, limiting himself to performing locally. After his graduation in 1942, he opened at the Capitol Lounge in Chicago and played Midwest venues. He moved to Los Angeles in 1943 for a three-year engagement at the Café Gala on the Sunset Strip. In the mid-1940s he played shows in Milwaukee and St. Louis and was an opening act at the Blue Angel in New York. Next he went to Phoenix, Arizona, where he played at two venues and cut his first (private issue) record. In 1951 Short made his screen singing debut in the musical *Call Me Mister* and played the piano in an episode of *I Love Lucy*. Short now traveled widely and honed a large catalog of songs by George

Gershwin, Duke Ellington, Noël Coward, Cole Porter, and Richard Rodgers and Lorenz Hart as well as underrated black composers such as Eubie Blake. Short's elegant baritone voice was heard in clubs in Paris and London, at the Black Orchid in Chicago and the Café Gala in Los Angeles, and on his ten-inch debut record for Atlantic Records *Bobby Short Loves Cole Porter*. From 1956, when Short began an extended engagement at the Beverly Club, New York City was his home and center of activity. More Atlantic recordings and engagements at the New York venues the Red Carpet and Le Cupidon followed.

In 1957 Short signed with the Blue Angel as the top act with a weekly salary of $1,000. During his five-year stay there he took summer engagements in other cities and recorded several more albums. Short's future seemed assured, but a poor business decision nearly ruined him. A French restaurant he had bought with a partner closed after fifteen months, costing him all of his savings. Another cause for concern, however, was musical.

Times were changing in American popular music. The arrival of the Beatles, the growth of television, and the widening of the "generation gap" in America were followed by a sudden decline in popularity for Short's style of music. Out of necessity he performed in Chicago, Boston, and London, appeared in an off-Broadway revue, and made more modest recordings. But if this represented a "dry spell" for Short, things were soon to change for the better.

George Feyer had been the pianist at New York's Carlyle Hotel for many years. In the spring of 1968 the hotel was looking for a replacement to cover Feyer's vacation. Atlantic Records president Ahmet Ertegun recommended Short and, in the process, helped create a New York institution. Short proved so popular with the patrons of the 120-seat Café Carlyle that the hotel installed him as the headliner. The Carlyle, at which Short held court for the next thirty-six years with the rich and the famous, is regarded as his signature engagement.

The workload was heavy, three shows, six nights per week, for eight months of the year (later contracts reduced it to two nightly shows for six months). Atlantic celebrated Short's new fame with a double album, *Mabel Mercer and Bobby Short at Town Hall*. In 1971 Short remade his youthful *Bobby Short Loves Cole Porter* disk as a double album and performed its songs live for a large audience at Avery Fisher Hall. He wrote a memoir of his youth,

Black and White Baby (1971), and now an icon of New York high society, he was featured in magazine and television ads. Television also beckoned. In 1979 Short appeared in the ABC miniseries *Roots: The Next Generations*, and he later guest starred on *The Love Boat*, *In the Heat of the Night*, *Central Park West*, *Frasier*, and *7th Heaven*. In 1986 Short immortalized his Café Carlyle act on film in Woody Allen's *Hannah and Her Sisters*. He also performed at the White House for Presidents Richard Nixon, Jimmy Carter, Ronald Reagan, and Bill Clinton.

An avid classical music fan, he annually attended the Salzburg Festival. Although he regularly vacationed in the south of France, Short never forgot his hometown. He performed in Danville several times for charity, returning again on 2 March 2001 for Bobby Short Day. When accused by black activists of pandering to upscale white tastes, Short countered that he had lived his life in rejection of racism. He led a drive to build a Duke Ellington Memorial at 110th Street and Fifth Avenue in Harlem. He never married but adopted a nephew, Ronald Bell.

Through the 1990s Short continued to perform and record prodigiously. Short also received three Grammy nominations. In 2000 the New York Landmarks Conservancy designated him a "Living Legend." But his long career was winding down, and he announced that he would retire from the Café Carlyle with a farewell performance on New Year's Eve 2004. He agreed to return to celebrate the Café's fiftieth anniversary the following May, but in March he passed away from leukemia. He was buried beside his parents at Atherton Cemetery in Danville and remembered as the best cabaret singer of his generation.

FURTHER READING
Short, Bobby, with Robert Mackintosh. *Bobby Short: The Life and Times of a Saloon Singer* (1995).
Obituary: *New York Times*, 22 March 2005.

DAVID BORSVOLD

Shorter, Susie Isabel Lankford (4 Jan. 1859–27 Feb. 1912), educator, writer, clubwoman, and religious worker, was born in Terre Haute, Indiana, to the Reverend Whitten Strange Lankford, pastor of the Allen Chapel African Methodist Episcopal (AME) Church, and Clarrisa Carter Lankford. The eldest of five children, Susie Isabel learned the precepts of Christianity and the beliefs of the AME as she listened to her father's sermons. The Reverend Lankford had high expectations for Susie Isabel.

He took her to Wilberforce University in Ohio, where she was taught by the talented instructors that America's first black college president, Bishop Daniel A. Payne of the AME, had assembled. In 1873, at age fourteen, she left Ohio when her mother died, and she assumed responsibility for overseeing her four younger siblings and the household.

The family moved to Baltimore when Rev. Lankford was appointed to the Bethel AME Church. Susie prepared meals and welcomed traveling clergy until her father remarried and his new wife assumed responsibility for hospitality at the parsonage. Shortly thereafter, Susie Lankford returned to Wilberforce, where she completed classes in botany, rhetoric, French, music, algebra, and arithmetic during the next two years. After completing the requirements in 1875 at Wilberforce, Lankford accepted a teaching position in Rockville, Indiana. She remained there for two years and then in 1877 relocated to teach in Richmond, Indiana.

The Reverend T. H. Jackson, a theology professor at Wilberforce who had dined with the Lankford family while Susie was in Baltimore, encouraged his Ohio colleague, Joseph Proctor Shorter, to propose to Lankford. Even though Joseph Shorter was fourteen years older than Lankford and had been her mathematics instructor during her years at Wilberforce, they were married during the Christmas holidays in 1878. Rev. Jackson performed the ceremony for his friend. Over the years, eight children were born, but only three—Lee Jackson Shorter, Joseph Prattis Shorter, and Susie Pearl Shorter Smith—outlived their parents. The couple proved compatible, sharing a common faith and background and having mutual respect for each other's gifts and graces. Joseph Shorter's father, the Reverend James L. Shorter, had helped Bishop Daniel Payne develop Wilberforce before becoming the ninth bishop of the AME Church. Shorter viewed teaching as his calling, but he was also an adept administrator and an active layperson in both the local church and on the financial board of the AME General Conference.

Susie Shorter managed her household and proved a loving mother of eight, as well as an exemplary faculty wife who extended hospitality to visiting dignitaries and sick or struggling college students. A businesswoman who ran a shop called the College Inn, she also became a caring teacher who provided free kindergarten classes in her home for neighborhood children and became an energetic clubwoman and church volunteer. As president of the Ladies' College Aid Society of Wilberforce University she helped many students stay in school and complete their studies.

During her married life Shorter also carved out time for writing and gained visibility as a journalist. The *Christian Recorder* published several of her occasional papers and news briefs, and she published a booklet entitled *Heroines of African Methodism* that she prepared for the observance of Bishop Daniel Payne's eightieth birthday on 24 February 1891. *Heroines*, in addition to providing a general overview of black women in America and a summary of specific women in the AME Church, was a manifesto of Christian womanhood. At first glance her words suggest a traditional role in which wives are subordinate to husbands; however, on a closer reading her views sustain a vision of limitless potential for women. In Shorter's thinking, women transformed by God were servant-leaders and agents of change who achieved their goals through merciful service, optimistic attitude, and impeccable character.

Shorter's book related the story of the first black person that John Wesley baptized in England in 1759, a woman who became the first black class leader in West India Isle. Shorter proudly cited the accomplishments of female composers, musicians, poets, sculptors, artists, elocutionists, store managers, teachers, lawyers, physicians, and surgeons who used their skills and talents to improve society. She highlighted the unsung wives of ministers and reminded male pastors of their responsibility to attend to their own families and the children while they sought salvation for their parishioners. Shorter encouraged young women to prepare themselves to be self-supporting economically as well as to become "queen of a household." It is probable that the *Heroines of African Methodism* also influenced the AME Conference to ordain female pastors and elect a female bishop. Shorter's book asserted the need for women to be preachers as well as teachers and warned that the church could languish and die if it failed to receive the gifts that women preachers represented.

In 1892 JULIA RINGWOOD COSTON, a journalist who edited and published the world's first fashion magazine for black women, convinced Shorter to write a column in *Ringwood's Afro-American Journal of Fashion* called "Plain Talk to Our Girls." Shorter also penned the words for the theme song of the Ohio Federation of Colored Women's Clubs, entitled "Federation Song" and sung to the tune of "Glory, Glory, Hallelujah." A version of the song has been sung by other state federations and at the National Annual Meetings of the National Association of Colored Women's Clubs since the late 1890s. Shorter died in Wilberforce, Ohio, two years after her husband's death.

FURTHER READING

Brown, Hallie Q., ed. *Homespun Heroines and Other Women of Distinction* (1926).

Majors, Monroe A. *Noted Negro Women: Their Triumphs and Activities* (1893).

Scruggs, Lawson A. *Women of Distinction: Remarkable in Works and Invincible in Character* (1893).

Wesley, Charles Harris. *The History of the National Association of Colored Women's Clubs: A Legacy of Service* (1984).

ARTHUREE MCLAUGHLIN WRIGHT

Wayne Shorter at his home studio in Los Angeles, Ca., on 9 May 1996. (AP Images.)

Shorter, Wayne (25 Aug. 1933–), saxophonist and composer, was born in Newark, New Jersey, the son of Joseph Shorter, a welder, and Louise Paige, who worked for a furrier. Wayne grew up in a middle-class black community. He showed an original, creative bent even as a youngster; he read science fiction and was nicknamed "Mr. Weird" by his friends. His interest in jazz developed when he heard THELONIOUS MONK on the radio and grew when his father urged him to play the clarinet when he was sixteen; he switched to the tenor saxophone the following year and played at area high school dances. He graduated from the Newark High School of Music and Art in 1952 and enrolled as a clarinet major at New York University, where he received a B.S. in music education in 1956.

Shorter participated in jam sessions while in college and played briefly with HORACE SILVER before being drafted. Stationed at Fort Dix, New Jersey, he played in army bands and frequented clubs in New York City, where he heard JOHN COLTRANE several times. After his discharge in October 1958, he spent much time with Coltrane at Coltrane's New York City apartment, playing and talking about music. Shorter joined Maynard Ferguson's band for a short while, but he came of age when he was a member of ART BLAKEY's Jazz Messengers from 1958 to 1963. There he made his initial mark as a soloist and composer and served as the group's music director from 1961 to 1963. While playing with Blakey, Shorter also recorded three albums for Vee-Jay records. During these years he produced a completely original synthesis of his two main influences: SONNY ROLLINS

and Coltrane. Though his general style remained within the parameters of hard bop, he played with uneven, unusual phrasing and with far greater harmonic and rhythmic freedom. In 1961 Shorter married Irene Nakagami; they had a daughter, Miyako, before they divorced in 1969. In September 1964 Shorter joined the MILES DAVIS Quintet with TONY WILLIAMS on drums, HERBIE HANCOCK on piano, and Ron Carter on bass; this group was the longest lived and perhaps the most creative of Davis's career. Shorter excelled as a soloist on the group's albums and in their numerous concert appearances from 1964 to 1969, and he also blossomed into one of the most original, influential composers of his generation. Tunes like "E.S.P.," "Nefertiti," and "Sanctuary" became staples of Davis performances and jazz standards. But it was on the several albums that Shorter recorded as a leader for Blue Note during these years that his writing skills were most visible and where he perfected his use of extended tonality and asymmetrical phrasing. Albums like *Speak No Evil* (1964) were meant to evoke visions of folkloric landscapes and were filled with "tonality-disturbing ambiguities, about to move in one direction but sometimes stopping to float like the elements in … 'misty landscapes'" (Don Heckman, liner notes to *Speak No Evil*). Such philosophical reflections were also typical of Shorter's writing and remained so throughout his career; he wrote *The All-Seeing Eye* (1965), for instance, as a depiction of God's act of creation.

Other Blue Note albums from this period include *JuJu* (1964), *Night Dreamer* (1964), *Soothsayer* (1965, released 1978), *Etcetera* (1965, released 1980),

Adam's Apple (1966), and *Schizophrenia* (1967). This was Shorter at his peak. With Carter on bass, Hancock on piano, Curtis Fuller on trombone, James Spaulding on alto sax, and Joe Chambers on drums, Shorter constantly challenged listeners, pushing the borders between post-bop and free jazz. He never again moved so far in this direction. *Super Nova* (1969) featured John McLaughlin and Sonny Sharrock on electric guitars, Miroslav Vitous on bass, Chick Corea on piano and keyboards, Jack DeJohnette on drums, and Moreira Airto on percussion, with Shorter himself doubling on soprano sax. The album was a mix of fusion and Latin jazz that was unlike anything else being played at the time, with Shorter's soaring soprano and McLaughlin's and Sharrock's dissonant, stabbing guitars over a roiling percussive base. *Odyssey of Iska* (1970) and *Motto Groso Feio* continued in the same vein, and 1974's *Native Dancer* featuring vocalist Milton Nascimento was a joyous celebration of Brazilian jazz fusion.

At the same time Shorter was taking the electronic instruments and rock rhythms of Davis's "Bitches Brew" music along a more psychedelic path in cofounding with former Davis keyboard player Joe Zawinul the group Weather Report in late 1970. Weather Report was the best-known and most aesthetically successful jazz fusion group of the decade. In a series of hugely popular albums from 1971 to 1986, most notably *I Sing the Body Electric* (1972), *Mysterious Traveler* (1974), and *Black Market* (1976), the group created atmospheric, sensuous, and rhythmically powerful music that increasingly incorporated earthy, funky dance rhythms. Particularly on the earlier albums, Shorter's melodic soprano soared above the rhythmic foundation to create a joyous lyricism that held enormous appeal for rock audiences seeking more adventurous listening experiences.

Shorter also toured and recorded in the late 1970s with VSOP, essentially a revival of the 1960s Davis group with Freddie Hubbard replacing Davis on trumpet. After leaving Weather Report in 1985, Shorter made a series of recordings that saw him searching for new musical direction, but albums such as *Atlantis* (1985), *Phantom Navigator* (1986), and *Joy Ryder* (1988) lacked the creative excitement of his earlier efforts. He appeared as a sideman on recordings by Joni Mitchell, Carlos Santana, and Steely Dan, and he played with classical clarinetist Richard Stolzman and the New Japan Orchestra. Shorter formed new groups in 1990 and again in the mid-1990s and often played in reunion bands with Hancock; the pair toured as a duo in 1997.

Though his playing and composing seemed to get stronger as the 1990s progressed, it was really with the formation of a new quartet, Footprints, that Shorter rediscovered his creative muse. The album *Footprints Live* (2001) was accorded universal critical acclaim. The pianist Danilo Perez, the bassist John Patitucci, and the drummer Brian Blade were Shorter's tightest, most communicative mainstream group since the late 1960s, and they responded brilliantly to his unusual demands. Much of what the group played was composed, but Shorter expected them to deconstruct and reassemble the tunes on the spot—creating a tension and an electric excitement that few jazz ensembles could match. And Shorter's own playing, moreover, was as strong as ever. The 2002 recording "Alegria" has an impressive compositional breadth, embracing folk song, arrangements of classical pieces by Hector Villa-Lobos, and reinterpretations of Shorter's own earlier compositions.

Shorter also began to focus increasingly on compositions for larger ensembles. He returned to an opera that he had begun in the 1950s, "Sacajawea," wrote music for the classical vocalist Renee Fleming, and made plans for collaborations with various European orchestras. In fall 2000 he performed a commissioned work at the Montreux Jazz Festival for a thirty-piece woodwind group, a brass ensemble, and his own quartet with the percussionist Alex Acuna. In June 2003 he appeared at Carnegie Hall with his quartet, a tap dancer, and a chamber orchestra. In his seventies, Shorter appeared ready to embark on an entirely new phase of his career.

Along with Sonny Rollins, Shorter is the most significant tenor saxophonist of the last forty years and is one of the most respected jazz composers of the past half century. His bluesy, syncopated tenor playing contrasts with the beautiful, singing tone of his soprano saxophone. His compositions have been described as "complex, long-winded, endlessly winding," words that accurately suggest the meditative, sinuous quality of so much of his work (Yanow, *The All Music Guide to Jazz*, 1151).

Shorter suffered through unspeakable tragedy. His father was killed in a car accident returning from watching him perform in Philadelphia in the 1960s. He had married Ana Maria Patricio in 1969, and the couple's daughter Iska, born in that year, suffered serious brain damage from a childhood vaccination and died of a grand mal seizure in 1983.

Ana Maria herself, on her way to join Wayne on tour in Italy, died with a niece on Pan Am flight 800 when it exploded off the New York coast in 1996. But aided by his strong Buddhist faith, Shorter always maintained a sense of optimism and pride in his life and in his playing and writing. He remarried in 1999, to the Brazilian dancer and actress Carolina dos Santos, and he spoke eloquently of the role of music in his own life: "When an artist creates he can feed the soul, heal the soul, make the soul well" (*Down Beat*, December 1968). Like Rollins, Coltrane, and many others in the history of jazz, Shorter always understood the larger purpose of the music: "Let us speak of music … a necessary indulgence—to give good and sustenance to the travelers as they move on through all their odysseys" (Liner notes to *Odyssey of Iska*, Blue Note, 1970).

FURTHER READING

Heckman, Don. "Wayne Shorter and Herbie Hancock," *Down Beat* 64 (Dec. 1997).

Koransky, Jason. "Lighting the Future," *Down Beat* 70 (Aug. 2003).

Martin, Mel. "Wayne Shorter," *Saxophone Journal* 16 (Apr. 1992).

Mercer, Michelle. *Footprints: The Life and Work of Wayne Shorter* (2004).

Szwed, John. *So What: The Life of Miles Davis* (2002).

Tingen, Paul. *Miles Beyond: The Electric Explorations of Miles Davis, 1967–1991* (2001).

Woodard, Josef. "Hancock and Shorter," *Jazz Times* 27 (Sept. 1997).

Woodard, Josef. "The Artful Dodger's Return," *Jazz Times* 25 (Nov. 1995).

Yanow, Scott. "The Wayne Shorter Interview," *Down Beat* 53 (Apr. 1986).

RONALD P. DUFOUR

Shultz, Arnold (Feb. 1886–14 Apr. 1931), guitarist and fiddler, was born in a mining camp near Cromwell, in Ohio County, Kentucky. He was the firstborn son of David, who was born into slavery in 1844, and Elizabeth, a freeborn sixteen-year-old.

In 1900 when Shultz was fourteen, his half brother Ed, who worked on one of the many riverboats that cruised the Green River, gave him a guitar and a few lessons. Shultz honed his skills by becoming a member of the Shultz family band, playing guitar and fiddle in old-time British dance tunes. The region was quite rich musically, and one imagines that he also learned from such other notable black musicians in the area as Jim Mason, Amos Johnson, and Walter Taylor—as well as from traveling tent, medicine, and minstrel shows, and the wide variety of music performed on the showboats that docked at cities along the Green. Shultz himself, in fact, is remembered to have worked as a musician on these boats.

Shultz became a restless, itinerant wanderer who was away from the region for months at a time. It is highly likely that he traveled extensively during his years of maturation, enjoying, and perhaps performing with, the different kinds of musicians that worked on the many steamboat lines that cruised the Mississippi from Saint Paul to New Orleans and, especially, the Ohio from Cairo to Pittsburgh, docking at such cities as Evansville, Louisville, Cincinnati, and Owensboro, which was only a few miles from Cromwell.

Indeed, from 1919 to 1922 Shultz could have heard such remarkable musicians as LOUIS ARMSTRONG, BABY DODDS, and JOHNNY ST. CYR, all of whom played in FATE MARABLE's band that worked on the Streckfus excursion line out of Saint Louis. Moreover, one supposes that Shultz heard the outstanding Louisville jug bands—Clifford Hayes's fiddling and Cal Smith's guitar from the Dixieland Jug Blowers and Phil Phillips's guitar work with Phillips's Louisville Jug Band—as well as Bob Coleman's Cincinnati Jug Band. Whatever his sources, Shultz assimilated the music of the 1920s—popular (both old standards and contemporary), blues, rags, religious music, old-time fiddle tunes and breakdowns, and jazz—as well as several instrumental techniques: flat-picking, finger style, and the open-tuned slide method on the guitar and both long-bow and short-bow fiddling styles. He became, in other words, a textbook example of a "musicianer," one who specializes in a wide variety of instrumental styles.

As he got older Shultz began to spend more time in the region, wandering around like a minstrel with his huge guitar attached to his shoulders with a rope. He played at street corners, railroad crossings, company stores, family gatherings, taverns and roadhouses, house parties, square dances (both black and white), and churches. Tex Atchison, who later became the fiddler for the Western swing band the Prairie Ramblers, has said that when he was a young boy his mother would give him a dime for the movies, which he would in turn give to Shultz to play him a tune. Shultz, who carried his guitar on his back, would execute a kind of twisting motion with his hips that brought the guitar around into playing position in one fluid move. Shultz's fiddling also impressed Atchison: "It had a *lot* of influence on me. ... I picked up that [swing] stuff from Arnold Shultz, hearing him play that stuff. When I got to playing [with the Prairie Ramblers] that would come back to me. ... Arnold Shultz was fifty years ahead of his time" (author's interview with Atchison, 9 Aug. 1979). Atchison's bluesy fiddling became a strong component of the Ramblers' jazzy Western swing style that made the group a favorite on both records and coast-to-coast broadcasts of the National Barn Dance on Chicago's powerful radio station WLS during the 1930s.

Tex Atchison was also struck by Shultz's ability to play the guitar in such a way that four major elements of music—rhythm, melody, bass, and harmony—were produced simultaneously by only his thumb and forefinger, a style surely derived from ragtime piano playing: "I watched him play quite a bit. I was very interested in Arnold's pickin' because it was something I had never heard. ... He played his own rhythm. He was the first that had ever done that, to play the lead and his own rhythm at the same time" (author's interview with Atchison). Atchison later replaced Shultz in a local dance band fronted by Forrest ("Boots") Faught, who confirmed Atchison's assessment: "[Shultz] absolutely played the first lead guitar that I had ever heard played. ... And people were amazed: 'Lookey there—that man's leading that music on that guitar and playin' his own accompaniment!'" (author's interview with Faught, 22 June 1978). In order to keep a raglike bass line operative continuously, Shultz was required to play chords out of first position, which led to a rich and complicated harmonic texture based on substitutions, inversions, and accidental chords. Shultz was of course not the first musician to play ragtime on a guitar, but it was essentially his approach that passed to such local players as Kennedy Jones, Ike Everly, Mose Rager, and the world-famous Merle Travis and Chet Atkins.

Remarkably Shultz also informed a third substyle of country music, bluegrass. Bill Monroe, whose particular form of old-time string-band music was to become known as bluegrass (named for his band the Blue Grass Boys but also suggesting his emphasis on African American blues), was also from Ohio County. As a young man Monroe, too, came under the influence of Shultz's superb musicianship: "There's things in my music, you know, that come from Arnold Shultz—runs that I use in a lot of my music [on the mandolin]. ... In following a fiddle piece or a breakdown, he used a [straight] pick and he could just run from one chord to another the prettiest you've ever heard. ...

Then he could play blues and I wanted some blues in my music too, you see" (Rooney, 23–24). Monroe even played with Shultz, accompanying his fiddling with a guitar.

Arnold Shultz was indeed a cultural hero, a bringer of culture, who brought back to his region a variety of music and instrumental techniques that enriched not only the lives of his fellow western Kentuckians but also those of the national community.

In the spring of 1931 Shultz fell ill while working in Evansville, Indiana. He returned to his home at the time in Morgantown, Kentucky, where he died on 14 April, having just turned forty-five. The cause of death was heart disease, according to official records. Many of Shultz's family and friends believe, however, that his whiskey was poisoned by fellow musicians jealous of all the attention given Shultz. He was buried in an unidentified grave in the all-black Bell Street Cemetery in Morgantown. In 1994 a monument to Shultz was erected at the entrance to the cemetery; above and below an image of a guitar are the lines, "He was famous for his guitar picking" and "Dedicated to thumb picking and finger cording."

In 1998 Shultz was inducted into the National Thumb Pickers Hall of Fame in Drakesboro, Kentucky, for his contributions to the famous Travis guitar style, but he equally belongs in the bluegrass and Western swing halls of fame. He was an extraordinarily talented walking musician who contributed substantially to the development of three distinct substyles of American country and western music.

FURTHER READING

Chevan, David. "Riverboat Music from St. Louis and the Streckfus Steamboat Line," *Black Music Research Journal* 9 (1989).

Lawrence, Keith. "The Greatest (?) Guitar Picker's Life Ended before Promise Realized," *John Edwards Memorial Foundation Quarterly* 17 (1981).

Lawrence, Keith. "A Regional Musical Style: The Legacy of Arnold Shultz," in *Sense of Place: American Regional Cultures*, eds. Barbara Allen and Thomas J. Schlereth (1990).

Rooney, James. *Bossmen: Bill Monroe and Muddy Waters* (1971).

WILLIAM E. LIGHTFOOT

Shuttlesworth, Fred Lee (18 Mar. 1922–5 Oct. 2011), civil rights activist and minister, was born Freddie Lee Robinson in Mt. Meigs, Montgomery

County, Alabama, the eldest of Alberta Robinson and Vetter Green's two children. In January 1927 Alberta Robinson married William Nathan Shuttlesworth, a onetime miner, small farmer, and small-time bootlegger, and her children took their stepfather's last name.

Shuttlesworth attended Rosedale High School, and starting in the early 1940s studied theology at Cedar Grove Academy Bible College and Selma University, and pursued a teaching certificate at Alabama State College. In 1941 he married Birmingham native Ruby Lanette Keeler, a nursing student, whom he had met when both worked as orderlies at Birmingham's Southern Club. In 1950 he became pastor of the First (African) Baptist Church in Selma, a position he left in 1952 after disputes with church lay leaders. In 1953 he took the pastorate at Birmingham's Bethel Baptist Church. From the Bethel pastorate Shuttlesworth would become one of the most significant if oftentimes overlooked leaders of the civil rights movement.

Shuttlesworth's significant first foray into civil rights issues, and his first of dozens of confrontations with the white authorities in Birmingham, came in July 1955 when he petitioned the Birmingham City Council for black police officers. He organized more than two dozen local ministers to support his call, but the city officials did not relent, finally rejecting his requests in September. Later that year Shuttlesworth attended meetings of the Montgomery Improvement Association, which organized that city's historic bus boycott, in order to show support for its campaign.

In February 1956 Shuttlesworth accompanied Foster Autherine Lucy during her effort to become the first black student at the University of Alabama in Tuscaloosa, leading to riots at the state's most prestigious university. In June he founded the Alabama Christian Movement for Human Rights (ACMHR), the organization with which he would be most closely associated during the civil rights era. The ACMHR became necessary because on 1 June 1956 Alabama circuit judge Walter B. Jones issued an injunction against the National Association for the Advancement of Colored People (NAACP), an organization which Shuttlesworth served as the state's membership secretary, on the grounds that the organization had failed to register as a "foreign corporation," effectively banning that organization in the state. Within a week Shuttlesworth established the ACMHR, which would become something of a proxy organization taking the place and fulfilling the responsibilities of the NAACP

in Alabama. From that point on Shuttlesworth expanded his civil rights activities, including pressing for the desegregation of city buses, encouraging qualified black candidates to try to take civil service exams, pursuing litigation when local authorities denied those applications, and challenging segregation laws in the city.

As a result of his heightened visibility and his steadfast pursuit of civil rights, Shuttlesworth's home was bombed on Christmas Day 1956. Although the house suffered significant damage, Shuttlesworth escaped without harm, and the next day he led a group of African Americans who challenged Jim Crow laws on city buses, leading to the arrests of twenty-one men. In response to the bombing, Shuttlesworth's congregation showed their support for him by building him a new parsonage and posting guards outside the house to dissuade other attacks. Birmingham's white supremacists were growing increasingly furious with Shuttlesworth and other leaders, and their increasing use of violence would earn the city the nickname "Bombingham."

In 1957 Shuttlesworth accelerated his activism. In January he attended the founding meeting of the Southern Leadership Conference on Transportation and Nonviolent Integration at Ebenezer Baptist Church in Atlanta. Within a few weeks the organization would change its name to the Southern Christian Leadership Conference (SCLC) with MARTIN LUTHER KING JR. at its helm. Shuttlesworth would soon become the organization's secretary.

Shuttlesworth continued to agitate for change in local bus seating laws, spoke at a major civil rights prayer pilgrimage in Washington, D.C., and challenged the city's segregated school system more than three years after the Supreme Court's decision in *Brown v. Board of Education* putatively struck down school segregation. When Shuttlesworth attempted to enroll his two daughters, Pat and Ricky, at all-white Phillips High School on 9 September 1957 a white mob set upon Shuttlesworth and his family. His wife and daughter Ricky sustained minor injuries. Shuttlesworth suffered a mild concussion. All of these activities would earn Shuttlesworth the dubious honor of being named 1957's "newsmaker of the year" by the *Birmingham World*. The designation would only garner Shuttlesworth greater harassment and more serious threats. The next two years saw Shuttlesworth engage in an increasingly tendentious war of words against Birmingham's ironically titled Commissioner of Public Safety,

Theophilus Eugene "Bull" Connor, an ardent segregationist with ties to Birmingham's active and prominent Ku Klux Klan chapters. Shuttlesworth's leadership of boycotts of Birmingham's city buses in October 1959 gave Connor the pretext to arrest his nemesis, who turned himself in voluntarily and would serve five days in jail. This would be the first of many arrests for Shuttlesworth.

Shuttlesworth was tremendously impressed with the student sit-in movement that began in Greensboro, North Carolina, on 1 February 1960 and spread quickly throughout the South. Shuttlesworth encouraged civil rights leaders to embrace and support the new student-centered phase of the movement and often found that he was disappointed by the tepid responses he received from some of the most prominent leaders of the era. Shuttlesworth encouraged Birmingham's black college students to initiate their own sit-in movement, and when they followed his lead at five Birmingham businesses at the end of March, Connor had Shuttlesworth arrested again.

A few weeks later Shuttlesworth was one of the defendants named in *Sullivan v. New York Times*, a libel case brought by segregationist leaders in order to drain the resources of the movement and to make coverage of it prohibitively difficult. In November, Shuttlesworth and his codefendants, Reverend RALPH DAVID ABERNATHY, Reverend Solomon Seay, and Reverend JOSEPH LOWERY were found responsible for libel with damages assessed at half a million dollars. (The Supreme Court would eventually overturn the decision in March 1964.)

In May 1961 when the Freedom Riders passed through Alabama and the violent intransigence of some of the state's whites became clear for the world to see, Shuttlesworth played a vital role. In planning the Freedom Rides JAMES FARMER and other leaders of the Congress of Racial Equality made sure to develop close contacts on the ground to provide housing and to address crises as they emerged. Shuttlesworth proved to be perhaps the most able of all of these contacts, and on several occasions he served as a protector and guardian angel of the Freedom Riders. He arranged to have them shuttled out of harm's way in Anniston, similarly rescued battered riders in Birmingham, lodged and nursed the wounded with the help of Ruby and the rest of his family, and generally stood up against the violent onslaught that the Freedom Riders evoked from Anniston to Birmingham to Montgomery over the course of just more than a week.

In 1961 Revelation Baptist Church in Cincinnati began an aggressive courtship of Shuttlesworth to take over its pulpit. Shuttlesworth was torn and refused the offer at first, but the Revelation officials appointed him anyway. In June he announced his acceptance of the post, which he would begin in August. Shuttlesworth would split his time between Birmingham and Ohio for the next few years, including 1963, the most explosive year in Birmingham's history.

On 3 April 1963 the SCLC launched Project C (for "Confrontation") with students from Miles College engaging in sit-ins at the lunch counters of five downtown department stores. Nationally, Martin Luther King Jr. would become the most public face of the Birmingham protests as he was of the movement as a whole by 1963, but Shuttlesworth proved to be the most visible local leader in the rapidly escalating campaign that increasingly drew violent reactions from Connor's police forces. The events in Birmingham in 1963 finally inspired President John Kennedy to propose a comprehensive civil rights bill, but his November assassination placed that responsibility in the hands of his successor, Lyndon Johnson, who would sign the Civil Rights Act of 1964, demanding desegregation of all public facilities, on 2 July, but not before Shuttlesworth would renew calls for challenges to the status quo in Birmingham.

By 1965 civil rights leaders had accelerated their push for voting rights, and when the nation turned its eyes to Selma, Alabama, Shuttlesworth was already there. He marched and spoke at Selma as the crisis developed, culminating in the successful Selma-to-Montgomery March and eventually Lyndon Johnson's signing of the Voting Rights Act of 1965.

The Revelation Baptist Church in Cincinnati split in 1966, largely over Shuttlesworth's leadership, and Shuttlesworth took over the dissident faction, the Greater New Light Baptist Church, which he pastored until he retired in 2006. In 1970 he and Ruby divorced (she would die less than a year later of heart failure) and in November 2006 he married Sephira Bailey. Although he never achieved the fame or status of Martin Luther King Jr., Shuttlesworth continued to crusade for justice well into the twenty-first century. In 2004 he became president of the SCLC but resigned soon after, dissatisfied with the direction that the once-vital organization had taken. His Shuttlesworth Housing Foundation, which he established in 1988, has helped hundreds of low-income families purchase their own homes.

In 1992, when the Birmingham Civil Rights Institute and Museum opened its doors across the street from the 16th Street Baptist Church, officials unveiled a statue to stand sentry in front of that testament to the bravery and struggle of those who sacrificed for the civil rights movement. That statue is of Fred Shuttlesworth. He died in Birmingham, Alabama, at the age of 89.

FURTHER READING

Shuttlesworth's papers are located at the Martin Luther King Jr. Center for Nonviolent Social Change in Atlanta.

Eskew, Glenn T. *But For Birmingham: The Local and National Movements in the Civil Rights Struggle* (1997).

Manis, Andrew M. *A Fire You Can't Put Out: The Civil Rights Life of Birmingham's Reverend Fred Shuttlesworth* (1999).

Thornton, J. Mills. *Dividing Lines: Municipal Politics and the Struggle for Civil Rights in Montgomery, Birmingham, and Selma* (2002).

White, Marjorie, and Andrew Manis, eds. *Birmingham's Revolutionary: The Reverend Fred Shuttlesworth and the Alabama Christian Movement for Civil Rights* (2000).

Obituary: *New York Times,* 5 October 2011.

DEREK CHARLES CATSAM

Sidat-Singh, Wilmeth (3 Mar. 1918–9 May 1943), athlete, was born Wilmeth Webb in Washington, D.C., the son of Elias, a pharmacist, and Pauline Miner. In 1925 Elias died of stroke, and Pauline subsequently remarried. Her new husband was Samuel Sidat-Singh, a medical doctor of West Indian descent. He adopted Wilmeth and moved the family to Harlem, New York, where Wilmeth was raised and attended school. Even as a young man, Wilmeth showed great promise as an athlete. By the time he was attending high school at New York's DeWitt Clinton, he was a basketball star. In 1934 he led his team to a New York Public High School Athletic League championship. He was offered a basketball scholarship to Syracuse University, to which he matriculated in 1935. He was also recruited by the school's football coach, and soon he was playing on the gridiron as well as the hardwood.

College sports at the time were still heavily segregated. Sidat-Singh was an African American by birth—and might have been forced to sit out games against teams that refused to play against African Americans (though not blacks from anywhere else)—but his surname led some to assume that he was a "Hindu." This odd notion was further advanced by Syracuse supporters (Sidat-Singh himself excluded; he seems never to have taken part in any ploy to pass himself off as anything but what he was) who wished to find a reason for Sidat-Singh to remain on the field. Soon, however, the ruse was exposed. Syracuse was scheduled to play a football match against the University of Maryland, which insisted on segregated play. Some time before the game, however, SAM LACY, the famed sports reported for the Baltimore *Afro-American,* revealed Sidat-Singh to be an African American, and the young star was forced to sit out the contest. The Orangemen lost.

The story got picked up in the press—the black press, especially—and Sidat-Singh became something of a cause célèbre. By the next season, when Syracuse again found Maryland on its schedule, the publicity was such that the Terrapins were forced to retract their objection. Sidat-Singh took the field, and the result was as 55–0 thumping of Maryland. Again, the black press took notice, this time in jubilation at Sidat-Singh's triumph. He appeared in his football uniform on the cover of the October 1938 *Crisis.* His fame on the rise, Sidat-Singh came to the attention of more and more sportswriters, black and white. He was allowed to take the field against Duke, which had formerly held a contract forbidding him to play. He took part in exhibition games against National Football League (NFL) teams. Still, when the time came to look forward to a professional career Sidat-Singh was cut off from the NFL and the NBA, which did not at the time draft black players. He graduated from Syracuse in 1939 with a degree in zoology and returned to his home city of Washington, DC.

Over the next several years, Sidat-Singh played for a number of barnstorming basketball teams. In 1940 he joined the Washington Renaissance then joined the roster of the Lichtman Bears when the Rens fell to financial troubles. He also played football for the U Street Lions, and even tried his hand at softball and tennis. But it was with the Bears that he had his greatest postcollegiate success, becoming one of the Negro barnstorming league's most efficient and well-known players and soon playing to packed houses wherever the team went. His scoring average was twenty points per game, an extraordinary achievement in the game as it was played at the time.

In 1942 Sidat-Singh enlisted in the Washington, D.C., police force, apparently feeling the need to take a greater part in his community following the attack on Pearl Harbor. Still, he continued playing basketball, and that same year led the Bears to a perfect season, 22–0. Following the season, he quit basketball and the police force and joined the Tuskegee Airmen. He soon found himself stationed to Selfridge Field in Harrison Township, Michigan. In 1943 he was flying a training mission over Lake Huron when the engine of his P-40 Warhawk suddenly failed. Witnesses later claimed to have seen Sidat-Singh attempting to clear the aircraft. He was reported missing, and his body was recovered nearly two months later. His parachute was snagged on part of the airplane.

Sidat-Singh was interred at Arlington Cemetery. The news of his passing attracted great attention in the African American community. Sidat-Singh's family was visited by some of the great black athletes of the time, including JOE LOUIS. It was not until 2005, however, that Syracuse retired Sidat-Singh's basketball jersey. Only four other Orangemen had been so honored.

FURTHER READING

Isaacs, Neil. *All the Moves: A History of College Basketball* (1975).

McKenna, Dave. "The Syracuse Walking Dream." *Washington City Paper*, 23 May 2008.

JASON PHILIP MILLER

Sifford, Charlie (2 June 1922–), golfer, was born Charles Luther Sifford in Charlotte, North Carolina, one of six children of Roscoe Sifford, a laborer, and Eliza. He was introduced to golf at the age of nine while working as a caddy at the local Carolina Country Club, where he learned the game during numerous early morning rounds. Sifford claimed his first title at a caddy's tournament in 1934, bringing home ten dollars and a case of Pepsi Cola. Financial difficulties and racial problems in Charlotte both on and off of the course forced him to drop out of his segregated high school during his junior year and move to live with an uncle in Philadelphia, Pennsylvania, in 1939. Sifford soon found a job as a shipping clerk for the National Biscuit Company, and he honed his golfing game at the public Cobbs Creek links.

During World War II, Sifford served in the Pacific theater with the 79th Signal Heavy Construction team from 1943–1946. After being discharged, he returned to Philadelphia and gave up his factory job to teach and play golf full time. One of his first and most successful students was the singer BILLY ECKSTINE, who hired the twenty-five-year-old as a chauffeur, valet, and instructor. From 1947–1953 Eckstine was Sifford's patron, encouraging and sometimes bankrolling the young golfer. Sifford married Rose Crumbley in 1947; the couple had two sons.

Although many athletic color barriers fell after World War II, there were few prospects for a talented black golfer in the late 1940s. Unlike professional football, baseball, basketball, and tennis organizations, the Professional Golfers Association (PGA) continued to draw the color line and to resist all attempts at repealing its constitution's "Caucasian clause," which restricted membership to white players. In 1948 the pioneering African American golfers TED RHODES and Bill Spiller unsuccessfully sued the PGA to gain access to the tour, and while the lawsuit brought needed publicity, the organization refused to alter its stand.

With the PGA off-limits, Sifford joined Spiller and Rhodes in the United Golf Association (UGA), an African American organization founded in 1925. Like its white counterpart, the UGA sponsored a regular schedule of events and a national championship. Sifford found immediate success, winning the Negro National Open each year from 1952 through 1956 and adding another title in 1960. Purses on the UGA tour, however, paled in comparison to the money available on the heavily sponsored PGA, and Sifford, like most black professionals, had trouble earning a living. In 1955 he teamed with the Burk Golf Company of Ohio to produce a set of "Charlie Sifford" signature clubs, which he peddled while golfing around the country.

The golf clubs were not big sellers, but a change in PGA policy improved Sifford's situation. The organization continued to deny membership to African Americans, but in 1952 it agreed to allow blacks with sponsors' exemptions to compete in sanctioned events. Only a handful of tournaments, mostly in California, invited African American competitors, but as one of the best black players in the country, Sifford managed to compete in about a dozen PGA events a year, frequently finishing in the money. In 1957 he became the first African American to win an integrated tournament at the Long Beach (California) Open.

Sifford and other talented black golfers, including Rhodes, Spiller, and Howard Wheeler, continued to hound the PGA, which faced mounting public pressure to eliminate its prejudicial membership requirements. In 1959 the organization attempted to affect a compromise by granting Sifford "approved tournament player" status that allowed him to compete in any tour event for which he qualified. Two years later California attorney general Stanley Mosk threatened to forbid the PGA to hold any of its tournaments on his state's public courses unless it rescinded the color line. In November 1961, fourteen years after JACKIE ROBINSON's rookie season with the Brooklyn Dodgers, the PGA finally deleted the "Caucasian clause" from its constitution. Soon afterward Sifford was the first African American to earn a PGA membership card. Years later he recalled his long struggle: "All I had was a stupid head, a raggedy golf game and determination to be a golfer; one of the best in the world, not a *black* golfer" ("Golf Pays Debt to Real Pro," 50). Although he was thirty-nine years old when he officially joined the PGA, Sifford could still compete with the best. In his first eight years on the tour, he won more than $200,000 (compared with just $17,000 before 1961), and in 1967 he won the Hartford Open. Two years later he shot a first-round 63 en route to capturing the prestigious Los Angeles Open.

Life was not always easy on the road. By the late 1960s there were only about ten other black golfers on the PGA tour, and nearly all private country clubs still refused membership to African Americans, creating a hostile atmosphere in certain clubhouses. Sifford and others sometimes still faced opposition when competing in southern tournaments. At an event in Greensboro, North Carolina, in 1969, a group of unruly white spectators abused Sifford with racial epithets and threw beer cans at him. Tournament officials had the group arrested, but it was a stark reminder of the long history of discrimination in white golfing circles.

For Sifford, though, the loneliness of the road and the occasional racial harassment were not the most frustrating aspects of the PGA tour. In the mid-1960s he lamented the slow pace of integration and counseled patience:

Golf has been the white man's game forever ... and the black man's just coming to it now. ... You know you can't play the game where they won't let you play, and they didn't let us play *no*where for a long time. It ain't easy catching up now. Not without money and without real good golf courses to play on ... and without good instruction. ... We got the opportunity to play golf—we just got a lot of catching up to do, that's all (Johnson, 58).

Sifford retired in the mid-1970s and became the club professional at Sleepy Hollow Country Club in Bricksville, Ohio. A founding member of the PGA Seniors' Tour, he won the Seniors' Championship in 1975 and continued to play competitively into the 1980s. In 2004 Sifford became the first African American member of the World Golf Hall of Fame.

FURTHER READING
Sifford, Charlie, with James Gallo. *Just Let Me Play* (1992).
Charlie Sifford: To Be the First Black into the World Golf Hall of Fame. http://www.afrogolf.com/charliesiffordHOF.html (2006).
Dawkins, Marvin P., and Graham C. Kinloch. *African American Golfers during the Jim Crow Era* (2000).
"Golf Pays Debt to Real Pro," *Ebony*, Apr. 1969.
Johnson, William. "Call Back the Years," *Sports Illustrated*, 31 Mar. 1969.
Sinnette, Calvin H. *Forbidden Fairways: African Americans and the Game of Golf* (1998).
"Top Negro Golfer," *Ebony*, June 1956.
                                        GREGORY BOND

Silver, Horace (2 Sept. 1928–), pianist and composer, was born Ward Martin Tavares in Norwalk, Connecticut, to John Tavares Silver, from the Cape Verde Islands who worked at the Norwalk Tire Company and played several instruments by ear, and Gertrude Edmonds Silver. Ward was baptized Horace Ward Silver. His father was of Portuguese descent and exposed Horace to Cape Verdean folk music from an early age. Horace began to study the piano when he was about twelve, largely because he was friendly with the girl next door who was taking lessons. In 1946, Silver graduated from Norwalk High School. He eventually became more serious about music, particularly when he heard the JIMMIE LUNCEFORD Band at a local amusement park. He decided he wanted to become a musician and bandleader and began to buy recordings of the COUNT BASIE and Dorsey Brothers bands. Silver was especially influenced by BUD POWELL and THELONIOUS MONK on the keyboard; but he remembered that his grandmother lived a block away from a storefront sanctified church, and the frequent exposure to the church's gospel sounds on his daily visits undoubtedly shaped his early musical tastes.

In 1950 the tenor saxophonist Stan Getz appeared in Hartford as guest soloist with Silver's trio, and Getz hired the group to tour with him for a year. Silver made several recordings with the group. He moved to New York City in 1951 and freelanced with

COLEMAN HAWKINS, LESTER YOUNG, ART BLAKEY, and others, appearing often enough at Birdland to become a de facto house pianist at the club. He also played on weekends at the Paradise Club with a group led by tenor saxophone player Big Nick Nicholas that often included CHARLIE PARKER, GENE AMMONS, SONNY STITT, and other bop stalwarts.

In 1952 Silver recorded a session with the tenor saxophonist Lou Donaldson on Blue Note Records. When Donaldson canceled a follow-up session at the last minute, Silver stepped in to record a trio session with the bassist Gene Ramey and the drummer Blakey. It was the beginning of a long relationship (twenty-eight years) with Blue Note Records, the label most associated with the style Silver helped establish, hard bop. In February 1954 Silver co-led a quintet with Blakey, featuring the trumpeter Clifford Brown, and recorded *A Night at Birdland*, and in November he recorded *Horace Silver and the Jazz Messengers*, with the saxophonist HANK MOBLEY and with Kenny Dorham replacing Brown on trumpet. This latter session cemented Silver's growing reputation. The album included "The Preacher" and "Doodlin'," two of his best-known tunes, and showcased the essential elements of the hard bop style that he pioneered: a funkier, earthier sound, with gospel- and blues-tinged playing that drew a new audience to the music. Silver himself noted that bop was becoming a little too sophisticated for the average listener; he sought to introduce simpler, more beautiful melodies into his compositions. This group continued to play together in 1954 and 1955 under the name the Jazz Messengers, with Donald Byrd replacing Dorham at the end of 1955, and recorded the two-volume *Live at the Café Bohemia* in November 1954.

In mid-1956 Silver formed his own quintet, leaving the leadership of the Messengers to Blakey. Beginning with *Six Pieces of Silver* (1956), the pianist recorded about twenty highly popular albums over the next six years. *Finger Poppin'* (1959) featured bluesy, swinging pieces like "Juicy Lucy," spare, poignant ballads, and Brazilian rhythms in tunes like "Swingin' the Samba." *Blowing' the Blues Away*, recorded the same year, contains some of his strongest compositions, including "Peace" and "Sister Sadie." These were the first albums from Silver's longest-running quintet, a group that featured the saxophonist Junior Cook and the trumpeter BLUE MITCHELL. *Song for My Father* (1964), a transitional album recorded just as this group was breaking up, is one of Silver's most sophisticated sessions, particularly notable for the creative interplay between the

tenor saxophonist JOE HENDERSON and the trumpeter Carmell Jones. Silver conceived the bossa nova rhythms of the title tune during a carnival visit to the composer Sergio Mendes in Brazil. The follow-up record, *Cape Verdean Blues* (1965), contains some of Silver's most modernist compositions, highlighted by the interplay between Henderson, the young trumpeter WOODY SHAW, and the veteran bop trombonist J. J. JOHNSON on three of the tracks. The album is laced with Latin-tinged rhythms and calypso melodies; though it is clearly a hard-bop recording, Silver took his music as far as he ever would toward his Afro-Latin heritage. Despite changing personnel over the next six years, Silver's music lost little of its rhythmic or melodic power. Of particular note are the albums *The Jody Grind* (1966) and *Serenade to a Soul Sister* (1968).

In 1970, Silver married Barbara Jean Dove. They had one child, Gregory Paul Silver and divorced in 1975.

For most of the 1970s and 1980s Silver shifted his musical focus. In the early 1970s he wrote lyrics and music for three albums collectively titled *The United States of Mind*. A mix of fusion, soul, mysticism, and African spirituality, they remain of their time, contributing little to the pianist's jazz heritage. In 1973 he returned to a more standard jazz format, this time with a series of albums featuring brass, woodwinds, percussion, strings, and voices. These recordings varied in critical and commercial success, and by the late 1970s Silver had moved into semiretirement.

In 1981 Silver returned to music and founded the Silveto label, whose productions focused on spiritually minded compositions; the label's subsidiary, Emerald, recorded the hard-bop material that Silver now began to play again. He toured with new groups in 1983 and 1984, reverting to his mentorship role and recruiting such future stars as the tenor saxophonist Ralph Moore, the trumpeters Brian Lynch and Dave Douglass, and the alto saxophonist Vincent Herring. In 1987 the singer Andy Bey became a regular member of Silver's groups. In 1992 Silver toured briefly in the summer, but almost died from complications following hernia surgery in early 1993. He was back on tour in 1994 with the Horace Silver Brass Ensemble.

Silver's comeback was genuinely affirmed with the 1993 recording *It's Gotta Be Funky* (Columbia), packed with new compositions played by a trio and a six-piece brass ensemble. He followed that up with 1994's *Pencil Packin' Papa*, with more new compositions and again featuring a six-piece brass section. In 1995 he recorded *Hard Bop Grandpop* (GRP), a truly exciting collection of ten new compositions and Silver's best album in years. It featured a stellar cast that included Ron Carter on bass, Lewis Nash on drums, Claudio Roditi on trumpet, Michael Brecker on tenor saxophone, Ronnie Cuber on baritone, and Steve Turre on trombone. Silver's next recording, *A Prescription for the Blues* (1997), continued to draw from the best mainstream talent available, including Carter, Michael Brecker, Randy Brecker on trumpet, and Louis Hayes on drums. *Jazz Has a Sense of Humor* (1998) followed, concentrating this time on younger players like the saxophonist Jimmy Greene and the trumpeter Ryan Kisor. This is well played, exhilarating funk driven by Silver's simple, bluesy piano style, dedicated to FATS WALLER. Finally, in 2003 Silver issued one of the most unusual albums in his discography, *Rockin' with Rachmaninoff*. As Silver tells it, the pianist had a dream in 1990 that DUKE ELLINGTON and Sergei Rachmaninoff met in heaven and became friends and mutual admirers, Ellington introducing Rachmaninoff to the jazz greats who lived there. Silver translated the story into a stage musical, and with the help of Los Angeles mayor TOM BRADLEY, he staged for a three-day run in Hollywood in 1991. Silver recorded the music in August of that year, but then Silveto Records ceased operation, and the recording sat on the shelf until released by Bop City records. It is typically ebullient Silver music, featuring the vocalists Bey and Dawn Burnett.

Silver was one of the most important composers and ensemble leaders in twentieth and twenty-first century jazz as well as an accomplished and original pianist. A mentor to dozens of important musicians, he was also one of the few jazz musicians to record his own material almost exclusively. His playing and composing combine simplicity, melodic beauty, and rhythmic power, and he produced many tunes that became jazz standards, notably "The Preacher," "Doodlin'," "Senor Blues," "Sister Sadie," "Peace," and "Song for My Father," all of which share the catchy themes and blues and gospel influences central to the hard-bop style. His own pianism combines blues phrasing in the right hand with "a grumbling left-hand bass that is unlike the style of any other player" (Alvarez, www.allaboutjazz.com). Silver has also published several books, most notably *The Art of Small Combo Jazz Playing, Composing, and Arranging* (1995). In 2003 he established the Horace Silver Foundation to give a $10,000 annual award to a young jazz

pianist. But Silver's true contribution lies in his music, best described in his own words. He wrote lyrics for many of his songs, though most have not been recorded; the best-known exception is DEE DEE BRIDGEWATER's 1995 tribute *Love and Peace: A Tribute to Horace Silver*. The best statement of Silver's soul, though, is in his *A Prescription for the Blues* (2007):

A Prescription for the Blues.
Here's What you have to do.
Just get your head into some music.
And let your feet move, too.
If you'll forgive, you'll be forgiven.
The blues won't bother you.

FURTHER READING

Lyons, Len. *The Great Jazz Pianists: Speaking of Their Lives and Music* (1983).

Morgenstern, Dan. "That Durable Horace Silver," *Down Beat* (Dec. 1965).

Rosenthal, David H. *Hard Bop: Jazz and Black Music, 1955–1965* (1992).

Shipton, Alyn. *Handful of Keys: Conversations with Thirty Jazz Pianists* (2004).

Williams, Martin T. *The Jazz Tradition*, 2d ed. (1983).

RONALD P. DUFOUR

Simeon, Omer (21 July 1902–17 Sept. 1959), jazz clarinetist and saxophonist, was born Omer Victor Simeon in New Orleans, Louisiana, the son of Omer Simeon, a cigar maker. His mother's name is unknown. His family moved to Chicago in 1914. Four years later he began taking lessons from the clarinetist LORENZO TIO JR.

After working with his brother Al Simeon's Hot Six, he joined Charlie Elgar's Creole Orchestra as an alto saxophonist and clarinetist in 1923, later taking up soprano saxophone as well. The band played mainly in Milwaukee at the Riverview Ballroom and the Wisconsin Roof Garden, but it also worked in Chicago. There Simeon met JELLY ROLL MORTON, and after returning to Milwaukee with Elgar he commuted to Chicago to play in the first sessions by Morton's Red Hot Peppers, in 1926. The first and greatest record of this session, *Black Bottom Stomp*, exemplifies Simeon's prominent, busy, cleanly articulated, bluesy playing, bright in the clarinet's high range and full-bodied in its lower register. On one title, "Someday Sweetheart," Simeon's part was a compositional gimmick; he reluctantly agreed to play a slow melody on a rented bass clarinet, thereby making an early and inconsequential claim for the instrument's place in jazz. Otherwise, these are all classic performances by the clarinetist.

In April 1927, when KING OLIVER's Dixie Syncopators played one night at the Wisconsin Roof, Simeon left Elgar to join Oliver. They toured colleges, performed in St. Louis, and then finished the month with two weeks at the Savoy Ballroom in New York, during which time they recorded. On these titles Simeon's tone is even more brilliant than it was with Morton, his clarinet sounding almost like a violin ("Showboat Shuffle") and his soprano saxophone almost like a clarinet ("Willie the Weeper"), possibly because of the tinniness of the recording fidelity rather than any fundamental change of approach. As a soprano saxophonist, his slow, slippery blues playing is featured on "Black Snake Blues."

Leaving New York, Oliver's group played assorted one-night stands before becoming stranded in Baltimore in May 1927 without further work. Simeon rejoined Elgar at the Eagle Ballroom in Milwaukee and at Dreamland in Chicago. In the summer of 1928 he returned to New York to join LUIS RUSSELL at the Nest Club for about three months. He also replaced RUSSELL PROCOPE in Morton's band for a recording session, performed with Morton's band for one week at Rose Danceland, and again recorded with Oliver.

In the fall of 1928 Simeon joined Erskine Tate in the pit band at the Metropolitan Theater in Chicago in order to be with his family. He remained with Tate until 1930, while working on occasion with Elgar at Chicago's Savoy. During this period he recorded regularly with JABBO SMITH's small groups. These sessions afford an extended opportunity to hear Simeon playing clarinet, alto sax, and tenor sax in a freewheeling style, paired with Smith's own audacious approach, as on the deceptively named "Take Your Time" (they do not), and in pretty, deliberate melodies serving as a foil for Smith's playing, as on "Sweet and Low Blues." After playing in DAVE PEYTON's orchestra at Chicago's Regal Theater, Simeon became the lead alto saxophonist in EARL HINES's orchestra at the Grand Terrace in March 1931. Except for a two-week stint with FLETCHER HENDERSON in 1936 as a replacement for BUSTER BAILEY, and a long stay in the big band of HORACE W. HENDERSON after a dispute over money between Hines and his sidemen (Aug. 1937–Sept. 1938), Simeon remained with Hines until 1940. He was, Hines said, "a very quiet sort of fellow, and very serious about his work. He always stayed by himself and didn't hang out with the wilder guys." On Hines's recordings he seems to have fashioned an improvisatory style in which rhythm and volume operated in spurts and bursts of sound. "Rock and Rye" from 1934 is characteristic, and it additionally provides a typical example of him leading the saxophone section through a florid line in rhythmic unison.

In 1940 Simeon joined a big band led by Hines's former trumpeter Walter Fuller, again at the Grand Terrace. After playing with COLEMAN HAWKINS in 1941 he returned to Fuller from late that year until the summer of 1942, playing mainly at the Happy Hour in Minneapolis. He was in JIMMIE LUNCEFORD's big band from 1942 until 1950, with Eddie Wilcox taking over its leadership after Lunceford's death in 1947. "Back Door Stuff" from 1944 offers a beautifully fluid, bluesy solo on clarinet.

While touring with Lunceford, Simeon became involved in the New Orleans jazz revival, most notably by recording with KID ORY in Hollywood in 1944, including "Do What Ory Say," and 1945. In 1951 he joined WILBUR DE PARIS's band, which toured Africa in the spring of 1957 but mainly held residencies in New York City, where Simeon died of cancer.

Simeon's place in jazz would be assured had he done nothing other than play clarinet for Morton on one of the most significant bodies of recordings in the music's history. As it stands, this was only the beginning—albeit an illustrious one—of a career as a versatile performer in early jazz and swing styles.

FURTHER READING

Simeon, Omer. "Mostly about Morton," *Selections from the Gutter: Jazz Portraits from "The Jazz Record,"* ed. Art Hodes and Chadwick Hansen (1977).

Dance, Stanley. *The World of Earl Hines* (1977).

Lomax, Alan. *Mister Jelly Roll: The Fortunes of Jelly Roll Morton, New Orleans Creole and "Inventor of Jazz"* (1950).

Wright, Laurie. *Mr. Walter C. Allen and Brian Rust's "King" Oliver* (1987).

This entry is taken from the *American National Biography* and is published here with the permission of the American Council of Learned Societies.

BARRY KERNFELD

Simkins, Modjeska (5 Dec. 1899–5 Apr. 1992), civil rights activist, was born Mary Modjeska Monteith in Columbia, South Carolina, the eldest of eight children of Henry Clarence Monteith, a brick mason, and Rachel Evelyn Hull, a teacher. She was named for her aunt Mary and for Helena Modjeska, a Polish-born actress famous for her Shakespearean roles. Modjeska's childhood was loving but strict. From an early age she was expected to perform chores around the family home and farm and to set an example to her younger siblings. Her parents also instilled in her a rigorous work ethic, a deep religious faith, and a powerful sense of race pride and race consciousness. Modjeska's father had once faced down a white man in Alabama who had taunted him with a finger severed from a black lynching victim. Her mother was active in the Niagara Movement and brought the teenage Modjeska to meetings of the Columbia branch of the National Association for the Advancement of Colored People (NAACP). Both parents also believed passionately in the importance of education and enrolled Modjeska in one of Columbia's few private schools for blacks, Benedict College, in 1905. Modjeska remained there through high school and graduated from the college proper with an AB in 1921. She taught medieval history at Benedict from 1921 to 1922.

Schooled in the prevailing ethos of racial uplift and community service, Modjeska Monteith followed the example of her mother and several aunts by becoming a public school teacher. She taught at the BOOKER T. WASHINGTON School in Columbia from 1922 until her marriage seven years later to Andrew Simkins, when she was forced to quit because married women were not allowed to teach in the city's schools. In a 1976 interview she recalled that the Columbia school board was probably happy to be rid of her because of her outspoken views, notably her refusal to assign students a state history textbook that she deemed racist. Andrew Simkins, who owned real estate and a gasoline service station in Columbia, was financially secure and, unusual for his times, was also supportive of his wife's desire for a career outside of the home. Twice a widower, he brought five children to the marriage and employed a housekeeper to look after them and the home, an arrangement that enabled his wife to take a full-time position as director of Negro Work for the South Carolina Tuberculosis Association (SCTA) in 1931. The couple later had three children together.

Simkins's work with the SCTA educated her about the deep-rooted problems of poverty and ill health faced by African Americans throughout South Carolina, one of the nation's poorest states. In urban areas such as Columbia and Charleston, low wages, high unemployment, poor sanitation, and substandard housing had long been the norm, while in rural communities the economic uncertainties of sharecropping were compounded by a lack of clinics and hospitals. Tuberculosis, pellagra, and other diseases were common. The severe economic depression of the 1930s and declining cotton sales made matters worse and made Simkins's task nearly impossible. Though the SCTA was perpetually short of funds, she worked tirelessly to provide tuberculosis testing in black schools, churches, and even factories and cotton fields, if landlords and mill owners permitted. Simkins also studied health education at the State Normal College in Ypsilanti, Michigan, and taught classes on the latest health education techniques to teachers, physicians, and nurses at South Carolina State College in Orangeburg.

In the eleven years that Simkins worked for the SCTA she came into contact with a range of black leaders who shared her frustration about black Carolinians' lack of economic opportunities and continuing second-class citizenship. When Levi G. Byrd, a plumber from Cheraw, South Carolina, helped found a state branch of the NAACP in 1939 to combat these ills, Simkins, long active in the Columbia NAACP chapter, took a leading role and was soon elected to the state executive board. The only woman on that board, she was elected secretary of the South Carolina Conference of the NAACP in 1941. Simkins's white conservative employers at the SCTA were unhappy about her prominent political profile in an organization that directly challenged segregation. When in 1942 they asked her to choose between her health education work and the NAACP, Simkins replied that she would "rather see a person die and go to hell with tuberculosis than to be treated how some of my people [are] treated" (Woods, 109). That characteristically undiplomatic answer prompted the SCTA to cut her budget, forcing Simkins to resign her SCTA post later that year.

Now focused solely on NAACP matters, Simkins joined with the Reverend James Hinton and the journalists OSCEOLA MCKAINE and JOHN MCCRAY to make South Carolina a hotbed of civil rights activism in the 1940s. Under the leadership of Simkins and Hinton, the South Carolina NAACP grew from only eight branches in 1939 to almost one hundred branches by 1950. As secretary of the Teachers Defense Fund between 1943 and 1944, Simkins also took charge of the legal campaigns to secure equal salaries for black and white teachers in Columbia and Charleston. Although the Teachers Defense Fund won both court cases in 1945, many black teachers opposed the campaigns for fear of economic reprisals by their employers, much to Simkins's annoyance. Indeed, she was often critical of "black Quislings," "sell-outs," and other "misleaders" whom she found overly cautious (Chappell, 65). Her fearlessness was famous, but it was sometimes hard for others to live up to her high ideals.

Like many well-to-do southern blacks, Simkins was a registered Republican who viewed the state Democratic Party as irredeemably racist. But she was also active in South Carolina's Progressive Democratic Party (PDP), founded in 1944 following the U.S. Supreme Court's *Smith v. Allwright* ruling, which had declared the all-white political primary unconstitutional. In particular she supported the PDP's goal of securing a fourth term in 1944 for the Democrat Franklin Roosevelt and regarded his presidency as a "shot in the arm for Negroes" (Sullivan, 144). In 1946 Simkins attempted to register in South Carolina's Democratic Party primary. Rejected by election officials, she worked with the PDP and the NAACP to mount a legal challenge to state laws that had attempted to circumvent *Smith v. Allwright*. Despite vigorous opposition the campaign was ultimately successful in 1948, when thirty-five thousand black voters were able to register in that year's Democratic Party primary.

Simkins's involvement in NAACP and PDP activities brought her into the orbit of several regional and national civil rights organizations. In 1942 she attended a conference in Durham, North Carolina, that led to the formation of the Southern Regional Council (SRC), the largest interracial civil rights organization in the South. Simkins was active in promoting the SRC's activities in Columbia but increasingly chafed at the organization's timidity when it came to challenging segregation. She found a more congenial home in the interracial Southern Conference for Human Welfare (SCHW) and its successor, the Southern Conference Educational Fund (SCEF), which elected Simkins vice president in 1952. Both the SCEF and the SCHW, as well as the predominantly black Civil Rights Congress, which she joined in 1946, were committed to racial integration and included among their members a number of Socialists, Communists, and other progressives who shared Simkins's goal of a more equitable South. Disillusioned by the civil rights platforms of both the Republican and Democratic parties in 1948, Simkins backed the Progressive Party and its presidential candidate Henry A. Wallace, a staunch liberal who won less than 3 percent of the national vote.

Simkins was also prominent in the NAACP's efforts after 1950 to challenge the separate and highly unequal South Carolina school system, where the state spent ten dollars per white child for every one dollar that it spent on a black child. The resulting Clarendon County case, *Briggs v. Elliot*, was one of several included in the Supreme Court's *Brown v. Board of Education* (1954) decision, which declared segregated schools inherently unequal and thus unconstitutional. In several southern states, however, the NAACP's victory provoked economic reprisals. In 1955, spurred on by prosegregationist White Citizens Councils, landowners in Orangeburg County, South Carolina, evicted several black tenants who had signed school desegregation petitions. Other NAACP supporters were denied credit and loans, and some were fired from their jobs. Simkins took the lead in a nationwide campaign to raise and distribute food, clothing, and money to these families. Through her position at Columbia's Victory Savings Bank, where her brother was president and where she worked from 1956 to 1982, Simkins was also able to secure low-interest loans for the victims of these economic reprisals.

Although relatively shielded personally from economic retaliation, Simkins was much more vulnerable to charges in the white-owned press claiming that she was a Communist. She was not, but neither was she willing to disavow her friendships with the Communists PAUL ROBESON and BENJAMIN J. DAVIS or her work for allegedly Communist-front groups like the SCHW. Exhausted by the pressures placed on his organization by these red-baiting attacks on Simkins, the NAACP state president James Hinton asked her to resign as secretary of the South Carolina Conference in 1957.

After 1957 Simkins took a less prominent role in the national civil rights movement but was still active at the local level. She ran for local political office in Columbia three times in the 1960s and again in 1983, but she was defeated each time. In later years she came to be known as the matriarch of the South Carolina civil rights movement. That kindly description reflects her influence on later civil rights leaders like BENJAMIN CHAVIS and JESSE JACKSON, but it masks her determined, even obstinate, radicalism. Simkins, who died at the age of 102, had no illusions that radical social change was easy or that those who held power could easily be persuaded to share it. She compared herself often to Job, "in great struggle against … the rulers of darkness" and "against spiritual wickedness in high places" (Chappell, 66).

FURTHER READING
Modjeska Simkins's personal papers are housed at the South Caroliniana Library, Columbia, South Carolina, and at Winthrop College in Rock Hill, South Carolina. A transcript of an interview of Simkins by Jacquelyn Hall (28–31 July 1976) is in the Southern Oral History Program Papers at the Southern Historical Collection, Chapel Hill, North Carolina.

Chappell, David L. *A Stone of Hope: Prophetic Religion and the Death of Jim Crow* (2004).

Sullivan, Patricia. *Days of Hope: Race and Democracy in the New Deal Era* (1996).

Woods, Barbara A. "Modjeska Simkins and the South Carolina Conference of the NAACP, 1939–1957," in *Women in the Civil Rights Movement: Trailblazers and Torchbearers*, eds. Vicki L. Crawford, Jacqueline Anne Rouse, and Barbara Woods (1990).

Obituary: *Charlotte Observer*, 10 Apr. 1992.

STEVEN J. NIVEN

Simkins, Paris (18 Feb. 1849–26 Sept. 1930), politician, lawyer, and fraternal leader, was born in Edgefield County, South Carolina, the son of Charlotte Simkins, a slave, and her owner Arthur Augustus Simkins, a newspaper publisher and scion of the local planter aristocracy. In the early 1850s Paris's father was prominent in organizing the Democratic Party in South Carolina, assisted by Preston Brooks, Edgefield's U.S. congressman, who in 1856 famously beat the Massachusetts Republican Charles Sumner with a cane on the Senate floor. Sumner had apparently insulted Brooks's kinsman. It is unclear how Arthur Simkins viewed his son Paris, though he most likely opposed the actions of another of his slaves, a coachman, who hid with the boy in the woods to secretly and illegally teach him to read and write. Paris's education was briefly interrupted at the outbreak of the Civil War in 1861, when he was sent with his father, an officer in the Confederate army, to work as a barber. At the end of the war, having witnessed several battles, including Gettysburg, Simkins returned to freedom in South Carolina, where he opened a barbershop and continued his efforts to gain an education, receiving instruction from a local minister.

In the immediate aftermath of emancipation, Simkins emerged as a leading critic of the black codes and other efforts to reassert white supremacy in Edgefield County, writing to the U.S. major general Daniel E. Sickles in 1866 to demand greater federal protection of the freedmen. In addition to being Edgefield's postmaster and a lieutenant colonel in the black state militia founded by PRINCE RIVERS of neighboring Hamburg, South Carolina, Simkins was also prominent in religious affairs, founding the Macedonia Baptist Church in Edgefield in 1868. Agreeing with his father that property holding was the foundation of liberty, he purchased land and owned six hundred dollars in real estate and one hundred dollars in personal property in 1870. Simkins's prominence in local politics was confirmed in 1872 with his election from Edgefield County to the South Carolina State House of Representatives. Serving until 1876, at which point he chaired the House Ways and Means Committee, his political skills were recognized even by South Carolina's white press, which was generally hostile to all black legislators during Reconstruction. Politically Simkins belonged to the wealthier, more moderate, native-born faction of black Republicans and was prominent in bringing embezzlement charges against Niles Parker, a white Massachusetts-born Union officer infamous for his corrupt tenure as South Carolina's state treasurer.

Like that of many other Reconstruction-era legislators in South Carolina, Simkins's political career was halted in 1876 by the vicious and violent race-baiting election campaign of former Confederate leaders, which "redeemed" the state from Republican rule. He was a victim of the so-called Edgefield Plan, which involved the intimidation of African American candidates and likely voters, often at gunpoint, as well as outright voter fraud and which served as a model for other white redemption campaigns in the South. Fearing the popularity of Simkins and his fellow Republican Laurence Cain, Democrats trumped up murder charges against the two men and then, when the charges did not stick, stuffed the ballot boxes with votes for white Democrats. Simkins, who had won election easily in black-majority Edgefield in 1872, lost four years later by a margin of two to one. He later testified before a U.S. congressional committee that he had refrained from campaigning in 1876 because of a thousand dollar bounty placed on his head by his opponents and that such abuses were widespread throughout the state.

Shortly before his election defeat, Simkins graduated from the University of South Carolina Law School at Columbia, where he, Cain, Walter Raleigh Jones, and three others were the first African Americans to matriculate in 1873. Simkins does not appear to have practiced law, however, until 1886, when he was admitted to the South Carolina bar. He was at that time still employed as Edgefield's postmaster and was working as a secretary for South Carolina governor John C. Sheppard, a Democrat who had "defeated" him in the fraudulent 1876 poll. Although he was never allowed to testify inside a South Carolina courtroom, Simkins applied his legal training to drawing up the legal papers for the Mutual Aid and Burial Society, which he served as president. Like WILLIS MOLLISON and other black lawyers in the post-Reconstruction South, he was also active in fraternal affairs, most notably in founding the Edgefield County chapter of the Knights of Pythias. The name of Simkins's wife has not been recorded, but the couple had sixteen children. During Reconstruction his half brother, Andrew Simkins, served as Edgefield County's first African American superintendent of education.

By the time Simkins died in Edgefield County, Reconstruction was a distant memory for most South Carolinians. Had it not been for the ending of Republican rule in 1876, he might have expected to found a political dynasty of black Simkinses to match his white forebears, who were Palmetto State leaders in the decades after the Revolutionary War. Simkins did, however, pass on his political activism to his grandson, C. B. Bailey, who in 1938 sued to reintegrate his grandfather's alma mater, the University of South Carolina Law School. While Bailey's application was rejected, like PAULI MURRAY's similar effort that same year to integrate the University of North Carolina Law School, his case helped prepare the groundwork for CHARLES HAMILTON HOUSTON and the NAACP's ultimately successful campaign to desegregate law schools. In 1984 Paris Simkins's Edgefield home was added to the National Register of Historic Places.

FURTHER READING

Burton, Orville Vernon. *In My Father's House Are Many Mansions: Family and Community in Edgefield, South Carolina* (1985).

Harris, J. William. *Plain Folk and Gentry in a Slave Society: White Liberty and Black Slavery in Augusta's Hinterlands* (1985).

Underwood, James Lowell, and W. Lewis Burke Jr., eds. *At Freedom's Door: African American Founding Fathers and Lawyers in Reconstruction South Carolina* (2000).

STEVEN J. NIVEN

Simmons, Calvin Eugene (27 Apr. 1950–21 Aug. 1982), symphony conductor, was born in San Francisco, California, the son of Henry Calvin Simmons, a dockhand and church official, and Mattie Pearl (maiden name unknown), a registered nurse and church musician. His mother's work as a choral conductor and pianist attracted the boy to music. By the time he was eight he had begun to perform in public and the next year joined the San Francisco Boys Chorus, directed by Madi Bacon, which was called on for occasional performances with the San Francisco Opera. Bacon offered young Simmons his first conducting lessons. While at a summer camp he began the study of theory with William Duncan Allen, trying his hand at composition during his mid-teens. At age sixteen he was appointed pianist for the San Francisco Boys Chorus and won the attention of Kurt Herbert Adler, who granted him access to the opera rehearsals. In commemoration of the death of MARTIN LUTHER KING JR., he conducted Mozart's *Requiem* while still in high school.

Simmons began his college days as a student at the University of Cincinnati, from 1968 to 1970. There he was befriended by the vocal coach SYLVIA OLDEN LEE and the conductor Max Rudolf, whose textbook he had studied while still in junior high school. When his conducting teacher left Cincinnati the next year for a post at Philadelphia's Curtis Institute of Music, Simmons followed. In addition to the continuation of his work in conducting, he was accepted in the piano studio of Rudolf Serkin. During this time he served as pianist to Maria Callas, who, like many, initially thought him a servant because he was black.

Following graduation in 1972 Simmons made his formal debut as conductor in San Francisco's production of *Hänsel und Gretel* (with which he also made his Metropolitan Opera debut in 1978). As assistant director of the Western Opera Theater he gave performances on tours from Arizona, where operas were presented to a Navaho audience, to Alaska, where they were performed for Eskimo children in a village of fewer than one hundred residents. This was consonant with his dedication to the presentation of music to new audiences, including many concerts for children and even opera productions on the street corners of San Francisco. In 1974 he was engaged by England's Glyndebourne Opera Company with the London Philharmonic Orchestra, principally for performances of Mozart's *Così fan tutte* and *Le nozze di Figaro*, both at the Glyndebourne estate and on tours. He moved to the Los Angeles Philharmonic

Orchestra as assistant to Zubin Mehta in 1975 with a grant from the Exxon Corporation and made his first recording with that ensemble.

In 1978 he was appointed music director of the Oakland Symphony, becoming the second African American—after Henry Lewis with the New Jersey Symphony Orchestra in 1968—to have full artistic authority over an American orchestra. In this post he was both aggressive and imaginative in selling the orchestra to a large public, raising the orchestra's standards as well as its budget. Frequently engaged as a guest conductor for most of the major orchestras, he was selected to lead the debut of *Juana la loca*, an opera by Gian Carlo Menotti, with Beverly Sills in her final opera performance, and of that Shostakovich opera which, as *Lady Macbeth of Mtsensk*, had infuriated the Soviet government. His St. Louis performance of *Così* in 1982 created a sensation, and numerous bookings reached into the future. Among the soloists for this production were two newcomers to the opera scene, Jerry Hadley and Thomas Hampson. "A more provocative and consistent *Così* you are not likely to come across in a lifetime of opera-going," stated a review in the *New York Times*. That summer, while relaxing at Lake Placid, his canoe overturned in the icy waters, and Simmons was drowned.

His funeral was held in San Francisco's Grace Cathedral. Musical tributes were offered by a string quartet from the Oakland Symphony and by the mezzo-soprano Marilyn Horne. The orchestra's hall was subsequently named in his honor when its schedule was resumed; the orchestra then became known as the Oakland East Bay Symphony.

Simmons was well known for his irrepressible and spontaneous humor, which often was manifest at unexpected moments. Though he took music seriously he enjoyed playing pranks in public and was quick to improvise, particularly when this could ease tensions. His antics, however, did not diminish the respect he earned from such figures as Elizabeth Schwarzkopf, Birgit Nilsson, and the appreciative critics who attended his American and European performances.

FURTHER READING

Wolfe, Rinna Evelyn. *The Calvin Simmons Story; or, "Don't Call Me Maestro"* (1994).

Obituary: *New York Times*, 24 Aug. 1982.

This entry is taken from the *American National Biography* and is published here with the permission of the American Council of Learned Societies.

DOMINIQUE-RENÉ DE LERMA

Simmons, Ellamae (26 Mar. 1918–) nurse, physician, and educational activist, was born in Mount Vernon, Ohio, the youngest of four children of Augustus "Gus" Simmons, a farmer, and Ella Sophia Cooper Simmons, a practical nurse. As part of the fledgling black middle class of early twentieth century America, Gus and Ella Simmons provided a financially secure and happy environment for their children. Looking back, Dr. Simmons had only pleasant memories of her early years, memories of extended family gatherings, learning to play the piano, friendships, hay rides, and dating one of the few black students at the high school (African Americans made up only 2 percent of Mount Vernon's population and 3 percent statewide).

An outstanding student with a special talent for the sciences, Simmons decided to follow in her mother's footsteps and pursue a career in nursing. In 1936, after graduating in the top 3 percent of her high school class, she applied to Ohio State University (OSU). Although her grades were more than adequate for admission, she was turned down by OSU's School of Nursing on the grounds that it lacked the facilities to train and house African American women. Although disappointed, Simmons was not one to brood. Behind her shy, soft-spoken demeanor was a self-confident young woman with the fierce determination of a bounty hunter. As she demonstrated throughout her life, once she set her sights on something, nothing got in her way. In the following year she applied to the all-black Hampton Institute (now University) School of Nursing in Virginia, where she was accepted and even received a small scholarship.

No one at the school had a greater impact on Simmons's future than Dr. Rupert A.B. Lloyd. He was the first black physician she had ever met. A surgeon, Lloyd was on the faculty of the Institute and had patients at nearby Dixie Hospital (a segregated facility), where Hampton student nurses trained. While Simmons made ward rounds, she interacted with Dr. Lloyd, who recognized her potential and advised her to go to medical school.

In 1940, after graduating Hampton at the top of her class, she set her sights on becoming a physician. With the outbreak of World War II, however, Simmons, like millions of other Americans, had to put her career plans on hold. In December 1942 she joined the U.S. Army Nurse Corps, a strictly segregated organization, reflecting the U.S. military itself. During her first few years, Simmons was stationed at black army hospitals in Louisiana and Texas. In 1945, after promotion to first lieutenant, she was ordered to Fort Des Moines, Iowa, where she participated in a historic event: the integration of the first U.S. Army hospital. As far as Simmons remembered, the experiment was highly successful. Neither white nurses nor white patients offered resistance to desegregation, which in 1948, thanks to President Harry S. Truman's Executive Order 9881, became the official policy of the U.S. military.

Mustered out of the service in March 1946, Simmons got right back on her career track. With the support of the GI Bill, she applied for admission to OSU to complete her pre-med requirements. OSU was willing to admit her, but refused to provide her housing on campus. A decade before, Simmons had been up against a similar situation with OSU, but now this twenty-seven-year-old ex-army nurse was not going to back down. After speaking to various administrators, Simmons was offered a room (no roommate permitted) in Baker Hall. She accepted the offer and thereby became the first African American woman to live on campus at OSU.

Within two years, Simmons fulfilled her premed requirements and graduated with a degree in biological sciences. After several rejections by OSU's Medical School (it allowed only one nonwhite to enter each year), in 1954 Simmons was finally accepted to one of the few black medical schools in the country, Meharry Medical College in Nashville, Tennessee.

Once her husband, Dr. John Williams (whom she had married two years before), had secured a residency in psychiatry at a hospital in Washington, D.C., Simmons transferred to another African American medical institution, Howard University College of Medicine, located in the capital. Despite efforts on both sides to make a go of the marriage, various personal issues had taken their toll, severe enough that the couple divorced soon after Simmons's arrival in Washington. Blessed with a felicity of putting aside disappointment, she focused her boundless energy on her medical studies, receiving her M.D. degree in 1959.

During her residency at National Jewish Hospital in Denver, Colorado, Simmons decided to specialize in chest medicine. This in turn led to an interest in asthma, allergy, and immunology, which brought her into contact with the chief of the department, Dr. Irving Itkin, who promised to make her the outstanding allergist in the nation. Following her year of residency in chest medicine, Simmons spent two additional years under Itkin's tutelage, and whether mentor or student realized it, this was a groundbreaking event in African American and medical history: Simmons became the first black female physician to be trained in clinical asthma, allergy, and immunology.

Nor did Itkin's influence end there. Once Simmons completed her residency, Itkin recommended her to another leading authority in the field, Dr. Benjamin Feingold, chief of the allergy department at Kaiser Permanente Medical Group in San Francisco, one of the largest health maintenance organizations in the country. In January 1965 Simmons interviewed for a position at Kaiser. After three straight days of meetings, Feingold turned her down, insisting that she lacked experience. Simmons stood her ground, declaring that she had never applied for anything that she had not been fully qualified for. Then she went to the heart of the matter, accusing Feingold of race and gender bias. Unaccustomed to being spoken to in that manner, Feingold was nonetheless impressed by Simmons's spunk. Also, Feingold was Jewish and may have experienced his share of prejudice. Simmons got the job and shattered yet another barrier: she was the first African American female physician to be employed by the Kaiser Permanente Medical Group.

After retiring from Kaiser in 1989 Dr. Simmons volunteered her services at a nonprofit clinic in Richmond, California, made several trips to Africa, and became an enthusiastic advocate for lifelong learning. More commonly known on college campuses as "Continuing Education," the program offers classes to the community at large, especially senior citizens. In 2005 Dr. Simmons helped launch such a program at her alma mater, Hampton University.

Indeed, this ordinary, soft-spoken African American girl from a small town in Ohio, who left home at age eighteen to pursue a career in nursing, had compiled an extraordinary record of achievement. In the words of the California Legislative Black Caucus, Dr. Ellamae Simmons's "path through life and its challenges and obstacles [serve as] inspiration and guidance [for] this generation and generations to come" (Resolution, No. 147, 26 March 2008).

FURTHER READING

The above is based largely on a series of oral interviews conducted with Dr. Simmons by Gerald S. Henig and Lori Henig in November and December 2008. The tapes are in the author's possession.

Another invaluable primary source is an oral interview conducted by Martin Meeker in 2008, sponsored by the Kaiser Permanente Oral History Project. A transcript of the interview is in the Regional Oral History Office, the Bancroft Library, University of California, Berkeley, California.

Philips, Alison L. "Alumna Encourages Others to Be Life-long Learners," *Hampton: The Alumni Magazine of Hampton University*, Summer 2008.

Resolution by the California Legislative Black Caucus, Member Resolution, No. 147, 26 Mar. 2008.

GERALD S. HENIG

Simmons, Howard L. (17 Apr. 1938–), educator, was born in Mobile, Alabama to Eugene Simmons, a cement finisher, and Daisy Davis Simmons, a cook, and educated in that city's public schools. He completed the first through seventh grades at Crichton Colored School, where he drew attention to himself as a standout student. After one year at Dunbar Junior High, Simmons completed the ninth through twelfth grades at Mobile's Central High School, graduating third in his class in 1956. He has stated that his commitment to learning began at a very early age:

> I've always been interested in books, reading and words, and origins of words, which led me to the library. In high school, I would miss gym class to go to the library. I was there so often that the librarian put me to work. I processed books, accessioned them, which was exciting to see new books coming in, and the librarian let me help classify them. Because I knew where everything was in the library, I helped students, explaining to them what they should be using (National Forum on Information Literacy, http://www. infolit.org/star_3.html).

Getting accepted to and being able to enroll in Spring Hill College was an accomplishment for Simmons, given the lack of opportunities for African Americans in the Deep South in the 1950s. As a young college student, his passion for reading intensified. He continued working in the library and helping students, even questioning the conventional system of reserving library books: "Why should anyone want to be limited to just what was on reserve? I argued with faculty that if students were to really learn, they needed to go beyond the reserve system. A few were convinced! I guess I was interested in information literacy even then" (National Forum on Information Literacy, http:// www.infolit.org/star_3.html).

Simmons received his bachelor's degree in secondary education and Spanish in 1960 and began teaching at Lakeshore High School in Belle Glades, Florida, that same year. He left Florida the following year to become a Spanish instructor at his former high school in Mobile and eventually enrolled in Spring Hill College again to satisfy a desire to learn the Russian language. It was a desire that would lead Simmons to pursue a master of arts degree in teaching Slavic language and literature (Russian) from Indiana University, which he earned in 1965. After spending a summer attending the Russian Language Institute in the Soviet Union, he launched a career in higher education at St. Louis Community College in St. Louis, Missouri, and was quickly promoted to chair of the foreign language department, while at the same time teaching Russian and Spanish at a local high school.

Simmons realized a passion for certification of instructional programs in 1967 while serving on his first Middle States Commission on Higher Education (MSCHE) site visit at State University of New York at Farmingdale. It was to have a profound impact on young Simmons, who would serve on a second visit held at Delaware Technical and Community College the following year, after which he relocated to an area near the MSCHE headquarters, where he landed an associate dean of instruction position at Northampton Community College in Pennsylvania in 1969.

His career took him to Washington, D.C., in 1972, when he accepted a prestigious American Council on Education (ACE) Fellowship at their main office. During his year there, Simmons published a monograph and conducted a study that examined the political influence of Washington-based higher education organizations on federal public policy. Following his fellowship year at ACE, he returned to his position at Northampton Community College and enrolled in the doctoral program in design and management of postsecondary education at Florida State University. Moving within close proximity to MSCHE in Newark, New Jersey, finally paid off for Simmons in 1975, when he became its associate director. That same year, he completed his doctoral studies, earning a Ph.D.

Dr. Simmons worked at MSCHE until 1987, when he went on a year-long sabbatical to Arizona State University, also conducting research with colleagues from Temple University in Pennsylvania at that time. When he returned to MSCHE in 1988, he became the first and, to date, the only African American male to serve as the executive director of the organization. He coauthored a book that examined diversity within MSCHE, which would be the impetus for the commission's eventual clarification of the use of diversity in MSCHE accreditation standards, the measurement by which all institutions would be assessed. The standards were approved and adopted by member institutions, making diversity an integral part of each MSCHE criterion. Because he was a staunch advocate for libraries and information literacy, both became essential elements of the accreditation process under Dr. Simmons's leadership.

Simmons remained executive director of MSCHE until 1995 when he returned to Arizona State University as department chair and a tenured faculty member. It was around this time that he began consulting with various higher education institutions, including the University of the Virgin Islands, and later Sojourner–Douglass College and Morgan State University, both in Baltimore, Maryland. Named professor emeritus by the Arizona Board of Regents in 2000, Simmons began what some consider the final chapter in his long and illustrious career in higher education, taking a full-time position as professor and chairperson of the Department of Advanced Studies, Leadership and Policy in the School of Education and Urban Studies at Morgan State University. While at Morgan, he assisted with the development of the research doctorate and master's programs in higher education. He also chaired the university's self-study assessment, which helped the institution gain reaccreditation in 2008.

Simmons served as a member of the Board of Educational Affairs Advisory Council of the American Psychological Association and as a member and past chairman of the Accreditation Commission for Acupuncture and Oriental Medicine. Simmons completed an appointment as an Educational Testing Service Historically Black College and University (HBCU) research scholar for 2003–2004, with particular responsibility for studying the contributions of HBCUs to American higher education. He also served as a member of the Commission on Accreditation of the Council on Chiropractic Education. Among his awards and recognitions are honorary degrees from Kings College and Sojourner–Douglass College.

Simmons' areas of interest have primarily been information literacy, diversity and multiculturalism,

accreditation, assessment, and quality assurance. He continued to write and speak on many of these topics into the twentieth century, publishing articles such as "Is It Time for a New Look at Academic Organization in Community Colleges?" (with R. C. Richardson, *Community College Review*, 1989); "External Agents Fostering Multiculturalism" (ed. Leonard A. Valverde and Louis A. Castenell Jr., in *The Multicultural Campus: Strategies for Transforming Higher Education*, 1990); "Information Literacy and Accreditation: A Middle States Association Perspective" (ed. D. W. Famer and Terrence F. Mech, in *Information Literacy: Developing Students as Independent Learners*, 1992); "The Concern for Information Literacy: A Major Challenge for Accreditation" (ed. Edward Garter, in *The Challenge and Practice of Academic Accreditation*, 1994); and "Librarian As Teacher: A Personal Review" (ed. Alice Bahr, in *Future Teaching Roles for Academic Librarians*, 2002).

FURTHER READING

Mendoza, C. M. *Dr. Howard L. Simmons: An Intellectual Biography of the First Black Executive Director of the Middle States Regional Accrediting Body* (unpublished doctoral dissertation, Morgan State University, Baltimore, 2009).

Murphy, J. B., S. R. Blanshei, J. F. Guyot, H. L. Simmons, J. Segall, R. H. Chambers III, and J. Sleeper. "The Progress of Affirmative Action: Accreditation and Diversity, the Accreditation of Baruch College by the Middle States Association." *Minerva Journal*, 30 (1992): 4.

Simmons, H. L., L. W. Bender, and C. L. Myers. *Involvement and Empowerment of Minorities and Women in the Accrediting Process: Report of a National Study* (1986).

ADRIEL A. HILTON

Simmons, Joseph. *See* Reverend Run.

Simmons, Philip (9 June 1912–22 June 2009), master blacksmith, was born in Wando on South Carolina's Daniel Island, the eldest of six children. Little is known about his parents, whose relationship ended when he was young. His mother, Rose Simmons, unable to solely support her family, relocated to nearby Charleston, where she was employed as a domestic worker. The Simmons children were reared by their maternal grandparents, William and Sarah Simmons. At age eight the future artisan departed for Charleston by ferry, leaving behind his birthplace, an agricultural and fishing community comprised mostly of Afro-Caribbean descendants.

In downtown Charleston, Simmons, who proudly identified himself as a Geechee (Sea Islander), resided with his mother. Working odd jobs to earn additional family income, Simmons also spent a number of summers back on Daniel Island, where he performed familiar tasks like farming and fishing. Just as his grandparents and great-grandparents (who were former slaves) had profoundly influenced his values and strong work ethic, his time in Charleston would indelibly impact his career path.

On walks to school Simmons admired Charleston's beautiful wrought iron gates and fences, some of the American South's finest examples. As he explored other streets Simmons eventually discovered the blacksmith shop of Peter Simmons (no relation) on Calhoun Street near the waterfront. Fascinated by the elder Simmons's skills and desiring to learn the trade, he eagerly became an apprentice at around age thirteen. Five years later Simmons was a very capable blacksmith, striking out on his own in the early 1930s.

In 1936 Simmons married Erthly Porchie, with whom he fathered three children. Following the unexpected death of his wife, two sisters and a trusted friend helped him raise the children. Simmons never remarried.

Early in his career Simmons forged functional items, including horseshoes and fireplace pokers, for which there remained a steady demand. Around 1938 he began creating ornamental ironwork. His first important client, the businessman Jack Krawcheck, had him fashion an iron gate for his King Street clothing store. Simmons used scraps, due to World War II iron shortages, to craft what would be the first of more than thirty commissions by the Krawcheck family.

For a short while in the late 1940s Simmons sought to supplement his income by dabbling in various ventures that all ended in financial failure. His ultimate decision to earn his living exclusively as a blacksmith was a wise one. By 1950 Simmons was the only blacksmith listed in Charleston's *City Directory*. His reputation would become widely known, and his career spanned seventy-seven years.

Some of Charleston's most prominent residences and institutions are adorned with Simmons's embellished gates, fences, window grills, and balconies, and entire streets bear the signature of his distinguished, self-expressive work. The "snake" gate at the Thomas Gadsden House, 329 East Bay Street, is generally regarded as Simmons's masterpiece. Initial attempts to craft a lifelike snake motif were futile, but Simmons's persistence rendered the desired effect. His biographer John Michael Vlach declared, "Philip made here a distinct and unique contribution with this piece, which initiated a new chapter in the saga of Charleston blacksmithing" (54).

Simmons's creations have been acquired by buyers from as far away as France and China, and are contained within the collections of the Smithsonian Institution, the National Museum of American History, and the National Museum of African American History and Culture in Washington, DC; the Museum of International Folk Art in Santa Fe, New Mexico; the Atlanta History Center; and the South Carolina State Museum in Columbia, South Carolina. Simmons was awarded the prestigious National Heritage Fellowship by the National Endowment for the Arts in 1982, and inducted into the South Carolina Hall of Fame in 1994. His other awards included the Order of the Palmetto (1998), the Elizabeth O'Neill Verner Governor's Award for "Lifetime Achievement in the Arts" (2001), and an Honorary Doctorate of Fine Arts (2006) from the historically black South Carolina State University.

Active in the St. John's Reformed Episcopal Church as well as the Boy Scouts and YMCA, Simmons would become a positive paternal figure to a number of boys, and was frequently viewed as a mentor and trusted advisor within his community. Under his tutelage, several young men learned the art of blacksmithing.

Simmons died in his sleep at the age of ninety-seven in an assisted living facility, where he had moved in 2008 due to health issues. In August 2010 his Blake Street residence and shop, frequented by thousands of tourists during his long career, opened as a museum following extensive renovations by the Philip Simmons Foundation with support from the city of Charleston.

FURTHER READING

Behre, Robert. "Once-Endangered Home, Shop of Legendary Blacksmith Now a Museum," *Post and Courier* (Charleston), 16 Aug. 2010.

Hunt, Stephanie. "A Tribute to Philip Simmons," *Charleston Magazine*, June 2009.

Vlach, John Michael. *Charleston Blacksmith: The Work of Philip Simmons* (1981).

Wilson, Charles Reagan, and William Ferris, eds. *The Encyclopedia of Southern Culture* (1989).

Obituary: *Post and Courier* (Charleston), 23 June 2009.

GREG FREEMAN

Simmons, Robert W., Sr. (1822–1892), civic leader, politician, and barber, was born in Fredericksburg, Virginia. He claimed, in an autobiographical sketch published shortly before his death, to be the son of Streshley Simmons, a black veteran of the War of 1812, and Rosetta Waring (*Historical Hand*, 33). A tradition among Robert's descendants, however, held that his actual father was "a master" (white plantation owner). Certainly Simmons's facial features appeared mulatto, and he is listed as such in three federal censuses. No documentation is known for the earliest period of Simmons's life. However, it is known that in April 1841 he immigrated to Parkersburg, (West) Virginia, on the Ohio River and successfully established himself as a barber, which would remain his lifelong vocation. On 19 January 1843, he married Susan King. By 1858, the couple had become parents of nine children.

Simmons's rise to local, state, and regional prominence began on 6 January 1862, when he and six other black Parkersburg men met to consider the need to educate the town's black youth. The men doubtless were encouraged in this bold enterprise by the atmosphere of political and social change, sparked by the Civil War, that had begun to transform life in western Virginia—which would become the state of West Virginia in 1863. Under the name of the Colored School Board of Parkersburg, Virginia, which Simmons served as secretary, the seven formed a "day school" for black children. As the monthly tuition of one dollar was optional, it was essentially free to all who wished to attend. The first challenge facing the Colored School Board was finding a building to house the planned school. To meet this need, oral tradition states that Simmons traveled to traveled to Washington where he gained an interview with Abraham Lincoln. The president allowed the board the use of one of the U.S. Army's Parkersburg barracks, "a large dilapidated frame building" on the outskirts of town (*Historical Hand*, 230).

The establishment of the school led to a sudden burst of cultural activity, planned and carried out by African Americans for African Americans, which flew into the face of the entrenched Southern tradition of restricting educational opportunities for black Americans. Thus, as the new school's initial enrollment of forty students grew rapidly, the board faced "violent opposition" from some members of the white community (*Historical Hand*, 230). By forming the new school, Simmons and his friends were only responding to a very real need.

Wood County's black population exploded in the 1860s, jumping from 255 (79 free and 176 enslaved) in 1860 to 713 ten years later. With this growth came more urgent needs of cultural, political, and moral leadership. African Americans had to confront these needs if they were to adapt to the new world and the opportunities that the Civil War had opened to them. Simmons stepped forward to fill this void.

The fledgling school, financed in large part by Simmons and his cohorts, managed to survive until it came under the protection of West Virginia's public school system in 1866. Parkersburg's "Colored School" stands as a milestone in American history as well as in Simmons's career, for it is credited as the first institution of learning south of the Mason-Dixon Line and it was operated by blacks for blacks and only the second such school in the United States, after Cincinnati's Gaines High School ("Parkersburg's Colored Schools," *Daily State Journal* [Parkersburg, W. VA], 26 Apr. 1888). In addition to promoting education, Simmons also became superintendent of a Sabbath school for Parkersburg's black children in 1863, the first of its kind in West Virginia.

The work of Simmons and other black civic leaders came to an astonishing fruition several decades later. By the 1880s, Parkersburg's African American community had created a refined and cohesive cultural world, the boundaries of which were defined by church, school, and fraternal lodge. Its copying of white Victorian society's manners and mores was exemplified by the existence of literary societies and the holding of "coming out" parties for adolescent girls. Later, the early and mid-twentieth century would witness a high percentage of college enrollment for Parkersburg's black youth.

Simmons also served the town's black community by relentlessly fighting for black suffrage. The adoption of the Constitution's Fifteenth Amendment was, as a local newspaper remarked, "the crowning glory of his life" (*Daily Times*, 31 Mar. 1870). Simmons's importance in this achievement was demonstrated when West Virginia's Senator, Arthur I. Boreman, sent him a special telegram on 30 March 1870 from the national capital announcing passage of the bill. Simmons's importance on the state's political scene, based upon his organizing the black vote, was illustrated by the marks of distinction accorded him and by the positions to which he was elected. He became a member of West Virginia's first Republican convention, was appointed as a delegate to two Republican national conventions, was appointed U.S. consul to Haiti by President Grant (declined), assisted in the unveiling of the Freedman's Monument in Lincoln Park, Washington, D.C., was elected chair of the State Central (Colored) Committee, and served as a delegate to West Virginia's first black convention.

Toward the end of his life, Simmons added yet another facet to his career by working as a journalist under the pen name of "Rombert." His articles, written with style and a consummate command of the language, covered such diverse local topics as economic development, cultural activities, and history. Simmons came to embody one of West Virginia's rarest political figures: he was a successful black leader in the violent, prejudice-charged, postbellum period, and this role demanded the highest skills of anyone who would aspire to it. He met these challenges with courage and grace, and he partially bridged the gap between the races by earning, as his obituary, published in one of Parkersburg's leading newspapers, stated, "the respect of not only his own people but of all who know him" (*Parkersburg Weekly Sentinel*, 23 Jan. 1892). His importance in history was recognized anew in 1999 when the federal government named Parkersburg's new main post office "Simmons Station" in his honor.

FURTHER READING

Researchers of Robert W. Simmons Sr. are dependent chiefly on public records and newspaper accounts, as a 1909 flood destroyed his personal papers. An interview taped in 1983 of his great-granddaughter provides some valuable family information. It and the only known likeness of Simmons, an 1860s tintype, are preserved in Parkersburg's Blennerhassett Museum.

Historical Hand-Atlas ... and Histories of Wood and Pleasants Counties, West Virginia (1882).

A History of Education in West Virginia (1904).

Matheny, Herman E. *Wood County, West Virginia, in Civil War Times With an Account of the Guerrilla Warfare in the Little Kanawha Valley* (1987)

Obituary: Parkersburg Weekly Sentinel, 23 Jan. 1892.

RAY SWICK

Simmons, Roscoe Conkling Murray (20 June 1878–27 Apr. 1951), orator, politician, and writer, was born in Greenview, Mississippi, the son of Emory Simmons, a principal of a black school in Hollandale, Mississippi, and Willie Murray. He grew up in Aberdeen, Mississippi, and worked for a time as Ohio senator Mark Hanna's office boy. In 1895 he entered Tuskegee Institute in Alabama, studying under BOOKER T. WASHINGTON, who had married Simmons's aunt, MARGARET MURRAY WASHINGTON. After graduating in 1899, he took a job as a reporter for the *Pensacola Daily News* and a year later moved to the Washington, D.C., *Record*, where he began his political involvement. Simmons worked for a time as a teacher in Holly Springs, Mississippi, and once tried selling cigars, but his ambitions lay in journalism and politics. When his uncle offered him a teaching position at Tuskegee Institute, Simmons declined, replying, "I have been called to teach, but the rostrum and the public hall will be my classroom" (*Chicago Defender*, 5 May 1951).

Simmons continued to work in journalism as a reporter for the Mound Bayou, Mississippi, *Demonstrator* from 1902 to 1904 and, from 1904 to 1913, as editor and contributor to three New York publications: the *Age*, the *Colored American Magazine*, and the *National Review*. Simmons campaigned in New York for William Howard Taft's 1908 run for the Republican presidential nomination and in exchange received party funding for his *National Review*. In his political and journalistic activities during this period, Simmons received funding and direction from his uncle Booker and often acted as a promoter of Tuskegee. In 1912 Simmons established a national reputation as an orator while campaigning for Theodore Roosevelt among blacks in New York City and in the South. After hearing him speak, William Jennings Bryan reportedly predicted Simmons would become one of the world's greatest orators. Simmons developed a long-lasting alliance with the *Chicago Tribune* publisher Joseph Medill McCormick, who later became a senator from Illinois. In 1913, at the urging of Washington, Simmons left the *Age* to start his own newspaper, the *Sun*, in Memphis, Tennessee. The paper, which extolled the Tuskegee philosophy of self-help, folded after one year.

Shortly after the *Sun*'s demise, Simmons began working for ROBERT SENGSTACKE ABBOTT's *Chicago Defender* as a columnist and promoter. The relationship proved mutually beneficial. Simmons became one of the highest paid employees in black journalism, and the *Defender*'s circulation increased dramatically, becoming the first black-owned mass-circulation newspaper. Simmons toured the South, recruiting distribution agents and speaking to crowds that sometimes numbered in the thousands. He plugged the *Defender* while speaking on the events of the day. "We go forth," he told a Memphis audience during World War I, "to make the world safe for democracy. After that job is well done we will make the United States safe for the Negro" (*Chicago Defender*, 7 July 1917). Even whites, according to the 1 June 1918 *Defender*, thought Simmons's wartime speeches were "surcharged with loyalty and patriotism, delivered by a master of all the arts and graces of the genuine orator."

Simmons continued with the *Defender* until 1925, when he was implicated with three others in a scheme to expropriate funds. Abbott did not bring formal charges and a few years later rehired Simmons, who was released again in the mid-1930s, when the Depression forced staff reductions. Simmons then parlayed his friendship with the McCormick family into a job as feature writer and columnist for the daily *Chicago Tribune*. His column, "The Untold Story," highlighted cooperation between blacks and whites.

Simmons made his greatest mark as a political orator on behalf of conservative Republican candidates. He visited Presidents Theodore Roosevelt, Warren Harding, and Herbert Hoover in the White House and became a fixture at Republican National Conventions, where he delivered speeches from the podium. He acted as chairman of the party's Colored Speakers' Bureau in 1920, 1924, and 1928; seconded the nomination of Hoover in 1932; and was a delegate to the Republican National Convention several times. While promoting the Republican presidential nominee Alf Landon in 1936, he declared, "My countrymen, on one side are *Landon* and *Liberty*; on the other side are *Roosevelt* and *Ruin*" (Boulware, 132).

Trezzvant W. Anderson, writing for the *Pittsburgh Courier*, 5 May 1951, called Simmons a "silver-tongued orator who wove a spell of beauty and delight." A professor of speech called his speaking style "impressive ... without being pretentious" (Boulware, 132). Yet Simmons's oratorical talents were not enough to win him a political office. In 1930 he lost his bid to take the Republican nomination for U.S. congressman from Chicago's incumbent, Representative OSCAR S. DE PRIEST, the only black member of Congress. Two years later Simmons lost a race for the state senate.

Simmons's racial philosophy of "undefeated *patience*" (Boulware, 131) tied him to the earlier period when Washington was influential and left him out of touch with an increasingly militant and Democratic black majority. As most black voters joined Franklin D. Roosevelt's New Deal coalition, Simmons remained loyal to the Republicans until his death and became irrelevant to the black struggle for equality. During his prime, however, he had been a major spokesman for African Americans to leading Republicans, a key figure in the development of African American journalism, and a spellbinding orator.

Simmons married twice. With his first wife, whose name is not known, he had one child. With his second wife, Althea, a schoolteacher, he had two children. He died in Chicago.

FURTHER READING

Boulware, Marcus H. "Roscoe Conkling Simmons: The Golden Voiced Politico," *Negro History Bulletin* 29 (Mar. 1966).

Ottley, Roi. *The Lonely Warrior: The Life and Times of Robert S. Abbott* (1955).

Obituaries: *New York Times*, 29 Apr. 1951; *Baltimore Afro-American*, *Chicago Defender*, and *Pittsburgh Courier*, 5 May 1951.

This entry is taken from the *American National Biography* and is published here with the permission of the American Council of Learned Societies.

WILLIAM JORDAN

Simmons, Russell (4 Oct. 1957–), entrepreneur, music executive, and promoter, was born in Queens, New York, to Daniel and Evelyn Simmons, both graduates of Howard University in Washington, D.C. Simmons's father was a politically active schoolteacher who worked for the New York Board of Education; his mother was an artist and recreation director for the New York City Department of Parks. Simmons had two brothers; his older brother, Danny, became an artist, while his younger brother, Joey, became the rap artist popularly known as "Run" (Reverend Run) of the music group Run-D.M.C. Simmons and his brothers grew up in the middle-class Queens neighborhood of Hollis, attending integrated schools in the politically charged 1960s, and were influenced by their father's social activism, protesting racial discrimination, and promoting black empowerment. Simmons's mother encouraged him to embrace both the arts and entrepreneurship, but despite his sound upbringing and his parents' strong family values, Simmons was drawn as an adolescent to the thriving New York City drug culture. His brother Danny was a heroin user; Simmons himself was caught up in the lucrative business of selling of marijuana locally, and he became involved for a time in a minor street gang called the Seven Immortals.

Simmons was lucky—by the time he enrolled at City College of New York City in Harlem in 1975, many of his friends had been killed or sent to prison. Hip-hop was just emerging in the underground New York music scene, and Simmons quickly became both a fan and a promoter of the music. Despite being close to completing a degree in sociology, he left college in 1979 to become a full-time music promoter. That year he and fellow promoter Rudy Toppin launched Rush Productions. In the late 1970s there were no rap records, so Rush Productions organized shows and parties, charging admission to live performances by rap artists. Though only in his early twenties, Simmons began managing the rapper Curtis Walker, also known as Kurtis Blow, and his brother Joey's group, Run-D.M.C., and producing their recordings. In 1985 Simmons and Rick Rubin formed Def Jam Recordings, a label that went on to sign several notable hip-hop and rap icons, including Run-D.M.C., LL Cool J, Public Enemy, and the Beastie Boys. Simmons was attracted to hip-hop because "hip-hop is an attitude, one that can be nonverbal as well as eloquent. It communicates aspiration and frustration, community and aggression, creativity and street reality, style and substance" (Simmons, 5). In the late 1980s Simmons toured the world with Run-D.M.C., whose popularity had spread internationally, bringing in more than a million record sales.

Simmons also developed an interest in film and television, and teamed up with the black producer George Jackson to produce *Krush Groove* (1985), a fictional account drawn partly on Simmons's rise in the hip-hop industry, and *Tougher Than Leather* (1988), starring Run-D.M.C. as themselves in a series of gang-related adventures. *Def Comedy Jam*, which Simmons coproduced with Stan Lathan, was a highly successful television comedy show that aired on HBO from 1991 to 1998, and the producers subsequently formed the Simmons Lathan Media Group. Simmons produced more films in the late 1990s, including *The Addiction* (1995), a vampire film directed by Abel Ferrara, the comedy *The Nutty Professor* (1996), starring EDDIE MURPHY, and *Gridlock'd* (1997), a comedy crime drama starring the rapper TUPAC SHAKUR.

In spite of Simmons's forays into film, the early 1990s were rocky for Def Jam. The company was having financial and marketing difficulties with its joint venture partner, Sony, who had signed on as the company's distributor and was positioning itself to take over Def Jam. In 1995 Simmons was able to close a deal with PolyGram, which became a major equity owner in Def Jam, and he used the influx of cash to sever ties with Sony. By the time Simmons sold off his stake in Def Jam in 1998 for $130 million, the company was an industry leader and had secured many of hip-hop's royalty, including JAY Z, DMX, Foxy Brown, and Warren G.

Realizing the enormous cross-marketing potential of hip-hop, Simmons launched a number of business initiatives. In 1991 he founded Phat Fashions, which began as a five-hundred-thousand-dollar boutique selling urban clothing and accessories. Simmons teamed up with the fashion expert Mark Beguda to create Phat Farm, a men's clothing line in 1992. In 1993 Simmons met Kimora Lee at a fashion show, while he was developing Phat Fashions. Lee was a seventeen-year-old fashion model who had worked for most of the high-profile fashion designers and had developed an insider's knowledge of the industry. Simmons put Lee in charge of launching Baby Phat, a separate women's and children's clothing line under Phat Fashions, whose growth quickly outstripped Phat Farm and was a testament to her fashion and marketing prowess. By 2002 Phat Fashions had earned $263 million, and Simmons sold the company in early 2003 for $140 million to Kellwood Corporation, though he and Lee retained their management responsibilities.

As an entrepreneur, Simmons was always seeking new markets for hip-hop's urban culture. One of his most influential mentors was the real estate mogul Donald Trump, under whose guidance he was able to build the prominence of the Def brand and use it to market his new ventures. Simmons embarked on a steady stream of business ventures, including an advertising agency, dRush (1999); an Internet company, 360 Hip Hop (2000); Russell Simmons signature i90 cell phones with Motorola (2002); Rush and Baby Phat prepaid VISA cards (2003); and DefCon3 energy soda (2003). The Simmons Lathan Media Group expanded into Broadway shows, launched *OneWorld* magazine, and created *Def Poetry Jam*, a live poetry and music television show.

In his early forties, Simmons found himself making the transition to becoming a family man, a philanthropist, and a social advocate. Simmons married Lee in 1998, and the couple had two daughters. Although they divorced in 2006, their business relationship continued. He made several fundamental changes in his lifestyle; he quit smoking and drinking, became a vegetarian, and started practicing yoga. Simmons's spiritual awareness grew, and in 2007 he published a self-help book entitled *Do You!: 12 Laws to Access the Power in You to Achieve Happiness and Success.*

In 1995 he cofounded the Rush Philanthropic Arts Foundation with his brothers, and used his wealth and celebrity to develop underrepresented and minority artists and to provide opportunities in the arts for disadvantaged urban youth. Simmons knew firsthand how destructive drugs were in the black community, and thus he became politically active, collaborating with Democratic politicians to reform the harsh Rockefeller drug laws, enacted in 1973 when Nelson Rockefeller was governor. The National Urban League appointed Simmons as a trustee in 2002, and he started a national literacy program for black youth. Simmons and the Simmons Jewelry Company courted controversy in 2006 when it emerged that the company had taken an industry-paid trip to Africa at the same time as the release of the film *Blood Diamond.* In response, Simmons asserted that the diamond trade "contributes to the overall self-empowerment of African people and communities" (*New York Times*, 18 Oct. 2006).

Simmons is widely regarded as the hip-hop pioneer and magnate responsible for introducing hip-hop and urban culture into mainstream America. According to Simmons, "Hip-hop has, in fact, changed the world. It has taken something from the American ghetto and made it global. It has become the creative touchstone for edgy, progressive and aggressive youth culture around the world. That's why my business is bigger than it's ever been. And, I believe, we're far from through" (Simmons, 9).

FURTHER READING
Simmons, Russell. *Life and Def* (2001).
Aspan, Maria. "A Hip-Hop Mogul Is the Diamond's New Best Friend," *New York Times*, 18 Oct. 2006.
George, Nelson. *The Death of Rhythm and Blues* (1988)
George, Nelson. *Hip Hop America* (2003).
Gueraseva, Stacy. *Def Jam, Inc.: Russell Simmons, Rick Rubin, and the Extraordinary Story of the World's Most Influential Hip-Hop Label* (2005).
Ogg, Alex. *The Men Behind Def Jam: The Radical Rise of Russell Simmons and Rick Rubin* (2002).

AYESHA KANJI

Simmons, Ruth J. (3 July 1945–), educator and university president, was born Ruth Jean Stubblefield in Grapeland, Texas, the youngest of twelve children of Isaac Stubblefield and Fannie, maiden name unknown. Her parents were cotton sharecroppers who moved the family to Houston, Texas, when Ruth was seven years old. In Houston, Isaac worked in a factory and served as minister of Mount Hermon Missionary Baptist Church while Fannie worked as a domestic for white families. As a child Simmons learned from her family that though they were poor in material possessions, they were rich in spirit and potential.

Simmons's mother had a tremendous influence on her development. By watching her mother iron clothes and scrub floors for wealthy whites, she said, "I was given the privilege to observe a remarkable woman take pride in her work and carry herself with extraordinary dignity, and with extraordinary kindness" (Simmons, 23). When asked what made her capable of becoming such an important and groundbreaking leader in education, she credited her mother's example. When Ruth Simmons was fifteen her mother died, and Vernell Lillie, a drama instructor at Phillis Wheatley High School, became one of a series of teachers who helped fill the void left by the loss. Lillie became a role model for Simmons, inspired her to excel academically, and encouraged her to apply for a scholarship at Dillard University, where she could find other nurturing teachers and an outlet for her theatrical talent.

With each success Simmons gained confidence and began to realize that she could achieve anything. While at Dillard, Simmons spent a summer studying at the Universidad Internacional in Saltillo, Mexico, and during her junior year participated in a student-exchange program with Wellesley College in Massachusetts. There she discovered that she could compete with students from more privileged backgrounds. She also had her first experience with the black consciousness movement of the 1960s and, because of it, felt compelled to do her part to dismantle white supremacy in all its forms. In 1967 Simmons received her B.A. in French, summa cum laude, and went on to study French in Lyon, France, on a Fulbright Fellowship. When she returned in 1968, she married Norbert Simmons, a lawyer, with whom she would have two children; the couple divorced in 1989. She briefly worked as an interpreter at the U.S. Department of State in Washington, D.C., and then entered Harvard University, where she earned an M.A. and, in 1973, a Ph.D. in Romance languages and literature. Her

Ruth J. Simmons, the president of Brown University addresses new students, 4 September 2001. (AP Images.)

first faculty appointment was as assistant professor of French at the University of New Orleans, where she also entered academic administration when she was appointed associate dean of the College of Liberal Arts in 1975.

Simmons became visiting associate professor of Pan-African studies at the University of Southern California, Los Angeles in 1978 and was quickly promoted to assistant and then to associate dean before being appointed director of Butler College at Princeton University in New Jersey in 1983. Her research on French-speaking African and Caribbean nations focused on writers such as Aime Cesaire and David Diop and led to the publication of *Haiti: A Study of the Educational System and Guide to U.S. Placement* (1985). Even as she made professional and scholarly strides, Simmons maintains that her priority during these years was rearing her two children, Khari and Maya. After seven years at Princeton, Simmons traveled to Spelman College in Atlanta, Georgia, where she served as provost for two years; she then returned to Princeton to become its vice provost.

During her tenure at Princeton she was asked by the university to prepare a study of racial problems on campus that came to be known as the "Simmons Report"; it became a model for other institutions. As the acting director of the Afro-American studies program in 1985, she was instrumental in recruiting the author TONI MORRISON and the renowned philosopher CORNEL WEST to the faculty. In 1995 Simmons assumed the presidency of the highly prestigious Smith College in Northampton, Massachusetts, the largest women's college in the United States. She was Smith's first African American president. There she established the nation's first engineering program at a women's college, founded a journal, *Meridians*, focusing on the careers of minority women, and nearly doubled the college's endowment.

In November 2000 Simmons made history again by being named president of Brown University. When she arrived on campus, she said: "I'm not a social worker. I'm here to lead a great university into even greater academic achievement" (*Providence Journal-Bulletin*, 18 July 2001). She engaged such difficult issues as a controversy over the rights and responsibilities of free speech in an academic environment, a campaign to unionize graduate teaching assistants (which she opposed), raising faculty salaries, and establishing need-blind admissions. While her decisions did not always please everyone, her thoughtful and amiable manner quickly endeared her to every segment of the university. In September 2011, Simmons informed the Brown community of her intention to step down as president at the end of the academic year, 2011–2012. She planned to return to teaching at Brown as professor of comparative literature and Africana studies.

As her star rose with each achievement, Simmons received greater attention for being the first African American woman to reach new heights. She accepted her role as a leader in the fight for social justice for women and minorities with grace and aplomb. In the realm of civic activities, Simmons often left the ivory tower to deliver motivational speeches to students in inner cities and rural areas. She used her position on such corporate boards as Pfizer Inc. and the Goldman Sachs Group to champion her belief that true corporate responsibility does not end with producing profits for the shareholders, but extends to helping produce a safe and just world for children, the holders of the future. Her philosophy is that ethics and civility are learned skills that sustain a civilization. In Rhode Island she became a strong advocate for educational programs that target women, because, as she said, "when you educate women, you educate families" (Davis). Simmons's life and accomplishments have themselves become the best example of the beliefs she espouses to others. As such, she has established a trajectory that points ever upward toward greater service.

FURTHER READING
Simmons, Ruth. "My Mother's Daughter: Lessons I Learned in Civility and Authenticity," *Texas Journal of Ideas, History and Culture* 20, no. 2 (Spring/Summer, 1998).
Passi-Klaus, Susan. "From Inner City Roots to Ivy League President: Ruth Simmons' Story," *Sharing Gods Gifts: Black College Fund* n.d. (8 July 2003).

JOHNNETTA B. COLE

Simmons, William James (26 June 1849–30 Oct. 1890), Baptist leader, educator, and race advocate, was born in Charleston, South Carolina, the son of enslaved parents, Edward Simmons and Esther (maiden name unknown). During his youth, Simmons's mother escaped slavery with him and two of his siblings, relocating to Philadelphia, Pennsylvania. Simmons's uncle, Alexander Tardieu (or Tardiff), a shoemaker, became a father to the children and a protector and provider for the fugitive slave family. He moved them among the cities of Philadelphia, Roxbury, Massachusetts, and Chester, Pennsylvania, constantly eluding persistent "slave catchers," before permanently taking residence in Bordentown, New Jersey. While Simmons never received formal elementary or secondary school education, his uncle made a point of teaching the children to read and write. As a youth Simmons served as an assistant to a white dentist in Bordentown. At the age of fifteen he joined the Union army, participating in a number of major battles in Virginia and finding himself at Appomattox in 1865. After the war, Simmons once again worked briefly as a dental assistant. He converted and affiliated with the white Baptist Church in Bordentown in 1867, announced his call to the ministry, and ventured to college with the financial support of church friends.

Simmons attended Madison (later Colgate) University in 1868. Leaving Rochester University in New York after a brief stay because of eye trouble, Simmons enrolled at Howard University in Washington, D.C., in 1871 and earned B.A. and M.A. degrees, in 1873 and 1881, respectively.

To secure additional requisite funds for living expenses while pursuing his education, Simmons taught school in Washington, D.C., serving for a time as principal of Hillsdale Public School. In August 1874 he married Josephine A. Silence of Washington, a union that produced seven children.

For five years the family lived in Florida, where Simmons, after attempting a living from investments in lands and orange farming, returned to teaching, becoming principal of Howard Academy. He also pastored a church and became deputy county clerk and county commissioner. After returning to Washington for several years of teaching, the young Baptist relocated once again in 1879, this time to Lexington, Kentucky, to pastor the First African Baptist Church. In 1880 the fledgling Normal and Theological Institution chose Simmons as its president, and under his leadership it attained university status in 1884. The name of the institution was changed to State University of Louisville, Kentucky, and in 1918 was changed once again to Simmons University. The school offered the only college education for blacks in the state, after the Kentucky legislature outlawed integrated education at Berea College in 1905, and was the only African American institution of higher learning offering undergraduate, law, and medical degrees. Prizing vocational training as well as classical education, Simmons established the Eckstein Norton Institute in Cane Spring, Kentucky, in 1890.

Simmons played major roles in a number of black Baptist conventions, including the Baptist Foreign Mission Convention, established in 1880 to pursue African missions. His role in the formation and presidency of the American National Baptist Convention (ANBC) in 1886 laid the foundation for the emergence in 1895 of the enduring National Baptist Convention, which resulted from a merger of the ANBC and two other groups. Appointed missionary to the South by the predominantly white, northern-based American Baptist Home Mission Society in 1887, Simmons organized churches and advocated black Baptist unity.

Simmons participated in a number of black state conventions and assemblies of race leaders dealing with critical issues facing African Americans, and he remained vigorously opposed to and outspoken about Jim Crow segregation and all forms of racial discrimination, especially as exercised by state and local governments. Though essentially a Republican he called for blacks to place their interests above any particular political party. In the 1880s he suggested that the state governments, not the federal government, were increasingly the places to work for racial progress.

While many Baptist leaders strongly opposed the organization of women's conventions, Simmons heartily encouraged and supported such groups, opening the organizing session of Kentucky women that led eventually to the establishment of the Baptist Women's Educational Convention of Kentucky. In 1882 the Baptist leader founded the *American Baptist* newspaper, in which he as editor called for racial and denominational unity. In addition Simmons established a publication, *Our Women and Children*, calling for racial progress, particularly for women and youth. Significantly, Simmons opened the pages of the magazine to an ecumenical array of women writers who published articles dealing with domestic life. Simmons achieved lasting fame for his *Men of Mark*, published in 1887, showcasing the triumphs of black males, most of whom had surmounted the horrors of childhood enslavement with the clear intention of banishing the increasingly academically respectable notion of black innate inferiority and of promoting a thirst for education among black youth. Interestingly, Simmons planned a sequel outlining the achievements of prominent women, but his premature death interrupted those plans. He died in Cane Spring.

With his contributions to denominational unity and missions, racial unity and progress, gender equity, journalism, and politics, Simmons, despite his relatively short life, emerged as one of the major American leaders of the nineteenth century.

FURTHER READING

Simmons, William J. *Men of Mark* (1887; repr. 1968).

Fitts, Leroy. *A History of Black Baptists* (1985).

Higginbotham, Evelyn Brooks. *Righteous Discontent: The Women's Movement in the Black Baptist Church, 1880–1920* (1993).

Pegues, Albert W. *Our Baptist Ministers and Schools* (1892).

Washington, James M. *Frustrated Fellowship: The Black Baptist Quest for Social Power* (1986).

Obituary: *Louisville Courier-Journal*, 31 Oct. and 3 Nov. 1890; *New York Age*, 8 Nov. 1890.

This entry is taken from the *American National Biography* and is published here with the permission of the American Council of Learned Societies.

SANDY DWAYNE MARTIN

Simms, Evelyn (18 Apr. 1932–20 July 2002), jazz singer, was born Evelyn Lucille Simms in Odum, Georgia, the daughter of William Simms and Rosalie Stanton. Simms was the youngest of nine children and migrated north with her father when she was only six months old because his employer, the Central of Georgia Railway, had gone into receivership and at this time white brotherhoods were seeking to displace black railroad workers all over the South through intimidation and violence. William Simms took his young daughter to his mother's home in South Philadelphia, Pennsylvania, and eventually brought his wife and the rest of his children north to settle in their own home on Latona Street. He obtained work as a machinist at the Philadelphia Navy Yard and remained there for the rest of his working life. Evelyn's mother worked as a maid at the Rittenhouse Hotel on and off while raising her large family.

Along with delivering the African American newspaper the *Philadelphia Independent*, Simms sang in the youth choir at Mount Hebron Baptist Church at Fifteenth and Wharton streets until she was in her late teens. While attending Bok Vocational High School for commercial art Simms went to a Tuesday night dance with a girlfriend when she was sixteen and sat in to sing with the Benny Fields Band at the Old Mercantile Hall. In the band were such soon-to-be-famous musicians as JOHN COLTRANE and Benny Golson in the reed section, Johnny Coles on trumpet, and Bill Doggett on piano. The bassist Jymie Merritt was in the audience and immediately asked her to come work with him in the Alex Cogwell Band, but Simms's mother said no because she was too young. Yet Simms was determined to make music her life and left Bok Vocational to pursue singing full-time. She soon went with Coatsville Harris, and then she met a musician who would become her lifelong friend, the organist SHIRLEY SCOTT.

In 1951, at the age of nineteen, Simms married Lonnie Shaw, who played baritone sax and flute with the LIONEL HAMPTON Band, Hank Crawford, Arnett Cobb, and Bobby Blue Bland. They were married until Shaw died in 1990, and they had five children.

In 1954 Simms went on tour with ERSKINE HAWKINS and stayed six months traveling around the country until pregnancy forced her to the sidelines. Throughout the 1950s Evelyn Simms stayed close to home to raise her big family while her husband toured the country. Playing with local powerhouse players like Al Grey, Buddy Tate, Don Patterson, Charlie Rice, Tommy Flanagan, RAY BRYANT, Barry Harris, and Beryl Booker in local clubs like Joe Pitt's Bar, the Showboat, Ridge Point, and the 421 Club, Simms became a local legend that everyone knew deserved wider recognition. Like many women in the 1950s and 1960s, Simms strongly felt that her career should always come after her family and her husband's musical career. With Shaw's frequent absences, Evelyn Simms assumed the role as head of her family, working consistently yet being there for her children. She reluctantly had to turn down jobs with CAT ANDERSON and Benny Goodman.

From 1960 to 1962 Simms worked with the drummer GEORGE EDWARD "BUTCH" BALLARD in a nightclub called the Underground at Broad and Spruce in downtown Philadelphia, which featured an up-and-coming young drummer-turned-comic named BILL COSBY. In 1962 she toured with DIZZY GILLESPIE and DICK GREGORY after Gillespie had heard Simms and the trumpeter LEE MORGAN when they opened for him three years before at the Tioga Theater. Simms told the jazz columnist Nels Nelson for the *Philadelphia Daily News*, "Lee came in that afternoon and just blew the top off the place, just wiped Diz out. Diz didn't forget Lee and he didn't forget me." Nelson called Simms "the undisputed main event of jazz singing in Philadelphia," and Simms spent the next two decades playing the main jazz clubs in town, making short tours to Canada with the drummer Mickey Roker, opening for artists like HARRY BELAFONTE and Dave Brubeck, and appearing at jazz festivals within driving distance of Philadelphia so that she could take care of her family. In April 1990 Simms's husband died of complications from AIDS, which he had contracted during his long history of heroin addiction. Simms nursed Lonnie Shaw for two years and later cared for her youngest son, Barry, who died in the same way.

In 1989 Simms released her one and only recording that she made as a leader. It was done live in the studio one night after she finished singing at the Borgia Café at 1:00 in the morning. It was called *On My Own*, and for it she won that year's Best Jazz Vocalist and Best Jazz Recording at the Philadelphia Music Awards. Later, in 2000, Simms was prominently featured on a double CD set called *Live at Ortliebs' JazzHaus*, the premier jazz club in Philadelphia and the heart of the Philadelphia jazz community. *JazzTimes* called her "a big-voiced, hearty vocalist," and jazz radio host Bob Perkins said that Simms was "America's greatest chanteuse." In 1990 Simms did her first tour overseas, traveling to South Africa with the organist Shirley Scott. They both insisted on playing before integrated audiences.

By 1998 Evelyn Simms was singing with the big band Philadelphia Legends of Jazz, but was fighting a long battle with asthma. She left the band in 2000 with many accolades for her mentorship of younger singers; one that was especially touching was given onstage by the singer Rachelle Ferrell when she was appearing at the Keswick Theater in concert. Simms was in the audience.

Evelyn Simms played every major venue in Philadelphia, including the Academy of Music and the Mann Music Center. She also was interviewed on camera for a PBS special on the history of Philadelphia jazz. Stylistically she drew on many sources such as BILLIE HOLIDAY, BETTY CARTER, and LOUIS ARMSTRONG, but she had a unique sound that drew listeners in and captivated them. Simms embodied the music of Philadelphia. The *New York Times* writer Bill Kent asked Simms what made Philadelphia a special town for jazz, and she said, "The music made this town ... and the music is still here. I say, let the music make this town again. I say, let's fix it up right. Let's run SUN RA for mayor. That's right, the man from Saturn himself. Just put him on the ticket. I'll be the first one to push the button."

FURTHER READING

Lloyd, Jack. "Legends Keeping Alive the Golden Age of Jazz," *Philadelphia Inquirer*, 31 Mar. 1995, 23.

Nelson, Nels. "It's a Powerhouse," *Philadelphia Daily News*, 18 Feb. 1994, 60.

Roberts, Kimberly C. "Evelyn Simms to Be Saluted by Peers," *Philadelphia Tribune*, 16 Jan. 2001.

SUZANNE CLOUD

Simms, Hilda (15 Apr. 1918–6 Feb. 1994), actor and performer, Hilda Moses was born in Minneapolis, Minnesota, to Emil, an engineer, and Lydia Marie (Webber) Moses, a homemaker. One of twelve children, as a child she predicted to her siblings that one day she would be on the stage.

After completing her early education at St. Margaret's Academy, she graduated from South High School in Minneapolis in 1938. She studied teaching and dramatics at the University of Minnesota, having earned a two-year teaching fellowship, but she left school due to lack of funds. In 1943 she graduated from Hampton Institute, Virginia, earning a BS. At Hampton, she made her acting debut as the character Cathy in a staging of the Emily Brontë novel *Wuthering Heights*.

In 1941, she married Williams Simms and took on the stage name Hilda Simms. Two years later she arrived in New York, where she pursued acting while juggling jobs as a painter's model, a writer, a dance teacher, and a secretary to the president of a film company. She performed on radio and became affiliated with the American Negro Theatre (ANT) and, in accordance with the bylaws of the troupe, she spent her first months working sound, props, and doing publicity. In June 1943, she made her first acting appearance in the ANT production of the Phoebe and Henry Ephron play *Three's a Family*.

Formed in the early 1940s by a committee that included the actor FREDERICK DOUGLASS O'NEAL, the playwright ABRAM HILL, and Austin Briggs-Hall, the ANT mounted productions of such plays as Hill's *On Striver's Row* in the basement of the 135th Street Library in Harlem. The goal of the ANT, conceived as a cooperative, was to maintain a place where black artists could hone their craft. In 1943 the group adapted a play about a white Pennsylvania mill family, written by a struggling young writer named Philip Yordan. The play was called *Anna Lucaskca*.

With a cast that included Simms, CANADA LEE, ROSETTA LeNOIRE, and O'Neal, *Anna Lucasta*, rewritten for a black cast, opened on 16 June 1944. The production received such critical praise that the cramped room, which held only 200 seats, filled to capacity with each performance. Five weeks after its opening, the entire production was moved to the Mansfield Theatre on Broadway, where it ran for more than 900 performances. *Anna Lucasta* was the first successful Broadway dramatic play with an all-black cast that did not deal with racial issues. Unfortunately, the unparalleled success of *Anna Lucasta* would negatively alter the course of the collectively organized ANT. In a sense, the group fell victim to its own success. As lawyers wrangled over who should profit from *Anna Lucasta*, the ANT succumbed to financial problems and actors left the troupe to promote their careers.

But the role of Anna made Simms a star. She accompanied the *Anna Lucasta* company as it toured Chicago in 1945 and London in 1946. She remained in Europe for several years where she studied at the University of Paris at the Sorbonne from 1950–1952, appeared in plays, and performed on radio and television. In Paris, she appeared on stage as the nightclub singer Julie Riccardo.

Simms's husband had greatly objected to his wife's onstage persona as the prostitute Anna Lucasta. Her popularity as a G.I. pin-up girl no doubt worsened matters, and the couple divorced.

While in Chicago in 1946, Simms performed the part of Juliet in the 1946 Harry Wagstaff Gribble production of Shakespeare's *Romeo & Juliet*, an adaptation that featured black Capulets and white Montagues. The part of Romeo was played by Italian American actor, Richard Angerolla. The couple wed in 1948 in Europe. The marriage ended in 1963.

For a time, Simms was one of black America's most popular entertainment figures. The *Chicago Defender* crowned her "Chicago's First Lady of the Stage." In 1951, she was honored for her work on behalf of the war effort, and in 1957 she was awarded a commendation from the Friends of the National Council of Negro Women. Her face graced the covers of fanzines, and her activities were detailed in organs of the African American press. It didn't hurt that Simms was slender, smart, and stunning, with large sultry eyes, luxurious hair, and fair skin. Indeed, at a time in the history of black America when a "high-toned" complexion was considered an asset, Simms seemed to have it all: striking features, a creamy hue, and flair. *Jet* magazine featured her on its cover in 1959, with an article titled, "Hilda Simms: Beauty, Brains, and Talent." Unfortunately, these attributes greatly limited her success in Hollywood pictures. Indeed, she was too fair of face, graceful, and cultured to be typecast in the standard roles afforded to African American female film actors. Beyond the infrequent cameos afforded to performers such as LENA HORNE or DOROTHY DANDRIDGE, postwar Hollywood had little use for a dignified and handsome black woman artist such as Simms.

In 1953 Simms returned from Europe to appear in the highly anticipated feature film *The* JOE LOUIS *Story*. Independently produced and financed by the former publicist and writer Stirling Siliphant and directed by Robert Gordon, the film presented a highly fictionalized biography of "the Brown Bomber," the African American boxing champ Joe Louis. In 1937 Louis became the youngest heavyweight champion in the history of professional boxing, and in 1953 he was still a national hero and popular figure. Simms was cast as Marva, Louis's wife.

In 1958 Simms was cast as Blanche in an off-Broadway, mixed-race version of the Tennessee Williams drama *A Streetcar Named Desire*. For reasons never clearly explained, Williams mysteriously closed down the production just weeks before its September opening. In 1959 Simms performed the one-woman show *An Evening with Hilda Simms*. In 1960 Simms appeared as the character Miss

Dewhurst in the short-lived Robert Rossen play, *The Cool World*, which featured ALICE CHILDRESS, JAMES EARL JONES, Raymond St. Jacque, and Billy Dee Williams. In 1961, she toured a one-woman show called *Love Letters of Famous Courtesans*. In 1963 she played the character Laura Wright Reed in the LANGSTON HUGHES play *Tambourines to Glory*, which included cast members Rosetta LeNoire, LOUIS GOSSETT, and Robert Guillaume. In March 1970 she performed in a revival of the Jean Giraudoux play *The Madwoman of Chaillot*, originally produced in New York in 1948.

Simms appeared regularly on local radio, including the half-hour WOV (New York) program *New World A-Coming*, which dramatized such subject matter as Reconstruction, blacks in the Revolutionary War, and the history of the American Negro Theatre. In the late 1950s she was the host of the New York–produced WOV (New York) morning show *Ladies Day with Hilda Simms*, and, she could also be heard on the Chicago-based, ABC radio program, *International Showcase* (1953). Additionally, she lent her talents to recordings and performed, along with O'Neal, on the *Great Negro Americans* spoken-word record series.

For Simms, acceptance in Hollywood was elusive. After the popular praise of *The Joe Louis Story*, she made only one more appearance in a Hollywood picture, *Black Widow* (1954), starring Ginger Rogers, Van Hefflin, Gene Tierney, and George Raft. In 1959 United Artists produced a film adaptation of the play *Anna Lucasta*. Simms, who was largely responsible for the original play's success, was passed over, and the part was given to EARTHA KITT.

In 1955, as African American performers struggled to find acceptance and opportunity on the new medium of television, Simms appeared alongside the up-and-coming young actor SIDNEY POITIER in the Philco Television Theatre production of the Robert Alan Aurthur play *A Man Is Ten Feet Tall*. NBC television received praise from many viewers who were appreciative of the program's depiction of racial harmony; however, the show also brought vitriol-laced letters, many from southern viewers, who thought Simms (who played Poitier's wife) to be white. Simms was particularly angry about the controversy and promised never again to appear on NBC. To add to the insult, when the teleplay was adapted into the 1957 feature film titled *Edge of the City*, Simms was passed over and the role of the wife went instead to RUBY DEE.

During the 1960s, Simms earned the role of Nurse Ayers in a number of episodes of the some-times-controversial CBS medical drama *The Nurses* (1962–1965), but it was also around this time that she took on another role, that of civil rights advocate. Her focus was on discrimination within the entertainment industry and the lack of opportunity for black performers. In 1962 she testified before the House Committee on Education and Labor, headed by New York congressman ADAM CLAYTON POWELL JR. Simms, joined by a host of notable black performers, voiced her dissatisfaction on a number of issues, including the dearth of parts for black actors on television and film, and the negative typing of African American life and culture in the various entertainment mediums. Simms was particularly critical of bias in theatre. She told *Variety*, "Of course, there are Negro plays. Well, damn Negro plays. ... I say it's immoral when we see casting notices and know bloody well it's no use applying because there are no Negro parts." In 1968, she told the *New York Times*, that she was "scandalized and shocked," that during the State Division of Human Rights (NY) two-day hearing on the lack of minority representation in the film industry, no casting directors nor producers had been called to testify. "These are the people we have to put the pressure on," she told the commission.

In 1970 Simms earned a master's degree in Sociology from City College in New York. That same year she was appointed creative arts director of the New York State Human Rights Division, where she continued to advocate on behalf of black artists. She also worked for drug treatment programs in New York and ran a theater for actors struggling with drug addiction. In 1971, she starred in the New York Theatre of the America's production of the Alfredo Dias Gomes play, *Journey to Bahia*, which opened on 25 June.

By the time of her death, Simms was still mostly remembered for her seminal role as Anna. She died of pancreatic cancer at the age of seventy-five.

Simms was an intelligent, attractive, and multitalented black woman whose acting career suffered under the weight of America's postwar racial climate. Her employment in Hollywood consists of only two films, and her stage career was stymied by racial bias. Simms should be recognized, however, not only for her stellar performance in the ground-breaking play *Anna Lucasta* but also for her decades of protest against discrimination, her advocacy, and her effort to create improved opportunities for blacks in the entertainment industry.

FURTHER READING

Bogle, Donald. *Brown Sugar: Over 100 Years of America's Black Female Superstars.*

Bogle, Donald. *Toms, Coons, Mulattoes, Mammies, & Bucks.*

Chanen, David. "Hilda Simms, 75; actress had talk show, human rights post," *Star Tribune*, 9 Feb. 1994.

Gent, George. "Movie Unions Are Accused of Job Discrimination." *New York Times*, 28 Aug. 1968.

"Hilda Simms: Beauty, Brains and Talent." *Jet* (17 Sept. 1959).

"Negro Stars from Coast To Coast Through the Camera," *Chicago Defender*, 2 Feb. 1945.

"Networks Deny Employment Bias," *Variety*, 31 Oct. 1962.

Obituaries: *Jet*, 7 Mar. 1994; *New York Amsterdam News*, 12 Feb. 1994; and *New York Times*, 8 Feb. 1994.

PAMALA S. DEANE

Simms, Willie (16 Jan. 1870–26 Feb. 1927), jockey and trainer, was born William Simms in Augusta, Georgia, the son of former slaves, whose names are unknown. Enticed by racing silks as a boy, he ran away from home to become a jockey. He worked for C. H. Pettingill's stable in New York for two years, until the trainer Con Leighton "discovered" him riding in Clifton, New Jersey, in 1887 or 1888.

For Simms's first important race, Leighton assigned him to ride the two-year-old Banquet, a 20-1 underdog, in the 1889 Expectation Stakes. Banquet defeated both the favorite, Bellisarius, ridden by Edward "Snapper" Garrison, and Banquet's preferred stablemate, Chaos. Later, at Monmouth Park in New Jersey, Simms guided Chaos, now a 30-1 underdog, to victory over favored Banquet. Freelancing in 1891 Simms enjoyed great success at Saratoga. In 1892 P.-J. Dwyer hired Simms, who won the Champion Stakes aboard Lamplighter. After signing with the Rancocas Stable later in 1892, Simms rode Dobbins in the famous 1893 dead-heat match race with the record money-earner Domino.

In 1895 Simms signed with M. F. Dwyer, who sent him to England for four months. Simms's "American" riding style, which featured extremely short stirrups, a whip, and spurs, was different from that of the English jockeys. The English ridiculed him and his high seat as "the monkey on a stick." In April he became the first American riding an American-owned and trained horse to win an English race when he finished first in the Crawford Plate at Newmarket on Richard Croker's Eau Gallie. He later had an easy win riding Banquet at Newmarket.

Although Simms achieved some success, English jockeys did not initially copy his more efficient riding style. Two years later, however, after Tod Sloan won twenty races in England riding in the same fashion, the English switched to the more efficient style.

Simms won the Kentucky Derby on Ben Brush in 1896, and Plaudit in 1898; the Preakness on Sly Fox in 1898; and the Belmont Stakes on Comanche in 1893, and Henry of Navarre in 1894. His other major stakes wins included the 1895 Champagne Stakes and the 1897 Suburban Handicap on Ben Brush, the 1893 Ladies' Handicap on Naptha, and the Lawrence Realization on Daily America in 1893, and Dobbins the following year. Simms earned twenty thousand dollars in 1895 and, investing it well, became one of America's wealthiest jockeys. In his career in the United States, he rode 1,173 winners (25 percent) in 4,701 races, placed second 951 times, and finished third 763 times. On three different occasions he won five out of six races in a day. After retiring as a rider in 1902 he trained horses until 1924.

Simms, a bachelor, died of pneumonia in Asbury Park, New Jersey. Characterized in the *Thoroughbred Record* as one of the best jockeys in America in 1895, he was known for his "most excellent judgment, especially on horses that require a lot of coaxing and placing. He had beautiful hands and is especially quick and clever in an emergency." In 1977, following ISAAC MURPHY's induction twenty-two years earlier, he was inducted into the National Museum of Racing Hall of Fame.

FURTHER READING

Hotaling, Edward. *Great Black Jockeys* (1999).

Lambton, George. *Men and Horses I Have Known* (1924).

Saunders, James Robert, and Monica Renae Saunders. *Black Winning Jockeys in the Kentucky Derby* (2002).

Obituaries: *New York Times*, 1 Mar. 1927; *Thoroughbred Record*, 5 Mar. 1927.

This entry is taken from the *American National Biography* and is published here with the permission of the American Council of Learned Societies.

STEVEN P. SAVAGE

Simon, Marguerite Francis (30 Oct. 1912–), educator, was born in Memphis, Tennessee, the youngest of four children of Edward Lee Simon and Laura (Dickerson) Simon, both of whom were college graduates. Her father, a graduate of Atlanta University, was a printshop owner in Memphis and later a woodworking and shop instructor at Washington High School in Atlanta. Her mother, a graduate of LeMoyne Normal Institute in Memphis, was a teacher. Her family relocated to Atlanta, Georgia, in 1923, when Marguerite was in the fifth grade. She started school in Atlanta at the South Atlanta Public School that was located on the campus of Clark University, later transferring to Oglethorpe Elementary. She began her secondary education at Knowles High School, later finishing high school at the laboratory school of Spelman Seminary (which later operated as the Atlanta University Laboratory School), all prior to her enrollment in Spelman College to pursue her undergraduate education. Simon graduated from Spelman College in 1935 with a degree in biology at a time when college-educated, African American women were anomalies, especially in the natural sciences, and, despite their educations, faced limited career choices.

Simon decided to teach, and her progressive but realistic father fully supported his daughter's decision, as he desired a work environment for her that would decrease her exposure to the negative aspects of segregation. Simon attended Atlanta University during the 1936–1937 school year and also worked as a graduate assistant in biology at Spelman College. Though intent upon becoming a teacher, she had no relevant experience. She appealed to the Spelman College dean of women, Jane Hope Lyons, for a recommendation to support her application for a teaching position within the Atlanta public school system.

Despite her bachelor's degree and Georgia high school teaching certificate, Simon was denied employment with the school system. Bowed but not bent, she relentlessly pursued teaching positions in other school systems. Her perseverance paid off, and she obtained a teaching position in Milledgeville, Georgia, in a preschool classroom. Her exemplary work in that classroom was rewarded with a promotion to the third-grade classroom, teaching core subjects the following school year. For the next several years, Simon taught in rural schools in the South, gaining teaching experience related to her undergraduate major—biology. She taught science in Evergreen, Alabama, where the school lacked running water and the science equipment was wanting. Despite such limitations, she worked diligently to teach her students the rudiments of the science curriculum and often improvised to provide her students with the education they needed.

In 1942 Simon returned to Atlanta, once again in hopes of obtaining a teaching position within the public school system of the city. While Simon was serving as a "supply teacher" (equivalent to a substitute teacher, most often replacing teachers who were volunteering with the war effort) at the Crogman School in Atlanta, Edna Callahan, one of her former physical education teachers at Spelman, asked her to serve as her permanent replacement teaching physical education when Callahan left the school mid-semester of the 1942–1943 school year to join the Women's Army Corps (WACs). Callahan had remembered Simon's love of children, her teaching abilities, and her experience in organizing "field days" in the Spelman College elementary school, and thought that Simon would be a good fit for the position

Simon was elated at the prospect of teaching at Spelman yet was concerned about her ability to leave her current teaching assignment prior to the conclusion of the school year as well as her lack of experience in teaching physical education. Despite these concerns, Spelman's president Florence Read made a call to the Crogman School to request Simon's release from her teaching duties. Her request was granted, and Simon began her career as a physical education teacher at Spelman on 24 March 1943. Simon's new position as instructor of physical education was a challenge as the Georgia State Department of Education's policy was that all students take courses in physical education from kindergarten through high school. In addition Spelman required four years of daily physical education instruction for all its students at a time when such rigorous and intense physical education instruction was not required by many women's colleges. In an effort to develop herself professionally, Simon took graduate courses in physical education and health science during the summers at the University of Colorado in an attempt to learn all she could to be effective in her new position.

Simon was again forced to improvise in her teaching as the war drained many resources and made even common items such as physical education uniforms and jump ropes scarce. Determined that her students receive the proper instruction in the most appropriate manner, Simon recruited alumnae and students to sew the Spelman student gym uniforms and used window cords and twine, borrowed from Spelman's physical plant, to make gym equipment.

In 1951 Spelman completed construction of a gymnasium, the Florence Matilda Read Health and Recreation Building (Read Hall), named for its fourth president. This building and Simon's contributions combined to provide a recreational facility with activities specifically targeted to the African American female students of Spelman at a time when African Americans in general and women in particular were denied access to public facilities in the South with similar offerings. Simon, along with her colleagues, created the Spelman College Department of Physical Education and Health, and laid the foundation for the department's curricular development and fulfillment of other requirements toward full membership in the National Collegiate Athletic Association.

Simon, who never married or had children, retired from her post as physical education teacher at Spelman in 1979, but continued to be an active alumna and former faculty member, participating in Spelman Alumnae Association events and serving as the de facto historian of the institution. She remained an avid contributor to her church in Atlanta as a Sunday school teacher and a community volunteer. On 6 April 2005 Spelman named the gymnasium in Read Hall the Marguerite F. Simon Gymnasium, in honor of her leadership in physical education and health not only at the institution but as a representation of the example she has set and the path she blazed for African American women in general.

FURTHER READING

Johnson, Patricia F. "Wise Words from Miss Simon." *The Spelman Messenger: The Alumna Magazine of Spelman College*, 117, no. 2 (Fall 2004).

Read, Florence M. *The Story of Spelman* (1961)

Watson, Yolanda L., and Sheila T. Gregory. *Daring to Educate: The Legacy of the Early Spelman College Presidents* (2005).

YOLANDA L. WATSON SPIVA

Simone, Nina (21 Feb. 1933–21 Apr. 2003), singer, musician, and songwriter, was born Eunice Kathleen Waymon in Tyron, North Carolina, the sixth of eight children of John Divine Waymon and Mary Kate (Irvin) Waymon. Eunice's father, called J.D., with whom she maintained an especially close relationship throughout her life, had built several small businesses including a barbershop, a dry cleaners, and a trucking business, but he lost everything during the Depression. Eunice's mother became the family breadwinner, working as a cleaning woman and seamstress and, beginning when

Eunice was three years old, a Baptist minister. Mary Kate Waymon spent a good deal of time on the road preaching, and Simone later described her mother as detached, with her top priorities being church and God. Eunice's musical talent appeared at a very early age, and by the age of six she was the regular pianist at her family's church. That same year she began lessons in classical piano, paid for by a local white family for whom her mother worked as a housekeeper. After a year Eunice's piano teacher set up the Eunice Waymon Fund to pay for her musical training. Contributions came from neighbors, and at age eight Eunice began giving public recitals, in part as a way to thank her benefactors. At age twelve Eunice began boarding fifty miles away in Asheville at the Allen High School for Girls, an integrated private school. After graduating in 1950 as valedictorian she studied at the Juilliard School in New York on a one-year scholarship, after which her plans for a career in classical music were derailed with her rejection by the Curtis Institute of Music in Philadelphia, Pennsylvania. Eunice moved in with her parents, who had moved to Philadelphia, and began giving private music lessons. In the summer of 1954 she landed a job playing piano at a boardwalk bar in Atlantic City for ninety dollars a week, where for the first time she sang and played popular songs in public. Eunice took a stage name—"Niña," or "little one" in Spanish, a nickname from a former boyfriend and "Simone" from the glamorous French actress Simone Signoret—so that her mother would not find out about the new job. By 1956 Simone was playing clubs in Philadelphia and then in New York City. She finally told her mother about her new career; "I was out in 'the world,' as she called it, and there was no forgiving that unless I repented" (Simone, 54).

In 1957 Simone signed with Bethlehem Records, a decision that she later claimed cost her millions in lost earnings. Simone's debut album, *Jazz as Played in an Exclusive Side Street Club*, also known as *Little Girl Blue*, was released the following year. It featured "Don't Smoke in Bed" and "Plain Gold Ring," songs that quickly become standards in her repertoire. It also yielded Simone's only top-20 hit, "I Loves You Porgy," from George Gershwin's musical *Porgy and Bess*. Simone and her new husband, Don Ross, moved to New York City, though they divorced in 1959. That year saw the simultaneous release of Bethlehem's *Nina Simone and Her Friends* and *The Amazing Nina Simone*, on her new label, Colpix. Later that year Colpix's release of the live album *Nina Simone at Town Hall*, which

Nina Simone performing at Avery Fisher Hall in New York City on 27 June 1985. (AP Images.)

included "Black Is the Color of My True Love's Hair," "The Other Woman," and "Summertime," pushed Simone into the spotlight. Audiences, especially Greenwich Village regulars, embraced the singer and the press took notice. Living in Harlem and playing in the Village, Simone enjoyed both epicenters of music and politics, hanging out with jazz and folk musicians, writers, and comedians. Simone started headlining at the Village Gate in 1960, and her seventh album, *Live at Village Gate*, was released in 1962.

In 1961 Simone married Andrew Stroud, a police officer with three children from previous marriages. The couple moved to Mount Vernon, a New York City suburb, and in 1962 had a baby, Lisa Celeste Stroud. Andrew Stroud was a physically and emotionally forceful man, and after becoming Simone's manager and agent he pushed her to capitalize on her growing fame. A blackboard in their kitchen read, "Nina will be a rich black bitch by …" followed by a date that Stroud constantly pushed back. Within a few years Simone had became an international star, touring eight months a year and releasing album after album, including *Nina Simone Sings Ellington* (1962), *Nina Simone at Carnegie Hall*

(1963), and *Folksy Nina* (1964). By 1964 Simone had a full-time office in New York City, and thirty-seven people in addition to her family were financially dependent on her career.

Simone's commitment to the civil rights movement was galvanized by the violent events of 1963, especially the murders of DENISE MCNAIR, CAROLE ROBERTSON, ADDIE MAE COLLINS, and CYNTHIA WESLEY, the four young girls killed in the bombing of the Sixteenth Street Baptist Church in Birmingham, Alabama, and the assassination of MEDGAR EVERS in Jackson, Mississippi, which inspired her to write "Mississippi Goddam," the first of her political songs. For the next seven years Simone "sang for the movement," as she called it, playing benefits, going on marches, and writing protest songs, including "Brown Baby," "Images," "Go Limp," "Old Jim Crow," "Sunday in Savannah," "Backlash Blues," "Four Women," and "Why? (The King of Love Is Dead)," written after the assassination of MARTIN LUTHER KING JR. She credited her political education to her friends JAMES BALDWIN, LANGSTON HUGHES, Miriam Makeba, STOKELY CARMICHAEL, and especially LORRAINE HANSBERRY, whom she honored by writing the song "To Be Young, Gifted and Black," the title of which was taken from Hansberry's posthumously published play.

Simone's political awakening brought about a new relationship with her audiences. Simone was always an emotional performer, but in her early years she focused primarily on the music, often playing with her eyes closed. As her dedication to the movement deepened, she forged a new level of spiritual connection with her music and with audiences. In performance she tried to hypnotize her audience, creating and controlling their mood. Casting this spell, as she referred to it, took a great of preparation, both mental and logistical. Simone was highly sensitive to the particulars of each performance venue and responsive to the disposition of each audience. As a result she gained a reputation as an extraordinary—if unpredictable—live performer.

Simone signed with Philips Records in 1963, and the label released *Nina Simone in Concert* (1964), which included the first recording of "Mississippi Goddam," followed by *Broadway, Blues, Ballads* (1964), *I Put a Spell on You* (1965), *Pastel Blues* (1965), *Let It All Out* (1966), *Wild Is the Wind* (1966), *Silk and Soul* (1967), and *High Priestess of Soul* (1967). *Nina Simone Sings the Blues* (1967), her first album with RCA, included her unforgettable cover of BESSIE SMITH's "I Want a Little Sugar in My Bowl." In 1968 the label released *Nuff Said* (1968), which Simone recorded two days after the murder of Martin Luther King Jr., followed by *Nina Simone and Piano* (1969), *To Love Somebody* (1969), *Black Gold* (1970), *Here Comes the Sun* (1971), *Emergency Ward* (1972), and the prophetically titled *It is Finished* (1974).

Simone's relentless touring and recording schedule combined with her intensely emotional style of performance took their toll. "Singing disturbed me in a way I never had experienced with classical music," she later divulged in her autobiography. "The tunes stayed in my head for hours—sometimes days—at a time and I couldn't sleep or ever simply calm down" (Simone, 83). By 1967 while on a national tour opening for BILL COSBY she began experiencing hallucinations and periods of dissociation. She finally broke down in tears on stage at the Montreux Jazz Festival in 1968. The assassinations of King, MALCOLM X, and Robert Kennedy, the conviction of her friend H. RAP BROWN, the escalation of the war in Vietnam, and racial violence at home exacerbated Simone's feelings of exhaustion, depression, anger, and isolation.

Simone's personal life had also reached a breaking point. She and Stroud divorced in 1970, in part over escalating financial woes that included severe debt and unpaid taxes. Financially, professionally, and emotionally insecure, Simone went to Barbados in 1971, beginning a decade of self-imposed exile in Liberia, Switzerland, Holland, and France. The decade was filled with ill-fated love affairs, strained family relationships, aborted performances, and financial problems, culminating in a conviction on tax evasion and a suicide attempt. Simone voiced her disgust with the U.S. recording industry at the Midem International Music Market trade show in 1977, lecturing record executives, "I am a genius. I am not your clown. Most of you people are crooks. I am an artist, not an entertainer, and five record companies owe me money." Her only album releases during this period were *Baltimore* (1978) and *Fodder on My Winds* (1982), both for small labels.

Simone began reconnecting with American audiences with the release of *Nina's Back* (1985), but her career truly reignited in 1987 when her 1958 recording of "My Baby Just Cares for Me" was used in a British television commercial for Chanel No. 5 perfume. As the song climbed the British pop charts, Simone began touring and recording again, releasing *Live & Kickin* (1987) and *Live at Ronnie Scott's* (1987), the first of a host of new, rereleased, and greatest hits collection albums released before her death.

Beginning with Luc Bresson's film *La Femme Nikita* (1990), in which her music is a key expression of the protagonist's character, Simone's songs have been featured in a number of feature films. The author of an autobiography in 1991 and the subject of a French documentary in 1992, Simone mellowed only slightly. In the mid-1990s she was fined for causing and leaving the scene of an accident and was fined a second time and placed on probation for shooting a rifle at two teenage neighbors. By the late 1990s she was touring major festivals, generally closing her set with the aptly named "My Way." Simone died in 2003 at her home in southern France after battling cancer. Less than three months after her death RCA released the *Nina Simone Anthology*, a collection of thirty-one tracks from six labels.

Audiences continue to be drawn to Simone's regal presence, her singular vocal style with its haunting vibrato, and her skillful use of timing and silence. A fusion of jazz, pop, gospel, classical, blues, and folk, Simone's sound defied categorization. Whether inaugurating her own protest songs, reinventing blues, jazz, and gospel standards, or interpreting the songs of Bob Dylan, George Harrison, the Bee Gees, The Beatles, Leonard Cohen, Cole Porter, DUKE ELLINGTON, Jacques Brel, Frank Sinatra, or BILLIE HOLIDAY, Simone delivered each song anew.

FURTHER READING

Simone, Nina, with Stephen Cleary. *I Put a Spell on You: The Autobiography of Nina Simone* (1991).

Obituary: *New York Times*, 22 Apr. 2003.

LISA E. RIVO

Simpson, Carole (7 Dec. 1940–), broadcast journalist, anchorwoman, and college instructor, was born Carole Estelle Simpson in Chicago, Illinois, the youngest daughter of Lytle Ray Simpson and Doretha Viola Wilbon Simpson.

Simpson's father, a talented artist, became a sign painter and later a mail carrier to provide a stable life for his family. Her mother was a seamstress who worked from the family's home. Together they used their financial resources to support voice lessons for Simpson's sister, Jacqueline, nine years her senior.

Simpson, who preferred reading and devoured books at the public library, spent five years taking piano lessons with the intent to become Jacqueline's accompanist. "I hated the piano," Simpson said. "I took it for five years, but I hated it."

Jacqueline decided to get married and give up a music career after graduating from college, causing Simpson to become driven to make her parents "proud." "I think that's a very strong influence on my drive, my determination, my ambition, which now is second nature to me, but then I think that was the beginning of it."

As a result, Simpson set her sights on excelling at school. During her time at Hyde Park High School in the Woodlawn area of Chicago, Simpson participated in stage plays, which helped her develop self-confidence and a strong, clear speaking voice. During her junior year she got involved with the school newspaper, where she was "the gossip columnist for all the homerooms."

Simpson liked seeing her words in print, and when her English teacher suggested she consider a career as a reporter, Simpson decided to become "a colored Lois Lane." That desire and a 3.5 grade point average were not enough to get Simpson into Northwestern University's Medill School of Journalism, where she was told outright she would never get hired because of her race and gender. The admissions director suggested she major in English instead.

Undeterred, Simpson entered the University of Illinois in 1958 and attended school there before transferring to the University of Michigan in 1960. She graduated in 1962 as the only African American among the sixty journalism graduates. Her first job out of college was as a journalism instructor and director of the information bureau at the Tuskegee Institute in Tuskegee, Alabama.

It was while at Tuskegee that Simpson first got broadcasting experience. Each month she would conduct an interview with an African student for *Voice of America*, which was then broadcast in a number of African countries. She continued her broadcasting experience while working on a graduate degree at the University of Iowa. While there, Simpson became the first woman to broadcast news on the Iowa City station, WSUI. "The whole community heard it," she said. "And I loved it, because I got to write and I got to report, and then I had this added thing of being able to go on the air with my material, and people hearing you and hearing your name and saying your name. ... From then on it was broadcast journalism. I just thought it was the neatest stuff in the world."

When she left Iowa in 1965, the civil rights movement was at its peak and she found herself in demand. When she was about to accept a newspaper job in St. Louis, WCFL, a major radio station in Chicago, invited her for an interview. Impressed with the test story she was given, the station offered Simpson a job on the spot, making her the first woman to broadcast hard news in Chicago, then the second-largest market in the nation behind only New York.

Her tenacity helped her score a scoop with Dr. MARTIN LUTHER KING when he brought his civil rights campaign to Chicago in 1966. He refused to say publicly what he planned to accomplish while in the city and no one from his campaign would speak to her. She not only found out the hotel where he was staying, but also found out his room number with the help of colleagues and then camped out in the hallway all night to get the story.

When King saw she had stayed the night, he told her he was there to "attack the segregated housing patterns" of the city, and WCFL was the first station to report his intent. From that beginning, Simpson reported on protest marches, riots, and other hard news stories all over the country. In September 1966, she married Eugene Marshall, an engineer she met while at the University of Michigan. The couple had two children, Mallika Joy and Adam.

In 1968 Simpson joined WBBM radio, a CBS affiliate and one of the first all-news radio stations in the country. In the two years she spent at the station, she covered the 1968 Democratic Convention in Chicago and the Chicago 7 conspiracy trial. At the end of the trial, a very pregnant Simpson sat in the back row of the courtroom and casually followed a bailiff out of the room as the judge polled the jurors. Her exit started a stampede of the other fifty national journalists covering the trial, but the judge ordered the doors bolted, giving Simpson a fifteen-minute jump on the story. "It was this joke that the nation had been scooped by a black, pregnant woman," she said, noting even CBS television had to credit WBBM Radio for the first word on the verdict (Geimann).

By 1970 she had moved to WMAQ-TV, the NBC affiliate in Chicago, where she spent six months as a special correspondent and two years as the weekend anchor. This job not only made her the first woman to anchor the news in Chicago, but also exposed her to network leaders, resulting in her move to the NBC affiliate in Washington, D.C., in 1974. During this same time, Simpson was recruited to teach journalism classes at the Medill School of Journalism, the same school that had rejected her as a student in 1958.

She moved in 1980 to ABC, where she became the first African American woman to anchor the evening news when she filled in for Peter Jennings during his vacation. As a general assignment reporter, Simpson covered such major events as the 1986 fall of the Philippine president Ferdinand Marcos; George H. W. Bush's 1988 presidential campaign; the 1989 student protests at Tiananmen Square in Beijing, China; the 1990–1991 Persian Gulf War; and the 1991 Senate hearings on the nomination to the U.S. Supreme Court of CLARENCE THOMAS.

From 1982 to 2003, Simpson served as anchor of ABC's *World News Saturday* and *World News Sunday*. She shared an Emmy for her coverage of the 1990 release of Nelson Mandela from a thirty-seven-year sentence in a South African jail, and in 1992 she moderated the second presidential debate among George H. W. Bush, Bill Clinton, and Ross Perot.

Throughout her career, she headed many committees to assist executives at resolving career path concerns of minority and women employees. Simpson retired from ABC News in 2006. Since 2007 she has taught and been leader in residence for the Journalism Department at Emerson College in Boston. Simpson has also served as a commentator for National Public Radio and CNN. In late 2007 her public endorsement of the presidential campaign of Senator Hilary Rodham Clinton (D-NY) caused some conservative critics to accuse her of "liberal bias" and question her political independence, even though Simpson was no longer an ABC anchor. Simpson offered her resignation to Emerson College, but college officials refused to accept it.

FURTHER READING

Chepesiuk, Ron, and Gale Teaster-Woods. "Making a Difference: African-American Leaders Rap about Libraries." *American Libraries* (Feb. 1995): 138–141.

Geimann, Steve. "Sacrifice and Commitment." *Quill* (June 1994): 24–28.

"Journalism Professor Keeps Job after Endorsing Clinton." *Editor & Publisher*, 20 Nov. 2007.

Stainback, Sheila. "*Soaring On-Air.*" *Essence* (Apr. 2000): 80–84.

CLARANNE PERKINS

Simpson, Georgiana Rose (31 Mar. 1865?–27 Jan. 1944), educator and first African American woman to receive a Ph.D. in the United States, was born in Washington, D.C., the daughter of David and Catherine Simpson. Little is known about her parents other than that her father was born in Maryland and her mother in Virginia. Georgiana was the oldest of six children and she had three brothers and two sisters. She attended segregated public schools in Washington, D.C., and in 1885 graduated from the Miner Normal School, a training college for black elementary school teachers. From the 1870s through to the 1940s, the Miner Normal School, which eventually became Miners Teacher College, was responsible for training the majority of black elementary school teachers in Washington, D.C. In the nineteenth century, African Americans had few educational opportunities, but the white educator Myrtilla Miner solicited funds from abolitionists, including Harriet Beecher Stowe, and opened a school in Washington, D.C., to train African Americans as teachers. In 1863 the U.S. Congress incorporated the school, and it evolved into a competitive teachers college, especially under the leadership of Dr. Lucy Moten, an African American who ran the school from 1883 to 1920. Eventually the school became part of the University of the District of Columbia. After graduating from Miner, Simpson taught in a Washington, D.C., elementary school and continued her education through private instruction. In 1896 Simpson traveled to Rostock, Germany, where Rostock University, founded in 1491, was located. She studied German language and literature, but it is not clear if she attended the university or received private instruction. When Simpson returned to the United States in 1897, she became assistant principal of the Miner Normal School, working with Dr. Lucy Moten.

In 1901 she left Miner to teach German at the District's famed Dunbar High School, where she taught for thirty years. Dunbar High School had evolved from the M Street High School, the first high school in Washington for African Americans, which began in the basement of a church in 1870. The school, though lacking adequate space and equipment, became one of the premier high schools in the nation. It later relocated to better facilities and was renamed Dunbar High School. Most universities in the North recognized the academic excellence of Dunbar graduates and waived the special entrance examination that was the usual requirement for African American students.

While teaching at Dunbar, Georgiana attended summer sessions at Harvard University, Clark University, and the University of Chicago. In 1911 she received an AB from Chicago. In 1920 she received a M.A. and a Ph.D. from the University of

Georgiana Rose Simpson, educator and the first African American woman to earn a Ph.D. in the United States, in an undated photograph. (University of Massachusetts, Amherst.)

Chicago, graduating cum laude in 1921, making her the first black American woman to receive a Ph.D. Segregation prevented black academics from gaining professorships in universities and colleges, so many of those scholars and academics taught at Dunbar High School. By 1923 three of Dunbar's teachers held a Ph.D.—one of these was Georgiana Simpson.

Her studies at white universities in the United States subjected her to prejudice, and while studying at the University of Chicago, her accommodations in a university residence caused some southern students to threaten to resign. In the University of Chicago archives there is a handwritten autobiographical account by Sophonisba Breckinridge, a white educator at Chicago at the time, that reports that after Georgiana Simpson arrived at the residence hall, she was asked to take her meals in her room, as many of the southern students could not conceive of "eating in the same room with a colored

student." Days later they complained that Georgiana had a room in what was a "whites only residence." Breckinridge reports in her papers that the controversy drew the attention of Harry Pratt Judson, president of the university. Breckinridge informed Judson that none of the university literature stated the residences were only for whites. Nevertheless, Judson met with Simpson, and while no record remains of their meeting, Georgiana moved out of the university residence. Where she resided while doing her academic work at the University of Chicago is unknown. In addition to racial prejudice, Simpson experienced false charges stemming from the anti-German hysteria that swept the United States during World War I. Because Simpson taught German, witch-hunters charged her with being pro-German and investigated her activities to determine her loyalty to the United States. Simpson prevailed and retorted that it was smart to study the language and culture of the enemy.

Simpson wrote her doctoral dissertation on the German poet Johann Gottfried von Herder's concept of *das Volk* or "folk." Throughout her teaching career, Dr. Simpson advocated for teaching African and African American history. She did postdoctoral work in French and consequently edited *Toussaint L'Ouverture*, a book, published in 1929, on the Haitian independence leader. She was a friend of FREDERICK DOUGLASS, and upon his death, she lived with his widow, Helen Pitts Douglass, and worked to make the Douglass home in the Washington, D.C. neighborhood of Anacostia a historical site. In 1931 Dr. Simpson left Dunbar High School and became an associate professor of German at Howard University, and in 1937 she became a full professor. She retired in 1939. In addition to her work at the university, she was a member of Alpha Kappa Alpha, the American Dialect Society, the American Association of Teachers of German, and the American Association of University Professors.

According to her obituary in *The Journal of Negro History*, she was a lifelong member of the First Congregational Church in Washington, D.C. Dr. Simpson is described in her obituary as "a scholar" and "a woman of Christian character" living "according to Christian ideals." She was a vegetarian, believing physical health important to good character. Simpson died on 27 January 1944 in her home. Although she often traveled and studied at various universities, she lived and taught in Washington, D.C., all her life. In 1976 the National Association of Black Professional Women awarded her a posthumous achievement award.

FURTHER READING

Information on and the papers of Dr. Georgiana Rose
Simpson are located at the Moorland-Spingarn
Research Center, Howard University, Washington,
D.C. The papers of Sophonisba Breckinridge are
located at the Special Collections Research Center,
The University of Chicago Library, Chicago,
Illinois.

Fitzpatrick, Sandra, and Goodwin, Maria R. *Guide to
Black Washington* (2001).

U.S. Census, 1880, District of Columbia, Washington,
Series T9; Roll 121, page 167.

Obituary: *The Journal of Negro History*, 29, no. 2.
(April 1944).

LINDA SPENCER

Simpson, Lorna (1960–), artist, was born in the
Crown Heights section of Brooklyn, New York.
She became a key practitioner of contemporary
conceptual photography. Her enigmatic text-image
combinations share common threads with the work
of conceptualists such as John Baldessari and post-
modernists such as Barbara Kruger, yet they add a
racial dimension, inviting the viewer to probe the
stereotypes embedded in images of black women.

Simpson's early career followed the track of
traditional black-and-white photography. While
earning a BFA from the School of Visual Arts in
New York in 1982, she photographed subjects from
her neighborhood. She studied a more conceptual approach to visual art as a graduate student
at the University of California at San Diego, where
she earned an MFA in 1985. In that same year she
was awarded a National Endowment for the Arts
Management Grant. On returning to New York she
was given a warm reception in contemporary art
circles, earning a National Studio Program Award
from the cutting-edge P.S. 1 Contemporary Art
Center in 1986 and a Workspace Grant from the
Jamaica Arts Center in Queens in 1987.

Like the painter JACOB LAWRENCE, Simpson is a
storyteller of the African American experience. But
different from the linear narratives that Lawrence
researched in history books and then interpreted
in a figurally abstract style, Simpson created crisp,
realist images and elliptical stories that seem
gleaned from conversations or unspoken thoughts.
According to the philosopher and cultural critic
BELL HOOKS, "Simpson's work uncovers the forgotten or repressed narratives of the African American
experience" (hooks, 137).

Consider the example of *Water Bearer*, a 1987
image of a black woman pouring water from two
containers. The motif is classical: a female figure
clothed in a simple, drapelike garment and pouring water, much like a bearer of libations in ancient
Greek art. That Simpson's subject turns her back to
the viewer, however, signals that the image requires
more than a strictly formal appreciation. In fact,
most of Simpson's photographs show only frag-
ments of the body. A text beneath the photograph
reads: "She saw him disappear by the river. … They
asked her to tell what happened… Only to discount
her memory." This caption and photograph have
the air of a bad dream from the Jim Crow South:
they suggest a fugitive on the run and the denial of
truth about racist violence and terror. In the minds
of critics, the truncated body and the turned back
often presented in Simpson's work signal both racial
marginalization and agency. Viewers rarely see her
subjects' faces, and as a result the subjects reflect
the invisibility and anonymity of blacks—and black
women in particular—in white, male-dominated
society, and they assert a defiant attitude as well. The
black woman in *Water Bearer*, bell hooks declared,
was not permitted to be a "subject in history." But
hooks found that her pose was not simply passive:
"she turns her back to create her own space that is
self-defining, self-determining" (hooks, 137).

In the early 1990s Simpson's career advanced rapidly. She was included in the 1990 Venice Biennale
and received the prestigious Louis Comfort Tiffany
award that same year. Her 1994 solo exhibition
Standing in the Water at the Whitney Museum of
American Art met with widespread critical acclaim.
In 1995 she began her long-standing affiliation with
the Sean Kelly Gallery with another acclaimed solo
exhibition.

Simpson expanded her visual vocabulary.
In addition to the human figure, wigs, hair, and
other objects that carry potent meaning within
African American culture became central elements in her work. Consider the case of *9 Props*,
a series of photographs of household objects such
as a vase, cup, or goblet. Each prop is reminiscent
of JAMES Van Der Zee Harlem Renaissance–era
photographs that depict the black middle class surrounded by signs of prosperity. In *9 Props*, however, there are no figures. According to the critic
Eleanor Heartney, these images signal the absence
of the black middle class in contemporary society
(Heartney, 85).

Critical reception of Simpson's work evolved to
consider the complexity of identity politics. A series
entitled *Public Sex*, for example, features a number of
images with no obvious racial subtext (and, strangely

enough, no human figures). Printed beneath one photograph of a skyscraper (*Clocktower*, 1995) is lengthy text—apparently a phone conversation between two employees—that describes plans for a romantic escapade in a disused conference room. In Heartney's analysis, *Clocktower* spoke to a "more universal sense of melancholy. … The furtive encounters suggested by the text seem part of the emotional isolation of modern urban life" (Heartney, 85). The race of the absent participants in these liaisons is unknown. The critic Kellie Jones, however, views this as a sign of the embattled condition of the black female body: "after centuries of rape and abuse under slavery … it is not surprising that Simpson would choose to isolate explorations of sexuality from the physical presence of the body" (Jones, 69).

Simpson added film to her artistic repertoire in 1997. During a residency at the Wexner Center for the Arts in Columbus, Ohio, that year, she completed *Interior/Exterior, Full/Empty*, a series of short films that were projected on gallery walls. Like *Clocktower*, the films offer sexually suggestive situations, often involving a woman speaking to an anonymous and unheard person on the telephone. In *Interior/Exterior, Full/Empty* Simpson makes her audience voyeurs who spy on isolated and sometimes unseen protagonists.

In 1998 Simpson was nominated for the Hugo Boss prize, and she won the Whitney American Art's Cartier Foundation Award in 2001. Her career reached a pinnacle in 2007 when her work was the subject of a 20-year retrospective at the Whitney Museum of American Art. Simpson's insightful pairings of word and image, which bring to the fore issues of race, class, and gender, made her one of the most influential contemporary artists. Her provocative texts succeeded not merely by making pictures meaningful but also in showing how meaning is distilled from them.

FURTHER READING

Bhabha, Homi. "Gestures/Reenactments," *Artforum* (Feb. 1995).

Heartney, Eleanor. "Figuring Absence," *Art in America* (Dec. 1995).

hooks, bell. "Lorna Simpson: Waterbearer," *Artforum* (Sept. 1993).

Jones, Kellie, Thelma Golden, and Chrissie Iles. *Lorna Simpson* (2002).

Robinson, Jontyle Theresa, ed. *Bearing Witness: Contemporary Works by African American Artists* (1996).

EDWARD M. EPSTEIN

Simpson, O. J. (9 July 1947–), football player, sportscaster, and actor, was born Orenthal James Simpson in San Francisco, California, to Jimmie Simpson, a cook, and Eunice Durden, a nurse's aide. The child disliked his unusual first name, which was given to him by an aunt who had heard of a French actor named Orenthal. Sometime during his childhood—accounts differ as to when—he began using his initials "O. J.," which friends later adapted to "Orange Juice" and, later, to "Juice." When O. J. was four, Jimmie Simpson abandoned his wife and family, leaving Eunice to raise four children in a two-bedroom apartment in the run-down Potrero Hill public housing projects near San Francisco's Chinatown. Eunice Simpson worked long hours to provide for her children, but it was often a hard struggle. When O. J. contracted rickets as an infant, for example, he was left bow-legged and in need of leg braces that his mother could not afford. Eunice improvised by connecting an iron bar to a pair of O. J.'s shoes and making him wear it for several hours a day until he was five. Despite his early handicap, Simpson displayed a precocious athletic ability. He played Little League baseball and hoped one day to emulate his idol, the San Francisco Giants' centerfielder WILLIE MAYS. Like many of his contemporaries in Potrero Hill, Simpson was also drawn to local youth gangs and joined one of the project's most notorious, the Persian Warriors, in junior high school. Styling himself as the "baddest cat" in the neighborhood, he ran afoul of the law a few times, mainly for fighting or petty theft. Simpson was arrested at fifteen for stealing bottles from a liquor store, for which he had to spend a week at a juvenile detention center. Shortly afterward he received an unexpected visit from Willie Mays, who hoped to steer the gifted teenage athlete away from a life of crime. Mays made a great impression on Simpson, who warmed to the ballplayer's easy manner and was even more impressed by the trappings of Mays's success, especially his large, expensively furnished home. From that point on, if not before, the prospect of great material reward and of becoming a celebrity would shape Simpson's powerful drive to succeed as a professional athlete.

After suffering a hand injury in junior high school, however, Simpson abandoned baseball in favor of track and then football, starring for Galileo High School initially as a defensive lineman but later as a fullback. In his senior year—1965—his dominating speed and strength earned him all-city honors, but his poor academic record meant that

O.J. Simpson during his double-murder trial in Los Angeles on 21 June 1995. (AP Images.)

no major college program recruited him. Instead, Simpson attended the City College of San Francisco between 1965 and 1967, where he set a junior college record by scoring 54 touchdowns and rushing for 2,445 yards in only two seasons. That record ensured the attentions of several major colleges, from which he selected the University of Southern California. He went on to lead the Trojans to the Rose Bowl in 1967 and 1968.

Most commentators viewed Simpson as the most exciting and explosive running back to emerge for at least a decade, and his two-season total at USC of 35 touchdowns and 3,295 yards gained in rushing earned him the Heisman Trophy in 1968. Shortly after he received that award, Simpson's wife, Marguerite Whitley, gave birth to a daughter, Arnelle. The couple, who married in 1967, would have two more children, Jason and Aaren, the latter of whom drowned in a swimming pool accident in 1979, the year his parents divorced.

Under the rules of the newly instituted National Football League draft, the NFL's poorest team, the Buffalo Bills, picked Simpson, the nation's top collegiate player, for the 1968–1969 season. Although he resented leaving the Sun Belt glamour of Southern California for upstate New York, and tried on several occasions to get out of his contract, Simpson remained in Buffalo until 1977. But in his first four seasons, even he could not prevent the hapless Bills from crashing to forty-two defeats and two ties, while winning only twelve games. Simpson's personal statistics were also less stellar than had been expected of him—he averaged only five touchdowns in each of his first four seasons.

Simpson's fortunes took an upswing in 1973, however, when the former Bills coach Lou Saban returned to Buffalo and restructured the team to play to Simpson's strengths, namely, to get the football to him and let him run. With an intimidating offensive line blocking for him, "the Juice" ran for 2,003 yards in 1973, breaking JIM BROWN's record for a season by 140 yards. Though Simpson won the bulk of the headlines and plaudits, he was the first to recognize that the "Electric Company," as the linemen were known, had been crucial in "turn[ing] on the Juice" (Wood, 43).

Simpson enjoyed exceptional seasons in 1974, when the Bills made the postseason for the only time in his career (they lost to Pittsburgh in the AFC divisional play-offs), and in 1975, when he scored a career-high twenty-three touchdowns, which was then a record. In 1976 the Bills returned to their losing ways under a new coach, but Simpson managed to be selected for the Pro Bowl, as he had been in every season since 1972. The following season, Simpson's last for Buffalo, was also his poorest by far. He played in only seven games because of injuries and scored no touchdowns. In 1978 Simpson returned to San Francisco to play for the 49ers, though it was clear by then that he had run out of juice. Nonetheless, when he retired in 1979, Simpson trailed only Jim Brown in rushing yards and was widely regarded as the NFL's most dominating running back of the 1970s. He was inducted into the NFL Hall of Fame in 1985.

Unlike many high-achieving professional athletes with similar goals, Simpson had little difficulty adjusting to a new career in broadcasting. Indeed, he had established himself with ABC Sports as a freelancer during his time at Buffalo and also worked for that network during the 1976 Olympics. Beginning in 1978 he worked as a commentator and host for NFL football on NBC, switching to ABC's *Monday Night Football* from 1983 to 1986, before returning to NBC in 1989. Simpson also had supporting roles in the television series of ALEX HALEY's *Roots* (1977) and in several high-grossing Hollywood movies, notably *The Towering Inferno*

(1974) and *The Naked Gun* (1989), but he rarely earned much critical praise.

It was, however, his appearance in a series of commercials for the Hertz car rental company during the 1970s that consolidated Simpson's reputation as a household name. Even those who never watched football came to recognize the affable Simpson, dapper in a three-piece business suit, sprinting, shimmying, and vaulting his way through a busy airport to catch his Hertz rental car. Simpson was eager to please corporate America. Unlike his contemporaries MUHAMMAD ALI and KAREEM ABDUL-JABBAR, he was not politically active, nor did he appear dangerously "militant" to whites. He did, however, help craft his own Horatio Alger life story of making it from Potrero Hill to the Hollywood Hills, and he donated to charitable causes. As a result, corporate America loved Simpson, too. His contracts with Hertz, General Motors, RCA, Wilson Sporting Goods, and several other companies helped make him the first African American celebrity to be marketed as "colorless," with an appeal that appeared to transcend race.

By the early 1990s Simpson's income from football, the movies, and his media career had given him the affluent, celebrity lifestyle that he had dreamed of since visiting Willie Mays as a teenager. He had remarried in 1985, to Nicole Brown, whom he had first met eight years earlier. The tabloids made some sport of the fact that Nicole was white and much younger than Marguerite, who was black, but it did little to dent Simpson's popularity. Simpson and Brown had a son and a daughter, but the breakdown of their marriage became public in January 1989, when Brown called the police to Simpson's mansion in the Brentwood section of Los Angeles and alleged that her husband had beaten her and threatened to kill her. In May of that same year Simpson was sentenced to two years' probation for spousal abuse and ordered to attend counseling sessions. Simpson's conviction did not affect his television and film career, nor did he lose any of his corporate sponsors, but his marriage ended in divorce in October 1992.

On 17 June 1994, five days after Nicole Brown and her friend Ronald Goldman were found stabbed and murdered near Brown's Brentwood apartment, the Los Angeles police charged O. J. Simpson with the crime. Simpson fled, leading the police on a bizarre, fifty-mile, slow-speed chase on the Los Angeles freeway in a white Ford Bronco driven by his boyhood friend A. C. Cowlings. A note written by Simpson before he fled suggested that he intended to commit suicide. Television networks and news channels such as CNN filmed the chase live from helicopters, capturing the scores of well-wishers urging, "Go, Juice, Go," as though they were extras in a TV movie or a Hertz commercial rather than bystanders in what was, regardless of Simpson's innocence or guilt, a brutal murder case. When the police finally caught up with Simpson, he denied responsibility for both murders.

After a trial that lasted more than nine months and dominated the nation's tabloids and talk shows, a Los Angeles jury cleared Simpson of both murders in October 1995. The racial makeup of the jury—nine blacks, two whites, and a Hispanic—and the contrasting responses of most African Americans and most whites to the verdict provoked as much controversy as the trial itself had done. Most whites were convinced by the physical and DNA evidence presented by the prosecution, and by the star's history of spousal abuse, that Simpson was guilty. Though many blacks were also convinced of Simpson's guilt, African Americans generally were more willing to doubt that the prosecution had proved its case beyond all reasonable doubt. Many had significant reservations about the role of the Los Angeles police officers in investigating the murders, notably Detective Mark Fuhrman, who was widely regarded as racist.

Though much was made at the time in the media, and also among prominent intellectuals, about the Simpson trial's racial symbolism and significance, public interest in Simpson dissipated remarkably quickly. Several of the scores of legal advisers, policemen, witnesses, and assorted Simpson trial hangers-on did, however, parlay their momentary vogue into a range of book and television deals. Simpson, for his part, continued to maintain his innocence, and in *I Want to Tell You: My Response to Your Letters, Your Messages, Your Questions* (1995), he vowed to find the killers of Ron Goldman and Nicole Brown. The Goldman and Brown families insisted that Simpson was the murderer and launched a wrongful-death civil lawsuit against him in 1996. In February 1997 the mainly white jury found Simpson guilty and liable to pay $33.5 million to the victims' families. Further controversy was raised with the cancellation of Simpson's book, *If I Did It* (2006), which described how he would have killed his ex-wife and her friend, if he were in fact the murderer. Though the verdicts in the criminal and civil trials were different, the two-and-a-half-year saga of the O. J. Simpson trials ensured that the former Heisman Trophy winner and Buffalo Bills star would be remembered by history less for what he did on the gridiron than for what he did—or did not do—near his former wife's Brentwood apartment in June 1994. This reputation resurfaced in 2007, when Simpson was accused of kidnapping and armed robbery following an incident in Las Vegas in which he and several associates raided a hotel room and took sports memorabilia items from two collectors. Simpson claimed that he was recovering possessions that had been wrongfully taken from him, and that the authorities had ignored his pleas for help because of his notoriety. In 2008, a jury found Simpson guilty of all counts, and sentenced him to at least nine years in a Nevada prison. The Nevada State Supreme Court upheld the conviction in 2010, meaning that Simpson would not be eligible for parole until 2017.

FURTHER READING

Simpson, O. J., and Pete Axthelm. *O.J.: The Education of a Rich Rookie* (1970).

Morrison, Toni, and Claudia Brodsky Lacour, eds. *Birth of a Nation'hood: Gaze, Script, and Spectacle in the O. J. Simpson Case* (1997).

Toobin, Jeffrey. *The Run for His Life: The People v. O. J. Simpson* (1996).

Wood, Peter. "What Makes Simpson Run," *New York Times*, 14 Dec. 1975.

STEVEN J. NIVEN

Simpson, Valerie (26 Aug. 1946–), songwriter, singer, and producer, was born in the Bronx, New York. Her father was a subway conductor and amateur pianist, and her mother was a clerk for the city government. Simpson's brothers Ray and Jimmy were also active in the music industry, the former as a singer, most famously with the Village People, and the latter as a producer and mix artist.

Simpson's early musical development was guided by her activities in the church. She began singing as a child in the choir of the Footsteps of Christ Spiritual Church, where her grandmother was a minister, and studied piano from the age of seven. While still a student at Morris High School, she began singing and playing piano for the choir at Harlem's White Rock Baptist Church, and it was there, in 1964, that she met Nickolas Ashford, an aspiring dancer from Michigan who had experience writing gospel tunes for his church's junior choir. The two struck up a friendship, and Simpson asked Ashford if he would help her write songs for her gospel group, the Followers of Christ. While the group was performing at the Sweet Chariot,

a short-lived gospel nightclub, their songs caught the attention of Glover Records, the imprint of the legendary A&R man and producer Henry Glover. Though the pair initially resisted the idea of writing secular songs, their shared ambition to be professional musicians eventually won out. They sold five songs to the label, and Glover released their own versions of two of the tunes, "I'll Find You" and "Lonely Town," under the name Valerie and Nick.

None of the songs Glover turned was a hit, but Simpson was encouraged enough that she abandoned her plans to become a secretary and began picking up whatever work she could find in the music business. She sang commercial jingles and, with Ashford, became a fixture at the renowned pop hit factory the Brill Building. In 1965 the duo was signed to a staff songwriters' contract with Scepter Records. Their songs, frequently written in collaboration with Jo "Joshie" Armstead, were recorded by ARETHA FRANKLIN, the Shirelles, Maxine Brown, and Candy and the Kisses. They also worked regularly as backup vocalists, appearing on records with Bobby Hebb, JERRY BUTLER, and Dee Dee Warwick. In 1966 Ashford and Simpson placed their first hit song, "Let's Go Get Stoned" (based on the gospel song "Let's Serve the Lord") with RAY CHARLES. The song's success attracted the attention of the Motown songwriter Brian Holland, who brought the team to Hitsville.

Ashford and Simpson's years at Motown were perhaps the pair's most productive songwriting period. Though the Motown system pitted them against better known songwriters like the Holland-Dozier-Holland team to place tunes with top artists, they soon landed an assignment writing for the label's newest duet pairing, MARVIN GAYE and Tammi Terrell. The first song they wrote for the duo, "Ain't No Mountain High Enough," was a smash hit and convinced BERRY GORDY JR. to allow them to take on production responsibilities, making Simpson the label's first female producer. Their first Gaye-Terrell production, "Ain't Nothing like the Real Thing," another of their own compositions, also became a number one hit. They continued to work with Gaye and Terrell until the latter's death in 1970, and Simpson is unofficially credited with standing in for the mortally ill Terrell on several later hits, including "Good Lovin' Ain't Easy to Come By" and "What You Gave Me."

In addition to the longstanding collaboration with Gaye and Terrell, Ashford and Simpson helped establish DIANA ROSS as a solo artist, writing and producing all of the tracks on her solo debut *Diana Ross* (1970), including the classic "Reach out and Touch (Somebody's Hand)" and a hit version of "Ain't No Mountain High Enough." Ashford and Simpson's production work for Ross continued even after they left Motown, culminating with *The Boss* (1979), and they composed two of Ross's numbers for the film musical *The Wiz* (1978), "Is This What Feeling Gets?" and "Can I Go On?"

Though Motown offered a tremendous opportunity to grow as a songwriter and producer, Simpson found the label less accommodating for her development as a recording artist. She released two solo albums, *Exposed* (1971) and *Valerie Simpson* (1972). Though "Sinner Man" from *Exposed* was a Grammy nominee for best rhythm and blues female vocal performance, the albums received little attention at the time, primarily, Simpson felt, because of Motown's failure to promote them. They subsequently were recognized as voicing a womanist complement to the frequently masculinist protest of early 1970s soul. Heavily influenced by Simpson's gospel roots, songs such as "I Don't Need No Help" and "One More Baby Child Born" articulated the sentiments of black female personae struggling with motherhood, self-assertion, and love.

In 1973, disappointed with Motown's unwillingness to promote them as performers, Ashford and Simpson signed with Warner Brothers and soon became one of the best-known rhythm and blues acts of the time. Unlike many of their Motown peers, they were as influential in the postdisco era as during the 1960s. They successfully incorporated disco elements into their traditional rhythm and blues sound on *Is It Still Good to Ya* (1978) and *Stay Free* (1979), both of which went gold. In 1981 they moved to Columbia Records, where they recorded five more albums, including *Solid* (1984), which featured the anthemic, gospel-influenced track of the same name that became their signature song. They also continued to write and produce for some of the most successful rhythm and blues artists of the 1970s and 1980s, including TEDDY PENDERGRASS and Chaka Kahn.

Much of Ashford and Simpson's songwriting and recording during these decades explored the themes of spiritual and sensual love that had characterized their earlier work. By the time they arrived at Warner Brothers, those songs reflected a new relationship between them, as their professional partnership blossomed into romance. They set aside their mutual concerns that it might affect their work and moved in together in 1972 and married in 1974. In the end, their personal relationship enhanced their professional fortunes, giving their songs and live performances a sense of intimacy and honesty. They remained married for more than thirty years and had two daughters.

Ashford and Simpson continued to write, record, and perform well into the 2000s, presiding over a business empire that included their own production company and record label, a publishing company, the New York nightclub Sugar Bar, and a back catalog of compositions that, in 1999, fetched as much as $25 million in bonds secured by future royalty earnings. They hosted a drive time interview and music show on New York's KISS-FM during the late 1990s and performed in a critically acclaimed engagement at the Regency Hotel in 2006 and at the Apollo Theater in 2007. Among the few artists to transition smoothly from the era of classic northern soul to disco and beyond, Ashford and Simpson also were among the most prolific and talented songwriters and artists of the late twentieth century.

FURTHER READING

"Ashford, Nickolas, and Simpson, Valerie," *Current Biography* (1997).

Bessman, Jim. Liner Notes, *The Very Best of Ashford and Simpson* (2002).

Neal, Mark Anthony. *What the Music Said: Black Popular Music and Black Public Culture* (1999).

Norment, Lynn. "Ashford and Simpson," *Ebony* (Feb. 1979).

DIANE PECKNOLD

Sims, Clifford Chester (18 Jun. 1942–21 Feb. 1968), soldier and Medal of Honor recipient, was born Clifford Pittman at Port St. Joe, Florida. Orphaned while a young boy, Sims was homeless for a time in Panama City before living with several relatives over the years. In 1955 he was adopted by James and Irene Sims of Port St. Joe, Florida. He subsequently attended George Washington High School, and it was there that he met his future wife, Mary.

Soon after his graduation in 1960, Clifford Sims enlisted in the army at Jacksonville, Florida. After completing his initial boot camp training, he was sent to Fort Bragg, North Carolina, for further training as an airborne soldier, with Mary accompanying him. The couple was subsequently married on 25 December 1961, and together raised Mary's niece Gina as their own child. While the details of Sims's early military career are unknown, it is clear that he quickly proved himself a talented soldier and a natural leader, rising to the rank of sergeant by 1967, the highest rank attainable for an enlisted man. Clifford Sims's service during the Vietnam War was important for several reasons. While the heroism exhibited in combat that earned him our nation's most exalted military decoration is reason enough to remember Sims's military service, he is also important in that his service was indicative of the overall contribution made by African American servicemen to the war effort. Black soldiers were once restricted from army leadership positions by institutionalized racism, but the Vietnam War was the first modern conflict in which they served on an equal footing with white soldiers, especially on the field of battle. Indeed, black platoon sergeants, men such as Sims, RODNEY MAXWELL, DONALD LONG, and MATTHEW LEONARD, are outstanding examples of their fine service. Sergeants in the army have long been the backbone of the service, with a tradition of not only leading their men, but training, mentoring, and looking out for them no matter what the situation. Regarding Clifford Sims, his commanding officer, Lieutenant Colonel Richard Tallman, would later say of him, "He was intensely loyal to his men, and never put his own interests above theirs. Just five days before he died he was assigned the task of securing an LZ during heavy fighting. He assured that his men were properly positioned and behind suitable cover. And he made certain the wounded were expeditiously evacuated. Yet he never considered cover for himself during a full six hour period during which he was under harassing sniper fire. His devotion was to his duty and to his men" (Williams, 4).

In August 1967 Sergeant Clifford Sims was sent to Fort Campbell, Kentucky, to join the newly formed Company D, 2nd Battalion, 501st Infantry Regiment, 101st Airborne Division, nicknamed the "Delta Raiders, and was subsequently deployed to Vietnam with his unit on 13 December 1967. Just three months into his tour of duty, Sims was serving as a squad leader with Company D on 21 February 1968 during an operation near Hue. The company was assaulting a heavily fortified enemy position when strong enemy fire was encountered. Sims subsequently led his squad in an attack to relieve the 1st Platoon, which was in peril, then moved his men to provide cover fire for the company command group and to provide support for the 3rd Platoon, which was also under pressure. After moving his men but a short distance, Clifford Sims spotted a brick structure, in which enemy ammunition was stored, that was on fire.

He quickly moved his men from the area, but while doing so two of his men were wounded by exploding ammunition. Had Sims not taken this quick action, however, many more of his men would have become casualties. Continuing to move his squad through the heavily wooded area under constant enemy fire, Sims was approaching an enemy bunker with his men when he heard the noise of a booby trap being triggered to the front of their position. Sims reacted quickly yet again by warning his men and, without regard for his own safety, throwing himself on the explosive device. Taking the full force of the blast in order to protect the men in his squad, Sergeant Clifford Sims was mortally wounded by the explosion.

On 2 December 1969, the Sims family, including his widow Mary, received Clifford Sims's Medal of Honor from Vice President Spiro Agnew during a White House ceremony. Clifford Sims was buried in the Barrancas National Cemetery in Pensacola, Florida, where a Medal of Honor headstone marks his final resting place. The Clifford Sims Parkway in Port St. Joe and the Clifford Sims Veterans Nursing Home in nearby Springfield, Florida, have been named in his honor.

FURTHER READING

Hanna, Charles W. *African American Recipients of the Medal of Honor* (2002).

Williams, Despina. "Veterans Reflections: Clifford Chester Sims." *Star*, 26 May 2009. http://www.starfl.com/articles/sims-18233-hogan-school.html

GLENN ALLEN KNOBLOCK

Sims, Howard "Sandman" (24 Jan. 1917–20 May 2003), tap dancer, was born in Fort Smith, Arkansas, but spent most of his youth in Los Angeles. The ten children in the Sims family made extra cash by "street tapping." Street tappers danced on plywood or cardboard on street corners and took pride in creating unique tap combination steps; the more difficult the step, the better the audience reaction. The best dancers kept the choice corner stages where the tips were best, and Sims learned to protect his sidewalk dance stage by performing extremely complicated steps and challenging other tappers to repeat the step sequence.

Sims began boxing as a child and made money in the sport until the second time he broke his hand. After a tap dancing tour of South America, Sims left Los Angeles for New York in 1947 where his image became familiar to visitors at the Apollo Theater in

Harlem. His performances won so many nightly talent contests that the Apollo created a limit on the number of contests one performer could win on any given night. Sims's tap dancing, mime, and acting skills were featured on the Apollo stage from the mid-1950s when he worked as the assistant executioner (the "executioner" escorted acts from the stage when either their performances ran long or the audience indicated the quality was below its standards). Sims soon took over as the main executioner, a role he would play until the 1980s, acquiring distinctive costumes and a persona that entertained audiences. Sims was so well known to Apollo regulars that he was featured in two television specials, *Uptown: A Tribute to the Apollo Theater* (1980) and *Motown Returns to the Apollo* (1987). Sims was also a guest on several episodes of the 1987 television series *Showtime at the Apollo*.

Sims described himself as a "hoofer," after his preferred style of dance. Hoofers used a full foot, flat shuffle action in tapping. Tappers, such as Fred Astaire and Gene Kelly, tapped with the body weight on the toe of the foot, adding the heel only as accent taps. Sims performed in an era when hoofers were plentiful, and in an effort to create a memorable and unique performance he developed a style, for which he received the nickname, "Sandman," that used sand on his shoes. He claimed he first had the idea when he stepped into a rosin box before his boxing matches. His first dancing was done on a rosin board, but the technique wore out too many shoes. He experimented with sand glued to the bottom of his shoes but found the sound unsatisfactory. Eventually Sims placed sand on a board and danced on it with standard tap shoes. While working at the Apollo, Sims also gave tap lessons to earn extra money. His most successful students included Ben Vereen and GREGORY HINES. Sims's online biography claims that boxers ARCHIE MOORE, SUGAR RAY ROBINSON, and MUHAMMAD ALI hired him to coach them in boxing footwork.

The popularity of tap dancing fluctuated over the decades, and Sims was forced to find work in other venues, including owning a restaurant on 125th Street in Harlem and hosting an amateur hour talent show at a bowling alley nearby. Amid his multiple careers he married a woman named Solange, with whom he had three children, Howard, Jr., Mercedes White, and Diane Jones.

A revival of interest in tap dancing, led by Gregory Hines, Hinton Battle, and SAVION GLOVER, brought the spotlight back to "Sandman" Sims in the 1970s. The 1979 film *No Maps on My Taps*, narrated by Sims, documented the importance of tap dancing to American theater and culture and described the lives and dance techniques of tappers such as BUNNY BRIGGS, CHUCK GREEN, JOHN WILLIAM SUBLETT, and Sims himself. He was also seen in the 1989 documentary *Tap Dance in America* that interviewed a new generation of tap dancers, including Battle, Hines, Glover, and Tommy Tune, discussing the influences of earlier dancers.

Sims joined with other veteran tap dancers in a series of public performances beginning in 1969. At the age of nearly seventy in 1986, he acted in a play by Sandra Hochman called *The Sand Dancer*. His tapping was in demand all over the world during the late 1970s and 1980s, and he performed in fifty-three countries as an unofficial representative of the U.S. State Department. He danced for New York mayors Edward Koch and DAVID DINKINS, as well as U.S. Presidents Jimmy Carter, Ronald Reagan, and Bill Clinton. Sims was an annual guest on Jerry Lewis's Labor Day Telethon for funding for muscular dystrophy.

Sims won a National Heritage Fellowship presented by the Folk Arts Program of the National Endowment of the Arts in 1984. He hoped to spark interest and to ensure the longevity of tap dancing by presenting master classes to youth. His $5,000 prize from the fellowship was used to create an outdoor summer tap school for children ages five to twelve living in New York City. He also worked with local basketball programs, including *Each One, Teach One*, to give children an outlet for afterschool activities. Sims assisted in the organization, coached teams, and worked as a referee. He received the Smithsonian, LIONEL HAMPTON, and the Bronx Borough President Awards and presented a program at the Fourth Annual Young People's Tap Conference in 1998.

Sims's movie roles included playing the role of the Hoofer in *The Cotton Club* (1984) and the part of the Crapshooter in *Harlem Nights* (1989). In his final television appearance, he portrayed himself in an episode entitled "Mr. Sandman" on the *Cosby Show* in February 1990.

Sims died in the Bronx, after having been ill for some time with Alzheimer's disease, diabetes, and ulcers. The Feet First Foundation was established in 2005 by his son Howard Sims Jr., after his father's death to maintain his legacy by teaching tap dance. Tap Mobile, one of the foundation programs, was a free (or minimal-cost) pilot project in an afterschool arts program at a public school in Harlem. The foundation's goal was to expand Tap Mobile to

Sims's hometowns of the Bronx, Los Angeles, and Ft. Smith, Arkansas.

FURTHER READING

Frank, Rusty E. *Tap! The Greatest Tap Stars and Their Stories, 1900–1955* (1994).

Haskins, James. *Black Dance in America* (1990).

PAMELA LEE GRAY

Sims, Naomi (30 Mar. 1949–1 Aug. 2009), fashion model, entrepreneur, and writer, was born in Oxford, Mississippi, the daughter of John Sims and Elizabeth Parham. Her father left the family when Sims was a baby, and her mother suffered a nervous breakdown when Sims was eight. She spent her childhood living with different foster families in Pittsburgh, Pennsylvania, separated from her sisters and mother. This isolation, coupled with Sims's self-consciousness about her dark skin and tall stature—she stood five feet ten inches at age thirteen—made her an insecure teenager. Nonetheless, Sims was urged by friends and family to try modeling. After graduating from Westinghouse High School in Pittsburgh, Sims moved to New York and enrolled in the Fashion Institute of Technology, where she studied merchandising and textile design. She also took evening classes to study psychology at New York University.

In New York, Sims did not immediately try to become a model, but financial need pushed her in that direction. Still, Sims did not think she was beautiful and judged herself by harsh general cultural standards as too dark, too skinny, and too tall. But her foray into the fashion world coincided with the black power movement and its proclamation that black was beautiful.

When Sims visited the modeling agencies in New York, however, she was told that there was no work for African American models. She was also told she that did not fit the type. Without a modeling agency or industry contact behind her but determined to make it as a model, Sims made a bold move by calling Gosta Peterson, a prominent fashion photographer, and asking him to meet her. He agreed, and this meeting led to an assignment for the *New York Times*. In 1967 she landed her first job, a cover of the *Times* fashion section, a first for an African American woman. Sims's career took off, and she signed with the Wilhelmina Cooper modeling agency. Sims became the first black model to appear in an AT&T commercial, the first black model to land the cover of a major women's magazine (*Ladies Home Journal*), and the first black model to appear in *Vogue*. She also appeared on the cover of *Life* magazine in 1969, at the age of nineteen. With her smooth dark skin and long legs, Sims's "new" look broke the color barrier that had existed in the fashion world.

Sims was becoming an "it" girl. Warner Brothers studio took notice and offered her the title role in *Cleopatra Jones*, a 1973 blaxploitation film that became popular with black and white audiences. According to her Web site, Sims flew to Hollywood to read the script but was outraged by what she perceived as stereotypes of black men and women throughout the script. She rejected the offer and wrote a complaint letter to the studio. (The title role went to Tamara Johnson, another model, who also starred in the movie's sequel).

After a successful six-year modeling career that included appearances on the covers of almost every fashion magazine in the world, Sims wanted to take her life in a new direction. She grew bored with the superficiality of the modeling industry and in 1973 quit the profession to start her own business manufacturing high-quality wigs for black women. Sims was only twenty-four years old. Also in 1973 she married Michael Findley, an art dealer of Scottish heritage; they had one son.

The idea of producing wigs for African American women grew from her difficult experience of trying to create different looks for her photos. She believed wearing wigs would have eased the problem, but there were no wig manufacturers who catered to black women. For years Sims experimented with synthetic fibers, taking the fiber used in white wigs and baking it at a low temperature. Eventually this produced the results Sims wanted—a texture similar to that of black women's hair. She patented the synthetic fiber, Kanekalon Presselle, and approached several wig manufacturers before getting into business with Metropa Company. The first line of the "Naomi Sims Collection" went into production soon after. Although some businesses questioned the marketability of wigs that catered to black women, within the first year sales of Sims's wigs reached $5 million.

Sims reveled in her new role as an entrepreneur. She designed the wigs, wrote the advertisements, and traveled around the country to promote her wigs. Soon Sims parlayed her sharp business acumen into a writing career, publishing several books on fashion, health, and beauty: *All about Health and Beauty for the Black Woman* (1976), *How to Be a Top Model* (1979), *All About Hair Care for the Black Woman* (1982), and *All About Success for the*

Black Woman (1982). Her first book was a best-seller. Naomi Sims Beauty Products was incorporated in 1985, and Sims served as chairperson of the board. She expanded her business interests to include perfume, skin care products, and cosmetics for black women. As a leading authority on beauty, Sims reclaimed the "black is beautiful" theme with her magazine covers and photo spreads and also with her contributions to fashion and cosmetics. She paved the way for others, such as Beverly Johnson, Iman, Naomi Campbell, and Tyra Banks, to have successful modeling careers. As cosmetics companies became more aware and inclusive of the needs of women of color, Sims's passion created more choices for black women. Sims passed away in Newark, New Jersey in August of 2009.

FURTHER READING

Lurie, Diane. "Naomi," *Ladies Home Journal* (Nov. 1968).

Schiro, Anne-Marie. "For Skins of All Shades, New Cosmetics," *New York Times* (15 May 1987).

Summers, Barbara. "Naomi Sims," *Essence* (Jan. 1986).

Obituary: *New York Times*, 3 Aug. 2009.

MARTHA PITTS

Sims, Thomas (c. 1828–c. 1905), fugitive slave and litigant, was born to unknown parents in the late 1820s. In court documents tied to his famous 1851 fugitive slave case, Sims maintained that he was born in Florida, but both the agents of the slaveholder claiming him and the later public records listed Georgia as his place of birth. Sims also asserted that his father had purchased his freedom as a child, but Massachusetts courts never accepted this claim and instead found him to be the slave of James Potter. If Sims was Potter's slave, it is unlikely that the two ever interacted personally: the South Carolina-born Potter owned massive plantations outside of Savannah as well as several hundred slaves, and he generally left their management to various agents. Potter also had strong affinities for the North: he graduated from Yale, all of his children were born in Philadelphia, and the family spent most of their time at Palmer House, a large home in Princeton, New Jersey, now owned by Princeton University.

During the late 1840s, Sims worked as a mason in and around Savannah—perhaps living with his mother and a sister and hiring his time. In February 1851, he stowed away on the *M. & J. C. Gilmore* and, although he was caught by a mate soon after the ship anchored in Boston's harbor, managed to steal a small boat and escape. He took a room in a boarding house at 153 Ann Street, found work as a waiter, and supposedly wired family in Savannah for funds. This seems to have tipped off Potter's agents, and one, John B. Bacon, quickly left for Boston. He arrived on 3 April 1851, the same day Sims was arrested. Sims resisted and stabbed one of the deputy marshals, Asa O. Butman (who would later also take fugitive ANTHONY BURNS into custody), in the thigh.

Abolitionists in Boston were still seething over the passage of the Fugitive Slave Law in 1850 and reflecting on their rescue of fugitive slave SHADRACH MINKINS (only months before) from the same return to slavery that now loomed over Sims. Word spread quickly of Sims's capture, and white abolitionists like Samuel E. Sewall began a series of legal actions fighting for Sims's liberty. Simultaneously, Boston police greatly increased their presence at—and even placed chains around—Boston's courthouse to keep growing crowds of protestors back. Sims' legal advocates (Sewall, as well as Charles J. Loring, Charles Sumner, Robert Rantoul, and Richard H. Dana Jr.) tried unsuccessfully to "recover" Sims through gaining a writ of habeas corpus from both Massachusetts Chief Justice Lemuel Shaw and later U.S. District Judge Peleg Sprague. Abolitionists like Theodore Parker and Wendell Phillips gave stirring speeches demanding Sims's liberty, and the Boston Vigilance Committee (including prominent African Americans like LEWIS HAYDEN AND LEONARD A. GRIMES) considered a range of possible escape plans for Sims, who was held on the courthouse's third floor under the guard of U.S. Marshal Charles Devens. Although similar efforts had contributed to the successful rescue of Minkins and would loom large during the later Anthony Burns case, all were frustrated in the Sims case. Sims's supporters even petitioned the Massachusetts Legislature to intervene, and they made a last-ditch effort to keep Sims in Massachusetts to stand trial for stabbing Butman, all to no avail.

The mayor of Boston called on the paramilitary Boston Light Guards, City Guards, and New England Guards to watch the courthouse, and the federal government placed troops at the nearby Charleston Navy Yard on alert. Proceedings before Commissioner George Ticknor Curtis—the same "cotton Whig" commissioner who presided over the initial phases of the Shadrach Minkins case—continued apace, and Curtis found Sims to be the slave of Potter and ordered his return late on 11 April. In the early morning hours of 12 April, a mass of Boston police and armed "volunteers" and city guards, as well as a detachment of federal troops now being referred to as the "Sims Brigade," escorted Sims from the courthouse to Long Wharf, where the brig *Alcorn* was anchored and waiting. Sims was on his way back to slavery before dawn.

Sims was reportedly back in Savannah by 20 April; there, he was held in the city jail, publicly whipped, and then eventually sent first to Charleston, South Carolina, and then to New Orleans, Louisiana, where he was purchased by a mason from Vicksburg, Mississippi. Some abolitionists—including Lydia Maria Child—made efforts to raise funds to purchase Sims, but, although April 1852 saw commemorative events within the abolitionist community in Boston and although WILLIAM COOPER NELL reported on Sims's believed whereabouts in a 14 November 1856 column in the *Liberator*, the movement largely set Sims aside as a lost cause. Sims later claimed that he lived in Vicksburg for a dozen years, working as a bricklayer and later as a peddler among the soldiers in the area.

Abolitionist periodicals reported that Sims—along with his wife, their eight-year-old child, and three other men—escaped in May 1863 and headed for Boston. On his way, he reportedly met with Ulysses S. Grant to share details of Confederate troops in Mississippi. The August 1863 issue of *Douglass's Monthly* reported that his master was advertising for his return.

After 1863, Sims seems absent from the public record until 1877, when he contacted Charles Devens, the same U.S. Marshall who guarded him in Boston and who had been named U.S. Attorney General under Rutherford B. Hayes. Devens apparently got Sims a job as a messenger for the Justice Department, and Sims is listed in the 1880 Federal Census of Washington, D.C., as a "gov. clerk" (104D). He was living with a new wife, thirty-five-year-old Emma, and the family of barber Charles Jackson. He is also listed in 1880–1883 city directories as a "messenger" living at 733 11th Avenue NW; these listings spell his last name "Simms" and give his middle initial as "M." Sims was apparently fired after Devens left the Attorney General's Office, probably in one of the waves of Chester Arthur's reevaluation of patronage jobs. Charles Adams reported that Sims was still in Washington in 1889 working as a mason, and Sims does appear in city directories—always at 733 11th Avenue NW and usually with the middle initial "M." and the last name "Simms"—throughout the rest of the nineteenth

century. All but the 1899 directory, which lists him as a machinist, mark him as a bricklayer. It seems likely that he is the Thomas M. Simms at the same address in the 1900 Federal Census, although this Thomas Simms's birthdate is listed as May 1843.

Details of his death have yet to be uncovered, and the importance of his case has been somewhat overshadowed by attention to Shadrach Minkins and Anthony Burns.

FURTHER READING
Campbell, Stanley. *The Slave Catchers: Enforcement of the Fugitive Slave Law, 1850–1860* (1970).
Levy, Leonard W. "Sims' Case: The Fugitive Slave Law in Boston in 1851." *Journal of Negro History* 35 no. 1 (Jan. 1950).
Trial of Thomas Sims, on an Issue of Personal Liberty (1851).

ERIC GARDNER

Singletary, Mike (9 Oct. 1958–), professional football player and coach, was born in a poor section of Houston, Texas, the youngest of ten children of Charles Singletary, a Pentecostal minister, and Rudell (maiden name unknown). Mike was a sickly child, plagued by constant illness, especially bronchitis or pneumonia, and it was not at all unusual for him to be rushed to the hospital in the middle of the night. Family life was also difficult. His father was a strict disciplinarian, a stern man who considered athletics—among many other activities—contrary to his notions of proper Christian spirit comportment. When Mike was twelve years old, however, Charles Singletary ran off with another woman and abandoned his family. For many years afterward Mike's relationship with his absentee father was strained. The same year his parents split up, Mike's brother Grady, then twenty-two, was killed in a multicar accident touched off by a drunk driver, and Mike's mother was left to pick up the pieces and support her large family. Mike, then in junior high school, was allowed (or, according to some accounts, took advantage of his father's sudden departure) to join the football team. He played linebacker, the only position he ever played throughout his long and storied career. Despite the fact that he had often been ill as a child and was unaccustomed to physical exertion, he quickly distinguished himself for the ferocity of his play.

Singletary attended Evan E. Worthing High School in Houston and then entered Baylor University on a scholarship in 1977, where as a

Mike Singletary was named to the National Football League's Hall of Fame on 24 Jan. 1998. (AP Images.)

freshman he racked up ninety-seven tackles. His coach, Corky Nelson, taught the somewhat under-sized Singletary (he was just 6 feet, 1 inch and 232 pounds) to hit, which he put to good use during his years at Baylor. There Singletary became known, quite literally, for cracking his opponents' helmets. During his illustrious college career, the intense and indefatigable Singletary averaged fifteen tackles a game, setting an amazing school record at 662 total, including 232 as a sophomore. He was named to the All-Southwest Conference Team for three years and was twice named an All-American. During a 1978 game against Arkansas, he accounted for thirty-five tackles. When he graduated from Baylor in 1980 with a bachelor's degree in management, he had been named to the All-Southwest Conference Team of the 1970s (the only junior to be so honored) and of the 1980s. Singletary entered the 1981 National Football League (NFL) draft but was not taken by the Chicago Bears until the second round as the thirty-eighth overall pick. Most teams considered him too small to play the professional game, but Singletary had managed to impress the Bears' scouts with his play and his attitude, which was professional, focused, and confident. When he entered training camp, he was determined to prove that he had deserved to be taken in the first round and that he deserved to start; he started the season's seventh game at the middle linebacker position. In his third game he scored ten tackles and forced a fumble against the Kansas City Chiefs. By the season's end he had

cemented his place as a starter and had begun to be compared to Bears defensive greats of the past, in particular Dick Butkus, widely considered one of the greatest and most savage players in the history of organized football.

In all Singletary played twelve seasons with Chicago, starting 172 games and missing just two. Under the direction of head coach Mike Ditka and defensive coordinator Buddy Ryan, Singletary amassed 1,488 career tackles, and he was the first or second leading tackler in all but his rookie season. He was elected to ten Pro Bowls and was named to the NFL 1980s All-Decade Team. When Ryan suggested Singletary's weight might take him out of certain defensive packages, Singletary dropped twenty pounds and continued playing in the new scheme. In nearly every sense he became the heart of what was becoming an unstoppable defensive unit. In 1984 Singletary married Kim (maiden name unknown), whom he had met at Baylor; they had three children.

Then came the 1985–1986 season. The popularity of the NFL had suffered a bit after the long players' strike and shortened season of 1982, and the Chicago Bears—filled with colorful, television-ready personalities like the quarterback Jim McMahon, the defensive lineman William "the Refrigerator" Perry, and the running back WALTER PAYTON—seemed to be the perfect salve for frustrated and disappointed fans. With Singletary leading one of the greatest defenses in the history of the NFL, the Bears surged to a 15–1 record, with Singletary accounting for 109 solo tackles and another fifty-one assists. The Bears had won many of their regular season games by close margins, but during the playoffs the number one ranked defense clamped down even harder; the New York Giants went down to defeat 21–0, the Los Angeles Rams 24–0. In Super Bowl XX the Bears romped all over the badly outmatched New England Patriots (even Perry scored a touchdown) 46–10, with the player nicknamed the "Minister of Defense" or "Samurai Mike" tying a Super Bowl record with two fumble recoveries. Later many of his teammates credited Singletary for a pregame locker room motivational speech—a wild, barking, top-of-his-lungs call to arms—for setting the game's jarring, smashmouth defensive tone.

Singletary won AP and UPI Defensive Player of the Year honors in 1985. His team was now widely considered one of the greatest single-season units in the history of the NFL, but Singletary was depressed and unhappy. During this time his religious faith, already strong, deepened even further. He reconciled with his father after many long and bitter years. Singletary played for the Bears until the end of the 1992 season. He was again named NFL Defensive Player of the Year in 1988, and the Bears won their division and went to the playoffs nearly every year, but Singletary never played in another Super Bowl. When he left the team in 1992, the Bears retired his jersey number 50.

Singletary became a motivational speaker, commercial pitchman (especially in the Chicago area), and coach. He served as linebacker coach for the Baltimore Ravens in 2003 and became assistant head coach for the San Francisco 49ers in 2005. In the middle of the 2008 season, Singletary took over as head coach, but was fired in 2010 after failing to make the playoffs. He later joined the coaching staff of the Minnesota Vikings.

One of professional football's most respected and beloved figures, Singletary was inducted into the College Football Hall of Fame in 1995 and the Pro Football Hall of Fame in 1998. For this and for the success of his career and his popularity among professional football fans everywhere, he credited his belief in himself and his faith in God. "Being a champion is more than being a winner," Singletary told the 2 September 1998 *Baptist Standard* magazine. "Being a champion is being obedient."

FURTHER READING

Singletary, Mike, with Armen Keteyian. *Calling the Shots* (1986).

Neft, David S., and Richard M. Cohen. *The Football Encyclopedia: The Complete History of Professional NFL Football, from 1892 to the Present* (1991).

JASON PHILIP MILLER

Singleton, Alvin (28 Dec. 1940–), composer, was born Alvin Elliott Singleton in the Bedford-Stuyvesant area of Brooklyn, New York. He was the oldest of three siblings. His mother, Annie Laurie Singleton, taught elementary school, and his father, also named Alvin Singleton, drove a city bus. Singleton attended New York City public schools. He began piano lessons at the age of ten, and he soon discovered a love for the music of J. S. Bach as well as the joy of musical improvisation—an inclination, he would later note, that infuriated his parents. Singleton sang in the choir of the United Methodist Church, which he credited as having been a strong and positive influence in his early years.

While attending John Marshall Junior High School, Singleton formed a jazz ensemble with five neighborhood friends, one of whom had an uncle who played drums for the singer Dinah Washington. Singleton began arranging music for the group. Although he had no intention of becoming a composer at that time, his fellow jazz players considered his arrangements to be true compositions in their own right owing to their idiosyncratic chord changes.

After graduating from high school in 1959, Singleton began working at an accounting firm on Madison Avenue and taking evening classes toward an associate degree in accounting. Singleton felt stifled, however, by the accounting career that lay ahead of him, so he began taking classes part-time at the New York College of Music, which was soon to be incorporated into New York University. After nearly five years of work, he quit his accounting job and turned his attention completely to music.

Singleton began studying music full-time and his life became saturated with music. He studied counterpoint with William Pollack and composition with Paul Creston. Starting in November 1963, Singleton worked part-time at the music division of the New York Public Library and then became an usher and ticket-taker at Lincoln Center. There he heard many inspiring performances, among them a particularly stirring rendition of Gustav Mahler's Second Symphony conducted by Leonard Bernstein. Soon thereafter Singleton decided that he would become a composer. In 1967 he completed his bachelor of music degree in composition and music education from NYU.

Between college and graduate school, Singleton studied privately with the composer Hall Overton to solidify his technical foundation in composition. Overton observed a jazz-like organization in his student's music, and he encouraged the young composer to recognize and develop this strength. During this rich educational period Singleton also took classes with two prominent teacher-composers: Charles Wuorinen at Columbia University and Roger Sessions at Juilliard.

Singleton chose to do his graduate studies at Yale University, where his teachers included Mel Powell and Yehudi Wyner. He became active politically and musically, and, together with three other black students in the music school, he established the Black Students Union in the late 1960s and early 1970s. The union urged the administration to recruit African American students, and it was influential in the hiring of the first black professor at Yale's Graduate School of Music, Carman Moore, who began teaching a course on the history of black music.

After graduating from Yale with a master of musical arts degree in 1971, Singleton traveled to Rome as a Fulbright Scholar to study with Goffredo Petrassi at the Accademia Nazionale di Santa Cecilia. Although it was something of a culture shock, Europe suited him so well that he moved to Graz, Austria, in 1973 and stayed in Europe for over a decade. There were many opportunities for composers, and Singleton was well supported by the artistic community and especially Austrian Radio, which commissioned and recorded several of his works. Singleton gained recognition as an outstanding composer with performances at festivals of the International Society for Contemporary Music in Brussels, Belgium, and Graz, Austria. He also won important honors, including the Darmstadt Kranichsteiner Musikpreis in 1974 for his work for three string instruments, *Be Natural*, and a grant in 1981 from the U.S. National Endowment for the Arts.

In May 1985 the legendary musical director of the Atlanta Symphony Orchestra, Robert Shaw, chose Singleton as composer-in-residence. The composer had not expected to return permanently to the United States, but he accepted the offer enthusiastically and moved to Georgia in August of that year. Singleton served as composer-in-residence for three years, writing some of his greatest works for orchestra, including the critically celebrated *Shadows* (1987) described by Richard Dyer of the *Boston Globe* as a modern *Bolero* (13 Jan. 1995).

Singleton went on to become the resident composer at Spelman College (1988–1991) and served as the UNISYS composer-in-residence with the Detroit Symphony Orchestra (1996–1997). In 1996 he was the only classical composer commissioned by the Atlanta Committee for the Olympic Games to write for the event. From 2002 to 2003 he was the composer-in-residence with the Ritz Chamber Players of Jacksonville, Florida, and in 2003 he became composer-in-residence with "Music Alive," a national organization that provides support to youth and adult orchestras of all sizes. In 2003 he also became artistic adviser for *IMPROVISE!*, the American Composers Orchestra festival that emphasizes orchestral improvisation. Singleton also served as visiting professor of composition at Yale University and won a 2003 Guggenheim Fellowship.

In addition to being recognized for his musical blend of spontaneity, ingenuity, and rigor, Singleton's pieces have received attention for addressing important social issues and historical events. His 2000 trio *Jasper Drag*, for example, recalled the dragging death of James Byrd Jr., in Texas. The 1977 percussion work *Extension of a Dream* recalled the tragic fatal beating of the South African anti-apartheid activist Stephen Biko. Similarly the title of his 1994 orchestral work *56 Blows*, premiered by the Philadelphia Orchestra, reflects the number of times RODNEY KING was struck by Los Angeles police in 1992.

Singleton also composed lighter musical works, among them the improvisatory 2001 *Vous Compra*, one of his most explicitly jazz-inspired pieces, in which the trumpet player and pianist engage in a conversation of improvised playing that revolves around fundamental harmonic and melodic material written by the composer.

Throughout his richly diverse career, Alvin Singleton maintained an uncompromising, dramatic, and original musical voice. He is revered as one the finest and most vital African American composers of contemporary classical music.

FURTHER READING

Washington, Richard. "Singleton, Alvin (Elliott)," in *Contemporary Composers*, eds. Brian Morton and Pamela Collins (1992).

Wyatt, Lucius. "Conversation with Alvin Singleton, Composer," *The Black Perspective in Music* 11.2 (1983).

DISCOGRAPHY

Extension of a Dream (Albany Records Troy 527).

Shadows; After Fallen Crumbs; A Yellow Rose Petal (Nonesuch 9 79231–2).

Somehow We Can (Tzadik 7075).

JEFFREY L. BIRK

Singleton, Benjamin (15 Aug. 1809–1892), black nationalist and land promoter known as "Pap," was born into slavery in Nashville, Tennessee. Little is known about the first six decades of his life. In his old age Singleton reminisced that his master had sold him to buyers as far away as Alabama and Mississippi several times, but that each time he had escaped and returned to Nashville. Tiring of this treatment, he ran away to Windsor, Ontario, and shortly thereafter moved to Detroit. There he quietly opened a boardinghouse for escaped slaves and supported himself by scavenging. In 1865 he came home to Edgefield, Tennessee, across the Cumberland River from Nashville, and supported himself as a cabinetmaker and carpenter.

Although Singleton loved Tennessee, he did not see this state in the post-Civil War era as a

Benjamin Singleton (third figure from left), black nationalist and land promoter, in an undated photograph. (Library of Congress.)

hospitable place for African Americans. Since coffin making was part of his work, he witnessed firsthand the aftermath of the appalling murders of African Americans by white vigilantes: "Julia Haven; I made the outside box and her coffin, in Smith County, Tennessee. And another young lady I know, about my color, they committed an outrage on her and then shot her, and I helped myself to make the outside box (Senate Report 693, vol. III, 382–83). Singleton dreamed that he and other African Americans would possess their own land, so that they could be independent of whites, but the high price of land in Tennessee made large-scale purchases of land impractical. He observed that "the whites had the land and the sense, and the blacks had nothing but their freedom" (228).

Although Singleton stated that he was a Ulysses S. Grant Republican, African Americans were never able to win a significant political role in the reconstruction of Tennessee, and he was less interested in politics than in economics. Nourishing his dream of black landownership, he increasingly focused on locations outside the state. His attention was drawn to Kansas, John Brown's former state and the locus of much land settlement since Congress had passed the Homestead Act in 1862. He envisioned the establishment of communities of African Americans who had left the South for the free soil of Kansas.

He made his first scouting expedition to Kansas in 1873 and found that "it was a good country." Along with several friends, he formed the Edgefield Real Estate and Homestead Association to encourage African Americans' purchase and settlement of land outside the South. Singleton printed and widely distributed fliers that advertised Kansas land, mailing them to African Americans in every southern state. As a result of his promotional activities, hundreds of African Americans in Kentucky and Tennessee decided to move to Kansas in 1877 and 1878. At least four black Kansas communities founded during this time, in Cherokee, Graham, Lyons, and Morris counties, owed their origins largely to his efforts. Singleton himself lived for most of 1879–1880 in the colony of Dunlap in Morris County. In addition, some Tennessee migrants settled in Kansas cities such as Topeka, where the African American community became known as "Tennessee Town." Singleton seems to have made little money from his land promotion, but that was not his aim. He saw himself as a prophet who was fulfilling God's plans rather than as a businessman. "I have had open air interviews with the living spirit of God for my people," he stated, "and we are going to leave the South."

In 1879 approximately 20,000 destitute African Americans left Mississippi, Louisiana, and Texas to settle in Kansas. Although Singleton's fliers had circulated in these states, the fresh wave of "Exodusters" seems not to have been occasioned by his publicity but by political repression and economic hardship in the states they left and by millenarian hopes for their destination. These new migrants suffered much hardship in Kansas, too, as they struggled to find work. A national controversy erupted over the reasons for the exodus, with Democrats accusing Republicans of encouraging the migration for political gain. Singleton excoriated black leaders such as FREDERICK DOUGLASS who spoke out in opposition to the exodus. He felt that after many years of receiving patronage from their white friends, middle-class black men like Douglass "think they must judge things from where they stand, when the fact is the possum is lower down the tree–down nigh to the roots." He appeared in 1880 as a witness before a committee of the U.S. Senate that was investigating the exodus. Unshaken by the Democrats' cross-examination, he garnered much publicity for his claim that he was the "whole cause" of the Kansas migration. His claim was in fact greatly exaggerated, but he nevertheless won fame as "the Moses of the Colored Exodus." By late 1880, however, he no longer advocated African American migration to Kansas, arguing that the state could not absorb any more impoverished immigrants. Still, after the initial hardships of relocation, many of the migrants achieved some success and preferred their new home to the South.

Singleton lived most of the remaining years of his life in the Tennessee Town neighborhood of Topeka, where he settled in 1880. He founded and actively supported a number of short-lived political associations, including the United Colored Links, an organization that sought race unity in order to build up factories and other industries controlled by African Americans, and to fashion a coalition with white workers through the Greenbacker party. In the mid-1880s he actively supported a proposal by Bishop HENRY MCNEAL TURNER of the AME church that African Americans should return to Africa and build up industry and governments there. This plan, in Singleton's words, would enable "the sons and daughters of Ham [to] return to their God-given inheritance, and Ethiopia [to] regain her ancient renown." African Americans, he said, would find that their needs could only be met by a separate black nation. Unlike his successful promotion of Kansas migration, Singleton was never able to instigate migration of African Americans to Africa. After years of poor health, he died in St. Louis. Against all odds, Singleton was able to achieve part of his dreams. A black nationalist who attempted to provide African Americans with economic independence, he was able to foster the establishment of several all-black communities in Kansas through his exceptionally strong sense of a God-given mission. He fell short of his goal of true freedom for his people, however, as the lack of money and the strength of racial prejudice proved to be too much to overcome.

FURTHER READING

Singleton's scrapbook and press clippings are held in the manuscript collection of the Kansas State Historical Society, Topeka.

Athearn, Robert. *In Search of Canaan: Black Migration to Kansas, 1879–1880* (1978).

Bontemps, Arna, and Jack Conroy. *They Seek a City* (1945).

Hamilton, Kenneth Marvin. "The Origins and Early Promotion of Nicodemus: A Pre-Exodus, All-Black Town," *Kansas History* 5 (1982): 220–42.

Painter, Nell Irvin. *Exodusters: Black Migration to Kansas after Reconstruction* (1977).

This entry is taken from the *American National Biography* and is published here with the permission of the American Council of Learned Societies.

STEPHEN W. ANGELL

Singleton, John (6 Jan. 1968–), director, screenwriter, and producer, was born in Los Angeles, California, the son of Shelia Ward, a sales representative, and Danny Singleton, a real estate agent and estate planner. Ward gave birth to John while she was still a teenager, and although she and Danny Singleton never married, they maintained a congenial relationship and shared custody of their son. While not able to entirely detach himself from the predicaments of the urban ghetto, John, with a thirst for knowledge instilled by his parents, managed to find another outlet, namely film. When Singleton was nine, his father took him to 1977's epic film *Star Wars*. Singleton was immediately enamored with the moviemaking process and decided then and there to be a filmmaker. Creating cartoon flip books that resembled animated films, he began practicing his new passion for storytelling through images. At the age of eleven he moved into his father's house on a more permanent basis. The new living situation provided him with the discipline and structure that few of his peers received from male role models. While still in high school, Singleton took classes on cinematography and upon graduation immediately enrolled in one of the premiere institutions for film production, the University of Southern California (USC).

In the Filmic Writing Program, Singleton finetuned his screenwriting talents and became a standout student. Twice during his tenure at USC, Singleton was awarded the Jack Nicholson Award for best feature-length screenplay, paving the way for a bright future. Concurrently Singleton interned for Columbia Pictures and was soon signed by the Creative Arts Agency, marking the first time a student was recruited to the powerful industry agency and providing the young screenwriter and director with important industry access.

Written in just a few weeks, Singleton's script for a semiautobiographical film about a trio of friends in South Central sparked interest from agencies while the young writer was still in school. Columbia Pictures made the winning bid on the script just a month after Singleton's graduation. A twenty-two-year-old with seemingly little influence, Singleton wielded what he had, a brilliant script, and convinced the studio to allow him to direct his own film. "So many bad films had been made about black people, and most of them had been done by people who weren't African American. I wasn't going to let some fool from Idaho or Encino direct a movie about living in my neighborhood" (Simpson, 61). Singleton won a $6 million budget and almost complete autonomy. His gritty and often violent (although the ultimate message was nonviolence) *Boyz n the Hood* (1991) catapulted the young director's career and ushered in a new era in black film.

John Singleton on the Piazza Grande square in Locarno, Switzerland on 4 Aug. 2001. (AP Images.)

Within the black community the film was an overwhelming sensation, realistically portraying both the positives and the negatives of a subset of society that had never been adequately represented on-screen. With no clean-cut SIDNEY POITIERS, no black caricatures or sidekicks, *Boyz* was a character-driven, three-dimensional tale of young black men living in America's inner cities. White audiences also embraced the drama, and the film earned more than $57 million at American box offices. Although *Boyz* received a fair amount of criticism for its explicit violence and language as well as real-life violence at the theaters during its opening weekend, Singleton's unrelenting narrative made it an innovation in the film industry.

SPIKE LEE's *Do the Right Thing* had opened the door to black directors, but Singleton's freshman effort kicked the door down. Starring the unknowns Cuba Gooding Jr., the rapper ICE CUBE, and the future screen star Morris Chestnut, *Boyz n the Hood* jump-started the careers of these three young black actors and solidified those of LAURENCE FISHBURNE and ANGELA BASSETT.

Leaving the country for the first time to promote *Boyz* at Cannes, Singleton also experienced the film's success within the industry's elite. The following year the director was nominated for Academy awards for Best Screenplay and Best Director. Not only was Singleton the first black man nominated for Best Director but he was also the youngest person nominated up to that time. In 1992 Singleton and his girlfriend Tosha Lewis had a daughter.

Immediately defined as one of Hollywood's rising stars, Singleton followed *Boyz* with *Poetic Justice*, which he wrote, directed, and produced. A road movie starring Janet Jackson and TUPAC SHAKUR, the film had undertones inspired by the

Los Angeles riots of 1992 and, although thematically similar to *Boyz*, represented a more feminine turn for the writer and director. Casting musicians again, Singleton continued to meld hip-hop with film, a tradition that greatly appealed to African American and white youths. Although neither as critically nor as financially successful as *Boyz*, *Poetic Justice* proved that Singleton's writing and directing continued to appeal to moviegoers and to yield a profit for studios. For Singleton, though, his success with *Poetic Justice* (as with all of his efforts) was not defined by the film's popular reception but by his ability to create a script with a message, a film that not only spoke to the black community but also succeeded as art. As a filmmaker Singleton also consistently reached out to the black community in more concrete terms, hiring a crew that was more than half black—not often the case on big-budget films.

Still in his early twenties, Singleton was an Oscar-nominated writer and director with a vast knowledge of the history of film and a serious approach to his art. "Film encompasses all the other arts—painting, photography, dance, theater—not too many people take all that into consideration. This little ghetto kid from South Central learned at an early age and that's why I'm making films" (Lee, 38). Despite his seriousness regarding film, Singleton was also well known for his childlike tendencies—reading comic books and playing video games on set. Singleton also utilized unconventional practices with his actors. During *Boyz n the Hood*, he shot an actual gun for a scene to make it more realistic. For *Poetic Justice*, Singleton sent Jackson to work at a beauty parlor for a day in preparation for her role as Justice. His combination of youthful vigor and age-old wisdom made Singleton a near legend just a few years after graduation from film school. In 1994 he married Akosua Busia; they had one daughter.

Singleton's next writing, directing, and producing effort was *Higher Learning* (1995). Although it covered typical college issues of personal relationships and sexuality, the film primarily addressed racism at the university level and was a moderate success. Singleton's integration of white cast members into the film and its departure from the South Central setting of his two previous films demonstrated his ability to expand his filmmaking formula, which he continued to develop with *Rosewood* (1997).

Undoubtedly Singleton's most distinctive film, *Rosewood*, about the massacre of more than four hundred innocent blacks in rural Florida in 1923, was based on a true story that had been suppressed for years. The film achieved critical success, even earning the director a Golden Bear nomination at the 1997 Berlin Film Festival, but it failed to fare well with mainstream audiences, who were more interested in African American stories in contemporary cities than in historical settings. Also in 1997 Singleton and Busia divorced.

Singleton's remake of *Shaft* (2000) brought him back to commercial glory and was fairly well received by audiences and critics. The following year *Baby Boy* (2001), often considered the third in a trilogy of South Central films, was released. Starring the young singer Tyrese as a morally torn young drug dealer, the film generated perhaps even more controversy than Singleton's earlier films. *Baby Boy* not only incorporated harsh language and violence but also explicit sexuality. Within the gritty peripherals, however, was a tale of heroes and antiheroes—characters trying to reconcile their moral decisions with their beliefs in God and in themselves. Singleton considered it one of his most profound films. Two years later he directed *2 Fast 2 Furious* (2003), the sequel to *The Fast and the Furious* (2001). His first foray into the action genre produced the highest grossing film for a black director to that time.

Singleton's effort impressed critics across the globe and audiences across the spectrum. His subsequent writing and directing efforts addressed the most profound and prevalent issues for African Americans. Regardless of subject matter, era, theme, or scale, Singleton created memorable and daring films that altered not only the black film movement but also the internal and external perceptions of black and white America.

FURTHER READING

Bogle, Donald. *Toms, Coons, Mulattoes, Mammies, & Bucks: An Interpretative History of Blacks in American Films* (2003).

Collier, Aldore. "Higher Learning in Hollywood," *Ebony* (Apr. 1995).

Lee, Kendra. "The Art of Higher Learning," *YSB*, 31 Jan. 1995.

Moon, Spencer. *Reel Black Talk: A Sourcebook of 50 American Filmmakers* (1997)

Simpson, Janice C. "Not Just One of the *Boyz*," *Time* (23 Mar. 1992).

Wood, Joe. "The Greenback Bind of the Assimilated Black Artist," *Esquire* (Aug. 1993).

ALEXIS WHITHAM

Singleton, William Henry (c. 1843–7 Sept. 1938), slave, Civil War veteran, author, and itinerant minister, was born in New Bern, North Carolina. His mother was Lettice Nelson, a slave on John Nelson's plantation at Garbacon Creek in eastern North Carolina; his father was a white man believed to be William Singleton. As a young child of four, William was sold by his owner and thus separated from his mother and two brothers for the first time.

Singleton was purchased by a Georgia widow who speculated in slaves, buying people cheaply when they were young and selling them at a premium when they had reached adulthood. He was given the common tasks of a slave child: running errands and carrying goods. Around the age of six, Singleton decided to escape the constant whippings and his bondage in Georgia and return to New Bern. He was able to ride a stagecoach from Atlanta to Wilmington, North Carolina, by pretending to be the slave of a white woman riding the stage. Why she agreed to participate in this ruse is unclear. From Wilmington he made his way by foot and horse and eventually arrived at his mother's house on the Nelson plantation. For several years William hid in his mother's house, sometimes in a root cellar beneath the floorboards. When he was finally discovered, William was sold again, and again he ran away, this time hiding in the woods. After several other sales and escapes, Singleton was finally allowed to remain on the same plantation with his mother. In his autobiography, *Recollections of My Slavery Days* (1922), Singleton described his life as a plantation slave, the Methodism learned on the plantation that he would embrace the rest of his life, the restrictions on his education, and the cruel knowledge of the relationship between white planters and their enslaved women (in particular his speculations about his own white father).

In 1858 Singleton began to hear rumors of war and abolition. In 1859 he became the manservant of Samuel Hyman, a young military cadet. He was rented to Hyman due to disruptions on the plantation and, perhaps, because of his own interest in learning the basics of military practice and theory. After North Carolina seceded from the Union on 20 May 1861, Singleton accompanied his young master in battle in New Bern and then Kinston, North Carolina. Hyman was a member of the First North Carolina Cavalry. In 1862 Singleton made his escape from Hyman and the Confederate army and returned to New Bern (now under Union control) and the headquarters of Major General Ambrose

Burnside. Singleton became the personal servant of Colonel Leggett of the Tenth Connecticut Regiment, not as a slave but not yet as a freeman. Under federal law Singleton remained contraband property. While in service to Leggett, Singleton saw a number of battles and chafed at his inability to defend himself as a soldier.

Singleton left Leggett's employ to form his own all-black regiment and also spent some time as Burnside's servant. While working for Burnside, Singleton met Abraham Lincoln and discussed his dissatisfaction with the exclusion of black men from the Union forces. He conducted exercises and drilled his recruits using cornstalks for rifles, much to the consternation of Union forces in New Bern. After the Emancipation Proclamation went into effect on 1 January 1863, Singleton knew his black regiment would soon be allowed to fight. Finally on 28 May 1863 his troops were accepted into the U.S. Army. Singleton became a sergeant in the First North Carolina Colored Regiment, later called the Thirty-fifth Regiment, U.S. Colored Troops. The commander of this unit was James C. Beecher, brother of the abolitionist Henry Ward Beecher. The cornstalks were replaced with actual firearms; Singleton and the rest of his men were mustered to Charleston Harbor, South Carolina. Singleton fought in battles in South Carolina, Georgia, and Florida. On 30 November 1864 he was injured in the battle of Honey Hill in Florida. He received an honorable discharge from the army on 1 June 1866.

After his military service Singleton left New Bern for the final time. He chose to move to New Haven, Connecticut, where he began a long career of thirty-one years as a coachman for various members of the Trowbridge family. Singleton became an active member in the African Methodist Episcopal (AME) Zion church in Connecticut and for the first time learned to read and write. In 1868 he married Maria Winston. They had one daughter. During his time in New Haven Singleton became a deacon and an elder in the church.

After Maria's death in 1898 Singleton became an itinerant Methodist minister and moved to Portland, Maine, to preach. In Portland he met and married Charlotte Hinnan in 1899, and he moved with her to New York City in 1903, then to Peekskill, New York, in 1906. The couple had no children. Singleton held a variety of jobs during his time in New York and was a well-known citizen of Peekskill. After Charlotte's death in 1926, Singleton moved back to New Haven. He married Mary Powell in 1929. Singleton died at age ninety-five while attending a Grand Army of the Republic reunion in Des Moines, Iowa. He marched in the parade and died of a heart attack an hour later.

Singleton lived many lives as an enslaved man and as a freeman. He wrote his autobiography to explain his struggles as an American icon. The overall themes of his life were resistance and perpetual motion and an absolute refusal to be denied his place in American society. At the conclusion of his autobiography, Singleton wrote:

> I am a citizen of this great country and have a part in directing its affairs. When Election Day comes I go to the polls and vote, and my vote counts as much as the vote of the richest and best educated man in the land. Think of it! I who was once bought and sold and whipped simply because it was thought I had opened a book (52).

FURTHER READING

Singleton, William Henry. *Recollections of My Slavery Days* (1922; rpt. 1999). Available at http://docsouth.unc.edu/neh/singleton/menu.html, with introduction and annotations by Katherine Mellen Charron and David S. Cecelski (1999).
Cecelski, David S. *The Waterman's Song: Slavery and Freedom in Maritime North Carolina* (2001).

TIMOTHY J. MCMILLAN

Singleton, Zutty (14 May 1898–14 July 1975), jazz drummer, was born Arthur James Singleton in Bunkie, Louisiana. No information on his parents is available. Singleton was given his nickname "Zutty"—a Creole term meaning "cute"—during his earliest years. As a child he moved with his family to New Orleans, where he grew up and attended public school.

An uncle, Willie "Bontin" Bontemps, a banjoist-guitarist, encouraged Singleton's childhood interest in the rich musical life of New Orleans. Singleton first performed on drums (1915–1916) with Steve Lewis's band and with a band led by John Robichaux. A U.S. Navy hitch came during World War I. Following his discharge (probably in 1919), Singleton played with groups led by such well-known local figures as PAPA CELESTIN and Big Eye Louis Nelson, played with the Tuxedo and Maple Leaf marching brass bands, and was leader of his own group.

Around this time Singleton became close friends with the trumpeter LOUIS ARMSTRONG. (One chronicler tells of Armstrong's rejecting an attractive offer to play in New York City unless Singleton was hired, too.) Late in 1921 Singleton joined Armstrong in FATE MARABLE's Mississippi riverboat band. Singleton was associated with Marable for nearly two years, markedly improving his technique and musical knowledge by playing the band's relatively complex written arrangements each night. He performed in Marable's sole recording, "Frankie and Johnny," in 1924.

From 1923 until 1925 Singleton moved between New Orleans and Saint Louis, playing mostly with Robichaux's theater orchestra in his hometown and with Charlie Creath's band upriver. The date of Singleton's marriage is uncertain, but probably around this time he became engaged to, or married, the pianist Marge Creath, the bandleader's sister; they remained husband and wife for more than four decades and had at least one daughter.

In 1925 Singleton moved to Chicago, which was a thriving jazz center. He first replaced the drummer BABY DODDS in Vernon Roulette's band, played in 1927 with other groups, and played with the great clarinetist Jimmie Noone at the Nest. From Noone's trio he moved to Clarence Jones's band, where he joined Armstrong. For a short spell he was in a small group with Armstrong and the pianist EARL HINES, and in 1928 Singleton and Armstrong shifted over to CARROLL DICKERSON's band.

The recordings that Singleton made with Armstrong's Hot Five and Hot Seven in 1928 sealed his fame in jazz history. On 27 and 28 June he recorded six sides with Armstrong and Hines (plus clarinet, trombone, and banjo), including the jazz classics "West End Blues" and "Sugar Foot Strut." On 29 June and 5 July Armstrong made three more recordings with Singleton, and five months later they made ten more. At the December 1928 sessions Singleton found that he could compensate for primitive recording techniques by placing a microphone under the snare and playing brushes to capture a fuller drum effect. Each Armstrong recording can be distinguished for some Singleton highlight, but generally his cymbal work, snare accents, and effortless drive keyed the soloists whom he accompanied to greater melodic variety and swing.

By age thirty Singleton was recognized by musicians as one of the two pioneers of jazz drumming. The other, accurately described by critics as the father of jazz drums, was Baby Dodds, who established his name and inimitable style first. Dodds's basic drumming approach was dense and heavy, a hand-to-hand, rudimentary technique. Some critics speak of Dodds's "tempestuous," "savage," "jungle" rhythms. He used devices such as bells, woodblocks, and whistles for maximum coloristic effects. Dodds invariably played the snare with wooden drumsticks, never brushes, and his backing of soloists was moderately complex and polyrhythmic.

Singleton's style was far different. He discarded the novelty devices that Dodds freely employed, he integrated the ride and hi-hat cymbals into his overall playing, and most noticeably he used an evenly spaced, steady beat (2/4 in those days) throughout each tune. To attain rhythmic and sonic variety Singleton explored offbeats and accents that he could meld into a constant, pulsating flow. Singleton's approach, rather than Dodds's, pointed the direction that mainstream jazz drumming took in the years ahead.

Less well recognized are Singleton's innovations, evidenced when he played with Noone in Chicago. Singleton devised and developed the chorus-long jazz drum solo there. His solos added flair and variety to the jazz trio's playing, and they avoided nonmusical, crowd-catering displays. Singleton typically structured a solo around a song's melodic phrasing—in effect, a theme-and-variation approach.

During the 1930s Singleton worked and recorded with a Who's Who of jazz instrumentalists and singers. Early in the decade he played with FATS WALLER at Connie's Inn in New York. He also worked with DUKE ELLINGTON alumni BUBBER MILEY and Otto Hardwick, with the trumpeter Tommy Ladnier, and in Chicago with Carroll Dickerson at the Grand Terrace and with his own groups at the Three Deuces, the New Deal Club, and the Flagship. From September 1936 through November 1938 Singleton performed in New York with the trumpeter ROY ELDRIDGE, with Mezz Mezzrow, and at Nick's with SIDNEY BECHET. Then, until early 1943, Singleton led his own trio or sextet at Nick's, the Village Vanguard, Kelly's Stable, and Jimmy Ryan's; often he used SIDNEY DE PARIS as his trumpeter.

Singleton's move to Los Angeles in April 1943 marked a major transition in his professional career. Although he frequently performed in local jazz clubs, his steady income came from film studio jobs and as a featured regular on Orson Welles's weekly radio broadcast. Singleton was seen onscreen in two feature films, *Stormy Weather* (1943) and *New Orleans* (1946).

Singleton's recording colleagues in the 1930s and 1940s included the pianists Waller, Joe Sullivan, Art Hodes, and JELLY ROLL MORTON (at some of Morton's final sessions); the reedmen Bechet, Pee Wee Russell, EDMOND HALL, Joe Marsala, and BUSTER BAILEY; the

brass players Jack Teagarden, RED ALLEN, and Wingy Manone; and others such as LIONEL HAMPTON, SLIM GAILLARD, and Mildred Bailey.

Singleton's career as a vital jazz performer was concentrated in his first two playing decades. He always remained a thoroughgoing professional, but from the 1940s until the end of his playing days he was basically repeating high points of his jazz life. With the postwar Dixieland revival he found ready work in New York at Nick's, the Stuyvesant Casino, and the Metropole Café on Broadway, where he led a group in 1959. In the 1960s he worked for long stretches at Jimmy Ryan's, and he appeared at several festivals.

In 1970 Singleton suffered a stroke that left him unable to maintain a full-time musical schedule. He died in New York City.

Many critics contend that Singleton's playing directly influenced Gene Krupa, Ray Bauduc, SID CATLETT, and George Wettling. Although other drummers who generally followed his stylistic path were more technically skilled and imaginative, Singleton's achievements as one of the leading early jazzmen will last as long as the sounds of the Armstrong Hot Five and Hot Seven recordings can be heard.

FURTHER READING

Kernfeld, Barry, ed. *The New Grove Dictionary of Jazz* (1988).

Lyons, Len, and Don Perlo. *Jazz Portraits: The Lives and Music of the Jazz Masters* (1989).

Schuller, Gunther. *Early Jazz: Its Roots and Musical Development* (1968).

Obituary: *New York Times*, 15 July 1975.

This entry is taken from the *American National Biography* and is published here with the permission of the American Council of Learned Societies.

ROBERT MIRANDON

Sinkler, William H., Jr. (24 Dec. 1906–22 Sept. 1960), surgeon, was born in Summerville, South Carolina, the son of William H. Sinkler Sr., a teacher, and a mother whose name is unrecorded. After completing his early education, Sinkler attended Haines Normal Institute in Augusta, Georgia, graduating in 1924. He then entered Lincoln University in Oxford, Pennsylvania, where he received an AB in 1928. Active in campus life and an excellent student, he decided on a career in medicine. He enrolled at the Howard University Medical School in Washington, D.C., and continued to experience academic success. Elected a member of Kappa Pi honorary society, he received his M.D. degree in 1932.

After his graduation from Howard, Sinkler moved to St. Louis, Missouri, where he successively completed one year as a junior intern (1932–1933), one year as an assistant resident (1933–1934), and two years as a resident surgeon—an internship and residency—at City Hospital No. 2. From its opening in November 1919, City Hospital No. 2 had served as a source of treatment for indigent African American patients and was one of the few locations in the country where African American medical school graduates could pursue postgraduate medical instruction and training. Sinkler made an early impression on the surgical profession by performing a delicate operation on a patient who had sustained a stab wound in his heart. At a time when few heart operations were performed by any surgeons (white or black), this procedure brought Sinkler to the attention of his peers nationwide.

In 1936 Sinkler established a private surgical practice in St. Louis, and in the following year he married Blanche Vashon, the daughter of a prominent local family; the couple had one son. In 1938 Sinkler was appointed a consultant in chest surgery at Koch Hospital in St. Louis by Ralph Thompson, the city hospital commissioner. Sinkler was the first African American surgeon to hold such a post, and he was successful enough to merit appointment as medical director and associate chief of staff at nearby Homer G. Phillips Hospital (HGPH) in 1941. Replacing Henry E. Hampton in the post, Sinkler assumed responsibility for patient medical care, physician training, and the supervision of attending physicians at the recently opened (1937) facility, which had been created to replace City Hospital No. 2—which had proved inadequate to the needs of the African American community.

Having received the unanimous endorsement of his peers at the Mound City Medical Forum at the time of his appointment, Sinkler soon made his presence felt at Phillips. Within two years of its opening, the hospital was accepting nearly half of the African American graduates of U.S. medical schools for postgraduate training. While committed to excellence in HGPH's training programs and to the African American physicians who participated in them, patient care at the extremely busy facility was not neglected; Sinkler made sure that those under him treated all patients, whether indigent or not, with the same degree of dignity and professionalism. Working with his chief of surgery, Robert Elman (who was white), Sinkler went beyond the walls of HGPH, helping to develop postgraduate medical training for African American surgeons at institutions outside the St. Louis area. His most notable success in this area came in 1941, when (with several colleagues) he successfully obtained Rosenwald Foundation grants that enabled several promising young surgeons to obtain advanced specialized training elsewhere.

During his nearly twenty years (1941–1960) of service to Homer G. Phillips Hospital, Sinkler influenced in some manner more than one-third of the black physicians receiving postgraduate medical training in the United States. As chief of surgery after Elman's death in 1956 he served as a model for young African Americans who aspired to a career in medicine. Sinkler was one of the first black members of the American College of Surgeons (1948) and in the following year became a member of the International College of Surgeons as well. He was the first black surgeon appointed to the faculty and the surgical service at the Washington University School of Medicine in St. Louis (serving from 1950 to 1960) and the first to operate at St. Louis's Cardinal Glennon Children's Hospital, the Barnes Hospital (Washington University), and the Jewish Hospital of St. Louis.

Sinkler received numerous awards as a result of his achievements. In 1953 he received the Insignia of the Haitian National Order for his work with Haitian physicians (several of whom received training at Phillips), and he received the Distinguished Alumni Award from Howard University in 1959. While he actively participated in numerous professional societies, including the Missouri Medical Society, the Mound City Medical Society, the St. Louis Medical Society, and the American Medical Association, he was most active with National Medical Association, serving as vice chairman of its surgical section from 1941 to 1949 and as chairman of the section in 1950. He also published numerous scholarly articles throughout his career, which appeared in the *American Journal of Surgery*, the *Archives of Surgery*, and the *Journal of the National Medical Association*. Sinkler died of heart disease in St. Louis, Missouri.

William Sinkler was instrumental in the development of Homer Phillips Hospital as a training ground for aspiring physicians and surgeons. Although the hospital closed in 1979, his influence on the training of countless African American medical professionals remains as solid testimony to his role as a pioneering African American surgeon and educator.

FURTHER READING

"Sinkler Receives Honorary Degree," *Journal of the National Medical Association* 47, no. 2 (Mar. 1955).

Organ, Claude H., Jr., and Margaret M. Kosiba, eds. *A Century of Black Surgeons: The U.S.A. Experience,* vol. 1 (1987).

Obituaries: *Journal of the National Medical Association* 52, no. 6 (Nov. 1960); *Journal of the American Medical Association* 175, no. 2 (Jan. 1961).

This entry is taken from the *American National Biography* and is published here with the permission of the American Council of Learned Societies.

EDWARD L. LACH JR. AND
FRANK O. RICHARDS

Sipuel, Ada Lois. *See* Fisher, Ada Lois Sipuel.

Sissle, Noble (10 July 1889–17 Dec. 1975), vocalist, lyricist, and orchestra leader, was born in Indianapolis, Indiana. His early interest in performance was influenced by his father, George Andrew, a Methodist Episcopal minister and organist, and by his schoolteacher mother, Martha Angeline, who stressed good diction. When he was seventeen the family moved to Cleveland, Ohio, and Sissle attended the integrated Central High School. Sissle had begun his professional life by joining Edward Thomas's all-male singing quartet in 1908, which toured a Midwest evangelical Chautauqua circuit. Upon graduating from high school, Sissle toured again, this time with Hann's Jubilee Singers. After brief enrollments at DePauw University and Butler University in Indiana, Sissle got his show business break when he was asked by the manager of the Severin Hotel to form a syncopated orchestra in the style of JAMES REESE EUROPE. Syncopated orchestras (also known as "society orchestras" and "symphony orchestras") played dance arrangements, restructured from the violin-based music of traditional dance orchestras, to feature mandolins, guitars, banjos, and saxophones. As the music historian EILEEN SOUTHERN notes, the syncopated orchestra sound was not "genuine ragtime, but it was nevertheless a lusty, joyful music, full of zest" (347). Sissle's pioneering work with syncopated orchestras formed the basis for his important contributions to the newly developing sounds of American popular music, dance music, and musical theater. In the spring of 1915 Sissle was offered a summer job as a vocalist and bandolin player for Joe Porter's Serenaders. He moved to

Noble Sissle, composer and cocreator of such celebrated American musicals as *Shuffle Along*. (Library of Congress/ Carl Van Vechten.)

Baltimore, where he met his first and most significant collaborating partner, EUBIE BLAKE, who had published his first piano rag at the age of fifteen and honed his craft by studying great ragtime pianists. When Blake met Sissle, he said: "You're a lyricist. I need a lyricist." Soon Sissle and Blake, with Eddie Nelson, wrote their first hit. "It's All Your Fault" was recorded by the singer Sophie Tucker and netted the trio two hundred dollars. In the fall and winter of 1915–1916 Sissle played with Bob Young's sextet in Baltimore, Palm Beach, and other Florida venues. After playing in E. F. Albee's Palm Beach Week show at the Palace Theatre, New York, Sissle took a letter of introduction from the white socialite Mary Brown Warburton to James Reese Europe. Europe invited Sissle to join his Clef Club Symphony Orchestra. Sissle persuaded Europe to find work for Blake, and Sissle himself had his own small orchestra gig in New Jersey.

When Sissle and Europe joined the army in 1917 upon the entry of the United States into World War I, the band they formed, the 369th U.S. Infantry Jazz

Band, toured as the Hell Fighters. Their command performance in Paris, France, in 1918 electrified the crowd of thirty thousand. During their tour of duty, Europe and Sissle wrote songs together and sent them back to Blake (who, at thirty-five, was too old to enlist), who put them to music. Such songs as "Too Much Mustard," "To Hell with Germany," "No Man's Land Will Soon Be Ours," and "What a Great, Great Day" clearly reflected the patriotic fervor of the period. With the end of the war, Sissle, Blake, and Europe began discussing a new musical. The tragic murder of Europe at the hands of a disgruntled band member in May 1919 cut short his participation in the musical genre. Sissle and Blake went on to become true songwriting partners in New York. The words of the hit song "Syncopation Rules the Nation" became a reality as they put the roar in the "Roaring Twenties."

Encouraged by Europe's former managers, Sissle and Blake reworked their material from the Clef Club shows and became the Dixie Duo on the Keith Orpheum vaudeville circuit. Blake banged out songs on an onstage upright piano, instead of a more traditional minstrel instrument such as the banjo or violin. However, the Dixie Duo's performances were greatly influenced by blackface minstrelsy. Sissle and Blake, and other African American duos such as BERT WILLIAMS and GEORGE WILLIAM WALKER (billed as "Two Real Coons"), existed on the narrow band between blackface minstrelsy and vaudeville. The racist and sexist joke material of minstrelsy was still standard, as was the glorification of plantation life "befo' de War." Progress was made beyond the stereotype through the innovations of ragtime music and by adopting sophisticated dress. By playing ragtime music but not performing in blackface, Sissle and Blake further separated black popular entertainment from its artistic dependency on minstrelsy.

In 1920, after seeing Sissle and Blake perform at an NAACP benefit performance in Philadelphia, Pennsylvania, Aubrey Lyles and Flournoy E. Miller asked them to collaborate on a new musical. Miller and Lyles, a vaudeville comedy duo who had met while students at Fisk University in Nashville, were interested in developing one of their comedic routines, "The Mayor of Dixie" (c. 1918), into a musical comedy. Miller believed blacks could and should perform in white theaters, but only in musical comedy. From 1910 to 1917 all-black musical shows had begun to define Broadway as the place for black talent. However, after 1917 black theater

had experienced, in the words of JAMES WELDON JOHNSON, a "term of exile."

By 1921 Sissle and Blake had completed their development work in black popular music and theater and were ready to introduce their sound to mixed audiences. They did so in two musical theater productions, *Shuffle Along* (1921) and *Chocolate Dandies* (1924, initially titled "In Bamville"), which moved black musical theater further from its roots in blackface minstrelsy and vaudeville.

Shuffle Along was actually a hodgepodge of material gleaned from the work of Miller and Lyles and the Dixie Duo of Sissle and Blake. But with the song "Love Will Find a Way," Sissle and Blake wrote the first romantic love song between two African Americans performed on Broadway. During the opening night performance in New York City, Miller, Lyles, and Sissle stood waiting by the stage door as Lottie Gee and Roger Matthews sang the song, ready to flee if the audience turned violent; they didn't, and the show was an overwhelming hit. Another landmark aspect of *Shuffle Along* is that the Sixty-third Street Theatre allowed blacks and whites to sit together in the orchestra seats. It also introduced the Broadway audience to a host of great African American performers, both during its New York run and its subsequent tour. In addition to Miller, Lyles, Sissle, and Blake, such notable performers as Gee, Gertrude Saunders, ADELAIDE HALL, JOSEPHINE BAKER, FLORENCE MILLS, and PAUL ROBESON were in the cast at various points. Orchestra members included WILLIAM GRANT STILL, the composer, as an oboist. But the great success of *Shuffle Along* also depended on prescribed conventions. Its creators were extremely anxious about introducing jazz music and dance to Broadway; Blake worried that "people would think it was a freak show." For example, the orchestra members had to memorize their parts, because, as Blake stated, white people were uncomfortable with seeing blacks read music. The creators of *Shuffle Along* had to strike a fine balance between the skill and professionalism integral to creating a great musical comedy, and the white audience's unease with the presentation of such a piece being written, composed, directed, and performed by blacks.

After the tremendous triumph of *Shuffle Along*, Miller, Lyles, Sissle, and Blake had difficulty deciding what to do next and opted to go their separate ways. Sissle and Blake wrote twelve songs for the musical *Elsie* (1923); they were jobbed in for the music only and had no influence on the production. They then worked on a new musical that became *Chocolate Dandies*. With a cast of 125, *Dandies* was an elaborate musical modeled on the revues of Florenz Ziegfeld and George White. Written by Sissle and Lew Payton, with music by Sissle and Blake, *Dandies* was Sissle and Blake's attempt to build a musical from the ground up. Staged in the South, *Dandies'* Bamville is a town where all life is centered on a racetrack. It recognizes the performance legacy of blackface minstrelsy and also pokes fun at it, as in Sissle's lyrics for the most overtly minstrelsy-influenced number in the show, "Sons of Old Black Joe": "Though we're a dusky hue let us say to you / We're proud of our complexion." Sissle and Blake were able to create a musical comedy that was enjoyable but also mildly critical of musical theater's racist history. And their cast reflected, again, some of the greatest performers of their day, including Johnny Hudgins, Baker, VALAIDA SNOW, Gee, and Sissle, with Blake leading the band. In the end, *Chocolate Dandies* was not more economically successful for Sissle and Blake than *Shuffle Along*, but they considered it their greatest collaborating achievement.

After *Chocolate Dandies* closed in May 1925, with a loss of sixty thousand dollars, Sissle and Blake returned to vaudeville. A European tour soon followed, and the pair toured England, Scotland, and France billed as the "American Ambassadors of Syncopation." They were commissioned to write songs for Charles B. Cochran's (the Ziegfeld of England) revues. Sissle wanted to continue living in England, but Blake was unhappy with life there, so they returned to the United States, with Sissle resentful that he could no longer work for Cochran. In 1927 Sissle returned to Europe, where he toured France and England. With the encouragement of Cole Porter, he formed an orchestra for Edmond Sayag's Paris café Les Ambassadeurs, performing as the Ace of Syncopation. Sissle's band included many expatriate black musicians, including SIDNEY BECHET. In 1930 the Duke of Windsor played drums with Sissle's orchestra when it played for the British royal family in London. The orchestra took its first American tour in 1931, playing at the Park Central Hotel in New York and on a CBS nationwide radio broadcast. Meanwhile, Sissle and Blake reunited with Flournoy Miller to write *Shuffle Along of 1933*. The revision proved to be unpopular in the Depression-laden times, running for only fifteen performances in New York and touring briefly. Sissle returned to his orchestra in February of the same year, touring from 1933 through the late 1940s. Sissle also wrote and helped stage a pageant in Chicago, *O, Sing a New Song*, choreographed by the young KATHERINE DUNHAM. LENA HORNE, Billy Banks, and Bechet all toured with Sissle at various points during this period. Sissle married his second wife Ethel in 1942 and became a father with the birth of Noble Jr. and Cynthia. (His first wife was Harriet Toye, whom he'd married on Christmas Day of 1919; their relationship had ended by 1926.) During World War II he toured a new version of *Shuffle Along* with the USO. After 1945 Sissle became increasingly involved in life away from the stage. He was a founder and the first president of the Negro Actors Guild and became the honorary mayor of Harlem in 1950. Both Sissle and Blake were involved with the Broadway production of *Shuffle Along 1952*. Developed as a star vehicle for PEARL BAILEY (who dropped out of the production), *Shuffle Along 1952* was changed through "modernization" and was an artistic and box office failure, and Sissle himself was injured when he fell into the orchestra pit during a rehearsal. His last recording, *Eighty-six Years of Eubie Blake*, was recorded with Blake in 1968.

Sissle died in Tampa, Florida. With James Reese Europe and Eubie Blake, and in his own work as an orchestra leader, Sissle created the sounds of syncopated dance music, ragtime, and musical theater that defined American music in the first third of the twentieth century.

FURTHER READING

Kimball, Robert, and Bolcom Williams. *Reminiscing with Noble Sissle and Eubie Blake* (1973).

Krasner, David. *A Beautiful Pageant: African American Theatre, Drama, and Performance in the Harlem Renaissance, 1910–1927* (2002).

Southern, Eileen. *The Music of Black Americans: A History* (1997).

Obituary: *New York Times*, 18 Dec. 1975.

DISCOGRAPHY

The Eighty-six Years of Eubie Blake (1969).

James Reese Europe and the 369th U.S. Infantry "Hell Fighters" Band, Featuring Noble Sissle (1996).

Sissle and Blake's Shuffle Along. Selections (1976).

ANNEMARIE BEAN

Sisson, Jack (c. 1743–1821), Revolutionary War soldier, was also known as Tack Sisson, Guy Watson, or Prince. His place of birth and the names of his parents are unknown. In fact, little record exists of his whereabouts, activities, or circumstances before or after the exploit for which he is noted—the July 1777 abduction of Brigadier General Richard Prescott, commander of the British garrison at Newport, Rhode Island. Sisson was among the forty volunteers Lieutenant Colonel William Barton raised from his regiment with the intention of seizing a British officer of sufficient rank that he might be exchanged for the captured American general Charles Lee. Some accounts suggest that Sisson was Barton's servant. Sisson steered one of the whaleboats that made their way with muffled oars from Tiverton, Rhode Island, toward Prescott's lodgings at the Overing House near Newport. Escaping the attention of British ships, the force landed on the night of 9–10 July and overpowered a sentry outside Prescott's quarters. Finding the door to the British general's room locked, the short but powerfully built Sisson, it was said, butted it twice with his head, breaking open a panel and allowing the latch to be lifted from the inside. Prescott, dressed in not much more than his nightshirt, was spirited away without any casualties or even a single shot fired. His capture led eventually to the release of General Lee.

The American press celebrated the exploit, one of the solitary bits of good news that patriots received in those dismal months. A ballad circulated at the time placed Sisson at the center of events, though it did not accord him the respect his contribution merited or even call him by his proper name:

A tawney son of Afric's race
Them through the ravine led,
And entering then the Overing house,
They found him in his bed
But to get in they had no means
Except poor Cuffee's head,
Who beat the door down, then rushed in
And seized him in his bed.
Stop, let me put my breeches on,
The general then did pray.
Your breeches, massa, I will take,
For dress we cannot stay.
(Kaplan, 58)

It is unclear to what extent the emphasis on Sisson's use of his skull as a battering ram partook of a longstanding penchant among many white Americans for making lame jests about the imagined hardness of black people's heads.

In the wake of Prescott's capture, Barton was promoted to colonel, while Sisson enlisted in the Rhode Island First Regiment, which recruited approximately two hundred black soldiers, both slave and free. What Sisson did after the war is unclear, but he reportedly celebrated holidays by appearing on parade grounds in his old uniform. Some sources describe him as unhappy that his role in the capture of Prescott was not better known. On 3 November 1821 the *Providence Gazette* reported the death of Sisson, "aged about 78 years," in Plymouth, Massachusetts. Even though he has become an elusive figure, Sisson stands as an emblem of black people's contributions to American freedom through those long decades during which few of them could partake fully of its benefits or could even win from many of their white contemporaries a decent respect for their efforts.

FURTHER READING

Falkner, Leonard. "Captor of the Barefoot General," *American Heritage* 11 (Aug. 1960).

Kaplan, Sidney, and Emma Nogrady Kaplan. *The Black Presence in the Era of the American Revolution*, rev. ed. (1989).

Quarles, Benjamin. *The Negro in the American Revolution* (1961).

Williams, Catharine. *Biography of Revolutionary Heroes* (1839)

Wright, Donald R. *African Americans in the Colonial Era: From African Origins through the American Revolution* (1990, repr. 2000).

This entry is taken from the *American National Biography* and is published here with the permission of the American Council of Learned Societies.

PATRICK G. WILLIAMS

Sizemore, Barbara Ann (17 Dec. 1927–24 July 2004), educator and theorist, was born Barbara Ann Laffoon in Chicago, the only child of Sylvester Walter Laffoon and Delila (Alexander) Laffoon. Her parents were both graduates of the Indiana State Teacher's College. Her father's occupation is unknown, but her mother worked as a domestic for a dentist who was also the president of the Northwestern University Alumni Association, a connection that would later facilitate Barbara's entry into that university. Barbara's father died in a car accident when she was eight years old, and her mother was remarried in 1940 to Aldwin E. Stewart. Barbara was reared in Terre Haute, Indiana, where she attended BOOKER T. WASHINGTON Elementary School. After graduating from Wiley High School at the age of sixteen, Barbara earned both her undergraduate (B.A.)

and graduate (M.A.) degrees from Northwestern University; the former degree was in classical languages (in 1947), and the latter in elementary education in 1954. Sizemore began her teaching career in Chicago in 1947, upon completion of her bachelor's degree, but in 1963 she left teaching to become one of the first African American women in the city to serve as a school principal—at Antonín Dvořák Elementary School—a rare accomplishment when prejudice against women and African Americans permitted few black women to rise so high in school administration. In 1965 she became the principal of Forrestville High School. She then held a series of principalships before becoming superintendent of Washington, D.C. schools in 1973, the first African American woman to head a major school system. During her two-year tenure, she attempted to reform the District of Columbia public school system to become more responsive to the needs of black students as well as those of other minority populations through the implementation of policies and programs that, for example, questioned the validity and necessity of standardized testing for minority students. However, her heavy emphasis on the academic achievement of African American students and the need to decrease the achievement gap between these students and their Caucasian counterparts was not always viewed favorably. Her unpopular stances on education policy issues related to African American students, her unequivocal educational philosophies regarding the same, and her nontraditional administrative style led to her being fired by the district's elected school board in 1975. In a 1975 interview given to the *Washington Post*, Sizemore, when questioned about her firing remarked that, "I did not understand that in order to be superintendent of schools I was to give up my higher mission." She had made it clear in public speeches prior to her firing that she had "a higher calling than educating children, and that was uplifting my race."

Following the fallout from the Washington, D.C., superintendency, Sizemore embarked upon a consulting career with various educational agencies and school systems from 1975 to 1977. In 1977, she joined the faculty of the University of Pittsburgh's Department of Black Community Research, Education, and Development, as professor and later as interim department chair, where she remained until 1992. In 1979, while at the University of Pittsburgh, she earned her doctoral degree in educational administration from the

Barbara Ann Sizemore was the first African American woman to head the public school system in a major city. (Austin/Thompson Collection, by permission of the Moorland-Spingarn Research Center.)

University of Chicago. Her critically acclaimed first book, *The Ruptured Diamond: The Politics of the Decentralization of the District of Columbia Public Schools*, appeared in 1981.

During her tenure at the University of Pittsburgh, Sizemore engaged in an intense study of schools situated in low-income, high-crime areas with predominately African American students. In 1983 she released a widely heralded paper based on this study, which was sponsored by the National Institute of Education (Washington, D.C.), entitled "An Abashing Anomaly: The High Achieving Predominantly Black Elementary School." The funders had commissioned the project during the 1979–1980 school year to examine three impoverished public schools in Pittsburgh, Pennsylvania, and the organizational factors that contributed to their production of high student achievement. In this paper, Sizemore contended that high-achieving, predominantly black elementary schools were anomalies in the Pittsburgh public school system of 1979, because standard operating procedures within the district allowed low-achieving black elementary schools to proliferate. This monumental study called standard practices into question, and called for reforms that would mitigate these schools' continued existence in light of successful reforms in the three schools included in the study that proved the availability of viable alternatives.

The findings of this study also suggested that the teaching of poor students required a different methodology to facilitate their success on standardized tests, which she called the "Structured Ten Routines." The ten routines were: assessment, placement, pacing and acceleration, monitoring, measurement, discipline, instruction, evaluation, staff development, and decision making. She used these routines as the basis for the creation of a cutting-edge achievement model and educational strategy that she named School Achievement Structure (SAS). This model was one that she found could accelerate the academic achievement and educational excellence of African American students in underachieving schools, as was the case of the three schools in her study.

From 1992 to 1998 Barbara Sizemore was dean of the DePaul University School of Education, where she championed her intervention mechanism on the local, regional, and national levels. Sizemore's SAS strategy emphasized the ten "core routines" for teachers of impoverished students and was founded on the tenet of administrative independence with an emphasis on grammar, vocabulary, and standardized test preparation. Schools that followed Sizemore's "routines" experienced great success through increases in their students' test scores and subsequent positive impacts on their student educational outcomes. Sizemore retired in 1999 at the age of seventy-one.

She was married twice, first to Furman Sizemore, a marriage that ended in divorce, and then to Jake Milliones, a former president of the Pittsburgh, Pennsylvania, school board, who died in the 1980s. Two of Sizemore's six children also have become respected academicians.

During her career Sizemore received numerous awards recognizing her contributions to educational practice and theory, including the Maude G. Reynolds Classical Language Scholarship (1944–1947), the Danforth Fellowship (1965–1967), the Chicago Board Fellowship (1965–1967), the African Heritage Studies Association's 1992 Edward Blyden Award, and the YWCA's 1995 Racial Justice Award.

FURTHER READING

Sizemore, Barbara A. "The Madison Elementary School: A Turnaround Case," *Journal of Negro Education*, 57, no. 3 (Summer, 1988).

Sizemore, Barbara A. *Walking in Circles: The Black Struggle to School Reform* (2007).

Arnez, Nancy L. *The Besieged School Superintendent* (1981).

Bradley, Ann. "Barbara Sizemore Stresses Test Preparation to Help Poor Black Children," *Education Week*, 15, no. 25 (March 13, 1996).

Mabunda, L. Mpho, ed. *Reference Library of Black America*. 5 vols. (1997).

Watson, Bernard C. "Interview with Barbara Sizemore," *Cross Reference: A Journal of Public Policy and Multicultural Education*, 1, no. 3 (May–June 1978).

YOLANDA L. WATSON SPIVA

Sklarek, Norma Merrick (15 Apr. 1928–), architect and educator, was born in Harlem, New York, the only child of Walter Merrick, a doctor, and Amy (Merrick) Willoughby of the West Indies. Sklarek was a precocious child who demonstrated a keen interest in science and math. She also had a natural talent for fine art, which she expressed through sketches, murals, and painted furniture. Her parents recognized her talents at an early age and encouraged her participation in activities that would develop her natural skills. Sklarek often spent time with her father fishing, house painting, and doing carpentry work—unconventional activities for most girls in the 1930s.

After she received her primary education at a Catholic elementary school, Sklarek transferred to the New York Public school system from which she graduated. A high math test score earned her admission to the prestigious Hunter High School—an all-girls magnet school in Brooklyn. Sklarek's excelled in all of her courses, but she did particularly well in math and science.

When Sklarek was ready to graduate from high school, she had no interest in the careers considered by most young women of the era: nursing, teaching, and social work. Her father suggested that she consider the field of architecture. Although it was traditionally a male profession, and there were no licensed African American women architects at that time, Sklarek agreed. Architecture embodied all of the subjects she was passionate about: art, math, and science.

During her first year at Barnard College, Sklarek took liberal arts courses to prepare for applying to the Columbia University School of Architecture. Compared to high school, college was an academic challenge, and she had to work extra hard to earn good grades. Yet after a year of rigorous study, Sklarek considered leaving college. After careful consideration and discussing the issue with her parents, Sklarek decided to stay at Barnard and continue her studies.

The following year Sklarek's hard work paid off. She was admitted to Columbia University's architecture program. Many of her classmates were World War I veterans who already held college degrees, and Sklarek was the youngest student in the architecture program and one of its few female students. In 1950 Sklarek graduated with a bachelor's degree in architecture from Columbia University in a class of twenty students, two of whom were women. Despite her achievement, she found it difficult to find work in the white, male-dominated field of architecture. After nineteen job applications in the private industry and as many rejections, Sklarek took a civil service job with the city of New York in the building department. Sklarek did not feel challenged by her work assignments for the city of New York, and she thought that her skills were underused. Dissatisfaction with her job motivated her to take the four-day, thirty-six-hour architecture licensing examination in 1954. Few applicants passed the test on the first try, but Sklarek did, becoming the first licensed African American woman architect in the United States.

Sklarek was offered a position with Skidmore, Owens, and Merrill (SOM), a prestigious architectural firm with a national reputation. At SOM she found what she had been seeking: a company that was truly interested in her ability, not her race or gender. Sklarek was given great responsibility and assigned challenging projects that corresponded with her capabilities. During this time she also taught evening architecture courses at the New York City community colleges.

In 1960, at the suggestion of friends, Sklarek relocated to Los Angeles. Shortly thereafter she began to work for another well-known architecture firm, Gruen and Associates. By 1962 Sklarek was licensed as an architect by the state of California; twenty years would pass before another African American woman would become a licensed architect in that state. In 1968 she was named director of architecture. Sklarek managed a number of building projects, including San Bernardino City Hall (1973), the Pacific Design Center (1976), and the U.S. Embassy in Tokyo (1976).

Sklarek worked at Gruen for the next twenty years. She and an associate, Rolf Sklarek, married. Rolf Sklarek designed the home their family lived in until 1968, the year of his death.

In 1980 Sklarek was awarded the College of Fellows by the American Institute of Architects (AIA) for her outstanding contribution to the architecture profession. At that time no other woman in the Los Angeles chapter had accomplished such a feat. Later that year Sklarek accepted the position of vice president with Weldon, Becket, and Associates, a Santa Monica-based architecture firm. During her employment there she managed the Terminal One design project at the Los Angeles International Airport, which was completed in time to accommodate visitors to the 1984 Olympics.

In 1985 Sklarek and two female colleagues cofounded Siegel, Sklarek, and Diamond, at the time the largest woman-owned architect firm in the United States. This bold step made Sklarek the first African American woman to co-own an architectural firm in the United States. But the firm closed, the owners citing many companies' reluctance to offer large architect projects to an all-female firm. In 1989 Sklarek went on to became a principal with another award-winning architectural firm—the Jerde Partnership International—noted for its public building designs, including the Las Vegas Bellagio Hotel.

During the decade of the 1990s Sklarek joined the AIA's National Ethics Council (NEC) and taught in the graduate architecture program at UCLA. Sklarek also worked the guest lecturer circuit where she visited prestigious universities like Hampton in Virginia, Columbia in New York, and Howard in Washington, which offered an architectural scholarship in her name.

Appointed by the governor of California to the California Architect Board (CAB) in 2003, Sklarek worked on the professional qualifications committee and the Regulatory Enforcement Committee, one of many boards she has served on. Sklarek also served as director of the University of Southern California Architects Guild, a member of the commission of the California State Board of Architectural Examiners, and as a juror for the National Council of Architecture Registration Boards (NCARB).

FURTHER READING

Ehrhart-Morrison, Dorothy. *No Mountain High Enough: Secrets of Successful African American Women* (1997).

Lanker, Brian. *I Dream A World: Portraits of Black Women Who Changed America* (1999).

Smith, Jessie Carney, ed. *Powerful Black Women* (1996).

Who's Who of American Women, 2004–2005 (2004).

Who's Who Among Black Americans, 1994/95 (1993).

ANGELA BLACK

Slater, Duke (19 Dec. 1898–15 Aug. 1966), football player and judge, was born Frederick Wayman Slater in Normal, Illinois, the son of the Reverend George W. Slater Jr. and Letha Jones. As a minister in the African Methodist Episcopal (AME) Church, Slater's father moved around so frequently that as a boy he was left to live for long periods with his grandparents in Chicago. During these visits he played "prairie" football, a pick-up form of the game, at Racine Avenue and Sixty-first Street, the neighborhood from which would spring his future team, the Chicago Cardinals. His old friends speculated that Slater received his nickname because of a mongrel dog named Duke, which he owned as a boy.

In 1913 his father accepted a position in Clinton, Iowa, where Slater attended high school and played football. When he asked his parents to buy him a helmet and a pair of football shoes, neither of which were supplied by the Clinton team, he was told that they could only afford one of the items. Slater chose the shoes; he subsequently played without a helmet through his career in high school, college, and the pros. After a spectacular four years as a tackle at Clinton High School, the six-foot two-inch, 210-pound Slater enrolled at the University of Iowa. Because so many able-bodied athletes were at war in 1918, Slater was allowed to compete as a freshman and almost immediately established himself as one of the nation's best college linemen. He was selected by an Iowa newspaper to the Iowa all-state college team in 1918 as well as in each of his three succeeding varsity years. In 1919 Slater was named by Walter Camp as a third team tackle on his All-America team. Slater was one of only a score of African Americans playing football at major white colleges in the postwar years. He was occasionally harassed by fans or singled out for extra rough play, but he seldom responded to the offenses. Because of his size, strength, and agility Slater was usually double-teamed and occasionally triple-teamed. Herbert "Fritz" Crisler, a former Michigan player and later a famed coach, who played against Slater in 1919 and 1920, remarked that "Duke Slater was the best tackle I ever played against. I tried to block him throughout my college career but never

once did I impede his progress to the ball carrier" (*Chicago Tribune*, 16 Aug. 1966).

In 1921, the year he graduated, Slater led Iowa to the most successful season that it had had yet. The Hawkeyes were undefeated (7-0), won the Western Conference (Big Ten) championship, and defeated a highly regarded Notre Dame team that had not suffered a loss in three seasons. Slater considered the 10-7 victory over Notre Dame his greatest day in sports. After the season he was named second team tackle on Walter Camp's All-America team but was selected first team All-America tackle on several other teams, including those picked by Walter Eckersall, the International News Service, and Walter Trumbull for the *New York Herald*.

After graduation Slater joined the Rock Island Independents of the recently renamed National Football League. With the exception of the three games in 1922 when he was loaned out to the Milwaukee Badgers who were coached by his friend FRITZ POLLARD, Slater played for Rock Island in the NFL from 1922 until 1925. He did not get a real chance to showcase his awesome talent because the Independents were mainly an NFL "road team." These road teams played a limited schedule against other NFL teams, were not serious contenders for the league championship, and played all or most of their games on the road. During the early 1920s when there were usually fewer than a half-dozen African Americans in the NFL, black players such as Dick Hudson, Jay Mayo "Ink" Williams, and Sol Butler found it easier to find employment with road teams.

Slater continued to play with Rock Island after it joined the recently created American Football League, founded in 1926 by Harold "Red" Grange and his business partner Charles C. Pyle. When the Rock Island franchise folded in early November, Slater was signed by the Chicago Cardinals of the NFL. He played the remainder of his career (1926–1931) with the Cardinals and established himself as one of the league's best tackles. He made unofficial all-NFL teams as tackle three times, in 1927, 1928, and 1929. In 1927 and 1929 he was the only African American player in the league. Grange, who played with the rival Chicago Bears after the demise of the AFL, considered Slater the greatest tackle of all time. Among his many thrills in the NFL, Slater rated as the most memorable the Cardinals' Thanksgiving Day 1929 40-7 victory over the Chicago Bears in which Ernie Nevers scored all forty points.

While playing pro football Slater attended law school in the off-season at the University of Iowa. He married Edda Searcy in 1926; they had no children. Slater received his law degree in 1928, was admitted to the Iowa bar the same year, and the Illinois bar the following year. After he retired from pro football in 1931 he opened a law practice in Chicago. In 1934 Slater was director of athletics and football coach at Douglass High School in Oklahoma City, but he returned to Chicago the following year and became involved in Democratic politics. After spending thirteen years in various governmental positions, including assistant corporate counsel for Chicago and assistant commissioner of the Illinois Commerce Commission, he was elected to the Chicago Municipal Court in 1948. Slater was only the third African American elected to that court in more than forty years. He was later advanced to the Superior Court and the Circuit Court. Among his many honors, Slater is in the College Football Hall of Fame. He was still a judge at the time of his death in Chicago.

FURTHER READING

A clipping file on Slater is in the Professional Football Hall of Fame in Canton, Ohio.

Chalk, Ocania. *Black College Sport* (1976).

Neft, David S., and Richard M. Cohen. *The Sports Encyclopedia: Pro Football, the Early Years* (1987).

Rathet, Mike, and Don R. Smith. *Their Deeds and Dogged Faith* (1984).

Obituary: *Chicago Tribune*, 16 Aug. 1966.

This entry is taken from the *American National Biography* and is published here with the permission of the American Council of Learned Societies.

JOHN M. CARROLL

Slater, Jackie Ray (27 May 1954–), football player, was born John Ray Slater in Jackson, Mississippi, the eldest of the five sons of John Slater, a rental car company employee, and Bessie (maiden name unknown). As a teenager Slater was physically gifted. By the time he was thirteen years old he was six feet one and weighed 245 pounds. The football coach at Blackburn Junior High School recommended that he pursue football. Slater later attended Jim Hill High School in Jackson, where he ran track, played basketball, and played football on both the offensive and the defensive lines.

Slater was the first of his siblings to experience legislated integration in school. After two years at Jim Hill High School (a school to which white students were bused) Slater and other black students were bused to Wingfield High School, a white school in the suburbs. On his first of day of football

practice at Wingfield, he got into a fight with two white teammates. "Those were turbulent and sometimes uncomfortable times," said Slater. "I can remember being terrified about going back to the locker room and having one of those guys hit me." Gradually the white and African American athletes began to accept and respect each other and function as a team. Slater also participated in the Fellowship of Christian Athletes at the high school, a group that had a great deal of influence on his character and faith (*Akron Beacon Journal*, 3 Aug. 2001).

By Slater's senior year, he was a well-known athlete in Jackson. However, the bigger universities in his home state, the University of Mississippi and Mississippi State University, were not interested in recruiting him. In contrast, the colleges in the smaller all-black Southwest Athletic Conference were highly interested in having Slater as a student athlete. Jackson State University sent their freshman running back WALTER PAYTON to the Slater household to recruit him. "I was coming off my freshman year at Jackson State," Payton said.

All they were talking about was this big tackle here in town, in Jackson, at Wingfield High—6 feet, 4½, 285 pounds, agile, great basketball player. They sent me to his house to pay a visit. He only lived five minutes away from the college. ... Of course a lot of my interest was selfish. Nothing better than recruiting another good offensive lineman. He was not at all cocky, always seeking information, kind of amazed at everything that happened. And dedicated. You could tell that right away (Zimmerman, 42).

Slater accepted the football scholarship to Jackson State because it was close to home. Although he had been an excellent pass rusher and run stopper as a defensive end, the head coach and offensive line coach decided that he should switch from defense to offense. But playing offensive tackle and blocking for Payton was not what Slater had in mind. There was no glory or statistics in playing offensive line, so Slater rebelled. "I decided I'd foil the coaches' plan by messing up so bad on offense that they'd have to shift me over to defense," said Slater. "But then I'd be in the huddle, and Emanuel Zanders would be explaining something to me, and he was so intense, so into it, that I figured I can't let a guy like this down" (Zimmerman, 42).

Slater devoted himself to blocking and excelled. He helped Jackson State win a share of the Southwest Athletic Conference title in three of his four years. The Tigers posted a record of 31–11 during his collegiate career. His teammates included such future National Football League (NFL) players as Payton, Robert Brazile, Leon Gray, Emanuel Zanders, and Donald Reese. After his senior year, Slater went on to earn postseason honors as an All-American, and he attracted the attention of the Los Angeles Rams.

In 1976 the Rams drafted him in the third round. In his first professional season he was used primarily as a backup player. Slater was well aware that life in professional sports could be uncertain, so he decided to use his degree in education and worked part-time as a substitute teacher during his first off-season. At the same time his physical training habits, which were always good, became even more intense. His teammates saw him still training when practice was over.

This extra effort later paid off. After three years of apprenticeship, Slater became a starter in 1979 and helped the Rams reach Super Bowl XIV. Although the Rams suffered a disappointing 31–19 loss to the Pittsburgh Steelers, Slater had a great individual performance. He protected the quarterback and kept All-Pro defensive end L.C. Greenwood without a sack.

Slater became known for his leadership skills as well as his work ethic. In his second season as a starter, he helped anchor a line that produced 6,006 yards of offense, the second most of any team that year. He was overlooked, however, when it came to postseason honors. But in 1983, after eight years in the NFL, Slater made All-Pro honors and appeared in his first of seven Pro Bowls. That year he helped block for Eric Dickerson, who rushed for a rookie record of 1,808 yards.

Slater became known as a symbol of longevity and durability. In a physically demanding sport with a grueling sixteen-game season and where the average career is barely four years, Slater's career spanned twenty seasons and 259 games. He blocked for twenty-four different quarterbacks and thirty-seven different running backs. As a powerful run blocker, he blocked for seven different one-thousand-yard rushers. He also blocked in 107 games in which a runner gained one hundred yards or more. As a pass blocker, twenty-seven Rams quarterbacks threw for three hundred yards or more while Slater was in the lineup. He appeared in eighteen playoff games, including five National Football Conference (NFC) championships and Super Bowl XIV. He was named Lineman of the Year three times by *USA Today*, and in 1992, in his seventeenth season at the age of thirty-eight, he was named the Rams' Most Valuable Player, an honor traditionally given to a younger player in a position with a large amount of popular statistics.

In 1995, at the age of forty-one, Slater retired from professional sports after playing twenty seasons with the Rams. His twenty seasons established a record for his position, and his career is the third-longest of any player in NFL history. A humble and deeply religious man, he gave much credit for his success to his faith, his colleagues, and his family, including his wife Annie, whom he met in college, and their two sons. On 4 August 2001 Slater received professional football's greatest honor when he was inducted into the Pro Football Hall of Fame. In his 2001 Hall of Fame induction speech, Slater recounted his memories of integration and what it was like to grow up in a Southern state during that time. "It shaped me a great deal," Slater said. He went on to say the following:

> When the races came together and forced integration in 1969, it was a pretty traumatic time. A lot people tried to fight it, and a lot of people tried to embrace it. I'd say I did my best to embrace it. It was a different time in the South. A lot of young people back there now take it for granted that they'll go to school here, or go to school there, do this or do that. It makes me feel real good to see the positive change that has taken place (Pro Football Hall of Fame, Class of 2001 Inductee Bio: Jackie Slater).

Payton, arguably the most successful running back in NFL history, summed up his evaluation of Slater by saying, "Of all the people I played with or against, he'd be one of the first three I'd pick if I were starting a team" (Zimmerman).

FURTHER READING
Akron Beacon Journal, 3 Aug. 2001.
Sporting News, 25 Dec. 1995.
Who's Who among African Americans, 17th ed. (2004).
Zimmerman, Paul. *Sports Illustrated*, 10 July 1995.

KEVIN ALAN WHITTINGTON

Slater, Morris. *See* Railroad Bill.

Slaughter, Henry Proctor (17 Sept. 1875–14 Feb. 1958), journalist, compositor at the Government Printing Office, collector of books and manuscripts on African American history, was born in Louisville, Kentucky, to Charles Henry and Sarah Smith Slaughter. Since Proctor is not his mother's family name, his parents may have chosen to name him after the one-time Kentucky governor of the same name, who died in 1830. Charles Henry Slaughter died when his son was six years old. Slaughter sold newspapers to support himself and his mother. She often heard him read aloud from printed descriptions of slave life, which, having been enslaved at birth, she knew were untrue, and told him so. The existence and frequency of slave uprisings were among the many details she exposed.

Slaughter graduated from Louisville Central High School; in keeping with Kentucky law at the time, students considered "white" were sent to other schools. He was salutatorian of his class, and soon after began an apprenticeship at the *Louisville Champion*. In 1894, he accepted a position as associate editor of the *Lexington Standard*, a two-year-old African American newspaper published until 1912. In 1896 Slaughter was appointed as a compositor at the U.S. Government Printing Office in Washington, DC, a job he continued to hold until he retired in 1937. He wrote news dispatches from the capital as a correspondent for the Bardstown-based *Kentucky Standard*, and for the *Louisville Courier-Journal*.

Slaughter received a bachelor of law degree in 1899 and a master of law degree in 1900, both from Howard University, but he never practiced law. He was secretary of the Kentucky Republican Club in Washington, D.C., and a committeeman at the inaugurations of presidents William McKinley, Theodore Roosevelt, William H. Taft, and Woodrow Wilson. During the planning of Theodore Roosevelt's inauguration in 1905, Slaughter was a member of the Sub-Committee for Colored Visitors of the Committee on Public Comfort, one of many committees responsible for the event.

Slaughter married Ella Russell, a library assistant at the Smithsonian Institute, 27 April 1904. In 1910, Slaughter lived at 2236 13th Street NW with his wife, his mother Sarah Slaughter, and lodgers Harriet Lee, a laundress for a private family, and Martha P. and William D. Johnson, a law office stenographer. Ella Russell Slaughter died on 2 November 1914.

Along with ARTURO SCHOMBURG, Slaughter was a coeditor of the *Odd Fellows Journal*, which was published by the Grand United Order of Odd Fellows (an Odd Fellows order for men of African descent), and was active in the Prince Hall Masonic lodge. Both were also members of the "Labor Day Bunch," a group of black men who were connoisseurs of good food and quality liquor, who met each Labor Day at Harrison's Café on Florida Avenue, NW, with WENDELL P. DABNEY, editor of the *Union*, presiding.

Sharing an interest in what later became known as black history, Schomburg often stayed at Slaughter's home when visiting Washington, D.C. Slaughter was among the mutually acquainted African American bibliophiles who met 28 December 1916 at the home of JOHN WESLEY CROMWELL to establish a Negro Book Collectors Exchange. The group also included Reverend Charles D. Martin, Dr. JESSE E. MOORLAND, DANIEL ALEXANDER PAYNE MURRAY, Lelly Miller, ALAIN LOCKE, and Schomburg. Although officers were elected, there is no record that the exchange, whose intended purpose was to centralize all literature written by "colored" people; provide a clearinghouse for Africana materials; and share, trade, or sell duplicate copies among members, was ever formally organized or met again.

Slaughter collected over 10,000 volumes of books and papers on the Civil War and slavery, which eventually filled every room and hallway of his spacious home on 13th Street NW. This collection may have included at least part of the three thousand items collected and catalogued by Bolivar, who died 12 November 1914. Inventoried by DR. DOROTHY PORTER WESLEY at the time the library acquired it, the collection included ten thousand books (including a complete set of the work of PAUL LAURENCE DUNBAR), one hundred thousand newspaper clippings, a complete set of issues of the Washington, D.C., weekly *Colored American* (published by E. E. Cooper), pamphlets, portraits, photographs, prints, letters, sheet music, and many rare items from Haiti.

Slaughter was elected to the American Negro Academy in August 1921, together with Locke, and Thomas M. Dent, a statistical clerk at the U.S. Department of Commerce. A gourmet cook, Slaughter was known for the elaborate meals he prepared for the academy's annual meeting. Sometime before 1920, a live-in servant named Julia Lewis became part of the Slaughter household, remaining into the 1930s. On 24 November 1925, Slaughter married Alma Level. The marriage eventually ended in divorce.

In 1945, Slaughter came into possession of the diary and correspondence of the historian GEORGE WASHINGTON WILLIAMS, author of *A History of the Negro Race in America from 1619 to 1880*, and *A History of Negro Troops in the War of the Rebellion*, upon the death of Williams's widow. The historian JOHN HOPE FRANKLIN relates in his biography of Williams that these materials were briefly provided to him by Slaughter, then withheld. In 1946, the collection was purchased by the Atlanta University Library for $25,000. Franklin found the diary and letters missing from the collection, and their fate is unknown.

Little is recorded about the last twelve years of Slaughter's life. He died in Washington, D.C., and was cremated.

FURTHER READING

Blockson, Charles L. *Damn Rare: The Memoirs of an African-American Bibliophile* (1998).

Josey, E. J., and Marva L. DeLoach. *Handbook of Black Librarianship* (2000).

Kent, Allen, Harold Lancour, and Jay Elwood Daily. *Encyclopedia of Library and Information Science: Volume 27* (1979).

CHARLES ROSENBERG

Slaughter, Moses (8 Apr. 1843–18 Feb. 1938), Union soldier, farm worker, and Union Army veterans' leader, was born Moses Fauntleroy, in Clarksville, Montgomery County, Middle Tennessee. He was one of ten children born to Emalina Fauntleroy. As the son of a slave woman, Moses was also born a slave. According to the 1900 U.S. Federal Census, Moses asserted that his parents were born in Virginia; however, no name was given for his father.

An elderly Moses Slaughter of Evansville, Indiana, was interviewed for the Indiana Writers' Project, Slave Narratives, conducted by the Works Progress Administration (WPA) in 1936–1938. The published interview is accessible in several formats, however, the descriptive source material has incorrect dates of certain events, likely due to an old man's declined health.

As the personal property of Joseph Murdock Fauntleroy, a prominent tobacco planter, the young Moses was separated from his family in 1854 when he was given as a wedding gift to Emily Frances A. Fauntleroy (Joseph's daughter) at the time she married Guilford H. Slaughter, a businessman and farmer in St. Bethlehem, Montgomery County.

Moses Slaughter was a teenager when Tennessee seceded from the Union in June 1861 and joined the Confederate States of America. Afterward the Confederates built Fort Henry on the Tennessee River and Fort Donelson on the Cumberland River near the Kentucky state line. Entry to the lower South was through Tennessee, making Middle Tennessee a strategic area in the Civil War's western theater. In February 1862 when General Ulysses S. Grant captured Forts Henry and Donelson, the Confederates abandoned Fort Bruce (Defiance) at Clarksville, county seat of Montgomery County. The Union Army rebuilt Fort Defiance and occupied it until 1865. Confederate evacuation of Nashville, the capital of Tennessee, on 23 February 1862, gave the Union Army control of Nashville, which became their headquarters for troop and supply movement. Fort Negley was built for Nashville's defense by December 1862 by thousands of local black laborers under the direction of Union Army engineer Captain James E. Morton.

On 26 October 1863, the nineteen-year-old farmer Moses Slaughter enlisted as a private in the 13 United States Colored Infantry (U.S.C.I), Co. K, at Clarksville in Middle Tennessee, where many former slaves were recruited as laborers and guards on the Nashville and Northwestern railroad, which extended from Nashville seventy-five miles to Johnsonville on the Tennessee River. Major General George H. Thomas called the 13 U.S.C.I. into action on 15 and 16 December 1864, in the Battle of Nashville, to defend Fort Negley, and prevent a Confederate raid of Union warehouses. Private Moses Slaughter was severely wounded at Overton Hill on 16 December from enemy cross fire. After the Confederates retreated the 13 U.S.C.I. pursued Confederate commander John B. Hood into Alabama. Slaughter was promoted to corporal on 1 November 1865, and honorably mustered out of military service on 10 January 1866 at Nashville.

Census records illuminate Slaughter's life in the decades that followed. His path reflected both the opportunities and the restrictions freedmen faced after slavery. Like many black southerners, he took advantage of the new right of mobility in search of a better life, and by 1876 had removed to Evansville, Indiana, following marriage to Virginia Smith, his second wife. Few African Americans resided in Evansville before the Civil War, although the city served as a recruiting hub for black enlistment during the conflict. In the 1870s and 1880s the population was swelled by black migrants from nearby Kentucky. There were 3,500 African Americans in Evansville by 1890, and 7,500 by 1900. The race riot of 1903 resulted from mounting tensions between blacks and whites in the port city.

Six children were born to the Slaughter union; four survived to adulthood. Elnora, the eldest, was born in 1878, and Dovie in 1879. The U. S. Federal Census recorded Moses Slaughter, age thirty-three, as head of household, working as a farmhand; while Virginia, age twenty-two, was keeping house. Moses Jr. was born in 1882, then Joseph in 1883. A daughter, Virginia, died at age two in February 1883. Lastly,

Henry was born in 1885. In short, by the 1880s, Moses Slaughter had achieved a settled family and working life—he would remain in Indiana the rest of his life. Though it does not appear that he yet owned property, the fact that his wife worked in the home suggested a degree of security. The survival of four of his six children likewise suggested good fortune and good health. The death of his wife, Virginia, in 1892, at only thirty-four, shows that life remained precarious for Moses Slaughter and many African Americans in the late nineteenth century. The 1900 Census sheds more light on Slaughter's life, stating that he was able to read and write.

From 1900 to 1936, Moses Slaughter upheld the principles of the Grand Army of the Republic (GAR), the first fraternal organization formed after the Civil War for honorably discharged veterans, by caring for the fallen and less fortunate with material self-help and psychological uplift. He conscientiously extolled the virtues of patriotism and the struggle to save the Union. An Application of Charter was sent to the commander of the Indiana Department of the GAR on 20 August 1900 with nineteen original members for a post to be established at Evansville, Vanderburgh County, Indiana. The Fort Wagner Post 581 was named for the courageous black soldiers in the 54th and 55th Massachusetts regiments that stormed the fortified Confederate position of that name on Morris Island in July 1863. Composed mostly of free blacks, these units included infantrymen from east-central Indiana as well as Sergeant Major LEWIS DOUGLASS and Charles Douglass, FREDERICK DOUGLASS's sons; James Caldwell, Sojourner Truth's grandson; and the first African American Medal of Honor recipient, WILLIAM H. CARNEY, among others. On 6 September 1900, Colonel C. C. Schreeder mustered, elected, and installed nine officers of the Fort Wagner Post 581. Regular meetings of the post were held on the first and third Thursday. Each year the Wagner Post participated in Memorial Day, Emancipation Day, and GAR conventions and performed in parades, reenactments, campfires, and speeches. Local Evansville newspapers reported on the organization's activities and events.

FURTHER READING

Humphreys, Margaret. *Intensely Human: The Health of the Black Soldiers in the American Civil War* (2008).

Lovett, Bobby L. "The Negro's Civil War in Tennessee, 1861–1865." *Journal of Negro History* 61, no. 1 (Jan. 1976): 36–50.

Lovett, Bobby L. "The Civil War: 'Blue Man's Coming.'" In *The African American History of Nashville Tennessee, 1780–1930: Elites and Dilemmas* (1999).

Shaffer, Donald R. "'I Would Rather Shake Hands with the Blackest Nigger in the Land': Northern Black Civil War Veterans and the Grand Army of the Republic." In *After the Glory: The Struggles of Black Civil War Veterans*, eds. Paul A. Cimbala and Randall Miller (2002).

CAROLYN WARFIELD

Sledge, Percy (25 Nov. 1941–), soul singer, was born in Leighton, Alabama. Sledge sang from an early age, but usually in an informal setting. He claimed to have been a member of the Singing Clouds along with his cousin (and fellow future recording artist) Jimmy Hughes. He was working as a hospital orderly when, in 1965, he was invited by his former high school teacher to join the local Esquires. The Esquires mostly performed locally, including a number of gigs on the white fraternity circuit.

By the end of the year, Sledge recorded "When a Man Loves a Woman," a massive hit that also happened to be one of the greatest, most emotive singles of the soul era. How exactly he came to do so, however, depends on the source. Sledge himself claims that producer and local deejay Quin Ivy caught one of his Esquires shows, at which he spontaneously invented the familiar melody on an impromptu "why did you leave me baby?" Ivy was so taken with Sledge's offhand inspiration that he invited Sledge to his Quinivy Studios in Muscle Shoals, Alabama, where Ivy refashioned it into the immortal chorus. Ivy recalled a no less magical version of things, in which Sledge dropped by Ivy's record store with a mutual friend, brought his group by the studio, and began the process of crafting the song, a process that would end up taking the entire fall. Ivy secured a distribution deal with Atlantic, and in 1966 the song became a million-selling, number-one single on the Billboard pop charts—unprecedented success for a slice of pure Southern soul.

With its devastatingly earnest vocals and sparse, almost solemn organ, "When a Man Loves a Woman" was the prototypical deep soul ballad, inspiring countless imitators over the next decade (including British rockers Procul Harum's "A Whiter Shade of Pale"). It more or less invented the genre, a sound that would loom large in the pop landscape for the rest of the decade. Muscle Shoals went from a sleepy outpost

Percy Sledge performs during the Rockport Rhythm and Blues Festival in Newport, R.I. in July 1996. (AP Images.)

to the epicenter of an entire musical movement. The town boasted a scene of like-minded singers, musicians, and producers working out this new style as they went along. Stax may have gone down in history as the home of Southern soul, but Muscle Shoals was its cradle. "When a Man Loves a Woman" also set the template for much of Sledge's subsequent career; while he failed to duplicate his initial triumph, he nevertheless produced affecting singles such as "Cover Me," "It Tears Me Up," and "Warm and Tender Love." Between 1966 and 1968, he cut four albums—*When a Man Loves a Woman, Warm and Tender Soul, The Percy Sledge Way,* and *Take Time to Know Her*—that compare favorably with better-known classics by his contemporaries OTIS REDDING and WILSON PICKETT. The unexpected stardom brought on by "When a Man Loves a Woman" also took a toll on the twenty-five-year-old, who was by no means ready for the demands of a career in the limelight. Following his first tour, he checked himself into the same

hospital that had recently employed him, suffering from nervous exhaustion. He continued to be managed for the next thirteen years by Ivy, whose place in history is inextricably linked to his most famous production.

By the end of the sixties, Sledge had all but disappeared from the U.S. charts. Soul had evolved into a more hard-edged, mischievous style, rendering his straight-faced pleading and sentimental airs somewhat old-fashioned. Sledge did, however, manage to find an audience overseas, becoming by many accounts the most popular soul singer in South Africa after an early seventies tour of the nation; the 1971's artificial live set *Live in South Africa* documented, at least in principle, the high esteem in which that country's audiences held the largely forgotten American singer. Stateside, he made one more bid for relevance by signing to Phil Walden's Capricorn label. The typically Sledge-ian "I'll be Your Everything" cracked the top twenty, but the album of the same name sold poorly, and Sledge disappeared from the major label business. He continued to tour, remaining a favorite in the South and overseas.

While some critics may dismiss Sledge as a one-hit wonder, they cannot deny the influence of "When a Man Loves a Woman," and his subsequent output was surprisingly consistent and heartfelt. In fact, interest in his signature hit helped relaunch Sledge's career. In the 1980s a number of movie soundtracks and television commercials featured the song, which was rereleased in 1987 and reached number two on the U.K. charts. Two years later the Rhythm and Blues Foundation presented Sledge with a Career Achievement Award, and in 2005 he was inducted into the Rock and Roll Hall of Fame. Sledge's constant touring continued throughout the 1990s, getting a boost from the revived interest in soul, the inception of the "oldies circuit," and the long-overdue recognition of his career as a whole. Strong releases like 1994's *Blue Night* and 2004's *Shining Through the Rain* proved that, although forever identified with "When a Man Loves a Woman," Sledge was capable of singing with that same power on other songs, too.

FURTHER READING
Guralnik, Peter. *Sweet Soul Music* (1986).

DISCOGRAPHY
It Tears Me Up: The Best of Percy Sledge (Rhino 70285).
When a Man Loves a Woman (Atlantic 8125).

NATHANIEL FRIEDMAN

Sleet, Moneta, Jr. (14 Feb. 1926–30 Sept. 1996), photojournalist, was born in Owensboro, Kentucky, the elder of two children of Moneta Sleet Sr. and Ozetta Allensworth, both teachers. Owensboro was a segregated town, but it fostered a close-knit black community that offered a safe environment in which to raise Moneta and his sister, Emmy Lou. Moneta's parents were college educated, and they instilled in their son a high regard for education and a deep respect for their racial heritage. By the time Moneta was ten years old, he had become the family photographer, shooting with a Brownie box camera. At Western High School, he joined the camera club, learning from his chemistry teacher how to develop pictures. He graduated in 1942.

Sleet enrolled at Kentucky State College in 1942 and majored in business while working as assistant to Dean John T. Williams, who was himself an accomplished photographer and from whom Sleet "learned a great deal … especially how to deal with people and portraiture" (Sleet, 7). Sleet joined the army in 1944 and served with the all-black Ninety-third Engineers unit in India and Burma. After returning from World War II in 1946, Sleet finished his B.S. degree and moved to New York City, where he took a course in photography at the School of Modern Photography. Sleet earned an M.A. in journalism from New York University in 1950, after a short stint teaching photography at all-black Maryland State College. That same year, he married Juanita Harris, a schoolteacher from Maryland. The couple had three children, Gregory, Michael, and Lisa, between 1951 and 1956. Although he often photographed his children, Sleet was particularly fond of a series of photographs that featured Michael at his school for children with special needs. Michael's mental disability encouraged the Sleets' involvement with the Association for the Help of Retarded Children.

Sleet took his first journalism job with the black press, sports writing and photographing for New York's *Amsterdam News* in 1950. Later, he joined the staff of *Our World* magazine, a black-owned and operated large-format news and feature magazine, where, under the editorial direction of John Davis, he learned the narrative possibilities of the picture essay. Davis guided Sleet by brainstorming with him and offering suggestions on possible shooting scenarios that might best communicate emotions and events through images.

By the time Sleet became a staff photographer for JOHN JOHNSON's (1918–2005) *Ebony* magazine in 1955, his political, artistic, and journalistic sensibilities had been honed. His position as staff photographer suited the family-oriented Sleet, because it offered him stability. He remained with the magazine for the next forty-one years. As a photographer at a black-owned, operated, and focused publication, Sleet felt he had a supportive vehicle through which he could communicate his commitment to African American equality and the black freedom struggle. Although he soon realized that he had little influence over how his images were employed by *Ebony*'s editors, Sleet was content that his photographs would be used in the service of-furthering the cause of civil rights. "My basic feeling," he later explained, "was, of course, I was observing … and trying to record, but I also felt a part of it because I'm black, and it was one way I could pay my dues. My contribution was to record and pass on, to whoever [sic] might see, what was happening" (interview with author, 1992).

In his first five years with *Ebony*, the civil rights movement was gaining strength in the United States. Sleet hoped his photographs would garner support from readers and mobilize them to act. His photos of ROSA PARKS and MARTIN LUTHER KING JR. during the 1956 Montgomery bus boycott and of participants in the 1963 March on Washington, D.C., and the 1965 Selma to Montgomery march humanized the civil rights struggle while documenting the events.

Sleet is perhaps best known for the photos he took at King's 1968 funeral, including the iconic image of BERNICE KING sitting in the lap of her mother, CORETTA SCOTT KING, for which he became, in 1969, the first African American recipient of the Pulitzer Prize in Photography. Outside the United States, Sleet covered the independence celebrations of the newly liberated African nations Ghana (1957), Nigeria (1961), Kenya (1963), and South Africa (1994). His portraits, including those of Haile Selassie, BILLIE HOLIDAY, THELONIOUS MONK, and MILES DAVIS, and his extraordinary series of landscapes in Surinam, Sudan, and Mali are admired for both their journalistic and artistic excellence.

Sleet's work first appeared in a museum exhibition at the Metropolitan Museum of Art's 1960 show *Photography in the Fine Arts, II.* Sleet has participated in a number of significant exhibitions, including *Black Photographers* (1974), *Tradition and Conflict: Images of a Turbulent Decade 1963–1973* (1985), *The Black Photographer: An American View* (1985), *A Century of Black Photographers, 1840–1940* (1989), *Black Photographers Bear*

Witness (1989), and *Reflections in Black: A History of Black Photographers 1840 to the Present* (2000). Sleet's first solo show was mounted in 1970 at the St. Louis Art Museum. One-person exhibitions followed at the New York Pubic Library (1986), the St. Louis Art Museum (1993), and the Schomburg Center for Research in Black Culture (1999). His photographs are held in the collections of the St. Louis Art Museum and the Schomburg Center for Research in Black Culture of the New York Public Library.

"The type of photography I do is one of showing from my point of view," Sleet said in 1992. "I must confess that I don't think I'm very objective. The area and the type of work I do is one of advocacy, I think, particularly during the civil rights movement because I was a participant just like everybody else. I just happened to be there with my camera. ... I felt and firmly believe that my mission was to photograph and to show the side of it that was the right side" (interview with author). Sleet received numerous awards over his career, including the Citation for Excellence from the Overseas Press Club of America (1957), a prize from the National Association of Black Journalists (1978), a commendation from the National Urban League (1978), and induction into the Kentucky Journalism Hall of Fame at the University of Kentucky (1989). He died in Baldwin, New York, in 1996.

FURTHER READING

Sleet, Moneta, Jr. *Special Moments in African American History 1955–1996: The Photographs of Moneta Sleet Jr.; Ebony Magazine's Pulitzer Prize Winner* (1998).
Smith, Cherise. "Moneta Sleet Jr. as Active Participant: The Selma March and the Black Arts Movement" in *New Thoughts on the Black Arts Movement* (2004).
Obituary: *New York Times*, 2 Oct. 1996.

CHERISE SMITH

Slew, Jenny (1719–?), slave who sued for freedom, was born to a white mother and a father of African descent, most likely a slave. Slew lived as a free woman until 1762, marrying several times. At the age of forty-three she was forcefully kidnapped from her Massachusetts home and enslaved by John Whipple Jr.

Three years after her capture Slew filed a civil suit, *Jenny Slew, Spinster, versus John Whipple, Jr., Gentleman*, against her would-be master, asserting through her counsel that as a child's legal status follows that of the mother, she was, like her white mother, a free woman. Though at the time most colonies denied slaves legal protection, Massachusetts allowed an enslaved individual, though still recognized as property, to bring a civil suit. As one of the first slaves to sue for freedom, Slew faced a panel of judges who had no precedent to follow. She accidentally filed her complaint in the incorrect jurisdiction, the Inferior Court of Common Pleas in Newburyport, which dismissed her petition on the grounds that, since Slew had been married, "Jenny Slew, Spinster," did not exist. Ironically, the assertion that Slew's marriages were legally significant implied that she truly was free. After losing the case, Slew was required to pay court costs.

Though the inferior court ruled in Whipple's favor, Slew continued to seek justice. In 1766 she submitted an appeal to the superior court, where she faced a trial by jury. The jury, though its members' names are not recorded, would have been composed of Whipple's peers: white "Gentlemen." The contested points were the same in both proceedings. Whipple asserted that Slew was unable to prove her right to liberty and that he possessed a bill of sale for her purchase. Even more importantly, however, he argued that as a married woman Slew's legal rights were nonexistent, subsumed under the authority of her husband, and that thus she lacked the right or ability to sue him. However, several factors complicated his argument. First, Slew was not married at the time of the trials. Second, and more significant, her marriages had all been to enslaved men and were thus legally questionable; Massachusetts, under a 1706 antimiscegenation statute, refused to legitimate marriages where one or both members of the couple were slaves. Thus, in contradiction of the earlier ruling, Slew was deemed a "spinster," independent and able to bring suit against Whipple. Ironically, her identity as a slave granted her a recourse to the law that she lacked as a woman.

The superior court ruled in her favor, granting Slew freedom and awarding her court costs as well as damages of four pounds. Slew may be the first person held as a slave granted rightful freedom through trial by jury. Her suit was followed by those of other slaves who sued for freedom, from Mum Bett (later ELIZABETH FREEMAN), whose 1781 case resulted in freedom, to DRED SCOTT's unsuccessful suit of 1856 and subsequent appeal to the U.S. Supreme Court, which was met by the court's devastating 1857 decision denying blacks citizenship.

FURTHER READING

Horton, James Oliver. "Freedom's Yoke: Gender Conventions among Antebellum Free Blacks," *Feminist Studies* 12, no. 1. (Spring 1986).

Lehman, Godfrey D. *We the Jury: The Impact of Jurors on Our Basic Freedoms* (1997).

Morris, Thomas D. "Villeinage … as It Existed in England, Reflects but Little Light on Our Subject: The Problem of the 'Sources' of Southern Slave Law," *American Journal of Legal History* 32, no. 2. (Apr. 1988).

SARA KAKAZU

Sligh, Clarissa (1939–), artist, was born Clarissa Thompson in Washington, D.C., to working-class parents Ethel Mozell Thompson, a domestic worker, and Clarence Thompson, a mailroom clerk. She and her five siblings grew up in a segregated, low-income African American community in Northern Virginia. As a child Sligh noted how African Americans were portrayed in the local *Washington Post* as criminals and on welfare, and collected family photographs to piece together her own history of a positive black American family experience. As a teenager, she realized that her family was treated differently because of her race, and her father placed additional restrictions and chores upon her that were not required of her teenage brothers. Her mother was active in the local National Association for the Advancement of Colored People (NAACP) and enrolled Sligh in the all-white Washington-Lee High School in Arlington, Virginia, because the Negro school did not offer business or academic courses. Sligh successfully challenged racial inequality as the lead plaintiff in the 1956 NAACP-sponsored desegregation case *Clarissa Thompson et al. v. Arlington County School Board*. The attendant publicity brought her to the attention of a white civil rights lawyer who helped her secure an academic scholarship. Sligh originally wanted to become a civil rights lawyer but was dissuaded from doing so after being told that there were very few practicing black lawyers. Instead, she earned a B.S. in mathematics in 1962.

After college Sligh worked for NASA as a computer programmer and soon married a fellow college-educated African American. Her marriage lasted only three years, and she and her daughter Tammy moved into her parent's home after her divorce. During this time Sligh began taking weekend painting classes at the Corcoran College of Art and Design but did not consider art

a viable profession. After seeing a performance by the African Guinea Ballet, she decided to travel to Africa and spent a year traveling across the continent with her four-year-old daughter in 1968. This experience inspired her to follow her passion, and she enrolled at Howard University, taking classes in painting, drawing, and art history while moonlighting as a computer programmer and earned a BFA in painting in 1972. She then moved to Philadelphia to pursue an MBA at the University of Pennsylvania and graduated from the Wharton School of Business in 1973. After earning her MBA, she moved to New York to work for Mobil Oil and later Goldman Sachs as a financial analyst. On Wall Street she again saw the same power imbalances that she had encountered as a child; she found the business world rife with racial and gender bias.

The constant battle to prove herself in the male-dominated financial world took its toll on Sligh. While living in New York City, she sought out other artists and developed her first significant body of work. Encouraged by the response to this work, she exhibited in group shows at New York's Parsons School of Design Gallery (1982) and P.S. 1 Contemporary Art Center (1984). She finally left the business world to pursue art full-time in 1984. Sligh returned to Washington, D.C., and Howard University to earn a MFA in 1999, studying with the only other African American woman artist she knew, LOIS MAILOU JONES.

Sligh produced painting, photography, film, mixed-media art, and installations. Her work combined her own history and her experiences uncovering the history of African American communities and people. She was the keeper of her family's photo albums as a child, often adding text to the pictures to provide a positive personal narrative in contrast to the negative representations of blacks in the media. This evolved into collaged mixed media that explored autobiographical and cultural themes of race, gender, and class.

Played House (1984), *Reunion* (1984), and *Who She Was* (1987) all drew on Sligh's research into African American history and linked her experiences and the larger narrative of multiracial America. She created a series of artist books, a unique text that combined written narratives with photographs, painting, and drawing: *What's Happening with Momma?* (1988), *Reading Dick and Jane with Me* (1989), *Hiroshima Hopes and Dreams* (1996–1997), *Voyage(r): A Tourist Map to Japan* (2000), and *Untitled (For Mama)* (2002).

Fashioned with the collage aesthetic that guided much of Sligh's work, these texts criticized oppressive social structures and prejudice. *Reading Dick and Jane with Me* reinterpreted the American primer through an African American viewpoint, *What's Happening Mama?* recounted the artist's memories of her sister's birth, and *Voyage(r)* and *Hiroshima* drew parallels between the treatment of African Americans and the treatment of Japanese during World War II.

Sligh's storytelling expanded from small artist books to entire mixed-media gallery installations with her images covering the entire gallery walls. *Mississippi Is America* (1989) addressed the murder of three civil rights workers killed twenty-five years earlier, *Sandy Ground* (1992) represented the experiences of free blacks settling in the North after the Civil War, and *Passages* (2001) describes the Middle Passage of Africans to slavery in the United States.

Sligh has won numerous awards for her work, including a National Endowment for the Arts and New York Foundation for the Arts Fellowship (1988), two Light Work Residency Fellowships (1990, 2000), and the Anonymous Was a Woman Award (2001). She exhibited at the Museum of Modern Art and at Art in General in New York, exhibited at the Galerie Junge Kunst in Trier, Germany, and lectured at the Visual Studies Workshop in Rochester, New York, and at the Toronto Photographer's Workshop.

FURTHER READING
Sligh Clarissa. "On Being an American Black Student," *Heresies: A Feminist Publication on Art and Politics* 7, no. 1 (1990).
Sligh, Clarissa. "The Plaintiff Speaks," in *Picturing Us: African American Identity in Photography*, ed. Deborah Willis (1994).
Sligh Clarissa. "Reliving My Mother's Struggle," in *Liberating Memory: Our Work and Our Working-Class Consciousness*, ed. Janet Zandy (1994).
Hall, Stuart, and Mark Sealy. *Different: Contemporary Photographers and Black Identity* (2001).
Harris, Alex, and Alice Rose George. *A New Life: Stories and Photographs from the Suburban South* (1997).
Marks, Laura U. "Reinscribing the Self: An Interview with Clarissa Sligh," *Afterimage*, 17:5 (1989).
Marks, Laura U. "Healing the Cultural Body: Clarissa Sligh's Unfinished Business," *Center Quarterly*, 50 (1992).
Neumaier, Diane. *Reframings: New American Feminist Photographers* (1996).

Williams, Carla. "Reading Deeper: The Legacy of Dick and Jane in the Work of Clarissa Sligh," *Image*, 38:3/4 (1995).
Willis, Deborah. "Clarissa Sligh," *Aperture*, 138 (1995).
JENNIFER LYNN HEADLEY

Slim, Guitar. *See* Jones, Eddie (Guitar Slim).

Sloan, Albert J. H., II (24 Sept. 1942–25 Nov. 2005), ordained minister and college president, was born in Atlanta, Georgia, the eldest child of Addie Sloan, an elementary school teacher, and Albert J. H. Sloan Sr., a Pullman porter and a salesman. As a boy, Sloan resisted his mother's desire for him to become a Christian Methodist Episcopal (CME) bishop. Instead, he had early aspirations of becoming a college president. Highly regarding the value of continued education, Sloan earned a bachelor of arts degree from Albany State University in Georgia. Ultimately heeding the call to Christian service and fulfilling his mother's wishes, in 1962 Sloan became an ordained minister in the CME Church, an organization founded by former slaves, and earned a master of divinity degree in 1969 from the Interdenominational Theological Center in Atlanta, Georgia.

Committed to the advancement of youth, Sloan began his professional career as a counselor at an Atlanta recreation center. Respected and reliable, he swiftly assumed the position of center director. In 1963, he entered the realm of academia as a counselor at Alabama State University, a historically black university founded in 1867 by former slaves, later joining the faculty ranks and eventually being employed as the assistant director of the Upward Bound Program.

In 1971, Sloan began his career at Miles College, a historically black institution founded in 1905 by the Colored Methodist Episcopal Church, located six miles west of Birmingham in Fairfield, Alabama, which would span over three decades. During his tenure at the college, Sloan's diverse qualifications earned him appointments as professor of religion and philosophy, director of public relations, team teacher for NASA at the U.S. Missile in Huntsville, Alabama, director of the Jefferson County/Miles College Elementary School Aid Act, dean of the chapel, and dean of students. Concurrently, Sloan earned a doctorate of jurisprudence from Miles Law School in 1982 and received a doctorate of humane letters from Faith Grant College in Birmingham, Alabama, and Texas College in Tyler, Texas. In addition, he was a 1970–1971 Ford Foundation Fellow for doctoral studies.

In the decades that followed the civil rights movement, in which Miles College played a key role, the institution had suffered its share of turmoil and was near extinction. The surrounding community began to decline as a consequence of riots, drugs, and gradual abandonment by wealthier residents. Meanwhile, the institution had barely endured wounds from the financial mismanagement and autocracy of past administrations. When in 1989 Sloan was appointed the thirteenth president of Miles College, student enrollment had already dramatically declined and the endowment was waning. During President Sloan's administration, student enrollment tripled, the campus size increased from thirty-two to fifty-two acres, and the endowment grew from $650,000 to more than $12 million. President Sloan presided over campus renovations, new construction, and the installation of multiple programs that would usher Miles into the twenty-first century. President Sloan became seriously ill and on 19 October 2005, Dr. George T. French Jr. was appointed interim president. On 25 November 2005, President Sloan died in the coronary unit at the Brookwood Medical Center in Alabama after complications that developed from an earlier surgery. His funeral services were held on Miles's campus at Brown Hall Auditorium and at the Boutwell Auditorium in Downtown Birmingham, Alabama. President Sloan was succeeded at Miles College by Dr. French Jr., who was appointed as the fourteenth president in March 2006.

President Sloan cultivated a legacy of service in academe and the CME Church. Dedicated to higher education, he was a member of the National Association of College and University Chaplains, the American Association of University Professors, the Editorial Board for the Study of Philosophy by the Collegiate Press, the Council for the Advancement of Private Colleges in Alabama, the National Bar Association, Delta Theta Phi Law Fraternity, the Board of Directors for the National Association for Equal Opportunity in Higher Education, the National Youth Summer Sports Program, the National Association of Independent Colleges and Universities, and the Region II National Collegiate Athletic Association Division II President's Council. Committed to the CME mission, President Sloan served as a pastor, National Youth President, Director of the Board of Christian Education for the Birmingham Conference, Dean of the Alabama Leadership Training School, Associate Justice for the Judiciary Council, and President of the President's Council of the Southern Intercollegiate Athletic Conference.

Furthermore, President Sloan assumed several civic roles as a member of the Community Affairs Committee of Operation New Birmingham and the Citizen's Supervisory Commission of Jefferson County. In addition, he was past president of the Fairfield Board of Education and on the Board of Directors for the Birmingham Civil Rights Institute, the Birmingham Opera Theatre, and Boy Scouts of America. President Sloan was a Master Mason and a member of the Omega Phi Psi Fraternity, Inc., the first African American national fraternity founded at a historically black college.

On 29 August 1970, Sloan was married to Emma Lillian Lee of Albany, Georgia, and together they had three daughters, Ashaki Nicole, Ashantee Denise, and Alescia Alexandria.

FURTHER READING

"Miles College celebrates 100 years," *Jet* (Nov. 2005).

Miles College Centennial History Committee. *Miles College: The First Hundred Years* (July 2005).

"Miles College President Albert J. H. Sloan II Succumbs in Birmingham at Age 63," *Jet* (Dec. 2005).

Mitchell, Sybil C. "Historical Black Colleges and Universities Featuring Miles College; A 20th Century Southern Gem," *Tri-State Defender* (Dec. 2005).

SAFIYA DALILAH HOSKINS

Sloan, Edith Barksdale (1935–24 Jan. 2012), humanitarian, political activist, and lawyer, grew up in the Bronx, New York. Her father, Odell Barksdale, was an electrician and a postal worker. Her mother, Elizabeth Watts Barksdale, was a retail buyer and a homemaker. Barksdale's parents, although not financially well-off, ensured that the Barksdale children were enriched culturally and socially by exposing them to a variety of experiences ranging from cooking, sewing, and piano lessons to attending political lectures and demonstrations. Early inspiration came from African American leaders, including MARY McLEOD BETHUNE and RALPH BUNCHE, whom her parents took her to see when they came to New York City. Young Edith Barksdale even met First Lady Eleanor Roosevelt and was ultimately inspired by Judge EDITH SAMPSON, the first black woman elected to preside over municipal court.

Barksdale graduated from Hunter College of the City University of New York in 1959. She received a bachelor's degree in international affairs. As a way to help others, and experience first hand the world she'd spent four years studying about, the young graduate accepted a position with the World Council Mission to Lebanon (1960), where she helped to teach English, math, and science. Shortly thereafter, she signed on with the Peace Corps in the Philippines, where she was instrumental in getting medical attention for needy children with physical deformities.

Barksdale was still overseas when she heard about two events in the fall of 1963 that further shaped her career: the bombing of the 16th Street Baptist Church in Birmingham, Alabama, that took the lives of four young black girls on 15 September and the assassination of President John F. Kennedy on 22 November. Barksdale decided that she would return to the United States and put herself on the front line of the fight for civil rights.

Immediately upon returning home, Barksdale signed onto a project for the Eleanor Roosevelt Memorial Foundation in New York. She worked as an intern for the New York Urban League housing director on code violations and assisted with the 1964 general election voter registration and education campaign. In 1965 Barksdale moved to Washington, D.C., and during this time married the attorney Ned Sloan. The couple had four sons.

Sloan became a public information specialist for the U.S. Commission on Civil Rights in 1965, for which she helped disseminate information addressing a variety of social concerns including voting, housing, legal, and educational rights to the general public. In 1967 she served as assistant manager of the National Conference on Race and Education (NCRE). A comprehensive national forum for issues of race and ethnicity in education, NCRE assisted higher education institutions to create inclusive academic environments, programs, and curricula, improve campus climate in regard to "race" relations, and expand opportunities and successful educational experiences for a diverse student body.

Sloan became executive director of the National Committee on Household Employment in 1971. It was through these offices that she worked to boost the minimum wage and improve the working conditions of domestic workers. In July of that year, six hundred women descended on Washington to take part in the first conference of National Household Workers. Sloan delivered the keynote address: "[W]e refuse to be your mammies, nannies, aunties,

uncles, girls, handmaidens any longer" (Biography Resource Center, 2005, 3). In addition to improving living circumstances Sloan's agenda included an attitude change for domestic and household workers through which they would begin to think of themselves as skilled technicians and valued service providers deserving equal rights and equal status with all other members of the American labor force.

In 1974 Sloan graduated from Catholic University Law School with a Juris Doctor degree. She was a member of the District of Columbia and the Pennsylvania Bar Associations.

Sloan accepted appointment by D. C. Mayor MARION BARRY to the District of Columbia's Office of Consumer Protection in 1976. For two years she worked on protection policies on the District cabinet and fought to have dangerous products removed from store shelves. Her crowning achievement was the recall and removal of carcinogenic flame-retardant pajamas, thus protecting the children of D.C. from a catastrophic health threat.

In 1978 President Jimmy Carter appointed Sloan to the Consumer Product Safety Commission (CPSC), a position she continued to hold even after Republican president Ronald Reagan took office in 1981. During her tenure, the CPSC may have averted more than one million possible injuries and removed hundreds of thousands of potentially lethal products from consumers' hands solely through the use of its authority to recall dangerous products. One example of the commission's good work is the enforcement of the child safety closure regulations on aspirin bottles, and containers of other drugs and various household products, that prevented approximately 40 deaths and 65,000 injuries among young children in 1980 alone (CPSC, 13 Mar. 1981). Sloan remained with the Commission until 1983.

In 1983 Sloan returned to the practice of law. She signed on with the law firm of Fortas, Porkop and Hardman. In 1989 Sloan became a full-time student at the Wesley Theological Seminary in Washington, D.C. It was her goal to become an ordained minister as another avenue to promote her humanitarian ideals. Throughout her career, Sloan was a caretaker for the health, safety, and well-being of others.

Sloan died of cardiac arrest at Holy Cross Hospital in Silver Spring, Maryland. She was 76.

FURTHER READING

"Edith Barksdale Sloan." *Notable Black Women*, Book 1. Gale Research (1992). Reproduced in Biography Resource Center (2005). Available at http://galenet.com/ document # K1623000404.

News from CPSC. U.S. Consumer Product Safety Commission Office of Information and Public Affairs, Washington, D.C., 13 Mar. 1981. Release # 81-012. Available at www.cpsc.gov/cpscpub/prerel/prhtml181/81012.html.

Obituary: *Washington Post,* 9 February 2012.

JOLIE A. JACKSON-WILLETT

Slowe, Lucy Diggs (4 July 1883–21 Oct. 1937), educator, feminist, and tennis player, was born in Berryville, Virginia, a farming community in Clark County. Following the premature deaths of her parents, Henry Slowe and Fannie Potter, the owners of the only hotel in Berryville, young Lucy joined the home of Martha Slowe Price, her paternal aunt in Lexington, Virginia. A few years later she and the Price family moved to Baltimore, Maryland, to improve their economic and educational opportunities. Looking back on her childhood, Lucy noted that her aunt had very pronounced ideas of dignity, morality, and religion, which she did not fail to impress upon Lucy and her cousin.

Always an excellent student, Lucy was salutatorian of her 1904 class at Baltimore Colored High School and the first female graduate of her high school to receive a college scholarship to Howard University. At Howard University she was active in numerous literary, social, musical, and athletic pursuits. In her senior year, she served as president of the women's tennis club and vice president of the Alpha Phi Literary Society and was a chaperone for female undergraduates. She graduated in 1908 as class valedictorian. Her involvement with extracurricular life at Howard sparked her interest in a career in education.

In 1908, while still an undergraduate at Howard, Slowe was a charter member of Alpha Kappa Alpha Sorority, Inc. She drafted its first constitution and was the first vice president. Slowe's relationship with Howard administrators is cited as a major reason why the constitution of Alpha Kappa Alpha Sorority, Inc., was approved. Slowe's values and aspirations helped shape the mission and traditions of America's first Greek letter organization for black women. New pledges of Alpha Kappa Alpha worldwide annually memorize her name as one of their sorority's founders.

At Howard, Slowe developed a love for the game of tennis. For many years she was considered one of the three top black female tennis players in America. In the summer of 1910 she, along with other male and female black tennis players, conducted one of the first recorded black traveling tours to introduce tennis to black communities across the nation. In 1917 she won the singles title at the first American Tennis Association (ATA) national tournament, an organization founded to promote black tennis. She was one of the founding members of the ATA, and by virtue of winning the first ATA national tournament, she became the first female black national champion in any sport. Slowe continued to play tennis well into her adult years and to encourage black children to play the game.

After graduation Slowe returned to Baltimore in September 1908 to teach English at her high school. During summers and extended school breaks she pursued a master's degree at Teachers College, Columbia University, in what is now known as educational administration. She completed her master's studies in 1916, developing lifetime relationships with faculty at Teachers College. She was a frequent visitor there, giving lectures and engaging her peers in the study of student personnel issues. Slowe attributed much of her success to her ongoing research in this field.

In 1916 Slowe was invited to return to Washington, D.C., to teach English at Armstrong High School and serve as "lady principal," or dean of girls. After three years at Armstrong High School, she was selected to organize Shaw Junior High School, Washington's first junior high for blacks. In 1920 she established an extension center of Columbia University at Shaw, which trained hundreds of black teachers. Many Washingtonians questioned the need for a black junior high school, but Slowe silenced her critics by creating a model school.

Slowe was appointed dean of women and associate professor of English at Howard University in June 1922. In an era when the enrollment of black women at colleges was on the rise, she shaped a new vision of what a college education could do for African American women. She developed a progressive student-life program for women, focusing on housing, health, social life, community service, and educational and vocational guidance. Slowe emphasized the need for women to be prepared for independent life and to take advantage of any and all professional opportunities. Moreover, she used Howard as a laboratory to train black female educators across the country. When Slowe assumed her position, she was the first female dean of women at Howard and the first formally trained student personnel dean on a black college campus.

At Howard, Slowe implemented a series of programs designed to provide a more equitable campus experience. She created a Women's Student League to provide a platform for leadership and self-governance, with mandatory membership for all female students. Slowe created cultural and social events that were previously unavailable to women at Howard University. She elevated the role of female staff under her supervision by teaching them how to counsel and mentor, rather than matron and monitor. Numerous Howard traditions were launched during the Slowe era, including the Christmas vespers service, a concert-lecture series, teas, coffee hours, current-events discussions, volunteer activities in the community, and book clubs. She also established an annual fund, raising money for needy women students. Her most lasting legacy was the creation of the Fourth Street campus, designed for women.

Slowe understood the importance of organizations. She founded or was active in many organizations dedicated to addressing the problems faced by African Americans. In 1935 Slowe was one of the founders of the National Council of Negro Women and served as its first secretary. She was also the leading force behind the creation of the National Association of Deans of Women and Advisors of Girls in Negro Schools, serving as president for many years. She served on numerous boards in and around Washington, D.C., and worked with the National Young Women's Christian Association and the Women's International League for Peace and Freedom. These organizations were an integral part of her efforts to improve the treatment and condition of black women college students.

The Jim Crow society of her day did dampen her belief in the benefits of an integrated society for blacks and whites. Slowe worked for social justice and integration. Her lifelong association with educators at Columbia's Teachers College provided her with opportunities to influence predominantly white institutions. Slowe once advised Boston College not to house black students in segregated housing, reflecting her belief that a college campus ought to be a place where people of different races learned from each other. She was an adviser to the Race Relations Group of the North American Home Missions of the National Student Council and thought that communication between racial groups was very important, both on and off the campus.

Not all of Slowe's ideas were readily accepted. Her work with the National Association of College Women was largely directed toward establishing higher academic standards for women, to steer them as much toward political science and natural sciences as education and home economics. Her belief that rules governing women at Howard ought to be reduced to a minimum and personal honor and responsibility increased to a maximum conflicted with the prevailing paternalist philosophy of the day. She unnerved some in the black community by challenging them to see their daughters as professionals and leaders, not just teachers and socialites. Her little known "memorandum on the sexual harassment of black women" was considered a betrayal by some and suicidal by others. Often at odds with male leadership in the black community, Slowe noted in a letter dated 22 May 1928, "I have had the courage of my convictions even though sometimes I have had to suffer personal discomfort for standing up for them."

Following an extended illness caused by influenza and kidney disease, Slowe died at the age of fifty-three in Washington, D.C. In recognition of her life, the District of Columbia Public Schools named an elementary school in her honor. Howard University named a dormitory for her, and a window at the university's Andrew Rankin Chapel also honors her. Beyond these tributes to a life serving others, Slowe deserves scholarly recognition from professionals in student personnel work as well as from feminists and historians of education. Her enlightened practices in student personnel work and her forward-looking attitudes about women and their place in both the university and society mark her as an activist and a thinker well ahead of her time.

In the introduction to *Ain't I a Woman: Black Women and Feminism*, BELL HOOKS writes: "At a time in American history when black women in every area of the country might have joined together to demand social equality for women and a recognition of the impact of sexism on our social status, we were by and large silent." Lucy Diggs Slowe was not silent. She devoted her life to joining with other women, black and white, to advance the educational, cultural, and social opportunities for women in general and black women in particular. She practiced, published, and preached her ideas, leaving a human and ideological legacy that helped open closed doors of education for all.

FURTHER READING

The Moorland Spingarn Collection at Howard
  University contains the personal papers of Lucy
  Diggs Slowe and the majority of the available
  biographical materials on her.

Ransom, Joanna Houston. "Innovations Introduced into the Women's Program at Howard University by the Late Dean Lucy D. Slowe", *Journal of the National Association of College Women* 14 (1937).

Turner, Geneva C. "Slowe School", *Negro History Bulletin*, Jan. 1955.

LEROY NESBITT JR.
DESMOND WOLFE

Slyde, Jimmy (2 Oct. 1927–16 May 2008), tap dancer and tap master, known for his innovative jazz style and breathtaking slides, was born James Titus Godbolt in Atlanta, Georgia, the only child of Titus Godbolt and Lillian Russell Godbolt. When the family moved to Boston, his father worked as a refueler for the Boston and Albany Railroad. Jimmy attended Christopher Gibson Elementary and Patrick Campbell Elementary, then graduated from Brighton High School, where he excelled in sports. After a few years on a football scholarship at Shaw University in North Carolina, where he majored in physical education, he returned to Boston to pursue his first loves—music and dancing.

As a boy, Jimmy had been enrolled by his mother in the New England Conservatory of Music in the hope that he would become a concert violinist. While he enjoyed the violin, at age twelve he heard rhythmic tapping coming from a nearby building, and that changed everything. It was the dance studio of the legendary Stanley Brown, who in his teaching combined rigorous tap dance basics and acrobatics with ballet, modern, primitive, and popular dance styles as well as the study of music. Decades later, Slyde recalled studying with Brown: "He was strict. Trying to earn his respect was a big impetus for me as a dancer. It was a wonderful, joyful time" (Bernstein, 2007).

Brown's studio attracted dancers at all stages, including the great "hoofers"—BILL "BOJANGLES" ROBINSON, JOHN BUBBLES, Derby Wilson, Avon Long, Bill Bailey, HENRY LeTANG, Tip Tap and Toe—as well as jazz, swing, and bebop musicians. Eddie "Schoolboy" Ford taught Slyde and Jimmy Mitchell how to slide, thus beginning their dancing partnership as the Slyde Brothers. In the 1940s they performed in the new entertainment genre called "Presentation," which emphasized music and featured an ensemble which included a big band, a comedian, singers, and tap dancers (Frank, 257).

The Slyde Brothers danced in clubs and burlesque theaters, performing with entertainers such as LOUIS ARMSTRONG and DUKE ELLINGTON.

Because racism in America excluded black performers from mainstream shows and films, they were forced to work the segregated black entertainment circuit. Slyde traveled the country with COUNT BASIE and others, sometimes doing seven shows daily. He experimented with different dance and musical styles, including Afro-Caribbean, and developed his unique style. Sali Ann Kriegsman described it as "at once poetry, music, storytelling, philosophy," with "uncommon lyricism, lucid, inventive, and immaculate rhythmic sensibility," and "taps clear as glass" (*Dance Magazine*, Nov 2005, 34).

Hoping for steady work, Slyde went to Hollywood in the 1950s, but he found few roles, and poverty forced his return east. In the 1960s he joined the Harlem Uptown All-Star Dancers and traveled with them to Europe. He lived and taught in Paris for six years, thriving in the city's more tolerant atmosphere and performing throughout Europe. His creativity as a tap artist grew and included his recording of tap percussion rhythms as music for listening—one of the first albums of its kind. He was also one of the original hoofers in the 1970s musical compilation *1000 Years of Jazz*, recorded in Amsterdam jam-session style, in which dancers' taps are their instruments.

African American Culture and History, edited by Jack Salzman (1995), reports that Slyde experimented with rhythm and tonality, "sliding into cascades of taps close to the floor. Sound was more important … than the step. Timing was crucial and music was his driving force." Discussing tap as music, Slyde said: "A tap dancer is also a musician, a percussionist. When I put my metal on wood, I get different tones. When clubs put carpets on the floor, they killed tap and made everything softshoe" (Bernstein, 2004, 76). About his trademark slides, he said "A slide is not a determinable motion because it can be any length. *Chhhooooooop!* How long is that? When people ask how I measure it, I don't. It's a matter of feeling and knowing your music and applying it" (Bernstein, 2004, 77). The rubato of his slides—the rhythmic flexibility within a phrase or measure—added something new, beautiful, and exciting to tap.

Slyde returned to the United States in the 1970s, but work for black hoofers was scarce. Performing when he could, he survived by teaching, and many young dancers speak gratefully of his generosity. He hosted a series of weekly tap jams at New York City clubs—La Cave and La Place—that attracted famous dancers. In the 1980s his career had a boost with appearances in films and television. A PBS special on American dance, staged at the White House, featured Slyde, as did a tribute to HARALD NICHOLAS and FAYARD NICHOLAS at Carnegie Hall. His film credits include *Round Midnight* (1986), and three films he appeared in which featured GREGORY HINES: *The Cotton Club* (1984), *About Tap* (1985), and *Tap* (1989). Slyde joined the tap dancer Steve Condos in developing a production of jazz tap improvisations for the Smithsonian Institution, which traveled throughout the United States and South America. He made his Broadway debut in 1989 in the musical *Black and Blue* (also in Paris), and was nominated for a Tony Award.

Slyde's tap rhythms were central in the soundtrack of *Brushstrokes*, the 1990 animated film against prejudice (without words) produced for the United Nations by the Emmy award-winning filmmaker and Aesthetic Realism consultant Ken Kimmelman, who also filmed rare footage of a rehearsal with Slyde tapping, accompanied by Major Holley's original jazz vocal effects.

In 1996 Slyde was responsible for bringing tap to the Jacob's Pillow Dance Festival. That year he received an honorary doctorate in performing arts from Oklahoma City University and also performed in *A Night at the Pops* with Baakari Wilder and in the Broadway hit *Bring in Da' Noise*. He appeared in Lincoln Center's *Majesty of Tap* with the tap legends BUNNY BRIGGS, Chuck Green, and Lon Chaney. Slyde received the National Endowment of the Art's prestigious National Heritage Fellowship Award in 1999. In 2003 he was awarded a Guggenheim Fellowship for choreography. He also performed at New York City's Tap Extravaganza with dancers of all ages, including the eighty-seven-year-old Ernest "Brownie" Brown (one of the original Copasetics tap group of the 1950s), the all-female company Rhythm ISS, Reggio "The Hoofer" McLaughlin, Andrew Nemr, Brenda Bufalino, and SAVION GLOVER.

Slyde said, "I would like to be known as representing surprise—the unpredictable—and humor as a tap dancer" (Bernstein, 2004, 77). In a career that had spanned more than six decades by 2007, his dancing continued to move, surprise, and thrill through musical recordings, films, video, and the Internet. He died in Hanson, Massachusetts, at the age of 80.

FURTHER READING

Bernstein, Alice. "Jimmy Slyde and the Beauty of Tap Dance," in *Aesthetic Realism and the Answer to Racism* (2004).

Bernstein, Alice. Personal interviews with Jimmy Slyde (unpublished, 2003 and 2007).

Frank, Rusty E. *Tap! The Greatest Tap Dance Stars and Their Stories, 1900–1955* (1994).

Sommer, Sally. "Interview with Jimmy Slyde," Oral History Project, Dance Collection, New York Public Library (unpublished, 1996).

ALICE BERNSTEIN

Small, Mary Jane Blair (20 Oct. 1850–11 Sept. 1945), ordained Methodist elder, minister, and denominational leader, was born in Murfreesboro, Tennessee, the daughter of Agnes Blair and an unknown father. It is possible that she attented Baltimore Catholic school operated by the black order the Oblate Sisters of Providence. Little information is available regarding her early life and after 1916. The years 1873 to 1916, nonetheless, witnessed significant contributions by this pioneering clergywoman. Small did not, however, embrace church membership until three days after she wed the Reverend John Bryan Small, a future bishop, in October 1873. As a minister's wife, she labored in parishes of the African Methodist Episcopal (AME) Zion Church in North Carolina, Pennsylvania, Connecticut, and the District of Columbia.

Women in most Christian churches during the later 1800s and the early 1900s had difficulty finding acceptance as practicing ministers. Indeed many women effectively preached without seeking ordination or attempting to pastor. As early as 1892 Small, however, began to work toward full ordination. Thanks to a change in the discipline of the AME Zion Church in 1876 that dropped the word *male*, Small secured a license as a missionary and evangelist in what was then the Philadelphia and Baltimore Annual Conference in 1892. Three years later she was ordained a deacon, becoming only the second female to attain this position in the AME Zion Church. John Small's election as bishop in 1896 enabled Mary Small, accompanying her husband, to fulfill a sustained desire to serve on the African mission field. Two years later Mary Small was ordained by Bishop Charles C. Pettey in the AME Zion annual conference. Many Zion members, especially male clergy, vigorously objected to her ordination, however, insisting that it contradicted scripture and Christian tradition. Although her opponents made plans to have the ordination of women officially prohibited at the upcoming denominational general convention in 1900, supporters of female ordination garnered the majority of the votes at that convention. Thus after 1898 no office in the AME Zion Church was officially closed to women, though subsequent practice did not always reflect equal opportunities for women preachers.

With Small's ordination as elder she attained a status that during this era few women, black or white, equaled. There were other denominations wherein women received ordinations for pulpit ministry between 1850 and 1890 (Congregationalist Church, Methodist Protestant Church, and African Methodist Episcopal Church), but those ordinations were either localized, carrying no mandatory recognitions in other congregations or annual conferences, or were rescinded by the denominational body. Thus the AME Zion Church's ordination of Small as elder stands as a significant watershed in women's advancement toward full equality in mainline Protestant churches, laying the foundation for later full acceptance of women ministers.

Small not only labored on the African mission field along with her husband but was also actively engaged in what became the Woman's Home and Foreign Missionary Society of the AME Zion Church. She served as president from 1912 to 1916. Significantly, her defeat by Rev. Dr. Florence Randolph in 1916 broke the custom of a bishop's wife serving as leader of the group. Small's husband died in 1905, and her influence in denominational leadership appears to have declined considerably after 1916. Apparently she never pastored a congregation. Possibly she resided for a while in a nursing home. She died in Pennsylvania in 1945, less than a month before her ninety-fifth birthday; her funeral was in the Bryan AME Zion Church (named in honor of her husband) in York.

FURTHER READING

Bradley David Henry. *A History of the A.M.E. Zion Church*, vol. 2 (1970).

Collier-Thomas, Bettye. *Daughters of Thunder: Black Women Preachers and Their Sermons, 1850–1979* (1898).

Martin, Sandy Dwayne. *For God and Race: The Religious and Political Leadership of AMEZ Bishop James Walker Hood* (1999).

Walls, William J. *The African Methodist Episcopal Zion Church: Reality of the Black Church* (1974).

SANDY DWAYNE MARTIN

Smalls, Robert (5 Apr. 1839–23 Feb. 1915), congressman, was born in Beaufort, South Carolina, the son of an unknown white man and Lydia, a slave woman who worked as a house servant for the John McKee family in Beaufort. Descendants of Smalls believed that his father was John McKee, who died when Robert was young. The McKee family sent Robert to live with their relatives in Charleston, where he worked for wages that he turned over to his master. Smalls apparently taught himself the rudiments of reading and writing during this period. Later he attended school for three months, and as an adult he hired tutors. In 1856 Smalls married Hannah Jones, a slave who worked as a hotel maid. They had three children, one of whom died of smallpox. The couple lived apart from their owners, to whom they sent most of their income. In 1861 Smalls began working as a deckhand on the *Planter*, a steamer that operated out of Charleston Harbor. By 1862 he was the craft's pilot. He knew the locations of Confederate armaments in the channels and on shore, and he knew of the U.S. Navy fleet anchored just outside Charleston Harbor. When he learned of the federal occupation of Beaufort, Smalls determined with several other slave sailors to guide the *Planter* to Union waters. Secretly loading their families on board, the men rushed the vessel out of Charleston Harbor under cover of darkness and surrendered it to the U.S. Navy. Congress awarded Smalls and his aides monetary compensation for liberating the *Planter* from Confederate hands. From occupied Beaufort, Smalls piloted the vessel, now outfitted as a troop transport, around the Sea Islands, carrying messages, supplies, and men for the Union army. He always maintained that eventually he was commissioned as a captain, but his papers were lost, and after the war he had difficulty proving his service when he tried to obtain a pension. He piloted other ships as well, including the ironclad *Keokuk* in an unsuccessful assault on the city of Charleston.

During the war Smalls and his family traveled to the North to elicit popular sympathy for the slaves' plight and to attest to the service ex-slaves might perform if the federal government would allow them the opportunity. Smalls began a store for freedpeople in Beaufort and, at the war's end, bought his former owner's house, where Smalls resided until his death, for unpaid taxes. By 1870 Smalls had six thousand dollars in real estate and one thousand dollars in personal property.

Smalls entered politics as a delegate to South Carolina's constitutional convention of 1868 and in the same year won election as a Republican to the state's general assembly. He served in that body until 1875, first as a representative and later as a

Robert Smalls, U.S. Congressman from South Carolina, photographed c. 1875. (Library of Congress.)

state senator. In 1874 Smalls was elected congressman from South Carolina's Fifth District, which included Beaufort. During his second congressional term in 1877, a South Carolina jury convicted him of accepting a bribe while he served in the state senate. Smalls had chaired the Printing Committee, which parceled out the state's printing. Evidence suggested that a leading printer bribed Smalls in return for state business. The judge sentenced Smalls to three years in the state penitentiary at hard labor. Smalls protested his innocence and appealed, losing before the state supreme court. He appealed to the U.S. Supreme Court, but before the case could be resolved, the Democratic governor, William D. Simpson, pardoned him in exchange for a federal agreement to drop an investigation into the Democrats' violation of election laws.

With his conviction blighting his reputation and the Democratic paramilitary group known as the Red Shirts terrorizing his constituents, Smalls lost a third bid for Congress in 1878. He ran again in 1880 but lost in an election characterized by fraud on the part of the Democrats. This time Smalls contested the result, and the House awarded him the seat. In 1882 he failed to receive his party's nomination after Democrats redistricted Beaufort into the Seventh District. When the victorious Republican died in office in 1884, however, Smalls was elected to serve the remainder of the term, and he won reelection to another term later in the year. He lost the seat permanently in 1886, as Democrats threw out ballots with impunity and extralegal violence kept black voters from the polls.

Hannah Smalls died in 1883, and Robert married Annie Wigg in 1890. They had one son before her death in 1895. Effectively excluded from local politics by the Democrats' electoral fraud and the state's disenfranchisement of African Americans in 1895, Smalls remained active in the Republican Party at the national level. Those contacts gained him appointment as collector of customs for the Port of Beaufort in 1889, a post he lost with the Democratic national victory of 1892. He regained the office in 1898 with the return of a national Republican administration. He served until 1913, despite growing lily-white sentiment in the Republican Party and the difficulties of discharging his duties in now-segregated Beaufort. Beset by several grave illnesses, Smalls died there, disillusioned by the reversal of the African American political gains for which he had worked in Reconstruction.

FURTHER READING

No single collection of Smalls's private or public papers exists, but his letters and documents are in other collections, notably the Frederick Douglass and Carter G. Woodson collections at the Library of Congress and the Governor Wade Hampton Collection at the South Carolina Department of Archives and History. His public career is documented in records of the South Carolina General Assembly, the U.S. House of Representatives, and the Veterans Administration at the National Archives.

Miller, Edward A., Jr. *Gullah Statesman: Robert Smalls from Slavery to Congress, 1839–1915* (1995).

Rabinowitz, Howard N., ed. *Southern Black Leaders of the Reconstruction Era* (1982).

Uya, Okon Edet. *From Slavery to Political Service: Robert Smalls, 1839–1915* (1971).

Williamson, Joel. *After Slavery: The Negro in South Carolina during Reconstruction, 1861–1877* (1965).

Woodson, Carter Godwin. "Robert Smalls and His Descendants," *Negro History Bulletin* 11 (Nov. 1947): 27–33.

This entry is taken from the *American National Biography* and is published here with the permission of the American Council of Learned Societies.

GLENDA E. GILMORE

Smallwood, Thomas (22 Feb. 1801–1883), abolitionist and slave narrative author, was born to James Smallwood in Prince George's County, Maryland. Smallwood's 1851 slave narrative, the *Narrative of Thomas Smallwood, (Coloured Man) Giving an Account of His Birth, the Period He Was Held in Slavery, His Release, and Removal to Canada, Together with an Account of the Underground Railroad*, is the only slave narrative published in Canada by an ex-slave from the United States.

Smallwood, along with his sister, were born into slavery. He became the property of Reverend J. B. Ferguson for the sum of $500; the price paid for his sister is unknown. Ferguson bequeathed the Smallwood siblings to his wife and children with the stipulation that they were to gain their freedom at the age of thirty.

Ferguson and his wife taught Thomas Smallwood the alphabet. Smallwood vividly described the way literacy made him "a walking curiosity in the village where I lived. When passing about the village I would be called into houses, and the neighbors collected around to hear me say the alphabet and to spell 'baker' and 'cider'" (35). Smallwood claims he learned how to spell words of "two syllables" from Webster's *Spelling Book*. Smallwood cited slaves' mass illiteracy and the denial of education as the most pronounced form of oppression waged against bondsmen and women and people of African descent in the United States. He hoped his discussion of illiteracy would serve as an access point for his readership so that they could "glimpse into the abyss of intellectual darkness" (35) that perpetuated slavery. Smallwood gained further education from John McLeod, a Scottish resident of Prince George's County, Maryland, who hired Smallwood as a laborer after he gained freedom.

Smallwood's slave narrative provides minimal autobiographical information about his enslavement; one must therefore examine additional documents produced later in his life in conjunction with his slave narrative to gain a fuller picture of his family life. Smallwood relegated his discussion of enslavement to a single opening paragraph. To circumnavigate the details of his life as a slave he wrote, "It is needless for me to go into detail of the vicissitudes through which I passed during that period, more than to say, about five years before the time I was to be freed I hired myself from my master for the sum of $60 per year" (35).

Smallwood quotes many prominent European intellectuals, political leaders, romantic philosophers, and poets such as John Milton, Napoleon Bonaparte, William Wordsworth, William Cowper, and Lord Byron, who wrote about oppression and critiqued forms of enslavement in either the feudal system in Europe or the transatlantic slave trade. Smallwood states he did this because "I do not wish that my solitary opinion concerning slavery should be forced upon mankind." Instead of simply relying on his own "treasure house of memory" he conjured these revered intellectuals "like an archangelic host, rallying at the command of some mighty leader, on the ethereal plains" in order to align his condemnation of slavery with a larger body of work that would be respectable to a larger audience (23–25). In his preface, Smallwood also retells the story of DAVID WALKER, a freeborn black abolitionist from North Carolina whose parents were enslaved. In 1829 a Boston printer published and distributed Walker's abolitionist pamphlet entitled *Walker's Appeal, in Four Articles; Together with a Preamble, to the Coloured Citizens of the World, but in Particular, and Very Expressly, to Those of the United States of America*. Smallwood highlighted Walker's narrative, as he believed the abolitionist movement overlooked his work.

Smallwood mentions his wife only in passing, and never divulges information on his children in his narrative in order to protect the anonymity of his family while still participating in the Underground Railroad. Smallwood was married to a woman named Elizabeth, a freeborn Virginian who worked as a laundress. Through her employment, Elizabeth was acquainted with Charles Turner Torrey, a white radical abolitionist in Washington, D.C., who claimed to have assisted over four hundred people escape slavery in the Washington, D.C., area between 1841 and 1844. Elizabeth worked as a laundress for the boarding house where Torrey lived (at Mrs. Padgett's boarding house on 13th Street, N.W., which catered to abolitionist participants). Smallwood had four children, who were undisclosed in his slave narrative, living with him in Toronto. He had three sons: William, a bookkeeper and law student; Joseph, who worked as a plasterer; and Thomas, a sawdresser. His daughter, Virginia, worked as a hairdresser. Smallwood focused his account on his free life after he gained freedom in 1831, at the age of 30, a year after his marriage to an unnamed bride. They relocated to Washington, D.C., where he worked as shoemaker until 1842 while participating in the Underground Railroad. Of this time, Smallwood claimed, "I was the sole proprietor of the so-called underground railroad of that section [Washington, D.C.], it had been started without the assistance of any earthly being save Torry, myself, my wife, and the lady with whom he boarded. Torry having gone North, the burden and responsibility of consequences rested entirely on me" (46).

The bulk of the narrative focuses on his activism and subsequent disillusionment between 1822 and 1830 with the African Colonisation Society. Smallwood, upon gaining his freedom, was a fervent supporter of the organization in Maryland, as he believed their main objection was the immediate and complete emancipation of all slaves in the United States. Smallwood believed the organization advocated the integration of former slaves into American society "together with all others, in an elevated position" (36). When he learned that the Colonisation Society was a proponent of emigration to Africa, Smallwood felt "deceived" and focused his activism on delegitimizing the African Colonisation Society in Maryland. He then invested his efforts into directly assisting runaway slaves with the Underground Railroad from 1831 to 1843, when he himself emigrated to Canada.

In Canada, Smallwood became a leading community organizer and abolitionist in Ontario and Drummondville (contemporary Niagara Falls), which is chronicled in a 16-page leaflet *Report of the Convention of the Coloured Population, Held at Drummondville, Aug., 1847.* At this convention, Smallwood served on three leadership committees: nominating, business, and finance. JOSIAH HENSON, a fellow black abolitionist; ex-slave in Charles County, Maryland; and author of *The Life of Josiah Henson, Formerly a Slave, Now an Inhabitant of Canada, as Narrated by Himself* (1849); worked beside Smallwood. Throughout the convention, Smallwood is given the prefix "Rev.," suggesting that he was a preacher; an occupation not mentioned in his autobiography. In April 1863, a similar convention was held in Toronto. Both Smallwood and his son Thomas W. F. Smallwood served on the committee that drafted the "Address to the Colored Citizens of Canada," which supported the Union in the United States during the Civil War.

His abolitionist work in Canada accelerated after the passage of the Fugitive Slave Act of 1850.

Smallwood portrays the Canadian black abolitionist community as broken into factions throughout his narrative, counteracting representations of Canada as a complacent safe haven for fugitive slaves. Most of the community strife, which at times focused directly on Smallwood, concerned whether or not participants in the Underground Railroad took payment from slaves attempting to flee the United States. Smallwood, throughout his narrative, stresses that he is a self-made man and denies taking bribes or payment from his involvement with abolitionist organizations or the Underground Railroad. In a letter by the author that prefaces his text, he clearly stated, "I have written this for the sake of pecuniary gain. Such is not the case; but to defend myself against those who are not just enough to 'render unto Caesar the things which are Caesar's. I have laboured night and day at my calling, therefore I have no need of charity at the hands of anyone" (34). Smallwood was also considered an agitator by fellow abolitionists in Canada. In 1856 he filed a lawsuit against MARY ANN SHADD CARY, a freeborn black abolitionist woman originally from Delaware who relocated to Canada. She founded *The Provincial Freeman*, a newspaper run out of King Street in Toronto. Smallwood filed the lawsuit on behalf of her subscribers when in the summer of 1856 she unexpectedly stopped production. Smallwood dropped the lawsuit when production resumed.

Thomas Smallwood died in 1883 in Canada. His narrative is emblematic of the black exodus to Canada, which increased after the passage of the Fugitive Slave Act. Smallwood's narrative gives historians an important glimpse into the world of black abolitionism in urban centers such as Toronto, where other fugitive slaves such as HENRY BIBB took up residence.

FURTHER READING

Smallwood, Thomas. *A Narrative of Thomas Smallwood, (Coloured Man) Giving an Account of His Birth, the Period He Was Held in Slavery, His Release and Removal to Canada, Etc. : Together with an Account of the Underground Railroad* (1851).

Davis, Charles T., and Henry Louis Gates. *The Slave's Narrative* (1985).

Report of the convention of the coloured population, held at Drummondville, Aug., 1847 (1847).

Ripley, C. Peter, et al., eds., *The Black Abolitionist Papers, Vol. II: Canada, 1830–1865* (1992).

Russell, Hilary. "Underground Railroad Activists in Washington, DC." *Washington History* 13, no. 2 (Fall/ Winter, 2001/2002): 28–49.

RHAE LYNN BARNES

Smiley, Tavis (13 Sept. 1964–), television and radio personality, political commentator, author, and social advocate, was born in Gulfport, Mississippi, the eldest of ten children, four of whom were adopted, to Emory G. Smiley, a noncommissioned officer in the United States Air Force, and Joyce M. Smiley, a missionary and apostolic Pentecostal minister. Smiley grew up in the Kokomo, Indiana, area and attended Indiana University in Bloomington. He was a member of the Kappa Alpha Psi fraternity and graduated in 1986 with a degree in law and public policy. While he was at Indiana University, a close friend of Smiley's was killed by local police, who claimed to have done so in self-defense. This act of violence changed the course of Smiley's life, and he began to lead protests against the police in defense of his friend, which set Smiley on a path of social advocacy.

During Smiley's senior year of college, he accepted an unpaid internship in the office of the Los Angeles mayor TOM BRADLEY. Upon graduation, Smiley returned to Los Angeles and worked as a top aide for Bradley until 1990. In 1991, when his tenure in the mayor's office ended, twenty-six-year-old Smiley ran for a seat on the Los Angeles City Council. Although he lost the election, his early political aspirations convinced him that many in the community agreed with his platform on social advocacy.

After losing his bid for political office in Los Angeles, Smiley entered the field of radio commentary and broadcasting. He debuted on station KGFJ in Los Angeles with short segments called *Just a Thought*, where he talked about social and political issues such as discrepancies in housing and home loans, unequal access to education, and acts of injustice within the criminal justice system. In 1993 he premiered as a local talk show host on KABC-TV and Radio. Proficient at combining political commentary with issues of race, class, and inequality, Smiley garnered national attention for his local show, and in 1994 *Time* magazine named him one of the nation's fifty young leaders of the future.

In 1996 Smiley became host and executive producer of *BET Tonight with Tavis Smiley* on Black Entertainment Television. Because he was still hosting his Los Angeles radio show, for the next five years Smiley flew from Los Angeles to Washington, D.C., each week to tape the show, for which he earned consecutive annual NAACP Image Awards in 1997, 1998, and 1999 for best news, talk, or information series. In 1996 *Vanity Fair* inducted Tavis Smiley into its hall of fame for his skill at asking difficult and important questions.

Smiley became more successful at broadcasting in radio and on television as his technique of educating and informing the public from a position of social advocacy increased in popularity. His national reputation enabled him to get interviews with President Bill Clinton in the midst of the Monica Lewinsky scandal, Cuban president Fidel Castro, and Pope John Paul II. The increased recognition and fame also paved the way for Smiley to turn up the volume on his social advocacy efforts for people of color, the underprivileged, and the downtrodden. In 1996, he joined the radio team of the *Tom Joyner Morning Show*, which at the time had an audience of more than 5 million, as a political commentator. Smiley and TOM JOYNER used the radio program as a launching pad for national advocacy campaigns aimed at righting injustices in the African American community. As a result of their advocacy, Christie's International Auction House in New York was prohibited from selling artifacts connected with the enslavement of blacks in America, CompUSA began to advertise their products on black radio to a black audience, and voter registration increased in the African American community. The program, with the help of Congressman JOHN CONYERS, was instrumental in ROSA PARKS's being awarded the Congressional Gold Medal in 1999.

In 1998 Smiley formed The Smiley Group (TSG) as a California corporation under which he housed all of his conglomerate entities. One such entity, the Tavis Smiley Foundation (TSF), was founded in 1999, dedicated to enlightening, encouraging, and empowering America's black youth. The foundation brought together potential young black leaders for leadership training seminars in cities across the nation. In 2000 Smiley founded the event production company Tavis Smiley Presents (TSP) as a forum to host substantive town hall meetings, seminars, and thought-provoking discussions with the best and brightest African American minds in the country. One such event took place during black history month in February of each year, where leaders would come together through a forum called the State of the Black Union to discuss many of the important political, social, and spiritual issues most important to the black community. Smiley believed that if through these discussions, which he moderated, Americans could figure out how to make black America better, all of America could be better.

It was out of this forum that the Covenant with Black America was born, and in 2006 The Smiley Group, in conjunction with Third World Press, published a 254-page book, *Covenant with Black America.* It focused on issues such as health care, crime, housing, education, and technology in the form of a national plan of action to address the primary concerns of African Americans. By May of 2006, *Covenant with Black America* had reached the number one position on the *New York Times* best-seller list and was touted as the first nonfiction book by a black publisher in America ever to reach the best-seller list and to occupy the number one position. Tavis Smiley went on to host a *Covenant* tour in fifteen cities across the United States.

In 2002, Tavis Smiley made history by becoming the first African American to host his own signature talk show on National Public Radio. *The Tavis Smiley Show* showcased his ability to bring to the public's attention issues affecting people of color and the underprivileged. Smiley, however, left NPR at the end of his contract in 2004, dismayed by what he saw as NPR's poor effort to advertise and open up their market to a wider listening audience, namely people of color who were not affluent. His show *The Smiley Report* later returned him to public radio and was distributed by Public Radio International.

In January 2004, *Tavis Smiley*, a late-night television show hosted by Smiley and the first program in the history of PBS to be broadcast from the West Coast, launched with the tag line "Late night just woke up." Smiley once again made history in 2004 by becoming the first American to ever simultaneously host signature talk shows on both the Public Broadcasting Station, with *Tavis Smiley*, and on National Public Radio, with the *Tavis Smiley Show.* His PBS show won the 2005 and 2006 NAACP Image awards for outstanding TV news, talk show, or information series or special.

An accomplished writer, Tavis Smiley authored a number of books and even acquired his own book imprint, Smiley Books, with Hay House. His book *Keeping the Faith: Stories of Love, Courage, Healing, and Hope from Black America* (2002) won the NAACP Image Award for best nonfiction book in the literary category, beating out other prominent authors such as MAYA ANGELOU and ZORA NEALE HURSTON.

Smiley received a number of prestigious awards, including the Mickey Leland Humanitarian Award from the National Association of Minorities in Communications in 2000, and a host of honorary doctoral degrees, including one from his alma mater, Indiana University, in 2004. In that year, Texas Southern University announced the development of the Tavis Smiley School of Communications and the Tavis Smiley Center for Professional Media Studies. At the age of forty, Tavis Smiley became the youngest African American to ever have a professional school and center named in his honor on a college or university campus.

In 2006 Smiley left NPR to host a new Tavis Smiley show on the more left-leaning Public Radio International. Four years later he joined public intellectual CORNEL WEST on a new radio talk show for PRI, *Smiley and West.* Along with West, Smiley emerged as one of the most pointed African American critics of the BARACK OBAMA administration, particularly for what Smiley saw as an avoidance of issues most relevant to people of color.

KAREN BEASLEY YOUNG

Smith, Albert Alexander (17 Sept. 1896–3 Apr. 1940), painter, printmaker, and jazz musician, was born in New York City, the only child of immigrants from Bermuda Albert Renforth Smith, lifelong chauffeur to newspaper publisher Ralph Pulitzer, and Elizabeth A. Smith, a homemaker. After graduating from Public School No. 70 in 1911, Smith attended the DeWitt Clinton High School for two years. He began studying art under Irene Weir in 1913 and was the first African American to receive a Wolfe scholarship at the Ethical Culture Art High School. In 1915 Smith became the first African American student at the National Academy of Design, where he studied painting under Douglas Volk, etching with William Auerbach-Levy, and mural painting with Kenyon Cox. There he won honorable mention and the Suydam Bronze Medal in his first- and second-year classes (1915, 1916), two prizes from the academy poster competition, and the Suydam Medal for charcoal work in a life-drawing class (1917). He also published an illustration, *The Fall of the Castle*, which depicted African Americans marching up a hill ready to dismantle a fortress labeled "Prejudice," in the National Association for the Advancement of Colored People magazine *The Crisis* in 1917.

When the United States entered World War I, Smith enlisted in the 807 Pioneer Band of the American Expeditionary Force and served overseas for two-and-a-half months. In 1919 he received an honorable discharge from the army and returned to the National Academy of Design, where he was awarded a John Armstrong Chaloner Paris Foundation first prize for painting from life, as well as a first prize in etching. In 1920 *The Crisis* published Smith's drawings, *The Reason* (depicting a Southern African American fleeing North, while a black man hangs from a tree in the background) and *They Have Ears But They Hear Not* (which showed a chained black man on trial before a Southern white judge and jurors wearing earphones). That year he also produced an etching called *Plantation Melodies*, which showed folks enjoying banjo, fiddle, guitar, and harmonica music in front of a cabin. *The Crisis* published the image and a column about the artist, and the print won a prize from the children's magazine *Brownies Book*.

Smith worked briefly as a chauffeur before expatriating to Europe in 1920. During his first two years abroad, he worked as a musician by night and an artist by day, producing mostly images of tourist spots in France. He exhibited these at the Salon of 1921 in Paris and at the New York Public Library in 1921 and 1922. His drawing *Plantation Melodies* was exhibited in 1922 at the Society of Independent Artists in New York and the Tanner Art League in Washington, D.C., where it earned a gold medal. The drawing would also later be exhibited at the New York Public Library.

Smith spent the first half of 1922 in Italy. His art began to celebrate black achievements and racial uplift, as in his print of *René Maran*, the black French novelist who won the Prix Goncourt in 1921. He executed a series of portrait etchings of great black leaders, perhaps at the request of ARTHUR SCHOMBURG, librarian at the 135th Street branch of the New York Public Library. Smith sent Schomburg rare books and materials on black culture he found throughout Europe.

Also in 1922 Smith moved to Montmartre, the center of black expatriate life in Paris. He played the banjo at many of the nightclubs in this neighborhood where he would maintain residence for the rest of his life. During most of 1923 and 1924, Smith lived in Belgium, performing in Brussels and studying printmaking at the Académie des Beaux-Arts in Liège under François Maréchal. He also began to draw magnificent scenes of ancient Ethiopia, such as *Visions of Ethiopia* (1923) and *The Builders of the Temple* (1924), which appeared on covers of *The Crisis*.

Smith's prints of European tourist scenes were exhibited at the Brooklyn Society of Etchers from December 1924 to January 1925. Back in France, Smith continued drawing tourist scenes and themes of racial discrimination and racial uplift until 1926. During the following two years, Smith mostly drew anonymous Europeans, especially the Spanish and the French, after having traveled to Seville, Bilbao, and Madrid earlier that year.

In the late 1920s and early 1930s, Smith worked primarily in Paris, performing on radio and in the nightclubs La Coupole, Zelli's, and the Café de Paris. Only two of his etchings depicted the French cabaret atmosphere, *Montmartre, Paris* and *Bal Musette*, both from 1928. Smith honored the origins of the banjo in the *chera masingo* in the drawing *A Fantasy Ethiopia* (1928) and the Abyssianian ten-stringed harp, the *beganeh*, in an oil painting, *Ethiopian Music* (1928), which was published on the cover of *Opportunity* magazine. Around this time, the Harmon Foundation in New York embraced Smith's work, showing two dozen of his pieces between 1928 and 1933 and awarding him a bronze medal in 1929. That same year, his work was also shown at the Smithsonian Institution in Washington, D.C. More common in his work were caricature-like black banjo players in stock settings, such as *Do That Thing*, *Temptation*, and *Dancing Time*, all from 1930.

After a short trip to Italy, Smith was rejected for a Guggenheim Fellowship in 1934, as he had been previously in 1929. While Smith's artistic productivity slowed in the mid-1930s, he exhibited every year at the American Artists Professional League in Paris from 1935 to 1938. In 1937 his interest in portraiture revived and he produced a watercolor series of great black historic leaders, including painter HENRY OSSAWA TANNER (also an expatriate in Paris) and novelist VICTOR SÉJOUR, as well as black Cubans, Haitians, Ethiopians, Spanish, and Frenchmen. In 1939 Smith's work was included in the Contemporary Negro Art exhibition at the Baltimore Museum of Art, and he created a series of drawings with Arabian themes; however, these pieces were apparently lost. In 1940 Smith died suddenly of a brain clot in Haute-Savoie, France, at the age of forty-four. In his lifetime he produced more than 220 prints, drawings, and paintings, many which have been in the Library of Congress and the New York Public Library.

FURTHER READING

Allen, Cleveland G. "Our Young Artists," *Opportunity* (June 1923).

Leininger-Miller, Theresa. "Playing to American and European Audiences: Albert Alexander Smith Abroad, 1922–1940," *New Negro Artists in Paris: African American Painters and Sculptors in the City of Light, 1922–1934* (2001).

McGleughlin, Jean. "Albert Alexander Smith," *Opportunity* (July 1940).

Weintraub, Laurel. "Albert A. Smith's *Plantation Melodies*: The American South as Musical Heartland," *International Review of African American Art* (2003).

THERESA LEININGER-MILLER

Smith, Amanda Berry (23 Jan. 1837–24 Feb. 1915), evangelist, missionary, and reformer, was born in Long Green, Maryland, the daughter of Samuel Berry and Mariam Matthews, slaves on neighboring farms. By laboring day and night, Samuel Berry earned enough to buy his freedom and that of his wife and children, including Amanda. By 1850 the family had moved to a farm in York County, Pennsylvania. Their home was a station on the Underground Railroad.

Samuel and Mariam Berry stressed the value of education and hard work. Taught at home, Amanda learned to read by age eight; later she briefly attended a local school in which white students were given priority. At age thirteen she entered household service, living with a series of white employers in Maryland and Pennsylvania. She married Calvin M. Devine in 1854 but soon regretted his lack of piety and his indulgence in alcohol. After a period of fasting and earnest prayer, she experienced conversion in 1856 and envisioned a life devoted to evangelism. Devine enlisted in the Union army in 1862 and died fighting in the Civil War. The couple had two children, but only one reached adulthood.

Amanda moved to Philadelphia and by 1864 had married James Henry Smith, a coachman who was an ordained deacon in the African Methodist Episcopal (AME) Church. He later reneged on his prenuptial promise that he would undertake active ministry, and his unkindness and religious skepticism seemed to hinder her spiritual growth. She continued working as a domestic and taking in laundry. Their three children died young.

Close but not always harmonious ties with other devout women introduced Amanda Smith to the Holiness movement that swept nineteenth-century Protestantism. Advocates of Holiness urged believers, regardless of sex, race, social status, or church affiliation, to testify publicly about their spiritual experience. Irresistibly drawn to the movement's controversial tenet that entire sanctification—purification from intentional sin—was attainable by faith, she fervently sought this transformative blessing. In 1865 the Smiths moved to New York City, where James found work, but three years later Amanda declined to accompany him when he relocated again to take a well-paid position. During a Methodist church service in September 1868, she "felt the touch of God from the crown of my head to the soles of my feet." Walking home, she shouted praises and sang with joy at being sanctified, "married to Jesus" (Smith, 77, 81).

Smith expanded her religious activities after James died in 1869, supporting herself and her surviving child during midnight hours at the washtub and ironing table. By her own testimony she wrestled with fears and temptations presented by Satan; she constantly prayed to learn God's will for her by interpreting randomly chosen Bible verses, dreams, and internal voices. In 1870 she determined to trust providence and went to work full-time organizing groups for testimony and spiritual nurturance, praying with the sick, and singing and preaching at camp meetings and urban revivals. Participating in national Holiness camp meetings enlarged her network of friends. Although she periodically encountered resistance to female preachers, clergymen of various denominations invited her to address large racially mixed and all-white audiences. Her own AME Church, like most denominations, withheld ordination from women, and Smith did not press for institutional authorization or financial support. Confident that God had ordained her, she accepted individuals' donations and hospitality. She was the most widely known of the nineteenth century's black women itinerant preachers.

In 1878 Smith felt called to England, Ireland, and Scotland to participate in temperance revivals and Holiness conventions. After traveling on the European continent in 1879, she proceeded overland to India. There she worked with James M. Thoburn, Methodist Episcopal bishop of India, who had previously observed her in the United States. Thoburn affirmed, "I have never known anyone who could draw and hold so large an audience as Mrs. Smith" (Smith, vi). In 1882 she went to West Africa to help "civilize" the natives and to cultivate mainstream Protestant values among black Americans who had immigrated to Liberia. Cooperating with Baptists,

Congregationalists, and Presbyterians in potentially competitive situations, she proselytized, promoted temperance and Western-style education, and started a Christian school for boys.

Returning to the United States in 1890, Smith resumed preaching and activism despite her failing health. With her own savings and supporters' contributions, she founded a home for black orphans in Harvey, Illinois. It opened in 1899 and was later named the Amanda Smith Industrial School for Girls, operating until it burned in 1918. Exhausted by years of fund-raising, Smith retired in 1912 to Sebring, Florida, where she died in a home a donor had built for her.

Through her evangelical work, Amanda Smith gained an international reputation and rose to be one of the most famous African American women of the late nineteenth century. The careers of Smith and contemporary women evangelicals and reformers reinforced the proposition, unwelcome in some quarters, that females could function without male control. The black Methodist Episcopal clergyman Marshall W. Taylor portrayed Smith as an exemplar of their race's progress and "a Christian of the highest type," unmatched by any living person, black or white (Taylor, 57–58).

Smith's *Autobiography* is valuable to scholars of black women's writing and to historians of the Holiness, temperance, and foreign missions movements; the roles of women in the Methodist Episcopal and AME churches; and blacks' experiences and perspectives during the Reconstruction era and ensuing decades of heightened interracial tension. Smith's description and interpretation of conditions in Liberia and Sierra Leone reflect certain Anglo-American views of "heathen darkness" and "superstitions" (Smith, 346, 451), but she firmly rejected the assumption that black people were inferior. General readers will find this book a circumstantial, often engaging account of the joys and rigors of a life committed to improvement.

FURTHER READING

Smith, Amanda. *An Autobiography: The Story of the Lord's Dealings with Mrs. Amanda Smith, the Colored Evangelist* (1893; repr. 1988).
Cadbury, M. H. *The Life of Amanda Smith* (1916).
Humez, Jean M. "'My Spirit Eye': Some Functions of Spiritual and Visionary Experience in the Lives of Five Black Women Preachers, 1810–1880" in *Women and the Structure of Society*, eds. Barbara J. Harris and JoAnn K. McNamara (1984).
Taylor, Marshall W. *The Life, Travels, Labors, and Helpers of Mrs. Amanda Smith, the Famous Negro Missionary Evangelist* (1886).
This entry is taken from the *American National Biography* and is published here with the permission of the American Council of Learned Societies.

MARY DE JONG

Smith, Andrew Jackson (3 Sept. 1843–4 Mar. 1932), Civil War soldier and Medal of Honor recipient, was born into slavery in or near Eddyville, Kentucky. His mother was an enslaved woman named Susan, while his father was his master, Elijah Smith. Little is known about Andrew Smith's life, except that he remained enslaved until sometime between late 1861 and February 1862.

When Andrew Smith found out that his master had enlisted in the Confederate Army and intended to take him with him, he ran away to seek his freedom. Family tradition states that he, as well as another slave, walked through the rain for twenty-five miles before coming to a Union Army encampment at Smithland, Kentucky. Smith became the servant of Major John Warner of the 41st Illinois Regiment and subsequently worked at the regiment's headquarters in Paducah, Kentucky. From February to April 1862, Smith performed orderly duties with the regiment, including personal service to Major Warner; one of his stated duties was, in the event of Warner's death, to return his personal effects to his home in Clinton, Illinois. When the 41st Illinois moved southward from Kentucky and deeper into the Confederacy, Smith went with them.

While his precise actions during this time are unknown, as a servant of Major Warner, Smith likely experienced some portion of the severe action in which the 41st Illinois took part at Fort Donelson, where the regiment gained its first combat experience and suffered heavy casualties. Smith soon thereafter accompanied Major Warner and the 41st Illinois to Pittsburgh Landing, Tennessee, arriving there on 10 March 1862. During the subsequent Battle of Shiloh on 6–7 April, Smith supplied Warner with fresh mounts after the major had two horses shot out from under him during the bloody battle. The battle was so fierce that the 41st Illinois's regimental commander was killed, with command of the unit subsequently falling to Major Warner. Indeed, as part of the last line of defense in the Union left wing, the 41st Illinois was personally directed by General Ulysses S. Grant, and Smith was there to witness the events. So close was he to the battle, in fact, that he was struck by a spent ball that entered his temple and penetrated his skin only, stopping in the middle of his forehead. The ball was later removed by a regimental surgeon, leaving Jackson with a scar and an exciting story to tell for years thereafter.

While Smith could claim a respectable amount of service after the Battle of Shiloh, he was not yet done serving the Union cause. He returned to Clinton, Illinois, with Major Warner by November 1862, but when he learned of President Lincoln's decision to allow black troops to join the army in early 1863 he immediately sought to join the 54th Massachusetts Regiment, the first unit of black soldiers in the North raised for service in the Union Army. So many African Americans enlisted in the 54th that its roster was quickly filled. The 55th Massachusetts Regiment was subsequently formed to handle the extra men, including Smith and over fifty other black men from Illinois.

The service of African Americans such as Smith, ROBERT BLAKE, and CHARLES VEALE was extremely important to the Union. Not only did these men prove to be capable and, in many cases, valiant soldiers, their large numbers (over 178,000 strong) significantly added to the North's available manpower and thus enabled the Union Army to survive the heavy casualties it incurred. The use of black soldiers in the Civil War also marked a clear change in the conflict, hastening its evolution from what many insisted was a dispute over state's rights to the fight to end slavery. Significantly, of the large numbers of African Americans who fought in the Civil War, two-thirds came from slaveholding states, many of whom, like Andrew Smith, were "contrabands," men who had run away from their masters to join the Union cause.

Smith joined the 55th Massachusetts Regiment at Readville, Massachusetts, in the spring of 1863. After his first formal training as a soldier, he departed with the rest of his regiment to South Carolina in late July. The soldiers were first employed on Folly and Morris Islands, near Charleston, building fortifications and making patrols while under fire from nearby Confederate forts. In February 1864 the 55th moved to Florida to take part in operations at Olustee, and later at James Island, South Carolina, where the unit saw its first real battle. On 30 November 1864 the men of the 55th Massachusetts took part in the Battle of Honey Hill in South Carolina. During this engagement, Corporal Andrew Smith was serving in Company B when the regiment made an advance over swampy ground toward the Confederate position.

During the action the company's color bearer was killed by shellfire; as he fell, Smith caught him with one hand, and with the other caught the regimental flags. He subsequently carried the colors for the remainder of the battle and was himself wounded. For his actions, Smith was later promoted to color sergeant, an important position in the army in a day when men were taught to follow their unit's colors during an engagement, both for tactical and inspirational purposes.

Because the commander of the 55th Massachusetts Regiment was severely wounded early on during the engagement, he did not witness the remainder of the battle and was thus unaware of Smith's actions, omitting them in his official action report. Had he done so, Smith would almost certainly been recommended for the Medal of Honor. Instead, Color Sergeant Smith served until his discharge from the army on 29 August 1865, and later returned to Clinton, Illinois. He purchased land in Eddyville, Kentucky, and had a long and prosperous life, dying in Grand Rivers, Kentucky. Among the friends he made in the army was the 55th's regimental surgeon, Dr. Burt Wilder, who corresponded with Smith for the remainder of his life and made an attempt to gain Smith the Medal of Honor. However, because of the inaccuracies of the original battle report, Smith's nomination for the Medal of Honor was turned down in 1916.

The award finally came in 2001, nearly 137 years after the Battle of Honey Hill, when the Medal of Honor was at last approved for Andrew Jackson Smith and presented to his descendants by President Bill Clinton on 16 January. Smith was not only the last African American soldier from the Civil War to be awarded the Medal of Honor, but his recognition also set a record of sorts, marking the longest period between a soldier's valorous deed and the actual award of our nation's highest military decoration.

FURTHER READING

Burkholder, Janeen. "Second Posthumous Medal of Honor Award Brings Attention to First from Clinton." *Clinton Journal.* http://www.webcitation.org/5r3j0HwbI.

Hanna, Charles W. *African American Recipients of the Medal of Honor* (2002).

GLENN ALLEN KNOBLOCK

Smith, Anna Deavere (18 Sept. 1950–), performer, author, director, teacher, and social activist, was born and grew up in Baltimore, Maryland, where

Anna Deveare Smith at the 2003 *Glamour Magazine* Women of the Year awards, held at the American Museum of Natural History on 10 Nov. 2003. (AP Images.)

a diverse population—Poles, Italians, African Americans, Jews, Catholics, Protestants, rich and poor—but each community kept largely to itself. Smith's worldview expanded in junior and senior high school, where she was active at the YMCA in downtown Baltimore. She found herself in an environment with more flow among races, ethnicities, religions, and classes. She also began to lay the groundwork for her artistic life. Studying high school French, she listened for hours to recordings, repeating word-for-word what she heard. Later in life Smith made plays by taping, listening with great care, and repeating what she heard with deep, embodying empathy.

Churchgoing within the African American community had a significant impact on Smith's development. Her mother and siblings went to church regularly. Her father did not attend, which according to Smith "may have been a good thing, because his behavior about church and most things left me with many unanswerable questions which is what prepared me for drama as a form of expression. I don't believe a play should give answers, and I don't believe education should give answers. I think both should lead us to our own questions and energize us to find the answers—in other words to put us on life-long quests of our choosing" (Smith, personal communication). During her teenage years Smith was active in her church, which was a focus for the burgeoning civil rights movement. Church also struck Smith aesthetically—the music, people's varying physical features and colors, different from each other but all African Americans, the ways they dressed, the generational differences. Watching and participating, Smith honed her ability to understand the experiences of others. Later, in her mature artistic work, Smith used these skills to portray on stage and in film people of very different cultures, ethnicities, races, and experiences.

After graduating from Beaver College (now Arcadia University) in Glenside, Pennsylvania, in 1971 and earning an MFA in acting from San Francisco's American Conservatory Theater in 1976, Smith launched her career as a teacher and actor; writing and social activism were soon to follow. In 1978–1979 she was an assistant professor of acting at Carnegie Mellon University. From 1983 to 1986 she was an instructor in acting at New York University. In 1986 she became an assistant professor of drama at the University of Southern California. From 1990 to 2000 she was at Stanford University, where in 1994 she became the Ann O'Day Maples Professor of the Arts. In 2001 she moved to New

her father, Deavere Young Smith Jr., was a self-employed coffee merchant and her mother, Anna Young Smith, was an elementary school teacher and then principal. The oldest of five children (two brothers, two sisters) Smith's principle influences were her family, neighborhood, and church. Until junior high school, Smith's world was almost entirely black. She attended an all-black elementary school and worshipped at an all-black Methodist church. She adored her maternal grandmother, Pearl B. Young, and her paternal grandfather, Deaver Young Smith Sr., and was fascinated by her cousins, aunts, and uncles with their fancy clothes, makeup and jewelry, dancing, and partying. They showed the young Smith life as a kind of theater. Baltimore in the 1950s was segregated not only in terms of race but also according to ethnicity and income. The city had

York University as university professor and professor of performance studies at the Tisch School of the Arts. Smith also began teaching at NYU's Law School in close collaboration with Shad Professor of Law Peggy Cooper Davis, director of NYU's Lawyering Program. In 1997, to advance the relationship between art and society, Smith inaugurated at Harvard University the Institute on the Arts and Civic Dialogue (IACD). Moving to NYU in 2001, the IACD convened an international group of artists working to bring about social change.

From the early 1980s onward, in a series of works under the overall title of *On the Road: A Search for American Character*, Smith created, developed, and deployed a remarkable performance style that made her a major force on the national American stage. In these works, many of them one-woman shows in which she portrayed a wide variety of actual people, Smith explored the American character, race relations, and communities in conflict. Dozens of figures—drawn from life and researched through face-to-face interviews—populated these works. "I was trying to define the geographic and social diversity of the country one person at a time by acting them out" (Smith, pers. comm.). The main acting technique she chose to employ was incorporation. This method is close to what African, Native American, Asian, and other traditional healers and performers do. Using both the tape recorder and the much older technique of careful listening and observation, Smith went far beyond "interviewing." She combined investigative reporting with the practice of a shaman: probing people's knowledge and feelings and then reproducing their behaviors in empathetic detail. In communities torn by violence, hatred, and fear, Smith was able to meet people of every different persuasion who opened up to her because she gave each her focused attention. Smith presented people of different races, ages, genders, ethnicities, habits, ideologies, religions, and opinions to the public respectfully, often with humor but never with parody. Her accomplishment was to enact the complexities and ambivalences of social and political life. Smith learned not to lose herself but rather to "double": to be simultaneously the other and herself. She practiced as a mature artist what she learned and experienced as a youth in Baltimore.

Smith's major works include the first piece in the eponymous series, *On the Road: A Search for American Character* (1982; Clear Space, New York), *Aye, Aye, Aye, I'm Integrated* (1984; American Place Theatre, New York), *On Black Identity and Black Theatre* (1990; Crossroads Theatre, New Brunswick, New Jersey), *San Francisco From the Outside Looking In* (1990; Eureka Theatre, San Francisco), *Fires in the Mirror: Crown Heights, Brooklyn, and Other Identities* (1992; Public Theatre, New York), *Twilight: Los Angeles, 1992* (1993; Mark Taper Forum, Los Angeles), *Hymn* (1994; City Center, New York), *House Arrest* (1997; Arena Stage, Washington, D.C.), *Piano* (2000; Institute on the Arts and Civic Dialogue, Harvard University), and *Rounding It Out* (2002; Yale University). In 2007 Smith had a work in development titled *Let Me Down Easy*, dealing with the vulnerability and resilience of the human body based on Smith's interviews with sick people and their caretakers as well as champion athletes and sex workers in the United States, Rwanda, Uganda, South Africa, and Germany.

A superb actor in the conventional sense as well, Smith appeared in films such as *Philadelphia* (1993), *The American President* (1995), *The Human Stain* (2003), *Rent* (2005), and *Life Support* (2007) and in television series including *The West Wing*, *The Practice*, *Presidio Med*, and *100 Centre Street*. Smith's articles have been published in major newspapers and scholarly journals. Her books include the texts of her major plays as well as *Talk To Me: Travels in Media and Politics* (2000) and *Letters to a Young Artist: Straight-Up Advice on Making a Life in the Arts* (2006).

Smith's honors include more than twenty awards for her work as a performer, director, and playwright, among them a MacArthur "genius" Fellowship (1996), two OBIE (off Broadway) awards (1992, 1994), two Drama Desk awards (1993 and 1994), Hollywood–Beverly Hills NAACP Award (1994), Pulitzer Prize nomination in drama (1992), and two Tony nominations in 1994, one for best actress, the other for best play. A frequent speaker at colleges and universities, Smith has been awarded eighteen honorary degrees. In 2004 she joined the Board of Directors of the Museum of Modern Art, New York, chairing the committee on film.

For this hugely creative author, director, performer, and activist, performance has remained the core of her life. "I believe that performance is a form of fiction that sometimes tells a great truth," she wrote in 2007. "It's a life force to me, and I personally don't want to participate in the use of performance as merely a form of influence. I don't think performances can really 'win' anything. I think they can raise questions, unsettle things, come to no conclusions" (pers. comm.).

FURTHER READING

Guinier, Lani, and Anna Deavere Smith. "Rethinking Power, Rethinking Theater: A Conversation between Lani Guinier and Anna Deavere Smith," *Theater* 31, no. 3 (Fall 2001).

Kondo, Dorinne K. "(Re)Visions of Race: Contemporary Race Theory and the Cultural Politics of Racial Crossover in Documentary Theatre," *Theatre Journal* 52, no. 1 (Mar. 2000).

Martin, Carol. "Anna Deavere Smith: The Word Becomes You" (interview), *TDR* 37, no. 4 (Winter 1993).

Thompson, Debby. "Is Race a Trope?: Anna Deavere Smith and the Question of Racial Performativity," *African American Review* 37, no. 1 (Spring 2003).

RICHARD SCHECHNER

Smith, Barbara (1946–), writer, activist, editor, speaker, was born Barbara Smith in the central part of Cleveland, Ohio. Smith's mother died at age thirty-four, exactly one month before Smith's tenth birthday; her father, she writes, was a "total mystery" to her. Smith and her twin sister, Beverly, were reared in a modest, working-class home by their mother, maternal grandmother, and great-aunt Phoebe. When Smith was six years old she and her family moved into a two-family house that her aunt LaRue and uncle Bill had bought, and she lived there until she was eighteen and went away to college. It is this house that Smith most vividly remembers as home and from which she learned many of the fundamentals of black feminism before such a term even existed. As Smith watched the women in her family struggle with dignity, strength, and perseverance against a segregated society marred by inequalities, she developed a growing awareness of how both racism and sexism affected the lives of African American women.

Smith became active in the civil rights movement in the early 1960s while she was still in high school, and then in college she became active in black student organizing and in the anti–Vietnam War movement. She designed an interdepartmental major in sociology and English at Mount Holyoke College in 1965 that allowed her to study African American writers independently and also to write her own political analyses of neglected social issues affecting the African American community. She had long loved reading, a pastime advanced by her aunt LaRue's unlimited access to books as an employee of the Cleveland Public Library, and by the seventh grade she had begun to enjoy writing as well.

After graduating from Mount Holyoke in 1969, Smith continued to study African American literature on her own in graduate school because it was not taught in the department at the time, but the development of women's studies journals where she could send her work and her decision to come out as a lesbian in the mid-1970s helped solidify her commitment to writing. She now felt that she had nothing to hide about her identity, and this feeling, along with her growing involvement in black feminist organizing, propelled her to write.

In the 1970s Smith became discontented with the black nationalist movement's avoidance of issues affecting black women and frustrated by the sexual politics that she felt limited many women's aspirations. She became increasingly involved in the women's movement in the 1970s but felt alienated by the white-dominated movement's inattentiveness to racism and by its narrow definition of feminism. As she suggested in her talk "Racism and Women's Studies," delivered at the first annual National Women's Studies Association conference in 1979, "The reason racism is a feminist issue is easily explained by the inherent definition of feminism. Feminism is the political theory and practice to free all women: women of color, working-class women, poor women, physically challenged women, lesbians, old women—as well as white economically privileged heterosexual women. Anything less than this is not feminism, but merely female self-aggrandizement" (Smith, *Truth*, 96). This expanded definition remains influential today and continues to be used by others who seek to broaden the aim and scope of feminism.

Smith's important critiques of the black nationalist and feminist movements found a widening audience in 1974 when she cofounded the Combahee River Collective, a black feminist group that did political organizing in Boston, Massachusetts, until 1980. The group took its name from the South Carolina river that was the site of a military action led by HARRIET TUBMAN, heralded for freeing hundreds of slaves. In 1977 the collective drafted a political statement espousing its political position and its commitment to struggle against interlocking racial, sexual, heterosexual, and class oppressions. This statement was widely anthologized in the years to follow and has been cited both as a model of coalition political work and as one of the first written documents to identify the simultaneity of these oppressions and their relevance for black feminism.

Smith was a forerunner in and major contributor to the eventual building of African American women's studies, black feminism, and the growing body of black feminist and womanist theory. Her landmark essay "Towards a Black Feminist Criticism" was published in 1977 and has since been regarded as a major catalyst in furthering the study of black women's literature in the United States. In it she calls for a viable, autonomous black feminist movement and argues for the ongoing study of literature by black women and black lesbian writers who had long been dismissed in literary study. Also in 1977 Smith was invited by the *Conditions* magazine collective to coedit a special issue on black women. In November 1979 *Conditions: Five, the Black Women's Issue* appeared as one of the first widely distributed collections of black feminist writing in the United States, and its early sales set a record in feminist publishing. Smith's desire to ensure that the issue remained in permanent form led her to edit the anthology *Home Girls: A Black Feminist Anthology*, published in 1983. Reissued by Rutgers University Press in 2000, the anthology explores the development of black feminism and the varied dimensions of black women's lives and writing.

In 1980 Smith cofounded Kitchen Table: Women of Color Press with AUDRE LORDE and helped keep it in operation until she relinquished her duties as publisher in February 1995. The establishment of the press grew out of the founders' shared desire for an outlet to publish and promote work by women of color. In 1982 Smith coedited the landmark collection *All the Women Are White, All the Blacks Are Men, but Some of Us Are Brave: Black Women's Studies* with GLORIA T. HULL and Patricia Bell Scott, one of the first texts to bring together personal narratives, literary criticism, bibliographies, and other resources geared toward establishing black women's studies programs in colleges and universities nationwide. Smith also coauthored with Elly Bulkin and Minnie Bruce Pratt *Yours in Struggle: Three Feminist Perspectives on Anti-Semitism and Racism* (1984) and was general editor of *The Reader's Companion to U.S. Women's History* (1998).

Smith has received a number of honors and accolades for her writing and activism, starting when she became the first woman of color to be appointed to the Modern Language Association's Commission on the Status of Women in the Professions in 1974 when she was a graduate student. She received the twenty-five-thousand-dollar Stonewall Award for service to the lesbian and gay community awarded by the Anderson Prize Foundation in 1994, was named one of *Advocate* magazine's Best and Brightest Activists for lesbian and gay rights in 1999, received the Church Women United's Human Rights Award in 2000, and was featured in *Essence* magazine's thirtieth anniversary issue as one of forty-six black women trailblazers in 2000. Smith was a scholar-in-residence during 1995–1996 at the Schomburg Center for Research in Black Culture in New York City and was a fellow at the Bunting Institute of Radcliffe College during 1997. Smith has also been interviewed for a number of television programs and films, including MARLON RIGGS's documentary *Black Is, Black Ain't* (1992).

Smith has long lectured widely on topics centered on race, class, gender, and sexuality at college and university campuses throughout the United States, and she has frequently been a keynote speaker at various academic and activist conferences and meetings. In 2000 Smith's *The Truth That Never Hurts: Writings on Race, Gender, and Freedom*, was released. The collection brings together many of her earliest writings and demonstrates her ongoing commitment to the struggle against homophobia, racism, sexism, imperialism, and poverty. Smith's later work has continued to argue against a tendency to see women as marginalized by gender alone and instead encourages a national, social, and political dialogue on how multiple forces of oppression affect the lives of African American women and all members of society.

FURTHER READING

Smith, Barbara. "Building Black Women's Studies," in *The Politics of Women's Studies: Testimony from Thirty Founding Mothers*, ed. Florence Howe (2000).

Smith, Barbara. *The Truth That Never Hurts: Writings on Race, Gender, and Freedom* (2000).

Smith, Barbara, and Beverly Smith. "Across the Kitchen Table: A Sister-to-Sister Dialogue," in *This Bridge Called My Back: Writings by Radical Women of Color*, eds. Cherríe Moraga and Gloria Anzaldua, 2d ed. (1983).

AMANDA J. DAVIS

Smith, Barbara (24 Aug. 1949–), entrepreneur, life-style expert, author, and model, was born Barbara Smith near Pittsburgh, Pennsylvania, the daughter of William H. Smith, a steel worker, and Florence Claybrook Smith, a part-time maid. She has described her parents as the original Bob Villa and

Martha Stewart, referring to the television handyman and the multimedia domestic guru, respectively, and was greatly influenced by the home her parents established. She assisted them in the family's vegetable and flower gardens. While in high school, Smith studied cooking, sewing, nutrition and fashion. During the same time, she took classes at the John Robert Powers modeling school in Pittsburgh on the weekend. She completed her modeling studies shortly before she graduated from high school. After graduation, Smith moved to Pittsburgh where she worked hard to launch her modeling career. It was not easy, but in the late 1960s, after a national search, TransWorld Airlines selected Smith as its first African American ground hostess—RUTH CAROL TAYLOR was the first African American flight attendant, for Mohawk Airlines in 1958. During this time, Smith also returned to school to learn to teach modeling and she applied to model in the Ebony Fashion Fair. She was finally selected in 1969 after her third attempt and moved to New York City.

In 1971, she signed with the Wilhelmina Modeling Agency and began using her first initial when she would call the agency for assignments as "B. Smith." While represented by the agency, she did runway modeling, appeared on fifteen magazine covers, including five for *Essence* and one for *Ebony*, and numerous television commercials and catalogs. In July 1976, she became the first African American model to appear on the cover of *Mademoiselle* magazine. As a model, she lived in Paris, France; Milan, Italy; Vienna, Austria; and Los Angeles, California; in addition to New York. Traveling around the world allowed her to hone her cooking skills by adding international cuisine to her repertoire.

As she neared the end of her modeling career, Smith, whose love of cooking and entertaining friends created an interest in running a restaurant, began developing her skills by first being a hostess at Ark's America, a fashionable restaurant in Manhattan. Later, she became a floor manager at the restaurant. In the mid-1980s she formed a partnership with Michael Weinstein, owner of Ark and opened her first restaurant, B. Smith's, in November 1986 in Manhattan's theater district. In 1988 she married Donald Anderson and launched *B. Smith with Style*, a syndicated television show. The marriage did not last, but as of 2008 the television show was still available on cable networks. In 1992, she married Dan Gasby, a television producer, and adopted his daughter Dana. In October 1994, she opened a second B. Smith's restaurant in the refurbished Union Station in Washington, D.C. The next year, Smith extended her empire by publishing *B. Smith's Cooking and Entertaining for Friends*, the first such book aimed at the African American audience. In 1997, she opened a seasonal B. Smith's in Sag Harbor, New York, where she had a summer home. In 1999 she relocated the flagship Manhattan restaurant to Restaurant Row. In October of the same year she published her second book *B. Smith: Rituals and Celebrations*.

By 2001, Smith expanded her enterprise by launching a home décor line exclusively for Bed, Bath & Beyond. The line included bedding, bath towels, rugs and wall art. In 2005, she became the face of Betty Crocker cornbread mix and in 2006 deepened her relationship with General Mills by becoming the spokesperson for "Serving Up Soul," an African-American marketing initiative. In March, 2006, she published her third book *Food that Says Welcome; Simple Recipes to Spark the Spirit of Hospitality*.

By the first decade of the twenty-first century, Smith was recognized as a "lifestyle expert" and in some quarters called a black Martha Stewart. In 2007 she launched a furniture collection, "At Home with B. Smith," with Clayton Marcus, a division of La-Z-Boy Corporation. The forty-piece upholstered furniture collection, the first designed by an African American woman for national distribution, included three groupings called Central Park South, Sag Harbor, and Mosaic Treasures. The groupings reflect Smith's homes throughout her career. She also joined forces with the Journey for Control campaign. The campaign supported by Merck & Co. featured Smith preparing old dishes in new healthy ways to make them diabetes friendly. With three family members suffering from diabetes, Smith was familiar with the needs for healthy presentations of favored dishes.

In April 2008 the "B. Smith Furniture Gallery Program" was launched. The home furnishings accessories supplement the upholstered furniture groupings introduced in 2007. A second furniture collection was introduced in Fall 2008, which added a fourth grouping, "Glam," to her other upholstered groupings. In early 2009 she was scheduled to publish a fourth book and launch a women's jewelry line in conjunction with Zalemark Inc.

FURTHER READING
Blades, Nicole, "Queen B. Smith." *Ebony* (May 2007).
Evans, Gary. "Comfort Colors Take Center Stage."
　Furniture Today (7 Dec. 2008).

Gray, Steven. "Betty Crocker Adds B. Smith to Package of Cornbread Mix, and Sales Take Off." *Wall Street Journal* (14 Nov. 2006),

Koncius, Jura. "The View from High Point." *Washington Post* (18 Oct. 2007).

Reed, Julia. "Can B. Smith Be Martha?" *New York Times*, sec. 6, p. 26 (22 August 1999).

Vaz, Valerie. "My Time," *Essence.* (Aug. 1989).

CLARANNE PERKINS

Smith, Bessie (c. 15 Apr. 1894–26 Sept. 1937), blues recording artist and performer, was born in Chattanooga, Tennessee, the third of seven children, to William Smith and Laura (maiden name unknown). The exact date of Bessie's birth is unknown, partly because in the rural and poor place in which she was born the official records of African Americans were given little care. The abject poverty in which Bessie's family lived contributed to the death of her eldest brother, who died before Smith was born, and her father, a part-time Baptist preacher, who died shortly after her birth. By the time Bessie was eight or nine, her mother and a second brother had died. Viola, the oldest sister, raised the remaining brothers and sisters.

There are a number of gaps in the record of Smith's career, some of which have been filled by myth. There is evidence that she began singing when she was nine—performing in the streets of Chattanooga for nickels and dimes with her brother Andrew, who played the guitar. Her first professional opportunity came when her oldest surviving brother, Clarence, arranged an audition for a traveling show owned by Moses Stokes, which included, among others, MA RAINEY. Legend has it that Rainey kidnapped Smith, teaching her how to sing the blues while taking her throughout the South. Actually, Smith did not need Rainey's coaching, since she had a natural talent, with unparalleled vocal abilities and a remarkable gift for showmanship. No one knows how long she stayed with Stokes's show, but there is evidence that Smith spent a long time performing at the 81 Theater in Atlanta, Georgia. Her shows there earned her only ten dollars a week, but her audiences were so taken by the power of her voice that they would throw money on the stage. Records show that she had begun touring with the Theater Owners' Booking Association and Pete Werley's Florida Blossoms troupe by 1918. Aside from singing, her performances for these shows included dancing in chorus lines and performing comedy routines. As Smith made her rounds in the southern circuits, she

Bessie Smith on 3 Feb. 1936. (Library of Congress/ Photographed by Carl Van Vechten.)

gathered increasing numbers of adoring fans and became known to producers like Frank Walker of Columbia Records, who hired her years later and supervised her 1923–1931 recording sessions.

Smith met and married Earl Love, a man about whom little is known, except for the fact that he came from a prominent black southern family and that he died shortly after his 1920 marriage to Smith. After his death, Smith moved to Philadelphia, Pennsylvania, where she met Jack Gee, a night watchman, whom she married in 1923 and with whom she adopted a child, Jack Gee Jr. Smith and Gee's marriage was passionate but tumultuous and they separated in 1929.

During the early 1920s Smith's career developed rapidly. She began performing at the Standard Theater in Philadelphia and Paradise Gardens in Atlantic City, and by 1923 she had recorded her first song, "Downhearted Blues," for Columbia Records. Though another blues singer had recently recorded and popularized the song, Smith's version sold seventy-eight thousand copies in less than six months. Following this success, Smith recorded seven more songs, this time with the piano accompaniment of FLETCHER HENDERSON. Smith then toured the South, where she was greeted as the star she was quickly becoming.

Like most blues singers of her time, Smith sang of love and sex and, in particular, of the challenges black men and women face in romantic relationships. But Smith was able to evoke the vigor of sex and the joy and sorrow of love in ways few others could match. Her slow tempos and deeply felt inflections enraptured her audiences, who remained largely African American. When she sang of love, she sang of love lost, often to infidelity and sometimes to death. But while she expressed the grief of such loss, she also projected the image of the loud-talking mama who would not take life passively. Smith drew easily on her own life to project this image. Her life with Gee was plagued by infidelity, though Gee was not the only guilty party; Smith was known for her affairs, some of them with women. No one knows when Smith began to have female lovers; some assume, without any actual evidence, that the first was Ma Rainey. By 1926 there was public knowledge of her relationship with a chorus girl from her troupe.

Smith sang her life story, and audiences and listeners felt that she was singing theirs. Her music did so well that it was said that people who did not have money to buy coal bought Bessie Smith records. By 1925 she had recorded nine more, with a young cornet player named LOUIS ARMSTRONG. By the end of her career, Smith had sold between 8 and 10 million records and recorded a total of 160 sides.

Yet Smith never forgot what she had left behind in the South. In her "Back Water Blues," she poetically evokes the sorrow of a people forced out of their homes by floods in the Louisiana backlands, while presenting a subtle statement of social protest. She also testified to the poverty that plagued African Americans in northern urban centers. In "Poor Man's Blues," which she wrote and which some consider her finest record, Smith eloquently exposes the "cruel irony of poverty in the land of riches" (Harrison, 70). Smith sang about the sickness and despair—often accompanied by alcoholism and drug addiction—that afflicted communities besieged by racism and inequality, and she sang of the rage that resulted from these ills. "Her blues could be funny and boisterous and gentle and angry and bleak, but underneath all of them ran the raw bitterness of being a human being who had to think twice about what toilet she could use" (Shapiro and Hentoff, 127).

Smith met the world with a bold toughness of spirit. She generally gave people—no matter their race or background—a tongue-lashing if they gave her trouble and sometimes she actually used physical force. She literally beat pianist CLARENCE WILLIAMS because he had been pocketing money that should have been hers. Her boldness, coupled with her immense talent, allowed Smith to earn as much as two thousand dollars per week. However, with artistic and monetary success came problems. Smith, who had always had a taste for alcohol, began to drink heavily when she became estranged from her husband. By the time she and Gee separated, her drinking had begun to make her temperamental and unreliable as an artist. She turned from a "hardworking performer who ran her shows with military discipline into a mean drunk who thought nothing of breaking a contract or leaving a troupe stranded penniless in some godforsaken town" (Albertson, 111). She also squandered the money she made. While some of her profligacy with money was due to the fact that she was generous—Smith was a renowned for giving money to friends in need—much of it was also a result of her destructive behavior.

Her problematic behavior, the impact of the Depression, changes in musical tastes, and the negative effect of the advent of radio on the record industry conspired to bring about Smith's decline. By 1931 Columbia Records was forced to drop her, as the sales of her records had decreased dramatically. Smith attempted to revise her repertoire, and in 1929 she starred in a Broadway show and acted in the motion picture *St. Louis Blues* in order to save her career. But the efforts proved fruitless—while she could still pack shows, her record sales continued to drop. Yet the power of her art was still evident. "Nobody Knows You When You're Down and Out," which she recorded that same year, captures the sorrow of her own decline as it speaks to a larger truth.

Smith died in a car crash in Clarksdale, Mississippi, in 1937, still trying to regain her professional footing. According to popular myth, she died because a whites-only hospital refused to admit her. The truth is that Smith could have been taken sooner to the African American hospital where she died, but it is unlikely that she could have survived given the seriousness of her injuries. Known as the Empress of the Blues, Smith laid the foundation for all subsequent women's jazz and blues singing, influencing hundreds of musicians and singers, among them Louis Armstrong, BILLIE HOLIDAY, and MAHALIA JACKSON. Ironically, no one from the music industry attended her funeral. In contrast, the number of adoring fans attending was seven thousand strong, and she continues to be loved today.

FURTHER READING
Albertson, Chris. *Bessie* (1972).
Davis, Angela Y. *Blues Legacies and Black Feminism* (1998).
Harrison, Daphne D. *Black Pearls: Blues Queens of the 1920s* (1988).
Shapiro, Nat, and Nat Hentoff, *The Jazz Makers* (1957).

DISCOGRAPHY
The Bessie Smith Collection, (Columbia CK 44441).
Bessie Smith: Empress of the Blues (Charly Records CDCD 1030).
The Bessie Smith Story (vols. 1–4, Columbia CL 855–858).

GLENDA R. CARPIO

Smith, Charles Spencer (16 Mar. 1852–1 Feb. 1923), politician, civic leader, writer, and bishop, was born in Colborne, Canada, the son of Nehemiah Henry Smith, a commissary sergeant of a black regiment in the English army. Little is known about his mother. Smith spent his childhood and adolescence in Bowmanville, Canada, where he attended public school and worked as an apprentice in furniture finishing. After completing public school, he moved to the United States and pursued a medical degree at Meharry Medical College in Nashville, Tennessee. From 1869 to 1871 he was a teacher with the Freedman's Bureau in Kentucky, Mississippi, and Alabama. Smith was the first African American preacher to obtain a medical degree in the United States, but he never actively practiced. His call to the ministry outweighed his desire to practice medicine. Therefore Smith turned to the African Methodist Episcopal (AME) Church to exercise his talents, becoming one of the few formally educated preachers in that church.

Smith converted to Christianity and followed the call to the ministry in 1871. In 1872 he was ordained to the ministry of the AME Church by the quarterly conference in Jackson, Mississippi. His ministry developed under the leadership of Bishop T. M. D. WARD, Bishop Wayman, and Bishop DANIEL ALEXANDER PAYNE. Bishop Ward appointed Smith to serve in Alabama, where he became active in politics. In 1874 Smith was elected to the Alabama State House of Representatives, where he served until he lost his reelection bid in 1876. His battle for reelection centered on questions of racial equality

and enfranchisement (Hill, *Sable Son of God*, 18). Smith married Kate Josephine Black in March 1876; they had one child.

Smith preached in many AME churches as well as in various economic and interracial settings. He was noted for his great oratorical skill and rhetorical eloquence. At age seventeen Smith gave a discourse on the Fifteenth Amendment, which granted blacks the right to vote. In 1873 he organized an Independence Day celebration that drew twenty thousand people and delivered a speech in which he eloquently expressed the need for racial harmony. His sermons to whites focused on acceptance of the biblical precepts of love and righteousness and the human dignity rooted in spiritual freedom. He believed that these precepts of Christian morality would not only develop self-respect in the hearers but also would make the African American race respectable in the eyes of whites and thereby improve race relations.

In 1882 Smith was appointed corresponding secretary and treasurer of the newly established AME Sunday School Union, founded to publish religious literature specifically for African American children. The union's office was in the basement of Smith's home in Bloomington, Illinois. Following the death of his wife in 1885, Smith moved to Nashville, Tennessee, where he bought the first Sunday school building for $9,000 in 1888.

Smith developed administrative skills by working closely with Payne as general officer of the Sunday School Union. Smith also served as chairman of the Boards of Trustees of Morris Brown College (Atlanta, Georgia) and of Paul Quinn College (Dallas, Texas). While at Morris Brown, Smith raised $25,000 for the celebration of the college's quartocentennial at a time when blacks possessed very little. In 1912, while chairman of the Paul Quinn board, he raised $50,000 for Christian education. His contribution to the financial stability of these two educational institutions was enduring. Segregation motivated Smith to hold high aspirations and to stand as a herald for black progress.

In 1884 Smith was chairman of the Illinois Colored Men's State Central Committee. On 29 April 1884 he organized the Conference of Representative Colored Men in Pittsburgh, Pennsylvania, to discuss means of influencing the federal government to provide protection for blacks in the South against Ku Klux Klan terrorism and to agitate for civil rights in the North. In that year Smith was elected as an alternate to the National

Republican Convention. In December 1888 Smith married Christine Shoecraft, a schoolteacher. They had one son.

Smith followed a similar role after World War I. He anticipated the problems black soldiers would face upon returning to their homeland and as chairman of the Bishop's Council of the AME Church in 1919, he helped form the Commission on After-War Problems to deal with all postwar problems affecting the religious, moral, educational, and economic interests of the members and adherents of the AME Church in particular and the race in general. Smith predicted that the Klan would meet black soldiers returning from France with lynching, burning, and other violence. During the latter months of 1919, there were approximately twenty-five race riots. Smith believed that to establish peace in the world, the church should help direct and strengthen morality by directing international affairs toward embracing supreme spiritual values. He also believed the church must serve as the moral conscience of nations and be ready at all times to stand up to humans and reveal its vision of peace.

As early as 1877 Smith advised blacks that electoral activity rather than armed resistance should be used in the struggle for civil rights. In 1899 he delivered one of his most highly acclaimed lectures, in which he encouraged blacks to use moral persuasion in their struggle for civil rights. He strongly believed that with an undiminished faith in God, blacks could withstand the injustices of whites and would be prepared spiritually for the eventual political struggle. In another speech in 1903 Smith reiterated his opposition to armed resistance and stated, "The man, White or Black, North or South, who advocates the use of dynamite or other violent means by the Negroes in the South is an enemy to both God and man" (Hill, *Charles Spencer Smith*, 21–22).

Smith was one of the most prolific religious writers of his era and one of the few black religious leaders to make an impact on the literary world in the late nineteenth century and early twentieth century. *Glimpses of Africa* (1895), a travel narrative of Smith's trip in 1884 to the west and southwest coasts of Africa, received popular acclaim in the literary world. His intention was to compare the condition of the blacks in the United States with that of their kinspeople abroad.

Smith's other scholarly contributions were in black church history. During his final years he served as church historiographer (1920–1923) and wrote *History of the African Methodist Episcopal Church* (1922), which served as a supplement to Payne's outstanding publication *History of the African Methodist Episcopal Church* (1891). Smith's writings included unpublished manuscripts and speeches on the history of the African Methodism. Among these were "The Life of Daniel A. Payne" (1894), "Dedicatory Services of the Publishing House of the A.M.E. Church Sunday School Union" (1894), "History of the A.M.E. Church 1844–1852," "Biographical Sketch of the Life of Reverend John Turner," "A Sketch of African Methodism in Tennessee," "Footprints of the A.M.E. Church in Foreign Lands," and "The First Decade of African Methodism in Arkansas and in the Indian Territory." Smith died in Detroit, Michigan.

FURTHER READING

A series of Smith's papers, c. 1875–1923, are in the Bentley Historical Library, University of Michigan, Ann Arbor.

Hill, Kenneth H. *Charles Spencer Smith: A Portrait; Sable Son of God* (1993).

Hill, Kenneth H., and Laura Okumu. *Selected Works of Charles Spencer Smith, M.D., D.D.* (1997).

University of Michigan, Bentley Historical Library, "Charles S. Smith papers ca. 1875–1923," http://www.hti.umich.edu/cgi/f/findaid/findaid-idx?c=bhlead&idno=umich-hbl-85413.

University of North Carolina, "Documenting the American South," http://docsouth.unc.edu/church/cssmith/bio.html.

MARY L. YOUNG

Smith, Chris (12 Oct. 1879–4 Oct. 1949), songwriter and vaudeville performer, was born Christopher Smith in Charleston, South Carolina, the son of Henry Mirtry, a shoemaker, and Clara Browne.

A baker by trade, Smith learned to play the piano and guitar by himself and showed much interest in and took part in local entertainment. He left Charleston with his friend Elmer Bowman to join a medicine show while they were "still in short pants," as he told Edward B. Marks. Smith and Bowman went to New York sometime in the 1890s and formed a vaudeville act billed as Smith Bowman. Smith began to publish songs in the late 1890s, and his "Good Morning Carrie!" (1901), written with Bowman, was his first major hit.

In the late 1890s and the 1900s Smith was an important member of the community of black entertainers in New York, home to a flowering of black theatricals, developments in the popular music publishing business, and the growing popularity of ragtime music. Smith was closely affiliated with Gotham-Attucks Music Co., one of the first black-owned publishing houses. Gotham-Attucks represented many songwriters and performers, including WILL MARION COOK, BERT WILLIAMS, CECIL MACK, Alex Rogers, WILLIAM TYERS, JAMES REESE EUROPE, Tom Lemonier, TIM BRYMN, Henry S. Creamer, and FORD DABNEY. With Cecil Mack, the head of the firm, Smith formed a successful songwriting team, scoring hits such as "He's a Cousin of Mine" (1906). Smith was also a close associate of Bert Williams, supplying many songs throughout Williams's career. Several of Smith's songs were featured in the Williams and GEORGE WALKER show *Bandanna Land* in 1908. During this period Smith's songs were also popularized by white stars such as May Irwin and Marie Cahill.

From early on, Smith was acquainted with the firm of Jos. W. Stern & Co., the major publisher of Smith's songs throughout most of his career. Edward B. Marks, the cofounder of the firm, indicated in his autobiography that he had known Smith since 1895 and praised the longevity of Smith as a successful songwriter.

Many of Smith's works during the early period of his career were ragtime songs, a new genre of popular song introduced to the mainstream in the late 1890s. Ragtime songs were noted for their vigorous syncopation. This kind of song played an important role in the development of black musical comedies and in the prosperity of Jos. W. Stern and other Tin Pan Alley publishers in the 1900s. Smith's songs were also noted for their combination of rhythmic vitality, interesting, often unusual harmonies, and felicitous lyrics.

In the 1910s Smith was active in vaudeville, teaming with George Cooper and Billy B. Johnson. In 1913 Smith produced his most famous song, "Ballin' the Jack," whose popularity can be understood in the context of the modern dance movement of the early 1910s. This song is noted for Smith's use of ingenious harmonies and for James Burris's lyrics describing dance steps, and it was later revived on many occasions, including the 1942 motion picture *For Me and My Gal*, starring Judy Garland and Gene Kelly, and *On the Riviera* (1951), starring Danny Kaye.

In the early 1920s Smith was engaged in the realm of private entertainment as well as in songwriting. According to the trumpeter REX STEWART, Smith belonged to the Clef Club cliques, which "were the aristocracy... the bigwigs who played Miami Beach, Piping Rock, Bar Harbor, and all the other posh resorts where society gathered to follow the sun." At this time Smith was associated with some important blues and jazz musicians of the day, such as PERRY BRADFORD, MAMIE SMITH, CLARENCE WILLIAMS, and W. C. HANDY. Smith also collaborated with the comedian Jimmy Durante.

Although Smith was a prolific songwriter until the mid-1920s, he did not become a member of the American Society of Composers, Authors, and Publishers (ASCAP) until 1931. In the 1930s and 1940s the number of Smith's new compositions declined, but he continued writing songs until his death in New York City. Little is known about his personal life. He was married and had at least two daughters, but other specifics are not known.

Smith is representative of the generation of black musicians who entered the entertainment field in New York around the turn of the century. They wrote songs in a distinctly black musical idiom and led successful careers in both songwriting and performing. Most of his collaborators came from the same pool of black talent and included Elmer Bowman, Cecil Mack, Harry Brown, Billy B. Johnson, John Larkins, James Burris, Tim Brymn, and Henry Troy, many of whom provided lyrics to Smith's melodies.

Well-known works other than those mentioned above are "I Ain't Poor No More" (1899), "Shame on You" (1904), "All In, Down and Out" (1906), "Down among the Sugar Cane" (1908), "You're in the Right Church but the Wrong Pew" (1908), "There's a Big Cry Baby in the Moon" (1909), "Come after Breakfast" (1909), "Constantly" (1910), "Honky Tonky Monkey Rag" (1911), "Beans, Beans, Beans" (1912), "I've Got My Habits On" (1921), "Cake Walking Babies from Home" (1924), and "Of All the Wrongs You've Done to Me" (1924).

Another important aspect of Smith as a songwriter is his opposition to the use of the derogatory term *coon* in the popular songs of the late 1890s. According to TOM FLETCHER, a black entertainer and one of Smith's close associates, Smith's refusal to use the term in the song "Good Morning Carrie!" started the turn away from "coon songs" around the turn of the century.

FURTHER READING

Fletcher, Tom. *100 Years of the Negro in Show Business* (1984).

Marks, Edward B. *They All Sang: From Tony Pastor to Rudy Vallee* (1934).

Shim, Eunmi. *Chris Smith and the Ragtime Song* (1993).
Obituary: *Amsterdam News*, 8 Oct. 1949.
This entry is taken from the *American National Biography* and is published here with the permission of the American Council of Learned Societies.

EUNMI SHIM

Smith, Clara (1894–2 Feb. 1935), blues and vaudeville singer, was born in Spartanburg, South Carolina. Nothing is known of her parents, including their names, or of her childhood. In about 1910 she began touring the South as a vaudeville performer. Probably in 1920 she joined the new Theater Owners' Booking Association circuit, in which context the guitarist LONNIE JOHNSON recalled working with Clara and MAMIE SMITH (no relation) in New Orleans. He said that Clara was "a lovely piano player and a lovely singer" (Oliver, 135).

In 1923 Smith came to New York and began singing in Harlem clubs and began a recording career that stretched to 1932. She became the most frequently recorded classic blues singer after BESSIE SMITH (also no relation). Disks from 1923 include "I Never Miss the Sunshine," "Awful Moanin' Blues" (documenting her nickname, "Queen of the Moaners"), and "Kansas City Man Blues." In 1924 she recorded "Good Looking Papa Blues," "Mean Papa, Turn in Your Key," "Texas Moaner Blues," "Freight Train Blues," and "Death Letter Blues." That same year she opened the Clara Smith Theatrical Club in New York while resuming her extensive touring. Visits to the West Coast reportedly extended into 1925, and she performed in Nashville, Tennessee, although she also worked at a theater in Harlem and recorded regularly in New York that year. Cornetist LOUIS ARMSTRONG was among Smith's accompanists on "Nobody Knows the Way I Feel 'Dis Mornin'," "My John Blues," and "Shipwrecked Blues," a morbidly chilling account of drowning and one of the earliest examples of a twelve-bar blues consistently in a minor key. Further sessions from 1925 include "My Two-Timing Papa" and two uninspired duets with Bessie Smith. Later that year the two Columbia Records blues stars became drunk at a party and got into a fistfight, with Bessie severely beating Clara; this fight ended their friendship and their collaborations.

In 1926 Smith married Charles "Two-Side" Wesley, a manager in the Negro baseball leagues; no children are mentioned in biographies or in Smith's obituary. Her recordings from 1926 include "Whip It to a Jelly," "Salty Dog," "My Brand New Papa," and two gospel songs. She had her own *Clara Smith Revue* at the Lincoln Theatre in 1927, and she continued working in Harlem theater revues until 1931. She recorded "Jelly Look What You Done Done," "Gin Mill Blues," and "Got My Mind on That Thing" (all 1928); "It's Tight Like That" and "Papa I Don't Need You Now" (both 1929); and two vaudeville vocal duets with Lonnie Johnson, "You Had Too Much" and "Don't Wear It Out," these last two under the pseudonym Violet Green (1930).

Smith sang with Charlie Johnson's Paradise Band at the Harlem Opera House in 1931 and that year appeared in Philadelphia, Pennsylvania, in the African American cowboy show *Trouble on the Ranch*. She worked in Cleveland from around 1931 to 1932 before returning to New York, where she joined the drummer PAUL BARBARIN at the Strollers Club in about 1934. She also worked for six months at Orchestra Gardens in Detroit. Smith had just returned to Detroit from further performances in Cleveland when she suffered heart trouble. Hospitalized for eleven days, she died of a heart attack. By the time of her death Smith was evidently separated from her husband, who could not be located.

Smith's singing straddled vaudeville and down-home blues styles. Her voice was slightly raspy. Moaning blue notes abounded, as for example in the session with Armstrong, but she enunciated lyrics clearly, using a southern African American pronunciation. In her first years of recording Smith favored lugubrious blues and vaudeville songs, but it may be obvious from titles listed above that she later followed a fashion for perky, risqué songs.

Smith was the subject of one of the finest contemporary descriptions of classic blues singing, written by Carl Van Vechten:

As she comes upon the stage through folds of electric blue hangings at the back, she is wrapped in a black evening cloak bordered with white fur. ... Clara begins to sing:

All day long I'm worried;
All day long I'm blue;
I'm so awfully lonesome,
I don' know what to do;
So I ask yo', doctor,
See if yo' kin fin'
Somethin' in yo' satchel
To pacify my min'.
Doctor! Doctor!

Her tones become poignantly pathetic; tears roll down her cheeks.

*Write me a prescription fo' duh Blues
Duh mean ole Blues....*

Her voice is powerful or melancholy, by turn. It tears the blood from one's heart" (106–108).

FURTHER READING

Bourgeois, Anna Stong. *Blueswomen: Profiles of 37 Early Performers with an Anthology of Lyrics, 1920–1945* (1996).

Oliver, Paul. *Conversation with the Blues* (1965).

Stewart-Baxter, Derrick. *Ma Rainey and the Classic Blues Singers* (1970).

Van Vechten, Carl. "Negro 'Blues' Singers: An Appreciation of Three Coloured Artists Who Excel in an Unusual and Native Medium," *Vanity Fair* (Mar. 1926).

Obituary: *Chicago Defender*, 9 Feb. 1935.

This entry is taken from the *American National Biography* and is published here with the permission of the American Council of Learned Societies.

BARRY KERNFELD

Smith, Damballah (14 Jan. 1943–1992), artist, illustrator, and activist, was born Dolphus Smith Jr. to Dolphus Smith Sr., a construction worker, and Lottie Hall, a schoolteacher, in Philadelphia, Pennsylvania. Dolphus Sr. and Lottie had met and married in their native Georgia and migrated north for better jobs and greater opportunity. Dolphus Jr. was the eldest of their four children: he had two brothers, Ronald Earl (deceased) and Thomas, and a sister, Raziyah.

The family established itself in a working-class community in North Philadelphia, and they took advantage of all that the city had to offer. Lottie, who had been keenly interested in literature and the arts, gave up teaching and devoted herself to her family. She kept abreast of cultural events, poetry (especially the works of PAUL LAURENCE DUNBAR), and art exhibits that might interest and inspire her children. They attended dance performances by the Dance Theatre of Harlem, the Paul Taylor dance troupe, and CARMEN DE LAVALLADE. Dolphus Jr. was mesmerized by the dancers' lithe movements and became increasingly devoted to the art.

Smith attended the Allison Elementary School, not far from the family home, and later the Dobbins Vocational High School in North Philadelphia. At an early age he exhibited an artistic bent and temperament and was independent and rebellious. His mother encouraged his artistic talent, and he spent his time doodling and, eventually, drawing. Each summer the Philadelphia Saving Fund Society held an art contest for elementary to high school students. In 1948 when Dolphus Jr. was five years old he entered the contest and won first prize. As he got older he neither liked nor wanted to attend school and often played hooky, spending his days in city parks where he would draw the animal and human figures he observed. His truancy went largely undetected, and he soon enlisted his two brothers and sister periodically to join him in the park. He also spent time with the dancers who came to Philadelphia to perform, and years later he proclaimed that he "danced in his work" as an artist.

Smith graduated from high school in 1963 and enrolled at the Philadelphia College of Arts (later defunct). In his spare time he studied art history as well as the works of famous African American artists at Philadelphia's Academy of Art. During his senior year he also studied painting and printmaking at the Art Students League in New York. He won several minor arts awards and had solo exhibitions of his work at Hinkley-Brohel Gallery in New York and at the Goldstein Gallery and Gallery 252, both in Philadelphia. In 1967 he graduated from the Philadelphia College of Art and moved to Washington, DC.

Created in the 1960s climate of social upheaval and civil rights struggle, Smith's early works depict urban strife and provide social commentary on the inner-city blues. Smith changed his name to Damballah to identify himself with African and the African diaspora heritage. In African mythology and the Haitian Vodun religion informed by it, Damballah is the all-powerful serpent god who created all the waters of the earth when he shed his skin in the sun, and the god who created the earth's hills and valleys, the stars and planets of the heavens, and metals from stone; he also used lightning to form sacred rocks and stones. When the god Damballah created water, the sun created the rainbow, called Aida-Wedo, whom Damballah wed.

In his work Smith explored Afrocentric subjects and themes. He said that he wanted to "understand the needs of the African community and express a cultural extension through imagery that has developed from my African ancestry." He noted that in much of his work, a bird appears as "a messenger from higher powers in African art. Our ancestors are always with us, always supporting us."

Smith was known for his brilliant watercolor drawings and colorful graphic art in pastel and pen and ink. In 1969 Smith arranged an exhibition at the Black Man's Art Gallery in San Francisco. In 1975, as his reputation began to grow, he showed at Coppin State College in Baltimore, Maryland. His first Washington, D.C. show was held at the Miya Gallery in 1977 and was followed by a second in 1979. In 1980 his art was featured in a gallery located in the Washington mayor's office. During these years he also participated in group exhibitions at his alma mater, the Philadelphia College of Art; he also exhibited at the Afro-American Festival for the Psychiatric Institute of Washington, at the National Conference of Artists' Black Family Exhibit at the John F. Kennedy Center, and at the Phelps Stokes Fund Mobile Exhibition at Savannah State University in Georgia. Although Smith was exhibiting in the late 1970s and early 1980s, he struggled to make a living from his art.

In subsequent years Smith's fortunes improved. In 1984 his work entered the Evans-Tibbs Collection, now part of the permanent collection of the Corcoran Gallery of Art in Washington, D.C. His work is also held by the National Cultural Foundation, the African American Scholars Council, the U.S. Public Information Agency Collection, the Afro-American Museum of History and Culture in Philadelphia, the National Exhibition of Contemporary African American Art, and many private collectors around the country.

In 1988 Smith was selected to illustrate the brochure and pamphlets for the first National Black Arts Festival, held in Atlanta. Through this commission he met and collaborated with other African American artists, art critics, art historians, and curators, among them Ed Spriggs, director of Atlanta's Hammonds House.

Smith won another high-profile commission in the late 1980s when the American Red Cross selected him to design HIV/AIDS education posters for distribution in African American communities. By 1990 AIDS had become one of the leading causes of death among African Americans. Smith mined the rich legacy of African art and history, ultimately choosing six proverbs tied to the goals of the Red Cross's African American HIV/AIDS awareness program. For example, one poster, reproduced on the organization's Web site, bears the Cameroonian proverb, "Knowledge is better than riches." The accompanying figures are animated, dramatic, and powerful. In many of the posters there seem to be characters within characters within characters, each expressing some part of the being's soul. Explaining his inspiration and goals, Smith said:

The images which have evolved from my life force have always been spiritual/cultural. The infinity of ancestral spirits has been a central recurring theme in my work. Through the line, color and textures that give shape to these images, I have sought to evoke the subtlety and polyrhythmic intensity of African music which conducts our spirit through the 'Diaspora.'

In 1992 Smith, whose art was an important tool in Red Cross lectures, community forums, and other settings for health education—for HIV/AIDS education in particular—succumbed at age forty-nine to an AIDS-related illness.

FURTHER READING
Lewis, Samella. *Black Artists on Art* (1977).
National Black Arts Festival. *Selected Essays: Arts and Artists from the Harlem Renaissance to the 1980's* (1988).

LUTHER BROWN

Smith, Damu (1952–2006), activist, was born LeRoy Wesley Smith in St. Louis, Missouri, to Vernice and Sylvester Smith. His family included three brothers and a sister. Smith's experiences growing up in a working-class family, enduring many hardships, and deprivations as a child, developed within him a lifelong commitment to improving living conditions for those in poverty.

Smith came to activism in 1969, while still in high school. During a field trip to Cairo, Illinois, at the age of seventeen, he toured African American neighborhoods where white supremacists had recently opened fire on several houses, and attended a Black Solidarity Day rally where he listened to speeches by AMIRI BARAKA, NINA SIMONE, JESSE JACKSON, and JULIAN BOND. As a first-year student at St. John's University in Minnesota he led an occupation of the school's administrative offices to demand a black studies program. Expressing his growing politicization, Smith, while at St. John's, changed his name to Damu Amiri Imara Smith, meaning blood, leadership, and strength in Swahili.

Outside of school, Smith's earliest activism included organizing against police brutality, gun violence, and government injustice. This work led Smith to become active in the 1970s and 1980s with a diversity of progressive organizations, including the National Alliance Against Racist and Political Repression, the National Black Independent Political Party, the National Wilmington 10 Defense Committee, and the United Church of Christ Commission for Racial Justice. As associate director of the Washington Office of the American Friends Service Committee, Smith was an outspoken voice in the campaign for a nuclear weapons freeze in the late 1970s and early 1980s.

Smith first came to national and, indeed, international prominence for his work in the fight against apartheid in South Africa. As executive director of the Washington Office on Africa and, later, as cofounder of Artists for a Free South Africa, Smith became a leading figure in the U.S. Wing of the global antiapartheid movement during the mid to late 1980s.

Among Smith's most significant contributions to social and environmental justice was his work in identifying the links between environmental destruction, racism, and poverty and his efforts to expose and confront toxic contamination by major corporations of African American and poor communities. Smith's work dramatically shifted the emphasis of environmental politics away from concerns with wilderness and leisure, which preoccupied much of mainstream environmentalism, and toward a recognition that environmental problems were in many ways matters of class and racial inequalities.

In addition to serving as the first coordinator for environmental justice with the Southern Organizing Committee for Economic and Social Justice, Smith worked for a decade as a toxics campaigner for Greenpeace USA. With that organization, Smith organized Toxic Tours of the South, in which he brought celebrities such as the writer ALICE WALKER and the actor Mike Farrell to observe the horrendous conditions existing in several notorious environmental hotspots in Mississippi and Louisiana. Between 1991 and 1992, Smith visited forty cities and towns in nine states to observe the effect of chemical dumping and other environmentally destructive corporate practices on African American and poor communities. One tour included a visit to "Cancer Alley" an area in Louisiana that earned its name from its high level of cancer deaths due to chemical contamination. Unfortunately, while the high proportion of deaths related to contamination was part of local and regional lore, governmental organizations had done nothing, prior to Smith's visit, to ameliorate the situation. Smith and Greenpeace played an important part in assisting local grassroots organizations in their efforts to confront Shell Oil over its dumping practices. In addition his efforts helped to force the highly toxic Shintech PVC plant to leave Norco, Louisiana.

In 1999 Smith initiated a project, the National Emergency Gathering of Black Community Advocates for Environmental and Economic Justice, that would have a profound effect on the composition and direction of the environmental justice movement in the United States. The largest environmental justice conference in U.S. history, the gathering laid the groundwork for the formation of the National Black Environmental Justice Network, the first national network of African American environmentalists.

In 2001, in the face of impending military deployment in Iraq, Smith left Greenpeace to form Black Voices for Peace, a group committed to organizing African American opposition to U.S. militarization and aggression in the Middle East and beyond. Black Voices for Peace called for the transfer of the billions of dollars earmarked by the Bush administration for global military operations toward universal health care, education, environmental protection, housing, and jobs.

Smith's work with Black Voices for Peace included support for Palestinian liberation and calls for an end to the Israeli government's occupation of Palestinian lands. Smith supported calls for an international peace force to separate the Israeli Army from Palestinians. He did not accept attempts to justify Israeli Army actions as a legitimate response to acts of terrorism. In his view it was essential to remember that one side was an occupier with a vast military and financial arsenal at its disposal while the other side, whose communities were being occupied, suffered most of the casualties.

It was during a Palm Sunday peace march in Palestine in 2005 that Smith fainted and had a seizure. Smith was subsequently diagnosed with stage four colon cancer.

Smith faced his battles with the disease that would eventually claim his life with the same activist determination and commitment with which he confronted struggles over social injustice. Indeed, rather than treat his illness as a personal trouble to be addressed privately, and to which all of his time would be given, Smith used the situation as an opportunity to campaign against the injustices of the American health care system and the dire need for a national health insurance program. Because his life had been devoted to movements for social justice, Smith found himself, like millions of poor and working-class Americans, with no health insurance and few resources to cover medical expenses and living costs. Despite his weakened condition over the last year of his life, and the medical need to rest his body, Smith unselfishly made himself available to speak publicly on behalf of the millions of Americans who lack health insurance.

Perhaps the most important and durable legacy of Smith's lifetime of activism was his capacity to build bridges across social movements that have traditionally been focused on single issues or the specific needs of their own, often distinct, constituencies. Whether building bridges between environmentalists and labor activists or antipoverty organizers and supporters of Palestinian liberation, Smith showed a consistent willingness and ability to find common ground among those seeking social justice, refusing to view social movements in isolation. Smith was survived by his daughter Asha Moore Smith and his partner Adeleke Foster.

FURTHER READING

"Damu Smith: Bush Doesn't Know Anything About Freedom," *Democracy Now*, 24 Jan. 2005.

"Activist Damu Smith: Fighting Colon Cancer and Systemic Racial Disparities in American Healthcare," *Democracy Now*, 1 Aug. 2005.

JEFF SHANTZ

Smith, Eddie Lee, Jr. (23 Jul. 1929–25 Jan. 2001), mayor, was born in Fayette County, Tennessee, to Eddie Lee Smith Sr., a farmer, and Lucy Sales Smith, a homemaker. He was educated in rural schools for black children. In the early 1930s his parents moved the family to Marshall County in northwest Mississippi, eventually settling on eleven acres that became part of the town of Holly Springs. The Smiths were founding members of the town's black Pentecostal church, now known as Christ Temple, and they instilled in their twelve children, including Eddie Jr., a sense of personal piety and pride.

Smith attended high school in Holly Springs at Rust College in the 1950s, and he also served in a medical unit when he enlisted as a conscientious objector during the Korean War. When he returned for undergraduate classes at Rust College, he was deeply impressed by the distinguished black men he saw running the campus and determined that he wanted to be a "Rust man" himself. He graduated from Rust in 1956 and worked for a year as the principal of one of the segregated schools in Marshall County. Starting in the early 1960s, Smith worked for more than two decades as an administrator at Rust, beginning as the public relations director. He went on to become the school's business manager

and later the director of grants and contracts. In 1957 he married his college sweetheart, Luberta Eugene Elliott, a music educator, and they had three sons: Edwin, Carlton, and Lee.

Smith was extensively involved in the struggle for civil rights. He helped organize meetings of the National Association for the Advancement of Colored People (NAACP) in northern Mississippi, and he was monitored by the Federal Bureau of Investigation for promoting black voter registration through the NAACP and the Council of Federated Organizations, of which the NAACP was a part. His employment at Rust gave him job security he did not have as a civil rights advocate employed by Marshall County Public Schools, at that time still controlled by defensive whites. He was among the first African Americans in Holly Springs to register to vote in that period of deep resistance and tumult. He also ran for Marshall County school superintendent in the late 1960s. Though Smith was not elected, his candidacy was effective in getting more black voters registered and participating in the democratic process.

Before Smith's elections to office, Holly Springs's record of African American elected officials was inconsistent and troubling. Though it had two African American colleges—Rust and Mississippi Industrial College—and, consequently, a sizeable number of educated black citizens, not since HIRAM REVELS during the Reconstruction era had there been black elected officials in the county. In 1977 Smith ran successfully for the position of alderman for Ward I of Holly Springs, becoming the first African American to serve in such a capacity in the town. Two years later he earned his master's degree in business administration from the University of Miami (Florida). In 1985 he made his first bid for the mayor's office, losing by only 109 votes.

In 1987 he left Rust College to pursue other business interests, with frustrating results. One year later, Smith saw the opportunity for a successful mayoral campaign. Undeterred by death threats, he ran his campaigns with grassroots support, mostly from the black community. Smith also refused funds from those who would have sought political favors. His commitment to the integrity of the election was consistent with his understanding of himself as a statesman, an elected official, and a public servant—never a "politician."

In the June 1989 mayoral race, when the initial returns surprisingly indicated that Smith had lost, the town was in an uproar, with rumors of rigged voting machines swirling. But when the votes were recounted by court order, Smith emerged victorious. He was reelected both in 1993 and 1997.

The town prospered during his tenure. His leadership was essential to several projects, including the establishment of the Ida B. Wells Family Art Gallery, in a building built by the activist-journalist's father. A new road and multipurpose building bear Smith's name, and he also jumpstarted a wave of African American-owned enterprises in Holly Springs and mentored a new generation of elected officials and entrepreneurs in the town. Black and white citizens alike had mixed responses to some aspects of his legacy. Perhaps the most controversial of his contributions was his endorsement of Marshall County's 1,000-bed prison run by Wackenhut Corrections Corporation, which opened in Holly Springs in 1996. Whereas Smith primarily saw the prison as an opportunity for employment of citizens in his economically depressed community, others saw it as a warehouse for young blacks and a capitulation to the growing for-profit prison industry. Throughout his almost twelve years as mayor, however, he maintained an open door policy, and he enjoyed the respect, admiration, and favor of the vast majority of his constituency.

His activities on the state and national level were numerous as well. He was secretary of the Presidential Scholars Foundation during the Clinton Administration (1993–2001), and a member of the White House Commission on Presidential Scholars (1993–2001). He was also chairperson of the Tennessee Valley Authority Board of Commissioners and was involved in the Mississippi Mayors Association, the Mississippi Conference of Black Mayors, the National Conference of Black Mayors, and the Mississippi Municipal League (1989–2001), of which he was president (1999–2000).

In the fall of 2000 Smith was diagnosed with kidney cancer. He went to Memphis the following January to have the kidney removed, and he died of complications hours after the surgery was completed, surrounded by his wife and sons.

Through his commitment to being mayor to all of the people of Holly Springs, Eddie Lee Smith Jr., was able to do what none had done before—he mobilized the political clout of the African American majority of the town while working collaboratively with the white minority. As a result, he provided a model of leadership that allowed for the increasing redistribution of jobs and resources while maintaining racial harmony.

FURTHER READING

"Holly Springs and Mayor Eddie L. Smith: M(ississippi) M(unicipal) L(eague) Feature Municipality," *Mississippi Municipalities* (Aug./Sept. 1999).

McAlexander, Hubert H. *A Southern Tapestry: Marshall County, Mississippi, 1835–2000* (2000).

CARLTON ELLIOTT SMITH

Smith, Emmitt, Jr. (15 May 1969–), football player, was born in Pensacola, Florida, the second of five children of Emmitt Sr., a city bus driver, and Mary. Emmitt Jr. watched his father play semiprofessional football for the Pensacola Wings of the Dixie League and knew from an early age that he would be a football player. When he was four, he announced that he would play for the Dallas Cowboys, and by the time he was eight he was playing in and dominating organized football leagues.

Smith attended Escambia High School, leading the football team to a state championship his sophomore year. In his junior year, Escambia won the state title again and was named the top-ranked high school football team in the country. Smith was named the *USA Today* and *Parade* magazine high school player of the year. He finished his high school career with 8,804 rushing yards, second all-time in high school football, and never missed a practice or game to injury.

Though scouts thought he was a great runner— described as quick, explosive, and having great vision—most considered him too small at five feet, ten inches for college football. Smith took the criticism personally, making him more determined to not only play college football but also excel at it. In 1987 Smith went to the University of Florida at Gainesville, with the promise of becoming the starting tailback, which happened the third week of his freshman season during a nationally televised game against Alabama. He silenced his critics with a 1,341-yard season, becoming only the second freshman to place in the top ten in Heisman Trophy voting.

During his sophomore year his numbers dropped as Florida switched to a pass-oriented offense and he suffered the first serious injury of his career, a knee injury, missing five games. He returned the next season healthy, though the team faced probation for recruiting violations, causing head coach Galen Hall to resign midseason and the remainder of the coaching staff to resign at the end of the season. Faced with the team's turmoil, Smith decided to forego his senior year and enter the upcoming National Football League (NFL) draft in April 1990, the first draft for which nonseniors were eligible. Despite playing only three seasons, Smith left Florida with fifty-eight school records, including all-time rusher, and he had been named All-American each season.

Smith faced the same criticisms as he entered the draft that he faced in college, with many scouts saying he was too slow or too small for the NFL. Despite this, the Cowboys selected Smith as the seventeenth overall pick. He immediately set out to prove his critics wrong, rushing for 937 yards and winning the AP Rookie of the Year honors and the first of many Pro Bowl selections in 1990. The following season, the Cowboys hired a new offensive coordinator, Norv Turner, who built the offense around Smith. He responded by winning two straight rushing titles, with 1,593 yards in 1991 and 1,713 yards in 1992, and leading the Cowboys to a victory over the Buffalo Bills in Super Bowl XXVII. With the victory, Smith became the first running back in NFL history to win a rushing title and a Super Bowl in the same season.

The Cowboys and Smith were locked in a heated contract dispute at the start of the 1993 season. Smith signed after missing the first two games, but was bitter over how Cowboys owner Jerry Jones treated him. When quarterback Troy Aikman signed a record contract during the season, Smith was livid—not at Aikman, but at how differently Jones treated Aikman. Smith never called Jones a racist, but he wondered if his race played a role. Despite missing two games, Smith rushed for 1,486 yards and a third rushing title, earning the NFL's Most Valuable Player (MVP) award. The final game of the season epitomized his career. With home field advantage in the playoffs on the line, Smith carried the Cowboys to victory over the New York Giants. He rushed thirty-two times for 168 yards and caught ten passes for sixty-one yards, all while playing most of the game with a separated shoulder. The football broadcaster John Madden called Smith's effort one of the gutsiest performances he ever saw. Smith capped the season by leading the Cowboys to a second consecutive Super Bowl title over the Buffalo Bills. He rushed for 132 yards and two touchdowns in the game, earning MVP honors.

At the start of the 1994 season, Smith knew he had one goal left in the NFL—surpassing WALTER PAYTON as the all-time leading rusher. The Cowboys, led by the "triplets" Smith, Aikman, and the wide receiver Michael Irvin, won one more Super Bowl in 1996 before declining from playoff contender to perennial loser. Through the decline, Smith continued to amass impressive rushing statistics well into his thirties, past the usual prime for a running back. Smith finally broke Payton's record on 27 October 2002 at Texas Stadium in a game against the Seattle Seahawks. An eleven-yard run over left end pushed Smith past Payton's record 16,726 yards. Smith finished the 2002 season with the Cowboys and played two additional seasons with the Arizona Cardinals before retiring in February 2005. He finished his career with 18,355 rushing yards, an NFL record some believe may never be broken, as well as records for consecutive one thousand-yard seasons (11) and career rushing touchdowns (164), all from a running back many considered too small or too slow to play professional football.

During his playing days, Smith planned for life after football. In May 1996 he completed his degree from Florida, a B.S. in health and human performance, becoming the first member of his family to receive a college degree. In 1999 he founded EJ Smith Enterprises, an investment and real estate company. He married the former Miss Virginia and ex-wife of the comedian Martin Lawrence, Patricia Southall, in 2000; they had four children. Following his retirement from football, Smith turned to his real estate business full time, partnering with the Staubach Company, owned by legendary Cowboys quarterback Roger Staubach, to form Smith/Cypress Partners, focusing on retail real estate development projects. In 2005 Smith was inducted into the Dallas Cowboys Ring of Honor alongside Aikman and Irvin. In 2006 he was inducted into the Florida Football Ring of Honor and the College Football Hall of Fame. Smith won the third season of *Dancing with the Stars* with professional dancer Cheryl Burke in 2006. In 2007 he joined ESPN as a studio analyst for the network's NFL pregame coverage. Smith was inducted into the Pro Football Hall of Fame in 2010, following an introduction at the ceremony by Jerry Jones. In an emotional and inspirational acceptance speech, Smith thanked his teammates and family.

FURTHER READING

Smith, Emmitt. *The Emmitt Zone* (1994).
Savage, Jeff. *Emmitt Smith: Star Running Back* (1996).

MICHAEL C. MILLER

Smith, Ferdinand Christopher (?–1961), international labor activist, was born in Jamaica and came to live in the United States after years of service as a maritime worker, most notably with the Luchenbach Steamship Company. Little is known about the early years of his life prior to his arrival in the United States. Despite his lack of American citizenship, Smith was an outspoken and active public figure, organizing openly and militantly for the rights of workers and in opposition to discrimination, whether on the basis of race, nationality, or belief. A lifelong member and supporter of the Communist Party, which he joined in the early 1930s, Smith made important and lasting contributions to the development and mobilization of a radical and militant element within the labor movements in the United States and Jamaica. Recognizing the importance of union contributions to broader struggles within working class communities, Smith played an important part in ensuring that union support went into building some of the organizations that would go on to play crucial roles in the civil rights movement in the United States.

Smith was a founding member of the National Maritime Union (NMU) in 1937 in New Jersey, and at its first convention won election as Secretary-Treasurer, the union's second-in-command. His election to this post meant that Smith held the highest union office of any African American at that time. Despite holding such a high-ranking office, Smith maintained his commitment to building a union controlled and run by rank-and-file members. This was a continuation of the work he had done in fighting against undemocratic and authoritarian practices within the International Seaman's Union, a predecessor to the NMU.

During the 1936–1937 strike of East Coast maritime workers, Smith was elected to the strike committee. He played a large part in organizing the African American, Jamaican, and Filipino workers of the United Fruit Company, Clyde Mallory Lines, and the Cuban Mail Line, effectively stopping owners from using divisions within the workforce to break the strike.

He then played a key role within the International Seaman's Union to remove conservative officials and bring the union under rank-and-file control. This struggle saw Smith take on the powerful head of the stewards division, David Grange, who had a well-earned reputation for intimidating workers. Smith was elected as a trustee of the marine Cooks and Stewards Union of the Atlantic Gulf and was charged with negotiating with the American Federation of Labor to ensure democratic elections.

Through the efforts of Smith and other members of the Communist Party within the NMU, the union set a course to organize all maritime workers, regardless of race, national background, or craft. Smith continued the work of the Industrial Workers of the World, a revolutionary union that had made huge strides in organizing sea and dock workers during the early 1900s. To build unity among a diverse workforce, the NMU developed an antidiscrimination policy for all union activities, elections, and offices. It worked to end all discrimination and practices of blacklisting in the industry, finally winning recognition for a nondiscrimination policy in the contract the NMU signed with ship owners in 1944, largely owing to Smith's efforts. The NMU also fought against discrimination suffered by maritime workers' families in their home communities.

During World War II, Smith worked to ensure the commitment of the NMU to the struggle against fascism. This meant, in opposition to many other leftists, advocating the support of maritime workers for the allied war effort. Smith actively campaigned on behalf of Franklin Roosevelt's bid for reelection to a third term as president, touring the shipyards and industrial centers to agitate for a vote for President Roosevelt.

Following the war, Smith became an increasingly outspoken critic of antilabor government policies that signaled the emergence of a new red scare. He condemned the Marshall Plan, arguing that it was partly a cover for U.S. military aggression globally, and challenged the requirement of the Taft-Hartley law that forced a non-Communist oath upon all union officials.

Smith's outspoken positions on crucial issues of the day, his effectiveness as an organizer, and his popularity among rank-and-file members made him a target of not only politicians and capitalists, but also his fellow officials within the union movement, his own union included. When the Congress of Industrial Organizations (CIO), the union federation to which the NMU belonged, initiated a purge of Communists from its ranks, many of the most militant and active union members, including those who had organized and participated in the major strikes of the 1930s that had built the CIO, found themselves marginalized, excluded, and unemployed. Many who, like Smith, lacked American citizenship were deported. NMU president Joe Curran, whose association with Smith dated to membership on the strike committee of 1936–1937, capitulated to pressures coming from ship owners and initiated the expulsion of leftist members from the NMU. Due to his particularly high profile and his lack of U.S. citizenship, Smith was especially vulnerable. A 1948 government report showed that Smith had been under surveillance as one of the CIO Executive Board members who supported the third-party presidential candidacy of Henry A. Wallace. That report, which made reference to Smith's recent arrest, noted that Smith had been under government surveillance for more than a decade. In 1951 Smith was deported to Jamaica.

Upon his return to Jamaica, Smith took up the struggles of poor workers, becoming the country's most prominent communist and labor advocate. His activities made him something of an embarrassment to the social democratic government of Norman Manley, which was caught between its nationalist aims and growing pressures from the United States to align itself with American interests during the cold war.

Smith remained a staunch supporter of the Soviet Union until his death in 1961, even after the crushing of the Hungarian Revolution in 1956, an event that led many members from around the world to leave the Communist movement. Smith was eventually forbidden from leaving Jamaica lest his opposition voice and organizing capabilities undermine the government's position.

Despite the significance of Smith's many contributions, and his own prominence during his day, history has rendered him a largely overlooked and underappreciated figure. Smith also had made significant contributions to the foundations of the American civil rights movement, supporting many of the institutions, including the National Negro Congress, the Southern Conference on Human Welfare, and the Southern Negro Youth Congress. These organizations set the foundation for the civil rights struggles that would transform the United States only a few years after Smith's deportation.

FURTHER READING

Buhle, Paul. "Red Seas," *Monthly Review* (2006).

Horne, Gerald. "Black Thinkers at Sea: Ferdinand Smith and the Decline of African-American Proletarian Intellectuals," *Souls* 4 no. 2 (2002).

Horne, Gerald. *Red Seas: Ferdinand Smith and Radical Black Sailors in the United States and Jamaica* (2005).

Rydell, Roy. "Fighting Jim Crow on the High Seas," *People's Weekly World* (1999).

JEFF SHANTZ

Smith, George Walker (28 Apr. 1929–), minister, educational administrator, and civic activist, was born in Hayneville, Alabama, the son of Will Smith, a sharecropper, and Amanda (Tyler) Smith, a laundress. Valedictorian of his Miller's Ferry, Alabama, Presbyterian high school class, George worked his way through Knoxville College in Tennessee majoring in chemistry with a minor in biology and German. A member of Kappa Alpha Psi fraternity, he was awarded his bachelor's degree in 1951, the same year that he married Irene Hightower; they eventually had three children.

Smith was taking graduate courses in education at Alabama State University while teaching high school in the rural town of Annemanie, Alabama, when a series of incidents of extreme racial brutality persuaded him to leave his job and his home state and enter the ministry, a career path that he had earlier rejected. In 1953 he enrolled at the Pittsburgh Theological Seminary in Pittsburgh, Pennsylvania, where he was one of only two African Americans in training. Smith far surpassed the low expectations of his white classmates and wound up tutoring some of them in the study of Hebrew. He did an extended practicum at the wealthy and predominantly white Third Presbyterian Church in the Squirrel Hill neighborhood of Pittsburgh. Upon earning his divinity degree in 1956 he moved to San Diego, California, where he founded the first black Presbyterian church in the city, the Golden Hill United Presbyterian Church (renamed Christ United Presbyterian Church in 1981).

In 1959 Smith became the first black member of the local Kiwanis and began building a multiracial base that would further his political ambitions in a city that was only 6 percent African American. In 1963 Smith, by then a respected figure in the predominantly black and Mexican American southeast section of the city, narrowly won a race for a seat on the San Diego board of education representing District E, which had a sizable African American and Latino population. It was the first time in the city's history that an African American had won election to public office. His fellow board members elected him school board president on three occasions before he retired from service in 1979. It was during his tenure, in 1969, that the board instituted a voluntary school integration program. Three years later he helped convince the board to adopt an affirmative action plan that encouraged firms receiving district contracts to hire minority workers. In 1974 he led the board in establishing district goals for minority employment and promotion.

334 SMITH, HARRY CLAY

On occasion he confounded both liberals and conservatives, taking stands against busing to achieve school integration and against tuition tax credits for parents sending their children to private schools.

Smith's high-profile position on the school board made him the most recognized African American in the county, and he frequently appeared on television and at social and political functions. Having been denied the right to vote by white Democrats in Alabama, Smith registered as a Republican in 1953 and remained loyal to and active in the party. Although the overwhelming majority of blacks in San Diego were Democrats, Smith's party affiliation did not affect his popularity among African Americans, and it boosted his acceptability among San Diego's white majority, which was predominantly conservative and Republican and whose votes were crucial in citywide elections.

Smith participated in regional Republican events, and during the presidential administration of Richard Nixon he was appointed to the White House Conference on Children and Youth, the National Advisory Commission on Juvenile Justice, and the White House Committee on Education and the Arts. Smith's involvement with public education reached its zenith in 1976 when he was elected president of the thirty-thousand-member National School Boards Association and was named chairman of the Council of Great City School Districts. Smith's liberal and progressive views were often at odds with the majority of his associates in the Republican Party. This was certainly the case when in 1966 Smith directly challenged the gubernatorial candidate Ronald Reagan's views on civil rights and fair-housing legislation.

Smith was a prime force in the city's southeast communities, cofounding the first minority-owned commercial bank, the Pacific Coast Bank, in 1971, serving for several years as chairman of the local United Negro College Fund drive, and as a charter member of the San Diego chapter of Alpha Phi Boule, a fraternity of black professionals. More significant, however, in terms of Smith's legacy of public service was his founding of the Catfish Club. The club began in 1970 as the Colored Folks Club and comprised Smith and two friends who loved fishing and discussing politics. The group quickly became a highly visible multiracial group that sponsored weekly catfish and red snapper lunches, featuring speeches by city, county, and state political and cultural leaders in politics. In 1976 the club was renamed the Catfish Club. For three decades Smith acted as spokesperson of the group, introducing speakers who were expected to field questions from audiences typically numbering two hundred. By the early 1980s the Catfish Club had become widely known to the citizens of the region as a nonpartisan venue focusing on topics of current concern. Initially the forums convened at Smith's church, but they later moved to the studios of the television station KNSD.

Frustrated in his attempt win a seat on the San Diego County Board of Supervisors, Smith was kept busy attending to a host of civic activities. In 1987 he was appointed to head the city's first police review board to monitor investigations of alleged police misconduct, and in 1992 following the Los Angeles race riots Smith, along with the local white activist George Mitrovich, cofounded the San Diego Coalition for Equality. The recipient of numerous honors and awards, Smith received an honorary doctor of humane letters degree from San Diego State University in 2002 and was given the 2004 annual Gloria Penner Civic Service Award by the League of Women Voters of San Diego. He officially retired from the ministry in 2000 but continued to preside over the Catfish Club. In 2002 he published his autobiography.

FURTHER READING

Smith, George Walker. *The Conscience of the Community* (2002).

Di Veroli, Robert. "Long-Time Leader Dr. George Smith Honored for Numerous Contributions," *San Diego Union*, 22 Nov. 1986.

Glanton, Dahleen. "Catfish Club to Honor Founder Smith," *San Diego Union*, 8 May 1986.

ROBERT FIKES JR.

Smith, Harry Clay (28 Jan. 1863–10 Dec. 1941), newspaper editor and politician, was born in Clarksburg, West Virginia, the son of John Smith and Sarah (maiden name unknown), occupations unknown. Accompanied by his sister and widowed mother, he came to Cleveland in 1866 and remained there for the rest of his life. A self-taught cornet player, Smith played in several bands while attending high school. After graduating in 1883 he and three friends established the *Cleveland Gazette*. Smith, who remained a lifelong bachelor, soon bought out his partners and became sole proprietor and editor. The first significant African American newspaper in the city, the *Gazette* was published weekly until Smith's death, at which time the newspaper went out of existence. Known for its militant editorial stance on racial issues, the *Gazette* circulated widely throughout Ohio before World War I. After 1917 its influence steadily declined as a result of competition from other African American newspapers in Cleveland.

Smith was one of the most eloquent, most consistently militant race leaders of his era. Throughout his career he used the *Gazette* as a forum to attack segregation and racial discrimination in all its forms. He continually urged blacks to use political pressure, legal action, or boycotts in the struggle against racism. Smith was a leader in the successful campaign to end segregated schools in Ohio in 1887. He was a founding member of the Afro-American League in 1890 and was one of the first to criticize BOOKER T. WASHINGTON when in his famous Atlanta Cotton Exposition address of 1895 the headmaster of Tuskegee Institute seemed to accept the validity of racial segregation in the South.

Smith entered Republican politics in 1885 when, in return for the editor's support of Joseph B. Foraker for governor, Smith was appointed deputy state inspector of oils, a patronage position he held for four years. He was elected three times to the Ohio General Assembly, serving from 1894 to 1898 and 1900 to 1902. In the state legislature Smith became known as a vigorous advocate of civil rights legislation. He was one of the main sponsors of the Ohio Civil Rights Act of 1894, which prohibited discrimination in public accommodations, and the Anti–Mob Violence Act of 1896, one of the first state antilynching laws.

In the late 1890s Smith gradually became alienated from the mainstream of the Republican Party as well as from other, more conservative African American politicians in the state. Though formally remaining in the party, Smith grew increasingly independent and sometimes refused to support Republican candidates—an unusual position for an African American editor at that time. In 1908 the *Gazette* urged blacks to vote for "anyone but [William Howard] Taft," primarily in protest against Theodore Roosevelt's summary dismissal, two years before, of a black regiment in Brownsville, Texas, on unproven charges of rioting.

Smith had participated actively in the anti-Bookerite Niagara Movement of 1905 and was named to the National Association for the Advancement of Colored People's select Committee of One Hundred soon after that organization was established in 1910. In 1912 he led an unsuccessful battle against the establishment of the Phillis Wheatley Association, a facility for homeless African American girls,

calling it a "jim crow hotel." From 1915 to 1917 he led a campaign to block the showing of the racist film *The Birth of a Nation* in Cleveland. When white mobs attacked black residents of Chicago and other cities during World War I, Smith urged blacks to arm themselves and retaliate if necessary. He was subsequently investigated by the young J. Edgar Hoover, who in his 1919 Justice Department report on black radicalism labeled the editorial stand of the *Gazette* "vicious."

By the time of the Great Migration of African Americans to northern industrial centers (1916–1919), Smith was one of a dwindling group of black leaders who adamantly refused to distinguish between segregation undertaken by the state and self-segregation by private organizations founded by and on behalf of African Americans. Perhaps because as a young man Smith had studied and worked alongside whites on a basis of equality, he strongly opposed the trend toward self-help and racial solidarity that was becoming popular among other black leaders at the time. During the decade following World War I, he opposed the creation of a separate black YMCA and vehemently attacked a proposal, which failed largely for lack of funds, to build a private hospital in Cleveland primarily for African Americans. Occasionally, Smith urged blacks to support black businesses, but this was virtually the only exception to a lifelong opposition to racial separatism of any kind. African Americans, the editor stated in 1914, should "be trying to wipe out color lines, rather than be trying to multiply them."

In the early 1920s the administrations of Presidents Warren G. Harding and Calvin Coolidge angered Smith because of their military occupation of Haiti and refusal to end the segregation of African Americans in some departments of the federal government. In 1924 Smith opposed Coolidge and set up an Independent Colored Voters League to support Robert La Follette, the Progressive Party presidential candidate. At the local and state level, too, Smith grew dissatisfied with the Republican Party's declining interest in civil rights and its failure to support more blacks for public office. In 1921 he ran unsuccessfully for city council as an independent against Thomas Fleming, the only African American member of the council at that time but a supporter of the city's dominant white machine. Smith also campaigned for the Republican nomination for secretary of state in 1920 and governor in 1922, 1924, 1926, and 1928. He received few votes but broke new ground by being the first African American to seek statewide office in Ohio. In the late

1920s and early 1930s Smith encouraged black insurgency in the local Republican Party, but unlike most African Americans in the North he did not shift his allegiance from the Republican to the Democratic Party during the Depression. Franklin D. Roosevelt's failure to deal with segregation and lynching in the South kept Smith within the Republican fold for the remainder of his life. For Smith, racial issues had always taken precedence over economic ones.

Philosophically and personally, Smith had much in common with WILLIAM MONROE TROTTER, the editor of another African American weekly, the Boston *Guardian*. Both men were uncompromising integrationists who refused to change with the times, and after World War I both found themselves increasingly relegated to the role of the principled but ineffective gadfly. Like Trotter, Smith was prone to personalize the struggle for racial equality. A rugged individualist who owned his own business, he was often reluctant to cooperate with other black leaders or organizations. Smith supported the formation of the NAACP, for example, but had little to do with the local Cleveland branch of the association, even when it supported his positions. Ironically, the same maverick traits that made Smith outspoken in the struggle for racial equality also restricted his ability to advance his own principles. He died in Cleveland.

FURTHER READING

Davis, Russell H. *Black Americans in Cleveland* (1972)

Kusmer, Kenneth L. *A Ghetto Takes Shape: Black Cleveland, 1870–1930* (1976).

Penn, I. Garland. *The Afro-American Press and Its Editors* (1891).

Simmons, William J. *Men of Mark: Eminent, Progressive, and Rising* (1887).

This entry is taken from the *American National Biography* and is published here with the permission of the American Council of Learned Societies.

KENNETH L. KUSMER

Smith, Hilton (27 Feb. 1912–18 Nov. 1983), baseball pitcher, nicknamed Smitty, was born Hilton Lee Smith in Giddings, Texas, the son of John Smith, a schoolteacher, and Mattie (maiden name unknown). After attending Prairie View A&M College for two years, the hard-throwing right-hander started his baseball career with the Austin Senators in 1933. That same year he married Louise Humphrey, with whom he had two children, both sons. In 1934 Smith joined the Monroe (La.) Monarchs of the Negro Southern League, before touring with the Bismarck

(N.D.) team in 1935 and 1936. While pitching for the Bismarck club, he compiled a 5–0 record in the highly regarded National Baseball Congress Semi-Pro Tournament held in Wichita, Kansas. His perfect performance at the National Baseball Congress tournament prompted a contract from the Kansas City Monarchs, whom he joined in 1936. The next year Smith pitched a no-hit, shutout game against the Chicago American Giants, striking out six batters, walking one, and allowing only two balls to be hit out of the infield, in a 4–0 Monarch victory.

Smith led the Negro League in wins for five seasons (1938–1942), more than any other pitcher in league history, and during the 1941 season he never lost a game. JOHN "BUCK" O'NEIL, a teammate and manager of Smith's, recalled in an interview:

> Hilton Smith was unbeatable there for a spell, from 1938 to 1942. Unbeatable! He had more natural stuff, a good rising fastball and an excellent curveball with good control. My land! He would have been a 20-game winner in the major leagues with the stuff he had. We played against an all-star team the year Stan Musial came up in 1941. Satchel Paige and Bob Feller pitched three innings. Musial hit a home run off Satchel on the roof of that stadium. But Musial and Johnny Mize said they'd never seen a curveball like Hilton's curveball.

When the Brooklyn Dodgers signed JACKIE ROBINSON to a major league contract in 1945, Smith was thirty-three years old. Although Smith entertained offers from major league clubs, he refused to take a pay cut to start in minor league baseball. As one of the premier pitchers in the Negro League, Smith was drawing a top salary of eight hundred dollars a month, twice the amount he was being offered to play in a league only very cautiously beginning to integrate. Smith retired from the Monarchs in 1948. But a year later, at the age of thirty-seven, he joined the integrated semipro Fulda team from Minnesota. On opening day Smith struck out twelve batters and won the game with a triple, with two runners on base, in the ninth inning.

Smith pitched in seven Negro League East-West all-star games; only LEON DAY pitched in more (nine). As an all-star Smith also was second in most innings pitched, with nineteen, and second in most strikeouts, with thirteen. In postseason play, Smith won a game in the 1942 Negro World Series and another in the 1946 series, compiling an ERA of 1.29. Based on statistics compiled by the Society for American Baseball Research, he completed his Negro League career with seventy-two wins against only thirty-two losses. He ranks third in highest strikeouts per innings ratio, behind Satchel Paige, also of the Monarchs, and Leon Day of the Newark Eagles.

Smith played winter ball with equal success. In two seasons in Cuba (1937–1938 and 1939–1940) he compiled a 10–5 record. While in Venezuela he won eight and lost five games for the league-leading Vargas club. Proof of his overall effectiveness is evident in exhibition games against white major league teams, where Smith fashioned a 6–1 won-lost record. In 1946, as a member of the Satchel Paige All-Stars, he beat the Bob Feller All-Stars, 3–2.

After the end of his baseball career Smith coached major league hopefuls in the young-adult Casey Stengel League for fifteen years, while working at the Sheffield Steel (later Amco Steel) plant in Kansas City, Missouri. Until his death he also scouted for the Chicago Cubs of the National League. He was active in his Baptist church and helped supervise a Boy Scout troop. Smith died in Kansas City.

In 1993 the Negro Leagues Baseball Museum in Kansas City, Missouri, conducted a survey, polling Negro League veterans to determine the greatest players in the league's history and how they should be ranked. Among pitchers Smith finished with the third highest number of votes behind Paige and Day. Recognition by his peers only partially served to bring Smith out of the shadow of his teammate Paige. When asked about Paige's overwhelming popularity in comparison to his own, Smith simply replied, "When Paige got the publicity, we all ate good." Nevertheless, many players considered Smith the better pitcher because of the variety of his pitches and his superb control. Known generally for his fastball, he was in his day most famous for his curveball. In 2001 he was inducted into the National Baseball Hall of Fame in Cooperstown, New York.

FURTHER READING
Clark, Dick, and Larry Lester. *The Negro Leagues Book* (1994).
Holway, John B. *Voices from the Great Black Baseball Leagues* (1975).
Porter, David, ed. *Biographical Dictionary of American Sports* (1987).
Riley, James A. *The Biographical Encyclopedia of the Negro Baseball Leagues* (1994).
Obituary: *Kansas City Star*, 20 Nov. 1983.
This entry is taken from the *American National Biography* and is published here with the permission of the American Council of Learned Societies.

LARRY LESTER

Smith, Homer (c. 1910–18 Aug. 1972), journalist, postal systems specialist, and African American expatriate in the Soviet Union from 1932 to 1946, was born in Minneapolis, Minnesota. His parents' names are not known. Fed up with Jim Crow in the South and discrimination and racism in the North, Smith joined hundreds of highly ambitious African Americans in the 1920s and 1930s who were anxious to test out the idea that there were societies outside the United States that would welcome all those of goodwill, no matter the color of their skin. Many blacks turned their attention to France as a result of experiences of World War I, where the French had expressed solidarity with African American servicemen. For others, the quest was directed to the new Soviet Union, a country that overtly offered sanctuary to oppressed people. As Smith wrote in his memoirs, "I read avidly the reports of the Soviet experiment…the classless society that was abuilding in Russia…which stood for social justice for all oppressed peoples. Who, I thought, was more oppressed than the American Negro?" (2). Smith's journey to the USSR and fourteen-year tenure there not only brought an opportunity to test this alternate society, but had a powerful effect on him, as this was the crucible in which he would forge his career as a journalist.

Living in the USSR in turbulent times, Smith reported under the pen name "Chatwood Hall" and provided a unique window into the many social developments of the evolving Union of Soviet Socialist Republics. He was also particularly mindful to report on the remarkable hospitality that African Americans were being accorded. He witnessed an energetic society that courted people from around the world who would bring their skills to modernize the USSR. He, himself, had been hired to help restructure the Soviet postal system in Moscow. His job was so important that he was provided with a large office, several staff members, and the office equipment he requested in short order—though much of this was in short supply elsewhere. The Soviets were pleased with Smith's work and expanded his responsibilities to include regional post offices outside the capital city as well. Smith's legacy was to bring new levels of efficiency to postal services, including a more reliable postal money order system, and the institution of the first special delivery system in the Soviet Union.

Besides himself and his contributions to the postal system, Smith's reports highlighted the experiences of African American artists, such as LANGSTON HUGHES and WAYLAND RUDD, and the contributions of engineers and technical specialists, such as Richard Williams and Robert Robinson, and agricultural specialists, such as GEORGE TYNES and John Sutton.

Within three years of his arrival, Smith had left his job with the post office to work as a correspondent full time. By 1935 he had witnessed early signs of the purges among the administrative staff of the central office and thought he would be safer working as a journalist than as an employee of the Soviets. Smith was at the Eighth All-Union Congress of the Soviets that launched the Soviet Constitution in 1936. He rode out World War II with the Russian people and was also the only black journalist posted in the USSR during the war. Also, as the only black person reporting from the Russian-German front, he was the first African American to be accredited a war correspondent for the Associated Press (AP) when so named in 1944.

When Smith contemplated his journey to the USSR, he was not sure that this would be his path to a career in journalism, but he clearly understood its potential. The Mason-Dixon Line might have fallen far south of Minnesota, and African Americans could, as did Smith, have access to journalism studies, but finding a job with any of the major presses had been virtually impossible. His white classmates, people with whom he took classes and with whom he worked on the student newspaper, had much better prospects. In fact, twelve years after he had moved to the Soviet Union, he encountered a fellow student from the University of Minnesota, the journalist Harrison Salisbury, who also acknowledged that their paths had diverged. It was only in the USSR, and during World War II, that the two—a white journalist and a black one—were now on the same level as correspondents.

At the time he contemplated going to the USSR, Smith also lacked a track record as a professional journalist, but he did two things that showed careful thought and planning. He knew he had to offer a skill that would be of interest to the Soviets and generate an invitation; but he also knew that the black press in the United States did not have enough staff for foreign posts. He had been working in the post office, like many college-educated African Americans hoping to eventually find work in their chosen profession. And it was this training

in the postal service that attracted the Soviets. He also knew that the Associated Negro Press did not have any journalists in the USSR, so he offered his services to them and thus gained an outlet for his writing and a journalist's status to present to the Soviets.

Evidence suggests that having received a positive response from the Soviets in 1932, he was directed to join a group of African Americans being formed by LOUISE THOMPSON to go to the USSR to work on the film *Black and White*. This group, which eventually numbered twenty-two, included the black poet and writer LANGSTON HUGHES, the singer and actor Wayland Rudd, and nineteen others. Most saw this as an opportunity to have a well-paid job and a temporary escape from the double worries of the Great Depression and of being black in a racist country. Some others saw this as a bridge to a new life and were contemplating never returning to the United States. While most returned within one year, Smith ended up staying fourteen years before he moved to Ethiopia with his Russian wife. Hughes stayed a full year, and two others, Lloyd Patterson and Wayland Rudd, remained in the Soviet Union for the rest of their lives. Though various sources place Smith among the *Black and White* film group, Smith, himself, writes of the group's experiences in his memoirs as though he had not been one of them. It is highly likely that he had traveled over with this group only for reasons of expediency, rather than having a strong interest in making the film.

Smith was not naive about the potential liabilities of tying his future to the Soviet experiment, but he felt his options were too few in the United States. While his deeply religious parents were not happy with the prospect of their son going to a "godless" country, he did not indicate that they were unaware of the stultifying effects of racism on their son's ambitions. However, Smith was mindful that his parents and others whom he cared about in the United States might experience some repercussions for his having decided to go to the USSR. Thus, he was careful to continue to use his pen name "Chatwood Hall" all the years he was abroad. As a result, his pieces, which appeared in the *Chicago Defender*, the Pittsburgh *Courier*, the NAACP's *The Crisis*, the Baltimore *Afro-American*, and *Time* magazine, among other publications, did not automatically connect him to family and friends in the United States.

Smith never gave up his American citizenship, as did the other long-term expatriates to the USSR.

The fact that he was working as a foreign correspondent helped him avoid the pressure coming from the Soviet government in the late 1930s that the expatriate community either take up Soviet citizenship or leave the country. When Smith did finally leave the Soviet Union, in October 1946, he was torn between his admiration for the Russian people who had treated him well, despite the many hardships they faced, and his disappointment with the Soviet system he saw developing in the postwar period. But, he was also looking forward to a job in the editorial department of the English Section of the Ethiopian Government's Press and Information Office, which he had secured with the help of the Ethiopian minister to Russia. He also planned to continue his work for the AP, although now from Africa. However, Smith still had one additional hurdle to jump: while the Soviets could not prevent him from leaving, they could prevent his Russian wife of eight years, Marie Petrovna, from going with him. But Smith prevailed, sending letters to the highest Soviet officials and bombarding the Soviet embassy in Addis Ababa with visits. A year later, again with the help of the Ethiopian minister to Russia, Smith's efforts were rewarded with notice that she had been given exit permission.

Smith and his growing family stayed in Ethiopia until 1962, when Smith returned to the United States. He published his memoir on his Soviet experience, *Black Man in Red Russia,* in 1964. In 1963 Smith was hired as an editor in the social studies department of the Chicago-based Lyons and Carnahan publishers. Little else is known about Smith after his return to the United States; however, his contributions as a groundbreaking black foreign correspondent were posthumously recognized in 2002, when the National Association of Black Journalists bestowed on him its "NABJ Legacy Award."

FURTHER READING

Smith, Homer. *Black Man in Red Russia* (1964).

Blakely, Allison. *Russia and the Negro: Blacks in Russian History and Thought* (1986).

Boyle, Sheila Tully, and Paul Bunie. *Paul Robeson: The Years of Promise and Achievement* (2005).

JOY GLEASON CAREW

Smith, Ida Van (21 Mar. 1917–13 Mar. 2003), teacher, aviator, and flight instructor, was born Ida Van Larkin in Lumberton, North Carolina, to Theodore D. Larkin, a businessman, and Martha J. Keith, a housewife and seamstress. Ida Van's love for flying began in childhood when her father took her to the airfield to watch the barnstormers who toured the country in the 1920s. But when her father tried to get someone to teach her to fly he was told that there were no instructors. Smith was an intelligent, eager student who graduated as valedictorian in 1934 from the Redstone Academy, a private Presbyterian school for blacks. That fall she entered the Barber Scotia Junior College in Concord, North Carolina, and later attended Shaw University in Raleigh, North Carolina. She graduated in 1938 from Shaw with a degree in education.

After graduation she took a job as a schoolteacher in Marietta, North Carolina, and married Willie E. Simms, a railroad porter, with whom she had grown up in Lumberton. The couple moved to New York City around 1940, and Smith began to teach in the public school system in Queens. During her ten-year marriage to Simms she bore four children—Jacquelyn, William, Sy Oliver, and Carlton—before they divorced in 1948. She later married Edward D. Smith, another North Carolina native.

Jacquelyn Thompson, Smith's oldest child, remembered her mother talking about flying, but she knew that her stepfather would not allow it until the children were grown. Smith eventually stopped talking about flying, and her family assumed that she had forgotten about it. "But then she got very ill—she had cancer," Thompson related. "When she recovered she got up and said it was time to do what she had always wanted to do" (author's interview with Thompson).

It was 1967, Smith's children were grown, she was divorced again, and she had just enrolled in a doctoral program at New York University. One day she walked out of school, drove to LaGuardia Airport, and signed up for her first flying lesson. From that day forward, flying became her life. Smith spent the summer with her parents in Fayetteville, North Carolina, to complete training for her pilot's license.

Smith saw something that summer that reminded her of her own fascination with flying: a group of children watching her. "The kids heard there was a black woman out at [the] airport. ... When I would land the plane ... they would waylay me ... and they would ask me so many questions" (Gubert, 260). Smith arranged to meet the children at set times, and these meetings sparked the idea of a club to teach children about flying.

When Smith returned to New York she established her first Ida Van Smith Flight Club. The club first met in her home; Smith talked about flying and had the kids sit at a cockpit instrument panel set up in her living room. She demonstrated how to plan routes and wind triangles with simple geometry and a calculator. She later moved the program into the public schools, and as the number of clubs grew she began a monthly workshop at York College, where aviation professionals came to talk about their careers.

Smith's own skills improved. She became a certified ground instructor and later earned her instrument flight rating, allowing her to fly in inclement weather. She logged hours with trips all over the country, participating in fly-ins with Tuskegee Airmen. During these trips Smith always attracted children. She invited them to sit at the controls of her plane and sometimes took them for a quick flight. She gathered names and addresses to send information. To help run her clubs she recruited any local aviators she could find. All in all Smith established eleven clubs, eight in New York State and one each in Fort Worth, Texas, Lumberton, North Carolina, and on the island of Saint Lucia in the Caribbean.

Over the years Smith introduced more than six thousand children to flying. Many of her students went on to become military and commercial pilots, flight engineers, mechanics, and air traffic controllers. Additionally, she wrote columns on flying for several Long Island newspapers, published a children's book in 1988 about her life called *Fly with Me Coloring Book (A True Story)*, and hosted a local cable television show about flying.

Smith's passion for flying affected many, but her desire to see every child succeed was even more profound. As she explained, "When I met the kids, I always said to them, 'We're not trying to make pilots out of everyone, but we want you to know that you can be a pilot if you want to be, or whatever else you want to pursue in life, you can do it'" (Gubert, 261).

Smith retired from teaching in 1977 but continued to fly and promote aviation. She garnered many local awards for her work with inner-city youth. In 1978 she was awarded the World Aerospace Education Organization Award by the International Women's Conference. In the same year the Federal Aviation Administration agreed to fund her aviation careers program for three high schools in New York and New Jersey, later adopting her program for its own use. In 1979 Smith received the Bishop Wright Air Industry Award, recognizing contributions to American aviation. In 1984 she was inducted into the International Forest of Friendship—the first African American woman to be inducted. Smith

was also featured in the 1997 exhibit "Women and Flight" at the Smithsonian's National Air and Space Museum in Washington, D.C., and in a permanent display at the International Women's Air and Space Museum in Dayton, Ohio. In 1998 she received the Award of Achievement for her contributions to aviation education from the International Ninety-Nines, an organization of women pilots to which she belonged. Smith was also an honorary member of the Tuskegee Airman's Black Wings and the Negro Airmen International. After Smith married Benjamin E. Dunn, a historian from Los Angeles, the couple retired to Lumberton in the early 1990s.

FURTHER READING
"Aviation's Pied Piper," *Ebony* (Nov. 1978).
Gubert, Betty Kaplan. *Invisible Wings: An Annotated Bibliography on Blacks in Aviation, 1916–1993* (1994).
Gubert, Betty Kaplan, Miriam Sawyer, and Caroline M. Fannin. *Distinguished African Americans in Aviation and Space Science* (1992).
Innis, Doris Funnye, and Juliana Wu, eds. *Profiles in Black: Biographical Sketches of 100 Living Black Unsung Heroes* (1976).
                    DOUGLAS FLEMING ROOSA

Smith, Isaac Hughes (c. 5 May 1854–6 July 1915), businessman, teacher, banker, philanthropist, and state legislator, was born in Craven County, North Carolina, the son of Thomas and Harriet Smith. His birth status is uncertain; he may have been born a slave, but was educated at an early age by a benevolent white family, who helped arrange for him to attend the private Saint Augustine's College in Raleigh, North Carolina, after the Civil War.

Smith began his career as a schoolteacher in New Bern, the Craven County seat, but his relentless energy and business acumen soon propelled him into the world of residential and commercial real estate, in which he accumulated a substantial personal fortune. By the time of his death, his worth was estimated to exceed $100,000, much of it in land, buildings, and stores he owned in the so-called Smithtown section of New Bern.

Smith began buying, selling, and renting these properties soon after his return from college, while still teaching. His success in these early ventures prompted him to expand his business interests, which included insurance, money lending, and the town's first black-owned commercial bank. He was also an investor in the well-known Coleman Manufacturing Company of Concord, North Carolina. By the 1890s, his influence had grown well beyond the business world, and Smith now began to express himself politically, first as an early supporter of drafting William McKinley as the Republican nominee for president in 1896 and then as an avid supporter of former congressman Daniel Russell, North Carolina's controversial gubernatorial nominee. Russell, who soon became the state's first Republican governor in a generation during the "fusion" era, when Republicans and a third party, the Populists, held control of the state legislature, had alienated many black leaders by public statements of unflattering opinions about black capabilities.

Smith nevertheless contributed significant sums of money to Russell's campaign coffers in 1896, as one of a handful of black leaders to support Russell, before or after his election. In 1898, Smith chose to run for the North Carolina House of Representatives, narrowly winning his election against a vitriolic white-supremacist candidate, who singled him out for libelous ridicule. Representing predominantly black Craven County in the 1899 General Assembly, now overwhelmingly controlled by Democrats, Smith, with his penchant for unorthodox statements and maverick stands, quickly alienated his own party. He was publicly expelled from the Republican caucus shortly after the legislature convened in January 1899, purportedly for betraying the party through his attempts to appease Democrats.

The state's victorious Democrats were already seeking a constitutional amendment that would disenfranchise almost all African American voters by making illiteracy a disqualifier to voting, if a majority of state voters agreed to the change. Modeled after Louisiana's notorious "grandfather clause," which exempted illiterate, white men whose fathers or grandfathers had been able to vote (and thereby excluding black men, whose grandfathers who had been slaves), the North Carolina plan effectively prevented black men from qualifying by establishing a cutoff date of 1867, before blacks had gained suffrage in the state. Smith, who hoped to head off the amendment through compromise, voted in favor of other related Democratic measures, angering his GOP colleagues of both races.

They have read me out of my own party," Smith protested in vain, in a lengthy statement read on the floor of the House and printed in the state's largest newspaper. "They have denounced the only one of them who has done what he has a right to do under the Constitution—vote as he thinks just and proper. ([Raleigh] *News and Observer*, 10 Jan. 1899)

Smith, one of just four black house members in 1899, was perhaps the body's most outspoken member, and certainly one of its most energetic, introducing a range of farsighted bills and resolutions, none successful, dealing with such subjects as equal pay for state witnesses and public officials; establishing compulsory education for all children in Craven County between the ages of six and eleven; and seeking the selection of at least one black trustee for each of the state's segregated black institutions. He sought to have Craven County returned to the "Black Second" congressional district, from which it had been removed during redistricting in the early 1890s. He did succeed in convincing the legislature to petition the U.S. Congress for compensation of savings lost by black investors in the failure, late in the Reconstruction era, of the congressionally chartered Freedmen's Savings and Trust Company. Approximately half the black depositors received partial compensation for their lost funds.

On 24 December 1875, he married Visie Dudley of Craven County, and the couple had one son, Livingston Smith. After her death, Smith was married on 30 June 1898 to Carrie Marie Rhone (b. 1872) and fathered five more children, including two daughters, Harriet and Henrietta, and two sons, Arnold and Isaac H. Smith, Jr.

After the final adjournment of the legislature in mid-1900, Smith retired from public life, disenchanted with Governor Russell and his party. He was the last African American legislator elected from Craven County for nearly a century. Even with his brief career of public service over, his business interests prospered, and Smith intensified his involvement in civic and fraternal affairs. A member of the Knights of Pythias and grand orator of the Negro Masons of North Carolina, he was also an active member of St. Cyprian's Episcopal Church in New Bern.

After his death in 1915, from complications of diabetes, an obituary in the state's largest newspaper described Smith as "one of the wealthiest Negroes in North Carolina and one whose career has been as spectacular as any other colored man in the state" ([Raleigh] *News and Observer*, 8 July 1915).

His will, probated the same week, was widely publicized in the press, both for its size and its eclectic nature. In it, Smith appointed a trustee to run his businesses and made detailed provisions for a wide array of institutions, societies, and individuals, including his wife's mother and sisters and the children of his former Episcopal rector, as well as weekly stipends to his widow and their surviving children. Specific bequests of $500 each went to Shaw University in Raleigh and the National Religious Training Schools (later North Carolina Central University in Durham), while bequests of $1,000 were to be divided among New Bern's many black churches and the town's fraternal societies, including the Masons and the Odd Fellows.

FURTHER READING

Kenzer, Robert C. *Enterprising Southerners: Black Economic Success in North Carolina, 1865–1915* (1997).

Obituary: Raleigh *News and Observer*, 8 July 1915.

BENJAMIN R. JUSTESEN

Smith, Jabbo (24 Dec. 1908–16 Jan. 1991), jazz trumpeter, trombonist, and singer, was born Cladys Smith in Pembroke, Georgia, to Ida (maiden name unknown), who ultimately became a schoolteacher. The name of his father, a barber, is unknown. Cladys was given his unusual name to complement that of an infant cousin, Gladys. After her husband's death in 1912 Ida Smith moved to Savannah, Georgia, and in 1914 she placed Cladys in the Jenkins Orphanage Home in Charleston, South Carolina. After two years of musical tutelage, in 1918 he was assigned to play cornet in one of the orphanage's several brass bands. In 1922, while touring with the band in Jacksonville, Cladys ran away and played for three months in Eagle Eye Shields's jazz band before he was caught and returned to the orphanage. After a few more instances of rebelliousness, in 1924 he was expelled from the home. Smith moved to Philadelphia, Pennsylvania, and worked in Harry Marsh's band for three months, during which time his fellow bandsmen, amused by the name of an Indian character in a William S. Hart movie, started calling him "Jabbo."

After leaving Marsh's band Smith went to Atlantic City, where he worked for one month with another Jenkins Orphanage alumnus, the trumpeter Gus Aiken. He played with the pianist Charlie Johnson from the fall of 1925 through January 1928, working extended residencies in Harlem and occasional college dances before leaving over a salary dispute. He also participated in two recording sessions with Johnson, and on one freelance date with DUKE ELLINGTON he took BUBBER MILEY's place as soloist on "What Can a Poor Fellow Do?" and "Black and Tan Fantasy." Between February and November 1928 he played with FATS WALLER and Garvin Bushell in JAMES P. JOHNSON's pit band

for *Keep Shufflin'*, leaving when the murder of the revue's backer, the gambler Arnold Rothstein, forced the show's cancellation during a Midwest tour. Smith remained in Chicago and joined Charlie Elgar's orchestra at the Dreamland Ballroom.

Between January and August 1929 Smith recorded a brilliant series of small band performances under his own name for Brunswick, all the while working through 1930 as the house trumpeter at the Sunset Café, where he played in a succession of different orchestras, including those of CARROLL DICKERSON, Sammy Stewart, EARL HINES, DAVE PEYTON, Tiny Parham, and Jimmy Bell. At the same time he worked at the Vendôme Theater with Erskine Tate and the Dreamland with Elgar and led his own six-piece band at My Cellar. Throughout this period Smith was one of the most highly regarded trumpeters in Chicago, considered by some to be the equal of LOUIS ARMSTRONG. On the basis of his recordings, his reputation among musicians spread even beyond the Midwest. However, his quick rise to prominence coupled with a lack of maturity led to a cocky self-assurance marked by heavy drinking and unreliability. In late 1930 Smith moved to Milwaukee, but he continued to travel back and forth between the two cities, going from one band to another. As a result of his increased irresponsibility and failure to live up to his earlier promise, he went unrecorded for five years and dropped into almost total obscurity. In 1936 he signed a two-year contract with the CLAUDE HOPKINS Orchestra, then on tour from its regular stand at the Roseland Ballroom in New York City.

In the spring of 1939 he started rehearsing with SIDNEY BECHET's new group, and when Bechet decided to move on, he turned the leadership over to Smith, who then secured a job for the band at the Midway Inn at the New York World's Fair. After the fair closed in 1940 Smith disbanded the group and, over the next four years, played in a variety of groups at the Alcazar in Newark, New Jersey. In 1944 he rejoined Hopkins briefly and then a year later settled in Milwaukee, where he worked as both a sideman and leader of his own sextet. Trying to maintain a stable life after his 1948 marriage, he started working days in a drug store, and in 1955, with the end of a long engagement at the Flame Bar, he took a job with the Avis Rent A Car, where he worked full time for the next thirteen years. Smith remained relatively inactive musically until early 1961, when local jazz record collectors learned of his whereabouts and urged him to return to music. He appeared in a concert staged by the Milwaukee Jazz

Society in June and started working again locally and in Chicago. Smith's embouchure, though, was in poor shape for lack of practice as well as dental problems, but he was still able to sing and play trombone, an instrument he had learned as a child at the Jenkins Orphanage.

He played trombone and piano and sang occasionally in the late 1960s and early 1970s, and he appeared at the Breda Jazz Festival in Holland in 1971 and 1972. In 1975 he was voted into the Jazz Hall of Fame at the Newport-New York Jazz Festival, and in 1977 he appeared in London and once again at Breda. Later that year he played at New Orleans's Preservation Hall, an engagement that led to his joining the company of *One Mo' Time*. The show opened in New York City at the Village Gate in October 1979 with Smith playing trumpet in Orange Kellin's small jazz band and singing two of his own numbers onstage. In 1981 he suffered the first of three strokes but recuperated sufficiently to return to the show after a brief layoff. In March 1982 he played ten concerts in France, Italy, and Switzerland with the Hot Antic Jazz Band, but following that tour he suffered his second stroke, recovering in time to play at the Nice Jazz Festival in 1982 and again at Breda. By the next year he could no longer play, but he performed as a singer both in Europe and at several New York City clubs. In 1986, on the strangest booking of his career, he appeared with the avant-garde trumpeter DON CHERRY at Jazzfest Berlin. Although almost completely blind as a result of his strokes, he continued to sing and write songs until his death at home in New York.

During his peak in the late 1920s Jabbo Smith was considered by many musicians to be Louis Armstrong's only serious competition. Although he can be heard to his advantage on the records he made with Charlie Johnson, Duke Ellington, and the Louisiana Sugar Babes (the recording name of James P. Johnson's *Keep Shufflin'* band), it is on the twenty sides he made in 1929 as leader of Jabbo Smith's Rhythm Aces that his astonishing gifts can most be appreciated. Designed by Brunswick to compete with the highly successful Okeh records by Louis Armstrong's Hot Five and Hot Seven, this series presented Smith with a challenge his talent and ego could not resist. All but one of the titles were released promptly, but despite the high regard in which fellow jazz musicians held such remarkable performances as "Jazz Battle," "Take Your Time," "Sweet 'n Low Blues," "Take Me to the River," "Ace of Rhythm," "Sau-Sha Stomp," "Decatur Street Tutti," and "Lina Blues," they failed to bring the success hoped for, most likely because of poor promotion and distribution by Brunswick. Smith and the clarinetist OMER SIMEON were at their best on such brightly paced original themes as "Jazz Battle" and "Ace of Rhythm," where, in a series of increasingly heated solos and ensembles, they played with a crackling excitement rarely heard on records before. Typically, the trumpeter's pyrotechnics were met head on by Simeon's sharply articulated, blues-intoned clarinet to a breathtaking effect of unrelieved intensity. But with the onset of the Depression, while the public could still respond to Armstrong's proven talent and charisma, it could not also support the efforts of an ambitious contender, however gifted.

Smith's incendiary tone, range, technical fluency, and imaginative phrasing contained the seeds that would later emerge fully grown in the playing of ROY ELDRIDGE and DIZZY GILLESPIE. But for all of these virtues, he lacked Armstrong's deeply moving vibrato, breadth of tone, and sense of structure, not to mention his inventiveness and originality. However, Smith's singing, as is evidenced on many of these sides, was almost on a par with the master's. Unfortunately this promising artist never again achieved the high plateau he set in 1929, and when he recorded as leader in 1938, after nearly a decade of obscurity, his playing, although technically polished, was so devoid of creativity that some believed it the work of a different musician. Smith regained some of his earlier powers, though, for a final series of recordings in the late 1970s and early 1980s.

FURTHER READING

Balliett, Whitney. *Jelly Roll, Jabbo, and Fats* (1983).

Chilton, John. *A Jazz Nursery: The Story of the Jenkins' Orphanage Bands of Charleston, South Carolina* (1980).

Deffaa, Chip. *Voices of the Jazz Age* (1992).

Schuller, Gunther. *Early Jazz: Its Roots and Musical Development* (1968).

Obituary: *New York Times*, 18 Jan. 1991.

This entry is taken from the *American National Biography* and is published here with the permission of the American Council of Learned Societies.

JACK SOHMER

Smith, James Lindsay (c. 1883), writer and preacher, was born in Northern Neck, Northumberland County, Virginia, to Rachel and Charles, on the property of Thomas Langdon, on which they were enslaved. Over the course of her life, Smith's mother gave birth to eleven children and labored as a cotton spinner. His father managed the Lancaster County plantation his owner had acquired through inheritance. When Smith was a young boy, he was injured while carrying lumber and remained crippled for his entire life because his owner did not think Smith's life was worth enough to call a doctor. As a result of his disability Smith worked in the house with the women, knitting and carding. Later in his life he was apprenticed to a shoemaker, which proved to be the source of his livelihood in all the places he settled. For a brief time Smith was hired out to a ship's captain, but he was treated poorly there, and he retreated to his old family home as soon as the opportunity presented itself.

Back in Virginia, Smith converted to Christianity and soon took to preaching in the Methodist Church. He described himself as a zealous preacher who could entice even the most wayward souls to turn to the church. NAT TURNER's rebellion shook Virginia in 1831, and black people were barred from holding meetings for fear that they might incite insurrections. Still, Smith insisted on holding religious meetings, feeling called by God to do so.

Having felt his entire life that freedom was his right, he decided to run away with two friends. After one failed attempt the previous year, Smith succeeded in escaping the South in 1838, but his journey was not without hardship. On the road to freedom his friends realized that his disability was slowing them down and left him to find his own way north. He managed to meet back up with them before they crossed over into Philadelphia, Pennsylvania, but once across, his two friends boarded boats bound for Europe, while Smith stayed in the United States. He met with various abolitionists in Philadelphia, where he was given a letter of introduction to the abolitionist printer DAVID RUGGLES in New York. Smith did not feel completely safe in Philadelphia, so he moved north, first to Hartford, Connecticut, then to Springfield, Massachusetts, where he met the area's prominent abolitionist and preacher the Reverend Dr. Samuel Osgood (to whom Ruggles had provided a letter of introduction). Through him Smith was given the opportunity to begin a career as a shoemaker. Smith sought out an education and attended school in nearby Wilbraham. Later Osgood invited him to give lectures across the northern states to encourage abolitionist sentiments in white audiences.

In 1842 Smith married Emeline Minerva Platt, and they subsequently had four children, three daughters and a son. In the same year he and his wife moved to Norwich, Connecticut, where they reared their children despite prejudices against them that made it particularly difficult for the children to receive a fair education. Regardless of these setbacks, his children were extremely successful, his son taking up his father's profession as a shoemaker and his three daughters all graduating from school; two of them became teachers.

During the Civil War Smith continued his work in the church while many of the young members of his congregation left to fight in the war. He was ordained a deacon at the New England Conference; the position did not pay a salary, so he continued to support himself through his shoemaking, which had become quite lucrative. After the war had ended, in June of 1867, Smith, motivated by his own curiosity, set off on a journey to see for himself what his hometown in Virginia looked like as a free state. His discoveries were both encouraging and discouraging. After his thirty-year absence, many of the buildings and structures in Virginia looked dilapidated and neglected. However, he found that though the former landed gentry of the South was destitute, the former slaves were prospering and improving their lots at a rapid pace. Smith visited his old home repeatedly through his adulthood, attempting to understand better the social and political dynamics of the region and to investigate the cause of such increased migration from the South to the North.

Smith and the people of Norwich organized a celebration in May of 1870 on the occasion of the passing of the Fifteenth Amendment. CHARLES LENOX REMOND, the famous African American abolitionist and orator, delivered an address at this event, which marked the enfranchisement and citizenship status of people of African descent in America.

In 1881 Smith published the story of his life, and in it he included his own historical accounts of the war and the effects of the war on the South. He praised the black infantry, including the famous Fifty-fourth Massachusetts Regiment and the Twenty-ninth Connecticut, the state's only black unit, for their bravery and loyalty to the cause of ending slavery and maintaining the unity of the nation. He also devoted large sections of the text to encouraging further growth in the African American community and to improving educational standards.

FURTHER READING

Smith, James Lindsay. *Autobiography of James L. Smith: Including Also, Reminiscences of Slave Life, Recollections of the War, Education of Freedmen, Causes of the Exodus, Etc.* (1881).

LAURA MURPHY

Smith, James McCune (18 Apr. 1813–17 Nov. 1865), abolitionist and physician, was born in New York City, the son of slaves. All that is known of his parents is that his mother was, in his words, "a self-emancipated bond-woman." His own liberty came on 4 July 1827, when the Emancipation Act of the state of New York officially freed its remaining slaves. Smith was fourteen at the time, a student at the Charles C. Andrews African Free School No. 2, and he described that day as a "real full-souled, full-voiced shouting for joy" that brought him from "the gloom of midnight" into "the joyful light of day." He graduated with honors from the African Free School but was denied admission to Columbia College and Geneva, New York, medical schools because of his race. With assistance from black minister PETER WILLIAMS JR., he entered the University of Glasgow, Scotland, in 1832 and earned his B.A. (1835), M.A. (1836), and M.D. (1837) degrees. He returned to the United States in 1838 as the first professionally trained black physician in the country.

Resettled in New York City, in 1838 or 1839 Smith married Malvina Barnet, with whom he was to have five children, and successfully established himself. He set up practice in Manhattan as a surgeon and general practitioner for both blacks and whites, became the staff physician for the New York Colored Orphan Asylum, and opened a pharmacy on West Broadway, one of the first in the country owned by a black.

Smith's activities as a radical abolitionist and reformer, however, secured his reputation as one of the leading black intellectuals of the antebellum era. As soon as he returned to the United States, he became an active member of the American Anti-Slavery Society, which sought immediate abolition by convincing slaveholders through moral persuasion to renounce the sin of slavery and emancipate their slaves. By the late 1840s he had abandoned the policies of nonresistance and nonvoting set forth by William Lloyd Garrison and his followers in the society. Instead, Smith favored political abolitionism, which interpreted the U.S. Constitution as an antislavery document and advocated political and ultimately violent intervention to end slavery. In 1846 Smith championed the campaign for unrestricted black suffrage in New York State; that same year he became an associate and good friend of Gerrit Smith, a wealthy white abolitionist and philanthropist, and served as one of three black administrators for his friend's donation of roughly fifty acres apiece to some three thousand New York blacks on a vast tract of land in the Adirondacks. He became affiliated with the Liberty Party in the late 1840s, which was devoted to immediate and unconditional emancipation, unrestricted suffrage for all men and women, and land reform. In 1855 he helped found the New York City Abolition Society, which was organized, as he put it, "to Abolish Slavery by means of the Constitution; *or otherwise*," by which he meant violent intervention in the event that peaceful efforts failed (though there is no indication that he resorted to violence). When the Radical Abolition Party, the successor to the Liberty Party, nominated him for New York secretary of state in 1857, he became the first black in the country to run for a political office.

In his writings, Smith was a central force in helping to shape and give direction to the black abolition movement. He contributed frequently to the *Weekly Anglo-African* and the *Anglo-African Magazine* and wrote a semiregular column for FREDERICK DOUGLASS's *Paper* under the pseudonym "Communipaw," an Indian name that referred to a charmed and honored settlement in Jersey City, New Jersey, where blacks had played an important historic role. He also wrote the introduction to Frederick Douglass's 1855 autobiography, *My Bondage and My Freedom*, and he often expressed his wish that Douglass relocate his paper from Rochester to New York City. Douglass considered Smith the "foremost" black leader who had influenced his reform vision.

Smith's writings focused primarily on black education and self-help, citizenship, and the fight against racism; these themes represented for him the most effective means through which to end slavery and effect full legal and civil rights. He was a lifelong opponent of attempts among whites to colonize blacks in Liberia and elsewhere and a harsh critic of black nationalists who, beginning in the 1850s, encouraged emigration to Haiti and West Africa rather than a continuation of the fight for citizenship and equal rights. Although he defended integration, he also encouraged blacks to establish their own presses, initiatives, and organizations. "It is emphatically our battle," he wrote in 1855. "Others may aid and assist if they will, but the moving power rests with us." His embrace of black self-reliance in the late 1840s paralleled his departure from the doctrines of Garrison and the American Anti-Slavery Society, which largely ignored black oppression in the North—even among abolitionists—by focusing on the evils of slavery in the South. Black education in particular, he concluded, led directly to self-reliance and moral uplift, and these values in turn provided the most powerful critique against racism. He called the schoolhouse the "great caste abolisher" and vowed to "fling whatever I have into the cause of colored children, that they may be better and more thoroughly taught than their parents are."

The racist belief in the innate inferiority of blacks was for Smith the single greatest and most insidious obstacle to equality. In 1846 he became despondent over the racial "hate deeper than I had imagined" among the vast majority of whites. Fourteen years later he continued to lament that "our white countrymen do not know us"; "they are strangers to our characters, ignorant of our capacity, oblivious to our history." He hoped his own distinguished career and writings would serve as both a role model for uneducated blacks and a powerful rebuttal against racist attacks. As a black physician, he was uniquely suited to combat the pseudoscientific theories of innate black inferiority. In two important and brilliantly argued essays—"Civilization" (1844) and "On the Fourteenth Query of Thomas Jefferson's Notes on Virginia" (1859)—he incorporated his extensive knowledge of biology and anatomy to directly refute scientific arguments of the innate inferiority of blacks.

The driving force behind Smith's reform vision and sustained hope for equality was his supreme "confidence in God, that firm reliance in the saving power of the Redeemer's Love." Much like other radical abolitionists such as Douglass and Gerrit Smith, he viewed the abolition movement and the Civil War in millennialist terms: slavery and black oppression were the most egregious of a plethora of sins ranging from tobacco and alcohol to apathy and laziness that needed to be abolished in order to pave the way for a sacred society governed by "Bible Politics," as he envisioned God's eventual reign on earth. He strove to follow his savior's example by embracing the doctrine of "equal love to all mankind" and at the same time remaining humble before him. He likened himself to "a coral insect ... loving to work beneath the tide in a superstructure, that some day when the labourer is long dead and forgotten, may rear itself above the waves and afford rest and habitation for the creatures of his Good, Good Father of All." Following his death in Williamsburg, New York, from heart failure, his writings and memories remained a powerful source of inspiration, a "rest and habitation" to future generations of reformers.

FURTHER READING

The Gerrit Smith Papers, housed in the George Arents Research Library at Syracuse University and widely distributed on microfilm, include thirty letters from James McCune Smith to Gerrit Smith that contain valuable information. *Frederick Douglass' Paper* contains more essays by Smith than any other contemporary publication.

Blight, David W. "In Search of Learning, Liberty, and Self Definition: James McCune Smith and the Ordeal of the Antebellum Black Intellectual," *Afro-Americans in New York Life and History* 9, no. 2 (July 1985): 7–25.

Ripley, C. Peter, ed. *The Black Abolitionist Papers*, vols. 3–5 (1991).

Stauffer, John. *The Works of James McLune Smith: Black Intellectual and Abolitionist* (2006).

This entry is taken from the *American National Biography* and is published here with the permission of the American Council of Learned Societies.

JOHN STAUFFER

Smith, Joe (28 June 1902–2 Dec. 1937), jazz cornetist and trumpeter, was born Joseph E. (or C.) Smith in Ripley, Ohio, the son of Luke Smith, a Cincinnati brass band leader from whom he received his first tutelage. Nothing is known of his mother, but all six of his brothers also studied trumpet, the most well-known being Russell Smith, who later played lead trumpet with FLETCHER HENDERSON and other top swing bands. During his teens Joe played with local bands and left town with a traveling show, but after becoming stranded in Pittsburgh he returned home.

Around 1920 he went to New York and worked with the drummer Kaiser Marshall in a dance hall on Forty-eighth Street, following which he returned to Pittsburgh for local jobs. In January 1922 he went to Chicago to join Fletcher Henderson's Black Swan Jazz Masters and then toured with ETHEL WATERS. He recorded a session with Waters in May 1922. After concluding the tour in July he replaced BUBBER MILEY in MAMIE SMITH's (no relation) Jazz Hounds. It was in this group that he first played with COLEMAN HAWKINS, later an important fellow sideman in Henderson's orchestra. While with Mamie Smith he toured the Loew's theater circuit in Canada and as far west as California but left her act in New York in early 1923 to work locally with Billy Paige's Broadway Syncopators and do free-lance recording dates. In March 1924 he toured as musical director and featured soloist with NOBLE SISSLE and EUBIE BLAKE's *In Bamville* revue, which in September opened in New York at the Colonial Theater as *The Chocolate Dandies*. Not wishing to travel again, Smith left the show in November, and from that time until April 1925 he worked in New York venues accompanying another Sissle and Blake star, the (African American) vaudeville performer Johnny Hudgins, who often performed in blackface.

In the spring of 1922 Smith began recording blues accompaniments for Ethel Waters, Mamie Smith, MA RAINEY, ALBERTA HUNTER, and BESSIE SMITH, as well as a host of other lesser-known singers. As was true of most New York-based trumpeters of the early 1920s, Smith was under the influence of Johnny Dunn, but to his credit he quickly abandoned Dunn's staccato attack and raggy phrasing and instead adopted a more relaxed rhythmic flow with a broad, expressive tone and acquired an ear for melodic nuance. He is especially winning on Waters's "Tell 'Em about Me" and "Smile!" and at his best on almost all of Bessie Smith's titles, most notably "Weeping Willow," "The Bye Bye Blues," "The Yellow Dog Blues," "At the Christmas Ball," "Money Blues," "Baby Doll," "Young Woman's Blues," "Alexander's Ragtime Band," and "There'll Be a Hot Time in the Old Town Tonight." On these records Smith defines his conception of blues accompaniment as something quite different from that of LOUIS ARMSTRONG, who was equally prolific in this capacity and with many of the same artists. Whereas Armstrong by the sheer force of his own surging creativity tended to outshine rather than support the singers he was hired to accompany, Smith, with his plaintive, burnished tone, complemented their lines with linking phrases, often to compellingly poignant effect. Not only did he play with much less vibrato and timbral drama than Armstrong, but he also avoided the upper register in which Armstrong excelled. Where Armstrong was the epitome of raw, unfettered, blues-based expression, Smith was spare, refined, and polished. Indeed it was most likely these qualities and the contrast they afforded her own passionate style that accounted for the preference shown him by Bessie Smith.

In mid-April 1925 Smith replaced Howard Scott in Fletcher Henderson's brass section, and for the next seven months he played alongside Armstrong both at the Roseland Ballroom and in the recording studios. His most characteristic early playing with the band is heard on "Memphis Bound," "What-Cha-Call-'Em Blues," and "TNT," where his alternating solo spots with Armstrong clearly demonstrate the marked stylistic differences between the two. Following Armstrong's return to Chicago in early November, Smith stepped to the fore more frequently on numbers such as "The Stampede," "Fidgety Feet," "Sensation," "Variety Stomp," and "The St. Louis Blues." Throughout Smith's tenure with the band, Henderson and the arranger DON REDMAN used his pure toned, lyrical style as a contrast to the hotter, earthier approaches of Armstrong and, after his departure, REX STEWART, Tommy Ladnier, and Bobby Stark. But Smith also possessed a talent for mimicry, so it is not surprising to observe his direct nod to Armstrong on Bessie Smith's May 1926 "Hard Driving Papa" and "Lost Your Head Blues" and to Bix Beiderbecke, a much closer stylistic model, on Henderson's January 1927 "Ain't She Sweet."

In late September 1928 Smith and his brother Russell left Henderson to join Allie Ross's Plantation Orchestra in the touring company of Lew Leslie's famous *Blackbirds of 1928*. In late June 1929 Smith and Kaiser Marshall appeared in a JAMES P. JOHNSON–led band in the Bessie Smith film, *St. Louis Blues*. In the summer Smith joined the Detroit-based McKinney's Cotton Pickers and first appeared on record with them in November, when he soloed on "Gee, Ain't I Good to You" and "The Way I Feel Today." Between January and July 1930 his expansive tone, both muted and open, was documented on "Words Can't Express," "If I Could Be with You One Hour Tonight," "Travelin' All Alone," and "Okay Baby." (Although long attributed to Smith, the muted solo on "I Want a Little Girl" was actually the work of George "Buddy" Lee, a recent addition to the band.) Unlike the role he enjoyed on the blues records or with Henderson, on the Cotton Pickers' arrangements Smith was rarely given fully improvised solos, his parts largely being restricted to straight exposition of the melodies, albeit enhanced by his expressive handling of the plunger mute.

In late 1930, while the band was on tour in New England, Smith, long a heavy drinker, chose to drive Kaiser Marshall's car to an engagement in Bridgeport instead of riding with the others on the band bus. With the band's valet and the saxman/singer George "Fathead" Thomas as passengers, Smith reportedly drove so recklessly that the car went off the road and crashed in a ditch. Although Smith escaped unhurt and the valet survived numerous fractures, Thomas was critically injured and died a few days later, a tragedy that only exacerbated the remorseful Smith's already severe drinking problem. In the words of the banjoist/singer Dave Wilborn, "Joe brooded over Fathead's death, and drank continually from then on. He quickly slipped downhill and eventually lost his mind."

Following the accident Smith left the Cotton Pickers and joined Marshall's band in Boston, but he returned in August 1931 and recorded one short but characteristic solo that September on "Wrap Your Troubles in Dreams." By this time, though, his behavior had become increasingly erratic and unreliable, and he left the band on New Year's Eve. In early 1932 he moved to Kansas City, where he may have worked for a while with BENNIE MOTEN. In February 1933 he was playing with Clarence Love's band at El Torreon Ballroom, but he was so ill that when Fletcher Henderson happened to see him while on tour he convinced Smith to return to New York, hoping that he would regain his health and ultimately rejoin the band. However, this proved in vain, for not only was Smith suffering from acute alcoholism but he was also mentally unstable. He was placed in a sanatorium on Long Island, but after further deterioration he was transferred to Bellevue Hospital in New York, where he died of paresis, an advanced stage of syphilis. There is no record of marriage or children.

Unlike Armstrong, Beiderbecke, and Bubber Miley, the three most influential stylists of the 1920s, Smith did not attract legions of disciples. His artistry lay not so much in creativity or innovation as in his establishment of an alternate temperament with which to play blues and, by extension, ballads. It has been said that he was probably the first "cool" jazz trumpeter, preceding MILES DAVIS by some twenty-five years, but that claim ignores the contemporaneous presence and influence of Beiderbecke and Red Nichols, who were each admired and widely emulated by both black and white jazzmen of the 1920s. But neither of these were bluesmen, and Smith was an anomaly within a mainstream established by KING OLIVER, Armstrong, and Miley. He was also a remarkable synthesizer, whose greater sensitivity enabled him to break away completely from the rhythmically restrictive mold of Johnny Dunn and develop a tone that soon became the envy of many. Although Smith did not leave any direct stylistic descendants, the influence of his wistful tone and economical phrasing can be heard in the playing of BUCK CLAYTON, BILL COLEMAN, FRANKIE NEWTON, and DOC CHEATHAM.

FURTHER READING
Allen, Walter C. *Hendersonia: The Music of Fletcher Henderson and His Musicians: A Bio-Discography* (1973).
Chilton, John. *McKinney's Music: A Bio-Discography of McKinney's Cotton Pickers* (1978).
Schuller, Gunther. *Early Jazz* (1968).
Shapiro, Nat, and Nat Hentoff, eds. *Hear Me Talkin' to Ya* (1955).
This entry is taken from the *American National Biography* and is published here with the permission of the American Council of Learned Societies.

JACK SOHMER

Smith, John (1854–?), a sailor in the U.S. Navy and Medal of Honor recipient, was a native of the island of Bermuda in the West Indies. Nothing is known about his life other than his military service and the fact that he immigrated to the United States by 1879, probably making his arrival in New York.

By 1879 John Smith had enlisted in the U.S. Navy at New York, and by September of that year was assigned to the screw sloop *U.S.S. Shenandoah* as part of its recommissioning crew. The *Shenandoah*, with a crew of about 175 officers and enlisted men aboard, John Smith included, subsequently departed New York for Rio de Janeiro, Brazil, on 8 September 1879, arriving there on 1 December. Designated as the flagship of Rear Admiral Andrew Bryson and his South Atlantic Squadron, the *Shenandoah*'s task was to protect American interests in the region. Just over a year after the ship's departure from the United States, it was anchored in port at Rio de Janeiro on 19 September 1880, when one of its crewmen, Fireman 1st class James Grady, fell overboard and was in danger of drowning. Seaman John Smith, without regard for his own personal safety, jumped overboard and saved Grady. For this act of bravery, John Smith was awarded the Medal of Honor just over four years later on 18 October 1884. While almost nothing is known about John Smith, his rating of seaman at the time that he earned the Medal of Honor, higher than that of either landsman or ordinary seaman, is an indicator that he was an experienced sailor; perhaps he had joined the navy some years prior to 1879, or possibly he was a merchant sailor in the Caribbean prior to joining the navy. Either way, he was surely a man who knew his profession well by 1880.

The service of men like John Smith, ROBERT SWEENEY, and WILLIAM JOHNSON in the U.S. Navy during this time period is important for several reasons. While the deeds that earned them the Medal of Honor alone make them worthy of remembrance, they also belong to a unique group of men who earned the medal for acts of heroism in peacetime conditions, a practice that was later discontinued.

Following his action that earned him the Medal of Honor, little is known about John Smith. He continued serving aboard the *Shenandoah* in South American waters until his ship departed Montevideo, Uruguay, for the return to its home port of New York, arriving there on 29 April 1882, after several stops in the Caribbean. After its return, the *Shenandoah* was subsequently decommissioned and its crew assigned to other stations. While Smith's later ship assignments are unknown, he was still in the navy when his Medal of Honor was approved in 1884. After this, John Smith disappears from history.

FURTHER READING
Hanna, Charles W. *African American Recipients of the Medal of Honor* (2002).

GLENN ALLEN KNOBLOCK

Smith, Joshua Bowen (1813–5 July 1879), abolitionist and caterer, was born in Coatesville, Pennsylvania. Little is known of his childhood except that he obtained an education in the local public schools through the influence and financial support of a wealthy Quaker woman.

Smith moved to Boston in 1836 and found employment as a headwaiter at the Mount Washington House. Over the following decade, while serving tables, he made the acquaintance of Francis G. Shaw, Charles Sumner, and other notable whites on the periphery of the antislavery movement. Many of these men became his lifelong friends. Smith also worked briefly as a personal servant for the Shaw family before joining the staff of Henry L. W. Thacker, a local black caterer. In 1849 Smith opened his own catering establishment. Over the next twenty-five years he developed a successful business and gained a sizable personal fortune

by serving gatherings of the local elite, as well as catering various functions at Harvard College, antislavery bazaars, and commemorations of the Emancipation Proclamation. He gained a reputation among Bostonians as "the prince of caterers."

In the 1840s Smith emerged as an important figure in the local abolitionist crusade. Through his friendships with Shaw and Sumner, he became a close acquaintance and ally of William Lloyd Garrison, George Luther Stearns, Theodore Parker, and other prominent abolitionists. He remained a devoted follower of Garrison for nearly three decades. He regularly attended and sometimes chaired antislavery gatherings in Boston's African American community. And he actively participated in the struggle to end segregation in the city's public school system. But Smith expended the bulk of his energies in aiding and protecting fugitive slaves who reached Boston. After the arrest in 1842 of George Latimer, a slave from Virginia, Smith helped found and served as vice president of the New England Freedom Association, an all-black organization devoted to providing runaway slaves with food, clothing, shelter, transportation, and legal aid. Some of the actions taken by the Freedom Association were not only illegal but also occasionally violent. When the interracial Boston Committee of Vigilance was formed in 1846 he became a vocal member of its executive committee. He served briefly as the committee's agent, interviewing and arranging assistance for fugitives who came to the members' attention.

After passage of the Fugitive Slave Act of 1850, which created a federal apparatus for the capture and return of runaway slaves, Smith encouraged Boston's blacks to resist the efforts of slave hunters and federal agents to enforce the law. He urged slaves in the city to purchase revolvers and, if necessary, to use them to prevent their recapture. He pressed local free blacks to protect the fugitives in their midst. At one antislavery gathering, speaking from the pulpit of Boston's African Meeting House, he brandished a bowie knife and a pistol, declared his intent to wield them to protect runaways, and demonstrated the proper method for their use. Smith became an active member of the newly created Boston Vigilance Committee (the successor to the Committee of Vigilance in 1850), personally feeding, clothing, and transporting to Canada several slaves who reached Boston. He even used his catering business to further these efforts. In his duties as a caterer he could keep a watchful eye on the movements of slave hunters in the city, and he could also provide temporary employment to a number of runaways. Smith refused to cater an affair for Senator Daniel Webster of Massachusetts, protesting Webster's vocal support of the act.

Smith welcomed the coming of the Civil War, seeing in it an opportunity to overthrow the institution of slavery. In 1861 he was selected by Governor John Andrew as the caterer for the Twelfth Massachusetts Regiment, the first volunteer unit raised in the state during the war. Because of his devotion to the Union cause, he agreed to perform the task for a lower price than that charged by other Boston caterers. During the ninety-three days the regiment trained in Boston prior to leaving for the South, he furnished daily rations for the officers and enlisted men. His expenditures amounted to $40,378. This proved to be Smith's financial undoing. The governor initially refused to pay the bill, citing inadequate legislative appropriations for the purpose. Although the catering bills of all other units were paid by the state, Smith received only $23,760.80, and then only after the federal government made funds available to the state for that purpose. He petitioned the state for payment of the balance several times before his death, but the debt remained unpaid. Despite personal frugality and keen business skills, he never recovered his lost fortune.

Even with his precarious finances, Smith remained an important figure in Boston's African American community after the war. Well respected by local whites, he was selected in 1867 as the first black member of St. Andrew's Lodge of Freemasons of Massachusetts. A Republican Party stalwart, he represented Cambridge in the Massachusetts Senate in 1873 and 1874 and was one of the few blacks to attend national party conventions during that time. Smith died at his Cambridgeport residence after an illness lasting several months. He was survived by his wife, Emiline (maiden name unknown); their only child, a daughter, had preceded him in death. Hundreds of leading Bostonians turned out to pay their respects at his funeral. At his death his generosity became even more apparent: he left debts some thirty times greater than the value of his estate, in large part on account of his unpaid expenditures for the Twelfth Massachusetts Regiment and decades of contributions to the abolitionist cause.

FURTHER READING

Bartlett, Irving H. "Abolitionists, Fugitives, and Imposters in Boston, 1846–1847," *New England Quarterly* 55 (1982).

Cook, Benjamin F. *History of the 12th Massachusetts Volunteers* (1882).

Horton, James Oliver, and Lois E. Horton. *Black Bostonians: Family Life and Community Struggle in the Antebellum North* (1979).

Ripley, C. Peter, ed. *The Black Abolitionist Papers*, vol. 3 (1991).

Obituaries: *Boston Evening Transcript*, 7 and 8 July 1879; *Boston Evening Traveler*, 8 July 1879.

This entry is taken from the *American National Biography* and is published here with the permission of the American Council of Learned Societies.

ROY E. FINKENBINE

Smith, Lovie Lee (8 May 1958–), professional football coach and the first African American to secure a Super Bowl berth, was born in Big Sandy, Texas, one of five children of Mae, a furniture maker, and Thurman Smith. His parents thought they were going to have a girl and planned to name her after Smith's great aunt, Lavana. When Smith was born, his parents modified the name Lavana and christened him "Lovie." Growing up in tiny Big Sandy (with a population of five hundred) wasn't always easy. Smith's father was an alcoholic and often unemployed and his mother suffered from diabetes. His father's drinking, in particular, as well as his mother's early religious instruction and discipline, informed Smith's own strict Christian beliefs, personal behavior, and what would later become his unusual coaching style.

Smith attended Big Sandy High School, where he excelled in both academics and athletics. He was a member of the National Honor Society and played defense on the school's Big Sandy Wildcats football team, which during Smith's tenure went on to win three state championships and were undefeated for three consecutive seasons. Smith was named all-state three times. After his graduation in 1976, Smith matriculated at the University of Tulsa where he played linebacker and safety for the Hurricanes. There Smith was twice named All-American for his superior defensive play. When he was a junior, his father shocked him by phoning to say he had given up alcohol; his father remained sober until his death twenty years later. Smith graduated in 1979, and two years later he married a fellow Tulsa student, Maryanne (maiden name unknown), whom he met on a blind date. Such was the nature of Smith's CME Methodist religious conviction that he refused to dance with his wife at their wedding reception. The couple went on to

Lovie Smith. The Chicago Bears coach looks on from the sidelines during a game against the Atlanta Falcons, 19 December 2005. Lovie Smith was the first black football coach to have a team in the Super Bowl. (AP Images.)

have three children. After college Smith intended to play in the NFL but went undrafted and instead focused on coaching. He returned to Big Sandy, where he secured the head coaching position at his old high school in 1980, remaining until 1981. He went on to hold a number of jobs as a linebacker's coach at Tulsa from 1983 to 1986 and as a defensive coach at the University of Wisconsin (1987), University of Kentucky (1992), and Ohio State University (1995), among several others. In 1996 he was hired as linebacker coach for the NFL's Tampa Bay Buccaneers, and it was there that Smith met the team's head coach TONY DUNGY. The Bucs, one of the NFL's more hapless squads, had long suffered from a poor defense; but during Smith's tenure with the team, things began to improve. Soon the Tampa Bay franchise had one of the league's most efficient defensive units. It was only a matter of time before the team's defense and its coaching staff came to the attention of other teams around the league. In 2001 Smith was offered the defensive coordinator job with the St. Louis Rams. Hailed around the league as the "Greatest Show on Turf," the Rams were a spectacular, high-scoring offensive unit, but had one of the league's poorer defenses. Smith reversed

this trend, moving the team from twenty-third in total defense to number three in his short time with the team. In 2001 the Rams represented the NFC in Super Bowl XXXVI, but were defeated by the underdog New England Patriots, 20–17.

Successful defensive coordinators were frequent candidates for head coaching positions throughout the NFL. Smith came to the attention of the Chicago Bears, who were seeking a replacement for outgoing coach Dick Jauron. Smith interviewed with the team and was offered the job, thus becoming one of the few black head coaches in the NFL. The Chicago Bears, despite their long and storied tradition and the team's glory years under head coach Mike Ditka in the mid-1980s, had a long and ignominious history of baffling personnel decisions and poor front office management. In 1998, for instance, the Bears, to much ridicule, lost their prospective head coach, Dave McGinnis, when they announced his hiring before McGinnis had decided to take the job. McGinnis instead went to the Arizona Cardinals. Then the team endured a seemingly endless carousel of quarterbacks that had become the stuff of NFL legend. Perhaps worse yet, the much-vaunted Bears defense, the so-called Monsters of the Midway, had fallen into disrepair and lingered near the bottom of the league standings. Smith, however, felt confident that he could turn the team around, and he quickly gave voice to his three major goals as head coach: to beat the Bears' longtime rivals, the Green Bay Packers; to win the NFC North Division; and to win the Super Bowl. Smith's first season with the team saw him complete the first of these goals. Despite a poor 5–11 record in 2004, the injury-ridden Bears managed to defeat the Packers. The following season, however, saw significant improvement in almost every phase of the team's game. Despite again losing their starting quarterback Rex Grossman to injury, the Bears relied on defense and the play of rookie quarterback Kyle Orton to seize the division title and compile an 11–5 record before losing to the Carolina Panthers in an NFC divisional matchup. Smith was named the Associated Press Coach of the Year, and his success with the Bears and his imperturbable sideline demeanor, soft-spoken manner, and Texas drawl made him one of the NFL's most widely recognized head coaches.

The Bears' success continued during the 2006 season, as they were 13–3 during the regular season, had one of the league's top defenses, again beat the Green Bay Packers, won their division, and secured the NFC's top play-off seed. The Bears then won two play-off games against the Seattle Seahawks and the New Orleans Saints to advance to the Super Bowl. Because the NFC Championship game was scheduled earlier in the day than the AFC bout, Smith became the first African American NFL head coach to secure a Super Bowl bid. Smith's close friend, Dungy, coach of the Indianapolis Colts, would become the second black coach to do so just a few hours later. The two teams met in Super Bowl XLI on 4 February 2007 after a week of intense media attention, even by Super Bowl standards. Indeed, that Super Bowl stood as the third most-watched U.S. television broadcast of all time. Though the Bears started the game strong with a substantial opening runback by return specialist Devin Hester, the Bears went down to defeat, 29–17. Following two successful seasons with the Chicago Bears, Smith was signed to a four-year, $22 million deal. In the 2010-11 season Smith led the Bears to the NFC Championship game, but lost to the Green Bay Packers.

Outside of football, Smith was active in a number of charitable causes, especially the American Diabetes Association. The disease blinded his mother in 1990, and a number of Smith's siblings also suffered from the disease. With his wife, Smith has organized and maintained a scholarship program for poor children who wished to attend college.

FURTHER READING

Aron, Jaime. "Still Big in Big Sandy," *Associated Press* (Jan. 2007).

Bell, Jarrett. "Stubbornness May Help Bears Coach Smith Live Out Boyhood Dream," *USA Today* (Dec. 2006).

Solomon, Jerome. "Made in Texas," *Houston Chronicle* (Jan. 2007).

JASON PHILIP MILLER

Smith, Lucy (14 Jan. 1875–18 June 1952), pastor and church leader, was born Lucy Madden in Woodstock, Georgia, to parents about whom little is known except that they were farmers. Smith was born poor, one of six children her mother raised by herself. She had a conversion experience at age twelve and walked twelve to fifteen miles to attend a Baptist church. At thirteen she began attending school four months a year. In rural counties black families worked during the farming season, and black children were allowed to go to school only when there was no farming to be done. Consequently Smith received a limited education.

In 1896 she married William Smith, with whom she had nine children. In 1908 they moved to Athens, Georgia, where she took in sewing for a living. In Athens, her husband abandoned the family, and Lucy later relocated to Atlanta.

In 1910 Lucy Smith moved to Chicago, where she first joined the famous Olivet Baptist Church before switching to the Ebenezer Baptist Church. In 1914 she moved her membership to Stone Church, an interracial Pentecostal congregation. By then Chicago had become one of the early centers of American Pentecostalism because of William F. Durham (1873–1912), pastor of the interracial North Avenue Mission. Durham was a dynamic white preacher who drew hundreds of Chicagoans into Pentecostalism. While attending Stone Church, Smith received the gift of healing and on 1 January 1916 started prayer meetings in her home with the help of Viola Smith, her eldest daughter, and other saints. The prayer service grew into a church that soon required more space. Meanwhile Smith's husband had joined her in Chicago, and he remodeled Smith's house to accommodate the growing congregation.

Smith's first healing was performed on a white man, and from the beginning her ministry was interracial. She named her congregation All Nations Pentecostal Church, reflecting her strong desire to promote fellowship among the various races in the city. All Nations included white immigrants, Native Americans, native-born Euro-Americans, and African Americans.

All Nations grew and moved from location to location in search of larger facilities. In 1926 it erected its first building at 3716 Langley Avenue in Chicago. Smith ordained both men and women to the ministry and later incorporated a new denomination as All Nations Pentecostal Church. In founding a new denomination with herself as the female overseer, Smith was following the path blazed by MARY L. TATE, a powerful Pentecostal leader who had founded the Church of the Living God the Pillar and Ground of the Truth in Alabama in 1908.

In 1933 Smith pioneered a radio program, the *Glorious Church of the Air*, that was heard as far away as Mexico. Her numerous healings brought great fame to All Nations. Combining broadcasting and healing was rare among black women clergy, and it is likely that Smith was influenced by Aimee Semple McPherson, a white female preacher who pastored a large congregation in Los Angeles and promoted faith healing through radio.

Smith's radio program drew even more people to a church that was already well-known for its social work. During the Great Depression, All Nations reached out to poor whites and black southern migrants by providing shelter, food, and clothing in the black self-help tradition that led mainline Chicago churches, such as Olivet and Ebenezer, to provide assistance to black migrants. Smith also planted numerous churches, and by 1936 All Nations reported affiliates in New York, Pennsylvania, Michigan, Nebraska, and Alabama.

All Nations enjoyed continuous growth and sold its building to the city of Chicago to make way for the Ida B. Wells Housing Project. In 1937 Smith bought land at 518 East Oakwood Boulevard and built a new church edifice in two years. In the interim, All Nations worshipped with a local black Methodist church, demonstrating both the respect Smith enjoyed among male clergy and her ecumenical inclinations. All Nations' pastor visited many black Baptist and Methodist congregations with her renowned choir. In fact, All Nations became an early center of gospel music that promoted great singers such as MAHALIA JACKSON and Smith's granddaughter Lucy Collier. In turn black ministers from various faiths were invited to All Nations. In an era when a growing sector of the African American population was asking for an educated ministry, Smith, who did not complete high school, gained the respect of Chicago's clergy through her entrepreneurial skills and successful ministry.

Smith's ministry continued to flourish in the new church building. Soon the local membership reached the impressive number of five thousand, which made it one of the largest congregations pastored by a black woman in America. All Nations also grew outside Illinois and spread over thirty-five states. Smith was so successful as a faith healer that she claimed to have healed two hundred thousand people during her lifetime. When her health declined, she in 1950 installed her daughter Ardella Smith as pastor over her local church, and Ardella Smith became the new leader of the denomination at Lucy Smith's death.

In time the Chicago All Nations congregation split, the Oakwood building burned, and Ardella Smith joined the Catholic Church. Ministers and churches that were part of All Nations joined other organizations. Nevertheless, Lucy Smith's legacy has survived through her spiritual heirs, who now belong to other denominations. Smith is an example of what an empowered black woman could accomplish.

FURTHER READING

The Lucy Collier Papers are in the Vivian G. Harsch Research Collection of Afro-American History and Literature, Carter Woodson Branch of the Chicago Public Library, Chicago.

All Nations. *Yearbook of the Second Annual Convention of the Langley Ave. All Nations Pentecostal Church* (1928).

Vicini, Tina. "Life Story of Rev. Lucy Smith," *Herald American*, 25 June 1952.

Wallace, Best. "Smith, Lucy Madden," in *Women Building Chicago 1790–1990: A Biographical Dictionary*, eds. Rima Lunin Schultz and Adele Hast (2001).

DAVID MICHEL

Smith, Lucy Harth (24 Jan. 1888–20 Sept. 1955), racial activist and educator, was born in Roanoke, Virginia, the daughter of Daniel Washington Harth Jr., a minister and lawyer, and Rachel Emma Brockington. In 1904 Lucy attended the normal department of the Hampton Institute in Virginia, completing both the high school and college courses in four years. Subsequently she accepted an elementary school teaching post in Roanoke. Two years later, after her marriage to Paul Smith, a school administrator, Lucy left the labor force; the couple had five children.

In 1917 the family relocated to Lexington, Kentucky, where Paul Smith became principal of the BOOKER T. WASHINGTON Elementary School. The next year Lucy Smith returned to public education, serving as a teacher and as assistant principal alongside her husband. In 1932 she graduated magna cum laude from Kentucky State College in Frankfort, Kentucky. After her husband transferred to another local school in 1935, Smith herself became principal of the Booker T. Washington Elementary School, a position that she held for twenty years.

Like many college-educated black women with families, Smith forged a distinguished career of public service while raising her children. In 1943 she completed her formal education, earning a master's degree in education from the University of Cincinnati. In her thesis she investigated the career of the noted African American scholar and inventor GEORGE WASHINGTON CARVER.

Smith actually pursued two careers: racial activist and educator. An active clubwoman, Smith served as president of the Kentucky Association of Colored Women and chaired the executive board of the National Association of Colored Women's

Clubs. Through her work with these organizations and with the public schools Smith addressed the problems of black children in a segregated society.

In the spirit of Progressivism, Smith was a persistent advocate of the right of black children to equal access not only to education but also to recreation and good health. In 1944 Smith organized and secured private funding for the summertime Health Camp for Colored Children in central Kentucky. The Community Chest of Lexington later supported this endeavor. Smith also was a member of the Governor's Committee on Youth and Children.

Smith made major contributions as an educator through her work as a public school administrator and as an active member of various professional associations and through her activities as a curriculum reformer. Although principalships at the elementary level became somewhat more common for white women in the post–World War II era, relatively few women of any color held administrative posts in the 1930s and 1940s. Principals were accorded great honor in black communities—principals of either gender. Thus Smith occupied a significant position among African Americans in Lexington.

Smith was active in professional organizations at both national and local levels. She served as a regional vice president and trustee of the American Teachers Association and held the presidency of the Lexington Teachers Association. She also became the first woman president of the Kentucky Negro Education Association.

For thirty years, from 1925 to 1955, Smith was numbered among the most dedicated members of the Association for the Study of Negro History and Life. The association's *Journal of Negro History* (Apr. 1956) described Smith as "a perennial figure at the association's annual meeting." Smith's role was both administrative and scholarly. As a longtime member of the executive committee she participated in policy-making decisions, and as a historian she chaired numerous paper sessions.

Smith's most notable contribution to the association remains her persistent and compelling advocacy of the inclusion of black history in the curriculum of the public schools. In an address at the annual meeting in November 1933 she concluded that both whites and blacks benefited from the introduction of black history into the curriculum. She believed that an accurate recounting of African American history would not only alter the attitudes of thoughtful whites but also inspire great pride within black students (*Journal of Negro History*, Jan. 1934). During the darkest days of World War II, at the association's annual meeting in November 1942, Smith's lecture concluded that through exemplary military participation and support of the war, African Americans in the United States belonged in the "front ranks as citizens" (*Journal of Negro History*, Jan. 1943). Smith died in Lexington, Kentucky.

Although Smith did not enjoy unquestioned success as a racial activist and educator, she remains a significant figure as one of few college-educated African American women who were unafraid to speak out and to take action to enhance opportunities for African American children in the South. In its account of her career and involvement with the association, the *Journal of Negro History* (Apr. 1956) ranked Smith with the inimitable MARY MCLEOD BETHUNE, stating, "Where [Bethune] built institutions, Lucy Harth Smith became a crusader in inspiring colored people to look to their past for sources of hope in the achievements and contributions of Negroes to civilization and history."

Smith received many honors for her work. The *Louisville Defender*, an African American newspaper, included her among the most outstanding black Kentuckians. The Kentucky Human Rights Commission named her in 1973 to its Gallery of Great Black Kentuckians. In 1974 the Kentucky Education Association honored her service by inaugurating the Lucy Harth Smith–Atwood S. Wilson Award for Civil and Human Rights in Education.

FURTHER READING

"Proceedings of the Annual Meeting of the Association for the Study of Negro Life and History," *Journal of Negro History*, 1928–1955.

Obituary: *Journal of Negro History* 41 (Apr. 1956): 177–178.

This entry is taken from the *American National Biography* and is published here with the permission of the American Council of Learned Societies.

CAROLYN TERRY BASHAW

Smith, Lucy Wilmot (16 Nov. 1861–Jan. 1890), journalist and educator, was born in Lexington, Kentucky, the only child of Margaret Smith, who raised her on her own. It is uncertain whether Smith was born into slavery. Though her mother and she were poor and struggled to make ends meet, Smith managed to get an education, and by the age of sixteen she had begun to support her mother and herself by working as a secretary to WILLIAM JAMES SIMMONS, the president of the State University of

Louisville. Later, after she graduated from the Normal Department at the State University in 1887, she worked as a faculty member.

Through her connection to Simmons, Smith also began working as a journalist. Simmons was an editor of the *American Baptist*, a newspaper owned by black Baptists, and in 1884 Smith began writing "The Children's Column" for the publication. When Simmons became the founding editor of a new women's magazine, *Our Women and Children*, in 1886, he hired Smith as editor of "The Children's Column." There she worked alongside two other women from Kentucky, fellow State University professor Mary Cook and renowned journalist and antilynching crusader IDA B. WELLS BARNET. In addition to her work as an educator and a journalist, Smith, along with Cook, served as a leader in the black Baptist church and also sat on the Board of Managers for the Baptist Woman's Educational Convention of Kentucky from its inception in 1883.

She wrote a series of short articles about female journalists for the New York newspaper *Journalism* that was later republished in other papers, such as the *Boston Advocate* in 1889. The article "Women as Journalists," appeared in the *Indianapolis Freeman* on 23 February 1889; it explored the themes that appeared in much of her writing: the twin causes of encouraging women to better themselves and promoting racial uplift. Smith argued in this article, that black women had an advantage over white women because black women had worked side by side with black men in the past and had remained working side by side in the present as well. This, she claimed, was especially true in journalism. Other women, however, had to struggle to gain acceptance from men, which kept them from moving forward as quickly.

The theme of racial uplift for women also permeated what came to be Smith's best-known work, the speech she gave at the newly formed American National Baptist Convention (ANBC) in St. Louis in August 1886. Simmons was the president of the convention, which, according to the historians EVELYN BROOKS HIGGINBOTHAM (1993) and Shirley Wilson Logan (1999), seemed to be more open to the role of women than the other two black Baptist conventions. Smith in fact was elected the official historian for the ANBC in 1887 an unprecedented position for a woman to hold within the world of the male-dominated conventions.

In her speech "The Future Colored Girl," Smith emphasized the need for women to continue to further their educations but also not to shy away from "honest work." Smith cited numerous examples from different cultures of women who had attained leadership positions to underscore her message. She also stressed the need for better, more independent jobs for women, encouraging southern women not to leave home for the North when they could stay in the South and create agrarian jobs for themselves. Lauding female writers again, Smith called for more women to write, publish, and edit material specifically for women. Though she was addressing a mostly male audience, Smith urged that women and girls should learn what men and boys always had: the value of hard work. Smith's purpose was twofold: racial uplift and female independence. Encouraging women and girls to find their own financial security through their own work, she was implicitly calling upon the mostly male audience to allow women to stand as their equals. Near the end of her speech she used the analogy of a bird with one wing that can fly only by pairing with another bird of its own kind. The two must work together in order to soar into the sky. Smith's message was for and about "the future colored girl," but it was also all of those in the audience: to really lift themselves up, they would have to work with each or they would get nowhere.

Smith's words were not idle ones, since she herself worked as both an educator and a journalist throughout her life. The causes of racial uplift and suffrage were those she supported strongly and which she wrote about often. And her voice was one among many of her contemporaries. Smith was one of several female journalists of the time who received recognition for her work. She is also one of several women celebrated in a chapter in I. GARLAND PENN's book *The Afro-American Press and Its Editors* (1891). At the time of her death at age twenty-nine, Smith, who never married, was the principal of the Model School at the State University of Louisville. Her colleague Cook eulogized her by pointing out how Smith's life, through her writing and her speeches, was spent in the service of her religious faith and in racial uplift.

FURTHER READING

Dann, Martin. *The Black Press, 1827–1890: The Quest for National Identity* (1971).

Dunnigan, Alice Allison. *The Fascinating Story of Black Kentuckians: Their Heritage and Traditions* (1982).

Higginbotham, Evelyn Brooks. *Righteous Discontent: The Women's Movement in the Black Baptist Church, 1880–1920* (1993).

Logan, Shirley Wilson. *"We Are Coming": The Persuasive Discourse of Nineteenth-Century Black Women* (1999).

AMY SPARKS KOLKER

Smith, Luther (27 Sept. 1920–9 Dec. 2009), Tuskegee Airman and prisoner of war, was born Luther Henry Smith Jr. in Des Moines, Iowa, the second child of Luther Henry Smith Sr., a black-eyed pea salesman, and Ida. His father's sales territory included the Midwest, and visiting Des Moines, Iowa, he found that since there were so few African Americans, the effects of segregation and discrimination were minimal and opportunities for economic progress were strong. Smith's mother was from Dubuque, Iowa. Her father had been a trader who later made his home in Des Moines. Smith's parents met in 1918.

Young Luther exhibited an interest in aviation as a child. At the age of seven he drew a picture of an airplane and, showing it to his second grade teacher, announced that it was a picture of the airplane in which he planned to fly his family to Africa. At the age of thirteen he walked or hitchhiked the five miles to the Des Moines airport, where he helped the mechanics and attendants refuel and service airplanes. In 1934 a newspaper article, "America's Youngest Greaseball," was written about him. The interviewer asked about his interest in aviation, and Smith stated he wanted to someday be a licensed pilot.

Such an aspiration seemed unattainable for an African American youth of that era, so Smith decided to seek a career in engineering with the intention of technically preparing himself to someday become a military aviator should the opportunity arise. He enrolled at the University of Iowa in 1938 and completed two years in mechanical engineering before entering the military.

While working at the Des Moines airport, Smith met Howard Gregory, who ran the Des Moines Flying Service flying school. Gregory asked Smith if he would be interested in applying for flight training. Smith applied, was accepted, and passed all the qualifications to enter the Civilian Pilot Training Program. He received his private pilot's license in 1941.

Smith learned of the aviation opportunities at Tuskegee from the *Chicago Defender* and the *Pittsburgh Courier*. He left Iowa for Tuskegee in September 1942 and graduated in Class 43-E on 29 May 1943. In July of the same year Smith and his fellow members of the 332nd Fighter Group were assigned to Selfridge Field, Michigan, to embark on fighter training. In January 1944 Smith was sent overseas to Taranto, Italy, and was assigned to do sea and harbor patrol. These duties were considered secondary rather than part of the primary war effort.

On Friday, 13 October 1944, Smith embarked upon his 133rd mission. The mission was to escort bomber planes to Blackhammer in southeastern Germany, and it was to be the longest mission Smith had ever flown. The mission began in the routine fashion, with the bombers escorted safely to and from the target. Before returning to the base, the objective was to fly over the enemy's base to find a target.

Smith saw two German bombers he tried to hit. He hit the first and, against military practice, went back to try to hit the second. He hit the second as well and decided to return once again to get footage from the gun camera. There was a sudden explosion, his plane caught fire, and Smith was forced to eject from the airplane. The plane fell into a tailspin while he was partially out of the cockpit. His foot became entangled, his oxygen mask came off, and he lost consciousness. After he regained consciousness and lost it for a second time, he was found by German soldiers.

Smith was taken to a prisoner of war camp and, because of the unavailability of adequate medical facilities and supplies, suffered tremendous damage to his leg. He was soon transferred to a hospital in Austria, but the damage to his leg was permanent. As the highest ranking officer in the hospital, Smith received respect from the Germans that he did not receive in the United States.

When the war ended on 10 May 1945 Smith was released from the German hospital and sent to a hospital in Naples until he was well enough to travel back to the United States. He was then transferred to Kellogg General Hospital in Battle Creek, Michigan. He was discharged from the hospital and from the army as a captain in September 1947.

Smith then returned to the University of Iowa. He taught courses in the use and application of power generation for electrical engineering students, and he graduated with a B.S. in mechanical engineering in 1950.

After over sixty job interviews, Smith secured a position at the General Electric Company in Philadelphia, Pennsylvania, where he participated in the development of two patents, helped create rockets for the space program, and worked on special assignments for the U.S. Air Force. He also worked for two years as the Equal Employment

Opportunity manager for General Electric and helped develop a more diverse workforce. He retired from General Electric in 1988.

In 1994 his friend Howard Gregory nominated Smith to the Iowa Aviation Hall of Fame. In 1995 Smith was selected as one of seven World War II veterans to travel to England, Czechoslovakia, and Russia with President and Mrs. William J. Clinton and Vice President and Mrs. Albert A. Gore to celebrate the fiftieth anniversary of VE day. Later in 1995 Smith was instrumental in having a plaque erected at Arlington National Cemetery in Washington, DC, that reads: "To the Tuskegee Airmen of World War II, For Their Great Achievement of Flying 200 Missions as Strategic Bomber Escort Without the Loss of a Single Bomber Aircraft to Enemy Aircraft."

Smith died in Bryn Mawr, Pennsylvania from infection-related complications.

Obituary: *Philadelphia Inquirer*, 12 Dec. 2009.

LISA BRATTON

Smith, Lydia Hamilton (14 Feb. 1813–14 Feb. 1884), housekeeper for Thaddeus Stevens, was born in Gettysburg, Pennsylvania, the daughter of a black mother surnamed O'Neill and a white father. She took Hamilton as her surname. Even though Lydia Hamilton Smith was merely a housekeeper, she became widely known because of her employment with Thaddeus Stevens. When Thaddeus Stevens came to Washington in 1849 as a Whig representative to Congress from Lancaster, Pennsylvania, he was known as an implacable foe of slavery. He labored tirelessly to make the slavery-ending Thirteenth Amendment (1865) a permanent part of the United States Constitution. He also played a major role in the enactment of the Fourteenth Amendment (1866).

After moving into a house on South Queens Street in Lancaster, Stevens decided that he needed a housekeeper. He first attempted to employ a woman by the name of Anna Sulkey, but Anna became the wife of Dennis Martin, a black barber who lived in town. She declined the offer, but told Stevens about her cousin, Lydia Smith. Lydia had been married to Jacob Smith, who was a teamster and a musician. They had two children, William, born in 1836, and Isaac, born in 1847. Lydia's husband, Jacob, died in Gettysburg in 1848. She was a widow with two small children when she began working for Stevens. When Congress was in session, Smith also came to Washington as Stevens's housekeeper. She was with him when he died in 1868 and was accorded a place of honor in his funeral procession. After Stevens's burial, Lydia returned to Washington, D.C., and operated a boarding house in the center of the downtown area. The house was located at 515 Fourteenth Street, N.W. She also may have operated boarding houses in Philadelphia and Lancaster, an unusual feat for any woman in 1868.

Lydia died in Washington, D.C., in 1884. Her obituary appeared in the *Washington Evening Star* on 15 Feb. 1884. The headline of the obituary read as follows: "The Death of Lydia Smith. A colored woman who became famous as Thaddeus Stevens's housekeeper." The obituary continued: "Mrs. Lydia Smith, a colored woman, who obtained a national reputation through her connection with the late Thaddeus Stevens, 'the great commoner,' died early yesterday morning at her home on Fourteenth Street opposite Willard's, aged sixty-nine years. She was stricken with paralysis while attending to some legal business. She never afterwards recovered her speech or consciousness. She was remembered in the will of Thaddeus Stevens with a bequest of $5000 in cash and property in Lancaster and in this city." Lydia, a Catholic, was a member of Saint Mary of Assumption Catholic church in Lancaster, Pennsylvania. In her will, she directed that she be buried in her lot in Saint Mary's Cemetery.

FURTHER READING

Brodie, Fawn M. *Thaddeus Stevens: Scourge of the South* (1959).

Brubacker, Jack. *Lancaster New Era* (Sept. 1994).

Hoch, Bradley R. *Thaddeus Stevens in Gettysburg: The Making of an Abolitionist* (2005).

Trefousse, Hans L. *Thaddeus Stevens: Nineteenth-Century Egalitarian* (2001).

Worden, Amy. *Philadelphia Inquirer* (Aug. 2001).

Obituary: *Washington Evening Star*, 15 Feb. 1884.

WILLIAM A. ALLISON

Smith, Mabel Louise "Big Maybelle" (1 May 1924–23 Jan. 1972), singer of blues, pop, R&B, and rock n' roll, was born in Jackson, Tennessee, to Frank and Alice Smith. Smith began her musical training as a child, singing gospel at church. Even at a tender age she was clearly possessed of a notable talent, as evidenced by her first-place win at a talent contest in Memphis at the age of eight and her discovery, at age twelve, by band leader Dave Clark. Clark's tutelage prepared Smith for a touring spot with the International Sweethearts of Rhythm swing band, America's first integrated, all-female music group. Smith later performed boogie woogie with pianist

"Big Maybelle," in an undated publicity photograph. (Photofest.)

Christine Chatman's orchestra, with whom she made her first recording on the Decca label in 1944.

With a rich, barreling, thoroughbred's voice, Smith's was a vocal instrument made for the blues. Yet she came of age at a time when the era of touring female blues singers of the black theater, tent show, and cabaret circuit, such as MA RAINEY and BESSIE SMITH, was coming to an end. As African Americans found stability and greater prosperity in northern cities such as Chicago, New York, and Detroit, the plaintive blues lament of the (usually male) sharecropper was shelved along with painful memories of segregation, economic privation, and social tension. Thus, for female singers in particular, sassy, female-empowered blues recordings became a launch pad toward pop success, rather than the limited career of the old bluesmen.

By 1947 Smith had migrated to Cincinnati, Ohio, and had recorded three singles with trumpeter HOT LIPS PAGE's revue on that city's King Records label. Smith was anointed with the appellation "Big Maybelle," for both her large voice and her stature, by producer Fred Mendelsohn, who signed her to Columbia Records' African American, or "race record" subsidiary Okeh in 1952. Smith found success that year with the traditional blues single "Gabbin Blues" (Don't Run My Business), which climbed high on the rhythm and blues charts, and was for Okeh, along with a single by Chuck Willis,

one of the label's most lucrative hits. This success was followed by the release of other popular singles, "Way Back Home," "My Country Man," "Jinny Mule," and "Rain Down Rain." Smith's popularity was cemented during her tenure at Okeh. In 1953 Cash Box magazine crowned her the number three rhythm and blues singer after Faye Adams and DINAH WASHINGTON.

Like other African American blues rooted singers of her time, Smith's extraordinary performances on wax were at once coveted and summarily copied by fledgling white rock n' rollers of the day without the extension of recognition or gratitude. Smith's rousing "Whole Lotta Shaking Going On," produced by QUNICY JONES early in his career, was immortalized in 1955, two years before the white Louisianan Jerry Lee Lewis made it his signature anthem. White rockabilly performer Roy Hall and his Cohutta Mountain Boys had recorded the song first, in 1954, although as in many blue songs, there is much dispute about the original author. Hall claimed credit (and later received royalties) for composing "Whole Lotta Shaking" even though a Decca sample copy of Hall's original recording solely credits Dave "Curlee" Williams, a black songwriter who worked with Hall, as composer. Hall also recorded another Smith classic for Okeh, "One Monkey Don't Stop No Show," with no documented credit to Smith or the individuals who composed the song.

Coaxed away from Okeh to the more refined Savoy label by Mendelsohn, Smith recorded a handful of pop gems in the late 1950s, backed by top New York session musicians. Her impeccable 1956 recording of "Candy" was a hit, proving her appeal as a crossover artist, a milestone that led to the recording of other pop staples such as "All of Me" and "Until the Real Thing Comes Along." This high point in Smith's career also marked appearances at Harlem's famed Apollo theatre and in the 1958 documentary Jazz on a Summer's Day, in which Smith's barn-burning performance of "I Ain't Mad At You" is captured in color by filmmaker Bert Stern. Smith's body of work in the late 1950s lives on as a testament to the fluency and versatility she would maintain throughout the remainder of her career. While easily assuming the poise needed to carry glossy pop tunes, Smith continued to demonstrate her prowess as a blues shouter and classic rock n' roller at Savoy, with up-tempo numbers such as "Tell Me Who" and "Ring Ding Dilly."

Smith's career slowed during the 1960s. She no longer held a secure place at Savoy, and the decade found her recording with a variety of labels such as

Rojac, Brunswick, and Chess, among others. Still, she continued to maintain a unique resourcefulness and openness to new sounds and styles of music, even recording a signature version of The Beatles' *"Eleanor Rigby"* for Rojac in 1968. Although stylistically she moved beyond the reaches of blues music with success, the rigors and temptation of the hard-living blues lifestyle that claimed Billie Holiday and adversely affected ETTA JAMES ultimately held Smith in a time capsule, and she struggled for years with a serious drug addiction that would eventually be a catalyst in her 1972 death by diabetic coma in Cleveland.

Smith's last chart-topping success was her 1967 cover of ? and the Mysterians "96 Tears," composed by Rudy Martinez of the aforesaid band. The 1983 release of *The Okeh Sessions*, distributed by Epic, won the W. C. Handy Award for "Vintage or Reissue Album of the Year," and her crossover smash "Candy" was awarded the Grammy Hall of Fame Award in 1999. Although her formidable, lightening voice may not have adapted to early rock n' roll with the commercial success of LAVERN BAKER or RUTH BROWN or to pop with a measure of acclaim equal to that of DINAH WASHINGTON, "Big Maybelle" has left an indelible mark on the cadence, phrasing, and roaring delivery of American blues, rock n' roll, R&B, and pop music. Credited as an inspiration to ARETHA FRANKLIN and Janis Joplin, among others, Smith's influence lives on through the performers who continue to emulate her style, whether knowingly or not.

FURTHER READING

Bogdanov, Vladimir. *All Music Guide to the Blues* (2003).

Deffaa, Chip. *Six Lives in Rhythm and Blues* (1996).

Doyle, Peter. *Echo and Reverb* (2005).

Hardy, Phil. *The Faber Companion to 20th Century Popular Music* (2001).

Keil, Charles. *Urban Blues* (1966).

Morrison, Craig. *Go Cat Go! Rockabilly Music and Its Makers* (1998).

Santelli, Robert. *The Big Book of Blues: The Fully Revised and Updated Biographical Encyclopedia* (2001).

Weissman, Dick. *Blues, The Basics* (2005).

Williamson, Nigel. *The Rough Guide to the Blues* (2007).

DISCOGRAPHY

Big Maybelle. *Roots of Rhythm: Sophisticated Ladies* (2000).

Big Maybelle. *The Complete Okeh Sessions 1952–1955* (2008).

Big Maybelle. *Jazz on a Summer's Day* (2009).

Big Maybelle. *Saga of the Good Life and Hard Times* (2009).

CAMILLE A. COLLINS

Smith, Mamie (26 May 1883–c. 30 Oct. 1946), blues and vaudeville singer and film actress, was born Mamie Robinson in Cincinnati, Ohio. Nothing is known of her parents. At the age of ten she toured with a white act, the Four Dancing Mitchells. She danced in J. Homer Tutt and Salem Tutt-Whitney's The Smart Set Company in 1912 and then left the tour the next year to sing in Harlem clubs and theaters. Around this time she married William "Smitty" Smith, a singing waiter who died in 1928. At the Lincoln Theatre in 1918 she starred in Perry Bradford's musical revue *Made in Harlem*, in which she sang "Harlem Blues."

In 1920 Bradford persuaded a New York recording company, Okeh, to take a chance and record Smith, despite racist threats of a boycott. In February, Smith recorded Bradford's songs "That Thing Called Love" and "You Can't Keep a Good Man Down," accompanied by a white band; this disk was not immediately released because of an industry-wide patent dispute. In August, with a hastily organized African American band that came to be known as Smith's Jazz Hounds, Smith recorded "It's Right Here for You" and "Crazy Blues." The latter tune, a retitled version of "Harlem Blues," sold spectacularly well. Further female blues singers were sought after and recorded, and a new marketing category, "race records," was under way in the industry.

Bradford organized a touring Jazz Hounds band. Trumpeter Johnny Dunn and reed player Garvin Bushell were among Smith's accompanists in 1920. Trumpeter Bubber Miley replaced Dunn, perhaps early in 1921. Tenor saxophonist COLEMAN HAWKINS joined that summer, while Bradford placed Smith on the Theater Owners' Booking Association circuit and continued directing recording sessions. Immensely popular, Smith made huge earnings in royalties (reportedly nearly one hundred thousand dollars) and performance fees (often more than one thousand dollars per week), enabling her to purchase a lavishly furnished house on 130th Street. Dan Burley of the *Amsterdam News* reported, "There were servants, cars, and all the luxuries that would go with being the highest paid Negro star of that day" (24 Feb. 1940, 20). Smith bought a building on Saint Nicholas Place, which she later lost in the stock market crash, and another home in Jamaica, New York.

Because of Bradford's financial and touring disputes with Smith's second husband, Sam Gardner, and with her boyfriend and band manager, Ocey (or Ocie) Wilson, Smith's contract was sold to a white manager, Maurice Fulchner, and Bradford left Okeh for the Columbia label to work with the singer EDITH WILSON. Later, Burley wrote, "Mister Bradford came to serve a summons on the blues queen on account of certain 'misunderstandings' having to do with his songs. Reports are that Mr. Bradford jumped roofs for a block and a half after Mamie got her gun" (9 Mar. 1940).

Late in 1922 Smith recorded "I Ain't Gonna Give Nobody None o' This Jelly-Roll" and "The Darktown Flappers' Ball." She continued to tour nationally with her Jazz Hounds. Hawkins remained with her until 1923, and in that year he may have worked alongside reed player SIDNEY BECHET with Smith at the Garden of Joy in New York. Featured in her own shows, Smith performed in theaters through the 1920s and into the 1930s. Among her recordings were "Goin' Crazy with the Blues," "What Have I Done?" (both from 1926), and "Jenny's Ball" (1931).

In 1929 Smith married a Mr. Goldberg (given name unknown), one of the brothers who managed and owned the Seven Eleven troupe in which she performed. No account of her marriage mentions children. She appeared in the film short *Jailhouse Blues* (1929) and costarred in *Fireworks of 1930*, a short-lived revue written and performed by FATS WALLER and JAMES P. JOHNSON. She worked with the band of the pianist and singer Fats Pichon from 1932 to 1934 and toured Europe around 1936, at which time she also led her Beale Street Boys at the Town Casino in New York. At some point in the 1930s Smith sang with ANDY KIRK's big band.

Smith starred in a series of low-budget African American films: *Paradise in Harlem* (1940) with LUCKY MILLINDER's big band, *Mystery in Swing* (1940), *Murder on Lenox Avenue* and *Sunday Sinners* (both 1941), and the soundie, a film short for video jukeboxes, *Because I Love You* (c. 1942), again with Millinder. Smith last sang in a concert at the Lido Ballroom in New York in August 1944. Confined to Harlem Hospital during a long illness, she died in New York.

Among classic female blues and vaudeville singers, Smith is celebrated more as a racial pioneer than as a great performer. Bushell recalled that "Mamie was a very fine-looking lady, had a nice personality, and was a bit higher cultured than a lot of the singers. She wasn't a low, gutbucket type of singer that they were wanting on records. ... She usually had a husband who was a big bruiser, taking all her money" (22). Derrick Stewart-Baxter wrote that "her voice lacked the richness of the truly great women artists who were to follow her into the recording studios. ... Seldom was she really involved in what she was singing, and at times she lapsed into the sentimental. ... There may appear to be an outward toughness, but occasionally the marshmallow at the roots comes to the surface" (10).

But Smith unquestionably had a special stage presence. The singer VICTORIA SPIVEY recalled seeing her for the first time:

Miss Smith walked on that stage and I could not breathe for a minute. She threw those big sparkling eyes on us with that lovely smile showing those pearly teeth with a diamond the size of one of her teeth. Then I looked at her dress. Nothing but sequins and rhinestones, plus a velvet cape with fur on it. We all went wild. And then she sang—she tore the house apart. Between numbers while the band was playing she would make a complete change in about a minute, and was back in record time for her next selection. Her full voice filled the entire auditorium without the use of mikes like we use today. That was singing the blues! I was really inspired and kept plugging to become a singer (quoted in Stewart-Baxter, 16).

This talent comes across reasonably well in Smith's late-career film roles, where she repeatedly steals the show, acting and singing in a manner that seems refreshingly natural and comfortable by comparison with and in spite of her consistently mediocre associates.

FURTHER READING

Burley, Dan. "'Crazy Blues' and the Woman Who Sold 'Em," *Amsterdam News*, 17 Feb. 1940, continued as "The 'Crazy Blues,'" 24 Feb. 1940, 3 Mar. 1940, and 9 Mar. 1940.

Bushell, Garvin, and Mark Tucker. *Jazz from the Beginning* (1988).

Charters, Samuel B., and Leonard Kunstadt. *Jazz: A History of the New York Scene* (1962; rpt. 1981).

Chilton, John. *Who's Who of Jazz: Storyville to Swing Street*, 4th ed. (1985).

Placksin, Sally. *American Women in Jazz, 1900 to the Present: Their Words, Lives, and Music* (1982).

Stewart-Baxter, Derrick. *Ma Rainey and the Classic Blues Singers* (1970).

This entry is taken from the *American National Biography* and is published here with the permission of the American Council of Learned Societies.

BARRY KERNFELD

Smith, Margaret Charles (12 Sept. 1906–11 Nov. 2004), midwife, was born to Beulah Sanders in Eutaw, Alabama. Perhaps very young, and unable to look after a baby, Beulah Sanders asked a local woman, Margaret Charles, to raise her child, because she had adopted and raised nine others. In her 1996 autobiography Margaret Charles Smith refers to her adoptive mother as both her "mama" and her grandmother, but it is unclear if Mrs. Charles was the biological or the adoptive mother of Beulah Sanders. Margaret Charles had been born in slavery in 1836 and sold to a family in the Alabama black belt for three dollars when she was thirteen. Smith never knew who her father was, and she "never did ask" because when she was a child, "you couldn't say things to old people, like children say to old people now, 'cause you got your tail tore up" (Smith, 27). Although her grandmother was also evasive about what happened to Beulah Sanders, Smith later discovered that her mother died soon after giving birth, perhaps of suicide.

Margaret Charles Smith was raised in a sturdy log cabin on land purchased for fifty cents an acre by her grandmother's husband, Henry Charles, after Emancipation. The land was swampy and heavily wooded, but the Charles family, aided by their neighbors, had cleared the worst of it by the time Smith was born. As a child she witnessed the strong sense of community among her neighbors at logrollings, at the cotton harvest, and, most notably, when someone was sick, dying, or pregnant. "Some come daytime and wash, iron, scrub, do anything, clean the house up, stay all night. Then tomorrow the next group come in, wash and scrub, put on peas and greens, whatever" (Smith, 26).

Although she admired such communal work habits, and in later life regretted their passing, Smith soon learned that children were also expected to participate. From an early age she pulled home her grandmother's nine cows from a nearby swamp every evening, did daily chores around the household and farmyard, and helped her adopted siblings to haul and sell lumber to white customers in Eutaw. She learned also to respect her elders, which meant accepting strict discipline at home, where she was frequently on the receiving end of her grandmother's "whoopings," and from the teachers at her one-room colored school, which was open only three months a year. During the summer months of her early teens, she began working as a cook, maid, and waitress at a vacation resort in the Tennessee mountains.

Despite an early exposure to hard work and physical pain, the sixteen-year-old Smith was not at all prepared for her first experience of childbirth, even though an experienced midwife attended the birth. She recalled that "instead of bearing, I raised and twisted a whole lot. I was down on the hard floor, and that floor was killing me. I wasn't able to walk in about two weeks after that baby," a son she named Houston (Smith, 47). Adamant that she wanted nothing to do with the baby's father, who "wasn't worth a shit nohow," she went back to housecleaning soon after the birth but shared child rearing duties with her grandmother (Smith, 44).

Smith gave birth again four years later on Christmas Eve 1926, but this time she delivered the baby on her own. Having gone into labor while cleaning for a white family, she rushed across the street to her cramped quarters, where her second son, Spencer, was born half an hour later. During both pregnancies, and in the weeks immediately following childbirth, she learned from her grandmother, midwives, and other women in the black community the various herbal remedies and traditional practices that eased the pains of labor, sped recovery, and brought good luck and health to mother and child. These included avoiding seeing sick or hurt animals during the early months of pregnancy, using jimsonweed to help with fever, and drinking bamboo briar tea to bring on contractions. Her grandmother also taught her to take the clothes she wore during labor and smoke them over a fire six or seven weeks after giving birth. This would give a woman the strength to go back to work. The folklore of Alabama midwives also recommended that women not work in the cotton fields for six weeks after giving birth, maintaining that the whiteness of the cotton would ruin their eyesight.

Three years after her grandmother died in 1943, Smith married Randolph Smith, a sharecropper she had known since childhood. One year later, seventeen years after the birth of Smith's second son, the couple's only child, Herman, was born. Fiercely independent, Smith continued to keep her own home but brought meals to her husband, who lived in a rented house nearby. Increasingly she wearied of helping her husband chop and plow his cotton in addition to doing her own farmwork and housework, particularly since Randolph Smith, like most black sharecroppers in Greene County, was unable to get out of debt to his white landowner no matter how hard he labored.

In 1949, determined to feed and clothe her family and to help her husband out of debt, Smith enrolled in midwifery classes at the Greene County Health Department. She also participated in the rigorous training program for lay midwives at Tuskegee University. The greatest influence on Smith's career, however, was the practical experience she had learned earlier from Ella Anderson, a friend, neighbor, and experienced midwife whom she assisted for more than a year. Because of the increasing interference and regulation of midwives by the Alabama department of health, Miss Anderson and many other midwives quit. Smith did not, even though she received no pay for the first year and was poorly paid in the years that followed. "After I took the oath to be a midwife," she recalled, "I just decided to stay around and do what they said" (Smith, 76).

Smith worked as a midwife in rural Alabama from 1948 to 1976, delivering more than 3,500 babies, but she was haunted throughout her life by the handful of children who died stillborn, including her very first delivery. Most of the women Smith cared for in her early years as a midwife gave birth at home, often in cramped and unsanitary homes. In the decades before desegregation, local white hospitals refused to accept black patients, while Tuskegee's maternity facilities, though among the best in the state, were more than two hundred miles from Greene County. Yet remarkably, despite the poverty and inadequate access to health care of her overwhelmingly African American patients, Smith never lost a single mother. She also earned the lifelong gratitude of mothers such as Augusta Duncan, who appreciated Smith's willingness to stay with her patients for as long as she was needed, both before and after they gave birth. She recalled, "couldn't no doctor in town or anywhere else" make "me feel any better than Mrs. Smith in assuring me that everything was going to be all right, and it was" (Smith, 84).

Much of Smith's success stemmed from her willingness to ignore health-board rules requiring that newborns be given separate sleeping quarters and prohibiting the use of herbal remedies. Since the only separate quarters available in many rural black homes was a cardboard box, she usually let the child lie in bed with the mother. Despite her misgivings Smith eventually stopped using herbal remedies when the state authorities made it a criminal offense. She nonetheless also recognized that "a midwife just can't say, 'you've got to do so-and-so'-" (Smith, 90). Thus while accepting that geophagy—eating clay or dirt—resulted in extremely difficult births for both mother and child, she recognized that rural Southern mothers of both races had done so for centuries and would not simply end the practice because medical authorities now prohibited it. Indeed, she even mailed boxes of Alabama earth to expectant mothers who had migrated to Chicago and other Northern cities and craved their native soil. For Smith, warm baths, massage, and exercise were essential for the mother during labor, but so too were patience, faith, and kind words from the midwife. "That means all of it," she believed. "Kindness whipped the devil" (Smith, 89).

The 1960s civil rights movement gradually ended the most blatant signs of racial discrimination in the Alabama black belt, but it did little to end racial inequality when it came to economic opportunity. By 1970 Greene County had more families living in poverty—most of them black— than any other county in Alabama, traditionally one of the nation's poorest states. Smith struggled, along with most of her neighbors. Because Alabama midwives were ineligible for Social Security, and because expectant black mothers were increasingly attended by obstetricians in hospitals, she made ends meet by continuing to farm her few acres. She also worked as a midwife in Birmingham, Tuscaloosa, and even Georgia, usually for white couples, and she helped care for the elderly. In 1976 the state of Alabama enacted legislation that essentially ended lay midwifery in the state. From a high of more than 2,600 midwives in the 1940s when Smith had begun "catching babies," fewer than 150 midwives, all of them black, remained in Alabama by 1976. Practically all of them had their midwifery permits revoked, including Smith in 1981.

Ironically, the ending of lay midwifery in Alabama coincided with a growing national movement to increase the number of full-time midwives. In the 1980s and 1990s a new generation of African American midwives drew upon the experiences of traditional midwives like ONNIE LEE LOGAN of Mobile, Alabama, who published her autobiography, *Motherwit*, in 1989, and Smith, whose own memoir, *Listen to Me Good*, appeared seven years later. In her final years, Smith at last received the accolades that her work as a midwife had long deserved. Among those organizations to honor her were the Black Women's Health Project Conference in Atlanta in 1983 and the Congressional Black Caucus in 2003.

In the intervening decades she lectured at midwifery conferences in Alabama, Georgia, Tennessee, and Oregon. She was also featured in a 2002 documentary about her life, *Miss Margaret*. One month before her death at age ninety-nine in November 2004, she attended the Third Annual Black Midwives and Healers Conference in Portland, Oregon, to accept their 2004 lifetime achievement award for outstanding dedication to midwifery and for services to her community.

FURTHER READING

Smith, Margaret Charles, and Linda Janet Holmes. *Listen to Me Good: The Life Story of an Alabama Midwife* (1996).

Obituary: Associated Press, 15 Nov. 2004.

STEVEN J. NIVEN

Smith, Marvin and Morgan Smith (16 Feb. 1910–9 Nov. 2003) and (16 Feb. 1910–7 Feb. 1993), artists who worked in photography and painting, were identical twin brothers born in Nicholasville, Kentucky, the only children of Charles Smith and Allena Smith, both sharecroppers. Raised in the rural town of Nicholasville, the Smith brothers divided their time between working in the fields alongside their parents and attending primary school. After Charles Smith took a job in the railroad industry, the family moved to Lexington, Kentucky, where Marvin and Morgan attended Paul Laurence Dunbar High School.

At Dunbar, the twins thrived, receiving special attention for their aptitude in painting and sculpture and for their skills on the football field. Through their respective jobs assisting prominent members of Lexington's white community, the Smith brothers met local photographer Matthew Archdeacon, who purchased a camera for them.

In 1933 the brothers graduated from high school; they were the first members of their family to do so. Although a number of historically black universities and colleges offered them football scholarships, the Smith brothers opted to pursue their artistic aspirations in Cincinnati, Ohio. Shortly after arriving in Ohio in 1933, they realized that greater opportunities could be found elsewhere and headed to New York.

The Smiths lived in Harlem and aligned themselves with local artists and arts organizations. In the Harlem Renaissance heyday of the 1920s, the neighborhood had been teeming with business, artistic, and social prospects; but the neighborhood was hit hard during the Great Depression. Organizations that supported the arts, such as the philanthropic Harmon Foundation, reduced their funding, and the number of individual patrons dwindled. In spite of the diminished opportunities available, the Smiths found employment with the Works Projects Administration (WPA). They took free classes with sculptor AUGUSTA SAVAGE at the Savage School of Arts and Crafts, where they worked with other artists, including JACOB LAWRENCE, GWENDOLYN KNIGHT, and ROBERT BLACKBURN. At the Savage School, the Smiths met identical twins Anna and Florence McClean. The two sets of twins married— Marvin to Florence and Morgan to Anna—in a joint ceremony in 1936. The four resided together in a midtown Manhattan apartment, but both couples ultimately divorced on their anniversary, either in 1937 or 1938, and the Smith brothers returned to Harlem. In 1948 Morgan married Jamaica-born coloratura soprano Monica Mais; they had one daughter, also named Monica.

The Smiths joined "306," a group of artists, performers, and writers who assembled at the studio of artist CHARLES ALSTON at 306 West 141 Street in Manhattan. Marvin continued to work at the New York Parks Department, but continued to hone his craft; and as a result, he won awards for his painting from the Federal Art Project (FAP). In 1937 Morgan Smith assisted Alston, Vertis C. Hayes, Sara Murrell, and Georgette Seabrooke (Powell) on an FAP-funded commission for Harlem Hospital's Nurses' Residence. The artists painted mural-size paintings on canvas and wall frescoes that represented African American history, culture, and achievement.

In the 1930s the Smiths began to submit their photographs to regional African American daily newspapers, such as Baltimore's *Afro-American*, the *Pittsburgh Courier* and New York's *Amsterdam News*. In 1937 Morgan entered the *New York Herald Tribune* amateur photography contest, sponsored by Kodak. His entry, *Robert Day Playing Hi-Li* (1937), won first place and received front page placement in the *Amsterdam News*; subsequently, Morgan was offered a full-time position as the paper's staff photographer.

Morgan and Marvin worked together as newspaper photographers, developing a realist style to highlight Harlem's unsung heroes, document the public and honorable private lives of black celebrities, and recognize African American achievement despite discrimination and adversity. The Smiths' images were in stark contrast to the images of other photojournalists, who overwhelmingly showed the devastating effects of poverty and racial inequality in Harlem.

In 1938 the Smiths opened their first photography studio in Harlem. The following year, they moved M. Smith Photo Studio to a second-story space at 243 West 125th Street, a location next door to the famous Apollo Theatre. On 125th Street, they witnessed and documented the social temperature of Harlem. They photographed street corner preachers, political rallies, and ADAM CLAYTON POWELL JR.'s strikes and protests against racially biased Harlem stores and unfair housing ordinances.

The Smiths experienced racism firsthand. Although M. Smith Photo Studio was one of the most popular (and profitable) independently owned businesses on 125th Street, their landlord, Frank Schiffman, refused to rent the ground floor to blacks, effectively limiting the possibility of expansion and advertising benefits for tenants of color. Continually resilient and industrious, the Smiths began to display their work on the ground floor.

Marvin Smith joined the U.S. Navy during World War II and made history by becoming the first African American to attend the Naval Air Station School of Photography and Motion Pictures in Pensacola, Florida. While his brother was away, Morgan Smith continued to offer his services to newspapers and began crediting his photographs to M. Smith or M. & M. Smith, underscoring their lifelong artistic collaboration. Morgan also began to work more closely with political organizations by freelancing for Adam Clayton Powell Jr.'s weekly newspaper, the *People's Voice*. After his discharge from the navy, Marvin Smith left for Paris, where he pursued his interest in abstract painting and met and worked with Pablo Picasso. In New York, Morgan learned sound recording, and was employed by W. E. B. DuBois and local bands. Eventually, he landed a position as a news and sound technician for the American Broadcasting Company. When Marvin returned to Harlem from France in 1952, he began working as a set and prop designer for television networks such as NBC and FOX. The Smith brothers concentrated less on their photography in the ensuing years, a time when technological advancements contributed to the decline of studio photography. In 1968 the M. Smith Photo Studio closed and the brothers retired from photography in 1975.

FURTHER READING

Smith, Marvin P. *Harlem: The Vision of Morgan and Marvin Smith* (1998).

Willis, Deborah, and Howard Dodson. *Black Photographers Bear Witness: 100 Years of Social Protest* (1989).

Willis, Deborah. *Reflections in Black: A History of Black Photographers, 1840 to the Present* (2000).

Obituary: *New York Times*, 12 November 2003.

MAKEBA G. DIXON-HILL

Smith, Mary Levi (30 Jan. 1936–), educator and university president, was born in Hazelnut, Mississippi, one of seven children of William Levi, a Church of God in Christ minister, and Byneter Markham Levi. Her father, whom Smith cited as her primary role model, encouraged his daughters to stay in school so they could become self-reliant. In 1953 Smith enrolled in Jackson State College (now Jackson State University) with the intention of becoming a nurse. After taking a dislike to the laboratory work and practical requirements of nursing, she shifted her focus to teaching. In 1957 Smith married Leroy Smith, whom she met at Jackson State; they would have two sons and a daughter. A month after her marriage, Smith graduated from college.

She began her career in education as an elementary school teacher in the public schools of Mississippi, Alabama, and Tennessee. Smith's collegiate career began at Tuskegee University. Smith and her husband spent their summers at the University of Kentucky in Lexington, his hometown, working on their master's degrees. She earned both her Master of Arts and Doctor of Education in curriculum and instruction from the university.

In 1970 she was appointed assistant coordinator of the EPDA In-Service Reading Program for Classroom Teachers of Kentucky at Kentucky State University in Frankfort. By 1974 she had been promoted to assistant professor, and she quickly rose in the ranks of the College of Education. She became the chairperson of the Division of Education, Human Services, and Technology in 1981; in 1983 she was chosen as the dean of the university's College of Applied Sciences. The Kentucky State University faculty recognized Smith as a leading educator and awarded her the outstanding faculty award in 1985. In 1988 she was appointed vice president of academic affairs and in less than a year she became interim president of the university upon the resignation of the president.

Smith served in the interim position for fourteen months until the new president began his term. Because of many controversial decisions, the new president was released, and Smith was named the eleventh president of Kentucky State University in October 1991, becoming the first female president in the university's 105-year history. She also became the first African American woman in the state to serve as a university president. During her presidency she focused on improving the financial stability of the university and establishing the campus's technology infrastructure.

Smith was recognized throughout her career with many honors. She was named an outstanding alumnus of Jackson State University in 1988 and was recognized by both the Alpha Kappa Alpha Sorority and Delta Sigma Theta Sorority for her accomplishments. In 1989 AKA's Phi Lambda Omega chapter of Louisville presented her with the Torchbearers and Trailblazers Education Award. This was followed in 1990 by her own Frankfort Alumnae Chapter of Delta Sigma Theta Sorority bestowing on her the Citizen Award. That same year she received the Lexington YWCA Women of Achievement Award and the NAACP's Woman of the Year Award. In 1994 Smith received the Woman of Achievement Award from the Frankfort Business and Professional Women and the Professional Achievement Award from the *Louisville Defender* newspaper. She was inducted into the University of Kentucky Hall of Distinguished Alumni in 1995.

Smith retired from Kentucky State in 1998. After forty-five years of marriage, in 2002 her husband died. In 2005 she published her memoirs, *In Spite of the Odds: Using Roadblocks, Pot Holes, and Hurdles as Stepping Stones to Success.* Following her retirement she remained active in local community groups, including the Frankfort Alumnae Chapter of Delta Sigma Theta and her church, St. John African Methodist Episcopal Church.

FURTHER READING

"Mary Levi Smith," in *Notable Black American Women, Book II*, ed. Jessie Carney Smith (1996).

"Mary Levi Smith," in *Kentucky Women: Two Centuries of Indomitable Spirit and Vision*, ed. Eugenia K. Potter (1997).

Smith, Mary Levi. *In Spite of the Odds: Using Roadblocks, Potholes, and Hurdles as Stepping Stones to Success* (2005).

Who's Who of American Women, 21st ed., (1998).

KAREN COTTON MCDANIEL

Smith, Maxine Atkins (31 Oct. 1929–), civil rights activist, was born in Memphis, Tennessee, the youngest of three children of Georgia Rounds Atkins and Joseph P. Atkins Sr., a postal worker. After graduating from high school at age fifteen, she entered Spelman College and became acquainted with MARTIN LUTHER KING JR., who was a student at Morehouse College. She graduated from Spelman in 1949 with an AB in biology. Because the University of Tennessee did not accept black students, the state of Tennessee paid her expenses to Middlebury College in Vermont, where she received a master's degree in French in 1950.

Smith began her career as an assistant professor of French at Prairie View A&M University in Prairie View, Texas, where she taught from 1950 to 1952; she relocated to Florida A&M in Tallahassee, Florida, in 1952. The following year she married Vasco Albert Smith Jr., a native of Memphis and eventually a full partner in her later activism. Smith was a captain in the air force, and from 1953 until 1955 he was stationed at Scott Air Force Base in Illinois, just east of St. Louis.

Smith and her husband had eagerly anticipated returning to Memphis from St. Louis. However, despite the 1954 *Brown v. Board of Education* Supreme Court decision, which ruled separate schools for blacks and white were illegal, no movement had been made in Memphis to comply, and the city and its schools remained segregated. Shortly after their return to Memphis in 1955, they became active members of the local NAACP branch. They were part of a younger generation of NAACP leaders, including H.-T. Lockard; Benjamin L. Hooks; A. W. Willis Jr.; Jesse H. Turner Sr.; and Laurie Sugarmon, all of whom gave new life to the black freedom struggle in Memphis by attacking the Jim Crow system through legal, political, and protest activity. Maxine taught at the historically black LeMoyne College (now LeMoyne-Owen College) from 1955 to 1956. Her teaching career ended after their son Vasco Albert Smith III was born in 1956.

Smith, along with Laurie Sugarmon (known later as Miriam DeCosta-Willis), applied to the all-white Memphis State College graduate program in 1957 but were denied admission because of their race. After hearing about the incident, Memphis NAACP branch officials called them to serve on the board. Smith soon became a full-time volunteer and its membership chair and coordinator of voter registration and education. W. C. Patton, a voter registration director for the national NAACP office, mentored her, and their efforts led to an unprecedented number of black Memphians being registered to vote in the late 1950s. "This was pre-sit-in movement," Smith explained. "We saw the ballot as the voice of our people."

Inspired by the Greensboro, North Carolina, sit-ins in February 1960, LeMoyne and Owen College students began their own sit-ins that following

March in Memphis. Their actions kicked off a twenty-month direct-action movement, which Smith coordinated. Not only students but also adults of all economic levels protested, and Memphis probably had more sit-ins than any other Southern city. They challenged segregated facilities and accommodations, including schools, buses, parks, libraries, museums, restaurants, transportation terminals, and churches. In November of 1961 leaders called off the protests after public and private facilities were desegregated.

Meanwhile, the Memphis NAACP branch became the largest one in the South, and Smith became its executive secretary in 1961. Along with their nonpartisan NAACP activity, Smith and other NAACP leaders worked through black political organizations as a means of gaining civil rights, and the Shelby County Democrat Club became the strongest of these local organizations. They also were members of the Bluff City and Shelby County Council of Civic Clubs, which also pressed for social improvements. This network of the NAACP branch, Democrat Club, and civic clubs had overlapping leadership and membership and was so powerful that other major civil rights organizations did not have a strong presence in Memphis.

Throughout the 1960s Smith and other civil rights activists continued to fight for equality on all fronts. Though all legal barriers to integration were removed by 1965, the Memphis NAACP, through a combination of litigation and direct action, worked tirelessly to eradicate remaining discriminatory practices in city government, hotels, hospitals, law enforcement, and housing. Voter registration numbers steadily rose, and blacks were elected to public office for the first time since the Reconstruction.

Smith also played a crucial role in the major local movements of the late 1960s. Sanitation workers went on strike in February 1968 to protest poor working conditions, and Smith was an influential member of the strike's coordinating committee. When Martin Luther King Jr. came to Memphis that April to support the strike, he was murdered. Not satisfied with persistent racial inequities in schools, Smith helped lead the "Black Monday" movement in 1969. Because schools were funded on the basis of average daily attendance, local NAACP leaders convinced black students and teachers to protest by staying home from school on Mondays. As a result, an agreement was reached that led to more blacks in administrative positions, including Smith's election as the first black member of the Memphis Board of Education in 1971 and the appointment of the district's first black superintendent, Willie Herenton, who became the city's first black mayor. Smith remained on the board until 1995, having served as its president for two terms.

In addition to her school board duties, Smith carried on with her NAACP and other political activities. She partnered with the business community to put on annual fund-raisers for the NAACP branch, and she remained active in politics, keeping in frequent contact with national, state, and local elected officials. When she stepped down as executive secretary of the Memphis NAACP branch in 1995, she left a formidable legacy. Not only had the branch received top state and regional awards annually but also received the organization's highest national honor, the Thalheimer Award, for every year except one during her tenure.

After her retirement from the NAACP branch and school board, Smith persisted in her social justice efforts and continued to accumulate honors. The many boards she joined included the national board of directors of the NAACP and the Board of Regents for the State of Tennessee, which controlled the schools that once denied her admission. She also chaired the NAACP's education division. During her lifetime, she received more than 160 awards and citations, including the nation's top urban education honor, the Richard R. Green Award. She also received two honorary doctorates and the National Freedom Award from the National Civil Rights Museum. No one was more closely associated with the Memphis civil rights struggle than Maxine Smith.

FURTHER READING

The Maxine A. Smith/NAACP Collection is located in the Memphis and Shelby County Room at the Memphis–Shelby County Public Library and Information Center, in Memphis, Tennessee. Her papers also may be found in the National Association for the Advancement of Colored People Papers both on microfilm and in the Manuscript Division of the Library of Congress in Washington, DC.

Beifuss, Joan Turner. *At the River I Stand: Memphis, the 1968 Strike, and Martin Luther King* (1989).

Duke, Kira V. "To Disturb the People as Little as Possible: The Desegregation of Memphis City Schools," master's thesis, University of Tennessee at Knoxville (2005).

Green, Laurie Beth. *Battling the Plantation Mentality: Memphis and the Black Freedom Struggle* (2007).

Gritter, Elizabeth. Interview with Maxine A. Smith. Transcript (Oct. 2000).

Gritter, Elizabeth. "Local Leaders and Community Soldiers: The Memphis Desegregation Movement, 1955–1961," honors senior thesis, American University, 2001.

Gritter, Elizabeth. Interview with Maxine A. Smith. Transcript (July 2004).

Hoppe, Sherry L., and Bruce W. Speck. *Maxine Smith's Unwilling Pupils* (2007).

Thomas, Bill, and Joan Beifuss. Interview with Maxine A. Smith (June 1968).

Tucker, David M. *Memphis Since Crump: Bossism, Blacks, and Civic Reformers, 1948–1968* (1980).

ELIZABETH GRITTER

Smith, N. Clark (31 July 1877–8 Oct. 1933), music educator, conductor, performer, and composer. Accounts of Smith's early life frequently contain unconfirmed or erroneous information. Leavenworth, Kansas, was his probable birthplace, and its 1870 census identified a three-year-old Clark Smith. The "N" does not stand for Nathaniel, as it is frequently cited, but for Noah (1880 census and *Leavenworth Herald*, 28 Aug. 1897). His parents were Kentucky-born Daniel Smith, and Missouri-born Margaret (Maggie) Davenport Smith. City directories identify Daniel's occupation as blacksmith and laborer. Smith indicated that his father had served in the military, but the National Archives could not verify this assertion. Educated in Leavenworth, Smith initially pursued a career in journalism. The 1880 census identified the fourteen-year-old as a "printer," and in 1888 he co-founded the *Leavenworth Advocate* newspaper. He also demonstrated his musical talent and capable leadership in community activities, and established a connection with the Hoffman Music Company, reportedly the largest music house west of Chicago.

Smith sold his interest in the Advocate Publishing Company in 1889 and married fourteen-year-old Laura Alice Lawson. (*Leavenworth Advocate*, 3 Aug. 1889). At this juncture, he shifted his vocation to music and became a church choir director in Columbia, Missouri, where his only child, Anna Lauretta, was born in 1893. By 1894 the family had settled in Wichita, Kansas, a larger community with greater opportunity. There he immediately became involved in a variety of musical activities. One of his earliest published compositions, the 1895 "Frederick Douglass Funeral March," honored the man he had met at the 1893 Chicago Columbian Exposition who significantly influenced his career.

FREDERICK DOUGLASS inspired him to explore the roots of his African musical heritage and its subsequent impact upon American music. The quest became a passionate dedication.

In 1885 Smith became musical director for Western University, a misnamed, small, struggling secondary school in Kansas City, Kansas. He also worked as an arranger and principal copyist for the Hoffman Music Company in its Kansas City, Missouri, branch. Hoffman published his "Pickaninny Band March," written for a youth band he organized, which John Philip Sousa reportedly called "the best kid band in the world" (*Leavenworth Herald*, 2 Nov. 1885). Smith's group received widespread accolades and played the Redpath Chautauqua circuit in 1898 (*Kansas City (Kansas) American Citizen*, 3 Mar. 1898). The following year the M. B. Curtis All Star Afro-American Minstrels engaged Smith's group to participate in a tour of Australia and New Zealand that featured ERNEST HOGAN, Billy McClain, ANNA MADAH HYERS (the "Bronze Patti"), and magician Carle Dante (Henry Sampson, *The Ghost Walks* [1988], 179).

Smith then moved to Chicago and worked for the Lyon & Healy music firm. Company administrators recognized his potential, contributed generously to his continuing education, and made contacts on his behalf to Chicago Musical College, from which he received unconfirmed undergraduate and graduate degrees (c. 1925). Although it proved to be short-lived, Smith and J. Bernie Barbour established what some contend to be the first black-owned music publishing house (*Indianapolis Freeman*, 2 Jan 1904). About this time Smith published *The Elements of Music*, a primer of traditional European theory with instructions explaining the rudiments of music and the art of singing by note. His expertise was recognized when he actively participated in Samuel Coleridge-Taylor's 1906 Chicago concert (*Chicago Tribune*, 2 Dec 1906).

Smith enlisted for three years as bandmaster for the Eighth Infantry, Illinois National Guard, in 1904. When his service ended, BOOKER T. WASHINGTON recruited him as bandmaster at Tuskegee Institute, where he received the rank of "captain."

He resigned in 1913, prompted by the arduous nature of the band tours and Washington's criticism of his music selections. But the experience at Tuskegee clarified Smith's career path; for the rest of his life he would teach music in public high schools that received federal assistance for military training programs. Once again he taught at

Western University where he rose to the rank of "major." In 1916 he accepted a teaching position at Lincoln High School in Kansas City, Missouri, and in 1925 became bandmaster at Chicago's Wendell Phillips High School. ROBERT S. ABBOTT, founder of the *Chicago Defender*, engaged Smith to create a marching band for his newsboys. Sumner High School in St. Louis, Missouri, became his final teaching position 1931–1935.

A significant aspect of Smith's legacy may be a consequence of his authoritative, distinguished bearing, coupled with his extraordinary teaching talent. He exercised stern classroom discipline, placed rigid demands upon his students, and strongly emphasized, in his own words, "conceptive and creative conceptive ability," which, he maintained should be the principal aim of the student (*Kansas City Call*, 1 Apr. 1922). Smith's educational philosophy, fused with the emerging generation's attraction to jazz provided his students with essential skills, and more than forty of them became professional musicians. As featured speaker, he commented on the origins of jazz at a 1922 Chicago memorial service for JAMES REESE EUROPE and challenged those who condemned the genre (*Chicago Defender*, 27 May 1922). Smith's personal commitment, however, operated within mainstream tradition.

In 1922, Smith accepted an offer from the Pullman Company, manufacturer of sleeping railroad cars, to organize Pullman porters into singing and instrumental groups. His responsibility extended to several northeastern sites, and while in New York he was invited to speak on African folk songs and melodies. Throughout his career Smith shared his knowledge and interest in African music through lectures, articles, public performances, and weekly broadcasts from St. Louis radio station KMOX, carried by the Columbia Broadcasting System (*St. Louis Argus*, 15 Feb. 1931). His dedication to amalgamating African and American traditions in contemporary compositions and performances brought him into working relationships with African emigrants in Chicago and St. Louis.

Throughout his career Smith worked with nationally recognized professional musicians. For Chicago's 1934 Century of Progress exposition, twenty-one contemporary composers collaborated to produce the featured attraction, *O, Sing a New Song*, a musical drama depicting the history of the African American. This extraordinary production brought together the illustrious talents of NOBLE SISSLE, Onah B. Spencer, Will H. Vodery, Henry Thacker Burleigh, Will Marion Cook, W. C. Handy, J. Rosamond Johnson, William Grant Still, and HARRY LAWRENCE FREEMAN. Critics regarded Smith and Freeman as representatives of scholarly musical endeavors and authorities on traditional African music (*Chicago Daily News*, 23 Aug. 1934). Prince Modupe Paris from Sierra Leone, director of the African exhibit, praised Smith for his exceptional knowledge of African Music (*St. Louis Argus*, 30 Sept. 1932).

Smith retired in 1935 and returned to Kansas City, his permanent residence, intent upon publishing his recent compositions. While conducting an orchestra at the local musician's headquarters he suffered a stroke and died shortly thereafter. His obituary appeared in many newspapers, including the *New York Times* (9 October 1935) and the *Chicago Defender* (12 October 1935). Smith was named one of fifty prominent Chicago citizens in 1929, and the WPA included him on its list of "Distinguished Negroes of St. Louis" in the 1930s.

Throughout his life Smith provided programs and entertainment for various civic and religious activities, and wherever he lived newspaper reports praised his work and applauded the performances of his choirs, ensembles, orchestras, and bands that frequently played his original compositions and arrangements. More than one hundred copies of Smith's published music have been identified. Three compositions received Wanamaker prizes: *Negro Folk Suite;* the Prelude from his five-part *Negro Choral Symphony;* and his arrangement of "Swing Low, Sweet Chariot." Smith pioneered in creating music that glorified his exalted concept of the African American tradition.

FURTHER READING

Copies of Smith's music are held by the Library of Congress, Special Collections; Miller Nichols Library, University of Missouri–Kansas City; Center for Black Music Research, Columbia College, Chicago; and Arthur B. Spingarn Collection, Howard University. A fire of undetermined date apparently destroyed most of Smith's personal papers.

Buckner, Reginald T. "Rediscovering Major N. Clark Smith," *Music Educators Journal* 71 no. 6 (Feb. 1985).

Ohman, Marian M. *Journal of the Illinois State Historical Society* 96 no. 1 (Spring 1903).

Pohly, Linda L. "N. Clark Smith's influence in Wichita: Toward a More Complete Biography," *Bulletin of*

Historical Research in Music Education 19, no. 2 (Jan 1998).

Scarborough, Ann. "Nathanial Clark Smith and the Development of Kansas City Jazz," (master's thesis, Sonoma State University, 1998).

DISCOGRAPHY

Two selections from Smith's *Negro Folk Suite* appear on the album *Black Music: The Written Tradition*, conducted by Michael Morgan, produced by Samuel A. Floyd, and recorded by the Black Music Repertory Ensemble in 1989.

MARIAN M. OHMAN

Smith, Nate (23 Feb. 1929–31 Mar. 2011), civil and labor rights activist, was born in Pittsburgh, Pennsylvania. In 1941, at the age of twelve, Smith ran away from home and joined the U.S. Navy. The navy did not discover their mistake in enlisting the underage Smith until he had reached the age of fourteen, by which time Smith had successfully passed through boot camp and sailed to Europe. During his two years in the navy, Smith would learn two skills that would greatly influence the course of his life: boxing and heavy equipment operation.

Upon his return to Pittsburgh in 1943, the fourteen-year-old Smith chose not to return to school. Instead he decided to devote himself full time to boxing. In two years as a middleweight fighter Smith participated in more than one hundred professional fights. He also met and developed a friendship with Edgar Kaufmann, a Pittsburgh department store owner and boxing fan who would go on to sponsor Smith's fight career as well as supporting his later efforts to integrate the building trades.

At age sixteen, having decided to end his fight career due to the damage his young body was taking, Smith turned to the other primary skill he acquired in the navy and tried to get a job as a heavy equipment operator. In the 1940s, however, construction unions, which controlled hiring for construction sites, were not yet integrated. Only the lowest paying and least desirable jobs were available for African American workers. In order to obtain his union card, Smith left tickets to a championship boxing match in the union office hoping that this would secure membership within the racially exclusionary union. As a result, he managed to secure a job as a heavy equipment operator with Local 66 of the International Union of Operating Engineers (IUOE).

Seeing few other African American workers in the craft unions, Smith began investigating union hiring practices. The response he received most often from the union leadership was that there were no trained minority workers. As a result Smith quickly set to work, using his weekends to train African Americans to operate cranes, bulldozers, and other heavy machinery. Soon, Smith decided to borrow against his home to pay for backhoes and scrapers, and in 1969, with additional financial backing from his friend Edgar Kaufmann, launched Operation Dig to offer formal training in heavy equipment operation. Also that year, Smith formed his own construction company, Nate Smith Enterprises, winning several contracts to work on stadiums, schools, and roads, always using integrated crews.

By 1971 ninety African American workers held union cards in western Pennsylvania and were employed on construction sites across the region. The program was such a success that similar initiatives were established across the United States, and in 1970 Smith was chosen by *Ebony* magazine as one of the one hundred most influential African Americans in the country.

Despite the important early victories won by Operation Dig, racism within the unions persisted, and white workers expressed fears about losing their jobs to African American workers. Because the workers being trained through Operation Dig were not being hired, in 1973 Smith helped to initiate the Black Construction Coalition; this organization, along with the NAACP and other civil rights organizations would confront unjust hiring practices. Out of the Black Construction Coalition grew the Pittsburgh Plan (1976), which was an effort of unions, community organizations, and local government to ensure the integration of the building trades.

Since Smith had been an active participant in the civil rights movement, he brought the lessons he learned marching in the South with Jessie Jackson to his attempts to organize in the building trades. Smith was also influenced by the black power movement and drew upon the practices of militant direct action in order to ensure that his struggles in the construction industry were successful. In the early and mid-1970s the Coalition was able to organize marches in Pittsburgh of almost a thousand people and the demonstrations did not shy away from open conflict with police who attempted to interfere with their goal. Marchers were beaten and jailed, but this punishment did not prevent them from participating in future demonstrations. Soon, more subversive tactics would be used by the Coalition.

Job sites where African Americans were being refused employment began to experience "accidents."

Smith himself recounts dangling a job supervisor out of a tenth floor window when he reneged on his promise to hire ten African American workers—Smith threatened to drop him if the workers were not hired. The ten black workers were soon hired on the spot.

The greatest successes, however, came when the Coalition carried out mass direct actions at the construction sites. The Coalition's most famous accomplishment was when they managed to temporarily shut down construction of Three Rivers Stadium, which was to be the home of Major League Baseball's Pittsburgh Pirates and the NFL's Pittsburgh Steelers. During demonstrations at the stadium site, Smith made national headlines by placing himself in front of a bulldozer to demand more jobs for African American workers. Overall, the Black Construction Coalition halted work on ten major construction projects.

During the 1990s Smith and contractor Gill Berry initiated a training program, Berry Enterprises in Partnership with Organized Labor, to help youth develop the skills needed to gain a union apprenticeship. In the late 1990s and 2000s Smith devoted his energies toward encouraging minority youth to pursue the opportunities that he himself helped to create in the building trades. He served as a board member of Renaissance III 2000 Inc., a preapprentice training program for women and people of color pursuing construction-related careers. Through this organization, sponsored by twenty-three trade unions, Smith also acted as a mentor and tutor for students in public schools in Pittsburgh and the surrounding region interested in careers in the building trades. He encouraged students to pursue careers in areas such as carpentry and electrical and operating engineering that have traditionally been less accessible to African Americans.

Over the years, Smith received numerous death threats and was once shot in the leg by someone aiming to stop his activism. Still, even close to his eightieth birthday he remained active in the ongoing struggle to place young women and minority workers into union jobs. Smith's work was formally honored with a plaque at Freedom Corner, Pittsburgh's main civil rights memorial. He died in Monroeville, Pennsylvania, at the age of 82.

FURTHER READING

"Pittsburgh labor activist Nate Smith pushes for more young minorities in building trades," *Jet* (Mar. 29 2004).

Plastrick, Stanley. "Confrontation in Pittsburgh," *Dissent* (Jan.–Feb. 1970).

JEFF SHANTZ

Smith, Nolle R., Sr. (26 Mar. 1889–9 Feb. 1982), engineer, tax expert, and U.S. State Department economic adviser to the Virgin Islands, Ecuador, Haiti, and Brazil, was born in a tent at Crow Creek Ranch, Cheyenne, in the Territory of Wyoming. Smith's mother, Melissa (Boulware) Smith, was the Missouri-born daughter of an African American mother and a Choctaw Indian father. Smith's father, Silas Peter Smith, was of Scottish-Irish parentage and had spent his early life in the trans-Mississippi West where he reputedly served as a scout for General George Armstrong Custer. Nolle (pronounced in Choctaw fashion, according to his mother, "Nulle") was one of nine children raised principally on Smith-owned ranches and dairy farms in the Cheyenne, Chugwater, and Casper regions of Wyoming. Smith's parents had settled in the frontier zone of Wyoming with the hope that their mixed-race children would there have a better chance of attaining the American dream of equality. After Smith's 1907 graduation from high school, he attended the University of Nebraska where he played football and earned a B.S. degree in Civil Engineering in 1911. Smith applied to West Point during his sophomore year but was denied entry. He believed that this rejection was based on his race.

After graduation from the university, Smith turned to Wyoming senator Francis E. Warren, a family friend, for career advice. Warren advised Smith to go to Hawaii where engineers were badly needed and where racism would not hold him back. Initially unwilling to leave the mainland, Smith delayed such a move, and between 1911 and 1914 he worked, instead, as a civil engineer in Wyoming and Colorado and as an assistant deputy county assessor in Denver. Smith's satisfaction with the Denver position was short-lived because of the openly expressed racism he encountered there, so he reconsidered the move to Hawaii. While he was reluctant to be seen as "running away," he was frustrated with American society's inability to judge him on his individual qualities and capabilities. Smith's insistence on individual merit and his desire to forge a reputation separate from a group identity would be a constant in his life. Frequently labeled by others in his wide-ranging public career as "an outstanding Negro," Smith just as frequently asserted that his own goal was to be "an outstanding

American" (*Honolulu Advertiser*, 20 Aug. 1971). Hawaii offered Smith the opportunity to pursue this goal; as he informed a sociologist researching black life in Hawaii in the 1940s, "There are obstacles, but they are more easily overcome here than elsewhere" (Lee, 437).

Smith arrived in Hawaii in 1915 with introductions from Senator Warren to prominent businessmen who were originally from Wyoming. "None had been [in Hawaii] more than ten years, but Bob Shingle, son of a Wyoming railroad conductor, was now head of Waterhouse Trust, Charlie Bond was postmaster of Honolulu, Bob Breckons was U.S. district attorney for Hawaii, and Ed Towse was editor and publisher of his own newspaper. After an exchange of Wyoming news and reminiscence, Bob Breckons told Nolle what his responsibilities would would be" (Gugliotta, 79). In Honolulu, he worked as an engineer in both the private and public sectors and as dock superintendent for the city's largest shipping firm, the Matson Navigation Company.

On 4 July 1916, Smith married Eva B. Jones, originally from San Francisco. An accomplished pianist, Jones also hosted, under the name Eve Cunningham, a Honolulu radio program during the 1930s that featured children's stories and music.

In 1920 Smith founded the Smith Construction Company. Wanting his family who resided on the mainland to experience the racial *aloha* of Hawaii (its lack of overt racial prejudice), Smith brought his parents and younger siblings to Hawaii to live with him, his wife, their daughter Iwalani, and their son Nolle Jr. Two additional daughters were born between 1920 and 1924, Leinani and Tsulan. Smith's mother remained in Hawaii until her death in 1965; Smith's father returned to Denver, Colorado, in the 1930s, following the death of his younger son, Donald, in an auto accident.

In 1924 the family moved to Honolulu's Kalihi area and settled in what was then a predominantly Portuguese district. Smith quickly became known in the community, volunteering as a basketball coach at a nearby settlement house, and serving as president of the Kalihi Valley Improvement Club. A lifelong Republican, Smith entered politics in 1928 and won a seat in the territorial house of representatives, serving from 1929 to 1932.

In 1932 Smith was appointed secretary of the Hawaii Bureau of Government Research. Although it was a privately funded organization, the research bureau was closely associated with the territorial budget bureau and other governmental entities.

The budget bureau specialized in investigations and reports on ways to make government agencies and institutions more "efficient," a social and political watchword of the day. One step in improving government efficiency was the development of a territorial civil service system. To this end, Smith was sent in 1936 on a three-month tour of mainland cities to gather information on civil service plans applicable to local governments, and he presented his findings to Governor Joseph Poindexter later that year. Three years later, a civil service bill for Hawaii passed.

Amidst political controversy, Smith was passed over for the directorship of the new territorial civil service commission, but a position was created for him at the territorial Bureau of the Budget as director of statistics and research. He held this position until 1942, when he assumed the directorship of the Hawaii Civil Service Commission for one year. His brief tenure was made problematic not only by wartime conditions in Hawaii following the attack on Pearl Harbor in 1941, but by what one Honolulu newspaper termed, "feuds and frictions" (*Honolulu Star-Bulletin*, 6 Feb. 1943). Smith returned to private business interests between 1943 and 1947.

From 1947 to 1954, Smith worked as assistant director of the Hawaii Chamber of Commerce's Tax Study Committee. During this period Smith also played a minor role in the McCarthy-era Red Scare that swept all parts of the nation, including Hawaii. In 1952, Smith was given a seat on the Territorial Loyalty Board, and in 1953 he was a government witness, testifying against a teacher, John Reinecke, who was charged with conspiring, as a leader of the Communist Party of Hawaii, to advocate the overthrow of the U.S. government. Smith was called as a government rebuttal witness, and he testified that Reinecke's reputation as a loyal American was "bad" (*Honolulu Advertiser*, 8 May 1953). John Reinecke was one of the so-called Hawaii Seven; convicted in 1953, all seven were acquitted on appeal in 1958.

At age sixty-five, Smith began work with the U.S. State Department. Following a year as tax consultant and commissioner of insular affairs for the government of the Virgin Islands, between 1955 and 1963 Smith served as an economic adviser for foreign aid programs in South America and the Caribbean. In newspaper interviews at the time, Smith emphasized the Cold War, anticommunist thrust of his USAID assignments in Ecuador, Haiti, and Brazil. When he returned to Honolulu in 1964, Smith became a partner in a ranch with his son.

Smith died in Honolulu one month short of his ninety-third year.

FURTHER READING

Records pertaining to Smith's work within the territorial government of Hawaii may be found at the Hawaii State Archives, Honolulu.

Gugliotta, Bobette. *Nolle Smith: Cowboy, Engineer, Statesman* (1971).

Harlocker, Nancy. "A Man Who Never Quit," *Honolulu Advertiser*, 20 Aug. 1971.

Lee, Lloyd L. "The Negro in the Hawaiian Community," *American Sociological Review* 13, no. 4 (Aug. 1948).

JANINE RICHARDSON

Smith, Otis W. (12 May 1925–5 Feb. 2007), pediatrician, civil rights and community activist was born Otis Wesley Smith in Atlanta, Georgia, to Ralph Horatio Smith, a baker, and Gertrude Wyche Smith, a housekeeper. Smith's early life and his decision to become a physician were greatly influenced by the untimely death of his father following complications during surgery. Young Smith prayed for his father's recovery and promised he would become a physician for Atlanta's African American community.

Smith attended BOOKER T. WASHINGTON High School, the first public high school for African Americans in Atlanta. In high school Smith, an avid sports enthusiast, was only allowed to participate in boxing; however, his opportunities to participate in sports flourished when he entered Morehouse College as a freshman in 1943. He majored in biology and worked part time at the Butler Street Young Men's Christian Association (YMCA) where he played basketball in the afternoon with MARTIN LUTHER KING JR. on a team called the City Slickers. At Morehouse, Smith was a member of all four of the school's varsity teams and the only Morehouse athlete documented to have received a letter in basketball, football, baseball, and track. His determination to seize every opportunity to score points in basketball earned him the nickname "Will Shoot." Smith was awarded a B.S. in biology from Morehouse in 1947.

In the three-year interim between college and medical school, Smith taught high school science and mathematics, and he enrolled in graduate courses in biology at Atlanta University. Smith entered Meharry Medical College in Nashville, Tennessee, in 1950. As with many African American students during the mid-twentieth century, funding for postgraduate study was extremely limited. This situation led to an unusual and little known coalition between Dr. BENJAMIN E. MAYS, president of Morehouse College, and Margaret Mitchell, author of *Gone With the Wind*, to finance the medical education of a number of Morehouse graduates. In 1946 an unannounced fund was established at Morehouse with money from Mitchell to "further medical education among Negroes" (Johnson and Pickens, 12). Smith, one of the recipients of financial support from the fund, learned of his benefactor years later in a confidential conversation with Mays. Smith also received funds to help pay for his final year in medical school from the Georgia Board of Regents, with the proviso that he practice medicine for at least fifteen months in a rural area of the state. This decision would later play a pivotal role in the life of the young doctor. After graduating from Meharry, Smith married Gwendolyn Melba Harris on 13 June 1954. Harris had graduated from Meharry as a registered nurse and the couple would have one son, Ralph Hugh Smith. Upon completion of his internship and initial residency at Homer G. Phillips Hospital in St. Louis, Missouri, Smith established a medical practice in Fort Valley, Georgia. He later completed a residency in pediatrics at Homer G. Phillips in 1963.

In the early 1960s, as the civil rights movement gained momentum, Smith sought to fulfill his commitment to the Georgia Board of Regents to practice medicine in a rural area. He chose Fort Valley, a small town in middle Georgia that had been without an African American physician for several years. After establishing his practice in the rural community, an incident occurred that could have ended Smith's career as well as his life. While talking to one of his patients on a telephone party line, Smith was abruptly interrupted by a white woman who wanted him to relinquish the telephone for her use. A heated and racially charged exchange occurred with the woman that led to Smith's arrest. Smith was sentenced to eight months on a chain gang for using inappropriate language to a white woman with the option to apologize and avoid incarceration. Smith refused to apologize and remained in jail until a visit from his mentor and friend Dr. Benjamin Mays. Mays convinced Smith to apologize because, as he told Smith, his life was "too valuable" to lose (Blake, *Atlanta Journal-Constitution*, Aug. 1994, D3). Smith agreed to apologize and returned to Atlanta where he established a practice and became the beloved pediatrician of generations of Atlanta's kids.

In the mid-1960s, Smith became engaged in efforts to desegregate hospitals in Georgia and was named Chairman of the Implementation Committee of the Atlanta Medical Association. The committee visited hospitals that received Medicare funding and compiled evidence of racial discrimination and noncompliance with the federal guidelines of Title 6 and the Medicare program. Smith and the committee presented their findings to the Department of Health Education and Welfare (HEW) and met with HEW officials in Washington 6 July 1966 to discuss implementation of Title 6. Following a delay in implementation of the guidelines by HEW, Smith sent two telegrams to President Lyndon B. Johnson dated 29 July 1966 and 17 August 1966, stating the gravity of the situation in view of racial tension in the South at that time. The White House referred both telegrams to the Secretary of HEW for action. The successful efforts of Smith and the Implementation Committee culminated with an invitation from HEW to attend a White House announcement of the integration of hospitals throughout the nation. Also in 1966 Smith became the first African American physician certified by the American Academy of Pediatrics to practice in Georgia. He was named Physician of the Year by the Atlanta Medical Association in 1969.

Four years after being named Physician of the Year by the Atlanta Medical Association again in 1983, Smith retired from medical practice in 1987 and focused his attention and energy on community activism. In 1988 he was elected president of the Atlanta Chapter of the NAACP to succeed JULIAN BOND. As local NAACP president, Smith sought to alleviate some of the social ills in Atlanta's African American community and increase membership in the organization. During the 1980s and 1990s he served on numerous boards for medical, educational, civic and religious organizations, including the Fulton and DeKalb Hospital Authority, the Morehouse School of Medicine, Meharry Medical College, and the Sickle Cell Anemia Foundation of Georgia. Smith was also a board member of Turner Seminary of the Interdenominational Theological Center, and on the board of directors of the Concerned Black Clergy; and he was a member of the board of trustees of his church, the Saint Mark African Methodist Episcopal Church.

Smith's activism also extended to his involvement in the project to renovate the house where Margaret Mitchell wrote Gone With the Wind. In the early 1990s Smith contributed $10,000 to restore the Mitchell house, a contribution that served as the foundation for fund-raising efforts. He became a founding member and later board chairman of the Margaret Mitchell House and Museum. After a number of setbacks, including arson, the renovated Margaret Mitchell House was opened to the public in May 1997. Some in Atlanta's African American community questioned Smith's participation in the project, noting its connection to the history of slavery. Smith was undaunted by the criticism and stated that by telling Mitchell's story, he sought to repay the woman who helped finance his medical education and that of several other physicians. Similarly, Smith was known for his own "behind the scenes" philanthropy. Beginning in 1994 he provided scholarships at Morehouse College to assist deserving medical students, many of whom did not know their benefactor. According to his wife Gwendolyn, Smith "preached the theme of giving back to the community" (Georgia General Assembly Senate Resolution 317, Feb. 2007). He also urged young people to prepare themselves to go back to their communities and help "bring someone forward" (Georgia General Assembly Senate Resolution 317, Feb. 2007).

Just as a young Smith had promised his dying father years before, Smith's commitment to improving health care in Atlanta was fulfilled during nearly fifty years of medical service and community activism. Throughout his career Smith received many awards and citations for his achievements, and he received citations from three Georgia governors, including one from Georgia Governor Roy Barnes in 1998. In recognition of his service to health care, on 23 July 1998 the Fulton and DeKalb Hospital Authority dedicated a building located on Martin Luther King Jr. Drive as the Otis W. Smith, M.D. Health Center, a satellite facility of the Grady Health System. In 1985 Smith received the Turner Broadcasting "Trumpet Award" for outstanding community service, and he was the recipient of the first Benjamin E. Mays Service Award from Morehouse College in 1989. That same year he also received the NAACP Freedom Hall of Fame and Nash-Carter Awards. In February of 2007 Smith died in Atlanta of complications from Alzheimer's disease. Many remembered him as warm hearted, charismatic and beloved by family, friends, and the many young people who were his patients; he was also remembered for his fight against racial injustice. As a final tribute, on 26 February 2007 Smith was inducted into the International Civil Rights Walk of Fame at the Martin Luther King Jr. National Historic Site in Atlanta, Georgia.

FURTHER READING

Copies of documents used to prepare this biography are from the Lyndon Baines Johnson Library, Austin Texas, White House Central Files Archives, Box 3 and Box S 406.

Blake, John. "Protégés Pay Tribute to a Mentor and Scholar," *Atlanta Journal Constitution* (Aug. 1994).

Crenshaw, Holly. "College Park: Otis Smith, 81, pioneer doctor, rights activist." *Atlanta Journal-Constitution* (Feb. 2007).

Durcanin, Cynthia. "NAACP Elects Dr. Otis W. Smith As Its President," *Atlanta Journal-Constitution* (Dec. 1988).

Georgia General Assembly Senate Resolution 317. "Smith, Dr. Otis W., condolences" (22 Feb. 2007).

Johnson, Ira Joe, and William G. Pickens. *Benjamin E. Mays & Margaret Mitchell: A Unique Legacy in Medicine* (1996).

ROSALYN MITCHELL PATTERSON

Smith, Owen L. W. (18 May 1851–5 Jan. 1926), minister, magistrate, and diplomat, was born Owen Lun West Smith in Giddensville, Sampson County, North Carolina, the son of Ollen Smith and Maria (Hicks), both slaves. Although Owen was only ten years old when the Civil War broke out in 1861, he served for part of the war as the personal servant of a Confederate officer, most likely his owner or a son of his owner. Several accounts suggest that Smith was present at the Battle of Bentonville in North Carolina near the war's end in March 1865. Some of these accounts insist that he was still a body servant for a Confederate soldier. Others claim that that by the age of thirteen, in 1864, Smith, like many eastern North Carolina slaves and some "buffaloes"— poor whites hostile to the area's wealthy and all-powerful slave owners—had fled the Confederate lines to join the Union army, which at that time controlled much of that region of North Carolina. After Bentonville, Smith, by all accounts in the Union army by this time, marched to Goldsboro, North Carolina, where he joined up with the advancing troops of General William T. Sherman and others. He marched with them to Alexandria, Virginia, and Washington, D.C., where in May 1865 at the age of fourteen he participated in a parade marking the end of the Civil War.

Owen Smith took advantage of the new opportunities open to African Americans under Reconstruction. He returned to his mother's home in New Bern, North Carolina, in 1865 to attend a private school run by a minister in the African

Methodist Episcopal Zion (AME Zion) Church. Smith's studies continued over the next four years under the tutelage of a Northern teacher (whose name and race are now unknown) in nearby Pitt County, where he learned Greek, Latin, and French. To pay for his studies he worked on a Pitt County farm owned by a white Northerner. Although he had intended to move to New Orleans, Smith found himself at the age of twenty a schoolteacher in Pickens County, South Carolina, where in 1873 he was appointed magistrate by the Reconstruction governor, Franklin J. Moses. In 1874 Smith entered the University of South Carolina's law school in Columbia—where his classmates included the future diplomats RICHARD T. GREENER and T. McCANTS STEWART—but he was forced to abandon his legal studies in 1877 when South Carolina once again prohibited African Americans from attending its flagship state university.

The end of Reconstruction does not appear to have deterred Smith's legal ambitions. He practiced law for a while in North Carolina, where he had returned in the late 1870s to teach and to dabble in politics. In October 1880, however, Smith was saved at a camp meeting of the AME Zion Church, and four months later he was licensed as a preacher in Whiteville, North Carolina, where he served as deacon until late 1883 when he pastored several congregations throughout eastern North Carolina. In 1885 he was ordained as the pastor of Saint John's AME Zion Church in Wilson, North Carolina, and was active in strengthening that denomination throughout the state. He served as secretary of the denomination's Sunday school convention, as corresponding editor of the state's most popular black newspaper, the *Star of Zion*, and beginning in 1890 as presiding elder of the AME Zion Church in New Bern. In 1898 Livingstone College, an institution founded and supported by the AME Zion Church, awarded Smith a Doctorate in Divinity in honor of his work for the denomination.

In spite of his professional successes Smith's personal life was troubled. His first marriage, to Lucy Ann Jackson, lasted thirteen years, but it was childless and ended in tragedy when a mentally disturbed relative shot and killed his wife in July 1891. Six months later Smith married Adora Estelle Oden; their three children died before reaching adulthood. While in Liberia the Smiths adopted a daughter, Carrie Emma Johnson, who died at age seventeen in Winston-Salem, North Carolina, while she was studying to be a missionary. In 1909, three years after Adora's death, Smith married a third time, to Cynthia Ann King Isler, who had four children from a previous marriage.

The persistence of black electoral power in North Carolina in the 1890s propelled Owen L. W. Smith from the pulpit to politics. In January 1898 the Republican president William McKinley nominated Smith as U.S. minister resident and consul general to Liberia, one of only two diplomatic posts for which blacks were at that time eligible (the other was minister to Haiti, a post held by FREDERICK DOUGLASS, among others). Representative GEORGE H. WHITE of New Bern and North Carolina's Second Congressional District, the only African American in the U.S. Congress at that time, vigorously supported Smith's candidacy, as did several white North Carolina Republicans. Despite strong opposition to the appointment by white supremacist Democrats, Smith's appointment was confirmed by Congress, and he arrived in Monrovia in early May 1898.

Upon being presented to the president of Liberia at Monrovia on 2 May 1898, Smith gave a traditional ceremonial address in which he declared himself the official representative "not only of The United States as a whole, but also of eight million human beings, descendants of the sons of Ham, constituting a part of that great whole whose sympathies are coeval with yours, and whose forefathers once dwelt upon this grand old continent" (Ingram, 7). Smith's goal as minister resident and consul general to Liberia was to improve trade and commercial links between the two republics. He looked forward to a day when "the businessman of America, the tourist, or the pleasure seeker, shall no longer look upon the passage from America to Africa as hazardous, but rather as a matter of business, attended with pleasure or profit" (Ingram, 8).

The prospects of such friendly commerce was limited, however, by the policies of the Liberian president William D. Coleman, who assumed office in 1896 with plans to extend Monrovia's political and economic influence into the undeveloped interior of Liberia. Smith reported in dispatches to the State Department in Washington in late May 1898 that Coleman's policies were opposed by the "masses of the people of Liberia" (Ingram, 11). In particular Smith noted that Coleman favored the Mandingo tribe, who lived in the Liberian interior but who were prevented from trading with Monrovia by the Golah people, whose lands lay between the Mandingo and Monrovia. The Golah, who had earlier defeated the Mandingo in war, placed a blockade on commerce between them and the Liberian

capital and successfully resisted government efforts to subdue them and their allies. The broad opposition to Coleman's aggressive policies, which Smith appeared to share, ultimately resulted in the president's forced resignation in 1902.

Smith's dispatches to Washington indicated that racial violence in America in the late 1890s was even more disruptive to the prospect of trade between Liberia and the United States. He would have been particularly aware of developments in North Carolina, where a race riot in Wilmington in 1898 resulted in the deaths of many African Americans, including the newspaper editor ALEX MANLY, and the destruction of black property. The escalating number of Southern lynchings of blacks and the successful efforts of several Southern states to disenfranchise African Americans had the effect, in Smith's view, of dissuading Liberian businessmen, many of them formerly American citizens, from trading with the United States. He informed the secretary of state John Hay in August 1899 that Liberian merchants were seeking closer alliances with European merchants instead.

Upon the assassination of President William McKinley in 1901, Theodore Roosevelt assumed the presidency and appointed a new consul general to Liberia to replace Smith early in 1902. Although Smith had been gone for only four years, race relations in his home state had been transformed in the meantime. The fusion government that had joined black and white Republicans and white Populists had been replaced by conservative, white supremacist, Democratic Party control. A new state constitution, passed amid great violence and intimidation of black voters in 1900, greatly restricted African American voting rights and resulted in the defeat of Congressman George White, Smith's benefactor. North Carolina would send no other African Americans to the U.S. Congress until 1992. Any political ambitions that Smith may have harbored were therefore moot upon his return. In his final years he devoted his energies to fraternal affairs and to the AME Zion Church, particularly as pastor of Saint John's Church in Wilson, North Carolina.

Smith died at his Wilson home in 1926, at age seventy-four. At each stage of his life he took maximum advantage of the opportunities available to him, as a slave who ran off to join the Union troops, as a freedman who benefited from the opening of Southern education to African Americans, as a Christian who rose through the ranks of a new black denomination, the AME Zion Church, and as a Republican who enjoyed the benefits of limited black political power in North Carolina in the 1890s.

FURTHER READING

Ingram, E. Renée. "Reverend Dr. Owen Lun West Smith: From Minister to Minister Resident and Consul General," *Journal of the Afro-American Historical and Genealogical Society* 20, no. 1 (2001).

Padgett, James A. "Ministers to Liberia and Their Diplomacy," *Journal of Negro History* 22, no. 1 (Jan. 1937).

STEVEN J. NIVEN

Smith, Ozzie (26 Dec. 1954–), baseball player, was born Osborne Earl Smith in Mobile, Alabama, to Clovis Smith, a truck driver, and Marvella Smith, a homemaker. When Ozzie was six, his parents moved with their five children to the Watts section of Los Angeles. Smith took up baseball at a young age, and rarely went anywhere without a ball in his hands. Developing his hand-eye coordination by spending hours fielding a rubber ball thrown against his house, Smith eventually played shortstop at Locke High School, which he entered in the fall of 1969. His small frame kept him from being noticed by baseball scouts, many of whom were interested in Smith's teammate and future Hall-of-Famer EDDIE MURRAY.

Graduating from high school in 1973, Smith enrolled that fall at California State Polytechnic University at San Luis Obispo on a government grant, and made the baseball team as a walk-on. Taught to switch-hit by his college coach, he turned down an offer from the Detroit Tigers during his junior year, but signed with the San Diego Padres after being selected in the fourth round of the 1977 amateur draft. Smith had a good college baseball career: he became the team's starting shortstop during his freshman year, was named to the All-California Collegiate Athletic Association first team (for California's best players) twice, and set Cal Poly records for stolen bases in a season and in a career. He began playing for the Padres' Walla Walla, Washington, Class-A affiliate immediately after graduating in 1977. That summer Smith hit .303 in Walla Walla, leading the Northwest League in stolen bases and runs scored; he also topped all shortstops in fielding percentage and assists. After being noticed that fall in the Arizona Instructional League, Smith was chosen to be San Diego's starting shortstop for the 1978 season. Padres skipper Roger Craig was effusive with praise for Smith, who ended up leading the team in games played. Smith

Ozzie Smith, St. Louis Cardinals' shortstop, during a World Series game in Kansas City, Mo., 26 October 1985. (AP Images.)

finished his first season with unimpressive offensive statistics, but his acrobatic fielding became known around the league. Smith's impressive midair, barehanded grab of a ground ball hit by Atlanta Braves outfielder Jeff Burroughs became known as "The Play": Burroughs had hit a groundball up the middle, and Smith dove to where it would be heading; instead, the ball took a wicked hop off a rock, changing course and caroming into the air, so while he was essentially horizontal, getting ready to snag the ball where it ought to be—given its natural trajectory—Smith reached to his other side and grabbed it with his bare hand. It was considered one of the all-time best defensive plays in the sport, and set the standard for shortstops' fielding prowess. Buoyed by his defensive play and forty stolen bases, Smith finished second in National League Rookie-of-the-Year balloting. When he performed a back flip on the field during Fan Appreciation Day toward the end of the season, he started a much-loved ritual that lasted throughout his career. While his defensive play with the Padres won him two Gold Gloves in 1980 and 1981, and brought him to an All-Star Game appearance in 1981 and the nickname "The Wizard of Oz," Smith's offensive output remained lackluster. He had proven his ability to steal bases, but with a batting average hovering around .230, the Padres couldn't justify giving him a raise. When contract negotiations stalled, San Diego traded him in February 1982 to the St. Louis Cardinals for Garry Templeton.

Now with manager Whitey Herzog and his slap-and-run offense on the Astroturf of Busch Stadium, Smith and the Cardinals thrived. In 1983, his first year in St. Louis, Smith made his second All-Star Game appearance and won his third Gold

Glove while helping the Cardinals to a World Series victory over the Milwaukee Brewers. With Smith and speedy outfielders Willie McGee and Vince Coleman, the Cardinals were a divisional contender throughout the 1980s, winning two more pennants in 1985 and 1987. Although they lacked a power hitter for much of the decade, Smith's own offense blossomed until he became a formidable weapon in St. Louis's attack. He raised his batting average in five consecutive seasons beginning in 1983, and Smith hit his first career left-handed home run to win Game Five of the 1985 National League Championship Series against the Los Angeles Dodgers.

Smith enjoyed his finest offensive year in 1987, when he combined his expert fielding with a .303 batting average, 104 runs scored, and forty-three stolen bases for a second-place finish in that year's MVP voting. For the second time in three years, however, the Cardinals were denied another World Series win, falling to the Minnesota Twins in seven games.

Smith remained with the Cardinals into the 1990s, and while his speed and offensive skills began to show signs of regression, he maintained his discipline and defensive wizardry. In 1991 a thirty-five-year-old Smith broke the record for fewest errors as a shortstop in a single season with only eight. He received his thirteenth and final Gold Glove in 1992, and also recorded his two thousandth hit and his five hundredth stolen base. He won St. Louis' Man of the Year Award that same year and the Branch Rickey Award in 1994. After missing the All-Star Game in 1993, fans overwhelmingly voted to bring him back in 1994. Also that year, he broke the record for most assists by a shortstop. In 1995 he won the ROBERTO CLEMENTE Award for his contributions to community service, including his involvement with children's organizations like Ronald McDonald House, the Boys' Club of St. Louis, and Annie Malone's Children and Family Center of St. Louis.

Smith's final campaign in 1996 brought some heartache; along with his impending divorce from his wife Denise, he had to fight for playing time after the Cardinals traded for shortstop Royce Clayton. Despite outperforming the younger Clayton offensively and defensively during spring training, Smith found himself relegated to a back-up job by new manager Tony LaRussa, with whom Smith began a bitter and public feud. Smith announced his retirement in June, and made his fifteenth and final All-Star Game appearance that July, receiving a standing ovation during his first at bat from fans and players alike. At the end of the season, he received a special tribute at each stadium the club visited, culminating in Ozzie Smith Day in St. Louis on 28 September 1996.

Smith's interests outside of baseball kept him busy throughout his career. His grace and sharp style allowed for an easy transition to television, as Smith soon took over for Mel Allen on the television show *This Week in Baseball*, and he also became a baseball analyst and columnist for CNN/SI in 1998. However, the dispute with LaRussa stayed with Smith, and in his retirement, he distanced himself from the franchise, implying that he would have better ties once management (i.e., LaRussa) changed.

Smith was overwhelmingly voted into the Baseball Hall of Fame on his first year of eligibility in 2002. The only player to be selected that year by the writers, Smith made an eloquent speech combining the layers of a baseball and the mythology of the "The Wizard of Oz." Smith correlated the layers of a baseball—the two rubber centers, the twine, and the horsehide cover—with the Wizard of Oz characters' desires. The three characters whom Dorothy meets in Oz are looking for attributes that would make them whole; in this way, the layers of the baseball represented for Ozzie the attributes that made him whole, closely linked to the movie. The rubber centers represented faith in God and faith in himself; the twine represented the people who were his protection and inspiration in life; and the outer shell was durability and resilience. Smith's journey from Alabama, to Watts, and finally to Major League Baseball remained an inspiration for inner-city children trying to make it out of poor neighborhoods through sports and the hope of academic scholarships. Along with his success on the diamond, Smith's continued involvement in charities and kids' organizations led him to be a hero not just in his adopted hometown of St. Louis, but also in numerous cities in America. In his newly created role of Education Ambassador for the Hall of Fame, Smith used his charity Play Ball with Ozzie Smith to raise funds for the museum's educational programs and scholarships.

FURTHER READING

Smith, Ozzie, with Rob Rains. *Wizard* (1988).
Smith, Ozzie, with Rob Rains. *Ozzie Smith: The Road to Cooperstown* (2002).
Berkow, Ira. "To Cooperstown with Glove, the Wizard," *New York Times,* July 2002.
Geffner, Michael P. "Cardinal Singe," *Sporting News* (July 1996).

ADAM W. GREEN

Smith, Patricia (6 June 1955–), journalist and poet, was born in Chicago, Illinois, the daughter of Otis Douglas Smith and Annie Pearl, who both worked at the local Leaf Candy Company. Raised on the disadvantaged West Side, Smith never felt deprived or ashamed of the community in which she lived. An only child, Smith's needs were met and, most often, exceeded. Smith attended Jacob Beidler Elementary School, Morton Upper Grade Center, and Carl Schurz High School.

As a teenager Smith concluded that newspapers were "magic" because they informed the community and their reports changed daily. With most of Smith's family believing that a black woman must be one of two things, either a nurse or a teacher, her journalistic ambitions were not taken seriously. As far as journalism and reporting were concerned, Smith's mother would repeatedly say, "Only white men do that." Her father, on the other hand, was not only supportive but also excited about his daughter's career choice. A self-trained poet, Otis Smith was the first person Patricia knew who wrote creatively and read vigorously. Each morning Patricia saw and heard her father reading the local newspaper. In 1979, when Patricia was twenty years old, Otis Smith was murdered in a botched robbery.

Upon her high school graduation, Patricia Smith enrolled at Southern Illinois University. However, she dropped out during her sophomore year after accepting a position at the *Chicago Daily News*. During her freshman year in college, at the age of twenty-one, Smith gave birth to her only child. From 1977 to 1978 Smith was a typist and freelance copier at the *Chicago Daily News*. The newspaper folded in 1978, and from 1978 to 1991 Smith worked at the *Chicago Sun-Times*.

During her time as a feature writer at the *Chicago Sun-Times*, Smith was introduced to performance poetry when she attended Chicago's Neutral Turf Poetry Festival. Winning championship after championship, Smith quickly became a celebrity staple on the performance-slam poetry scene. In 1990 she was awarded an Illinois Arts Council Literary Award.

In 1991 Smith married Michael Brown, whom she met on the Chicago poetry and newspaper circuit. The pair moved to Boston, bringing with them the Chicago-style slam poetry. That year Smith accepted a position at the *Boston Globe* as an arts and entertainment critic.

Smith was nominated for the Pulitzer Prize for Journalism in 1998 for her reporting at the *Boston Globe*. The nomination, however, was quickly retracted after evidence of fabricated stories surfaced. Throughout the controversy, Smith had frequent physical and mental breakdowns. At this time poetry became the voice through which she assessed her personal and professional lives. On 18 June 1998 Smith resigned her position at the *Globe* after admitting that at least four of her columns were partially fabricated.

Smith was a firm believer that there is no distinction between creative writer and journalist, and her transitions from poet to reporter and reporter to poet were seamless. The only difference, Smith insisted, is the way the words were written down. Further, poetry unleashed the formulaic reporter's voice, releasing irrational thought. "Writers should be impassioned by the craft. There is no need to restrain ourselves when it comes to craft," Smith urged.

Breaking fresh ground in performance poetry, Smith experimentally performed alongside musicians. These collaborations led to the formation of her band Bop Thunderous. Smith also performed as a lead vocalist with Paradigm Shift, a jazz band that played with the legends MILES DAVIS and CHARLIE PARKER.

Winner of the U.S. National Poetry Slam multiple times, Smith performed with GWENDOLYN BROOKS, RITA DOVE, Viggo Mortensen, WALTER MOSLEY, Sharon Olds, and NTOZAKE SHANGE, among others, throughout the United States and Europe. Smith appeared on HBO's *Def Poetry Jam* and was featured in the nationally released film *SlamNation* (1998).

Smith's poetry was published in literary journals, including the *Paris Review*, and anthologies, including *The Outlaw Bible of American Poetry* (1999) and *Aloud: Voices from the Nuyorican Poets Café* (1994). Smith's essays were included in the anthologies *Rise Up Singing: Black Women Writers on Motherhood* (2004) and *A Question of Balance: Artists and Writers on Motherhood* (1995).

Tía Chucha Press published Smith's first book of poetry, *Life According to Motown*, in 1991. Her second book of poetry, *Big Towns, Big Talk* (1992), won the Carl Sandburg Literary Award. Her short poetry film *The Undertaker* (1997) won awards at the Sundance and San Francisco film festivals and the renowned Cable Ace Award as part of the Lifetime Network's first-ever Women's Film Festival. Several of Smith's poems were adapted to theater, one of which was produced by the Nobel Prize winner DEREK WALCOTT. Additionally Smith taught courses on poetry, performance poetry, and memoir writing.

With Charles S. Johnson, author of *The Middle Passage* and a National Book Award winner, Smith cowrote *Africans in America* (1998), a history of slavery in the United States to accompany a four-part PBS series. *Janna and the Kings* (2003), Smith's debut children's book, won the New Voices Award.

Smith wrote on diverse themes and took pride in her varied poetic technique and approach. Poets, Smith argued, should not be boxed in but always seek unexpected entry points and unexpected things to write about. She continued to find alternative language manipulation and self-expression. In 2003 Smith married Bruce DeSilva, a journalist for the Associated Press.

FURTHER READING

Much of this biography is drawn from a telephone interview with Patricia Smith on 30 June 2005.

Kennedy, Dan. "Patricia Smith Breaks Her Silence," *Boston Phoenix* (1998).

LaBrecque, Ron. "Touch of the Poet," *Columbia Journalism Review* (1997).

NICOLE SEALEY

Smith, Pine Top (11 June 1904–15 Mar. 1929), boogie-woogie pianist and singer, was born Clarence Smith in Troy, Alabama, the son of Sam Smith and Molly (maiden name unknown). Clarence's nickname, spelled as Pine Top or Pinetop, came from a boyhood game of hanging a wire from treetop to treetop and talking through tin cans, as though the wire were a telephone line. From 1918 to 1920 Smith lived in Birmingham, where he taught himself to play the piano. He moved to Pittsburgh, Pennsylvania, in 1920 and from that home base toured as a pianist and tap dancer in various revues, mainly with lesser-known entertainers but also with MA RAINEY. While back in Pittsburgh he met Sarah Horton, whom he married in 1924; they had two children.

At the suggestion of the pianist Charles "Cow Cow" Davenport, Smith moved to Chicago in the summer of 1928. His family followed soon after. He played at parties and successfully auditioned for J. Mayo Williams, producer for Brunswick Records. From December 1928 to March 1929 Smith made a series of solo recordings, singing, speaking over music, and playing vaudeville songs and boogie-woogie blues. (In a few pieces Williams added his own voice, in conversation with Smith.) Eight titles were released posthumously, including "I'm Sober Now," "Now I Ain't Got Nothin' at All," and two versions each of "Pine Top's Blues" and "Pine Top's Boogie Woogie." During a fight at a party at a Masonic lodge in Chicago, Smith was killed by a stray bullet.

The precise origins of boogie-woogie piano playing will never be known. Certainly Jimmy Yancey developed the style well ahead of Smith, and MEADE LUX LEWIS recorded a version of "Honky Tonk Train Blues" a year before Smith's first session. Nonetheless "Pine Top's Boogie Woogie" is the landmark recording in the popularization of the style, and as such it—perhaps more than any other piece—provided a foundation on which rhythm and blues and rock and roll were built. Both takes of this title feature a reiterated, rollicking left-hand bass line that traces out the blues progression and right-hand melodies made from brief and catchy blues phrases, trills, and repeated syncopated chording (after the manner of the "Charleston" rhythm). Also in each take Smith gives joyful instructions to dancers, including colorful stops and starts that give the performance a special energy absent from many subsequent boogie-woogie pieces of unvarying rhythmic character. During the national craze for boogie-woogie music in the late 1930s, "Pine Top's Boogie Woogie" was recreated numerous times in versions as diverse as pianist ALBERT AMMONS's solo tribute and Deane Kincaide's big band arrangement for Tommy Dorsey's orchestra. "Pine Top's Boogie Woogie" thus served as a template for the boogie-woogie style and subsequent stylistic developments.

FURTHER READING

Harrison, Max. "Boogie Woogie," in *Jazz: New Perspectives on the History of Jazz by Twelve of the World's Foremost Jazz Critics and Scholars*, ed. Nat Hentoff and Albert J. McCarthy (1959).

Russell, William. "Boogie Woogie," in *Jazzmen: The Story of Hot Jazz Told in the Lives of the Men Who Created It*, ed. Frederic Ramsey Jr. and Charles Edward Smith (1939; rpt. 1977).

This entry is taken from the *American National Biography* and is published here with the permission of the American Council of Learned Societies.

BARRY KERNFELD

Smith, Relliford Stillmon (30 Nov. 1889–28 June 1965), physician, was born in Americus, Georgia, the son of Dennis Smith, a laborer, and Mollie Daniels. Smith came from a poor family, and he worked hard during his youth at a variety of menial jobs—including as a service industry employee, a domestic, an office worker, and a railroad employee—to help support himself and his parents. He received his elementary and secondary education at the Americus Institute, then in 1906 he began studies at Shaw University in Raleigh, North Carolina, where he earned a B.S. in 1910. During the summers he worked as a bookkeeper and a butcher in the city markets of Americus.

Smith attended Leonard Medical College of Shaw University from 1910 to 1914 and received an M.D. in 1914 from the University of West Tennessee College of Medicine and Surgery. He earned a graduate degree at Meharry Medical College in Nashville, Tennessee, in 1916. While in graduate school Smith worked during the summers as a Pullman porter and a steamboat waiter. Smith began the general practice of medicine in 1916 in Americus, Georgia, after he passed medical licensing examinations in Georgia, South Carolina, Maryland, and the District of Columbia. In 1918 he entered the U.S. Army Medical Corps, and from 1918 to 1919 he served as assistant regimental surgeon at New Receiving Camp Infirmary, Camp Wheeler, Georgia. After an honorable discharge, he established a medical practice in Macon, Georgia. In 1920 Smith married Gertrude Savage. They had children, but the exact number is unknown.

Smith was keenly aware of the value of graduate training for physicians, especially black physicians, who because of racial barriers were restricted to a black world. Throughout his career he took advanced graduate courses whenever possible, including numerous sessions at the Medical College of Georgia, the Grady Hospital of Emory University Medical School, the Mayo Clinic in Rochester, Minnesota, the Howard University School of Medicine, and the Johns Hopkins University School of Medicine. When taking courses focused on public health, Smith became personally acquainted in 1938 with the U.S. surgeon general, Thomas Parran, and Assistant Surgeon General R. A. Vonderlear. Through these relationships Smith convinced the U.S. Public Health Service to grant modest stipends, beginning in the summer of 1938, to each black physician who attended the Howard University medical school postgraduate course in venereal diseases. Without this aid many black physicians would not have been able to afford to attend the sessions.

Smith served as a local medical examiner for the Guaranty Life Insurance Company (1919–1965) and was a member of the company's board of directors for more than twenty years. He overcame repressive racial and financial barriers to gain local, state, and national recognition as an excellent medical practitioner, an effective advocate for medical improvement, and a reliable civil rights spokesman for black physicians. For example, the annual medical seminars hosted by the Medical College of Georgia, which Smith attended for seventeen consecutive years, permitted black physicians to attend, but would not give them certificates verifying their presence or the courses they had taken. Smith protested this, and beginning in 1935, the college changed its policy.

Smith actively participated in many civic and professional organizations, including the Macon Academy of Medicine, Dentistry, and Pharmacy, which he served as president; the Georgia State Medical Association of Physicians and Pharmacists; the John Andrew Clinic, Tuskegee Institute; the Macon County Academy of Medicine and Surgery, which he served as president; and the Tremont Baptist Church. In spite of an excellent reputation, extraordinary medical preparation and knowledge, and recognition by the U.S. Public Health Service, Smith was not permitted to join the "whites only" Bibb County Medical Society. Fifty-one years after Smith had been awarded a medical degree, when racial barriers were finally dropped in 1965, the Bibb County Medical Society invited Smith to join.

Smith for many years served the National Medical Association (NMA) in almost every capacity possible. He was the fifty-eighth president of the organization, as well as its vice president, vice speaker of the house of delegates, six-year member of the board of trustees, three-year chairman of the budget committee of the board, six-year member of the judicial counsel and for three years its chairman, and twenty-four-year member of the house of delegates. Because of his excellent sense of organization, his ability as a team player, and his hard work, Smith was considered one of the NMA's best presidents.

Smith's first wife died in 1946, and in 1947 he married Cynthiabelle Blacke Gordon. They had no children. He died in Washington, D.C.

FURTHER READING

Cobb, W. Montague. "Relliford Stillmon Smith, M.D. 1889–1965," *Journal of the National Medical Association* 58 (Mar. 1966).

"The President Elect," *Journal of the National Medical Association* 49 (Nov. 1957).

Sammons, Vivian Ovelton. *Blacks in Science and Medicine* (1990).

This entry is taken from the *American National Biography* and is published here with the permission of the American Council of Learned Societies.

BILLY SCOTT

Smith, Robert Lloyd (6 Jan. 1861–10 July 1942), educator, politician, and reformer, was born to Francis A. and Mary H. (Talbot) Smith, free black schoolteachers in Charleston, South Carolina. Little is known about his childhood, other than that at some point he lost his right arm, presumably in an accident. It can be assumed, moreover, given his parents' occupations, that the household was a cultured one. Smith pursued education as a career, following in his parents' footsteps. He studied at Avery Normal Institute and then enrolled in the University of South Carolina in 1875, but he had to transfer to Atlanta University in 1877 after South Carolina legislators closed the university to black students. Smith finished his bachelor's degree in 1879 and taught in public schools in Georgia and South Carolina before relocating to rural Colorado County, Texas, in 1885. It is not certain what subjects he taught, but it is believed that Smith studied under Horace Bumstead, who taught natural sciences and math at Atlanta. Smith, who became principal of Oakland Normal School, and Nathan Hill Middleton, a doctor and fellow South Carolinian, sought to improve conditions for rural residents in Freedmanstown, the black settlement near Oakland, Texas, by helping those residents to become economically independent from the crop lien system of agriculture, to pursue education, and to live a morally upright life, centered on family values. They both eventually married daughters of William H. Isaacs, one of few land owning blacks in the area. Smith married Francis Isabella "Belle" Isaacs in 1890, and they raised two children, Olive Bell Smith Hardeway and Roscoe Conkling Smith. After Middleton drowned in 1900, Smith raised and educated Vivian Middleton-Rhodes, one of Middleton's daughters.

Smith, most likely with the assistance of Middleton and the Isaacs family, formed the Farmers' Improvement Society of Texas (FIS) in 1891 to help farmers avoid debt. He expected farmers to invest their hard-earned funds in the FIS mutual benefit fund and in real estate. Such goals appealed to a growing group of middle-class blacks that included his in-laws. Smith administered the organization; Belle Smith coordinated the Women's Barnyard Auxiliary; and William Isaacs Jr., Belle's brother, developed the FIS cooperative purchasing system. Such activism helped farmers transition from sharecropper to tenant to farm owner, and gain personal security and influence in local decision making. This improved the quality of life for these farmers because members of economically stable farm communities could hire educators, ministers, tradespeople, doctors, and even lawyers to work in their interest. Smith invested himself in the community, serving as president of the Farmers' Improvement Bank, in Waco, Texas, and directing a factory that produced overalls. He held a life membership in the National Negro Business League.

Smith began his influential political career on the wave of reform efforts in a quest to offer rural blacks an alternative to populism. The Colored Farmers' National Alliance and Cooperative Union had originated in nearby Houston County, Texas, in 1886. It offered blacks who had been excluded from the Farmers' Alliance because of their race a voice in local, state, and national politics. Smith's FIS, on the other hand, appealed to partisan Republicans, both white and black. Colorado County Republicans thanked Smith for his uncontroversial goals of economic security through private property ownership, self-improvement, and local activism by electing him twice as their representative to the Texas state legislature, in 1895 and 1897. During the 1896 campaign Smith even ousted the influential black Texas Republican, NORRIS WRIGHT CUNEY, as the party leader.

Smith and the FIS illustrate the ways that rural blacks used grassroots politics to secure improvements without challenging segregation. For example, Smith did not contest public school segregation when he sat in the Texas legislature because African Americans exercised some control over their own schools. Eliminating black schools would have diminished the little authority that blacks had in the color-sensitive South. He supported construction of a public institution of higher learning for black youth and black control of public school administration. Smith challenged other aspects of segregation, however, as the 1896 U.S. Supreme Court decision *Plessy v. Ferguson* legalized separation of races in places of public accommodation. He opposed separate waiting rooms in depots, and he pursued civil liberty causes as well, supporting antilynching legislation and an amendment to the 1874 Landlord and Tenant Act to prevent landlords from exacting more from tenants than the harvest warranted. Ultimately, he favored free access to the vote, even as blacks were systematically denied the franchise. Such visibility led to his service on the Anna T. Jeanes Foundation board, the board of education of the Methodist Episcopal Church, the Commission on Inter-Racial Cooperation, and the Texas branch of the Negro Business League.

Smith left elected politics in 1901 but served as U.S. marshal for the Eastern District of Texas from 1902 to 1909. During this time he also devoted his energies to expanding the FIS, starting a juvenile branch in 1907, and opening the FIS Agricultural College between Wolfe City and Ladonia, Texas, in 1908. FIS members lobbied United States Department of Agriculture (USDA) officials to allow their children to participate in corn clubs as their white peers did. White farmers had been offered the latest agricultural research in boll weevil prevention and diversified agriculture through experiment station research and interaction with experts available through white land-grant colleges, such as the Agricultural and Mechanical College of Texas (now Texas A&M University), and through the USDA's program in cooperative demonstration work. Similar educational resources did not exist through land-grant institutions serving African Americans, such as Prairie View Normal and Industrial College (now Prairie View A&M University). The USDA believed that if they could attract the children to information on scientific agriculture, then the parents would be brought into the program, and Smith and the FIS followed this idea, trying to get black youth involved in corn clubs and homemakers' clubs, and through them, interest the parents in agricultural sciences and higher standards of living associated with the Golden Age of Agriculture (1909–1914).

By late 1909 black agents had been hired in some states by General Education Board funds, which created a problem in public versus private funding of agricultural reform. Smith walked the line between these polarities, furthering private reform through the FIS and its school, but also calling for more public support. The black agents, who worked in Alabama, Virginia, and Mississippi, provided the same information to black farmers that previously only white farmers had been able to access through contact with experts and access to USDA publications. Smith knew of this work because of his personal relationship with BOOKER T. WASHINGTON, who had facilitated their hiring. Texas Agricultural Extension Service (TAEX) administrators, however, stalled in hiring blacks to work as agents to black farmers in Texas. The white agricultural agents satisfied individual demands, but did not make their services—advice on crop cultivation and stock improvement techniques, marketing, farm management, sanitation, pesticide and herbicide use, and soil conservation practices—more generally available even as the number of black farmers in Texas increased, especially in cotton cultivation. Texas ranked fifth in the nation in the number of black farmers in 1910, but no provision allowed for their inclusion in programs provided by TAEX.

After 1914, and the passage of the Smith-Lever Act, which guaranteed state extension officials authority over national funds appropriated for extension work, the TAEX created a segregated division in August 1915 to serve black farmers and their families. The division operated out of Prairie View State Normal and Industrial College, and Smith, already a leading rural reformer, assumed the responsibility as state leader. He and the other two employees, Jacob Ford and MARY EVELYN V. HUNTER, quickly built the program by meeting with families, often FIS members, in private homes, churches, schools, and at FIS convocations and fairs.

Initially Smith welcomed the visibility that the FIS gained through cooperating with extension work. However, the public reform quickly co-opted the FIS programs, sapped FIS members' limited resources, and prompted a steady decline in FIS membership. Smith resigned his position with TAEX on 30 June 1919 and returned full time to his duties as FIS grand president. Following his first wife's death in 1918, Smith married Ruby Loda Cobb in 1919. They raised and educated Mildred Isaacs-Rhombo (or Rambo). He and Ruby Cobb spent the next twenty-nine years trying to keep the FIS solvent. Though debilitated by inadequate cash flow during the Great Depression, the FIS did not dissolve until Smith's death in 1942.

FURTHER READING

An autobiography and other Robert L. Smith papers, along with records of the Farmers' Improvement Society of Texas, are housed in the Smith-Cobb Family Papers, Texas Collection, Baylor University, Waco, Texas. Information about Dr. Nathaniel Hill Middleton is housed in the Nesbitt Memorial Library, Columbus, Texas.

Carroll, Robert. "Robert Lloyd Smith and the Farmers'
Improvement Society of Texas," master's thesis,
Baylor University, 1974.

National Encyclopedia of the Colored Race, vol. 1 (1919).

Pitre, Merline. *Through Many Dangers, Toils, and
Snares: Black Leadership in Texas* (1997).

Reid, Debra A. *Reaping a Greater Harvest: African
Americans, the Extension Service, and Rural Reform
in Jim Crow Texas* (2007).

Rice, Lawrence D. "Robert Lloyd Smith," *New
Handbook of Texas* (1996).

Who's Who in Colored America, 3rd ed. (1930–1932).

Obituary: *Waco Messenger*, 17 July 1942.

DEBRA A. REID

Smith, Stephen (c. 1795–14 Nov. 1873), businessman
and minister, was born near Harrisburg, Dauphin
County, Pennsylvania, the son of an unknown
father and Nancy Smith (maiden name unknown),
a Cochran family servant. On 10 July 1801 Thomas
Boude, a former revolutionary war officer from
Columbia, Lancaster County, Pennsylvania, purchased the boy's indenture. As Smith grew to manhood he proved so able that Boude eventually made
him manager of his entire lumber business.

On 3 January 1816 Smith borrowed fifty dollars to purchase his freedom from Boude. Later
that year Smith married Harriet Lee, a domestic
servant in the Jonathan Mifflin home; they had no
children. Free of his indenture, Smith entered the
lumber business for himself, while his wife ran an
oyster house. In 1820 his one-and-a-half lots were
valued at three hundred dollars; thirteen years later
he owned six houses and lots worth three thousand
dollars, stocks and bonds of equal value, "a pleasure carriage," a horse, and a cow. His lumberyard
became one of the largest on the Susquehanna
River. This success aroused the envy of some whites;
an anonymous hate letter in 1835 accused him of
inflating property prices with his excessive bids.

When the race riots of 1834–1835 broke out in
Columbia, Smith's place of business was a target.
Windows were broken, his desk rifled, and papers
scattered. His property and life in jeopardy, Smith
offered his holdings for sale, but after six months
with no takers, he withdrew the offer. His financial strength enabled him to weather the 1837
bank panic. With his business partner, WILLIAM
WHIPPER, a relative and an equally astute merchant, Smith's Columbia investments included nine
thousand dollars in a bridge company and eighteen
thousand dollars in a bank. Moving to Philadelphia
in 1842, he increased his holdings of houses, lots,

stocks, and bonds and expanded his lumber and
coal business. By 1849 Smith and Whipper had an
inventory of "several thousand bushels of coal," over
two million feet of lumber, "and twenty-two of the
finest merchantmen cars running on the railroad
from Columbia to Philadelphia and Baltimore"
(Worner, 185). When his partnership with Whipper
ended, his wife's nephew, Ulysses B. Vidal, joined
him in the coal business.

Smith's business dealings were not his sole occupation. In 1832 he purchased a church building in
Columbia and founded the Mount Zion African
Methodist Episcopal (AME) Church. Six years later
he was ordained an AME minister.

Early on, Smith turned his talents to race
rights and reform. He was a well-known participant in the Underground Railroad; Whipper told
William Still that it was known "far down in the
slave region, that Smith & Whipper, the negro lumber merchants, were engaged in secreting fugitive
slaves" (Still, 739). Smith opposed the colonization movement and supported the early strivings
of Whipper's American Moral Reform Society in
1834–1835. A frequent convention-goer and mass-
meeting participant, he fought for the abolition of
slavery, the removal of "white" from the state constitution, and the integration of Philadelphia's railway
cars. Smith supported the temperance movement
and was an officer in a number of black organizations, including the Odd Fellows, Social, Civil, and
Statistical Association; the Grand Tabernacle of the
Independent Order of Brothers and Sisters of Love
and Charity; and the Union League Association. He
hosted John Brown for a week in 1858 and, along
with JAMES WORMLEY and HENRY HIGHLAND
GARNET, had a leadership role in the movement to
erect a Lincoln memorial monument.

An occasional victim of white persecution, he
had also earned the respect of many whites and
worked with them in his business and charitable
endeavors. His race views were unequivocal but
moderate. In 1855 he was aware "that the colored
people of the city of Philadelphia could not obtain
[an] opportunity to learn mechanical trades. But,"
he added, "wherever a colored man understood a
trade, he was sustained in Philadelphia" (Foner and
Lewis, vol. 1, 262). As time went on, Smith became
more pessimistic. He discouraged black attempts to
integrate the Philadelphia railway cars because he
doubted such attempts would receive the support
of the city's white citizens.

During the Civil War, though a member of
Bethel AME Church, Smith served for a year or

so as pastor in charge of the Zion AME Mission Church. He worked with Bethel's committee to collect food, clothing, and money for contrabands in Washington, D.C. He helped to organize one meeting and chaired a second at which FREDERICK DOUGLASS spoke, urging black recruits for the army and equal rights for all men and women. A short-term trustee of Wilberforce University, he headed a committee to raise funds for that institution.

After Appomattox, Smith continued his business and church activities. Not assigned a parish, he occasionally preached and frequently spoke ("in his usual animated and forcible style") in and around the city. He and his wife regularly summered in Cape May. His major charitable interest centered on a home for the elderly and the Olive Cemetery. He bought the cemetery at a forced auction for payment of debts and rejoiced when in 1863 the state supreme court resolved a seven-year-old management dispute in his favor. The next year Smith and some white Quakers established the Philadelphia Home for the Aged and Infirm. In 1870 a new building was dedicated, a gift of Stephen and Harriet Smith. By bequest the Smiths endowed the home with almost $250,000.

Beyond this, his denomination, including Bethel Church, benefited from his continuing generosity and special gifts. He built the Zion AME Mission Church in 1857 and contributed to the establishment of an AME Church in Cape May. With nine others Smith put up one thousand dollars to buy the vacated Institute for Colored Youth building and convert it into a meeting hall with stores for black retailers.

As an individual Smith was quiet but stubborn. In 1856 he chastised the editor of the *Christian Recorder*, Jabez Campbell, for criticizing an AME General Conference ruling, asserting that the editor should "vindicate her [that is, the church's] acts, defend her organization, discipline and laws." Be patient, he urged; "try them, and if they do not suit, repeal them" (*Christian Recorder*, 4 Mar. 1856). Five years later the AME district conference settled another dispute between the two men in Smith's favor. At the 1864 general conference, some Bethel members protested his seat for unstated reasons but their claim was denied. Early in 1873 Wilberforce University's president, Bishop DANIEL PAYNE, stung by rumors of Smith's lack of confidence in him, published an offer to resign if Smith would endow the institution with a $100,000 gift. Smith's terse response praised Payne "as a man of learning and a Christian gentleman," but questioned his abilities to manage finances (*Christian Recorder*, 6 Mar. 1873).

This was probably Smith's last public statement before illness incapacitated him. After his death in Philadelphia, he was praised as "the ablest financier and the wealthiest man among the colored people," and "one of the best-known colored citizens of Philadelphia" (*New National Era*, 4 Dec. 1873; *Philadelphia Public Ledger*, 15 Nov. 1873). Smith's life was a rags-to-riches saga, unique in the nineteenth-century black community. He tried to live his Christian creed, courageously patient under persecution, moderate in materialism, and sensitive to the less fortunate.

FURTHER READING
Foner, Philip S., and George Walker, eds. *Proceedings of the Black State Conventions, 1840–1865*, vol. 1 (1979).
Quarles, Benjamin. *Black Abolitionists* (1969)
Still, William. *The Underground Rail Road* (1872)
Worner, William F. "The Columbia Race Riots," *Lancaster County Historical Society Papers* 26, no. 8 (Oct. 1922).
Obituaries: *New National Era*, 4 Dec. 1873; *Philadelphia Inquirer*, 19 Nov. 1873; *Philadelphia Public Ledger*, 15 Nov. 1873.
This entry is taken from the *American National Biography* and is published here with the permission of the American Council of Learned Societies.

LESLIE H. FISHEL

Smith, Stuff (13 Aug. 1909–25 Sept. 1967), jazz violinist, singer, and comedian, was born Leroy Gordon Smith in Portsmouth, Ohio, the son of Cornelius T. Smith, a barber and musician, and Anna Lee Redman, a schoolteacher. Smith's birth certificate gives 13 August, but he celebrated his birthday on 14 August, for reasons unknown (though perhaps superstition); he also was known to many as Hezekiah (or by the nickname Hez), but this name is not on the certificate.

Smith was raised in Massilon, Ohio, from age nine, at which point he was playing in his father's band. His father wanted him to follow his sister Helen, who studied classical violin at Oberlin Conservatory, but Smith heard Joe Venuti and Eddie Lang perform locally and was smitten by jazz. Around 1925 he won a musical scholarship to Johnson C. Smith University in Charlotte, North Carolina, but he never graduated. In 1926 and 1927 he toured with Aunt Jemima's Revue, at which time he acquired his nickname through his habit of calling someone "Stuff" if he could not remember a name. Smith's first wife, a dancer whose name is unknown, had died in childbirth. He married Marion Armeta Harris around 1927; they had one child.

By this time Smith was becoming familiar with LOUIS ARMSTRONG's recordings, which he felt provided a much greater influence than Venuti's comparatively lightweight work. Smith joined ALPHONSO TRENT's orchestra in Lexington, Kentucky, late in 1927 for southwestern and midwestern tours. He served as the orchestra's conductor and master of ceremonies, thereby developing skills that would later bring him stardom in New York City. Leaving Trent in Davenport, Iowa, in 1928, Smith went to New York, where he joined JELLY ROLL MORTON, but after two weeks he left because Morton's band played too loudly for the violin to be heard. Smith traveled to Little Rock, Arkansas, to rejoin Trent and to contribute solos to Trent's few recordings, including "Nightmare" and "Black and Blue Rhapsody" (5 Dec. 1928). He remained with Trent until 1930, touring Canada and the Northeast and making his recording debut as a solo vocalist on "After You've Gone" (Mar. 1930).

With the birth of his son, Smith left Trent to spend several years with his family in Buffalo, New York. There he formed a group that included the trumpeter Peanuts Holland from Trent's band, the tenor saxophonist JOE THOMAS (Joseph Vankert), and later the trumpeter Jonah Jones. In January 1936 Smith formed what immediately became an extremely popular sextet at the Onyx Club in New York, where he began using an amplified violin. Together with the leader, the sextet featured Jones and the drummer COZY COLE. They played swing tunes and novelties, well represented on record by "I'se a Muggin'," "After You've Gone," "You'se a Viper," "Old Joe's Hittin' the Jug," and "Knock, Knock, Who's There?" (all from 1936).

Smith's great admirer, the Danish baron Timme Rosencrantz, reports, "Often at the Onyx, after the music started, he would tell risqué stories over the microphone. There was one about Adam and Eve in the Garden of Eden, that used to make the management panic. I've seen him stop in the middle of a solo when a young and beautiful woman entered the room and point out to the audience the woman's anatomical qualities" (Barnett and Løgager, 56). Together with this verbal outrageousness, Smith's acclaimed sextet presented childlike vocal melodies married to Harlem jazz talk and other silly lyrics (including some wonderfully awful puns in knock-knock jokes); Cole's swinging drumming; Jones's swinging and melodically lyrical trumpet playing in the Armstrong mold; and most significantly, Smith's always-swinging and sometimes delightfully weird violin improvisations.

While at the height of his fame at the Onyx, Smith, billed with BILLIE HOLIDAY, became jealous of her emerging popularity and in a well-publicized incident succeeded in having her fired; later in life they resolved their difficulties, becoming friends and sometimes working together.

The pianist Clyde Hart had joined the sextet by the time that Smith recorded "Upstairs" in May 1937. That month the group traveled to Hollywood to perform in the musical *52nd Street*, but they were excluded from the film because they violated their contract by taking an engagement at the Famous Door in Hollywood from the summer of 1937 to early 1938. Around March 1938 Smith went bankrupt, disbanded, and briefly joined Holland's orchestra in Buffalo. By May, Smith had re-formed his band, which worked steadily into 1942, mainly in New York and Chicago. Smith's group in 1942 included former members of FATS WALLER's band; they fired the leader "when his eccentricity went beyond reason" (Barnett, 90). Smith divorced his wife around 1940. He married Helen Rogers in the early 1940s; they had no children.

In the spring of 1943 Smith formed a trio with the pianist Jimmy Jones and the string bassist John Levy, and after performing in Chicago and making national radio broadcasts the trio went to New York in September 1944 for recordings and a tenure at the Onyx through the spring of 1945. The pianists ERROLL GARNER and BILLY TAYLOR each briefly followed Jones in the trio. Over the next decade Smith led lesser-known groups based in Chicago on occasional tours from coast to coast. He recorded with the trumpeter DIZZY GILLESPIE's sextet in 1951 and with the keyboard player SUN RA sometime before 1953. Divorced again in 1950, Smith married Arlene Janzig about 1955; they had no children.

Smith's career was revived in the mid-1950s by a series of excellent recordings for Norman Granz. These albums include *Ella Fitzgerald Sings the Duke Ellington Song Book* (1956), Nat King Cole's *After Midnight* (1956), Smith's own *Have Violin, Will Swing* and *Stuff Smith* and, with violinist Stephane Grappelli, *Violins No End* (all from 1957). He toured Europe in the spring of 1957 with Granz's Jazz at the Philharmonic, but he did not complete the tour because of illness. He performed several times on the television series "Art Ford's Jazz Party" in 1958. Recording for Granz again he made the album *Cat on a Hot Fiddle* in 1959. Settling for a time in Los Angeles he performed regularly, including appearances at the Monterey Jazz Festival in 1961 and 1962.

Smith played at the Royal Tahitian Room in Ontario, California, from 1963 to 1964. He returned to New York to perform with the pianist Joe Bushkin's group at the Embers, but illness ended this affiliation. Early in 1965 he left his wife and settled in Copenhagen, where he found his playing in great demand. He underwent a serious operation in Paris in mid-August; a doctor described Smith as a "medical museum," a consequence of decades of wild and careless living. Nonetheless he immediately resumed playing. He had an illegitimate child with Margaret Fossum Poulsen, but in his final year Smith lived with Eva Løgager. He made the renowned album *Violin Summit* at a jam session with the violinists Svend Asmussen, Grappelli, and Jean-Luc Ponty at a concert in Basel, Switzerland, on 30 September 1966. He recorded the album *Black Violin* in Germany the next year. Still touring Europe extensively, Smith died while in Munich.

Even at his peak in the 1930s Smith did not routinely depart from the norms of jazz swing soloing, but whenever he wished he could invent melodies offering a then-unknown level of dissonant pitch selection and dissonant intonation in relationship to blues and pop harmonies, as if the free jazz era had suddenly been unleashed a quarter century too soon. This type of playing may be heard not only on 1936 novelty tunes such as "You'se a Viper" and "Old Joe's Hittin' the Jug" but also in as sedate a setting as "My Blue Heaven" (recorded in 1939). Speaking of their trio of 1943 Jimmy Jones said, "Stuff's a strange guy, you know. He wants to play what he wants to play. Cut out from the melody, depart from the chords. It's a wrong note, maybe, but Stuff makes it right, and we had to make it right with him. ... I got so I knew his moods, his harmonic tricks, when he would suddenly switch tempo or change key" (interview with Barry Ulanov, Barnett, 109). Because of this melodic impetuousness, as well as his raucous approach to tone quality (including explorations of amplified sound) and vibrato, and his hard-driving sense of swing rhythm, Smith is regarded as one of the greatest jazz violinists.

FURTHER READING

Barnett, Anthony. *Desert Sands: The Recordings & Performances of Stuff Smith: An Annotated Discography & Biographical Source Book* (1995).
Dance, Stanley. *The World of Swing* (1974; repr. 1979).
Glaser, Matt, and Stephane Grappelli. *Jazz Violin* (1981).
Morgenstern, Dan. "Jazz Fiddle," *Down Beat* (9 Feb. 1967).
Shaw, Arnold. *The Street That Never Slept* (1971; repr. as *52nd Street: The Street of Jazz*, 1977).
Obituary: *New York Times*, 2 Oct. 1967.
This entry is taken from the *American National Biography* and is published here with the permission of the American Council of Learned Societies.

BARRY KERNFELD

Smith, Tommie (6 June 1944–), Olympic track-and-field gold medalist and world record holder, was born in Clarksville, Texas, to James Richard, a sharecropper, and Dora Smith. Tommie, the seventh of twelve children, grew up on a farm where his family raised hogs and cows and picked cotton. Like many black Texans hoping to escape the misery of the Jim Crow South, the Smiths moved to the San Joaquin Valley of California and settled in Lemoore. There, Smith's athletic track career began in the fourth grade, when he raced the fastest kid at his school, his older sister, Sallie, and won. He struggled academically but nonetheless decided in the sixth grade that he wanted to be a teacher. Recognizing the lack of attention given to his own learning difficulties, he hoped that he might serve students more effectively. Smith grew rapidly as he entered his teenage years, and he excelled at a variety of sports. In ninth grade, by which time he was already six feet, two inches tall, he ran the 100-yard dash in only 9.9 seconds; cleared the high jump at 6 feet, 5 inches; and recorded 24 feet, 6 inches in the long jump. He improved his 100-yard-dash time in 1963, when he ran the sprint in 9.5 seconds and the 220-yard dash in 21.1 seconds. Most Valuable Athlete awards in basketball, football, and track and field during his sophomore, junior, and senior years of high school earned Smith an athletic scholarship for the three sports at San Jose State University. Smith majored in social science and teaching at San Jose State and was also enrolled in the Army Reserve Officers Training Corps.

After attempting to compete as a three-sport athlete during his freshman year of college, he opted to focus on track and field for Coach Bud Winter. As a sophomore in 1965, Smith ran the 220-yard sprint in 20.0 seconds, tying the world record. Known for his powerful acceleration and for wearing dark sunglasses in his races, Smith soon emerged as a

Olympians Tommie Smith (center) and John Carlos protest racism and segregation in the United States by staring down and raising their fists to salute black power during the playing of the "Star Spangled Banner" after Smith received the gold medal and Carlos the bronze medal for the 200-meter sprint at the Summer Olympic Games in Mexico City, 16 October 1968. (AP Images.)

world-class sprinter and as a critical member of "Speed City," the nickname given to San Jose's track program. In 1966 Smith cut his 220-yard-dash time to 19.5, establishing a world record. He won the AAU and the NCAA titles in the 200-meter dash in 1967 and repeated his AAU title win the next year. Smith married the heptathlete Denise Paschal in 1967; their son, Kevin, was born in 1968.

That same year, Smith captured the world's attention by raising his fist in a "black power" salute on the victory podium at the 1968 Mexico City Olympic Games. Smith's actions took place during a time of turmoil on many college campuses as students protested the Vietnam War and demanded equality for women and racial minorities. African American athletes, both college and professional, became involved in these protests, while critics denounced collegiate athletic programs for exploiting African American athletes. At Smith's college, San Jose State,

the sociology instructor HARRY EDWARDS encouraged black athletes to become politically active on campus and to fight for equality. Edwards established the Olympic Project for Human Rights and encouraged Smith and some of his teammates to consider the power of the platform that sport provided for the civil rights struggle.

In November 1967 Smith attended the Western Regional Black Youth Conference held in Los Angeles. At that conference Edwards organized a meeting of black collegiate athletes to discuss the possibility of boycotting the 1968 Olympic Games. Coming from a world-class sprinter, Smith's declaration that he would support the boycott garnered significant attention. In an interview published in *Life*, Smith spoke of the difficulties African American students faced on predominantly white college campuses. Smith also addressed the need for athletic departments to hire black coaches and trainers in a *Newsweek* cover story, "The Angry Black Athlete." He began to receive hate mail in response to his statements.

After much deliberation, Smith decided not to boycott the Olympics, but he was still the subject of great media scrutiny at the U.S. Olympic Trials hosted in Los Angeles. Smith qualified in his specialty, the 200 meters. With the threat of the boycott resolved, the International Olympic Committee's (IOC) president, Avery Brundage, informed the black athletes who made the team that he would not tolerate any trouble. In the qualifying heats of the 200 meters, Smith wore tall black socks as his means of making a statement. He felt pain in his hamstrings but was determined to compete in the finals. On 16 October 1968 Tommie Smith won the gold medal in the 200 meters at the Olympic Games with a world-record time of 19.83 seconds. His San Jose State teammate John Carlos finished third.

Before the medal ceremony, Smith approached Carlos to discuss a nonviolent protest during the award ceremony. Smith wore a black glove on his right hand, with Carlos wearing the left glove. They each wore black socks with no shoes. As the American national anthem began to play, Smith and Carlos bowed their heads and raised their gloved fists in the air. The image was seen around the world, and the response was immediate. Some teammates were very supportive, while other American athletes criticized the use of the award platform as a place of protest. Others thought that sport was not the place for politics. Smith told the media that his raised fist with the black glove represented "black power" in America, and his black scarf represented black pride. His black socks with no shoes represented black poverty in racist America.

The U.S. Olympic Committee (USOC) did not want to make Smith and Carlos into martyrs, but they were pressured by Brundage and the IOC to punish the athletes. Smith and Carlos were suspended from the team, banned from the Olympic Village, and sent home. Brundage and the USOC warned the pair's teammates that further protests would result in the same punishment. Even so, several black athletes expressed solidarity with Smith and Carlos. The 4×400–meter relay team wore black tams on the victory stand but did stand at attention during the national anthem. The long jumpers BOB BEAMON and Ralph Boston, who won gold and bronze medals, respectively, wore black socks on the victory stand as a protest. Other teammates were less forgiving. Years later they remained critical, believing that the actions of Smith and Carlos reflected poorly on the entire team and overshadowed the accomplishments of the other members of the 1968 squad.

Following the Olympics, Smith returned to San Jose State for his final semester of college. Along with Carlos, he was both celebrated and denounced on campus for his black power protest; the ROTC even demanded that Smith return his military uniform. Smith graduated with a B.A. degree and later earned a master's degree in sociology from the Goodard-Cambridge Graduate Program for Social Change in Cambridge, Massachusetts. Upon graduation from San Jose State, Smith played football on the taxi squad of the Cincinnati Bengals, earning three hundred dollars a week. He recorded only one reception, for forty-one yards, in a professional game. Cut after the 1971 preseason, Smith played one month for the Hamilton Tiger-Cats of the Canadian Football League. Jack Scott, the radical athletic director at Oberlin College in Ohio, hired Smith in 1972 to coach track and field. Denied tenure at Oberlin in 1978, Smith relocated to California to coach the men's track-and-field team at Santa Monica College. That same year, he married his second wife, Denise Kyle. They have three children, Danielle, Timothy, and Anthony.

Smith's achievements on the track have left a lasting imprint on the record books. He is the only man to simultaneously hold eleven world records. His records of 10.1 seconds in the 100 meters, 19.83 seconds in the 200 meters, and 44.5 seconds in the 400 meters still rank high on the all-time lists. His 19.83 seconds in the 200 meters, set at the 1968 Olympic Games, stood until 1979 and was an Olympic record until 1984. He has received numerous honors for his athletic accomplishments, including induction into the National Track and Field Hall of Fame in 1978, the California Black Sports Hall of Fame in 1996, and the San Jose State University Sports Hall of Fame in 1999. Although it was once viewed as controversial and confrontational, the image of Tommie Smith and John Carlos giving the black power salute has come to be celebrated in recent years. San Jose State plans to erect a statue of the salute commemorating the two former student athletes.

FURTHER READING
Smith, Tommie and David Steele. *Silent Gesture: The Autobiography of Tommie Smith* (2007).
Bass, Amy. *Not the Triumph, but the Struggle: The 1968 Olympics and the Making of the Black Athlete* (2002).
Edwards, Harry. *The Revolt of the Black Athlete* (1969).
Wiggins, David K. "'The Year of Awakening': Black Athletes, Racial Unrest and the Civil Rights Movement of 1968," *International Journal of the History of Sport* 9 (1992).

MAUREEN M. SMITH

Smith, Trixie (1895–21 Sept. 1943), blues and vaudeville singer, was born in Atlanta, Georgia. Nothing is known of her parents or of her childhood. Having studied at Selma University in Alabama, she went to New York City around 1915 to perform in clubs and theaters. She was at the New Standard Theater in Philadelphia in 1916, and she toured on the Theater Owners' Booking Association circuit, probably in 1920 and 1921.

While performing at Harlem's Lincoln Theatre and recording for the Black Swan label from 1921 to 1923, Smith furthered her fame by entering and winning a blues contest at the Manhattan Casino on 20 January 1922. Her recordings included "Trixie's Blues" (c. 1921; by some accounts she recorded it after winning the contest) and two titles accompanied by the cornetist LOUIS ARMSTRONG in 1925, "The World's Jazz Crazy and So Am I" and "Railroad Blues." In 1932 Smith appeared in the film *The Black King*. She continued working as a singer and actress in New York until 1933 and then in national tours until 1935. As the New Orleans jazz revival was just beginning to get under way she had an opportunity to record an outstanding session with the reed player SIDNEY BECHET's group in 1938, including "My Daddy Rocks Me." Smith made one further title, "No Good Man," with a jazz trio in 1939. She died in New York City.

Although little is known of Smith's life, she is remembered for her few recordings, which document her stature as one of the best classic blues and vaudeville singers. In her early work Smith's voice is high-pitched and penetrating. On some titles she seems uncomfortable singing blues. But "Railroad Blues" is dramatic and convincing, and it shows a fully idiomatic command of sliding blue notes. She articulates lyrics clearly yet retains some black English pronunciation. Thus her historical place among African American singers is midway between those who attempted to assimilate completely into the mainstream of American popular song, like ETHEL WATERS, and those who upheld rural southern traditions, like MA RAINEY—and whose pronunciation could verge on the indecipherable.

By the time of her 1938 recordings with Bechet, Smith's voice remained as penetrating as it did when it sounded more girlish, but it had acquired a full-bodied timbre. Whether this change reflects her physical maturity or whether it reflects a dozen or so years of improvement in recording fidelity is hard to determine. It may be that better microphones captured what had been in her voice all along.

A far more significant development is represented by an excerpt from the lyrics of "My Daddy Rocks Me," the two-sided (six-minutes-long) 78-rpm record from the session with Bechet:

My daddy rocks me, with one steady roll.
There's no slippin' when he once takes hold.

. . .

I looked at the clock, and the clock struck ten.
I said, "Glooooooory, Aaaamen."
He kept rockin' with one steady roll.

. . .

I looked at the clock, and the clock struck
   eleven.
I said, "Now daddy, ain't we in heaven!"
He kept rockin' with one steady roll.

Through her extroverted and heavy manner of delivering this irreverent blend of sex and religion, Smith claims her place in a path leading from the risqué African American cabaret singing of the 1920s to the soul music of the 1950s and 1960s.

FURTHER READING

Dixon, Robert M. W., and John Godrich. *Recording the Blues* (1970).

Harrison, Daphne Duval. *Black Pearls: Blues Queens of the 1920s* (1988).

Stewart-Baxter, Derrick. *Ma Rainey and the Classic Blues Singers* (1970).

This entry is taken from the *American National Biography* and is published here with the permission of the American Council of Learned Societies.

BARRY KERNFELD

Smith, Venture. *See* Broteer (Venture Smith).

Smith, Wendell (27 June 1914–26 Nov. 1972), sportswriter, was born in Detroit, Michigan, the son of John Henry Smith, a chef for the industrialist Henry Ford, and Gertrude (Thompson) Smith. He was the only African American student enrolled in Detroit's Southeastern High School and was a member of the school's baseball team. He earned a B.S. in education from West Virginia State College, where he played basketball and served as sports editor of the newspaper.

Upon graduation in 1937 he accepted a position at the *Pittsburgh Courier*, a prominent black weekly newspaper. After only a year he became the sports editor. In addition to covering the Pittsburgh Crawfords and the Homestead Grays, baseball teams in the Negro Leagues, he also reported on the National League's Pittsburgh Pirates, the local white baseball team. Smith used his position to campaign for racial integration, particularly the integration of baseball, which had been segregated since 1884.

Smith began his integration efforts by interviewing Pirate players and managers and members of visiting National League teams, asking whether they believed that African American ballplayers could compete with white professional ballplayers. In 1938 he polled National League players and managers about the prospect of integration in Major League Baseball and found that 75 percent favored integration, 20 percent opposed the idea, and 5 percent expressed no opinion. In 1939 Smith, his publisher Ira Lewis, and PAUL ROBESON appeared at a meeting of major league owners to present their findings and promote the integration of the national pastime. The baseball establishment never responded.

Smith continued his campaign through his columns in the *Pittsburgh Courier*, which were sometimes picked up by wire services and reprinted by other newspapers. When the Boston Red Sox and Braves were seeking permission from the Boston city council to play baseball on Sunday, which was not allowed because of surviving blue laws, Smith used this political situation as an opportunity to advance integration. He convinced a Boston city councilman that he would pick up black votes by pressuring the local professional teams to give tryouts to black ballplayers as a condition for advancing their requests for Sunday baseball.

In 1945 Smith selected the Negro Leaguers Sam Jethroe, JACKIE ROBINSON, and Marvin Williams to travel to Boston for the tryout, which failed to produce either national publicity or a contract offer. On the return trip to Pittsburgh, Smith and the players stopped off in New York to meet with Branch Rickey, the general manager and president of the Brooklyn Dodgers. Rickey developed an interest in the young, educated Robinson and signed him to play for Montreal, the Dodgers' highest minor league team, in 1946.

Smith followed Robinson closely in 1946 and in 1947 when Robinson joined the Brooklyn team, becoming the first African American since 1884 to play in Major League Baseball. The close relationship between the sportswriter and the ballplayer culminated in Robinson's selecting Smith to write his autobiography, *Jackie Robinson: My Life Story*, which was published in 1948. Smith later ghostwrote books for the baseball stars ROY CAMPANELLA and ERNIE BANKS. In 1949 Smith married Wyonella Delores Hicks.

After his unsuccessful attempts to gain membership in the Baseball Writers' Association while working at an African American newspaper, Smith's white peers finally granted him admission when he left the *Courier* in 1947 to work as a sportswriter for the *Chicago American*. He continued his campaign for integration in Major League Baseball by pushing for the desegregation of housing, dining accommodations, and playing fields during spring training in Florida. At the same time he attempted to keep the Negro Leagues alive by encouraging African Americans to continue their patronage of the Negro Leagues and by trying, unsuccessfully, to persuade the baseball establishment to use the Negro Leagues as part of Major League Baseball's minor league system. After the integration of the major leagues, the Negro Leagues, deprived of the most talented black players, folded within a few years.

During his tenure at the *Chicago American* Smith earned recognition as one of America's preeminent boxing writers. He was the ghostwriter of JOE LOUIS's autobiography, and the Hearst newspapers recognized Smith as its top sportswriter in 1958. He left the *Chicago American* in 1963

and joined WBBM-TV in Chicago as a news and sports reporter. In 1964 he switched Chicago televisions stations and became the sports reporter for WGN. Smith also wrote a sports column for the *Chicago Sun-Times* from 1969 to 1972. Smith's other professional activities included stints on the governing boards of the Chicago Press Club in 1964, the Chicago Headline Club in 1964, and the National Academy of Television Arts and Sciences in 1965. He also served as president of the Chicago Sportscasters Association from 1969 to 1972 and of the Chicago Press Club in 1972.

Jackie Robinson, who claimed that he would not have made it to the major leagues without Smith's efforts, died in 1972, just a month before Smith. The *Chicago Tribune* baseball writer Jerome Holtzman led a two-year campaign that culminated in 1993 with the Baseball Writers' Association bestowing the J. G. Taylor Spink Award posthumously to Smith. In 1994 Wendell Smith, who was instrumental in breaking Major League Baseball's color line, became the first African American enshrined in the writers' wing of the National Baseball Hall of Fame.

FURTHER READING

Wendell Smith's papers are housed in the National Baseball Hall of Fame Library in Cooperstown, New York.

Reisler, Jim. *Black Writers / Black Baseball: An Anthology of Articles from Black Sportswriters Who Covered the Negro Leagues* (1994).

Tygiel, Jules. *Baseball's Great Experiment: Jackie Robinson and His Legacy* (1983).

Weaver, Bill L. "The Black Press and the Assault on Professional Baseball's 'Color Line,' October, 1945–April, 1947," *Phylon* 40 (Winter 1979).

Wiggins, David K. "Wendell Smith, the *Pittsburgh Courier-Journal*, and the Campaign to Include Blacks in Organized Baseball, 1933–1945," *Journal of Sport History* 10 (Summer 1983).

Obituary: *New York Times*, 27 Nov. 1972.

PAUL A. FRISCH

Smith, Will (25 Sept. 1968–), rapper, actor, producer, was born Willard Christopher Smith Jr. in Philadelphia, Pennsylvania, the second of four children of Caroline Smith, a school board employee, and Willard C. Smith Sr., the owner of a refrigerator company. Smith was a bright child who was very popular at the city's Julia Reynolds Masterman Laboratory and Demonstration School. Even though Smith attended a Catholic school, his family was Baptist. He grew up in a neighborhood populated mostly by Orthodox Jews and Muslims. This inevitably helped Smith learn how to be personable with almost anyone. As a teenager Smith attended Overbrook High School in West Philadelphia. There he began rapping, modeling himself after GRANDMASTER FLASH, and acquired the nickname "Prince" from his teachers because of his charm.

In 1984, at the age of sixteen, Smith met Jeff Townes (a.k.a. DJ Jazzy Jeff) at a party. Together they formed the rap duo DJ Jazzy Jeff and the Fresh Prince in the 1986. The duo quickly became a household name in the burgeoning hip-hop music scene spreading throughout the nation. In 1987 the duo's single, "Girls Ain't Nothing but Trouble," from their debut album, *Rock the House*, became a hit, reaching number eighty-three on the U.S. charts, and number twenty-four on the rap and hip-hop charts. In 1988 their second album, *He's The DJ, I'm The Rapper*, was the first hip-hop LP to go double platinum. The wholesome, articulate humor of their next single, "Parents Just Don't Understand," solidified their place in the hip-hop industry. That same year the duo won their first Grammy Award, which was also the first Grammy ever given for the category of Rap. They gained both parental approval and commercial crossover success because their style was not as abrasive as that of most of their fellow rappers in the late 1980s.

Close to bankruptcy for not having paid taxes in 1990, Smith was approached by NBC to do a sitcom with producer Benny Medina. Immediately Smith found a second career as an actor, and *The Fresh Prince of Bel-Air* was born. On the show Smith got a chance to work with other stars such as James Avery, Alfonso Ribeiro, and the actress and singer Tatyana Ali. The show was an instant success and became a TV staple in living rooms across America. Smith won another Grammy in 1991 for his hit single "Summertime." In 1992 Smith married Sheree Zampino, an actress whom he had met at a taping of *A Different World*; the couple had a son, Willard Christopher III, that same year. The couple would divorce in 1995.

During *The Fresh Prince*'s television run, Smith became involved in film. His first role was in *Where the Day Takes You* (1992), about young runaways in Hollywood, also starring Rikki Lake, Alyssa Milano, and Sean Astin. The next year he had a more notable dramatic role as a gay con man in the film *Six Degrees of Separation*, starring alongside Stockard Channing, Donald Sutherland, and

Ian McKellen. Smith's acting career took a giant leap in 1995 with his role in the action film *Bad Boys*, costarring Martin Lawrence. When *The Fresh Prince of Bel-Air* ended in 1996, Smith was starring in a number of films while simultaneously solidifying his music career as a solo artist. In 1996 Smith played a brave fighter pilot in the hugely successful film *Independence Day*, which also starred Bill Pullman, Jeff Goldblum, Judd Hirsch, Randy Quaid, and Vivica A. Fox. Following that performance, which earned him an MTV Movie Award, he costarred with Tommy Lee Jones in the smash hit *Men in Black* (1997). That same year, Smith married actress Jada Pinkett. Smith's first two solo albums went platinum on the strength of the number one hit "Men in Black" (the theme song to the movie) and 1998's number-one hit single "Gettin' Jiggy Wit' It." Smith then starred in the 1998 movie *Enemy of the State*, also starring Gene Hackman, Jon Voight, Regina King, and Lisa Bonet. Smith's second child, Jaden Christopher Syre, was born that same year, and his third child, Willow Camille Reign, was born in 2000.

Smith had several lead roles in successful movies during the early twenty-first century, including *The Legend of Bagger Vance* (2000), *Ali* (2001), for which he won an Academy Award for Best Actor; *Men in Black II* (2002), *Bad Boys II* (2003), and *Made in America* (2003). In 2003 Smith produced a program with wife Jada Pinkett Smith called *All of Us*, which was a show inspired by his own family.

Later in the decade, Smith lent his voice to the highly successful animated *Shark Tale* (2004); he would also star in *I, Robot* (2004) and *Hitch* (2005). After signing to the Interscope label, Smith's 2005 *Lost & Found* album produced "Switch," which became yet another number-one hit single for Smith. "Switch" was such a success that he was asked to perform the song at the 2005 Nickelodeon Kids' Choice Awards, the 2005 Black Entertainment Television awards, and at the second game of the 2005 NBA Finals (San Antonio vs. Detroit). Also in 2005 Smith hosted the Live 8 concert in his hometown of Philadelphia and later performed with DJ Jazzy Jeff.

In 2006 Smith was nominated for an Academy Award for his starring role in *The Pursuit of Happyness*; he also starred in the feature film *I Am Legend* in 2007. Over the years, Smith developed a solid reputation as one of Hollywood's best comic and dramatic leads.

Smith branched out from his acting and singing to produce films through his production company,

Overbrook Entertainment, with partner James Lassiter. The company has produced a number of feature films, television shows, and albums, including *Jitney*, an off-Broadway play (2001), *All of Us*, a television series (2003–2007), the films *Ali* (2001), *I, Robot* (2004), *Hitch* (2005), and *The Pursuit of Happyness* (2006), and the album, *The Evolution of Robin Thicke*, by Robin Thicke (2006). In addition, with his brother Harry Smith, he owns Treyball Development Company, which deals in luxury housing developments for the city of Philadelphia. Smith still owns a home in his hometown of Philadelphia, and he and his family split their time between Philadelphia and Miami, Florida.

FURTHER READING

Robb, Brian J. *Will Smith*: *King of Cool* (1999).

WILLIAM E. BANKSTON

Smith, Willi (29 Feb. 1948–10 Apr. 1987), fashion designer, was born Willi Donnell Smith in Philadelphia, Pennsylvania, the son of Willie Lee Smith, an ironworker, and June Eileen (Bush) Smith, a homemaker. He had two siblings, a brother Norman and a sister Doris, known as Toukie. As a child Smith showed an interest in art and, encouraged by his parents, also took an interest in clothing design. He attended Mastbaum Technical High School, where he studied commercial art. In 1962 he studied fashion illustration at the Philadelphia Museum College of Art but knew almost immediately that he would rather be a fashion designer. At seventeen his ambitions took him to New York City and the Parsons School of Design. During his two years at Parsons, he worked as an illustrator for designers like Arnold Scaasi. When he left Parsons in 1967, he freelanced for the Bobbie Brooks Company and did additional work at Talbott and Digits, both sportswear manufacturers. By 1969 his name was on the Digits label.

Smith joined an elite group of designers who gained access to the fashion industry after racial barriers were relaxed in the late 1950s, a group that included artisans like Anne Lowe, who designed Jacqueline Bouvier Kennedy's wedding dress, and Stephen Burrows, the first African American to win the Coty American Fashion Critics' Award, often referred to as the industry's "Oscar." Smith was touted as the most successful African American fashion designer of the twentieth century by the late fashion editor Liz Rittersporn of the *New York Daily News*. Certainly he was considered one of the industry's most talented designers. In a field

known for its competitiveness, where up-and-coming designers, especially African Americans, often found it difficult to secure financial backing and a broad audience for their designs, Smith more than met these challenges. His sense of style and his willingness to innovate made him a visionary in the world of fashion. As a result success came quickly. In 1972 he became the youngest designer to be nominated for a Coty Award.

Given his early achievements, Smith soon decided to branch out on his own. His first company, undertaken as a joint venture with his sister Toukie Smith, who began her modeling career with her brother, was short-lived. But in 1976 Smith joined forces with Laurie Mallet, a former colleague from his time at Digits, to form WilliWear Ltd., with Smith in the roles of designer and vice president. Because the two entrepreneurs had little capital between them, they had to improvise. To complete their first collection Smith and Mallet went to India, where fabric was cheaper. With no money for buttons, Smith produced wrap-around coats that became the signature pieces of the collection. Those coats also signaled his emerging style: vibrant colors, natural fabrics, a relaxed fit, and street-smart appeal.

Smith's willingness to improvise was a mark of his genius and spread to other areas of the business, most notably marketing and promotion. WilliWear, for example, shied away from high-powered runway presentations. Instead, the company used its urban-inspired showroom, replete with fire hydrants, brick walls, and police barricades, as a backdrop for the models sporting his designs. Moreover, the business did not embark on large-scale advertising campaigns. Instead, Smith's clothes quickly found favor with fashion editors, department store buyers, and specialty chain stores. Neither jeans nor evening wear, his designs filled a ready niche in large part because they were fashionable and affordable. According to the *New York Times* Smith once said, "I don't design clothes for the Queen, but for the people who wave at her as she goes by." As a result his clothes were casual, comfortable, and fun. It was this focus on ease and simplicity that set the tone for the relaxed clothing styles of the late 1980s and 1990s.

Smith was one of the first designers to use video in his showroom presentations. He was also one of the first to design for both women and men under one banner; he added the menswear line to his collection in 1978. And he was one of the first designers to link fashion design to visual arts, often incorporating the work of other artists into his designs. In 1984, for example, the company produced a line of T-shirts featuring the work of twenty artists; the shirts were sold in cardboard frames to highlight their artistic qualities.

In 1983 Smith's hard work finally earned him the Coty Award. Only the second African American to win this prize, he also received the Cutty Sark Menswear Award two years later. In 1985 he turned to costume design, creating the uniforms for workers on *The Pont Neuf Wrapped, Project for Paris*, an artistic venture by the artist Christo. In that same year Smith did designs for the BILL T. JONES/Arnie Zane Dance Company's *Secret Pastures*, an avant-garde dance production. He worked in the same capacity of costume designer on the 1988 SPIKE LEE film *School Daze*. Throughout his career Smith designed textiles for Bedford Stuyvesant Design Works, upholstery for Knoll International, and patterns for Butterick and McCall's. He was also a lecturer in art history at the Fashion Institute in London.

In 1987 Smith died unexpectedly from complications of AIDS after a trip to India, where he contracted pneumonia and shigella, a parasitic disease. At the time of his death, annual sales at WilliWear were nearly $25 million. The company continued, with stores opening in both New York and Paris after his death. Moreover his pioneering legacy lives on in the rise to prominence in the 1990s of other African American designers such as Anthony Mark Hankins and design companies such as Karl Kani, FUBU, and Sean John. After Smith's death a panel commemorating his life was created for the Names Project AIDS Memorial Quilt. In 2002 he was honored with the installation of a bronze plaque on New York City's Seventh Avenue, otherwise known as Fashion Avenue.

FURTHER READING

Alexander, Lois K. *Blacks in the History of Fashion* (1982).

Gregory, Deborah. "Then: Brothers on Seventh Avenue—African American Fashion Designers," *Essence* (Nov. 1991).

Martin, Richard. "Smith, Willi." In *Contemporary Fashion* (1995).

Milbank, Caroline Rennolds. *New York Fashion: The Evolution of American Style* (1989).

Obituary: *New York Times*, 19 Apr. 1987; *Washington Post*, 19 Apr. 1987.

ELEANOR D. BRANCH

Smith, William Gardner (6 Feb. 1927–5 Nov. 1974), novelist and journalist, was born in Philadelphia, Pennsylvania, the son of Leon Vernon Hemsley and Edith Smith, who in 1934 married Douglas Stanley Earle, a custodian, and had with him three more children. Smith grew up in Philadelphia and attended Benjamin Franklin High School, where he fenced, edited the school newspaper and yearbook, and graduated second in his class. In 1943, while a high school senior, he began working full time as a reporter at the *Pittsburgh Courier*. Upon graduating from high school in 1944, though he received scholarship offers from Howard University and Lincoln University, Smith decided to stay on at the *Courier* as a full-time reporter.

In January 1946, seven months after the official end of World War II, Smith was drafted into the U.S. Army and worked in Berlin for eight months as a clerk. Returning to Philadelphia, he attended Temple University under the GI Bill while working on his first novel. *Last of the Conquerors*, about black soldiers who experience an ironic liberation from racism while stationed in Germany, was published in 1948 to significant acclaim. Smith married Mary Sewell, his girlfriend since high school, in 1949. The couple had no children. Smith's second novel, *Anger at Innocence*, was published in 1950.

In 1951, after a summer at Yaddo, Smith and his wife moved to Paris, where he continued to write for the *Pittsburgh Courier* and worked as a foreign correspondent for *Jet* and *Ebony* magazines. Although the Smiths had hoped that time abroad would reinvigorate their marriage, after less than a year in Paris they decided to separate; they divorced in 1957. Whereas his wife returned to the United States, Smith remained in Paris, where he wrote full time and became a fixture of the black expatriate community that congregated at the Café Tournon near Smith's flat and included JAMES BALDWIN, BEAUFORD DELANEY, OLLIE HARRINGTON, GORDON HEATH, and CHESTER HIMES.

After three productive but not very lucrative years of writing, Smith took a position in 1954 as an editor and translator at the Agence France-Presse (AFP), where he worked intermittently for the rest of his life. His third novel, *South Street*, considered among the earliest protest novels, was published in 1954. During that time Smith completed another manuscript, "Simeon," about an idealistic young lawyer working his way up in the corrupt world of Philadelphia politics; it was never published and is now lost.

Despite a prohibition on foreign residents' involvement in domestic politics, Smith voiced criticism of French policy and military actions in Algeria. In 1957 Richard Gibson, a fellow AFP journalist and friend, published antiwar letters in *Life* magazine and the *London Observer* under the name Oliver Harrington. Smith distanced himself from the resulting scandal ("the Gibson affair"). In 1960 Smith completed a manuscript on recent French politics, "Pink Ballets," which was accepted by a French publisher but never released.

On 31 October 1961 Smith married Solange Royez, with whom he had two children. Smith's fourth novel, *The Stone Face*, a semiautobiographical work about a black expatriate in Paris and his encounter with the plight of Algerians in France, was published in 1963. In 1964 Smith moved to Ghana to help create a television station in collaboration with SHIRLEY GRAHAM DuBois. He worked in Accra as director of Ghana's Institute of Journalism, taking the name Kofi Abaka Smith. After the fall of the Kwame Nkrumah government on 24 February 1966, Smith and his family were forced to leave Ghana for France, where Smith returned to work at the AFP.

Made a senior editor at the AFP, Smith in 1967 returned to the United States for the first time in sixteen years to gather material for a book on the black power movement and to visit family and friends. *Return to Black America*, published in 1970, included material based on Smith's observations in the United States and his time in Ghana. In 1970 Smith and Royez divorced. Later that year Smith married Ira Reuben; they had one child. In September 1973 Smith was diagnosed with cancer. After undergoing radiation therapy, he died at a clinic in Thiais, near Paris, leaving behind a respected body of work on black experiences at home and abroad.

FURTHER READING

Hodges, LeRoy S., Jr. *Portrait of an Expatriate: William Gardner Smith, Writer* (1985).

Stovall, Tyler. *Paris Noir: African Americans in the City of Light* (1996).

Obituary: *New York Times*, 8 Nov. 1974.

ALEX FEERST

Smith, Willie "the Lion" (25 Nov. 1897–18 Apr. 1973), jazz pianist, was born William Henry Joseph Bonaparte Bertholoff in Goshen, New York, the son of Ida Oliver, a domestic worker, and Frank Bertholoff. In 1900 Ida expelled Frank from the household; he died the next year, and she married John Smith, who took the family to Newark, New Jersey, where he worked as a meat-wagon driver and later a mechanic. Willie attended Newark High School, where he excelled as an athlete.

Having begun to play the family's home organ by ear, Smith received lessons from his mother, a church pianist and organist. He worked for tips as a dancer but preferred piano and, after winning an upright piano in a contest, devoted himself to it, practicing pop songs and ragtime. From around 1911 he entertained in saloons in Newark. Although his music was informed by his background in the African American Baptist Church, Smith had been befriended by a Jewish family and had embraced Judaism, learning Hebrew as a child and becoming a bar mitzvah at age thirteen; later in life he served as a cantor at a synagogue in Harlem.

In the summers of 1915 and 1916 Smith worked in saloons in Atlantic City, New Jersey, initially as a replacement for EUBIE BLAKE. He also began to play professionally in New York City. The pianist Arthur Eck taught Smith to read music, and in exchange Smith improved Eck's improvisatory skills. At age nineteen Smith married Blanche Howard Merrill, a pianist (not the vaudeville songwriter of the same name); they separated after one year. Smith enlisted in the army in November 1916 and the following July was sent to France, where he played bass drum in Lieutenant TIM BRYMN's Regimental Band and where, by one account, his energy as a gunner earned him his nickname (Artie Shaw, however, attributed the nickname to the growls that Smith vocalized while playing piano). Late in 1919 Smith was discharged and returned to New York City. Reunited with his lifelong friend JAMES P. JOHNSON, whom he had met in 1914, and soon joined by their younger colleague FATS WALLER, he became a pioneer and a virtuoso in a new jazz style that came to be known as stride piano, a swinging and sometimes improvised offshoot of classic ragtime that features irregular patterns in which the left hand "strides" between the instrument's bass range and mid-range.

Smith performed at Leroy's in Harlem in 1919 and 1920. In August 1920 he organized and performed in the band that accompanied the singer MAMIE SMITH on the historic recording "Crazy Blues." Its success touched off a craze for "classic blues" (female African American blues and vaudeville singers with jazz bands), and it established a new marketing category that soon acquired the name "race records." As a member of the Holiday in Dixieland troupe, Smith performed in New York in April 1922 and then set out on a brief tour. In 1923, while working in Chicago, he heard some of the great New Orleans jazz musicians.

Back in Harlem by year's end, Smith performed at the Garden of Joy and then at the Capitol Palace, where future jazz soloists BUBBER MILEY and Jimmy Harrison sat in with the band. Many nights, after the Capitol Palace closed, he went to the Rhythm Club, where the house band was led by SIDNEY BECHET and where emerging giants of jazz came to improvise. Smith took over the leadership and hired the soprano saxophonist JOHNNY HODGES when Bechet left in the spring of 1925. When the Rhythm Club moved, Smith stayed at the same location, now renamed the Hoofers' Club, and he changed the format from an open jam session to a tightly organized quartet that included the C-melody saxophonist Benny Carter. Smith played and acted in the drama *Four Walls* at the John Golden Theater on Fifty-eighth Street in New York City beginning in September 1927. When after 144 performances the show moved to Chicago, he, as usual, chose to stay in New York.

Throughout the mid- to late-1920s, Smith, Johnson, and Waller were in constant demand as solo pianists at rent parties in Harlem. Although the three friends were energetic to excess and lived wild lives, Smith, like Johnson (and unlike Waller), was nonetheless concerned with meticulous show-business mannerisms and a stylishly elegant and orderly presentation: a fine suit, a derby hat, and a cigar were fixtures of his appearance. He was intelligent, inquisitive, and opinionated, and (anticipating the 1960s) he was sensitive to good and bad "vibrations," which would determine his involvement in a given situation.

Smith spent about two years in the early 1930s at another Harlem club, Pods' and Jerry's (officially the Catagonia Club but known by the owners' nicknames). He discouraged sitting in, after the chaos of the Rhythm Club, but he made exceptions for talents like Bechet and the young Artie Shaw; Shaw played without pay for the experience of performing with Smith. At Pods' and Jerry's he met his future wife, then a married woman, Jennie Williams, also known as "Silvertop" or "Jane." Her maiden name, details of the marriage, and the number of their children, if any, are unknown.

Smith began working steadily for Joe Helbock on Fifty-second Street, and with the end of Prohibition in 1933, Helbock made the venue into a legitimate nightclub, the Onyx. Smith worked as intermission pianist at the nearby Famous Door from 1934 to 1935. During

these years he recorded and broadcast with EVA TAYLOR in CLARENCE WILLIAMS's band. He may be heard as a soloist on "Somebody Stole My Gal" from a session on 3 October 1934 by a group of Williams's musicians recording under the name of the Alabama Jug Band. Also during this period Smith commenced formal studies with the pianist Hans Steinke, and he began to write pieces exhibiting an amalgam of jazz, blues, and European influences.

In 1935, with personnel drawn from Williams's circle, Smith made his first recordings as a leader, including his composition "Echo of Spring." After further sessions of his own in 1937, he agreed to a recording contract with the musically ponderous organist Milt Herth, an association he detested. In January 1938 he recorded two more compositions, "Passionette" and "Morning Air," in a duo with drummer O'Neil Spencer; these are firmly based in the irregularly leaping and swinging patterns of stride and thus exhibit Smith's usual approach to performance. For the Commodore label in January 1939 he made his most famous recordings: fourteen unaccompanied titles comprising popular songs and his own compositions, including "Concentratin'," "Fading Star," "Sneakaway," and "Finger Buster," as well as versions of some previously recorded pieces. The fourteen recordings summarize his twofold approach, alternately centered in the mainstream of the flamboyant stride piano tradition and exploring a sensitive twist on that tradition. In the best known of these, titled "Echoes of Spring" for the Commodore session (rather than "Echo of Spring"), his exuberant style is modified by a delicacy that hints at turn-of-the-century French piano impressionism and by a simple, repeated, loping accompanimental figure that perhaps owes more to boogie-woogie piano than to the complexities of stride. The Tommy Dorsey and Artie Shaw orchestras performed arrangements of Smith's compositions in the 1940s, thereby bringing him a somewhat greater audience, although he was never famous outside the jazz world.

Smith worked in a trio with Bechet in the spring of 1939. In November, as members of the Haitian Orchestra, they recorded an odd session of arranged merengues, rhumbas, and Haitian melodies, notable for pioneering the concept of Caribbean jazz but not for the result. In 1940 he accompanied the blues singer Joe Turner, but unfortunately this pairing was a mismatch: Smith's musically florid and emotionally fluffy blues playing is temperamentally unsuited to Turner's raw style. In 1941 he recorded with Bechet's New Orleans Feetwarmers.

In the 1940s Smith worked at the Man About Town Club on Fifty-first Street and in dixieland bands in Lower Manhattan, including the Pied Piper, where in 1944 he served as the pianist in the trumpeter Max Kaminsky's band while also engaging in legendary solo contests with the intermission pianist, his friend James Johnson. Smith also made regular trips to perform in Toronto. Hard living finally took its toll, and he ceased working temporarily. He returned to performing to tour Europe and North Africa from December 1949 through February 1950 and recorded for the Royal Jazz label in Paris. By this time he had arthritis in his fingers, and it slowly worsened over the years, but only the expert and cranky listener will find fault with these performances. His career continued unabated, and he recorded new versions of the Commodore solos for Royal Jazz in December 1950. Despite the strong compositional element in his own pieces, the re-creations are substantially different from the originals of 1939. His dramatic, texturally thick, bent-for-hell readings of several of the popular songs, including "Stormy Weather," "Tea for Two," and "Between the Devil and the Deep Blue Sea," demonstrate the sort of playing that must have given the competition fits.

During the 1950s Smith worked regularly at the Central Plaza, and the film *Jazz Dance* captures him there in 1954. He hated the crass tastelessness of the music (the band was notorious for playing loudly and without regard for the sensitive aspects of musical taste), but he stayed at the Central Plaza until 1958. In the spring of that year he appeared in the third show ("Ragtime") of the television series *The Subject Is Jazz*. Smith ceased performing in nightclubs and turned instead to colleges, country clubs, festivals, benefit concerts, and other less demanding work. He toured and recorded again in Europe in 1965 and 1966. In the spring of 1969 he was filmed playing in New York for the French documentary *L'Aventure du jazz* (1970). He died in New York City.

Smith was one of the most formidably talented stride pianists. Although not an innovator of the stature of Johnson, Waller, and ART TATUM, he was a central figure for a half century in the development and subsequent international dissemination of stride and related early jazz styles.

FURTHER READING

Smith, Willie "the Lion," with George Hoefer. *Music on My Mind* (1964; repr. 1975).

Obituary: *New York Times,* 19 Apr. 1973.

DISCOGRAPHY

Collison, John. "Willie 'the Lion' Smith." *Storyville*, nos. 132 (1 Dec. 1987), 133 (1 Mar. 1988), 134 (1 June 1988), 135 (1 Sept. 1988), 136 (1 Dec. 1988), 137 (1 Mar. 1989), 138 (1 June 1989).

This entry is taken from the *American National Biography* and is published here with the permission of the American Council of Learned Societies.

BARRY KERNFELD

Smith, Willie Mae Ford (23 June 1904–2 Feb. 1994), gospel singer and evangelist, was born Willie Mae Ford in Rolling Fork, Mississippi, to Clarence Ford, a railroad worker, and Mary Williams, a restaurateur. The seventh of fourteen children, Willie Mae had varying experiences in her early life as the family moved frequently throughout the Midwest. Clarence Ford worked hard to give his children a stable home. He and his wife were devout Christians whose interest in gospel singing extended beyond their music making in the home to area churches in and around Memphis, Tennessee, where the family moved shortly after Willie Mae's birth.

The vibrant black community and musical environment of Memphis introduced Willie Mae to the two genres that would greatly influence both her musical development and the course of her life—blues and gospel singing. Willie Mae's experience with the blues, considered by most Protestant blacks to be the "Devil's music," came in the form of singing blues songs on the streets of Memphis for money. Not unlike the Reverend GARY DAVIS and other early blues singers, Willie Mae would later claim that only through salvation in the church was she rescued from this life of sin. She overcame the moral reservations associated with the secular music genre, and through the blues influence she developed the robust and resonating quality of her contralto voice. Willie Mae gained further experience in church, singing the long-meter hymns and spirituals that her mother enjoyed. As a small girl she was placed upon a table in the church; from this stage she enthralled her first audiences.

In 1917 the family settled in St. Louis, Missouri. Encouraged by her father, Willie Mae became the leader of a female quartet that included her sisters Mary, Emma, and Geneva. The Ford Sisters patterned themselves after popular male quartets of the day and earned a reputation throughout Missouri and Illinois. The group presented the "new" sound in gospel music—female groups that sang both a cappella and with piano accompaniment. The Ford

Sisters reached a high point in their career when they performed at the National Baptist Convention in 1922. Because the National Baptist Convention was the largest body of black Protestants in America, the concerts that took place at these events influenced the latest trends in black gospel across the country. The Baptist musical tradition was quite conservative compared with those of Pentecostal and Holiness churches, but by 1922 the convention was just beginning to accept the new type of singing. The Ford Sisters' reception at the convention was lukewarm, and despite efforts to keep the group functioning, domestic responsibilities proved more pressing than their desire to sing. By the mid-1920s the group had disbanded.

Willie Mae had discontinued her education after the eighth grade and was determined to become successful as a singer; therefore, she continued singing when her sisters could not, ultimately becoming a consummate soloist. In time, her reputation for soulful, spirit-filled performances earned her a place of distinction both in the St. Louis area and at the annual National Baptist Convention. There is uncertainty as to the date of her marriage; most sources cite either 1924 or 1929 as the year in which she married James Peter Smith, who owned a small moving company. The union produced two children, Willie James and Jacquelyn, who would often accompany their mother when she performed in and around St. Louis. When the Depression threatened James's business, Willie Mae began traveling more widely, conducting musical revivals to supplement the family income.

On one of these occasions she met the gospel composer and former blues pianist THOMAS A. DORSEY. Impressed by Smith's voice, Dorsey invited her to Chicago in 1932 to help organize the National Convention of Gospel Choirs and Choruses (NCGCC), which brought together directors and choirs from Baptist churches throughout the United States. Each year an annual convention was held in a different city, where new compositions were presented that directors could teach to their local choirs. Smith's participation in the NCGCC placed her at the center of a musical movement that would diversify the marketing of gospel music and expand its audience beyond the traditional venues.

By 1936 her role in Dorsey's gospel dynasty was secured when he appointed her the principal teacher of singing and the director of the soloist bureau of the convention. Smith's devotion to the Dorsey convention did not, however, prevent her from performing on her own, and she continued to travel extensively throughout the late 1930s and early 1940s. In 1937 her performance at the National Baptist Convention of an original composition, "If You Just Keep Still," gained her particular attention. From 1937 onward Smith spent a great deal of time on the road, while her husband raised their two children. She performed frequently in churches in Cincinnati, Buffalo, Detroit, Kansas City, Atlanta, and small towns around the Midwest and the South.

Her performance style changed considerably during the late 1930s and early 1940s when she joined the Church of God Apostolic, one of many Pentecostal denominations emerging during this period. She took on as accompanist a young woman named Bertha, whom she and James adopted. The combination of Smith's robust voice and Bertha's piano style was formidable and had a marked influence on the performance style of a number of gospel soloists and groups. Smith began to integrate into her performances elements of the singing styles of Sanctified churches, including rhythmic bounce, expressive timbres in the voice conveyed through melodic embellishments, slides, moans, groans, percussive attacks of words, phrases, and distinctive harmonies.

Central to Smith's performance was her inclusion of sermonettes, five- to ten-minute sermons delivered before, after, and even during a song. The emotional quality of these sermonettes was intensified by her physical enactment of the text, though this, at times, brought the criticism of ministers and deacons who objected to her movements as undignified. Nevertheless, audiences packed the churches where Smith performed, and her popularity grew.

Although her live performances were highly successful, Smith never achieved the popularity that gospel recordings had helped her counterparts ROBERTA MARTIN and MAHALIA JACKSON attain. During the 1940s she concentrated on preaching and singing, openly acknowledging her "calling" to preach the gospel, though a woman preacher was not readily accepted in many black churches. Her career took a turn following the death of her husband in 1950. Soon afterward, Bertha grew disenchanted with traveling and eventually gave up her position as accompanist. Smith was never fully able to establish with other accompanists the musical rapport she had had with Bertha, and she began performing less frequently in order to devote more time to her domestic responsibilities.

"Mother Smith," as she came to be known in congregational and church circles, began teaching gospel singing after the 1950s and mentored a number of noteworthy vocalists, including the O'Neal Twins, Edna Gallmon Cooke, and Brother Joe May, who reportedly was the first to call her "Mother." In the 1970s she resurfaced to record several albums on the Savoy label and appear at the Newport Jazz Festival, and was featured in the 1982 film *Say Amen, Somebody* that solidified her place in gospel history. In 1988 she received the Heritage Award from the National Endowment of the Arts and a year later appeared in Brian Lanker's book *I Dream a World: Portraits of Black Women Who Changed America*. On 2 February 1994, at the age of eighty-nine, Willie Mae Ford Smith died of congestive heart failure in a St. Louis nursing home.

Ford's contribution to the gospel world was multifaceted. She defined the role of the female soloist at a time when gospel music was dominated by male quartets and groups. She effectively translated a blues-derived style into gospel singing and brought the regional traditions of St. Louis to national attention. More important to the gospel genre, perhaps, was her introduction of the sermonette and song format that became popular years later with the singers SHIRLEY CAESAR and Dorothy Norwood.

FURTHER READING

Boyer, Horace Clarence. *How Sweet the Sound: The Golden Age of Gospel* (1995).

Dargan, Thomas, and Kathy White Bullock. "Willie Mae Ford Smith of St. Louis: A Shaping Influence upon Black Gospel Singing Style," *Black Music Research Journal* 9 (Fall 1989): 249–270.

Heilbut, Anthony. *The Gospel Sound: Good News and Bad Times* (1985).

DISCOGRAPHY

Going on with the Spirit (Nashboro 7148).

I Believe I'll Run On (Nashboro 7124).

The Legends: The O'Neal Twins, Thomas Dorsey, the Barrett Sisters, Sallie Martin, Willie Mae Ford Smith (Savoy SL-14742).

TAMMY L. KERNODLE

Smitherman, Andrew Jackson (c. 27 Dec. 1883–20 June 1961), journalist, was born in Alabama, one of at least six children of James, a storekeeper, and Elizabeth (Phillips) Smitherman. "A.J." as he was known, worked for a time in coal mines around

Birmingham and went to school in Birmingham and Bessemer, Alabama, and attended high school in Louisiana. He later attended the University of Kansas and Northwestern University and studied law at LaSalle University Extension School of Chicago, although it is not known whether he graduated from any of these programs. Like many others seeking opportunities not available to African Americans in the former Confederate states, the Smitherman family moved to Oklahoma in about 1908, where three years later A.J. Smitherman began working for the eastern Oklahoma town of Muskogee's weekly newspaper, the *Muskogee Cimeter*. Around 1911 he briefly published the *Muskogee Star*, a paper that concentrated on ideas of economic progress, racial uplift, and racial pride. Perhaps because of his earlier training as a lawyer, his emphasis was on demanding full civil rights for African Americans. He married Ollie B. Murphy of Servier County, Arkansas, on 29 June 1910, and they had at least three sons (Delmas M., Antenor, and A. Toussaint) and three daughters (Carole Embrose, Guelda Baxter, and Aprilyn Williams).

Around 1914, Smitherman moved on to Tulsa where he founded the *Tulsa Star*, a weekly newspaper. For a short time in or around 1920 the paper may have been published as a daily. Through editorials in the *Tulsa Star* and in his actions around Tulsa, Smitherman contributed to the development of a strong, self-conscious black community. Every week the paper ran front-page stories about the struggles throughout the country to prevent lynchings and riots and to compel public officials to finance both black and white schools equally and to end segregated Jim Crow public accommodations. Smitherman, however, went beyond simply retelling those stories. In 1918 he traveled to Bristow, a town near Tulsa, after hearing that a lynching was about to take place and then stood alone against a mob. According to Smitherman's account, he drove them off. Additionally, he claimed credit for assisting in the defeat of the Oklahoma grandfather law, which the United States Supreme Court struck down in 1915. And in 1919 he filed a lawsuit after he was forced into inferior and segregated accommodations on a railroad car. On his editorial pages, Smitherman emphasized self-help and urged African Americans to support the Democratic Party. He hired DAISY SCOTT to draw editorial cartoons for his paper that emphasized the unequal treatment that African Americans endured in Oklahoma. After Claude Chandler, a young black man, was lynched in Oklahoma City in 1920, Smitherman, clearly frustrated, challenged Oklahoma City's quiescent black community: "The proper time to afford protection to any prisoner is before and during the time he is being lynched, and certainly not after he is killed" (*Tulsa Star*, Sept. 1920). Later that month he wrote that when the young man was in jail, "and while there was danger of mob violence any set of citizens had a legal right—it was their duty—to arm themselves and march in a body to the jail and apprize the sheriff or jailer of the purpose of their visit and to take life if need be to uphold the law and protect the prisoner" (*Tulsa Star*, Sept. 1920).

In Smitherman's words one could find the motivation for Greenwood (the black section of Tulsa) to prevent a threatened lynching of Dick Rowland in May 1921, who was falsely accused of attempting to assault a young white woman in a downtown Tulsa elevator. When word reached Greenwood that there might be a lynching, Smitherman met with other perhaps a dozen (or maybe more) leaders of the Greenwood community such as J. B. STRADFORD, and they all pledged to prevent Rowland's lynching. Around nine that evening, a contingent of World War I veterans from Greenwood went to the courthouse to help protect Rowland. At the courthouse there was a confrontation between the men from Greenwood and Tulsa's police officers and the white mob assembled there to witness (and perhaps participate in) a lynching. The riot was on.

The next morning, members of the Tulsa police force, working in conjunction with a hastily deputized mob of around 250 men and the local units of the Tulsa National Guard, rounded up every Greenwood resident they could lay their hands on and took them into custody. Then followed the looting and burning of Greenwood, which was orchestrated in part, it now appears, by the special deputies and perhaps in part by a few police officers. In the aftermath, Smitherman, fearing a biased prosecution for inciting rioting, fled to Boston, where he published a poem about the riot. Among the stanzas, Smitherman records the early successes of the Greenwood community, holding off those men bent on burning down the community:

Like a flash they came together,
Word was passed along the line:
"No white man must cross the border;
Shoot to kill and shoot in time!"
"Ready, Fire!" And then a volley
From the mob whose skins were white

"Give 'em hell, boys," cried the leader,
"Soon we'll put them all to flight."
But they got a warm reception
From black men who had no fear,
Who while fighting they were singing:
"Come on Boys, The Gang's all Here."
Rapid firing guns were shooting.
Men were falling by the score.
'Till the white men quite defeated
Sent the word, "We want no more."
Nine P.M. the trouble started,
Two A.M. the thing was done.
And the victory for the black men
Counted almost four to one. (Brophy, 41)

After about a year in Boston, Smitherman moved to Springfield, Massachusetts, where he founded the Springfield *New World*, and then moved on to Buffalo, New York, in 1925, where he founded the *Buffalo Star* in 1931 (known subsequently as the *Empire Star*). While there, Smitherman nurtured young journalists, including ISHMAEL REED. Smitherman died in 1961 in Buffalo, where he was still publisher of the *Empire Star*. Smitherman lived through extraordinary times, stretching from the Tulsa riot in 1921 to the Supreme Court's monumental 1954 decision in *Brown v. Board of Education*. At the time of his death, Smitherman said, "I'm never licked," which is an appropriate summary of a determined and heroic life.

FURTHER READING

Smitherman, A.J. "The Facts Remain the Same," *Tulsa Star* (Sept. 1920).

Smitherman, A.J. "Misguided Oklahoma Patriots," *Tulsa Star* (Sept. 1920).

Brophy, Alfred L. *Reconstructing the Dreamland: The Tulsa Riot of 1921—Race, Reparations, Reconciliation* (2002)

O'Dell, Larry. "Protecting His Race: A. J. Smitherman and the *Tulsa Star*," *Chronicles of Oklahoma* (Fall 2002).

ALFRED L. BROPHY

Smitherman, Geneva (10 Dec. 1940–), linguist and educator, was born in the rural outskirts of Brownsville, Tennessee. Her education began at the age of four in a one-room schoolhouse. She reminisced: "My father, a self-educated, self-made man, would always say that with education, a person could accomplish *anything*. Believing that, I threw myself into school with a passionate zeal after we moved to Detroit. I was double-promoted in the regular school year, and I advanced grade levels by attending summer school every year" (personal interview). One month after her fifteenth birthday, Smitherman entered Wayne State University in Detroit, where she earned a B.A. (1960) and an M.A. (1962) in English and Latin. While teaching English and Latin in the Detroit Public Schools for five years, she also earned a Ph.D. in English at the University of Michigan (1969). Her original goal had been to take charge of the Detroit Public Schools. But through study groups and community work in the 1960s black liberation movement, she was introduced to what was later called the African American intellectual tradition with its focus on race, racism, religion, and slavery, as well as class and gender, and she became active in campus struggles to establish African American studies in the academy.

In 1971 Smitherman became a member of the first group of faculty in Harvard University's Afro-American Studies Department, founded in response to the activism of Harvard's black students. Two years later she left Harvard to work in the newly established Wayne State University Center for Black Studies, serving as program coordinator, associate director, and director (1973–1980). At Wayne State she was also director of the linguistics program, professor of speech communication, and interim associate dean of liberal arts. She held visiting professorships at Montclair State College; the University of Michigan; Pennsylvania State University; California State University, Northridge; Oxford University; and the University of Ghana-Legon.

In 1989 Smitherman began teaching at Michigan State University. She was appointed University Distinguished Professor of English and became director of the African American Language and Literacy Program. She was director of My Brother's Keeper, a middle school male mentoring program at the Detroit Public Schools' Malcolm X Academy. She cofounded the doctoral program in African American and African studies and served on its executive committee through 2007.

Smitherman focused on educating the professional and lay public about linguistic-cultural issues and the language rights of marginalized groups. She said: "As the daughter of a Baptist preacher, I was already baptized in the linguistic fire of my people, but it was through the Black Liberation and Black Arts Movements that I learned about and studied that fire. My work, my mission has always been about the speech—and the speakers"

(personal interview). She appeared on television and radio and published scholarly articles arguing that language is fundamental to the struggle and liberation of oppressed peoples and calling for reforms in the teaching of language and literacy. To demonstrate the power and cultural richness of the African American verbal tradition, her writing reflects the flavor of black language, for example, "English Teacher, Why You Be Doing the Thangs You Don't Do?" (*English Journal*, 1972) and "White English in Blackface, or Who Do I Be?" (*Black Scholar*, 1973). Her first book, *Talkin and Testifyin: The Language of Black America* (1977), written for public and academic readers from the black perspective, showcased issues of language, culture, identity, history, politics, and education and was widely reviewed.

Smitherman played a major role in *Martin Luther King Junior Elementary School Children et al. v. Ann Arbor School District Board* (1979), also known as the Black English case. Working for two years with Michigan Legal Services on behalf of the plaintiff children, she researched the language patterns of the children, analyzed the children's academic records, coordinated the team of linguists and educators who served as expert witnesses, served as an advocate for the children, and testified at length during the trial. With her assistance, the legal team successfully established the case for a language barrier under the existing law, thus ensuring that school children would not be unfairly penalized for speaking what is considered a nonstandard dialect of American English. In keeping with her commitment to bring language awareness to the nonacademic public, she published "Black English: So Good It's Bad" in *Essence* in 1981.

In 1971 Smitherman was appointed to the newly created Students' Right to Their Own Language Committee of the Conference on College Composition and Communication (CCCC), an organization concerned with instruction in rhetoric and composition at colleges and universities. In 1974 the committee adopted a policy statement in support of the language rights of marginalized, nonmainstream students that was intended to serve as a guide to college writing and rhetoric instructors. In 1987 she became chair of the CCCC Language Policy Committee and a member of the National Council of Teachers of English Language Commission, where she continued to promote students' right to their own language. In 1999 the CCCC presented her with its Exemplar Award in recognition of this work.

Beginning in 1995 Smitherman extended her language research and educational activism to South Africa in conjunction with that country's new constitutional recognition of eleven official languages. She received Spencer Foundation funding for a program in language research for English faculty at North West University-Mafikeng, which South Africa labeled a "historically disadvantaged" institution.

In 2001 Smitherman received the National Council of Teachers of English David H. Russell Research Award for her book *Talkin That Talk: Language, Culture, and Education in African America* (2000). Other publications include *Black Language and Culture: Sounds of Soul* (1975), *Black Talk: Words and Phrases from the Hood to the Amen Corner* (1994, 2000), and *Word from the Mother: Language and African Americans* (2006). Her honors include the Richard Wright-Woodie King Award for her work with the playwright ED BULLINS; the Educational Press Association Award for Excellence in Educational Journalism for her "Soul 'n Style" columns in the *English Journal*; and the James R. Squire Award from the National Council of Teachers of English, established in 1967 to recognize a scholar who has had a "transforming influence and has made a lasting intellectual contribution" to the profession.

FURTHER READING

Smitherman, Geneva. "CCCC's Role in the Struggle for Language Rights," *College Composition and Communication* (1999).

Smitherman, Geneva. *Black Talk: Words and Phrases from the Hood to the Amen Corner* (2000).

Smitherman, Geneva. *Word from the Mother: Language and African Americans* (2006).

Villanueva, Víctor, and Geneva Smitherman. *Language Diversity in the Classroom: From Intention to Practice* (2003).

BETHANY K. DUMAS

Smyth, John H. (14 Jul. 1844–5 Sept. 1908), lawyer, diplomat, educator, and editor, was born John Henry Smyth in Richmond, Virginia, the son of Sully Smyth, a slave, and Ann Eliza Goode Smyth, a free African American. Smyth was also born free because at the time of his birth, slave codes decreed that a child's status followed that of the mother. Ann Smyth then paid Sully Smyth's owner $1,800 to gain her husband's freedom, but Virginia law prohibited her from freeing him, and she willed her husband to Smyth.

Another African American woman in Richmond taught him Smyth how to read, and he was able to take advantage of better educational opportunities beyond Virginia's borders. In Philadelphia African American youth attended private schools as early as 1770 and public schools as early as 1822. When he was seven years old, Smyth's parents sent him to Philadelphia where he attended a Quaker school until his father died in 1857. Smyth then left school and worked as an errand boy at a dry goods store and as a newsboy but the following year, 1858, Smyth attended the Pennsylvania Academy of the Fine Arts in Philadelphia. At the academy, Smyth was especially interested in landscape and figure painting. Although detailed information about Smyth's life is not readily available, he may well have been the first African American to attend the academy; however this has yet to be ascertained.

In 1859 when Smyth was fifteen, he enrolled in the Institute for Colored Youth (now known as Cheyney University of Pennsylvania), which was founded by Quakers in 1837. Ebenezer Bassett, who later became the first African American diplomat when he was appointed minister resident and consul general to Haiti in 1869, was the school's principal during Smyth's time there. He graduated on 4 May 1862 at the age of eighteen. Three years later, after working several jobs including as a laborer at a Philadelphia china factory and a sutler's clerk for the army, Smyth traveled to London where he hoped to meet the tragedians IRA ALDRIDGE and Samuel Phelps and become an actor. He did not meet Aldridge and whether he met Phelps is uncertain, but the trip also proved unsuccessful because Smyth was unable to afford acting lessons. He returned to the United States and worked as a manual laborer before he began teaching first in Philadelphia, then Wilkes-Barre, and finally Pottsville, Pennsylvania.

Smyth then attended the Howard University School of Law and he received his degree in 1870. That same year he married Fannie Ellen Shippen, who was a minister's daughter from Washington, D. C.; they had a son and a daughter. Smyth was employed as a clerk in the War Department's Bureau of Refugees, Freedmen, and Abandoned Lands (the Freedmen's Bureau), which provided assistance to former slaves, before he became a clerk in the Census Office of the Department of the Interior. From 1872 to 1873, he worked at the Treasury Department, and then became a clerk at the Freedmen's Bank, in Washington. Freedmen's, established by Congress in 1865, was the United States' first African American bank, which had more than thirty branches in various states. Smyth transferred to the Wilmington, North Carolina, branch and worked as a cashier until the bank's demise in 1874.

After he passed the law examination administered by members of North Carolina's Supreme Court in Raleigh, Smyth began practicing law. In 1875 Smyth attended North Carolina's Constitutional Convention. One year later, Smyth returned to the District of Columbia where he practiced law and served as a clerk in the office of the Comptroller of the Treasury. In 1876 he supported Rutherford Hayes's candidacy for president of the United States. After FREDERICK DOUGLASS and other individuals recommended Smyth for a diplomatic position, Hayes appointed him the U.S. minister resident and consul general to Liberia on 23 May 1878. He remained in office until 22 December 1881 when Henry Highland Garnet succeeded him. Garnet died on 13 February 1882; consequently, President Chester Arthur reappointed Smyth to the position on 12 April 1882, and Smyth remained in the office until 14 December 1885. During his tenure as a diplomat in Africa, the U.S. government permitted Smyth to work with the German Consulate in Monrovia and the Belgian Consulate in Liberia. Smyth's diplomatic activities were not unheralded; Liberia College presented him with an honorary LLD degree, and on 28 December 1885, Hilary R. W. Johnson, president of Liberia, appointed Smyth a knight commander of the Liberian humane order of African redemption.

Smyth returned to the U.S. and sold real estate in Washington, D.C., until 1892, when he assumed editorship of The Reformer, an African American newspaper based in Richmond, Virginia.

In 1897 Smyth, along with several other African American men, founded the Negro Reformatory Association of Virginia after discovering that African American male juvenile offenders in Virginia were jailed in a different manner than white male juvenile offenders. While their white peers were allowed to attend reformatory schools, African American boys were incarcerated. The Negro Reformatory Association received donations from residents of Virginia as well as other East Coast states and purchased the Broad Neck plantation in Hanover, Virginia. Smyth, who headed the Negro Reformatory Association, founded and led the Manual Labor School, which opened in Hanover on 12 September 1899 and was one of the first reformatory schools in the South for African American boys as well and girls in the South. Until his death in 1908, Smyth was the school's chief administrator, and he strove to instill a heightened work ethic in the youth by requiring them to work on the Manual Labor School's farm.

Smyth's greatest contributions were to Virginia's youth. Since 1920 the Manual Labor School, now known as the Hanover Juvenile Correctional Center, has been operated by the state of Virginia. In Smyth's honor, the center's secondary school is known as the John H. Smyth High School, and a Hanover County highway marker on Route 301 near the intersection with VA 605 commemorates Smyth's achievements.

FURTHER READING

Carter, Linda M. "John H. Smyth," in Notable Black Men, Book II, ed. Jessie Carnie Smith (2006).

Coppin, Fannie Jackson. Reminiscences of School Life and Hints on Teaching (1913).

Dumas Malone, ed. "John Henry Smyth," in Dictionary of American Biography, vol. 17 (1935).

Foner, Eric. Freedom's Lawmakers: A Directory of Black Officeholders During Reconstruction (1996)

Simmons, William J. "Hon. John H. Smythe," in Men of Mark: Eminent, Progressive and Rising (1887).

LINDA M. CARTER

Snaër, François-Michel-Samuel (c. 1833–c. 1896), musician and composer, was born in New Orleans, Louisiana, the son of Anne Emerine Beluche Snaër and François Snaër. His family immigrated to New Orleans from St. Domingue via Cuba before 1818 and was of mixed African, French, and German ancestry. His mother was purportedly the daughter of the Caribbean pirate René Beluche, and his father was a wealthy grocer and church organist. The young Snaër played more than a dozen musical instruments, including violin, cello, piano, and organ. He was also a prolific composer. Little is known about Snaër's life before the Civil War other than his first song, "Sous sa fenêtre," was written sometime around 1851, when he was eighteen. As a member of the free black population in New Orleans before the Civil War, many of whom spoke French, identified with French culture, and had a certain amount of wealth, Snaër's status lay between the city's white and slave population. This would change when the Louisiana legislature passed a law defining anyone with a drop of African blood as a Negro. After the Civil War, New Orleans free blacks and Creoles of color lost their status and rights, a condition that continued throughout

Reconstruction and the late nineteenth century as New Orleans Creoles of color experienced tightening racial restrictions. The relative autonomy they'd enjoyed before the Civil War began to erode.

Documentation for the musical activities of New Orleans Creole-of-color musicians becomes more available after 1865. Samuel Snaër often performed with other Creole of color musicians, including Basile Jean Barès and Victor-Eugène Macarty. Some of these performances were benefits for groups in support of black male suffrage as well as for orphanages, but most were held for profit at the Théâtre d'Orléans. The stage of this theater was first opened to performances by Creole-of-color musicians after emancipation, but only during the summer off-season when many white residents fled the city's heat and frequent yellow fever epidemics. Snaër composed pieces and led the orchestra for these performances that included not only locally produced music but also imported operas, plays, and recitations; they were performed for mixed audiences.

Snaër's known unpublished compositions include orchestral polkas, waltzes, mazurkas, quadrilles, an overture, vocal duets and trios, a drinking song, an Allegro for Grand Orchestra, and several dances. Two masses he wrote were published (whether or not he wrote others is unknown) in JAMES MONROE TROTTER's *Music and Some Highly Musical People*. The latter were likely composed for his job as organist at St. Mary Catholic Church. Snaër was notorious for sharing his original compositions (after which they were often not returned to him and subsequently lost) instead of working toward getting them published, hence few of these still remain in existence. This did not seem to hinder his performance career, due to his ability to play his pieces precisely from memory.

There are only three known published pieces by Snaër (not counting the masses mentioned above, since those constituted, according to James Trotter, merely an illustration of the composer's ability to "scientifically arrange good music"): "*Rapelle-toi: Romance pour voix de tenor*," "*Le chant du déporté: Melodie pour voix de baryton*," and "*Sous sa fenêtre*," all published in 1865 or 1866 by Louis Grunewald in New Orleans. The lyrics to all three pieces were written in French by local white lyricists, including the celebrated Creole poet Louis Placide Canonge. It seems that Snaër made his living mostly by performing, conducting, and teaching music. Although his compositions were based on European models and published with French titles, some music scholars have suggested that

forms used in these pieces contained elements later used in jazz. His extant pieces, however, do not use African or Caribbean influences in ways similar to Gottschalk, who as a white Creole composer could more easily borrow such forms with less chance of losing his legitimacy as a composer, especially in the atmosphere of hardening racism that dominated the time. Snaër was remembered by contemporaries as a shy individual who, by the time of his death in New Orleans, was locally known better as a great chess player than as a musician.

FURTHER READING

Snaër's three published pieces are held at Tulane University, Howard-Tilton Memorial Library, Louisiana Collection, Sheet Music Collection.

Blassingame, John W. *Black New Orleans, 1860–1880* (1973).

Sullivan, Lester. "Composers of Color of Nineteenth-Century New Orleans: The History Behind the Music," *Black Music Research Journal* 8 (1988).

Trotter, James M. *Music and Some Highly Musical People* (1881; rpt. 1968).

ANN OSTENDORF

Sneed, Floyd (22 Nov. 1942–), musician and drummer, was born in Calgary, Alberta, Canada, the son of Napoleon and Willa Sneed, of whom little is known. Music was an integral part of Floyd's life from an early age. His parents were active in their local church playing the guitar and the piano and singing, and Floyd first became interested in drumming at the young age of five.

His educational accomplishments are not now known, but by 1961 Sneed was fully committed to drumming. He was already a fixture on the local music scene when his sister Maxine bought him his first drum set. Sneed's first job as a drummer was for Conway Twitty. The country singer's regular drummer was sick for their concert in Calgary, and Sneed was contacted as an emergency replacement. Soon thereafter he joined his first group, Little Daddy and the Bachelors, a band fronted by African American vocalist Tommie "Little Daddy" Melton and whose guitarist was Tommy Chong, who had married Maxine Sneed and would later achieve fame as part of Cheech and Chong. The band played blues and funk in the Vancouver area for several years before Floyd Sneed formed his own band, called Heatwave, and moved to Los Angeles, California, in 1966. The following year Sneed and his band traveled to Hawaii and performed in the Honolulu area for ten months before returning to Los Angeles.

Like many other musicians, Sneed hoped he would be discovered in Los Angeles' thriving music scene. By sheer chance he landed at the right place at the right time. He later related that while working in a Los Angeles club, the Red Velvet on Sunset Boulevard, Joe Schermie, the bass player for Three Dog Night, walked by the club and heard this beat going on inside. Joe paid admission to the club and entered to find out who the drummers were. Once inside, he discovered that it was Floyd Sneed and invited him to come down and audition to join the band. The band had just formed, and the drums were the remaining slot to be filled, and Sneed would prove to be just the drummer they wanted.

In 1968 Sneed joined the then-unknown band Three Dog Night. The seven-piece band consisted of three singers (Danny Hutton, Chuck Negron, and Cory Wells), the bassist Joe Schermie, the guitarist Michael Allsup, and the keyboardist Jimmy Greenspoon, and was now complete with Sneed as its drummer. Sneed was optimistic that a change in the music scene was coming: "I wanted to get out of the soul type bands I had been in, and into an ... across the board and 'open' type of music. I saw an opportunity with these guys and the timing was perfect" (Jeansonne, 4). With the addition of Sneed, Three Dog Night became a racially mixed group. Although integrated bands were still quite rare at the time, there were a few others, notably Booker T. and the MGs (featuring BOOKER T. JONES on organ, AL JACKSON JR. on drums, the white guitarist Steve Cropper, and the white bassist Donald "Duck" Dunn) and the JIMI HENDRIX Experience (in which Hendrix, who had briefly played with Sneed's former group, Little Daddy and the Bachelors, when they changed personnel and achieved some measure of success under the name Bobby Taylor and the Vancouvers, was joined by the bassist Noel Redding and the drummer Mitch Mitchell, both white Englishmen).

Three Dog Night achieved spectacular success. From 1969 to 1975 the group recorded thirteen albums and had twenty-two top forty hits, three of which reached number one ("Joy to the World" and "Mama Told Me (Not to Come)," both in 1970, and "Black and White" in 1972). Indeed Three Dog Night was one of the bands that defined the era of the late 1960s and the early 1970s, and an important part of their sound was Sneed's drumming. Most notable was the "Lafrican" style he developed, combining Latin and African beats into one style that was distinctly his own. Negron later commented that "we had a drummer who was not skilled in basic, fundamental sound drumming but was totally unique, and when he did his drum solo, that's when the crowd got on its feet" (Jeansonne, 5).

Perhaps symbolic of Sneed's presence in Three Dog Night was the recording of their smash hit "Black and White" in 1972. While the soulful vocals on the song belonged to Negron, Sneed provided the unusual backbeat. Hutton commented: "I don't know how to explain why Floyd was such a great drummer, but 'Black and White' is proof of it. ... He was the only drummer I've ever seen play the cowbell at the same time as everything else.... And what he was playing was so incredible and off the wall. It was a big part of why the record was a hit" (Jeansonne, 17).

After Three Dog Night broke up in 1976, Sneed went on to other musical projects. He played with the Ohio Players on tour for nine months and later was part of a short-lived group, SS Fools, which recorded one album in 1976 before its demise. Three Dog Night reunited to record a final album in 1984, and Sneed toured several times with various members of the group. By 2002 he had formed a new band, K.A.A.T., and was again touring and recording. He also pursued other interests, including making an instructional drum video and painting.

FURTHER READING
Jeansonne, Bruce. "Featured Drummer ... Floyd Sneed," *Vintage Drummer* (Fall 2001).
GLENN ALLEN KNOBLOCK

Snoddy, Dilsey (c. 1790–c. 1875), enslaved servant of John Snoddy, Spartanburg, South Carolina. Her place of birth and the names of her parents are unknown. John Snoddy and his family emigrated from County Antrim, Ireland, in 1773, and by the time of the 1790 census, he owned ten slaves. When his will was executed in 1808, John owned eighteen slaves including a "boy Bill and girl Dilsey" (Spartanburg County Probate Records, #1756), who were bequeathed to his son Isaac and noted as already in Isaac's possession. Dilsey was eighteen years old and valued at $400. This made her one of the most valuable slaves in the estate, along with a man named George ($482.50), and a woman named Fan and her child, Ransom ($500). Dilsey's attributed value strongly suggests that she was a skilled house servant rather than a field hand. Isaac, his wife, Jane, their children, and their slaves lived in the Beech Springs (now Wellford) area of Spartanburg County. Their home was located on a major thoroughfare, and from about 1810 to 1840, it served as a way station for the stagecoach. Dilsey may have worked with the white Snoddy family and other slaves to prepare and serve meals to passengers during stopovers.

On 7 May 1858, Dilsey and two other slaves were examined by the session and received as members of Nazareth Presbyterian Church. During the 1850s, Nazareth had about two hundred members, including sixty "colored" members enslaved to local masters, not all of whom were themselves members of the church. (Membership by "examination" indicated that the applicant was interviewed by session members regarding her faith rather than transferring membership from another church.) There is no indication of separate churches for enslaved African Americans in this area until after emancipation ("The Roll of Nazareth Church: Adult Roll of Black Members," 52–53).

After Isaac's death, Dilsey remained with his widow, Jane, until Jane's death in 1864. The estate inventory recorded fifteen slaves, including a "Negro woman Dilce (old)," appraised at $50, compared with $2,500 for a man named Jim. Dilsey became the property of Isaac and Jane's only surviving son, Samuel Miller Snoddy, for the final year of the Civil War. After Emancipation, Dilsey Snoddy remained in Beech Springs. The 1870 census enumerated her at age eighty, and indicated that she lived with Pompey Vernon, age seventy-four, described as "mulatto" and a farmer; Sudy Vernon, age forty-five, who "keeps house;" and Emma Vernon, age ten. Dilsey's status in the Vernon household is not indicated, but it is likely that she was connected by kinship.

Of the countless thousands of enslaved African Americans, very few lives have been documented in any detail. Those for whom partial biographies can be constructed provide data for a better understanding of the complex subject of American slavery. Dilsey Snoddy survived a long life under slavery to emerge a free woman near its end.

FURTHER READING

Primary documents include Spartanburg County (South Carolina) Probate Records, Spartanburg County Library; and Nazareth Church roll books and session records, Presbyterian Historical Society, Montreat, North Carolina.

LAUREL HORTON

Snoop Dogg (20 Oct. 1971–), rapper, actor, and record producer, was born Cordavar Calvin Broadus Jr., in

Snoop Dogg performs at the Wembley Arena Pavilion in London, England on 12 July 2005. (AP Images.)

Long Beach, California, to unwed parents, Vernell Varnado, a singer and postal worker, and Beverly Tate, whose occupation is unknown. As a child he acquired the nickname "Snoopy" because of his physical similarities to the popular Peanuts cartoon character. His name later evolved to Snoop Doggy Dogg. After his parents separated, Broadus remained with his mother and two stepbrothers. He showed an early interest in music, following the example of his uncle, Bootsy Collins, a bassist in the funk band Parliament-Funkadelic. He showed great promise playing piano in church. He also became interested in rap music.

While attending Long Beach Polytechnic High School in the late 1980s, Broadus gained some attention as a promising basketball player. However, an active gang life in Long Beach often distracted him from athletics and academics. He joined a local gang, the Rollin' 20 Crips. The Crips were one of the country's most notorious gangs, originating in Los Angeles and maintaining an intense rivalry with another famous gang, the Bloods. Often involved in criminal behavior, Broadus left home at sixteen and periodically lived with different relatives and friends.

Soon after his graduation from high school, Broadus was arrested on drug charges, and he spent the next three years of his life in and out of the prison system on three separate drug possession charges. His musical abilities, however, helped him escape a life of crime. He often recorded homemade rap tapes with childhood friends. He received his first big break through friend and rap partner, Warren Griffin. Known as Warren G, Griffin was the stepbrother of rapper Dr. Dre, who was a key member of the controversial, infamous rap group N.W.A. Griffin gave one of Broadus's homemade rap tapes to Dr. Dre, and Dre's interest helped spark Broadus's career in rap music. Broadus soon took on the stage moniker of Snoop Doggy Dogg and was often referred to as simply "Snoop Dogg." Snoop Dogg made his initial splash in the world of rap music on the soundtrack of the film *Deep Cover* and the 1992 Dr. Dre album *The Chronic*. His lazy drawl, laid-back style, and risqué gangster-themed lyrics contributed to his mass popularity. Dr. Dre's hip-hop hits "Nothin' but a 'G' Thang" and "Dre Day" prominently featured Snoop Dogg and became top-ten hits in the summer of 1993. These singles were among the first hardcore rap songs to cross over into the pop market. Snoop Dogg's nonaggressive, lackadaisical lyrical style appealed not only to black youths but also to white suburban kids. Consequently, he rose to instant stardom and in 1993 released his first solo work, the controversial *Doggystyle*. Death Row Records, managed by CEO Suge Knight, released the album, and it became one of the top-selling albums in hip-hop history. In 1993 Rolling Stone magazine readers and critics voted Snoop Dogg best rapper and he won an MTV Award for best rap video with "Doggy Dogg World." With his thin, six-foot four-inch frame, he introduced graphic lyrics to go with his diverse hairstyles, ranging from long, braided hair to cornrows, which became fashionable among black men.

Trouble, however, continued to follow him. Police had arrested the singer in 1993 while he was recording his solo debut album. They charged Snoop Dogg with being an accomplice in the shooting death of a rival gang member. Snoop Dogg's legal problems inspired the short quasi-documentary film, *Murder Was the Case* (1994), directed in part by Dr. Dre and accompanied by a Snoop Dogg soundtrack. In 1996 the courts acquitted him of all murder charges. That year his recording company released his sophomore album, *Tha Doggfather*, which also proved to be controversial. Critics charged that he and his record label, Death Row, glorified the criminal lifestyle and objectified women. The violence associated with hip hop resulted in an alleged battle between West Coast and East Coast rappers. It was supposedly this public conflict that resulted in the violent deaths of two of the biggest rappers in hip hop: the East Coast rapper NOTORIOUS B.I.G. and the West Coast rapper TUPAC SHAKUR. Shakur had been a friend and Death Row labelmate of Snoop Dogg. The deaths of these rappers and the incarceration of Suge Knight, CEO of Death Row, resulted in Snoop Dogg eventually leaving the label and signing a new contract with No Limit Records, the New Orleans, Louisiana–based record company founded by rapper and entrepreneur Percy Robert Miller, known as Master P.

Despite contract disputes and murder conspiracy theories, in 1997 Snoop Dogg married his childhood sweetheart, Shantay Taylor. No Limit released *Da Game Is To Be Sold Not Told*, his debut album for the company. He released three additional albums for the label and eventually returned to his West Coast roots, working with independent producer Dr. Dre. Snoop Dogg also ventured beyond his hip-hop career into numerous film and television roles, appearing in 2001's *Training Day* and *Baby Boy and Bones*, and in *Starsky & Hutch* and *Soul Plane* in 2004, and making several guest appearances on two television series, *Monk* and *Entourage*, in 2007.

Snoop Dogg's public persona no longer focused on his hardcore, violent lyrics but instead presented him as a comical and talented crossover personality. He was used to advertise with Chrysler, AOL, Boost Mobile cellular company, Orbits Gum, and numerous other national and international companies. Beyond his fame and celebrity, Snoop Dogg actively participated in the lives of his three children, Corde, Cordell, and Cori, despite the fact that he and his wife divorced in 2004. In 2003 Snoop Dogg served as the offensive coordinator for his son's team, the Rowland Raiders; then in 2005 he formed the Snoop Youth Football League (SYFL), which reached approximately 2,500 kids in ten local chapters throughout Southern California. Snoop Dogg was accused of sabotaging other leagues of talented young players through his SYFL that also has numerous corporate sponsors and celebrity appearances. Snoop Dogg also created the Snooperbowl, the championship game for these football leagues as an active part of his effort to keep young people away from drugs and gangs. In the early years of the twenty-first century, he provided approximately two million dollars annually for extra curricular activities for children throughout Southern California.

Controversy continued to be part of his life. On 26 April 2006, Snoop Dogg and members of his entourage were arrested and removed from the first-class lounge of British Airways. As retaliation for the removal, some members of the group vandalized the airport's duty-free shop, which led to the arrest of Snoop Dogg and other men. This incident resulted in Snoop Dogg being banned from British Airways. Another incident on 11 May resulted in Snoop Dogg being denied entry to the United Kingdom. Following these events, Snoop Dogg was arrested in October in California, in November after performing on NBC's *Today* show, and on 12 March 2007 in Sweden; several other criminal infractions caused his visa request to enter the United Kingdom to be rejected resulting in the cancellation of many scheduled European appearances. Although Snoop Dogg remained a controversial figure, he also made great strides as a rapper, producer, actor, entrepreneur, coach, and more.

Snoop Dogg remained dedicated to the West Coast through his coordination of the Protect the West Conference, which had an agenda to build dialogue, boost economic progress, and cultivate peace among West Coast rappers who often were affiliated with conflicting gangs. As hip hop continued to grow and evolve, Snoop Dogg remained a pivotal influence in music, film, commercials, clothing, and videos.

FURTHER READING

Chang, Jeff. *Can't Stop, Won't Stop: A History of the Hip Hop Generation* (2005).

Keyes, Cheryl L. *Rap Music and Street Consciousness* (2004).

Quinn, Eithne. *Nothin' But A 'G' Thang: The Culture and Commerce of Gangsta Rap* (2004).

KATRINA D. THOMPSON

Snow, Valaida (2 June 1903–30 May 1956), jazz singer, lyricist, jazz trumpeter, band director, dancer, and actress, was born in Chattanooga, Tennessee, to Etta Snow, a Howard University–trained musician, and John Snow. Little is known about John Snow, but it is thought that he may have been white. Snow had at least two sisters, named Alvaida and Lavaida; she may have had other siblings as well. Snow began performing early in life but first achieved widespread recognition performing in Barron Wilkins's productions in New York in 1922. By 1924 she had appeared in a number of variety shows and musicals, including *Ramblin' Round* (1923), *Follow Me* (1923), and *In Bamville* (1924), the last by NOBLE SISSLE and EUBIE BLAKE. *In Bamville* was later renamed *Chocolate Dandies* and featured JOSEPHINE BAKER. In 1926 she traveled to London as the understudy for FLORENCE MILLS in *Blackbirds* (she would perform in *Blackbirds* again in London in 1929 and 1934). She soon traveled the world, playing locales such as Hong Kong, Rangoon, and Cairo. In Paris she performed with Maurice Chevalier, who became a close friend. In

1931 she was in a hit show on Broadway in New York, *Rhapsody in Black*, which starred ETHEL WATERS. Snow also directed the show's sixty-piece orchestra. In short, she was a multitalented and ubiquitous figure on the American and international musical theater scene in the 1920s and 1930s.

Snow was also an exceptional trumpet player. At a time when it was rare for women to play wind instruments, especially brass (something still rare today), Snow's playing was reportedly comparable to that of the greatest trumpet player alive at the time, LOUIS ARMSTRONG. Two prominent contemporary critics, Krin Gabbard and Will Friedwald, have slightly different takes on her approach to playing like Armstrong, with Gabbard claiming she developed a "distinctly Armstrongian style" and Friedwald claiming she "mimicked" Armstrong (Lusane, 168). At any rate, her Armstrong-like trumpet playing led to her nickname, "Little Louis." Armstrong himself on one occasion had the chance to check out Snow's trumpet playing and other talents. In a 1928 performance in Chicago at the Sunset Café, Snow played the trumpet, sang, and then followed up with a specialty dance number, in which seven pairs of shoes were placed in a row at the front of the stage, and she did a dance in each pair for one chorus. The dances and shoes to match were: soft-shoe, adagio shoes, tap shoes, Dutch clogs, Chinese straw sandals, Turkish slippers, and the last pair, Russian boots. "When Louis Armstrong saw the show one night, he continued clapping after others had stopped and remarked, 'Boy I never saw anything that great'" (Reitz, 158).

In 1934 Snow married Ananais Berry, a dancer. Around this time she performed with EARL HINES in Chicago at the Grand Terrace. Also that year, she wrote a piece in the *Chicago Defender* opposing interracial relationships. In 1936 she toured with big band pioneer FLETCHER HENDERSON. Snow was apparently rather flashy, and there are reports (repeated by the pianist BOBBY SHORT) of her wearing orchid-colored dresses and being driven around in an orchid-colored Mercedes-Benz with a chauffeur and pet monkey also dressed in orchid uniforms.

Snow also had a brief film career. She appeared in the French films *L'Alibi* (1936) and *Pièges* (1939), and the English film, *Take it From Me* (1937). Snow's career took an unfortunate turn around 1940. A miscalculation of the political situation in Europe led her to continue performing there (primarily in Denmark and Sweden) when many black American stars such as COLEMAN HAWKINS had returned home. In early 1941 Snow's work permit in Denmark was revoked, possibly due to involvement with narcotics. Shortly thereafter she was imprisoned in the Wester-Faengle internment camp in Copenhagen. According to the political scientist Clarence Lusane who described Snow's life, in an understatement, as "imperfectly known," this was "clearly not a 'concentration camp'" *per se*, as is often reported in accounts of Snow's life (Lusane, 169). According to Rosetta Reitz, Snow's elaborate wardrobe and $7,000 in travelers' checks were seized (Reitz, 159). Snow claimed to have suffered a beating during her imprisonment that left her with a head wound and permanent scar.

Snow managed to return to the United States, via Portugal, in late 1942. She was apparently emaciated and in very poor health. In 1943 she married her manager and caretaker Earle Edwards. It is not clear when or if she divorced Ananais Berry. Snow revived her career in the mid-1940s, performing with bands such as the Sunset Royal Orchestra and Buzz Adlam's. She also came into prominence again as a soloist. The *New York Times* published a report of her 1949 performance at Town Hall in Manhattan, noting that her performance included everything from "early American folk songs" to pieces by Howard Arlen, George Gershwin, and "a group of sacred songs by Schubert" (*New York Times*, 21 May 1949).

By 1950 Snow's career was flagging, but she was honored that year in a ceremony at the popular New York jazz club Small's Paradise, which also honored major figures such as W.C. HANDY, BILLY ECKSTINE, ETHEL WATERS, CAB CALLOWAY, among others. In 1956 Snow suffered a stroke after a show at the Palace Theater in New York. She died three weeks later at Kings County Hospital in Brooklyn. Snow's life was fictionalized in Candace Allen's 2005 novel, *Valaida*.

FURTHER READING

Snow, Valaida. "I've Met No Color Bar," *Chicago Defender* (Oct. 1934).

Charles, Mario A. "The Age of a Jazzwoman: Valaida Snow, 1900–1956," *The Journal of Negro History* (1995).

Lusane, Clarence. *Hitler's Black Victims: The Historical Experiences of Afro-Germans, European Blacks, Africans, and African Americans in the Nazi Era* (2003).

Reitz, Rosetta. "Hot Snow: Valaida Snow (Queen of the Trumpet Sings and Swings)," *Black American Literature Forum* (1982).

PAUL DEVLIN

Snowden, Elmer (10 Sept. or 9 Oct. 1900–14 May 1973), banjo, guitar, and saxophone player, was born in Baltimore, Maryland. His parents' names are unknown and his exact birth date varies depending on the source. In 1915 he began his career in his hometown playing a New Orleans–derived jazz with EUBIE BLAKE and later with the pianist Gertie Wells, to whom he was married for several years during the early 1920s. By 1921 he had moved to nearby Washington, D.C., where he jobbed with Louis Thomas and CLAUDE HOPKINS and his own eight-piece group, which played alternately with DUKE ELLINGTON's trio. Snowden also appears to have played banjo with Ellington's group earlier, from 1919 to 1920, but this is not reported conclusively. Snowden's Washington band included SONNY GREER on drums, ARTHUR WHETSOL on trumpet, and Otto Hardwick on sax. The three would later be long-term members of the Ellington orchestra.

Bolstered by the belief that FATS WALLER was to join the group as featured artist, Snowden and band moved their operation to New York City in 1923. The Waller association proved to be a false start, but all ended happily in 1924 when Ellington joined the band on piano, replacing the no-show Waller. This began an arrangement wherein Snowden was nominal leader responsible for financial matters and managerial details, while Ellington was responsible for conducting rehearsals, planning music, and "setting moods," which probably meant just "counting off" the beat for each number, during performances. At this time the band's name was changed to the Washingtonians in recognition of their geographical past. Key members of the Snowden/Ellington group were BUBBER MILEY on trumpet (who replaced Whetsol), Charlie Irvis on trombone (soon to be replaced by JOE NANTON), Hardwick on reeds, Fred Guy on banjo and guitar, and Greer on drums. From 1923 until 1927 the band was nominally based in the Hollywood Club (renamed the Kentucky Club in 1924) at Forty-ninth and Broadway.

The Snowden/Ellington co-op connection reached an ignominious end in early 1927 when members of this talented group discovered that Snowden, as their business representative, had on occasion cut himself a disproportionate share of the collective proceeds. It was after Snowden's departure in December 1927 that Ellington enlarged the band, now called The Duke Ellington Orchestra, and began his historic appearances at the famed Cotton Club in Harlem.

Snowden was reported by his contemporaries to have been an exceptional banjo player, an instrument whose time in the jazz world had, alas, run out. He also possessed a keen nose for talent, and his New York network gave him entrée to some of the hottest jazz talent of the Prohibition era. During the late twenties and early thirties he led groups operating in Harlem and Greenwich Village through which passed names destined to play momentous roles in their art's history. At one time he could boast as many as five bands working under his imprimatur in the New York City area. In an impressive succession his sidemen included COUNT BASIE (whom he reputedly fired), Hopkins, JIMMIE LUNCEFORD, CHICK WEBB, Benny Carter, Fats Waller, ROY ELDRIDGE, and SID CATLETT. Snowden and this array of jazz giants played dates at the "in" clubs: the City, the Hot Feet, the Bamville, the Nest, and Small's Paradise. At the Nest during the 1930s Snowden's group featured the cornetist REX STEWART, who would later achieve artist status with the Ellington orchestra. During the band's tenure at Small's, in 1930–1931, its lineup included Catlett, Gus Aiken, DICKY WELLS, Al Sears, and Hardwick. At this venue Eldridge, on trumpet, had replaced Stewart. The last-named roster was the band featured in a 1932 Warner Bros. film short, provocatively titled *Smash Your Baggage*.

Snowden's career as a performer and leader did not prosper on schedule. In addition to the gradual replacement of banjos by guitars in bands' rhythm sections, he encountered legal difficulties in the early 1930s with the New York City Musicians' Union. The circumstances were serious enough to lead to his expulsion from Local 802 of the American Federation of Musicians for eight years. This direct professional barrier added to the difficulties musicians commonly experience in their club-to-club, date-by-date existences, soured him on the performing life of New York. He thus moved to Philadelphia, Pennsylvania, in 1933 to teach banjo, mandolin, and reed instruments, maintaining only modest professional status as a part-time performer and leader. During the two decades of 1940 to 1960, after settling his union problems, he occasionally led small groups for limited engagements in clubs in Canada and the northeastern United States. These sorties were sandwiched between short runs in New York City at Jimmy Ryan's and the Metropole.

In 1963 Snowden moved once again, this time with high hopes for a new start, to Berkeley, California, replacing the steel strings on his old banjo with the gut of a guitar. He played the Monterey Jazz Festival that summer with an unlikely yet smashingly successful quartet consisting of old-timers Darnell Howard and POPS FOSTER and the young bebop drummer TONY WILLIAMS. That success behind him, he took a job at the Berkeley School of Music, teaching there for three years and playing night dates around the Bay Area with the trombonist Turk Murphy. Before returning for good to the East Coast he led his own groups at the Cabale in Berkeley and at the Coffee House in San Francisco. He joined a European jazz tour in 1967, then returned to his adopted hometown of Philadelphia, where he died. His last big public performance took place at the fledgling Newport Jazz Festival in 1968.

Ralph Gleason tells a touching story about a kind of last roundup meeting between Snowden and Ellington in 1963 shortly after the Monterey Festival, where both had played but on different days. The meeting took place between sets in Ellington's dressing room in San Francisco's Basin Street West, many years after the two aging pros had last seen each other. Gleason says:

> The two of them, Duke, the piano player who went on to the heights of show business success, and Snowden, the man who gave him his first job and had gone down steadily ever since, just radiated love and delight at seeing each other. For an hour they sat there, Duke on the cot and Snowden on the chair, and reminisced. 'Remember the night …?' 'How did such and such go?' 'What ever happened to …?' It was a magic moment and I felt privileged to be present as they played the game of Remember When, each trying to catch the other out by bringing up an old nickname or the title of a song neither one of them had played for forty years.

FURTHER READING

Dance, Stanley. *The World of Swing* (repr. 1974, 2001).

Gleason, Ralph J. *Celebrating the Duke: And Louis, Bessie, Billie, Bird, Carmen, Miles, Dizzy and Other Heroes* (1995, repr. 1975).

Ulanov, Barry. *Duke Ellington* (1946).

This entry is taken from the *American National Biography* and is published here with the permission of the American Council of Learned Societies.

WILLIAM THOMSON

Snowden, Frank Martin, Jr. (17 July 1911–18 Feb. 2007), Howard University professor of five decades, international authority on blacks in the ancient

Mediterranean, and "dean" of African American classicists, was born in York County, Virginia, the son of Alice (née Phillips) and Frank Martin Snowden Sr., a War Department employee. The transatlantic turmoil of the 1910s swept the Snowdens from the rural South to Boston, Massachusetts. In 1917, the year the United States entered World War I, they joined increasing numbers of southern blacks who migrated to the brimming industrial centers of the North as military production needs peaked. For the Snowdens, at least, the move to New England was a success. Later in life, Frank Junior did not recall experiencing any discrimination as he grew up in racially diverse Roxbury, Massachusetts.

In 1922 Frank passed the entrance examination to the highly selective Boston Latin School. The institution rigorously discarded those whose performance was considered subpar, but primed the rest for a college career. While adult America relished in the Roaring Twenties, teenaged Frank Snowden acquired the uncompromising study habits and deep appreciation for Greece, Rome, and their languages that would enable his scholarly career. When he graduated in 1928 Snowden won prizes for excellence in Latin, Greek, and ancient history.

Next, Snowden applied to Harvard, was accepted, and earned scholarship support for all five successive years of study. At Harvard, he deepened his lifelong love for the classics and perfected his remarkable command of ancient languages, winning the Bowdoin Prize for an essay he composed in Attic Greek. He determined to walk in the footsteps of the educators and set his mind to a teaching career. Accordingly, the home-boarder enrolled in the graduate program in classical philology after he completed his undergraduate studies in 1932 and earned a Master of Arts degree in 1933.

It was upon leaving Harvard that Snowden first experienced the bitter racial resentments of his day. He applied to the Boston Public School System and made history as the first African American to exceed the qualifications of all other applicants in Latin and French, yet job offers for black teachers had already been scarce before the stock market crash of 1929. It took some efforts from his father and his Harvard friend RALPH BUNCHE to convince twenty-two-year-old Frank Jr. to accept an offer from "Virginia State College for Negroes" to teach at a reduced salary, one of the few options available during the Great Depression even to an Ivy League graduate.

Frank Snowden deeply dreaded the descent into Jim Crow territory. Arriving on campus in Ettrick,

Virginia, he learned that his fears were not unjustified. Nearby Fredericksburg was completely segregated. Snowden and his fellow blacks had to sit on the balcony in the local theater, were not allowed into restaurants, and had to drink from "colored" water fountains. He made the best of unacceptable circumstances and focused his energies on the classroom. In addition to teaching an overload of Latin classes, Snowden, upon popular request, also devoted his Saturday evenings to Greek study groups. As a result of his devotion, enrollments in Latin increased steadily. At Virginia State, Frank also met Elaine Hill, a high school art teacher, whom he married in 1935. They raised a daughter, Jane, and a son, Frank Martin III.

When Frank Snowden was offered a more prestigious joined position at Atlanta University and Spelman, the city's all-black women's college, the young Latinist successfully bargained for a spousal appointment for his new wife. In 1936 the couple moved to Georgia and joined a faculty that then included the civil rights giant W. E. B. DuBois and Snowden's Harvard friend William H. Dean Jr. While Snowden's academic prospects improved at the successful all-black school, his luck with white southerners did not. Taxi drivers rejected his patronage, an airport restaurant condemned him from the dining area to the kitchen (where he refused to eat), and professional photographers would not take pictures of his little daughter. He fought back by calling for boycotts of discriminatory tailors, convincing the *Atlanta Constitution* to capitalize the word "Negro," and publicizing his teaching successes. Once, driving into North Carolina with two students, Snowden was overcharged twenty-eight cents in gasoline. When he complained, the proprietor of the gas station threatened to club him to death with a blackjack. Snowden only backed down when the owner poured fuel over the back of the classicist's car and threatened to set it on fire. The students could not contain their relief as their teacher sped off.

Frank and Elaine Snowden were justifiably relieved to leave the Deep South for Washington, D.C., when Howard University extended a teaching offer in 1940. During World War II, Frank heard reports of his father serving in Germany and encountering Jim Crow style segregation forbidding him to ride in the same train coaches as Nazi POWs. In 1944—undeterred by continued discrimination—Snowden finished his Harvard Ph.D. thesis, written in Latin and entitled "Slaves and Freedmen in Pompeii."

The dissertation proved the cornerstone to his scholarly fame. Encouraged by academics from a variety of fields, Dr. Snowden expanded his focus from the slopes of Mount Vesuvius to encompass all extant archaeological and literary evidence about blacks in the ancient Mediterranean. The thesis he put forth in a number of articles was that the ancients knew no color prejudice. The Greeks and Romans enslaved blacks and whites alike, and some Africans rose quite high in the ranks of society. Racism, according to Snowden, is deeply entrenched, but not universal and can therefore be overcome.

Even as Snowden's success in classical scholarship undercut contemporary assumptions of blacks' intellectual inferiority, he faced harsh realities that made him doubt immediate improvements in U.S. race relations. In the 1940s, he publicly challenged a Washington school superintendent whose segregating methods compromised the quality of Jane's education. He often managed to use the D.C. press to his advantage. In 1946 the National Theatre excluded Snowden's students from a production of Jean Anouilh's *Antigone*, staged for the express purpose of celebrating the recent victory of U.S. liberty over the tyranny of the axis powers. Snowden attacked this hypocrisy in letters to the *Washington Post*, and the National Theatre eventually dropped its segregating policies.

In 1949 Snowden received a Fulbright travel grant. Returning to Italy (after a previous visit in 1938), he immersed his family in the cultures his scholarship had revolved around at a distance. Throughout the 1950s, Snowden traveled all over Europe, Northern Africa, and even into the Soviet Union, while convincing Howard University, at home, to enlarge its classics department. The State Department paid for a sixth-month lecture tour in 1953, which included talks on race relations ancient and modern and led him from Nigeria via Greece to Austria. One memorable night found a sleepy Snowden in Lagos, amid swarms of malaria-infested mosquitoes, clarifying points from an earlier overcrowded lecture. His success with Italian audiences in particular led to his appointment as cultural attaché to the U.S. Embassy in Rome from 1954 to 1956. In ensuing years, the State Department also sent him to India and Brazil.

Though his travels and interests spanned the globe, Snowden never forgot his wards in Washington, sending students like DEBBIE ALLEN, ANDREW YOUNG, and countless others on to careers in law, acting, or theology. They remembered him for striking recitations, from memory, in Ancient Greek and Latin. *Time Magazine* subsequently hailed Snowden's success as a refutation of such Soviet charges of racism and lack of cultivation as were hurled at the United States during the Cold War.

And Snowden's political sympathies indeed did not lie with all who attacked white supremacy and U.S. imperialism. The chair of the Howard Department of Classics became dean of the College of Liberal Arts in 1956 and as such attracted the scorn of social revolutionaries and Vietnam War protesters in the 1960s. When Snowden was hanged in effigy in 1968, he quickly resigned his deanship.

As he visited the world's museums, Snowden had tirelessly collected material for his studies of blacks in antiquity, which culminated in two seminal books. His *Blacks in Antiquity: Ethiopians in the Greco-Roman Experience* (1970) won the American Philological Association's Charles A. Goodwin Award of Merit in 1971. The influential *Before Race Prejudice: The Ancient View of Blacks* of 1983 presents the most developed argument for his thesis of Greek and Roman racial tolerance. Although Snowden himself has been criticized for idealizing the past, he had no tolerance toward those who, he felt, sacrificed academic integrity to the advancement of their race. Martin Bernal's *Black Athena* (1987) and more radical Afrocentrist writings attracted Snowden's vociferous scorn, as he accused them of ignoring inconvenient evidence disproving their claims that the likes of Cleopatra and Hannibal had been black.

In 1990 Snowden retired from service at Howard University. Unwilling to stop teaching, even at more than seventy years of age, he joined the Classics Department of Georgetown University. Yet he was no longer able to accept an offer to lecture in post-Apartheid South Africa, and the 1992 visiting appointment he held at Vassar College was the last of his career.

Frank Snowden was awarded the National Humanities Medal in 2003. Photographs from the ceremony show a nonagenarian Snowden—trim, stern-faced, and impeccably clad, the medal's red strap complementing his bronze skin, thin white mustache, and black suit—holding a cane and gazing at the camera through robust glasses. President George W. Bush grasps the laureate's wheelchair. Snowden's career was the capstone to a dogged tradition of black professional classicism that dates back to the early days of emancipation. Unlike his predecessors, he had his scholarly merits recognized by his white colleagues and did not require a more liberal brand of twenty-first-century classicists to unearth his achievements. Dr. Snowden lost his wife of seventy years in 2005 and died of congestive heart failure two years later, at age ninety-five, in a D.C.-based assisted living facility.

FURTHER READING

Snowden, Frank, Jr. "A Lifetime of Inquiry: Frank Snowden Jr." *Against the Odds: Scholars Who Challenged Racism in the Twentieth Century*. Ed. Benjamin P. Bowser and Louis Kushnick with Paul Grant (2002).

Obituaries: *New York Times*, 28 Feb. 2007; *Washington Post*, 22 Feb. 2007.

MATHIAS HANSES

Snowden, Isaac Humphrey (1826–June 1869), printer and physician in Liberia, Africa, was born in Boston, Massachusetts, the son of the Reverend SAMUEL SNOWDEN AND LYDIA W. SNOWDEN.

Isaac H. Snowden grew up in Boston as a free black man in a home where his father was a well-known and well-respected antislavery activist. It is likely that he attended the Abiel Smith School built in 1834–1835 to house the school for African American students. Snowden later became involved in the Young Men's Literary Society, composed of the most promising young African American men in the city, for the purpose of improving and strengthening their intellectual abilities. He served as president in 1847.

Snowden initially made his living as a book, newspaper, and fancy job printer. Following in his father's footsteps, he was involved in the antislavery and equal rights movements and was often elected as one of the secretaries of the various meetings held by these groups.

Snowden married a young woman named Caroline, who, as historian WILLIAM C. NELL states in his 1855 *Colored Patriots of the American Revolution* (99), was a descendant of the famed PRINCE WHIPPLE from Portsmouth, New Hampshire. It is possible that Caroline was related to Whipple's daughter, Elizabeth Smith, because Isaac and Caroline named their only child Lydia Elizabeth (b. 28 August 1849), perhaps after her grandmothers.

In the fall of 1850, following the death of Snowden's father, Isaac H. Snowden, Daniel Laing Jr., and MARTIN ROBISON DELANY became the first African Americans to be admitted to Harvard University's Medical School. Snowden and Laing, who had already been studying with Dr. Henry Clarke, a surgeon on the staff of Massachusetts General Hospital, were being sponsored by the Massachusetts Colonization Society in preparation for traveling to Liberia, Africa, to serve as physicians for the African Americans who were emigrating to that country as a part of the colonization movement. This is somewhat ironic on the part of Snowden because his father was a very outspoken opponent of that movement. It appears, however, that the only way in which Snowden and Laing could practice medicine at the time was to agree to emigrate, partly because there were already several black physicians in Boston struggling to make a living. Further, their willingness to emigrate seems to have been a major factor in the decision to admit Snowden and Laing to Harvard.

But their tenure at the medical school was destined to be short. As the result of a protest raised by a number of students, although by no means a majority, the faculty determined that allowing African Americans to study in the same classrooms as white students was disruptive and not in the best interests of the school. Thus, Delany, Laing, and Snowden were only permitted to finish out the winter semester of classes in which they were already enrolled.

Snowden attended one series of lectures at Dartmouth Medical School in Hanover, New Hampshire, in 1851 and then completed his medical studies with Dr. Clarke in Boston. He did reapply to Harvard once again in 1853, still under the auspices of the Massachusetts Colonization Society, but was once again refused admittance.

Despite Snowden's involvement with the antislavery and equal rights movements in Boston, there is no record that there was any outcry or protest regarding the action of the Harvard Medical School by either the Massachusetts Colonization Society or the antislavery groups.

On 24 May 1854, Isaac H. Snowden and Daniel Laing Jr., having completed their medical education, sailed to Liberia on the ship *Sophia Walke*—Snowden to serve in Sinou County and Laing on the St. Paul River. The following year, Dr. Snowden returned to the United States and on 24 December 1855 he sailed back to Liberia on the barque *Lamartine*, bringing with him his mother, wife, daughter, and a sister, Mrs. A. A. Williams.

On 29 November 1856, Dr. Snowden's sister, Mary Jane Triplett, and her two daughters, Anna Maria and Helen Lorinda, sailed to Liberia on the *Mary Caroline Stevens* and joined his family at Greenville in Sinou County. Mrs. Triplett became matron and nurse for the establishment there and her daughter, Anna Maria, was a schoolteacher. By January 1861, Dr. Snowden's brother, Charles, had also sailed to Liberia with plans for his wife, Isabella, and their two children, Isabella E. R. B. and Thomas, to emigrate as soon as a suitable home could be built for them. Charles died from dropsy, however, in March, and his family remained in Newport, Rhode Island.

The records of the American Colonization Society (ACS) include many letters written from Dr. Snowden to his contacts in the Colonization Society, most particularly to the Reverend William McLain in Washington, D.C. These letters chronicle the grueling story of free African Americans, raised in nineteenth-century Boston, attempting to adjust to their new life in Liberia with few of the amenities they had previously enjoyed.

It was only after many, many years of repeated requests that Snowden finally received materials that had been promised him to build a decent home for his family. During the Civil War years, the ACS was so short of funds that there were many times when Snowden drew only a partial salary and was unable to even purchase enough food to feed his family, and he expressed concern that they might die of starvation. Often, needed medicines were in short supply, especially when boxes that were destined for Sinou County never arrived or were diverted to other areas. The lack of additional emigrants from the United States made it difficult for many of the communities to survive and flourish. Nevertheless, Snowden's letters also reveal his commitment to the ACS and their attempts to provide a new life for African Americans in Liberia.

Dr. Snowden died at the age of forty three, after many years of declining health, having served for fifteen years as a physician in Liberia. The only record of his death seems to be a report from ACS Agent Henry W. Dennis, in a letter to William McLain, dated 10 August 1869.

FURTHER READING
African Repository and Colonial Journal (1855–1869).
Nell, William C. *The Colored Patriots of the American Revolution* (1855).
Nercessian, Nora N. *Against All Odds: The Legacy of Students of African Descent at Harvard Medical School before Affirmative Action 1850–1968* (2004).
Records of the American Colonization Society, http://www.footnote.com.
Wesley, Dorothy Porter, and Constance Porter Uzelac, eds. *William Cooper Nell: Nineteenth-Century African American Abolitionist, Historian, Integrationist* (2002).

PATRICIA J. THOMPSON

Snowden, John Baptist (14 May 1801–8 Sept. 1885), minister and author, was born a slave in Anne Arundel County, Maryland, the son of Fanny and Nathan Snowden, slaves belonging to Nicolas Harden and Ely Dorsey, respectively. John's maternal grandmother, Sarah Minty Barrikee, was stolen from a coastal African village in Guinea in 1767 or 1768. There she had a husband and child whom she never saw again. The Hardens were Catholic and introduced her to Christianity through their Catholic faith. Sarah regaled her children and grandchildren with stories about Africa and the traditions of her people until her death in 1823 or 1824. Thomas Collier, a white Englishman, was John's maternal grandfather. Family lore has it that only the antimiscegenation laws of the period prevented them from marrying. Little is known of John's paternal lineage except that his paternal grandfather was a slave named John Snowden and is therefore responsible for the family name.

Fanny Snowden was a religious woman who had nine children, of whom John was the seventh. She died in 1815 after giving birth to John's youngest sister. John's father Nathan, as the property of Ely Dorsey, lived seven miles away in Elkridge Landing. Despite the distance and the fact that he did not share Fanny's religious convictions, Nathan managed to be a frequent presence in John's life until he died shortly after John's mother.

As a child Snowden was big and strong for his age and full of spirited vitality tempered by religious mores that fostered an uncritical acceptance of the institution of slavery as reflecting God's will and the natural order of things. Hence in his autobiography, *From Whence Cometh* (1980), which traces three generations of the Snowden family, Snowden stated with pride, "I was obedient to my owner, always ready to obey their commands" (Snowden, 18). Yet he painfully recalled his frostbitten feet for lack of shoes during the winters of his youth, the coarseness of his clothing that grated on his body, and the unremitting work that consumed most of his days. Serious and solitary, Snowden preferred to perform tasks that would leave him alone with his thoughts rather than in the company of other slaves or under the watchful eye of a master or overseer.

Snowden had five owners during his period of bondage. He saw one sister sold off to New Orleans, and the threat of a similar fate helped convince slaves in border states like Maryland that their lot was far better than that of slaves on large cotton and tobacco plantations deeper in the South. Most of Snowden's owners were related by birth or marriage, and he was transferred from one owner to another by will or dowry. As a testament to his exceptional behavior and high moral character, Snowden related that he was "never whipped save once by any of my owners"—though he later came to regard slavery as "a great crime, one that man should give account of in the day of judgment" (Snowden, 25).

In 1820 Snowden heard several sermons that moved him profoundly, and in April of that year, while felling trees in the woods, he had a conversion experience that permanently changed his life. He claimed that in 1821 he had a vision similar to that of the Hebrew prophet Isaiah in which God called him to preach. He began to pursue this vocation by first becoming a Methodist exhorter, a person who expounded on scripture and rallied the devout. In 1826 he delivered an inspiring sermon before a competency panel at the Methodist Quarterly Conference. His oration was based almost entirely on verses he had learned by heart because he could not yet read. The deciding clerics were so impressed that they granted Snowden a license to preach, and his reputation as a minister grew.

Like many other slaveholders, Elisha Bennet's wife, the mistress of the plantation, did not approve of Methodist theology and practices that stressed the potential of human perfection (many were in fact called "perfectionists") through faith, the strict moral disciplines of abstinence from alcohol and smoking, or the egalitarian and socially radical belief in universal salvation without regard to race—doctrines that often were taught at interracial and spirit-filled camp meetings. In an effort to break Snowden's faith, the mistress treated him harshly and went so far as to strip him of his bed covering to force him to renounce his belief. Snowden described her as being "the worst thing the devil ever made," a remark uncharacteristic of his general penchant for understatement, from which one can infer that she also prohibited him from preaching or receiving additional religious instruction. However, Snowden was so transformed by his epiphany that he kept his faith a secret rather than renounce it and defiantly continued his religious education on his own.

In a manner reminiscent of Maryland's most famous ex-slave, FREDERICK DOUGLASS, Snowden achieved literacy by observing the white children who sometimes studied in his presence. They were often amused and encouraged by his interest and in this way became unwitting tutors. Also like Douglass, Snowden used what little money he could earn independent of his master to pay white children to explain things he did not understand and to purchase the books that he could not legally own. Although it was against the law to teach a slave to read or write, Catherine Lynch surreptitiously schooled Snowden for a small fee because she believed that he wanted to become literate in order to read the Bible. It was only after he learned to read the Bible for himself that Jesus's story took definite shape in his mind.

Belying his rather benign description of slavery, Snowden refused to marry while he was a slave or to marry a woman who was still in bondage because such a family would be at the mercy of unpredictable masters. Instead he decided to earn enough money to purchase his own freedom. Snowden worked without stint weaving baskets and hickory brooms, distilling peppermint drops, and trapping partridges, all of which he could sell for a few cents each. In December 1830 Bennett told Snowden that he was worth $1,000, far more than Snowden had saved. But realizing that Snowden was so intent on being free that he might run away if he had no hope of emancipating himself and recognizing that Snowden had served him well and might continue to do so for a short while longer, Bennett agreed to free Snowden for $200 and ten additional months of work.

In May 1831 Snowden married Margaret Coone, who had been born a slave in Westminster, Carroll County, Maryland, in 1809. When her German owner, Grand Adams, died, Margaret and her mother were manumitted and were left all the property and money that was not bequeathed to the Catholic Church. Even though they were later defrauded of most of their inheritance, Margaret was a remarkable woman who had an excellent business sense, was a well-respected nurse and midwife in her community, and was fluent in German, Pennsylvania Dutch, and English. In addition Snowden boasted that Margaret could "shear the sheep, cord the wool, spin the yarn, and knit the socks. She could plow the ground, sow the flaxseed, pull the flax, thresh it, put it out to rot, break the flax, and spin it" (Snowden, 33–34). They had fourteen children, six of whom preceded them in death.

Snowden had wanted to raise his family in Philadelphia, where free people of color had greater opportunities for education and economic advancement. But he and Margaret had deep roots in Maryland, and in his sermons Snowden routinely associated sin and debauchery with city life while extolling the virtues of tilling the soil and working by the sweat of one's brow. Most of their children were homeschooled. Their son Thomas Snowden eventually earned degrees from Howard University and Boston University before becoming the first black professor of theology at Centenary Biblical Institute, now Morgan State University.

John Snowden was the only black Methodist minister in western Maryland until Bishop Levi Scott, with Snowden, formed the Washington Conference in 1864 as a body that would organize and advocate for black Methodists within the predominately white Methodist Episcopal Church. By this time large numbers of black Methodists were so frustrated with the slow rate of ordaining black ministers and the prevalence of subtle and overt forms of racism that they were leaving the church en masse to join the African Methodist Episcopal (AME) Church founded by RICHARD ALLEN in 1816. Snowden was one of those stoic black ministers who remained within the Methodist Episcopal Church. He served it for over forty years; for twelve years he worked a circuit of seven congregations, which sometimes required him to walk as far as thirty miles to make engagements.

Snowden died at the age of eighty-four of what was probably pneumonia. He never gained fame or acquired great wealth, but because he wrote a detailed memoir that was later published by his grandson, Houston D. Snowden, he provided an important portrait of black faith, fortitude, and self-determination during a bleak period in U.S. history.

FURTHER READING:

Snowden, John Baptist. *From Whence Cometh, 1767–1977* (1980).

Obituaries: *Democratic Advocate* and *American Sentinel*, Sept. 1885.

SHOLOMO B. LEVY

Snowden, Samuel (c. 1775–8 Oct. 1850), Methodist Episcopal minister and antislavery activist, was born in Maryland apparently as a slave. Little is known of Samuel Snowden's early life though there are a number of references to his having been a former slave. In an address before the fourth New England Anti-Slavery Convention held in Boston, Massachusetts in 1837 he talks about his experience as a slave in the cornfields but gives no further information about when and where that was or how and when he came to be a free man.

Snowden first appears in the North in Portland, Maine, in the early 1800s where he was described in land records, first as a laborer and later as a yeoman (a small farmer who tills his own soil). On 3 January 1808 Snowden married Nancy Marsh from Monmouth, Maine, and they had at least one child, a daughter Isabella. Though no death record has been found, apparently Nancy died (perhaps in childbirth) since Portland City Vital Records report that on 20 June 1813 Snowden married Rebecca Gerrish of Portland.

During these years Snowden became a member of the Chestnut Street Methodist Episcopal Church (MEC) in Portland and eventually obtained a license as a local preacher. The history of the Methodist Episcopal Church at Brown's Hill in Cape Elizabeth, Maine, near Portland, reports that he preached there as well. Snowden must have been a powerful preacher for his reputation apparently spread as far as Boston. In 1818 he was recruited by Colonel Amos Binney and Thomas Patten, Esq., members of the predominantly white Bromfield Street MEC in Boston, to pastor the growing number of African Americans who were attending their church.

That same year Snowden moved with his family to live on the north slope of Beacon Hill where many of the African Americans in the city lived. He became the pastor of the May Street MEC, the only permanent Methodist Episcopal Church for African Americans in New England until the very early 20th century. At the 1818 annual conference of the New England Conference of the MEC Snowden was finally (after some difficulties) ordained as a deacon, the first African American pastor to be ordained in the New England Conference. Becoming known fondly as "Father Snowden" he served his church as a deacon until his death, as African Americans were not allowed to be ordained as elders and receive full clergy rights until 1864.

Despite several early and contemporary references to Snowden's church as the African Methodist Episcopal Church, the May Street MEC never joined the African Methodist Episcopal (AME) denomination established in 1816 in Philadelphia. Because it remained under the oversight of the Bromfield Street MEC until after 1900, some members did break away to form an AME and later an African Methodist Episcopal Zion Church in Boston, but Snowden and his congregation always remained a part of the Methodist Episcopal Church.

After moving to Boston Snowden became active in the antislavery movement that was growing there in the city and was an outspoken opponent of the American colonization movement. He was an active member of the Massachusetts General Colored Association (MGCA) organized in the city in 1826. DAVID WALKER, the best known member of the MGCA and author of *Walker's Appeal to the Colored Citizens of the World,* which called for an end to slavery and urged slaves to become actively involved in fighting for their freedom, was a member of Snowden's church and a good personal friend as well.

In 1831 Snowden, along with Robert Roberts, JAMES BARBADOES, and the Reverend HOSEA EASTON (Roberts's brother-in-law) represented Boston at the first National Convention of Free People of Color in Philadelphia. Snowden also became a strong supporter of William Lloyd Garrison. When the New England Anti-Slavery Association was organized in 1832 Snowden was the only African American appointed to their first panel of counselors. Antislavery meetings were often held at the May Street MEC and Snowden and his church became well known for assisting runaway slaves. On the day of his death in 1850 thirteen fugitive slaves arrived on Snowden's doorstep seeking sanctuary (*The Liberator*, 3 January 1851). His daughter Isabella continued to provide refuge for runaway slaves for some time after his death.

Father Snowden was also known for his particular ministry to black seaman and for his rescue of a number of these men who might have been sold into slavery in the South had it not been for his intervention.

At the time of his death in Boston Samuel Snowden was married to a woman named Lydia from Rhode Island; therefore, it seems likely that his second wife, Rebecca Gerrish, must also have died. His will identifies six children who were living at the time: Isabella Holmes, Mary Jane Triplett, Joshua Cook Snowden, ISAAC HUMPHREY SNOWDEN, Charles Allen Snowden, and Thomas Smith Snowden. His son Isaac was one of the first African Americans to be admitted to Harvard Medical School in 1850, along with Daniel Laing Jr., and MARTIN DELANY. The three were expelled, however, at the end of the semester due to significant protests from the white students. Isaac H. Snowden eventually completed his education and in a rather ironic twist of fate eventually sailed to Liberia as a physician under the auspices of the Massachusetts Colonization Society.

In a final tribute *The Liberator* (3 January 1851) stated, "It seems appropriate that the *Liberator* should contain something more than a passing notice of the excellent man whose name heads this article, so well and widely known as 'Father Snowden.' Aside from the associations of his mission as a Methodist clergyman in this city, the detail of his anti-slavery character would both interest and instruct, furnishing an incentive to others to work while their day lasts for the redemption of man. He was active in season and out of season in his endeavor to undo the heavy burdens, and in helping the oppressed go free."

FURTHER READING

Hinks, Peter P. *To Awaken My Afflicted Brethren: David Walker and the Problem of Antebellum Slave Resistance* (1992).

Horton, James Oliver, and Lois E. Horton. *Black Bostonians: Family Life and Community Struggle in the Antebellum North* (1999).

New England Anti-Slavery Convention. *Proceedings of the fourth New-England Anti-Slavery Convention, held in Boston, May 30, 31, and June 1 and 2, 1837.* (rpt. 1837).

Thompson, Patricia J. "Samuel Snowden: Preacher, Anti-Slavery Activist, and Minister to Mariners," *Maine's Visible Black History: The First Chronicle of Its People*, ed. H. H. Price and Gerald E. Talbot (2006).

PATRICIA J. THOMPSON

Solomons, Gus, Jr. (27 Aug. 1940–), dancer, teacher, and choreographer, was born in Boston, Massachusetts, to parents whose names and occupations are now unknown. Little is known of his early life, but he received a B.A. in architecture from the Massachusetts Institute of Technology (MIT) in 1961. While attending MIT, Solomons took dance classes at the Boston Conservatory of Music with Jan Veen for the Laban dance technique and Robert Cohan for the Graham technique. At the same time he studied ballet with E. Virginia Williams, founder of the Boston Ballet Company, and took dance classes from May O'Donnell, a member of Martha Graham's troupe of American modern dancers. Solomons then joined a Boston dance group, the Dance Makers, and began his own career as a choreographer.

Solomons moved to New York City in 1962, where he shared a studio with a group of dancers that became known as Studio 9. Before founding his own dance company in 1971, he worked as a member of dance companies directed by Graham, Joyce Trisler, Pearl Lang, and Donald McKayle and gave solo performances with Trisler, Lang, McKayle, and Paul Sanasardo. Solomons worked with the Merce Cunningham Company in 1964 but left the troupe in 1968 after an injury. With Cunningham, Solomons created roles in two important dance pieces, *Winterbranch* and *Rainforest*. In 1965 Solomons joined the Martha Graham Company, but he left after only one season. The Solomons Company/Dance was formed in 1971 to feature its founder's choreographic work. He was credited with more than twenty solo works for the McKayle, Graham, and Cunningham companies, and he choreographed more than 165 dances for his own company.

In addition to his dance performances, Solomons worked off-Broadway in the production of *Joan, an Opera*, an Al Carmine production. His television work includes *Exploring* on NBC and *City in Motion Space Game* on Boston's public television station WGBH, which was awarded a prize for innovative work with dual-screen video in a dance piece.

Solomons's degree in architecture was a critical element in his dance theory, and the design of structures played an important part in much of his choreography. The musical accompaniments to his works used speech and synthesized music, frequently including human sounds rarely associated with dance or music. *Chryptych*, presented in St. Mark's Church in New York, integrated dancers as part of the church structure by moving them through the reflection of the stained glass and subtly intimating religious statuary. Solomons referred to his own choreography as "kinetic autobiography." Dance historians describe his choreographic interpretation as expressions of architecture, game forms, and geography. While many other black dancers and choreographers focused on the context and message of the piece, Solomons was adamant that his dance design allow the dancers room for interpretation. He spoke of his choreography as "energy-as-motion" rather than an interpretation of anger and a response to social oppression. The Berkshire Ballet and the Alvin Ailey Repertory Ensemble performed Solomons's choreography. He also created a role for Martha Clarke's production of the *Magic Flute* at the Canadian Opera and Glimmerglass Playhouse in 1994, as well as the lead dance role in *The Harlem Nutcracker* in 1997 for Donald Byrd's company The Group. Becoming a dance critic in the early 1980s, Solomons wrote

dance reviews for *Dance Magazine*, the *Village Voice*, and *Gay City News*. He was named senior editor at DanceInsider.com, and his writings on dance appeared in the *New York Times* and the *Chronicle of Higher Education*, from the 1980s into the early twenty-first century.

Over the course of his career, Solomons danced with Nathan Trice's company Rituals, Alan Danielson, Complexions, Johannes Wieland, and the Contemporary Dance Company in Fort Worth, Texas. He lectured and taught master classes at universities through the United States, including the University of California, Santa Cruz; California State University, Long Beach; Hunter College, CUNY; and Goucher College. He accepted the position of dean of the School of Dance at the California School of the Arts but resigned when the duties of the office restricted his ability to accept outside engagements. He served as distinguished visiting dance professor at Washington University in Saint Louis in 2004. In 1995 Solomons was appointed associate professor of dance at the Tisch School of the Arts at New York University; he became a full professor in 2005. Receiving a position as a Phi Beta Kappa Visiting Scholar, he lectured at U.S. universities affiliated with the Phi Beta Kappa honor society during the 2006–2007 academic year. In addition to his teaching appointment at Tisch, Solomons taught at Virginia Commonwealth University and the Silesian Dance Festival in Poland. A frequent judge and panelist for arts councils, advisory boards, and private foundations, Solomons received fellowships and grants of his own from Riverside, Cary Charitable Trust, the National Endowment for the Arts, the New York State Council on the Arts, the New York Foundation for the Arts, and the Harkness Foundation. He also received a number of awards and honors, including a Bessie, the New York Dance and Performance Award in 1999–2000 for Sustained Achievement in Choreography. His alma mater MIT awarded him the first Robert A. Muh Award for a distinguished alumnus in 2001. Solomons was given the Joy Ann Dewey Beinecke Endowed Chair for Distinguished Teaching and the Balasaraswati at the American Dance Festival in 2004. Additionally he was featured in several dance documentaries, and he worked in the film *Romance and Cigarettes* as a singer and dancer in 2005.

Solomons wrote and lectured frequently about the role of the older dancer and believed that experienced dancers could and should still contribute to the field as teachers, as administrators, and equally importantly, as performers who adapt to the body's changing range of movement. Senior dancers, in his view, offer a more mature interpretation than do younger dancers. Solomons performed with the dancers CARMEN DE LAVALLADE and Dudley Williams in the repertory company Paradigm. He was a pivotal figure in postmodern and experimental dance, and his belief that dance can be a lifelong profession changed the way older dancers are perceived by both peers and audiences.

FURTHER READING

Long, Richard A. *The Black Tradition in American Dance* (1989).

McDonagh, Don. "Gus Solomons, Jr.," in *The Complete Guide to Modern Dance* (1976).

Performance Lab. Dana Foundation, Gus Solomons Jr., available online at http://www.theperformancelab.org/section_do/DANA_GUS2.htm.

Public Broadcasting Service. Great Performances: Free to Dance Biographies. Gus Solomons, Jr. Available at http://www.pbs.org/wnet/freetodance/biographies/index.html.

PAMELA LEE GRAY

Somerset, James (c. 1741–after 1772), slave who challenged his status in as English court and in the process undermined the legality of slavery in Great Britain, was born in Africa. Captured as a young boy, he was taken to America on a British slaver, arriving sometime in the spring of 1749. In August, Charles Stewart or Steuart purchased Somerset, who was between eight and ten years old. Stewart, a Scottish-born merchant, later became the chief of customs for all of Britain's North American colonies from Virginia to Canada. Somerset lived in America for about two decades and then was taken to England in November 1769. Unlike most bondsmen in Virginia, Somerset did not work in the tobacco fields. Rather, he was Stewart's personal servant and valet. Stewart purchased fine clothing for Somerset, including silk stockings, and gave him some spending money. Scattered records suggest that Stewart had some affection for Somerset, treating him kindly, even generously, as a trusted servant and valet. Stewart owned a few other slaves in Virginia, but Somerset was the only one he took with him when he traveled to Massachusetts and other colonies.

In November 1769 Stewart moved to England, taking Somerset with him. Somerset continued as Stewart's servant and valet. There is no indication that Stewart mistreated Somerset or physically abused him. In February 1771 Somerset was baptized under the name of James Summersett, but he later adopted the more conventional spelling, Somerset. The church records described him as an "adult black" aged "about thirty."

What appeared to Stewart as a harmonious master-servant relationship ended abruptly in October 1741, when Somerset left Stewart and refused to return. On 26 November 1771 Stewart had Somerset seized, planning to ship him to the British Caribbean, where he would have been sold. However, this never happened. Friends of Somerset contacted the British abolitionist Granville Sharp, who sought a writ of habeas corpus form the Court of King's Bench. This case raised, for the first time, the status of the fifteen thousand or so slaves then in Great Britain. Most were servants, like Somerset, brought to the mother country by colonial officials like Stewart, by slave traders, or by absentee sugar planters who owned lands and slaves in the Caribbean but lived in Britain.

Chief Justice William Murray, Lord Mansfield, strenuously urged the parties to settle the case. In the May 1772 term of court Mansfield noted that half a dozen or so similar cases had been brought before the British courts, but they had always been settled. Mansfield reminded both sides that "on its [Somerset's case] first coming before me, I strongly recommended it here. But if the parties will have it decided, we must give our opinion." Mansfield was strongly hinting that it was time for the case to be settled. He warned, "Compassion will not, on the one hand, nor inconvenience on the other, be to decide; but the law." Mansfield noted that in England "contract for sale of a slave is good," but this case was different because "the person of the slave himself is immediately the object of enquiry." The legal question was whether British courts should enforce a status created by "American laws." Mansfield noted the great "difficulty of adopting the relation, without adopting it in all its consequences." If a slave could be held in England, then all the consequences of slavery might follow, including whippings, jailing of runaways (like Somerset), and, although he did not say so, sexual abuse of slaves by masters. Giving the lawyers one more chance to settle the case, Mansfield declared, "If the parties will have judgment, fiat justitia, ruat coelum [let justice be done though the heavens may fall] let justice be done whatever the consequence." He noted the complications of former slaves suing for wages, hinted at the social problems of fifteen thousand recently freed blacks living in Britain, and noted the potential lost of some £700,000 sterling for the slave owners. It was clear that Mansfield thought the smartest course was for Stewart to end the litigation by letting Somerset leave. Mansfield concluded this phase of the litigation by noting: "In these particulars, it may be matter of weighty consideration, what provisions are made or set by law. Mr. Stewart may end the question, by discharging or giving freedom to the negro."

Stewart did not take the hint. His lawyers were paid for by wealthy Britons connected to the sugar trade who wanted to resolve the status of the slaves they brought to England. However, their lawyers should have understood that Mansfield was not likely to decide in their favor, because he ended the May hearing by urging Stewart to free Somerset. Perhaps the elite lawyers for the sugar interests simply did not believe a group of reformers would actually beat them in this case. It is also likely that Stewart was not interested in settling the case in any way that would help Somerset. Stewart was a kindly master, and he had apparently convinced himself that Somerset was happy in his status and owed Stewart his gratitude and affection. He, after all, had virtually raised Somerset. Perhaps he had raised Somerset too well, given him ideas that he was entitled to the same measure of happiness and self-direction that Stewart had. Somerset felt he was entitled to his liberty—he had given Stewart more than two decades of faithful service, and Stewart was not entitled to his life; Stewart doubtless felt Somerset owed him gratitude for raising him and protecting him from the burdens of field work as a slave.

At the June term Mansfield reviewed the case and reduced the issue to the simple and narrow question: Could a slave owner maintain control of a slave in England, against the will of the slave? Mansfield concluded he or she could not. The chief justice wrote:

> So high an act of dominion must be recognized by the law of the country where it is used. The power of a master over his slave has been extremely different, in different countries. The state of slavery is of such a nature, that it is incapable of being introduced on any reasons, moral or political; but only positive law, which preserves its force long after the reasons, occasion, and time itself from whence it was created, is erased from memory, it's so odious, that nothing can be suffered to support it, but positive law. Whatever inconveniences, therefore, may follow from a decision, I cannot say this case is allowed or approved by the law of England; and therefore the black must be discharged.

With this opinion Somerset was set free, and he walked out of the courtroom and out of the historical record. Presumably he melted into London's growing community of slaves and free blacks, who lived among other members of the city's working and servant class.

Scholars know little about Somerset's life before or after the case. But his life illustrates two enduring aspects of slavery. First, that even the most pampered and well-treated slaves wanted their liberty, and many, like Somerset, were willing to sacrifice material well-being and some security for freedom. Second, Somerset's life illustrates FREDERICK DOUGLASS's observation half a century later that if a master gave someone a little bit of freedom, he or she would only want more. Somerset doubtless had substantial physical mobility in England and probably when living in America as well. It enabled him to make friends with free people, to find people to help him when he left Stewart, and ultimately to believe he could fend for himself as a free person.

The meaning of Somerset's case has been contested. It did not lead to an immediate end to slavery in Britain, and for the next half a century some slaves were taken there. But the case did give slaves in Britain a legal claim to freedom if they were savvy enough to make the claim. The case also created a powerful precedent for the idea that slavery could only exist where positive law created it. Many American states adopted the *Somerset* precedent, freeing slaves that entered their jurisdiction. However, the U.S. Supreme Court rejected it in *Dred Scott v. Sandford* (1857).

FURTHER READING

Davis, David Brion. *The Problem of Slavery in the Age of Revolution, 1770–1823* (1975).

Finkelman, Paul. *An Imperfect Union: Slavery, Federalism, and Comity* (1981).

Paley, Ruth. "After Somerset: Mansfield, Slavery, and the Law in England, 1772–1830," in *Law, Crime, and English Society, 1660–1830*, ed. Norma Landau (2002).

Somerset v. Stewart, 1 Lofft 1, 20 *Howell's State Trials* 1, 98 Eng. Rep. 499 (1772, G.B. King's Bench).

Weiner, Mark S. "New Biographical Evidence on Somerset's Case," *Slavery and Abolition* 23 (Apr. 2002): 121.

Wiecek, William M. *The Sources of Antislavery Constitutionalism in America, 1760–1848* (1977).

Wise, Steven M. *Though the Heavens May Fall: The Landmark Trial That Led to the End of Human Slavery* (2005).

PAUL FINKELMAN

Somerville, John Alexander (c. 1882–11 Feb. 1973), civil rights activist, religious pioneer, dentist, and investor, was born in Kingston, Jamaica, the youngest son of Thomas Gustavius Somerville, an Anglican minister. Little is known about his mother. He was educated in the Jamaican public schools, where he learned that social status and racial attitudes often triumphed over equality, and between 1897 and 1900 he attended and graduated from Mico College in Kingston with a teaching degree.

Rather than strain against the prevailing practices, Somerville left home for the United States in December 1901, at age nineteen, in the company of a childhood friend, seeking both adventure and a future devoid of racial intolerance. Arriving in San Francisco with some money from his father, Somerville quickly settled in Los Angeles, a city whose prospects he considered promising. Even in Los Angeles, however, he felt the pangs of America's racial prejudice. He was most stunned when he was forced to worship in a segregated church, which was entirely foreign to his previous experiences and his understanding of Christian teaching. He spent the remainder of his life challenging the un-Christian practices he both endured and witnessed, chastising national and local religious leaders for extolling equality while remaining silent on racism and racial violence.

For the next couple of years Somerville worked at various odd jobs. He formed connections with several prominent whites while working in business and real estate, finally setting his sights on dentistry as a career in which he could serve both whites and blacks and which would give him the prestige he sought. In the fall of 1904 he enrolled at the University of Southern California (USC) School of Dentistry. In his second year there he was the subject of a meeting of the School of Dentistry's student body in which his classmates protested his enrollment. In spite of the adversity, in 1907 Somerville became the second African American to receive a degree from USC and the second African American to pass the California dental licensing exam.

Somerville subsequently set up a private practice in Los Angeles, where he served whites and blacks, rich and poor, and became a leading figure in the African American community. While enrolled at USC, he had become a member of the Wesley Methodist congregation and met Vada Watson at a social function at the Azusa African Methodist Episcopal Church. Watson was born and raised in Los Angeles and had attended USC as an undergraduate for three years. After an extended courtship, they married in 1913. Two years later Vada followed in her husband's footsteps and enrolled in USC's School of Dentistry. In 1918 she became the school's first African American female graduate and the state's first black female dentist. Somerville immediately set her up as a partner in his practice, and she quickly became a civic leader of local and national importance in her own right.

In 1909 Somerville applied for citizenship. In preparation for the exam, his studies of the American system of government made him keenly aware of the contrast between the lofty ideals stated in the nation's founding documents and the daily realities of white supremacy—the nation promised so much but delivered so little. This was, he noted, in stark contrast to his experiences in and knowledge of the British system, which promised little but did deliver on those promises. Along with his wife, Somerville became a founding member of the Los Angeles branch of the National Association for the Advancement of Colored People (NAACP) in 1913 in a meeting held in their home. For more than a decade Somerville served as the organization's vice president, and later he became executive director, eventually gaining an appointment to the National NAACP Board of Directors. He described the Los Angeles chapter as "militant" in its refusal to give into racial prejudice. Under his leadership the group pursued an agenda centered on the integration of education and the city's playgrounds and on equal opportunities for black children in sports, extracurricular activities, and medicine.

Somerville took an active role in politics and claimed to have voted in every election following his attainment of citizenship in 1910. His views determined his party affiliation, not the other way around, and until the late 1920s he identified with the Progressives. He supported Hiram Johnson as governor of California and was a staunch advocate for Theodore Roosevelt and the Bull Moose Party, lobbying in support of the party's efforts throughout the black community and often canvassing for its candidates.

With the onset of the Great Depression, Somerville turned to the Democratic Party, which was in tune with many of his personal beliefs concerning government activism and leadership in addressing and correcting social problems. During the Depression he met George Creel, former director of the Committee on Public Information, who, along with Aubrey Williams, head of the Federal

Emergency Relief Administration, called him to Washington to discuss racial issues. With the backing of Creel, Williams appointed Somerville as an adviser to the California State Emergency Relief Administration, where he worked to assure equality of status and appropriations for African Americans in the agency's programs. In 1934 he ran for the Sixty-second Assembly District seat in the Democratic primary, the apparent front-runner until the late entry of other black candidates. Somerville was not able to carry the election with support from the African American community alone, and he lost to a twenty-seven-year-old Democrat, AUGUSTUS FREEMAN HAWKINS, who courted not only the black constituents but also the whites and had the backing of the Reverend General Jealous Divine (more commonly known as FATHER DIVINE) and his Peace Mission Movement followers. In 1962 Hawkins became the first African American member of Congress from California. Nonetheless, Somerville was not finished with politics. In 1936 he was the first African American in California elected as a delegate to the Democratic National Convention, held in Philadelphia, Pennsylvania.

During World War II and the cold war, Somerville used his stature to challenge claims that African Americans were Communists and to denounce the charges as fear-mongering and racist. Rumors of a massive black conversion to Communism as a means of upsetting the social order were just one more way, he pointed out in both his political campaigning and his later autobiography, for those who were seeking to maintain segregation and sustain entrenched racism to justify their beliefs.

Somerville was a constant critic of racism and American hypocrisy, something that he felt his immigrant-turned-citizen status helped him better understand. In an attempt to stop racial profiling by lenders in real estate transactions, the racial stratification of city neighborhoods, and the dearth of both public and private facilities in which blacks could dine, sleep, and congregate, he became a leading investor in black neighborhoods. In 1928 he borrowed heavily from his fellow black businessman Louis Blodgett of Liberty Savings and Loan Company to build the Somerville Hotel on the city's east side so that black workers and migrants to the city would have a place to stay. Almost immediately the site gained respect within the African American community and was chosen as the site for that year's NAACP National Convention. Despite his personal financial losses, which also caused him to lose ownership of the Somerville Hotel (which became the Dunbar Hotel) during the Depression, the Forty-first Street and Central Avenue neighborhood in which he invested became the center of African American business in Los Angeles. His investments included the construction of apartment buildings on Berlin Avenue (named the Vada Arms in honor of his wife) and loans to local black businesspeople.

Somerville worked tirelessly to establish interracial congregations, eventually leaving Saint Philips Episcopal Mission after he helped organize the interracial Church of Christian Fellowship in 1948. He also played a significant role in shaping racial attitudes in postwar Los Angeles. As the first African American member of the Los Angeles Chamber of Commerce and the city's police commission, he fought against the spread of racism and illegal practices as both whites and blacks migrated to California in increasing numbers. He worked with the agencies responsible for oversight of the federal Fair Employment Practices Act to see that blacks were given equal treatment under the law and in the resulting programs. Somerville retired from active business and civic life in the 1950s and died at the age of ninety-one. His pursuit of social justice, equality, and civil rights based on his religious values for more than fifty years formed an essential foundation for the advances and successes of the civil rights movement of the 1960s.

FURTHER READING

Somerville, J. Alexander. *Man of Color: An Autobiography* (1949).
Beasley, Delilah. *The Negro Trail Blazers of California* (1919).
Flamming, Douglas. *Bound for Freedom: Black Los Angeles in Jim Crow America* (2005).
Taylor, Quintard. *In Search of the Racial Frontier: African Americans in the American West, 1528–1990* (1998).

J. D. BOWERS

Sorrell, Maurice B. (13 Dec. 1913–22 June 1998), award-winning news photographer, was born in Washington, D.C., to Lillian E. McLane and Roscoe Sorrell. His father died when Maurice was five, and Maurice and his brother were raised by their mother. As a teen Maurice developed an interest in photography while observing and assisting his uncles, who were amateur photographers. He took up the camera and began to consider photography as a career. He began by photographing family gatherings and events around the neighborhood. While attending public schools in Washington, he also was responsible for taking class pictures. Sorrell graduated from Shaw Junior High School and Armstrong Senior High School, but his family could not afford to send him to college.

Sorrell took a job as a skilled assistant at the U.S. Bureau of Engraving and Printing. But racism frustrated his ambitions for starting a career in photography, and his superiors prevented his reassignment as a photographer's apprentice at the bureau. Later he applied for a position as photographer at the Pentagon but became a darkroom technician there instead.

In June 1946 Sorrell married Beatrice Wyms, a nursing student at Freedmen's Hospital on the campus of Howard University. That same year he purchased a 4x5 Speed Graphic camera and began photographing weddings, babies, and family events. On the weekends Sorrell photographed couples in nightclubs along Washington's U Street corridor while his wife collected fees. He developed the prints in a makeshift darkroom in the bathroom, and the customers came by his home the following day to pick them up. Despite the obstacles he faced on his job, he continued to hone his skills in photography.

Sorrell sought to further develop his skills by enrolling in a three-year photography program offered by the U.S. Department of Agriculture. In 1957, at the age of forty-four, armed with professional training and encouraged by his wife and by the success of his part-time photographic work, he established himself as a full-time photographer and left the Pentagon. Shortly afterward he was hired as a staff photographer for the *Washington Afro-American* newspaper, shooting local events and crime scenes. He was also a member of the Prince Hall Masons and became their official photographer.

Sorrell's career then began to take off. In 1962 JOHN H. JOHNSON, founder of Johnson Publishing Company, which published *Jet* and *Ebony* magazines, was impressed by Sorrell's photograph of the singer MARIAN ANDERSON and hired him to work in the company's Washington office. Although Sorrell was based in the nation's capital, his assignments took him all over the country. Between 1962 and 1994 he photographed many memorable and historic moments of the civil rights era, sometimes at risking his life. In 1964, for instance, Sorrell

and the *Jet* reporter Larry Still hid in the back of a hearse between coffins and rode to a funeral home in Meridian, Mississippi, to cover the story of the murdered civil rights worker JAMES EARL CHANEY. It was rumored that Ku Klux Klan members had learned of their arrival and had set up roadblocks to prevent them from getting the story. The hearse was indeed stopped, but Klan members did not search the rear of the car. Other assignments were not as dangerous but still left a powerful impression on Sorrell. In 1965 he went to Selma, Alabama, to cover the march to Montgomery for voting rights. In 1968 he was in Memphis photographing MARTIN LUTHER KING JR. and was there the night King was killed.

To get some of the images he is best known for, Sorrell faced unsympathetic sheriffs with police dogs, angry mobs, gunshots, and tear gas but still maintained a high level of decorum. Johnson sometimes referred to his reporters and photographers as "ambassadors of the Black race" in that they represented more than just themselves out in the field. Sorrell also found it necessary to fight discrimination within the profession. After several failed attempts to gain entry to the elite White House News Photographers Association, he was belatedly admitted as its first black member. This was due to the prompting of the *Jet* reporter Simeon Booker, who during a press conference the year before had asked President John F. Kennedy why there were no black photographers in that association.

Sorrell's photographic legacy amounts to a who's who of black America. Dignitaries, celebrities, politicians, and entertainers have stood in front of his cameras. His images of the Supreme Court justice THURGOOD MARSHALL, the singers JAMES BROWN and LENA HORNE, the congressional members Charles Diggs, SHIRLEY CHISHOLM, and ADAM CLAYTON POWELL JR., the funeral of President Kennedy, SAMMY DAVIS JR. receiving an honorary degree from Howard University, and MICHAEL JACKSON with President George Bush at the White House graced the pages of *Jet* and *Ebony*. Sorrell informed the world of what it meant to be black in America.

Sorrell retired in 1994 after thirty-two years with *Jet* and *Ebony*. In 1997 the Exposure Group African-American Photographers Association honored Sorrell with its Lifetime Achievement Award, which now bears his name. Also in 1997 Howard University hosted a one-man exhibition, Photographs by Maurice Sorrell: Ambassador of the Black Race, which featured more than sixty images representing fifty years of his work. He died from heart failure.

FURTHER READING

Sorrell's funeral program, which includes "Obituary of Maurice Sorrell," 29 June 1998, is in the Photographers Vertical File, Prints and Photographs, Moorland-Spingarn Research Center, Howard University.

Gilliam, Dorothy. "Celebrating a Life Time of Being in Focus," *Washington Post* (5 July 1997).

Wells, Donna Marica. Personal interview with subject, Washington, D.C. (Dec. 1985). Unpublished.

DONNA MARCIA WELLS

Southerland, Ellease (18 June 1943–), writer, poet, and educator, was born in Brooklyn, New York, the third of fifteen children of Monroe Penrose Southerland, a minister and baker, and Ellease (Dozier) Southerland, a homemaker. The family had its origins in the South but had moved to New York in search of a better life. Reading and playing music were regular pastimes in the Southerland household, and, although they endured hard times financially, the children were supported in their learning. Young Ellease decided to become a poet at the age of ten and even conducted poetry sessions at her father's church. She attended John Adams High School in Queens and graduated in 1961.

While an undergraduate student at Queens College, part of the City University of New York (CUNY), Southerland won the John Golden Award for Fiction in 1964 for her novella *White Shadows*. She graduated with a B.A. in English in 1965, the same year that her mother died of cancer at the age of forty-five. Southerland had a strong bond to her mother, who was her first editor. Her love and the impact of her early death are recurring themes in Southerland's writings. As the oldest daughter, Southerland took a job with the New York City Department of Social Services in 1966, where she worked until 1972, to help support her younger siblings. In 1973 she entered academia, teaching English at the Community Educational Exchange Program at Columbia until 1976 and black literature at the Borough of Manhattan Community College (CUNY) until 1993. In 1975 she began to teach literature of African peoples and creative writing at Pace University, where she earned tenure as a full professor in the Department of English in 1999.

In the early 1970s, while working at the Department of Social Services, Southerland began to publish poetry regularly in magazines such as the *Journal of Black Poetry* and *Black World*. In 1972 she won the GWENDOLYN BROOKS Poetry Award, given by *Black World* for her poem "Warlock," which appeared in that magazine. Poems about the horrors of war and the short story "Soldiers" (*Black World*, 1973) reflected her experience of the bone-shaking sirens of the Korean War when she was a little girl and having loved ones in the Vietnam War.

In 1974 Southerland received her MFA in creative writing from Columbia University. The following year she published the poetry collection *The Magic Sun Spins* (1975), which included previously published poems like "Black Is" and "Warlock." Its major themes revolved around family, tradition and self-perception, and condemnation of war.

Southerland first visited Nigeria in 1971, and she bought a summer home in Enugu in 1997. She was made a fellow of the University of Nigeria at Nsukka in 1998, spoke on radio programs there, and contributed to *Okike* (*African Journal of New Writing*), which is based at the University of Nsukka. Her deep love of Africa, its people, its folk traditions, and her African roots were important themes in her prose and poetry, expressed in such poems as "Night in Nigeria." She was also fascinated by ancient Egypt hieroglyphs, and in her university classes she emphasized Africa's contribution to world culture. In 1996 she changed her family name, which had been that of the slave owners of her ancestors, to Ebele Oseye (Ebele means "mercy" in Igbo, a Nigerian language, while Oseye means "the happy one" in Benin, another Nigerian language).

Even though Southerland had entered the literary world with poetry, she was first and foremost known for her semiautobiographical novel *Let the Lion Eat Straw* (1979). The book tells the story of Abeba, who is born an illegitimate child in rural North Carolina and gets uprooted at age six to live in New York with her ever-criticizing mother. Her lifetime is shaped by hardship, austerity, an abusive uncle, and the suffering from her madness-stricken husband, Reverend Daniel Torch. But it is also a life full of hope, joy, and love, and a story of female strength. The novel is an homage to Southerland's mother, who, like Abeba, abandoned a potential career as a pianist to become the committed wife and mother of large family, and who died an early death. Southerland's intertwining of her own family experience with elements of fiction made this story rich and truly touching. Her condensed, almost lyrical style of writing received much critical acclaim. Her first novel was likened to works by TONI MORRISON, and MAYA ANGELOU called her a "seer of the interior human landscape." In 1979 *Let the Lion Eat Straw* was voted Best Book for Young Adults by the American Library Association.

It was not until 1998 that she published her second novel, *A Feast of Fools*, which is the sequel to the Torch family story. The main character is Kora Ada, the oldest daughter of Abeba, who becomes a social caseworker after her mother's death to help support the family. The relationship of American-born Kora Ada and Nigerian-born Ibe Ikenna takes the reader to Africa, reuniting African Americans and Africans. *A Feast of Fools* is, among other things, "a portrait of the artist."

In addition to her novels, short stories, and poetry, Southerland wrote numerous essays and articles. Among her well-recognized essays on literature is "The Influence of Voodoo on the Fiction of ZORA NEALE HURSTON" (in *Sturdy Black Bridges*, 1979). Southerland also recollected her family experience in the autobiographical article, "I Got a Horn, You Got a Horn" (in *A World Unsuspected*, 1987). In *This Year in Nigeria* (2000), she shared her travel experiences in Africa, reporting on her own bewilderment at cultural and political differences, as well as her falling in love with the country and her feelings of coming home. Other writings discussed social developments in both the United States and in Africa, criticized racism, and emphasized the importance of art in society, like her essay "The Responsibility and Power of Art" (in *The Heritage Series of Black Poetry, 1962–1975: A Research Compendium*, 2007). In 2006 Southerland began working on her collection of essays *Put Your Grammar in Your Mouth*, together with her next volume of poetry, *A Silver Hieroglyph*. The major themes of the poetry in this volume are her deep rooting in African culture and her appreciation for the cosmos.

Southerland had many speaking engagements throughout the United States and regular reviews in *Quarterly Black Review of Books*, and she became publisher of Eneke Publications in the 1990s. Many of Ellease Southerland's writings are deeply personal, sharing her experience and insights into life. She skillfully blends biographical facts with fiction, and her multi-layered themes, strong characters, and stories are rich with symbolism, mythology, and spirituality. It is this synergy combined with African folk tradition that makes her work unique. In her narrations and poetry she brings vivid images to life in an unobtrusive and yet almost real fashion, without ever employing vulgarity or artificial action. According to the author, celebration of life is the most important theme in her writings.

FURTHER READING

Barnwell, Cherron A. "Ellease Southerland," in *Contemporary African American Novelists: A Bio-Biographical Critical Sourcebook*, ed. Emmanuel S. Nelson (1999).

Brookhart, Mary Hughes. "Ellease Southerland," in *Afro-American Fiction Writers after 1955, Dictionary of Literary Biography*, vol. 33, eds. Thadious M. Davis, Trudier Harris (1984).

Brookhart, Mary Hughes. "Ellease Southerland," in *The Oxford Companion to Women's Writing in the United States*, eds. Cathy N. Davidson, Linda Wagner-Martin (1995).

Metzger, Linda, et al., eds. "Ellease Southerland," in *Black Writers: A Selection of Sketches from Contemporary Authors* (1989).

BÄRBEL RENATE BROUWERS

Southern, Eileen (19 Feb. 1920–13 Oct. 2002), concert pianist and musicologist, was born Eileen Jackson in Minneapolis, Minnesota, the daughter of Walter Jackson, a musician and chemistry teacher, and Lilla Gibson. She grew up in the Midwest, primarily Chicago, with her mother and two sisters. Her parents divorced when Jackson was eight, but she remained close to her father. Her interest in music was sustained in her mother's South Side home, which was a meeting place for African American musicians and entertainers, most notably LOUIS ARMSTRONG. Despite her contact with popular and jazz musicians, Jackson's musical training and orientation remained rooted in the traditions of classical European music. A student of works by Bach, Beethoven, and Debussy, she played her first piano recital at the age of twelve and performed at Orchestra Hall in Chicago at the age of eighteen. She graduated from Lindblom High School in Chicago and at the same time studied piano at the Chicago Musical College.

Jackson continued her education at the University of Chicago, earning a B.A. in 1940 and an M.A. in 1941. Her master's thesis was titled "The Use of Negro Folksong in Symphonic Form." She went on to teach music at several historically black institutions of higher learning, including Prairie View A&M State College in Texas and Southern University in Baton Rouge, Louisiana. In 1942 she married Joseph Southern, a professor of business administration.

They had two children. The Southerns moved to Mississippi in 1945 to teach and serve as the heads of the music and business administration departments at Alcorn A&M College. In 1947 they moved to Orangeburg, South Carolina, where Southern taught music at Claflin University and her husband taught business at South Carolina State A&M College. In addition to her teaching duties and scholarship, she continued performing and competing as a concert pianist. She toured and performed on college campuses in both the North and the South as well as in cities in the Great Lakes region. Southern studied at the Julliard School of Music and at Boston University. In 1948, after being awarded first prize in a national piano competition, she performed in New York City at Carnegie Hall.

In 1951 Southern moved to New York with her family. She taught in the New York public school system while pursuing a Ph.D. in historical musicology at New York University. In 1960 Southern received an appointment to the faculty at Brooklyn College. She completed her doctoral studies in 1961 and became the first African American woman to receive a Ph.D. in musicology from an American institution. (CORTEZ REECE was the first African American man to receive such a degree.) She wrote her dissertation about a fifteenth-century manuscript known as the "Buxheim Organ Book." This became the foundation for her first book, *The Buxheim Organ Book*, published in 1963 by the Institute of Mediaeval Music. Southern left Brooklyn College in 1968, moving to York College of the City University of New York (CUNY), where she was chair of the music department until 1975. In an interview with Samuel Floyd Jr., Southern stated that while she was at York College the attitudes of her colleagues about black music spurred her to undertake the groundbreaking research in the field of black music for which she is best known.

Wishing to teach a course on black music as a response to black student uprisings, Southern described her colleagues' response to her idea as skeptical at best. "What is there to learn about black music? There's nothing there—just jazz and the spirituals; how can you find enough material to make a course?" were among the questions and comments she received. The answers were forthcoming in *The Music of Black Americans* (1971), Southern's comprehensive interdisciplinary study of black music in the United States. Unlike earlier texts on black music by WILLIAM MONROE TROTTER, MAUD CUNEY-HARE, and ALAIN LOCKE, Southern's study was written by a trained

musicologist and therefore found its way into the established disciplinary conversation concerning American musicology. As such the publication of *The Music of Black Americans* stands as a milestone in American scholarship, hailed by Samuel Floyd Jr. as a "watershed event" (Floyd, 7).

The Music of Black Americans and its companion text, *Readings in Black American Music* (1971), which Southern compiled, proved to be invaluable both for advancing the study of black music and for demonstrating the scholarly importance of African American studies. Southern made another major contribution to the field by cofounding with her husband the journal *Black Perspectives in Music* in 1973, the first journal dedicated to the study of black music. As editor of this journal until 1990, Southern continued to solidify her reputation as a pioneer in American scholarship. In 1974 Southern was invited to teach at Harvard University. She served as the chair of that institution's African American studies department in 1975. She went on to become the first African American woman to receive tenure at Harvard. More importantly, she brought African American studies into the institution's larger intellectual conversation. Writing about the experience in her essay "A Pioneer: Black and Female," Southern explained that she looked at W. E. B. DuBois as her role model. "Like him I went to Harvard because it was a great opportunity for me as a black female scholar, and I accepted the reality of racial and sex discrimination (Sollors, 502). She retired from the Harvard faculty in 1986.

Southern remained an active scholar after leaving the classroom, revising *The Music of Black Americans* and overseeing the publication of its second and third editions in the 1980s and 1990s. She coedited *African-American Traditions in Song, Sermon, Tale, and Dance, 1600s–1920* (1990), an annotated bibliography, with Josephine Wright, and the two collaborated again in *Images: Iconography of Music in African-American Culture, 1770s–1920s* (2000). A recipient of the National Humanities Medal in 2001, Southern also won an ASCAP–Deems Taylor Award, the SOJOURNER TRUTH Award, and the National Association of Negro Musicians' Distinguished Achievement Award (1986), among her many accolades. After her retirement she lived in Port Charlotte, Florida, until her death.

FURTHER READING

Floyd, Samuel, Jr. "Eileen Jackson Southern: Quiet Revolutionary," in *New Perspectives on Music:*

Essays in Honor of Eileen Southern, ed. Josephine Wright (1992).

Sollors, Werner, Caldwell Titcomb, and Thomas A. Underwood, eds. *Blacks at Harvard: A Documentary History of African-American Experience at Harvard and Radcliffe* (1993).

Obituary: *New York Times*, 19 Oct. 2002.

MICHAEL A. ANTONUCCI

Sowell, Thomas (30 June 1930–), conservative economist, political writer, and educator, was born in Gastonia, North Carolina, to Willie (maiden name unknown), a domestic, and Henry Sowell, who died before his son's birth. Because they already had four other children, Thomas's parents, even before he was born, asked for help in rearing the baby. Henry turned to his aunt, Molly Sowell, who was sixty; she and her husband named the baby Thomas Hancock Sowell, nicknamed "Buddy," and raised him as their own. Willie Sowell died a few years later in childbirth, and Sowell did not know until he was an adult that his aunt and uncle were not his real parents. He was a fourth grader when in the 1930s the family moved to Harlem, New York, where Sowell grew up and attended the prestigious Stuyvesant High School. He dropped out in the tenth grade to go to work, and for four years he labored at such jobs as deliveryman, Western Union messenger, and factory worker. He left home at seventeen but eventually earned his high school equivalency diploma. On 30 October 1951 Sowell was drafted into the Marine Corps. After training at Parris Island, he reported to the Naval Air Station's photography school in Pensacola, Florida, in February 1952. He served for two years at Camp Lejeune in North Carolina and worked in the photo lab, and he was a pistol instructor and photographer in the Korean War. After leaving military service in 1953, he entered Howard University on the GI Bill and worked part time as a photographer and civil service clerk in the General Accounting Office. After three semesters at Howard, he transferred to Harvard University, where he earned his AB in economics in 1958, graduating magna cum laude. He wrote his senior thesis on Karl Marx's political philosophy. Sowell then earned a master's degree in economics in 1959 at Columbia University. In 1968 he earned a Ph.D. in economics at the University of Chicago, where he studied under two Nobel Prize-winning economists, George Stigler and Milton Friedman.

In 1962 Sowell began his career as an intern then as a labor economist in the U.S. Department of Labor. From September 1962 to June 1963 he was

Thomas Sowell, prior to his appearance on the NBC Television show "Meet the Press" on 20 Sept. 1981. (AP Images.)

an instructor in economics at Rutgers University and Douglass College. He was a lecturer in economics at Howard University from September 1963 to June 1964. From 1965 to 1972 he taught economics at a number of other institutions, including Cornell University, Brandeis University, Amherst College, and the University of California, Los Angeles (UCLA). From 1972 to 1974 he was project director at the Urban Institute. In 1974 Sowell was promoted to full professor of economics at UCLA, where he taught until 1980. During those six years at UCLA he was also an adjunct scholar at the American Enterprise Institute (1975–1976) and a fellow at the Center for Advanced Study in the Behavioral Sciences at Stanford University (1976–1977). In 1980 Sowell became the Rose and Milton Friedman Senior Fellow in Public Policy at the Hoover Institution at Stanford.

In 1980, with the new conservative Republican president Ronald Reagan in office, Sowell organized the Black Alternative Conference in San Francisco, where some one hundred business and education leaders advocated right-wing policies. Sowell was offered a cabinet post in the new Reagan administration, but he declined. He did, however, accept a post on the White House Economic Advisory Board in February 1981, but he resigned shortly afterward because the commute from his house in California to Washington, D.C., proved too lengthy.

Beginning in 1971 with *Economics: Analysis and Issues* and continuing with one book almost every year, Sowell published extensively on economics, culture, the middle class, education, and race. In the late 1970s and early 1980s Sowell's writing centered on studies of American racial and ethnic groups in such works as *Race and Economics* (1975), *American Ethnic Groups* (1978), *Markets and Minorities* (1981), *Ethnic America: A History* (1981), and *The Economics and Politics of Race: An International Perspective* (1983). Sowell's research on cultural history produced the trilogy *Race and Culture: A World View* (1994), *Migration and Cultures: A World View* (1996), and *Conquests and Cultures* (1998). In 2000 he published his memoir, *A Personal Odyssey.* Sowell says at the end, "The whole point of looking back on my life, aside from the pleasures of sharing reminiscences, is to hope that others will find something useful for their own lives." It is a book about growing up black, but it is also a book about struggle, perseverance, and ideals.

Sowell received a number of awards and honors. In 1990 he won the Francis Boyer Award from the American Enterprise Institute, in 2002 the National Humanities Medal, and in 2003 the Bradley Prize for intellectual achievement. He married Alma Jean Parr and divorced in 1975; the couple had two children: John (c. 1965) and Lorraine (1971). Sowell later married Mary M. Ash, an attorney. On 19 May 2000 he launched the Thomas Sowell website at www.tsowell.com, which includes the full range of his beliefs and interests, including photos, columns, speeches, favorite quotations, and thoughts on writing.

Sowell wrote nearly forty books and numerous articles and essays in scholarly journals. His nationally syndicated column, which began in 1984, appeared in more than 150 newspapers, and he was an occasional columnist for numerous anthologies and periodicals, including the *Wall Street Journal, American Economic Review*, the *New York Times*, the *Washington Post, Ethics, Education Digest, Forbes Magazine, Newsweek*, and the *Los Angeles Times.* Some of his columns appeared in book form, such as *Is Reality Optional?* (1993).

In the *New York Times Book Review*, Fred Barnes, editor of the conservative *Weekly Standard*, called Sowell a "free-market economist and perhaps the leading black scholar among conservatives" (Metzger, 528). An academic economist who wrote on a variety of topics, including social and political history, ethnicity, and the history of ideas, Sowell took a conservative, often controversial approach, criticizing such liberal causes as gay marriage, affirmative action, federally funded health care, and liberal judicial activism. He argued against the federal government's role in eliminating discrimination and contended that many of the so-called black leaders hindered true economic and social progress for blacks.

FURTHER READING

Sowell, Thomas. *A Personal Odyssey* (2000).
Cortez, John P. "Thomas Sowell 1930—Economist, Writer," *Contemporary Black Biography* (1992).
Jones, Daniel, and John J. Jorgenson, ed. "Sowell, Thomas 1930," *Contemporary Authors, New Revision Series*, vol. 61 (1998).
Metzger, Linda, ed. *Black Writers: A Selection of Sketches from Contemporary Authors* (1989).
Wiloch, Thomas. "Sowell, Thomas 1930," *Contemporary Authors, New Revision Series*, vol. 26 (1989).

GARY KERLEY

Spann, Otis (21 May 1930–24 Apr. 1970), blues pianist and vocalist, was born in Jackson, Mississippi, and began playing piano at the age of eight. Nothing is known of his parents or his early life. He joined local bands as a teenager. His principal influence was the Chicago-based pianist Big Maceo, whom he met in either 1946 or 1947 when Spann migrated to Chicago. He became Big Maceo's protégé, and performed locally with guitarist Morris Pejoe. In 1952 Spann joined the groundbreaking band of MUDDY WATERS, which included the harmonica player LITTLE WALTER JACOBS, second guitarist JIMMY ROGERS, and drummer Fred Below. The group first recorded together for the Chess label in September of 1952, and their second session produced the classic "Blow Wind Blow." He remained a key ingredient of Waters's sound for nearly the rest of his life, not leaving to work on his own until 1969. Waters so trusted Spann that he often left him in charge of rehearsals and breaking in new musicians. Their collaboration is memorably audible on such classics of the blues canon as "Hoochie Coochie Man," "I'm Ready," "I Just Wanna Make Love To You," and

"Got My Mojo Workin'." Spann also toured with Waters in Europe, and made a notable impression on the music press and on audiences outside the blues community when the ensemble appeared at the 1960 Newport (Rhode Island) Jazz Festival.

As was the case with any number of artists affiliated with the Chess label, Spann appeared on more than just the Waters releases. He accompanied such diverse and noteworthy artists as HOWLIN' WOLF, Little Walter, SONNY BOY WILLIAMSON (RICE MILLER), Jimmy Rogers, CHUCK BERRY, and BO DIDDLEY. For labels other than Chess, he played alongside JOHN LEE HOOKER, BUDDY GUY, James Cotton, Johnny Young, Johnny Shines, and WILLIE MAE THORNTON.

Spann was a convincing and effective vocalist, yet Chess somehow failed to recognize that skill. The only single of Spann's that Chess ever released was "It Must Have Been the Devil" (1954), which featured guitar accompaniment by B.B. KING. Subsequent sessions for the company were recorded in 1956 and 1963, but those were not released.

Spann recorded his first solo effort for the Candid label in 1960, *The Blues Is Otis Spann*. It was a striking debut on which he was accompanied by ROBERT LOCKWOOD JR. on guitar. He subsequently cut another session, *Portrait in Blues*, for the Denmark-based Storyville label in 1963 and another for British Decca the following year, *The Blues of Otis Spann*. Muddy Waters and a young Eric Clapton appear on the latter recording. The harmonica player from the Waters band, James Cotton, performed on his 1965 Prestige release *The Blues Never Die*. Spann recorded two albums for the Bluesway subsidiary of ABC Paramount Records, *The Blues Is Where It's At* (1967) and *The Bottom of the Blues* (1968).

Spann's final session with Muddy Waters was the concept recording *Fathers and Sons* (1969), which paired black musicians with some of the most successful and proficient white musicians in the genre: harmonica legend Paul Butterfield and ace guitarist Mike Bloomfield. Subsequent to leaving Waters, Spann released a similarly themed album with members of Fleetwood Mac called *The Biggest Thing Since Colossus*.

Spann died of cancer in 1970 at the young age of forty. A posthumously released live recording, *Last Call* (2000), caught him at the top of his form and introduced his considerable talents to a younger generation. In 1972, his widow, Lucille Spann, was presented with a plaque by Muddy Waters at the Ann Arbor (Michigan) Blues and Jazz Festival.

The plaque read, "The people of Ann Arbor in recognition of the talent, the genius of the late Otis Spann, sweet giant of the Blues, formally dedicate the Ann Arbor Blues and Jazz Festival 1972 in the grounds upon which it stands to the memory of this great artist." Spann was inducted into the Blues Foundation Hall of Fame in 1980.

FURTHER READING

Gordon, Robert. *Can't Be Satisfied: The Life and Times of Muddy Waters* (2002).

Oliver, Paul, ed. *Blackwell Guide to the Blues* (1991).

DAVID SANJEK

Sparrow, Simon (1925–26 Sept. 2000), artist and preacher, was born to a West African father and a Cherokee mother in Africa, although the exact date was not recorded. After two years the family moved to the United States and settled on the Cherokee Indian Reservation in North Carolina, where Sparrow's maternal grandfather lived. Sparrow later claimed the man was a tribal chief. Sparrow grew up in an area that was settled by Cherokees and the descendants of slaves. At seven he began preaching to the forest animals, then he began speaking in tongues and speaking to his family's Pentecostal church. In his youth he drew stick figures in the sand, then recorded images on scraps of paper. One day he discovered pieces of plywood and began to use them to for his sketches. A passing man offered to buy one, but Sparrow angrily refused—he had not made pictures to sell. At age twelve Sparrow set out on his own for Philadelphia, where he took a job as a dishwasher at a restaurant and sometimes drew portraits of customers. In 1942 he lied about his age to join the U.S. Army, and the same year he married Johnnie Roper. They had six children. Sparrow was assigned to Fort Dix in New Jersey, and much to his relief he never saw combat during World War II.

After his discharge from the army, Sparrow moved with his growing family to New York, where he worked as a singer, a housepainter, a pizza chef, and briefly a professional wrestler called "the Green Lantern" to make a living while he preached and painted. But the stress of preaching, creating art, and trying to make a living took a toll on his marriage, and he and his wife divorced in 1946. Throughout this difficult period Sparrow continued to paint, adopting a realistic style. Sometime in the early 1960s a fire destroyed his apartment house and all of his art except one miraculously undamaged painting. Sparrow took this as a sign from

God that he should abandon realism and paint only spiritual subjects.

In 1968 Sparrow married Jocelyn Reed, who was more than twenty-five years his junior, and moved with her to Madison, Wisconsin, where her family lived. He continued his preaching on the streets of Madison, wearing a homemade robe and carrying his tattered Bible. Although Sparrow was functionally illiterate, he could recite any verse from memory. He was also fond of sitting in the student union of the University of Wisconsin, where he talked about religion with students while he drew.

By the early 1980s the art world had begun to take notice of Sparrow's work. Some of his art was featured in the Madison Art Center, and throughout the 1980s and 1990s examples of his work appeared in other museums, including the Smithsonian Institution in Washington, D.C., and the Museum of American Folk Art in New York. Sparrow's work communicated his spiritual convictions and seemed to show the figurative influence of his father's Yoruba heritage. He worked both in pastels and on three-dimensional creations known as assemblages. The pastels are bright with primary colors and feature spirit-like faces and birds. The assemblages are fantastic conglomerations of beads, marbles, buttons, plastic toys, and glitter forming strange images of faces and all-seeing eyes. The most spectacular of these is certainly a late 1990s Buick totally encrusted with religious figurines, animal statues, glitter, and wood-burned placards bearing biblical passages. Completed in 1997, it became an exhibit at the Art Car Museum in Houston, Texas.

Sparrow achieved extraordinary renown and even received an invitation to Bill Clinton's presidential inauguration. But fame and money meant little to Sparrow. His preaching was more important to him, and he convinced a friend, Darryl Markowitz, to record his thoughts in *The Standard of the Foundation of the Understanding of Life*. Sparrow spent the last two years of his life in a nursing home, where above his bed hung a portrait he had painted of his wife Jocelyn.

FURTHER READING

Ever More, April 18–July 16, 2006, Minnesota Museum of American Art, http://www.mmaa.org/Ever_More.html.

Illuminating: Light as Context, November 23–December 17, 1997, Hyde Park Art Center, http://www.hydeparkart.org/exhibitions/1997/12/illuminating_light_as_context.php.

Krug, Don, and Ann Parker. *Miracles of the Spirit: Folk, Art, and Stories from Wisconsin* (2005).

Schmeltzer, Paul. "Paul Schmeltzer Examines the Mystery Art and Ministry of Simon Sparrow," *Raw Vision* 34, http://www.rawvision.com/back/sparrow/simonsparrow.html.

Schmeltzer, Paul. "The Seen and the Unseen: The Life, Death, and Mystery Art of Simon Sparrow," *Outsider* 5 (Winter 2001), http://www.art.org/theOutsiderMag/simon-sparrow.htm.

JOSEPHA SHERMAN

Spaulding, Asa Timothy (22 July 1902–5 Sept. 1990), businessman and civic leader, was born in Columbus County, North Carolina, to Armstead Spaulding and Annie Lowery (Bell) Spaulding, who together owned a farm and ran a general store. He was born into a family that had produced several prominent political and business leaders, including his great-uncle, Dr. AARON MCDUFFIE MOORE, a founder of the North Carolina Mutual Life Insurance Company in Durham, and his second cousin, CHARLES CLINTON SPAULDING, who was the Mutual's general manager and later its president. Asa's mother was a descendant of Henry Berry Lowry, a leader of resistance to the Ku Klux Klan in the 1870s. His parents ensured that Asa learned business principles at an early age by making him plant and look after his own one-acre cotton patch. It was his grandfather, however, a Sunday school superintendent for more than four decades, who instilled in the young boy a basic philosophy that guided him throughout his life—namely, that the solution to most problems can be found by reading the Bible.

Asa Spaulding showed a precocious aptitude for numbers and mathematics. When his grade-school classmates were still learning basic counting, he was practicing multiplication tables up to twenty. His reputation as the brightest student in Columbus County brought him to the attention of his uncle Aaron Moore, who in 1919 encouraged him to move to Durham—a move that another ambitious young man from Columbus County, C. C. Spaulding, had made exactly a quarter of a century earlier. Asa enrolled at Dr. JAMES SHEPARD's National Religious Training School and Chautauqua for the Colored Race (now North Carolina Central University) in Durham and worked for the Mutual during his summer vacations. He graduated with several student awards in 1923 and returned home to his native Columbus County to serve as the principal and teacher in a rural school, just as his uncle

Aaron Moore had done in the 1880s. Spaulding's intellectual curiosity and his desire to learn more about both mathematics and the business world encouraged him to take a take a leave of absence from teaching in 1924 while he studied at Howard University in Washington, D.C., and continued to work for the Mutual.

In 1927 Spaulding moved north, and with financial support from C. C. Spaulding he enrolled at New York University (NYU), where he studied mathematics. Spaulding's first experience of life outside the South proved bittersweet. He found intellectual stimulation and academic success at NYU and took some satisfaction in personally dispelling the myth of white intellectual superiority when several of his white colleagues approached him for help with their studies. "They are willing to admit their 'inferiority' for the time being. Isn't it strange," he wrote to his friend William Kennedy in 1927 (Weare, 165).

Spaulding also enjoyed living in Harlem during the peak of the Harlem Renaissance, and he regularly attended ADAM CLAYTON POWELL SR.'s Abyssinian Baptist Church. He did not, however, enjoy the daily journey of more than a hundred blocks from his shared room in Harlem to NYU in Greenwich Village, and he chafed at the lack of job opportunities that he found in the city. Unlike in Durham, Spaulding's talents and connections mattered far less to employers in New York than did his race. With what he called at the time a "burning passion to be of loyal, upright service to my group," Spaulding determined that he should return to Durham and the Mutual after he finished his studies (Weare, 165).

After graduating magna cum laude from NYU in 1930, Spaulding moved first to the University of Michigan in Ann Arbor, where he graduated two years later as the first African American to receive a master's degree in actuarial mathematics, a relatively new discipline. Spaulding's experience in the Midwest was at best mixed. He found more explicit racial prejudice than in North Carolina or New York, as well as a far greater sense of racial isolation. Upon graduation Spaulding worked briefly for an actuarial consulting firm in Indianapolis before returning to North Carolina to put into practice at the Mutual the actuarial science that he had learned at NYU and Michigan. Shortly after arriving in Durham in June 1933, Spaulding married Elna Bridgeforth of Tuskegee, Alabama; the couple would have four children, Asa Jr., Patricia Ann, Aaron, and Kenneth.

A history of the North Carolina Mutual notes that "virtually every dimension of the business improved" after Spaulding's arrival at the height of the Great Depression (Weare, 163). At the same time that President Franklin Roosevelt was establishing the New Deal's innovative programs to regenerate the American economy, Spaulding brought to the Mutual the new insights of actuarial science to address the company's financial woes. Actuarial science combined statistics, business theory, and a little morality; its complex calculations and formulas punished policyholders considered a poor risk, such as the elderly and the sick, while rewarding younger and healthier policyholders.

By analyzing the Mutual's entire financial operations Spaulding discovered, for example, that the Mutual paid out a disproportionate number of claims to policyholders who had been insured for less than five years. He responded to this problem by increasing the benefits paid to claimants who died decades after taking out policies with the Mutual, while cutting benefits paid to claimants who died shortly after signing up for their policies. Spaulding also instructed the company to pay out only one-quarter of the policy value to beneficiaries who died within a year of paying premiums. Over five years Spaulding promoted these new policies of risk selection in columns for the *Whetstone*, the Mutual's magazine, and in seminars for the company's hundreds of insurance agents. In 1938, at age thirty-five, he became the youngest officer on the Mutual's board, an appointment that reflected his skills at placing the company on a sound financial footing.

Asa Spaulding remained at the North Carolina Mutual during the prosperous era of World War II and the 1950s, steering it through the death of C. C. Spaulding in 1952 and assuming the presidency of the company seven years later. By then, under the guidance of Spaulding and his close friend William Kennedy, the company had expanded its operations to New Jersey and other northern and midwestern states, reflecting the population shift of its primarily African American base of policyholders. Trained to analyze risk and to predict future outcomes, Spaulding believed that the Supreme Court's 1954 *Brown v. Board of Education* decision signaled the potential death knell for companies such as the Mutual that depended on segregated markets. Spaulding's hopes for an integrated future must have been dampened somewhat by his defeat in a race for Durham County commissioner just weeks after the *Brown* ruling. Thanks to the get-out-the-vote efforts by the Durham Committee on Negro Affairs, Spaulding won 98 percent of the black vote, but he attracted almost no support from whites.

In the 1950s Spaulding began to take a strong interest in international relations. He served as an official representative of the U.S. government at a UNESCO conference in New Delhi, India, in 1956 and helped organize one of the first state visits by a postcolonial African leader to the United States in 1959 when Sekou Toure of Guinea visited North Carolina. Asked about his impression of the American South, Toure responded that he was most impressed by the size and ambitions of Negro institutions, especially the Mutual.

By the 1960s the federal government finally responded to black demands for integration and equality, and white insurance firms began to compete with the Mutual and other black companies for customers. Such competition further persuaded Spaulding to court white customers and to attract white tenants to share the Mutual's gleaming new offices, which were formally opened by Vice President Hubert Humphrey in April 1966. This decision angered some black Durhamites who viewed the new Mutual as having betrayed its African American past. Shortly after Spaulding stepped down as president in 1971, the wisdom of his decision to seek new markets became apparent. That year the Mutual became the first black-owned company to reach one billion dollars in annual insurance business, primarily by securing lucrative group policies from white corporate clients such as IBM and General Motors. The company's profits were also boosted, however, by advertising campaigns that appealed to black pride and greatly increased the ranks of its African American policyholders.

In 1971 Spaulding narrowly lost a race to become Durham's first African American mayor, and thereafter he focused primarily on business and community affairs. Since 1964 he had been a major shareholder in several large, historically white corporations, and in 1972 he became active in the Association for the Integration of Management (AIM), which lobbied to increase the presence of African Americans in corporate boardrooms. Spaulding and the research chemist PERCY JULIAN were also prominent in the National Negro Business and Professional Committee, which helped raise money for the NAACP's Legal Defense Fund. Spaulding also formed his own consulting company and during more than seven decades in

Durham remained an active member of the city's White Rock Baptist Church. He died in Durham at the age of eighty-eight.

FURTHER READING

The Asa Timothy Spaulding Papers are housed in the JOHN HOPE FRANKLIN Research Collection of African and African-American Documentation at Duke University in Durham, North Carolina. A smaller set of Asa Timothy Spaulding Papers, 1943–1974, can be found at the State of North Carolina Archives in Raleigh, North Carolina.

Kennedy, William J., Jr. *The North Carolina Mutual Story: A Symbol of Progress, 1898–1970* (1970).

Surface, Bill. "The World of the Wealthy Negro," *New York Times*, 23 July 1967.

Weare, Walter B. *Black Business in the New South: A Social History of the North Carolina Mutual Insurance Company* (1973).

Wise, Jim. *Durham: A Bull City Story* (2002).

STEVEN J. NIVEN

Spaulding, Charles Clinton (1 Aug. 1874–1 Aug. 1952), businessman and civic leader, was born in Columbus County, North Carolina, one of ten children of Benjamin McIver Spaulding and Margaret (Moore) Spaulding, who together ran a prosperous farm. The Spauldings were descendants of a tight-knit, self-reliant, and fiercely independent community of free people of color who had settled in southeastern North Carolina in the early nineteenth century. Benjamin Spaulding was also an accomplished blacksmith and furniture maker, and he served as county sheriff during Reconstruction. GEORGE WHITE, the last African American to represent a Southern district in Congress until the late 1960s, was a neighbor. Like his nine siblings Charles Spaulding learned the dignity of labor from an early age. He recalled in an unpublished autobiography that when not working with their father tending crops, the children were to be found helping their mother scrub the floors of their cabin or keeping the farmyard as pristine as a farmyard can be kept.

As the second eldest son, however, it became clear to Spaulding that he would have to leave the family farm to make his way in the world. In 1894 he moved to Durham to live with his uncle, AARON MCDUFFIE MOORE, the city's only African American physician and pharmacist. Spaulding completed his high school equivalency two years later and worked variously as a bellhop, waiter, dishwasher, and office assistant before taking over the management of a cooperative grocery store in 1898. For a young man of Spaulding's ambition Durham was the right place at the right time. Once a sleepy village, Durham was by the 1890s a bustling, industrious city whose tobacco factories drew thousands of black and white workers from the surrounding countryside and produced vast profits for white businessmen like James Buchanan Duke.

Enterprising African Americans such as Aaron Moore and JOHN MERRICK could only dream of Duke's millions. But imbued with the entrepreneurial ethos of BOOKER T. WASHINGTON they readily understood the business opportunities made possible by the city's rapidly expanding black population and by the prevailing white preference for racial segregation. Because white insurance companies such as the Prudential, for example, refused to insure African Americans, Merrick and Moore founded the North Carolina Mutual and Provident Association in Durham in 1898. Two years later, with the company floundering, they turned to Spaulding to reorganize the Mutual singlehandedly.

Over the next three years Spaulding's natural flair for salesmanship, his boundless energy, and his tenacious optimism transformed the company's fortunes. He began his workday sweeping and mopping the Mutual's floors, spent his mornings and afternoons hawking insurance policies door to door and street corner to street corner, and worked well into the night attempting to balance the company's books. The long hours that Spaulding worked left little time for a personal life, but in 1900 he married Fannie Jones, with whom he had four children before her death in 1919. Though the Mutual flirted with bankruptcy on several occasions, by 1903 Spaulding had earned the trust of hundreds of policyholders and had secured insurance agents in fifty towns in North and South Carolina. That year Spaulding finally awarded himself a set salary—fifteen dollars a week—and also launched an innovative company magazine, the *North Carolina Mutual*, which published testimonials from satisfied customers and helped to build the company's reputation for trustworthiness.

The Mutual's greatest achievement lay in making life and sickness policies affordable to the great mass of African Americans, with premiums beginning as low as only five or ten cents a week. By 1907 Spaulding presided over a new, imposing brick headquarters, which serviced the needs of more than 100,000 policyholders. Advertising itself as "the Greatest Negro Insurance Company

in the World," the Mutual encouraged the formation of other black-owned businesses in Durham and with Spaulding at the fore helped establish and support a hospital, a library, a college, a literary club, three newspapers, and even a baseball team for African Americans in Durham. In 1911 Spaulding's efforts at the Mutual earned the endorsement of his hero, Booker T. Washington, who praised the entrepreneurial spirit of black Durhamites in a national newsweekly. W. E. B. DuBois echoed these views a year later and contrasted the favorable climate for black businesses in Durham with the hostility of whites to black business development in Atlanta.

By the time that E. FRANKLIN FRAZIER dubbed Durham "the Capital of the Black Middle Class" in the early 1920s, the Mutual had a presence in eleven Southern states and employed 1,100 workers. Spaulding, who married Charlotte Garner in 1920, assumed the presidency of the Mutual in 1923 upon the death of Aaron Moore and retained that position until his own death twenty-nine years later. In the 1920s and 1930s Spaulding emerged as the most powerful black businessman of his era. In addition to his leadership of the Mutual he was prominent in the National Negro Business League (NNBL), which had been founded by Booker T. Washington in 1900. When the NNBL was on the verge of collapse in the late 1930s, Spaulding rescued it, although almost at the cost of his health.

In 1924 Spaulding founded the National Negro Finance Corporation (NNFC) in the hope that it could pool black capital and expertise in a central location and provide loans for black entrepreneurs. In 1927 Secretary of Commerce Herbert Hoover endorsed the NNFC's goals and praised Spaulding's efforts in Durham, but this early experiment in government-supported black capitalism was a victim of the Depression. That the Mutual survived the Depression years while so many other companies failed was thanks in part to Spaulding's skills in lobbying Congress to provide loans through the Reconstruction Finance Corporation. A more significant role was played by Charles's second cousin, ASA TIMOTHY SPAULDING, the nation's first black actuary, who masterminded the company's successful modernization after joining the Mutual in 1933. Indeed, C. C. Spaulding gathered around him a cadre of talented executives, including the board's only female member, Viola Turner. But as Turner recalled, "nobody ever doubted that 'Papa' was in charge" (Weare, 170).

The Mutual's secure business footing enabled Spaulding to pursue his broader social and political goals. He continued to fund and support libraries, schools, colleges, and youth groups throughout the South, and he served as a trustee of Howard University in Washington, D.C., Shaw University in Raleigh, and the North Carolina College for Negroes (NCCN) in Durham. In 1932 Spaulding registered as a Democrat and had the ear of several prominent New Dealers, including First Lady Eleanor Roosevelt. He also enjoyed unprecedented access to, and influence on, several governors, state legislators, and other members of North Carolina's white political elite.

Yet such connections and his wealth could not always protect Spaulding from the worst excesses of Jim Crow racism, most notably in 1931 when a white man attacked and beat him in a Raleigh drugstore. The NAACP national secretary WALTER WHITE also criticized Spaulding in 1933 for sabotaging an early legal challenge to segregation when NAACP activists sought admission for the Durham native Thomas Hocutt to the pharmacy school on the University of North Carolina's flagship white campus at Chapel Hill. Remembering the bloody violence of the Wilmington race riot three decades earlier, Spaulding feared that such a blatant challenge to segregation would provoke a violent white backlash, and he joined with the NCCN president JAMES SHEPARD to block Hocutt's admission. Spaulding later tried to parlay his opposition to Hocutt into increased public spending on black education, but white lawmakers ignored his entreaties.

The Hocutt case marked a turning point in Spaulding's evolving political liberalism. Afterward he proved more willing to work with the state and national NAACP, most notably in helping to fund and organize a campaign for equalizing teachers' salaries and spending on North Carolina's separate and woefully unequal educational system. In 1935 he also helped establish and served as chairman of the Durham Committee on Negro Affairs (DCNA), which became the most effective local political and electoral organization in the South prior to the Voting Rights Act of 1965. By the end of its first year in existence the DCNA had increased the number of registered black voters from a paltry fifty (including Spaulding) to 1,000, and by 1939 this number had tripled. By the late 1940s the DCNA had proved so adept at registering black voters, getting them to the polls, and getting them to vote for committee-approved candidates that Durham's white politicians routinely sought support from the committee, recognizing that its endorsement could provide the margin of victory.

The DCNA also enabled Spaulding to voice some of the more radical views that he kept from his white business associates in Durham, Raleigh, and elsewhere. A sociological study of the DCNA during World War II recorded Spaulding's praise of his ancestor, Henry Berry Lowry, a mixed-race Lumbee Indian who led a guerilla war against the Ku Klux Klan in North Carolina during Reconstruction. "Lowry was different," Spaulding told a DCNA meeting. "He wasn't afraid. I think we need some Negroes like that. We got to fight to … get justice" (Weare, 241). In the 1940s Spaulding became more outspoken in condemning the racism of police officers in Durham, and he lobbied behind the scenes to secure reprieves for African Americans condemned to the electric chair.

The North Carolina Mutual remained Spaulding's abiding passion, however, and well into his seventies he boasted that he still worked ten hours a day. Nevertheless Spaulding always managed to find time for a game of pool, and he carried his portable cue with him on business trips. Though he only had to look as far as the unpaved streets and dilapidated housing of Durham's black neighborhoods to see evidence of capitalism's failures, Spaulding remained an unabashed capitalist. "What we want is not Negro businesses but businesses [run] by Negroes," he told *Time* in 1950, adding that "all businesses will fail" unless "we combat godless communism" (Weare, 276). Spaulding died in Durham in 1952 on his seventy-eighth birthday; his funeral was the largest in the city's history.

FURTHER READING

The Charles Clinton Spaulding Papers are housed in the John Hope Franklin Research Collection of African and African-American Documentation at Duke University in Durham, North Carolina.

Kennedy, William J. *The North Carolina Mutual Story* (1970).

Weare, Walter B. *Black Business in the New South: A Social History of the North Carolina Mutual Insurance Company* (1993).

Wise, Jim. *Durham: A Bull City Story* (2002).

STEVEN J. NIVEN

Spaulding, Jane Morrow (?–1965), social activist, was born in Kentucky and moved to Nashville, Tennessee, as a child. Nothing is known of her parents or her early life; even the actual date of her birth is uncertain. She attended Fisk University, but the records of the university do not confirm that she graduated. On 7 February 1918 she married Albert Lee Spaulding, a physician; the couple had one child, Albert Lee Spaulding Jr., who also became a physician.

Jane Morrow Spaulding's life is an excellent example of a long tradition of family and community service by African American women. "Lifting as we climb" was not only the motto of the National Association of Colored Women's Clubs, it was also the motto of Jane Morrow Spaulding, who spent her public life working tirelessly to improve the lives of African Americans on the local, state, and national level. Participation in women's clubs gave middle-class African American women the opportunity to aid those in need and to serve in leadership positions, which gave them confidence and collective self-esteem.

Spaulding has been described as "the most prominent person in the field of social service" within the African American community in West Virginia. The Spauldings had moved to West Virginia around the time of their marriage; Albert Spaulding's medical practice was in Charleston. Jane Spaulding became a member of the Charleston Woman's Improvement League, the oldest club for African American women in West Virginia, sometime around 1920. Through this group, Spaulding worked to improve the lives of African American women and girls. She was a very active member and by 1940 had been elected president of the organization. Spaulding understood the needs of the poor in West Virginia, and as president she was instrumental in providing a variety of programs to assist the needy, including supporting scholarships for students, helping to improve living conditions for the poor, and establishing a daycare center for preschool children. The Mountaineer Club of Charleston, a social club for African American men, raised money to help support the day-care. Also under her leadership the club acquired its first permanent headquarters, "The Club House," in 1940. As president of the Charleston Woman's Improvement League, a local women's club that was an affiliate of the National Association of Colored Women's Clubs, she traveled the state participating in community functions and speaking on issues confronting African Americans.

Club women such as Spaulding also participated in politics, campaigning for candidates and working to get out the vote. The majority of African American voters in West Virginia who voted during the 1940s were members of the Republican Party. Involvement in the Charleston Women's Improvement League and in the Republican Party became the foundation for Spaulding's social activism on the national level. During the New Deal she was appointed director of the Negro division of the West Virginia Relief Administration and served in this position for four years. She used her contacts with local and state politicians from her club work to bring federal dollars to West Virginia to assist the poor and to ensure that African Americans were included in as many social programs as possible, including homestead subsistence, vocational training centers, self-help and cooperative enterprises, rural rehabilitation, road-building projects, and housing programs.

In the post–World War II era, Spaulding found opportunities for international travel that broadened her perspectives on social issues. In 1951 she represented the U.S. Council of Women at the triennial conference of International Council of Women in Athens, Greece, and served as a national organizer for African American voters who supported Citizens for Eisenhower-Nixon. Spaulding declared her support for Eisenhower early in the campaign, and she participated in the women's division in the national headquarters of the Citizens for Eisenhower during the 1952 campaign. Her activities on behalf of the Republican Party led to a political appointment in 1953 as assistant to Oveta Culp Hobby, the first secretary of the Department of Health, Education, and Welfare. In this position Spaulding's assignments were in the areas of education, social security, child welfare, and health. Her position as Hobby's assistant apparently included some clerical work and some work assisting Hobby with various projects. She attended the meetings of the Human Rights Commission of the United Nations in Geneva, Switzerland. Spaulding remained in this position for about nine months. She resigned her position as assistant to Hobby in January 1954 to accept a position with the War Claims Commission.

Spaulding was an example of the view of many black clubwomen that they and all black women of the middle class have a vested interest in improving the lives of underprivileged women. She used her position at a member and as president of the Charleston Woman's Improvement League to assist hundreds, if not thousands, of African American women and girls. Through her social activism Spalding helped to lay the foundation within the African American community that would enable future generations to reach the middle class. At the same time, Spaulding's involvement in community work helped her forge a career for herself. By marriage to a physician and through her own social activism, Spaulding became a member of the black middle class. Her status in the community was documented in an edition of *Ebony* magazine in which she was listed as one of the ten best-dressed African American women in 1953. She received numerous awards for her public service. In 1953 Spaulding was the recipient of the Woman of the Year award of the Philadelphia, Pennsylvania, branch of the National Council of Negro Women. Like so many other social activists, Spaulding dedicated herself to her life's work but did not pay attention to documenting that work. Hence, no archival record of her service activities survived. She died in 1965, but the exact date and circumstances of her death are not known.

FURTHER READING
Davis, Elizabeth Lindsay. *Lifting as They Climb* (1933).
"Negro Group Head Scores Mrs. Hobby," *New York Times*, 30 Dec. 1954.
Perry, Patsy B. "Jane Morrow Spaulding" in Jessie Carney Smith, ed. *Notable Black American Women, Book II* (1996).
"Welfare Worker Named Hobby Aid," *New York Times*, 15 Apr. 1953.
Wesley, Charles Harris. *The History of the National Association of Colored Women's Clubs* (1984).
FLORA BRYANT BROWN

Speaks, Sara Pelham (7 Nov. 1902–23 Aug. 1984), political and civic activist, lawyer, and civil rights advocate, was the daughter of ROBERT A. PELHAM, the former editor and publisher of the *Washington Tribune*, and Gabrielle Lewis Pelham, a pianist and the first honorary member of the Delta Sigma Theta Sorority. Her sister was Dorothy Pelham Beckley, the Deltas' second national president. Speaks was a graduate of the prestigious Dunbar High School in Washington, D.C., and the University of Michigan, where she received a bachelor's degree in science in 1924.

Prior to her marriage in 1926 to Dr. F. Douglas Speaks, with whom she had one son, she taught in South Carolina and did social work in Washington, D.C. In the late 1920s Speaks assisted her father in organizing the Capital News Service, an African American news agency in Washington. She worked in journalism for three years before moving to New York City with her husband. There Speaks was an active member of the New York Urban League and the Delta Sigma Theta Sorority. She also served as president of the New York State Federation of Business and Professional Women's Clubs and chair of the Anti-Discrimination Committee in the late 1930s. In 1936 she received a law degree from New York University. A committed Republican, Speaks campaigned for the GOP in the 1932, 1936, and 1940 elections; during the 1940 election she was director of women's activities for the Eastern Division of the Republican Party.

Speaks's relationship to electoral politics was deeper than just that of a campaigner. She was twice a candidate. In 1937 Speaks ran for the New York State Assembly in the Republican Party primary. She won the primary against her opponent by a razor-thin margin. With only one woman in the state assembly at the time, female candidates had an uphill battle, and Speaks was no exception. She lost in the general election to the Democratic incumbent, William T. Andrews, although the election was decided by less than three hundred votes.

In the wake of her defeat Speaks jumped right back into her legal practice and maintained her active involvement in the Republican Party. In 1938 she attended the National Republican Party Committee meetings to help draft the party's platform. Two years into President Franklin Delano Roosevelt's second term, the popular New Deal Democrats appeared difficult to beat. Speaks expressed concern about the Republican Party's shift away from its original mission as a party of freedom and equality and noted that black voters would reconsider their move to the Democratic Party if the Republicans demonstrated genuine commitment to racial equality.

In 1944 a new U.S. congressional district was formed in upper Manhattan, and Harlem made up a significant majority of the area. The Democrats and the American Labor Party (ALP), which was strong in New York at that time, chose as their candidate the popular and well-known minister of the Abyssinian Baptist Church, ADAM CLAYTON POWELL JR. The Republicans turned to the respected and committed party activist Speaks to challenge him. New York was about to send its first African American member to Congress. Moreover, in accepting the GOP nomination, Speaks became the first black woman chosen to run for Congress by one of the major political parties.

The campaign drew a great deal of attention in Harlem. Speaks and Powell had dramatically different campaign styles that reflected their divergent ideas about how politics should be done. Speaks suggested that Powell's style was short on substance and long on emotional and inflammatory appeal. She also argued that he would be a renegade and a loner in Congress, and that to get anything done, one had to work with others, especially when you were a member of a minority group. Her political platform was an articulation of her commitment to racial justice. She promised to fight for the abolition of the poll tax, antilynching legislation, and effective laws against Jim Crow. Powell, however, was equally committed to these issues.

Speaks's campaign garnered support from a number of key activists in Harlem. Not only did the *New York Amsterdam News* endorse her, but she also received backing from large groups of women from both major parties. A number of influential people in the community had serious reservations about Powell, including Herbert Bruce, a Tammany Hall district leader in Harlem; Eardlie John, chairman of the labor and industry committee of the NAACP; and William T. Andrews, a Harlem assemblyman and Speaks's opponent for the state assembly in 1937. At least some of them openly gave Speaks their support. Enough Democrats wanted Speaks to win that they collected signatures and assured that her name was entered in the Democratic primary in addition to the Republican. In a particularly New York fashion, Speaks and Powell both ran on multiple-party ballots—Speaks on the Republican ticket for which she was first nominated, and then the Democratic ticket as well; and Powell on the Democratic and ALP tickets, and then on the Republican ticket to counter Speaks's entry into the Democratic primary.

Although she was an ardent advocate for racial equality, had actively fought for improved services in Harlem, and had the stature for the job, Speaks proved the less convincing candidate to the Harlem audience to serve as the first New York African American in Congress. When the votes were counted in the August primary, Powell won on all three ballots. He had been a charismatic campaigner, he had a huge base of support in his church, and he had served in the New York City Council. He was ultimately too strong a candidate for the Republican challenger to defeat.

Speaks's public career came to a dramatic and premature close in 1948 when she was disbarred by the appellate division of the New York Supreme Court for alleged misconduct in her dealings with clients. The disbarment followed a headline-making exposé of alleged police graft by Speaks.

She remained active in Republican Party politics and in organizations that fought for racial equality. She did not, however, run for office again. Speaks died in New York in 1984 at the age of eighty-one.

FURTHER READING

Articles on Sara Pelham Speaks can be found in the *New York Times*, the *New York Amsterdam News*, the *New York Age*, the *Chicago Defender*, and *Time* magazine.

Lewinson, Edwin R. *Black Politics in New York City* (1974).

Obituary: *Washington Post*, 26 Aug. 1984.

JULIE GALLAGHER

Spear, Chloe (c. 1750–3 Jan. 1815), Boston freedwoman, was born in Africa. Spear is known to scholars primarily through the *Memoir of Mrs. Chloe Spear*, written by "A Lady of Boston" in 1832. According to the *Memoir*, Spear was kidnapped from the African coast when she was about twelve years old. Her captors carried her to a slave ship headed for Philadelphia, where Captain John Bradford purchased her and took her to his home in Boston.

Bradford was a merchant and, during the American Revolution, the Continental agent for Massachusetts. The *Memoir* depicts him as a harsh master and Chloe as an obedient slave. For the deeply religious author of the *Memoir*, Bradford's most reprehensible fault was his failure to bring up his slaves in the Christian faith. Bradford also claimed that "it made negroes saucy to know how to read" (Lady of Boston, 26). When he discovered that Chloe had been getting reading lessons, he threatened to whip her if she ever went to the schoolmistress again. Nevertheless, Chloe continued to read her psalter in secret and became increasingly drawn to Christianity. During the Revolutionary War, the Bradford family moved from Boston to Andover. There Chloe befriended a devout Christian, a Mr. Adams, who became her religious instructor and spiritual counselor. Upon her return to Boston, Chloe became a member of the New North Congregational Church.

In 1776 Chloe married Cesar Spear, servant to Nathan Spear; they had several children. According to her obituary, Bradford had promised to free her, but before the manumission took effect, she was emancipated by Massachusetts law. In fact, Massachusetts passed no such legislation ending slavery. It is likely that Spear negotiated her freedom with her master in the early 1780s, when several Massachusetts legal decisions were interpreted as invalidating slavery under the state constitution. In any event, following her emancipation, Spear continued to work as a paid servant to the Bradford family, to whom she remained close even after she went to live with her husband. Cesar was a cooper by trade, but he and Chloe also ran a boardinghouse in the North End. In the postwar economic climate, black men often had difficulty finding regular work as craftsmen or manual laborers. Black women could secure more consistent income, since the demand for domestic labor was relatively constant. Chloe worked as a washerwoman to keep the Spears afloat. The author of the *Memoir* characterizes Chloe as hardworking, self-sacrificing, and thrifty, in contrast to Cesar, who encouraged his wife to buy herself fine silk dresses. Instead, she put aside the money he gave her along with savings she carefully accumulated from her own work until she amassed seven hundred dollars, enough money to buy a small house.

Deeds and probate records confirm that the Spears bought a house on White Bread Alley, near Hanover Street, in Boston's North End in 1798. They did not live there long before Cesar fell seriously ill; he died in 1806. The *Memoir* suggests that her husband's death released Chloe from a difficult marriage. Cesar apparently did not share his wife's religious devotion, and as a widow Chloe had the freedom to participate more fully in spiritual activities. Her home became a meeting place for black and white Bostonians to pray and discuss religion. "So happy was her talent in conversation with persons, in the early stages of religious conviction, that in seasons of revival in the neighbouring towns, she was frequently invited to visit them, and was instrumental of good," the *Memoir* reported (Lady of Boston, 77).

Spear's religiosity was ecumenical. Though she had originally joined a congregational church, she also attended Baptist services and befriended Rev. Thomas Gair, who baptized her into his Second Baptist Church in 1788. Spear probably also participated in activities at Boston's African Baptist Church. One of the attendees at her funeral was that church's minister, Rev. Thomas Paul, whom Spear "was much in the habit of calling her *son*" (Lady of Boston, 90). Spear was buried in the Granary Burying Ground in the tomb belonging to her former master's family. Her one-line death notice in a Boston newspaper described her as "a colored woman, highly respected" (*Columbian Centinel*, 7 Jan. 1815), and her bequests confirmed her status as a respected member of Boston's black community. In her will she left money to her surviving grandson and to eight black Bostonians, many of whom had ties to the Second Baptist Church. She also left part of her $1,400 estate to the church's fund for the poor and to the Massachusetts Baptist Missionary Society.

If "A Lady of Boston" had not written her lengthy *Memoir of Mrs. Chloe Spear*, it is unlikely that scholars would have more than a passing interest in this former slave's life. Authored by a white woman years after the death of its subject, the *Memoir*, like other narratives commemorating the lives of people of color, is "fraught with conflicting literary, social, and racial politics" and "thoroughly mediated" by its author's own priorities (Brown, 38). The preface to the book announces that proceeds from its sale would "be devoted to the *benefit of Schools in Africa*" (Lady of Boston, iii). The author's educational agenda was also an evangelical one. Near the end of the book, she quotes the favorite Bible verse of missionaries to Africa, "Ethiopia shall soon stretch out her hand unto God" (Ps. 68:31 AV), and praises "the efforts now making for the civilization of Africa, and for spreading the gospel in that populous country" (Lady of Boston, 106).

The content of the *Memoir* itself was part of an evangelical project directed closer to home. The author ends each of the four chapters of Spear's biography with a didactic section plumbing Spear's experience for evidence of God's providence and examples of how to live a Christian life. While the *Memoir's* author clearly believed that people of all races and nations could become exemplary Christians, she also exhibited the racial chauvinism that most nineteenth-century white northerners shared. She exhorts her white readers to take heed of Spear's story, warning, "How dreadful then will it be in that solemn day, when we shall all appear before the judgment seat of Christ, should any, who may have read this little history, be found unprepared for his coming, while this uncultivated African shall sit down in the kingdom of heaven" (Lady of Boston, 45).

Despite its biases and possible distortions, the *Memoir of Mrs. Chloe Spear* provides an unusually rich account of the life of a former slave in the North, including many details corroborated by other sources. The text cannot be classified strictly as a slave narrative because its author's intent is more evangelical than abolitionist. Furthermore, unlike most narratives of southern slaves, the *Memoir* does not even purport to be autobiographical, but the author does claim to have recorded stories that she had earlier heard Spear recount herself. For all that the *Memoir* tells about Chloe Spear's life, the identity of the book's author is uncertain. Some sources attribute it to Rebecca Warren Brown, who used the pseudonym "A Lady of Boston" for her children's book about the general Joseph Warren, issued in 1835 by the *Memoir's* publisher. Other bibliographies cite the author as Mary Webb, a founder of the Boston Female Society for Missionary Purposes and the Boston Children's Friend Society. Webb also tried to start a school for African American children in the North End and directed the Sabbath school at the Second Baptist Church. Given her membership in Spear's church and her interest in educating black children in Spear's neighborhood, it is likely that she and Spear knew each other personally.

Spear accumulated more property than did most blacks (and even many working-class whites) in the Boston of her day. Her social network, especially within the city's interracial community of Baptists, seems to have been deep. The simple fact that someone bothered to write a 108-page account of her life made her particularly unusual. But many of the details described in that account—including those corroborated by other sources—reflect experiences common to former slaves in the region. Many other black New Englanders knew the convergence of the American Revolution and personal emancipation, the difficulty of making a living out of low-paying and exhausting domestic work, and the significance of faith communities to spiritual and social life. While Spear's successes were remarkable, the challenges she faced were typical for the first generation of freed people in Massachusetts.

FURTHER READING

Brown, Lois. "Memorial Narratives of African Women in Antebellum New England," *Legacy* 20 (2003): 38–61.

Horton, James Oliver, and Lois E. Horton. *Black Bostonians: Family Life and Community Struggle in the Antebellum North*, rev. ed. (1999).

A Lady of Boston. *Memoir of Mrs. Chloe Spear, a Native of Africa, Who Was Enslaved in Childhood, and Died in Boston, January 3, 1815* (1832).

Piersen, William D. *Black Yankees: The Development of an Afro-American Subculture in Eighteenth-Century New England* (1988).

Obituary: *Massachusetts Baptist Missionary Magazine*, Mar. 1815.

MARGOT MINARDI

Spears, Arthur K. (16 Nov. 1943–), linguist, anthropologist, and activist, was born in Kansas City, Kansas, to Mack Spears Sr. and C. R. Spears. Both his parents were from enterprising, educated, upper-middle-class families. Mack Spears Sr. taught at Lincoln University, at Sumner High School, and at the black branch of the segregated Kansas City, Kansas, Community College. He received a master's degree in business at the University of Kansas in the early 1930s and was active in bringing the AFL Teachers Union to the public schools in Kansas City, Kansas, and in managing his father's estate and other businesses in the twin cities of Kansas City, Kansas, and Kansas City, Missouri. Becoming one of the key business leaders in the black community, he initiated various projects, including the first black housing development, the eponymous Spears Crest, built on a portion of a tract of property he owned. Mack Spears Sr. died during Arthur Spears's early childhood. Arthur Spears's mother, C.R. Spears (who married R. B. Edwards several years after Mack Spears Sr.'s death), was the daughter of Bishop John Wood, of the Fifth Episcopal District of the African Methodist Episcopal Zion Church, and J. E. Wood, originally from Tennessee.

Spears's parents, who served as role models, nurtured his quest for high achievement and his sense of social responsibility. Educated in the racially segregated public schools, where his parents had taught, Spears entered Sumner High School in 1958. Sumner, along with Dunbar High School in Washington, D.C., and others throughout the United States, was one of the storied all-black high schools that provided the black communities with the majority of its high achievers before the advent of integration. Some all-black schools were more academically challenging and nurturing than their white counterparts, not because of superior facilities or material resources, but because the best and the brightest of the black community became teachers.

After graduating as an honor student from Sumner High School in 1961, Spears enrolled at Kansas University, in Lawrence, Kansas. While there, he was active in many organizations, including the Civil Rights Committee, one of the leading civil rights organizations in the state pursuing desegregation; the Inter-fraternity Council; Alpha Phi Alpha Fraternity; and various honor societies. During his college years, he spent three summers in France, as a student (1962), as a summer intern at an automotive supply depot of Automobiles Peugeot and the cement manufacturing company Ciments Lafarge (1963), and as an intern at the U.S. Department of State in 1964. The 1965 college yearbook indicates that his peers selected him as one of the outstanding seniors. He graduated in 1965 with honors and a triple major in political science (international relations option), French, and Spanish.

Spears had studied French with the assistance of his mother, who had learned French in high school and college, and while still in grade school, he became proficient. By the time he entered high school, where the first language courses were offered, he was not allowed to take advanced French, since it was inconceivable that a pupil from the segregated black area of Kansas City could speak French. Thus, Spears endured French I and II, the only French courses offered. He also took two years of Spanish. He was fluent in Spanish by the time he entered college. His appetite for languages greatly increased with courses at Kansas University in German and Serbo-Croatian, the latter's forty-seven (as the language was taught) verb conjugations and seven nominal cases furnishing him with a grammatical feast, so he added these two languages to his studies.

After he completed a number of foreign language literature courses, Spears realized that his real interest was not foreign language literature, but the nuts and bolts of grammar and usage. His summers in France had brought to his attention the gap between the literary language of the texts he had been reading and the contemporary French language. Spears states, "On several occasions in France I used words, expressions, and verb tenses that were bookish, archaic, and/or socially inappropriate. No attention was given in the French courses at Kansas to levels of usage. So, for example, during my *stage* (internship) at Automobiles Peugeot right outside Paris, I picked up expressions from blue collar workers at the factory that I then proceeded to use at the suburban villas of elite French families—with correction, as one could imagine." According to Spears, "I had planned to take the introductory linguistics course but had heard negative reports about how it was taught by a white American professor (as was 99.9% of the faculty). In talking one day with the only American (white) professor who seemed not to be overtly racist (and who had assigned me an A), I learned that I could do a kind of honors independent study and could choose to focus on linguistics in that course" (unpublished correspondence with author, 12 June 2006).

After Spears's 1965 graduation with a bachelor's degree in political science as one of his majors, he won a Fulbright grant to study in Montevideo, Uruguay. He had selected political science because of interest, but perhaps more because at the time students of color were being recruited by the State Department to become diplomats. Subsequently, Spears spent a year and a half in Uruguay (1965–1966). He also studied in Santiago, Chile, and traveled extensively. During that period, he added Portuguese as the sixth language in his repertoire, after, in order of acquisition, English, French, Spanish, German, and Serbo-Croatian.

During his Fulbright year, he received acceptance from the Johns Hopkins School of Advanced International Studies and some other international relations programs, but quite surprisingly, from no graduate foreign language program. Consequently, when Spears returned to the United States, he enrolled in the international relations master's program at Johns Hopkins, temporarily relinquishing the idea of becoming a linguist or language scholar. However, he felt the imperative to return to language as his primary interest. He then pursued a second master's degree, in linguistics, entering Northwestern University (to which he had applied because of its extensive offering of courses in Bantu and in Swahili in particular, which was the rage among civil rights–oriented black youth) in the fall of 1968. He graduated in 1969. Wishing to continue his studies, Spears enrolled in the Ph.D. Program in Linguistics at the University of California, San Diego, in 1969, receiving his degree in 1977.

Spears, the first of the second cohort of black linguists to earn Ph.Ds in linguistics in the United States (see, for example, LORENZO DOW TURNER), has forged a rich and varied career agenda. His first position as a professor was at the University of California, Santa Cruz. In 1983, he joined the faculty of the City College of the City University of New York (CUNY) as a professor of anthropology. In 1984 he was appointed to the doctoral faculty in anthropology at the CUNY Graduate Center, and in 1985 he was appointed to doctoral faculty in linguistics there. As of 2007 he served as chair of the Anthropology Department (the City College, CUNY) and continued on the doctoral faculty in the linguistics and anthropology programs at the Graduate Center. In 1992 and 1993, Spears served as an exchange professor at the Université de Paris VIII, Département des études de pays Anglophones. Since 1967, he has been a contract interpreter in Spanish, French, and Portuguese for the U.S. Department of State. He is active in numerous professional organizations, among them the American Anthropological Association, the Association of Black Anthropologists, the Associação de Crioulos de Base Léxica Portuguesa e Espanhola, the Linguistic Society of America, and the Society for Pidgin and Creole Linguistics, in which he served as vice president (2005–2007) and president (2007–2009).

Spears's research can be categorized in four related areas: (1) African American English; (2) pidgin and creole languages, focusing on Haitian and other French-lexifier creoles; (3) language and education; and (4) race and ideology. In addition to writing prolifically, he advances the disciplines of linguistics and anthropology by serving on editorial boards, holding office in organizations of the professions, and through the mentoring of a host of younger linguists and anthropologists. He is the founder and first editor of *Transforming Anthropology*, the journal of the Association of Black Anthropologists.

An internationally recognized expert on African American language and particularly its relation to African languages and Atlantic creole languages, Spears has repeatedly expanded the boundaries of knowledge about black language forms through numerous publications and has disseminated research on African American English and creoles through frequent media appearances, including on *The Story of English* (BBC), Black Entertainment Television, National Public Radio, WBAI, and Inner City Broadcasting's WLIB.

Among Spears's publications are "African American Language Use: Ideology and So-Called Obscenity," in *African American English*, edited by Salikoko S. Mufwene, John Rickford, Guy Bailey, and John Baugh (1998); and "Directness in the Use of African-American English," in *Sociocultural and Historical Contexts of African American English*, edited by Sonja L. Lanehart (2002). His books include *The Structure and Status of Pidgins and Creoles* (coeditor with Donald Winford, 1997), *Race and Ideology: Language, Symbolism, and Popular Culture* (editor, 1999), and *Black Linguistics: Language, Society, and Politics in Africa and the Americas* (coeditor, 2003). While Spears speaks a number of languages, he is fluent in five: "Network" American English, African American English, French, Spanish, and Portuguese. A versatile multitasker, he is perhaps the only linguist in the world who is writing and publishing in four languages.

MARGARET WADE-LEWIS

Speed, Ella (1865 or 1866–3 Sept. 1894), was probably born Ella Cherwiss in New Orleans, Louisiana. She was an African American woman whose death in New Orleans at age twenty-eight is the subject of the ballad "Ella Speed" (also known as "Alice B." and "Po' Li'l Ella"). With her husband Willie Speed, she had a son and possibly other children.

For several years before her death, Ella Speed was a prostitute. In the spring of 1894, while an "inmate" at "Miss Lou" Prout's sporting house at 40 South Basin Street, a luxurious parlor house built nearly thirty years earlier for the renowned madam Kate Townsend, Speed met Louis "Bull" Martin, an Italian American born in July 1866. A short, stocky bully and small-time thug, Martin lived with his parents and worked as a bartender at Trauth's Saloon near the Dryades Street market. In August 1894 he was arrested for beating up an elderly African American man, possibly a paper carrier, on the street. He had faced charges of assault and battery previously.

Martin was quite taken with Speed and began to spend considerable time with her. At the end of June 1894, he received a letter from "A Lady Friend" telling him that he was a "sucker" to believe what Speed told him, that he was "the only one" she loved (*Times Democrat*, 4 Sept. 1894); Dan O'Neil and Leon Meyers were others. Despite Speed's denials, Martin was enraged. His obsessive jealousy led to constant bickering, and he began to threaten Speed with physical harm. In response she laughed. Prout was not amused. She first cautioned Speed about Martin and then asked her to leave. In early August Speed relocated to an upstairs room in the house operated by "Miss Pauline" Jones at 137 Customhouse Street (later 829 Iberville Street). The front facade of this building, including the fancy ornamental ironwork and gallery (balcony), has been preserved.

On 21 August Speed sent Martin a handwritten note. She was not feeling well, perhaps suffering from a dental problem that would shortly send her to bed under Martin's care for a few days. She apologized for "the way I treated you" but stated:

> [I]f I did not love you I would not care what you done or were you went to or who you had and I know you are the same way … now darling I will awaite for you at your same hour, and dont you go any wher else I am as ever yours untill death from you devote girl Ella Kiss ÷ Kiss ÷ Kiss ÷ Hug ÷ Hug ÷ Hug ÷ Pleas pay the boy Answer (Criminal District Court, Parish of Orleans, Section A, case no. 22559 A).

Jones later told a reporter that Speed often said that she had no "liking" for Martin—her "affections … were for another"; she "simply went with him for the money he gave her" (*Daily Picayune*, 4 Sept. 1894).

On Sunday evening, 2 September, Martin called on Speed. Around 9:00 P.M. he arranged for a coupe to take them to Lake Pontchartrain's West End, a resort area made famous by LOUIS ARMSTRONG's 1928 recording of KING OLIVER's "West End Blues." They returned to Jones's around 2:30 Monday morning, having consumed some liquor. After drinking beer and wine with Jones, they retired to Speed's room upstairs and ordered in three dozen oysters and two bottles of white wine, augmented by a third bottle when another inmate joined them. Jones's furniture had been seized for nonpayment and was about to be sold at auction. Inmates of the brothel had to be out by midweek. Conversation during the evening included discussion of Speed's situation. According to others, Martin proposed "going housekeeping" by setting Speed up in a small cottage (*Daily Picayune*, 4 Sept. 1894). According to Martin, he told her he was going to Chicago.

Martin went to bed around 5:00 A.M.; Speed joined him later. Around 8:45 A.M., Speed awakened Martin complaining of a headache and wanting something to drink. Twice Martin went downstairs in his underwear and sent out for whiskey cocktails, requesting that the second round be strong.

Around 9:30 A.M., Jones was awakened by a woman's screams. She ran from her room, adjacent to Speed's, into the hallway. Speed was standing in the doorway of her room, her chemise seeming to be "on fire" near her left breast. She said: "Oh, Miss Pauline! Help me! Help me!" and "Louis shot me!" Martin appeared with a pistol in his hand and said, "Look out there, Miss Pauline!" (State of Louisiana, City of New Orleans, Second Recorder's Court, 25 Sept. 1894). Frightened, Jones ran downstairs.

Paul Brelet, a civil sheriff's deputy, was guarding the furniture. After hearing a gunshot and a scream, he saw Jones rushing down the stairs. As Brelet went up, Martin, fully dressed, passed him coming down. Martin left through the front door and turned toward Dauphine Street. When Brelet got to the top of the stairs and saw Speed lying on the floor, unable to speak, he blew his whistle for police. A waiter from the Bon Ton Saloon saw Martin walking on Customhouse Street with tears streaming down his face.

A large crowd gathered as the police did their work. The coroner confirmed that Speed died from internal wounds caused by gunshot. In her room were found photographs of P. B. S. PINCHBACK,

governor of Louisiana briefly from 1872 to 1873, and other prominent African Americans.

A massive manhunt was mounted. Martin eluded it but turned himself in early the next morning and was jailed to await trial in early May 1895.

The trial was presided over by Judge John H. Ferguson, who would shortly gain fame as a principal in *Plessy v. Ferguson* (1896), the Supreme Court case that legally established "separate but equal." Martin's defense was that he shot Speed accidentally. Charged with murder, he was convicted of manslaughter. It was difficult to convict a white man of murdering a black woman.

Ferguson gave him the maximum sentence of twenty years in prison. By 1901 he had been released and was back at bartending and thuggery.

It seems likely that the ballad "Ella Speed" arose shortly after the crime.

Come all you pretty girls and take heed,
Don't you die the death of Ella Speed,
You may be runnin' around, and having you a
    lot of fun,
Some man gonna shoot you down, just like
    Martin done.
(Edmond "Doc" Souchon, *Night Train*, NTI CD
    7080, 1996).

About a year after Speed's death, in the Broadway show *The Widow Jones*, May Irwin sang the "Bully Song," words and music by Charles E. Trevathan, who said he based it on a song he had learned from a southern African American. The timing of these events, tune similarity, occasional recovery of "Bully" lines as part of "Ella Speed," and aptness of "looking for that bully" (manhunt for "Bull") suggest that "Ella Speed" was the song on which Trevathan based the "Bully Song," which has entered tradition as "Bully of the Town."

The name "Ella Speed" has been applied to characters or objects in several works of fiction (*Speed of Light*, Gwyneth Cravens [1979]; *The Talisman*, Stephen King and Peter Straub [1984]; "Ella Speed," Ron Goulart, in *Fantastic Science Fiction Stories* [1960]) as well as to a least one rock band, one thoroughbred horse, and one sailboat.

FURTHER READING
New Orleans newspapers for early September 1894 and May 1895 provide details of Speed's death and Martin's trial, and pertinent police and court records (Case No. 22559, Section A) are in the New Orleans Public Library.

Cowley, John, and John Garst. "Behind the Song ('Ella Speed')," *Sing Out!* 45 no. 1 (2001): 69–70.

Garst, John. "The Deed That Bill Martin Done," *Blues and Rhythm* (Oct. 2003).

JOHN GARST

Speer, Guilford (c. 1808–9 Nov. 1889), shoe- and harness-maker, businessman, and community leader, was born in Georgia to parents whose names and occupations are unknown. Called simply "Guilford," he was enslaved to Benajah Birdsong in Jasper County, Georgia. Birdsong died in 1824, and his widow inherited Guilford before she married James Spier, an Upson County merchant-farmer, in 1827. Guilford came to live and work in Thomaston, the legal and commercial center of Upson County.

Guilford married his first wife, Ellen, after she arrived in Thomaston from Columbia County about 1830. Their child, Susan, was born about 1831. Ellen and Susan were both slaves of George Cary, a onetime Georgia congressman, and, after his death, of his son John J. Cary. The younger Cary's chronic financial distress was a long-standing threat to Guilford and Ellen's family.

Spier moved Guilford to his farm, Hurricane Place, about three and a half miles from town. Guilford labored on the farm by day but worked in his own shoe shop at night. About 1836 Guilford took up with another slave at Hurricane Place, sixteen-year-old Viney, with whom he had four sons, Frank, Charles, Benjamin, and William (WILLIAM GUILFORD). Guilford's connection with Viney ended after William was born in 1844, perhaps because Guilford moved back to Thomaston to work full time at the harness- and shoe-making business.

By the 1850s Guilford had hired his time from his owner, meaning that he arranged his own work and kept all profits over and above a prearranged amount paid to Spier. Georgia law strictly forbade slave owners from allowing slaves to hire their time, but many owners flouted this law. Guilford operated the "Guilford shoe and harness shop" on Thomaston's courthouse square, purchasing leather supplies in his own name and selling a variety of shoes, harnesses, horse collars, and saddles. This enterprise directly contravened Georgia law, which denied that a slave could "control a … shop, and carry on and conduct the business thereof" (*Henry, a Slave, v. The State*, 33 *Georgia Reports*, 441). Guilford rented his shop from the county sheriff, a further example of how whites winked at laws that did not serve their personal interests.

Guilford was a relatively privileged slave because his skill and business acumen profited his master and other whites, but freedom to manage his own employment conferred no protection on his enslaved family. To pay creditors John J. Cary sold Guilford's daughter Susan and his grand-child Caroline. They were transported to Minden, Louisiana, in 1855, and Guilford did not see Susan again for thirty years.

In November 1856 the sheriff seized Ellen to pay more of John J. Cary's perennial debts. Guilford had lost his daughter to the interstate slave trade, and only money could prevent the same fate from befalling his wife. Under Georgia law the notion of a slave purchasing another slave was as impossible as a slave hiring his own time or operating his own business; nevertheless, on 6 January 1857, when Cary sold Ellen for $686 cash, Guilford "bought his wife and paid for her" (*Barred and Disallowed Case Files of the Southern Claims Commission, 1871–1880*, claim of Guilford Speer, commission 10515, office 400, report 3, 1873). Ellen died sometime during the Civil War, and Guilford subsequently married Magamie Rogers. There were no children from this union.

By 1862 James Spier and his widow were dead, and their estate administrator hired Guilford out to members of the Sandwich family, Thomaston businessmen. The Sandwiches let Guilford run his own shop while they acted as his agents in matters requiring legal authority. Fire on 30 August 1863 destroyed three sides of Thomaston's downtown square, including Guilford's shop, but he resumed business in an unburned part of the village at a house owned by William O. Sandwich that also served as Guilford's home.

Asked in later years about his loyalty to the Union during the Civil War, Guilford described himself as "a man of inoffensive manners" who publicly "did not have a great deal to say" but who wanted the North to win the war and free the slaves. A prominent Thomaston lawyer said that whites "tolerated" Guilford's opinions because "[h]e was always polite and kind towards those opposed to him" (*Southern Claims Commission*, claim of Guilford Speer). When Major General James H. Wilson's Union cavalry invaded and liberated Thomaston on 19 April 1865, Emancipation was a bittersweet victory for Guilford. Federal soldiers pillaged his shop of saddles, harness, shoes, and other leather goods valued at $463.50. They even ransacked his house, stealing his quilts and bedspread.

After Emancipation Guilford entered the public record as Guilford Speer. A Republican, he played a visible part in reordering politics and civil relations during Reconstruction. In 1866 he served as president of the short-lived Upson County branch of the Georgia Equal Rights and Educational Association. The local Freedmen's Bureau agent wrote that whites expressed "dissatisfaction ... on account of the meetings of the Equal Rights Association, but ... I attended one of their meetings last night by invitation from their President & their speeches exhibited kindness for the Whites. ... And so long as they demean themselves as law abiding men I shall protect them" (National Archives, RG 105, *Records of the Assistant Commissioner for the State of Georgia, Bureau of Refugees, Freedmen and Abandoned Lands, 1865–69*, Unregistered Letters Received, James W. Greene to Davis Tillson, 25 May 1866). Emboldened, Speer and his sons, Charles Speer and William Guilford, who were also officers in the association, penned a protest to the Freedmen's Bureau over inequitable treatment of freedmen in the county courts.

In 1868 Guilford Speer's name appeared among the trustees who purchased a house and lot for Thomaston's recently established African Methodist Episcopal (AME) Church, which doubled as a school for freedmen and a Republican Party meeting place. When Guilford Speer registered to vote on 12 July 1867, his son William Guilford was a registrar. As his last known public act Speer served as an Upson County election manager for the 1870 race in which William Guilford unsuccessfully ran for state senator.

Speer had survived fifty-seven years of slavery by cultivating the patronage of powerful local white men; therefore when Congress withdrew military protection from the South, ended Reconstruction, and left Upson County whites still dominant in political and economic power, Speer left politics and devoted his energies to business.

Guilford Speer prospered after Emancipation. Besides the Thomaston business he managed a second shop owned by the Spier estate in nearby Barnesville, Pike County. When legal arbitration awarded him title to the Barnesville property in 1867, Speer sold it and then bought his Thomaston home and shop from his old employer, W. O. Sandwich, at a sheriff's sale in 1870. Speer ran his Thomaston harness-making business for many years until his mind failed.

When Guilford Speer died 9 November 1889 at about the age of eighty-one his funeral was well attended. His wife Magamie had predeceased him in 1883; he was survived by at least two of his children, Susan Drake and William Guilford.

FURTHER READING
The Thomaston-Upson Archives, Upson County, Georgia, hold documentation for Guilford Speer's life: the Birdsong family Bible; probate records (1858–1866) for James and Alzina Spier; and interrogatories in Upson Superior Court, January term 1892, *William Guilford, Heir at Law, v. J. S. King, Administrator*. Further materials can be found in the Upson County tax digests and deed books through 1889 and in Superior Court Minute Book F, 100–101.
Obituary: *Thomaston Times*, 15 Nov. 1889.

DAVID E. PATERSON

Spence, Eulalie (11 Jun. 1894–7 Mar. 1981), playwright, drama critic, actress, and elocution teacher, was born in the British West Indian territory of Nevis, the eldest of the five daughters of Robert Spence, a planter, and Eno Anna Spence (née Lake), both natives of neighboring British colonies. The family migrated to the United States in 1901 following a hurricane that devastated the island's sugar industry and settled in New York City where Robert, like many black Caribbean immigrants of that era, experienced great hardship finding suitable employment. After high school, Eulalie attended the Normal Department of New York Training School for Teachers, and in 1914 started her career as a schoolteacher. The 1920 federal census found her living in Manhattan with her now widowed mother, and her four siblings.

Although her first production, *Being Forty*, appeared as early as 1924, Spence's entry into the theater arts began in earnest in 1927 with the performance of *Fool's Errand* by W.E.B. DuBois's theatrical group the Krigwa Players in the National Little Theater Tournament held in New York City for the David Belasco Cup. Not only did this play win a prize, it was also staged in a Broadway theater—a rare achievement for a work by a black playwright. The year 1927 turned out to be one of Spence's most successful as many of her plays such as *Hot Stuff*, *The Starter*, and *Undertow* won awards sponsored by African American journals especially the *Crisis*, the official organ of the NAACP, and *Opportunity*, a publication of the National Urban League.

Spence parted company with the Krigwa Players in 1929 after years of disagreement with DuBois about the role and the responsibility of the

African American dramatist. The mentor of the Harlem "propaganda" school proposed that black drama should examine "the manner in which Negroes are treated by white people in the United States," and that its primary objective should be the improvement of the race. Spence, however, repeatedly expressed the view that the playwright's priority is dramaturgy rather than any social or political agenda. "To every art it's [sic] form," she wrote, "thank God! And to the play, the technique that belongs to it" (*Opportunity*, 180). Spence also rejected racial conflict as an appropriate subject for the theater, especially for dramatists whose aim is a varied cosmopolitan audience, entertainment, and universal goodwill: "Hammering away at an old illness and injury, whether it is of eighty years, or one thousand, does no good at all. ..." It's defeating because "theater that has universal good and joy and welcome and understanding ... opens the door of humanity a little wider" (Hatch interview).

But, as critics such as Yvonne Shafer and Adrienne C. Macki have observed, some of the emphases in Spence's work contradict her reputation as an artist who repudiated a dominant and influential aesthetic of the Harlem Renaissance. In reality, Spence subtly confronts the socioeconomic realities of African American existence. In plays such as *The Hunch*, *Hot Stuff*, and *The Starter*, she reimagines Harlem as a site of resilience and normalcy and captures the fullness and complexity of black life, while celebrating its vibrancy and survival in the face of racial and economic marginalization. Her representations of black culture avoid any romanticizing or degrading excess. The black playwright, she insisted, should "portray the life of his people, their foibles, if he will, and their sorrows, ambitions and defeats" (*Opportunity*, 180). In some ways, Spence might be said to be restaging race without "difference," redeeming blackness from traditional stereotypes. Additionally, she has been praised for inscribing positive images of the African American woman in many plays that center on black female protagonists and address gender dynamics in the Harlem community. However, *Her* (1927), Spence's most ambitious and visionary work, transcends both race and gender in its exploration of alienation and dispossession in American society and achieves a wider resonance.

When her association with the Krigwa Players ended, Spence joined the Lighthouse Players of the New York Association for the Blind, which staged *La Divina Pastora*, "a Spanish miracle play," in 1930

and again in 1931. Her last work, *The Whipping* (1934), is a dramatization of Roy C. Flannagan's novel of the same name about the Ku Klux Klan. Set in Virginia, the lengthy three-act drama features another strong female role, and even though it contains no major black characters, evokes some elements of African American culture to indict— implicitly—the black experience in the American South. Paramount Studios bought the rights for the play but opted not to film it; for some unknown reason, a production scheduled for Danbury, Connecticut, in July 1933 with the famous Queenie Smith in the leading role was also canceled.

After these disappointments, Spence returned to her academic pursuits, graduating with a B.S. from New York University in 1937, and two years later, with an M.A. in speech from Columbia University where she had continued her association with the stage. In 1958 she retired from her post as teacher of English and elocution at Eastern District High School in Brooklyn, which she had held since 1927. Her most famous protégé was the director Joseph Papp, founder of the New York Theater Festival. Spence, who applied for U.S. naturalization in 1920, died in Gettysburg, Adams County, Pennsylvania in 1981.

Eulalie Spence authored at least fourteen plays, some of which were published as well as staged, and are still being performed in the early twenty-first century. She is celebrated as a skillful exponent of the comic one-act play and as a consummate dramatist who, despite a commitment to stagecraft and her often repeated reservations about the social compulsion of black creativity, utilized the Harlem stage to renegotiate African American identities and to interrogate American racial and gender ideologies. But perhaps Spence's most significant accomplishment was her role in the establishment of drama by black women as a viable art form during a movement dominated by the prose and verse of African American men.

FURTHER READING

Eulalie Spence's papers are housed at the Schomburg Center for Research in Black Life, New York Public Library, in Harlem, New York.

Spence, Eulalie. "A Criticism of Negro Drama as It Relates to the Negro Dramatist and Artist," *Opportunity*, June 1928.

Spence, Eulalie. Taped Interview with Joshua Carter, 1973. (Recorded Sound Division, Schomburg Center for Research in Black Culture, New York Public Library, New York).

Spence, Eulalie. Taped Interview with James V. Hatch, 22 Aug. 1973. (Included in the Hatch-Billops Archives at the Schomburg Center for Research in Black Culture, New York Public Library, New York).

Brown-Guillory, Elizabeth. *Their Place on the Stage: Black Women Playwrights in America.* (1988).

Giles, Freida Scott. "Willis Richardson and Eulalie Spence: Dramatic Voices and the Harlem Renaissance." *American Drama* 5 (Spring 1966).

Macki, Adrienne C. "Talking B(l)ack": Construction of Gender and Race in the Plays of Eulalie Spence." *Theater History Studies,* 27 (1 Jan 2007).

Perkins, Kathy A., ed. *Black Female Playwrights: An Anthology of Plays before 1950* (1989).

Roses, Lorraine Elena, and Ruth Elizabeth Randolph. *Harlem Renaissance and Beyond: Literary Biographies of 100 Black Women Writers, 1900–1945* (1990).

Shafer, Yvonne. "Eulalie Spence (1894–1981)," in *American Women Playwrights, 1900–1950* (1991).

CARL A. WADE

Spencer, Anne (6 Feb. 1882–27 July 1975), poet, librarian, and teacher, was born Annie Bethel Scales Bannister in Henry County, near Danville, Virginia, the daughter of Joel Cephus Bannister, a saloon owner and former slave, and Sarah Louise Scales. The only child of divorced parents, at the age of eleven Annie was sent to Virginia Seminary in Lynchburg, where she excelled in literature and languages. After graduating in 1899 she taught for two years, then in 1901 married fellow student Edward Spencer and lived the rest of her life in Lynchburg.

Outwardly it was a pleasant life that Spencer spent with her husband, a postal worker, and their three children in a comfortable house built in part by Edward. For twenty years (1925–1945) Anne Spencer was a librarian and part-time teacher of literature and language at the all-black Dunbar High School, named for the poet PAUL LAURENCE DUNBAR. The Spencers often entertained in their home well-known visitors to the city who, because of their race, were denied lodging in local hotels.

Their son CHAUNCEY SPENCER, who was born in 1906, remembered houseguests such as LANGSTON HUGHES, PAUL ROBESON, W. E. B. DuBOIS, GEORGE WASHINGTON CARVER, and THURGOOD MARSHALL. Adjoining the house was "a beautiful garden tended by my mother," her son wrote. "As soon as mother, 'Miss Anne,' arrived home from her job as a librarian, she would head for the garden. … Either she was working with her flowers, which

she cross-bred, or she'd be reading and writing in the garden house. This was my mother's world, the only world in which she felt comfortable" (Spencer, 42). The garden house, called "Edankraal," and the main house are maintained as historic sites.

A less tranquil side of Anne Spencer's life was her indignation toward racial and social injustice and her lifelong efforts to improve the lot of blacks. Her biographer, J. Lee Greene, records her successful campaign to replace the all-white faculty at a black high school with black teachers and "her outspoken opposition to tokenism when school integration came to Lynchburg" in the 1960s (85). Her letters to newspaper editors and city officials, as well as her refusal to patronize segregated city buses and streetcars, earned her grudging recognition as an uncompromising foe of Jim Crowism. "My mother was full of fire," her son recalled (Spencer, 17).

Anne Spencer had scribbled poems since school days, but her career as a poet began when she met JAMES WELDON JOHNSON during his stay at the Spencer home in 1918 while he was helping to establish a local chapter of the National Association for the Advancement of Colored People. "He released my soul," she was to say (Greene, 78). Johnson recommended her to H. L. Mencken, and the two writers jointly sponsored the publication of her poem "Before the Feast of Shushan" in *Crisis: A Record of the Darker Races* (Feb. 1920). Based on the Book of Esther, the poem is a monologue by King Ahasuerus about his wife Vashti. Eleven Spencer poems were published between 1920 and 1931 in magazines such as *Crisis*, *Palms*, and *Opportunity*, which were associated with the Harlem Renaissance movement. Her poems have been frequently included in anthologies, beginning with Johnson's *The Book of American Negro Poetry* (1922, with five Spencer poems) and including *The Norton Anthology of Modern Poetry* (1973) and *Four Hundred Years of Virginia, An Anthology* (1985). Yet her poems published in her lifetime number less than thirty, and her biographer could account for only about fifty extant poems of the hundreds that Spencer remembered writing. Forty-two poems, including twenty-two previously unpublished, are printed in the appendix of the biography.

This slim surviving body of work has nonetheless established Anne Spencer as a significant American black poet of the twentieth century. Her themes are universal. She uses traditional forms: sonnets, epigrams in varied rhythm and rhyming schemes, and elegies such as "For Jim, Easter

Eve," recalling Johnson. She published little poetry after his death in 1938. Most of Spencer's poems are short, with only "At the Carnival" (fifty lines) and "Before the Feast of Shushan" (forty-one lines) running much beyond twenty lines.

Spencer read widely and felt deeply. Her tribute to lost poets, "Dunbar," first published 1920, is in the voice of Paul Laurence Dunbar:

Ah, how poets sing and die!
Make one song and Heaven takes it;
Have one heart and Beauty breaks it;
Chatterton, Shelley, Keats and I–
Ah, how poets sing and die!

In its four rhyming quatrains and concluding couplet, "Life-long, Poor Browning Never Knew Virginia," published in 1927, sums up Browning's Italian exile, his pantheistic existence in nature after death, and his possible reunion with Elizabeth Barrett Browning. A touch of Gerard Manley Hopkins's sprung rhythm is in her description of a half-inch brown spider in "Po' Little Lib" (1977): "M O V E S thru the grass, O god / if it chance / For the drought driven air turns leaf into lance."

Greene indicates that "as a private poet, Anne Spencer did not see racial protest as her métier in poetry" (138). An exception is "White Things," with its two intricate rhyming stanzas about a lynching.

Anne Spencer loved gardens, books, freedom, and the life of the mind—and when she died in Lynchburg she left a slender golden legacy in her poems and in her restored garden.

FURTHER READING
Spencer's papers are in the archives at Alderman Library, University of Virginia.
Greene, J. Lee. *Time's Unfading Garden: Anne Spencer's Life and Poetry* (1977).
Spencer, Chauncey. *Who Is Chauncey Spencer?* (1976).
This entry is taken from the *American National Biography* and is published here with the permission of the American Council of Learned Societies.

DORA JEAN ASHE

Spencer, Chauncey Edward (5 Nov. 1906–21 Aug. 2002), aviation pioneer, was born and raised in Lynchburg, Virginia, the son of Edward Alexander Spencer, a postman and real estate developer, and ANNE BETHEL (SCALES) SPENCER, a teacher, librarian, and writer. Anne Spencer was an important, if now little known, poet and editor associated with the Harlem Renaissance and the NAACP. Her Lynchburg home and legendary garden became a way station for eminent blacks traveling between the North and the Deep South at a time when hotel facilities for African Americans were few and far between. From a young age Chauncey Spencer was used to rubbing elbows with celebrities. The likes of W. E. B. DuBois, THURGOOD MARSHALL, PAUL ROBESON, LANGSTON HUGHES, JAMES WELDON JOHNSON, and ADAM CLAYTON POWELL SR. were guests in the Spencer home during his youth. "Of all of them, I think I was most impressed by Paul Robeson," Spencer wrote in his 1975 autobiography. "I remember thinking that Robeson was a man who didn't need a door, who could walk through a wall."

Separating the facts of Spencer's life from fiction is no easy task, if only because some of the verifiable facts are so outlandish. His relationship with OTABENGA provides but one example. Otabenga, a Congolese Pygmy, had been brought to the United States to be exhibited at the 1904 Louisiana Purchase Exposition in St. Louis, Missouri, and in 1906 was displayed at the monkey house of the Bronx Zoo in New York City. Outraged black New Yorkers arranged to have him removed from the zoo and placed in an orphanage. In 1910 he was entrusted to the black community of Lynchburg, where at first he flourished. Otabenga learned some English and basic reading skills, took a job in a tobacco factory, and taught some of what he had learned in the forests of the Congo to black boys around the woods of Lynchburg. Otabenga, whom the children knew as "Otto Bingo," taught Chauncey Spencer, who was then known as "Woogie," how to trap small game and hunt with a bow and arrow (according to one account Otabenga learned the latter talent not in the Congo but in St. Louis, from the Apache leader Geronimo, who was also on exhibit at the Exposition). Sadly Otabenga, convinced that he would never be able to return home, committed suicide in 1916.

A graduate of Lynchburg's Virginia Theological Seminary with a degree in sociology, Spencer held a variety of odd jobs throughout the late 1920s and early 1930s. A marriage to his high school sweetheart Elvira Jackson lasted a very short time. Spencer entered the all-black Coffey School of Aviation in Chicago in 1934 and soon began working in barnstorming shows as a daredevil pilot and parachute racer.

He is best remembered for a publicity flight that he made from Chicago to Washington, D.C., in May 1939 with his fellow pilot Dale Lawrence

White. Spencer and White embarked on the flight to Washington to draw attention to blacks in aviation and dramatize the exclusion of blacks from military flight training. The *Chicago Defender* and the Jones brothers, noted Chicago numbers runners, sponsored the flight. Spencer and White rented a true jalopy of a Lincoln-Page biplane, and after at least two harrowing unplanned landings they piloted it safely to Washington. There they met with Edgar Brown, lobbyist for the all-black United Government Employees union. Brown took the pair to the Capitol, where Congress was considering a bill to expand the Civilian Pilot Training (CPT) program, which would train a massive cadre of pilots who could be converted to military fliers in wartime. Civil rights organizations, historically black colleges, and black newspapers were pushing to include African Americans in the training program.

According to Spencer—the story has not been corroborated—he, White, and Brown were walking through a Capitol hallway when a short white man stopped them and asked, "Hello, Edgar, how are you?" The man was Senator Harry S. Truman (Democrat of Missouri), and after being introduced to Spencer and White he asked if he could see their airplane. Amazed that two blacks could coax such a machine all the way from Chicago, Truman said (again, according to Spencer), "If you had guts enough to fly that thing I see there, that plane, I got guts enough to get you into the Air Corps." In any case the CPT bill that passed later that year did include a provision for training blacks at Tuskegee Institute and six other historically black colleges. This program formed the foundation of the famed Tuskegee Airmen experiment in World War II.

During and immediately after World War II, Spencer, now married to the former Anne Howard, worked as a civilian employee relations officer at Wright-Patterson Air Force Base near Dayton, Ohio. While serving in that position, Spencer later claimed, he conducted undercover investigations of racial discrimination at the Tuskegee army air field in Tuskegee, Alabama, at the behest of WILLIAM H. HASTIE, civilian aide to the secretary of war. Details of the investigation are sketchy, but Spencer himself credited the mission with having changed policies at Tuskegee for the better. His work at Patterson field involved implementation of President Franklin Roosevelt's executive order 8802 of 1941 prescribing fair employment in the military and defense industries without regard to race. Spencer found his position doubly difficult: "Many Negroes wanted special favors" from Spencer because of his skin color, he wrote. "And then, of course, there were those in authority in the Air Force who warned me not to do my job. They wanted integration in name only." But Spencer persevered, and in 1948 he received the U.S. Air Force's Exceptional Civilian Service Award, the service's highest civilian commendation.

In 1953 Spencer found himself the victim of redbaiting. He was suspended from his position in the air force and was charged with nineteen counts of untoward activity, the most serious of which were having been employed in the 1920s as a female impersonator and having attended a 1950 Communist Party rally at which Paul Robeson had appeared. Spencer had worked briefly as a female impersonator at a Harlem theater in 1926 or 1927—he had quit the job, he said, when he learned that his father was traveling to New York to pay him a visit—and his lawyer denied that the portrayal "was in any manner homosexual or perverted." Spencer also admitted having seen the old family friend Robeson perform in 1950, but he claimed that the performance had nothing to do with politics. The secretary of the air force officially cleared Spencer of the charges in 1954, but his career with the service was effectively ended.

In 1959 Spencer moved his family to San Bernardino, California, where he was active in the local branch of the NAACP. In that capacity he waged prodigious rhetorical battles against black nationalists and especially against those who tried to introduce black studies programs in the town's public schools. "I'm not going back to segregation—to Black studies, to Black dormitories, to Black schools. I've worked all my life for integration and now we're retreading our steps," he complained in his 1975 memoir. Spencer became San Bernardino's police commissioner and later served as deputy city administrator in Highland Park, Michigan. He retired to Lynchburg in the late 1970s and established the Anne Bethel Spencer House and Garden as a state historic landmark.

As Spencer reflected on his improbable life he drew increasingly from a family trait that his mother had called a "colossal reserve of constructive indignation" to sound off on issues of American race relations. In later years he referred to himself as "the bigmouth." Spencer told and retold the story of his 1939 flight and other exploits in a boomingly digressive style, demanding attention for the pioneers who had opened the field of aviation to people of all races. What most vexed Spencer at the end of his life was Americans' continued use of racial terminology. "It galls me that I have to be called black or African-American or Negro … in these United States," he told a reporter in 1993. "I am an American." Spencer died in 2002, survived by Anne, his wife of sixty-two years, and six of their eight children.

FURTHER READING

Separate oral history interviews with Chauncey Spencer are housed in the archives of the Virginia Museum of Transportation, Roanoke, Virginia, and in the National Park Service's Tuskegee Airmen Oral History Project, Tuskegee, Alabama.

Spencer, Chauncey. *Who Is Chauncey Spencer?* (1975).

Laris, Michael. "Freedom Flight," *Washington Post Magazine*, 16 Feb. 2003.

J. TODD MOYE

Spencer, Margaret Beale (5 Sept. 1944–), developmental psychologist and educator, was born Margaret Beale in Philadelphia, Pennsylvania, the daughter of Elizabeth Rebecca (Keith) Beale, a public library aide, and Junius Alton Beale, a Philadelphia local government worker. Beale's parents divorced when she was six years old, after which time she and her older sisters—Gwendolyn Rebecca and Maryann—were raised by their mother. Spencer described her family as nurturing and supportive, providing her with the motivation and values that enabled her to succeed in both her personal and her professional life. Much of her early formal education was at the Thaddeus Stevens School of Practice (now the Masterman School in Philadelphia). After high school she enrolled at Temple University, where she received her B.S. in pharmacy. Her ultimate intention was to go to medical school and prepare for a career in pediatrics.

After college graduation Beale worked in a hospital as a pharmacist and worked with children. From these experiences she redirected her life plans and career goals. At the hospital she witnessed resilience in very sick patients, many of whom were children. Her day-to-day encounters with these youngsters, and her marvel at their strength under very difficult circumstances, led her to move from the biomedical to the social sciences. She was also troubled by the ways that the poor, especially African American children, were viewed almost exclusively in the context of deviance and pathology. When the University of Kansas offered her a doctoral fellowship, she seized the opportunity to pursue a new career path.

In 1967 she married Charles L. Spencer, an M.D. and Ph.D. specializing in internal medicine and geriatrics at the University of Pennsylvania. When her husband was offered a position in Chicago, Spencer left the University of Kansas after receiving her M.A. in psychology in 1970 and moved to the University of Chicago. She applied to the doctoral program at Chicago at the suggestion of her adviser and mentor Frances Degen Horowitz, and she received her Ph.D. in human development and in developmental psychology in 1976.

Spencer combined the roles of student and mother. Her first child was born while she was enrolled in the doctoral program at the University of Kansas, and she began her doctoral studies at Chicago with two children aged four months and eighteen months. A third child was born three years later.

In Spencer's view, her most significant accomplishment was her simultaneous engagement in the roles of parent and of developmental psychologist. Her work gave her a sense of mission that further fueled her long-term desire to do well in her parenting. Spencer was an exemplary model of one who has successfully combined family and work, and she credited her family with providing her with a sense of mission and directedness in looking at issues of resilience in poor and African American children. Through her work Spencer came to understand that the professional literature largely ignored African American children. The absence of nonpejorative images and portrayals provided motivation for her lifework in developmental psychology.

Spencer's early work built on the pioneering work of the psychologists KENNETH BANCROFT CLARK and MAMIE PHIPPS CLARK on black children's racial identification and preferences. She surmised that those who referenced or used the Clarks' work would not take into consideration, and indeed ignored, the normative human development theory that was necessary to add meaning to the Clarks' findings. Spencer contended that the interpretation of the Clarks' work that suggested self-hatred among black youngsters should have reflected larger influences. Because children are "learning machines," they would absorb American perspectives on and references to race. However, this does not mean that they would internalize society's messages and engage in self-hatred.

Spencer's professional endeavors, spanning thirty years, reflected her assessment that black children engage in normal human development processes. Her contribution to the field of applied psychology and human development lies in the formulation of phenomenological variant of ecological systems theory, or PVEST. PVEST merged the individual's experiences with an ecological systems approach, advancing previous theories, in particular Bronfenbrenner's ecological systems theory that took into account the impact of cultural environments or contexts on self perceptions by which individuals make meaning of their experiences. PVEST was an interactive perspective that incorporated cultural context, experience, self-valuation and worth, and the meaning one gives to one's personal qualities and behaviors.

This dynamic approach represented a significant contribution to the field of developmental psychology as a theory of human development that, while applicable to all humans coping under varying conditions, also included diverse groups and afforded a special contribution to the study of developmental processes and outcomes of highly stigmatized groups. Spencer's approach substantially aided the study of African American adolescents in areas including psychosocial wellness and academic achievement.

Spencer was the founding director of the Center for Health Achievement Neighborhood Growth and Ethnic Studies (CHANGES). By combining the perspectives of human development and cultural context, the center provided students and faculty with opportunities to collaborate on research activities focusing on resiliency among racially, ethnically, socioeconomically, and academically diverse adolescents and families. The goal of the center was to explore and develop models of resiliency for youth gleaned from the vantage point of a variety of academic disciplines. Students who worked with the center were trained to think in interdisciplinary terms.

At the University of Pennsylvania, Spencer was also the director of the interdisciplinary studies in human development (ISHD) program in the Graduate School of Education and the director of the W. E. B. DuBois Collective Research Institute. Her professional legacy included developing the theory of humanization versus demonization of youth of color and poor children in the field of human development, and putting forth the notion that human development rules governed children's response to context. Her work also demonstrated the importance of context, and that policy and practice represent part of the problem of children of color and poor children. Her studies afforded the field a theory of human development that was culturally inclusive. Finally, she highlighted the

continuing impact of racism, privilege, and power on theorizing and analyzing human development in cultural context.

Spencer wrote scores of articles and book chapters, and coedited three books. She received dozens of grants from federal funding agencies like the National Science Foundation and the National Institute of Mental Health. She also served on several professional committees and editorial and organization boards. She received numerous awards from professional and academic associations and organizations, including the American Psychological Association 2005 Senior Scholar Award for Distinguished and Scholarly Contributions in the Public Interest. She was part of the small cadre of African American scholars who in the late twentieth century began to craft a new, revisionist literature on a variety of topics related to black life and culture from a nonpejorative perspective.

FURTHER READING
Spencer, M.B., G.K. Brookins, and W. Allen, eds. *Beginnings: Social and Affective Development of Black Children* (1985).

SUSAN D. TOLIVER

Spencer, Peter (Feb. 1782–July 1843), founder of the Union Church of Africans, was born a slave in Kent County, Maryland. Much of his early life is shrouded in obscurity. There is no record of his parents' names. Freed upon the death of his master, he moved to Wilmington, Delaware, sometime in the 1790s and received a basic education in a free African school supported by Quakers.

In Wilmington, Spencer soon established a reputation as a shrewd businessman with unblemished honesty. The 1814 *Wilmington Directory* listed him as "a labourer" residing at the corner of French and Chestnut streets, and his work as a mechanic resulted in strong business ties with both blacks and whites. The intelligence, sound practical sense, and great dignity of character he displayed in the business arena and as a property owner were matched only by his deep religious faith and personal piety.

Spencer joined the Asbury Methodist Episcopal Church, a predominantly white congregation in Wilmington. He quickly emerged as a leader and lay preacher, devoting special attention to the black members of Asbury. As black membership increased, tensions developed over segregated seating arrangements and the efforts of white Methodists to control the spiritual lives of black members. Unwilling to accept an inferior status,

Spencer and William Anderson led some of the black parishioners out in June 1805 and organized Ezion Methodist Episcopal Church. The new church, named for the port of Ezion-Geber, where Solomon kept a fleet of ships, was to function in connection with Asbury and the mostly white Methodist Episcopal Conference. When Spencer, Anderson, and their followers sought to choose their own pastors, they encountered strong opposition in December 1812 from James Bateman, a white elder from Philadelphia who had been appointed at Ezion. The two sides appeared in a Wilmington court, but Spencer and the other charter members soon abandoned the case, left Ezion, and took steps toward complete ecclesiastical separation and independence.

Spencer became a staunch advocate of black religious freedom and of religious nationalism among his people. In July 1813 he and his followers purchased a lot from Quakers and organized the Union Church of Africans, a body also called the Union Church of African Members, the African Union Church, the African Union Methodist Church, and the Union Methodist Connexion. Incorporated under the Delaware law of 1787 that authorized free religious bodies, the Union Church of Africans drew up articles of association, dated 18 September 1813, four days after Spencer and Anderson were ordained as elder ministers. The document was signed by some forty charter members, six of whom were women. Spencer's wife, Annes, would later emerge as a significant force in the new church, a development not surprising in view of its acceptance of women as licensed preachers.

Spencer became the first pastor of the Union Church of Africans, and his personality gave it character and direction. The church soon expanded with the addition of congregations in Christiana, Delaware, and Kennett Square, Pennsylvania. In contrast to African Methodist leaders like RICHARD ALLEN (1760–1831) and JAMES VARICK, Spencer rejected the Methodist Episcopal structure in favor of a more democratic arrangement. His church's structure consisted of one lay order, known as ruling, or lay, elders, which constituted the central policy-making board in each congregation. There were three orders of preachers: elder ministers, deacons, and licensed preachers. Also in contrast to other African Methodist leaders, Spencer rejected the itinerary in favor of the stationed pastorate and chose the loosely associated church system over the strong traditional Methodist connectional

system. He was similar to other African Methodist leaders in retaining the doctrine of the Methodist Episcopal Church as embodied in its general rules, articles of religion, and discipline.

Spencer combined strong pastoral leadership with a devotion to the educational, moral, social, and economic uplift of people of African descent. Under his guidance, the Union Church of Africans established a regional base with thirty-one congregations in Delaware, Maryland, Pennsylvania, New Jersey, and New York. A school was organized in connection with each congregation; Spencer taught the values of personal morality, the monogamous and stable family life, temperance and sobriety, economic self-sufficiency and cooperation, and Christian social responsibility. To further promote strong family life, black unity, and communal liberation, he inaugurated in 1813 the Big August Quarterly, a socioreligious festival of African Union Methodists in Wilmington that was still occurring annually at the beginning of the twenty-first century.

Spencer's involvement in the independent African Methodist movement extended beyond his own church. Between 1813 and 1816 he participated in a movement in Attleborough, Pennsylvania, that resulted in a separate African Methodist congregation. When Richard Allen called for a general meeting of African Methodists in Philadelphia in 1816, Spencer was among those invited. Disagreements with Allen concerning church polity and detailed matters of the discipline, however, prevented him from joining Allen's African Methodist Episcopal Church. Besides, his own denomination was already organized, and he saw no need to unship matters a second time.

Spencer's name remains prominent in black church history and the black freedom movement. His strong stand against colonization and in favor of emancipation and the abolition of slavery stands as testimony to his significance as both a Christian leader and a proponent of equal rights and social justice. He stood tall among those imbued with a black nationalist consciousness in his time. His vision for his church and his people as a whole found expression in the 1822 and 1839 editions of his church's hymnal and in *The Doctrine and Discipline of the African Union Church* (1813).

Spencer died in Wilmington. Eight years after his death, a dispute erupted within the ranks of his church, resulting in a major schism in 1855–1856. Both the African Union Methodist Protestant Church and the Union American

Methodist Episcopal Church claim Spencer as their founder.

FURTHER READING

Baldwin, Lewis V. *The Mark of a Man: Peter Spencer and the African Union Methodist Tradition* (1987).

Ramsey, Jacob F. *Father Spencer, Our Founder: His Work for the Church and the Race* (1914).

Russell, Daniel J., Jr. *History of the African Union Methodist Protestant Church* (1920).

Obituary: *Delaware State Journal*, 28 July 1843.

This entry is taken from the *American National Biography* and is published here with the permission of the American Council of Learned Societies.

LEWIS V. BALDWIN

Spikes, Dolores Margaret Richard (24 Aug. 1936–), mathematician and university president, was born Dolores Margaret Richard in Baton Rouge, Louisiana, to Lawrence Granville Richard, a worker in the chemical division of the Exxon refinery, and Margaret Patterson. Spikes attributed her academic success to her father's love of reading and her parents' insistence that she and her sisters attend college. Her father attended primary school and got his general equivalency diploma (GED) after his children graduated from college. Her mother had a little more formal schooling, having completed tenth grade. Spikes attended Southern University in Baton Rouge on a scholarship and graduated in 1957 summa cum laude with a bachelor of science. The following year she attended the University of Illinois at Urbana on a fellowship and earned a master's degree in 1958. Just weeks after graduating she married Herman Spikes, a fellow mathematician and a classmate from Southern University. They had one child.

Spikes returned to Louisiana, where she taught at the Southern University Baton Rouge campus. She also taught biology, chemistry, and general science at Mossville High School in Calcasieu Parish in western Louisiana. Her instruction allowed the students to participate in statewide science competitions for the first time. In 1965, when her husband moved the family to Baton Rouge for a job, Spikes enrolled in the Ph.D. program in mathematics at Louisiana State University (LSU). In 1966 she received a National Science Foundation Science Faculty Fellowship to help fund her studies. In 1968 she received a three-year Ford Foundation Fellowship that allowed her to work on her Ph.D..

In 1971 Spikes became the first African American and the first graduate of Southern University to get a Ph.D. in pure mathematics from LSU. She said of this accomplishment, however, that, she was "not proud of that fact. I regard it as a shame—a blight on the state of Louisiana and on education in general" (Kenschaft, "Black Women in Mathematics in the United States," *Journal of African Civilizations*). She also said that a lack of role models was a significant hurdle to overcome. Ultimately she finished her degree in pure math with a specialty in commutative ring theory. The title of her dissertation was "Semi-valuations and Groups of Divisibility." Her research, conducted under the direction of Jack Ohm, dealt with algebraic rings, Abelian groups, and group theory. Spikes was the twelfth African American woman to get her Ph.D. in pure mathematics.

Shortly after getting her Ph.D., Spikes was promoted to associate professor at Southern University, where she had continued to teach when not actively working on her dissertation. She participated in forming a faculty senate at Southern in response to student uprisings and subsequent shootings. She became a full professor in 1975, and in 1978 she served as president of the faculty senate.

While still a faculty member in the Mathematics Department, Spikes was appointed assistant to the chancellor of Southern University at Baton Rouge in 1981 on a part-time basis. She became a full-time assistant to the chancellor the following year. In 1985 she became the executive vice chancellor and vice chancellor for academic affairs for the university. From 1986 to 1987 she attended Harvard University's Institute for Educational Management, and the following academic year she served as chancellor of Southern University at New Orleans. In 1988 Spikes became the first woman in the United States to head a university system when she became the sixth president of the Southern University and A&M system, one of the largest predominantly African American university systems in the United States. At the same time, due to a legal battle threatening to merge all Louisiana schools into one university, she was made chancellor of Southern University at Baton Rouge. This appointment meant that if the Southern University system was broken up, she would remain in charge of one of the schools. In 1989 Spikes received the Thurgood Marshall Educational Achievement Award.

On becoming president of Southern, Spikes found herself in the unenviable position of overseeing a budget deficit of $5.2 million. She addressed this by firing sixty employees, reducing all salaries over $20,000 (including her own), simultaneously increasing faculty teaching workloads, and compressing the university's course offerings while attempting to raise $1 million from Southern University alumni.

During her tenure as president Spikes was responsible for overseeing tremendous growth on the university campuses. One of her legacies was settling a twenty-year desegregation lawsuit in 1994. She defended the outcome against opposition from high-profile detractors like NAACP president Rupert Richardson. She maintained that keeping the school primarily African American was preferable to combining it with the other Louisiana public colleges and universities with one governing board. An outcome of the settlement involved changing Southern's admissions policy from one of open enrollment, which allowed anyone with a high school diploma to attend, to one of selective admission, which requires students to have either a 2.2 (in a 4.0 system) average from high school, or have a score of 17 on the American College Test (ACT), or have a combined score of 820 on the Scholastic Aptitude Test (SAT). When this policy was announced in 1996, a quarter of the student body enrolled at that time would not have qualified.

President Bill Clinton appointed Spikes to his Board of Advisors on Historically Black Colleges and Universities in 1994. In that capacity she advised both the president and his secretary of education on how to strengthen those institutions through federal programs and funding as well as private sector participation. In 1997 President Clinton named her a member of the U.S. Naval Academy Board of Visitors.

In early 1997 Spikes left Southern University to become the eleventh president of the University of Maryland Eastern Shore (UMES), an historically black university in Princess Anne, Maryland. This position put her closer to Washington, D.C., where she served on many committees and boards. At UMES she was instrumental in starting new programs and getting several new buildings constructed. Concerned about the issue of hazing in African American fraternities, Spikes called for strict punishments, including suspension for the victims and expulsion for those students responsible for carrying out the beatings. She believed that unless students had a reason to report the abuse, the "cycle of hazing" would continue (Paul, Karin, and Jamilah). Spikes served on countless committees, many pertaining to historically

African American institutions and issues of interest to women in academia. She was vice chair of the Kellogg Commission on the Future of State and Land-Grant Universities. From 1990 to 1992 she served on the Commission on Women in Higher Education, which advised the American Council on Education (ACE). Her other positions included vice chair (1990–1992) and chair (1993–1994) of the Council of Presidents/Chancellors of 1890 Land-Grant Institutions; director and elected class representative, Harvard University Institute of Educational Management (1987–1992); senior associate to the University of the North West, Mmabartho, South Africa; member of the National Agricultural Research, Extension, Education, and Economics Advisory Board, U.S. Department of Agriculture; and Louisiana representative on the Board of Directors of the Public Broadcasting Corporation (1995–1997). After she retired from UMES in 2002 for health reasons, Spikes was named a Kellogg Leadership Fellow and was appointed to the Louisiana Board of Ethics.

FURTHER READING

Dolores Margaret Richard Spikes, Ph.D., University of Maryland Eastern Shore, http://www.adec.edu/clemson/spikes_bio.html (accessed 29 July 2005).

"EM's Tribute to Black Women of Distinction," *Ebony Man* (Nov. 1989).

"Four UMES Students Arrested, Face Felony Charges," *Black Issues in Higher Education* 15, no. 7 (1998): 8.

Kenschaft, Patricia C. "Black Women in Mathematics," *Association for Women in Mathematics* 10, no. 3 (1980).

Kenschaft, Patricia C. "Black Women in Mathematics in the United States," *American Mathematical Monthly* 88, no. 8 (1981): 592–604.

Kenschaft, Patricia C. "Black Women in Mathematics in the United States," *Journal of African Civilizations* 4, no. 1 (1982): 63–83.

Paul, Ruffins, Chenoweth Karin, and Evelyn Jamilah. "Curing the Madness," *Black Issues in Higher Education* 15, no. 9 (1998): 16.

Sapp, Sherry. "Saying Goodbye," *Advocate*, 29 Dec. 1996.

ANN ZEIDMAN-KARPINSKI

Spiller, Isabele Taliaferro (18 Mar. 1888–14 May 1974), music educator and performer, was born Cary Isabele Taliaferro in Abingdon, Virginia, the daughter of Granville L. Taliaferro and Josephine Outlaw Taliaferro. She was educated in Philadelphia public schools, graduating from Girls

Commercial High School, then earned a teaching certificate from the New England Conservatory of Music (Boston). Her early professional experience remains obscure. In 1912 she joined a famous vaudeville act, the Musical Spillers, eventually marrying its leader, WILLIAM NEWMEYER SPILLER. The act was already a vaudeville favorite by this time, and soon she was touring with them throughout the Americas. Originally a trio, the act stabilized as a sextet, evenly divided between men and women, shortly before she joined.

Isabele Taliaferro Spiller remained with the Musical Spillers from 1912 to 1925, playing multiple instruments and acting as the primary teacher of new members of the band. The Spillers were best known as a saxophone ensemble, a novelty at the time, but under the highly disciplined regime established by its leaders, each of its members was also expected to master either the cornet (or trumpet) or the trombone, to play percussion instruments such as the xylophone, to dance (sometimes while playing a musical instrument), and to perform other vaudeville specialties. Such versatility was not unusual in show business at the time. The excellence with which the Spillers performed their synchronized routines won them great acclaim.

The Musical Spillers were as important as an academy as they were as a vaudeville act: a finishing school for talented youngsters. Isabele Spiller was the primary teacher and disciplinarian in her husband's ensemble, and was remembered as a stern, even ferocious, taskmaster by her one-time student and band member REX STEWART. Later a noted cornet soloist with the Duke Ellington Orchestra, Stewart joined the Spillers as a fourteen-year-old novice in 1921. Like the other band members, he was expected to excel at several instruments and serve as an all-around entertainer. The tightly drilled act was always impeccably arrayed in matching uniforms. Attendance at rehearsals, punctuality, hard work, and personal discipline were prerequisites for membership. Anyone keeping irregular hours or indulging in the temptations of night life was harshly disciplined, and usually immediately dismissed. The group performed carefully choreographed dances while playing, regardless of how large and heavy their instruments.

Isabele Spiller's career in show business was noteworthy but pales in significance compared with her later career as a music educator. This began in earnest in 1926, when she and her husband established the Musical Spillers School in their home in Harlem, a row house on West 138th Street. Spiller joined the National Association of Negro Musicians in 1926 and also joined the Negro Actors Guild during the 1920s. She also resumed her own musical education, enrolling at Teachers College at Columbia University to qualify for a teacher's certificate (1930). She also took private lessons with Melville Charlton, a leading African American organist. He had been her future husband's musical mentor a couple of decades earlier. The Spillers' pupils went on to win numerous prizes in competitions held by the Music Education League at Carnegie Hall and other leading venues.

William Spiller did not take as naturally to a settled existence as Isabele did, and he returned to the road as an entertainer in 1928, remaining an active performer through the 1930s. By 1928 Spiller had branched out well beyond her private school, becoming the director of music at the Brooklyn YWCA (a segregated institution) from 1928 to 1930, and then director of music at the Columbus Hall Center from 1929 to 1932. She was also active in musical life at the Concord Baptist Church of Christ.

During these years Spiller began to gain wider attention as the author of articles on music pedagogy. These were published in music educators' trade publications such as *Jacobs' Orchestra Monthly*, and also in such prestigious journals as *The Etude* and *The Metronome*. Among her publications were: "Balancing the School Orchestra," *Jacobs Orchestra Monthly*, August 1927; "Drum Instruction in Public Schools and How to Begin," *The Metronome*, November 1927; "A Well Balanced Symphony Orchestra in the School," *The Metronome*, January 1928; "Selecting an Instrument for the School Child," *The Metronome*, August 1928; and "The Rhythmic Educational Value of the Toy Symphony," *The Etude*, October 1928.

Spiller was already establishing herself as one of New York's significant music teachers by the early 1930s. Through her publications, she began to gain a nationwide profile as an expert on teaching music, particularly to children.

Spiller's career as an educator reached new heights during the New Deal era. She was a high-profile educator with New York's Federal Music Project from 1933 to 1941, as she proudly put it: "Supervisor of the 5 Boros of the Woodwind Brass & Percussion, which included Rhythm Bands, Drum, Fife, and Bugle Corps, Bands and Orchestra for the Federal Music Project." Another New Deal–related supervisory position took her to the Breeze Hill Civilian Conservation Corps Camp during 1936 and 1937. Spiller was also put in charge of the music education projects at the 1939 World's Fair in New York. She also found time to teach at the Moorland YMCA in Plainfield, New Jersey, from 1938 to 1940. During World War II she won a scholarship permitting her to further her education at the Juilliard School of Music, and she was appointed music chairman for the West Harlem-Riverside Neighborhood Council in 1942. Spiller was then named conductor of the Wadleigh Senior High School Orchestra, a post she held from 1942 to 1952. Her final major appointment was as the organizer and conductor of the Harlem Evening High Orchestra, from 1952 to 1958, after which she retired.

In her later years Isabele Spiller was the doyenne of Harlem's musical scene, by a wide margin its most famous music educator. By the time of her death at the age of eighty-six, she was a legendary figure in African American music. Her sole survivor was her sister Bessie Taliaferro (1889–1991); she had lived with Isabele in the Harlem home they bought with William Spiller in 1920, and had herself been a member of the Spillers act at one time.

While she was a noteworthy figure in African American vaudeville entertainment for fifteen years, in the end, Isabelle Taliaferro Spiller's greatest significance lies in the degree to which she professionalized musical training among African Americans. She served as a pioneer of the race at the highest levels of music education and an inspiration to several generations of music students.

FURTHER READING

There are two primary repositories of the papers of the Spillers: (1) Isabele Taliaferro Papers, Moorland-Spingarn Research Center, Howard University, Washington, D.C. and (2) The Isabele T. and William N. Spiller Papers, Schomburg Center for Research in Black Culture, New York Public Library.

Lotz, Rainer. "The Spillers." In *Black People* (1997). Details some of the Spillers's tours in Europe.

Stewart, Rex. *Boy Meets Horn* (1991).

ELLIOTT S. HURWITT

Spiller, William (4 May 1876–3 Sept. 1944), vaudeville entertainer, was born in Virginia, probably in Goodson (now Bristol). His father, Richard, was a minister and teacher; his mother, Mary Still, came from a distinguished New Jersey abolitionist family.

Spiller began his education in his parents' school, the Spiller Academy in Hampton, then went on to the Hampton Institute, a leading African American college. His most influential teacher there was Melville Charlton, later an important church organist and teacher in New York.

William Spiller joined the brass band of Mahara's Minstrels, under the leadership of W.C. HANDY, in 1899. Initially, Spiller played the alto horn (a brass instrument sometimes used in place of a trumpet or trombone) with Handy's band, but he soon discovered a tenor saxophone Handy had purchased, and, according to the latter, appropriated it for his own use. The tenor saxophone became the linchpin of Spiller's performing career for the next four decades. In the summer of 1900 Spiller was with Rusco & Holland's Big Minstrels playing the Midwest. In 1903 he was residing in Chicago, where he played in one of the first African American symphony orchestras, organized by the former regimental bandleader Nathaniel Clark Smith. This was one of the few performing ventures he went into that would have pleased his respectable parents; in becoming an entertainer, he opened a rift with this father that took years to heal.

In 1906 Spiller began touring at the head of a band which in its early years was called variously the Three Musical Spillers, the Three Spiller Musical Bumpers, and the Three Bumpers. Already in this early period the group was known for its versatility, comprising variously a saxophone trio, a brass trio, and a xylophone act. In this last configuration they won praise for their rendition of "St. Louis Rag" by TOM TURPIN. Their 1906–spring 1909 tours were limited to the northeast United States and Ontario, but in 1909–10 they began to cover the Midwest and West Coast as well. They received very positive write-ups, and their success was soon sufficient that they grew to a five-piece band. In 1908 SCOTT JOPLIN, the greatest ragtime composer, dedicated his classic "Pineapple Rag" to the group, which included Joplin's friend Sam Patterson from 1906 to 1910. From around 1909 to 1912 the act also included William "Cricket" Smith, a cornetist who like William Spiller had earlier worked with Mahara's Minstrels. He would later win fame in the bands of James Reese Europe and FORD DABNEY. In 1910 the group grew to its best-known configuration of six players, although this fluctuated widely over the decades to follow; at one point the act featured thirteen performers. Around 1911 the Spillers stabilized at six players, generally divided evenly between men and women.

In 1912 the Spillers band saw its most important personnel change with the addition of Isabele Taliaferro, whom William later married. The version of the group she joined was on the cusp of international headliner status. As reviewed in London in 1912, their eighteen-minute act was immensely varied, including Joplin's "Pineapple Rag" in a saxophone arrangement (the original was for solo piano), the sentimental song "Love Me and the World Is Mine," and the famous "Miserere" section from Giuseppe Verdi's opera *Il Trovatore*, all rendered in the syncopated style of ragtime. Contrary to an impression given by some later pianists, this was not a frenetic up-tempo pop music; like his friend Scott Joplin, William Spiller insisted that ragtime should be played at a moderate tempo to be properly appreciated. The reviewer for London's *Hippodrome* (Christmas 1912 issue), particularly praised the Spillers' harmonies, and remarked that "symphony must be the key-note to real Rag-time," a statement that highlights the harmonic cohesiveness of the group. The Spillers' effectiveness depended on the classical technique and ferocious discipline that the leaders instilled in their band.

Once they hit the big time, the Spillers became attractive to the impresarios (often themselves entertainers) of white vaudeville, their act being interpolated into longer variety shows. Among the mainstream outfits the Spillers toured with, they spent the longest stretches with the comedians Clark & McCullough (four years) and the juggler Jean Bedini (1919–1922). Some of these white acts spilled over into burlesque, which ranked lower in respectability than the vaudeville circuit, though the Spillers' propriety was never compromised. The Spillers appeared on bills with numerous "legitimate" white vaudeville headliners as well.

The Spillers were famous above all for their exceptional versatility; the ensemble could move with ease from a saxophone sextet to a three-cornet/three-trombone group, and its members were expected to sing, dance, and tell jokes as well. In addition William Spiller played xylophone solos with another member of the band accompanying him on the larger marimba, while the remainder of the ensemble formed a backing ensemble, at times consisting of multiple percussion instruments linked together across the stage. William Spiller was especially renowned for performing a trombone solo while dancing; having a gimmick of this type was essential in the highly competitive realm of vaudeville. The tightly drilled act was always impeccably arrayed in matching uniforms.

Attendance at rehearsals, punctuality, hard work, and personal discipline were prerequisites for membership. The act had to be highly organized: they traveled with so much baggage, ranging from costumes to the immense bass saxophone and marimba, that they needed their own baggage handler on the road.

The Spillers also became famous as a training ground for younger talent, described in the *Jacobs Band and Orchestra Magazine* as a "Circumnavigating Conservatory." One future jazz star who got his start with them was REX STEWART, later a cornet soloist with the Duke Ellington Orchestra. He joined the Spillers as a fourteen-year-old in 1921. The roster of performers in the Musical Spillers changed repeatedly during its long run. When Stewart joined, the personnel included the future big band-leader Willie Lewis on first alto saxophone, Seymour Todd on C-melody sax, Isabele Spiller on first tenor sax, Stewart on second tenor, Fred Pinder on baritone and bass saxes, and the leader William Spiller on bass sax. Eventually the group stopped calling themselves the Six Musical Spillers, as their number had more or less stabilized at seven members. The configuration of the band during a 1924 tour of upper New England and southern Canada was soprano, two alto, two tenor, baritone, and bass saxophones. This was the band at the end of its initial two-decade run; they disbanded in 1926, when William and ISABELE TALIAFERRO SPILLER founded a music school in their home in Harlem.

William Spiller was a highly respected figure in Harlem's musical circles. He was a founding member of the Colored Vaudeville Benevolent Association in 1909, and in later years he became an early member of the Negro Actors Guild. But unlike his wife, William Spiller was not content teaching, and he returned to the road in 1928. For most of the next decade he was peripatetic and appears not to have spent much time in the Harlem home he bought with his wife in 1920. William Spiller's tours during this last phase of his career took him repeatedly to Europe, with engagements in England, France, Belgium, the Netherlands, Switzerland, Germany, Italy, and Bulgaria. During 1930 he made London his home base; in 1932 he was resident in Paris. He also toured in Argentina, Brazil, and Uruguay during this period. Apparently he took ill during a final European tour; his last known performances were in Italy early in 1940. He lived out the remainder of his life in retirement in New York.

It is unfortunate that the Six Musical Spillers were never recorded, although this was the fate of many leading black entertainers of their time. It is possible that their music sounded something like that of the Six Brown Brothers, a saxophone sextet (white) who in all likelihood modeled their act on that of the black group. (The Brown Brothers recordings have been reissued on an Archeophone label CD.)

Only one original composition by Spiller is known, "New York Tango Blues" (1914) originally self-published, then taken up by the firm of Pace & Handy, cofounded by Spiller's friend and former bandmaster W. C. Handy. Its title takes commercial advantage of two of the most popular genres of the era. It is among the earlier pieces to feature the designation "blues" in its title, but exhibits, apart from some flatted notes, few of the salient musical features of what was becoming an important American musical form. It lacks the tango rhythm, despite its title. It is noteworthy that Handy's own "St. Louis Blues," which features a tango as the second of its three strains, appeared in the same year as Spiller's piece; also that at the time blues often referred to an up-tempo entertainment music and not (as is generally assumed today) a lugubrious, mournful music, but that Spiller's piece specifies that it be played slowly. Though published only in a solo piano version, the piece was no doubt performed as a saxophone sextet, in keeping with the photo on the sheet music's cover; it is easy to imagine such a band playing synchronized routines to the repeated chains of parallel octaves and thirds, perhaps with an air of mock seriousness.

The prime of William Spiller's career was almost entirely defined by the era in which the popularity of black vaudeville was at its height, roughly the first two decades of the twentieth century. Although he remained active in music until nearly the end of his life, by the 1930s his type of entertainment was very much a thing of the past. Yet in the years around 1910–15, when the idea of a saxophone ensemble was a new and exciting one, he was on the cutting edge of an entertainment wave that would make other, white performers, arguably his imitators, quite popular. Spiller pioneered the use of the saxophone as an entertainment vehicle; it would go on to become a ubiquitous instrument in jazz and soul music.

FURTHER READING
There are two primary repositories of the papers of Isabele T. and William N. Spiller: (1), Moorland-Spingarn Research Center, Howard University, Washington, D.C., and (2) Isabele T. and William N. Spiller Papers, Schomburg Center for Research in Black Culture, New York Public Library.
Lotz, Rainer. "The Spillers." In *Black People* (1997).
"Stage" pages of the *[Indianapolis] Freeman*, 1899–1924.
Stewart, Rex. *Boy Meets Horn* (1991).

ELLIOTT S. HURWITT

Spillers, Hortense J. (24 Apr. 1942–), literary scholar and writer of fiction, was born Hortense Jeanette Spillers in Memphis, Tennessee, the eldest child of Curtis and Evelyn (Taylor) Spillers.

She began her scholarly career at Melrose High School in Memphis, from which she graduated in 1960. She began her studies at Bennett College in Greensboro, North Carolina, to continue at Memphis State University, where she received both a B.A. in English literature (1964) and an M.A. in English and American literature (1966). Having grown up in a Baptist community, the African American sermon was to become a focus of her graduate work and after two years of teaching at Kentucky State College (now Kentucky State University) Spillers entered the graduate department of English and American literature of Brandeis University in the fall of 1968. There she continued her teaching throughout the period of graduate study, particularly in the African-American Studies program at Brandeis (1972–1973). Spillers also lectured in American and African American literature at Wellesley College in Massachusetts. On 17 May 1974 she completed her graduate studies and was awarded a Ph.D. for her dissertation, "Fabrics of History: Essays on the Black Sermon."

Full-time devotion to a career of scholarship followed with a joint appointment in English and black studies at Wellesley College, which she held for five years (1974–1979). Her career continued through appointments at the University of Nebraska (1979–1981); Haverford College in Haverford, Pennsylvania (1981–1988); Cornell University (1988–1990), where she was the Frederick J. Whiton Professor of English; and Emory University (1990). A major force in African diasporic literary and cultural criticism, she has taught in the English Department at Vanderbilt University in Nashville, Tennessee, since 2006.

She has been the recipient of various awards, among them the National Magazine Award for Excellence in Fiction and Belle Letters (1976), postdoctoral fellowships from the National Endowment for the Humanities and the School of Criticism and

Theory at the University of California in Irvine (1976), the Rockefeller Foundation (1980–1981), and the Ford Foundation (1985–1986). Professor Spillers was also Senior Fellow for a term at the Society for the Humanities, Cornell University (1988), and seminar leader and lecturer at the School of Criticism and Theory, Dartmouth College (1990).

Professor Spillers has emerged as a premier scholar of literary criticism and theory, with a focus on African American literature and studies of race and gender. Her essays, articles, and reviews have been published in various academic journals and anthologies and along with HENRY LOUIS GATES JR., Houston Baker, and Kimberly Benston, among others, Spillers has been a major force in shaping the direction of African American literary criticism since the 1980s.

Spillers's writings are noted for their insurgent spirit and compelling prose. In addition to her scholarly work, Spillers has engaged in political activism. Her 2002 article, "Inauguration Day 2001," appeared in the journal *boundary 2* and signaled a concern over American policy in the era of George W. Bush.

Professor Spillers has also produced scholarship on the black sermon, documenting it as a "mode of discourse by which African-Americans envisioned a transcendent human possibility under captive conditions" (Spillers, *In Color*, 84). She argues that the sermon, illustrative of the peculiar relationship blacks have to America given the country's legacy of enslavement, has imbued African American life with a grammar of its own: a symbolic order that emerged through an almost violent formation of identity, effected by the slave trade, which attempted to destroy African cultural practices. The structure of the sermon speaks to the experience of being black in the New World, as an oral and musical vernacular form (interestingly, *verna* translates into "slave" in Latin) encompassing the need to speak out against the silencing of African American people that is not wholly a phenomenon of the past. As a result, those of African ancestry in America are neither fully "here" as an American nor "there" as an outsider/African.

In *The American Grammar Book*, Spillers explores the "grammar" ordering the life meanings lives of black women in America, as well as those of mixed race. Interracial figures, Spillers argues, are neither/nor propositions without historic locus or materiality; they are identifiable only by their violent appropriation by dominating racial/sexual forces. What the interracial figure in general and the African American woman in particular paradoxically conceal and reveal are the strategies of violence (the master/slave encounter, for example) responsible for the experience of alterity that underwrites the experience of African Americans in the United States currently. Alterity, as a form of cultural unmaking, hearkens to the Middle Passage that in effect left enslaved persons, and especially women, suspended in anonymity.

Professor Spillers is the author of various texts that speak out against the distortion of blacks in America through both extensive readings and rewritings of the larger grammar of American history. In 1985 she and Marjorie Pryse edited *Conjuring*, a landmark anthology that showcased the most groundbreaking scholarship on black women's literature in its time, announcing black women's place in the annals and protocols of American literary history. Spillers's Afterword in this collection, entitled "Cross-Currents, Discontinuities," advocates poststructuralist flexibility in deriving a sense of black tradition. Spillers has further practiced the poststructuralist approach to literary history as a section editor for the much lauded *Norton Anthology of African American Literature* (1996), with editors-at-large Henry Louis Gates Jr. and NELLIE Y. MCKAY.

FURTHER READING

Abel, Elizabeth, Barbara Christian, and Helene Moglen, eds. *Female Subjects in Black and White: Race, Psychoanalysis, Feminism* (1997).
"Hortense Spillers." *Notable Black American Women, Book 1* (1992).
Lane, Christopher Lane, ed. *The Psychoanalysis of Race* (1998).
Reproduced in Biography Resource Center (2009). http://galenet.galegroup.com/servlet/BioRC.

ADEBE DERANGO-ADEM

Spinks, Leon (11 July 1953–), boxer, was born in the rough-and-tumble Pruitt-Igoe housing project in St. Louis, Missouri, to Leon and Kay Spinks. He was the oldest of seven children. It was not an easy upbringing. Violence in Spinks's neighborhood was endemic and after being mugged and bullied, he was given the nickname "Mess Over," in reference to the opinion that he was an easy target. Home was little better. His father, an absentee who finally vanished when Spinks was ten, was often physically abusive to his children, once hanging Spinks from a nail and beating him. Spinks's mother taught Bible classes

ALI		SPINKS
	AGE	
36		25
	*WEIGHT	
220		205
	HEIGHT	
6 ft. 3 in.		6 ft. 2 in.
	REACH	
80 in.		76 in.
	CHEST (Normal)	
44 in.		40½ in.
	CHEST (Expanded)	
46 in.		42 in.
	BICEPS	
15 in.		15½ in.
	WAIST	
34 in.		32¼ in.
	THIGH	
26 in.		24 in.
	CALF	
17 in.		15½ in.
	WRIST	
8 in.		7 in.
	FIST	
13 in.		12½ in.

*Estimated

The tale of the tape describes the matchup between world heavyweight champion Leon Spinks and challenger Muhammad Ali. The duo met for their championship bout in the Superdome in New Orleans, Louisiana, on 15 September 1978. (AP Images.)

out of the family home. When he was fourteen Leon developed an interest in boxing—in no small part as a means of self-defense—and, along with his brother Michael, became a frequenter of the local gym.

Spinks dropped out of school in the tenth grade and joined the U.S. Marines, with whom he continued his young fighting career as a member of the All-Marine Team. Stationed at Camp Lejeune, North Carolina, he soon developed a reputation as a brawler and an effective one at that. Spinks secured the Corps light heavyweight championship three times. His trademark gap-tooth smile was the

result of head butt during a camp smoker. Not long after the time of his enlistment, Spinks married a woman named Nova (maiden name unknown). The couple had three children. In one bizarre incident, he was mistakenly shipped out to Vietnam, where he spent two terrified weeks before being rerouted home and back to boxing.

In 1974 Spinks competed in the World Amateur Boxing Championships, that year held in Havana, Cuba. Spinks took a bronze medal in the light heavyweight division. Two years later, in 1976, he was selected to represent the United States in the

Summer Olympics games at Montreal, Canada. On the boxing team, he joined SUGAR RAY LEONARD and his own brother Michael. When the Spinks brothers both won gold, they made history as the first brothers to do so in the same event during the same Olympics. Following the games Spinks was granted an early hardship discharge. He was out of the Marines and ready to embark on his professional career.

A year later, in 1977, Spinks made his debut in Las Vegas against a slugger named Lighting Bob Smith. He won that first fight and went on to reel off a number of wins until, not much more than a year later, he found himself at the top of the ranks of potential heavyweight challengers. At the time the television networks broadcast fights quite regularly, and Spinks quickly became a familiar face. In 1978 he faced MUHAMMAD ALI in a Las Vegas title bout. Ali was widely considered past his prime and Spinks defeated him in a fifteen-round decision in which he badly outfought his opponent. Spinks had done what no other fighter had managed; he had taken a title belt away from Ali. After just eight professional bouts, he was the heavyweight champion of the world.

It was the highlight of a career that seemed to decline as quickly as it ascended. Shortly after his fight with Ali, Spinks began to run afoul of the police. Too much fame too quickly and too much partying and drugs brought trouble. He was arrested four times, once for possession. Within just a few months, Spinks refused to fight KEN NORTON, then the number-one challenger, and was stripped of his world championship title when the World Boxing Council (WBC) responded by taking back its belt. Meanwhile, Ali was demanding a rematch, and the two agreed to a bout with the WBA title on the line. The fight was held in New Orleans, Louisiana, on 15 September 1978, and this time Ali was better prepared for the much younger Spinks. He took back the title in a fifteen-round decision.

Spinks continued boxing. He was knocked out in the opening round of his only fight in 1979. Two years later he had another title shot, this time against LARRY HOLMES, but Holmes knocked him out in the third round. Most of the rest of his career was spent slugging it out with small-timers. He retired in 1995. For his career, Spinks held a record of twenty-six wins (fourteen by knockout), seventeen losses (nine by knockout), and three draws.

In 1990 Spinks's son, Leon Calvin (himself a professional fighter), was murdered in St. Louis in what appeared to be a gang-related shooting. Out of the fight game, Spinks drifted from job to job. He worked in one of former Bears' coach Mike Ditka's restaurants in Chicago, but soon lost that job for missing too many shifts. He was homeless for a time and often found himself in the local city shelters. He and his wife divorced and Spinks moved to Columbus, Nebraska, where he lived a quiet life, working in fast food restaurants and as a janitor at the local YMCA.

FURTHER READING
Doogan, Brian. "The Big Interview: Leon Spinks," *Sunday Times*, 1 Oct. 2006.
Grossfield, Stan. "Leon Spinks Is Down, Not Out," *Boston Globe*, 21 Dec. 2005.
"Leon Spinks: The 'Boy' Who Did a Man's Job on Muhammad Ali," *Ebony*, May 1978.

JASON PHILIP MILLER

Spinks, Michael (13 July 1956–), boxer, was born in St. Louis, Missouri, one of seven children born to Kay Spinks, an ordained minister, and a father of whom little is known. Michael's father was reportedly abusive, although elder brother Leon bore the brunt of his father's often brutal behavior. Spinks's doting mother barely kept the family together through welfare subsidies and teaching Bible school after her husband left the family in 1965.

Like Leon, Michael Spinks used his fists to fight his way out of his poor neighborhood in St. Louis. The tall and deceptively lanky Spinks fought as a middleweight in the amateur ranks, eventually amassing an impressive record of ninety-three wins and only seven losses, with a third of those victories coming through knockout. In 1975 he lost a close decision for the National Amateur Athletic Union (AAU) Middleweight Championship, but the next year he won both the National Golden Gloves Championship and a berth on the U.S. Olympic boxing team. He thus became part of what many have called the greatest U.S. boxing team in Olympic history. His teammates included his brother Leon Spinks (fighting as a light heavyweight), SUGAR RAY LEONARD, Leo Randolph, and Howard Davis Jr. Each of these fighters brought home a gold medal, and the U.S. team also picked up a silver and bronze medal at the games. Leon Spinks and Leo Randolph went on to become world champions after turning professional. Leon gained momentary fame in February 1978 by beating MUHAMMAD ALI for the heavyweight title. He lost it in a rematch with Ali seven months later. Michael Spinks won his gold medal with a technical knockout over a fighter from the Soviet Union. With nothing left to accomplish at the amateur level, Spinks became a professional boxer in 1977. After five fights and five wins against less than stellar opposition, Spinks quickly moved up to more difficult opponents. He decisioned Gary Summerhays in October 1977 and did the same to Tom Bethea in February 1978. At this point, however, his rise to the top was slowed somewhat by a nagging knee injury that would plague him the rest of his career. He fought just once more in 1978 and then did not have another bout until November 1979; both fights ended with Spinks's knocking out his overmatched opponents.

In 1980 Spinks came back with a vengeance. After two quick victories against unknowns, he rattled off a series of impressive wins. He decisioned future super middleweight champion Murray Sutherland, crushed former light heavyweight titlist John Conteh in nine rounds, and destroyed perennial contender Yaqui Lopez with just one punch in the seventh round. Spinks continued his rampage into 1981, battering three-time light heavyweight champ Marvin Johnson to the canvas in just four rounds. By this time, his lethal right hand had acquired its own nickname—the "Spinks Jinx." In July of that year, after just sixteen fights as a professional, Spinks was matched against the slick-boxing Eddie Mustafa Muhammad for the World Boxing Association light heavyweight title. Demonstrating that he was a fine boxer, and not just a puncher, Spinks floored Muhammad late in the fight and then cruised to a unanimous points victory.

Over the course of the next four years Spinks fought ten more times as a light heavyweight. He knocked out eight of the men he fought, including Murray Sutherland in a rematch, Jerry Celestine, Vonzell Johnson, Oscar Rivadeneyra, and Johnny Davis. In 1983, he engaged in his first "superfight," battling World Boxing Council king Dwight Braxton for the unified world light heavyweight championship. The "Camden Buzzsaw," as he was known, was a rugged fighter who usually wore down and eventually knocked out his opponents. Spinks confounded Braxton in the fight by turning in a brilliant display of jabbing and punching, and then quickly moving out of Braxton's punching range. Despite suffering a controversial knockdown in the eighth round, Spinks easily rolled to a unanimous decision and was now the undisputed light heavyweight champion of the world.

Spinks defended the unified title just four times in the next two years. In 1985, like so many light heavyweights before him, he decided to make the move to the bigger money available in the heavyweight division. Instead of taking some "tune-up" fights at the higher weight, Spinks underwent a strenuous program of physical conditioning and weight gain to prepare for the biggest fight of his life. In September 1985, he became the first light heavyweight champion in the history of boxing to successfully challenge for the heavyweight title when he out-boxed and out-hustled Larry Holmes for the International Boxing Federation championship. At the time, Holmes was considered the best heavyweight in the world and entered the fight with Spinks with a record of forty-eight wins and no defeats. In fact, one of the publicity angles of the fights was that Holmes would tie Rocky Marciano's record of 49-0 with a win over Spinks. Utilizing the same strategy he used against Braxton, Spinks moved in and out, alternately slugging and jabbing, and the much bigger Holmes became increasingly frustrated. Spinks earned a unanimous decision in what many called the upset of the year in boxing.

Spinks was now an undefeated heavyweight champion himself, with a record of twenty-eight victories and no losses. He gave Holmes a rematch in early 1986, and although the fight was closer, Spinks emerged with a split decision win. After a meaningless defense of the title in late 1986, Spinks gave up the IBF title to fight another superfight against Gerry Cooney. Cooney, who was unfairly labeled a "great white hope" by some sportswriters, was an awkward but powerful puncher who had earlier challenged Holmes for the heavyweight title. Any questions about how effective the "Spinks Jinx" would be against heavier opponents were erased when Spinks smashed Cooney to the canvas in five rounds.

By 1988, there was really only one fight left for Spinks, against the young and dangerous MIKE TYSON, who, by the age of twenty-two, had already captured the WBA, WBC, and IBF titles. The bout, such as it was, lasted only ninety-one seconds. Spinks came into the ring wearing a knee brace and the look of someone who was being led to a firing squad. A terrific blow from Tyson sent him crashing halfway through the first round and the fight was over.

Spinks wisely decided on retirement after the Tyson debacle, finishing with a splendid record of thirty-one victories and only one defeat. He briefly dabbled with a film career, appearing in the 1989 movie *Speed Zone!* Most of his time, however, was spent as a boxing promoter, working with his old manager Butch Lewis. In 1994, Spinks was elected to the International Boxing Hall of Fame. In 2002, *The Ring* magazine named him as the third greatest light heavyweight in the history of boxing.

FURTHER READING

Ashe, Arthur R. *A Hard Road to Glory: A History of the African-American Athlete since 1946* (1988).
"Leon Spinks Becomes a Somebody," *Time*, 27 Feb. 1978.
"Michael Spinks," *The Ring*, Sept. 2002.

MICHAEL L. KRENN

Spivey, Victoria (15 Oct. 1906–3 Oct. 1976), blues singer, songwriter, and record label founder, was born Victoria Regina Spivey in Houston, Texas, the daughter of Grant Spivey, a straw boss on Texas wharfs and a string player, and Addie Smith, a nurse. She was one of eight children in a musical family. Her father and brothers were members of a local string band, and her three sisters, Addie "Sweet Peas," Elton "Za Zu," and Leona, also were singers. Spivey began playing piano at an early age and soon was performing with various local groups, including Henry "Lazy Daddy" Filmore's Blues-Jazz Band and L. C. Tolen's Band and Revue. There followed appearances in vaudeville houses and theaters throughout Texas, Missouri, and Michigan. As a teenager she played piano for silent movies at the Lincoln Theater in Houston.

In 1926 Spivey went to St. Louis with the goal of meeting Jesse Johnson, a recording talent scout. After hearing her audition, Johnson awarded Spivey a contract to record four tunes for the Okeh label. One of them, "Black Snake Blues," a Spivey original, established her as a blues singer. Within the first month the record sold 150,000 copies, leading to a New York City recording date. Six Victoria Spivey discs were released in 1926 alone. Over the course of her career she would record on several other labels, including Victor, Vocalion, Decca, Bluesville, GHB, Folkways, and later in life, her own label, Spivey Records. Typical of Spivey's Texas singing style were off-tones, drops, moans, wails, and flat tones, which she used to great effect when performing. Often billed as "The Queen of the Blues" or as Queen Victoria Spivey, she collaborated, over the course of her career, with such stellar artists such as KING OLIVER, LOUIS ARMSTRONG, LONNIE JOHNSON, Porter Grainger, RED ALLEN, EDDIE DURHAM, J. C. HIGGINBOTHAM, SIDNEY DE PARIS, Lee Collins, LUIS RUSSELL, ALBERT NICHOLAS, POPS FOSTER, ZUTTY SINGLETON, Eddie Barefield, and MEMPHIS MINNIE.

Returning to St. Louis in 1927, Spivey worked as a staff writer for the St. Louis Publishing Company. That same year she appeared in the musical revue *Hit Bits from Africana* in New York City. In 1929 she made her film debut in the King Vidor film *Hallelujah*. She appeared in two other musical revues in those early years, *4-11-44* in New York City in 1930 and, on tour in Texas and Oklahoma, *Dallas Tan Town Topics* in 1933.

Spivey is believed to have had four husbands—among them, Reuben Floyd, whom she apparently married sometime around 1928 and with whom she remained until the early 1930s. However, her most significant marriage was to dancer Billy Adams, whom she married sometime around 1934 and with whom she had a long professional association until their relationship ended in 1951. Spivey and Adams performed in the highly successful Ole Olsen and Chic Johnson musical revue *Hellzapoppin* on Broadway in 1938–1939 and then on tour for an additional three and a half years. During the late 1930s and the 1940s Spivey and Adams worked the vaudeville circuit and appeared at various exclusive clubs, lounges, and theaters in Chicago, Cleveland, St. Louis, and New York City, including the Apollo Theater.

Spivey was comparatively inactive during the 1950s, but in the 1960s her musical career revived, and the decade was filled with various artistic endeavors. She toured widely, both in the United States and abroad, appearing at blues festivals, on radio and television, and on college campuses, and as a blues historian she contributed to *Record Research* magazine. Her most noteworthy accomplishment of the period, however, was the establishment of her own record company, Spivey Records, which reissued many of her own recordings, brought out of retirement other classic blues singers, in particular, LUCILLE HEGAMIN and ALBERTA HUNTER, and provided recording opportunities for a cadre of younger blues artists, with whom Spivey frequently shared recording sessions. Of the Spivey reissues, the most outstanding was *Victoria Spivey Recorded Legacy of the Blues* (1969), which features Spivey recordings made between 1927 and 1937 with the backing of trumpet greats such as King Oliver and Louis Armstrong.

Other highlights of Spivey's professional activity in the 1960s and 1970s included an appearance on "Lyrics and Legends" on New York television station WNET in 1963; at the American Folk-Blues Festival tour in England and Europe, also in 1963; at the Chicago Blues Festival in 1969; on the PBS show "Free Time" in 1971; and at the Philadelphia Folk Festival, broadcast on PBS in 1974. In the early 1970s she served as a blues adviser to the Conn Instrument Company of Chicago, and in 1976 she was featured in the BBC-TV documentary *The Devil's Music—A History of the Blues.*

A prolific songwriter (many of her songs were considered to be blues "tone poems"), Spivey contributed to the blues repertoire such titles as "Arkansas Road Blues," "Big Black Belt," "Blood Hound Blues," "Garter Snake Blues," "You're Going to Miss Me When I'm Gone," "No. 12, Let Me Roam," "Black Belt Blues," "Big Black Limousine," and "Organ Grinder Blues." According to one blues historian, "Spivey produced nearly 1,500 songs, many of them never credited to her" (Placksin, 33). During her final years, she was able to both inform and clarify for blues aficionados and researchers. Her recall faculties were excellent and she had lived through the various eras and had heard and often performed with the legends. In 1970 Broadcast Music Incorporated (BMI) awarded Spivey a Commendation of Excellence "for long and outstanding contributions to the many worlds of music." She died at the Beekman-Downtown Hospital in New York City. According to her obituary in the *New York Times*, she was survived by two daughters.

FURTHER READING

Bourgeois, Anna Stong. *Blueswomen: Profiles of 37 Early Performers, 1920–1945* (1996).

Harrison, Daphne Duval. *Black Pearls: Blues Queens of the 1920s* (1988).

Placksin, Sally. *American Women in Jazz, 1900 to the Present: Their Words, Lives, and Music* (1982).

Stewart-Baxter, Derrick. *Ma Rainey and the Classic Blues Singers* (1970).

Obituary: *New York Times*, 7 Oct. 1976.

This entry is taken from the *American National Biography* and is published here with the permission of the American Council of Learned Societies.

ANTOINETTE HANDY

Spottswood, Stephen Gill (18 July 1897–2 Dec. 1974), bishop of the African Methodist Episcopal (AME) Zion Church, was born in Boston, Massachusetts, the only son of Abraham Lincoln Spottswood, a porter, and Mary Elizabeth Gram. The family was religious. Spottswood received a B.A. from Albright College in Reading, Pennsylvania, in 1917 and a ThB from Gordon Divinity School in Boston

in 1919. He attended Yale Divinity School in 1923–1924. In 1919 he married Viola Estelle Booker; they had five children. That same year he joined the NAACP.

During the 1920s and 1930s Spottswood served as pastor of churches in Massachusetts, Maine, Connecticut, North Carolina, Indiana, and New York. During his tenure as pastor of John Wesley AME Zion Church in Washington, D.C., from 1936 to 1952, he enlarged the congregation from six hundred members to more than three thousand and became increasingly prominent in denominational circles. From 1947 to 1952 he was head of the Washington, D.C., branch of the NAACP. He served as the head of the AME Zion Home Mission Department and in 1952 was elected bishop of the Tenth Episcopal District. In 1953 his wife was killed in a fire in Washington.

In 1954 Spottswood became a member of the board of directors of the NAACP, and in 1961 he was elected chairman, initially to complete the term of ROBERT CLIFTON WEAVER. A moderate who emphasized economic betterment, Spottswood devoted many of his speeches and sermons to building a better society based on legislation and voting. He participated in sit-ins and boycotts aimed at desegregating public accommodations.

In 1969 Spottswood married Mattie Brownita Johnson Elliott. He retired as bishop in 1972, though he continued in the top leadership post of the NAACP until his death. Widely respected for his dynamic, compassionate leadership, personal warmth, and commitment to the quest for freedom and equality, he was best known for his keynote speeches at the opening sessions of NAACP national conventions, particularly his 1970 address in Cincinnati when he branded the presidential administration of Richard Nixon as antiblack. He died at his home in Washington.

FURTHER READING

Spottswood's papers are at the Amistad Research Center, Tulane University, New Orleans, Louisiana.

"Bishop Stephen Gill Spottswood," *Crisis*, Feb. 1975.

Kellogg, Charles Flint. *NAACP: A History of the National Association for the Advancement of Colored People* (1967, 1997).

Moore, Jacqueline. *Leading the Race: The Transformation of the Black Elite in the Nation's Capital, 1880–1920* (1999).

Obituary: *New York Times*, 3 Dec. 1974.

This entry is taken from the *American National Biography* and is published here with the permission of the American Council of Learned Societies.

MILTON C. SERNETT

Sprague, Rosetta Douglass (c. 24 June 1839–1906), activist, was born Rosetta Douglass in New Bedford, Massachusetts, the daughter of FREDERICK DOUGLASS and ANNA MURRAY DOUGLASS. Both of her parents—the man who would become America's most famous escaped slave and a woman who seems to have been born free—came from Maryland and were building a life in the North after her father's escape. The growing family moved to Lynn, Massachusetts, while Rosetta was still young.

Sprague's childhood must have been difficult. While all extant sources agree that her mother's focus was on her family and domestic circumstances, by 1845 her father, still a runaway, was an important African American in the abolitionist movement and was lecturing across the North. That status led to fears of capture, and he fled to England, where he stayed until his freedom was purchased. Left in Lynn, Anna Murray Douglass had to be, in essence, self-sufficient during his long absences; to support herself and her children, she took in shoes for binding. In addition to providing the essentials for her children, she seems to have loved them deeply.

Frederick Douglass, though, showing the first stirrings of a desire to "cultivate" his children, removed Sprague from her mother's care when she was seven and sent the young child to live in Albany, New York, with Abigail Mott and Lydia Mott, cousins of the abolitionist activists Lucretia Mott and James Mott. Soon after Frederick Douglass's return to the United States in April 1847, he moved to Rochester, New York, and the family—including Sprague—followed. In August 1848 Sprague passed the entrance examination for Lucilia Tracy's small Rochester school and, after her tuition was paid, began attending. Tracy did offer her instruction, but in the earliest example of pronounced racism she experienced, Sprague was not allowed to be in the same room with the other (white) pupils. Sprague and the other Douglasses were devastated, yet the other children were willing to accept her. Tracy seemed swayed by Frederick Douglass's urging to include her fully, but one parent objected. Rosetta was dismissed, leading to one of Douglass's most scathing early editorials.

As she grew into adolescence, Sprague was tutored privately and learned to negotiate the complex Douglass home. Frederick and Anna Murray Douglass's relationship became more distant, and Anna Murray Douglass had especial difficulties in the often racist Rochester. The British abolitionist Julia Griffiths entered the scene, seeming only to emphasize Anna Murray Douglass's slave background and illiteracy. Sprague grew to remember her mother as a disciplinarian during this period, and, in the midst of Douglass's affairs and the influences of Griffiths and later Ottila Assing, their relationship was sometimes strained. Sprague also filled the roles of reader and amanuensis for her mother, reading Frederick Douglass's letters and other documents and attempting to teach her mother to read. In the midst of this as well as Frederick Douglass's break with William Lloyd Garrison, his increasing national prominence, and his use of the home as an Underground Railroad station, the family also had to cope with the death of the youngest Douglass child, Annie.

Sprague had briefly attended the Oberlin College Academy in 1854 and, hoping to be a teacher, finally left Rochester in 1862. She began in Philadelphia, Pennsylvania, where she boarded with the family of the caterer Thomas J. Dorsey and taught in an African American school. Rosetta bridled under the Dorseys' strictness, struggled to balance teaching in a Sabbath school with her father's animus against the organized church, and seemed uncomfortable with most free African Americans (her dark skin color ostracized her from some elitist mulatto circles and her background and bearing from other free blacks). She left within the year. When Myrtilla Miner refused to hire her for her school for black children in Washington, D.C., Sprague moved to Salem, Massachusetts, where she stayed with the family of her mother's brother Perry Murray. Poor, Murray and his wife, Lizzie, shared many values with Anna Murray Douglass, and tensions finally drove Sprague from their home. She stayed only a bit longer in Salem, where she passed examinations to become a teacher and taught briefly. She returned to Rochester in 1863 and married Nathan Sprague.

Nathan Sprague led a troubled life. He served briefly in the Union army but won no distinction. The Spragues lived with Frederick Douglass until 1867, when Nathan purchased a house in Rochester. But he became almost immediately involved in a conflict over the title. He hoped to start a business as a hackman but failed quickly. Frederick Douglass eventually secured him a job in the post office, but he was caught removing the contents of the mail and imprisoned for a year.

The Spragues had seven children. At least at first, Rosetta Sprague was a hesitant mother, and Anna Murray Douglass cared for the first child, Annie, while Sprague managed her father's office. For a time in the late 1860s and early 1870s, Nathan's sister Louisa Sprague lived with the family and seems to have helped Rosetta Sprague, though Rosetta also seems to have spent at least some time with her mother. By 1872 the full family was living with Anna Murray Douglass, and they barely escaped the fire that destroyed the Douglass home.

Frederick Douglass, already leaning toward settling in Washington, D.C., gave up on Rochester. The Spragues stayed in Rochester through their daughter Alice's death in 1875, and in 1877 they too finally moved to Washington. Nathan Sprague continued to move from job to job and even went as far as Omaha, Nebraska, in 1879 in yet another scheme for success. Caring for her large family, constantly having to ask her father for funds, and dealing with her difficult husband, Rosetta Sprague suffered two more blows in the 1880s. Her mother was stricken with paralysis and then died on 4 August 1882. Less than two years later her father married the white woman Helen Pitts, of whom Sprague disapproved. Nathan Sprague dabbled in real estate, and Rosetta Sprague worked as a clerk in the register of deeds office, a patronage job secured by her father.

Sprague worked actively to educate her children. Her daughter Annie died in November 1893. Her four remaining daughters all taught for at least a time and became active clubwomen; her son Herbert worked for a time as a butler before becoming a painter. Sprague, like her daughters, became active in the African American club movement and other civic activities. In 1896 she was a founding member of the National Association of Colored Women (NACW), and her keynote address to this group's first meeting, "Anna Murray Douglass—My Mother as I Recall Her," remains one of the best extended discussions of Anna Murray Douglass; it was posthumously published in the *Journal of Negro History* (Jan. 1923). But much of the end of Sprague's life was distant from her father's fame; her grave in Rochester's Mount Hope Cemetery was not "rediscovered" until 2003.

Sprague is primarily remembered as her father's sometime assistant, for her role in founding the NACW, and for her memorial to her mother. She struggled throughout her life not only in the shadow of her father but also in the much larger shadow of racial discrimination.

FURTHER READING

Several of Sprague's letters, especially those to her father, are in the Frederick Douglass Papers at the Library of Congress.

McFeeley, William S. *Frederick Douglass* (1991).

ERIC GARDNER

Springer Kemp, Maida (12 May 1910–29 Mar. 2005), labor leader and Pan-Africanist, was born Maida Stewart in Panama, the daughter of Adina Stewart Carrington, a beautician, and Harold Stewart, a worker on the Panama Canal Zone project. At the age of seven she immigrated with her parents to the United States and settled in Harlem, and soon after they arrived, her parents separated. From 1923 to 1926 Springer attended the Manual Training and Industrial School for Colored Youth in Bordentown, New Jersey, a boarding school renowned for its teaching staff but encumbered by the industrial model of education advocated by BOOKER T. WASHINGTON. Not until 1927 did the school expand beyond its focus vocational training by offering a more academic curriculum that could lead to a high school diploma. The commandant of the school was LESTER GRANGER, with whom Springer would later share a friendship and working relationship when he served as executive director of the National Urban League from 1941 to 1961. Her science teacher and another later associate was WILLIAM HASTIE, who would become the first black judge to serve on the U.S. Court of Appeals. In 1928 Maida Springer married Owen Springer. The marriage ended in divorce in 1955 and produced one child, Eric Winston Springer, who became a cofounder of the first law firm with a national reach to practice exclusively in the health-care field.

Springer's childhood was imbued with the spirit of black protest. With her mother she regularly attended the meetings of MARCUS GARVEY's Universal Negro Improvement Association (UNIA) and observed the street-corner orations of black leaders protesting against lynch law, police brutality, and widespread discrimination and segregation. As a union leader with the International Ladies' Garment Workers' Union (ILGWU) in the 1930s, Springer would collaborate in civil rights and labor activism with two of the chief street-corner orators of her childhood, A. PHILIP RANDOLPH and FRANK CROSSWAITH. Randolph became head of the Brotherhood of Sleeping Car Porters in 1925 and a vice president of the American Federation of Labor and Congress of Industrial Organizations (AFL-CIO) in 1955, and

Crosswaith worked as an organizer for the porters' union and the ILGWU. Springer came to view the labor movement as a potential force for uplifting the status of all workers after listening to a speech given by Randolph in 1932, in which he extolled the benefits of interracial unionism despite the hostility of many white union members. In 1933, after Springer was cheated out of two weeks' pay by an employer, she joined the ILGWU's Local 22, the dressmakers' local, which later boasted a membership of thirty-two nationalities. Under the mentorship of Charles "Sasha" Zimmerman, the local's manager, Springer held various union offices including educational director, staff member of the Dress and Waistmakers' Joint Board, business agent, and labor organizer.

With her appointment in 1945 as a delegate on a goodwill labor exchange tour to England, Springer gained the distinction of becoming the first black woman to represent American labor abroad. However, the racism directed against her in the nation's capital during the preparatory meetings for the trip almost caused her to quit in anger. Known as a Southern city, Washington generally practiced segregation and exclusion toward blacks. Springer could not stay in a hotel with the white delegates or gain easy access to taxis and restaurants. MARY McLEOD BETHUNE convinced Springer to continue as a delegate by challenging her to remember the gains for black people that could ensue from this trip. Bethune herself was familiar with the challenges and benefits of activism—she was a close confidant of First Lady Eleanor Roosevelt, the head of the National Council of Negro Women (NCNW), and the director of the Negro Division of the National Youth Administration—the highest federal office held by a black woman up to that time. From 1970 to 1974 Springer would serve as a vice president of the NCNW. She was also a lifelong member of the NAACP.

While on her goodwill tour in England, Springer met GEORGE PADMORE, who was in the midst of preparations for the fifth Pan-African Congress, which was an organization that would define the tactics and strategies that African independence movements would soon inaugurate. Padmore was a leading theoretician for the anticolonial movements, and over the years he helped to integrate Springer into the Pan-African network. During this trip, Springer met Ras Makonnen, a financial backer of Pan-African movements, who introduced her to Jomo Kenyatta, the future president of independent Kenya. Kenyatta's challenging questions to her concerning U.S. workers' knowledge of Africa led Springer to devote herself to bringing about American labor support of African trade union development and anticolonialism. Many of the later AFL-CIO anticolonial resolutions have the imprint of her influence through her collaboration with Randolph, a strong advocate for African affairs on the AFL-CIO council.

Springer first visited Africa in 1955, when she traveled to Ghana, serving as an AFL observer. She did not have the higher status of a delegate since she was not an ICFTU representative, or an African trade unionist and the only woman attending a seminar on African workers issues held by the International Confederation of Free Trade Unions (ICFTU), the non-Communist International Labor Organization. After Springer attended the 1957 ICFTU African Regional Conference and served, in the same year, as a special AFL-CIO representative in East Africa, she gained a wide reputation as an advocate for African aspirations and as a valued labor consultant. Because she was older than most of her young African labor colleagues, Springer was affectionately called "Mama Maida." From 1960 to 1966 she worked for the AFL-CIO as an international representative and became a principal liaison between African labor movements and the AFL-CIO and an advocate for African independence. She worked particularly closely with Julius Nyerere, the future president of Tanzania, as well as Rashidi Kawawa, head of the Tanganyikan federation of labor and later vice president and prime minister of Tanzania, and Tom Mboya, head of the Kenyan Federation of Labor and later a government minister and putative successor to Kenyatta as president, before he was assassinated in 1969. Among the labor educational programs and projects for which she was responsible while working with the AFL-CIO, the Institute of Tailoring and Cutting, a Kenyan trade school established in 1963, has had the greatest long-term impact, through its focus over many years of upgrading the skills of thousands of garment workers.

Springer's work bolstered the reputation of the AFL-CIO on the African continent, particularly in comparison to the European unions that many Africans deemed as compromised by colonialism. However, the coming of independence and the popularity of the nonaligned movement resulted in African nations shifting away from the Cold War constrictions of the West, and Springer's influence began to wane as African labor movements, under pressure from their governments, disaffiliated from the ICFTU.

In 1965 Springer married James Horace Kemp, a prominent Chicago labor leader who would serve as national president of the NAACP just before his death in 1983. She returned in the mid-1960s to the garment workers as the general organizer for the Southeast region, and from 1969 to 1973 she worked as Midwest director of the A. Philip Randolph Institute in Chicago, helping to expand voter education and registration in general. Springer Kemp returned to international affairs in the late 1970s, as a staff member of the African-American Labor Center (AALC), an AFL-CIO regional institute, and as an AFL-CIO consultant. One of her most challenging tasks with the AALC was serving as drought program coordinator for the seventeen affected West African countries in the Sahel.

Springer Kemp was recognized internationally by other labor leaders as a role model who could bring more women into the labor movement. In 1977 she helped to coordinate the first Pan-African Conference on the Role of Trade Union Women, and from 1977 to 1981 she worked with the Turkish Federation of Labor to establish a women's bureau. In 1979 in Indonesia she participated in putting together a seminar for women workers that was designed to increase female activism. During the last years of her life, Springer Kemp turned to the children of Africa. During the 1990s in Tanzania she established a scholarship in her mother's name to help girls who had no other means to continue in school. She also helped to raise money for the Maida Fund, an AFL-CIO–sponsored program established in 2000 with a grant from UNITE, the successor union of the ILGWU, to help East African children, often AIDS orphans, quit dangerous and exploitative agricultural work and return to school.

Maida Springer Kemp is known for the integrity and fortitude with which she, a black female, approached the challenging task of working in a male-dominated and often racist labor movement during the turbulent years of the cold war. Her legacy of activism in civil rights, Pan-Africanism, women's leadership development, and workers rights is a testament to the eclectic nature of her humanitarian efforts and to her abiding belief in social justice.

FURTHER READING

Murray, Pauli. *The Autobiography of a Black Activist, Feminist, Lawyer, Priest, and Poet* (1987).

Orleck, Annelise. *Common Sense & A Little Fire: Women and Working-Class Politics in the United States, 1900–1965* (1995).

Richards, Yevette. *Maida Springer: Pan-Africanist and International Labor Leader* (2000).

Richards, Yevette. *Conversations with Maida Springer: A Personal History of Labor, Race and International Relations* (2004).

YEVETTE RICHARDS JORDAN

Spyglass, Elmer (1 Nov. 1877–16 Feb. 1957), singer, instrumentalist, diplomat, was born in Springfield, Ohio. The exact circumstances of his birth and upbringing are uncertain. Spyglass himself once gave his year of birth as 1878; but on another occasion, he mentioned it as being 1877. Elmer was not the natural child of his mother, Elizabeth Spyglass (born Elizabeth Johnson in Kentucky in 1843); he was probably adopted by Elizabeth and her husband, the blacksmith Augustus Spyglass (born in Jefferson County in 1846).

At age five, Augustus taught his son to play organ at the local church, and Elmer later joined the choir. At age ten, he spent the money he earned as a rose-picker on sheet music and music lessons. In 1897 he graduated from Springfield High School and sang at the graduation ceremony. That same year he became cofounder of St. John's Baptist Missionary Church and directed the choir. He worked as a waiter, a catering employee, and a packer in order to earn money for further training. He organized an amateur choir and conducted it before an audience at Pittsburgh's Carnegie Music Hall (probably the first African American to do so). From 1905 to 1906 Spyglass studied at the Toledo Conservatory of Music. Sponsors collected the $400 he needed to travel to Europe for further voice studies in Germany.

In 1906, upon arrival in London, he was out of money and was forced to sing in music halls (the English equivalent of American vaudeville) for a living. From then on he toured these music halls of Europe as an entertainer and concert singer, accompanying himself at the piano. He appeared in Brussels, London, and Berlin; in Paris he performed with Sarah Bernhardt and Mistinguett, known as "Queen of the French Music Hall." He also had appearances in Italy, Hungary, Austria, Belgium, the Netherlands, and Romania. Also in 1906 he married Mary Alice Stewart (born on 11 July 1878 in Springfield, Ohio). The marriage did not last, and Mrs. Spyglass returned to her mother in 1912.

Spyglass's performances were apparently always well received; a typical review would read much like the following one he received in Germany: "J. Elmer Spyglass is an interesting and amusing negro. This American baritone has a very pleasing and powerful voice and his grotesque comic is not repulsive but pleasing. His song, which he delivered right in the middle of the audience, went down very well, as did his negro folk songs, accompanied by his own piano" (Oberbreyer, *Der Artist*, 13 Apr. 1913, 1470). In 1914, the year his mother passed away, Spyglass paid a brief visit to his family in the United States.

Despite the war, he immediately returned to Europe in the company of his widowed father in 1915. He resided in the Netherlands during World War I. During this period, several music-sheet covers featured his photo, including the 1919 composition "Waardeering," for which he provided words, music, and a dedication to the Dutch people who provided him safe haven during the war. He worked from his base at Rotterdam until 1925, when he resumed his touring schedule, beginning with stints in Germany and Switzerland, then Scandinavia.

Around 1931 he would retire from his singing career and settle in Frankfurt am Main in Germany. In 1939 he moved to Nice, France; but upon the outbreak of World War II, he returned to Germany to access his savings he had invested there. According to his own testimony he was never maltreated; although, as an American citizen, he had to make weekly reports to the police after Germany declared war on the United States in 1941. After his home in Frankfurt was destroyed during an Allied bombing raid, he moved to nearby Schwalbach. When Frankfurt was taken by the U.S. Army in 1945, he served as a translator for the occupation forces and, in 1946, became receptionist at the U.S. Consulate. The 3 November 1947 issue of *Life* magazine covered Spyglass in a lengthy illustrated article that detailed his experiences in Germany and his work for the Consulate.

In 1952 the U.S. Consulate celebrated Spyglass's seventy-fifth birthday. On this occasion he broadcasted in German for the Hessischer Rundfunk radio station, headquartered at Frankfurt am Main, and for the Armed Forces Radio Network in English. On 9 November 1954, when Spyglass was seventy-seven years old, the city of Schwalbach made him an honorary citizen. Elmer Sypglass died at his home in Schwalbach, shortly before his eightieth birthday. The funeral took place at the Frankfurt central cemetery. According to his last will and testament, his ashes were taken to Yellow Springs near Springfield, Ohio, where he was laid to rest next to his mother's grave.

Spyglass is one of many talented African American artists whose dream to conquer the concert stage never reached fruition. Because of his years spent in Europe Spyglass had become conversant in many languages besides English, including Dutch, Flemish, French, Italian, Danish, Spanish, and various German dialects. He performed in all those languages a repertory that consisted of African American material (spirituals, most notably), as well as European folk songs, popular tunes, *lieder*, operetta tunes, and even operatic arias. He always maintained a dignified appearance. Although he had lived as a black American alien in racist Nazi Germany during the war, the U.S. occupation forces in Frankfurt were satisfied that he was a thoroughly honorable gentleman who had always been loyal to the Allied cause.

FURTHER READING

Lotz, Rainer E. *Black People: Entertainers of African Descent in Europe and Germany* (1997).

Lotz, Rainier E. "Elmer James Spyglass: Singer, Instrumentalist and Diplomat—An Update (parts 1 and 2)," *Doctor Jazz* (Dec. 2006, and Mar. 2007).

Martin, Peter, and Christine Alonzo, eds. *Zwischen Charleston und Stechschritt—Schwarze im Nationalsozialismus* (2004).

RAINER E. LOTZ

Stagolee (16 Mar. 1865–11 Mar. 1912), the archetypal "bad man" of song, toast, and legend, was born Lee Shelton somewhere in Texas. Shortly after Shelton murdered William "Billy" Lyons in 1895, blues songs began to appear recounting the event, giving rise to the figure of Stagolee. Little is known about Shelton's origins and childhood except the name of his father, Nat Shelton. The date of his birth is known only from his prison death certificate. The elegant style of his signature in his arrest records suggests that he had some schooling. Although he became the mythical Stagolee—a "bad mother" who shot somebody just to see him die—Lee Shelton was of ordinary stature. Prison records describe him as being five feet, seven and one-half inches tall. His hair and eyes are described as black, his "complexion" as "mulatto." Under the column "marks and scars," the authorities listed the following: "L[eft] eye crossed. 2-scars [on] R[ight] cheek. 2 scars [on] back head. 1-scar on L[eft] shoulder blade" (Brown, 38).

The *St. Louis Star-Sayings* of 29 December 1895 refers to Lee Shelton as "Stag" Lee; the coroner's report on Lyons calls him "Stack" Lee. The name "Stag" carries connotations of male sexual potency, but it also has associations with "Stagg Town," which was widely used to refer to a black settlement or district, especially one characterized by poverty, crime, vice, and prostitution. Alternatively, or additionally, Shelton's nickname may be related to that of the *Stack Lee*, a riverboat belonging to the Lee Line. Given the reputation of the riverboats for gambling, high living, and prostitution, this too has fitting connotations for Shelton. The trisyllabic versions of his name, spelled variously as Stagolee, Stagger Lee, Stackalee, Stackerlee, and Stack-o-lee, probably derive from the rhythmic requirements of the ragtime and blues in which the story was first couched.

In *Gould's St. Louis Directory* for 1894, "Stack L. Shelton" is listed as a waiter living at 1314 Morgan Street. In 1897 he appears as "a driver," living in a-somewhat better neighborhood on North Twelfth Street. Some years later, the *St. Louis Post-Dispatch* called him "formerly a Negro politician" and said he was the "proprietor of a lid club for his race" (17 Mar. 1911). A "lid club" was an establishment that "kept a lid" on such criminal activities as gambling, while serving as a front for other illegal activities, including prostitution. At least until 1911, Shelton ran the Modern Horseshoe Club on Morgan Street, in the city's red-light district. There is no reason to doubt that he ran the club as a gambling saloon, and its name certainly suits his profession as a driver. As a carriage driver, or "hack-driver," Lee Shelton would have been able to direct both black and white male visitors to St. Louis to their choice of bordello. The most prestigious underworld nightclubs in "Deep Morgan" were the Chauffeurs Club, the Deluxe Club, the Jazzland Club, the Cardinal's Nest, and the Modern Horseshoe. By the 1920s these were also the best blues clubs in the city. It is no wonder, then, that "Stagolee" is a blues song, since Lee Shelton was himself the owner of a famous blues café.

On Christmas night 1895, according to eyewitnesses, the extravagantly dressed Shelton entered the Bill Curtis Saloon on the corner of Morgan and Thirteenth streets and asked, "Who's treating?" Someone pointed out Billy Lyons, and the two drank and laughed together until an argument began, during which Shelton grabbed Lyons's derby hat and broke the form. Lyons in turn grabbed Shelton's hat—identified in many of the songs as a Stetson, the very symbol of masculinity. Shelton demanded his hat back, and Lyons refused. Shelton pulled his .44 revolver and hit Lyons on the head with it. According to an eyewitness, George McFaro, Lyons then pulled out a knife and taunted Shelton, "You cockeyed son of a bitch, I'm going to *make* you kill me." Shelton backed off, took aim, and shot. He walked over to the dying Lyons, said, "Nigger, I told you to give me my hat," snatched his hat, and walked out (Brown, 21–24).

The *St. Louis Star-Sayings* suggests that the killing may have been "the result of a vendetta" (29 Dec. 1895). Five years earlier a stepbrother of Lyons had killed a friend of Shelton's. Further motivation may have arisen from the rivalry of various politically motivated "social clubs" organized ostensibly for the moral uplift of young black men. Shelton was leader of the recently formed Four Hundred Club, with Democratic Party ties, and Lyons had connections with a group led by Henry Bridgewater, a prominent black Republican and saloon owner. Motive, however, is not a problematic theme of the Stagolee blues; indeed, most versions focus on the mere taking of his hat as the catalyst that provokes Stag's deadly reaction. Even the suggestion of the bluesman Mississippi John Hurt that it was a magic hat goes beyond the necessities of the mythical narration. The archetype of "badness" needs no deeper rationale.

Shelton was arrested at three o'clock on the morning of the 26th. By Friday, 27 December, he had hired a white lawyer, Nat Dryden, one of the best lawyers in St. Louis (although an alcoholic and an opium addict), and the first lawyer in Missouri to gain the conviction of a white man for murdering a black. At an inquest that day, Judge David Murphy signed a warrant against Shelton for first-degree murder. After being bound over to a grand jury on 3 January 1896, Shelton was released on a four-thousand-dollar bond, a considerable sum in 1896. The trial began on 15 July, during which Dryden argued that Shelton shot Lyons in self-defense. Three days later, after twenty-two hours of deliberation, the jury was unable to agree on a verdict. Shelton was again released on bond and apparently returned to running the Modern Horseshoe.

Nat Dryden died after a drinking binge in August 1897, before a second trial was held. There are no records of that second trial, but on 7 October 1897 Shelton began a twenty-five year sentence at the Missouri State Penitentiary. He was paroled on Thanksgiving Day 1909, but two years later he was in trouble again, "accused of robbing the home of

William Akins, another Negro, last January, beating Akins on the head with a revolver and breaking his skull" (*St. Louis Post-Dispatch*, 17 Mar. 1911). Shelton was sentenced to five years and returned to prison on 7 May 1911. When he reentered prison, he was suffering from tuberculosis and his weight dropped to 102 pounds. Under pressure from other Democrats, Governor Herbert S. Hadley granted the weakened Shelton another parole; however, the Missouri attorney general objected, and Shelton died in the prison hospital on 11 March 1912.

But well before he died, Stagolee himself may have heard the song that gave rise to his mythic status. One version was collected in Memphis in 1903, and in 1911 hoboes were singing a version in Georgia. A circus performer heard it in the Indian Territory in 1913, at about the same time a white youngster hunting with his father heard Negroes singing it in Virginia's Dismal Swamp. Indeed, the rapid spread of these songs exemplifies the workings of the oral tradition, and different details—the name of Shelton's wife or girlfriend (Lilly or Nellie), the name of the judge, even the name of a bartender who witnessed the shooting—survive in different renditions. In evidence of its widespread popularity among black and white audiences, several jazz and dance orchestras, including Fred Waring's Pennsylvanians, recorded versions in the early 1920s. In its opening stanzas, Mississippi John Hurt's 1928 classic blues rendition captures perfectly the tone of the implacable heartlessness of its hero: "Police officer, how can it be? You can arrest everybody but cruel Stagolee. That bad man! O, cruel Stagolee. Billy de Lyons told Stagolee, 'Please don't take my life, I got two little babes and a darlin' lovin' wife.' That bad man! O, cruel Stagolee. 'What I care about your two little babes, your darlin' lovin' wife? You done stole my Stetson hat, I'm bound to take your life.' That bad man! O, cruel Stagolee. "Stagolee" became a staple of the blues repertoire and has been recorded by over two hundred musicians in styles ranging from blues to jazz, R&B, and rock and roll, including versions by MA RAINEY (1925), DUKE ELLINGTON (1927), CAB CALLOWAY (1931), BIG BILL BROONZY (1946), SIDNEY BECHET (1946), Lloyd Price (1959), JAMES BROWN (1967), the Clash (1979), and Bob Dylan (1993). In the Jim Crow atmosphere of the early twentieth century, Stagolee became a trope for the resentment felt by people marginalized by the dominant white society. For over a century, Stagolee has remained a symbol of rebellion—oppositional, subversive, underground, and largely invisible—as part of the unofficial subculture of prostitutes, gamblers, criminals, and other "undesirables" (Brown, 120). The tale is variously told, but the character of Stagolee continues to exemplify what it is to be "bad," whether "bad" is meant as a compliment or an insult.

FURTHER READING

Barlow, William. *Looking Up at Down: The Emergence of Blues Culture* (1989).

Brown, Cecil. *Stagolee Shot Billy* (2003).

CECIL BROWN AND
JOHN K. BOLLARD

Staines, Ona Maria Judge (c. 1774–25 Feb. 1848), slave of President George Washington, was the daughter of Andrew Judge, a white indentured servant who came to North America from England in 1772, and an enslaved woman named Betty. Andrew Judge worked at the Washingtons' Mount Vernon estate for a term of four years before becoming free. Betty was originally a slave of Martha Washington's first husband. Upon his death and Martha's subsequent marriage to George Washington, Betty came to Mount Vernon, where she met Judge. Though Ona's father was free, the children of slave women in Virginia were, as virtually everywhere else in the New World, legally considered the property of their owners and remained in bondage.

Betty was an expert seamstress for the Washington family. Like her mother, Ona Judge was assigned to work in the Washington mansion performing domestic duties, and she learned sewing skills from her mother. She became such a skilled seamstress that George Washington described her as being "a perfect mistress of her needle" (Gerson, 2). Judge's status as a slave grew because of her skills. She eventually became Martha Washington's personal servant. Though her living conditions were better than those who worked in the fields at Mount Vernon, Judge was by no means satisfied with her position; she received no formal education and was never taught to read. Once Washington became president, the family residence alternated between New York, Philadelphia, and Mount Vernon during the year, and Judge was forced to be away from her family and friends for extended periods. However, Judge was most troubled by the fact that she would always remain a slave, knowing that upon the death of the president and his wife she would become someone else's property. This was a burden she was not willing to bear.

Ona Judge made her bid for freedom in May or June 1796 during Washington's final months in office in Philadelphia. The timing was perfect; the Washington household was a beehive of activity for the move back to Mount Vernon, and it would be easy for Judge to escape from the Executive Mansion in such a diverse city as Philadelphia. Judge also had support in Philadelphia of free blacks whom she had come to befriend during her time there. She realized that once back in the South, such an opportunity would be much more difficult. In preparation for her flight, Judge took her belongings to a friend's house beforehand. She left the Executive Mansion forever one evening while the Washingtons were having dinner. By the time her absence was noticed, Ona Judge had already gained passage on the merchant sloop *Nancy*, commanded by Captain John Bowles of Portsmouth, New Hampshire. Whether or not Bowles knew that she was a runaway slave is unknown, but it seems likely that he did; Judge stated in 1845 that she "never told his name till after he died, a few years since, lest they should punish him for bringing me away" (Adams). By July 1796, Ona Judge was living in Portsmouth as a free woman.

Though it is unknown whether Judge chose a ship heading to New Hampshire by design or by chance, her choice proved sound; Portsmouth had a vibrant African American community led by such individuals as Cuffee Whipple, the brother of Revolutionary War veteran PRINCE WHIPPLE, and a number of other well-established families. By 1797 Judge met and married a black mariner named John Staines and they had two children: Eliza and Nancy, the latter perhaps named after the vessel that carried Judge to freedom.

Ona Staines's continued freedom was not a certainty. The Washington family discovered her whereabouts, and in November 1796 George Washington wrote to Portsmouth's collector of customs, Joseph Whipple, requesting his help, even the use of deception if needed, to have Ona Staines returned. Whipple politely refused to help, but in 1798 Washington sent his nephew, Burwell Bassett Jr., to Portsmouth to persuade her to return. Though the two met in person, Staines adamantly refused to return to Mount Vernon. When Bassett returned yet again to take her by force, she was warned of his arrival by New Hampshire senator John Langdon and fled to nearby Greenland, New Hampshire. There she found refuge with the free black family of John and Phillis Jack. JOHN JACK was a Revolutionary War veteran, while Phillis was a midwife who may have presided at the birth of Staines's first child. Ona Staines remained with the Jacks until Bassett left Portsmouth empty-handed.

Though Staines returned to her home in Portsmouth for a few years, when her husband perished at sea in 1803, she moved back to the Jack household and lived there as a free woman for the remainder of her days. Though Staines's years of freedom were financially difficult, when she was questioned about this late in life, she responded that "I am free and have, I trust, been made a child of God" (Adams).

In addition to the drama of her successful escape, the life of Ona Judge Staines is also significant because it demonstrates in a very personal way the flaws of our nation's founding fathers. No matter what is written in the Declaration of Independence and the Constitution, the true intent and thoughts of its great creators were ambiguous at best when it came to freedom and equality for people of color. The Washingtons certainly valued and may have had a personal regard for Staines, but the man who freed America from British rule could not see fit to give her the personal freedom she desired.

In her last years, Ona Staines, who outlived her own daughters, remained with the Jack daughters. Impoverished, she was supported by the town of Greenland in her remaining years. Upon her death she was buried in the Jack family cemetery in a peaceful spot of land that has now reverted to wilderness.

FURTHER READING

Adams, Rev. T. H. "Washington's Runaway Slave, and How Portsmouth Freed Her," *Frank W. Miller's Portsmouth New Hampshire Weekly*, 2 June 1877.

Blassingame, John W., ed. *Slave Testimony: Two Centuries of Letters, Speeches, Interviews, and Autobiographies* (1977).

Gerson, Evelyn. *Ona Judge Staines: Escape from Washington* (2000), http://seacoastnh.com/blackhistory/ona.html.

Wiencek, Henry. *An Imperfect God: George Washington, His Slaves, and the Creation of America* (2003).

GLENN ALLEN KNOBLOCK

Stakeman, Randolph (12 Dec. 1949–), educator, scholar, and documentary filmmaker, was born in Brooklyn, New York, the elder child of Randolph and Evelyn (Turnipseed) Stakeman. He had one sister, Gail. Dr. Stakeman's father was a building superintendent; his mother was a bookkeeping clerk until 1960. Then, from 1961 to her death in 1993, Evelyn Stakeman fostered dozens of children, including young women and their babies.

Stakeman attended New York City public schools through tenth grade; then completed two years at Phillips Exeter Academy in Exeter, New Hampshire. He received his bachelor of arts degree from Wesleyan University in 1971 and his masters from Stanford University in 1976. He completed his Ph.D. in history at Stanford in 1982.

When an undergraduate, Dr. Stakeman took European, American, and African history during the same semester. Each course covered the same time period, allowing him to see relationships between wide-ranging world events. The knowledge that not only are all things changed from place to place but that they are all interrelated guided his teaching and scholarship throughout his career.

He married Catherine Jackson in 1973. They had one son, Jackson, born in 1981. Catherine was a social worker for several years, an assistant professor of social science at the University of Southern Maine, and then became the executive director of the Maine Chapter of the National Association of Social Workers. His son Jackson was a freelance photographer and documentary filmmaker.

From 1978 to 1982, while writing his doctoral dissertation, *The Cultural Politics of Religious Change: A Study of the Sanoyea Kpelle in Liberia*, Stakeman was an instructor of history at Bowdoin College in Brunswick, Maine. After attaining his doctorate he was made assistant professor of history at Bowdoin, being promoted to Associate Professor of History in 1988. He was the Director of the Africana Studies Program for sixteen years, from 1989 until his retirement in 2005.

Dr. Stakeman's research took him to Africa several times. His first trip was to the Republic of Liberia on the west coast of Africa where he gathered information for his Ph.D. dissertation. His later research concentrated on the African American influence on United States foreign policy in black countries such as Liberia and Haiti. His work revealed the NAACP's active lobbying in the 1920s that exposed abuses in Haiti, influenced the 1920 U.S. presidential election, and eventually precipitated the country's eventual pull-out from Haiti. He was unable to return to Liberia when that nation suffered political crises.

Dr. Stakeman considered his work at Bowdoin College to be one part teaching and one part scholarship. As he and his wife met other members of Maine's African American community such as GERALD TALBOT, that state's first black legislator, he felt an obligation to tell their virtually unknown stories. In articles, papers, and presentations he used demographic statistics from federal censuses to bring to life the social and economic realities of the early black population in Maine, enlightening blacks and whites alike to the state's diversity.

Later Dr. Stakeman compiled the names of Maine African Americans together with the towns in which they lived from the federal censuses. His *A Black Census of Maine 1800–1910* was printed in draft form June 1997 and soon became an important resource for academic researchers and genealogists alike.

In 1999 Dr. Stakeman helped set up a study abroad program for Bowdoin College in Cape Town, South Africa. The course work was designed to give students an opportunity to work for the public good while obtaining real world experience. South Africa was new to multiracial democracy, which was simply laid over the country's previous apartheid structure. Dr. Stakeman taught the first group in 2000, endeavoring to help students, many of whom were white, contact blacks in a country where the races were still largely separated. He returned in 2003 and 2005.

During his six-month stay in South Africa in 2003, Dr. Stakeman saw an exhibit at the Naval Museum in Simon's Town that told the story of forced removal of the black and mixed-race communities after the town was declared "whites only" in 1967. Always quick to use technology to supplement classroom teaching, he made a documentary with his son, Jackson, to illustrate how those displaced overcame the psychological and economic effects of relocation. *Heritage Day* won the 2007 Emerging New England Documentary Artist Award at the Woods Hole Film Festival.

Before his retirement from Bowdoin College, he partnered with his son to make a film about the Mellon Mays Undergraduate Fellowship Program. The program encourages underrepresented minority groups to become academics by pairing students with faculty mentors. Dr. Stakeman and his son visited twelve campuses where they talked to students, program alumni, and staff. Campuses ranged from Heritage University on the Yakima Indian Reservation in Toppenish, Washington, to Harvard University. The film was an important tool in supporting the program and attracting participants.

In 2008, Dr. Stakeman explored multiculturalism in another documentary. *Azalech and Me* documented the adoption of a young Ethiopian, Azalech, by minister Ann Lovejoy Johnson and how that action affected Johnson's mostly white congregation at St. Phillip's Episcopal Church in Wiscasset, Maine.

Although retired from Bowdoin College, Dr. Stakeman saw an opportunity to create a working model of his "blended teaching" methods that integrated online tools with classroom teachings. In the fall of 2008 he designed and taught *The Racial Argument in Historical Perspective*, a course in argumentation and critical thinking. The first year seminar covered key points in American history including slavery, American Indians, nonwhite minorities, Japanese American internment during WWII, the civil rights movement, ending with that year's Barack Obama presidential campaign. He shared with Bowdoin staff his multimedia approach of merging new technologies with traditional college teaching, helping the school remain relevant to tech savvy students.

Throughout his career Dr. Stakeman chose to actively educate his students and the general public about multicultural issues in positive and innovative ways, whether educating Mainers about their rich black history by analyzing early census records page by page, facilitating minority participation in academia through video, or teaching teachers to use the Internet effectively.

Dawn Staley balances a ball on her finger during practice in Raleigh, N.C., on 17 March 2007. (AP Images.)

FURTHER READING

Stakeman's *The Black Population of Maine, 1764–1900* and *The Cultural Politics of Change: A Study of the Sanoyea Kpelle in Liberia* are available at the Bowdoin College Library, Brunswick, Maine. Further information regarding Dr. Stakeman is available on the Bowdoin College Web site at http://www.bowdoin.edu.

Price, H. H., and Gerald E. Talbot. *Maine's Visible Black History: The First Chronicle of Its People* (2006). Web site available at http://www.visibleblackhistory.com.

BARBARA A. DESMARAIS

Staley, Dawn (4 May 1970–), professional basketball player, college coach, author, and foundation president, was born Dawn Michele Staley in Philadelphia, Pennsylvania, to Clarence and Estelle Staley. The youngest of five children, Staley grew up playing sports with neighborhood boys on the streets of North Philadelphia.

Staley enjoyed success at every level of athletic competition, beginning with her high school basketball career. She led Dobbins Tech to three Philadelphia Public League titles and was named *USA Today* Player of the Year during her senior season in 1988. Staley went on to the University of Virginia, where she led the Cavaliers to three National Collegiate Athletic Association (NCAA) Final Four tournaments in her four seasons in Charlottesville. Standing only five-feet six-inches tall, Staley relied on her quickness, intelligence, and unmatched intensity to succeed as a point guard. She was named National Player of the Year in 1991 and 1992. She graduated from Virginia in 1992 with a degree in rhetoric and communication studies. At the time of her graduation the United States did not have an established women's professional basketball league, so Staley played professionally in Italy, France, Brazil, and Spain from 1992 to 1995. The American Basketball League for women was founded in 1996, and Staley was assigned to the Richmond Rage in the first round of the draft. She ended her three-year stint in the ABL ranked third in career assists. Staley was one of the first high-profile players to defect to the newly formed WNBA in 1999. Staley's professional basketball career continued after the WNBA was established, as she was selected by the Charlotte (North Carolina) Sting in the first round. Being a player with a marquee name, Staley played an integral part in the early success of the league. Displaying her versatility as a player, she came within one rebound of recording the league's first triple-double when she had thirteen points, ten assists, and nine rebounds in a game at Detroit during her first season. She was named to the Eastern Conference All-Star team during the 2001, 2002, and 2003 seasons. In addition to her on-court success Staley participated in many service activities in the Charlotte area. In recognition of her work in this area, 24 July 2004 was named Dawn Staley Day in Charlotte by the city's mayor.

As Staley was enjoying success in her professional career, she was also becoming one of the most successful women in U.S. Olympic history. During the 1996 Olympic Games in Atlanta, Georgia, Staley won the first of her three Olympic gold medals. She averaged 4.1 points and 3.5 assists per game as the U.S. women's team cruised to Olympic gold. Staley went on to win her second gold medal at the 2000 Olympic Games in Sydney, Australia. The crowning achievement of her Olympic career came when she was selected to serve as the flag-bearer during the opening ceremonies at the 2004 Olympic Games in Athens, Greece. Citing her outstanding service to the U.S. Olympic team, the captains of fourteen different teams selected Staley as the person to lead the entire U.S. delegation into the stadium. In recognition of her years of international competition, she was named to the USA Basketball Executive Committee in 2005. She had been involved with fifteen USA Basketball teams since being named to her first squad—the 1989 USA Women's Junior World Championship Team.

Because Staley viewed education and athletics as vehicles for social change, she sought to provide academic and athletic opportunities for at-risk youth in North Philadelphia, and in 1996 she created the Dawn Staley Foundation. The foundation's programs were geared toward eleven- to fourteen-year-old girls who, like Staley herself, come from disadvantaged backgrounds. The foundation's After School Program provided literacy and computer classes, health-education workshops, and field trips. The foundation also sponsored a summer basketball league and a year-round mentoring program. Staley's concern for the well-being of young women took a literary form as well when she wrote a series of books, loosely based on her life, designed to inspire young women to find their passions and to make healthy lifestyle choices.

Given Staley's desire to mentor youth, it was only natural for her to turn to coaching. In 2000 Staley assumed the role of head coach of the women's team at Temple University, located just blocks from her childhood home. The challenge was a formidable one as Staley took over a struggling program. Prior to Staley's tenure as head coach, the Temple women's team had not had a winning season in the previous ten years. Staley did not take long to turn the program around, and the team posted a 19-11 record during her first season. During the 2003–2004 season she led the Temple University Owls to their first NCAA tournament win in the program's history. During that season the Owls had a twenty-five-game winning streak and was ranked number fifteen in the country, the highest-ever for the women's program. At the conclusion of the 2004–2005 season Staley was named the Atlantic 10 Coach of the Year for the second straight year.

Through her foundation and her work at Temple University, Staley had an indelible impact on the lives of many young women in Philadelphia and beyond. Philadelphia, in return, recognized and honored Staley for these achievements. In 1997 she became the first woman to receive the prestigious John Wanamaker Award, an award given annually to the Philadelphia-area athlete, team, or organization that has excelled in their respective sport. Staley joined boxer JOE FRAZIER and former Phillies pitcher Steve Carlton as the only two-time award winners when she was selected a second time in 2005. In addition Staley was given a larger-than-life tribute that touched her deeply. On the corner of Eleventh and Market Streets, five miles from her childhood home, a seven-story mural of Staley was painted on the side of a building. The mural was a fitting tribute to this consummate role model and educator, a person who was a consistent voice for improving the lives of the city's youth.

FURTHER READING

Cherner, Reid. "Staley: Dream Believer," *USA Today*, 7 Dec. 2004.

Grundy, Pamela, and Susan Shackelford, *Shattering the Glass: The Remarkable History of Women's Basketball* (2005).

Smallwood, John. "Dawn's Dream a Reality," *Philadelphia Inquirer*, 14 Apr. 2005.

THOMAS A. MOGAN

Stallings, George Augustus, Jr. (17 Mar. 1948–), church founder and former Catholic priest, was born in New Bern, North Carolina, the oldest of six children of George Augustus Stallings Sr. and the former Dorothy Smith, a convent housekeeper. Stallings's early upbringing took place in the Catholic faith, but his grandmother introduced him to black Baptist worship, which led him to aspire to become a Protestant preacher. His mother, however, persuaded him to become a Catholic priest. He completed Asheville Catholic High School and later matriculated at Saint Pius X Seminary in Erlanger, Kentucky, where he was awarded a B.A. in philosophy in 1970. Later that year Stallings enrolled at the North American College in Italy. In Rome he obtained three degrees from the Pontifical University of Saint Thomas Aquinas: an STB in 1973, an M.A. in pastoral theology in 1974, and a STL in 1975.

In 1974 Stallings was ordained at Our Lady Queen of Peace Church in Washington, D.C. He served as associate priest there for two years, the first of three pastorates he held in Washington. In 1976 he was given full pastoral charge of the Saint Teresa of Avila parish. At Saint Teresa, Stallings restructured the worship service by introducing a gospel choir and a painting of Christ as a black man and preaching like a Baptist preacher. By injecting more African American culture into the liturgy Stallings was following the dictates of the Second Vatican Council (1962–1965) that encouraged Catholic clergy to be more sensitive to native cultures.

Stallings was also inspired by religious developments in the United States. In using a gospel choir he was following in the footsteps of Father William L. Norvel's Saint Benedict the Moor Church, the first black Catholic parish in the Washington area to organize a gospel choir. Similarly Albert Cleage Jr. had been widely promoting the idea that Jesus Christ was black through his book *The Black Messiah* (1968). By 1969 Father James Patterson Lyke of Memphis's Saint Thomas Church was already celebrating Christmas with a black baby Jesus.

Like many other black ministers, Stallings addressed the social needs of the community by serving on the boards of MUSCLE (Ministries United to Save Community Life Endeavors), a housing development corporation, and CONSERV, an organization that served the homeless. His growing reputation led him to serve for one year as president of the National Black Catholic Clergy Caucus. Under Stallings Saint Teresa grew from two hundred to two thousand members and became highly regarded in Catholic circles. In 1988 he went to Rome for further study but returned early and was not reassigned to Saint Teresa, as he had wished. James Cardinal Hickey, archbishop of Washington, appointed him director of evangelism for the archdiocese. Stallings kept asking for to be reassigned to a parish, but Cardinal Hickey put his request on hold after receiving allegations of sexual

misbehavior with young boys against Stallings. Then he told Stallings he would not be reassigned to a parish until he sought medical care, which Stallings refused to do. Disappointed Stallings announced plans to open his own church and on 21 June 1989 Cardinal Hickey fired him as evangelism director and banned him from celebrating the Eucharist throughout the Washington area.

Stallings opened Imani Temple African American Catholic Congregation (*imani* means "faith" in Swahili) in Southeast Washington on 2 July 1989. Stallings publicly maintained that racism in the American Catholic Church had compelled him to establish the temple; however the *Washington Post* in its 4 September 1989 issue publicly revealed that a former altar boy at Saint Teresa alleged that he had sexual relations with Father Stallings, which was denied by the priest. Those revelations would later hurt Stallings's ministry and cause a decrease in membership at Imani Temple. Stallings's initial vision was to offer American blacks a version of Roman Catholicism that integrated African culture, African American gospel singing, and Baptist-style preaching. Imani Temple's inaugural service drew seventeen hundred people and experimented with a liturgy that included the summoning of ancestors and a gospel choir from Saint Teresa. Within a few months two Imani Temples were operating in Washington and one more in Norfolk, Virginia. In January 1990 Stallings canonized Dr. MARTIN LUTHER KING JR., making him the first saint of Imani Temple. The previous August, Bruce Edward Greening from Norfolk became the first Catholic priest to join Imani Temple and he later opened the second Imani Temple in Washington.

In early 1990 Stallings was a suspended priest but still a member of the Catholic Church. He further enraged the Catholic hierarchy by publicly endorsing birth control and abortion, optional celibacy for priests, ordination of women, remarriage without annulment of the previous marriage, and elimination of the sacrament of penance. These new developments led Hickey to excommunicate Stallings and forced Greening to leave Stallings and return to the Roman Catholic Church with his three hundred parishioners. Pockets of African American Catholics were willing to try a black version of Catholicism but not at the risk of severing connections with Rome.

In 1990 Stallings was consecrated bishop by Richard Bridges of the Old Catholic Church, a predominantly white breakaway group. In September 1991 Stallings ordained Rose Marie Vernell, a former nun, as priest, and in that same month he himself was elevated to the rank of archbishop by Bridges. Despite his progressive orientation, Stallings proved unable to rally vast throngs of African Americans. Many were disappointed with his handling of fiscal matters and his radical liturgical innovations and troubled by the sexual allegations made public against him.

Between July 1989 and April 1990, church attendance at Stallings's local parish fell from two thousand to nine hundred and fifty. In late 1991 Trevor D. Bentley, slated to open an Imani Temple in Los Angeles, withdrew from the Stallings movement. Bentley rejected the practice of ancestor invocation that he associated with Vodun, and he was troubled that Stallings never produced financial statements. Similarly, Stallings broke ranks with Bridges when Bridges consecrated a black priest as bishop without his approval. In doing so Archbishop Stallings made himself the sole ruler of his denomination.

Stallings supported the Million Man March, a rally for black men that Minister LOUIS FARRAKHAN of the Nation of Islam organized in Washington on 16 October 1995. He ran unsuccessfully for councilman in 1997 and 1998. On 27 May 2001 he married twenty-four-year-old Japanese woman, Sayomi Kamimoto, who is the mother of his two children. By the end of 2006 Imani Temple had reported thirteen congregations in Louisiana, the District of Columbia, Maryland, Philadelphia, and Virginia.

FURTHER READING

Dedman, Bill, and Laura Sessions Stepp. "Priest, 300 Parishioners Quit Stallings," *Washington Post*, 9 Feb. 1990.

Gonzales, Enrique J. "Stallings to Declare Dr. King a Saint," *Washington Times*, 12 Jan. 1990.

Hyer, Marjorie. "Cardinal Bars Priest from Saying Mass; Stallings is Warned about Black Parish," *Washington Post*, 25 June 1989.

National Office for Black Catholics. *This Far by Faith: American Black Worship and Its African Roots* (1977).

"Rift in Stallings's Ranks," *Christian Century*, 6 Nov. 1991.

"Stallings Ordains Woman," *Christian Century*, 18–25 Sept. 1991.

Stepp, Laura Sessions, and Bill Dedman. "Ex-Altar Boy Says He Had Sex with Stallings; 1977 Relationship Lasted Months, Man Alleges," *Washington Post*, 4 Sept. 1989.

Stepp, Laura Sessions, and Bill Dedman. "Concerns about Stallings's Lifestyle Fueled Conflict," *Washington Post*, 30 Apr. 1990.

DAVID MICHEL

Stallworth, John (15 July 1952–), football player, was born Johnny Lee Stallworth in Tuscaloosa, Alabama. Stallworth grew up in Tuscaloosa playing baseball, basketball, and football in his neighborhood on a daily basis. However, Stallworth liked football best and was "always upset when football season was over" (O'Donnell). Despite his love for the game, Stallworth was not initially a gifted athlete because of pigeon toes that plagued him through the fifth, sixth, and seventh grades. He had to practice relentlessly in those pickup games to hone his skills and credits a book he read in ninth grade about a misfit who through perseverance became a hero. When he was a freshman at Tuscaloosa High School, his biggest influences were the University of Alabama's athletic program and the civil rights movement. Attending a high school that had been integrated only three years before his arrival, Stallworth described this time as "a little scary," citing fans watching games waving Confederate flags (Sauer). Despite this, Stallworth credited his team and school for forging unity and camaraderie across racial lines.

Stallworth's persistence paid off when he played football in college at Alabama A&M University. By the time he left for the NFL in 1974 Stallworth was the Bulldogs all-time leading receiver. He hauled in 103 career passes including 48 for 925 yards as a senior. Some of the highlights of his college career were being named All-Southern Intercollegiate Athletic Conference twice, catching passes for 261 yards in one game against Fisk, and being named Black College All America in 1973. When Stallworth was drafted in 1974, Alabama A&M honored him by retiring his jersey.

Stallworth was drafted by the Pittsburgh Steelers in the fourth round of the 1974 National Football League Draft. Widely considered among the best draft classes of all time, the Steelers 1974 draft included Stallworth and fellow Hall of Famers Lynn Swann, Jack Lambert, and Mike Webster. On 25 May 1974 Stallworth married Florastein Caudle; the couple would have two children, Johnny Lee Jr. and Natasha.

After serving as an understudy for one year, Stallworth was able to harness his leaping ability into success on the football field starting in his second season. Stallworth had an amazing NFL career by any standard. He played in six American Football Conference Championship games and enjoyed all four of the Steelers' legendary Super

Bowl victories in 1975, 1976, 1979, and 1980, scoring the winning touchdown in Super Bowl XIV in 1980 against the Rams with a memorable 73-yard touchdown. Stallworth holds Super Bowl records for average yards per catch (24.4 yards) and single game average (40.33 yards), both set in Super Bowl XIV. He played in four Pro Bowls in 1980, 1983, 1984, and 1985 and was voted Steelers MVP twice.

Despite his lengthy NFL résumé, Stallworth was the last member of the 1974 class voted into the Hall of Fame, finally inducted in 2002. Some claimed that Stallworth's lifetime statistics of 537 catches for 8,723 yards did not measure up to other Hall of Famers' statistics. Ultimately, however, it was the memorable quality of Stallworth's acrobatic catches that cemented his spot in the Hall of Fame. An indispensable part of the Steelers 1970s dynasty, Stallworth was inducted into the Hall in front of 20,000 fans, along with Jim Kelly, Dave Casper, Dan Hampton, and the late George Allen. After at last receiving validation from the Hall of Fame, Stallworth stated that: "With this recognition, I can put that part of my life to rest. There are no battles left to fight, no doubts left to remove, no unrealized expectations, and I thank God for that."

After he retired from the NFL, Stallworth began a new career that proved to be almost as successful as his playing on the field. In 1986, one year before he retired from the NFL, Stallworth, his wife Flo, and his business partner Sam Hazelrig started a company called Madison Research Corporation in an effort to make a successful run as government contractors. In 1997, after a decade of hard work, Madison Research was named one of the 500 fastest-growing companies in the United States, Stallworth was selected as the Small Business Administration's 1997 Regional Small Business Person of the Year, and in 1998 Madison won the Better Business Bureau's Torch Award for Business Ethics.

By 2007 Madison Research had operations in nine states throughout the country and employed over 650 people. Its annual revenue was more than $56 million dollars. The company held a number of coveted government contracts, including several with the military to maintain computers at the U.S. Army Space and Missile Command's Simulation Center in Alabama.

Stallworth's business success enabled him to provide students from historically black colleges (such as his alma mater, Alabama A&M) with internships to prepare them for the marketplace. Furthermore, Stallworth's company and its partners offered the students opportunities both to see how a large corporation operates and to get some hands-on experience.

FURTHER READING

Blount, Mel, with Cynthia Sterling. *The Cross Burns Brightly: A Hall-of-Famer Tackles Racism and Adversity to Help Troubled Boys* (1993).

Blount, Roy, Jr. *About Three Bricks Shy ... and the Load Filled Up: The Story of the Greatest Football Team Ever* (2004).

Chastain, Bill. *Steel Dynasty: The Team That Changed the NFL* (2005).

Mendelson, Abby. *The Pittsburgh Steelers: The Official Team History*, updated ed. (2005).

O'Donnell, Chuck. "From the Sandlots to the Shrine: For John Stallworth and the Rest of the Class of 2002 the Call to the Hall is a Culmination of Boyhood Dreams," *Football Digest*, August 2002.

Sahadi, Lou. *Super Steelers: The Making of a Dynasty* (1980).

Sauer, Patrick J. "How I Did It: John Stallworth, CEO, Madison Research," *Inc.com*, August 2006, http://www.inc.com/magazine/20060801/hidi-stallworth.html.

Wexell, Jim. *Tales from Behind the Steel Curtain* (2004).

DANIEL A. DALRYMPLE

Stance, Emanuel (1847–25 Dec. 1887), farmer, soldier, and Medal of Honor recipient, was born free in Carroll County, Louisiana, the son of sharecroppers. His parents' names are unknown. Before his enlistment at the age of nineteen as a private in the army, Stance worked crops like his parents, but as he later noted, farming did not agree with him. As a member of the Ninth U.S. "Buffalo Soldiers" Cavalry Regiment fighting in the Indian Wars in Texas, he became the first African American soldier after the Civil War era to receive the Medal of Honor for bravery and leadership.

Stance learned to read and write during his childhood or teenage years. He may have received some schooling in Freedmen's Aid Society Schools, which opened their doors during the early years of Union occupation of Civil War Louisiana, or perhaps later in Freedmen's Bureau schools during Reconstruction. In 1866 Stance left the fields of Carroll Parish and headed for New Orleans. It appears from Ninth Cavalry regimental returns that Stance, along with a large number of other field hands, joined the military at Lake Providence, Carroll Parish, on 2 October 1866 for an initial five-year enlistment.

The U.S. Army was recruiting black men for a new cavalry regiment to be designated the Ninth U.S. Cavalry Regiment. On 28 July 1866 Congress enacted legislation reorganizing the army to add six new African American regiments, including two cavalry and four infantry units. Following in the Civil War tradition, the army created segregated units. Enlisted men and noncommissioned officers in the new army regiments were to be black, while all officers would be white. On 3 August 1866 the Adjutant General's Office in Washington, D.C., ordered Major General Philip Sheridan, commander of the Department of the Gulf, to raise recruits for the Ninth Cavalry at a recruitment center in New Orleans. Army recruiters fanned out across the state from August to November looking for able-bodied men to fill out the ranks of the Ninth Cavalry. Repeated crop failures, waves of yellow fever and typhoid epidemics, bleak economic opportunities, and violent race relations between freed people and whites in Louisiana meant the recruiters had little difficulty finding volunteers, and Stance would have been an especially attractive prospect because of his literacy. From the regimental returns and enlistment papers of his fellow recruits, it appears that few of these new soldiers were literate. Stance may also have been promised rapid promotion for enlisting. He was promoted to sergeant in Company F by March 1867. He stood just over 5 feet 1 inch tall at the time of recruitment, and this also would have stood him in good stead as recruiters desired volunteers who would not weigh heavily on army horses.

Stance survived epidemics that swept the ranks of the Ninth Cavalry Regiment as well as a riot between black noncommissioned officers and white commissioned officers in the first few months of the new regiment's existence. Despite these setbacks, the regiment continued to organize, and at the end of March 1867 the regiment was transferred to Texas for its first frontier posting. Indian uprisings were breaking out throughout Texas and New Mexico that year, and the various companies (or troops, as they were unofficially called) of the Ninth Cavalry were spread among several different forts in Texas. Posted at Fort Davis in eastern Texas, Sergeant Stance proved to be an excellent leader, and more responsibilities were put on his shoulders by the officers of the Ninth Cavalry during 1867. He gained valuable combat experience leading small groups of enlisted men independent of white officers. In the fall of 1867 Stance led his first cavalry patrols against Indian raiders, again without the presence of white officers. From 1867 to 1869 Stance

and the enlisted men of Company F were engaged in almost constant patrols and skirmishes with Apache, Comanche, and Kiowa Indians.

The officers of the Ninth Cavalry stationed at Fort Davis recognized Stance's superb military talents and increasingly relied on him to command small patrols of six to ten men in the surrounding countryside. This recognition may have led them to overlook or excuse a darker side of Stance's personality that was emerging. The sergeant was proving to be an extremely strict disciplinarian, given to violence against enlisted men under his command, and he was gaining a reputation for temper. In 1869 he received a court-martial for a physical altercation with an enlisted man in the Fort Davis stables. It was the first of a series of infractions of military justice by Stance resulting in courts-martial, fines, and reprimands throughout the remaining eighteen years of his military career.

In 1870 Sergeant Stance and Company F, under the command of Captain Henry Carroll, were transferred to Fort McKavett, Texas, on the San Saba River. Company F was responsible for safeguarding mail delivery, protecting ranchers and their herds of cattle and horses, and guarding supply trains running between Fort McKavett and other forts. Of special importance was protection of Kickapoo Springs, twenty-six miles north of the fort, where there was a mail and stage station and where local ranchers watered their herds. Early in May local Indians became active in stealing horses. By Special Order Number 73, issued on 19 May, Sergeant Stance and a detachment of ten men from Company F were ordered on patrol along Kickapoo Springs to stop the raids.

According to Stance's 26 May report of his patrol, on 20 May he spotted a band of Indians moving into nearby hills with a herd of stolen horses. Stance ordered his detachment to charge, and after a brief skirmish, the Indians fled without the horses. The detachment rounded up nine horses, and Stance resumed his march toward Kickapoo Springs, where he camped for the night. Early the next morning he decided to return to Fort McKavett with the stolen horses. Just ten miles into their southern march the detachment spotted a band of twenty to thirty Indians preparing to attack a team of government contractors driving a herd of horses to resupply Fort McKavett. Once again Sergeant Stance ordered his detachment to charge. This time the Indians decided to make a stand and fight for the herd. However, as Stance states in his report, "I set the Spencers [carbine rifles] to talking and whistling about their ears so lively that they broke in confusion and fled to the hills." For the next eight miles, while the detachment escorted the government team, the soldiers engaged in running gun battles against the Indians, with Stance leading repeated mounted charges to drive off the Indians.

Captain Carroll sent a recommendation to the headquarters of the Military Division of the South that Sergeant Stance receive the Medal of Honor for his bravery and leadership during the Kickapoo Springs patrol. On 24 July 1870 Stance acknowledged receipt of his Medal of Honor. Over the next sixteen years he continued to serve well in the field with the Ninth Cavalry in Texas, New Mexico, and Nebraska. However, when not in the field, he ran into trouble for drunkenness, fighting, or other unsoldierly conduct and was repeatedly reduced in rank for this behavior.

In 1885 Company F was assigned to Fort Robinson, Nebraska, and Stance stayed out of trouble just long enough to be promoted to first sergeant in Company F. Unfortunately, it was not long before troubles started again in Company F, and there followed a series of brawls, fights, and incidents of insubordination during 1886 and 1887. On 25 December 1887, while walking back to Fort Robinson from Crawford, Nebraska, where he had celebrated leave, Stance was shot and killed by unknown parties. His body was found by a guard patrol early Christmas morning, and it was widely believed by officers and enlisted men of the Ninth Cavalry stationed at Fort Robinson that he was killed by a fellow soldier or soldiers of the regiment. The murder was never solved.

FURTHER READING

Stance's report on the patrol for which he won the Medal of Honor is Sergeant Emanuel Stance to Lieutenant B. M. Custer, Post Adjutant, Fort McKavitt, Texas, 26 May 1870, Records of the Adjutant General's Office, 1780's–1917: Letters Received, 720–S–1870 (Record Group 94), National Archives and Records Administration Building, Washington, D.C.

Kenner, Charles L. *Buffalo Soldiers and Officers of the Ninth Cavalry, 1867–1898: Black and White Together* (1999).

Leckie, William H., and Shirley A. Leckie. *The Buffalo Soldiers: A Narrative of the Black Cavalry in the West* (2003).

Schubert, Frank N. *Black Valor: Buffalo Soldiers and the Medal of Honor, 1870–1898* (1997).

MICHAEL F. KNIGHT

Stanford, Peter Thomas (1860–20 May 1909), a Baptist minister whose life took him from the United States to Britain, then back across the Atlantic with a mission to report on the rising tide of racially motivated lynching, was born in Hampton, Virginia, where by the laws of the state at that time, he inherited the enslaved status of his parents. His father was sold before he was born, and his mother taken away when he was four years old.

Freed and without parents at the close of the Civil War, he found shelter at the age of five at a Home for Black Orphan Children initiated by General Samuel Chapman Armstrong, who in 1868 also founded Hampton Institute. The young orphan then went to live with the family of Perry L. Stanford in Boston. At the age of twelve, he left the Stanfords, for what he later described as "some trivial matter," although Reverend Paul Walker recounts that "they treated him as a slave rather than an adopted son." He kept their family name as his own.

For a time he ran with a crowd of youth living semihomeless on the streets of New York City, collecting old clothes, shining shoes, and selling matches. He was attracted to religious revivals organized by Dwight L. Moody and Ira D. Sankey, and began formal education at Suffield Institute, in Suffield, Connecticut, with the help of Henry Ward Beecher, Henry Highland Garnett, and Harriet Beecher Stowe. Stanford was ordained a minister, and accepted as pastor of the Mt. Zion Baptist Church, Hartford, Connecticut, on 26 May 1878.

In 1880 he moved to Canada, where he was employed by the African Baptist Association, and served as pastor of the Horton Street Baptist Church in London, Ontario, then as editor of the *Christian Defender*. Moving to England, he arrived in Liverpool in May 1883. He began evangelizing in Leeds, Narnsley, and Leighley, then lived for a time in Bradford before settling in Birmingham in 1887, where he married Beatrice Mabel Stickley on 13 August 1888. The following year he published an autobiography, *From Bondage to Liberty*.

Stanford was called to accept the position of pastor at the Hope Street Baptist Church, a forerunner of the present Highgate Baptist Church, in 1889, a congregation he recalled as "composed largely of laboring people." Stanford also accepted the pulpit at a church on Priestly Road, in nearby Sparkbrook, for which he proposed the name Wilberforce Memorial Church, after the British evangelist William Wilberforce, responsible for much of the political agitation in Britain that led to the abolition of legalized slavery in all parts of the British Empire in 1833. (Many forms of peonage, contract labor, and debt-slavery continued thereafter).

A public meeting was held at Wilberforce Church on 28 May 1894, inspired by news of "outrages" committed in the United States against citizens of African descent, also referred to as "the lynch-law question." Stanford was called on "in the interests of the philanthropic and Christian public of England, to visit the States," investigate, and plead "with the prominent white Christians to induce them to exert their influence in preventing further reprisals, and in insisting upon the enforcement of law and order" (Stanford, i–ii).

Although he wrote that "Leaving my Birmingham Church was the greatest trial of my life," Stanford felt bound to undertake "the new duties thrust upon me" (Stanford, ii). Arriving in America, accompanied by his English wife, he found that appeals to "white Christians" proved unproductive. He had returned to a nation where the entire Southern Baptist Convention owed its separation from the General Baptist Convention to the former's heartfelt insistence that slavery was a divinely sanctioned institution, approved explicitly by the Bible. Slavery being officially banned by constitutional amendment, a large proportion of "white Christians" were dedicated to affirming "white supremacy" by other means.

However, Stanford did produce one of the most detailed contemporary accounts of the increasingly blatant terrorism being inflicted on the African American population at that very period, put in historical perspective as the "poisonous fruit of seed sown in the distant and near past." It was published as *The Tragedy of the Negro in America* in 1897 in Boston, by Charles A. Wasto, printer.

While still traveling the country, writing and speaking, he founded St. Mark's Congregational Church in Roxbury in 1896, the first church in the area dedicated to a membership of African descent. In 1897 he was additionally invited to accept the pulpit of Zion Congregational Church, Haverhill, Massachusetts. He accepted, with the understanding that he would often be absent due to his investigation, and "the expectation of my many friends in England of hearing from me on the lynching question," which would require a great deal of his time and attention. In 1899 Reverend and Mrs. Stanford founded the Union Industrial and Stranger's Home for homeless women and children in nearby Cambridge. Ten years later, he died of kidney failure, and was buried in Cambridge.

FURTHER READING

Stanford, Reverend P. Thomas. *The Tragedy of the Negro in America* (1897).

Walker, Paul. "The Revd Peter Thomas Stanford (1860–1909): Birmingham's Coloured Preacher." Ph.D. diss., Manchester University (2004).

CHARLES ROSENBERG

Stanley, Sara G. (c. 1836–1918), teacher of freedmen, was born in New Bern, North Carolina, the daughter of John Stuart Stanley and Frances Griffith, teachers who ran an antebellum private school in New Bern that was patronized by free blacks from throughout North Carolina. The Stanleys, free blacks related to a prominent slave-owning family of the same name, identified with their African American community. As a youth, Sara corrected people who mistook her for a white woman by explaining, "I am a colored woman having a slight admixture of negro blood in my veins."

Stanley was a pioneer for her gender and for her race in being an antebellum college student, studying at Oberlin College, Ohio, from 1852 to 1855. She left college before receiving her degree. Many North Carolina free blacks emigrated to Ohio at this time because of persecutions in the South, and this may have been why the entire Stanley family in New Bern emigrated to Cleveland in the late 1850s. With no income from their school, the family might have been unable to afford tuition for their daughter at Oberlin, or perhaps the family needed her to work as a teacher to provide income for the family.

Little is known about Stanley from the time when she left college until the end of the Civil War. "Sara G. Staley [*sic*]" gave an antislavery speech at the Ladies Antislavery Society, an African American association in Delaware, Ohio, in 1856, and the style of the extant speech suggests that this may well have been Sara Stanley. She was one of the few black women in the country with a college education, and it would not be surprising that she was asked to speak, despite her youth. The speech addresses the hatred and prejudice against African Americans—"fostered by religion and science united"—that threatened to annihilate the race. "In view of these things, it is self-evident and above demonstration that we, as a people, have every incentive to labor for the redress of wrongs."

In 1862 Stanley's reputation as a writer was such that she was asked to join the National Young Men's

Literary Association. That same year the *Weekly Anglo-African*, a national periodical, published her analysis of the poetry and the antislavery politics of John Greenleaf Whittier. Just as African American literary critics of the twentieth century hold writers to a political as well as to a literary standard, so did Stanley. "In the poetry of John G. Whittier, we find the nearest approximation to the distinctness of moral purpose, that earnest maintenance of universal freedom," she wrote approvingly.

It is not clear how Stanley supported herself after she left college, but it seems likely that she lived with her family in Cleveland and taught school. In the late 1850s the first black woman teacher in the Cleveland public schools was reputedly a well-educated woman named Stanley, although some have assumed that this was Maria Stanley.

In 1864 Stanley was accepted as a teacher by the Protestant-based American Missionary Association (AMA) to teach newly freed people in Norfolk, Virginia. In her application she stated her views on education and service:

> I know that no thought of suffering and privation, nor even death, should deter me from making every effort possible for the moral and intellectual salvation of these ignorant and degraded people; children of a beneficent Father, and heirs of the kingdom of Heaven. And I feel, moreover, how much greater my own spiritual advancement will be, for while laboring for them, while living a life of daily toil, self-sacrifice, and denial, I can dwell nearer to God and my Savior.

In a second letter of application she explains further that she feels "bound to that ignorant, degraded, long-enslaved race by the ties of love and consanguinity; they are socially and politically 'my people.'"

While teaching in Norfolk, Stanley spoke up against the AMA for maintaining racially segregated housing, because she believed that the deepest principles of action within the association should be spiritual—that the son of God could be seen in the "person of a Negro" as well as in others. While she did not expect to be the social equal of whites in the North, she expected better of whites in the South who were on a spiritual mission.

The AMA reassigned Stanley to a school in St. Louis, Missouri, in 1865 for personal reasons. (She was accused of having an affair with a married white male teacher in Norfolk, and had this been true, she would probably not have been retained as a teacher.) The first publicly elected school board in St. Louis refused to employ African American teachers, so the AMA moved Stanley to a private school in Louisville, Kentucky, in 1866. Her letters and annual reports were frequently included in AMA publications, which was unusual and is a tribute to her talent for writing and description. In one report to the AMA, Stanley described how her uneducated pupils bested a representative of the Freedmen's Bureau who was visiting her class. When the representative told them that education accounted for their difference from whites, the children corrected him by saying money, not education, accounted for the difference. When he said, "Yes, but what enabled them to obtain it?" he expected that they would give the answer he was looking for—education. "*How* did they get that money?" he asked. Stanley records, "A simultaneous shout burst forth, 'Got it off us; stole it off we all.'" Then she added her personal view: "A different answer might have been returned, but hardly a truer one as applied to the people of the South."

In 1868, when Stanley was teaching in Mobile, Alabama, she met and married Charles Woodward, a white Union veteran then managing the local freedmen's bank. The AMA urged that the interracial marriage take place in the North to avoid a possible violent reprisal by the Ku Klux Klan in Mobile. Stanley refused on principle. In 1869 her husband published a history of the Freedman's Bank, and Stanley—who at times assisted him as a cashier and was far better educated than he was—may have assisted him in writing the book.

The Woodwards had only one child, who died in infancy, and the 1870 census for Mobile lists Stanley as a white woman. The determination of race was left to the census taker, who may have assumed that she was white since she was married to a white man and since she had always appeared white to those who did not know of her African American heritage. Perhaps she did not correct the census taker because this could have caused problems affecting her own happiness or because she was less idealistic than in her youth, when she sometimes would go out of her way to challenge racism by telling whites who mistook her for white that she was black.

Since the primary source for information on Stanley is her letters and writings to the AMA, she became lost from historical view when she ceased to be a teacher for them. The next source on Stanley's life is her application for a federal pension as a veteran's widow. There she mentions working as an engraver in Philadelphia, Pennsylvania, becoming a widow in 1885, and teaching at Lucy Lainey's new school in Georgia in the 1890s. The pension record lists her death as 1918 but does not indicate where she died.

Stanley was known and appreciated within the nineteenth-century African American community as a speaker, writer, critic, and teacher. She was less prominent after her interracial marriage in 1870 until her death. Then, like many black women of achievement in the nineteenth century, she was lost to history until recent scholars were interested in the accomplishments of African American women. Stanley was a pioneer for her gender and race by attending college before the Civil War and by teaching within the white-dominated American Missionary Association.

FURTHER READING

Many of Stanley's unpublished letters can be found at the American Missionary Association Papers, Amistad Research Center, New Orleans.

Carraway, Gertrude Sprague. *The Stanley Family and the Historic John Wright Stanley House* (1969).

Franklin, John Hope. *The Free Negro in North Carolina, 1790–1860* (1943).

Lawson, Ellen Nickenzie, ed. *The Three Sarahs: Documents of Antebellum Black College Women* (1984).

This entry is taken from the *American National Biography* and is published here with the permission of the American Council of Learned Societies.

ELLEN NICKENZIE LAWSON

Stanly, John Carruthers (1774–c. 1845), former slave and wealthy North Carolina planter, was born a slave in Craven County, North Carolina, the son of an African Ibo woman who had been brought to America on a vessel owned by the merchant-shipper John Wright Stanly in the decade prior to the American Revolution. Described as a "dark-skinned mulatto," he was almost certainly the son of John Wright Stanly, although his apparent father did not acknowledge paternity. As a young boy he was turned over to Alexander Stewart, who captained the ship that brought his mother from Africa, and Stewart's wife, Lydia Carruthers Stewart, who taught Stanly to read and write and arranged for him to open a barbershop in New Bern as a teenager. Intelligent, gracious, and personable, Stanly quickly became a success, and as New Bern expanded commercially, he earned a good livelihood, even as a slave. In 1795 the Stewarts petitioned the Craven County court for a license of emancipation, explaining that twenty-one-year-old Stanly had always served them faithfully and well.

Once free, Stanly began to invest in land and slaves. He acquired two slaves to assist him in his barbering business and began attending sheriffs' sales to purchase human property at reduced prices. By 1798, as he said in a petition to the state legislature to ratify his emancipation license, "by honest & persevering industry" he had acquired "a considerable real and personal estate." He was already well known as the "barber of the town of New Bern," and soon expanded his real estate holdings both in the city and the countryside. He purchased valuable property at the intersection of Broad and Middle streets in the center of town and rural acreage in what was called Folly Tract on the west side of Neuse Road. He also started a family with an enslaved woman named Kitty, who gave birth to six children before she became ill with an undisclosed and debilitating disease. Stanly freed Kitty and his children during the early years of the nineteenth century.

Along with his many white acquaintances and using his growing wealth, Stanly continued to invest in town property, farmland, and slaves after 1800. He bought houses and lots in New Bern on Middle, Johnson, Queen, and Hancock streets, rented the houses and sometimes-vacant lots to local residents, and added to his rural landholdings by purchasing a 450-acre tract on the south side of the Neuse River. He bought slaves from dealers, at private sales, at auctions, and during confiscation sales at the county courthouse. Most of the slaves he purchased were field hands, unskilled laborers, or children. At the same time he hired skilled free blacks to construct buildings on his rural holdings, which by the 1820s included three plantations. Hiring white overseers, he produced turpentine, a profitable commodity used in the shipping industry. By 1828 his businesses and plantations were producing a substantial income, and Stanly possessed an enslaved labor force of 163 Africans and African Americans, which ranked him as the largest free black slaveholder in the South.

While maintaining business relationships with a number of whites, Stanly remained close to only a few trusted friends. They included his former owner Lydia Stewart, who paved the way for his purchase of two pews at the back of the city's First Presbyterian Church; the lawyer John H. Bryan, who not only served as Stanly's legal counsel but also maintained personal relationships with him and his family over many years; and his half brother John Stanly, a slaveholder, congressman, president of the Bank of New Bern, and speaker of the North Carolina House of Commons. In fact, it was Stanly's close relationship with his white half brother that precipitated his economic downfall. In 1828 he signed security notes for John Stanly, who had engaged in a number of highly speculative business ventures amounting to $14,962, a huge sum at the time. When his brother had a stroke and the notes were called for payment, John Carruthers Stanly lost a large number of his mortgaged slaves and a good portion of his plantation lands.

It is not known precisely when Stanly died, but his economic decline was precipitous. During the 1830s and the early 1840s, he possessed only a small proportion of his once great estate.

FURTHER READING

Schweninger, Loren. "John Carruthers Stanly and the Anomaly of Black Slaveholding," *North Carolina Historical Review* 67 (Apr. 1990): 159–192.

LOREN SCHWENINGER

Stanton, Alysa (2 Aug. 1963–), rabbi, was born in Cleveland, Ohio, into a Pentecostal family and spent her early years in the predominantly Jewish neighborhood of Cleveland Heights. On 6 June 2009 she was ordained by Hebrew Union College in Cincinnati, Ohio, and became the first African American woman to become a rabbi in either of the primary mainstream branches of Judaism (Reform and Conservative) most prevalent in the United States.

Stanton was six when her family moved to Cleveland Heights, and from an early age she was intrigued by spiritual matters. As a young child she asked her uncle Edward, a Catholic who sometimes attended services at a local synagogue, about the purpose of the *mezuzot* (parchment scrolls with inscriptions from the Torah) hanging from the front doors of many homes in the neighborhood. This same uncle also presented her with her first Hebrew grammar book. Although she grew up attending Pentecostal services with her mother, and had a grandfather who was a Baptist minister, Stanton's curiosity about other religions continued to flourish throughout her formative years. At nine she telephoned a local priest to inquire about Catholicism.

By the time she was eleven her parents had divorced, and Stanton moved with her mother and siblings to Lakewood, Colorado. After investigating various eastern religions, Stanton was in

Alysa Stanton poses in front of an ark in the synagogue at Hebrew Union College in Cincinnati in 2009. (AP Images.)

her early twenties and majoring in psychology at Colorado State University when she decided firmly on Judaism. At the completion of an intense period of study with a rabbi in Denver, Stanton became a Reform Jew in 1987.

She received a Master's of Education degree in counseling and multiculturalism in 1992 from Colorado State University, and her professional counselor's license in 1998. Prior to this, she had studied social psychology, neuropsychology, and interpersonal relationships at Lancaster University in England from 1983 to 1984, and received her Bachelor of Science degree in psychology from CSU in 1988.

Despite suffering hostility at her conversion to Judaism from members of her new congregation in Fort Collins, Colorado, and the doubt and aspersions of some friends, Stanton's spiritual quest was far from over. By the mid-1990s she had adopted a baby, a daughter Shana, and was practicing therapy—briefly counseling survivors of the Columbine high school massacre of 1999—when she assumed her first role as a congregational leader, becoming a cantor at Congregation Emmanuel in

Denver. Serving as a cantor, and the satisfaction that came with having a visible, service-oriented role within the community, was a major catalyst in Stanton's decision to become a rabbi. With the guidance and encouragement of the local rabbi and mentor Steven Foster, Stanton chose Hebrew Union College Jewish Institute in Cincinnati to pursue her ordination in the rabbinate.

While the Orthodox Jewish Community bans women from assuming leadership roles traditionally reserved for men, the Reform and Conservative branches began ordaining women as rabbis in the 1970s and 1980s. Still, for many Jews, the acceptance of a rabbi who is both female and African American has required some adjustment. Fortunately for Stanton, her rabbinical career has begun at a time when the American Jewish community is more ethnically and racially diverse than ever before. As of 2010, twenty percent of Jews in the United States are African American, Asian, Latino, or of mixed race.

Stanton's achievement is unique among mainstream sects of Judaism, but African American rabbis presiding over Black Hebrew communities that practice an amalgamation of Jewish and Christian teachings is nothing new. The Hebrew Israelite movement, in which various African American groups claim to be direct descendants of the ancient Israelites, has existed in the United States for well over a century. WENTWORTH A. MATTHEW, LEVI BEN LEVY, and FUNNYE C. CAPERS were among the leading black male rabbis of the twentieth century. Much like Rastafarianism in Jamaica and Black Muslims in America, the black Hebrew movement developed out the desire of blacks to have a spiritual destiny and identity separate from mainstream Christianity, to serve as something of a protective barrier and liberator from the social injustices and prejudice visited on them by white Christians.

While Stanton has ultimately received acceptance as a rabbi, her path to the rabbinate was far from smooth. The curriculum at Hebrew Union College required study in Israel. Initially, the Israeli government denied her a visa. Persistence led to her finally settling in Jerusalem with her daughter. There, Stanton and her child contended with open racism, which included the ostracism and beating of her daughter by Israeli kids. Another requirement of the rabbinate was a summer internship. Stanton found herself in a small congregation in Dothan, Alabama. Many members of the synagogue were not shy about lodging complaints on her arrival. Still, her ability to relate well to others prevailed,

and some of those who had initially opposed her were sad to see her go. These experiences helped prepare Stanton for her new role as leader of a predominately white synagogue, Congregation Bayt Shalom, in Greenville, North Carolina, a diverse congregation of both Reform and Conservative Jews. Stanton won the position of rabbi at Bayt Shalom over at least half a dozen other candidates, and was installed there in August of 2009.

FURTHER READING

Friedman, Emily. "Alysa Stanton Becomes First Female Black Rabbi." *ABC News.* 21 May 2009. http://www.abcnews.go.com

Gillick, Jeremy. "Post-Racial Rabbis," *Moment,* July/Aug. 2009.

Kaufman, David. "Introducing America's First Female Black Rabbi," *Time,* 6 June 2009.

CAMILLE A. COLLINS

Staples, Brent (13 Sept. 1951–), journalist and author, was born in the shipyard town of Chester, Pennsylvania, to Melvin Staples, a factory worker and truck driver, and Geneva (Patterson) Staples. He was one of nine surviving children who grew up in the working-class industrial town about twenty miles south of Philadelphia, Pennsylvania, during the 1950s and 1960s when street gangs were on the rise and illegal drug use began to soar. Those circumstances were partially caused by manufacturing plants' slamming doors shut under stringent post–World War II economic conditions, as Staples describes in his award-winning autobiography *Parallel Time: Growing Up in Black and White* (1994). He tells of facing overwhelming odds amid despair and tragedy that seemed to mount as he matured in the mostly black community with southern roots.

Although Staples's father Melvin made a decent salary, Melvin's turn to alcohol led to the dissolution of his marriage and placed additional stress on the family. Brent's parents had originally migrated from near Roanoke, Virginia, during the late 1950s, and they moved numerous times in Chester trying to avoid evictions, especially after Melvin left. As a result of his leaving, Brent felt bewildered and disoriented. "I grew up with the household always on the verge of collapse, the threat of eviction ever present, the utilities subject to cutoff at any moment" (Staples, 18).

Nonetheless, he recalled the sense of community that endowed well-meaning Chester neighbors with southern black values to chastise those with delinquent behavior, even occasionally Staples, who claimed that he avoided and rarely got into trouble. His younger brother Blake met a different fate. Staples graphically described Blake's tragic shooting death at age twenty-two during a hellish descent as a drug pusher and gangster in Roanoke, Virginia, where the family had briefly returned to live. His searing emotional prose reflected a synthesizing redemptive spirit intent on moving the reader:

> Blake is said to have cried out for his life as he lay on the ground. 'Please don't shoot me no more. I don't want to die.' ... His vowels were locked high in his throat, behind his nose. This voice kept him a baby to me. This is the voice in which he would have pleaded for his life (Staples, 5–6).

Staples was able to avoid such a fate thanks to his superbly inquisitive mind that initially had him wondering about his mental health. As a child he was being "morbidly vigilant about the past. Not the past of a year ago or even the previous day, but the past of the last few seconds. I handled memories over and over again, hoping to give them permanence" (Staples, 10). Only after watching a film about "the physics of time" passed to him by a teacher did he realize that he was not mad but was in fact a gifted thinker; he had promise that would one day lead to the topic of his doctoral thesis at the University of Chicago: the mathematics of thought. "The movie was a saving bolt from the blue," Staples wrote.

Staples majored in secretarial studies in high school and was sympathetic to the goals of the Black Panther Party; he also deeply identified with SIDNEY POITIER's brilliantly rebellious character Walter Lee Younger in the film version of LORRAINE HANSBERRY's classic play *A Raisin in the Sun*. Unsure whether he would attend college and likely headed for a life of some kind of factory work, Staples said that an inspiring conversation with a black teacher convinced him to attend the Penn Morton College (today Widener University) in Chester.

He excelled at college "with the help of a remedial-training and financial-aid program called Project Prepare, through which he participated in a kind of academic boot camp with 23 other black men" (*Current Biography Yearbook 2000*, 530). Graduating in 1973 with a bachelor's degree in behavioral science, he acquired a Danforth Fellowship for psychology graduate studies at the University of Chicago, where he received a master's

degree in 1976 and a doctorate in 1982. After graduating Staples returned to his hometown of Chester to teach as an adjunct professor at his undergraduate college, by then known as Widener University. Upon returning to Chicago, Staples wrote in-depth, first-person essays for the *Chicago Reader*, "a fat and sassy weekly, hungry for stories" (Staples, 235–236).

One of his most notable pieces concerned the gruesome killing of a neighbor stabbed by his wife. Meanwhile, to help pay the bills he worked part-time as a psychologist for a social services agency, and he sought adjunct positions at local colleges, an experience he later described as humbling and humiliating because he hoped one day to land a tenured position with an Ivy League school. "I woke up from my Ivy League dream at Roosevelt University," he wrote in his autobiography, noting that the market was saturated with doctoral graduates, ending his mission to become an Ivy League professor (Staples, 240).

He pinned his hopes on becoming a staff writer for the *Reader* but to no avail; he later landed a short contract with a Chicago magazine, as well as an apartment-sitting job, allowing him refuge for several months. Just after completing a story about the restoration of a painting at Chicago's Art Institute and facing homelessness, Staples received a letter from a *Chicago Sun-Times* editor who had been reading his work and wanted to hire him. Though he bemoaned having to write much shorter news stories, Staples could not turn down a starting weekly salary of about $465. After accepting a six-month tryout for the job, Staples sensed a looming rejection that seemed to be connected to his perceived arrogance rather than to what he believed to be very sufficient writing. But by 1983, after working extra hours and even contributing free book reviews, he had garnered enough support at the newspaper to hold on to his job.

Along the way Staples became angered by the racism that he encountered and bemoaned the extinction of the earlier local black Chicago jazz culture and neighborhood through gentrification and other forces. He would notice whites move out of his way, even crossing streets, apparently afraid of his appearance as a large-stature black man with a sizable "bush" hairstyle. The message was clear to him. They thought that he was threatening, something that prompted him mischievously to walk between tight-knit couples and others. Staples wrote prolifically and in detail about such encounters and also contributed to various jazz publications, including *Jazz Hot–Paris* and the influential *Down Beat*.

Remaining at the *Sun-Times* for two years and continuing his writing for the *Chicago Reader*, as well as contributing pieces to various jazz publications, Staples began to receive job offers in 1985 when the *Sun-Times* was bought by the Australian media magnate Rupert Murdoch. Black reporters were rare and at a premium, Staples noted. He interviewed at the *Austin American-Statesman* in Texas but was ecstatic at being called by the editor of the *Washington Post Magazine*. During interviews, however, Staples turned against the *Post* when he sensed that he would be relegated to covering ghetto stories. He also became angry concerning impolite questions about his "escape" from the ghetto (Staples, 260).

A few months later he found himself "in similar waters during an interview at the *New York Times*. When my anger began to rise, I opened my pocket watch, noted that I was late for my next interview, and left the room. The interviewer was stunned, but better to have fled than not. This time I got the job" (Staples, 261). By 1985, the year after his brother Blake was killed, Staples went to work as an editor for the *New York Times Book Review* before moving on to assistant metropolitan editor and in 1990 joining the editorial board, writing often about social issues and politics. Before he married the public relations executive Julie Williams Johnson on 16 September 2000, Staples wrote about his and her fears for her teenage son and other black males who were being unfairly tagged as criminals and killed by overzealous police ("How a Black Man's Wallet Becomes a Gun," 12 Mar. 2000). In the early twenty-first century Staples continued to write about victims of racism, educational inequities, incarceration, the racial digital divide, and even the commodification of jazz and the blues, earning him a reputation as the quintessential observer, chronicler, and commentator of the universality of the human experience.

FURTHER READING

Staples, Brent. *Parallel Time: Growing Up in Black and White* (1994).
Baker, James N. "Together and Apart," *Newsweek* (14 Mar. 1994).
Muwakkil, Salim. "A Bicultural Voyage into the Mainstream," *Chicago Sun-Times*, 6 Feb. 1994.
Nelson, Jill. "Hiding in Plain Sight," *Nation* (25 Apr. 1994).
Nicholson, David. "Parallel Time, Divergent Paths," *American Visions* (Apr.–May 1994).
Thompson, Clifford, ed. *Current Biography Yearbook* (2000).
White, Jack. "Between Two Worlds," *Time* (7 Mar. 1994).

DONALD SCOTT SR.

Staples, Mavis (10 July 1939–), gospel singer, was born in Chicago, the daughter of ROEBUCK "POPS" STAPLES, who held a variety of blue collar jobs including work in construction and meatpacking, and Oceola Staples, at one point a laundry supervisor at a Chicago hotel. Born after her parents migrated to Chicago from Mississippi, Staples grew up in an environment marked by a strong sense of faith and family. She was a child in kindergarten when her parents discovered the power in her voice. That power was subsequently honed by her exposure to a wide variety of music including the blues and soul, but especially to gospel. As a youngster, Staples and her sister, Yvonne, often spent part of the year in Mound Bayou, Mississippi, visiting their grandmother. In this small town, Mavis gained a deep appreciation for the link between music and spirituality. Yet it wasn't until she was eight years old that her father, an amateur blues musician, began to groom his children to be performers. Along with her two sisters, Cleo and Yvonne, and her brother, Pervis, she was taught the musical language of the Mississippi Delta, which formed the basis of the group's signature gospel sound. Finally in 1950, the family began to appear locally in churches and nightclubs, often traveling on the weekends to sing at Sunday services and eventually on a weekly Sunday radio show. The group became known as the Staple Singers.

The Staple Singers' first hit came in 1956 with the song "Uncloudy Day." The success of that single, which reached the top of the gospel chart, brought the group greater visibility, and soon they had even more invitations to perform. Mavis shared lead singing duties along with her father, but she was still in high school, so the group did not begin to pursue music full time until she graduated in 1957.

In 1963, as the civil rights movement began to peak, and inspired by the leadership of MARTIN LUTHER KING JR., the group began to sing so-called freedom songs. In a 2006 interview for the National Endowment for the Arts, Staples recalled, "we made a transition to what we called message songs. But we never got far away from gospel—we've always considered ourselves basically gospel singers. It's the message we put in our songs and our harmonies that made us so different" (Eckstein, 2006).

Mavis Staples performs at the Democratic National Convention in Boston on 29 July 2004. (AP Images.)

That difference lies in the multilayered nature of the music, which is deeply rooted in the gospel tradition but also imbued with aspects of R&B, country, and folk music.

Always committed to the life of the group, Mavis did not embark on a solo career until 1969, when her first solo album, *Mavis Staples*, was released on the Stax label. A second album, *Only for the Lonely*, followed a year later and reached number thirteen on *Billboard* magazine's R&B chart. With that album also came her first R&B hit, "I Have Learned to Do Without You." Staples's albums were accepted by gospel fans, even though the music was more secular and personally revelatory in nature. Staples would later tell the *Washington Post*, "Being a singer, you want to sing about your life. I'd gotten to be a woman, I was married and divorced, and heartbroken, and I wanted to sing some of those songs" (Harrington, 31 Oct. 2004, NO1). Because of a dispute over royalties, however, Staples would not record another solo album for Stax.

In the years leading up to this period, Staples had a secret relationship with legendary folk-rock singer-songwriter Bob Dylan that did not result in marriage—she feared what people might say if she married a white person. Ultimately, however, she did decide to marry and start a family. But in 1970, the marriage—to a Chicago mortician whom she has referred to as "Mr. Spencer"—was dissolved. Moreover, their union did not result in the birth of a child, and her desire for children eventually took a backseat to the group's success following the 1972 hit "I'll Take You There." That song was part of the larger triumph of the Staple Singers, who had eight top-forty hits during that period, including "Respect Yourself" in 1971 and two number one

hits, "I'll Take You There," which topped both the R&B and pop charts in 1972, and "Let's Do It Again" in 1976, which topped the R&B charts.

Sadly, the group lost much of its popularity in the 1980s because of a shift in musical trends away from inspirational soul music and toward disco. As a result, Staples did not release another album until 1984. In 1987 she was approached by the musician and pop star PRINCE's Paisley Park label. Two albums resulted from that association with Prince who produced both efforts, one in 1989 and the other in 1993. Neither album had broad commercial appeal. During this period Staples also appeared in the 1990 movie *Graffiti Bridge*, which was written and directed by Prince.

Toward the end of the 1990s a number of circumstances resulted in the full-scale rebirth of Staples's career. In 1996 she recorded the album *Spirituals and Gospels*, which was a tribute to her idol, gospel great MAHALIA JACKSON. In 1999 the Staple Singers were inducted into the Rock and Roll Hall of Fame. Perhaps more affecting, however, was the death of her father in 2000, and her sister Cleotha's subsequent diagnosis and death from Alzheimer's. Both incidents compelled her to rethink her identity as a solo artist; ultimately she was forced to face the prospect of performing alone onstage after nearly fifty years of performing with her family.

Meanwhile, the accolades kept coming. In 2003 she received a Grammy nomination for the song "Gotta Change My Way of Thinking," which was a collaboration with Bob Dylan. A year later, Alligator Records released Staples's album *Have a Little Faith* to critical acclaim. In 2005 Staples was honored again when the Staple Singers won a Grammy Lifetime Achievement Award. In 2006 she won a National Heritage Fellowship from the National Endowment for the Arts, the nation's highest honor in the folk arts.

A show business veteran for more than half a century, Staples's belief in justice, combined with the legacy of spirituality passed down from her father, and her powerful contralto vocals, has made her a legend in her own right. She recorded with a range of singers, including RAY CHARLES, Nona Hendryx, Los Lobos, and Dr. John. Staples was also sampled by a new generation of musicians, including hip-hop artist Ludacris, and she has inspired audiences with the example of her faith in the healing power of music and her commitment to address the myriad problems of the contemporary world. In carrying on the legacy of her father, she moved her audience with the uplifting power of her voice and the strength of her vision.

FURTHER READING

Dye, David. "Mavis Staples, Legend of the Soul," *National Public Radio*, 21 Feb. 2006.

Harriington, Richard. "The Gospel According to Mavis," *Washington Post*, 31 Oct., 2004.

ELEANOR BRANCH

Staples, Roebuck "Pops" (2 Dec. 1915–19 Dec. 2000), musician and member of the Staple Singers, was born Roebuck Staples in Winona, Mississippi, the seventh child of a plantation family. His parents' names are unknown. Musical from an early age, Staples became a friend and collaborator of blues pioneers like CHARLEY PATTON and ROBERT JOHNSON, and with these players he developed his signature guitar sound, thick and reverb heavy, that influenced many subsequent guitarists. Despite his blues associations, Staples was increasingly drawn to gospel music.

After moving to Chicago with his wife, Oceola, in 1935, following the Great Migration path with millions of other black Americans, he worked at an Armour meatpacking plant and joined the Trumpet Jubilees, a moderately successful member of Chicago's fertile gospel scene. When his children reached a suitable age Staples created an ensemble with the members of his family. His four children, Cleotha, Pervis, Yvonne, and Mavis, joined with him to form the Staple Singers, and "Pops" left the Trumpet Jubilees to launch his newly created group in 1951. Pervis, Yvonne, and Cleotha all possessed strong, church-trained voices that blended perfectly with their father's warm baritone, and MAVIS STAPLES quickly displayed an unusually powerful vocal instrument.

Recording a series of gospel sides for Vee-Jay Records in the late 1950s and early 1960s, the Staple Singers perfected a style that bridged the grittier sound of their Mississippi roots with the modern gospel popular in Chicago. Often accompanied only by the biting guitar of their father (now ubiquitously called "Pops"), the family's cries and moans with vocalizations and call-and-response patterns recalled early blues, work songs, or slave spirituals. The Staples' early albums are mostly composed of black gospel standards, like "Swing Low, Sweet Chariot" or "Won't You Sit Down (Sit Down Servant)," but they also contain some of Pops's original compositions. Perhaps most prominent among these is the ominous "This May Be the Last Time," which many now mistake for a traditional song. They became a popular touring act, and their performances included appearances at the mass meetings of the burgeoning civil rights movement. Particularly inspired by the work of MARTIN LUTHER KING JR., whom the group met in 1963, Pops Staples led his family's music in an explicitly message-oriented direction, translating the masked intensity of gospel into a more direct political style.

Throughout the 1960s the Staple Singers recorded for a variety of labels, and their work during this period is notable for their (sometimes uncomfortable) attempts to find a middle ground between the explicit gospel of their early work and the secular message music for which they became most famous. They recorded songs by folk-rockers like Bob Dylan or Buffalo Springfield, issued blatantly political recordings like *Freedom Highway* (1975), and continued recording gospel standards. Although Mavis was now their lead voice, Pops's voice and guitar remained central to their sound.

In 1967 the Staple Singers signed with the Memphis-based Stax Records and began the most successful period of their career. Under the guidance of the new Stax president Al Bell, a fan who saw the Staples family as the perfect embodiment of his politically minded vision, the group recorded a series of albums, first at Stax Studios in Memphis, then at Muscle Shoals Sound Studios in Muscle Shoals, Alabama. Often staying away from romantic love songs and the meditative laments of much of the era's rhythm and blues, they focused on creating records that blended southern soul's deep grooves with gospel themes of redemption and community. A string of hits followed, most famously "Respect Yourself," on which Pops shares the lead vocal, and "I'll Take You There," a semi-improvised, reggae-inflected track over which Mavis preaches a lesson of commitment and promise. The group was one of Stax's top artists throughout the period, and many, including Bell, viewed their 1975 departure from the company as a crushing blow to the company.

After leaving Stax, the Staple Singers signed with Curtom Records, the label owned and operated by the Chicago soul great CURTIS MAYFIELD. Mayfield and the Staples admired each other greatly, and their decision to record together seemed perhaps the last chance to restart the kind of uplifting, movement-fueled soul music that both had made their names producing. Instead the pair's first release was the soundtrack to the 1975 film *Let's Do It Again*. On this soundtrack, where the Staple

Singers perform songs written and produced by Mayfield, the music is a lush departure from the rootsy base of their previous work, and the themes are decidedly more romantic, even sexual. In fact, as the historian Craig Werner discusses in a work on Mayfield, Pops had to be convinced that this was not a sinful sellout; according to Mavis, it was only the deep respect that Pops held for Mayfield that convinced him. This proved a wise decision, as both the album and the song "Let's Do It Again" (an ode to sexual pleasure sung by Mavis and Pops) went to number 1 on the charts. Even though the group's work with Mayfield was ultimately short-lived and though they never repeated the success of *Let's Do It Again*, this triumph further marks the Staple Singers as among the era's great artists.

Throughout the 1980s and 1990s, the group recorded sporadically. Mavis Staples launched a successful solo career, and Pops Staples found success both as a recording artist (releasing two albums in the early 1990s) and as an actor (including an appearance in the film *Wag the Dog*). The Staple Singers were inducted into the Rock and Roll Hall of Fame in 1999. In December 2000 Pops Staples died following a concussion. His musical legacy reaches from the Delta blues of the 1930s through gospel in the 1950s to soul in the 1960s and 1970s. His intense singing and playing and his leadership of the Staple Singers mark him as a towering figure in American music.

FURTHER READING

Ankeny, Jason. "Pops Staples," in *All Music Guide to Soul: The Definitive Guide to R&B and Soul*, ed. Vladimir Bogdanov (2003).

Bowman, Rob. *Soulsville, U.S.A.: The Story of Stax Records* (1997).

Bowman, Rob. "The Staple Singers," in *All Music Guide to Soul: The Definitive Guide to R&B and Soul*, ed. Vladimir Bogdanov (2003).

Werner, Craig. *Higher Ground: Stevie Wonder, Aretha Franklin, Curtis Mayfield, and the Rise and Fall of American Soul* (2004).

Obituaries: *New York Times*, 22 Dec. 2000; *Guardian*, 29 Dec. 2000.

DISCOGRAPHY

The Staple Singers. *The Ultimate Staple Singers: A Family Affair, 1955–1984* (Ace Records 240).

Staples, Pops. *Father Father* (Pointblank Records 39638).

Staples, Pops. *Peace to the Neighborhood*, (Pointblank Records 92147–2).

CHARLES HUGHES

Stargell, Willie (6 Mar. 1940–9 Apr. 2001), baseball player, was born Wilver Dornel Stargell in Earlsboro, Oklahoma, the son of William Stargell and Gladys Vernell Stargell, giving him an ancestry both African American and Seminole Indian. He faced challenges growing up in the projects in Alameda, California, with his mother and stepfather Percy Russell after his father abandoned the family, but his mother later recalled that he was always "Mr. Good Guy." He played high school ball at Encinal High in Alameda; his teammates Tommy Harper and Curt Motton also became big leaguers. After a season at Santa Rosa Junior College, Willie was signed by Bob Zuk of the Pirates for $1,500 and pursued his dream of escaping from the projects through baseball. The low minors were intimidating, especially his first stop at Roswell, New Mexico, where he was threatened by drunk whites not sympathetic to integrated baseball. The conditions in which he played improved in Grand Forks, North Dakota, in 1960, Asheville, North Carolina, in 1961, and Columbus, Ohio, in the International League in 1962. His impressive power won him a call-up to the parent Pittsburgh Pirates in late 1962, and he remained a Pirate throughout his career. Although his leadership skills were immediately evident, Stargell happily took a back seat to Pirate team leader ROBERTO CLEMENTE for his first ten years with the club. Primarily a left fielder early in his career, he moved to first base in 1975 as his mobility declined and his size increased from 180 toward 240 pounds on a six-foot three-inch frame. He became famous for clouting prodigious home runs when he connected and for striking out frequently when he did not, and for his infectious enthusiasm whatever the result. He hit two homers out of Dodger Stadium, the first in 1969 (no other player managed even one until 1999). At one point he had the longest homer on record in half the National League parks. Dodger pitcher Don Sutton said, "He doesn't just hit pitchers. He takes away their dignity." He led the league in 1971 with 48 home runs and in 1973 with 44, on his way to a career total of 475. On the other hand, his lifetime tally of 1,936 strikeouts trailed only REGGIE JACKSON's among the century's eminent whiffers. Stargell played on his first pennant winner in 1971, but it was Clemente's World Series as the Pirates beat the Baltimore Orioles and Stargell batted only .208 after going hitless in the league championship series. However, when Clemente died in a plane crash following the 1972 season,

Willie Stargell stands in the batter's box during a game in Pittsburgh, Pennsylvania, 2 August 1980. (AP Images.)

the mantle of team leadership fell to the now-veteran Stargell.

Stargell presided over the dominant team in the National League East in the seventies. The Pirates won six of ten divisional titles, and they did it with a decidedly multicultural lineup. On 1 September 1971 they became the first major league team to field an all-black lineup, the result of aggressive recruiting during the 1960s among Latin and African American prospects. Stargell, with his own mixed-race background, provided a bridge among the various racial groups of players and managed to develop a harmonious atmosphere rare among big-league teams. "Pops," as the fatherly Stargell was dubbed, gave out "Stargell Stars" to players for outstanding contributions to the team, and his teammates were eager to get these symbols. The Pirates of the 1970s and Stargell himself reached a climax in 1979. He hit .281 with thirty-two home runs and eighty-two runs batted in (in only 126 games), and his natural leadership skills inspired the team to take the pennant. The team found its identity in the Sister Sledge song "We Are Family," a celebration of harmony that symbolized the distinctive quality of the 1979 Pirates. Then Stargell had his postseason as Clemente had had his in 1971. He batted .455 with two homers and six runs batted in, leading a sweep of Cincinnati. Then he hit .400 with three more home runs, leading the Pirates to a world championship from a three-games-to-one deficit against the favored Baltimore Orioles. He collected an unmatched array of awards for the season: he was co–MVP (most valuable player) for the season (with Keith Hernandez), MVP of the Championship Series, MVP of the World Series, *Sporting News* Player of the Year, and *Sports Illustrated* coathlete of the year (with Pittsburgh

quarterback Terry Bradshaw). Thereafter, injuries slowed him, and after three more abbreviated seasons, he retired in 1982 at age forty-two with a lifetime .282 batting average.

Stargell was an active community leader. During the Vietnam War, he vocally opposed American intervention. In 1972 he participated in a Nixon White House athletes-against-drugs effort. He founded and served as president of the Black Athletes Foundation, an organization set up to combat sickle-cell anemia. But above all, he was a truly beloved ballplayer. JOE MORGAN, a fellow Hall of Famer, said, "When I played, there were 600 baseball players, and 599 of them loved Willie Stargell. He's the only guy I could have said that about. He never made anybody look bad and he never said anything bad about anybody." Other teammates saluted him as a teacher and an infectiously joyous person. Sportswriter Claire Smith said, "There are Hall of Fame people, as opposed to Hall of Fame players. The former grace the game as much as the latter. And if you combine in one body both ingredients, you have something truly special. Willie Stargell was truly special."

Following his playing career, Stargell coached at the minor- and major-league levels, largely with the Atlanta Braves, before he returned to the Pirates in 1997 as a special assistant to general manager Cam Bonifay. He never achieved his dream of managing in the major leagues.

Stargell had two daughters in a first marriage. His second marriage, to Dolores Parker on 19 November 1966, ended in divorce after producing two daughters and one son. In 1993 he married a third time, this time to Margaret Weller of Wilmington, North Carolina, where they lived until his death. The very day Stargell succumbed to high blood pressure, kidney disorders, and a stroke, the Pirates opened their new PNC Stadium to inaugurate the 2001 season. Outside the new stadium stands a statue of the greatest of Pirate sluggers from their Forbes Field and Three Rivers Stadium days—Willie Stargell.

FURTHER READING
Stargell, Willie. *Willie Stargell* (1984).
Adelman, Bob, and Susan Hall. *Out of Left Field: Willie Stargell and the Pittsburgh Pirates* (1974).
Libby, Bill. *Willie Stargell: Baseball Slugger* (1973).
Obituaries: *Pittsburgh Post-Gazette*, *Philadelphia Inquirer*, *New York Times*, *USA Today*, and *Los Angeles Times*, 10 Apr. 2001; *Sports Illustrated*, 16 Apr. 2001.

This entry is taken from the *American National Biography* and is published here with the permission of the American Council of Learned Societies.

JOHN R. M. WILSON

Starks, Samuel W. (10 Mar. 1865–3 Apr. 1908), fraternal and community leader, was born in Kanawha County, West Virginia, the son of Lewis Starks, a cooper, and Mary Starks. While attending the public schools in Charleston, West Virginia, Starks worked as a cooper's apprentice, making and repairing wooden barrels, and later worked in shops along the Elk River.

Dissatisfied with the cooper's trade, he took a job as janitor in the offices of the Kanawha & Michigan Railroad. The constant clicking of the telegraph apparatus intrigued Starks, so he bought a minimal amount of telegraph equipment to practice on and convinced one of the operators to teach him how to operate it. Soon he was taking the place of absent operators, becoming the first black telegraph operator for the Kanawha & Michigan Railroad. A railroad official, a Colonel Sharp, soon noticed the ambitious young man and employed him to work as a telegraph operator at the Kanawha & Michigan Railroad's Columbus, Ohio, office. Starks was eventually put in charge of the Charleston office before transferring to the company's Corning, Ohio, office. Starks resigned when the company failed to promote him because of his race.

Hoping for better work opportunities, Starks moved to Chicago, where he attended the Bryant and Stratton Business School, completing courses in bookkeeping and stenography. After working as a bookkeeper in Chicago and Denver, he returned to Charleston and established his own company, a grocery. He attended the First Baptist Church, where he was ordained as a deacon in 1884 at the age of eighteen and became a founder and charter member of Capital City Lodge No.1, Knights of Pythias. In 1892 Starks organized the Grand Lodge of West Virginia and became its first grand chancellor, serving in that capacity for sixteen years.

Starks became increasingly politically active, challenging economic and political discrimination against blacks. In 1896 he joined with Dr. Henry Floyd Gamble, founder of the West Virginia State Medical Association and president of the National Medical Association, and other prominent African Americans to form the Colored Republicans Protective League of Charleston. The league united blacks into a political bloc and pressured the Republican Party to give blacks a more significant role within the party. Starks himself ran for a seat in the state legislature from Kanawha County in 1898. Although he was defeated in the primary, he remained loyal to the Republican Party and helped elect the entire ticket.

Starks's keen organizational skills led him to national prominence in the Knights of Pythias and made him one of the outstanding political leaders of West Virginia. After serving several terms as supreme vice chancellor of the Knights of Pythias, Starks was elected supreme chancellor in 1899. At that time the organization was in chaos, with its treasury depleted and the order divided into warring factions. In 1900 the order had fewer than 20,000 members and could not pay the expenses of its representatives to the biennial convocation. By Starks's death in 1908 the order had 150,000 members and owned a temple on State Street in Chicago worth $150,000 and a sanitarium for ill members at Hot Springs, Arkansas. In addition Starks established and became president of the Pythian Mutual Investment Company and the Pythian Temple and Sanitarium Commission. As supreme chancellor he oversaw twenty-six grand lodges and numerous subordinate lodges. In West Virginia alone, as grand chancellor of the state he watched over seventy-two subordinate lodges.

Starks often headed the Republican Party's political campaigns for blacks in the state. During the state elections in 1900 leading Republicans conferred with CHRISTOPHER PAYNE, West Virginia's first black state legislator, and decided to establish a newspaper "in the interest of the Party, for the benefit of the Negro" (Governor A. B. White's papers, West Virginia and Regional History Collection). In September 1900 Starks was tapped to be editor and manager of the new paper, the *Advocate*. Within ten days he had gathered the names of more than four thousand African American voters throughout the state, established contacts in towns and voting precincts with black communities, and made the slogan "Equal Rights and Equal Privileges" the cry of black voters across West Virginia. J. MCHENRY JONES, president of the West Virginia Institute, maintained that it was the first time that a black contingent was actively associated with party management. Following the Republican victory in the state, Starks, together with the Colored Republicans Protective League of Charleston and black constituents from across the state, demanded that state Republican leaders recognize the black community for its political work and its loyalty to the Republican Party.

Immediately following the November 1900 election Starks sent a letter to the governor-elect A. B. White requesting the position of state librarian. Starks was supported in his bid by prominent blacks across the state, many of whom wrote letters on his behalf. Starks traveled from city to city obtaining signatures of support from prominent whites, including U.S. senators Stephen B. Elkins and Nathan B. Scott, several state supreme court judges, congressmen, and newspaper editors, some of whom issued statements that did not mention Starks by name but stated that because of the unprecedented support of black voters it was only "just and right" that they be given recognition (A. B. White Papers).

Starks mailed more than fifty of the statements along with a letter written on the stationery of the Colored Protective League to Governor White in December. In March 1901 Governor White appointed Starks state librarian, the first African American to hold that position in the United States. In 1904 Starks was reappointed to the position. Despite party loyalty and his patronage position Starks continued to fight against discrimination. Starks appeared before the West Virginia house judiciary committee in February 1907 to protest House Bill 18, which proposed the segregation of railroad cars, and he played a vital role in keeping segregated railroad cars out of West Virginia.

Starks married twice and had no children. Little information is available about his wives beyond their first names. In the 1900 census Starks was living with his first wife, Fannie, his mother, and a nephew. Obituaries report that he was survived by his second wife, Lillian, his mother, and one sister. Upon his death in 1908, more than a thousand mourners from across the United States came to pay their last respects at the First Baptist Church of Charleston, where he was eulogized by the governor and by J. McHenry Jones, who stated, "He loved his race and never wanted for himself any privilege that it [the race] could not share. When injustice and prejudice bore hard on his race, his heart felt the blow, and those of us who were near him have seen him shed bitter tears over race oppressions that he could not cure" (*Advocate*, 11 Apr. 1908).

In 1911 the Knights of Pythias dedicated a thirty-two-foot granite monument, an obelisk, on Starks's grave to honor their former leader. Perhaps the former

West Virginia governor George Atkinson summed up Starks's life best when he said, "Out of nothing, save empty dignity and a few faint, faint promises, he has built the greatest organization among his people in this day" (Randall and Gilmer, 18).

FURTHER READING
The History and Manual of the Colored Knights of Pythias of NA, SA, E, A, A & A (1917).
Posey, Thomas. *The Negro Citizen of West Virginia* (1934).
Randall, James, and Anna Evans Gilmer. *Black Past* (1989).
Trotter, Joe William, Jr. *Coal, Class, and Color: Blacks in Southern West Virginia, 1915–1932* (1991).
Obituaries: *Advocate*, 11 Apr. 1908; *Charleston Daily Gazette* and *Charleston Gazette*, 3 Apr. 1908.

CONNIE PARK RICE

Starlins, Mark (?–c. 1784), Revolutionary War sailor in the Virginia State Navy, was born in Africa and forcibly brought to the colonies as a boy to work as a slave. Working for a master in an area along the James River in Virginia, Starlins would eventually gain an intimate knowledge of the river and its many inlets and tributaries; in fact, "Captain" would soon become his nickname. Although nothing is known of Starlins's life other than his military service, those that remember him recall him as "a devoted patriot" who "evinced a remarkable attachment" to America (Kaplan, 61).

"Captain" Mark Starlins's only recorded service in the American Revolution was aboard the armed schooner *Patriot* in the Virginia State Navy. In 1779, along with five other black sailors, Caesar Tarrant, David Baker, Jack Knight, Cuffee, and Pluto, Starlins took part in the *Patriot*'s capture of the Boston-bound British supply ship *Fanny*. While nothing else is known about Starlins's naval service, there is little doubt that he served as a pilot on the James River and perhaps later as a sailor on Chesapeake Bay and ocean-faring warships. Based on the recollections of Commodore James Barron, a young seaman in the Virginia State Navy at the end of the war (and later captain of the U.S. frigate *United States*), Starlins, though skilled, sometimes "allowed his patriotism to get the better of his judgment" (Kaplan, 61). Although we are left guessing by Barron's words as to the operations that Starlins may have participated in, there can be little doubt that, whatever they may have been, his tasks were carried out with much skill and daring and earned him a fine reputation "by all worthy citizens, and more particularly, by all the naval officers of the State" (Kaplan, 61).

Starlins's service is yet another example of the important African American contribution to the navy's war effort during the American Revolution. Though experiencing little success against the British Navy, the frigates of the Continental Navy were well served by black sailors such as SCIPIO AFRICANUS and CATO CARLISLE. The same is true of the privateer service, where many men such as JAMES FORTEN served valiantly. Men such as Starlins and Tarrant served with distinction in the state navies of such colonies as Massachusetts, Virginia, and New Hampshire. In particular, many blacks in coastal areas were skilled pilots and were highly familiar with the waters where both British and American warships operated. Some were no doubt pressed into the service of the British Navy; men such as SAMPSON served the enemy under unknown circumstances, and others such as Starlins "zealously volunteered their services in the patriotic cause" (Kaplan, 61).

Although Starlins was said to be a "noble African" that "lived and died a slave soon after the peace," and who toiled in obscurity, the actions of this "very singular and meritorious character" during the war have nonetheless elevated his status to that of a true American patriot (Kaplan, 61). Denied his own freedom, Starlins's service, and that of others like him, in dramatic and, perhaps, ironic fashion helped win the very freedoms that define America to this day.

FURTHER READING

Kaplan, Sidney, and Emma Nogrady Kaplan. *The Black Presence in the Era of the American Revolution* (1989).

Quarles, Benjamin. *The Negro in the American Revolution* (1961).

GLENN ALLEN KNOBLOCK

Starr, Edwin (21 Jan. 1942–2 Apr. 2003), soul singer and songwriter, was born Charles Edwin Hatcher in Nashville, Tennessee, to William Hatcher, a military serviceman, and his wife. Though at first they moved a great deal, the family settled in Cleveland, Ohio, after World War II. There Edwin attended Cennard High and East Technical School. Encouraged by his nonmusical parents, he enjoyed singing. His cousins were the soul singers Willie and Roger Hatcher. From 1955 to 1960, Edwin sang with a teen doo-wop group, the Future Tones, who released the single "All I Want Is You" (1957).

Hatcher was drafted into the U.S. Army from 1960 to 1962 and stationed in Canada, then Germany. He then toured for two years with the performer Bill Doggett's road show. Doggett introduced him one evening as Edwin Starr. The name stuck. In 1965 Starr went solo on Detroit's Golden World/RicTic Records. He soon broke onto the American and British charts with two singles of his own composition, "Agent Double O Soul" and "Stop Her on Sight (SOS)." Darrell Banks charted with Starr's "Baby Whatcha Got for Me" and the Shades of Blue with his "Oh How Happy."

In 1966, while Starr was performing in Great Britain, the Motown executive BERRY GORDY JR. bought Ric-Tic and turned its studio into Motown Studio B. Starr learned about the takeover from the Temptations while performing with them at Harlem's Apollo Theater. Outraged that Gordy did not consult or share profits with Ric-Tic's musicians, Starr initially declined to produce new work for Motown. He did allow its reissue of his Ric-Tic work as the LP *Soul Master* (1968). In 1969 Starr charted with the Motown singles "I'm Still a Strugglin' Man" and the Top Ten "25 Miles."

In 1970 Edwin Starr released the protest song "War," composed by the Motown producer Norman Whitfield and Barrett Strong, as a single. Whitfield and the Temptations had already included it on *Psychedelic Shack* (1969). But Motown forbade its release as a single, fearing political backlash against one of its most lucrative groups. According to Starr, the label did not feel it had anything to lose by having him record the single. Because of intensifying opposition to the Vietnam conflict, "War" quickly went to number one in the United States and number three in Britain. It won Starr a Grammy and became his signature song and one of Motown's best sellers ever. Peace advocates of all races felt that Starr's arresting baritone gave them a united voice, with his passionate, emphatic expression of sentiments like "WAR! What is it good for? Absolutely NOTHING! Say it again!"

Although he did not repeat the runaway success of "War," Starr recorded other acclaimed work for Motown, mostly notably his duets with Blinky (the gospel singer Sondra Williams) and the *Hell Up in Harlem* soundtrack. After his Motown contract expired in 1975, he moved to the English Midlands. He had long enjoyed performing for his appreciative and numerous British and European fans. He continued to record on a series of labels, while shifting more and more to live performances. In 1979 his disco songs "HAPPY Radio" and "Contact" reached the British Top Ten. By the 1980s, he owned a café and recording studio in Birmingham. In 1987, after the ferry *Herald of Free Enterprise* capsized in the English Channel, killing 193 people, he took part in the Ferry Aid recording of "Let It Be" to benefit survivors of the disaster.

In March 2000, Starr presented the BBC Radio 2 documentary series, "RESPECT—Soul and the Civil Rights Movement." He had long since become a frequent and popular performer in Motown revival concerts and other British and European live-music venues. His last performances were on 29 and 30 March 2003 to audiences of over sixteen thousand in Stuttgart, Germany. At his home in Bramcote, Nottinghamshire, England, he died from an apparent heart attack, two weeks after the U.S.-Iraq War started. He was survived by his longtime partner Jean, two children from previous relationships, and several grandchildren. He was married once before.

Edwin Starr's "War" secured him a powerful legacy, even at Motown. The label decided to record more social protest songs, including STEVIE WONDER's "Livin' in the City" and MARVIN GAYE's "What's Goin' On." Prominent musicians like Bruce Springsteen have covered "War." When the Gulf War began in 1991, the BBC banned the song. After the September 11, 2001 terrorist attacks, the American radio network Clear Channel also prohibited its DJs from playing the song. Despite—and perhaps because of such censorship, "War" has endured as a protest against military buildups and conflicts.

FURTHER READING

Walker, Bruce. "Starr, Edwin." *Gale Cengage Contemporary Musicians Volume 50*, edited by Angela M. Pilchak (2005).

Obituaries: BBC News Entertainment, 3 Apr. 2003; *Guardian*, 4 Apr. 2003; *Independent*, 4 Apr. 2003; *[London] Times Online*, 4 Apr. 2003.

MARY KRANE DERR

Staupers, Mabel Doyle Keaton (27 Feb. 1890–30 Sept. 1989), National Association of Colored Graduate Nurses executive officer, was born Mabel Doyle in Barbados, British West Indies, to Thomas and Pauline Doyle. In 1903 her family settled in Harlem, where her father became a brake inspector for the New York Central Railroad. Staupers attended public schools in New York and graduated from Freedmen's Hospital School of Nursing (now the Howard University College of Nursing) in Washington, D.C., in 1917. After graduation, she began her professional career as a private-duty nurse in New York, but she soon went to work as a nurse administrator in Philadelphia. In 1922 she returned to Harlem and began an illustrious career as a nurse and an administrator.

The Great Migration of African Americans from the rural South resulted in an increase of over 66 percent in Harlem's black population between 1910 and 1920. The attendant social problems of such rapid population change—inadequate housing, unemployment, and insufficient public health services—made Harlem a center for reform-related activism. Staupers, on behalf of the New York Tuberculosis and Health Association, undertook to survey the Harlem community to determine its public health needs. As a consequence of her final report, the Harlem Committee of the New York Tuberculosis and Health Association was created. Staupers served as its executive secretary for twelve years, during which time the Harlem Committee helped to create the city's first hospital for black tuberculosis patients and initiated a public health library and a variety of programs for children, adults, physicians, nurses, and social workers. By the late 1920s the committee had duplicated many of these programs and their publications in Spanish. Staupers's work with the Harlem Committee undoubtedly established her as an important person in the area of public health, but it was through her role as executive secretary and president of the National Association of Colored Graduate Nurses that she achieved a national reputation. The NACGN was founded in 1908 in New York City, and Staupers joined in 1916 while she was still a nursing student. During its early years the organization's leaders worked to improve and standardize nursing instruction and to raise the status of black nurses. After Staupers became executive secretary in 1934, the organization expanded, growing in membership from 175 to 821 by 1939. The NACGN was especially effective in its efforts to integrate the nursing profession, to improve black public health, and to cultivate leadership ability among black nurses while creating leadership roles for them. To reach these goals, Staupers and ESTELLE MASSEY RIDDLE OSBORNE, the NACGN's first president, gained financial support from the Rosenwald Foundation, the General Education Board, and other sympathetic people and organizations. These funds enabled nurses to conduct regional and national conferences, to publish and circulate papers and reports, and to serve as a liaison between black nurses and the agencies and institutions that trained, employed, and promoted them. An important goal for Staupers and other black nursing leaders was the complete integration of the American Nurses Association, for without full membership in the ANA no nurse could consider herself fully credentialed. Reaching this goal was no small accomplishment. ANA membership was gained either through state associations or through alumnae associations, yet most black nurses lived and worked in states that would not allow them to join, and the only black institution that had affiliate status with the ANA was Freedmen's Hospital Nursing School.

Staupers and her colleagues undertook a variety of steps to open the ANA to black nurses. In 1938, for example, she helped create the NACGN Advisory Council, composed of representatives of the major nursing and public health organizations and a variety of private philanthropic agencies and public institutions. This council became a vehicle for pressuring the white national organizations to open their doors to black members. Estelle Osborne recommended that in the South, where state laws precluded the formal association of black and white nurses, the ANA should recognize the black organization as an ANA affiliate. In the North a different strategy was required. Large numbers of black nurses in the North had graduated from southern schools and had migrated from states that excluded them from membership in the state affiliate. At the least, an "individual membership" category was necessary. Staupers began the effort to establish this new category in New York, with the hope that if the New York State affiliate opened its membership to black nurses, other northern states would follow suit. But before the ANA was integrated, World War II began, and the campaign to integrate nursing spread to a new front.

Although the war created an increased need for nurses, neither the army nor the navy accepted black nurses. The armed forces took their nurses from among American Red Cross Nursing Service applicants, so Staupers encouraged black nurses to submit Red Cross applications. She also coordinated a campaign to pressure the military to change its policy. When the War Department decided in 1941 to accept a maximum of fifty-six black nurses at segregated military camps, Staupers coordinated a massive protest movement. By 1944 there were almost three hundred black army nurses, but the army still had a quota, and the navy still had no black nurses. Staupers wrote letters to military

leaders on behalf of the NACGN, and she sent news releases to black newspapers publicizing the government's discriminatory policy. She lobbied the surgeon general of the army and worked to persuade members of Congress to pass bills explicitly prohibiting racial discrimination "in the selection, induction, voluntary recruitment, and commissioning of nurses" in the armed forces.

In the fall of 1944 Staupers met with President Franklin D. Roosevelt to detail the problems arising from the quota on black nurses in the army, the segregation of the camps in which they worked, and their work assignments, which were usually limited to caring for German prisoners of war. When the surgeon general of the army announced in early 1945 that a special draft for nurses might be necessary, Staupers was present and asked why they did not accept the black nurses who were willing to serve. She also helped coordinate a successful letter-writing and telegram campaign protesting proposed amendments to the Selective Service Act that would have allowed the drafting of nurses. Within two months Staupers's efforts had paid off. The army eliminated its quota for black nurses, and shortly thereafter the navy announced a "color-blind" recruitment policy.

During the war Staupers and members of the NACGN Advisory Council continued to put pressure on the ANA, and in 1942, following the example of the American Red Cross and the National League of Nursing Education, the ANA began to admit black nurses through their membership in the NACGN. Emboldened by the 1945 change in military policy, in January 1946 Staupers asked the ANA to directly admit black nurses from any state that denied them membership on the basis of race. The ANA agreed in September to admit qualified black nurses to the organization and its state affiliates. Although this process was not complete until 1948, Staupers considered her work done and stepped down as executive secretary of the NACGN.

The historian Darlene Clark Hine has written that it is likely that "the complete integration of black women into American nursing on all levels" would not have occurred without the work of Mabel Staupers" (Hine, 186). And, indeed, Staupers seemed indefatigable. Her work during the 1920s and early 1930s was critical to the creation of public health policies and programs in New York City. The historian Susan L. Smith notes that Staupers was also instrumental in establishing and organizing National Negro Health Week. She was a master coalition builder, linking black nurses and their organizations to other nursing groups and to philanthropic, government, civic, and social leaders throughout the country. She became the NACGN's last president in 1949 and led the process of folding the goals and objectives of the NACGN into the ANA.

Although the NACGN ceased to exist in 1951, Staupers continued to encourage black nurses to protect the gains they had made and to submit histories of black nurses to the Schomburg Collection for Research in Black Culture of the New York Public Library. Ten years later she would publish her own history of the NACGN, *No Time for Prejudice: The Story of the Integration of Negroes in Nursing in the United States* (1961). In one of her final acts as president of the NACGN, Staupers encouraged her members to participate in the profession in ways to make real the new policy of integration. On 15 March 1951 the headquarters of the NCAGN closed; the ANA was finally a fully integrated professional organization for nurses.

Although the NAACP awarded Staupers its prestigious Spingarn Medal in 1951 for her work in integrating the nursing profession, she did not "retire" from the profession after finishing her work as president of the NACGN. Almost immediately, she became a member of the Board of Directors for the ANA. Staupers remained active in the national black nursing sorority, Chi Eta Phi, and she received many honors for her life's work from universities, church groups, nursing organizations, and civic associations. She died in Washington, D.C.

FURTHER READING

Information on Staupers can be gleaned from the Mabel Keaton Staupers Papers in the Howard University–Moorland-Spingarn Research Center, Washington, D.C., and from the Mabel Keaton Staupers Papers, housed at the Schomburg Center for Research in Black Culture of the New York Public Library.

Hine, Darlene Clark. *Black Women in White: Racial Conflict and Cooperation in the Nursing Profession, 1890–1950* (1989).

Shaw, Stephanie J. *What a Woman Ought To Be and To Do: Black Professional Women Workers during the Jim Crow Era* (1996).

Smith, Susan L. *Sick and Tired of Being Sick and Tired: Black Women's Health Activism in America, 1890–1950* (1995).

Obituary: *New York Times*, 6 Oct. 1989.

STEPHANIE J. SHAW

St. Clair, Stephanie ("Queenie") (c. 1890–c. 1974), Harlem "policy queen" and advocate for immigrant and African American rights, was born in Martinique. She immigrated to New York via Marseilles, France. After settling in Harlem in 1913, she served as an advocate for renter's rights and fought to require police to have search warrants to enter a resident's home. She also became a passionate advocate for French-speaking immigrants in need of education and job opportunities. In 1922 St. Clair opened a successful "numbers" bank in Harlem.

According to the *Encyclopedia of African-American Culture and History*, the "numbers game" was a "pervasive form of gambling in African-American urban communities from around the turn of the century until the late 1970s" (Palmer, 2032). The numbers game—also referred to as "policy"—eventually folded in the 1970s with the advent of state lotteries and legal gambling. "Playing the numbers" initially involved placing a bet on the last three digits of the daily trade volume of the New York Stock Exchange. Later the winning numbers were taken from the winning horses at the racetrack. Number runners moved through the neighborhood on a daily basis, picking up bets written on small sheets of paper. At the end of the day there was a payout to those who chose a combination of the correct three-digit number.

St. Clair, who was nicknamed "Queenie" and "Madame St. Clair," built Harlem policy into a multimillion-dollar business, pumping a significant amount of money into the fragile economy. Her infamy began after she infiltrated the Forty Thieves, an extortion gang that dated back to the nineteenth century. As a result of her fierce reputation, St. Clair established herself as the leader of this once white-led organization. She invested nearly ten thousand dollars to open her own policy bank.

St. Clair charged nickels and dimes for residents to play the numbers. The affordability made the game immensely popular despite the dearth of wealth in the neighborhood. By the middle 1920s St. Clair's estimated worth was five hundred thousand dollars. She employed more than fifty runners and ten comptrollers for her flourishing business. Surprisingly she achieved this during the Great Depression of the late 1920s and 1930s.

ELLSWORTH RAYMOND "BUMPY" JOHNSON was the most well known of St. Clair's protégés. His involvement in the numbers game in Harlem grew so legendary that his life has been documented and dramatized far more often than has St. Clair's. In Francis Ford Coppola's film *The Cotton Club* (1984), Novella Nelson portrayed St. Clair. The character does not figure as significantly into the plot and cinematic turf war battles as does Bumpy Johnson, played by LAURENCE FISHBURNE. Fishburne later reprised the role in the 1997 film *Hoodlum*. In this film St. Clair (played by CICELY TYSON) plays a much larger role in the narrative. However, Bumpy Johnson still serves as the primary focus.

Both St. Clair and Johnson shared a passion for the arts and attended opera and events at Carnegie Hall. In addition, both made countless anonymous donations to help the Harlem poor. St. Clair lived at 409 Edgecombe Avenue, the most prestigious address in Harlem's Sugar Hill district.

As the policy business continued to grow and succeed, white outsiders began to overtake both St. Clair and Johnson. St. Clair took out full-page newspaper advertisements to highlight the graft and corruption by the police force and city judges.

Dutch Schultz, of German Jewish descent, became a successful bootlegger in the 1920s and 1930s. After the end of Prohibition in 1933, Schultz sought a new source of income. He seized on Harlem policy with hopes to overtake St. Clair's coveted business. Between 1931 and 1935 Schultz engaged in a bloody turf war with St. Clair and Johnson. Schultz, also a feared gangster, had strong alliances with the police and Tammany Hall. St. Clair fought Schultz's pressure but was in and out of jail beginning in the 1930s. Schultz eventually died in a Newark, New Jersey, hospital from gunshot wounds inflicted by rival gangsters. Before his death, St. Clair sent him a telegram: "As ye sow, so shall you reap" (Cook, 170). She provided evidence that led to a series of convictions of Schultz's people after his death.

Many white-owned Harlem businesses refused to hire African Americans. SUFI ABDUL HAMID, an activist, labor organizer, and speaker, worked to secure rights for African American workers using aggressive tactics, such as storekeeper intimidation. His 1 August 1938 *New York Times* obituary called him the "Harlem Hitler," referring to his anti-Semitic preaching against the Jewish shop owners in Harlem. To residents of Harlem, Hamid was a peerless advocate for their right to work.

In 1935 St. Clair married Hamid. However, they did not have a peaceful marriage, and it ended two years later. The 1938 *New York Times* obituary for Hamid referred to "Queenie" as Hamid's "'contract' wife." Although St. Clair did not kill Hamid, she

ambushed and shot him on 8 January 1938. Hamid died in a plane crash later that year.

On 18 January 1938 St. Clair was arrested for shooting Hamid. Definitive information concerning St. Clair's prison release from the Bedford Correctional Women's Facility in Bedford Hills, New York, is not available. After finishing her time at the facility, she kept a low profile. Upon her sentencing, the white mafia slowly took over policy in Harlem until legalized gambling and state lotteries were established in the 1970s. St. Clair's time and place of death cannot be confirmed.

FURTHER READING

Cook, Fred J. "The Black Mafia Moves into the Numbers Racket," *New York Times*, 4 Apr. 1991.

Jones, Catherine Butler. "409 Edgecombe, Baseball, and Madame St. Clair," in *The Harlem Reader*, ed. Herb Boyd (2003).

Lawrenson, Helen. *Stranger at the Party: A Memoir* (1975).

Palmer, Colin A., ed. *Encyclopedia of African-American Culture and History: The Black Experience in the Americas*, 2d ed. (2006).

Watkins-Owens, Irma. *Blood Relations: Caribbean Immigrants and the Harlem Community, 1900–1930* (1996).

DONNY LEVIT

St. Cyr, Johnny (John Alexander) (17 Apr. 1890–17 June 1966), guitarist, banjo player, and jazz musician, was born John Alexander St. Cyr in New Orleans, Louisiana, the second son of Gilbert St. Cyr and Josephine Granger, a seamstress and laundress. His parents separated when he was five, and he was raised by his mother, who taught him simple chords on her guitar. As a child he enjoyed playing music with his brother's friends Jackie Dowden and Jules Batiste. He took lessons from Jules and later performed with Jackie and Jules at fish fries and house parties. St. Cyr attended school in New Orleans, leaving after the fifth grade to become a plasterer's apprentice. He married his first wife at the age of seventeen, but little information about her is known.

In the early 1900s St. Cyr was part of a distinctly Creole music scene in New Orleans, performing at many functions including downtown balls, Saturday evening dances, and Sunday picnics at Lucian's Pavilion, Little Alice's, and other camps along the shores of Lake Pontchartrain. On Saturday afternoons he performed atop wagons in the streets of New Orleans, promoting the weekend festivities.

While St. Cyr is most famous for his "hot jazz" recordings with JELLY ROLL MORTON and LOUIS ARMSTRONG, he, like his colleagues, performed many styles of dance music, including quadrilles, schottisches, and waltzes. In New Orleans, St. Cyr played with many famous bands and musicians including the Superior and Olympia brass bands, A. J. PIRON, KID ORY, and OSCAR "PAPA" CELESTIN's Tuxedo Band. The Creole musicians with whom St. Cyr played were often serious, trained musicians who prided themselves on their technique, music-reading skills, and professionalism. For these reasons they rarely performed the blues music favored by non-Creole African American musicians working in New Orleans' uptown bars.

As his career developed St. Cyr began performing in Storyville, New Orleans's famed red-light district. While it is commonly assumed that jazz was born in the brothels of Storyville, there is little basis for this myth. The "houses" rarely even had pianos. Most musicians instead performed in the district's stylish cabarets. St. Cyr earned only one dollar a night in the cabarets, so as often as he could he played at the more lucrative functions held outside Storyville. St. Cyr began his career as a guitarist, but early on he became interested in the banjo, which was growing in popularity. In 1914, with the encouragement of A. J. Piron, St. Cyr built a banjo-guitar by attaching the neck of a guitar to the head of a banjo. Unlike the more common tenor banjo, St. Cyr's instrument had six strings and was tuned like a guitar. The banjo and the banjo-guitar had an advantage over the guitar since they were louder and more cutting, making them more effective in large bands as well as in early recordings. He played the banjo-guitar on most of his famous recordings of the 1920s.

In 1918 St. Cyr went to work as a riverboat musician for the Streckfus Line. This was a great step forward professionally, since St. Cyr could earn thirty dollars a week when the boat was docked in New Orleans and $52.50 when it was docked in St. Louis. He sometimes worked a three-hour morning shift, an afternoon shift from 1:00 to 6:00, and a late-night shift from 8:00 until 12:15. Working for the Streckfus Line was also a musical step forward: musicians referred to riverboat work as "going to the conservatory." The bandleader and pianist FATE MARABLE demanded much from his musicians, sometimes tutoring them in music reading and performance skills. Good music-reading skills were crucial, since, unlike the collectively improvising ensembles of New Orleans, Marable's band was strictly a reading band, and publishing companies often sent them the latest dance arrangements hoping Marable's famous orchestra would popularize them up and down the Mississippi. Aboard ship St. Cyr performed with many of the best New Orleans jazz musicians of the day, including the clarinetist JOHNNY DODDS, the bassist GEORGE "POPS" FOSTER, the drummer WARREN "BABY" DODDS, and the cornetist Louis Armstrong. When the riverboat was docked in St. Louis he also met musicians like the pianist and ragtime composer TOM TURPIN. St. Cyr stayed with the Streckfus Line through the summer of 1921, when he returned to New Orleans for a year and a half.

In September 1923 St. Cyr moved to Chicago to join the New Orleans cornet player JOE "KING" OLIVER; he stayed there until the Great Depression of 1929. He was one of the city's top performers, working regularly with the likes of Louis Armstrong, the clarinetist Jimmie Noone, and Jelly Roll Morton. These musicians set the standard for "hot" improvisational jazz. As in New Orleans, they performed at a variety of functions, though Chicago venues also included such opulent ballrooms as the Lincoln Gardens, which could accommodate up to one thousand dancers. While many clubs were segregated, some "black and tans," like the Apex Club, welcomed both black and white patrons, allowing rare opportunities for racial mixing.

In Chicago, St. Cyr participated in many landmark jazz recordings. In 1923 he recorded with Joe Oliver's Creole Jazz Band and in 1926 he recorded with Jelly Roll Morton's Red Hot Peppers. Though largely unimprovised, Morton's carefully arranged and rehearsed performances represented the apex of the New Orleans sound. Between 1925 and 1927 St. Cyr also played on Louis Armstrong's famous Hot Five and Hot Seven recordings, which heralded the transition from collective improvisation to a style that showcased virtuosic soloists.

Following the stock market crash of 1929 the music industry declined, so St. Cyr returned to New Orleans, where he worked as a plasterer and performed part-time with musicians like PAUL BARBARIN, ALPHONSE PICOU, and GEORGE LEWIS. In 1955 he moved to Los Angeles, resumed full-time performing, and made several recordings. From 1961 until his death in 1966 he performed at the Disneyland riverboat exhibit leading the Young Men from New Orleans, a traditional jazz band that featured a number of veteran musicians. During his long life he married twice, had two daughters, three sons, and many grandchildren.

FURTHER READING

Johnny St. Cyr's papers are housed in the Hogan Jazz Archive, Howard-Tilton Memorial Library, Tulane University in New Orleans, Louisiana. Materials for this biography were provided courtesy of the Hogan Jazz Archive.

St. Cyr, Johnny. "Jazz as I Remember It: Part One: Early Days," *Jazz Journal* 19 no. 9 (Sept. 1966).

St. Cyr, Johnny. "Jazz as I Remember It: Part Two: Storyville Days," *Jazz Journal* 19 no. 10 (Oct. 1966).

St. Cyr, Johnny. "Jazz as I Remember It: Part Three: The Riverboats," *Jazz Journal* 19 no. 11 (Nov. 1966).

St. Cyr, Johnny. "Jazz as I Remember It: Part Four: Chicago Days," *Jazz Journal* 20 no. 1 (Jan. 1967).

JOHN HARRIS-BEHLING

Stearnes, Turkey (8 May 1901–4 Sept. 1979), Negro League baseball player, was born Norman Stearnes in Nashville, Tennessee, the son of Will S. Stearnes and Mary Everett. Although his daughter once said that he acquired his nickname because he flapped his elbows when he ran, Stearnes believed a protruding stomach during childhood was the reason. One of five children, he pitched for Pearl High School until "around 15 or 16 years old," when his father died. He then worked at any job he could find, including slopping pigs, driving wagons, delivering groceries, and general cleaning.

In 1921 Stearnes played professionally with the Montgomery, Alabama, Gray Sox in the Negro Southern League, a sort of black minor league. After playing for a year in Memphis, Tennessee, he was picked up by the Detroit Stars of the Negro National League, one of the two major black leagues. The Stars players worked in an automobile factory when they were not playing ball for Tenny Blount, who ran the numbers racket in Detroit. The team played black league games five days a week and semipro games against white teams in Michigan and Canada the other two days.

The Stars' home, Mack Park, had a high fence in right field and fell away to a deep center field. Despite the size of the ballpark Stearnes hit seventeen home runs, second in the league, and batted .365 during a sixty-game rookie season. (The Negro Leagues played forty to sixty games a season, or about one-third as many as the white major leagues.) That fall the St. Louis Browns of the American League came to Detroit for a series

against the Stars; it was quite unusual for a major league team to travel in order to play against a Negro League team. The Stars won two of the three games, with Stearnes batting .500 in twelve plate appearances. The following year he led the league in home runs with a relatively low total of ten in sixty games, and he batted .358.

Physically, Stearnes was not a typical slugger. Weighing less than 170 pounds he whipped his short, thirty-five-inch bat from an odd left-handed stance, lifting the toes of his right foot off the ground. "Yeah, Turkey had a funny stance, but he could get [his bat] around on you," sighed SATCHEL PAIGE. "He could hit it over the left field fence, or the center field fence, or over the right field fence. Turkey Stearnes was one of the greatest hitters we had. He was as good as anybody ever played baseball." Also a fast runner, he often batted leadoff and was a wide-ranging center fielder.

Stearnes let his bat talk. "He wasn't a good mixer," the players said, "he never popped off." Sometimes he talked to his bat and even took it to bed with him, it was said. When pitchers threw at his head, he told them, "You make it harder for you. If the ball comes across, I'm gonna hit that ball. You don't scare me."

For the rest of the 1920s, the glory years of black baseball, Stearnes kept his batting average well over .300 and remained among the leaders in home runs. His best power season was 1928, when he drove twenty-four over the wall, the second highest total ever in the history of the black leagues.

With the onset of the Great Depression, in 1930 Stearnes and other midwestern Negro League players went east to try to make more money. He briefly landed with the New York Lincoln Giants but found pickings were just as slim there and had returned to Detroit by mid-1930. By then the Stars had moved to huge Hamtramck Park, which had a foul line 450 feet extending from home plate. Soon thereafter Stearnes became the first player to hit a home run over the park's outfield fence. He arrived in time to help the Stars win the second-half pennant in the Negro National League that season. The Stars then lost to St. Louis, the first-half winner, in a seven-game playoff. Stearnes's St. Louis rival, GEORGE "MULE" SUTTLES, batted .357 in the series; Stearnes led all batters with a .467 average and knocked in eleven runs.

In 1931 Stearnes moved to Kansas City. Although he hit only eight home runs that season, his record was good enough to lead the league for the fourth time. The next season he joined the Chicago American Giants, who played four blocks from the White Sox's Comiskey Park on the South Side. Even though home runs were hard to get in South Side Park, the Giants' huge ballpark, Stearnes led the league in doubles, triples, homers, and steals—a feat not equaled by any major leaguer of the time.

When Suttles joined the Giants in 1933, the two great rivals became teammates. Suttles hit cleanup, while Stearnes led off. While Suttles's batting fell off in the new park, Stearnes flourished. He batted .342 in 1933 and .374 in 1934 to lead the American Giants to the pennant. They lost the Negro League World Series to Philadelphia in seven games. Finally in 1935 Stearnes batted a rousing .434, one of the highest averages achieved in the Negro Leagues.

Stearnes played with the Philadelphia Stars in 1936, moved to Detroit, then came back to Chicago for two years before ending his career in Kansas City at the age of thirty-nine. He went out with a bang. In 1939 he led the league in batting with a .350 average and apparently led in homers as well (no one else seems to have matched his two home runs). In 1940 he topped everyone again with five home runs, the first player to end his career as a league home run champion. In 1946 Stearnes married Nettie Mae McArthur; they had two daughters.

After he left baseball Stearnes said, "I went to work." He engaged in twenty-seven years of heavy labor, initially at six dollars a day, on the rolling mills of the auto plants in Detroit, where he died.

During his career Stearnes ranked first in the Negro League in triples, second in home runs and doubles, and fifth in batting average and stolen bases. He also won three batting crowns and six home run championships. Against white big leaguers he batted .313 with four home runs in fourteen games. Stearnes hit with consistency as well as power, with a lifetime batting average of .352. "I never counted my homers," he once said. "I hit so many, I never counted them." The black leagues did not keep careful records either, but later scholarship has determined that Stearnes was probably one of the two top black home run hitters of his era, 1923 to 1940. Suttles narrowly outslugged him in total homers, 190 to 181, although the renowned JOSH GIBSON might well have been first if he had played more games. Reacting to the absence of Stearnes from the National Baseball Hall of Fame, JAMES "COOL PAPA" BELL said, "If they don't put Turkey Stearnes in the Hall of Fame, they shouldn't put *anybody* in!"

FURTHER READING
Bak, Richard. *Turkey Stearnes and the Detroit Stars* (1994).
Holway, John B. *Blackball Stars* (1988).
Peterson, Robert. *Only the Ball Was White: A History of Legendary Black Players and All-Black Professional Teams* (1970, repr. 1992).
Obituary: *Detroit Free Press*, 6 Sept. 1979.
This entry is taken from the *American National Biography* and is published here with the permission of the American Council of Learned Societies.

JOHN B. HOLWAY

Stedman, Cato (fl. late eighteenth century), Revolutionary War soldier, was a resident of Cambridge, Massachusetts, when the American War of Independence broke out in 1775. Though precise facts about Cato's background are unknown, local lore asserts that Stedman was a slave and was brought to America from Africa, while his surname suggests that he was possibly the slave of the Ebenezer Stedman family of Cambridge.

When British regulars set out from Boston in the early hours of 19 April 1775 to confiscate rebel supplies and munitions at Concord, Massachusetts, little did they realize that their expedition would result in "the shot heard around the world" at nearby Lexington after a historic confrontation with local militiamen. Although patriots were bloodied to the count of eighteen men left dead and wounded on the town green, morale was still high, and the day was far from over. After reaching Concord, the British troops had to retrace their steps and march back to Boston the way they had come. However, their return journey would not be so easy; the action at Lexington stirred up a hornet's nest of activity, and local militia units flooded into the area from near and far. Starting slowly at first and gradually building, the patriot militiamen lined the main road, later known as Battle Road, and sniped at the Redcoats from behind trees and stonewalls. This harassing fire degraded the British march into a disorganized affair that soon became a rout. Among the militiamen that fought that day were at least twenty-one blacks representing eleven towns; one of these was Stedman (Quintal, 236).

On 19 April 1775 Stedman, designated in official records as "a negro," served for one day in the Cambridge militia company commanded by Captain Samuel Thatcher, an old soldier who had fought in the French and Indian War. Militiamen were often called up for brief stints. One of Stedman's fellow soldiers this day was another black man, Cato Boardman. They would spend the day under the command of Colonel Thomas Gardner's militia regiment and, along with the Brookline militia, were stationed near Watson's Corner and Cambridge Bridge. Here, the militiamen offered the British forces a final dose of harassing fire until the enemy finally returned to their base at Charlestown Neck.

Nothing is known of Stedman's actions on this day, but it takes little imagination to picture the events that took place; early in the morning an exhausted messenger arrived in town to announce the Lexington action and that the British were coming. Captain Thatcher and other militia officers hurriedly sent word to their men to grab their guns and gear and quickly form up in the town square; also arriving, no doubt, were a number of boys and older men, as well as some of the town's free blacks and slaves, all anxious to join in the fight. Captain Thatcher probably knew most of these men, by reputation if not personally, and had some quick decisions to make. Those able to handle a musket and fit enough to withstand a long day's march, trustworthy men such as Stedman, were accepted, given a spare musket and ammunition and then went off to battle. Although little thought was apparently given to the blacks of Cambridge, there seemed to be no question as to their loyalty; but this was not the case in every town. Black men were usually called up for public service, such as militia duty, but seem rarely to have been allowed to handle arms while performing their duty. In nearby Arlington panic ensued when a rumor spread that blacks were starting an uprising, which caused desperate housewives to barricade themselves inside their houses armed with pitchforks. This event was all the more interesting because the town's citizens of color were known to be loyal, and three of them were militiamen who had fought that very day.

Perhaps given little consideration at the time beyond the events of the day, the inclusion of Stedman and blacks such as PRINCE ESTABROOK, both free and slave, in the patriot militia during the "Lexington Alarm" would set a precedent for African American military service. Indeed, blacks such as Stedman, JUDE HALL, LONDON DAILEY, and countless others would become mainstays in New England regiments and proved themselves dedicated and accomplished soldiers. Though George Washington would initially question their inclusion in the ranks upon taking command of the American Army in June 1775, he soon changed his mind; even a Hessian officer favorably commented in 1777 that many of these blacks were "strong and brave fellows" (Aptheker, 34).

In regard to the later service of Stedman, the fighting on 19 April 1775 would not be his last conflict. Two years later, in May 1777, Stedman was listed as a soldier in the company of Captain Reuben Slayton in Colonel William Shepard's Fourth Massachusetts Regiment. In this unit Stedman served for the duration of the war, participating in the fighting at Fort Ticonderoga and the Battle of Saratoga in 1777 and at the Battle of Monmouth and the Battle of Rhode Island in 1778; later he served garrison duty in the Hudson Highlands of New York until the regiment was disbanded in late 1783. That Stedman served alongside his fellow white soldiers in an atmosphere of soldierly brotherhood and racial tolerance can hardly be doubted. The sympathetic mindset of the regiment's commander, Colonel Shepard, toward the black men in his regiment is revealed in a letter he wrote in 1782 regarding one such black soldier, an aged conscript and slave named Prince Pierce. Angered by Pierce's "indigent" condition and his advanced age upon his arrival for service at Springfield, Shepard wrote to his master stating that "You must allow me to express my astonishment at the depravity of Mankind, lost to all sense of Humanity, Honesty, and True Religion, not urged by Necessity, but cruel avarice, to Rongfully [sic] distress the Human species because they Can! … his being worn out in private service, and no case for public, he is hereby Discharged, and ought … to fare sumptuously on his former earnings the few days he can live" (Quintal, 26).

Whether or not Stedman lived out his remaining days after the War of Independence in favorable circumstances is unknown, much like the details of most of his life. Though buried in an unmarked grave in Cambridge's Old Burying Ground, the memory of Stedman's service in Lexington on that historic day in April 1775 has nonetheless gained a lasting and well-deserved place in the history of the American Revolution.

FURTHER READING
Aptheker, Herbert. *The Negro in the American Revolution* (1940).

Kaplan, Sidney, and Emma Nogrady Kaplan. *The Black Presence in the Era of the American Revolution* (1989).

Quintal, George Jr. *Patriots of Color* (2002).

GLENN ALLEN KNOBLOCK

Steele, Carrie (c. 1829–3 Nov. 1900), children's home founder and director, was born into slavery in Georgia, as was her father. Her mother, also a slave, was born in Virginia. As a small child, Steele was orphaned. Unlike most slaves, Steele learned to read and write. After Emancipation she spent sixteen years as a train depot "matron" in Macon, Georgia. By 1880 Steele, one of Atlanta's first black property owners, resided in a two-room house at 112 Wheat Street near Piedmont Avenue. Wheat Street, later renamed Auburn Avenue, became black Atlanta's historic heart. The 1880 Federal Census recorded Steele's occupation as "dressmaker," her race as "mulatto," and her marital status as "widowed." The identity of Steele's first spouse, the date of their marriage, and the number of children they may have had together are unclear. Steele evidently had at least one child, Bob Steele, according to his obituary in the *Atlanta Constitution* (31 Aug. 1899). Born during 1843 in Milledgeville, Georgia, at age twenty-one, he moved to Atlanta. He married, had five sons, and became a prominent barber with an interracial clientele and a lucrative shop at 13 Marietta Street.

Between 1880 and 1882 Steele was hired as a car shed "stewardess," maintaining the facilities, keeping them clean, and assisting the travelers, for the Central Railroad of Georgia in downtown Atlanta's Union Depot. The hungry, abandoned babies and children she regularly found at the station moved her deeply. She vividly remembered her own experiences as an orphan. During her workday she gathered the children to play inside an empty boxcar, and each evening brought them home with her, giving them food, comfort, and a place to sleep. As she took in more children, she recognized the need for a larger living space than she could afford on her $100 per month salary alone. To raise funds, Steele penned and printed up her own life story, then sold it on the streets. There are no known surviving copies of this autobiographical booklet.

On 12 October 1888 Fulton County granted Steele a charter for a black orphanage, the Carrie Steele Orphan Home. She raised additional money from both the black and white communities. She also sold her Wheat Street residence to Henry A. Rucker, who later constructed the Rucker Building,

a black professional office complex, on the lot. In 1890 Steele retired from her railroad job and wed Joseph (or Josehia) Logan, a New Yorker who shared her passion for community service. After raising over five thousand dollars, Carrie Steele Logan secured a ten-year (later ninety-nine-year) lease from the city on four acres along Roy Street. There she built a three-story brick structure with room for fifty homeless children. It was dedicated in 1892. Steele Logan secured the Home's future financial health through contracts with the city and county to house local orphans.

Steele Logan's black contemporaries greatly admired her farsighted efforts that surely included but went beyond food, clothing, and shelter. Reverend E. R. Carter's *The Black Side* (1894) praised "the spacious and most beautiful campus" where the children attended school and acquired skills in, among other things, housekeeping, cooking, sewing, and farming. "They are taught, first of all, to pray … [E]ven the little ones of four years can repeat chapters in the Bible … Mrs. Logan … is wrapped up in her work … the greatest joy of her life … [A]ll should lend a helping hand to push forward the grand and glorious work" (Carter, 35–37). *Some Efforts of American Negroes for Their Own Social Betterment* (1898), edited by scholar W. E. B. DuBois, included staff member Minnie L. Perry's report on the Carrie Steele Orphan Home. By then the grounds included a hospital, and since 1890 it had "sheltered 225 souls" total (Carter, 60–61). "In short," Perry observed, "we are taking castaways, and through God's help, striving to make of them good citizens, who will be a blessing rather than a menace to the community" (Carter, 60–61). In her famous "lifting as we climb" speech to the organized woman suffrage movement's fiftieth anniversary celebration, pioneering feminist and civil rights leader MARY ELIZA CHURCH TERRELL mentioned the Carrie Steele Orphan Home. She placed it in its wider social context: the home was one of numerous charities and widespread advocacy movements that testified to black women's unflagging compassion, intelligence, resilience, and resourcefulness.

Steele Logan directed the orphanage until her death at age seventy-one from a paralytic stroke. Her tombstone was engraved with the words: "Mother of orphans. She hath done what she could" (Henson). Joseph Logan managed the orphanage until his own death on 15 November 1904. His epitaph read "Father of orphans." The Carrie Steele Orphan Home enjoyed substantial goodwill and support from both the black and white communities, and other socially concerned blacks stepped forward to fill in the leadership void. Thus the Home and its mission of serving the most vulnerable black children lived on. Upon the retirement of Clara Maxwell Pitts, executive director from 1908 to 1950, the facility was renamed the Carrie Steele-Pitts Home. Pitts's daughter and successor Mae Maxwell Yates moved the Home to 667 Fairburn Road NW, in Atlanta. In 1976 Ollivette Allison, a former resident of the Home and its first professionally trained staff social worker, became executive director.

In 1998 Steele Logan was named one of the Georgia Women of Achievement. Between 1888 and early 2007 the facility she established sheltered over twenty thousand children. In keeping with both changing social needs and its original mission, the Home's focus shifted away from orphans to wards of the state. This remarkable, unbroken record of service evokes a conserved fragment of Steele Logan's fund-raising booklet: "It is appointed to me in my old age to accomplish what I believe to be a great and glorious work, and one that shall live long after my poor frail body has dropped into the dust whence it came" (Perry, 60).

FURTHER READING

The Historic Oakland Cemetery, Atlanta, Georgia, and the Atlanta University Center's Robert W. Woodruff Library each hold a few archival materials on Carrie Steele.

Jordan, Casper L. "Carrie Steele," in *Notable Black American Women Book Two* (1996).

Terrell, Mary Church. *The Progress of Colored Women: An Address Delivered Before the National American Woman Suffrage Association at the Columbia Theatre, Washington, DC, February 18, 1898* (1898).

Obituary: "Carrie Steele Died Last Night," *Atlanta Constitution*, 4 Nov. 1900.

MARY KRANE DERR

Steele, C. K. (7 Feb. 1914–19 Aug. 1980), Baptist minister and civil rights leader, was born Charles Kenzie Steele in Gary, West Virginia, the only child of Henry L. Steele, a coal miner, and Lyde Bailor. From his youth Steele wanted to be a preacher. While still in elementary school, he conducted religious services for fellow students and delivered his first sermon at age fifteen. He began his ministerial studies at Morehouse College in 1934 and was ordained the following year. After completing his course work in 1938, he accepted a call to pastor the Hall Street Baptist Church in Montgomery, Alabama. There he met Lois Brock, the daughter of a successful contractor. The couple married in 1944; they had six children. In 1945 Steele moved to Augusta, Georgia, where he led the Springfield Baptist Church. In 1952 the Steele family moved again, this time to Tallahassee, Florida, where Steele assumed the pastorate of the Bethel Missionary Baptist Church.

Steele rose to prominence as the leader of the Tallahassee bus boycott. On 26 May 1956 Wilhelmina Jakes and Carrie Patterson, students at Florida Agricultural and Mechanical University (FAMU), were arrested when they refused to move from the "whites only" section of a city bus. The next day three thousand FAMU students rallied to protest the arrests and voted to boycott the buses. The protest spread beyond the campus as students persuaded older African Americans to join the boycott. On 29 May a group of black ministers and businesspeople met with city officials in a fruitless attempt to resolve the issue. That evening 450 people gathered at Bethel Baptist Church and decided to continue the boycott. They formed the Inter-Civic Council (ICC) to coordinate the protest, with Steele as president. The nine-member steering committee consisted of a dentist, a store owner, a funeral director, and six clergymen. The ICC offered a three-point proposal for resolving the crisis: (1) treating courteously all passengers, (2) hiring black drivers, and (3) seating passengers on a first-come, first-served basis. City commissioners told ICC representatives that courteous treatment had always been the bus company's policy and that hiring black drivers for routes in the black community would be considered. The city offered to permit seating on a first-come, first-served basis as long as members of different races did not occupy seats in the same row. Some members of the ICC favored accepting this compromise, but Steele held out for full integration, and the boycott continued.

Following the model established six months earlier during the Montgomery bus boycott, the ICC established car pools to convey residents who had stopped riding the buses. City officials decided the best way to break the boycott was to attack the car pools. At first the drivers were targeted by the police, who issued traffic citations at the slightest excuse. Steele himself was arrested three times in one day. When this harassment failed to slow the car pool, twenty-two drivers were arrested and charged with operating an unlicensed transportation system. The defendants argued that since no fares were collected, they had violated no law.

Judge John A. Rudd ignored this reasoning, found the defendants guilty, and fined them five hundred dollars each. The ICC ceased operating the car pool but continued the boycott.

The bus company suspended all operations on 1 July following a 60 percent decline in its revenues. In August it announced its willingness to hire black drivers and resumed limited service with only a few front seats reserved for whites, but the ICC rejected this scheme. On Christmas Eve 1956 Steele and two other ministers rode in the "whites only" section of a city bus without incident. When the city commission revoked the bus company's charter for not enforcing the segregation ordinance, the company sought a restraining order against the city.

Community tensions increased as the boycott continued. Steele and other ICC leaders received anonymous telephone threats, windows in Steele's parsonage were broken, and a cross was burned in front of Steele's church. The legal bickering between the city and the bus company dragged on for months. Full bus service resumed without fanfare in late 1957, and black riders began sitting wherever they pleased. Eventually the segregation clause was removed from the company's contract, and by May 1958 city buses were operating on a completely integrated basis.

The success of the Tallahassee boycott catapulted Steele into the front ranks of southern civil rights leaders. On 10 January 1957 he joined MARTIN LUTHER KING JR. at the Atlanta conference where the Southern Christian Leadership Conference (SCLC) was born. Steele was named vice president of the organization, a position he held for the rest of his life. During his tenure he was involved in planning SCLC's campaigns against segregation throughout the South. In 1963 he traveled to Albany, Georgia, and led a demonstration that resulted in his arrest. Steele toured northern cities to raise money for the ICC and SCLC, often at considerable personal sacrifice. In 1964 he underwent surgery to remove a cyst on his larynx that left his voice permanently damaged.

Steele's activism was not appreciated by all members of his congregation. Some felt he spent too much time working for civil rights and not enough time in the pulpit. For seven years he went without an increase in salary and in 1968 staved off an attempt to force his resignation. He remained as pastor of Bethel until his death in 1980.

Steele belongs in the ranks of African American ministers such as Martin Luther King Jr., FRED SHUTTLESWORTH, RALPH ABERNATHY, and JAMES LAWSON, who provided strategic vision and moral guidance for the nonviolent civil rights movement. His statue stands in front of the downtown Tallahassee bus terminal named in his honor.

FURTHER READING
Padgett, Gregory B. "C. K. Steele and the Tallahassee Bus Boycott," M.A. thesis, Florida State University (1979).
Padgett, Gregory B. "C. K. "The Push for Equality—A Bus Boycott Takes Root and Blossoms," *Florida Humanities Council Forum* (Winter 1995–1996).
Rabby, Glenda Alice. *The Pain and the Promise: The Struggle for Civil Rights in Tallahassee, Florida* (1999).
Obituary: *New York Times*, 20 Aug. 1980.

PAUL T. MURRAY

Steele, Claude (1 Jan. 1946–), psychologist and educator, was born Claude Mason Steele in Chicago, Illinois, the son of Shelby Steele Sr., a black truck driver, and Ruth Hootman, a white social worker. He was raised in Phoenix, Illinois, a working-class suburb of Chicago, along with two sisters and his identical twin brother, SHELBY STEELE JR., who became a well-known author and social commentator. Steele's parents were active in the civil rights movement and were founding members of the first chapter of the Congress of Racial Equality (CORE), which began at the University of Chicago. As a child, Claude attended protests and demonstrations with his parents and learned principles of nonviolence. Steele encountered racial discrimination himself through such experiences as having his maternal grandparents not welcome him into their home.

After high school Steele moved to Cleveland, Ohio, to attend Hiram College and study dentistry. However, an experience seeing the famed African American psychologist Kenneth Clark on television discussing the Harlem summer race riot in 1964 awakened his interest in psychology. Steele met Dorothy Munson at Hiram, and they married in August 1967; they had a son and a daughter. After graduating from Hiram, Steele applied to graduate school at Ohio State University and the Graduate Center of the City University of New York, where Clark was teaching. Because the graduate center lost his application, Steele enrolled at Ohio State, where he received his master's degree in 1969 in social psychology and his doctorate in 1971 in social psychology with a minor in statistical psychology.

After graduate school, Steele's first job was at Utah State University, where he began studying how people handle threats to their self-image. Steele left Utah after two years and joined the faculty at the University of Washington at Seattle, where he conducted research with colleagues on how alcohol influences cognitive and perceptual functioning. He began to develop his best-known research after his move to the University of Michigan in 1987. He analyzed how stereotypes about a group affect performance, which became known as stereotype threat theory. What motivated this line of research was Steele's observation that black college students' academic performance lagged behind that of their white counterparts even when the black students came from a middle-class background and were among the most academically prepared.

Steele undertook a series of experiments showing that black college students who took a standardized test performed worse when they were told that the test was a measure of their intellectual abilities and performed better when not given this prompt. He proposed that black students became so anxious about fulfilling the racial stereotype of black intellectual inferiority that they ended up performing poorly. Steele's research drastically shifted thinking about racial differences in academic performance and about stereotypes more generally. Steele not only analyzed the problem but also focused on creating solutions. He helped to develop a successful intervention program at the University of Michigan to help black students excel in college environments. After participating in the program, black students' grade point averages were similar to white students' and were about one point higher than those of black students not in the program.

Steele continued his work on stereotype threat and published dozens of articles on the issue. In 1991 he moved to join the faculty at Stanford University, where he later chaired the department for four years and was named the Lucie Stern Professor in the Social Sciences. Steele generalized his theory beyond race to show that other identity group stereotypes, such as gender stereotypes, affect performance. He also published works with colleagues on the type of feedback that minority students should receive from teachers to help them perform well, and he worked on other interventions in conjunction with his wife, who obtained a doctorate in education.

By 1996 Steele's work was receiving national acclaim. He was elected to serve as president of the Western Psychological Association and the Society for Personality and Social Psychology. His colleagues in psychology honored him with three of the most prestigious awards in the discipline—the Gordon Allport Prize in Social Psychology, the William James Fellow Award for Distinguished Scientific Career Contributions from the American Psychological Society, and the Distinguished Scientific Contribution Award from the American Psychological Association. In appreciation of his broader intellectual impact, he was elected to the American Academy of Arts and Sciences, the American Academy of Education, and the National Academy of Sciences, one of the highest honors that can be bestowed upon an American scientist. Likewise universities such as Yale, Princeton, and Chicago presented Steele with honorary degrees.

Steele's contributions extended beyond the academy, and he became a public voice on issues of race and education. In his expert testimony before the U.S. Supreme Court in 2003 on the affirmative action cases *Gratz et al. v. Bollinger et al.* and *Grutter et al. v. Bollinger et al.* Steele discussed the nature of standardized tests and the factors that may lead to racial differences in performance on such tests. He offered his support to universities considering race as one of many criteria used when admitting students. Moreover, he influenced public debate through his editorials and appearances in major national media, many times arguing a position opposite that of Shelby Steele Jr., who is known for his conservative writings.

FURTHER READING

"Claude M. Steele: Award for Distinguished Career Contributions to the Public Interest," *American Psychologist* (Nov. 2003).

Lehrman, Sally. "Performance without Anxiety," *Scientific American* (Feb. 2005).

SABRINA PENDERGRASS

Steele, Michael (19 Oct. 1958–), politician and Republican Party chair, was born Michael Stephen Steele at Andrews Air Force Base in Maryland and adopted by William and Maebell Steele. By the time Steele was five, his father had passed away; his mother later married John Tucker. He grew up in northwest Washington, D.C. At Archbishop Carroll Roman Catholic High School, Steele became interested in the theater and politics. He was a part of numerous organizations, such as the Glee Club and the student body council. In addition, he was a member of the National Honor Society. After graduating from high school in 1976, Steele continued

Michael Steele delivers a victory speech on 12 September 2006 in Greenbelt, Maryland, after winning the state's Republican primary for U.S. Senate. (AP Images.)

his education at the prestigious Johns Hopkins University in Baltimore, Maryland. He later acknowledged that he experienced some difficulties in his early undergraduate year, Steele earned a B.A. in international studies in 1981. He studied for the priesthood at Villanova, but left, believing that the seminary limited his ambitions. In 1991 he earned a J.D. from Georgetown University Law School, and began his career as a lawyer and politician. He married Andrea Derritt Steele in 1985, and they had two children, Michael II and Drew.

Steele entered law practice in 1991 with the Washington law firm of Cleary, Gottlieb, Steen, and Hamilton, specializing in corporate and financial law. This work gave Steele a solid understanding of how the financial, political, and corporate worlds intersected. Through his work on these issues, and business travel to England and Japan, he developed a nuanced understanding of Wall Street and the role of public policy in the economy. In 1997, after six years with the firm, joined the Mills Corporation, a real estate company in Virginia. A year later he

founded the Steele Group, which provided lobbying and consulting services. His strong interest in politics however, prompted Steele to become an active member of the Republican Party in Maryland and Washington.

As a child Steele took to heart the lessons of his mother that government was problematic, especially for African Americans. Further, her refusal of government assistance during the trying times following the death of her first husband taught Steele lessons that had a great impact on his life. The ideas of self-reliance resonated with Steele and, when Ronald Reagan was elected president in 1980, he became an active member of the Republican Party. During the 1990s, Steele served in a number of positions in the state of Maryland: chair of the Republican Central Committee in Prince George's County and chair of the Maryland State Republican Party in 2000. He was the first African American to serve as a state chairman. By the beginning of the 2000s Steele was a prominent figure in Republican circles, poised to gain higher office and stature.

In 2002, Steele successfully ran for lieutenant governor of Maryland. Central to his political platform was his support of the death penalty for violent offenders. This support has largely been confined to murderers and rapists. Steele proposed to study whether or not African Americans were unfairly being sentenced to death in comparison to others; however, he failed to produce a report detailing the alleged disparities. He also proposed reforming Minority Business Enterprise and chairing the governor's education initiative. In 2004, when BARACK OBAMA, then a candidate for the U.S. Senate from Illinois, captured the media's attention with his address to the Democratic National Committee Convention in Boston, Steele won kudos for his remarks to the Republican National Convention in New York City. Building on his visible tenure as lieutenant governor, where he was an active presence within the Maryland state government and a frequent visitor to locales around the state, and on his speech at the 2004 RNC convention, Steele announced his candidacy for the United States Senate in 2006 after the incumbent Democratic senator Paul Sarbanes announced his retirement. Steele lost the race against the Democratic congressman Ben Cardin by eleven percentage points. His respectable showing in a strongly Democratic state nonetheless enhanced his reputation within both state and national Republican circles. After his loss, Steele became even more active in the national Republican Party and made clear his interest in becoming chair of the RNC. He also became chair of GOPAC, a Republican political action committee, and practiced law at the Washington, D.C., firm of Dewey & LeBoeuf.

In January 2009, after several ballots and contentious debate, Michael Steele was elected chair of the Republican National Committee with 91 of the 168 RNC votes cast. Race was central to his election, since Michael Dawson, then-chair of the RNC, had a checkered past, including membership in a whites-only club. Politically, Steele has been difficult to pin down, as he has struck a moderate tone in Maryland yet conservative within the national party. He is the first African American elected to the post and only the second African American chosen to lead a major American political party. The first was RONALD BROWN, who led the Democratic National Committee from 1989 to 1993. Steele's early tenure as party chair proved controversial, however, as he faced criticism from numerous factions of the GOP. Republicans alleged that he was not properly using and directing party money. Specifically, critics noted that he began his tenure in 2009 with more than $20 million in the RNC budget, while only $4 million was left at the end of 2010. In one well-known incident, he was accused of signing off on an RNC-sponsored outing to a lesbian-themed bondage club that cost close to $2,000. His alleged improprieties, coupled with several controversial statements—such as his remark that the right-wing radio commentator Rush Limbaugh, a powerful conservative talk radio commentator, was simply an "entertainer"—led key financial backers of the G.O.P. to express increasing distrust of his leadership. Several neoconservative Republicans, notably William Kristol of the *Weekly Standard*, also attacked Steele for his statement in the summer of 2010 that the U.S.-led war in Afghanistan was a conflict of Obama's choosing. Steele nonetheless presided over a period of Republican resurgence following the Arizona senator John McCain's presidential loss to Barack Obama in 2008. As party chair during the 2010 midterm elections, he helped Republicans win the House, increase their seats in the Senate, and regain several governorships. Still, controversy continued to dog him throughout his tenure, and it was a surprise to many when, on 13 December 2010, he announced that he would run for reelection as RNC chair. In January 2011, recognizing after several ballots that he could not win, Steele removed himself from the five person field of candidates for the position of Republican Chair, and was replaced by Reince Priebus of Wisconsin.

FURTHER READING

Burton, Danielle. "10 Things You Didn't Know about Michael Steele," *U.S. News & World Report*, 7 Apr. 2008.

Stratton, Lashell. "Mr. Steele Goes to Annapolis: A D.C. Kid Can Grow Up to Be Lieutenant Governor," *The Common Denominator*, 7 Apr. 2003.

Sokolove, Michael. "Why Is Michael Steele a Republican Candidate?" *New York Times*, 20 Mar. 2006.

DARYL A. CARTER

Steele, Shelby (1 Jan. 1946–), author, professor, and political commentator, was born in Chicago, Illinois, one of four children of Shelby Steele Sr. and Ruth Steele. Steele's father, born into poverty in Kentucky in 1900, completed only the third grade before being pushed out of school to work in white-owned tobacco fields. He left Kentucky for Chicago in 1914 and met Shelby's mother, Ruth, a white social worker, while volunteering in the early 1940s for the Congress of Racial Equality (CORE), an organization composed mainly of white middle-class college students seeking to change racist attitudes through peaceful protest. Steele's father supported his family by working as a nonunion truck driver and earning extra income as a rental property owner, garage builder, exterminator, and paint salesman. Through reading and rigorous independent study, he achieved a high level of self-education.

Both of Steele's parents were devoted civil rights activists who believed in nonviolent passive resistance. Steele grew up "watching them struggle against an unapologetically racist America" (*White Guilt*, 17) and accompanying them to political marches and rallies in the 1950s. In his own writings Steele credited his racially mixed heritage and his parents' example of political activism as remarkable gifts that demystified his outlook on racial issues and facilitated his later cultural insights.

Raised in a black community just south of Chicago, Steele attended segregated schools until the sixth grade, when he was cruelly persecuted over several months by a white teacher after misreading a sentence on the first day of class. Plagued by self-doubt, Steele vowed not to let his parents know what was happening. When his brother told his parents of the situation, they organized a boycott of the school and the teacher was dismissed. Steele later theorized that his maltreatment conformed to a timeless pattern of racial discrimination that carried profound psychological affects for segregated blacks. Through his parents' exertions, Steele was able to switch schools the next year, becoming the lone black student in his junior high class. Among white students and teachers, Steele observed how the segregation-era educational system fostered negative stereotypes toward black Americans.

Steele's teenage jobs in Chicago included picking vegetables on the truck farms south of the city and three summer stints in the stockyards, followed by a period as a bus driver for the Chicago Transit Authority, a job he quit at age twenty-one as a gesture of identification with the black power movement immediately after hearing a militant speech by activist RICHARD CLAXTON (DICK) GREGORY.

Steele entered Coe College in Cedar Rapids, Iowa, where he was one of eighteen black students in his class. In 1965 he volunteered with the Summer Community Organization and Political Education (SCOPE) project, a voter registration effort connected with the Southern Christian Leadership Conference (SCLC). During his junior year of college, Steele met his future wife, Rita, at an activist meeting. They were married in 1967. During his senior year at Coe, Steele led a student protest that burst into the office of the college president and presented a list of "nonnegotiable demands" from black students. Though the demands were implemented, Steele later expressed regret for this action and explored in his writings what he perceived as the dubious long-term consequences of 1960s black militancy.

Steele graduated with a B.A. in political science in 1968 and went on to earn an M.A. in sociology from Southern Illinois University. He later attended the University of Utah, teaching black literature courses while he worked toward his Ph.D. in English, which he received in 1974. That year Steele accepted a position as a professor of English literature at San Jose State University, where he would remain until 1991.

In the 1980s Steele began publishing essays in journals such as *Harper's, Commentary,* and the *American Scholar,* quickly gaining a reputation for cogent and introspective analysis of race issues. In 1990 he won an Emmy Award and two awards for television documentary writing—the Writer's Guild Award and the San Francisco Film Festival Award—for his work on "Seven Days in Bensonhurst," a PBS *Frontline* documentary examining the racially motivated killing of Yusef Hawkins in Brooklyn, New York.

Steele won the National Book Critics Circle Award in 1991 for *The Content of Our Character: A New Vision of Race in America,* a series of commentaries on race that drew heavily on his personal experience. The book included the groundbreaking essay "On Being Black and Middle Class." This frequently reprinted article focused on the dilemma of blacks who have escaped poverty but are caught in a "double bind" produced by deep antagonism between their racial identity and a middle-class identity infused with "white" values.

Throughout *The Content of Our Character,* Steele called on blacks to rely on individual effort within the American mainstream—rather than collective action against the mainstream—as a means of advancement. He argued that blacks must learn to make the difficult but crucial distinction between actual victimization, which should be resisted with every resource, and self-destructive identification with the victim's status. "No illusion weakens [blacks] more," Steele stated, than "the illusion of deliverance by others" (174).

Steele's next book, *A Dream Deferred: The Second Betrayal of Black Freedom in America* (1998) maintained that the vast culture of collective entitlements instituted since the 1960s was as undemocratic as the racial and gender discrimination it was intended to redress. Quota-based affirmative action, for example, stigmatized its recipients, presupposed black helplessness, and diverted America's focus from the "real work" of integration. For his iconoclastic stances on issues of black development, Steele drew criticism from African American leaders, some of whom saw him as a racial apostate who ignored the systemic oppression of the black underclass.

Steele's third book, *White Guilt: How Blacks and Whites Together Destroyed the Promise of the Civil Rights Era* (2006), argued that the age of white supremacy had given way to an age of white guilt in which whites dissociate themselves from the racist past but cling to a spurious moral authority that comes from "helping" blacks through superficial race-based handouts. In this work, Steele thoughtfully addressed his controversial identity as a "black conservative," declaring that he accepted this label as the price of his intellectual freedom. Rejecting the interpretation of conservatism as "anti-black," Steele described his politics as a necessary corrective to failed liberalism and the true heir to the moral-democratic vision of the early MARTIN LUTHER KING JR.

In 1994 Steele became a research fellow of the Hoover Institution at Stanford University, where his work focused on multiculturalism, identity politics, and affirmative action. In 2004 he was awarded the National Humanities Medal, and in 2006 he received the Bradley Prize for his contributions to the study of race issues.

Steele's career courageously explored the meaning of race in America. His work profoundly invigorated the nation's cultural and intellectual dialogue while expressing eloquent, uncompromising resistance to monolithic definitions of African American identity.

FURTHER READING

Anderson, Michael. "Still Waiting," *New York Times*, 22 Nov. 1998.

Monroe, Sylvester. "Up from Obscurity," *Time* (13 Aug. 1990).

Monroe, Sylvester. "Nothing Is Ever Simply Black and White," *Time* (12 Aug. 1991).

Williams, Patricia J. "A Kind of Race Fatigue," *New York Times*, 16 Sept. 1990.

PATRICK CHURA

Stephens, Charlotte Andrews (1854–17 Dec. 1951), teacher, high school principal, and librarian, was the first African American public school teacher in Little Rock, Arkansas. She was born to slave parents, William Wallace Andrews (usually known as Wallace) and Caroline Sherman Andrews, in Little Rock. When he was four years old, Wallace Andrews had begun working in the home of Colonel Chester Ashley, later the U.S. senator from Arkansas and Little Rock's most prominent citizen. The Ashleys were unusually generous with their slaves, and the senator's wife, seeing Wallace's keen intellect, taught him to read. After Wallace Andrews married Caroline Sherman, Colonel Ashley worked with Caroline's owner to enable Caroline to hire her time out. This made it possible for the young couple to live together and gave them a home in which to live. Caroline Andrews ran a laundry business from her home to compensate her owners for permission to hire her own time. Shrewd and hard-working, she was able to pay her owners the required $10 a month and still have money remaining for her own expenses. Soon after their marriage, Wallace Andrews conducted prayer meetings in his home, after which he would offer reading lessons, despite the danger of teaching blacks to read in the antebellum South. He also taught his wife and Charlotte to read. He continued to teach and to be active in ministry, later becoming an elder in the AME church.

Charlotte was the third child born to the Andrews (a second child died soon after birth). As a young child, Lottie, as she was called, helped her mother with the laundry and worked at lessons with her father. In 1861, when she was seven years old, she was taken from her family by her mother's owners to serve as housemaid to an uncle who lived ten miles away. She stayed there until September of 1863, when Little Rock was captured by Union forces, and she was returned to her parents by a friend. The fall of Little Rock to the Union Army meant freedom for all African Americans in the area, and they expressed a keen desire to obtain the education that slavery had denied them. Wallace Andrews, with the help of a black Union veteran, began teaching school sessions in a black Methodist church building, which stood on land given to the church by the Ashleys in 1854. Beginning in 1863, the building also served as a school that admitted students of all ages, including adults, who paid twenty-five cents a week, if they could, to attend.

In the fall of 1864, Wallace Andrews traveled north to ask for support in establishing a school for African Americans. The twenty-five-cent tuition was more than most black families could afford, and Andrews was convinced of the need for a free school. He had served as commissioner for the Freedman's Bureau in Little Rock and had worked with newly freed slaves seeking services, such as employment, food, and shelter. Having served the black community in a leadership role for all of his adult life, he was well aware of the educational needs of the community, and he had ideas for attending to those needs. In addition, his contacts in the AME denomination would, he hoped, prove to be sources of support for a free school. He traveled to Louisville, Memphis, St. Louis, and various towns in Ohio, Indiana, and Illinois. According to his travel journal, he was able to collect a few books and a little over $100—clearly not enough to establish a school.

In 1865 Wallace Andrews attended the AME conference in Louisiana, Missouri, where he was ordained minister and commissioned to organized churches in the area between Fort Smith and Pine Bluff, Arkansas. In 1866 he organized a church in Pine Bluff, and after discovering that there were no educational opportunities for African Americans, and that none of them could read or write, he arranged for his own children, including twelve-year-old Lottie, to go to Pine Bluff and help him start a school. The school drew students of all ages, like the first black school in Little Rock, and Lottie taught the youngest children. Eventually, however, her mother believed that young Lottie should live at home and persuaded her husband to let Lottie return. Later that year, her father died in Pine Bluff.

In 1867, the Quakers, with the help of the Freedman's Bureau, built Union School. In 1869, one of the teachers fell ill, and Lottie Andrews, only fifteen years old, taught the rest of the term. During this time, the city of Little Rock established a public school system and bought the Union School property from the Quakers. At the end of the school year, Andrews and three other African American teachers were hired to teach the following year.

After teaching for one full year, Andrews used money she had saved to attend Oberlin College. The Little Rock school board gave her a year's leave of absence so she could attend her first year at Oberlin, and when she ran out of money, she returned to Little Rock to teach. She continued her studies at Oberlin, with intermittent breaks for teaching, until 1873. She studied Latin, English, music, history, geometry, and the Bible. Andrews returned to teach in Little Rock in 1873, and in 1876 she married John Herbert Stephens, a carpenter and a teacher. He also served as deputy sheriff and deputy constable for a time before the 1890s, when legal segregation expelled most blacks from public life. The couple had eight children, six of whom reached adulthood and received a college education.

Although she never received a degree, Charlotte Stephens continued her studies at various teacher's colleges and institutes throughout her life, including at the University of California in 1922. Stephens taught for seventy consecutive years in Little Rock before retiring in 1939. She taught all grades, but particularly high school English, Latin, and science. Among her many students were composers FLORENCE BEATRICE SMITH PRICE and WILLIAM GRANT STILL. She also worked as the librarian at Dunbar High School and Junior College and twice served as a school principal.

Following the example of her parents, Stephens devoted her life to education and leadership in the African American community. In addition to her long teaching career, she was a charter member of the National Association of Colored Women and the Arkansas Teachers Association. She was also a member of the Phyllis Wheatley Branch of the YWCA, and she was active in the National Association for the Advancement of Colored People. In 1910 an elementary school was named for her, becoming, for fifty years, the only school in Little Rock named for a woman. The building was replaced with a new one in 1950, a year before her death at the age of ninety-eight. This building was replaced in 2001, and continued to bear her name.

FURTHER READING

"Interview with Charlotte Stephens, Little Rock, Arkansas," *Slave Narratives*, CD-ROM (2000).
Terry, Adolphine Fletcher. *Charlotte Stephens: Little Rock's First Black Teacher* (1973).
Obituary: *Arkansas Gazette*, 19 Dec. 1951.

ANN O'BRYAN

Stephens, George E. (1832–24 Apr. 1888), abolitionist, activist, soldier, and journalist, was born in Philadelphia, Pennysylvania, to William and Mary Stephens, free African Americans who had fled Virginia's eastern shore in the wake of the NAT TURNER rebellion. Little is known of Stephens's early education, but he likely attended a combination of segregated primary schools in Philadelphia and the

Sunday school of the First African Baptist, a fervently abolitionist church that his parents attended. Prior to the war Stephens worked as a cabinetmaker, a skilled position that offered him elite status in the urban Philadelphia black community.

Stephens's antebellum exploits included a wide range of civic and political activities. In 1853 he helped found the Banneker Institute, an African American literary society and library, honoring BENJAMIN BANNEKER, the African American scientist and inventor. While working with the society he met influential white leaders including General Oliver Otis Howard—later head of Freedmen's Bureau—and the antislavery congressman William D. Kelley. In November 1857 he became a sailor on the USS *Walker* that was part of the U.S. Coast Survey, forced to abandon cabinetmaking because of limited job opportunities for skilled African American craftsmen. While roaming ashore in Charleston, South Carolina, he was arrested under the Negro Seaman's Act, which obligated vessels to confine all black seamen to the city jail while in port. Eventually a white officer of his ship secured Stephens's release, and he returned to Philadelphia in the spring of 1858. On the eve of the war Stephens's political activities included leading support rallies for John Brown in the aftermath of the Harpers Ferry raid. By the late 1850s Stephens had become increasingly depressed about the lot of African Americans in the United States and began advocating emigration to Haiti or elsewhere in the Western Hemisphere.

The outbreak of the American Civil War revived Stephens's hopes for ending slavery. He joined the Army of the Potomac as cook and personal servant to Benjamin C. Tilghman, colonel of the Twenty-sixth Pennsylvania Infantry with whom he served until January 1863. Stephens condemned the Emancipation Proclamation for not freeing slaves in the border South. Yet he believed that the Proclamation's call for black Union soldiers to be a vital step toward the goal of ending slavery, viewing military service as the only way for blacks to gain freedom and full citizenship. He supported of the efforts of the Massachusetts governor John A. Andrews to form the Fifty-fourth Massachusetts Volunteer Infantry, one of the earliest black regiments recruited in the Northern states. Stephens spoke at black churches in Philadelphia imploring men that "We do not deserve the name of freemen ... if we disregard the teachings of the hours and fail to place in the balance against oppression, treason and tyranny, our interests, our arms, and our lives" (*Weekly Anglo-African*, 18 Apr. 1863). Stephens deeply believed that the Fifty-fourth held the fate of all African Americans and joined the unit in February 1863. The popular black newspaper the New York *Weekly Anglo-African* continued to publish his correspondence, which began in 1859 and had continued while he was attached to the Army of the Potomac. Stephens, a reliable soldier, was quickly promoted to sergeant of Company B in April 1863. The War Department prohibited the promotion of blacks to line officers, keeping Stephens from attaining higher rank during the war.

In early June 1863 the Fifty-fourth arrived on the Sea Islands of South Carolina. From there, the regiment made its first raid on the coastal town of Darien, Georgia. The unnecessary destruction of the town, Stephens believed, would damage the regiment's reputation. On 18 July he participated in the disastrous attack on Battery Wagner on Morris Island, South Carolina, in which the regiment's famed commander Colonel Robert Gould Shaw was killed. As the Union army's Department of the South attempted to take Charleston proper, Battery Wagner guarded the approach to Fort Sumter in the harbor. During the famous charge of the Fifty-fourth on that installation, Stephens escaped along with a handful of his own company, but he was wounded, having a rifle shot out of his hands during the engagement. Of the six hundred enlisted men and twenty-three officers that the Fifty-fourth sent into battle, the unit lost 272 killed, wounded, and captured. Confederates lost only 181 men. Although the attack failed to carry Battery Wagner, the Fifty-fourth garnered national praise for demonstrating reliability and heroism and effectively ended the North's debate over the use of black troops. Stephens's devastated company, however, would not reach full strength again until January 1864. In the aftermath it was assigned fatigue duty as ditchdiggers and became increasingly demoralized. This dangerous duty, digging a trench to the front of the fort, took place in full view of the Confederate defenders who kept the Union soldiers under constant fire. During this long summer Stephens, disillusioned by the constant elevation of inexperienced white officers over veteran black soldiers, briefly considered a transfer to another regiment.

Stephens and other black soldiers in the Department of the South protested the War Department's policy of unequal pay (ten dollars a month for black soldiers compared to thirteen dollars for whites). His letters to the *Anglo-African* decried the double standard in pay, which he saw as an attempt to destroy black hopes for full citizenship. The men of the Fifty-fourth refused all pay for eighteen months, until granted equal pay. By December 1863 Stephens's wife, whom he had married in 1857, and family were destitute in Philadelphia, and only charity enabled them to pay the rent. In early February 1864 the regiment captured Jacksonville, Florida, and then fought bravely at the ill-considered Union assault at the Battle of Olustee, Florida. In the wake of the battle Confederates massacred many wounded black soldiers. In April 1864 Stephens returned to Folly and Morris Island, South Carolina. During the summer after the defeat at Olustee the pay issue led to several instances of mutiny and insubordination in the regiment. With the regiment bordering on anarchy in July 1863 Congress reversed earlier law and ordered full pay for black troops who had been free at the start of the war—this included Stephens. On 25 February 1865 the Fifty-fourth Massachusetts and George Stephens entered Charleston after rebel forces abandoned the city. They spent late March patrolling the coastal area from Savannah, Georgia, to Georgetown, South Carolina, and fought their last engagement at Boykin's Mill, South Carolina, on 18 April 1865. During his final months of service Stephens's promotion to first lieutenant was denied by the War Department on racial grounds. He returned to Boston in September 1865.

In late 1866 or early 1867 Stephens started a Freedmen's school near Port Royal, Virginia, having elected to cast his lot in the South to aid former slaves. This school did not survive, and he quickly returned to Philadelphia seeking funds. He returned south to organize the Tilghman School in Essex County, Virginia, and eventually received aid from the Freedmen's Bureau and the American Freedmen's Union Commission in Philadelphia. But in 1868 whites evicted the school, and the Freedmen's Bureau cut off funds. Stephens left Virginia in 1870 after running into financial problems and increased white violence. He settled in New York and remarried, this time to Catherine Tracy, a working-class Irish woman (Susan, his first wife, having died). He remained politically active in veterans' organizations during the 1870s and 1880s; in particular he was a member of the William Lloyd Garrison Post of the Grand Army of the Republic. Though Stephens died never having received his promotion, his second wife fought for and eventually won his commission to first lieutenancy in 1891.

FURTHER READING
Yacovone, Donald, ed. *A Voice of Thunder: The Civil War Letters of George E. Stephens* (1997).

BARTON A. MYERS

Stepin Fetchit. *See* Fetchit, Stepin.

Steward, Austin (1793–1865), antislavery reformer, was born in Virginia, the son of Robert Steward and Susan (maiden name unknown), slaves. About 1800 a well-to-do planter, William Helm, purchased the family. Escaping business reverses and debts, Helm moved to Sodus Bay on New York's Lake Ontario frontier and shortly thereafter, in 1803, to Bath, New York, taking young Austin with him. Hired out for wages, Steward entered the employ of a Mr. Tower in Lyons, New York, where he worked until 1812. Escaping, he went to Canandaigua, where he worked for local farmers and attended an academy in Farmington. While thus employed, Steward learned of New York's 1785 law banning the sale of slaves brought into the state subsequent to that date. Drawing upon the state's 1799 gradual emancipation statute as well as an 1800 court decision, *Fisher v. Fisher*, which ruled that hiring out a slave constituted an intentional and fraudulent violation of the 1785 law, he openly asserted his freedom and continued to hire his labor in his own name, despite challenges from Helm.

Sometime between 1817 and 1820 Steward moved to Rochester. In 1825 he married a Miss B. of Rochester, the youngest daughter of a close friend, who bore him eight children, and, overcoming white opposition, he ran a successful grocery business. During these prosperous years, Steward became an activist on behalf of other northern blacks, both de jure and de facto free, who were subject to prejudice and treated as second-class citizens. From 1827 to 1829 he was an agent for *Freedom's Journal* and the *Rights of All*, both black newspapers. In 1830 he served as vice president of the first Annual Convention for the Improvement of Colored People, held in Philadelphia, Pennsylvania.

Steward and his family moved to Upper Canada (now western Ontario) in 1831, where they joined a group of African Americans who had fled Cincinnati after the race riots of 1829. There they had established, under the leadership of their agent Israel Lewis, an organized black community called Wilberforce. Steward invested the savings from his grocery in the project and undertook a major role in its proceedings, replacing Lewis as its principal leader until the community collapsed six years later. His career there, however, was beset with ill fortune. He soon fought with Lewis over the handling of the community's finances and other matters until in 1836 Lewis was dropped as the community's principal agent. The brothers Benjamin Paul and NATHANIEL PAUL, who replaced him, proved equally unsatisfactory, the latter, who was sent to England to raise funds, never rendering a satisfactory account of his mission. By 1837 Wilberforce, wracked by internal dissension, had virtually ceased to exist, and Steward, his savings gone and his reform efforts blasted, returned to Rochester with his family.

Reestablishing himself in the grocery business, Steward prospered for a season, but the aftershocks of the 1837 panic and a disastrous fire finally destroyed the enterprise. Steward moved back to Canandaigua about 1842, where he taught school and continued his antislavery work as an agent for the *National Anti-Slavery Standard*. Although he gradually faded into obscurity, he was active for awhile in the emerging political antislavery movement. He served as president of the New York Convention of Colored Men in 1840, 1841, and 1845 and lobbied for black male suffrage on equal terms as white suffrage.

Steward, like most other black activists, remained on the periphery of the antislavery movement, whose inner circles kept even noted abolitionist FREDERICK DOUGLASS at a distance. Moreover, by the 1840s Steward, tainted by his association with the failed Canadian settlement and lacking a personal following, was pushed from the black national convention limelight by younger, more aggressive black leaders such as HENRY HIGHLAND GARNET, JAMES MCCUNE SMITH, and CHARLES B. RAY.

Steward is best remembered for his autobiography, *Twenty-Two Years a Slave and Forty Years a Freeman*, published in 1857. It provides only a sketchy outline of his life and addresses his understanding of the evils of slavery, but it testifies primarily to the vicissitudes that African Americans experienced even in the North in its depiction of the struggle of one exceptional black man against social and economic discrimination and exclusion from the full political and legal privileges that white citizens enjoyed.

Steward pressed to achieve full citizenship for himself and others like him. For example, he attempted, unsuccessfully, to enlist in the Steuben County militia during the War of 1812, embraced the popular temperance reform of the 1830s, and served a term as clerk of Biddulph Township during

his years in Canada. In the end, however, he always remained a marginal figure. His autobiography was his most effective undertaking; his strongest message was a plea to "those who have the power" to "have the magnanimity to strike off the chains from the enslaved, and bid him stand up, a Freeman and a Brother!" He died in Rochester, New York.

FURTHER READING
Steward, Austin. *Twenty-Two Years a Slave and Forty Years a Freeman* (1857), reprinted with an introduction by Graham Russell Hodges (2002); reprinted with an introduction by Jane H. Pease and William H. Pease (1969).
Pease, Jane H., and William H. Pease. *Black Utopia: Negro Communal Experiments in America* (1963).
Pease, Jane H. *They Who Would Be Free: Blacks' Search for Freedom, 1830–1861* (1974; repr. 1990).
Ripley, C. Peter, ed. *The Black Abolitionist Papers*, vol. 2 (5 vols., 1985–1992).
Winks, Robin. *The Blacks in Canada* (1971).
This entry is taken from the *American National Biography* and is published here with the permission of the American Council of Learned Societies.

WILLIAM H. PEASE AND
JANE H. PEASE

Steward, Emanuel (7 July 1944–25 Oct. 2012), boxing trainer, manager, and sports commentator, was born in Bottom Creek, West Virginia, the first child of Catherine Steward and Manuel Steward, a coal miner. His early childhood in rural Appalachia was characterized by typical boyhood pursuits of swimming and playing ball with his friends and exploring the hollows and hills around his home. He received his first pair of boxing gloves when he was seven years old. He took to boxing immediately, constructing his own punching bags, which he hung from a tree in his yard; he engaged in matches with any friends he could convince to fight him. At the age of eight, he was put into the ring in clandestine bouts against children from neighboring towns. In his first match against a well-known tough kid, he won a quick victory, which led to several other fights over the next three years. These matches were arranged by older men in the community and always included wagering on the young boxers. Although the race of these men is unclear, the scenario is similar in scope to the pursuit of boxing in isolated rural areas of the South. Matches in the late nineteenth and early twentieth centuries, where African American youths fought for the vicarious pleasure of others, were part of the notorious "Battles Royale" in which a number of boxers competed. The last one standing was declared the winner.

When Steward was eleven years old, in 1956, his parents divorced. His mother subsequently moved to Detroit, Michigan, taking Steward and his two sisters, Lavern and Diane, with her. To provide some discipline and direction and to allow him to continue pursuing his interest in the sport, Steward's mother signed him up in the local Catholic Youth Organization (CYO) boxing program. Steward, however, became involved in street fighting and had several run-ins with the police. When the CYO program was terminated, his mother encouraged him to box at the Brewster Recreation Center, which was famous for having produced JOE LOUIS and legendary trainer Eddie Futch. Steward quickly became a noted amateur fighter, compiling a record of 94–3; he also won the National Gold Gloves bantamweight title in 1963 at the age of eighteen. In 1969 his father sent Steward's half-brother, James, to Detroit and asked Steward to train the fifteen year old. They established their home base at the Kronk gym, part of the city's Kronk Recreational Center that was named for politician John F. Kronk. In the 1970s the small gym became a place of pride in Detroit's African American community because of the programs it offered to impoverished young men, and Steward's growing reputation added considerably to its prestige. He worked as a part-time trainer and attended Henry Ford Community College, graduating in 1970; soon after he began an apprenticeship program with the Detroit Edison Company. Eventually he became a supervisor and a master electrician, but after two years, he returned to the gym to pursue a career in boxing. His skill as a trainer had drawn wide attention in 1971 when the young neighborhood fighters he mentored captured seven championships in the Detroit Gold Gloves competition.

As Steward's abilities as a trainer became recognized, the reputation of the Kronk Gym continued to rise, and nationally ranked fighters joined local boxers in seeking him out for his expertise. He ended his employment as an electrician in 1972 and became a full-time trainer and manager. In 1977 Steward formed ESCOT (Emanuel Steward's Champions of Tomorrow) Boxing Enterprises Inc. and began training professional boxers. For Steward, his responsibilities in Detroit's inner-city neighborhoods, particularly for local youths, meant teaching life skills as well as boxing, and he encouraged those he trained to get an education. Although

he embraced traditional boxing strategies regarding punching and defense, Steward also believed that his boxers should learn proper dietary habits. He believed in working with each boxer's personal temperament, but he insisted on having total control during training camp. His techniques quickly saw results when, in 1980, Hilmer Kenty won the World Boxing Association (WBA) lightweight title, becoming the first of several world champions trained by Steward. That same year, Steward's most notable fighter, THOMAS HEARNS, won the WBA welterweight championship and would become one of the most renowned boxers of the decade. Frequently honored by a number of organizations and communities for his youth scholarship programs and his mentoring of impoverished youth, Steward was awarded the Southern Christian Leadership Conference Youth Development Award in 1983.

Over the course of the next twenty-five years, Steward managed or trained thirty-one professional world champions. Additionally, in a seminal year for American amateur boxing that saw the United States win eleven medals at the 1984 Los Angeles Olympics, Steward helped develop six gold-medal winners. And after becoming a popular commentator for HBO's boxing broadcasts in the 1990s, Steward donated a portion of his salary to the Kronk Gym. Steward was inducted into the Afro-American Sports Hall of Fame in 1992 and into the International Boxing Hall of Fame in 1996.

By the end of the 1990s, the Kronk Gym, once a socially thriving haven in a crowded, bustling community, was in decline, despite Steward's support. The city of Detroit reduced funding, and the Kronk Recreation Center fell into disrepair. Though Steward continued to promote the value of the gym to the city and to the boxing world, frequent vandalism made the facility difficult to maintain. But the changing demographic of the neighborhood also contributed to the gym's demise. As families moved away, new residents did not move in, and the remaining population was not large enough to effectively support the gym and Steward's programs. Steward helped establish "branches" of the gym in Tucson, Arizona, and Belfast, Ireland, and for a time, 1995–2005, he trained boxers in nearby Dearborn, Michigan, with the hope that his fundraising activities would reinvigorate the historic Kronk facility.

In 2000 Steward was named a Michiganian of the Year. In 2002 he was named the National Director of Coaching for USA Boxing, the governing body of American Olympic boxing. Steward also began designing improvements in boxing gloves and other boxing-related equipment. Around this time, Steward's other boxing-related activities involved setting up training camps and working as a training consultant to various boxers in preparation for title matches. In November 2006, Steward's beloved Kronk Gym finally closed its doors.

FURTHER READING

Anderson, Dave. *In This Corner: Great Boxing Trainers Talk About Their Art* (1991).

Lindell, Lindy. *Metro Detroit Boxing* (2001).

Roberts, James B., and Alexander G. Skutt. *The Boxing Register and International Boxing Hall of Fame Official Record Book*, 4th ed. (2006).

Sammons, Jeffrey T. *Beyond the Ring: The Role of Boxing in American Society* (1988).

Obituary: *New York Times*, 25 Oct. 2012.

KEVIN GRACE

Steward, Rebecca Gould (2 May 1820–8 June 1877), educator, and committed member of the African Methodist Episcopal Church, was born Rebecca Gould in Gouldtown, a small town in southern New Jersey named after the Gould family that had lived there for several generations. Rebecca came from the lineage of the founders of Gouldtown. Elizabeth Adams, an Englishwoman and the granddaughter of the proprietor of the colony, married into the Gould family, who were of African American descent. Rebecca's father, Benjamin, was a farmer, while Phoebe, her mother, remained at home to raise the children.

At the age of nineteen Rebecca married James Steward. They had six children: Margarette, William, Mary, Theophilus Gould, Alice, and Stephen Smith. In 1846 Rebecca and James joined the AME Church in Gouldtown, which was led by Reverend Alexander W. Wayman. She was baptized in 1851. As the movement to officially sanction female preachers in the AME Church gained strength, she held firm against the practice. Unconvinced that the Bible commanded infant baptism, a common Methodist practice, she refused to baptize any of her six children. Rebecca taught in the Sunday school and in an adult Bible class which met often at her home, led a weekly prayer meeting for women in the church, and was active in the church aid society. As a mother, in addition to raising her children, Rebecca read and studied extensively in her home.

In March 1869 Rebecca took ill and was confined to her bed for two years and to her home for five. During this period she wrote several articles for the official newspaper of the AME Church, the *Christian Recorder*, including a series entitled "Sanctification." She critiqued the holiness movement for holding special meetings for sanctification. She believed the practice undermined the centrality and importance of conversion in achieving salvation. Another article examining sanctification focused on covenants in the Old and New Testaments in the Bible. She also wrote an autobiographical account entitled "Two Years on the Brink of Jordan."

Her mother, Phoebe, died in May 1877. Just three weeks later Rebecca died in her hometown. Her funeral on 11 June 1877 was attended by prominent ministers in the AME Church including BENJAMIN T. TANNER and HENRY MCNEAL TURNER. THEOPHILUS G. STEWARD wrote and edited a book entitled *Memoirs of Mrs. Rebecca Steward* to honor his mother shortly after her death. This moving tribute memorialized his mother's work in the church and held her up as a shining example of true womanhood and the ideal race woman toward which females in the church ought to aspire. Even after her death, her life and work in the denomination impacted the discourse surrounding the ideology of domesticity and the role of women in the church.

FURTHER READING

Miller, Albert G. *Theophilus G. Steward, Black Theology, and the Making of an African American Civil Society, 1865–1924* (2003).

Steward, Theophilus Gould. *Memoirs of Mrs. Rebecca Steward, Containing a Full Sketch of Her Life. With Various Selections From Her Writings and Letters* (1877).

JULIUS H. BAILEY

Steward, Susan Maria Smith McKinney (1847–7 Mar. 1918), physician, was born in Brooklyn, New York, the daughter of Sylvanus Smith, a pork merchant, and Ann Springstead. She grew up in a farming community with her large, prosperous family. As a teenager she learned to play the organ, studying under two prominent New York City practitioners, John Zundel and Henry Eyre Brown. She became an accomplished organist, but she had other goals. The deaths of two of her brothers during the Civil War and the high death rates from a cholera epidemic in Brooklyn in 1866 may have influenced her choice of a medical career. Her versatile mind and disciplined approach earned her an

M.D. in 1870 from the New York Medical College for Women. She thus became the first African American woman to graduate from a medical school in the state of New York and only the third in the United States.

In 1874 Susan Smith married the Reverend William G. McKinney and then practiced under the name of Dr. Susan Smith McKinney. Two children were born of this marriage before her husband's death in 1892. Dr. McKinney conducted a private general practice at 205 DeKalb Avenue in Brooklyn from 1870 to 1895. Serving both white and black patients, she had another office in Manhattan. During the period of her medical practice in Brooklyn, she also served as the organist and choir director at the Bridge Street African Methodist Episcopal (AME) Church near her office.

In 1881 McKinney cofounded the Brooklyn Women's Homeopathic Hospital and Dispensary (later renamed Memorial Hospital for Women and Children), a hospital for African Americans, where she served as a staff physician until 1896. During 1887 and 1888 she was engaged in postgraduate study at the Long Island Medical College Hospital in Brooklyn. She was also on the staff of the New York Medical College and Hospital for Women in Manhattan from 1892 to 1896. From 1892 to 1895 she was one of two female physicians at the Brooklyn Home for Aged Colored People and served as a member of its board of directors. McKinney was an active member of the Kings County Medical Society and the New York State Homeopathic Medical Society.

In 1896 the widowed McKinney married the Reverend THEOPHILUS G. STEWARD, a U.S. Army chaplain with the Twenty-fifth U.S. Colored Infantry. She accompanied him for two years on tours of duty in Montana and Wyoming, where she gained medical licenses and practiced. In 1898, shortly before her husband's retirement from the army, she became a faculty member, teaching health and nutrition, and a resident physician at Wilberforce University, Wilberforce, Ohio, a school supported by the African Methodist Episcopal Church. She held both positions for twenty-two years until her death. Reverend Steward joined his wife at Wilberforce and became a member of the history faculty.

In 1911 Steward and her husband participated as delegates of the AME Church at the First Universal Races Congress at the University of London. She addressed the interracial group of delegates with a presentation entitled "Colored Women in America." In 1914 she presented a paper, "Women in Medicine," before the National Association of Colored Women's Clubs in Wilberforce, Ohio; it included a nearly complete list of African American women who had completed medical school and practiced in America up until that time.

With forty-eight years in the medical profession, Steward was a leading woman physician as well as a musician, public speaker, and devoted church-woman. The Susan Smith McKinney Steward Medical Society, the first organization of African American female physicians, founded in 1976 in the greater New York area, took the name of this pioneer. Steward died at her home on the campus of Wilberforce University.

FURTHER READING

Alexander, Leslie L. "Early Medical Heroes: Susan Smith McKinney-Steward, M.D. 1847–1918," *The Crisis* (Jan. 1980).

Seraile, William. "Susan McKinney Steward: New York State's First African-American Woman Physician," *Afro-Americans in New York Life and History* (July 1985).

This entry is taken from the *American National Biography* and is published here with the permission of the American Council of Learned Societies.

ROBERT C. HAYDEN

Steward, Theophilus Gould (17 Apr. 1843– 11 Jan. 1924), author, clergyman, and educator, was born in Gouldtown, New Jersey, the son of James Steward, a mechanic who had fled to Gouldtown as an indentured child servant, and Rebecca Gould, a descendant of the seventeenth-century proprietor of West Jersey, John Fenwick. His family's interest in history and literature supplemented his elementary school education in Bridgeton, and his mother encouraged him to challenge "established truths." He began preaching in 1862, was licensed to preach by the African Methodist Episcopal (AME) Church in 1863, and was appointed to serve a congregation in South Camden, New Jersey, in 1864.

In May 1865 Steward accompanied AME bishop DANIEL ALEXANDER PAYNE and others on a mission to South Carolina, where they reestablished the denomination, which had been banned from the state after the Denmark Vesey slave rebellion conspiracy of 1822. From 1865 to 1868 Steward nurtured new AME congregations in South Carolina. In 1866 he married Elizabeth Gadsden; before her death in 1893, they had eight children.

From 1868 to 1871 Steward was the pastor of the AME congregation in Macon, Georgia, which was later renamed Steward Chapel AME Church in his honor. From his base in Macon, Steward actively participated in the business and politics of Reconstruction. He worked as a cashier for the Freedmen's Bank in Macon and speculated in cotton futures. He helped to write the platform of Georgia's Republican Party in 1868 and served as an election registrar in Stewart County, Georgia. He organized a successful protest by freed slaves in Americus, Georgia, against compulsory labor contracts and attacked the practice of limiting jury service to white males.

Leaving Georgia in 1871, Steward spent the next twenty years as the pastor of AME congregations in Brooklyn, New York; Philadelphia, Pennsylvania; Wilmington, Delaware; and Washington, D.C. In 1873 he undertook a mission to Haiti, establishing an AME congregation in Port-au-Prince, and in 1877 he completed his first book, *Memoirs of Mrs. Rebecca Steward* (1877). From 1878 to 1880 he studied at Philadelphia's Protestant Episcopal Church Divinity School.

In the subsequent decade, Steward published two theological works, *Genesis Re-read* (1885) and *The End of the World* (1888). In these two books, he undertook Christian reinterpretations of the first and the last things—the doctrines of creation and of the eschaton. *Genesis Re-read* offered a liberal evangelical's assimilation of Darwinian evolutionary theory into Christian doctrine by arguing that evolution took place within a divine plan. *The End of the World* contested Anglo-Saxon triumphalism by contending that a final clash of nations would purge Christianity of its bondage to racism and give birth to "new nations," borne out of darkness to walk "in the light of the one great God, with whom there are no superior races and no inferior races."

Defeated in a bid for the presidency of the AME denomination's Wilberforce University in 1884 and at odds with its bishops because of repeated challenges to their authority, Steward won an appointment as chaplain to the Twenty-fifth U.S. Colored Infantry Regiment in 1891. His wife died in 1893, and three years later, in 1896, he married Susan Maria Smith McKinney, a widow and physician; they had no children. After service at Fort Missoula, Montana, and Chickamauga, Georgia, Steward and his regiment were sent to Cuba in 1898 at the beginning of the Spanish-American War. On his return to Brooklyn later that year, he addressed a celebration of the war's conclusion.

Steward wrote a novel, *A Charleston Love Story*, in 1899, but his main interest was military history. In addition to two pamphlets, *Active Service; or, Gospel Work among the U.S. Soldiers* (1897) and *How the Black St. Domingo Legion Saved the Patriot Army in the Siege of Savannah in 1779* (1899), he published *The Colored Regulars in the U.S. Army* (1899), a vindication of the service of African American soldiers in the Spanish-American War.

Sent to the Philippines in 1900, Steward was stationed in Manila, where he served as superintendent of schools for Luzon province. In 1902 he was transferred back to the United States with the Twenty-fifth Infantry Regiment and stationed at Fort Niobrara, Nebraska, and Fort Brown near Brownsville, Texas. In August 1906, white residents reported that soldiers from Steward's regiment had briefly roamed through Brownsville's streets, freely shooting up its cafes and dance halls, killing a civilian and injuring a police officer. The soldiers maintained their innocence and implicated no one, but President Theodore Roosevelt dismissed them from service without honor and barred them from future government service. Steward, who had retired from the army in 1907, did not join in the African American community's outcry against Roosevelt's arbitrary action. But in his autobiography he wrote, "I have yet to find one officer who was connected with that regiment who expresses the belief that our men were guilty."

In 1907 Theophilus and Susan Steward moved to Ohio, where he became vice president, chaplain, and professor of French, history, and logic and she became the college physician at Wilberforce University. Active in fund-raising efforts for Wilberforce, Theophilus Steward advocated military training for African American men as preparatory to their struggle for freedom. In 1911 the Stewards were the AME delegates to London's Universal Races Congress.

An active contributor to such newspapers as the *Cleveland Gazette* and the *Indianapolis Freeman*, Steward returned to familiar territory in his last books: family history in *Gouldtown, a Very Remarkable Settlement of Ancient Date* (1913), and military history in *The Haitian Revolution, 1791 to 1804* (1914). He published his autobiography, *From 1864 to 1914: Fifty Years in the Gospel Ministry*, in 1921.

FURTHER READING

Steward's papers are at the Schomburg Center for
    Research in Black Culture of the New York Public
    Library.

Miller, Albert George. *Elevating the Race: Theophilus G. Steward, Black Theology, and the Making of an African American Civil Religion, 1865–1924* (2003).

Seraile, William. *Voice of Dissent: Theophilus Gould Steward (1843–1924) and Black America* (1991).

This entry is taken from the *American National Biography* and is published here with the permission of the American Council of Learned Societies.

RALPH E. LUKER

Steward, William Henry (26 July 1847–3 Jan. 1935), journalist and educator, was born in Brandenburg, Kentucky, a son of the slaves Henry and Frances Steward, who were freed before the Civil War. In about 1860, the Stewards moved to Louisville, where William attended a private school run by the Reverend Henry Adams, pastor of the First African Church, who became one of the strongest influences in young Steward's life.

As a young man, Steward served as a schoolteacher at Frankfort and Louisville, before working for railroad companies, and in 1876, he became the first African American letter carrier for the Post Office Department in Louisville. An active member of the Fifth Street Baptist Church in Louisville, he was longtime secretary of the General Association of Colored Baptists of Kentucky. He also became active in local Republican politics, becoming the first black man to serve as a city precinct judge of registration and elections, and in 1877, a member of the city's Orphan Home Commission.

Steward was married in 1877 to the music teacher Mary E. Lee, also called Mamie, and they had three children: daughters Jeannette L. and Caroline A. and one son, William H. Steward Jr. Mrs. Lee also raised Steward's older daughter, Lucy, from a previous marriage; Lucy's mother's name is not known.

In 1879 Steward became the chairman of the board of trustees at the Baptist-affiliated State University in Louisville, an honor which he held for the rest of his life. Mamie became a music professor at the school, later renamed Simmons University (now Simmons College of Kentucky), and Steward himself served for a time as its interim president, in the early 1900s, while the school conducted a search for its next president. He also played a leading role in managing Louisville's black public schools from 1896 until 1910, helping choose teachers and principals for the schools until a new city board of education was created.

But much of his remarkable energy was poured into editing the influential *American Baptist* newspaper, which he founded in 1879 and published for the next fifty-six years. He was frequently called the "pioneer of colored Baptists in Kentucky," and although not an ordained minister, was often mistakenly referred to as a clergyman (Wright, 280). As lay editor of the *Baptist*, Steward achieved national standing as a journalist, serving as an early president of the National Afro-American Press Association, a distinction he earned three times.

In 1898 a new national civil rights organization—the National Afro-American Council, led by BISHOP ALEXANDER WALTERS and the journalist T. THOMAS FORTUNE—was formed, and Steward became one of the council's most active members in Kentucky. Selected as a member of the group's first national executive committee, on which he served until 1903, Steward became a national officer in 1900, when he was elected eighth vice president. When BOOKER T. WASHINGTON took control of the council in 1902, installing T. Thomas Fortune as president, Steward was elected second vice president, and was reelected a year later. Shortly after the death of the first vice president, William A. Pledger, Steward became acting president of the council in April 1904, when Fortune resigned, and gained the title in his own right at that year's national meeting in St. Louis, Missouri.

The council was initially successful in organizing African Americans nationwide to protect their interests from the encroachment of legal segregation, disfranchisement across the South, and mob violence. Yet even as Steward's star rose, the council began to decline, as members lost interest and left to form the Niagara movement and competing groups. When Bishop Walters returned to reenergize the failing group in Detroit 1905, Steward stepped aside, becoming executive committee chairman instead.

The council dissolved after 1907, leaving Walters and others to join W. E. B. DuBois in forming what became known as the NAACP after 1909–1910. Steward became a leader in the new Louisville branch of the NAACP in 1914, and remained on the local board until 1926, when a local dispute led to his removal. He then became active in the city's new Commission on Interracial Cooperation.

Steward was a close associate of Booker T. Washington, who invited him to attend the 1904 Carnegie Hall conference which created the Tuskegee-aligned Committee of Twelve. Until his death, Steward remained a stalwart voice for moderation in racial matters during the era of segregation in the twentieth century.

FURTHER READING

Simmons, William J. *Men of Mark: Eminent, Fair, and Rising* (1887; reprint, 1970).

Wright, George C. "William Henry Steward: Moderate Approach to Black Leadership." In *Black Leaders of the 19th Century* (1988).

BENJAMIN R. JUSTESEN

Stewart, Bennett McVey (6 Aug. 1912–29 Apr. 1988), politician, was born in Huntsville, Alabama, the son of Bennett Stewart and Cathleen Jones. After attending local public schools in Huntsville and Birmingham, he entered Miles College in Birmingham, where he earned a bachelor of arts in 1936. After serving as assistant principal of Irondale High School in Birmingham from 1936 to 1938 he became associate professor of sociology at Miles College. In 1938 Stewart married Pattye Crittenden; they had three children. Leaving teaching in 1940 to sell insurance, he eventually became an executive of the Atlanta Life Insurance Company and in 1950 was sent to Chicago to open an office there. Stewart remained in the insurance business for the next eighteen years before embarking upon a career in city politics. He was first employed as a city building inspector and concurrently served as a rehabilitation specialist for the city's Department of Urban Renewal. In 1971 Stewart was elected to the Chicago City Council as an alderman for the Twenty-first Ward, and in 1972 he held the dual office as Democratic committeeman; he remained in these posts until 1978.

As a member of the city council Stewart was involved in the power struggle that ensued following the death of Mayor Richard J. Daley in December 1976. Daley, considered the last of the old-time big city political bosses, ruled Illinois Democratic politics virtually single-handedly until his death. Stewart, a Daley "machine loyalist," first supported Alderman Wilson Frost to succeed Daley, but when Frost was pressured to take himself out of the running, Stewart seconded the nomination of Alderman Michael Bilandic, who was chosen interim mayor.

Stewart's own rise to higher political office came in October 1978 following the death of Representative RALPH METCALFE. He was tapped as his party's candidate to succeed Metcalfe by the ten Democratic ward committeemen from the First Congressional District. Though Stewart was an African American, his candidacy sparked controversy within the black community because of his ties to Daley and his successor. Daley was often criticized for perfecting the instruments of racial suppression and repressing civil liberties through the police force. The *Chicago Tribune* columnist VERNON JARRETT wrote that City Hall's choice of Stewart defied "political logic" and would "unnecessarily agitate the black community." "[Tom] Donovan [patronage boss at City Hall] and the other remnants of the Daley machine," he wrote, "are not only thumbing their noses at the black community, they are trying to deliver a message to even the most respected black leaders of their own party" (*Chicago Tribune*, 20 Oct. 1978).

Nonetheless, in the general election that followed three weeks after Stewart's nomination, the Democratic candidate was victorious, defeating Republican A. A. "Sammy" Rayner by a wide margin. He became a member of Congress on 3 January 1979 and served on the House Appropriations Committee, where he voted in favor of the massive financial bailout of the Chrysler Motor Corporation, which had employed more than 1,500 of his constituents from the First District. In addition he became a champion of his district's low-income citizens and received national recognition for his advocacy of emergency appropriations to provide low-income families with home heating assistance.

Despite his successes in Congress, Stewart was accused by his political opponents of financial mismanagement during his tenure with the Chicago Housing Authority (CHA). In response to this criticism he sought and received a study of the city agency by the U.S. General Accounting Office. The investigation cleared his name and concluded that poor management and bookkeeping, not actions attributable to Stewart, had caused the agency's near collapse.

With the CHA business behind him, Stewart focused his attention on fighting a proposed constitutional amendment prohibiting school busing. He attacked the proposal as "a subversion to the Fourteenth Amendment and an attempt to reestablish segregation in the United States" (Ragsdale and Treese, 140). His efforts helped defeat House approval of the proposed amendment. He also succeeded in securing congressional approval of a bill (originally introduced by his predecessor, Metcalfe) designating February as Black History Month.

Stewart served only one term in Congress, being defeated in the 1980 primary by the antimachine Democrat HAROLD WASHINGTON. Returning to Chicago he resumed his career in local politics, serving from 1981 to 1983 as an interim director of the Chicago Department of Inter-Governmental Affairs, to which position he had been appointed by Mayor Jane Byrne. He also served as one of Byrne's administrative assistants.

A skilled ward politician, Stewart did not distinguish himself until he went to Congress and became a champion for families on public assistance and other disadvantaged poor who could not help themselves. He assumed a leadership role in the House, opposing those who sought to "turn the clock back" to the segregated pre-1960s. Nonetheless, it was difficult for Stewart to shake his ties to the Daley machine, and he was considered by some critics to be nothing more than a "party hack." Perhaps his greatest recognition came as the man Harold Washington defeated, which was an important step in Washington's advancement toward becoming Chicago's first black mayor in 1983. Stewart died in Chicago.

FURTHER READING
Jarrett, Vernon. "City Hall Displays More Than Racism," *Chicago Tribune*, 20 Oct. 1978, and "A Tuesday Night on the South Side," *Chicago Tribune*, 10 Nov. 1978.
Ragsdale, Bruce A., and Joel D. Treese. *Black Americans in Congress, 1870–1989* (1990).
Obituary: *Chicago Tribune*, 28 Apr. 1988.
This entry is taken from the *American National Biography* and is published here with the permission of the American Council of Learned Societies.

LEO J. DAUGHERTY

Stewart, Charley (c. 1800–?), slave, jockey, and horse trainer, was born Charles Stewart, most likely in the first years of the nineteenth century, in Pocahontas, Virginia, the son of a free, mixed-race man named Charles Stewart, a sailor, and an enslaved woman, Sally Vaughan, who was owned by a man named Enoch Vaughan. Charley's parents were not married at the time of his birth. Enoch Vaughan died when Charley was a baby, and for several years he lived with the free members of his father's family, residing with his aunt Mary Stewart. When Charley was about twelve years old Enoch Vaughan's daughter Lizzie Pace sold him in order to pay her husband's gambling debts. Stewart later recalled that his father was out of town when this sale occurred and thus did not have the opportunity to buy his son. This was only the first of many heartbreaking—and permanent—separations from his family that Stewart suffered in his lifetime.

Stewart was sold to Colonel William Ransom Johnson, a prominent Virginia horseman and breeder of thoroughbred racehorses, whose nickname was "the Napoleon of the Turf." Johnson assigned Stewart to his thoroughbred stables because Stewart was small for his age and slight of build, making him good material for a jockey. At Johnson's stables in New Market, Virginia, Stewart was put under the tutelage of the English horseman Arthur Taylor to learn the business of raising and training racehorses.

Stewart began as a groom, rubbing down horses after they had been exercised. Soon he was training as a jockey and rode for Johnson's stables in many races. In 1823 he traveled north with Johnson's stable retinue for a vaunted set of North-South races between Virginia's Sir Henry, a horse trained by Johnson's stable, and New York's American Eclipse, a horse owned by Cornelius van Ranst. Stewart rode Johnson's Young Sir Archy but lost in a close race during an intense week of symbolic sectional conflict.

Because Stewart had demonstrated himself to be a good trainer and horseman he was put in charge of one of Johnson's training stables at New Market in the late 1820s. As head of the stable, Stewart was the supervisor of eleven slave grooms and two white workers. Among the horses he trained was the champion Bonnets o' Blue who won races in Charleston, South Carolina, in 1831. By 1832 Stewart was responsible for horse breeding as well as training. In this capacity he traveled unescorted to Germantown, Pennsylvania, with the stallion Medley so that the horse could service the stables of John Craig. At Germantown a portrait of Stewart with Medley was painted by the equine portraitist Edward Troye.

In 1833 Stewart was married for the first time to an enslaved woman named Betsey Dandridge. To secure the marriage he purchased Dandridge from her owner, Isaac Puckett, for $350, which was taken out of the cash reserves that Stewart had earned as one of Johnson's leading stablemen. According to the version of Stewart's biography published in *Harper's New Monthly Magazine* in 1884, the marriage was an unhappy one, and Stewart traded his wife and their two children to a horse trader for an old horse. Given that the source of this story was the Jim Crow-era press, the story quite possibly is untrue.

In 1837, the year that he may have traded his wife, Stewart, who was still a slave, was sent to Paris, Kentucky, to run a new training stable set up there in a partnership between William Ransom Johnson and John S. Hurt. Stewart traveled the backcountry of Kentucky, putting Medley to stud at local stables. In these years Stewart enjoyed a kind of quasi-freedom because, as he described, "I had my helpers and jockeys, grooms and stablemen under me, nobody was over me" (*Harper's*, 736). While in Kentucky he achieved a fair amount of fame within the horse-breeding community, and such eminent men as Wade Hampton II and Henry Clay Jr. made offers to Johnson to purchase Stewart, all of which were declined.

By 1840 Stewart married again, this time to Mary Jane Malloy, a mixed-race woman who was enslaved as a seamstress to a Mr. Robertson. After their marriage Malloy was required to pay a monthly rent to Robertson in order to live with Stewart. Mary Jane soon gave birth to their first child, John Stewart, but fell ill and died when the boy was less than one year old. Grieving, Stewart wrote to Johnson and asked to be allowed to leave Kentucky. Johnson agreed to sell Stewart to a new owner of his own choosing.

After a series of negotiations with Stewart, Alexander Porter, a judge from Louisiana, a U.S. senator, and the president of the New Orleans Jockey Club, purchased Stewart from Johnson for $3,500, a sum more than ten times the typical price of a slave in the New Orleans market at that time. Before removing to Louisiana, Stewart arranged to purchase his son John from Robertson, his late wife's owner, for $150.

In 1841 Stewart moved to Porter's sugar plantation, Oaklawn, in Franklin, Louisiana, on the Bayou Teche. Stewart moved to Louisiana without his son, leaving him in the care of his late wife's sister. He was unable to travel with the boy right away because John was still very young, and moreover there was some question about the boy's legal status as the slave of an enslaved man. Apparently Robertson cheated Stewart in this deal, for Stewart was not able to regain legal possession of his own child and never saw his son again after his move to Louisiana. As unusual as Stewart's position was and as much relative freedom as he had within the institution of slavery, Stewart was still enslaved.

At Oaklawn, Stewart was in charge of a staff of forty-five slaves and had a private home next to the stables. Stewart expanded the training and breeding operations of the Oaklawn stables, and his services were so in demand that he had to turn away requests from neighboring horsemen

to train their thoroughbreds. Judge Porter died in 1844, and Stewart's legal ownership passed to Porter's brother James Porter, attorney general of the state of Louisiana. Stewart continued to operate the stables at Oaklawn until James Porter's death in 1849. When James Porter's widow Mary took possession of the estate she ceased the training and racing activities of the stables, and Stewart's responsibilities were reduced to taking care of the family's horses and coach. Charles Stewart remained at Oaklawn with Mary Porter and her two daughters through the Civil War until 1881, when the now heavily indebted Porter family sold their home and its furnishings and moved to Europe.

Stewart was still living in a home on the grounds of Oaklawn in 1884 when the biographical article about him was published in *Harper's*. Some time after he arrived in Louisiana, Stewart married for a third time, and at the time of the *Harper's* article he had three grown children from this marriage living near him. The place and year of his death are unknown.

Charles Stewart led a life of remarkable achievements. He was a well-regarded horse trainer who earned the special trust and respect of the most prominent horseracing men of the South. By all accounts he excelled in his profession. Though facing considerable social and legal challenges as a slave, Stewart managed to carve out for himself a relative degree of practical if not legal freedom. He traveled unaccompanied around the Eastern Seaboard to various stables and racetracks. He was given the opportunity to choose his position when Johnson agreed to part with him. Stewart was also able to accumulate reserves of cash unheard of for the vast majority of slaves. That Stewart still suffered the loss of family members through the workings of the slave market shows only how remarkable was his relatively self-determined life.

FURTHER READING

Stewart, Charles. "My Life as a Slave," *Harper's New Monthly Magazine* 69, no. 413 (Oct. 1884).

Hotaling, Edward. *The Great Black Jockeys: The Lives and Times of the Men Who Dominated America's First National Sport* (1999).

ELIZABETH KUEBLER-WOLF

Stewart, Ella Nora Phillips (6 Mar. 1893–27 Nov. 1987), pioneering pharmacist, entrepreneur, and clubwoman, was born near Berryville, Virginia. Her parents, Eliza and Hamp Phillips, were sharecroppers, but the family's lack of financial resources did not stand in the way of their daughter's academic success. Phillips was an outstanding student who won five scholarships at Storer College in Harper's Ferry, West Virginia, where she enrolled at age twelve. After graduation, at age seventeen, she married her classmate Charles Myers, and soon gave birth to a daughter, who died at the age of two.

The couple divorced following the death of their child, and Ella Phillips went to work as a bookkeeper in a Pittsburgh, Pennsylvania, drugstore. Although some of her friends discouraged her, saying it had never been done by a black woman, she dreamed of attending pharmacy school. She was encouraged by a local physician who befriended her, and in 1916 she succeeded, becoming the first African American to graduate from the Pittsburgh University School of Pharmacy.

Ella Phillips found friends and allies in two Jewish classmates and soon took a position working at the Mendelsson Drug Company, which they owned. Before long she was promoted to manager at Howard's Drugstore in Braddock, Pennsylvania, which she later purchased with a loan from an insurance company and operated until 1918. From 1918 to 1920 she owned and operated Myers Pharmacy in Pittsburgh. When she married prominent pharmacist William Wyatt Stewart on 1 May 1920, at age twenty-seven, the couple moved to Ohio and opened a new drugstore together, Stewarts' Pharmacy. The store was unusual in that it was located in a predominantly white community in Toledo, where the Stewarts were extremely popular among their patrons.

Their store was also unique in that the couple made the location (and their spacious apartment above it) a lively hub for members of the local and national black community, including notable historical figures such as W. E. B. DuBois, MARIAN ANDERSON, CARTER G. WOODSON, PAUL ROBESON, and MARY MCLEOD BETHUNE, who often stayed in their rooms when they passed through town.

Ella Stewart is known as much for her medical accomplishments as for her tireless leadership as a preeminent clubwoman of her day. In her lifetime she was active with a wide range of organizations such as the Toledo Council of World Affairs, the NAACP, YWCA, American Academy of Political Science, Preschool Council of Toledo, League of Women Voters, Toledo Art Museum, Toledo Council of Churches, FREDERICK DOUGLASS Historical Association, and Delta Sigma Theta Sorority, to name but a few.

Perhaps through her contact with Mary McLeod Bethune, she was especially dedicated to the National Association of Colored Women (NACW), serving as treasurer for twelve years and as editor-in-chief of its *National Notes*. In addition Stewart used her editorial skills to update the club's historical biography, *Lifting as They Climb*. In 1948 she was elected president of the organization.

During the 1950s Stewart began to move in increasingly influential political circles, as she was first appointed to the women's advisory committee for the U.S. Department of Labor, and later toured twenty-three countries as a goodwill ambassador for the U.S. Department of State. Offering lectures in India, Indonesia, the Philippines, Japan, and China, she was appointed in 1963 to the executive board of the U.S. Commission of United Nations Educational, Social and Cultural Organization (UNESCO).

Stewart often referred to herself publicly as someone who never had children. Perhaps the pain of the loss of her child was too great even to mention, and one wonders if that tragedy may have sparked her initial medical curiosity. It is clear that she remained emotionally committed to children around the globe for the rest of her life, even becoming the first black woman to join the League of City Mothers in Toledo. Therefore, it was only fitting when the city of Toledo named a $3 million elementary school in her honor in 1961; she visited the Ella P. Stewart Elementary School often.

Prior to her death in 1987 at age ninety-four, Stewart was the oldest living black woman pharmacist in America.

FURTHER READING

The Ella P. Stewart Elementary School established a museum in Stewart's honor, which houses many of the global artifacts from her travels, as well as awards and personal memorabilia. Oral histories and additional papers can be found at Bowling Green State University in Ohio and the Toledo-Lucas County Public Library.

Davis, Elizabeth Lindsay. *Lifting as They Climb* (1996).

Wesley, Charles Harris. *The History of the National Association of Colored Women's Clubs*, (1984).

KRISTAL BRENT ZOOK

Stewart, Ellen (c. 7 Oct. 1920–13 Jan. 2011), fashion designer, director, producer, and theater founder, was born in Alexandria, Louisiana. The names of her parents are unknown; however, it has been recorded that her father was a tailor in Louisiana and that her mother was a schoolteacher in Detroit, Michigan. She had descended, she would later remark, from vaudeville people.

In 1950 Stewart moved to New York City from Chicago, intending to study fashion design at the Traphagen School of Design. Within three days of her arrival she secured jobs as a porter and as a seamstress for the lingerie designer Edith Lances at Saks Fifth Avenue, where she endured much racial discrimination. In her spare time Stewart explored New York's diverse neighborhoods. The Lower East Side—Orchard and Delancey streets in particular—had a lifelong effect upon her. It was there that she met the fabric salesman Abraham Diamond, who "adopted" Stewart into his Orthodox Jewish family. To save money Stewart designed and made her own clothes. Diamond noticed Stewart's keen interest in fabrics and her innate sense of design. Every Sunday, when she visited her new family, she would model her latest design, made with fabric that Diamond gave her.

Stewart's designs were discovered by a Saks patron who demanded that an outfit that Stewart was wearing one day be made available for purchase. Under the tutelage of Lances, who referred to Stewart as her "little genius," Stewart was promoted to executive designer of sportswear within just a few months of her arrival in New York, making her the first black American designer at Saks Fifth Avenue, with her own showroom and staff. Stewart remained at Saks until about 1958, and even after she left she continued to design on a freelance basis for Henri Bendel and Bergdorf Goodman.

One day while walking along East Ninth Street in New York's East Village, Stewart spotted a basement space for rent. At first she had the idea of opening up a boutique to carry her own line of clothing. Instead, a friend of hers, Fred Lights, and his fellow playwright Paul Foster convinced her to use the space as a theater where they could showcase their plays. The theater's original name was Café La MaMa (MaMa being Stewart's nickname). Stewart was the only black tenant in the building, and she suffered much racial harassment; she was even accused of running a prostitution ring because of the many people (mostly Stewart's white male-model friends) who were constantly entering and leaving the building. When a New York City Health Department inspector met with Stewart (he was a retired vaudeville performer himself), he persuaded her to obtain a restaurant license, which would enable her to operate the business legally. In 1961 Café La MaMa opened its doors.

In April 1963 a zoning ordinance forced La MaMa to move to 82 Second Avenue. It was at this point that Stewart decided to focus on presenting original plays. In November 1964 La MaMa moved again. Finally, in August 1967 Stewart's efforts and hard work paid off when La MaMa received a grant of sixty-five thousand dollars from the Rockefeller Foundation, enabling Stewart to purchase permanent space at 74A East Fourth Street. Stewart was also able to establish the first of La MaMa's resident theater companies, La MaMa Repertory Theatre.

Over nearly half a century Ellen Stewart and La MaMa fostered the careers of many internationally renowned theater artists, such as the Eastern European directors Jerzy Grotowski and Andrei Serban. Stewart was also responsible for having produced the British playwright Harold Pinter's first play and for developing the work of the black American playwright ADRIENNE KENNEDY.

Between 1961 and 1986 La MaMa received forty-nine Obie awards, presented to off-Broadway productions. Stewart herself received more than forty honorary degrees, awards, appointments, and designations, including a MacArthur Fellowship in 1985, the Paul Robeson Theater Lifetime Achievement Award in 1992, a special *Village Voice* Obie in 1975 and one for "Sustained Achievement" in 1980, and an Association for Theatre in Higher Education Lifetime Career Achievement Award in 1995.

In 1993 Stewart was inducted into the Broadway Theatre Hall of Fame, making her the first off-off-Broadway producer to be so honored. In addition, Stewart received honors from the emperor of Japan and from the Philippines president Corazon Aquino. In 1993 Stewart was granted honorary citizenship by the city of Spoleto, Italy, for her invaluable contribution of establishing La MaMa Umbria International, an artists' colony housed in a seven hundred-year-old convent that Stewart secured through funding from the MacArthur Foundation. She died in New York City on 13 Jan. 2011 from complications from a heart condition.

FURTHER READING

Horn, Barbara Lee. *Ellen Stewart and La MaMa: A Bio-Bibliography* (1993).

Obituary: *New York Times*, 13 January 2011.

C. M. WINSTON

Stewart, John (1785–17 Dec. 1823), licensed minister and Methodist missionary, was born in Powhatan County, Virginia, to parents of African and European ancestry. His mother and father, whose names and occupations are not known, were practicing Baptists of noted reputation. Nor is it known whether Stewart had any siblings. During his childhood Stewart received religious instruction from his parents and attended a winter school for African American boys. He was an excellent singer and worked as a dyer. In adulthood those acquainted with Stewart described his physical appearance as light-skinned, five feet eight inches and one hundred forty pounds (Love, 338).

In 1806 or 1807, at age twenty-one, Stewart left Virginia for Marietta, Ohio. During his travels Stewart was robbed of all personal belongings and upon reaching his destination struggled with poverty and with being away from his family. Stewart eventually found work as a sugar maker, which helped him earn money and provided him with opportunities to retire to the woods to read his Bible and to pray. But by 1814 Stewart, still longing for his family in Virginia, was battling with alcoholism, depression, and thoughts of suicide.

One evening in 1815 Stewart and a friend decided to spend another night in Marietta immersed in what they understood to be sinful activities. That evening his friend suddenly died, which forced Stewart to reflect on death and the state of his own soul. For many days Stewart wandered aimlessly in Marietta and finally decided to drown himself in the Ohio River. On his way to the river Stewart passed a meetinghouse where a group of Methodists were holding a religious service. Standing outside the front door Stewart listened intently to the singing and exhortation of the Methodist itinerant preacher Marcus Lindsey until he was ushered into the sanctuary to speak to the small assembly. His address impressed the audience, who invited Stewart to a Methodist camp meeting the following week. At the campground Stewart experienced a conversion to Christianity and dedicated his life to service in the Methodist Episcopal Church.

During the early nineteenth century, Christian revivals dotted the American landscape as a result of the work of traveling ministers and evangelists. At camp meetings and revivals, participants experienced a variety of physical manifestations, witnessed visions, and on occasion heard what they believed to be the voice of God or of a spiritual entity. Three months after his conversion to Christianity Stewart experienced a vision in which a bright halo appeared in the northern sky and two voices, one that of a woman and the other that of a man, beckoned him to take Christianity to the people of northwest Ohio. Shortly after this vision Stewart became violently ill and in his despair Stewart vowed that if God would heal him of his infirmities, he would commit his life to missionary work. Soon Stewart regained his health and fulfilled his promise to God, leaving Marietta armed with only a Bible and a hymnbook to preach Christianity to the Wyandot.

From 1816 to 1823 Stewart resided on a Wyandot Indian reservation established by the U.S. government in Upper Sandusky, Ohio. In December 1818 Stewart married Polly Carter of the nearby Negro Town; they had no children. Stewart is recognized as the first U.S. Methodist home missionary because of his work with the Wyandot nation. In order to provide Stewart with financial assistance and additional personnel, Methodists created The Missionary Society in 1819, the first missionary agency of the Methodist Episcopal Church in the United States.

The Wyandot had been a large and powerful nation from Canada and the Great Lakes Region of Michigan in the Northwest Territory. Negotiations between the U.S. government and the Indian Federation, including the 1795 Greenville Treaty, were often moderated by Wyandot leaders. But the War of 1812 and the continued expansion of white settlers into the region decimated both the Wyandots' numbers and their influence. Eventually many relocated to a U.S. reservation in western Ohio. In 1816 Stewart visited a remnant of the Wyandot in Upper Sandusky. Upon arrival he met Jonathan Pointer, an African American who as a child had been taken from his Virginia home by members of the Wyandot. Pointer and his wife were both fluent in the Wyandot language and worked as translators for Stewart in his task to convert the tribe to Christianity.

Stewart held meetings and preached to those in attendance concerning the necessity of avoiding the wrath of God, which might come upon them at any time. A few Wyandot accepted Christianity, but the majority did not trust Stewart, nor did they embrace his religion. Local chiefs initially refused to embrace Christianity and would not permit their people to abandon worship of the Great Spirit or the religious system in place at the village. Wyandot leaders also rebuffed what they considered attempts by Stewart to assail and exploit the rituals and customs of their Native American tradition. Stewart countered the arguments of the chiefs and proclaimed Christianity as an imperative for all nations, including Indian nations. He declared that a curse would fall upon the people if they did not change their ways. Though Stewart faced much initial resistance in his work with the Wyandot, many later converted to Christianity.

In 1819 Stewart received his credentials as a licensed minister of the Methodist Episcopal Church. Later that year, at the request of the Wyandot Tribal Council, the Methodist Episcopal Church established its first mission in North America at Upper Sandusky. In 1821 Stewart was commissioned as a resident missionary and provided with a cabin and land to raise crops. In 1823 Stewart died after suffering a bout with consumption. He was buried on his own property in an unmarked grave. The site became a shrine for the Wyandot, who often placed flowers on his burial plot. In 1834 Stewart's remains were exhumed and reinterred on the site of the Wyandot Indian mission. Stewart's grave in Upper Sandusky is now an official Methodist Heritage marker and the site serves as a religious shrine in memory of the first American Methodist missionary.

FURTHER READING

Love, N. B. C. "John Stewart: Pioneer Missionary of the Methodist Episcopal Church," *Ohio History* 17, no. 3 (1908).

Marsh, Thelma R. *Moccasin Trails to the Cross: A History of the Mission to the Wyandott Indians on the Sandusky Plains* (1974).

Mitchell, Joseph. *The Missionary Pioneer; or a Brief Memoir of the Life, Labours, and Death of John Stewart, Man of Color* (1827).

Sidwell, Mark. "The Fruit of Freedom," *Christian History* 18, no. 2 (1999).

                        CHRISTOPHER J. ANDERSON

Stewart, Maria W. (1803–Dec. 1879), political activist, lecturer, evangelical writer, and autobiographer, was born Maria Miller in Hartford, Connecticut, where she was orphaned by age five. Nothing is known about her parents. As a five-year-old girl, she was "bound out," or indentured, to a clergy family for ten years. She then moved to Boston, Massachusetts, where she supported herself as a domestic for the next ten years. Maria enjoyed no formal education but struggled through her youth and young adulthood to become literate and to gain an education. Until she was twenty years old, she attended Sabbath school classes, where she learned to read the Bible, and this served as a staple in her pursuit of learning.

Miller married James W. Stewart on 10 August 1826 in the Reverend THOMAS PAUL's African Baptist Church in Boston. In addition to taking his last name, Maria adopted Stewart's middle initial "W." The couple become involved in Boston's small, but growing black middle-class community, and like many of their entrepreneurial neighbors, they enjoyed financial security. James Stewart was a successful and independent shipping outfitter, whose business was situated in prime wharf space. Considerably older than Maria, he was, according to her witnessed claim for his service pension, "a tolerably stout well built man; a light, bright mulatto" (Richardson, 117). There was even a suggestion that his business peers thought him to be white until he married Maria, after which time he was listed as a black businessman.

Nevertheless, the Stewarts were not content with their own success and earnestly took up the cause of slaves and poor blacks. The political writer and activist DAVID WALKER, cofounder of the Massachusetts General Colored Association, one of the first black political organizations in the country, had a profound impact on the couple and on Maria especially. Walker's 1829 work, *Appeal to the Colored Citizens of the World*, one of the most influential black political documents of the nineteenth century, exposed the inhuman treatment of African Americans in general and slaves in particular. Walker was responding directly to the racist sentiments espoused by Thomas Jefferson in his 1826 *Notes on the State of Virginia*, which stated in part that blacks were descended "from the tribes of Monkeys or Orang-Outanges."

As owner of a "slop shop," or used-clothing store, Walker was able to distribute his pamphlet to every port along the eastern seaboard, the Caribbean, and other international ports in which the sailors docked, by planting his pamphlet in the pockets of clothing that he sold to mariners. Walker befriended James and Maria and used James's contacts, as the only black businessman in his trade, to distribute his pamphlet more widely, which he did by hiding the text in the folds of sails and in ship fittings.

Walker died in 1830, apparently of consumption, although rumors still persist that he was poisoned. James W. Stewart had died a year earlier. The two deaths were tremendously difficult for Maria Stewart and were exacerbated by the probate court's rejection of her husband's last will and testament.

As a result, she lost all rights and property interest in her husband's estate and was left widowed and poor. This period of turmoil and grief pressed Stewart to reconsider her faith, and by 1831 she had publicly professed her faith in Christ.

This epiphany marked Stewart's newfound and strident commitment to political action. She became a "warrior" and an advocate for "oppressed Africa." Her essay "Religion and the Pure Principles of Morality, the Sure Foundation on Which We Must Build" (1831) became the first political manifesto authored and published by an African American woman. While she does not advocate violence in the manner of her political mentor, Walker, she militantly advocates that blacks improve their skills, sharpen their minds, and heighten their expectations. Issues of freedom, liberty, and civil rights are central to the text's message, as is her insistence that her vehemence is holy. Her religious conversion catalyzed her political life and propelled her into the public arena.

Appearing with most of Stewart's writings, and, in fact, integral to these texts, are religious prayers and meditations on key issues in her life—gender, gaining education, race, and political concerns. God became, in Stewart's estimation, an intercessor for the race. A biblical sense of morality, time, and prophetic resolution drives her texts. This is made especially clear in her call to women to educate themselves and their children. Stewart was not suggesting that African American women pursue literacy as a middle-class nicety but that education was a political necessity. The race would benefit from schools, libraries, and innovation offered to its women. Stewart was to speak forthrightly about women's influence over husbands and children and the attendant obligation to be moral and progressive in their politics well before Elizabeth Cady Stanton's 1848 Seneca Falls meeting where interested social reformers met, initiating the Women's Right's movement.

Nevertheless, Stewart's "holy zeal" carried her beyond the political arena with which her Boston friends were comfortable. She demanded of men and women a responsibility for the health, morality, and economic and political fortunes of the race that they could not meet. As her friends fell away, she recognized that her time in the public sphere had come to an end. In her final address before friends and political acquaintances, she asked, "What if I am a woman?" (Richardson, 68), going to the heart of public disenchantment with her stridency. Stewart recognized that her zeal transgressed the norms for female, especially black female, behavior. Yet, she wrote, "brilliant wit will shine, come from whence it will; and genius and talent will not hide the brightness of its luster" (Richardson, 70). Her enthusiasm for the progress of African Americans was a call that could not be dampened by waning public opinion.

This same address, "Mrs. Stewart's Farewell Address to Her Friends in the City of Boston" (21 September 1833), served as a eulogy to her fiery public career. Stewart continued her activism in New York and Washington, D.C. In New York she attended the 1837 Women's Anti-Slavery Convention and was a member of a black women's literary society. In the District of Columbia, in the early 1870s, she served as matron of the Freedmen's Hospital and Asylum, a refuge for Civil War veterans, freed slaves, and their families. The Hospital and Asylum housed and trained the physically and mentally ill, the homeless, and those displaced by the significant cultural, economic, and social shifts brought on by the end of the war and Reconstruction.

In 1879 Stewart published *Meditations by Mrs. Maria W. Stewart*, which includes autobiographical information about her experiences during the Civil War. She died later that year while occupying the matron's position at the hospital and was buried on 17 December 1879, exactly fifty years after her husband, James, in Graceland Cemetery, Washington, D.C. Eulogized in *The People's Advocate*, a black newspaper circulated in Washington, D.C., she was remembered for her missionary work throughout Baltimore and Washington and for her generosity toward those in straitened circumstances.

Stewart was the first American woman to address a racially and sexually mixed audience publicly during an era when women's public speech was usually restricted to female audiences and African Americans generally did not address whites on political or moral issues. Her deep commitment to moral and religious purity and to the abolition of slavery led her to strident public advocacy in a manner uncommon for women of her day.

FURTHER READING

Hinks, Peter, ed. *David Walker's Appeal, to the Coloured Citizens of the World, but in Particular, and Very Expressly, to Those of the United States of America* (2000).

Logan, Shirley Wilson. *With Pen and Voice: A Critical Anthology of Nineteenth-Century African American Women* (1995).

Richardson, Marilyn, ed. *Maria W. Stewart, America's First Black Woman Political Writer* (1987).

Obituary: *The People's Advocate*, 28 Feb. 1880.

MARTHA L. WHARTON

Stewart, Rex (22 Feb. 1907–7 Sept. 1967), jazz cornetist, was born Rex William Stewart in Philadelphia, Pennsylvania, the son of Rex Stewart, a violinist and singer, and Jane Johnson, a pianist, who taught him music from the age of four. In 1914 he started playing alto horn and then cornet in a boys' band in Washington, D.C., where his parents had settled sometime earlier. After three years' experience with this group he played on the Potomac riverboats and then in 1920 joined Ollie Blackwell's Jazz Clowns to tour with Rosa Henderson's blues revue, *Go-Get-It*. When the show folded in Philadelphia he found work with the Musical Spillers, a family vaudeville act whose code of behavior Stewart violated so often that he was dismissed in 1923. Instead of returning home, though, he stayed in New York City to freelance in dozens of small Harlem clubs.

In the fall of 1924, after an engagement with Billy Paige's Broadway Syncopators, Stewart joined the banjoist ELMER SNOWDEN's band at the Balconnades, where he played with such talented young jazzmen as the trombonist Jimmy Harrison and the reedman PRINCE ROBINSON. When his idol LOUIS ARMSTRONG left the FLETCHER HENDERSON Orchestra in early November 1925, he recommended Stewart as his replacement. It took much coaxing from Snowden, but the younger cornetist finally agreed to join Henderson at the Roseland Ballroom the following May, only to believe himself still inadequate to the task nine months later, when he quit to join younger brother HORACE HENDERSON's Collegians at Wilberforce University in Ohio. In October 1928 Stewart returned to New York and resumed his place in the elder Henderson's band for another year or so. After a brief stint with Alex Jackson around 1930, he joined McKinney's Cotton Pickers in Detroit and stayed with them from August 1931 to early 1932, when he once again returned to Fletcher Henderson. From June 1933 until August 1934 Stewart led a twelve-piece band at the Empire Ballroom opposite the Roseland on Broadway, but he eventually left because of poor business. With further opportunities for leadership of his own band diminishing, Stewart worked for a few months with LUIS RUSSELL's band before joining DUKE ELLINGTON in December 1934.

With the exception of a brief period between April and October 1943, during which he worked with Benny Carter and formed his own band in Los Angeles, Stewart remained with Ellington until December 1945. After almost two decades of national exposure on both records and radio broadcasts and in theaters and ballrooms, Stewart attempted once again to go out on his own. In early 1946 he formed a seven-piece group, the Rextet, and worked in New York at the Three Deuces and Kelly's Stable on Fifty-second Street and the Savoy Ballroom and the Apollo Theater in Harlem as well as at the Savoy Cafe in Boston. He next went on tour for a few months with Norman Granz's Jazz at the Philharmonic and in October 1947 reassembled his Rextet for a European tour booked by the Hot Club of France; in June 1948 he disbanded the group and worked as a soloist with local jazz bands in Germany. Enjoying his newfound fame in Europe as a visiting jazz star, Stewart also took time to indulge another passion; he studied gourmet cooking at Le Cordon Bleu, ultimately earning a certificate of proficiency in December 1949. In the summer of that year he also had gone on a successful tour of Australia with Graeme Bell's traditional jazz band.

After securing a divorce from his first wife, Margie Slaughter, with whom he had at least three children, Stewart married Ruth Hansen around 1950. From 1950 to 1952 he worked sporadically in Philadelphia, New York, and Boston, using a farm he had bought near Troy, New York, as a home base. He also had a radio show on WROW and lectured on jazz at Dartmouth and Bennington colleges. In the spring of 1953 he formed a group starring the clarinetist ALBERT NICHOLAS to work at the Savoy in Boston, after which he spent a few more years freelancing. In the summer of 1957 Stewart was asked to assemble and direct a big band of Fletcher Henderson alumni to appear at the Great South Bay Festival on Long Island. Recorded in November and December, the music of the seventeen-piece Henderson All Stars featured Stewart with BUSTER BAILEY, J. C. HIGGINBOTHAM, COLEMAN HAWKINS, BEN WEBSTER, and other stars of the Swing Era. Also in December, along with RED ALLEN, VIC DICKENSON, Pee Wee Russell, and Hawkins, he appeared on the historic telecast "The Sound of Jazz." The next year Stewart restaged the Great South Bay Festival concert with slightly different personnel, and recordings were made in August 1958 shortly after his July appearance at the Newport Jazz Festival as leader of the Ellington Alumni All Stars.

From early 1958 through the summer of 1959, Stewart worked regularly at Eddie Condon's in New York City, and in 1960 he moved to Los Angeles to be close to his now-adult children. He found little work there, however, and once again accepted a job hosting shows on the all-jazz station KNOB. Always highly literate, despite a limited formal education, and a lively raconteur, Stewart also began writing his autobiography as well as articles on jazz for *Down Beat*, *Playboy*, *Evergreen Review*, *Melody Maker*, and *Jazz Journal*. In his later years he planned to complete the account of his career in music, but two European tours in 1966 and a few concerts in California occupied most of his time before his sudden death from a heart attack in Santa Barbara.

Although Stewart had been initially impressed by JOHNNY DUNN and BUBBER MILEY, it was Louis Armstrong's brilliant solos with KING OLIVER, CLARENCE WILLIAMS, Fletcher Henderson, and his own recording groups that served as the younger player's major inspiration. His own best early work can be heard on "The Stampede" (1926) and a number of other Henderson titles from 1928 to 1931, including "My Gal Sal," "Sugar Foot Stomp," "Clarinet Marmalade," and "Singin' the Blues"; the latter two were especially notable for his emulation of the white cornetist Bix Beiderbecke. Stewart can also be heard to advantage on McKinney's Cotton Pickers' "Rocky Road," "Never Swat a Fly," and "Do You Believe in Love at Sight?" where his heated, rhythmic style offers direct contrast to the sober lyricism of the lead trumpeter DOC CHEATHAM. By the time he joined Ellington, Stewart was a highly individualized stylist with an intense, hard-punching delivery increasingly characterized by the use of artfully controlled "off-notes" produced by the partial lowering of the cornet's valves. Although not featured nearly as much as COOTIE WILLIAMS, Ellington's star trumpeter, Stewart nevertheless contributed greatly to the varied texture that was the Ellington trademark. Among his many showcase performances, "Trumpet in Spades," "Braggin' in Brass," "Tootin' through the Roof," "Boy Meets Horn," "Morning Glory," and "John Hardy's Wife" are the most strikingly indicative of his powers, while his own small-band records during the same prewar period offer equally exceptional performances. In addition to the several films he appeared in as a member of the Ellington orchestra, Stewart also had an acting role in *Syncopation* (1942), in which he portrayed a fictitious New Orleans trumpeter.

FURTHER READING
Allen, Walter C. *Hendersonia: The Music of Fletcher Henderson and His Musicians* (1973).
Bruyninckx, Walter. *Swing Discography, 1920–1988* (12 vols., 1985–1989).
Dance, Stanley. *The World of Duke Ellington* (1970).
McCarthy, Albert J. *Big Band Jazz* (1974).
Stewart, Rex. *Jazz Masters of the Thirties* (1972).
Stewart, Rex. *Boy Meets Horn*, ed. Claire P. Gordon (1991).

DISCOGRAPHY
Rust, Brian. *Jazz Records, 1897–1942* (1982).
This entry is taken from the *American National Biography* and is published here with the permission of the American Council of Learned Societies.

JACK SOHMER

Stewart, Sallie W. (4 Jan. 1881–1951), clubwoman, educator, and real estate entrepreneur, was born Sallie Wyatt, the eldest of eight children, to Armstead and Eliza Jones Wyatt in Ensle, Tennessee. She migrated with her family to Evansville, Indiana, in the 1890s. Stewart overcame overwhelming odds to graduate valedictorian from Evansville High School at the turn of the century. She received her teacher's training at Evansville Normal School, University of Chicago, and Indiana University.

In 1903, when Stewart was twenty-two, Evansville erupted in a riot when an African American man was accused of shooting a white police officer at a drug store in Baptisttown, a poor, racially integrated area of the city. Whites threatened to kill every Negro in Evansville, forcing the governor to call up the state militia to restore order. The racial violence and intimidation prompted hundreds of black families to leave the already tiny black community. Stewart decided to stay and saw Baptisttown transform into a strictly segregated area during the first decade of the 1900s. Despite the deteriorating racial climate, Baptisttown became the vibrant center of African American community life in the city.

In 1910 she married successful businessman Logan Henry Stewart. Logan started a life insurance company and a real estate investment company in the early 1900s. He also helped organize the local Negro Business League. The local league proved instrumental in organizing the Cherry Street YMCA. The couple made a formidable team in their commitment to enhancing the quality of life for blacks in Evansville. Stewart was a significant influence in the economic, educational, and civic development of Evansville. As an active club-woman, she led efforts to improve social services and facilities for Baptisttown residents and to provide charity and assistance for poor families. As an educator, Stewart worked for fifty years to improve the curriculum, schools, and quality of education for African American students. As an entrepreneur, she broke down barriers for African American women in real estate and business. In 1915 Stewart and Reverend Hugh Shannon organized a small committee of black civic leaders, professionals, and business leaders to protest the showing of the films *The Birth of a Nation* and *The Nigger*. Having lived through a racial riot in 1903, Stewart believed the films could stir up racial hatred among whites, and she felt they would be highly offensive to African Americans. The committee evolved into a short-lived National Association for the Advancement of Colored People (NAACP) chapter, which elected Stewart secretary. The fledgling NAACP chapter, along with black principals and other community leaders, stressed the need for more pragmatic training in janitorial services, domestic science, gardening, and carpentry, rather than science or humanities. At the time, a contentious debate existed among African American educators regarding the efficacy of vocational or liberal arts education for working-class African Americans. Many educators stressed vocational education because they believed that by making African Americans useful and productive workers in American society, they would improve the image of the race in the eyes of whites and illustrate African Americans' fitness for full citizenship rights. Critics believed vocational education limited the intellectual development of the African American community, played into white stereotypes and prejudices, and impeded the movement to secure equal rights.

In reality, many educators openly supported vocational education to win financial support from white-controlled city and state governments and from elite foundations, but they also supported and provided a liberal arts education. Within and outside of the NAACP, Stewart pressed for better funding of African American schools and modernization of curriculum. She supported vocational and domestic science education to prepare students for jobs outside of the classroom. Stewart drew some criticism for her position, but she probably stressed vocational training above liberal arts education because the former position drew strong support and cooperation from the local white Chamber of Commerce. The chamber

influenced the school board to increase funding for Baptisttown schools and to build a new vocational high school. However, the improvements fell well short of equality with white schools. Regardless of the politics of vocational versus liberal education during her more than fifty years as an educator, Stewart's commitment to encouraging excellence in education remained unquestioned. Students who have cited her as an important influence include ELBERT FRANK COX, the first African American to earn a Ph.D. in mathematics.

In 1916 Stewart organized the City Federation of Colored Women's Clubs in Evansville. In 1917 Stewart's husband replaced her as secretary of the NAACP chapter, which disbanded soon after the outbreak of World War I. In 1918 Stewart and other African American teachers partnered with white teachers to raise money to establish a teachers' college in Evansville. Though they raised enough money to open the teachers' college, the college denied admission to African Americans—forcing African American educators to continue traveling more than one hundred miles to Indiana State Teachers College for certification and continuing education. The same year, Baptisttown residents persevered in their commitment to interracial efforts despite white Evansville's poor record on racial progress. African Americans heeded interracial calls to support the war for democracy abroad and American troops by planting over one thousand war gardens, establishing food conservation clubs and Junior Red Cross clubs in neighborhoods and schools, and raising $74,000 in Liberty Loans for the war effort. Stewart was central to these successes. As state organizer for the Indiana State Federation of Colored Women's Clubs, she traveled throughout the state, encouraging existing clubs to affiliate with the state and national organization and urging the formation of black women's clubs in communities where none existed. Stewart's work in the war effort, in the suffrage movement, and in fighting racism enabled her to extend her political vision beyond Evansville. Along with other club-women such as MARY ELIZA CHURCH TERRELL, she attended several meetings of the Women's International League for Peace and Freedom, founded in 1915 to promote peace and equal rights. She believed the League provided an international forum for improving the global image of African American women.

After World War I, Stewart advocated that African Americans exercise even greater leadership within their communities, but she was not averse to alliances with whites. In the early 1920s the Evansville Federation of Colored Women under Stewart's leadership helped to raise money among Evansville's white philanthropists for band instruments, football uniforms, and sports equipment for Douglass and Lincoln High Schools. In 1919 she organized the Day Nursery Association (DNA) to provide childcare for working mothers. The DNA expanded and opened a boarding house and recreational center for African American women. In 1925 Stewart and her long-time associate, fellow educator Fannie Snow, formally incorporated the DNA, with Stewart as president.

Education remained one of Stewart's most important commitments. She served as the dean of girls from 1924 to 1928 at Douglass High School and from 1929 to 1951 at Lincoln High School. She and other women educators popularized the study of African American life, history, and culture through their support of CARTER GODWIN WOODSON's Negro History Week, which began in 1926. Women supported the Association for the Study of Negro Life and History behind the scenes, despite the fact that no women were included in its formal program during the first ten years of its existence. However, in the late 1920s, women increased their visibility in the organization's activities. In 1928 Stewart presented a paper outlining the persistent influence of African culture on African Americans in a paper titled "Serious Thoughts on Race Appreciation." During the age of Jim Crow, Stewart carved out a place in academia in defiance of mainstream arguments of African American intellectual inferiority and despite gender conventions that deemed women unfit for academic scholarship and leadership in the larger academic community.

Stewart continued her work to improve social services in Baptisttown. Her efforts to improve African American health care bore fruit in 1928 when the Vanderburgh County Tuberculosis Association appointed her chair of its colored auxiliary. That year's health and neighborhood cleanup campaign resulted in the opening of a small cottage with room for eight African American patients at the all-white Boehne Hospital.

After her husband's death in 1929, Stewart refused to sell his lucrative real estate business or to allow someone else to manage it. She studied for and received a formal broker's license in 1930, making her the first African American woman in the country to gain a broker's license and to own a real estate brokerage firm. Her personal business successes won her prestigious positions as head of the Women's Auxiliary of the National Negro Business League in 1929 and on the Executive Committee of the National Colored Merchants' Association in the early 1930s. Stewart's business activities enhanced her growing national reputation. She served as vice president of the U.S. National Council of Women, an interracial federation of women's reform clubs.

In addition to her work for the state federation, Stewart was also active in the National Association of Colored Women Clubs (NACW) since 1918, including serving for two years as chair of the Executive Board and for four years as vice president at large. She wrote articles for the NACW's *National Notes* and founded the newspaper *Hoosier Women*, which provided a voice for Indiana's African American clubwomen. The NACW elected Stewart president in 1928 in a bitterly contested election following MARY McLEOD BETHUNE's retirement. The NACW's programs under Stewart's leadership from 1928 to 1933 stood in contrast to the activities of the women still active in the Garvey movement and with Bethune's National Council of Negro Women founded in the mid-1930s. Stewart argued that African American women should focus on social reform and families rather than political activism as the best strategy to uplift the black community. Stewart instituted a "Better Homes Projects" program, which included focus on home life and housing and also focused on the problem of delinquency among young women. Stewart also put her business skills to productive use, instituting a number of fiscal reforms while streamlining the NACW during the Depression.

During World War II, Stewart shifted gears and focused on the war effort. She served as head of the committee of hostesses serving black soldiers stationed at nearby Camp Breckenridge. As in the first World War, Stewart continued to face resistance to African American appeals for equal access and treatment. Stewart raised some public funds and used them to subsidize activities for African American soldiers, such as weekly Saturday night dances and Sunday morning breakfasts. She also raised funds for recreational facilities and sleeping quarters for soldiers and their families.

Having no children of her own, she provided in her will that $100,000 of her estate be used to help young black women. Stewart died in 1951.

FURTHER READING

Bigham, Darrel F. *We Ask Only a Fair Trial: A History of the Black Community of Evansville, Indiana* (1987).

Hine, Darlene Clark, ed. *Black Women in America* (2005).

Stetson, Erlene. "Black Feminism in Indiana, 1893–1933," *Phylon* (1983).

White, Deborah Gray. *Too Heavy a Load: Black Women in Defense of Themselves, 1894–1994* (1999).

SHENNETTE GARRETT

Stewart, Slam (21 Sept. 1914–10 Dec. 1987), jazz string bassist, bandleader, and educator, was born in Englewood, New Jersey. Nothing is known of his parents or his real name. He was raised as Leroy Elliott Stewart, but he said, without offering details, that a different name is on his birth certificate. His adoptive father was a caretaker and gardener. Stewart started on violin at age six or seven and switched to string bass while in high school in Englewood.

His father worked for Dwight Morrow, an affluent man whose daughter Anne married Charles Lindbergh. After Stewart graduated, Morrow helped send him to the Boston Conservatory of Music, where he studied string bass for one year while playing in local bands. At this time he began to imitate Ray Perry, who hummed in unison with violin bowing; Stewart's humming, situated an octave above his bowed bass, became his overused musical signature.

In 1936 he joined the trumpeter Peanuts Holland's band in Buffalo, New York. He returned to New Jersey and started playing in New York City clubs. Around 1937 he met the guitarist and singer SLIM GAILLARD at a jam session at an after-hours club in Harlem. The next day they played together on Gaillard's radio show on WMEW in New York. Martin Block, host of "The Make Believe Ballroom" on that same station, volunteered to manage the new duo, Slim and Slam, for which Stewart took up his lasting nickname. They toured theaters nationally and had a huge hit with the nonsense song "The Flat Foot Floogie (with the Floy, Floy)"; at the next World's Fair a copy of this disc was buried in a time capsule, together with a recording of John Philip Sousa's "Washington Post March."

Stewart also worked with the Spirits of Rhythm (spring 1939), Van Alexander's dance orchestra (1940), and his own trio at Kelly's Stable in New York (late 1940). Slim and Slam performed in the comedy film *Hellzapoppin'* (1941), but the duo broke up the next year, when Gaillard was inducted into the armed forces. Stewart played in FATS WALLER's group in the film *Stormy Weather* (1943), and while in California, the guitarist TINY GRIMES took Gaillard's place. A successful jam session with the pianist ART TATUM led to their joining Tatum in a trio from 1943 to 1944. Stewart had perfect pitch and was able to keep up with Tatum's impetuous habit of reharmonizing popular songs, playing them in different keys, or changing keys in the course of a tune. "He never did get me," Stewart told the interviewer Doug Long. "I was able to follow him right straight through."

Tatum's trio played at the Three Deuces in New York. Apart from Tatum, Stewart recorded "Afternoon of a Basieite" and "Sometimes I'm Happy" at a session with the saxophonist LESTER YOUNG in December 1943, and during 1944 he also worked at the Three Deuces with the pianist Johnny Guarnieri's trio, and he played in Grimes's quartet.

Late in 1944 Tatum went to Los Angeles, California, and Stewart took over the trio, with ERROLL GARNER serving as its pianist. The Three Deuces remained his home base, but he also toured extensively. Concurrently from late January to November 1945 Stewart was a member of the clarinetist Benny Goodman's quintet and sextet. During this same year he recorded "Groovin' High" and "All the Things You Are" with DIZZY GILLESPIE's amalgamated swing and bop group (February), two magnificently energetic duos with the tenor saxophonist DON BYAS, "Indiana" and "I Got Rhythm," in a concert at Town Hall (9 June); "Slam Slam Blues" with the vibraphonist Red Norvo (also June); and "Three O'Clock in the Morning" with Byas's quartet, including Garner (August).

In January 1946, after Garner had a hit record, "Laura," and went out on the road as a leader, Billy Taylor took Garner's place in Stewart's trio; they also worked as a quartet with the drummer Doc West. Stewart worked with Tatum again that spring. His trio continued with John Collins replacing Grimes in 1946 and MARY LOU WILLIAMS taking over the piano chair by the time of the movie *Boy! What a Girl* (1947).

After performing with Garner in France in May 1948, Stewart moved to Los Angeles and played on and off with Tatum during the late 1940s and early 1950s, with Everett Barksdale serving as their guitarist. Stewart worked in the trumpeter ROY ELDRIDGE's quartet (1953), continued leading a trio with Beryl Booker as his pianist from 1953 to 1955, and then toured as accompanist to the singer and pianist Rose Murphy from around 1956 into the 1960s. He was reunited with Gaillard for a performance at the Great South Bay Jazz Festival in summer 1958.

In the mid-1960s Stewart settled permanently in Binghamton, New York. After retiring temporarily owing to illness, he led his own trio in New York City late in 1968 and for work in Binghamton television studios. He rejoined Gaillard one last time for a quartet performance at the Monterey Jazz Festival with the organist MILT BUCKNER and the drummer JO JONES in 1970. He then toured Europe with Buckner and Jones in April 1971. While performing in San Francisco, California, with Tatum in 1951, Stewart had met a singer and pianist, Claire (maiden name unknown). They married around 1970 and had two children.

From the early 1970s onward Stewart taught at the State University of New York in Binghamton, gave programs on jazz history at Binghamton-area schools, and produced jazz concerts at the Roberson Center in Binghamton. He rejoined Goodman in June 1973 for the Newport Jazz Festival in New York and then toured steadily with the clarinetist until March 1976, including a trip to Europe in 1974. In February 1977 Stewart suffered a heart attack, followed by a stroke. He recovered to play at the Grand Parade du Jazz in Nice, France, in July 1977, and that same year he played at Hopper's in New York in a duo with the guitarist Bucky Pizzarelli. The duo performed regularly on the *Today* show on NBC during 1978.

Stewart rejoined Goodman occasionally in 1979 and for a last time as a guest soloist in June 1985. He toured internationally with the saxophonist ILLINOIS JACQUET (c. 1980–1981). In May 1984 he was awarded an honorary doctorate in music from SUNY Binghamton. He died in Binghamton. The date is given incorrectly as 9 December in the *New York Times* obituary; the funeral home confirmed the correct date, 10 December.

Having discovered a coarse, humorous sound, Stewart relentlessly hummed and bowed his solos through half a century of jazz. Unfortunately, a little of this gimmick goes a long way. It seems a shame that Stewart never tried to make his solos beautiful, deep toned, and heady, along the lines of an OSCAR PETTIFORD. Otherwise, in his principal role as an accompanist, plucking the instrument in a conventional jazz manner to keep rhythm and harmony in place, he ranks with any of the finest jazz bassists.

FURTHER READING

Oral histories of Stewart are at Yale University and at the Institute of Jazz Studies, Newark, N.J.

Burns, Jim. "Slim & Slam," *Jazz Journal* 21 (Sept. 1968).

Doran, James M. *Erroll Garner: The Most Happy Piano* (1985).

Jones, Max. *Talking Jazz* (1987).

Obituary: *New York Times*, 11 Dec. 1987.

This entry is taken from the *American National Biography* and is published here with the permission of the American Council of Learned Societies.

BARRY KERNFELD

Stewart, Thomas McCants (28 Dec. 1853–1 Jan. 1923), educator, minister, lawyer, and justice, was born in Charleston, South Carolina, the first of two children born to George Gilchrist Stewart, a blacksmith, and Anna Morris Stewart, a dressmaker, both free blacks. Stewart attended, but did not graduate from, Avery Normal Institute in the late 1860s, and he entered Howard University in 1869. He matriculated at the integrated University of South Carolina as a junior in 1874, and he graduated in December of the following year with bachelor of arts and bachelor of laws degrees. Stewart married Charlotte "Lottie" Pearl Harris in 1876, and they had three children: McCants (1877), Gilchrist (1879), and Carlotta (1881).

Stewart began his career practicing law in Sumter, and he taught math at the State Agricultural and Mechanical School in Orangeburg during the 1877–1878 school year. South Carolina congressman ROBERT BROWN ELLIOTT invited Stewart to join his Orangeburg law firm, where the young lawyer remained until Elliott, Stewart, & Straker dissolved less than a year later. After being licensed as an African Methodist Episcopal (AME) minister in October 1877, Stewart resigned from his teaching position, enrolled at Princeton Theological Seminary (he remained there until May 1880), and was ordained in the AME Church. Following his ordination, Stewart became pastor at Bethel AME in New York City's "Little Africa" section of Greenwich Village.

In addition to ministering to one thousand congregation members, Stewart filled other roles as an emerging African American leader. He promoted black nationalism in America and emigration for those nationalists who believed their goals could not be realized in the United States. As an Africanist, he advocated Christianizing and developing Africa. It was these convictions that led Stewart to leave Bethel for Africa in early 1883.

President EDWARD WILMOT BLYDEN of Liberia College hired Stewart as the Charles Sumner

Professor of Belles Lettres. The Stewart family remained in Columbia, South Carolina, during Stewart's two-year stint in Africa, and Lottie and the young children suffered from Stewart's financial neglect. Stewart and Blyden quickly clashed personally, the president accusing the professor of being lazy, uncooperative, outspoken, and insubordinate; additionally, Blyden believed that people of mixed race exploited Africans, and he seemed to resent that Stewart's skin was not as dark as that of the native Africans. Stewart and Blyden conflicted ideologically as well: while both men agreed on the importance of industrial training, Stewart saw the president de-emphasizing liberal arts education— one of the features of the job that drew Stewart to Liberia. Stewart returned to New York in 1885, publishing *Liberia: The Americo-African Republic* the following year. *Liberia* increased Stewart's reputation as an African American leader and allowed him to promote himself as an authority on Africa.

Stewart returned to the law in New York City and opened an office near the New York Stock Exchange, and he was admitted to practice before the state Supreme Court in 1886. Stewart specialized in civil law, and, while other members of the bar—both black and white—respected Stewart and his work, his client list and workload were modest. Stewart's most famous case was the Trainor Hotel suit in November 1891, in which Stewart successfully argued for the plaintiff—T. THOMAS FORTUNE, of the New York *Age* newspaper—that his civil rights had been violated when he was forcibly removed from the Trainor Hotel because the proprietor did not want to serve a black person. The Trainor Hotel suit garnered Stewart some national attention, including that of BOOKER T. WASHINGTON, who invited Stewart to give the commencement address at the Tuskegee Institute.

Stewart was elected to the Brooklyn school board in May 1891, and he devised a plan, adopted in 1893, to merge two schools to create an integrated public school. He believed consolidation was prudent for economic as well as racial reasons because separating black students meant operating separate schools; given the small number of blacks in Brooklyn public schools (about 450), that was not financially viable.

Sometime during the years that followed Stewart's return from Liberia, he and Lottie divorced, and, in 1893, Stewart married Alice M. Franklin, an accomplished elocutionist and dramatic reader. Stewart and Alice had three daughters: Anna, who was born in New York, and Gladys and Kapulani, both of whom were born in Hawaii.

In 1898, Stewart moved his family to Hawaii to take advantage of the economic and political opportunities there, as well as to escape what he saw as pervasive racial discrimination in the United States. He established a law practice in Honolulu, and the majority of his work focused on civil cases. By 1900, Stewart was involved in Republican party politics, and the Republican Territorial Central Committee appointed him to draft an act that would grant Hawaiian people greater autonomy in local government. Hawaii proved not to be the boon he had hoped, however. His legal practice was unremarkable, he did not become a prominent political figure, he received no significant political appointment, and his investment in sugar paid very little.

His Hawaiian hopes unfulfilled, Stewart moved to London in summer 1905. He hoped to use London as a base to trade with and invest in Liberia. While Stewart found London to be racially tolerant—he faced neither the race nor class discrimination that the majority of blacks in London encountered—and while Stewart's youngest three children thrived in London, he abruptly left England for Liberia since he was not successful. Combining his love for the law and affection for Africa, Stewart moved to Monrovia, the largest city in Liberia, in 1906. He set up a legal practice and served the government by revising the country's statutes in 1906 and 1911, by writing the legal code for justices of the peace in 1907, and by helping establish the National Bar Association. He first declined and then accepted an associate justiceship on the Liberian Supreme Court in 1911. Liberia's President Arthur Barclay also used Stewart as an envoy to secure a loan from the U.S. government. In October 1914, after hearing complaints about Stewart's criticisms of other Supreme Court justices and his acceptance of retainers from individuals, the legislature passed a joint resolution and removed Stewart from the Supreme Court.

Stewart returned to London in 1914, spending his time raising his three daughters and looking for new economic opportunities. He and his family moved to the Virgin Islands in February 1921, where he formed a legal practice with longtime resident CHRISTOPHER HARRISON PAYNE. In addition to his legal work, Stewart devoted energy to the Virgin Islanders' attempt to gain constitutional rights and to exercise greater local political control. Stewart died the first week of 1923, having contracted pneumonia following a two-month trip to the United States.

FURTHER READING

Broussard, Albert S. *African-American Odyssey: The Stewarts, 1853–1963* (1998).

Richings, G. F. *Evidences of Progress among Colored People* (1902).

Simmons, William J. *Men of Mark: Eminent, Progressive and Rising* (1887).

Thornbrough, Emma. *T. Thomas Fortune: Militant Journalist* (1972).

Wynes, Charles E. "T. McCants Stewart: Peripatetic Black South Carolinian," *South Carolina Historical Magazine* (Oct. 1979).

DAVID SCHROEDER

Stewart-Lai, Carlotta (16 Sept. 1881–6 July 1952), educator, was born Carlotta Stewart in Brooklyn, New York, to THOMAS MCCANTS STEWART, lawyer, minister, educator, and civil rights activist, and Charlotte Pearl Harris Stewart. In 1883 Stewart-Lai's father accepted a professorship at the College of Liberia and left his family in Brooklyn with no apparent means of support as he assessed liberal and industrial education models for the Liberian school. His absence and neglect led to a divorce from Charlotte, but by 1886 Stewart had resumed his legal practice in New York and he and his children would remain there throughout Stewart-Lai's childhood.

Stewart-Lai attended public school in New York before accompanying her father and stepmother Alice to Honolulu, Hawaii, in 1898. Entering the racially and ethnically diverse Hawaiian community with virtually no existing African American presence, the Stewarts were able to live unburdened by many of the racial prejudices they had known in the mainland United States. T. McCants Stewart wrote so glowingly of the prospects for racial equality in Hawaii that he inspired his friend and prominent activist T. THOMAS FORTUNE to go there as well. Stewart-Lai continued her education at Oahu College and was one of eight graduating seniors in 1902. She majored in English and finished college in only one year. After graduating, Stewart-Lai completed the requirements for a teaching certificate that she received later in 1902. She immediately was offered and accepted a position in the normal school's practice department where she began teaching in July of the same year. Stewart-Lai taught English in the normal school until 1909.

Carlotta Stewart-Lai taught in the Hawaiian public schools and served as a principal on the islands of Oahu and Kauai. (Austin/Thompson Collection, by permission of Moorland-Spingarn Research Center.)

Her annual teaching salary began at $660 in 1902, increasing to $900 in 1906 and $1,000 in 1908. After her father and stepmother left Hawaii in 1905, Stewart-Lai supported herself and supplemented her earnings by working as a typist during her spare time. Her income placed her comfortably in the black middle class, whether measured by Hawaiian or mainland standards, and she was able to offer some financial assistance not only to older brothers McCants and Gilchrist but also to her mother, all of whom lived in the United States. Charlotte Harris Stewart was estranged from the family when she and T. McCants Stewart divorced, and he forbade any of his children from contacting her after his 1893 remarriage. Stewart-Lai was able to subvert her father's orders to some extent, but was never able to provide her mother with substantial support or to visit her. After her father and stepmother left Hawaii in 1905, Stewart-Lai felt isolated from friends and family, and her mother's death in 1906 cast her into bouts of depression. During her first years in Hawaii, Stewart-Lai experienced both the benefits and the challenges of being a black woman in a community where African Americans comprised approximately 0.2 percent of the population. Because Hawaii had no established antiblack laws such as those in the Jim Crow South, or even a tradition of discriminatory practices that the Stewarts experienced in the North and the West, Stewart-Lai's life was unique among many of her African American counterparts. She taught in a multiracial school and had an active social life that was not defined by her race or the races of her friends and associates. Writing to her brother McCants in 1906 she described her leisure activities, which included taking classes, vacationing, surfing, attending parties, and watching Sunday baseball games (Broussard). In fact, she acted as coach of the junior and senior women's teams in her community. It was her prospects of career advancement, strong friendships, and social ties that compelled Stewart-Lai to remain in Hawaii when her family departed. Nevertheless, her continued alienation from family, some financial trouble stemming from the 1907 Banker's Panic (an economic crisis in the U.S. market), and emotional distress upon her mother's death made Stewart-Lai consider returning to the mainland.

Ultimately, she knew that a return to the United States would jeopardize her professional goals. Only in her mid-twenties, she had attained a respected position in the community and taught in a multiracial classroom. In 1909 her decision to remain in Hawaii paid rich dividends, as Stewart-Lai was promoted to the post of principal of an elementary school. This promotion came with a salary increase, and she was placed in a position that would have been even more unusual in the United States. While many African American women were schoolteachers and some were even principals during this era, few served as principals of racially integrated schools. The families Stewart-Lai taught hailed from Hawaii, the Philippines, Japan, Korea, Portugal, and the United States. Some of her students were white Americans and probably the children of military personnel, but it is unlikely that she had contact with more than a few black families before World War II, when black soldiers began arriving in Hawaii. In 1916 Carlotta Stewart married Yun Tim Lai, the manager of an automobile dealership on Kauai and a man of Chinese descent.

The lives of T. McCants Stewart's three children offer insights into the challenges that even elite African Americans faced. Stewart-Lai's brothers would follow in their father's footsteps by becoming lawyers and struggling activists. McCants attempted to set up legal practices in Minnesota, Oregon, and San Francisco, but never found sufficient work, restricted as he was to serving the African American portion of these communities. Facing mounting health problems and a failing career, McCants committed suicide in 1919. Gilchrist won some renown as a lawyer, writing a report on the unfair discharging of African American soldiers who rebelled at Brownsville, Texas, in 1906. He was also active in equal rights organizations such as the Niagara Movement and the Constitution League, but personal conflicts left him out of favor with his father.

Stewart-Lai inherited her father's devotion to education and economic self-sufficiency. However, by remaining in Hawaii she transformed his race-based educational passion into a multiracial one. Unlike her American family members, Stewart-Lai was not an activist for racially specific causes. In fact, she never joined a reform organization for any demographic group. One can explain this away by noting that Hawaii did not have chapters of the major African American reform organizations such as the National Association for the Advancement of Colored People or the Urban League. Nevertheless, Stewart-Lai's decision to remain in Hawaii as a part of her multiracial social circle makes for risky assumptions about her reform interests.

Stewart-Lai retired in 1944. She served forty years in the Hawaiian public schools. She lived much of the rest of her life on Anahola Bay, Kauai, before entering a nursing home where she died in 1952. One of the few African Americans to venture to Hawaii prior to World War II, and one of a handful of women principals of public schools, Stewart-Lai was an exceptional and adventurous person. She might not have joined reform organizations, but Stewart-Lai led a life of devotion to equal rights and racial integration for all people.

FURTHER READING

Broussard, Albert S. *African-American Odyssey: The Stewarts, 1853–1963* (1998).

Broussard, Albert S. "Carlotta Stewart-Lai," in *Black Women in America* (1994).

de Graaf, Lawrence B. "Race, Sex, and Region: Black Women in the American West, 1850–1920," *Pacific Historical Review* (May 1980).

Lee, Lloyd L. "A Brief Analysis of the Role and Status of the Negro in the Hawaiian Community," *American Sociological Review* (Aug. 1948).

AMBER MOULTON-WISEMAN

Still, James (9 Apr. 1812–c. 1885), distinguished herbalist, early medical practitioner of folk remedies, and known in New Jersey as the Black Doctor of the Pines, was a son of Charity and Levin Steel. Levin bought his own freedom and left the eastern shores of Maryland for New Jersey. His wife escaped slavery through the Underground Railroad and on joining her husband changed her given name from Charity to Sydney, and they changed their surname to Still. The couple made their way to Springtown, located in Greenwich Township in Cumberland County, New Jersey, established by freedmen around 1800. The Bethel African Methodist Episcopal Church can trace its beginnings in Springtown in 1810, and it played an important role in the Underground Railroad in this area. The Stills settled in the forests of the Pine Barrens of Southern New Jersey near Medford, in Burlington County, where Levin sawed wood and chopped lumber for a living. They had eighteen children, and three of his sons, Peter, William, and James, went on to have important careers related to the antislavery movement and in medicine. Peter Still, who was separated from his mother at the age of six and reunited with her forty years later, was the subject of a book, *The Kidnapped and the Ransomed* (1856). WILLIAM STILL headed the Philadelphia "station" of the Underground Railroad and documented his work in his massive volume titled *The Underground Rail Road: A Record of Facts, Authentic Narratives, Letters …* (1872). "Doctor" James Still, with neither official title nor medical certificates, was a self-taught physician and a notable spokesperson for the African American community in New Jersey during the nineteenth century. In 1877, at age sixty-five, he published *Early Recollections and Life of Dr. James Still* to reflect pride in his accomplishments.

James Still was born in a log cabin in Washington Township, later Shamong, Burlington County, in the town of Indian Mills, New Jersey. In his autobiography he writes that he wanted to be a doctor from three-and-a-half years of age. It was the chance visit of Dr. Fort, the city physician who vaccinated the children living in the Pine Barrens, who fired young James' imagination. As a youth, he was bound out, and during his indenture, James kept his dream alive by reading during his spare time, especially any botany books he could find.

His childhood consisted of heavy farmhand work, and he wrote that his formal education consisted of a total of three months instruction in reading, writing, and arithmetic. He writes that he was not able to get medical training because of poverty and discrimination: "… worst of all, I had not the right color to enter medical school."

Still's early friendship with the Lenni-Lenape Indians who settled in the Pine Barrens was instructive and added to Still's informal medical training. He had gone with them in earlier years on their herb-gathering excursions. Not only did they show Still what to "harvest," they also taught him how to use the plants for medicines. In 1833, at age twenty-one, he set out for Philadelphia in search of work. Traveling through South Central New Jersey to cross the Delaware River, he suspected that he might be taken for a runaway slave, but he had his indenture papers as a free man. On 25 July 1835, Still married Anna Angelina Willow, with whom he had one daughter, Beulah. Anna contracted tuberculosis and died on 12 August 1838, and the following year on 8 August Still married Henrietta Thomas. Three days after the wedding, his little daughter, Beulah, died. James and Henrietta had five children, and two surviving sons, Jimmie and Joseph, followed in their father's footsteps. James Still Jr. moved to Boston to become the third African American to graduate from Harvard Medical School, and Joseph Still used his father's formulas in his medical practice in Mt. Holly, New Jersey.

The self-taught "Dr." James Still is of historical interest because he was one of several early blacks who, without any formal training, established reputations as medical doctors and apparently were, by the customs of the times, permitted to practice without legal interference. Early New Jersey settlers came from miles around to be treated by Still. He developed a large office practice, and on long circuit rides with horse and buggy he covered a large territory visiting the "Pineys" deep in the woods, who had no one else to succor them. His patients were predominantly whites who welcomed his gentle remedies and unorthodox cures. Still was a distinguished herbalist at the time when most doctors relied on often questionable patent medicines. Throughout his life he read and investigated the healing powers of herbs and other plants. For his distilling business, the Pine Barren region provided such herbs as sassafras root, with which he treated piles, snakeroot, and spikenard and skunk cabbage roots, which he used to make a cough balsam. Still devoted a chapter of his book to the treatment of fevers, rheumatism, and cancers. He wrote that he did not believe in chemical drugs, particularly mercury, and he disapproved of surgery, water cures, and electric shock. His treatments might be best classified as humanitarian with a concern for the comfort of the patient; therefore his reputation for cures spread and his practice prospered.

Still lies in Colemantown Cemetery, in Mount Laurel, New Jersey, where a monument was erected after his death. In 2006, the New Jersey Department of Environmental Protection bought his 8.8-acre homestead in Medford to establish a museum and to protect and preserve for future generations the contribution of an early pioneer in nature's medicines and curatives, the Black Doctor of the Pines, James Still.

FURTHER READING

Beck, Henry Charlton. "The Doctor of the Pines," in *Forgotten Towns of Southern New Jersey* (1961).

Callas, Toni. "State DEP buys historic James Still homestead—NJ buys land of 'Black doctor of the Pines'—The James Still Homestead in Medford Will Become a Museum," *The Philadelphia Inquirer*, 1 Mar. 2006.

Cobb, William Montague, M.D. "'Dr.' James Still—New Jersey Pioneer, Medical History," *Journal of the National Medical Association* (Mar. 1963).

Fishman, George M. "Copy of Letters on Dr. James Still which Appeared in the Courier-Post, Camden, NJ, 16 May 1961," *Negro History Bulletin* (Apr. 1962).

Lang, Carole Ann. "James Still: New Jersey's Black Physician of the Pines," *Negro History Bulletin* (Oct.–Dec. 1980).

RICHLYN FAYE GODDARD

Still, William (7 Oct. 1821–14 July 1902), abolitionist and businessman, was born near Medford in Burlington County, New Jersey, the youngest of the eighteen children of Levin Still, a farmer, and Charity (maiden name unknown). Still's father, a Maryland slave, purchased his own freedom and changed his name from Steel to Still. His mother escaped from slavery and changed her given name from Cidney to Charity. With a minimum of formal schooling, William studied on his own, reading whatever was available to him. He left home at age twenty to work at odd jobs and as a farmhand. In 1844 he moved to Philadelphia, where he found employment as a handyman, and in 1847 he married Letitia George. They had four children.

In 1847 the Pennsylvania Society for the Abolition of Slavery hired Still as a clerk, and he soon began assisting fugitives from slavery who passed through the city. After the passage of the Fugitive Slave Act of 1850, the society revived its Vigilance Committee to aid and support fugitive slaves and made Still chairman. One of the fugitives he helped was Peter Still, his own brother who had been left in slavery when his mother escaped. Finding Peter after a forty-year separation inspired Still to keep careful records of the former slaves, and those records later provided source material for his book on the Underground Railroad.

While with the Vigilance Committee, Still helped hundreds of fugitive slaves, and several times he nearly went to prison for his efforts. In 1855, when former slaves in Canada were being maligned in the press, he and his brother traveled there to investigate for themselves. His reports were much more positive and optimistic than the others and helped counteract rumors that former slaves were lazy and lawless. Five years later he cited cases of successful former slaves in Canada in a newspaper article that argued for freeing all the slaves.

Although Still had not approved of John Brown's raid on Harpers Ferry, afterward Brown's wife stayed with the Stills for a time, as did several of Brown's accomplices. Still's work in the antislavery office ended in 1861, but he remained active in the society, which turned to working for African American civil rights. He served as the society's vice president for eight years and as president from 1896 to 1901.

Still's book, *The Underground Railroad* (1872), was unique. The only work on that subject written by an African American, it was also the only day-by-day record of the workings of a vigilance committee. While he gave credit to "the grand little army of abolitionists," he put the spotlight on the fugitives themselves, saying "the race had no more eloquent advocates than its own self-emancipated champions." Besides recording their courageous deeds, Still hoped that the book would demonstrate the intellectual ability of his race. Along with the records of slave escapes he included excerpts from newspapers, legal documents, correspondence of abolitionists and former slaves, and some biographical sketches. He published the book himself and sent out agents to sell it. The book went into three editions and was exhibited at the Philadelphia Centennial Exposition in 1876.

Although he had not suffered personally under slavery, Still faced discrimination throughout his life and was determined to work for improved race relations. His concern about civil rights in the

North led him in 1859 to write a letter to the press, which started a campaign to end racial discrimination on Philadelphia streetcars, where African Americans were permitted only on the unsheltered platforms. Eight years later the campaign met success when the Pennsylvania legislature enacted a law making such discrimination illegal. In 1861 he helped organize and finance the Pennsylvania Civil, Social, and Statistical Association to collect data about the freed slaves and to press for universal suffrage.

Still was a skilled businessman as well as an effective antislavery agent. He began purchasing real estate while working for the antislavery society. After leaving that position he opened a store where he sold new and used stoves and coal. In 1861 he opened a coal yard, a highly successful business that led to his being named to the Philadelphia Board of Trade. In 1864 he was appointed post sutler at Camp William Penn, where black soldiers were stationed.

Still's independent nature was illustrated in 1874 when he repudiated the Republican candidate for mayor of Philadelphia and supported instead a reform candidate. He explained his position at a public meeting and later in a pamphlet entitled *An Address on Voting and Laboring* (1874). He was also a lifelong temperance advocate, and as a member of the Presbyterian Church he established a Mission Sabbath School. His other civic activities included membership in the Freedmen's Aid Commission, organizing around 1880 one of the first YMCAs for black youth, and helping to manage homes for the aged and for destitute black children and an orphan asylum for children of black soldiers and sailors. Poor health forced him to retire from his business affairs six years before his death at his home in Philadelphia.

FURTHER READING

Part of William Still's journal of the Philadelphia Vigilance Committee, along with some personal correspondence, is in the Historical Society of Pennsylvania in Philadelphia.

Still, William. *A Brief Narrative of the Struggle for the Rights of the Colored People of Philadelphia in the City Railway Cars* (1867).

Gara, Larry. "William Still and the Underground Railroad," *Pennsylvania History* 28 (Jan. 1961): 33–44.

Norwood, Alberta S. "Negro Welfare Work in Philadelphia Especially as Illustrated by the Career of William Still, ..." M.A. thesis, Univ. of Penn., 1931.

Obituary: *Philadelphia Public Ledger*, 15 July 1902.
This entry is taken from the *American National Biography* and is published here with the permission of the American Council of Learned Societies.

LARRY GARA

Still, William Grant (11 May 1895–3 Dec. 1978), composer, orchestrator, arranger, and musician, once called the "Dean of Afro-American Composers," was born in Woodville, Mississippi, the son of William Grant Still, a music teacher and bandmaster, and Carrie Lena Fambro, a schoolteacher. His father died during Still's infancy. Still and his mother moved to Little Rock, Arkansas, where she taught school and in 1909 or 1910 married Charles Shepperson, a railway postal clerk, who strongly supported his stepson's musical interests. Still graduated from high school at sixteen, valedictorian of his class, and went to Wilberforce University.

Still's mother had wanted him to become a doctor, but music became his primary interest. He taught himself to play the oboe and clarinet, formed a string quartet in which he played violin, arranged music for his college band, and began composing; a concert of his music was presented at the school. In 1915, just a few months shy of graduation, Still dropped out of Wilberforce in order to become a professional musician, playing in various dance bands, including one led by W. C. HANDY, "the Father of the Blues." That year he married Grace Bundy, with whom he had four children. They divorced in the late 1920s.

A small legacy from his father, which Still inherited on his twenty-first birthday, allowed him to resume his musical studies in 1917, this time at Oberlin College's conservatory. World War I interrupted Still's studies, and he spent it in the segregated U.S. Navy as a mess attendant and as a violinist in an officers' mess. After being discharged in 1919, Still returned to the world of popular music. He had a strong commitment to serious music and received further formal training during a short stay in 1922 at the New England Conservatory. From 1923 to 1925 he studied, as a private scholarship pupil, with the noted French "ultra-modernist" composer Edgard Varèse, whose influence can be heard in the dissonant passages found in Still's early serious work. Still managed to make his way both in the world of popular entertainment and as a serious composer. He worked successfully into the 1940s in the entertainment world as a musician,

William Grant Still on 12 Mar. 1949. (Library of Congress/ Photographed by Carl Van Vecht.)

arranger, orchestrator, and conductor. As an arranger and orchestrator, he worked on a variety of Broadway shows, including the fifth edition of Earl Carroll's *Vanities*. He also worked with a wide variety of entertainers, including Paul Whiteman, Sophie Tucker, and Artie Shaw. Still arranged Shaw's "Frenesi," which became one of the best-selling "singles" of all time. He also conducted on the radio for all three networks and was active in early television.

Despite his many commercial activities, Still also produced more serious efforts. Initially these works, such as *From the Land of Dreams* (written in 1924 and first performed a year later) and *Darker America* (also written in 1924 and first performed two years later), were described by critics as being "decidedly in the ultra-modern idiom." He soon moved into a simpler harmonic milieu, often drawing on jazz themes, as in *From the Black Belt* (written in 1926 and first performed in 1927), a seven movement suite for orchestra.

Still's most successful and best-known work, *Afro-American Symphony* (completed in 1930 and first performed a year later), draws heavily on the blues idiom; Still said he wanted "to demonstrate how the blues, so often considered a lowly expression, could be elevated to the highest musical level." To some extent the symphony is "programmatic," since after its completion Still added verses by black poet PAUL LAURENCE DUNBAR that precede each movement. Still believed that his symphony was probably the first to make use of the banjo. The work was well received and has continued to be played in the United States and overseas.

Still was a prodigious worker. His oeuvre includes symphonies; folk suites; tone poems; works for band, organ, piano, and violin; and operas, most of which focus on racial themes. His first opera, *Blue Steel* (completed in 1935), addresses the conflict between African voodooism and modern American values; its main protagonist is a black worker in Birmingham, Alabama. Still's first staged opera, *Troubled Island* (completed in 1938), which premiered at the New York City Opera in March 1949, centers around the character of Jean Jacques Dessalines, the first emperor of Haiti. The libretto, begun by the black poet Langston Hughes and completed by Verna Arvey, depicts the Haitian leader's stirring rise and tragic fall. Still married Arvey in 1939; the couple had two children. Arvey was to provide libretti for a number of Still's operas and choral works.

Among Still's other notable works are *And They Lynched Him on a Tree* (1940), a plea for brotherhood and tolerance presented by an orchestra, a white chorus, a black chorus, a narrator, and a soloist; *Festive Overture* (1944), a rousing piece based on "American themes"; *Lenox Avenue*, a ballet, with scenario by Arvey, commissioned by CBS and first performed on radio in 1937; *Highway 1, USA* (1962), a short opera, with libretto by Arvey, dealing with an incident in the life of an American family and set just off the highway in a gas station.

Still received many awards. Recognition had come relatively early to him—in 1928 the Harmon Foundation honored him with its second annual award, given to the person judged that year to have made the "most significant contribution to Negro culture in America." He won successive Guggenheim Fellowships in 1934 and 1935 and was awarded a Rosenwald Fellowship in 1939.

Still's early compositions were in an avant-garde idiom, but he soon turned to more conventional melodic and harmonic methods, in what he later described as "an attempt to elevate the folk idiom into symphonic form." This transition may have made his serious work more accessible, but for much of his career he sustained himself and his family by pursuing more commercially successful endeavors.

Still dismissed the black militants who criticized his serious music as "Eur-American music," insisting that his goal had been "to elevate Negro musical idioms to a position of dignity and effectiveness in the fields of symphonic and operatic music." And at a 1969 Indiana University seminar on black music he asserted, "I made this decision of my own free will. ... I have stuck to this decision, and I've not been sorry."

During his lifetime Still broke many racial barriers. He was heralded as the first black man to have a major orchestral work played before an American audience, the first to conduct a major symphony orchestra (the Los Angeles Philharmonic) in an evening of his own compositions (at the Hollywood Bowl in 1936), and the first to conduct a major all-white orchestra in the deep South (the New Orleans Philharmonic in 1955 at Southern University). He is also credited with being the first black man to have an opera performed by a "significant" American company (the New York City Opera in 1949). He composed into his late seventies; the Fisk Jubilee Singers performed a piece by him at the Fisk University Centennial Celebration in 1971. He died in Los Angeles.

FURTHER READING

Arvey, Verna. *William Grant Still* (1939).

Haas, R. B., ed. *William Grant Still and the Fusion of Cultures in American Music* (1972; repr. 1995).

Smith, Catherine Parsons. *William Grant Still: A Study in Contradictions* (2000).

Still, Judith Anne, et al. *William Grant Still: A Bio-Bibliography* (1996).

This entry is taken from the *American National Biography* and is published here with the permission of the American Council of Learned Societies.

DANIEL J. LEAB

Stith, Charles Richard (26 Aug. 1949–), clergyman, founder of Organization for a New Equality, and former ambassador to Tanzania, was born in St. Louis, Missouri, the son of Charles J. Stith, a jazz musician and Dorothy Stith, a nurse. His parents later divorced. Stith's mother was very active in the Methodist church. She made church participation an integral part of Stith's upbringing. He had two younger siblings, Rebecca Fanning and James Butler.

A 1963 graduate of Soldan High School in St. Louis, he matriculated into the St. Louis junior college system. During a trip to build churches in Africa in 1969, Stith was inspired to enter the ministry and acquired an interest in international development and justice issues in Africa. He transferred to Baker University in Baldwin, Kansas, graduating in 1973.

During a conference at St. Paul School of Theology in Kansas City, Missouri, in which Stith participated as a student teacher, he heard the dean of Gammon Seminary in Atlanta, Dr. Major J. Jones, speak about ministry. Dr. Jones encouraged Stith to attend Gammon, and he later became his mentor, guiding him in his call to the ministry. In 1975, Stith completed his master of divinity degree at Gammon. Stith married Deborah Prothrow in the same year. He received a master's degree in theology from Harvard University two years later.

In 1977, Stith became the minister at Wesley United Methodist Church in Boston. In 1978, Percy Stith was born to Charles and Deborah Stith. Then in 1979, at age thirty, he became the youngest senior minister ever appointed to Union United Methodist Church, one of the oldest African American congregations in that city. Mary Stith was born in 1981 to the Stiths. In 1985, Stith founded the Organization for a New Equality (ONE), a nonprofit civil rights organization that concentrates on economic opportunities for minorities and women. This initiative was based on the premise that in the post–civil rights era, the next justice issues facing the next generation of African Americans (and other historic victims of discrimination) were economic.

Of note during his administration of ONE was his leadership in negotiating and brokering the first comprehensive community reinvestment agreement in the country. The agreement committed Boston financial institutions to $500 million in mortgage and commercial lending to low- and moderate-income and minority communities in Massachusetts. The movement to develop such agreements was initiated by ONE at a national conference it convened in 1985 at Howard University. Subsequently, he worked on the Community Reinvestment Act (CRA) Regulatory Agency Working Group, chaired by then comptroller of the currency, Eugene Ludwig. The CRA Working Group's mandate was to develop stringent standards governing lending practices of banks as required by the CRA. Ten years after the implementation of the regulatory changes spawned by the working CRA Working Group, the *New York Times* cited that these regulatory changes governing the lending practices by banks resulted in over $2 trillion in credit and capital being made available to low and moderate income families across America.

Stith's work as diplomat began in 1994, when President Bill Clinton invited him to be a part of the official delegation that oversaw the South African election. Stith, a longtime friend and supporter of the president, was appointed by Clinton several years after their meeting, to serve as the U.S. ambassador to the United Republic of Tanzania. His appointment came shortly after the August 1998 bombing of the U.S. embassy in Dar es Salaam. Through Stith's expertise as a conciliator, the embassy was able to repair the breach between Tanzania and the United States. While in Tanzania, he set new standards for U.S. embassies to promote U.S. trade and investment in Africa. These new policies marked an economic turning point in Tanzania that led to the country's signature on an Open Skies Agreement, the first between an African country and the United States. Open Skies Agreements are preconditions for airlines obtaining routes in the countries that are signatories to such agreements. This agreement led to the code-share agreements for Delta and Northwest Airlines.

In September 1999, Ambassador Stith also organized Tanzanian President Benjamin W. Mkapa's visit to the United States. Mkapa's trip was lauded as having the largest delegation of African business leaders to ever accompany an African head of state to a Western nation. On the heels of that milestone, Stith arranged "reverse trade missions" to London and Johannesburg to allow Tanzanian business representatives to meet with U.S. business interests with offices in those cities to encourage greater U.S. trade and investment in Tanzania. During Stith's tenure, the Tanzanian government became the first sub-Saharan African country to reach the decision of debt relief under the Heavily Indebted Poor Countries Initiative.

After his tenure as ambassador to Tanzania ended, Ambassador Stith joined the administration of Boston University and was charged by the chancellor to establish the African Presidential Archives and Research Center at Boston University. The center provided forums and current resources for exchange on political and economic development in sub-Saharan Africa.

Stith also served on the national advisory boards of Fannie Mae and Fleet InCity Bank, the editorial board of WCVB-TV, and the boards of West Insurance Inc., and Wang Center for the Performing Arts. In June 2001, Senate Majority Leader Tom Daschle appointed him to the U.S. Commission on International Religious Freedom.

He received many accolades and several honorary doctorates from the University of South Carolina, Clark Atlanta University, and Baker University. He was the author of *Political Religion* (1995) and various articles in national publications, such as the *New York Times*, *Denver Post*, *Boston Globe*, *Los Angeles Times*, and *Atlanta Journal Constitution*.

FURTHER READING

Carlson, Margaret. "Hero, Suspect, Suicide," *Time*, 15 Jan. 1990.

Hume, Ashley. "Stith Receives International Citizen Award, *Daily Free Press*," 5 Nov. 2003.

Stith, Charles. "George Haley Sworn in as New U.S. Ambassadors to Tanzania and Gambia in Africa," *Jet*, 5 Oct. 1998.

ALISHA LOLA JONES

Stitt, Sonny (2 Feb. 1924–22 July 1982), jazz alto and tenor saxophonist, was born in Boston, Massachusetts, the son of Edward H. S. Boatner, a music professor, and Claudine Tibou, who played and taught piano and organ; she later married Robert Stitt. Raised in Saginaw, Michigan, Sonny, whose given name was Edward, took up piano at age seven before turning to clarinet and alto saxophone. He received informal lessons from the local saxophonist "Big Nick" Nicholas and from the saxophonist WARDELL GRAY, who slept and practiced in Stitt's room when in Saginaw, there being no hotel for African Americans in the town.

During summer vacation from high school, Stitt led a band and toured Michigan with Nicholas and trumpeter THAD JONES. As members of Cornelius Cornell's band, they ranged as far as Tennessee. Stitt declined an offer to join the bandleader Ernie Fields when his mother, upset that Stitt had stopped attending school, insisted that he earn a diploma. After some time with the band of Claude and Clifford Trenier, he graduated. Stitt worked in Boston with Sabby Lewis's big band (c. 1942), and in Detroit he joined the 'Bama State Collegians (1942), touring to New York in 1943. During this period Stitt was deeply influenced by CHARLIE PARKER's alto sax playing, heard on recordings with pianist

JAY MCSHANN's big band. In New York, Stitt partic-ipated in bop jam sessions in clubs on Fifty-second Street and in Harlem. In July 1943 he joined TINY BRADSHAW's big band in New York and toured to St. Louis and Kansas City, where he met and briefly rehearsed with Parker, who said, "You sound too much like me."

Stitt first recorded in 1944 as a sideman with Bradshaw. Late in April 1945 he joined BILLY ECKSTINE's bop big band, in which the saxophon-ists John Jackson, DEXTER GORDON, Leo Parker, and Stitt were known as the unholy four for their wild behavior. Stitt recorded with Eckstine in May and probably went on the orchestra's ensuing tour of the Northeast and the South, but he had left Eckstine by the fall. In March 1946 he joined DIZZY GILLESPIE's big band, which performed in New York from April to June. Not the orchestra's main alto soloist, Stitt served in effect as Charlie Parker's replacement in a bop sextet drawn from the big band, Parker and Gillespie having parted company. In this setting Stitt made his first significant record-ings, including "Oop Bop Sh'Bam," on 15 May 1946. Three days earlier he had participated in the all-star Bebop Jam Session at Lincoln Square Center, and in June he left Gillespie to lead his own groups. Stitt made various further seminal bop recordings that year: with the trumpeter Kenny Dorham as coleader of the Bebop Boys, alongside trumpeter FATS NAVARRO in drummer KENNY CLARKE's group, and the following day as a member of Navarro and Gil Fuller's Modernists, who recorded two-sided 78-rpm versions of "Boppin' a Riff," "Fat Boy," "Everything's Cool," and "Webb City," afford-ing Stitt ample opportunity to show his talent as an improvising alto saxophonist.

Owing to troubles stemming from an addic-tion to narcotics, Stitt lost his New York City police cabaret card sometime in the mid- to late 1940s and was unable to take nightclub work in the city until the card was reauthorized in around 1950. Late in 1946 or early in 1947 he went to Chicago, where he played with the trumpeter MILES DAVIS and the tenor saxophonist GENE AMMONS in jam sessions and with the tenor saxophonist Johnny Griffin at ballroom dances. Stitt led bands at the Twin Terrace Café and at the Strode Hotel Lounge, employing the trumpeter Freddy Webster for the engagement at the Strode Hotel Lounge. In the summer Stitt moved to Detroit, and later that year he played in jam sessions with Gillespie, Davis, and Parker at the El Sino Club. Stitt returned to New York at the beginning of 1948.

Having taken up tenor saxophone as a means of getting away from the overwhelming influence of Parker's alto playing, Stitt made his first record-ings on tenor with the trombonist J. J. JOHNSON's Boppers on 17 October 1949. There followed on 11 December an outstanding session under his own name with the pianist BUD POWELL, the bassist Curley Russell, and the drummer MAX ROACH as his sidemen; they recorded versions of "All God's Chillun Got Rhythm," "Sonny Side," "Bud's Blues," and "Sunset" (actually the ballad "These Foolish Things"). This quartet expanded to include Davis, the trombonist Benny Green, and the baritone sax-ophonist Serge Chaloff for a Stars of Jazz concert at Carnegie Hall on 24 December.

That same fall in 1949 Ammons and Stitt formed a quintet that worked mainly at Birdland in New York from 1950 to 1951. Their finest recordings, made under Ammons's leadership in 1950, present the tenor saxophonists in improvisational battles in two takes of "You Can Depend on Me" and in three takes of "Blues Up and Down." Stitt also briefly tested the idea of playing baritone saxophone, fea-tured on Ammons's 1950 recordings of "Chabootie" and "Seven Eleven," and he continued to play the alto instrument, notably in his own quartet record-ing of "Imagination."

Stitt worked with Ammons intermittently to 1955. He rejoined Gillespie for three months early in 1958, and he toured Britain with Jazz at the Philharmonic in 1958 and 1959. By this time, perhaps years ear-lier, a first marriage had failed; details are unknown. In 1960 Stitt married Pamela W. Gilmore; they had two children. Stitt was the second in a succession of unsatisfactory replacements for the saxophonist JOHN COLTRANE in Davis's quintet, which he joined in September 1960 for a European tour. Stitt left Davis by early 1961. Ammons and Stitt performed in Chicago from late 1961 into February 1962. Stitt toured Japan in a sextet with Johnson and the trum-peter Clark Terry in 1964, played in Europe the same year, and played in Scandinavia in 1966 and 1967. As a member of the Giants of Jazz, Stitt toured with Gillespie, the trombonist Kai Winding, pia-nist THELONIOUS MONK, bassist Al McKibbon, and drummer ART BLAKEY in 1971 to 1972. In 1974 Stitt performed in *The Musical Life of Charlie Parker* at the Newport Jazz Festival–New York.

Throughout these years and continuing through the last decade of his life, Stitt worked mainly on his own as a leader and as a soloist, often employing whatever local accompanists were available rather than trying to maintain a group, and sometimes simply showing up at other people's jobs. In the company of other saxophonists he was almost fearsome. Extremely competitive, he delighted in devastating the competition as much as he delighted in making music. The alto saxophonist Art Pepper described Stitt sitting in at the Blackhawk in San Francisco while working with Jazz at the Philharmonic and challenging Pepper to a lightning-fast head-to-head duel on "Cherokee": "It's a communion. It's a battle. It's an ego trip. It's a testing ground." In addition to Ammons and Pepper, Stitt's worthy opponents included the tenor saxophonists EDDIE "LOCKJAW" DAVIS, Sonny Rollins, Paul Gonsalves, Zoot Sims, Ricky Ford, and Red Holloway.

Stitt recorded prolifically under his own name. Few saxophonists have had their career so thoroughly documented, and large portions of his work for the Roost and Verve labels in the late 1950s to early 1960s are sometimes dismissed critically as representing a workmanlike, uncaring Stitt. But the merely average mid-career Stitt session seems powerfully substantial compared to much of the saxophone playing associated with a revival of bop from the mid-1970s onward. Among many highlights is the album *Sonny Side Up*, co-led with Gillespie and Rollins for Verve (1957); this album includes "The Eternal Triangle" (another of the countless retitlings of "I Got Rhythm"), a tenor battle with Rollins in which Stitt and Rollins are even more closely matched in timbre and melody than in the earlier Stitt and Ammons duels. Other highlights include *Personal Appearance* (1957), *Boss Tenors*, co-led with Ammons (1961), *Sonny Stitt Plays Bird* (1963), and *Salt and Pepper*, co-led with Gonsalves (1963). Stitt's work during these years is also preserved in the documentary *Jazz on a Summer's Day* (1960) filmed at the 1958 Newport Jazz Festival. On the LP *What's New!!! Sonny Stitt Plays the Varitone* (1966), Stitt explored a then-new device for the electronic modification of saxophone pitch and timbre, but unlike his contemporary EDDIE HARRIS, Stitt soon lost interest in this area of saxophone sound. Generally speaking, his playing on his last fifty or sixty albums is perhaps a notch below his earlier productions, but there are many inspired exceptions, including *Tune-Up!*, *Constellation*, and *12!* (all from 1972), *In Walked Sonny* (1975), and *Good Life* (1980).

By the 1970s international travel had become a part of Stitt's working routine. He visited Europe many times, including an appearance at the 1974 Umbria Jazz Festival in Italy, captured in the film *Jazz in Piazza*, and a trip to England for duels with Holloway in December 1980. Stitt also performed and recorded in Japan, and he played in Israel and Brazil. Stitt replaced Pepper, who had just died, at the Kool Jazz Festival in New York in July 1982, shortly before his own death of lung cancer in Washington, D.C.

Michael James has noted that Stitt's alto saxophone recordings of 1946 raise a fundamental question about jazz criticism, in which individuality and original creativity are typically valued above all other considerations. Certainly Stitt was Parker's closest imitator, but he was also the most talented and well-rounded of the early alto saxophonists influenced by Parker. Stitt understood both the erudite side of Parker's playing and his deep connection to the blues, and the efforts in the mid- to late 1940s of such contemporaries as John Jackson, SONNY CRISS, and ERNIE HENRY seem halting by comparison with Stitt's. At such moments as the burst of notes in his solo during the opening theme of "Everything's Cool," Stitt's approach to improvisation is every bit as complex and swinging as Parker's, and to the question of imitation one is tempted to respond, "Who cares?" Without modifying his interest in improvising harmonically rich melodies with tremendous technical facility, Stitt in any event moved away from Parker upon taking up tenor saxophone. Apart from the obvious but crucial difference in instrumental timbre, one hears in Stitt's tenor improvisations—and also in his subsequent work on alto—a greater tendency to spin out long lines, evidently with the aim of maintaining a hard-driving rhythmic flow.

FURTHER READING

Enstice, Wayne, and Paul Rubin. *Jazz Spoken Here: Conversations with Twenty-two Musicians* (1992).

McRae, Barry. *The Jazz Cataclysm* (1967; rpt. 1985).

Salemann, Dieter, et al. *Sonny Stitt: Solography, Discography, Band Routes, Engagements—in Chronological Order* (1986).

Obituaries: *Los Angeles Times*, 23 July 1982; *New York Times*, 24 July 1982; *Village Vanguard*, 10 Aug. 1982.

This entry is taken from the *American National Biography* and is published here with the permission of the American Council of Learned Societies.

BARRY KERNFELD

Stockton, Betsey (c. 1798–24 Oct. 1865), educator and missionary, was born in slavery of unrecorded parentage. As a child Betsey was given by her owner, Robert Stockton, as a wedding gift to his daughter when she married the Reverend Ashbel Green, the president of the College of New Jersey (now Princeton University). Most of Betsey Stockton's early life was passed as a slave domestic in the Green home at Princeton, except for four years that she spent with Green's nephew Nathaniel Todd when she was an adolescent. At Todd's she underwent a period of training intended to instill more piety in her demeanor, which had not been developed in the affectionate, indulgent Green household. Stockton returned to the Green home in 1816 and was baptized in the Presbyterian church at Princeton in 1817 or 1818, having given evidence through speech and deportment of her conversion to Christian ways. At the time of her baptism Stockton was formally emancipated from slavery, since the Greens were abolitionists who believed that Christian baptism prepared her for freedom. Stockton became very well educated through their tutoring and the use of their enormous private library. So competent did Stockton become that the Greens finally placed her in charge of their entire household, and she remained as a paid domestic and family member.

Stockton often spoke to Green about her wish to journey abroad, possibly to Africa, on a Christian mission. Green introduced her to Charles S. Stewart, a young missionary, newly ordained in 1821, who was about to be sent by the American Board of Commissioners for Foreign Missions (ABCFM) to Hawaii. The ABCFM made special concessions to allow Stockton to join the mission because of her piety and interest in traveling and missionary work. Michael Osborn of the theological seminary at Princeton wrote a recommendation for Stockton, stating that she had a full and complete knowledge of all the Scriptures, the Jewish antiquities, the geography of the holy lands, and the larger catechism in addition to a keen understanding of English composition, literature, and mathematics. In short, she was well qualified for missionary endeavors. Through a special agreement between Green, the Stewarts, and the ABCFM, she joined the mission both as a domestic in the Stewart household and as a missionary. The agreement stated that although she was to assist Harriet Stewart domestically, Stockton was not to be called upon for menial work "more than any other member of the mission, or this might manifestly render her life servile, and prevent her being employed as a teacher of a school, for which it is hoped that she will be found qualified."

Stockton arrived in Hawaii in April 1823. She was part of the second company of Congregational missionaries sent to the islands to convert Hawaiians to Christianity. Upon their arrival in Honolulu, the company was greeted by an African from Schenectady, ANTHONY ALLEN, who was living in Hawaii. Allen presented the new arrivals, possibly because of the presence of Stockton, with gifts of food, including a whole goat for their trip to Lahaina, Maui, where they were stationed.

Stockton distinguished herself in Lahaina by offering education to the common people instead of erecting schools only for the *alii* (chiefs, or nobility). In the past, the Hawaiian chiefs had not allowed the missionaries to teach the commoners. By August 1824, however, the chiefs had determined that the missionaries could teach the lower levels of Hawaiian society as well. Charles Stewart's journal reveals the chiefs' new attitude:

> Indeed, till within a few weeks, they (*alii*) have themselves claimed the exclusive benefit of our instructions. But now they expressly declared their intentions to have all their subjects enlightened by the *palapala* (letters or learning), and have accordingly made applications for books to distribute among them. In consequence of this spirit, we have today been permitted to establish a large and regular school among their domestics and dependents.

Stockton's school was formed upon special request from commoners in Lahaina, as Stewart's journal entry of 20 August 1824 revealed:

> Now the chiefs have expressed their determination to have instruction in reading and writing extended to the whole population and have only been waiting for books, and an increase in the number of suitably qualified native teachers, to put the resolution, as far as practical, into effect. A knowledge of this having reached some of the *makuainana*, or farmers of *Lahaina* … including the tenants of our own plantation, application was made by them to us for books and slates, and an instructor; and the first school, consisting of about thirty individuals, ever formed among that class of people, has, within a few days, been established in our enclosure, under the superintendence of B—[Betsey], who is quite familiar with the native tongue.

The missionaries, including Stockton, believed that education among the common people would prove, as it had among the chiefs, "the most effectual means," as Stewart wrote, "of withdrawing them from their idle and vicious habits and of bringing them under the influence of our own teachings in morality and religion." Stewart praised Stockton's efforts: "B—[Betsey] is engaged in a fine school kept by her every afternoon in the chapel adjoining our yard," and she took part in all the social activities of the mission settlement.

In 1825 over 78,000 spelling books had issued from the mission presses, and by 1826, 8,000 Hawaiians had received instruction on Maui. Stockton's efforts to educate the commoners had borne fruit, and the missionary efforts combated drunkenness, adultery, infanticide, gambling, theft, deceit, treachery, death, and what Stewart called "every amusement of dissipation." The missionary and educational efforts that Stockton extended to the masses also had a democratizing effect on the Hawaiians, as, while the chiefly class taxed off most of the food the commoners produced, they could not take away promised salvation. As Stewart remarked of the commoners, "Their only birthright is slavery. … Surely to such, the message of salvation must prove indeed 'glad tidings of great joy.'"

> If, after the shortest and most perfect tuition, many are capable of composing neat and intelligent letters to each other, now, almost daily passing from island to island, and from district to district; so far from judging them not susceptible of attainments in the common branches of education, we need not fear to encourage a belief, that some may yet rejoice in the more abstruse researches of philosophy and science. They can be civilized, they can be made to partake, with missions of their fellow-beings, in all the advantages of letters and the arts. Nor is there more doubt, that they can be converted to Christianity.

The Stewarts decided to return to Cooperstown, New York, after two and a half years because of Harriet Stewart's poor health. Stockton accompanied them, leaving native Hawaiian teachers she had trained to take her place. She ran the Stewart household and assisted Harriet Stewart with her children until Harriet Stewart's death in 1830. Stockton continued to care for the Stewart children, perhaps until Charles Stewart remarried in 1835. Venturing forth on her own, she taught at an infant school in Philadelphia, journeyed to Canada where she established a school for Indians along the same lines as the school she had started in Hawaii, and then returned to Princeton to set up a school, which later became the Witherspoon Street Colored School, the culmination of her life's work. She labored there, supported by northern blacks and whites, and was committed to abolition in the area, until her death.

She was a strong role model for the less fortunate at every institution she established and administered. At her death, the *Freedom's Journal* of Cooperstown observed, "The superintendent and visitors of the public schools unhesitantly state that, in their inspections, they found no school better trained, better instructed, or with evidence of greater success than hers." Stockton was buried with the Stewart family at Lakewood, and her tombstone attests to that family's kinship with her: "Of African blood and born in slavery she became fitted by education and divine grace, for a life of great usefulness, for many years was a valued missionary at the Sandwich Islands in the family of Rev. C. S. Stewart, and afterwards till her death, a popular and able Principal of Public schools in Philadelphia & Princeton honored and beloved by a large circle of Christian Friends." Betsey Stockton had overcome bondage to distinguish herself as an educator of the disadvantaged and underprivileged.

FURTHER READING

The Hawaiian Mission Children's Society (HMCS) in Honolulu, Hawaii, contains the journal of Charles S. Stewart that describes Stockton's role in Lahaina, Maui. The HMCS collection also includes letters from contemporaries and diaries with references to her contributions.

French, Thomas. *The Missionary Whaleship* (1961).

This entry is taken from the *American National Biography* and is published here with the permission of the American Council of Learned Societies.

BARBARA BENNETT PETERSON

Stokes, Carl (21 June 1927–4 Apr. 1996), mayor, was born Carl Burton Stokes in Cleveland, Ohio, the son of Charles Stokes, a laundry worker, and Louise Stone Stokes, a domestic. Stokes's father died when he was a toddler, and he grew up in poverty as his mother struggled to provide for him and his older brother LOUIS STOKES. He attended local public schools before dropping out of East Technical High School in 1944. After a year spent as a street hustler, Stokes joined the U.S. Army, serving in post-World War II occupied Germany and rising to the rank of corporal. Following his 1946 discharge, he returned to Cleveland and finished his high school education in 1947. He was briefly enrolled at West Virginia State College (now University) before he went back home to attend Western Reserve University (now Case Western Reserve).

Still unsure of his future, Stokes dropped out of college and became an agent with the Ohio State Department of Liquor Control. After three years of battling corrupt saloon keepers, he decided on a career in law and entered the University of Minnesota. He graduated with a B.S. in law in 1954, but he realized that he needed additional training and returned yet again to Cleveland, where he attended Cleveland-Marshall Law School while working as a probation officer for the municipal court. Stokes received his LLB degree in 1956, the year he ended his childless marriage to Edith Shirley Smith, whom he had married in December 1951.

After gaining admittance to the bar in 1957, Stokes practiced law with his brother in the firm Stokes & Stokes. His attention, however, soon focused on a career in politics, and he spent countless hours doing volunteer work with such groups as the NAACP and the local Community Council. In 1958 he was appointed assistant city prosecutor by Mayor Anthony Celebrezze and that same year married Shirley Edwards, with whom he had three children.

After two failed attempts in 1958 and 1960, Stokes became the first African American Democrat to hold a seat in the Ohio State House of Representatives in 1962. Reelected twice, he served during his six years in office on the Public Welfare, Judiciary, and Industry and Labor committees and gained a reputation as a moderate who supported civil rights legislation while at the same time voting to empower the governor to employ National Guard troops in antiriot activities. In 1965, after considering a run for Congress, Stokes entered the mayoral race in Cleveland as an independent and lost a narrow election to incumbent Ralph Locher. By 1967, Cleveland (which had suffered through years of decline, along with many other industrialized northern cities) was in political turmoil. A race riot had erupted in the Hough area of the city in July 1966, and under Locher Cleveland's urban renewal program had become so hopelessly befuddled that the Department of Housing and Urban Development (HUD) suspended the city's allotment of federal funds. Having defeated Locher in the Democratic primary, Stokes went on to win a narrow victory over Seth Taft, the grandson of President William Howard Taft, and in the process became the first African American mayor of a major American city.

Stokes's election attracted national attention, and for a while Cleveland experienced a euphoric sense of uplift. Under his leadership, the city regained control of HUD funds (thanks in part to Stokes's friendly

relationship with Vice President Hubert Humphrey), and Stokes also took justifiable pride in creating increased opportunities for the poor to obtain decent, affordable housing. African Americans and other minority groups that had long been excluded from city jobs and contracts also found increasing opportunities during his administration. Almost alone among major cities, Cleveland remained riot-free in the aftermath of the assassination of Dr. MARTIN LUTHER KING JR. in April 1968. Shortly thereafter, Stokes helped engineer the creation of "Cleveland: NOW!" The program was meant to induce the business community and the general public to raise money to combat a variety of societal ills.

Despite his promising beginning, Stokes could not maintain the city's forward momentum in the face of nearly insurmountable urban problems and social upheaval. An ugly confrontation broke out in the Glenville section of the city in July 1968, leaving six citizens and three police officers dead. The riot ended Stokes's honeymoon with much of Cleveland's white community, many of whom apparently had felt that the election of an African American mayor might prevent such disturbances. Worse still was the revelation that a local African American militant leader, Fred Ahmad Evans, had used "Cleveland: NOW!" funds to purchase guns used during the disturbance. Although Evans was later sent to prison for his crimes, the damage had been done. Stokes had long sought to overhaul what he viewed as a corrupt, inefficient, and racist police department, but his exclusion of white officers from the Glenville riot scene and a series of disastrous appointments within the department left the city deeply discouraged.

Although Stokes was narrowly reelected in 1969, it was clear by the end of his second term that his effectiveness in office had dissipated. He moved to New York City and achieved another milestone by becoming the first African American television news anchor on a major network in the city. After his second marriage ended in divorce, he married Raija Salmoniv, a former Miss Finland, in 1977; the couple had one daughter.

Stokes returned to Cleveland in the early 1980s and served as a municipal judge there from 1983 to 1994. In 1995 he was appointed ambassador to the nation of Seychelles by President Bill Clinton, but he had to take a leave of absence after he was diagnosed with cancer of the esophagus. He died in Cleveland.

Colorful and charismatic, Carl Stokes could not during his relatively short tenure as mayor reverse the socioeconomic decline that had reduced his native city's identity from that of a thriving commercial and cultural center ("the Best Location in the Nation") to a byword for urban blight ("the Mistake by the Lake"). But as the first black mayor of a large American city, he succeeded in encouraging other African Americans to be competitive in electoral politics throughout the country.

FURTHER READING

Stokes's papers are held at the Western Reserve Historical Society in Cleveland.

Stokes, Carl. *Promises of Power: A Political Autobiography* (1973).

Porter, Philip W. *Cleveland: Confused City on a Seesaw* (1976).

Weinberg, Kenneth G. *Black Victory: Carl Stokes and the Winning of Cleveland* (1968).

Obituary: *New York Times*, 4 April 1996.

This entry is taken from the *American National Biography* and is published here with the permission of the American Council of Learned Societies.

EDWARD L. LACH JR.

Louis Stokes rose from poverty to become the first African American from Ohio to be elected to Congress. (AP Images.)

Stokes, Louis (Lou) (23 Feb. 1925–), cofounder of the Congressional Black Caucus, was born in Cleveland, Ohio, the eldest son of Louise Stone and Charles Stokes, two Georgia natives who came to the midwest during the Great Migration of the 1920s. His father, a laundry worker, became a member of the Future Outlook League, a group that helped increase job opportunities and improve working conditions for black workers in Cleveland. When his father died in 1929, Lou and his younger brother Carl were raised by their industrious mother in the Outhwaite Homes, Cleveland's first federally funded housing project. After graduating from Central High School in 1943, Stokes served in the U.S. Army from 1943 to 1946. He left the then segregated military and returned to Cleveland, Ohio, where he used funds from the G.I. Bill to complete a degree from what was then known as Western Reserve University in 1948. In 1953 Stokes graduated with a J.D. degree from the Cleveland-Marshall College of Law, one of the few law schools to admit African Americans. His brother Carl followed, graduating from the same law school in 1957.

During Stokes's fourteen-year law career he helped found two law practices, including Minor, Stokes and Stokes, along with his brother Carl and his mentor, Norman S. Minor, one of Ohio's outstanding criminal attorneys. While he honed his skills as a trial lawyer, representing many working-class clients from Cleveland's streets, he also became a renowned Constitutional attorney. In 1968 Stokes brought *Terry v. Ohio* before the United States Supreme Court, defending a suspect against a police search. Although Stokes lost the case, his defense helped to establish the notion that police racial profiling subverted the Constitutional rights of minority defendants.

Cleveland in the 1960s had a highly charged racial environment; and in the summer of 1966 the black community of Hough experienced a series of racially motivated outbreaks. Stokes became the head of the Legal Redress Committee of the Cleveland Chapter of the NAACP and he represented community residents and organizations in their fight against racism and police brutality.

By 1968 Stokes was widely recognized as the most prominent civil rights attorney in Ohio, and that year he brought *Lucas v. Rhodes* before the U.S. Supreme Court, a case that would forever change his life. The case attacked gerrymandering, the deliberate diluting of black voting districts in Cleveland by drawing boundaries to increase the likelihood that white candidates would prevail. Stokes won 74 percent of the vote in the new majority black district. The year prior to Lou Stokes's election to Congress, his brother CARL STOKES won election as mayor of Cleveland, making him the first African American to win a mayoral election in a major American city. The two founded the Black Elected Democrats of Cleveland to extend black political power throughout the city.

Stokes was sworn in as a member of Congress on 1 January 1969 with newly elected members William Clay (Missouri's first black congressman), and SHIRLEY CHISHOLM from New York, who was the nation's first black congresswoman (and later the first African American candidate for president of the United States).

Stokes would become the first African American to serve on the Appropriations Committee, which he later chaired. He was the first African American to chair the House Committee on Official Conduct (the House Ethics Committee).

Stokes was appointed in 1969 to the House Un-American Activities Committee, where he fought against the subversion of constitutional rights. As the first black member on the Committee on Standards of Official Conduct, he became chairman of the committee and presided over the Abscam bribery investigations that convicted one senator and five members of the House of Representatives. Stokes also led the investigation into the financial disclosures of Geraldine Ferraro, Democratic candidate for the U.S. vice presidency in 1984.

Stokes led a number of high profile congressional investigations, including the House Select Committee on Assassinations' investigations of President John F. Kennedy and DR. MARTIN LUTHER KING, JR. Stokes traveled to Cuba and questioned President Fidel Castro for six hours regarding the assassination of President Kennedy. The Cuban president denied any involvement in the murder. Stokes also cross-examined James Earl Ray, who had been jailed for the murder of Dr. Martin Luther King Jr.

In addition to investigating the circumstances surrounding the U.S. invasion of Grenada, Stokes also led the investigations of what became the Iran Contra hearings. Officials in the Reagan Administration destroyed information related to the sale of arms to Iran to finance a war in Nicaragua, directly subverting the directives of Congress. During the course of the hearings Stokes battled with Colonel Oliver North, who was later indicted, tried, and convicted of illegal actions. Stokes also fought attempts by Reagan Administration officials to weaken the Voting Rights Act.

One of his greatest legislative accomplishments was the 1989 passage of the Health Promotion and Disease Prevention for Minorities Act. This bill established a federal Office of Minority Health and authorized the Secretary of Health and Human Services to develop initiatives in minority health to prevent and control diseases and chronic health conditions. Stokes chaired an Appropriations Subcommittee that had jurisdiction over $90 billion of the federal budget.

Mr. Stokes left Congress at a time when partisan rhetoric and actions were increasing. His last recorded vote was against the impeachment of President Bill Clinton. Stokes was the first African American male congressman from Ohio and the first African American representative to complete thirty years of service, serving from 1969 to 1999. Stokes was also the first African American and only one of a select few congressmen to receive the Distinguished Service Award upon retirement.

FURTHER READING

Fenno, Richard. *Going Home: Black Representatives and Their Constituents* (2003).

FREDERICK H. BLAKE

Stokes, Louise (1913–25 Mar. 1978), Olympian in track and field and professional bowler, was born in Malden, Massachusetts, the eldest of six children of William Stokes, a gardener, and Mary Wesley, a domestic worker. Stokes began her running career during her time at Beebe Junior High in Malden when one of her basketball teammates suggested, because of her speed, that she join the local Onteora Track Club, sponsored by William H. Quaine, Malden's park commissioner. At the club, she soon began to excel in the sprints and jumping events.

At Malden High School, where she also played basketball, Louise repeatedly set records in track. She was awarded the James Michael Curley Cup as a junior for outstanding track performance of the year. She set the New England record in the 100 meters, and tied the world record in the standing broad jump, jumping eight feet, five and three-quarter inches. She was also competitive in the high jump. These outstanding performances brought her to the Olympic Trials a year later.

At the 1932 Olympic Trials in Evanston, Illinois, Louise's third-place finish in the 100 meters won her a spot on the women's 400-meter relay team for the Los Angeles Olympic Games, along with TIDYE PICKETT. Photos of the 1932 Olympic Track team include a determined-looking Stokes in the lineup along with Pickett, but coach George Vreeland selected only white women for the final relay team. Historian A. D. Emerson suggests that "the exclusion of Tidye Pickett and Louise Stokes from the 1932 Olympics remains a pivotal point in Olympic history where politics and racial tensions threatened any future possibilities for black female

Louise Stokes, in an undated photograph. (University of Massachusetts, Amherst.)

athletes to compete on a world stage in representing the United States in the Olympic games" (Emerson, 9). The exclusion of Stokes was a questionable call, as she had beaten Mary Carew, who was selected, in a majority of races, and they had tied for fourth in the Olympic Trials. Furthermore, when the Olympic team stopped in Denver on the way to Los Angeles, Stokes and Pickett were given a room separate from the rest of the team near a service area on an upper floor, and were served dinner in their rooms rather than at the banquet for the team. This blatant exclusion foreshadowed what happened later.

One aspect of the treatment of Stokes and Pickett was no doubt related to the dominant culture's uneasy relationship to women in sports, particularly sports that were considered "masculine" such as track and field. Stereotypical definitions of white femininity prevailed, so that women were considered too weak to participate in track,

or there was a stigma if they did. The women's 800-meter run at the 1928 Olympics, after which two untrained women lay down on the field in understandable exhaustion after their run, was the basis for a movement by the International Olympic Committee in 1929 to remove women's track and field from the 1932 Olympics. Participating in track and field was considered unseemly for middle-class white women, and the decision to exclude Stokes and Pickett from the final relay team was perhaps affected on some level by this, as officials may not have wanted to stigmatize the track team further by including women of color. Ironically, Babe Didrikson, who was the standout celebrity of the 1932 games, but who also suffered from a stigma because of her working-class roots and masculine self-presentation, missed her opportunity for solidarity and made it clear that she did not want black women on the team. There was enough tension surrounding the selection of the relay team that the NAACP sent a telegram to team captain Jean Shiley in Los Angeles, seeking to ensure fair treatment for Stokes and Pickett. It does seem clear that prevailing racist attitudes and practices combined with stereotypes about femininity to give Stokes and Pickett less than a fair chance. They spent the 1932 Olympics in the bleachers, watching their teammates win the gold medal in the 400-meter relay.

Stokes continued to compete after the 1932 Olympics, winning sprints at distances from 25 to 200 meters, as well as the high jump and broad jump. At the U.S. trials for the 1936 Olympics in Berlin, she placed fifth in the 100 meters but once again made the team as a member of the 400-meter relay. In what must have been devastating to Stokes, history repeated itself when at the Berlin games, Stokes found she had been replaced by a white runner. Despite the fact that she was not selected to compete in the finals, the town of Malden treated her as a hero with a welcome home parade upon her return.

Stokes planned to try out for the 1940 Olympic Games, but World War II precipitated the cancellation of the games. She retired from running, working as an elevator operator, and became a professional bowler. She founded the Colored Women's Bowling League in 1941 and was a preeminent bowler for the next thirty years. She married Wilfred Fraser in 1944 and had one son. The New England Amateur Athletic Union, for which she had contributed some of the pioneering performances by black women in track, honored her in 1974 by establishing Louise Fraser Day at Boston University. She continued to be an active leader in community youth sports in Malden and neighboring Medford until her death.

Louise Stokes Fraser was one of the first two African American women to earn a place on the U.S. Olympic team, clearing the way for the 1948 Olympians ALICE COACHMAN and Audrey "Mickey" Patterson Tyler to be the first black Olympic medalists. Her accomplishments mark the beginning of the long history of black female excellence in Olympic track and field.

FURTHER READING

Emerson, A. D. *Olympians against the Wind: The Black American Female Difference* (1999).

Pieroth, Doris H. *Their Day in the Sun: Women of the 1932 Olympics* (1996).

LESLIE HEYWOOD

Stokes, Maurice (17 June 1933–6 Apr. 1970), professional basketball player was born in Ranking, Pennsylvania, to Tero Stokes, a steel worker, and Myrtle Stokes (maiden name unknown). The Stokes family—Maurice, his twin sister, two brothers, and his parents—moved to the Homewood section of Pittsburgh when he was eight years old. Stokes played basketball at Westinghouse High School, where he led his team to back-to-back Pittsburgh City Championships in 1951 and 1952.

After receiving scholarship offers from ten colleges, Stokes surprised many by accepting a scholarship offer to play at tiny St. Francis College in Loretto, Pennsylvania. At six-feet seven-inches tall and 240 pounds, Stokes possessed uncharacteristic quickness for a man his size. Displaying dominance over the competition, he averaged twenty-two points and twenty-four rebounds for his career at St. Francis. He guided the school to the postseason on three occasions: to the National Collegiate Athletic Association (NCAA) Tournament in 1952–1953 and to the prestigious National Invitation Tournament (NIT) in 1953–1954 and 1954–1955. He led the Frankies on an improbable run in the 1955 NIT, which ended with him scoring forty-three points in an overtime loss to Dayton in the semifinals. The *New York Times* called Stokes's performance "one of the most dazzling individual exhibitions ever seen" in Madison Square Garden (*New York Times*, 18 Mar. 1955). He was named Most Valuable Player of the tournament, becoming the first person in college basketball history to be named MVP from a fourth-place team.

Stokes's professional career began in 1955 when the Rochester (New York) Royals made him the second overall pick in the National Basketball Association draft. When Stokes arrived in the NBA, the prevalent stereotype was that African American players were not very skilled offensively. Indeed DON BARKSDALE was the highest-scoring African American player to that date, and his top season scoring average was only 13.8 points. Stokes immediately shattered this image, scoring thirty-two points and grabbing twenty rebounds in his NBA debut. Maintaining this high level of play throughout his initial season, Stokes averaged 16.8 points and a league-leading 16.3 rebounds and was named NBA Rookie of the Year. In just his second season the big, strong power forward set an NBA record for rebounds in a season when he grabbed 1,256 boards during his sophomore campaign. Stokes displayed great versatility on the court as he handed out over 4.6 assists a game in his second season, ranking him third in the league in this category. Stokes's peers in the NBA had incredible respect for his game. Of his tremendous impact on the game, future Hall of Famer and fellow Pittsburgh native Jack Twyman would later remark, "He was MAGIC (JOHNSON) before there was Magic. He could play pivot, forward, or bring the ball down as a guard. He was all over the court" (Thomas, 179). The Royals' franchise moved from Rochester to Cincinnati after the 1956–1957 season. Stokes played remarkably well again during the 1957–1958 season and was selected to play in the NBA All-Star Tournament for the third consecutive time.

Stokes's promising career ended tragically on 12 March 1958 as the Cincinnati Royals were playing the Lakers in Minneapolis in the season finale. He went up for a rebound and was accidentally knocked to the ground, smacking his head against the hardwood floor. He was knocked unconscious for several minutes; however, after a brief rest he returned to finish the game. Three days later Stokes appeared lethargic in scoring twelve points and grabbing fifteen rebounds in a playoff loss at Detroit. He began to feel ill on the team's flight back to Cincinnati and was immediately rushed to the hospital where he fell into a coma and remained unconscious for several weeks. Stokes was diagnosed with post-traumatic encephalopathy, as the fall caused swelling in his brain. He emerged from the coma with full mental capacity; however he had lost all movement in his arms and legs. Although limited by his loss of mobility Stokes eventually learned how to type and paint. He even regained limited speech, although his speech remained painfully slow and difficult to understand. He underwent a grueling daily regimen of physical therapy and eventually took several

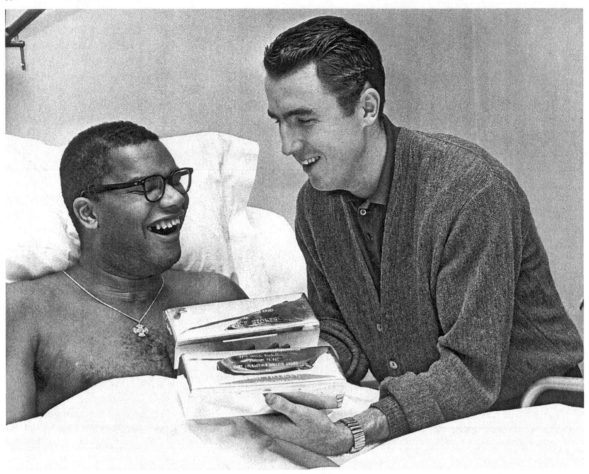

Maurice Stokes, left, in his hospital room with Jack Twyman and the trophies they received from the Philadelphia Sports Writers Association designating them as the "Most Courageous Athletes" on 9 Feb. 1962. (AP Images.)

small steps with the aid of hospital staff. When Stokes's family had difficulty paying for his medical bills, Royals teammate Jack Twyman stepped in to assist. Twyman became Stokes's legal guardian and handled his medical and legal affairs. The NBA refused to pay Stokes's medical bills, and Twyman successfully sued for workmen's compensation from the state of Ohio. Twyman organized fundraisers to help defray the costs, including a summer exhibition all-star basketball game at a resort in the Catskill Mountains. WILT CHAMBERLAIN and BILL RUSSELL were among the many NBA stars that played in the annual game. Although he rarely left the Good Samaritan Hospital in Cincinnati, Stokes was a frequent visitor to these games. Throughout his ordeal Stokes remained an inspiration to many younger players, especially to those of his alma mater. Each year the members of the St. Francis College basketball team visited Stokes in the hospital. Prior to

his death he was overwhelmed with the news that St. Francis was naming its planned field house in his honor. Demonstrating the love he had for St. Francis, Stokes requested in his will to be buried on campus. In 1970 Stokes died at the age of thirty-six from a massive heart attack.

Following Stokes's death Twyman worked hard to keep his friend's spirit alive. The Maurice Stokes Memorial Basketball Game continued until 1999, with the funds going to needy players from the NBA's early years. Twyman nominated Stokes annually for the National Basketball Hall of Fame to no avail. Stokes was finally voted into the Hall by the veterans' committee and was enshrined on 10 September 2004. He was presented for induction by NBA greats OSCAR ROBERTSON and Bob Petit, and the award was accepted on Stokes's behalf by Jack Twyman. Twyman presented St. Francis with Stokes's Hall of Fame jacket, trophy, and ring, which are permanently displayed in the Maurice Stokes Athletics Center on the campus of St. Francis.

FURTHER READING

Thomas, Ron. *They Cleared the Lane: The NBA's Black Pioneers* (2002).

Robinson, Louis, "Cincinnati's Stricken Giant: Maurice Stokes," *Ebony* 14 (April 1959), 38–42.

Tax, J. "A Brave Man and a Good Friend: Maurice Stokes," *Sports Illustrated* 12 (1 Feb. 1960), 10–15.

Obituary: *New York Times*, 7 Apr. 1970.

THOMAS A. MOGAN

Stone, Chuck (21 July 1924–), newspaper editor, columnist, and civil rights activist, was born Charles Sumner Stone Jr. in a segregated hospital in St. Louis, Missouri, to Charles Sumner Stone Sr., a business manager at Poro College in St. Louis, and Madalene (Chafin) Stone, a payroll director. The Stones moved to New England when Chuck was three, and he grew up with his three sisters, Irene, Madalene, and Anne, in Hartford, Connecticut. Stone trained to be a navigator and bombardier in World War II as part of the famous Tuskegee airmen squadron. After leaving the military he continued his education at Wesleyan University, where he was the only black student on campus. Stone graduated in 1948 with a B.A. in political science and economics, and he received an M.A. in sociology from the University of Chicago in 1951. He spent eighteen months studying law at the University of Connecticut. In 1956 he joined CARE and spent two years distributing food packages in the Gaza Strip and India.

In 1958 Stone married Georgia Louise Davis of Hampton, Virginia, who was the first black student to attend and graduate from Fryeburg Academy in Fryeburg, Maine. After receiving a B.A. in sociology from Colby College in Waterville, Maine, she spent her career editing, writing, and directing publications at the University of Delaware and the North Carolina Department of Labor. The Stones were married for forty-five years and had three children: two daughters, Krishna and Allegra, and a son, Chuck III.

During the early years of the civil rights movement Stone was the editor of three influential black newspapers: the *New York Age* from 1958 to 1960, the *Afro-American* in Washington, D.C., from 1960 to 1963, and the *Chicago Daily Defender* from 1963 to 1964. One of only two black correspondents covering the John F. Kennedy White House, Stone was named by *Newsweek* "the angry man of the Negro press" ("A Victim of Negro Progress," *Newsweek*, 26 Aug. 1963). In 1969 the *Washington Star* called Stone a "tough-minded militant" who "probably poured forth more angry rhetoric, ruffled more political moderates and simultaneously pacified and frightened more whites than most of Washington's other black leaders." In Chicago, Stone was eventually fired as editor-in-chief of the *Daily Defender* for refusing to soften his political stance and for publishing critical opinions about Mayor Richard Daley.

From 1964 to 1967 Stone served as chief administrative assistant to the U.S. representative ADAM CLAYTON POWELL JR. during the years that the Harlem congressman was chairing the House Education and Labor Committee. A principal player in the black power movement, Stone organized the national Black Power Conferences held in Washington, D.C., (1966), in Newark, New Jersey, (1967), and in Philadelphia, Pennsylvania (1968). Stone was friends with both MARTIN LUTHER KING JR. and MALCOLM X. When King offered him the position of executive director of the Southern Christian Leadership Conference, Stone declined, saying, "Martin, I'm not nonviolent. If someone throws a rock at me, I'm going to throw it back" (author's interview with Stone). Stone was one of the people whom Malcolm X called after his break with the Nation of Islam and ELIJAH MUHAMMAD. The two met and decided to take some pictures for memories; Malcolm X was gunned down two weeks later. From 1969 to 1970 Stone was a commentator on the *Today Show*. Then in 1972 he became a political columnist at the *Philadelphia Daily News* and later its first black senior editor.

Because Stone had a reputation in Philadelphia as a crisis mediator, between 1987 and 1991 more than seventy-five black murder suspects, fearing abuse by the police, agreed to surrender to him. On five occasions Stone helped to negotiate the release of hostages. The most noted incident was the dangerous takeover at the Graterford federal penitentiary on 1–2 November 1981 when four murder convicts tried to escape. After the ringleader of the group, Jo-Jo Bowen, threatened to execute six hostages, Stone was called in to negotiate. Stone was later named honorary federal warden by the U.S. Bureau of Prisons and testified before a U.S. Judiciary subcommittee on "three strikes" legislation. Stone also reported from Belfast, Ireland, from South Africa, and from Zaire for the *Philadelphia Daily News* in 1981. Twice nominated for the Pulitzer Prize for columns that he wrote for the *Philadelphia Daily News*, Stone was a leading critic of the 1985 decision of the Philadelphia mayor W. WILSON GOODE to bomb

Chuck Stone in the newsroom of the *Daily News* in Philadelphia, on 15 Feb. 1984. (AP Images.)

the headquarters of Operation MOVE, an action that resulted in the death of eleven people. Stone attended the Eastern Baptist Theological Seminary in Philadelphia from 1989 to 1991. In 1991 he left the *Philadelphia Daily News* and became the Walter Spearman Professor in the School of Journalism and Mass Communication at the University of North Carolina (UNC) at Chapel Hill.

Widely recognized as one of the twentieth century's most influential African American journalists, Stone was the first president of the Philadelphia Association of Black Journalists and was founding president of the National Association of Black Journalists. He wrote more than four thousand newspaper columns, magazine stories, and scholarly essays. In 1973 Stone's column was syndicated, and eventually it appeared in more than one hundred newspapers. Stone published many books, including *Tell It like It Is* (1968), *Black Political Power in America* (1970), and the novel *King Strut* (1970), based on the life of Adam Clayton Powell Jr. His other books include *The White Foundation's Role in Black Oppression* (1971), *A New Day, the Same Old Challenge: A Renewed Hope for Journalism Education in the 21st Century* (1992),

and the children's book *Squizzy the Black Squirrel: A Fabulous Fable of Friendship* (2003).

In 2002 Stone was a co-recipient of UNC's top faculty honor, the Thomas Jefferson Award. His numerous other awards include the 1993 Free Spirit Award from the Freedom Forum, five honorary doctorates, and induction into the National Association of Black Journalists' Hall of Fame.

FURTHER READING

Stone's papers are at the Rare Book, Manuscript, and Special Collections Library, Duke University, Durham, North Carolina.

Reed, Jeff. "Stone Continues to Leave His Mark on Carolina and Beyond," *Carolina Communicator: A Publication of the School of Journalism and Mass Communication at UNC-Chapel Hill* (Oct. 2002).

Stancill, Jane. "Journalism Veteran Has Learned by Teaching," *Raleigh News & Observer*, 25 Mar. 2005.

KAREN JEAN HUNT

Stone, Fred (9 Sept. 1935–10 Dec. 1986), progressive jazz and classical trumpet and flugelhorn player, composer, conductor, and teacher, was born in Toronto, Ontario, the son of bandleader and saxophonist Archie Stone. His father conducted the Casino Theatre Orchestra in Toronto (1936–1960).

Stone began studies on the flugelhorn when he was twelve years old. Between 1950 and 1955, he studied the trumpet with Donald Reinhardt in Philadelphia. By age sixteen he studied with Benny Louis and performed in dance bands in Toronto. He also played jazz and classical works with Canadian Broadcasting Company orchestras. His composition studies were with the noted Canadian jazz arranger and composer Gordon Delamont (1955–1960) and the eminent Canadian atonal music composer John Weinzweig (1960–1962).

Stone received his B. Mus. from Metropolitan College in London, Canada. He felt at home not only performing and composing for jazz bands, but also with classical symphony orchestras. Synthesizing improvisation and classical music's formal structures, he heard his compositions as works that formed a bridge between classical music and jazz. The composer Gunther Schuller coined the term "third stream" for such music. During the 1950s and 1960s Stone was flugelhorn soloist with many symphony orchestras, in which he performed third-stream works (e.g., the premiere of Norman Symonds's *Democratic Concerto* and *The Nameless Hour* with the Toronto Symphony Orchestra) (Canadian Broadcasting Corporation, 1969). During the 1960s he also worked with several studio ensembles in Toronto, organized his own jazz big band, and performed with it. He played with the Buffalo, Cleveland, Detroit, Ottawa, and San Diego Symphony Orchestras (1965–1970); the Boss Brass (1968–1970); and the Lighthouse, a jazz-rock band (1969–1970). During the 1960s through the 1970s Stone experimented and explored the sounds of the synthesizer and amplified horn in his compositions and also performed with the jazz bands of Phil Nimmons and Rob McConnell. He composed, orchestrated, and arranged music for all types of ensembles, including big bands, symphony orchestras, and small ensembles.

DUKE ELLINGTON first came into contact with Stone during the mid-1960s, when he was co-featured soloist on flugelhorn with Ron Collier's Orchestra at a concert in Windsor, Ontario. Ellington was very impressed with his playing and, through the help of Collier, who was also Ellington's arranger, Stone became a member of Duke Ellington's orchestra. He often sat between such jazz greats as COOTIE WILLIAMS, CAT ANDERSON, and MERCER ELLINGTON. Stone also traveled with Duke Ellington's orchestra on its 1970–1972 North American and European tours, the first and only Canadian to do so. He was interested in not only playing but also studying Ellington's method and technique. He was interested in observing how Ellington handled the different personalities and how he allowed each personality to be a unique individual in his band. Ellington's method was later used by Stone in his ensemble, Freddie's Band.

By 1972, after touring with the Duke Ellington Band, Stone became tired of being on the road and away from home. He notes that Ellington's touring regimen was very exhausting. Regardless of the fact that Ellington wanted him to remain with the band, Stone knew he did not want to spend his life as a sideman; he wanted to pass on his own ideas to others. He therefore devoted much of his time to teaching, first at community colleges in the Toronto area and then privately. He became artist in residence at Centennial College and later taught composition, improvisational theory, and trumpet and flugelhorn at Humber College (1972–1975) and George Brown College, which was associated with Blue Mountain College (1976).

In 1984 Stone founded and directed his twelve-member improvisatory orchestra of his young students. Naming his ensemble Freddie's Band, he and his students played both classical music and jazz. He used ideas and methods he learned from Duke Ellington and the idea of the "orchestra-is-my-instrument." On 2 November 1984 Freddie's Band successfully debuted at Toronto's Music Gallery.

Stone remained a dominant force on Toronto's young musicians of the 1970s and 1980s, especially those performing in Freddie's Band. Each semester, he taught about twenty to thirty students who played a variety of instruments. His aim was not to have his students copy or imitate styles of the past, such as solos by CHARLIE PARKER, but to study the quintessential features of the music, focusing on the creative process. The students in Freddie's Band knew what they were going to perform and rehearsed the method they would be using. When they played solos, it was more the shared energy of the group performing instead of competition between the soloist and ensemble.

Ellington's orchestra also recorded Stone's work *Maiera* on the album *Duke Ellington & His Orchestra, 1965–1972* (MusicMasters, 1965). Stone recorded several works and albums by Duke Ellington: *Mendoza*; *Up in Duke's Workshop*; *Love Is Just around the Corner* (Pablo, 1969); *Aristocracy à la Jean Lafitte* from *New Orleans Suite* (Atlantic, 1971); *The Afro-Eurasian Eclipse* (Fantasy, 1975); *The Intimate Ellington* (Pablo,

1977); and *The Best of Duke Ellington* (Pablo, 1980). Stone also performed with HARRY BELAFONTE, Percy Faith, and Henry Mancini. For Moe Koffman he composed *Uranus* (Anthem Records, 1983); *Troika* (Radio Canada International, 1990), and a tribute to Igor Stravinsky. In summary, he composed works for symphony orchestras, small ensembles, flugelhorn, and jazz orchestra. These include *Leah*; *Maiera* (1965); *Reflections on a Theme* (1969); *Sunshine and Pretty Things* (1969); *For Igor* (1972); *Tribute to Igor Stravinsky* (1972); *Ideal for Orchestra* (1974); *Stone Poem* (1974); and *Young People's Guide to the Jazz Orchestra* (1976). On 6 June 1984, the Composers Co-Op Jazz Orchestra (an ensemble organized by saxophonist Chris Chahley Nonet and eight musicians) presented a performance of Fred Stone's *Znorl* (an improvisatory work created by chance) at Harbourfront Centre's Brigantine Room, Toronto. The Humber College Big Band recorded *Leah* in 1986. *Ideal for Orchestra* was recorded by Moe Koffman with Stone as soloist. His major writing is *Treatise on Improvisation*.

In April 1982 Stone suffered a heart attack, from which he appeared to have recovered. In 1985 he organized the Parasol Arts Centre in Toronto, a performing arts conservatory. He was scheduled to perform on 13 December 1986 at the Parasol Arts Centre but heart problems prevented him from performing. But on 19 December 1986 he suffered another massive heart attack in Toronto, which led to his death at age fifty-one. At the time of his death, he intended to record an album in February 1987 of solo piano music and edit his essays for publication. His wife, Diane Stone, donated many of his personal papers, including biographical records, notes, notebooks, composition, recordings, and writings, to the National Library of Canada Archives.

Stone's music and performances contained the element of chance and spontaneity. Only a skeletal outline of the work to be performed was made, on which the performers based their improvisation. Hence, few of his compositions were ever published. Melody played an important role in his works and solos were used to add texture to the ensemble. Stone left a strong influence on many younger Toronto musicians.

FURTHER READING

Lambert, Eddie, and Mark Miller. "Stone, Fred(die)," in *The New Grove Dictionary of Jazz*, 2nd ed. (2001).
Miller, Mark. "After Playing with the Duke, Teaching May Sound Tame, But It Keeps Fred Stone Happy." *The Globe and Mail*, 2 Nov. 1984.
Miller, Mark. "Freewheeling Stone Gather No Moss." *The Globe and Mail*, 1 May 1985.
"Stone, Fred, 1935–1986: Music Archives at the National Library of Canada." http://www.collectionscanada.ca/4/7/m15-497-e.html.
Obituary: *The Toronto Star*, 11 Dec. 1986, D1.

BARBARA BONOUS-SMIT

Stone, Jesse (17 June 1924–14 May 2001), attorney, educator, was born Jesse Nealand Stone Jr. in Gibsland, Louisiana, Bienville Parish, son of Jesse Nealand Stone Sr. and Ola King Stone. His father was an educator in African American schools during the period of segregation in Webster Parish, where the family moved after the birth of their son. As a boy in Louisiana, Stone had witnessed an African American man tied to a tree and whipped nearly to death by a group of white men. He attended Webster High School in Minden, Louisiana, and upon graduating enrolled at Southern University in Baton Rouge, Louisiana, a historically black university, where he earned his undergraduate degree. Subsequently, he enrolled at the Southern University School of Law, established in 1947, where in 1950 he was among six students in the first ever graduating class from the university's law school. Also, among notable graduates of the Southern University School of Law are Annette M. Eddie-Callagain, the first African American to establish a law practice in Japan and the former Louisiana governor, Mike Foster, who is white. Stone moved to Shreveport, Louisiana, after earning his juris doctorate and began to practice law, thus, becoming the first African American attorney in the city since 1932. He specialized in civil rights and criminal cases; yet, maintained a general practice. Consequently, in the 26th Judicial District of Bossier and Webster Parish he became the first African American attorney to appear before the bench. Stone had to conduct cases in front of all white juries, many of which he won, until he successfully sued for the inclusion of African Americans in the jury stand.

Stone was actively involved in the civil rights movement. He served as an attorney for the NAACP and also worked with the Congress on Racial Equality (CORE) and the Southern Christian Leadership Conference. In 1960 he posted bail on behalf of four African American students arrested for attempting to secure library cards in an all-white facility, Shreveport Memorial Library, and he helped to gain release for four African Americans who had been beaten, in Shreveport, after attempting to eat lunch at the counter reserved for whites only in a store called H. L. Green's. He strategized with members of the NAACP on ways to address the threats from members of Ku Klux Klan members and incessant bombings of homes in the African American community. In the late 1960s and early 1970s Stone represented families in the Caddo and Webster parishes in school desegregation lawsuits; in the case of *Blain A. Gilbert et al. vs. Webster Parish School Board*, which led to desegregation of schools, he was the lead attorney. Stone had also worked with the civil rights attorney A. P. Tureaud on a number of cases. In the mid 1960s, Stone assumed a state leadership role as associate director of the Louisiana Commission on Human Relations, Rights and Responsibilities under the administration of the Louisiana governor John J. McKeithan.

In 1971, Stone was elected dean of the Southern University School of Law, where he had been a student only twenty years earlier. In 1972 he assumed the responsibility of assistant superintendent of education for the State of Louisiana and the same year he was appointed associate justice of the Louisiana Supreme Court, a post he maintained for two years. In 1974, Stone was elected as the fourth president of the Southern University System and served for eleven years until 1985. In 1985, Stone departed from his presidency and assumed a professorship in the recently renamed Law Center at Southern University until his retirement in 1986. Five years later, in 1991, he resumed his active affiliation with Southern University as a member of the Southern University Board of Supervisors through 1995.

Stone was married to Willa Dean Anderson and together they have a daughter, Shonda Deann, born 10 March 1963, like her father, an attorney. In 2001, Stone succumbed to a long illness and on 14 May he died in Shreveport, Louisiana, at the age of seventy-seven. His funeral was held in Shreveport on 18 May 2001. In 1990, the Law Center at Southern University honored Stone as the first inductee into their newly established Hall of Fame. In 1998, an endowed professorship was established at Southern University in his name. The Southern University in Shreveport named The Jesse N. Stone Lecture Hall on their campus in his honor. The main Southern University campus in Scotlandville named a street in tribute to Stone. The Shreveport Branch of the NAACP has established the Dr. Jesse N. Stone Pioneer Award to recognize outstanding service in the field of law.

FURTHER READING

Fairclough, Adam. *Race and Democracy: The Civil Rights Struggle in Louisiana, 1915–1972* (2008).

Farmer, James, and Don E. Carleton. *Lay Bare Heart: An Autobiography of the Civil Movements* (1998).

Rogers, Kim Lacy. *Righteous Lives: Narratives of the New Orleans Civil Rights Movement* (1995).

Obituary: *Jet*, 4 June 2001.

SAFIYA DALILAH HOSKINS

Stone, Sly (15 Mar. 1944–), pioneer of funk, was born Sylvester Stewart in Denton, Texas, to Alpha Stewart, a homemaker, and K.C. Stewart, a janitor. After moving from Texas to Vallejo, California, the Stewart children (Loretta, Sly, Freddie, and Rose; the youngest, Vaetta, had not yet been born) performed gospel music in the Church of God and Christ as the Stewart Four. The group released a single in 1952 called "On the Battlefield for My Lord"/"Walking in Jesus' Name." Sly took up the guitar at age nine. He studied music theory at Vallejo Junior College and performed in groups such as the racially integrated doo-wop group the Viscaynes as well as Joey Piazza and the Continentals. He also recorded two singles with his brothers as the Stewart Brothers and some others under the name Danny Stewart. He first adopted his stage name Sly Stone as a disc jockey for the San Francisco R&B radio station KSOL in 1966 (Stone had studied radio broadcasting at the Chris Borden School of Modern Broadcasting.) The name Stone would later be adopted by Freddie, Rose, and Vaetta as well. In 1967 the Stewart brothers were each involved in their own bands: Sly and the Stoners and Freddie and the Stone Souls. At the suggestion of the saxophonist Jerri Martini, Sly merged the bands into Sly and the Family Stone. Because Freddie and Sly both played guitar, Sly kept Freddie on guitar and took up the electric organ. The band also included Martini, Cynthia Robinson on trumpet, Gregg Errico on drums, and Larry Graham (later of the band Graham Central Station) on bass. Background vocals were provided by Little Sister, a gospel group consisting of Vaetta (now "Vet") Stone, Mary McCreary, and Elva Mouton. Rose Stone joined the band as keyboardist and vocalist in 1966. This was a revolutionary lineup for a band, both in its interracial composition and its incorporation of female instrumentalists. Soon after, the single "I Ain't Got Nobody" was released on Loadstone Records and became a regional hit. In the following year, the band's debut album, *A Whole New Thing*, did less well commercially but was well received by critics.

Sly Stone, with his bride Kathy Silva during their wedding ceremony at a rock concert in New York's Madison Square Garden on 6 June 1974. (AP Images.)

This first period of the band's life was a time of joyful, youthful optimism and genre mixing. The concept of the self-contained band, such as the Beatles, was new in black American musical culture; often freelance studio musicians backed established singers. Motown studio bands, for instance, were highly skilled yet often anonymous. Even highly established instrumental-oriented bands, such as the COUNT BASIE Orchestra, saw personnel come and go. Sly and the Family Stone was different in that it presented a self-contained band making music that was influenced by British rock and pop and psychedelia, yet idiomatically close to black America.

The band's second single and album, *Dance to the Music* (1968), enjoyed greater success. "Dance to the Music" was written by Sly at the suggestion of the record executive Clive Davis, who suggested that the band try a more popular and mainstream sound for greater commercial viability. Its third album, *Life!*, also in 1968, again suffered from low sales. *Stand!* (1969), a return to the pop feel of *Dance to the Music*, led the band back to the charts. These albums had a wide cultural influence. During this time, the band was touring and performing extensively. At the famous Woodstock concert in August 1969, Sly and the Family Stone delivered a noteworthy and culturally significant performance. Earlier that summer, a riot had broken out during their performance at the Newport Jazz Festival.

The band's final single of this period was "Thank You (Falettinme Be Mice Elf Agin)"/"Everybody Is a Star," released in December 1969. While "Everybody Is a Star" was along the same positive lines as the band's other songs, the cynical lyrics of "Thank You" made it clear that the optimism of the late 1960s was being replaced by the darker shades of the 1970s. With connections to both the hippie and black power movements, Stone's music reflected the change in the national political tone, the increasing violence of the Vietnam War protests, and the growing separatism and disillusionment of the Black Panthers. These pressures translated into personal terms for Stone, who was caught between his record company's demands for more of the buoyant pop-funk of "Stand!" and the Black Panthers' exhortations to take a more aggressively militant stance. Stone's constant drug use and discovery of PCP, and an increasingly frequent habit of not showing up to gigs or else refusing to play, added to the pressure, as did proliferating personal tensions within the band.

As a result, There's a Riot Goin' On (1971) was dramatically darker than previous releases and clearly reflected the change in tone that had taken place both in the small scale of Sly's life and in the larger picture of American culture as a whole. The album, which reached number one on Billboard's pop and R&B charts, contained the number-one single and later standard of R&B radio, "Family Affair," and featured Stone's protégé BOBBY WOMACK (who later helped Stone get treatment for drug abuse) on guitar. When asked if There's a Riot Going On was meant to be a political album, Stone replied "Well, yeah, probably. But I didn't mean it to be" (Kamp, 177). It paved the way for a wave of similarly sonically and lyrically bleak R&B hits over the next few years from artists such as CURTIS MAYFIELD, MARVIN GAYE, and War. Ironically, though, its use of synthesizers and drum machines and its rhythmic grooves also influenced the development of disco, arguably the decade's most articulate musical expression of abandon and hedonism. Over the course of two more records, Fresh (1973) and Small Talk (1974), the band continued to disintegrate, breaking up in 1975. Stone continued to record as a solo artist, though continuing to use the Family Stone name, until his final album, Ain't But the Right Way in 1983.

In 1974 Stone married Kathleen Silva on stage at a concert at Madison Square Garden in New York on 5 June. By October of that year they were divorced. The couple had one child, Sylvester Jr. Sly also had a daughter, Sylvette Phunn Robinson, with the Family Stone trumpeter, Cynthia Robinson.

Stone remained involved with music, with little success, through the 1980s. In 1993 Sly and the Family Stone was inducted into the Rock and Roll Hall of Fame. After that, Stone retreated dramatically from the public eye and lived a rather reclusive life. At the 2006 Grammy Awards ceremony, Stone reunited with most of the original Family Stone band, performing "I Want to Take You Higher." In April 2007, Stone performed at the Flamingo Hotel in Las Vegas.

Stone's music influenced many pop music performers of the late twentieth century. In 1991 the rap group A Tribe Called Quest sampled the break of Stone's "Sing a Simple Song," which was the b-side to their number 1 1968 single "Everyday People," itself sampled by the rap group Arrested Development in 1992. "Everyday People" was also to become part of a large advertising campaign by the carmaker Toyota.

FURTHER READING

Lewis, Miles Marshall. Sly and the Family Stone's There's a Riot Goin' On (2006).

Kamp, David. "Sly Stone's Higher Power." Vanity Fair (Aug. 2007).

Selvin, Joel. Sly and the Family Stone: An Oral History (1998).

PAUL DEVLIN

Stone, Toni (21 Jan. 1921–2 Nov. 1996), professional baseball player, was born Marcenia Lyle, one of four children, in West Virginia and spent her childhood in St. Paul, Minnesota. Her father was a barber and her mother a beautician. As a child, Marcenia was attracted to playing all kinds of sports; she abandoned softball for baseball as a teenager, because she found baseball a faster and more competitive game. She began playing with boys' teams in the St. Paul Catholic league and at one time saved Wheaties box tops so that she could play on teams that the cereal company sponsored across the country.

When the former St. Louis Cardinal manager Gabby Street came to St. Paul to head a baseball school, Marcenia asked for a tryout and kept pestering him until he gave her a chance to play. Street was impressed by her skill and her persistence and invited her to join his baseball school; he even paid for her cleats. Against her parents' wishes, Marcenia continued to pursue baseball after she graduated from St. Paul's Roosevelt High School, playing for a men's semipro team in St. Paul and then moving to San Francisco, where her sister was in the military. In San Francisco, she played for the barnstorming team the Sea Lions and gave herself the name Toni Stone, because, she reported, she thought it sounded like "Tom Boy."

In 1947 JACKIE ROBINSON became the first African American man to play baseball in the major leagues when Branch Rickey signed him to the Brooklyn Dodgers. As Major League Baseball began to integrate, the Negro Leagues deteriorated. More and more fans of the Negro Leagues turned their attention to Robinson and other African American players who followed him into the majors. The Negro Leagues faced financial problems and tried to increase box office revenues with creative marketing that included special exhibition play, comical stunts proceeding games, and raffles. Stone took advantage of this moment when black baseball was searching for ways to bring more fans through the turnstiles. While she was a serious player with a fierce dedication to the game, others saw her as novelty act. From 1949 to 1953 she played for a string of barnstorming, semipro, and minor league teams in the Negro Leagues. She played for the New Orleans Black Pelicans, the New Orleans Creoles, and the House of David. With increased attention from both fans and front office personnel, Stone began to believe that she might become the first woman to play professional baseball. "There was nothing else I was interested in," she told *Ebony*. "I dreamed about it every night."

In 1950 Stone married a former army officer, Aurelious Alberga, a man forty years her senior. Like her parents, Alberga opposed Stone's playing professional baseball. "He would have stopped me if he could," Stone later said. "But he couldn't" (Gregorich, 175). In 1953 Stone received a call from Syd Pollack, owner of the Indianapolis Clowns, a famous Negro Leagues team known for its comical high jinks as well as its superb play. Pollack offered Stone a contract to play second base and told reporters he was signing her not for publicity purposes but because she played a good brand of baseball. Pollack was also looking for a way to increase interest in his team, since he had lost the second baseman HANK AARON to the major leagues the year before. When Pollack asked Stone to play in a skirt, as female players did in the segregated white All-American Girls Professional Baseball League, she refused. She also would not consent to play in shorts and made it clear that she would dress in the same uniforms as her male teammates did.

During the 1953 season Stone hit .243 and played in fifty games. At five feet, seven inches tall and 148 pounds, Stone held her own physically and was noted for being fast on the base paths. She was clocked in the 100-yard dash at eleven seconds. Reporters noted that competitors treated her no differently from male players on the diamond: pitchers occasionally brushed Stone back with throws to her head, charging basemen slid spikes-up when she was covering second. Stone was proud of scars on her left wrist sustained when a runner tried to knock her down at second. "He was out," she noted (*New York Times*).

Not all players welcomed Stone. In reflecting on her career years later, she remembered that some players made it clear that women should not play professional baseball. "They'd tell me to go home and fix my husband some biscuits," she recalled (Gregorich, 174). But Stone stuck it out because she wanted to play and resented that sexism held her back. "A woman has her dreams, too," she told those who questioned why she stayed. "When you finish high school, they tell a boy to go out and see the world. What do they tell a girl? They tell her to go next door and marry the boy that their families picked for her. It wasn't right. A woman can do many things" (Thomas, 60).

The highlight of Stone's career came during her first season with the Clowns, when she got a single off the legendary pitcher SATCHEL PAIGE during an exhibition game in Omaha, Nebraska. Stone was almost as surprised as Paige and laughed all the way to first base. The clean single over second base was "the happiest moment of my life," she said (Gregorich, 174). In 1954 Pollack sold Stone's contract to the Kansas City Monarchs. That year Pollack added two women players to the Clowns' line-up: the second baseman CONNIE MORGAN and the pitcher MAMIE "PEANUT" JOHNSON. Stone drew little playing time in Kansas City. Frustrated with sitting on the bench, Stone wanted the Monarchs' manager, BUCK O'NEIL, to play her as much as the Clowns' manager, OSCAR CHARLESTON, had. "He'd let me get up there and hit," she said of Charleston (Gregorich, 174). But O'Neil did not give her much playing time. At the end of the season, Stone returned to San Francisco, where she worked as a nurse and cared for her ailing husband, who lived another three decades and died at age 103. Not playing professional baseball, she said, "hurt so damn bad I near had a heart attack" (Thomas, 60).

Stone continued to play recreational baseball until her early sixties and, after years of being forgotten by sports historians, she was delighted in 1985 to be inducted into the Women's Sports Foundation International Sports Hall of Fame. She also participated in National Baseball Hall of Fame events in 1991 that honored Negro League ball players. In 1995 a play entitled "Tomboy Stone," written by Roger Nieboer, was performed in St. Paul at the Great American History Theatre.

Toni Stone died of heart failure at age seventy-five in Alameda, California. A baseball field in her hometown of St. Paul was dedicated in her memory in 1997. Stone's lifelong commitment to baseball proved that women have always had the interest and the talent to play the sport. "Maybe I'll be the first woman to play major league baseball. At least

I may be the one who opens the door for others," Stone said hopefully in 1953. A half a century later, her dream has yet to be realized.

FURTHER READING

Berlage, Gai Ingham. *Women in Baseball: The Forgotten History* (1994).

Gregorich, Barbara. *Women at Play: The Story of Women in Baseball* (1993).

"Lady Ball Player: Toni Stone Is First of Sex to Play with Professional Team," *Ebony*, July 1953.

Thomas, Ron. "She Made It a League of Her Own," *Emerge*, May 1996.

Obituary: *New York Times*, 10 Nov. 1996.

MARTHA ACKMANN

Stout, Juanita Kidd (7 Mar. 1919–21 Aug. 1998), attorney and jurist, was born on a farm near Wewoka, Oklahoma, the only child of Mary Chandler and Henry Maynard Kidd, both schoolteachers. A precocious child, she entered a racially segregated elementary school in the third grade after being homeschooled by her mother in her early years. In 1931 Stout graduated as valedictorian of Page Junior High School and was again valedictorian for the 1935 graduating class at Frederick Douglass High School. Kidd graduated into a world in which racial segregation, enforced by law and custom, was the norm. She attended college at Lincoln University, a state-supported black institution in Missouri. While at Lincoln she joined Delta Sigma Theta, a black sorority founded in 1913, which provided her with an important and valuable network of friends and contacts for the rest of her life. In 1937 Kidd went to hear the case of Lloyd Gaines argued before the Missouri state court, and it altered her life. Gaines, a young black graduate of Lincoln University, had applied to the University of Missouri Law School but had been turned down because of his race. He sued the school, and CHARLES HAMILTON HOUSTON, Howard University law professor and civil rights litigator, argued the case for Gaines. Kidd probably had no idea that within a decade Houston would play a pivotal role in steering her toward her life's work.

While still an undergraduate Kidd transferred to the University of Iowa, and she graduated in 1939 with a bachelor's degree in music with a concentration in piano. Returning home to Oklahoma, she took a post as a music teacher at the segregated Booker T. Washington school in Seminole, Oklahoma, and after two years transferred to the black school, Booker T. Washington High School

Juanita Kidd Stout on 15 April 1965. She was the first African American woman elected to be a judge in the United States. (AP Images.)

in Sand Springs, Oklahoma. While at Sand Springs she met a young man and fellow teacher, Charles Otis Stout, to whom she became engaged, and when the outbreak of World War II required him to move to Washington, D.C., due to being drafted in 1942 and sent to Aberdeen Proving Grounds near Baltimore, she followed.

On 23 June 1942 Kidd and Stout were wed. That year, she also went to work for Houston, the lawyer she had heard argue the *Gaines* case several years earlier. At the end of the war in 1945 Charles Stout had ambitions for further success in education, so he returned to school to pursue a master's degree and then a doctorate at the University of Indiana. Perhaps influenced by working for Houston, Juanita began legal studies at Howard University in 1942, but she transferred to the University of Indiana Law School in 1943 to seek her J.D. while her husband pursued his graduate degrees in education, both living on his small income from the G.I. Bill. Three years in graduate school left them broke, and they both went to teach at Texas Southern University, a historically black institution in Houston, Texas. Stout applied for a job teaching in the law school but was turned down largely because of her gender and wound up teaching business law to undergraduates.

Within a year she was contacted by WILLIAM HENRY HASTIE, a black circuit court judge she had met while working in Washington, D.C. He wanted her to relocate to Philadelphia to work for him. So in December of 1949 she and her husband moved north again. Charles Stout found employment at Maryland State College as a dean while Juanita Stout took up residence in Philadelphia, an arrangement they maintained for more than a decade. He worked in Maryland during the week, rising to the position of dean, while commuting to Philadelphia on the weekends. Juanita Stout was, by all accounts a workaholic, hence, a long-distance marriage did not seem to have been troubling.

In 1954 Stout entered private law practice, but after a few years she went to work in the Philadelphia District Attorney's Office, eventually being promoted to chief of the Appeals, Pardons and Paroles Division. Here, her objective was to contest the efforts of convicted felons to have unfavorable decisions reversed and to oppose the granting of pardons or paroles to incarcerated felons.

Stout's time in the district attorney's office was cut short in 1959 when a sitting common pleas court judge died. Pennsylvania Governor David Lawrence appointed her to be interim judge pending an election to fill the unexpired term. In the regular election for the next full term, the Republican Party put a black attorney on the ballot. The Democrats countered by nominating Stout for the full term. She received more than four hundred thousand votes, winning in a landslide; she was sworn in on 23 October 1959 as one of the first black women in the United States to be elected to the bench. In 1969 she was elected to the Court of Common Pleas and was reelected in 1979. She served almost thirty years on the bench before being appointed to the Pennsylvania Supreme Court in 1988, becoming the first black woman to sit on a state supreme court.

During her years as a judge, she heard hundreds of cases, including one in which she sentenced a man to jail for flying a private plane drunk; but generally, she favored restitution rather than jail time if the circumstances allowed. Witnessing a reign of terror in poor neighborhoods by young hoodlums, she was determined to jail the major gang leaders and, as a result, became the recipient of death threats, necessitating police protection. She also had the satisfaction of seeing a young felon whom she had sentenced to eighteen months speak later of the sobering effect of the experience, leading him to embark on a path that eventually led to law school and a stint as her law clerk.

Mandatory, age-dictated retirement made Stout's tenure on the Pennsylvania Supreme Court brief, but she returned to the Philadelphia Court of Common Pleas and was still writing opinions in June of 1997—a little over a year before her death. Stout died in August of 1998.

During her lifetime Stout received numerous honors, including an honorary degree from Indiana University Law School, an award from the National Association of Women Lawyers in 1965, and an appointment by President John F. Kennedy in 1963 as Special Ambassador to the Kenyan independence celebration.

FURTHER READING

The Papers of Juanita Stout Kidd at the Library of Congress in Washington, D.C., provide a wealth of information on her life and career and are probably the best source of material on Kidd.

Notable Black American Women (1992).

"The Papers of Jessie Kidd Stout," *New York Times*, 24 Aug. 1998.

JOHN R. HOWARD

Stout, Renée (1958–), painter and sculptor, was born in Junction City, Kansas, but moved to Pittsburgh, Pennsylvania, at a young age with her parents and younger sister, Lauren. There, the artist grew up, drawing and painting since her earliest years, with her interest in art encouraged by a creative and supportive family. Stout attended Pittsburgh's Carnegie Mellon University, graduating with a degree in art in 1980. Throughout her high school and college years, Stout cultivated—and perfected—a precise, photographic realism, inspired by the works of Edward Hopper and others. A postcollege stint as a signmaker at a local thrift store helped the artist develop a facility for lettering and signage, along with a fondness for text that informs her work to this day.

An extremely versatile artist, adept at working in a range of materials and media, Stout most often explores the terrain between painting and sculpture in visually complex and cryptic multimedia collages, installations, and assemblages. Her eclectic incorporation of various media into her art dates back to her move from Pittsburgh to Boston in 1984, when she first began importing objects from the urban environment into her paintings. She continued this process with her subsequent relocation to Washington, D.C., in 1985, thereby transforming the detritus of another alien city into the raw materials of painting in ways that suggested the healing, redemptive power of art. By 1987, she had abandoned hyperrealist painting altogether for collage, found objects, and handwritten text that she used to create sculptural works focused on spirituality, healing, and the vagaries of love.

Since the mid 1980s, Stout's work has reflected her deep engagement with African and African Diaspora religions and imagery. In 1988, she made a breakthrough sculpture on this theme entitled *Fetish #2*, which was a life-size cast of her own body in the guise of a Kongo *Nkisi* (the sculptural container for efficacious medicine produced by the Kongo peoples of Central Africa). Included in an important exhibition, *Black Art/Ancestral Legacy: The African Impulse in African-American Art*, this bold work brought the artist significant critical recognition early on in her career. In 1993, Stout exhibited her own *nkisi*-inspired sculptures alongside a collection of historical *minkisi* at the Museum of African Art in Washington, D.C., before moving on to explore the broader legacy of Central African Kongo found throughout the Americas, which has been so famously documented by Yale art historian Robert Farris Thompson. Through reading Thompson, Stout traced Kongo practices in New World spiritualities such as Haitian *hoodoo* and New Orleans *vodou*, as well as in the local "root stores" of cities such as Washington, D.C. By focusing on the healing dimensions of these syncretic practices—on their function as coping mechanisms in a difficult world—Stout treats themes such as faith and human agency, as well as the parallels between art and spirituality.

Stout's work is often autobiographical and invariably literary, incorporating textual narratives peopled with invented characters like the healer Madame Ching or Dorothy and her roving Colonel Frank. She builds thematic bodies of work around these literary constructions, such as the tableaus and altar-like installations of her Madame Ching series (1992–1996). Stout's protagonists are not only the product of fantasy, however: they are partly exteriorized self-portrait and partly based on real people, like the Thompson-inspired wandering anthropologist Colonel Frank. Mississippi Delta blues singer Robert Johnson was another of Stout's protagonists, a historical personality who inspired a major exhibition of work entitled *Dear Robert, I'll See You at the Crossroads*. Here again, Stout looked back at Africa, invoking Kongo cosmography and the notion of the crossroads as a liminal meeting point between various worlds.

Reader's, Advisors and Storefront Churches was the artist's second major solo exhibition, a large 2002 midcareer retrospective that included Stout's locally engaged, politically inflected installations and paintings from 1997 to 1998. These works included a series of sculpted hand guns, both a response to the local endemic violence of Stout's Washington, D.C., neighborhood and a salute to international revolutionaries such as Winnie Mandela and Che Guevera, whom Stout perceived as using guns as a desperate last measure to fight inequality. This signal exhibition also tracked the artist's post-2000 return to oil painting—and to her early realism in particular—in heavily textual paintings of vernacular signage and fastidiously rendered bottles of herbs with loopy, handwritten labels accompanied by verbal promises of potency. These new paintings, a dramatic shift in direction from her earlier sculptural works, suggest a synthesis of Stout's early painterly realism with her longtime interest in African, Caribbean, and African American folk traditions of visuality, medicine, and spirituality.

FURTHER READING

Berns, Marla. *Renée Stout: Dear Robert, I'll See You at the Crossroads* (1995).

Harris, Michael. *Astonishment and Power: Kongo Minkisi and the Art of Renée Stout* (1993).

Owen-Workman, Michelle A., and Stephen Bennett Phillips. *Reader's, Advisors and Storefront Churches: Renée Stout: A Mid-Career Retrospective* (2002).

LEORA MALTZ LECA

Stovey, George Washington (1866–22 Mar. 1936), baseball player, was most likely born in Williamsport, Pennsylvania, the child of a white father and a black mother whose names and occupations are unknown. He was raised in the predominantly white environment of Williamsport, and his earliest baseball experience placed him among mostly white teammates. As a teenager in the early 1880s Stovey played on amateur teams in Williamsport, and there is evidence that in 1885 he left home to play for a team in Elmira, New York. Some accounts place him the following year with a Canadian team. At some point early in the 1886 season he played for a short stint with the Cuban Giants, an all-black team based in Trenton, New Jersey, where he immediately established a reputation as a superb pitcher. In a colorful account of the rising star one reporter wrote that his deliveries looked "as large as an alderman's opinion of himself" and that his pitches could not be hit "with a cellar door" (Zang, 53).

Stovey's performance attracted the attention of the Jersey City team in the Eastern League, which was then regarded as the highest level of minor league baseball. The Jersey City manager convinced Stovey to break his contract with the Cuban Giants (jumping from one team to another was common) and join his team. Stovey thus began his brief experience as one of a select group of African American baseball pioneers who took part in white-dominated organized baseball in the late nineteenth century.

Stovey's experience reflected the pioneering role of this generation of black ballplayers as well as the rapidly changing atmosphere that soon led to their exclusion from organized baseball for half a century. Between 1872 and 1898 some fifty blacks played for teams within organized baseball. Of this generation of players several names stand out. BUD FOWLER is generally recognized as the first black professional to play for a white baseball team. FRANK GRANT was a leading hitter in the International League and arguably was the best black player in organized baseball of his generation. FLEETWOOD WALKER was the first black player of his generation to play at the major league level—he spent the 1884 season catching for the Toledo team in the American Association, which was considered a major league at the time. And George Stovey is generally regarded as the outstanding pitcher of this group.

During his debut season in the Eastern League, Stovey established himself as a top pitcher. Yet his manager considered his star pitcher "head-strong and obstinate, and consequently hard to manage" (Hunsinger, 81). Probably because of this conflict, the following year Stovey moved to the Newark team of the International League, where he joined Fleet Walker. Together they formed organized baseball's first African American pitcher-catcher combination. Again Stovey performed extremely well, compiling a 33–14 record. He also played some outfield on days that he was not pitching, batting .255 in 54 games.

Stovey's performance in the 1886 and 1887 seasons gained the attention of the New York Giants of the National League, one of the two recognized major leagues of the time. "New York has been seriously considering the engagement of Stovey, Jersey City's fine colored pitcher," reported the 8 September 1886 issue of *Sporting Life*. The following year John Montgomery Ward, the star player for the Giants, apparently made an effort to have his club sign both Stovey and Fleet Walker. If such a deal was in fact considered, it was never completed, and the National League did not have its first black player until JACKIE ROBINSON's dramatic debut in 1947.

One of the reasons that Stovey never had the opportunity to move to the major leagues was that by 1887 white hostility toward the handful of black players in organized baseball, though always in existence, was escalating. "How far will the mania for engaging colored players go?" complained *Sporting Life*. "At the present rate of progress the International League may ere many moons change its name to 'Colored League'" (1 June 1887). In response to this sentiment the International League, which had African Americans on six of its ten teams, banned the admission of any more black players to the league. In the same season Adrian Constantine (Cap) Anson of the Chicago White Sox refused to play an exhibition game against Newark in which Stovey was scheduled to pitch. Not only was Anson one of the greatest players of his generation: he also was one of the most outspoken advocates of excluding African Americans from the game. Stovey avoided a confrontation by claiming that he had a stomach illness and could not play. A *Sporting Life* account from the-following year revealed that Stovey's sickness was feigned to avoid a confrontation with Anson (Peterson, 29).

Despite his winning thirty-three games, Newark dropped Stovey after the 1887 season. He continued to play baseball until 1896, pitching for at least two white teams, including teams in Worcester, Massachusetts, and Troy, New York, and several black teams, including the Cuban Giants, the New York Gorhams, and the Cuban X Giants. These early all-black teams, although occasionally affiliated with a league, more often barnstormed the country, playing games against competitors wherever they could find them. With the color line being drawn in organized baseball, these teams became a refuge for talented black players. The best of these teams—including the three teams on which Stovey played—were often on par with the top teams in organized baseball.

By the late 1890s Stovey had returned to his native Williamsport. He pitched occasionally for local amateur teams and sometimes offered his services as an umpire for local games. He apparently undertook his role as an umpire with particular enthusiasm and skill—one contemporary account praised his "fog horn voice" and the fairness of his decisions (Hunsinger, 82). He also earned a living off the field, working in a sawmill and in various odd jobs. The respect that Stovey earned from his mostly white neighbors was shown when in 1926 he found himself on the wrong side of the law, charged with violating a Prohibition law. Testifying on Stovey's behalf, the former mayor of Williamsport told the court: "George Stovey has more friends in Williamsport than any other colored man" (Hunsinger, 82). Stovey received a suspended sentence and a small fine. Stovey lived out the rest of his life in Williamsport.

FURTHER READING

Hunsinger, Lou Jr. "George W. Stovey," *National Pastime* 14 (1994).

Malloy, Jerry, ed. *Sol White's History of Colored Base Ball, with Other Documents on the Early Black Game, 1886–1936* (1995).

Peterson, Robert. *Only the Ball Was White: A History of Legendary Black Players and All-Black Professional Teams* (1992).

Zang, David W. *Fleet Walker's Divided Heart: The Life of Baseball's First Black Major Leaguer* (1995).

CHRISTOPHER W. SCHMIDT

Stowers, Freddie (1896–28 Sept. 1918), U.S. soldier and Medal of Honor recipient, was born in Sandy Springs, South Carolina, the son of Wiley and Annie Stowers. Freddie was the oldest son among the Stowers' children, including Minnie, Bettie, Alna, Edie, Mary, Leula, Georgina, Johnye, and three others who died young. The grandson of a slave, Freddie made a living as a farmhand and prior to his service in World War I was married with a daughter, Minnie, named after his oldest sister.

Freddie Stowers was drafted by the army in 1917, and like nearly 3,400 other African Americans called to service in the South was sent to Camp Jackson, South Carolina, in the newly formed 371st Infantry Regiment of the 93rd Division, one of two such units in the army, the other being the 92nd Division, manned by African American recruits and commanded by white officers. The first recruits for the 371st arrived from Florida in August 1917, but the vast majority of them, Stowers included, did not arrive in camp until October, by order of the War Department, until after the year's cotton crop had been harvested. While nearly half of these men were subsequently assigned to labor and support units, Stowers was among about five hundred men who were designated for combat duty and trained at Camp Upton, New York, before being sent to France as part of the American Expeditionary Force (AEF) in April 1918. Upon arriving in France, the men of the 371st were quickly assigned to French control and after undergoing further training and being fully reequipped with French rifles, machine guns, and even helmets, were assigned to the 157th French "Red Hand" Division under the command of General Mariano Goybet.

Thus assigned to the French "Red Hand" Division, Freddie Stowers and the men of the 371st Infantry Regiment soon went into action manning the trenches around the area of Verdun at Avocourt and Verrieres for over three months, during which time Stowers rose to the rank of corporal as a member of "C" company and commanded a rifle squad. In September the French division was transferred to take part in one of the last great offensives of the war in the Champagne region. On the first day of fighting, on 28 September 1918, Freddie Stowers and "C" company were ordered to assault Cote 188, a heavily defended hill near the town of Ardeuil. The black soldiers slowly but surely advanced on the Germans defending the hill, withstanding heavy mortar and machine gun fire. Nearly to the top, the Germans signaled their surrender, but this was nothing but a trick; as the black troops approached, the Germans machine-gunned the Americans and within minutes the company suffered the loss of half their men, including many officers. With these losses, command of Company C fell to Corporal Freddie Stowers, and he immediately led an advance on the German gun positions, shouting for his men to follow him. They successfully knocked out the machine gun nest in the first line of trenches and Stowers then regrouped his men and led a charge against a second enemy trench line. During this attack, Stowers was wounded by machine gun fire, but continued on until he was hit again. Though weakened by a loss of blood, Stowers urged his men to continue on and take the German gun position. As Stowers lay dying, his men did just that, taking the hill and driving the enemy to lower ground.

The service of men like Freddie Stowers, HENRY JOHNSON, and NEEDHAM ROBERTS in World War I was important for several reasons; not only were these men decorated for their heroism under fire (Johnson and Roberts were the first American soldiers to be awarded the French *Croix de Guerre*, Cross of War), but they are also indicative of the fine but forgotten service rendered by African American soldiers in the "Great War." Sadly, these men received more recognition from the French government than their own country: while the commander of the AEF, General John Pershing, had previously supported the development of black soldiers in the army before gaining high command, he did not support their use in combat units during the war due to the racial conditions then prevailing in the United States and related political considerations. The assignment of black American soldiers to French control was due both to the fact that they were in dire need of men and the fact that the French were well accustomed to using black soldiers in their army raised from among their colonial territories in Africa, mainly Senegal and the Sudan. While General Pershing advised the French not to praise too greatly the achievements of the African American troops under their command, the French ignored him by making numerous awards to them, including a unit citation and the Croix de Guerre to eighty-nine enlisted men of the 371st Infantry Regiment. Upon arriving home, the black soldiers that served overseas found matters even worse; not only was their service at best ignored, or in the worst case deemed a failure, but racial tensions had increased because of fears that returning African Americans would demand greater equality. During the subsequent antiblack race riots that occurred in 1919 in over two dozen American cities, black veterans were often targeted, and some were the victims of lynch mobs.

After his death, Freddie Stowers was buried at the Meuse-Argonne American Cemetery along with 133 other men from his regiment and was largely forgotten by all but his family and friends. He was recommended for the Medal of Honor, but the request was not acted on and lay forgotten for over seven decades. This was almost certainly due to the army's racist policies, as no black soldier was awarded the medal during the war. In 1990 Congress directed that the army conduct a review of its award policies from previous wars. As a result of subsequent research, including the discovery of the Medal of Honor recommendation and information collected at the battlefield site where Stowers performed his deeds of heroism, the Army Decorations Board approved a posthumous award of the Medal of Honor for Freddie Stowers. The medal was presented to his surviving sisters, Georgina Palmer and Mary Bowens, by President George H. W. Bush at a White House ceremony on 24 April 1991. Among those in attendance were Freddie Stowers' great-grandnephews, themselves members of the military: Staff Sergeant Douglas Warren and Technical Sergeant Odis Stowers.

FURTHER READING

Barbeau, Arthur E., and Florette Henry. *The Unknown Soldiers: African-American Troops in WW I* (1974).

Scott, Emmett J. *Scott's Official History of the American Negro in the World War* (1919).

GLENN ALLEN KNOBLOCK

Stradford, J. B. (1861–1935), businessman, lawyer, and civil rights litigant, was born John the Baptist ("J. B.") Stradford (also sometimes spelled "Stratford") probably in slavery at Versailles, Kentucky, the son of Julius Caesar Stradford. Little is known about Stradford's childhood. He studied at Oberlin College from 1882 to 1885 and Indianapolis Law School (later Indiana University–Indianapolis). He married Augusta, and they lived in Lawrenceberg, Kansas, among other places, before moving to Tulsa, Oklahoma, in 1899. Stradford owned and operated a rooming house, the Stradford Hotel, in Greenwood, the black section of Tulsa. Like other leaders of the Greenwood community (including fellow lawyers A.-J. SMITHERMAN and BUCK COLBERT FRANKLIN, the father of JOHN HOPE FRANKLIN), Smitherman was concerned with aggressively preventing lynching and other violence. In 1909 Stradford challenged Oklahoma's statute that permitted unequal treatment on segregated railroad cars. The statute permitted railroads to provide luxury accommodations to whites only; the railroads argued that there was insufficient demand for luxury accommodations among black travelers. Stradford, who had paid for first-class accommodations, boarded a train in Kansas and refused to move to the segregated car when the train crossed into Oklahoma. The railroad conductor had him arrested. Stradford took the case to the Oklahoma Supreme Court, arguing that the law was unconstitutional, even under the standards of "separate but equal" of the time, for the accommodations were unequal. But the Oklahoma Supreme Court denied his claim. In *McCabe v. Atchison, Topeka, and Santa Fe Railway* (1914) the U.S. Supreme Court, which had a broader sense of constitutional rights than the Oklahoma Supreme Court, ruled unconstitutional the same statute that Stradford had challenged earlier.

Stradford had already proven his willingness to challenge Oklahoma's Jim Crow system. On 31 May 1921 he met with other leaders of the Greenwood community in a back room in the Dreamland Theater to plot a response to the threatened lynching of a nineteen-year-old black man, Dick

Rowland, who was being held at the Tulsa County Courthouse on suspicion of attempted rape. Greenwood leaders often met in the Dreamland Theater to discuss the ideas of equality then in circulation in *The Crisis* and the *Chicago Defender*. Stradford and Smitherman often contemplated meeting threats of lynching with force. At one point that evening Stradford said "If I can't get anyone to go with me, I will go single-handed and empty my automatic into the mob and then resign myself to my fate" (Brophy, 31). Later that evening, a group of World War I veterans (perhaps accompanied by Stradford) crossed the tracks separating Greenwood from the white section of Tulsa and went to the courthouse. They were apparently acting on advice from Stradford (and advice had been published in Smitherman's *Tulsa Star*) to take action if a lynching appeared to be imminent. When the Greenwood men confronted the white mob at the Courthouse in an effort to protect Rowland, a riot broke out. The local authorities spoke of it as a "negro uprising," and by noon the next day most of the black section of Tulsa, which housed eight thousand people, was destroyed. Thousands were left homeless; Stradford's hotel was burned to the ground, and dozens, perhaps hundreds, of people died in the riot. There was talk among white Tulsans of prosecuting the radical leaders of Greenwood for their role in inciting the riot. Stradford, fearing arrest, fled first to Kansas and then to Chicago, where he lived the rest of his life. He never again set foot in Oklahoma.

Stradford's fight against Jim Crow Oklahoma was not yet over. He sued his insurance company and the City of Tulsa for losses sustained in the riot. He sued the insurance company because it refused to pay on its fire insurance policy citing a "riot exclusion" clause. He sued Tulsa for the role of its police force and the several hundred special deputies (white men who were hastily deputized on the evening of 31 May) in the riot. Much of what we know about the riot comes from testimony in Stradford's suit, filed in the city of Chicago. For reasons of jurisdiction, Stradford should have filed in Oklahoma; the Illinois courts could not grant relief against a governmental body (the city of Tulsa) outside the state. However, Stradford feared that if he appeared in Tulsa to prosecute his case, he would be arrested. He settled the suit against his insurance company when they returned the premiums he paid on his policy, which was far less than the damage he suffered. Tulsa never gave Stradford or any other Greenwood resident any reimbursement.

Stradford died in Chicago in 1935. His son, C. Francis Stradford, attended Columbia Law School and became a civil rights lawyer. Among his cases was *Hansberry v. Lee*, (1940), in which LORRAINE HANSBERRY's father successfully challenged racially restrictive covenants in their neighborhood in Chicago.

In 1996, in conjunction with Oklahoma State Representative Don Ross, Stradford's family successfully lobbied the Tulsa prosecutor to drop the charges against him. Shortly afterward, and partly inspired by the story of Stradford's wrongful prosecution, the Oklahoma legislature voted to create the Tulsa Race Riot Commission to study the riot. Their report in 2001 led to the 1921 Tulsa Race Riot Reconciliation Act, which acknowledged the costs of the riot and Oklahoma's Jim Crow system.

FURTHER READING

Brophy, Alfred L. *Reconstructing the Dreamland: The Tulsa Riot of 1921–Race, Reparations, Reconciliation* (2002).

Ellsworth, Scott. *Death in a Promised Land: The Tulsa Race Riot of 1921* (1982).

Final Report of the Oklahoma Commission to Study the Tulsa Race Riot of 1921 (2001).

ALFRED L. BROPHY

Straker, David Augustus (1842–1908), lawyer and judge, was born in Bridgetown, Barbados, the son of John and Margaret Straker, of whom little is known. His father John Straker died when David was less than a year old, and his mother cared for him until he reached age seven, when she enrolled him in a private school. He entered the Central Public School in Bridgetown at age thirteen. Although he was also serving an apprenticeship as a tailor, Straker was deeply attracted to intellectual studies. With the support of Robert P. Elliott, principal of the Central Public School, Straker abandoned tailoring for full-time classical studies, including instruction in Latin and French under the tutelage of a linguist, the Reverend Joseph N. Durant. He also studied history and philosophy under R. R. Rawle, principal of Codrington College, an Anglican grammar school in Bridgetown, which is now part of the University of the West Indies. At age seventeen Straker's accomplishments were such that he was appointed principal of St. Mary's School on Barbados. He also occasionally tutored to earn extra money.

In 1868 an Episcopal bishop in America wrote to the Codrington College administration inquiring whether the college had any well-educated blacks who might be willing to move to the United States to help with the enormous project of teaching basic literacy and mathematical skills to the recently emancipated black population of the South. Straker, who had planned to go to England to study law, seized the opportunity to work with the American freed people instead. In 1868 he arrived in Louisville, Kentucky, where under the auspices of the local Episcopal church he organized and taught classes for the city's large African American population. He was also intrigued by the possibility of becoming an Episcopal clergyman, and spent considerable time reading church history and studying theology.

In 1869 Straker learned that the newly-opened Howard University in Washington, D.C., whose mission was to provide postsecondary education for blacks, was to include a law school. He immediately applied and was admitted. While studying law, he worked as a clerk for General O. O. Howard, for whom the university had been named, assisting with the affairs of the U.S. Freedman's Bureau. Straker also earned money teaching classes in the university's Preparatory and Normal (teacher training) departments. He graduated with an LLB degree in Howard's first law class in June 1871, and was soon appointed as a clerk in the U.S. Treasury Department. He was quickly promoted to managing the international accounts between the United States and other countries with which the U.S. had enacted postal treaties. Straker also circulated among the capital's black intelligentsia. He endorsed the advancement of blacks' civil rights, and expressed his views in articles he wrote for FREDERICK DOUGLASS's newspaper, *New National Era*. He also began to build a name for himself by making public speeches.

In September 1871 he married Ann Carey in Detroit, Michigan; her parents, Thomas and Julia Carey, were leaders of the thriving black middle-class community there. The couple returned to Washington, D.C., where Straker's interests broadened to include the issue of women's suffrage. In April 1874 he gave a series of lectures at an African Methodist Episcopal church in Washington, D.C. on "Citizenship, Its Rights and Duties—Woman Suffrage." The topic was timely and controversial, since a narrow but vocal national movement was then developing that aimed to obtain the franchise for women, just as black men had secured it by a constitutional amendment in 1870. Straker endorsed the concept of voting rights for women, but noted that government could place limits upon any citizen's rights, if it did so using legal procedures. Similarly, Straker asserted that American blacks should share the social and political rights and privileges of whites not as a matter of natural entitlement only, but also by their own labors.

In 1875 Straker relocated from Washington, D.C., to Charleston, South Carolina, where he was admitted to the state's bar. He assumed the prestigious position of U.S. customs inspector at the port of Charleston. He also launched a legal practice and in 1876 was elected to the South Carolina state legislature. As a black, however, he was ejected from the state house by white lawmakers who opposed Reconstruction and questioned Straker's citizenship status. Although reelected in 1878 and 1880 he was prevented from taking his seat. Between 1880 and 1882 he continued his work for the Treasury at Charleston, but also remained politically active. In 1881 he led a delegation of black activists who met with President-elect James Garfield to protest the states' denial of blacks' political rights in the South. In the same year he was appointed dean of the newly-opened law school of Allen University in Columbia, South Carolina. This institution, dedicated to providing university-level education for African Americans, gave Straker an opportunity to teach courses in law and legal theory, at the same time that he took on important civil rights cases in his private practice. He pioneered the introduction of medical evidence and expert testimony in South Carolina's state courts. Under his tutelage, four black law students from Allen University were admitted to the South Carolina bar in 1882. Straker remained much in demand as a public speaker during the 1880s, traveling to New Orleans, Louisville, New York, and other major cities to speak on African Americans' civil and political rights.

In the mid-1880s Straker and his family moved to Detroit, where again he opened a law practice and quickly became a leader within the local black community. He continued to write, publishing historical and legal books and pamphlets, including a biography of the Haitian revolutionary Toussaint Louverture in 1886 and a treatise on African Americans and race politics in the South in 1888. He also edited a weekly edition of an African American newspaper, *The Detroit Advocate*. In 1889 Straker was asked to speak on "Law and Law Reform" to students at the prestigious University of Michigan Law School in Ann Arbor, Michigan, becoming the first black person to be formally invited to address students on the university's campus.

In 1890 Straker was retained as legal counsel by a well-known Detroit African American businessman, William W. Ferguson. While dining at a white-owned Detroit restaurant, Ferguson and a black associate had been denied service when they seated themselves in the "whites-only" area of the restaurant. Ferguson sued the restaurateur. The case went to the Michigan Supreme Court, where Straker became the first black lawyer to present arguments. Claiming that race-based segregation in public facilities was illegal under Michigan's constitution, Straker won a unanimous ruling from the Court in October 1890. The case created a legal precedent to which later civil rights lawyers across the nation regularly referred.

In 1894 Straker was elected as a Wayne County (Detroit) Circuit Commissioner, becoming the first black judicial official in Michigan history. He was empowered to act as a circuit court judge, and was able to take testimony and render rulings on a variety of cases. As one of Detroit's most prominent blacks, Straker was invited to submit a letter addressed to Detroit's future black population to a time capsule, which was sealed in 1901. While guarded about the struggle for civil rights that would lie ahead, he expressed an authentic optimism about the future of race relations in the United States. D. Augustus Straker, who had often been called the "black Irish lawyer" because of his British West Indies accent, died in Detroit in 1908. He is buried in Detroit's Elmwood Cemetery, the city's oldest (1846) and most prominent racially desegregated public cemetery.

FURTHER READING

D. August Straker published several books, pamphlets, and speeches, including: "Citizenship, Its Rights and Duties—Woman Suffrage, A Lecture" (1874); *Reflections on the Life and Times of Touissant L'Overture, the Negro Haytien* (1886); and *The New South Investigated* (1888). The text of Straker's 1901 time capsule letter is available through the Detroit Historical Museums and Society (www.detroithistorical.org).

Hawkshawe, Dorothy D. "David Augustus Straker, Black Lawyer and Reconstruction Politician, 1842–1908" (1974).

Phillips, Glenn O. "The Response of a West Indian Activist: D. A. Straker 1842–1908," *Journal of Negro History* (1981).

Simmons, William J. *Men of Mark: Eminent, Progressive, and Rising* (1887).

Smith, J. Clay, Jr. *Emancipation: The Making of the Black Lawyer, 1844–1944* (1973).

LAURA M. CALKINS

Strawberry, Darryl Eugene (12 Mar. 1962–), baseball player, was the third of five children born to Henry Strawberry, a postal worker, and Ruby Strawberry, a secretary for Pacific Bell Telephone. Born and raised in South Central Los Angeles, Strawberry was thirteen when his father left following a physical fight with his mother, his brother, and himself about his gambling and drinking. Strawberry attended Crenshaw High, where he starred on what has been considered, during his tenure there, one of the strongest high school baseball teams in history. Though he also played football and basketball, it was baseball that Strawberry was best known for: *Sports Illustrated* ran a short piece on him while he was a senior in high school quoting a major league scout who compared him to the Boston Red Sox legend Ted Williams.

Strawberry was drafted out of high school in 1980 with the first overall pick by the New York Mets, and was immediately a public relations sensation for his minor league teams, which hosted strawberry-themed nights at different stadiums. After he lived up to the tremendous hype for the Double-A Jackson (Mississippi) Mets in 1982, and with the team's fans clamoring for a young star, the Mets promoted Strawberry in May 1983. He hit twenty-six home runs that season en route to winning the Rookie of the Year award.

The lean and agile outfielder immediately became part of the nuclei of the Mets franchise, and, along with the pitcher Dwight Gooden, helped lead the team to contention, and finally, a World Series championship in 1986. Throughout his tenure with the Mets, Strawberry exhibited both easy speed and a legendary graceful swing, tallying up stolen bases, home runs, All-Star appearances, and MVP votes.

However, Strawberry, much like Gooden, was known more for his off-field problems and unfulfilled expectations. Even before he had played his first major league game, Strawberry was breathlessly anticipated by fans and the media as a potential Hall of Famer, one who could eventually hit six hundred home runs. But along with an inconsistent work ethic and altercations with teammates and his manager, Strawberry came under the influence of alcohol and hard drugs. In the bright lights of New York City, Strawberry was one of many Mets players who were known as late-night carousers; the substance abuse would plague Strawberry for the rest of his playing career.

In May 1989 Strawberry's first wife, Lisa Andrews, filed a divorce petition against Strawberry, citing a paternity suit from another woman. In January 1990 Strawberry was arrested after allegedly punching Andrews and threatening her with a gun. Following less than a month of time spent in a Manhattan alcohol-treatment center, Strawberry was back in spring training with the Mets.

After totaling 37 home runs, 108 RBIs, and a third-place MVP finish in 1990, Strawberry signed a lucrative five-year deal with the Los Angeles Dodgers; Crenshaw High welcomed him back to the city by throwing a high-profile homecoming for him in which they retired his uniform number. Following an All-Star 1991 debut season with the Dodgers, Strawberry missed most of 1992 and 1993, dealing with back injuries and surgery.

Strawberry's personal problems continued to plague him. After a drawn-out divorce to his first wife, Strawberry was arrested in September 1993 for hitting his girlfriend, Charisse Simons, who would become his second wife that December. In April 1994, a month after being named in a federal investigation on tax evasion, Strawberry went missing from the Dodgers before the final spring training game; when he was found, he admitted an addiction to cocaine, and attended the Betty Ford Clinic for a month. Three weeks after his release, the Dodgers reached a financial settlement to cut ties with him.

Strawberry soon signed with the Giants, but was released in February 1995 after testing positive for cocaine; two months later he was found guilty of tax evasion. The New York Yankees signed the troubled outfielder that summer, but released him following the season. Though saddled with penalties for failing to pay child support, Strawberry had a promising spring of 1996 with the independent league St. Paul Saints, and the Yankees resigned him. Joining his former teammate Gooden on the Yankees, Strawberry excelled in his part-time role, and hit three home runs in that postseason's American League Championship Series, helping lift the Yankees to a World Series victory.

Strawberry played parts of the next three seasons amid injuries, colon cancer, and a suspension following an April 1999 undercover sting that caught him for cocaine possession and prostitute solicitation. In early 2000 Strawberry once again tested positive for cocaine, and was suspended for the season, effectively ending his playing career.

Over the next five years, Strawberry continued to struggle with substance abuse, checking in and out of clinics and prison, then regressing on the outside. While recovering from another bout of colon cancer and drug troubles, Strawberry stayed connected with baseball as a spring training coach and player development instructor for the Mets and Yankees. Strawberry also made a foray into the reality show era, appearing on one season of *The Apprentice*.

Strawberry fathered six children in total: one out of wedlock, two with first wife Lisa (of whom, his eldest son, Darryl Jr.—or D.J.—became a professional basketball player), and three with his second wife Charisse, who divorced him in 2005. In 2006, he married his third wife, Tracy Boulware, whom he met at a Narcotics Anonymous recovery convention.

FURTHER READING

Strawberry, Darryl, with John Strausbaugh. *Straw: Finding My Way* (2010).

Sokolove, Michael. *The Ticket Out: Darryl Strawberry and the Boys of Crenshaw* (2004).

ADAM W. GREEN

Strayhorn, Billy (29 Nov. 1915–31 May 1967), composer, arranger, and pianist, was born William Thomas Strayhorn in Dayton, Ohio, the son of Lillian Young and James Nathaniel Strayhorn, who worked at a variety of jobs, including a "wire-puller" in a copper plant and a janitor. He was first raised in Hillsboro (later Hillsborough), North Carolina, and then in Pittsburgh, Pennsylvania. As a child he took piano lessons and played in the school orchestra. In his teens he studied harmony and the French impressionist composers, read the *New Yorker* magazine, and developed a taste for good times and fine clothes. His family, especially his mother and grandmother, encouraged and supported his study of classical music and his subsequent career in jazz. Strayhorn himself never married and had no children, and his closest friends during his high school years believed he was either asexual or homosexual because he did not date or discuss girls. In fact, as the biographer David Hajdu points out, Strayhorn was gay and took no great pains to hide it.

In 1934, the year he graduated from high school, Strayhorn heard DUKE ELLINGTON's band in a Pittsburgh theater. "I was hooked," he later recalled. While working in a drugstore Strayhorn studied arranging and continued to compose and play. In 1938 he again heard Ellington at a concert and upon venturing backstage managed to play some of his songs for Ellington, including "Lush Life." This encounter produced an invitation to visit New York City. Several weeks later Strayhorn played for Ellington "Something to Live For," which the bandleader considered a good vehicle for his new vocalist, Jean Eldridge. Shortly thereafter, when Ellington left on a European tour, Strayhorn studied the Ellington songbook under Mercer Ellington, Duke's son. Because of his shyness and his respect for Ellington, Strayhorn stayed in the background, preferring to socialize primarily with close friends such as LENA HORNE, Herb Jeffries, and BEN WEBSTER. Ellington's one admonition for Strayhorn was to "observe." Strayhorn's first work with Ellington consisted primarily of small group performances with Ellington band members or with Mercer's band, from which a few successful recordings ensued with JOHNNY HODGES and COOTIE WILLIAMS. Strayhorn also arranged some vocal and commercial dance numbers for the larger group. Young, sensitive, and polite, Strayhorn won recognition from the veterans of Ellington's band by being given nicknames, including "Weely," "Strays," and—from the Popeye comic strip—"Sweetpea."

Strayhorn was an important factor in Ellington's success. At the start of their association Ellington was arranging and composing all of his band's repertoire, dealing with personnel problems, and struggling to keep the band afloat in a changing musical environment. By 1939 Strayhorn had become an official member of the band and would occasionally fill in as pianist and assist Ellington with arranging and composing. Strayhorn's contributions included "The Kissing Bug," "Rain Check," "Satin Doll," "Take the 'A' Train" (which replaced "East St. Louis Toodle-Oo" as Ellington's theme song), "My Little Brown Book," and the introspective and sophisticated ballad "Chelsea Bridge." Strayhorn's importance is addressed in Ellington's autobiography:

> Any time I was in the throes of debate with myself, harmonically or melodically, I would turn to Billy Strayhorn. We would talk, and then the world would come into focus. The steady hand of his good judgment pointed to clear the way that was most fitting for us. He was not, as he was often referred to by many, my alter ego. Billy Strayhorn was my right arm, my left arm, all the eyes in the back of my head my brainwaves in his head, and his in mine (Ellington, 156).

Strayhorn was not the workaholic his partner was. Unlike Ellington, he would hit the town at night or see the sights during the day. This may explain his relatively low compositional output. Ellington is thought to have finished some overdue Strayhorn compositions and claimed them as his own. LAWRENCE BROWN evidently saw Strayhorn as "the power behind the throne," and MARY LOU WILLIAMS claimed that "Strayhorn loved Duke so much that he would just give him tunes" (Collier, 201). Strayhorn was in fact entrusted with much of the day-to-day rehearsing of the band and the final approval of master tracks in the recording studio.

Strayhorn's creativity came at a particularly good time because a dispute in 1939 between the American Society of Composers and Publishers (ASCAP) and the nation's radio stations led to a radio boycott of all ASCAP material. Duke Ellington, as a member of ASCAP, could not perform his own compositions over the air. Strayhorn did not belong to ASCAP nor did Mercer Ellington, leaving Duke free to perform their material plus arrangements of BMI tunes until the boycott ended in 1941. Strayhorn and Mercer Ellington rewrote the entire Ellington book in this period, a time Mercer later called "a golden era" for both of them. This period also witnessed a large volume of recordings by Ellington's band with Strayhorn as a sideman, including *I Want Something to Live For* (1939), *Lost in Two Flats* (1939), *After All* (1941), *Take The "A" Train* (1941), *Raincheck* (1941), and *Johnny Come Lately* (1942), as well as albums by others that included Strayhorn's music: Johnny Hodges's *Day Dream* (1940), *Passion Flower* (1941), and *Lotus Blossom* (1947).

Some of Strayhorn's musical traits can be heard in "Chelsea Bridge" (*Chelsea Bridge* [1941]), which features a sparse yet beautiful melody framed in an *aaba* format. The melody notes are often high extension chord tones such as ninths, elevenths, and thirteenths. A sudden modulation at the bridge contrasts with the darker harmonies of the *A* section (which begins with a Strayhorn trademark, a vamplike chord progression in the first few bars). "Lush Life" (JOHN COLTRANE, *Lush Life* [1957–1958]), a through-composed form (that is, none of the segments is repeated) built from imitative and related materials, begins with the familiar vamp. A distinctive feature is Strayhorn's use of fourteen-bar phrases, divided into two seven-bar units. The *B* section uses a line progression and a mostly linear melody in contrast with the wide intervals used in the opening verse. The melody is placed in higher chord extensions in the *C* section, where in the space of a few bars Strayhorn smoothly maneuvers between four distinct key centers. Strayhorn uses tritone substitution in the bass line to achieve linear motion. The *D* section is notable in its use of sequences, and the coda displays parallel chromatic harmony.

"Passion Flower" begins with the trademark vamp harmony and uses higher chord extensions in the chromatic melody. Strayhorn changes the harmony under a sustaining melody note at the end of the bridge, a device used in many of his tunes to gracefully change keys.

The strongest feature in "Upper Manhattan Medical Group" (on *Historically Speaking: The Duke* [1956]) is the memorable, swinging melody. Ellington said in his autobiography that Strayhorn was in the truest sense a "dancer." Even without melodies and chords, Strayhorn's phrasing and syncopation were musical. The chord structure in "U.M.M.G.," as this tune is often called, is more conventional than that of many of his other works, but Strayhorn intended the piece to serve as a simple yet original dance number.

Strayhorn's importance can also be gauged by his ability to mirror Ellington's compositional style. In later years Strayhorn became involved in some of Ellington's extended projects, writing and arranging parts of "The Perfume Suite," "The Liberian Suite," "The Far East Suite," and "Such Sweet Thunder" ("The Shakespearean Suite"). Although jazz writers have argued that Ellington's and Strayhorn's arranging and composing styles are indistinguishable, Gunther Schuller asserts that there are several identifiable Strayhorn characteristics: brighter and leaner orchestral texture, predominant higher-register sounds, voicings that tend to separate rather than coalesce, thinner textural sonorities, faster tempos that favor a staccato brass style, and the infusion of classical elements derived from composers of modern art-music such as Claude Debussy, Darius Milhaud, Maurice Ravel, and Igor Stravinsky.

Strayhorn left Ellington's employ in 1955, after he was approached with a proposal for a publishing partnership with Luther Henderson, but the business arrangement never gelled. Strayhorn then spent several months relaxing and partying in Paris, which at the time had attracted other African American jazz musicians, writers, and painters, including JAMES BALDWIN, KENNY CLARKE, HERB GENTRY, CHESTER HIMES, and Art Simmons. While in Paris, Strayhorn forged a close personal relationship with Aaron Bridgers, a lounge pianist. After returning to the Ellington band in 1956, Strayhorn toured regularly with the group until September 1965, when he began a series of painful cancer operations. But it was his buoyant optimism that enabled him to compose "Upper Manhattan Medical Group," anything but an exercise in introspection. During the hospital stays, the creative link with Ellington endured. Ellington recalled one example in his autobiography:

> Our rapport was the closest. When I was writing my first sacred concert, I was in California and he was in a New York hospital. On the telephone I told him … to write something … 'The title is the first four words of the Bible—In the Beginning God.' He had not heard my theme, but what he sent to California started on the same note as mine (F natural) and ended on the same note as mine (A-flat a tenth higher). Out of six notes representing the six syllables of the four words, only two notes were different (Ellington, 156).

After his initial improvement, Strayhorn's condition worsened. By the spring of 1967 he was receiving chemotherapy for cancer of the esophagus. He named his last composition "Blood Count." He died in New York City. A few months later the Ellington band recorded an album devoted to Strayhorn's compositions, *And His Mother Called Him Bill*. As the band packed up to leave the studio, Ellington contributed an impromptu solo piano performance of "Lotus Blossom."

Although complicated, Strayhorn's relationship with Ellington remained one of mutual respect and admiration, a relationship born and nurtured in the musical and personal sensitivity that they shared with each other. In Ellington, Strayhorn saw a compassionate, supportive father figure, unlike his natural father; in Strayhorn, Ellington saw a sensitive, polished arranger and composer who he could trust to create new music and to finish some of his own compositions. The relationship was mutually beneficial, resulting in an extended collaboration of legendary stature in the history of jazz.

FURTHER READING

Ellington, Duke. *Music Is My Mistress* (1973).

Hajdu, David. *Lush Life: A Biography of Billy Strayhorn* (1996).

Shapiro, Nat, and Nat Hentoff, eds. *Hear Me Talkin' to Ya* (1955).

This entry is taken from the *American National Biography* and is published here with the permission of the American Council of Learned Societies.

EDDIE S. MEADOWS

Streat, Thelma Beatrice Johnson

Streat, Thelma Beatrice Johnson (29 Aug. 1911– 21 May 1959), abstract expressionist artist, dancer, and educator, was born in Yakima, Washington, the second of five children of Gertrude Beatrice Carson and James A. Johnson, an interior decorator and inventor.

The family moved from Yakima to Boise, Idaho, and Pendleton, Oregon, finally settling in Portland, Oregon. They were often the only black family where they lived, and were subjected to racist taunts. Streat attended Boise High then graduated from Washington High School in Portland in 1932. She attended the [Portland] Museum Art School (now Pacific Northwest College of Art or PNCA) in 1934, and the University of Oregon from 1933 to 1936, but did not get a degree. Having started painting at the age of nine, Streat won honorable mention from the Harmon Foundation (set up by the white philanthropist William E. Harmon to support black artists) for a juried exhibit in New York City in 1929.

On 26 June 1935, Streat married Romaine Virgil Streat, and they moved to San Francisco. He was in the military, and after many long separations they divorced. She worked for the Works Progress Administration (WPA) Federal Art Project in 1941, in the Pickle Factory building in San Francisco, creating murals to promote black culture and history. She helped the Mexican muralist Diego Rivera paint the *Pan American Unity Mural*. Rivera wrote a letter praising her.

Streat worked in gouache, watercolor, tempera, and oil paints. Her first show was in 1939, at the San Francisco City of Paris galleries. Her paintings were exhibited at San Francisco's De Young Memorial Museum in 1941. *Rabbit Man* was the first work by a black woman to be exhibited at the Museum of Modern Art (MoMA) in New York City. MoMA purchased the painting on 7 May 1942, and included it in the New Acquisitions American Painting and Sculpture exhibition that year. Streat's paintings were also exhibited at the Raymond and Raymond Galleries in 1942. In 1943 *Robot* was part of the International Exhibition of Water Color at the Art Institute of Chicago. She had a solo show at the actor Vincent Price's Little Gallery in Beverly Hills California in 1943, exposing her work to Hollywood stars. In 1944 *Rabbit Man* was part of the Thirty American Artists exhibit at the New York Public Library.

In 1943 her controversial painting *Death of a Black Soldier* depicted a dying black soldier's thought about "whites only" signs at defense plants, Red Cross refusals to accept Negro blood, separate barracks in the army and navy, segregated restaurants, all while black Americans fought Nazism in World War II. Streat was threatened several times by the Ku Klux Klan when the work was shown. In 1946 Streat exhibited her paintings and danced at the San Francisco Museum of Art. Her dances were another way to express abstractly her themes of freedom, the difficulties of obtaining it, and black contributions in industry, agriculture, medicine, science, and transportation. They were often interpretations of black spirituals. The paintings were created as murals, then reproduced for distribution to schools and libraries.

Streat lived in Chicago in the 1940s, and taught children's art classes. In 1945 *Mother and Baby on Desert* was in the The Negro Artist Comes of Age show at the Albany (New York) Institute of History and Art. The show provoked a controversy about whether black artists should be treated separately or included in the mainstream of American artists.

On 12 December 1948, Streat married her manager, the playwright John Edgar Kline, who was white, in Seattle, Washington. (Washington was one of only twenty-one states at that time that allowed interracial marriages between blacks and whites.) She continued to use the surname Streat professionally. They moved to Honolulu, Hawaii, where she established Children's City, a multicultural arts center with free arts classes for underprivileged children. She performed and exhibited around the world promoting her theme of freedom and researching folk literature, dance, and industrial workers. Between 1946 and 1950 she visited Canada, Haiti, Ireland, England, South Pacific islands, Hawaii, Mexico, and France. After Streat performed on British television, Queen Elizabeth II requested a command performance; and Streat was the first American to have her own television show in Paris, France.

In 1953 Streat set up her easel on the rim of the Kilauea volcano in Hawaii and painted the eruption for six hours. That same year, Streat performed her one-woman musical-dance-drama-pantomime *Bringing Back Those Wonderful Days* at the Curran Theatre in San Francisco. In 1956 Streat and her husband set up another children's art school on Salt Spring Island in Vancouver, British Columbia, Canada. Salt Spring had been settled by former slaves in 1858, and was a refuge for black Americans seeking escape from racism.

Streat died of a heart attack in Los Angeles. Her murals have been lost, but there were posthumous exhibits of paintings in New York City and Portland, Oregon. Streat used her art to promote an understanding of black Americans' contributions to American history, and multiculturalism. She was one of only four black American artists to have solo shows before 1947, and her paintings were in the private collections of Eleanor Roosevelt, Charlie Chaplin, and Rivera among others. In 2010 Streat was awarded a posthumous doctorate by the PNCA. She was inspired by Native American and other folk cultures, and she used abstract expressionism and bold color to promote a multicultural image of the world and racial tolerance.

FURTHER READING

Streat's paintings are in collections at Reed and Johnson Colleges in Oregon and MoMA.

Bullington, Judy. "Thelma Johnson Streat and Cultural Synthesis on the West Coast American Art." *American Art* 19, no. 2 (Summer 2005): 92–107.

Butler, Cornelia H., and Alexandra Schwartz. *Modern Women: Women Artists at the Museum of Modern Art* (2010).

Wilson, Judith. "How The Invisible Woman Got Herself on the Cultural Map: Black Women Artists in California." In *Art, Women, California 1950–2000: Parallels and Intersections* (2002).

JANE BRODSKY FITZPATRICK

Street, John Franklin (15 Oct, 1943–), Philadelphia councilman and mayor, was born on 15 October 1945 in Norristown, Pennsylvania, to poor rural farmers. He was third child of James and Elizabeth Street. Street grew up without electricity or indoor plumbing and often helped his mother tend to the farm while his father was working at a brick manufacturing plant. After graduating from Conshohocken High School in suburban Philadelphia, he attended Oakwood College in Huntsville, Alabama. He worked his way through college and eventually graduated in 1964 with a degree in English. Street then attended Temple Law School and graduated with a Juris Doctor in 1975. To pay for tuition, he worked as a sidewalk vendor.

Four years later, John Street was elected as a Democrat to the Philadelphia City Council. For the next twenty years of his life, Street would represent the Fifth Council District, one of the most diverse, both racially and economically, in the city. In 1992 and again in 1996, he was unanimously elected as City Council president. During these two terms, Street worked on many projects that would eventually come to fruition during his terms as mayor. By working with then Mayor Edward G. Rendell, Street was able to institute a financial plan that turned a $250 million deficit into the largest surplus in city history. They were also able to reverse a thirty-year trend of job losses in Philadelphia. Lastly, Street passed a tax on alcohol that generates an extra $23 million for public schools annually. On 17 December 1998, John Street retired from the City Council to run for mayor of Philadelphia.

His opponent was Sam Katz, a white Republican and municipal finance expert. The race was extremely close, and many people believed Philadelphia would elect its first Republican mayor since 1947. Street received endorsements from Senator Edward Kennedy of Massachusetts and President Bill Clinton. John Street was elected mayor in one of the closest votes in Philadelphia history, winning by slightly less than 10,000 votes out of half a million votes cast. After being sworn in on 3 January 2000, Street immediately went to work. During his first term, Mayor Street made many changes to Philadelphia, especially in the poorer wards. He started the Neighborhood Transformation Initiative. Under this plan, old, abandoned buildings were demolished. He also instituted a privatization program that placed the worst of the Philadelphia public schools under the Edison Corporation. In addition to these major changes, the Philadelphia Parking Authority was taken over by the Pennsylvania state government, the Philadelphia Children Commission was started, and Street started the Office of Health and Fitness (this was in response to an article in *Men's Fitness* that dubbed Philadelphia as America's fattest city). Also, the new Philadelphia Eagles stadium, Lincoln Financial Field, was opened on 3 August 2003.

A major controversy emerged in 2003 when bugs were found in Street's mayoral office. The listening devices had been placed there by the FBI during an ongoing investigation into corruption in the Philadelphia city government. The FBI was gathering evidence against the treasurer and Street's top fund-raiser; they believed city contracts were being traded for campaign contributions. Street maintained his innocence throughout the entire investigation, claiming that the recordings would have "no corruption, no sex, and no profanity" (WHYY). Mayor John Street was never under formal investigation and it was never proved that he knew anything about the corruption taking place under him. Close to two dozen people were eventually arrested.

After what many people regarded as a successful first term, Mayor Street ran for reelection in a rematch with his opponent of 1999, Katz. This time

Street garnered close to 60 percent of the vote. During his second term as mayor, Street continued to build on the progress made during his first term. He started the Adolescent Violence Reduction Partnership to cut down on gang violence in the city. Street also passed a law that banned smoking in city buildings. His largest project during his second term was Wireless Philadelphia. This program was a huge initiative to provide Internet throughout the city. The goals of the project were to promote economic development and help overcome the digital divide. At first this project was hailed as a huge success but it turned into a total failure as the years went by. In addition to these programs, exactly eight months after the new Eagles stadium opened, Citizens Bank Park, home of Major League Baseball's Phillies, was opened on 3 April 2004. This building project generated much controversy in its early phases. Several different sites around the city were proposed to host the park, but were eventually turned down until a site at the South Philadelphia Sports Complex was eventually chosen.

Mayor Street did much to help Philadelphia during his tenure as mayor. He helped reduce crime rates and revitalize the city. It remains unclear whether that will be his lasting legacy, or if those successes will remain tainted by the corruption scandal of 2003.

FURTHER READING

Blockson, Charles L. *Philadelphia: 1639–2000* (2000).

Books LLC. *Mayors of Philadelphia, Pennsylvania: George M. Dallas, Ed Rendell, Frank Rizzo, John F. Street, Jonathan Dickinson, Michael Nutter* (2010).

"A Conversation with Mayor John Street." WHYY. 2004: http://www.whyy.org/tv12/street.html.

Mihaly, Mary E. *Insiders Guide to Philadelphia* (2007).

ARTHUR HOLST

Stringer, C. Vivian (16 Mar. 1948–), basketball coach, was born Charlaine Vivian Stoner in Edenborn, Pennsylvania, the oldest of six children of Charles "Buddy" Stoner, a coal miner by day and a talented jazz musician on weekends, and Thelma "Bird" Stoner. Siblings included Verna, Tim, Madeline, Richelle "Ricky," and Jack.

Stringer was named Charlaine after her father; she states in her memoir, "it's so much of a boy's name, which is why I never use it. Not that it matters—these days; pretty much everyone assumes that the *C* stands for *Coach*" (Stringer, 36). As a young girl in Edenborn, Stringer spent a lot of time playing football and basketball with the

Charlene Vivian Stringer, the head coach for women's basketball at Rutgers University, during the Big East Championship in Hartford, Conn., on 9 March 2004. (AP Images.)

boys and playing softball. "I always just wanted to play," Stringer said. "Playing for the sake of playing was enough for me" (Stringer, 29).

Since there were no girls' teams in her high school, Stringer decided to try out for the cheerleading squad, thinking that would get her close enough to the field to "encourage" the boys. Although she felt she "nailed" the routines, she was not selected for the team. When the president of the local NAACP discussed the tryouts with her father and the discrimination he felt had been at the root of her nonselection, her father encouraged Stringer to take a stand against the injustice (Stringer, 33). She did, and with friend Kathleen Morris and after an intense school board meeting, the two were added to the squad. Stringer later apologized for giving the impression in her autobiography that she and Morris had been the first African Americans on the cheerleading squad.

Education was extremely important to the Stoner family, so in 1966 Vivian left Edenborn to be the first in her family to attend college. During her first semester at Slippery Rock University, she was introduced to William D. Stringer, a young gymnast she had seen the year before during her high school visit, and decided he was the man she would eventually marry. She had a shaky first semester, but eventually graduated from Slippery Rock with a B.S. in health and physical education. She played basketball, softball, field hockey, and tennis during her time there. She earned a master's degree from Slippery Rock in 1972.

In 1971 she accepted a position as assistant professor of recreation, health, and physical education at Cheyney State College in Cheyney, Pennsylvania, where Bill had accepted a position. They married in September 1971 and eventually had three children, David, Janine, and Justin.

In addition to teaching, Stringer volunteered to coach basketball at Cheyney State, after volunteering to coach softball and volleyball when no one else would. She eventually became head coach at Cheney State, where she worked alongside a longtime mentor and friend JOHN CHANEY, who would later coach Temple University. Stringer built the women's program into a national powerhouse, taking the historically black college to the championship game of the first ever NCAA women's basketball tournament in 1982. Her fourteen-month-old daughter Janine contracted meningitis during that year. While coaching in the Final Four, Stringer flew between the tournament and Philadelphia, where her daughter fought for her life. The illness left her severely disabled.

By 1983 Stringer had posted a 251–51 win/loss record at Cheney State and caught the eye of the University of Iowa athletic department, which offered her their women's head coaching position. In late 1983, Stringer accepted the coaching job at Iowa, which was ranked 298 of 301 in the nation. She built Iowa into a powerhouse, going 29–2 in the 1987–1988 season. She won the Big Ten Conference title, and the program was ranked first in the nation for several weeks.

During that season, 22,157 fans packed Carver Arena for the Iowa versus Ohio State women's basketball game, a new single-game attendance record for national women's basketball games. Stringer would become the second coach and the first woman coach to advance teams from two different programs to an NCAA Final Four. However, her husband Bill, who had been her best friend and team exercise physiologist, died of a massive heart attack on Thanksgiving 1992.

Stringer returned to coaching in January 1993 and led the Hawkeyes to a 24–3 season. She lost in the semifinal game of the NCAA tournament and ended the year being named the Naismith Coach of the Year. She was also awarded the Carol Eckman Award, given to a coach who exhibits spirit, courage, coaching commitment, leadership, and service to women's basketball.

In July 1995 Stringer left Iowa, citing a need to get closer to her extended family in the East, and was named head coach at Rutgers University with what was another landmark contract. Negotiated by her brother Tim, who had become a lawyer, the contract made her not only the best-paid women's coach in the country, but also the highest-paid coach at Rutgers, surpassing the salaries of the head football coach and the head men's basketball coach.

In 2000 Stringer took the Scarlet Knights to the Final Four, the first time in Rutgers's history, and became the only coach ever to take three different programs to a NCAA Final Four.

Rutgers, under Stringer's leadership, went from 11–17 in 1995 to 28–6 in 2000 and the national semifinal game. In 2007, despite a 2–4 start to the season, Stringer took the Scarlet Knights team of five freshman and five upperclassmen, the first to win the Big East Tournament, to the Final Four again, losing the championship game to Tennessee, coached by the legendary Pat Summitt, a friend of Stringer's.

The day after the loss, shock-jock Dan Imus made disparaging and racist remarks about the team on his CBS-owned radio and television show *Imus in the Morning*, causing such controversy that he was fired for his comments. Throughout the controversy, Stringer and the Scarlet Knights remained poised and eventually accepted an apology from Imus.

Stringer has been highly recognized for her coaching and impact on women's basketball. She was inducted into the Women's Basketball Hall of Fame in June 2001. She was inducted into the Naismith Memorial Basketball Hall of Fame in September 2009. Fellow inductees that year included MICHAEL JORDAN and DAVID ROBINSON.

In April 2008 Nike built the C. Vivian Stringer Child Development Center at its World Headquarters in Oregon. The 35,000-square-foot facility included twenty-six classrooms and provided care, learning, and development for three hundred children. Stringer was the third woman, second coach, and first African American woman to have a building named after her on Nike's corporate campus.

In addition to leading U.S. basketball programs, Stringer has also coached on the international level, winning a bronze medal at the Pan American Games in Havana, Cuba, and served as an assistant coach for the gold medal–winning U.S. women's basketball team in the 2004 Olympics in Athens, Greece.

In 2010 the Rutgers Scarlet Knights lost in the first round of the NCAA tournament to Iowa, but Stringer, their creative coach and master recruiter, noted that she was looking forward to the next season. At the end of the 2010 college season, her career wins stood at over 830, the third highest among women coaches.

FURTHER READING

Stringer, C. Vivian. *Standing Tall: A Memoir of Tragedy and Triumph* (2008).

"Looking Down on Tall White Men." *The Economist*, 5 Aug. 1995, 26.

Rhoden, William C. "*Stringer's Long, Rewarding Trip to Hall of Fame.*" *New York Times*, 10 Sept. 2009.

Thomas, Katie. "*C. Vivian Stringer.*" *New York Times*, 30 Dec. 2007.

CLARANNE PERKINS

Stringer, Thomas W. (1811 [or 1815]–23 Aug. 1893), AME minister, Freemason, and Mississippi politician, was born in Maryland, but grew up in Ohio. He was described as a slightly heavy man of medium height with a light brown complexion. Although very little is known about his early life and family background, Stringer became a consequential political, religious, and fraternal leader. In tracing his career, one writer correctly surmised that wherever he went, "churches, lodges, benevolent societies, and political machines sprang up and flourished" (Wharton, 149).

Stringer joined the African Methodist Episcopal (AME) Church and was ordained in the Ohio Conference in September 1846. He subsequently moved to Canada and organized the first branch of the AME Church there. After the Civil War ended in 1865 Stringer moved to Vicksburg, Mississippi, where he served as pastor of Bethel AME Church. He was later appointed presiding elder and worked in that capacity until his death. According to one of his contemporaries, he "was known and loved by the ministers and laymen of this state as no other minister was ever known and loved." Furthermore, "wherever he went, the people, white and colored, and of all denominations, knew and respected him" (Adams, 191). Indeed, Stringer made a tremendous impact on African Methodism throughout Mississippi. Known as a great organizer, observers considered him to be one of the church's most capable missionaries. Stringer was personally responsible for converting many Mississippians to the AME Church. He traveled "passing over rough roads, through dense forests and malarial swamps, and enduring many hardships and much exposure," according to one source, "but he never shrank from duty, always punctually meeting his appointments and doing his duty" (Adams, 191).

Stringer also had a notable career in politics. According to historian Vernon Wharton, he was "the most powerful political leader of his race in the state until 1869" (Wharton, 149). Stringer served as a state senator in Mississippi starting in 1870. However, one of the highlights of his political career occurred before then when he served as a delegate at Mississippi's Constitutional Convention of 1868. One hundred delegates were at the meeting, and of that number eighty-four were white and only sixteen were black. Although fewer in number, the African American delegates tended to vote along similar lines as the native (white Republicans born in Mississippi) and Northern white Republicans who had control of the convention. Under Stringer's leadership, all black delegates, with the exception of "renegade" William T. Combash, opposed clauses in the state constitution that would have required property qualifications for membership in the state senate, restricted jury service to whites, and limited suffrage and citizenship.

Stringer took up a number of measures after being elected to the Mississippi legislature in 1870. He tried to secure a provision that would have required compulsory school attendance for all children, but the measure failed. Stringer also supported a clause in the Constitution that disfranchised Mississippians who had supported the Confederacy while holding any military rank above private. Nonetheless, overall, it was his work on the Constitution of 1868 that made the state government of Mississippi a more viable force than it had ever been. "Its greatly expanded powers and obligations, especially in matters concerning education and the judiciary placed the centralized machinery of the state in immediate contact with almost every citizen," wrote historian Wharton, and this shocked many whites "who had trusted their state government little more than they had that of the nation, and who had even been inclined to allow their county governments to become dormant" (150–151).

In October of 1868 Stringer called Bishop James A. Shorter to Vicksburg to formally recognize the AME Church in that state. At the resulting meeting, the Mississippi Annual Conference of the AME Church began. By the time the second state meeting occurred (held in Greenville), the church, under Presiding Elder Stringer's guidance, had grown exponentially. By that time the Mississippi Conference included thirty-five churches with nearly five-thousand members. In fact, the Mississippi Conference became so large that it split into regions.

Stringer also brought freemasonry to Mississippi, establishing the Stringer Lodge at Vicksburg in 1867, two years after he moved to the state. Stringer had served as the first grand master of the African American Masonic Order in Ohio and had been the District Deputy Grand Master of the territory west of Pittsburgh, Pennsylvania. After founding the Vicksburg Lodge, Stringer added chapters at Natchez and Jackson, with assistance from HIRAM REVELS and JAMES D. LYNCH. This move led to tremendous growth among black Freemasons throughout Mississippi, culminating with the establishment of the Most Worshipful Stringer Grand Lodge at Vicksburg in July 1876. On 26 March 1880 Stringer and T. M. Broadwater founded the African American order of the Knights of Pythias in Mississippi. Stringer served as its first supreme chancellor and the first grand chancellor of the state.

By 1877 the North Mississippi Conference consisted of nearly 5,300 members and sixty-two churches. Stringer's influence in the church increased so much that bishops routinely took advice from him at the annual conferences; and although he never ran for bishop, Stringer was more popular than many of them in the church. In 1880 the Stringer Grand Lodge started the Fraternal Life Insurance Benefit, which paid up to $700 to its beneficiaries. This insurance group would prove to be a long-term asset to the people of Mississippi.

Stringer not only made contributions to politics, the church, and the fraternal lodges of Mississippi, in 1890 he also became one of the founders of Campbell College, an AME Church school. The school held its first classes in the Bethel Hall located at the rear of Stringer's church in Vicksburg. Campbell College helped to provide training for African Americans during a time when Mississippi held the dubious distinction of being the Southern state that spent the least amount of money on black education. Stringer passed away in 1893.

In 1907 the Fraternal Life group paid $110,000 in claims and by 1908, over a decade after Stringer's death, the insurance provider had grown to fourteen thousand members and owned one thousand acres of land along the Yazoo and Mississippi Valley Railroad.

When BOOKER T. WASHINGTON visited Mississippi in 1908, CHARLES BANKS, his most trusted lieutenant in the state, began to collect information about the cities he had scheduled Washington to visit and was asked to give him names of prominent people who lived in each one. Banks told Washington about the tremendous legacy of Stringer and assured the Tuskegee leader that "a reference to him is easily a great hit anywhere in Mississippi, and especially in Vicksburg" (Jackson, 67).

Those who knew Stringer described him as encouraging and kind; they recalled that he exercised patience with older African Americans, especially former slaves who had no formal education. Nonetheless, he could be very strident with shiftless people and indolent ministers (Adams, 191). Stringer's reputation lived on long after his death.

FURTHER READING

Adams, Revels A. *Cyclopedia of African Methodism in Mississippi* (1902).

Jackson, David H., Jr. *A Chief Lieutenant of the Tuskegee Machine: Charles Banks of Mississippi* (2002).

Sewell, George A. *Mississippi Black History Makers* (1977).

Wharton, Vernon L. *The Negro in Mississippi 1865–1890* (1965).

DAVID H. JACKSON JR.

Strode, Woody (28 July 1914–31 Dec. 1994), film actor and athlete, was born Woodrow Wilson Woolwine Strode in Los Angeles, the son of Baylous Strode, a brick mason whose mother was a Blackfoot Indian, and Rosa Norris Strode, whose ancestors included Cherokees. Because of his imposing size—6 feet 4 inches and 215 pounds at his peak—and his physical strength and coordination, Strode first achieved renown as an athlete. At Thomas Jefferson High School in Los Angeles, he earned honors in both football and track and field (shot put, high jump, high and low hurdles), which resulted in an athletic scholarship to the University of California at Los Angeles. However Strode's scholastic credentials were insufficient, so he first had to prove himself academically. Over the next two years he took special classes, while also training for the Decathlon event at the 1936 Olympic Games, though he was not selected for the team. He finally entered UCLA in 1936. Once in college, Strode became one of the football team's star players, along with quarterback KENNY WASHINGTON and running back JACKIE ROBINSON. Strode was in such top physical condition that throughout most of his life he could complete one thousand sit-ups, one thousand push-ups, and one thousand knee bends each morning.

Strode majored in history and education at UCLA, but left school in 1940, several months shy of graduation, to earn money playing exhibition football and to work as an investigator for the Los Angeles District Attorney's office. One night Strode unexpectedly encountered Luukialuana "Luana" Kalaeloa, a Hawaiian princess whom he had first met while on a college football trip to the University of Hawaii in 1938, but who had moved to California to work as a nightclub dancer. The two were married in Las Vegas in 1941, and raised two children, a son and a daughter.

Strode lost his job as an investigator when the district attorney was voted out of office, but he continued playing football. He also began a new career as a professional wrestler, even using certain football techniques, such as the flying tackle and body block, in the ring. During World War II Strode joined the Fourth Air Force of the Army Air Forces, but spent three years playing football for the March Field Flyers in California before serving briefly in the Pacific. Following his discharge Strode returned to football, and in 1946 was signed by the Los Angeles Rams. African Americans had not played in the National Football League since 1933; Strode and Kenny Washington, who had played together at UCLA, thus broke the color line in professional football a year before Jackie Robinson did the same for professional baseball in 1947. Strode played just one season for the Rams before switching in 1948 to the Calgary Stampeders in the Canadian League, where he was named All-Pro. Unfortunately injuries he suffered on the playing field in 1949 forced his retirement from professional football.

Because professional wrestling was less hazardous, Strode resumed his career in the ring, participating in matches throughout the United States and Canada from the late 1940s to the late 1950s. Even though African American wrestlers were rare, Strode became one of the sport's headliners, often appearing on television, where he was noticed by Hollywood agents, who enticed him to try acting. His early roles were in the television series *Ramar of the Jungle*, and for feature films set in African jungles, such as *The Lion Hunters* (1951), *Bride of the Jungle* (1951), and *African Treasure* (1952). As Strode explained in his autobiography, "What they needed were some African warriors, and because of my physical presence, I fit the role better than the actors. With me, all they had to do was give me a loin cloth and put a spear in my hand" (Strode, 183).

Gradually, however, Strode earned distinction as an actor, particularly by working with such renowned directors as Cecil B. DeMille in *The Ten Commandments* (1956), Lewis Milestone in *Pork Chop Hill* (1959), Stanley Kubrick in *Spartacus* (1960), Richard Brooks in *The Professionals* (1966), Sergio Leone in *Once Upon a Time in the West* (1968), Francis Ford Coppola in *The Cotton Club* (1984), and John Ford in a series of films that Strode regarded as his most notable achievements: *Sergeant Rutledge* (1960), *Two Rode Together* (1961), *The Man Who Shot Liberty Valance* (1962), and *Seven Women* (1966).

In *Sergeant Rutledge* Strode played the title character, a buffalo soldier with the 9th Cavalry, who is falsely accused of murder and rape, but exonerated in the end. Strode's character maintains his honor, dignity, and professionalism throughout the film, in a performance that resonated with the civil rights movement at the time. Equally memorable were Strode's roles as the doomed gladiator in *Spartacus*, who commands great respect even in death, and as a stoic gunslinger in *Once Upon a Time in the West*, who (in one celebrated scene, filmed in extreme close-up) calmly gulps down the water that has collected on the brim of his large black hat. This latter role was one of several appearances Strode made in Italian films, including *Black Jesus* (1968), in which he played a rebel leader based on the slain Congolese nationalist leader Patrice Lumumba.

Following the death of his wife, Luana, of Parkinson's disease in 1980, Strode married Tina Tompson, the daughter of a Las Vegas minister, in 1982. Strode continued to take acting roles up until the time of his death from lung cancer in Glendora, California. Even though he was never a vocal exponent for civil rights and even though he would accept almost any role that was offered him—once telling *The New York Times* that "If the money was right, I'd play Mickey Mouse" (Hunter, D5)—Strode's pioneering achievements as football player, wrestler, and Hollywood actor served to illustrate the way he overcame racial barriers through talent, self-determination, and pragmatism. "It wasn't that Strode was mercenary," one film historian has concluded. "Rather, he believed that the way to break down prejudice was to demonstrate your ability and not depend upon someone's goodwill" (Manchel, 39).

FURTHER READING

Strode, Woody, and Sam Young. *Goal Dust: An Autobiography* (1990).

Burrell, Walter Rico. "Whatever Happened to … Woody Strode" *Ebony* (June 1982).

Campbell, Jim. "Woodrow Wilson Woolwine Strode," in *Scribner Encyclopedia of American Lives* (2001).

Hunter, Charlayne. "Woody Strode? 'He Wasn't the Star But He Stole the Movie.'" *New York Times*, 19 Sept. 1971, D5.

Manchel, Frank. "The Man Who Made the Stars Shine Brighter: An Interview with Woody Strode." *The Black Scholar* (Spring 1995).

Regester, Charlene. "From the Gridiron and the Boxing Ring to the Cinema Screen: The African-American Athlete in Pre-1950 Cinema." *Culture, Sport, and Society* (June–Oct. 2003).

Ross, Charles K. *Outside the Lines: African Americans and the Integration of the National Football League* (1999).

JAMES I. DEUTSCH

Strong, Ted (2 Jan. 1917– c. 1955), professional basketball and baseball player, was born in South Bend, Indiana. Theodore "Ted" Strong was quickly initiated into the culture of basketball for which Indiana was recognized. By the age of eighteen he already had gained the height and skill required to play professionally and quickly became the team captain of the Harlem Globetrotters. Strong's large hands gave him the unique ability to "palm" the ball; thus, he was deemed the team's "pitcher," hurling remarkably accurate full-court passes to teammates waiting under the basket. Like many other Globetrotters (sixteen players in the team's early history), Strong used the basketball season to get in shape for the upcoming baseball season; by age twenty he had been signed to play with the Indianapolis Athletics. Yet Strong would continue to be an integral part of the Globetrotters for more than a decade.

Strong, however, proved to be just as skilled in baseball—as he was immediately voted to the Negro League West's All-Star team in his first year with the Athletics In 1938 he was traded to the Indianapolis ABC's and again made the West's All-Star team that year. However, it wasn't until 1939, after Strong had been traded to the Kansas City Monarchs, that he truly began to excel and live up to his potential.

While playing for the Monarchs in the 1940s, Strong went to the East-West All-Star game five times, for three different positions (first baseman, shortstop, and outfielder). One year he was even named an All-Star at two different positions—first base and shortstop. Strong's contributions helped the Monarchs win four consecutive Negro League pennants, from 1939 to 1942. In 1946 the Monarchs won the pennant once again and faced the Newark Eagles in the Negro League World Series. At a crucial point, with the series tied three games apiece and a decisive game seven still to be played, both Strong and SATCHEL PAIGE (the Monarchs' scheduled starting pitcher for the final game), were no-shows, and the Monarchs dropped the game to the Eagles, 3–2. Allegedly, both Strong and Paige had been busy working out their contracts for the next season.

As an infielder, Strong was one of the best in the game. His large hands gave him the ability to field ground balls one-handed, a skill looked down upon by old-timers who accused Strong of showboating. It would seem, to some extent, that the "clowning" nature of the Globetrotters did make its way into Negro League baseball—and Strong may have been partly responsible. As a hitter, Strong was naturally right-handed but could also switch-hit. He hit for both power and average; and in 1946 he led the Negro American League in home runs and RBIs. Every year he played with the Monarchs he hit in the mid-.300s, and his career batting average was well over .300.

In fact, it would seem that the only passion Ted Strong possessed that matched his passions for baseball and basketball was his passion for alcohol; and, unfortunately, alcohol won out in the end. After JACKIE ROBINSON broke Major League Baseball's color barrier in 1947, Strong was thought to be another possible choice to further organized baseball's integration, but years of substance abuse had worn away his talents. It has been said that he could have been the greatest two-sport athlete ever were it not for his drinking. As Negro League All-Star Sherwood Brewer commented, "[Ted Strong] could do everything. He could hit from both sides, great arm, great speed, power, hit percentage-wise, but he couldn't take care of himself. He drank, stayed out at night. He just did everything off natural ability. He was never really in shape. If he had taken better care of himself, I think he could have been better than all of them." BUCK O'NEIL, the first

African American to coach in the major leagues, said of Strong, "He could have been anything. He was that natural. ... But he, well, let's just say that if somebody offered him a drink, he took it. He did not want to insult anybody."

After playing on the 1946 and 1947 teams that defeated All-Star George Mikan and the NBA World Champion Minneapolis Lakers, at age thirty-one, Strong quit the Globetrotters in 1948. After 1949 Strong played short stints with the Indianapolis Clowns and the Chicago American Giants. He did play some years in the minor leagues, trying to make his way into the majors, but drinking had taken its toll. Strong ended his career playing in the Manitoba-Dokata league in the 1950s. It is assumed that Ted Strong died in Chicago sometime in the mid-1950s, although official records of his death are not available.

BAILEY THOMAS PLAYER

Stubbs, Frederick Douglass (16 Mar. 1906–9 Feb. 1947), pioneering surgeon, medical researcher, hospital administrator, and community leader, was born in Wilmington, Delaware, the youngest child and only son of Dr. Jeannette Bacon Stubbs and Florence Blanche Williams Stubbs's three children. The elder Stubbs (commonly referred to as J. Bacon Stubbs) was a physician highly respected by Wilmington's blacks and whites. He served on the city's Board of Health, owned vast amounts of real estate, and financed the mortgages for several black-owned buildings. The younger Stubbs had exemplary role models in both parents: Academic excellence and social consciousness permeated every facet of their daily lives. Dr. J. Bacon Stubbs earned a B.A. from Virginia Normal and Industrial Institute (now Virginia State University) in 1891 prior to earning a medical degree from Howard University in 1894. His wife (more commonly referred to by her middle name, Blanche) was an educator with a Normal Certificate from Howard University (1892). Both parents were actively involved in operating the Thomas Garrett Settlement House in Wilmington, which provided vocational and academic opportunities for the city's black youth. In addition to having his parents as role models Stubbs was closely related through his maternal line to pioneering surgeon Dr. Daniel Hale Williams.

Frederick Stubbs was both industrious and studious as a youngster, reportedly saving $1,000 in earnings from newsstands he operated seven days a week. Blessed with an innate curiosity coupled with a brilliant mind, Stubbs graduated valedictorian from Wilmington's respected all-black Howard High School (1922).

To further prepare for college, Stubbs spent the 1922–1923 school year at the prestigious Cushing Academy in Massachusetts. In the fall of 1923 he entered Dartmouth College, where his record of academic excellence continued: Stubbs was elected to membership in Phi Beta Kappa and the Beta Alpha Omega biological fraternity. As a Rufus Choate Scholar, he had a prestigious summer internship in zoological research. Stubbs was also a member of the diving team and the Dartmouth Christian Association. In 1927 Stubbs graduated magna cum laude with a B.A. in zoology. In the fall of 1927 Stubbs matriculated at Harvard Medical School, where he was reportedly the first black student to stay in the campus medical dormitory—which met with resistance. Undeterred, Stubbs continued to excel academically, becoming the first black medical student inducted into the Harvard Medical School chapter of the medical honor society Alpha Omega Alpha. Stubbs graduated cum laude with an M.D. in 1931.

Even before Stubbs graduated from Harvard Medical School, he was being quietly scouted as a candidate for a trailblazing position in Cleveland, Ohio. The Cleveland City Hospital had never had a black intern; however, several groups, spearheaded by three black Cleveland city councilmen, were determined to change the status quo. After being granted permission to appoint a black intern, an all-out search was made for a highly accomplished inaugural candidate with impeccable character. On 1 July 1931, Dr. Frederick Stubbs became the first black intern appointed to the Cleveland City Hospital (*Norfolk Journal and Guide*, 11 July 1931)—and one of the first black interns appointed to any major teaching hospital in America (Tollett, 538). Teamed with the white intern James E. Morgan, Stubbs experienced the travails and triumphs of his first full year as a physician. Despite incidents of racial insensitivity and intolerance, Stubbs prevailed and excelled. Having an interest in surgery, Stubbs trained for an additional year in general and thoracic surgery under Dr. Samuel O. Freedlander at Cleveland City Hospital. In 1933 Stubbs completed a one-year surgical residency at Philadelphia's Frederick Douglass Memorial Hospital. Founded in 1895 by Dr. Nathan Mossell, Douglass was one of the country's oldest black-run hospitals. Stubbs served his surgical residency under Dr. John P. Turner, a graduate of the Leonard Medical School of Shaw University. Turner had done postgraduate work at the University of Pennsylvania and abroad. He was a highly respected surgeon and community leader who became Philadelphia's first black medical inspector of schools, board of education member, and police surgeon. Stubbs married Dr. Turner's daughter, Marion V. Stubbs, in June 1934, and they had two daughters. Stubbs entered private practice and in 1936 was appointed by the mayor of Philadelphia as assistant surgeon at Philadelphia General Hospital—the first black physician appointed to the hospital's staff. Stubbs later completed a thoracic (chest) surgery residency at Sea View Hospital in Staten Island, New York, from 1937 to 1938. Sea View was nationally known for its research and treatment of tuberculosis (Cobb, 25), and Stubbs is believed to be the first formally trained black thoracic surgeon in America. He returned to Philadelphia for leadership positions in surgery at both Douglass Memorial Hospital and Mercy, the city's other black-run hospital. He later played a critical role along with his father-in-law in the two hospitals' merger.

Stubbs's advanced thoracic surgery training brought extraordinary advances in the surgical treatment of tuberculosis to Philadelphia, garnering him national acclaim. His pioneering work at Douglass Memorial Hospital was featured in a 1940 *Time* magazine article. Stubbs authored articles in several respected medical journals. He became a diplomat of the American Board of Surgery (1943), an associate and later a fellow of the International College of Surgeons, and a fellow of the American College of Surgery (1946). He headed Philadelphia's City Health Center and was a dedicated preceptor for surgical residents. Stubbs also served as president of both the Philadelphia Academy of Medicine and Allied Sciences and the Pennsylvania State Medical, Dental, and Pharmaceutical Association. His other memberships included the National Medical Association and the American Medical Association.

Dr. Stubbs died of a heart attack aboard a train while traveling with his wife from New York City to Long Island. Many mourned the brilliant surgeon. At the time of his death he had been appointed acting chief of Philadelphia General Hospital's Division of Tuberculosis and had been tapped to lead and develop the Jefferson Medical School Hospital's tuberculosis division, with the privilege of naming his own staff (Cobb, 26). In lamenting the incalculable loss, the famed surgeon and hematologist Dr. CHARLES DREW stated in part, "He was one of this country's great young surgeons. I know of no one of any race who had accomplished more in so short a period of time. He wrote his own record by the life he lived" (Drew, 265).

FURTHER READING
Cobb, W. Montague. "Frederick Douglass Stubbs, 1906–1947: An Appreciation." *Journal of the National Medical Association* 40, no. 1 (1948): 24–26.
Drew, Charles R. "Annual Report of the Surgical Section of the National Medical Association." *Journal of the National Medical Association* 39, no. 6 (1947): 263–265.
Tollett, Charles A., Sr. "Frederick Douglass Stubbs, M.D., F.A.C.S." In *A Century of Black Surgeons: The U.S.A. Experience*, vol. 2. Ed. Claude H. Organ Jr. and Margaret M. Koshiba (1987).
Obituaries: *Norfolk Journal and Guide*, 15 Feb. 1947; *The Philadelphia Evening Bulletin*, 10 Feb. 1947; *Philadelphia Inquirer*, 10 Feb. 1947.

ELVATRICE PARKER BELSCHES

Stubbs, Levi (6 June 1936–17 Oct. 2008), singer, was born Levi Stubbles II in the north end of Detroit, Michigan, one of eight children born to foundry worker Levi Stubbles and his homemaker wife, Daisy. For a time, the family resided in a short-lived, ill-constructed development at Dequindre and Six Mile, nicknamed "Cardboard Valley." Brother Joe Stubbs, a member of the Falcons, Contours, and Originals singing groups, and cousin JACKIE WILSON paved Levi's way into music.

At Pershing High School in Detroit, Levi befriended and sang with Abdul "Duke" Fakir. At a mutual friend's birthday party in 1954, the two young men harmonized in an impromptu quartet with Northern High students Lawrence Peyton and Renaldo "Obie" Benson. They launched a group together, the Four Aims. By 1956, Levi changed his surname to Stubbs. The group renamed themselves the Four Tops to avoid confusion with the Ames Brothers. The Tops declined to follow the fashion of other young harmony groups who named themselves after birds, like the Flamingos. Levi Stubbs explained, "That sounds great at 14, 15, 16 years old, but at 35 …" (quoted in *The Washington Post*).

The Four Tops already envisioned a long run for themselves and indeed would perform together for over forty years. Stubbs sang lead in an impassioned baritone with a generous upper register. Obie Benson sang baritone, Duke Fakir first tenor, and Lawrence Payton second tenor.

After starting out at church socials and school dances, the Four Tops sang jazz standards at Detroit and then New York City nightclubs. They toured with prominent African American artists like COUNT BASIE, BETTY CARTER, DELLA REESE, AND BILLY ECKSTINE, an early mentor. Between 1956 and 1962, the Four Tops cut singles on the Chess, Red Top, Columbia, and Riverside labels. None of these charted.

In 1960, Levi Stubbs wed Clineice Townsend, a dancer from Detroit's Ziggy Johnson revue. They had five children: Deborah, Beverly, Raymond, Levi III, and Kelly. In 1963, after watching the Four Tops sing on the "Tonight Show," Motown Records head BERRY GORDY JR. signed them onto his Detroit-based label, originally as jazz artists, until he saw their pop potential. The Tops began to collaborate fruitfully with the in-house band, the Funk Brothers, the female backing group the Adalantes, and the songwriting team of Brian Holland, LAONT DOZIER, and Eddie Holland (HDH).

The Four Tops' first single on the Billboard pop charts was "Baby I Need Your Loving" (1964). According to Gordy, when Motown staff first heard them sing it, "Levi's voice exploded in the room and went straight for our hearts" (quoted in McCollum). As his Reuters obituary observed, "Stubbs' voice began to emerge as a special ingredient. While not as rough or tough as some of his fellow R&B singers, it seemed to touch an inner sensitivity and his vocal delivery reflected the kind of preaching style of gospel and church choirs."

The Four Tops charted over thirty times during their eight years with Motown, mostly between 1964 and 1967 when HDH still worked there. The Four Tops became worldwide soul stars and in-demand nightclub performers with such well-loved hits as 1965's "Ask the Lonely," "Same Old Song," and "I Can't Help Myself"; 1966's "Reach Out and I'll Be There" and "Standing in the Shadows of Love"; and 1967's "Sugar Pie Honey Bunch," "Bernadette," and "7 Rooms of Gloom." Even after HDH left the label, the Tops came out with the likes of "It's All in the Game" (1970), "Still Water" (1970), and, with the Supremes, a remake of IKE [TURNER] AND TINA TURNER's "River Deep Mountain High" (1971).

In 1972, Levi Stubbs declined Berry Gordy's offer of the leading man role opposite DIANA ROSS in the movie "Lady Sings the Blues." Stubbs turned down many such opportunities for a solo career because he did not want to be disloyal to the other Tops. The group switched to ABC Records. Collaborating with the songwriting and production team of Dennis Lambert and Brian Potter, they charted with "Keeper of the Castle" (1972) and "Ain't No Woman Like the One I Got" (1973). After moving to the Casablanca label in 1980, they had a pop chart comeback with "When She Was My Girl" (1981).

After returning to their old label, the Tops were featured in the 1983 television special "Motown at 25." The Four Tops then took to the road with the Temptations in many "Battle of the Bands" tours. In 1986, Levi Stubbs starred in the movie *Little Shop of Horrors* as the voice of Audrey II, the man-eating plant. The same year, British musician Billy Bragg released the song "Levi Stubbs' Tears." The Tops moved to Arista Records in 1988, but focused largely on their still-thronged live concerts. In 1990, they were inducted into the Rock and Roll Hall of Fame.

In 1995, Levi Stubbs was diagnosed with cancer. Two years later, Lawrence Payton died from liver cancer. In 1999, the Four Tops were inducted into the Vocal Group Hall of Fame. In 2000, Levi Stubbs experienced a severe stroke that led him to use a wheelchair. In 2004, he made his last public appearance, in a PBS TV special celebrating the Tops' fiftieth anniversary. By then, the Tops had charted nearly forty-five times and sold over 50 million records. Obie Benson died of lung cancer in 2005.

At age seventy-two, Levi Stubbs died peacefully in his sleep at his Detroit home. He was survived by his wife Clineice, their five children, eleven grandchildren, and ten great grandchildren, along with Duke Fakir, then the lone surviving original Top, and countless fellow colleagues and fans who admired his character as much as his talent. Longtime friend GLADYS KNIGHT praised not only his "emotional, crisp with energy voice," but also his profound humility and kindness (quoted in Associated Press). The funeral took place at Detroit's Greater Grace Temple and burial at Woodlawn Cemetery. In 2009, the Four Tops received a Lifetime Achievement Grammy award. The group continued with Duke Fakir, Lawrence "Roquel" Payton Jr., Motown stalwart Ronnie McNeir, and former Temptations singer Theo Peoples.

FURTHER READING

"Artist Chart History—The Four Tops," *Billboard Music Magazine*, http://www.billboard.com, accessed 17 June 2009.

Fields, Gaylord, "Four Tops Honored with Lifetime Achievement Grammy," *Spinner*, http://www.spinner.com, 8 Feb. 2009.

The Four Tops, http://www.thefourtopsoriginal.com/
  index.html, accessed 17 June 2009.
"Levi Stubbs," Internet Movie Database, http://www.
  IMDb.com, accessed 17 June 2009.
McCollum, Brian. "Stubbs Leaves Legacy of Sound,"
  Detroit Free Press, 18 Oct. 2008.
Obituaries: Associated Press (17 Oct. 2008);
  BBC News.com (28 Oct. 2008); Billboard.com
  (17 Oct. 2008);
Detroit News (18 Oct. 2008);
The Guardian (18 Oct. 2008);
Los Angeles Times (18 Oct. 2008); National Public
  Radio (17 Oct. 2008);
New York Times (17 Oct. 2008); Reuters (18 Oct. 2008);
USA Today.com (19 Oct. 2008).

SELECT DISCOGRAPHY
Catfish (ABC/Dunhill, 1976)
The Four Tops (Motown, 1964)
Four Tops' Second Album (Motown, 1965)
Four Tops Live! (Motown, 1966)
Indestructible (Arista, 1988)
Keeper of the Castle (ABC/Dunhill, 1972)
The Magnificent 7 (with the Supremes, Motown, 1970)
Reach Out (Motown, 1967)
Still Waters Run Deep (Motown, 1970)
Tonight (Casablanca, 1981)
On Top (Motown, 1966)

MARY KRANE DERR

Stuckey, Elma (15 Mar. 1907–25 Sept. 1988), poet, was born in Memphis, Tennessee, the daughter of Frederick Spencer Johnson, a cement contractor, and Mary Cornelius Stafford. The grandchild of slaves, the young Stuckey befriended a number of former slaves in her neighborhood and was fascinated by them. She was considered a sage by adults around her, and her father, after work each evening, would ask his wife, "What did Elma say today?" On one occasion, the principal of Manassas Elementary and High School chose her to welcome the superintendent of Memphis schools, adding, "You'll know what to say."

When Stuckey was eleven, she began to write poetry, and her parents gave her a book of poems by PAUL LAURENCE DUNBAR. Together with her five sisters, she entertained the family on Saturday nights by reading her poems—which she began to hide after a sister waved aloft a poem to be read. Her parents made it clear, however, that no one was to interfere with Elma's reciting of poetry, and in time her considerable gift in that regard became evident.

The Bible, which she read nightly to her father, became an influence that later surfaced, at times in starkly ironic ways, in her poetry. Another important influence was the Negro church, in which the Negro spiritual, rich in poetic language, could be heard. In addition, while growing up in Memphis's black musical world, she was exposed to jazz and the blues at a time when both were beginning to flower. In high school, she read Shakespeare, the Brownings, William Cullen Bryant, Edgar Allan Poe, and other poets, and she was introduced to the essays of Ralph Waldo Emerson, whose appreciation of irony resonated with her own.

Stuckey attended Lane College in Jackson, Tennessee, where an aunt was married to Bishop ISAAC LANE, founder and president of the college. Within a year she received enough credits to become a rural schoolteacher, a job she held in Aubine, Tennessee, where she met a number of personalities who would later enter her poetry. In 1928, after a year in Aubine, she returned to Memphis and married Ples Stuckey, who waited tables at a local hotel; the couple would have two children.

Outrages against blacks, common for generations following slavery, continued into the 1930s. A particularly gruesome one occurred in Memphis when the head of an African American was tied to the bumper of a car and dragged down Beale Street, on which Stuckey, then in her late twenties, was employed at Johnny Mills restaurant. Though she later wrote about injustices to Memphis blacks, in the thirties especially, her poetry took a philosophical turn and began exploring tragedy. In "Shadows in the Light," the opening lines read: "The dose of life is fatal in itself/Beginning indicates there is an end"; and in "Uncertainty," there are these lines: "Those who weep at morn at eve may laugh/ Who live today tomorrow may not be." Originally conceived as stanzas in a long poem to be called "Top Hat and Cane," the stanzas were published on their own, but the initial title indicates that the young poet considered her work to be, at the least, sophisticated and polished. During the thirties and early forties the poet read her work at numerous churches and at family gatherings. It was agreed by those who heard her read that she gave voice, and indeed life, to an extraordinarily rich and varied collection of characters.

Although employment in the defense industry at Firestone Rubber Company brought good wages, in 1945 the Stuckeys moved to Chicago in search of better opportunities. She quit one job, however, when it was arranged for her to be excused from jury duty, a precious right that Memphis blacks had not enjoyed since Reconstruction.

For years after her move to Chicago, Stuckey's output of poetry did not equal her productive years of the thirties and early forties, because in addition to her responsibilities in a new environment, her family members in Memphis and Grand Rapids, Michigan, were relying on her to such an extent, she once remarked, that if she were to write an autobiography she would call it *Send for Elma*. Still, she regularly wrote poems for funerals, retirements, birthdays, and other special occasions—"a shoe box full," as she put it. She wrote other poems of ironic humor, and some of biting satire, about the Illinois Department of Labor, where she worked for years as a supervisor before she retired at age sixty to write full time. Her son, who played Pound to her Eliot, occasionally changed a word or two in a poem, but she almost invariably returned to her original wording.

Many of the poems in Stuckey's *The Big Gate* (1976) are inspired by the lives and dreams of slaves, and the play of irony and subtlety is evident everywhere in this first book. "I don't know how I got onto this slavery kick," she once remarked. The title poem of the volume introduces twenty-two characters who tell tall tales of how they tricked "Ole Marsa." Since practically the entire poem came to Stuckey in a sustained flash, with each tale distinctive yet related to the whole, "The Big Gate" is about as close to jazz improvisation as poetry can be. Blues and Negro spiritual tones are also represented in her work, as Stephen E. Henderson notes in his introduction to *The Big Gate*: "Her voice comes alive in these lines. Read them and hear … the voices of the people who created the spirituals and the blues." By the time *The Big Gate* appeared in print, Stuckey was reading widely at universities such as Stanford, Berkeley, Illinois, Harvard, and Malcolm X.

The Collected Poems of Elma Stuckey (1987) appeared when she was eighty years old. Included is "Night and Sunshine," a long narrative poem in which a white man, Woodstock, kills his wife and only child, because of his love for a woman named Sunshine. He blames the murders on a black man, Will Jamison, whom he had sought out on Beale Street allegedly to do some work for him. After shooting Jamison, Woodstock screams, "A nigger has killed my wife and child! I shot 'im, I'm holding his bloody knife!"

A long poem about Aint Rachel, a former slave, infidel, and midwife, "Ribbons and Lace," is referred to by E.D. Hirsch Jr. in his introduction to *The Collected Poems* as "a masterpiece that should find its way into standard anthologies of American poetry." Further he writes that in the *Collected Poems* the themes of *The Big Gate* are deepened and "interspersed with more contemporary, yet equally universal themes." In Hirsch's view, the poet shares a spiritual affinity with William Blake: "Not because Elma Stuckey was influenced by Blake; that is unlikely. It is because they both build upon the strengths of the ballad form and the power of an apparent simplicity that resonates within a deeply complex religious tradition." According to Hirsch, "this moving, often humorous collection of poems shows again that Elma Stuckey belongs among authentic American poets of our century." While on a visit to read poetry, Elma Stuckey died in Washington, D.C.

FURTHER READING
Elma Stuckey's papers are at the Chicago Historical Society.
DeCosta-Willis, Miriam. "Southern Folk Roots in the Slave Poetry of Elma Stuckey," *CLA Journal* 4 (1995).
Roediger, David R. "An Interview with Elma Stuckey," *Black American Literature Forum* 10 (1976).
Obituary: *New York Times*, 30 Sept. 1988.
This entry is taken from the *American National Biography* and is published here with the permission of the American Council of Learned Societies.

STERLING STUCKEY

Stump and Stumpy, comedy dance team, was comprised of James "Stump" Cross (20 June 1919–25 Jan. 1981) and Eddie Hartman (dates unknown) and, later, Harold Cromer (1921). Raised in poverty in Philadelphia, at the age of twelve Cross teamed with Hartman to perform on the local radio showcase *The Horn and Hardart Kiddie Hour*. The pair was well received, they were signed by an agent, and by the time they were teenagers they were performing regularly as the comedy dance team Stump and Stumpy.

Stump and Stumpy's dance style was an athletic and synchronized combination of tap and swing, and they also sang and performed comedic sketches with a heavy emphasis on slapstick. Their introductory number, "Rhythm for Sale," set the tone for the act, with Eddie "Stumpy" Hartman singing and James "Stump" Cross clowning, the two men joining together for vigorous partner dancing while

Stump mugged to the crowd as if he were terribly bored. One reviewer called them "the fastest moving comedy act" (*Las Vegas Review-Journal*, 24 June 1955); this momentum was achieved by their dancing skills, their physicality, and the manic, improvisational nature of their performances.

They toured extensively but made their home in New York and were mainstays of Harlem's famed Apollo Theater. In April of 1938 they broke the Apollo's attendance records when they appeared on a bill headlined by the bandleader Cab Calloway, and they worked with Calloway again later that year at the Cotton Club in the revue *Jitterbus*.

Despite their stage success, they rarely worked in films. They appeared in *Ship Ahoy* (1942), a lavish MGM musical, and *Boarding House Blues* (1948), an inexpensively made film designed for black movie houses, in both pictures performing their routine "Rhythm for Sale." Cross appeared in *This Is the Army* (1943), where he sang "That's What the Well-Dressed Man in Harlem Will Wear," and, with a different partner, he danced a number identical to the comedic bored-then-explosive jitterbug that was Stump and Stumpy's opening number.

Attaining the rank of colonel, Cross toured the European theater with the USO stage production of *This Is the Army*. Returning from the war, in 1948 he split with the increasingly unreliable Hartman and reformed the duo with Harold Cromer. A dancer who had appeared with Stump and Stumpy in *Boarding House Blues* and whose specialty act, tap dancing while wearing roller skates, showed both athleticism and comic sensibility, Cromer became the new Stumpy. They continued performing at the Apollo and touring nationally, and they appeared on high-profile television programs like *The Ed Sullivan Show* and *The Milton Berle Show*. The act remained largely unchanged, although as the men became close friends their level of personal comfort was reflected in their increasingly spontaneous performances.

With their combination of a handsome entertainer and a wildly disruptive physical comedian, with the two men occasionally joining together in the chaos, Stump and Stumpy are thought by many to be the inspiration for the white comedy team of Dean Martin and Jerry Lewis. While their black counterparts spent the 1950s touring the nightclub circuit, Martin and Lewis moved from stage to screen and were among the decade's most lucrative headliners. It is difficult to ignore the similarities of the two acts, both in tone and in specific routines. One peculiar bit of business involved Cross pulling his coat around his elbows, his hat over his eyes, sticking cigarettes in his nostrils, and barking like a walrus, something Jerry Lewis would later do, beat by beat, on the *Colgate Comedy Hour*. When asked about Stump and Stumpy, Lewis said that he drew inspiration from many black comedians, although he admitted in the same interview that "comics are thieves" (*Frontline*). Harold Cromer agreed, saying "Martin and Lewis stole from me and Jimmy" (Fox, 181), but Cross put it more charitably. "Imitation," he told his daughter, "is the sincerest form of flattery."

Stump and Stumpy officially disbanded in 1963, although both partners continued their stage work. In 1981 James Cross passed away after a long illness, leaving behind his daughters Linda Cross Gravott and June Cross, who documented her life as an abandoned mixed-race child in both the book and the PBS *Frontline* episode *Secret Daughter*. Harold Cromer continued to make numerous appearances on stage and at tap dance symposia, becoming a much-loved elder statesman for his craft. Stump and Stumpy were inducted into the Tap Dance Hall of Fame in 2008, the first comedy team given this honor.

FURTHER READING

Cross, June. *Secret Daughter* (2006).
Fox, Ted. *Showtime at the Apollo* (1983).

MALCOLM WOMACK

Sublett, Frank Ellis, Jr. (5 Mar. 1920–27 Sep. 2006), pioneer black naval officer, was born in Murphreesboro, Tennessee, one of two children of Frank E. Sr. and Rosa Sublett, who were divorced in 1931. When Sublett was about five years old, the family moved to Highland Park, Illinois, and a year later to Glencoe, Illinois, another Chicago suburb. Sublett spent most of the rest of his life in Glencoe. His education in the first eight grades was in Glencoe, and he then went to high school in nearby Winnetka. He was among the very few black students in the high school, from which he graduated in 1938, but he later recalled that he encountered no prejudice there (Stillwell, 149). As a teenager he got his first exposure to service life when he attended Citizens Military Training Camp at Fort Riley, Kansas, for two summers. He spent the 1938–1939 school year at the University of Wisconsin, where he played end on the football team and threw the discus and shot on the track team. Subsequently, he spent a year each at Northwestern University in Evanston, Illinois, and George Williams College in

Chicago, but he did not earn a degree. The advent of World War II interrupted his studies, and he did not return to college after the war ended.

Sublett enlisted in the navy in July 1942 and received his recruit training at all-black Camp Robert Smalls, part of the large Great Lakes Naval Training Station complex north of Chicago. After boot camp he began occupational training as a machinist's mate. Until earlier in 1942, African American enlisted men in the navy had been limited mostly to serving as cooks and servants for white officers. With the opening of general service ratings to black sailors, the navy established the segregated Naval Training School at Hampton Institute, in Hampton, Virginia, a civilian trade school for African Americans. In December 1942 Sublett successfully completed machinist's mate training and was rated as a petty officer second class. In January 1943 he reported to a U.S. Navy section base machine shop in Boston and the following month reported aboard the *Queen of Peace*, a converted fishing boat that patrolled in the vicinity of Boston. In May 1943 he advanced to petty officer first class and returned to the Boston machine shop.

In January 1944 Sublett was one of sixteen enlisted men who reported to Camp Robert Smalls at Great Lakes to undergo training as the first group of African American officers in the history of the navy. They were drawn from the approximately 100,000 black sailors then on active duty, chosen on the basis of recommendations from white officers and after undergoing the scrutiny of FBI background investigations. It is likely that Sublett was recommended by Commander E. Hall Downes, a Naval Academy graduate who was officer in charge of the navy school at Hampton. He had observed Sublett's performance as a battalion commander in service school. Years later, in an oral history, Sublett said of Downes, "He gave me one heck of a good compliment one day. ... He told me that he wished one thing in life, and that would be that his son Hall would grow up to be as fine a gentleman as I" (Stillwell, 153). It was a rare thing for a white man to say to a black man in Virginia in 1943.

During the officer training, the sixteen men took a two-and-a-half-month cram course in such subjects as navigation, communications, gunnery, propulsion machinery, seamanship, naval history, and the navy disciplinary system. The members of the training class resolved to succeed or fail as a group, rather than compete with each other. Thus they pooled their knowledge in after-hours sessions.

All sixteen passed, but at the end of the course in March 1944 only thirteen became officers—twelve ensigns and one warrant officer. The other three students remained as enlisted men. Years later the pioneering officers became known collectively as the "Golden Thirteen."

Upon becoming an officer, Sublett and one of the other new ensigns, JOHN REAGAN, reported back to Hampton. Sublett was an instructor in small boat handling and also served as a role model for the thousands of sailors then in training. In July 1944 he reported to San Francisco, where he served successively in two harbor craft, the patrol boat *YP-131* and the yard oiler *YO-106*. At the time black officers were not allowed to serve in combat-type ships but could go aboard auxiliary vessels with crews of black enlisted personnel. Unlike some of his cohorts in the initial group of officers, Sublett did not put white sailors on report if they failed to salute him. That was a manifestation of his easygoing approach: "Live and let live," he would say (Stillwell, 149).

In July 1945 Sublett reported to Eniwetok Atoll in the Marshall Islands, where he was in command of a contingent of black stevedores who were loading and unloading ships as the navy geared up for the planned invasion of the Japanese home islands in the autumn of the year. He was then a lieutenant (junior grade) and could have remained on active duty but chose to get out for the sake of his marriage. In March 1944 he had married Eugenia Beck right after his commissioning. He left active naval service in February 1944 and returned to civilian life in Illinois.

In the postwar era Sublett settled into the automobile business to support his family and remained in it for thirty-four years. From 1946 to 1951, he was employed by Foley Buick in Wilmette, Illinois, and from 1951 to 1980 by Grant Dean Buick in Highland Park. In that time he did body work, served as a mechanic, sold parts, was an assistant service writer, and eventually became the first black service manager for a Buick dealership in metropolitan Chicago. After his retirement from that business, Sublett worked as a male model for an agency in the Chicago area. He did work for radio and television ads, industrial films, and print advertisements. Among his roles, he portrayed Harold Washington, Chicago's first black mayor, in a television commercial.

All told, Sublett was married three times, to Eugenia Beck, Frances Stephens, and Susan Bayerl Lopez; his first two marriages ended in divorce. He was the father of four children: Frank III, Michael, and Rosanne with his first wife Eugenia, and Nicole with his second, Frances. At the time of his death in 2006 he was the last surviving member of the original Golden Thirteen.

FURTHER READING

"Reminiscences of Frank E. Sublett, Jr., Member of the Golden Thirteen," U.S. Naval Institute oral history (1989).

Stillwell, Paul, ed. *The Golden Thirteen: Recollections of the First Black Naval Officers* (1993).

Obituary: *Chicago Sun-Times*, 12 Nov. 2006.

PAUL STILLWELL

Sublett, John William. *See* Bubbles, John.

Sudarkasa, Niara (14 Aug. 1938–), educator, Africanist, and anthropologist, was born Gloria Albertha Marshall in Fort Lauderdale, Florida; nothing is known of her parents. She attended Dillard Elementary School and Dillard High School. A student of high academic prowess and promise, she skipped grade levels because of her exceptional ability and mastery of her school work and was classified as a high school junior at the age of fourteen. At fifteen she was offered and accepted early admission to Fisk University in Nashville, Tennessee, on a Ford Foundation Early Entrant Scholarship. In 1955, while a student at Fisk, Gloria attended Oberlin College as part of an academic exchange program and was exposed to an educational setting that she perceived to be a better fit for her academic interests. Consequently she transferred from Fisk to Oberlin to complete her undergraduate degree.

Sudarkasa received her bachelor's degree in anthropology and English from Oberlin in 1957 and earned her master's degree in anthropology at Columbia University in 1959. She pursued doctoral studies in Yoruba language and culture, and in 1961 she traveled to England and Nigeria to conduct research toward the completion of her dissertation (it is reported that during this time she adopted the Yoruba name Niara Sudarkasa, though she never formally changed her name). She returned from her travels abroad to complete her studies at Columbia in 1962. Immediately upon her return to the university, while still completing the work for her degree, she assumed a faculty position, becoming the first African American woman to teach at the university. She earned her doctorate from Columbia in 1964.

Sudarkasa was also the first black woman appointed as assistant professor of anthropology at New York University in 1964 and the first African American appointed to the Department of Anthropology at the University of Michigan in 1969. At Michigan she was promoted to associate professor in 1970 and full professor in 1976, the first African American woman to earn tenure there. Additionally she directed the university's Center for Afro-American Studies and was a research scientist for Columbia's Center for Research on Economic Development. Her seventeen-year career with the University of Michigan culminated in 1986 with her final position at the university as associate vice president for academic affairs.

In 1977 while still at the University of Michigan, Sudarkasa married the inventor, sculptor, and contractor John L. Clark. They have one son.

In 1986 Sudarkasa embarked on a new chapter in her academic career. She left the University of Michigan to become the first woman president of Lincoln University in Pennsylvania. She worked indefatigably to increase student enrollment, to increase the institution's competitiveness in science, math, and engineering, and to strengthen the school's connection with the continent of Africa by enhancing its international curriculum and establishing various international programs. She served as president of the institution until December 1998. Her administration succeeded in increasing Lincoln's enrollment, and during her final semester, the institution boasted a historic high of 1,500 full-time registered students. Sudarkasa is also credited with increasing the institution's public image and presence in nearby Philadelphia through the creation of an "urban center" campus and companion urban studies program. According to published reports, Sudarkasa also successfully eliminated the institution's budget deficit, through the expansion of its endowment and increased alumni donations. These accomplishments were eclipsed, however, by Sudarkasa's hasty resignation from the institution following the controversial findings in a Pennsylvania auditor general's summary report, released on 9 September 1998 (six days prior to the announcement of her impending resignation), that the university had engaged in a number of financial improprieties, including a sustained pattern of mismanagement and waste in the department of the physical plant. That facility had been under the supervision of Sudarkasa's husband Clark as Lincoln's director of physical facilities from 1988 to 1995.

This public debacle did not preclude Sudarkasa from continuing her seminal work in anthropological studies. She became a distinguished scholar in residence at the African American Research Library and Cultural Center in Fort Lauderdale. A renowned anthropologist, Sudarkasa was an authority on the roles of African women, Yoruba trade and migration in West Africa, and African and African American family structure. She conducted fieldwork in Ghana, the Republic of Benin, Nigeria, the Caribbean, and the United States. Her extensive travels took her to twenty-seven African countries. Her books and articles included *Where Women Work: A Study of Yoruba Women in the Marketplace and in the Home* (1973), *Exploring the African American Experience* (1995), and *The Strength of Our Mothers: African and African American Women and Families: Essays and Speeches* (1996).

Sudarkasa was awarded thirteen honorary degrees from U.S. and African universities and was the recipient of over one hundred civic and professional awards. A former senior Fulbright research fellow (1961) and a member of the Council on Foreign Relations (1991), she also served on many local, state, and national boards, including an appointment to the Peace Corps National Advisory Council by President George H. W. Bush (1991). In 1992, she was one of five Americans who served on the fifteen-member Trilateral Task Force on Educational Collaboration, which sought to build educational coalitions among the United States, Canada, and Mexico through North American cooperation on higher education, research, and training. In 1993, she was appointed by President Bill Clinton to the White House Commission on Presidential Scholars. She was a lifetime member of Delta Sigma Theta Sorority, Inc., the National Council of Negro Women, and the NAACP. In 2001 Sudarkasa became the first African American to be installed as a chief in the historic Ife Kingdom of the Yoruba of Nigeria.

FURTHER READING

Sudarkasa, Niara. *Education Is Still the Key: Selected Speeches and Essays.* (1998).

Lanker, Brian. *I Dream a World: Portraits of Black Women Who Changed America* (1989)

Washington, Elsie. "Niara Sudarkasa: Educator for the 1990's—President of Lincoln University," *Essence* (May 1989).

YOLANDA L. WATSON SPIVA

Suggs, Eliza G. (11 Dec. 1876–29 Jan. 1908), writer and religious worker, was born near Providence, Bureau County, Illinois, the youngest child of two emancipated slaves, Malinda (Philbrick) and Reverend James Suggs, a Free Methodist minister. Eliza's parents had met near Ripley, Mississippi, after they were both sold to a Mr. Suggs. As teens, the couple married and experienced religious conversions and after the Civil War moved to Illinois. Under slavery, the Suggses had four children: Ellen, Lucinda, Calvin, and Franklin. Afterwards they had four more daughters: Sarah, Katharine (Kate), Lenora, and finally Eliza Gertrude. Between the ages of one month and six years Eliza inexplicably broke one bone after another. Moving about and even sitting up caused her intense pain. Years later doctors speculated that she had severe rickets. Twenty-first-century physicians might evaluate her for the genetic bone disorder osteogenesis imperfecta. Yet during her childhood, medicine offered neither diagnosis nor effective treatment. Her bewildered family sewed her burial clothes, but Eliza survived. Her bones stopped breaking, and she learned to sit comfortably and use her hands well. Her height stalled permanently at thirty-three inches, and she never walked.

As her sisters learned to read and write at school, they shared their newfound knowledge with Eliza at home. Despite her quick intelligence, joy in learning, and affectionate, sociable temperament, she was unable to attend school herself until age ten, when the family moved to Logan, Kansas, a town without a schoolhouse. To Suggs's delight, her sister Sarah, a budding teacher, created a school in a large room of the family's home. Early on Suggs began to distinguish herself as a religious worker. Unlike most majority-white denominations, Free Methodists advocated racial and gender equality, and from a young age Suggs assisted her father with his evangelism, performed secretarial work for religious associations, "presided over public meetings with marked dignity and ability," and "clearly and forcibly" testified at church services as her sister Kate raised her up (Suggs, 8, 12). Wherever she needed to move, her family and friends carried her there in their arms or wheeled her in a go-cart or carriage.

The Suggs family became part of an over tenfold increase—from 82 to 8,913 people—in Nebraska's black population between 1860 and 1890. In 1888, the family moved to Orleans, Harlan County, so that several daughters could attend the Free Methodist seminary there. The next year, Eliza

Suggs's father took ill and died. His widow received a pension, and the Orleans Seminary awarded Eliza free tuition. She thrived there, winning a silver medal in the Demorest temperance speech competition. Because alcohol abuse was linked to family trauma, racial and gender justice advocates like Suggs often equated or associated drinking with enslavement. As a slave James Suggs had drunk before his religious conversion. Drunken slavemasters had harmed Eliza Suggs's mother and maternal grandmother. From youth Eliza Suggs was aware of other alcohol-affected families, too.

By her teens Suggs was an avid reader and writer. At age thirty she self-published *Shadow and Sunshine* in Omaha. The book combines vivid, engaging autobiography and family memoir, prose, and poetry. It belongs to the slave narrative genre, yet its testifying voice comes from the first post-slavery generation. After testimonies and reminiscences from her Free Methodist leaders Burton R. Jones and C. M. Damon, *Shadow and Sunshine* offers the author's prose sketches of her father, her mother, and herself, and a general reflection on slavery. These texts are interwoven with family photographs as well as hymns and poems, several by Suggs herself.

The book is the main source of information about the Suggs family. Born in North Carolina in 1831, Suggs's father was sold away at age three from his parents and twin brother Harry, never to see them again. After arriving on the Suggs plantation in Mississippi by his teens, he learned to be a blacksmith, taught himself to read and write, and earned his own money through nighttime metalworking and gardening. Eliza Suggs's mother was born in 1834 to an Alabama slave couple who also had eight sons. A Mississippi slavemaster purchased the entire family, but they were sold off one by one upon his death. Although slaves' family relations still lacked all legal protection, the young James Suggs and Malinda Philbrick risked starting their own family. In 1864 James Suggs escaped and enlisted with the Union to fight "for his freedom and that of his family" (Suggs, 20–21). After suffering many trials apart, reuniting, and moving North with their children, James and Malinda Suggs celebrated their exodus with a legally recognized wedding in 1866. James Suggs gradually became a Free Methodist preacher, achieving his exhorter's license in 1874, and working his way up to ordained elder by 1884. He ministered materially and spiritually to both blacks and whites on the Great Plains, even after a dramatic racial profiling incident. Mistaken for a fugitive black murder suspect, he was arrested at a camp meeting in Marvin, Kansas, and imprisoned. His longtime Free Methodist mentors, notably C. M. Damon, negotiated his release.

Shadow and Sunshine also presents Eliza Suggs's experiences of disability in her own words. She reveals the strong contrast between the way she viewed her situation and the way others did. Out of pity, some people asked how she could enjoy her life. She confidently answered: "It is the sunlight of God in my soul that makes me happy. … In fact many pleasures come to me through the five senses, of which I have full use" (Suggs, 66). She wrote, too, about her abundant circle of family, friends, and community members, who matter-of-factly accommodated her bodily limitations. Much to her amusement, strangers often crowded about her, mistaking her for some odd sort of infant. They either baby talked at her—"Hello sir! Boo!"—or asked her companions, "Does she have feet? Can she use her hands?"(Suggs, 57–58). Some informed her companions that they could earn large profits by exhibiting her in freak shows, then rampantly popular in the United States, but Suggs, who had visited one before, felt strongly that: "God did not create me for this purpose" (Suggs, 65–66). Freak shows visually presented persons with disabilities, often women of color, as isolated, grotesque "others" (Thomson, 55–56). By contrast the words and photos in Suggs's book neither deny nor sensationalize her disabilities, and present her as a dignified, active participant in a rich, intergenerational liberation saga.

At age thirty-one Suggs died unexpectedly from an apparent lung hemorrhage. Reverend J.W. Edwards, the presiding minister at her funeral, described the thronged event as a "love-feast" and noted that Suggs, as carrier and teller of her parents' stories, "had developed in her traits of gentleness that drew people to her" (*The Free Methodist*, 18 Feb. 1908). She also developed these traits as the carrier and teller of her own inextricably connected life story.

FURTHER READING

Marston Memorial Historical Center, Free Methodist Church of North America, Indianapolis, Indiana, holds some archival materials on Eliza Suggs, her family, and their religious denomination.

Suggs, Eliza. *Shadow and Sunshine* (1906).

Damon, C. M. "Rev. James Suggs," *The Free Methodist*, 5 June 1889.

Snyder, Howard A., *Populist Saints: B. T. and Ellen Roberts and the First Free Methodists* (2006).

Thomson, Rosemarie Garland. *Extraordinary Bodies: Figuring Physical Disability in American Culture and Literature* (1997).

Obituary: *The Free Methodist*, 18 Feb. 1908.

MARY KRANE DERR

Sul Te Wan, Madame (12 Sept. 1873–1 Feb. 1959), actress, was born Nellie (last name unknown) in Louisville, Kentucky, to Cleo de Londa and Silas Crawford Wan, a native of Hawaii who died when his daughter was young. Nellie's mother was a washerwoman whose clients included several local actresses from whom Nellie caught the acting bug. Her first performing work was in an all-black novelty act at the Buckingham Theater and New Brunswick Saloon, a high-end vaudeville and burlesque theater owned by the brothers John and James Wallen, local Democratic political bosses who ran their businesses out of the back of the theater. Nellie and her mother moved to Cincinnati, Ohio, where, using the stage name Creole Nell, she found vaudeville work in Over-the-Rhine, Cincinnati's German-immigrant neighborhood that was home to many breweries and theaters, including vaudeville, burlesque, and legitimate venues. She also performed at Cincinnati's dime museum, one of a series of popular late nineteenth- and early twentieth-century establishments exhibiting exotic objects and specimens and offering live entertainment. Sul-te-Wan later joined the Three Black Cloaks Company and performed on the legitimate stage in a touring play starring Fanny Davenport during its Cincinnati engagement. Using the growing network of theaters catering to black audiences, she eventually organized and performed with her own vaudeville touring companies, The Black Four Hundred and the Rair Black Minstrels.

Around 1906 she married her fellow performer Onest Conley and five or six years later they moved to Arcadia, California, a suburb of Los Angeles. It is not known when she began using the professional name Madame Sul-te-Wan, but all her screen and radio credits use this name. Within two years of their arrival in California, Conley deserted his wife and their three sons, Otto, Onest, and James, aged seven years to three weeks old. With help from several African American aid organizations, Sul-te-Wan and her children moved to downtown Los Angeles while she worked at the Pier Theater in nearby Venice. When she heard that the filmmaker D. W. Griffith, who had also grown up in her hometown of Louisville, was casting African Americans for his current project, Sul-te-Wan personally convinced him to hire her on the movie, then filming under the title *The Clansman*. Released in 1915 as *The Birth of a Nation*, the resulting film was a significant flashpoint in both the history of cinema and in the African American experience, spurring the growth of the fledgling National Association for the Advancement of Colored People (NAACP) and the birth of race films. The impact of the events surrounding the film and her association with Griffith directly impacted Sul-te-Wan's subsequent film career.

Pioneering a new visual and narrative vocabulary, *The Birth of a Nation*, the longest and most expensive film that had yet been produced, was a milestone in film history, introducing crosscut editing, aerial shots, mobile camera takes, various rising effects, and the employment of new storytelling techniques that formed the basis of modern filmmaking. Based on Thomas Dixon's pro-South, pro-Ku Klux Klan novels *The Clansman* and *The Leopard*, the film was also maliciously antiblack, presenting devastating depictions of African Americans and a racist treatment of the historical events of the Civil War and Reconstruction, which it argued resulted in the subjugation of whites by malevolent blacks and "mulattos." Prior to the film's release, a committee consisting of members of the Los Angeles branch of the NAACP, the Ministers' Alliance, and the Forum, filed a protest with the local Los Angeles censor board. When the censor board nevertheless passed the film, the NAACP registered a protest with the L.A. City Council arguing that the film made "an appeal to violence and outrage" by its efforts to "excuse the lynchings and other deeds of violence committed against the Negro and to make him in the public mind a hideous monster." Intervention by the National Board of Censorship's executive committee resulted in the first series of edits to the film. While *The Birth of a Nation* proved an enormous popular and financial success, over the next fifteen years, owing to protests and pressure from African American groups and their allies, the film was repeatedly banned or edited by local politicians, community groups, or theater owners across the country, further obfuscating the details of the film's original version.

In an interview with the African American journalist DELILAH BEASLEY for her 1919 book, *The Negro Trailblazers of California*, Sul-te-Wan recalled that after her first day in front of the camera, Griffith, who launched the career of a number of stars, including Mary Pickford, Lillian and Dorothy Gish, and Mae Marsh, raised her pay from three dollars to five dollars a day and expanded her on-screen role, casting her "as a rich colored lady, finely gowned and owner of a Negro colony of educated colored citizens." In the film released nationally, however, the character Sul-te-Wan described is not in the film and all major African American parts are played by whites in blackface. Sul-te-Wan appears only as a bit player, her more substantial scenes having been cut either by Griffith or by censors. The extent of her original participation and contribution to the film is not known. After *The Birth of a Nation* Griffith put Sul-te-Wan on his company's payroll at five dollars day, making her one of the first African Americans under contract to a film studio. She also recalled that Griffith fired her when associates accused her of helping to organize protests against the film, but then he reinstated her after she hired the African American lawyer E. Burton Ceruti. Although some scholars have claimed that she remained employed by Griffith for the next seven years, the extent of her working relationship with the filmmaker remains unclear. Sul-te-Wan did appear in Griffith's next film, *Intolerance* (1916).

With limited work available to black performers, she continued to work in black vaudeville and occasionally on radio with L-KO. "I get bitter sometimes," she later confided to an interviewer, "because I don't work long enough to buy a handkerchief" (quoted in Cripps, 130). Sul-te-Wan managed, however, after her screen debut in *The Birth of a Nation*, to sustain a career as a film actor for forty-three years. Cast mostly as a bit player or extra and often uncredited for her performances, Sul-te-Wan portrayed mothers and grandmothers, slaves and midwives, and most often servants. Mammies, housekeepers, cooks, and maids were her bread and butter and like other black actors in Hollywood, she played African Americans, American Indians, "gypsies," "half-breeds," and "natives."

In the silent era she appeared in three films directed by Lloyd Ingraham, *Hoodoo Ann* (1916), *The Children Pay* (1916), and *The Lightning Rider* (1924), as well as *Stage Struck* (1917) starring Dorothy Gish, *Manslaughter* (1922) directed by Cecil B. DeMille, *Who's Your Father?* (1918), *The Narrow Street* (1925), and *Uncle Tom's Cabin* (1927). After the arrival of sound technologies Sul-te-Wan made the transition to "talkies" in small parts in *Sarah and Son* (1930) and *Queen Kelly* (1929), Erich von Stroheim's

uncompleted big-budget feature film, which was never completed having been halted mid-production by producer and star Gloria Swanson.

In the 1930s and 1940s she worked alongside many of the era's biggest Hollywood stars, including Barbara Stanwyck in *Ladies They Talk About* (1933), Fay Wray in *King Kong* (1933) and *Black Moon* (1934), Melvyn Douglas in *The Toy Wife* (1938) and *Tell No Tales* (1939), Jane Wyman in *Torchy Plays with Dynamite* (1939), and Douglas Fairbanks Jr. in *Safari* (1940). She worked in B movies, including *Pagan Lady* (1931), *The Thoroughbred* (1930), *King of the Zombies* (1941), and *Revenge of the Zombies* (1943) and under the groundbreaking directors G. W. Pabst in *A Modern Hero* (1934) and Preston Sturges in *Sullivan's Travels* (1941). Although her work in these films was often limited to small roles, Sul-te-Wan turned in larger supporting performances as "Voodoo Sue" in *Heaven on Earth* (1931), "Hattie" in *In Old Chicago* (1937), "Lily" in *Kentucky* (1938), "Naomi" in *Maryland* (1940), and, most significantly, "Tituba" in *Maid of Salem* (1937).

In 1934 Sul-te-Wan played a cook in *Imitation of Life*, one of the only Hollywood films of the period to directly explore racial themes. The film starred Claudette Colbert and LOUISE BEAVERS, with whom Sul-te-Wan had appeared in three previous films. She worked with most of early Hollywood's black actors, including HATTIE McDANIEL, Noble Johnson, Ben Carter, and George Reed, there is no record that she ever worked with OSCAR MICHEAUX, Noble and GEORGE JOHNSON of the Lincoln Motion Picture Company, or other black filmmakers producing race films, or films made specifically for black audiences. In 1954 Sul-te-Wan appeared as the grandmother of the title character played by DOROTHY DANDRIDGE in *Carmen Jones*, costarring HARRY BELAFONTE, PEARL BAILEY, and DIAHANN CARROLL and directed by Preminger. Playing Dandridge's grandmother on-screen led to persistent misidentification of Sul-te-Wan as the real-life mother of Ruby Butler Dandridge, Dorothy Dandridge's mother.

Sul-te-Wan continued working even into her eighties, appearing in *Something of Value* (1957) starring Rock Hudson, *The Buccaneer* (1958) starring Yul Brenner, and *Tarzan and the Trappers* (1958). In 1957 her career came full circle, when she was cast in *Band of Angels* (1957), directed by Raoul Walsh, whom she had met forty-two years earlier when he played John Wilkes Booth in *The Birth of a Nation*.

Publicity photos show a pretty, slight woman, beautifully dressed and bejeweled. After her divorce from Conley, Sul-te-Wan was briefly married to William Holt, a man she described as a "German count." In 1943, at the age of seventy, she married Anon Ebenthur, a white interior decorator twenty-two years her junior.

Sul-te-Wan died in 1959 at the age of eighty-six. At the time of her death she was living at the Motion Picture Country Home in Woodland Hills, California, home to Hattie McDaniel until her death in 1952 and Billy Bitzer, the innovative cinematographer who shot *The Birth of a Nation*, who died in 1944.

FURTHER READING

Beasley, Delilah L. *The Negro Trailblazers of California* (1919, repr. 1997).

Cripps, Thomas. *Slow Fade to Black: The Negro in American Film* (1977, repr. 1993).

LISA E. RIVO

Sullivan, Leon Howard (16 Oct. 1922–24 Apr. 2001), Baptist clergyman, civil rights leader, and human rights activist, was born in Charleston, West Virginia, the son of Charles Sullivan, a truck driver, and Helen Trueheart, a domestic. Because his parents were frequently away from home working, Sullivan was reared by his maternal grandmother, Carrie, to whose influence he credited his strong religious faith, firm determination, and lifelong philosophy of self-help.

One particular childhood experience helped inspire Sullivan's passion for social justice. At age eight, he bought a Coke at the local drugstore but was forbidden to sit down by a white clerk, who angrily informed him that blacks were always required to stand. Sullivan recounted this abuse to his grandmother, who encouraged him to help end such prejudicial treatment when he grew up.

Six feet, five inches tall and a gifted athlete, Sullivan received a basketball and football scholarship to the historically black West Virginia State College. When an injury ended his athletic career, he paid for his education by working in a steel mill. He also became a Baptist preacher at age seventeen and served part time as pastor at two local churches. After earning a B.A. degree in 1943, Sullivan became assistant minister to ADAM CLAYTON POWELL JR., New York congressman and pastor of the Abyssinian Baptist Church in Harlem. Sullivan oversaw church programs addressing youth issues, crime, and drugs. He also served, at age twenty-two,

under A. PHILIP RANDOLPH in the March on Washington movement, an experience that helped shape Sullivan's ideas regarding nonviolent direct action and community mobilization.

In New York, Sullivan met Grace Banks; they married in 1944 and had three children, Howard, Julie, and Hope. In 1945 Sullivan became pastor of the First Baptist Church in South Orange, New Jersey, and began experimenting with new models of church ministry, such as building homes for the poor and lobbying the city for better opportunities for blacks. He also continued his formal education at Union Theological Seminary and Columbia University.

In 1950 Sullivan moved to Zion Baptist Church in downtown Philadelphia, Pennsylvania, where he served as pastor for thirty-eight years, expanding his congregation from six hundred to more than six thousand members. He was nicknamed "the Lion of Zion" for his powerful preaching style and his intrepid manner of tackling seemingly intractable social issues. In Philadelphia, Sullivan studied the nature of corporate business in America, mainly through his participation in Americans for the Competitive Enterprise System and the Junior Chamber of Commerce. He perceived that in cities with substantial black populations, such as Philadelphia, minority purchasing power was integral to corporate profitability and that organized action by black consumers could thus redirect corporate conduct to socially responsible ends.

In 1958 Sullivan organized a network of four hundred African American preachers who exhorted their congregations to boycott businesses that declined to employ blacks in managerial and professional positions, adopting a slogan used by his mentor, Powell, in Harlem during the Depression: "Don't buy where you don't work." Within four years three hundred Delaware Valley employers adopted fair employment practices as a result of this campaign. This program became the model for the nationwide Operation Breadbasket movement, led by MARTIN LUTHER KING JR. and later by JESSE JACKSON.

Recognizing that "integration without preparation is frustration," Sullivan founded in 1964 a training initiative called Opportunities Industrialization Centers (OICs) to help the poor, including the long-term unemployed, school dropouts, and those with criminal records, develop the skills required for newly opening career possibilities. The first OIC was headquartered in one of the poorest neighborhoods in Philadelphia. Schoolchildren collected pennies to provide financing, and in the early years Sullivan remortgaged and then borrowed against his home to meet payroll. Sullivan developed OICs in 140 American cities, and it became the largest employment-training program in the nation.

OIC won the enthusiastic support of President Lyndon Johnson, who regarded it as a vital contribution to the War on Poverty and worthy of federal financial support. Sullivan also opened OICs abroad. Three million people thus far have been prepared by OIC for employment at some twenty thousand companies. Additional Sullivan initiatives created black-owned shopping centers, apartment complexes, assisted living centers, an aerospace manufacturing company, and other facilities, often through modest weekly contributions or investments by members of Zion Baptist Church and other supporters.

In 1971 Sullivan became the first person of color on the board of directors of a major American corporation when he joined General Motors (GM), then the largest company in the world and the largest American employer in South Africa. On his initial visit to South Africa in 1975, Sullivan witnessed first hand the dehumanizing consequences of apartheid. Further, on his return journey he was detained at the Johannesburg airport by the security police, who stripped him to his underwear and menaced him with a. 45-caliber pistol. At that moment Sullivan determined to take up personally the challenge of abolishing apartheid through nonviolent, economic measures.

The GM board agreed to Sullivan's unprecedented proposal that the company take the lead in organizing American corporations against apartheid. For two years, Sullivan held private meetings with the leaders of over one hundred companies, although on 1 April 1977 only twelve of them endorsed Sullivan's initial "Principles for U.S. Firms in South Africa." These principles challenged apartheid statutes by requiring workplace racial integration, fair employment practices, training and supervisory positions for blacks and other nonwhites, and eventually improved housing, schooling, recreation, and health facilities for workers. The media dubbed these antiapartheid measures "the Sullivan Principles," and the name permanently stuck.

Sullivan's principles were expanded five times over eleven years, bringing corporations into increasing conflict with the South African government and ultimately constituting a program of corporate civil disobedience against apartheid within the workplace and in the larger society. At the height of the campaign, 194 American companies subscribed to the principles, representing $500 billion in stocks and investments. This was perhaps the first time in history that companies organized to defy and undermine a nation's laws in order to overturn an unjust system of government.

Sullivan was criticized by some who favored corporate withdrawal from South Africa, but such detractors were generally unaware that Sullivan was continually laboring behind the scenes and conferring with corporate leaders to increase pressure on the South African government. He threatened, for example, to organize a worldwide boycott of South African diamonds. Sullivan endured such criticism in silence, and even weathered numerous death threats, believing that his approach was the best way to avoid a race and ideological war that could engulf all of southern Africa. On 7 May 1985 Sullivan issued a two-year deadline for the South African government to end apartheid or face the economic effects of the departure of American companies. Overriding President Ronald Reagan's veto, the U.S. Congress then passed the omnibus Anti-Apartheid Act of 1986, requiring American corporations to comply with the principles. Some seventy corporations left South Africa when the deadline passed. The South African government repealed the apartheid laws by 1991, and in successive years nonwhites were given the vote, and Nelson Mandela was elected president. Most of the corporations then returned. As a complement to the resistance to apartheid undertaken by South Africans themselves, Sullivan's principles made a unique contribution toward rendering apartheid financially unsustainable and provided models of integration for a new, postapartheid society.

The dismantling of apartheid allowed Sullivan to devote additional time to other initiatives. In 1983 he had founded the International Foundation for Education and Self-Help (IFESH), a private, nongovernmental organization addressing development issues, primarily in sub-Saharan Africa but also in Latin America and Asia. He moved to Scottsdale, Arizona, the foundation's headquarters, to become more directly involved in its work of building schools, training teachers, educating bankers, promoting agricultural development, and combating HIV/AIDS. He also convened a series of "African–African American Summits" to develop intercontinental strategies regarding Africa's distinctive developmental needs and opportunities. In his last major initiative, Sullivan expanded his original antiapartheid principles into a world-wide code of conduct termed the "Global Sullivan Principles of Social Responsibility" (GSP), which he announced in November 1999 at the United Nations. Seventeen months later, at the time of his death, over three hundred corporations, civic organizations, and academic institutions had endorsed the GSP.

In 1998 Sullivan published an autobiography, *Moving Mountains: The Principles and Purposes of Leon Sullivan*. Three years later, having recovered from leukemia a decade earlier, he succumbed in Scottsdale to a recurrence of the disease. Shortly after his death, family members, friends, and supporters created the Leon H. Sullivan Foundation, headquartered in Washington, D.C., to continue his work.

Sullivan was one of the most honored Americans of his time. In 1963 *Life* magazine named him one of the "100 Outstanding Young Adults in the United States." He received numerous awards, including fifty honorary doctorates and the 1971 Spingarn Award, the NAACP's highest honor for achievement. President George H. W. Bush conferred upon him the Presidential Medal of Freedom, President Bill Clinton presented him with the Eleanor Roosevelt Human Rights Award, and he was several times nominated for the Nobel Peace Prize. In 2000 the city of Charleston dedicated "Leon Sullivan Way," honoring a man who as a child could not even walk down certain streets simply because he was black. Representatives of scores of foreign countries attended his funeral in Arizona and a memorial service at the Zion Baptist Church in Philadelphia.

Sullivan was a relentless innovator who understood that blacks and other oppressed minorities hold in their own hands the economic power to resist injustice and secure political, social, and financial equality. His work went far toward helping corporations understand that their range of responsibilities extends beyond obeying the law and producing profits for shareholders. Through Sullivan's influence, many corporations now recognize their obligations to a more diverse set of "stakeholders," appreciating that addressing the needs of the disadvantaged and actively supporting economic, educational, and social development are not only key elements of responsible corporate conduct, but are also good for business itself.

FURTHER READING

Sullivan's papers are scheduled to be housed in the Library of Congress.

Sullivan, Rev. Leon Howard. *Moving Mountains: The Principles and Purposes of Leon Sullivan* (1998).

A Principled Man: Rev. Leon Sullivan. Marshall University and MotionMasters (Videocassette, 2000).

Obituaries: *New York Times*, 26 Apr. 2001; *Washington Post*, 29 Apr. 2001.

THOMAS J. WLY

Sullivan, Maxine (13 May 1911–7 Apr. 1987), singer and instrumentalist, was born Marietta Williams in Homestead, Pennsylvania. The names of her parents are unknown, and it remains unclear why or when she began using the surname Sullivan. In an interview Sullivan credited her uncle, Harry Williams, a bandleader, with influencing her musical career, which she began as an occasional singer with his band, the Red Hot Peppers, in small clubs in and around Homestead during the late 1920s.

Sullivan had no formal musical training and later claimed that she "never made a conscious effort to become a singer." During her late teens and early twenties she supported herself as a waitress, singing whenever she had the chance. Pittsburgh was nearby and afforded her more exposure when her uncle introduced her to pianist Jennie Dillard. She and Dillard worked together as a duo that was popular as the "filler" between band sets. In the early thirties they performed regularly at the Benjamin Harris Literary Club, a private, after-hours club that was a favorite spot for musicians and singers in the swing bands that played in Pittsburgh. She was thus exposed to influential musicians such as DUKE ELLINGTON, CAB CALLOWAY, EARL HINES, and FATS WALLER. Gladys Mosier, the pianist with the Ina Ray Hutton all-women's band, heard Sullivan at the club in 1937 and encouraged her to go to New York to try out for the big clubs. Sullivan and Dillard, who had developed a close professional relationship, followed Mosier's advice and moved in with Dillard's brother while they pursued performing opportunities. Sullivan brought with her a letter of introduction to the Mills Music Company from Shirley Heller, a member of a Pittsburgh theatrical company; she also made a connection with pianist-arranger Claude Thornhill through Mosier. By the end of their first week in New York, she and Dillard landed a job as the intermission act at the famed Onyx Club. Thornhill and Mosier put Sullivan under contract and sought ways to bring her to the attention of a larger audience.

When Sullivan began at the Onyx Club, the backup band included JOHN KIRBY on bass,

FRANKIE NEWTON on trumpet, BUSTER BAILEY on clarinet, and PETE BROWN on alto saxophone. Later, trumpeter CHARLIE SHAVERS replaced Newton, and RUSSELL PROCOPE replaced Brown. With Billy Kyle on piano and O'Neill Spencer on drums, Kirby formed his first sextet. Sullivan worked with the ensemble for nearly two years. In 1939 Thornhill signed the Kirby group, along with Sullivan, to record "Loch Lomond," which eventually became Sullivan's signature piece. Like most inexperienced performers, she did not know her contractual rights, and she agreed to a flat twenty-five dollar fee for the recording. Thornhill, who had adapted the public domain melody, garnered composer royalties, but Sullivan received the acclaim. Her mellow, graceful rendition demonstrated that she was a popular music vocalist of the highest order.

The recording's success aroused the ire of some song traditionalists who decried the "jazzing up" of old favorites, and a Detroit radio station refused to air it. The protest earned more attention for the song and the singer, and the Columbia Broadcasting System hired her and Kirby's band for a network radio show, *Flow Gently, Sweet Rhythm*. By this time Sullivan and Kirby were married, and their program achieved enough popularity to stay on the air for two years. Sullivan also starred in a Broadway show patterned after the program. These successes resulted in a substantial salary increase for Sullivan, who recognized that, while she was fortunate to be earning money in show business, her compensation was not equal with that of other performers. She said that she went from making "forty dollars a week at the Onyx Club to eighty and then one hundred fifty, which in the late 1930s was considered a great deal of money for anyone, ... for a colored girl it was a fortune. Yet, I was making less than singers with some of the large bands who had a lot less talent than I."

Sullivan and LOUIS ARMSTRONG starred on Broadway as Bottom and Tatiana, respectively, in *Swingin' the Dream* (1939), a variation on William Shakespeare's *A Midsummer Night's Dream*. The show ran for only thirteen performances, even though it featured Benny Goodman's sextet and an Eddie Condon–led group. Sullivan had gained enough attention to get a tiny part in the 1939 film remake of *St. Louis Blues*, starring Dorothy Lamour and Lloyd Nolan, but she soon experienced Hollywood's lack of respect for black talent. She said, "The movie had nothing to do with W.C. HANDY, and I played a waif washing clothes ... with the usual bandanna on my head." Sullivan's other Hollywood role was as another singing maid in *Going Places* (1938) with Louis Armstrong and Dick Powell. She returned to New York and resumed singing with Kirby and his band until their marriage dissolved in 1941. She then began to perform as a single. After touring with Benny Carter in 1941, Sullivan returned to her native state in 1942 for what she described as a brief break. She was back on the scene in New York by 1943, performing as a single with Goodman, Glen Gray and his Casa Loma Orchestra, and the Johnny Long and Henry Busse bands. With New York as her base, she performed regularly on the club circuit in Chicago, Philadelphia, and other cities for the next ten years.

Sullivan's marriage in the early fifties to Cliff Jackson, one of Harlem's great stride pianists, brought another change in her career. In 1956 she retired from singing to devote her energies to being a wife, mother, and PTA leader. She spent the next decade working in her daughter's school as a volunteer, serving as a school aide, and acting as secretary to the East Bronx Community Council. During that period she studied the flügelhorn and valve trombone and became reasonably accomplished on both instruments. She added an instrumental portion to her act because she felt she needed a gimmick to make her show more appealing to new and younger audiences.

She and Jackson performed around the city in community and public concerts, but she did not return to show business full time until 1970, when she appeared with Yank Lawson and Bob Haggart's The World's Greatest Band. Her singing was still refined, crystalline, and flowing, with the lilting swing that she had introduced in the thirties, but the surprise was her ability on valve trombone and flügelhorn. Nevertheless, it was her singing that kept her going into the late 1970s. She recorded several albums, including *It Was Great Fun* (1983), usually to the accompaniment of well-polished small groups. Her repertoire stuck to the popular ballads and standards that she interpreted best, such as the Duke Ellington songs "I Didn't Know About You," "Don't Get Around Much Anymore," and "I Got It Bad (and That Ain't Good)," and Hoagy Carmichael's "Skylark" and "Georgia On My Mind." She finally gained wide recognition from the music industry when her album *The Great Songs from the Cotton Club* was nominated for a 1986 Grammy Award.

In a career that spanned more than fifty years, Sullivan was an inimitable singer of jazz and popular ballads. Despite her petite size and quiet demeanor, she had a big voice and sang with great assurance. Although the public remembered her best for "Loch Lomond," other singers and instrumentalists admired her polished swing style and silky, refined, rich voice. She was a singer's singer whose artistry won the praise and respect of several generations of musicians and jazz lovers. She died in New York City.

FURTHER READING
Crowther, Bruce, and Mike Pinfold. *Singing Jazz: The Singers and Their Styles* (1997).
Friedwald, Will. *Jazz Singing: America's Great Voices from Bessie Smith to Bebop and Beyond* (1996).
Shaw, Arnold. *52nd Street: The Street of Jazz* (1977).
Travis, Dempsey J. *An Autobiography of Black Jazz* (1983).
This entry is taken from the *American National Biography* and is published here with the permission of the American Council of Learned Societies.

DAPHNE DUVAL HARRISON

Sumlin, Hubert (16 Nov. 1931–), blues guitarist, was born on a farm in Greenville, Mississippi. Raised in Arkansas in a family of thirteen children, Hubert dabbled with drums but switched to guitar when his older brother A. D. made a makeshift guitar by stringing wires on the wall. Hubert's mother Anne bought him a real guitar after he made a fuss. He played in church, but he offended his mother by playing in a bluesy style that was considered the "devil's music." He left home to play area juke joints and ended up playing in a band with harmonica player James Cotton. They played around the greater Memphis area, and he recorded with Cotton for the Sun record label in 1954. Sumlin married a woman named Alberta when he was just sixteen years old, but the union was never legalized and ended after twelve months. As a teenager, Hubert would go to hear HOWLIN' WOLF (Chester Burnett) and his band at Silkhairs, a juke joint in Seyypel, Arkansas, beside the Mississippi River. The underage Sumlin crawled under the club, which was raised up on cement blocks. He was enthralled with the music. Another time, Sumlin climbed a stack of Coca Cola crates behind a window at the back of the club. From there, he had a bird's-eye view of Wolf's powerful band. Suddenly, Sumlin fell through the window from his shaky perch and landed right on top of Howlin' Wolf. The club owner tried to throw Sumlin out, but Wolf insisted the boy stay. He sat

Hubert Sumlin performs with Little Feat during the Sixth Annual Jammy Awards at the Theater at Madison Square Garden in New York City on 20 Apr. 2006. (AP Images.)

Sumlin down on a chair between guitarists Willie Johnson and Pat Hare so Sumlin could take in the music while nursing a glass of water. He got an earful of wild blues guitar; and after the show, Wolf drove him home and asked Sumlin's mother not to punish him—he just wanted to hear the music.

Howlin' Wolf was already a legend throughout the South, having learned from CHARLIE PATTON who is generally regarded as the father of the Delta Blues. He had recorded sides at Sam Phillips's Memphis Recording Service for release on both the Chess and RPM labels by the time Leonard Chess convinced him to move to Chicago. His band, however, preferred to stay in Memphis, and after going to Chicago alone and establishing himself, Wolf asked Sumlin to join his band. Sumlin was twenty-one years old in 1954 when he boarded the train Wolf told him to take. He was met at the station in Chicago by OTIS SPANN, the great blues pianist, and put up in an apartment building owned by the Chess family.

Sumlin was soon accompanying Wolf on classic recordings such as "No Place to Go," "Evil," and "Forty Four." As the junior guitarist in Wolf's band, Sumlin would play with the more seasoned guitarists Willie Johnson and Jody Williams on tracks such as "Smokestack Lightnin'-" and "Sittin' on Top of the World." Though he recorded on Wolf sessions over the years with guitarists such as JIMMY ROGERS, FREDDIE KING, BUDDY GUY, and several others, Sumlin was the constant in Wolf's sound.

Wolf's band performed around Chicago several nights a week and continued to tour the South, where they drew large crowds. Though paternalistic with his band members, particularly with Sumlin, whom he treated like a son, Wolf was a rough taskmaster who demanded promptness and professionalism. He could resort to violence to get his point across. Recognizing that Sumlin still hadn't reached his full potential as a guitarist, Wolf once berated and humiliated him onstage, suggesting that he drop his pick and use his fingers instead. Sumlin left the stage for home, but when he returned, he had left his picks behind and used only his fingers. This allowed him to get even closer to his guitar and provide a more vocal-like sound to compliment Wolf's voice. His skittering, slippery style became the perfect foil to Wolf's sound. Indeed, aside from a seven-month hiatus in 1956, during which time Sumlin left Wolf for a stint in MUDDY WATERS's band, Sumlin was a mainstay in Wolf's band for the rest of Wolf's life.

In Chicago, he married Evelyn Cowans, who became the band's photographer and secretary. They were married for twelve years, but their relationship was tempestuous. Sumlin was quiet and shy off-stage, but he argued and fought with Evelyn continuously, and it was she who eventually knocked out Sumlin's front teeth.

By the early 1960s, blues music began losing favor with the younger African American audience. Waters's recording career hit a dry spell, but his only rival, Howlin' Wolf, continued to enjoy hit recordings such as "Wang Dang Doodle," "Back Door Man," and "Spoonful" (all WILLIE DIXON compositions), thanks in large part to the modern sound of Sumlin's guitar. These songs would be covered a few years later by blues singer KOKO TAYLOR and by rock groups such as the Doors and Cream. Sumlin had now become Wolf's featured guitarist and contributed his slithering style to such gems as "Built For Comfort," "300 Pounds of Joy," "I Ain't Superstitious," "the Red Rooster" (covered by the Rolling Stones), and the classic "Killing Floor." Influential rock acts took notice of Sumlin's unique and unpredictable guitar playing and imitated his sound. Howlin' Wolf and Sumlin were seen by a large white audience for the first time on the ABC music show *Shindig* in 1965, and they followed that appearance with a tour of Europe. In 1971 the pair flew to England to record the *Howlin' Wolf London Sessions* with British stars such as Eric Clapton, Steve Winwood, and the Rolling Stones' Bill Wyman and Charlie Watts. The resulting album was a hit, further exposing Wolf and Sumlin to a wider audience.

Howlin' Wolf passed away in 1976. Sumlin regained his footing after moving to Austin, Texas, and became a fixture at the famous Antone's blues club, where he would influence the up-and-coming Vaughan brothers, Jimmie and Stevie Ray. Sumlin began recording as a bandleader, including the albums *Heart and Soul* (1989), *Blues Anytime* (1994), and *About Them Shoes* (2003), which was his first record to reach the *Billboard* blues charts.

In 1982 Sumlin married Willie "Bea" Reed, a cousin of blues piano great Sunnyland Slim. In 1991 they bought a home in a Milwaukee suburb. Bea died in 1999. Sumlin survived the removal of a cancerous lung in 2004 and continued to play the blues at festivals and clubs all over the world. Over the years, his dynamic and eccentric style influenced countless legendary guitarists such as JIMI HENDRIX and Clapton.

FURTHER READING

Gordon, Robert. *Can't Be Satisfied: The Life and Times of Muddy Waters* (2002).

Harris, Sheldon. *Blues Who's Who* (1981).

Moanin' At Midnight: The Life and Times of Howlin' Wolf (2004).

MARK S. MAULUCCI

Summer, Donna (31 Dec. 1948–17 May 2012), singer and songwriter, was born LaDonna Adrian Gaines in Boston, the third of seven children of Mary Ellen Davis and Andrew Gaines. In 1955 the Gaines family moved out of the projects to a predominantly white working-class section of Boston. The family was religious, so it is not surprising that Summer's first public performance at age ten was in the Grant African Methodist Episcopal (AME) Church. Inspired by the records of the black gospel singer MAHALIA JACKSON, Summer developed a powerful but controlled singing style. Everything from jazz to gospel and rhythm and

Donna Summer during her concert at the Universal Amphitheater in Los Angeles, Ca., on 11 Aug. 1979. (AP Images.)

blues and rock interested her, and she longed for a singing career.

In 1967 Summer joined the otherwise all-white and all-male Boston rock band Crow. The band had a strong local following but broke up the following year. Summer quit school and moved to New York City to pursue a musical theater career. She accepted a role in the Munich production of *Hair*, a controversial antiestablishment musical. In Germany she received a warm reception. Europe in the 1960s exhibited more tolerant attitudes toward blacks than did the United States. After the end of *Hair*'s Munich run, Summer took a role in the Austrian production and honed her performance skills in several other musical theater productions. The early 1970s was a period of stress and transition for Summer. In 1972, she married an Austrian actor named Helmut Sommer after she became pregnant with their child Mimi. The couple divorced in 1974, but Donna kept Helmut's last name with an anglicized spelling. While waiting for divorce

proceedings to conclude, Summer began a relationship with the German painter Peter Muldorfer.

Summer wished to continue performing on the stage, but this changed when she linked up with the songwriting and production team of Pete Bellotte and Giorgio Moroder. After a few hit records in Western Europe, Bellotte, Moroder, and Summer crafted a smash hit in 1975 with "Love to Love You Baby." The sound was disco, a derivative of soul and funk music. Summer coyly sang little more than the title's five words accompanied by X-rated moaning. Despite initially disappointing European sales, Neil Bogart, president of Casablanca Records, released the single in America, where it reached number two of the Billboard Hot 100 chart. The record contributed to the mainstreaming of disco music.

The Casablanca marketing campaign played up the overt sexuality of "Love to Love You Baby," casting Summer as a cool sex goddess. She felt uncomfortable with the representation and stressed in interviews that she was merely playing a role. Nevertheless, the image dogged her in the press, even though follow-up recordings pointed to diversity in both her singing style and her musical tastes. Singles became central to Summer's success, but she was one of the first black female artists to make cohesive albums. She relied on her partners to compose such concept records as 1976's *Love Trilogy* and *Four Seasons of Love* and 1977's *Once upon a Time*. The late 1970s brought hit after hit for Summer, including "I Feel Love" (1977), "MacArthur Park" (1978), and "Last Dance" (1978). Her commercial and critical peak arrived with *Bad Girls* (1979), an acclaimed disco-rock fusion that yielded two number one pop hits—the title track and "Hot Stuff." The same year a duet with Barbra Streisand, "No More Tears (Enough Is Enough)," also topped the pop charts. Suffering from depression, anxiety, and an addiction to drugs, Summer became a born-again Christian. She credited this with helping her regain control of her life.

Summer's star status marked her as an anomaly during the disco era. Her songwriting contributions, which first included lyrics before extending to musical accompaniment, were also unusual. With disco's decline, Summer's career began to stagnate in the early 1980s. As she and her producers pondered her musical direction, she left Casablanca for the new Geffen Records. *The Wanderer* (1980) experimented with a hard-rock sound, but it only reached number thirteen on the *Billboard* albums chart. The renowned producer QUINCY JONES produced 1982's *Donna Summer*, but it barely managed to crack the Top 20. For *She Works Hard for the Money* (1983), Summer reunited with Bellotte and Moroder. The LP marked a brief resurgence of her explosive commercial and critical success.

Beginning in this period, Summer was harshly criticized in the gay community for some antihomosexual remarks she allegedly made to fans after a 1983 concert. Gay men represented a sizable portion of her audience, and they felt betrayed. Summer emphatically denied that she had made the disparaging comments. Summer's audience remained overwhelmingly white, although she felt that by the end of the 1970s she had built up a sizable black fan base. Many African Americans considered her detached from black culture. Others were offended by album art that lightened her skin (*On the Radio*) or showed her in white makeup (*Another Place and Time*).

Summer recorded little and toured occasionally during the 1990s. She spent most of her time with her husband, Bruce Sudano, who she wed in 1980, their two daughters, and Mimi. Summer also took up painting. In 1997 she received the Best Dance Recording Grammy Award for "Carry On," her fifth career Grammy win. She released her autobiography, *Ordinary Girl: The Journey*, in 2003. She continued to record new material and tour the world as she developed a generation of new fans.

Summer was one of the most successful black female singers of the late 1970s and early 1980s. She garnered fourteen Top 10 hits and four number one singles and sold tens of millions of albums. She will perhaps forever be known as the "Queen of Disco," but her talents as a vocalist and songwriter showcased her ability to transcend the limits of the genre. Her work with Bellotte and Moroder helped redefine the sound of popular music in the 1970s and deeply influenced the future of dance and electronic recordings.

Later in life, Summer was diagnosed with lung cancer unrelated to smoking. In 2012, she died of the illness in Naples, Florida. She was 63.

FURTHER READING

Summer, Donna, with Marc Eliot. *Ordinary Girl: The Journey* (2003).
Gilmore, Mikal. "Donna Summer: Is There Life after Disco?" *Rolling Stone* (23 Mar. 1978).
Howard, Josiah. *Donna Summer: Her Life and Music* (2002).
Obituary: *New York Times*, 17 May 2012.

ZACHARY J. LECHNER

Summers, Jane Roberta (5 May 1895–29 June 1992), community activist, was born Jane Roberta Whatley in Hayneville, Lowndes County, Alabama,

the eighth child and only girl of fifteen children born to Minerva Kendall Whatley and Calvin Whatley, a sharecropper and laborer. At an early age Jane worked to help support the family, and by the age of sixteen she was selling insurance for the Atlanta Mutual Benefit Association.

Summers's lifelong commitment to helping others was instilled at an early age by her parents, who had been born into slavery. A family story passed down through the generations had an enormous impact on young Jane. Relatives told how her father, Calvin, at the age of five carried water to his enslaved father, Simon, who had been beaten, tied to a tree, and left to die. Simon was subjected to this torturous punishment because he had protested the master's sexual abuse of his wife.

In 1922 Jane Whatley married George Summers, a skilled and prosperous tailor and haberdasher. She brought a son, Walter L. Whatley, to the marriage. Her husband, a widower, had three daughters. They together had one daughter, Mary Adeline, born in 1929 just days before the stock market crash. At the time of Mary's birth the family lived in Anniston, Alabama. The Summers were a prosperous family, as evidenced by their car and telephone, rare possessions for Alabama blacks at the start of the Depression and made possible because George's customers were affluent whites. However, after the stock market crash, suits were a luxury that his customers could forgo. Subsequently George lost his business and home, and the family was forced to split up, George and Jane leaving Alabama to seek employment. Like many other African American families of that era, they migrated north to Chicago around 1930.

In 1934 Jane Summers journeyed to Covington, Kentucky, to care for her ailing mother. She arrived with her daughter Mary in one hand and all of her possessions in a shopping bag in the other. She engaged in whatever honest employment she could find, including selling toiletries and women's clothing through a company called Fashion Frocks. She did hand laundry, worked as domestic in a private home, cleaned offices, and kept books for a tavern. She was never able to return to Chicago, and her husband George was never able to join her in Kentucky, although they maintained a relationship until his death in the late 1940s.

Summers believed strongly in the value of education, and she walked several miles from Covington to Cincinnati after working all day to attend night school. After completing a course of study in business, she became secretary to the manager of Covington's Jacob Price public housing community. Three years later she became manager, at the age of fifty. Some sources record that she was the first woman and the first African American to be manager of the Jacob Price project. According to her daughter Mary Northington, she was the second African American to serve in that role—a Robert Jackson had served in that capacity for about a year prior to Summers's appointment in 1945.

Summers remained at the job until her retirement at the age of seventy-five. She did not really retire, however; she just changed jobs. She helped convert the struggling Kenton County Community Action Commission into a vital service organization. At the age of seventy-seven she became a paralegal and worked with the Legal Aid Society to help low-income residents struggling with legal issues. It was not unusual for her to go to court with individuals to offer emotional support as well as legal assistance. Summers was also active in the NAACP, Northern Kentucky Interfaith Commission, Poor People's Coalition, Meals on Wheels, Kentucky Human Rights Commission, and Saint James African Methodist Episcopal Church.

During her six decades of membership at Saint James, she served in every capacity except pastor. She was also a tireless advocate for youth, the elderly, the imprisoned, the lonely, the unlettered, and the homeless of every race, creed, and color. If a young person needed money for college, she organized fund-raisers to earn money for tuition. She provided young couples with seed money to enable them to move out of public housing and into homes. She did whatever was needed at the moment, whether it was cleaning a house, tending the sick, taking food to the hungry, writing a letter, or supplying transportation.

Many terms have been used to describe Jane Summers, including guardian angel, mentor, and agent of God. At her induction into the Northern Kentucky Leadership Hall of Fame in 1992, the community activist Eddie Thompson Jr. summed up Jane Summers's contributions:

> Mrs. Summers lived a lifetime dedicated to helping others by advocating what she termed her early training [self-help], the same concept she taught to her family and those in the community who were willing to learn. Mrs. Summers believed not only in taking help to others in need, but in teaching others to care and fend for themselves.

There were twenty initial inductees into the Northern Kentucky Leadership Hall of Fame on the occasion of the Kentucky Bicentennial. Of those twenty only four were women and only two were African Americans. The *Kentucky Post* similarly captured her dedication when Summers was elected to the Gallery of Great Black Kentuckians in 2001: "Mrs. Summers left 'A legacy of which Covington can be proud and can use as a role model for generations to come'" (14 Nov. 2001).

By the time of Summers's death in Covington, Kentucky, at the age of ninety-seven, she had received many accolades. The Jane Roberta Summers Foundation was established in her honor in 1994; the mayor of Covington, Denny Bowman, proclaimed 5 May 1991 as Jane Summers Day; she was elevated to the Honorable Order of Kentucky Colonels by Governor Wallace G. Wilkinson in 1991; and that same year she was given a key to the city of Covington and was appointed trustee emeritus of Saint James. The NAACP recognized Summers in 1980, 1981, and 1992 for her efforts to eliminate racial discrimination and her devotion to the cause of freedom and dignity. The Northern Kentucky Community Action Commission for outstanding outreach service recognized her service in 1970, and she also was recognized by Northern Kentucky State College (now Northern Kentucky University) for her efforts in helping to establish the college in 1968.

FURTHER READING
Primary sources include Mary Northington's conversation with the author in Covington, Kentucky, on 1 July 2004, and a photocopy held by Mary Northington of Eddie Thompson Jr.'s "Speech at Northern Kentucky Leadership Hall of Fame Induction Ceremony" (c. 15 Nov. 1992).
Hicks, Jack. "Past and Present Leaders Inducted," *Kentucky Post*, 11 Nov. 1992.
Jennings, Mary. "20 Who Shaped Kentucky History," *Cincinnati Enquirer*, 3 Nov. 1992.
"Local Activist Added to Gallery," *Kentucky Post*, 14 Nov. 2001.
Obituary: *Kentucky Post*, 1 July 1992.

LOIS MASSENGALE SCHULTZ

Sumner, Francis Cecil (7 Dec. 1895–12 Jan. 1954), psychologist, was born in Pine Bluff, Arkansas, the son of David Alexander and Ellen Lillian, African Americans who had previously adopted the surname Sumner in honor of Massachusetts's antislavery senator Charles Sumner. Francis received his elementary education in Norfolk, Virginia, and Plainfield, New Jersey. His father was not satisfied with the secondary education in segregated schools, so he taught Sumner himself. Sumner passed a

Francis Cecil Sumner, psychologist, in an undated photograph. (University of Massachusetts, Amherst.)

written examination to gain admission to Lincoln University in Pennsylvania in 1911. In 1915 he graduated magna cum laude with honors in English, Greek, Latin, modern foreign languages, and philosophy. Sumner said that his sole ambition was to be a writer, but he also said that he knew he would have to fall back on teaching or something else as a means of livelihood. While at Lincoln University, Sumner corresponded with members of the psychology faculty at Clark University in Worcester, Massachusetts, including Clark's president, G. Stanley Hall. Hall was eminent among psychologists; his accomplishments included starting the *American Journal of Psychology*, leading the founding of the American Psychological Association (APA), and serving as the APA's first president. With Hall's sponsorship Sumner enrolled at Clark and earned a second B.A. (English) in 1916. In 1916–1917 Sumner returned to Lincoln University for graduate study, earning an M.A. while at the same time teaching psychology and German. He wished to further his education but was undecided as to whether to pursue psychology or German. In 1917, with Hall's encouragement and a senior fellowship, Sumner returned to Clark University to study psychology.

Sumner began his doctoral studies at Clark on 15 October 1917. A week later he passed the French and German examinations required for candidacy for the Ph.D.. Although he intended to study the psychology of race, he wrote instead "Psychoanalysis of Freud and Adler," a work completed by the end of the 1918 spring semester. (In 1909 Hall had been the first to bring Freud to the United States.) While seeking a publisher for his manuscript, Sumner asked Hall to consider it for the doctoral dissertation. Before Hall could examine the manuscript, Sumner was drafted into military service. The United States was involved in World War I, and Hall complied immediately with Sumner's request for a letter recommending that he receive officer training. However, it was too late, and Sumner instead became a sergeant in the 808th Pioneer Infantry and was sent to France. His letters home graphically portrayed the frightening experiences of being under bombardment. Following the 11 November 1918 armistice, Sumner's unit was detained in France until June 1919. He wrote to Hall of his fondness for France and of his desire to live there, but he returned to Clark University to complete his doctorate in psychology. Hall and the other members of Sumner's doctoral committee accepted with high praise the Freud and Adler manuscript as his dissertation. Published in 1923 as "Psychoanalysis of Freud and Adler; or, Sex-Determinism and Character Formation" (*Pedagogical Seminary*), Sumner's dissertation contrasted the two bitter rivals' theories of sex and character formation, in Sumner's words, by "throw[ing] the searchlight of psychoanalysis upon the lives of its very founders." Sumner received his Ph.D. on 14 June 1920, becoming the first black American to earn a Ph.D. in psychology.

In the academic year 1920–1921 Sumner was a professor of psychology at Wilberforce University in Ohio, and he taught during the summer of 1921 at Southern University in Baton Rouge, Louisiana. He married Frances H. Hughston in 1922; they had no children. After the marriage ended he married Nettie M. Brooker in 1946; this marriage too was childless. From 1921 to 1928 Sumner was on the faculty at West Virginia Collegiate Institute (later West Virginia State College). He was a persistent critic of practices that hindered the development of black education and intellectualism and a visionary for the advancement of education for African Americans. For example, Sumner advocated the consolidation of both the intellectual and material resources of the forty scattered, substandard black colleges and universities to form five strategically designed universities.

In 1928 Sumner accepted a position at Howard University in Washington, D.C., where he was appointed as the acting chair and, soon thereafter, the chair of the psychology department. He remained at Howard until his death. Initially the department consisted of Sumner and his assistant, Frederick P. Watts. In 1930 Max Meenes, a white man with a Ph.D. in psychology from Clark University, joined Sumner and Watts. For the next fifteen years Sumner, Watts, and Meenes were Howard's psychology department, and they enabled the university to become the leading institution in educating black psychologists. Although Howard did not confer the Ph.D. until nearly twenty years after Sumner's death, it was documented in 1975 that of the three hundred black American Ph.D. psychologists, sixty had received bachelor's or master's degrees from Howard.

Sumner was not considered a charismatic teacher, but KENNETH B. CLARK, perhaps the most recognized black American psychologist, attributed his own conversion to the study of psychology to Sumner. Clark earned bachelor's and master's degrees under Sumner's supervision, and he served as the first African American president of the APA (1970–1971). Clark and his wife, Mamie Phipps Clark (Meenes's master's student at Howard), published research on children's self-esteem that was instrumental in the 1954 Supreme Court decision in *Brown v. Board of Education* that declared segregation in public schools illegal. Recalling the occasion of Sumner's death, Clark said, "I felt it more deeply than I felt the death of my father."

Sumner's scholarly accomplishments included at least forty-five publications. Among his interests was the psychology of religion. He presented a paper titled "Mental Hygiene and Religion" at the First International Congress of Religious Psychology in Vienna in 1931. Inspired by his participation in the congress, he collected an extensive set of European works on the psychology of religion that led to his writing a large but unpublished manuscript, "The Structure of Religion: A History of European Psychology of Religion." In addition he wrote more than two thousand abstracts for *Psychological Abstracts* (this was before authors provided their own abstracts), mostly from articles in foreign language journals. These were outstanding accomplishments, considering that he taught five courses most semesters and handled the administration of the department. Sumner was a fellow of the APA, and his other professional memberships included the American Association for the Advancement of Science, the American Education Research Association, the Eastern Psychological Association, and the Southern Society for Philosophy and Psychology. Sumner has been recognized as the "father of black American psychologists." He died of a heart attack while shoveling snow at his home in Washington, D.C. A combat veteran of World War I, Sumner was buried with military honors at Arlington National Cemetery.

FURTHER READING
Some of Sumner's personal correspondence with G.-Stanley Hall and James Porter is at the University Archives in Goddard Library, Clark University.
Bayton, James A. "Francis Sumner, Max Meenes, and the Training of Black Psychologists," *American Psychologist* 30 (1975).
Guthrie, Robert V. *Even the Rat Was White: A Historical View of Psychology* (1976; rev. ed. 1998).
This entry is taken from the *American National Biography* and is published here with the permission of the American Council of Learned Societies.

ROGER K. THOMAS

Sun Ra (22 May 1914–30 May 1993), jazz bandleader, composer, and keyboard player, was born in Birmingham, Alabama. Nothing is known of his father; his mother ran restaurants. Sun Ra claimed that he was a visitor from Saturn and acted accordingly, often discouraging investigations into his earthly upbringing. His given name was Herman and his surname may have been Lee, but his siblings were named Blount, perhaps from a stepfather. He denied that his surname was really Blount, and yet this surname was documented early in his professional career. In childhood he received the nickname Sonny.

For his tenth birthday his mother bought him a piano. There seems no question, from observations of his later working methods, that he was gifted with an extraordinary ear for complex music, and his claim that he immediately taught himself to play piano and to read music may not be an excessive exaggeration. A few years later he studied with a renowned local high school music teacher, John T. "Fess" (as in pro*fess*or) Whatley, and he worked in dance bands.

After graduating from high school, he took the Alabama A & M swing band to Chicago for Christmas break and, as Sonny Blount, joined the Chicago musicians union on 15 December 1934.

During the academic year 1935–1936 he studied music education at Alabama A & M, his tuition and fees paid by a Birmingham doctor. Over the next decade Blount (or Sonny Lee) toured the South and Midwest, working at some point with the Sunset Royals, a swing band, and with Oliver Bibb's society orchestra, whose members dressed as eighteenth-century French aristocrats, wigs and all. Little else is known of this period. He may have served in the army, or perhaps he was a conscientious objector.

In 1946 Blount made his first recordings, accompanying the rhythm-and-blues singer WYNONIE HARRIS. He then left Birmingham permanently, joining one of the pianist and arranger FLETCHER HENDERSON's last bands at the Club DeLisa in Chicago from summer 1946 to May 1947.

Around 1950 he established the seed of his future band in rehearsals with a trio that included the saxophonist Pat Patrick. In 1951 he joined a secret society in Chicago:

> Whose members studied the occult, advocated a form of black nationalism, and frequently preached about outer space. ... In 1952, he proclaimed his vocation: that he was not human, but rather of an angel race; that he was to serve as the Cosmic Communicator, bringing the Creator's message to benighted Planet Earth. Accordingly, he changed his name to Le Sony'r Ra—Ra after the Egyptian sun god, Le from his last name, Sony for reasons both heliocentric and mundane, and an extra r to bring the total up to a lucky 9 letters. This is the name that appears on his passport. ... Sun Ra is technically his stage name. Upon changing his name, he began calling his band an Arkestra (a respelling that just happens to include "Ra" both forwards and backwards) (Campbell in Geerken and Hefele, eds., *Omniverse Sun Ra*, 11).

Sun Ra's earliest avant-garde efforts were not stylistic but organological, as he experimented with alternative, electric, and electronically modified keyboards, and programmatic, as he gave his pieces titles evocative in some way of ancient Africa and outer space. Initially these organological and programmatic elements operated within the context of swing, bop, and rhythm-and-blues.

The Arkestra grew gradually. Its most important permanent member was the saxophonist John Gilmore, who joined in 1954, shortly before the trombonist Julian Priester. Another accomplished soloist, the baritone saxophonist Charles Davis, joined in 1956. That year Sun Ra established his own record label, Saturn, whose chaotic but long-standing output included "A Call for All Demons" (1956), later issued on the album *Angels and Demons at Play*. Priester left late in 1957 or early in 1958, at which point two significant new members joined, the saxophonist and flutist Marshall Allen and the bassist Ronnie Boykins. They are heard, together with the trumpeter Hobart Dotson, the reed player James Spaulding, Davis (shortly before he left), Gilmore, Patrick, and a lesser-known trombonist and drummer in the ten-piece Arkestra that recorded the Saturn album *Jazz in Silhouette* (1958). As elsewhere during these early years, there are moments of unusual playing on this album, but given the band's understated approach and its instrumental combination of two brass, five winds, and rhythm section, listeners may find the overall sound surprisingly reminiscent of cool jazz. Sun Ra's music had not yet caught up with his program.

Around 1959 the Arkestra began to wear outlandish costumes and to present its chanting theme, "We Travel the Spaceways," first recorded on the album of that name (1959–1960). Robert Campbell suggests that Sun Ra's music of this period influenced, inspired, and in some instances perplexed future members of Chicago's avant-garde jazz organization, the Association for the Advancement of Creative Musicians, which was established in 1965. A considerable amount of this music, as heard on portions of *Lady with the Golden Stockings* (1958–1959; reissued as *The Nubians of Plutonia*), the 1960 tracks of *Angels and Demons at Play*, and other Saturn issues from these years, consists of slow, unremarkable, repetitive melodic improvising over static, droning accompaniments. Perhaps only devoted fans of Sun Ra will find these hypnotic, meditative pieces to be inspiring.

Sun Ra rehearsed the Arkestra constantly, but by 1961 opportunities for paid performances had diminished considerably. He left Chicago, going to New York City after a disastrous job in Montreal at which the misinformed club owner had expected to hear a rock-and-roll band. Scuffling for work, the Arkestra continued to document its development on record. The drummer Clifford Jarvis, who became another permanent member, first recorded with Sun Ra around 1960 and seems to have been in the group regularly from around 1963, as was the alto saxophonist Danny Davis, the bass clarinetist Robert Cummings, and the wind player and percussionist James Jacson, when the Arkestra recorded *Cosmic Tones for Mental Therapy, Volume II*. This album (of which there is no volume one) presents strikingly original and virtually unclassifiable pieces featuring an emphasis on low-pitched drums, blaring massed reeds and brass, and the leader's eerie keyboard sounds. The result sounds as if the erudite European avant-garde scene and a B-grade 1950s American sci-fi soundtrack had somehow come together.

In 1965, after Gilmore's return from several months with ART BLAKEY's hard-bop group, the Jazz Messengers, Sun Ra recorded three further outstanding avant-garde albums, *The Magic City* and *The Heliocentric Worlds of Sun Ra*, the latter in two volumes. On a number of these tracks he makes a further radical break from jazz tradition by exploring new combinations of instrumental tone colors without regard for a regular beat or meter.

Of his opportunities for public performance, Sun Ra's steadiest job was an engagement on Monday nights at Slug's Saloon in New York City from 1966 to 1972. June Tyson began to sing with the band in 1968. Sun Ra lost his lease in the late 1960s, and Allen's father gave the Arkestra a dilapidated house in Philadelphia, Pennsylvania, where they settled permanently. Around 1970 Sun Ra began to focus less persistently on his avant-garde stylistic stance, as he brought blues, swing, and bop back into the mix. This musical reassessment came hand-in-hand with an enhanced theatricality: he expanded the group to include dancers, acrobats, jugglers, fire eaters, a light show, singers, and more instrumentalists. Campbell argues that at this point Sun Ra lost his sense of the value of silence in his music, instead favoring loud, thick sounds and utilizing the new technology developed in rock music for public address systems, with microphones on every instrument, even when unnecessary.

The Arkestra performed at the Fondation Maeght in Saint Paul de Vence, France, in August 1970 and made its first European tour from October to November and a second European tour from October to December 1971, with a visit to Cairo before returning home. Cummings left the band in 1971, the bass clarinetist Elmo Omoe taking his place, and Patrick left in 1973. Boykins, having missed the earlier European performances, left after a concert in Paris in October 1973; Sun Ra never found a suitable replacement for his bassist.

For his fourth European tour in 1976, Sun Ra's nineteen-piece Arkestra (plus Tyson and three dancers) included the trumpeter Ahmed Abdullah, the trombonist Craigh Harris, Gilmore, Allen,

Davis, Omoe, Jacson, Jarvis, and, for a brief time once again, Patrick. They recorded at the Montreux Festival in Switzerland. Sun Ra toured West Africa in February 1977, and he began giving Halloween concerts, which led to the Arkestra's annual appearances in Greenwich Village Halloween parades.

In the mid-1970s Sun Ra attempted to reach the market for contemporary dance music, but he failed. Presumably the inherent loose edges (and sometimes, loose center) of his music was incompatible with the clean, glossy, tight sound of popular soul and disco tunes. At the same time, arrangements of Henderson's music became a regular part of his repertoire. The Arkestra also presented pieces associated with DUKE ELLINGTON, as well as standard popular songs of the swing era. In a parallel development, Sun Ra presented himself as an unaccompanied pianist in concert and on record from 1977 onward, playing blues and stride in combination with modern and free styles.

Sun Ra reached his largest audience with the Arkestra's five-minute performance on the television show "Saturday Night Live" in May 1978. He was the subject of director Robert Mugge's documentary film *A Joyful Noise* (1980), and his recorded output was celebrated in a Sun Ra festival on WKCR-FM in New York City in 1987, during which he taped an extensive interview. The Arkestra toured Europe at least once annually during the 1980s, while also revisiting Egypt in 1983 and making their first trip to Japan in 1988. Allen, Gilmore, Tyson, Olmoe, and Jacson continued as Arkestra stalwarts, with Patrick rejoining from 1985 to 1988. During this decade Sun Ra added tunes associated with BILLIE HOLIDAY to his repertoire, and in 1988 he began to perform tributes to Walt Disney characters.

In 1990 Sun Ra made seven European tours, even as his health began to fail. He was hospitalized for irregular heart rhythm in November and then suffered a stroke but resumed touring as soon as possible. He suffered another stroke in October 1992. The following January he returned to Birmingham, where he died. He had never married.

There is perhaps no better concise introduction to Sun Ra's world than Mugge's documentary *A Joyful Noise*, in which the members of the Arkestra, dressed in space/Egyptian costume, offer wide-ranging samples of their approach. Included in the film are Tyson's rendition of a sappy astral-pop-soul lyric, a conventional blues number, a swinging big-band march, a stiff, free bop requiem, and excerpts from a wild, free jazz improvisation that features astounding solos from Allen and Sun Ra, who at one point becomes a jazz whirling dervish, spinning rapidly while somehow maintaining a furious clustered melody on the synthesizer. Sun Ra was also a poet, and Mugge captures him lecturing in his elliptical way, including a moment in which he poignantly and concisely summarizes a philosophy of alienation and otherness by situating himself across the street from the president's home on Pennsylvania Avenue, stating that you can't have a White House unless you have a Black House.

Sun Ra was the spiritual and artistic leader of a cooperative, monk-like musical brotherhood whose members lived together under his direction, maintaining only a meager standard of living while devoting themselves to a jazz-based music for which rehearsals might be called at any hour and aiming thereby to offer to the world, through music, a sense of peace and an improvement in the condition of African Americans. (Reportedly women were not allowed in the house, and one wonders how the Arkestra's singer, Tyson, fit into this scheme.) In this setting Sun Ra became one of America's most creative musicians. His mid-1960s recordings are among the most important documents of free jazz, but more broadly speaking his personal innovations on keyboards and the Arkestra's diverse and theatrical repertoire were so idiosyncratic that they belonged less to any large-scale movements than to his own personal style, as was his aim. In inventing a musical fantasy world in which serious commentary and cerebral sound were inseparable from theatrical clowning, he felt that he was creating a place to exist that was far less absurd than the racist world into which Herman Blount had been born.

FURTHER READING

Campbell, Robert L. *The Earthly Recordings of Sun Ra* (1994).

Geerken, Hartmut, and Bernhard Hefele, eds. *Omniverse Sun Ra* (1994).

Jones, LeRoi [Amiri Baraka]. *Black Music* (1967; repr. 1980).

Pekar, Harvey. "Sun Ra," *Coda*, no. 139 (June–July 1975).

Obituary: *New York Times*, 31 May 1993.

This entry is taken from the *American National Biography* and is published here with the permission of the American Council of Learned Societies.

BARRY KERNFELD

Suttles, George "Mule" (31 Mar. 1900–9 July 1966), first baseman and baseball manager, was born in Brockton, Louisiana, to parents about whom nothing is known. A right-hander who stood six feet two inches tall and weighed around 220 pounds, Suttles began his baseball career with the Birmingham Black Barons in 1918. He stayed with the Black Barons until 1926, at which time he became a teammate of JAMES "COOL PAPA" BELL on the St. Louis Stars managed by Candy Jim Taylor. In 1926 Suttles hit a record twenty-seven home runs in eighty-seven league games, a feat unmatched by any other batter in Negro League history, including the prodigious slugger JOSH GIBSON. Suttles helped lead the St. Louis Stars to Negro National League pennants in 1928, 1930, and 1931, before the league fell victim to the Depression.

After the league folded in 1931, Suttles barnstormed with the Washington Pilots and the Detroit Wolves, before joining Robert A. Cole's Chicago American Giants of the Negro National League in 1933. He continued to excel as a top ball player under the tutelage of Giants manager Dave Malarcher. When the American Giants suffered a financial setback Suttles joined the Newark Eagles in 1936. The next season, the Eagles boasted of the "Million Dollar Infield" with Suttles at first base, DICK SEAY at second, WILLIE WELLS at short, and RAY DANDRIDGE at third; according to press accounts, had they been white players, the foursome's total value would have been around $1 million. Nevertheless, the Eagles finished that year in second place, five and a half games behind the powerful Pittsburgh Crawfords.

In the first Negro League all-star game of 1933, Suttles led his West squad to an 11–7 victory with a tremendous home run in the fourth inning off Pittsburgh Crawfords pitcher Sam Streeter. His second all-star home run came off the Hall of Fame pitcher MARTIN DIHIGO in 1935. He connected for this game-winning hit, with two on and two outs, in the bottom of the eleventh inning to capture a thrilling 11–8 victory for the West squad. Overall his performance in five East-West All-Star games (1933–1935, 1937, and 1939) netted him a .412 batting average. Attesting to Suttles's greatness against black baseball's best is his overall slugging percentage in Negro League all-star history: an extraordinary .882 average, the highest achieved.

Suttles played for twenty-five years, retiring from the New York Black Yankees in 1942. He credited his playing longevity to the philosophy of "Don't worry about the Mule going blind, just load the wagon and give me the lines." In 1943 he returned to his former team, the Newark Eagles, as manager but stayed only until 1944, when he retired permanently from baseball.

According to the baseball historian John B. Holway, in twenty-six games against white major league teams Suttles hit eleven home runs in only ninety-nine at bats, while hitting for a .374 average. Within the Negro Leagues he won the home run crown not only in 1926 but also in 1937, with twelve homers, and in 1938, with nine. Statistics compiled by the Negro Leagues Committee of the Society for American Baseball Research indicate that Suttles is the career leader in home runs, whereas the renowned Josh Gibson, often thought to have the highest career total, is in fourth place with 144 home runs in fewer at bats.

Suttles's home runs were legendary. In 1929 it was reported that Suttles hit a home run approximately six hundred feet in Tropical Park in Havana, Cuba. According to teammate Willie Wells, the ball traveled over a centerfield fence that was more than five hundred feet from home plate and sixty feet high. Afterward, a marker was placed on the landing spot, memorializing the tremendous blast. That same year, it was reported by the *Chicago Defender* that Suttles, then with the St. Louis Stars, hit sixty-nine home runs in league and nonleague games combined. When asked who was the hardest hitter of the time, BUCK LEONARD, the great first baseman of the Homestead Grays, said, "Mule Suttles. Yes, harder than Josh Gibson. In my opinion Mule could hit the ball just as far as anybody—Josh, John Beckwith, Babe Ruth or anybody!" Suttles reminded pitcher Laymon Yokely of a later player, Boog Powell of the Baltimore Orioles: "You better not get the ball away from him. He hit one off me once, and before I could straighten up, the ball went through my legs, through Dick Lundy at shortstop, and through Pete Washington in centerfield and rolled to the fence."

Remembered primarily as a power hitter, Suttles was an average fielder yet surprisingly agile and quick for someone of his large build. He was also known for swinging a fifty-ounce bat, a size unheard of in today's game. Teammates often described him as a jovial, fun-loving, yet gentle man who loved to tell stories. Suttles died in Newark, New Jersey.

FURTHER READING

Holway, John B. *Blackball Stars: Negro League Pioneers* (1988).

Riley, Jim. *Biographical Encyclopedia of the Negro Baseball Leagues* (1994).

This entry is taken from the *American National Biography* and is published here with the permission of the American Council of Learned Societies.

LARRY LESTER

Sutton, Percy (24 Nov. 1920–26 Dec. 2009), lawyer, government official, and entrepreneur, was born Percy Ellis Sutton in San Antonio, Texas, the youngest of fifteen children of Samuel J. Sutton and Lillian Smith, both schoolteachers. Education was a top priority in Sutton's household. All of the twelve surviving children finished college, and six of Sutton's siblings became teachers. Sutton was exposed to business early as well, since his family owned a funeral home.

After stints at Prairie View A&M College in Texas, Hampton Institute in Virginia, and Tuskegee Institute in Alabama without earning a degree, Sutton decided to enlist in the military and joined the Army Air Corps in New York, shortly after the U.S. entered the war in 1941. In the summer of 1943, walking through Times Square, he met Leatrice O'Farrel. They married in December of that year and would have two children, Pierre and Cheryl Lynn.

A month later Sutton was shipped out to Europe and became one of the Tuskegee Airmen, the famed all-black Ninety-ninth Pursuit Squadron that flew combat missions in World War II. For his work he won combat stars and was honorably discharged as a captain in 1945.

In 1945 Sutton returned to New York City and enrolled at Columbia University's School of Law. He subsequently transferred to the Brooklyn College of Law, where he earned his J.D. in 1950. During this period he supported himself and his family by working sixteen hours a day as a mail handler in the post office and as a conductor in the subway system. After graduating from law school Sutton decided to reenlist in the military just as the Korean War erupted. After serving three years as an Air Force intelligence officer in Washington, D.C., Sutton returned to Harlem and established a law firm with his brother Oliver and a former judge named George Covington.

He also became actively involved in the nascent civil rights movement. Beginning in the 1950s he was active in the New York branch of the NAACP, serving as president from 1961 to 1962. Sutton joined the Freedom Riders who journeyed from Atlanta, Georgia, to Montgomery, Alabama, in 1961 and

1962 and in 1963 Sutton's law firm represented over 200 civil rights workers in the South who had been arrested for protesting Jim Crow. Sutton also served as the legal representative for MALCOLM X from the late 1950s until Malcolm's assassination in 1965.

Active in local politics, Sutton became involved in a number of Harlem political clubs and meetings. In 1954 he ran for a seat in the New York State Assembly but lost. This was the first of eleven failed attempts to win an election. He finally won a seat in the assembly in 1964. Two years later, Manhattan Borough President CONSTANCE BAKER MOTLEY vacated her office to become a federal judge. The New York City Council chose Sutton to finish her term. He would serve as Manhattan's borough president for the next eleven years.

During this period Sutton also was active in business. In 1972 he incorporated Inner City Broadcasting, a pioneering minority-owned firm in the communications industry. That year it bought WLIB-AM for $1.9 million. It was the first black-owned radio station in New York City. A year later, Inner City bought WLIB-AM's sister station, WLIB-FM, for $1.1 million. Sutton changed the call letters to WBLS.

In 1977 he resigned as Manhattan Borough President in order to run for mayor of New York City, thus becoming the first major-party black candidate for the city's top position. Among the seven candidates running in the Democratic primary, however, he came in a disappointing fifth—a defeat especially bitter to Sutton because he did not get the backing he had anticipated from friends and supporters whom he had cultivated for years while Borough president.

After his defeat, Sutton never again ran for elected office, but he remained active in politics. He had close relationships with Congressman CHARLES RANGEL; Basil Paterson, who became New York's secretary of state in 1979; and DAVID N. DINKINS, who in 1989 would become the first black mayor of New York City. Collectively they were known as "The Gang of Four," a powerful force in New York politics. Sutton would also serve as a senior adviser to JESSE JACKSON in his 1984 and 1988 presidential bids.

No longer seeking public office for himself, however, Sutton focused his energies on his Inner City Broadcasting and WBLS, which by 1980 was the number-one station in New York and also one of the most popular radio stations playing black music in the nation. It remained one of the most successful stations for many years. By 2007 Inner City Broadcasting owned nineteen radio stations throughout the United States and ranked as of the one hundred largest black-owned businesses throughout that period.

Although radio broadcasting remained at the core of Inner City Broadcasting, Sutton expanded his business into other areas. Most notably, he paid $250,000 for the legendary Apollo Theater in 1981. At the time, the Harlem cultural landmark had been closed for five years and was in bankruptcy court, its future in doubt. Once Sutton gained control, he sought to restore the Apollo to its former glory. He revived the theater's famous "Amateur Night" and renovated its decaying facilities. Its revival begat the rebirth of 125th Street in Harlem.

In 1991 Sutton passed control of Inner City Broadcasting to his son, Pierre. He did not retire, but continued his legal work by working pro bono for selected clients. He remained actively involved in local politics and mentored a generation of young leaders. In the late 1990s the New York State Attorney General's Office looked into allegations of misconduct by Sutton and his work on the Apollo. Although he was eventually cleared, he lost control of the theater. At the age of eighty-six, in 2006, he co-founded Synematics, a high-technology company.

Sutton received numerous awards for his accomplishments. In 1987 he received the NAACP's highest honor, the Spingarn Medal. A year later he became the first recipient of the National Black Leadership Forum's Lamplighter Award. In September 2007 the U.S. House of Representatives voted to support Congressman Charles Rangel's proposal to rename a post office on 125th Street after Sutton. "Percy Sutton is an inspiration not only to the people of Harlem, but to the entire nation," Rangel said in a statement proposing the bill. "The renaming of the post office is one of the many honors we can do to recognize him for giving so much to so many" (http://www.house.gov/list/press/ny15_rangel/PercySutton021407.html). Sutton died in Manhattan on 26 December 2009.

FURTHER READING

"Charles Rangel and Percy Sutton Cleared of Wrongdoing in Apollo Theater Business Case," *Jet*, 27 Sept. 1999, 25.

Corry, John. "Percy Sutton's Rising Star," *New York Times* 2 Nov. 1973, 47.

Gross, Jane. "Sutton and Dinkins: Labor of Law and Love, *New York Times* 5 Aug. 1997, A1.

Riley, Clayton. "Percy Sutton: Power Politics–New York Style." *Ebony* 28 (November 1972): 165–75.

GREGORY BELL

Swails, Stephen A. (23 Feb. 1832–17 May 1900), soldier and politician, was born in Columbia, Pennsylvania, the son of Peter Swails, an African American boatman, and his wife Joanna Atkins Swails, who was usually listed as white; both were from Maryland. After living in Columbia and Manheim the Swails family moved about 1856 to Elmira, New York.

In 1860 Stephen A. Swails worked as a waiter at the Keyes Hotel in Cooperstown, New York, where he married Sarah Thompson, from a local black family; they had two children. On 8 April 1863 Swails enlisted in the newly formed 54th Massachusetts Infantry Regiment, one of the Union's first African American regiments, and was immediately promoted to first sergeant. On 18 July 1863 he fought in the attack on Fort Wagner, south of Charleston, South Carolina, that established the regiment's reputation for valor and led to the formation of the United States Colored Troops. Transferred to Florida, the regiment participated in the disastrous 20 February 1864 battle of Olustee, near Jacksonville. In his official report Colonel Edward N. Hallowell wrote that "Sergeant Stephen A. Swails, acting sergeant-major, deserves special praise for his coolness, bravery, and efficiency during the action; he received a severe but not mortal wound to the head" (*Official Records of the War of the Rebellion*, Series I, 35(1), 315). On 11 March 1864 Massachusetts governor Andrew took the unprecedented step of commissioning Stephen A. Swails as a second lieutenant in the 54th Massachusetts Infantry—no other African American soldier had ever been made an officer. The War Department refused to implement the commission, and in October 1864 formally ordered Swails not to wear his officer's insignia. Officers in the field protested, and Governor Andrew wrote the secretary of war that "Sergeant Swails, though not of white Caucasian blood, is a man of character and intelligence, a soldier of superior merit, a gentleman and worthy of the recognition of gentlemen. ..." (*Freedom*, 343–344). The War Department relented, and on 8 February 1865 Swails was officially mustered in as a second lieutenant, to be followed by other African American soldiers. He continued to perform with distinction and on 11 April 1865 led an attack behind enemy lines at the battle of Honey Hill, near Grahamville, Jasper County, South Carolina. On 8 June 1865 Swails was promoted to first lieutenant; a month later he was named the regiment's acting adjutant general.

At the end of the Civil War, the regiment was assigned to garrison duty in Charleston, until it was disbanded. Lieutenant Swails did not return north; he had formed a new attachment and on 18 April 1866 married Susan Aspinall, daughter of a free African American family in Charleston. Why he left his family back in New York is not yet known. His wife there remarried, and there is no further record of contact between them.

After two years with the Freedman's Bureau, Swails was named its special agent at Kingstree, capital of Williamsburg County northwest of Charleston—a county with a two-thirds African American population. With the advent of Reconstruction Swails began an active political career. As chairman of the Rules and Regulation Committee of the South Carolina Constitutional Convention of 1868, he helped draft a constitution based on universal male vote and providing for a race-blind public school system. In the 1868 elections he was elected senator from Williamsburg County and was easily reelected in 1870, 1872, 1874, and 1876. From 1872 he served as the State Senate's president pro tem. Further research is needed on his legislative activities, but he acquired a reputation as a strong and influential legislator. He was named major general in the newly established South Carolina National Guard, and a trustee of the University of South Carolina. On the national level Swails was a delegate to Republican Party national conventions in 1868, 1872, and 1876, and a member of its powerful Credentials Committee. In 1868 he became one of the first four African Americans to serve as presidential electors.

In Kingstree Swails built a home on Main Street for his wife and four children, was elected mayor, and served as Williamsburg County auditor. He was admitted to the bar in 1872 and practiced law, forming a partnership with a younger white attorney. For five years he was editor of the *Williamsburg Republican* newspaper. Following the withdrawal of federal troops, a white supremacist government in South Carolina forced Swails and a few remaining black legislators to resign in 1877. He ran again in 1878, but an armed white mob forced him out of his home under threat of death. His protests, carried personally to President Hayes in Washington, went unanswered. Swails was given a job in Washington with the Post Office and later the Treasury, but appears to have traveled freely to his family back in Kingstree.

In 1886 he received a military pension, and in 1887 was listed on the program for a 54th Massachusetts

Regiment reunion in Boston. As late as 1892 Swails was named to the National Executive Committee of the Republican National Association. He died at home in Kingstree in 1900. The Williamsburg County Historical Society in 1998 erected a memorial sign on the site of his home there, and in 2007 a marker was placed on his grave in Charleston.

FURTHER READING

No books or articles have been written about Swails. Biographic information is scattered throughout books on the Civil War and on the South during Reconstruction. Other information has been obtained from official records, including Swails's military pension file, and from newspapers, notably the *New York Times*. Further work is needed, especially as to Swails's life in South Carolina and Washington, D.C.

Berlin, Ira, ed. *Freedom: A Documentary History of Emancipation* (1982).

Blatt, Martin H., et al. *Hope and Glory* (2001).

Emilio, Luis. *A Brave Black Regiment* (1894).

Holt, Thomas. *Black over White: Negro Political Leadership in South Carolina during Reconstruction* (1977).

Williamson, Joel. *After Slavery: the Negro in South Carolina during Reconstruction* (1965).

Obituary: Kingstree *County Record*, 24 May 1900.

HUGH C. MACDOUGALL

Swan, Frederic W. (c. 1809–c. 1822), visionary, was born in Northfield, Massachusetts, one of several children of Elizabeth "Betsy" Swan. A sickly child who reported visions and dreams to family members, Frederic was the subject of a rare and virtually unique publication, *The Remarkable Visionary Dreams, of a Mulatto Boy* (1822). Little is known of this family or of Frederic's short life except that he had a brother named Calvin. Visions and dreams he experienced in his final illness occasioned an unusual publication, one of the few early American publications that transcribed the words of an African American child. It seems likely that his mother influenced the publication of his words to the degree that she should be considered at least a co-author. There were only a few African American women whose words were published before the early 1820s. This biographical sketch, written by a white minister, probably Amasa Taylor, the man who baptized Frederic, prefaced the transcription of Swan's dreams:

Nothing remarkable took place with him till he was eleven years old. He then being at work in the field with two other boys, and hearing them swear most profanely, it struck him with such horror, knowing that he was no better than they by nature, that he ran away from them to cry aloud to God for mercy. He was then at work for Mr. Asa Stratton in Northfield. He soon after came home, and became serious, and told his mother that at times his distress of mind was such that he knew not what to do. He then took to reading the Bible, and said he knew if he died as he then was he should go to hell. He appeared to have remarkable discoveries of the odious nature of sin, and that without religion he and all mankind must be miserable. He thus lived about two years, between hope and fear, and then was taken sick, and passed through many trials and temptations of mind, and dreamed a number of remarkable dreams before he was converted. In the fifth dream, it was stated that if he would read the Bible three months, he should be well, which appears to allude to the time of his obtaining heaven and immortal glory; for at the expiration of the three months, he fell asleep, as we trust, in the arms of Jesus. His soul was made happy in the love of God, at the time of dreaming the sixth dream, when he lost his load spoken of, and drank the wine from the angel's hand. He dreamed about once a week, generally on Monday. The dreams were copied by his mother and friends, in childlike language, as near as possible as he delivered them in short terms; for he was so weak that he could talk but a little at a time. He well knew many people that he saw in his dreams, in different places, both in happiness and in misery. He knew all the houses spoken of, and the people who live in them; and there were many things seen and done, which he would not have written, because of giving offence; but eternity will unfold the whole. I will remark, that after he was converted, although confined to his bed, he was baptized by Elder Amasa Taylor; and soon after died in the triumphs of living faith.

Swan's dreams and visions seem to have been initiated by his removal from his mother's house, when he left to work as an apprentice or an indentured servant. He returned home sickly and unhappy, and his dreams and visions commenced. Dreams were commonly considered a source of knowledge in early nineteenth-century folk religion. The dreams and visions condemned the sinful—possibly an indication that Swan's service was harsh. But they also conveyed a message to Swan's brothers, which could have been an indication that Elizabeth Swan influenced the content of the transcriptions. Frederic had visions of his brothers slipping into sin and into the devil's grasp. His visions also instructed his brothers to read the Bible as well as other books. Elizabeth Swan may have added those elements (or at least underscored them) as she passed her account of the dreams to Frederic and Frederic passed them to a transcriber. In rural New England in the early nineteenth century, literacy was paramount not only for practicing one's religion but also for participation in a market economy. Put simply, Elizabeth Swan seems to have used the final illness of one of her sons as the occasion to offer advice to her other sons on their economic and spiritual welfare.

Elizabeth Swan may have been an author or co-author of the pamphlet, since the account of Swan's dreams was "taken from the mouth of his mother" (Introduction, *Remarkable Visionary Dreams*). Elizabeth Swan herself was probably mulatto or black. Had she been white, she would probably have been literate and transcribed the dreams herself instead of repeating them to a third party. Had she been a white woman with a deceased mulatto child, it seems unlikely that his existence would have been published for posterity without at least omitting mention of his skin color. If Elizabeth Swan was mulatto or black, then *The Remarkable Visionary Dreams, of a Mulatto Boy* should be considered among the earliest prose authored by an African American woman in North America.

FURTHER READING
The Remarkable Visionary Dreams, of a Mulatto Boy, in Northfield, Mass., by the Name of Frederic W. Swan, Aged Thirteen Years, Together with a Sketch of His Life, Sickness, Conversion, and Triumphant Death. Taken from the Mouth of His Mother, His Father Being Dead (1822).

JOHN SAILLANT

Swann, Alonzo Alexander, Jr. (21 Sept. 1925–30 Jan. 2007), World War II veteran and Navy Cross winner, was born in Harrisburg, Pennsylvania, one of five children of Alonzo Alexander Swann Sr., a steelworker, and Mary (maiden name unknown). The family moved to nearby Steelton, where Alonzo graduated from high school in 1943. On 23 November 1943 he enlisted in the U.S. Navy. His honorable military service lasted less than three years, but the ramifications had an effect nearly fifty years later.

From the start Swann's service in the navy was unusual. Most African Americans in the Navy during this time were assigned to the Steward's Branch, where they served white officers, cleaning and taking care of their quarters, helping prepare and serve their meals, and other similar duties. However, during times of combat, stewards like Leonard Harmon and William Pinckney also became fighting men. In fact the large majority of black men in the navy in combat zones were rated as steward's mates or stewards, and most were trained in segregated facilities. Swann's first three months of duty, however, were spent at the Philadelphia Navy Yard in Pennsylvania, and he never received formal training as a steward. The reasons are unknown; perhaps his fair skin resulted in a simple clerical error in his assignment, or maybe a recruiting officer recognized the inherent flaw in assigning a man to the steward's rating based solely on the color of his skin.

Whatever the case, after his time in Philadelphia, Swann was sent to Shoemaker, California, where he awaited his first ship assignment. On or about 23 March 1944 he was among the approximately one hundred men of the Steward's Branch assigned to the aircraft carrier *Intrepid*. While his first job was serving the ship's officers, he was also assigned a general quarters station as part of a gun crew. He seemed blessed with an understanding officer corps that, recognizing his intellect, kept his steward's duties to a minimum. In 1995 Swann told the historian Richard Miller:

> I was neither trained for nor personally inclined for work in officer's country, and I spent most of my time working around the guns. But I lived with the other men in the steward division and that meant a close physical proximity to the naval aviators. ... Many of them were college athletes; and since we Blacks had a reputation ourselves for being good ball players, we spent a lot of off duty time with them on the hangar deck basketball court. Because we also had a reputation as gunners ... they were very interested in our ideas about gunnery. ... They appreciated what we had to tell them; and in my case at least, when my division officer (a non-aviator) was after me [for neglecting something in the officer's mess] they would quickly intervene and put him in his place (Miller, 8–9).

The *Intrepid* departed the United States on 9 June 1944, headed for Pearl Harbor and from there to the Marshall Islands. Swann was assigned to the all-black gun tub number 10, and the members of the unit soon honed their skills off Peleliu and the southern Philippines at Mindanao and in late October 1944 in the Battle for Leyte Gulf. On the night of 30 October the carrier's fighters were pounding Clark Field in the Philippines when the ship was attacked by a Japanese suicide bomber. The men of gun tub number ten stuck to their posts in the face of imminent peril, furiously firing on the plane in the hope of either bringing it down or diverting it from its course. In the final moments they achieved success, but diverted from its course, the enemy aircraft struck gun tub number ten. While the ship received no mortal damage, nine men were killed. Swann and six others were wounded.

For their courage and sacrifice, the African American stewards turned gunners—Brewer, Cody, Davison, Fleming, Gant, Giddens, Smith, and Taylor—were recommended for the Navy Cross, an award for bravery second in importance only to the Medal of Honor, by the ship's commander, Captain Joseph Bolger, on 4 December 1944. But on 16 January 1945 Bolger's superior, Admiral Marc Mitscher, reduced the award to a Bronze Star, a distinguished but lower level of award. That recommendation was received by the Board Awards Meeting on 21 February and was approved on 1 March 1945. Thus Swann and the men of the *Intrepid* were awarded the Bronze Star. Much speculation has focused on the reduction of the award. Because such awards were determined by whites in command positions, an element of bias was sometimes present. Downgrading of original award recommendations might have reflected a racial bias, or the heroic deed might not have met specific criteria. However, the awards reduction in the case of Swann and his shipmates, despite a lack of documentation, seems clear; if the *Intrepid*'s captain's recommendation was approved, the carrier crew would have included twenty African American Navy Cross winners. In an era when the navy was still segregated, the award of not just one such prestigious medal but twenty at once was almost unthinkable and something the navy was not yet prepared to accept.

Despite the downgraded award and the resulting dip in morale among his shipmates, Swann served on the *Intrepid* until the close of the war. He saw shore duty at the Naval Training Center Great Lakes in Illinois before receiving his discharge on 7 May 1946. With a Purple Heart and a Bronze Star, Swann returned to civilian life in Pennsylvania. He enrolled at Pennsylvania State University and graduated with a B.A. in political science. In 1950 he moved to Gary, Indiana, and worked for the city as an administrator. With five children from a previous marriage (about which little information is available), Swann married Gussie Mae Thomas on 4 October 1966. The couple had no children

together, but with her five children from a previous marriage, the blended family was a large but happy one.

However, Swann still burned from the indignity he had suffered at the hands of the navy and was determined to get the Navy Cross and the recognition he deserved. In 1985 he petitioned a navy review board to look into his case but was turned down. Subsequent calls and verbal appeals fell on deaf ears, so Swann took the navy to court. The case reached the U.S. District Court at Hammond, Indiana. On 16 December 1992, forty-eight years after his heroism, Swann was awarded the Navy Cross by court order. Swann's personal success had implications of a broader nature. His court case was an important step in righting the wrongs of a prejudicial past and also highlighted the contributions of African American soldiers and sailors. Navy Secretary Sean O'Keefe independently reviewed the case after the court order and issued the medal without further appeal. Swann was the subject of a Hero's Night organized by navy officials aboard his old ship, now a museum ship in New York, where Swann was awarded the Navy Cross. He was also honored at Carnegie Hall with a Marine Band concert.

With his court case over, Swann resumed a peaceful life as general director of the Gary Sanitation Department. Though he suffered periodic bouts of post-traumatic stress disorder, with the help of his family, friends, and fellow church members, he persevered and was the co-owner of the Casbah Lounge and a revered member of the Peace Baptist Church at his death. His courage and example paved the way for continuing efforts to gain the Navy Cross for the other members of gun tub number ten.

FURTHER READING

An unpublished manuscript by the naval historian Richard Miller, "The Last Heroes" (1996), has information about Swann and the *Intrepid*.

"Black Gets Navy Cross 49 Years after His War Heroism," *Jet* (15 Nov. 1993).

Knoblock, Glenn A. *Forgotten Sacrifice: African American Naval, Coast Guard, and Merchant Marine Casualties in World War II* (forthcoming).

Obituary: Harrisburg (Pennsylvania) *Patriot-News*, 10 Feb. 2007.

GLENN ALLEN KNOBLOCK

Sweatman, Wilbur Coleman (7 Feb. 1882– 9 Mar. 1961), clarinetist, bandleader, composer, and music publisher, was born in Brunswick,

Missouri, the youngest of three children born to Coleman Sweatman (b. ?1853 or 1859–d.?) and Matilda "Mattie" Sweatman (1857–1919). Coleman Sweatman ran a barbershop in Brunswick, but by 1885 had left his wife and family and relocated to St. Joseph, Missouri, leaving Mattie to run the barbershop business and Wilbur to be raised by his older sisters, Eva and Lula. Wilbur was taught music by his sister Eva, initially playing piano, but later taught himself to play violin, clarinet, trombone, and organ.

In the mid-1890s Sweatman joined the "Pickaninny Band" led by bandmaster and hugely influential music educator N. CLARK SMITH and with this group toured the Midwest. In 1899 Smith's Pickaninny Band was contracted to tour Australia and the Far East with the M. B. Curtis Afro-American Minstrel Company, with an all-star black cast headed by the comedian ERNEST HOGAN. Unfortunately, no evidence survives to confirm Sweatman's participation in this tour, but lack of reports of him working in the United States may suggest that he did make the trip. Curtis left the company stranded in Australia in August 1899, but thanks to the generosity of another black touring company, led by Orpheus McAdoo, sufficient money was raised for them to continue to New Zealand, eventually making their way back to America by Hawaii.

By 1901, after a short stint of working in the family barbershop, Sweatman moved to Saint Louis, an important city in the development of ragtime. In 1902 he chose to go on the road with P. G. LOWERY's concert band, which was working with Forepaugh & Sells Brothers Circus. Lowery's band was a sideshow feature (black musicians were not allowed to perform in the big top of white circuses until the 1970s) that also included singers, comedians, and acrobats, and Sweatman led the orchestra that accompanied these acts. According to contemporary newspaper reports, Sweatman was the youngest orchestra leader on the road.

At the end of the 1902 season, Sweatman joined Mahara's Minstrels, as assistant orchestra leader under the baton of W. C. HANDY, but left in about May 1903 with two key members of Handy's band to form his own band, which played at the Palace Museum in Minneapolis for a number of years. During his tenure as leader at the Palace Museum, Sweatman made what are thought to be the first recordings of a black orchestra in the United States—wax cylinder recordings made by the Metropolitan Music Company of Minneapolis.

By 1908 Sweatman had moved again, this time to Chicago, then the epicenter of the first pioneering efforts of self-directed black theatrical entertainment. Sweatman was an important and integral part of this movement, first as leader of the orchestra at the Grand Theater, and then, from 1911, as leader of the orchestra at the Monogram Theater. He married Hazel Venie Gilmore, cashier at the Grand Theater, on 29 June 1910.

In 1911 Sweatman's composition "Down Home Rag" was published by the Chicago music publisher Will Rossiter. Such was its success that a version with lyrics was published in 1913, and it was subsequently recorded by dozens of groups nationally and internationally, including James Reese Europe's Society Orchestra in December 1913 and black American group The Versatile Four in London in 1916. Sweatman was to compose many other rags and dance tunes over the years, most notably, "Old Folks Rag," "Boogie Rag," "That's Got 'Em," and "Battleship Kate," and in 1924 he formed his own music publishing company. In 1917 he was admitted to the American Society of Composers, Authors, and Publishers, the first African American composer working in the popular music idiom to do so.

In 1911 Sweatman was persuaded by the veteran minstrel comedian Tom Fletcher to try his hand in black vaudeville. Such was his success as a performer that by the following year he was working on the prestigious Keith-Albee mainstream vaudeville circuit and had relocated to New York. His specialty in vaudeville was his trick of playing three clarinets simultaneously, something which later jazz critics have used to besmirch Sweatman's reputation as a jazz musician. The fact that an act needed a memorable "hook" to get noticed and that he reserved this feat of dexterity for a straight rendition of the ballad "The Rosary" is not considered! Sweatman's pioneering role in presenting African American musical rhythms and compositions to white audiences cannot be underestimated, nor can the fact that he achieved success in mainstream vaudeville without ever resorting to the indignities of blackface make-up or the wearing of "plantation" costumes—both considered de rigueur for black performers in white theater at that time. Sweatman was to remain a national vaudeville headliner until the 1930s, when vaudeville, unable to combat the challenges of radio and talking pictures, went into terminal decline.

In late 1916 Wilbur Sweatman made the first records that can truly be described as jazz—clarinet solos of "Down Home Rag" and "My Hawaiian Sunshine"—for the little-known Emerson Phonograph Company, two months before the better-known Victor records of the Original Dixieland Jass Band. The phenomenal success of the latter group's first records saw a clamoring among record companies for "jass bands" of their own, and in 1918 Sweatman signed a lucrative recording contract with the Columbia Graphophone Manufacturing Company. The Columbia records by Wilbur C. Sweatman's Original Jazz Band sold in huge numbers—only the Columbia records of BERT WILLIAMS and Al Jolson outsold Sweatman's—and his fame spread even further. However, the arrival on the musical scene of smooth dance bands led by the likes of Paul Whiteman and Art Hickman soon turned popular tastes away from the rawer, frenetic performances of Sweatman, and by the end of 1920 Sweatman's contract with Columbia was terminated.

Despite his contract with Columbia not being renewed, Sweatman was still hugely popular in vaudeville, and he worked hard to keep his act fresh and up to date. This included bringing younger talent into his band, and in March 1923 he went on tour with a new group, including a group of Washington-based musicians freshly arrived in New York—the pianist DUKE ELLINGTON, drummer SONNY GREER and saxophonist [Otto] TOBY HARDWICK. Throughout the 1920s and early 1930s Sweatman's bands were a fertile breeding ground for talented young black jazzmen—musicians of the caliber of COLEMAN HAWKINS, JIMMIE LUNCEFORD, SIDNEY BECHET, FREDDIE KEPPARD, CLAUDE HOPKINS, WELLMAN BRAUD, COZY COLE, Teddy Bunn, and Ikey Robinson all worked for Sweatman, as well as singers and dancers such as Ada "Bricktop" Smith, Princess White, and Zaidee Jackson.

With the demise of vaudeville in the early years of the Great Depression, Sweatman sought other avenues of work, including supplying bands and entertainers on the then-popular Hudson River night boat cruises and residencies at roadhouses and restaurants. By the 1940s Sweatman was concentrating on his music publishing business, and a car accident in the 1950s curtailed his clarinet playing. Through his long friendship with SCOTT JOPLIN's widow, Lottie Joplin Thomas, Sweatman was made a trustee of the Lottie Joplin Thomas Trust, and after her death he became executor of both the Lottie Joplin estate and the Lottie Joplin Thomas Trust and ensured that the copyright on Scott Joplin's compositions was renewed as and when required. As well as handling the Joplin estate, he took into safe-keeping hundreds of Scott Joplin's unpublished manuscripts; however, a family dispute upon his death in 1961 meant that they have never been subsequently located.

Sweatman's long, varied, and illustrious career was overlooked by many jazz historians—mainly due to the fact that he worked in vaudeville for many years, but also because he distrusted white jazz writers of the 1950s and their pro–New Orleans "birthplace of jazz" agenda. Thus it is only recently that his pioneering work as bandleader, musician, composer and performer has been reevaluated, both by publication of a biography and by the reissue of his complete recorded output on CD.

FURTHER READING

Berresford, Mark. *That's Got 'Em: The Life and Music of Wilbur C. Sweatman* (2010).

Brooks, Tim. *Lost Sounds: Blacks and the Birth of the Recording Industry, 1890–1919* (2004).

Fletcher, Tom. *100 Years of the Negro in Show Business* (1954).

Handy, W. C. *Father of the Blues: An Autobiography*, ed. Arna Bontemps (1941).

Kunstadt, Len, and Bob Colton. "In Retrospect: Wilbur Sweatman." *The Black Perspective in Music* 16, no. 2 (1988).

MARK BERRESFORD

Sweatt, Heman Marion (11 Dec. 1912–3 Oct. 1982), civil rights plaintiff and social worker, was born in Houston, Texas, to James Leonard Sweatt and Ella Rose (Perry) Sweatt, whose occupations are unknown. Sixteen years before Heman's birth the U.S. Supreme Court had held in *Plessy v. Ferguson* that state-imposed racial segregation did not offend the Equal Protection clause of the Fourteenth Amendment, and hence the Texas in which Sweatt grew up was rigidly segregated. He attended the all-black Jack Yates High School, graduating in 1930, and went from there to the all-black Wiley College in Marshall, Texas, graduating in 1934.

The decade following his graduation from college saw Sweatt trying to find himself. He taught in a public school for a couple of years and then in 1937 entered the University of Michigan, matriculating in biology in hopes of attending medical school. He left after a year, returned to Houston, took a job with the post office, and in 1940 married Constantine Mitchell.

Heman Marion Sweatt, civil rights plaintiff and social worker, in a portrait from 1950. (Library of Congress.)

In the 1940s the ongoing struggle for civil rights and Sweatt's personal aspirations and dreams intersected. Houston's black community was active in the fight to end racial discrimination, and Sweatt came to know some of the most prominent activists. His barber was Richard Grovey, who led the fight against the all-white primary. In Texas—as in the other states of the old Confederacy—the Democratic Party dominated politics at all levels. Victory in the party's primary was tantamount to being elected to office; yet the party defined itself as a private association, able to select its own members, and excluded blacks from participation in its primaries. Grovey unsuccessfully challenged this practice in *Grovey v. Townsend*, a case decided by the Supreme Court in 1935. Sweatt's dentist, Lonnie Smith, was also a civil rights activist and took up Grovey's fight. In *Smith v. Allwright* the Supreme Court reversed *Grovey* and opened up the primaries to all eligible voters. Sweatt took part in

fund-raising drives to support the challenges to the all-white primary.

Sometime in the 1940s Sweatt approached an attorney about racial discrimination against employees of the post office. Blacks were systematically excluded from supervisory positions and were denied access to the jobs that would have prepared them to move up the career ladder. Involvement in the legal work necessary to prepare a case challenging post office discrimination piqued his interest in law, and Sweatt decided to apply to law school.

Sweatt's aspiration to attend law school coincided with a growing interest on the part of the local NAACP to challenge racial segregation in the state's university system. Under the direction of LULU BELLE WHITE the Houston chapter of the NAACP had become one of the largest and most dynamic in the South. With the encouragement of William Durham, a vigorous and effective black civil rights attorney, and with the support of White and the NAACP, on 26 February 1946 Heman Sweatt applied for admission to the University of Texas law school. After seeking an opinion from the Texas attorney general, the law school refused Sweatt admission, citing the state's constitution, which mandated racial segregation. On 16 May 1946 Sweatt filed in district court seeking to have the decision of the university president Theophilus S. Painter reversed. On 17 June 1947 the district court denied Sweatt's petition for a writ of mandamus but issued an order giving the state six months to create a separate, equal opportunity for blacks to study law in Texas.

Six months later the state had not made much progress, but when Sweatt returned to court the district court dismissed the case, holding that a resolution passed by Texas A&M—a white school that had been founded alongside a black school (today known as Prairie View A&M University)—to create a professional school for African American students satisfied the state's obligation. On 26 May 1947 Sweatt filed an appeal with the Court of Civil Appeals. That appeals court affirmed the district court decision, as did the Texas Supreme Court a short time later. State-level appeals were exhausted. In November 1949 the U.S. Supreme Court agreed to hear the case.

The state faced a stark legal problem, one that the NAACP lawyers CHARLES HAMILTON HOUSTON and THURGOOD MARSHALL hoped to use in toppling segregation. *Plessy v. Ferguson* (1896) allowed states to mandate racial separation provided that "equal" facilities were provided for blacks. Like most states of the old Confederacy, Texas had failed to provide professional schools for blacks. Several years earlier the Supreme Court had mandated integration of the University of Missouri's law school, given Missouri's failure to create a black law school. Texas now moved to create a black law school in order to be able to argue before the Supreme Court that it was honoring its obligation under *Plessy*. By the time the case finally reached the Supreme Court a black "law school" was in operation with a handful of students, a half dozen or so faculty members, and a tiny library.

As knowledge of the suit spread, the champions of segregation mobilized. Sweatt's life was threatened; both he and his wife received menacing phone calls; and their home was vandalized. Chronic stomach problems, possibly stress-related, became worse, and Sweatt was briefly hospitalized and suffered a heart attack.

Then in June 1950 the Supreme Court handed down its decision, rejecting Texas's claim that it had made progress toward providing a law school for black students. In its ruling the Supreme Court foreshadowed the major conclusion of *Brown v. Board of Education* (1954): separate is inherently unequal. It made no difference how much money and effort Texas put into creating a new black law school, the court said, because such a school could not be the University of Texas law school. It would lack the century-long history that lent prestige to that institution. It would lack the network of alumni in the legal profession in Texas that would give its graduates the contacts and mentoring essential to competent practice and professional success.

On 19 September 1950 Sweatt finally registered for classes at the University of Texas law school. But the struggle had taken a lot out of him. He missed classes early because of an appendectomy. The tension of the preceding years fractured his marriage: his wife left Austin, returned to Houston, and sought a divorce. After two years Sweatt dropped out of school and returned to Houston.

Shortly thereafter he received a grant to pursue a master of social work degree at the Atlanta University graduate school of social work. Upon earning his degree in 1954, he moved to Cleveland, Ohio, where he embarked on a long career with the National Urban League. In 1962 he returned to Atlanta to become assistant director of the Urban League's southern regional office, working on a variety of community development projects. In 1963 he married Katherine Gaffney, with whom he had two daughters, one adopted. Sweatt died in 1982 in Atlanta.

Five years after his death the University of Texas initiated an annual Heman Sweatt symposium on civil rights and established a $10,000 scholarship in his name at the law school.

FURTHER READING

Howard, John. *The Shifting Wind: The Supreme Court and Civil Rights from Reconstruction to Brown* (1999).

Kluger, Richard. *Simple Justice* (1976).

JOHN R. HOWARD

Sweeney, Robert Augustus (20 Feb. 1853–19 Dec. 1890), a sailor in the U.S. Navy and two-time Medal of Honor recipient, was a native of Montserrat, a French possession in the West Indies. When he immigrated to the United States is not known for certain, nor is anything known of his family background. While a number of accounts cite Sweeney as a native of Montreal, Canada, this is incorrect according to official military records.

By 1873 Robert Sweeney was in the United States, and on 1 December of that year he enlisted in the U.S. Navy from New Jersey for a period of three years. He would subsequently reenlist for another term of service in 1876, and during these first two terms he served aboard the *U.S.S. Vermont, U.S.S. Colorado, U.S.S. Pawnee, U.S.S. Dictator, U.S.S. Powhatan, U.S.S. Constellation,* and the *U.S.S. Franklin*. Though nothing is known of Sweeney's activities prior to joining the navy, he likely had no seafaring experience, as after eight years of service he was rated an ordinary seaman. On 17 September 1881 Sweeney signed up for a third term of navy service and was assigned to the *U.S.S. Kearsarge*; just over a month later, on 26 October, he earned his first Medal of Honor when he saved a fellow crewman from drowning after he fell overboard while the ship was at Hampton Roads, Virginia. With a heavy tide running, Sweeney himself was nearly overcome several times before reaching the drowning sailor. Once he reached the man, Sweeney was able to keep the man afloat in rough seas for nearly a half an hour before the *Kearsarge* could reach the men and bring them aboard. Two years later, Sweeney was serving aboard the *U.S.S. Yantic* at the New York Navy Yard in 1883, when he again saved a fellow sailor from drowning. The *Yantic* was tied up beside the *U.S.S. Jamestown* with a gangplank between them when on 20 December a cabin boy named A. A. George from the *Jamestown* fell off the gangplank. Sweeney and Landsman J. W. Norris from the *Jamestown* both quickly dove into the water and saved the boy. While both men were subsequently awarded the Medal of Honor, for Robert Sweeney it was his second such award.

Robert Sweeney is a significant figure in both naval and African American history. Not only is he the only African American to win the Medal of Honor twice, he is also one of just thirteen men from all branches of the military to have been awarded the medal for two different feats of valor. Sadly, the deeds of Sweeney, and men such as ALPHONSE GIRANDY and JOHN JOHNSON have been largely forgotten due to the fact that they occurred in peacetime; the Medal of Honor was awarded for feats of valor in noncombat situations until the advent of World War I, when the criteria for its award were changed.

Following the award of his second Medal of Honor, Robert Sweeney served in the navy for most of the remainder of his life. Interestingly, Sweeney enlisted in the army at New York on 9 December 1885 during an intermediate period between terms of naval service. What prompted his change in service branches is unknown, but he had a quick change of heart, as he deserted from the army just two days after enlisting. Shortly thereafter he joined the navy for his fourth and final term of service. Robert Augustus Sweeney ended his naval career on 18 June 1890 and, possibly worn out by his years of service, died at Bellevue Hospital in New York City just six months later on 19 December 1890. He was subsequently buried in Cavalry Cemetery, Woodside, New York, in an unmarked grave.

FURTHER READING

Hanna, Charles W. *African American Recipients of the Medal of Honor* (2002).

GLENN ALLEN KNOBLOCK

Sweet, Ossian H. (30 Oct. 1895–20 Mar. 1960), physician, was born Ossian Haven Sweet in Orlando, Florida, the eldest of nine surviving children of Dora DeVaughn and Henry Sweet. In the summer of 1898 the Sweets bought a plot of land in the town of Bartow, approximately forty-five miles east of Tampa, where they ran a successful farm and lumberyard. Ossian attended Union Academy (Bartow's all-black public school) through the eighth grade. In September 1909, at the age of thirteen, he began preparatory work at Wilberforce University in Xenia, Ohio, the nation's first black college. He was initially awarded a scholarship, but it was rescinded due to lack of funds. Sweet did odd jobs around campus to help cover expenses. He started the college program in the fall of 1913, concentrating in the sciences with the goal of entering medical school. Sweet earned his B.S. (a general science degree that focused on biology, chemistry, and mathematics) in the spring of 1917. He attended Howard University's College of Medicine in Washington, D.C., from which he graduated with an M.D. in the spring of 1921. In the summer of the same year, he moved to Detroit, where he had spent many summers since 1910 working as a bellhop and waiter.

Detroit had undergone dramatic changes since Sweet first arrived a decade earlier looking for summer work. While Michigan maintained civil rights statutes that prohibited segregation in schools and other public places, discrimination manifested itself blatantly in the real estate market. As a result the vast majority of the black population was confined to a dilapidated four-square-mile section of the city east of downtown known as Black Bottom. Sweet rented a room in the neighborhood and set up a medical practice in the back room of a pharmacy around the corner. He delivered much needed medical care to the residents of Black Bottom, and his practice thrived. In the spring of 1922 he joined the staff of Dunbar Memorial Hospital, founded in 1918 to serve Detroit's growing black community.

Later in 1922 Sweet met Gladys Mitchell at a formal dance at the local YWCA, and they married on 20 December of that year. The couple moved in to the home of Gladys's parents, who were among the few blacks in Detroit to live in a white, working-class neighborhood in the northeast side of the city. On 17 July 1923 Gladys gave birth to their first child, a boy. Tragically he was premature and died three days later. The Sweets did not give him a name.

Living with Gladys's parents allowed the Sweets to save money, and on 6 October 1923 they set sail for Europe, where Ossian planned to do postgraduate work. They spent the first few months at the University of Vienna, where Sweet attended lectures by Anton von Eiselberg, a pioneer in the field of neurosurgery. Then they moved to Paris, where Sweet had the opportunity to listen to Marie Curie lecture at the Sorbonne about the medical implications of her work on isolating radium. The Sweets enjoyed the comparative lack of racism in Europe and only suffered overt discrimination when Gladys became pregnant again and was denied access to the American hospital in Paris on racial grounds. Luckily there were no complications, and on 29 May 1924 their daughter Marguerite was born.

The Sweets arrived in Detroit in late June 1924 and moved back in with Gladys's parents as they searched for a house of their own. Conditions in Black Bottom had continued to deteriorate, and Sweet had no intention of moving his family into the ghetto. Unfortunately there could not have been a more inauspicious time than the summer of 1924 for a black family in Detroit to look for a house outside of Black Bottom. Racial tensions were at an all-time high, as Detroit's Ku Klux Klan boasted thirty-five thousand members, some of whom filled the ranks of the police department. More than once during the summer before the Sweets moved into their new home, white crowds attacked blacks who tried to move into all-white neighborhoods.

Determined not to be intimidated, the Sweets moved into their home on 8 September 1925, leaving the baby with Gladys's parents. Preparing for the worst, Sweet brought weapons and enlisted the help of his brothers Otis Sweet, a dentist, and Henry Sweet, a student at Wilberforce University who was spending the summer in Detroit. A cousin, John Latting, and six friends also joined the group. Around dusk a large crowd gathered outside the house, but it slowly dissipated during the night. The following night, 9 September, a larger crowd appeared in front of the Sweet home and this time began yelling obscenities and pelting the house with rocks, shattering windows. Shots rang out from the Sweet house, wounding a white man in the crowd, Eric Houghberg, and killing another, Leon Breiner. The police, who had been passive up until then, rushed into the house and arrested all eleven occupants, charging them with murder.

Having successfully challenged the residential segregation laws in Louisville, Kentucky, in 1917 and anticipating a Supreme Court battle over restrictive covenants in Washington, D.C., the National Association for the Advancement of Colored People (NAACP) saw the Sweet case as yet another compelling opportunity to use the courts to publicly affirm the rights of African Americans to live where they chose. WALTER WHITE, assistant secretary of the NAACP, asked the renowned attorney Clarence Darrow to take charge of the defense. Having recently defended John Scopes in the celebrated Dayton, Tennessee, "Monkey Trial," Darrow was an ardent fighter for progressive causes and racial justice. Furthermore White was convinced that, given public sentiment against the Sweets for killing a white man, a prominent white attorney was the defendants' only hope.

True to form, Darrow mounted a stirring defense, arguing that Sweet was an accomplished man who had earned the right to live wherever he chose and that the people gathered outside the Sweet household on 9 September constituted nothing less than a lynch mob—against which Sweet had every right to defend himself and his family. The defense attorney Arthur Garfield Hays called Sweet to the stand and, to great effect, asked him to recall the events of that evening and to discuss the incidents of racial violence nationwide that most haunted him. The first trial produced a hung jury, so Darrow asked that the defendants be retried separately. The prosecution decided to retry Ossian's brother Henry first, as he had admitted firing into the crowd during interrogation by the assistant prosecuting attorney Ted Kennedy right after the shooting. Again Ossian Sweet testified and performed impressively. Darrow delivered an unforgettable seven-hour closing statement, and after a brief deliberation, the jury acquitted Henry Sweet. Prosecutor Robert Toms then dropped the charges against the remaining ten defendants.

Shortly after the second trial, Sweet bought a drugstore in Black Bottom and set up a successful practice on the second floor. However, his personal life took a tragic turn. During Gladys's incarceration in the Wayne County Jail following the shooting, she contracted tuberculosis and later passed it on to their baby, who died in August 1926. Two years later Gladys succumbed as well.

In 1929 Sweet resigned his position at Dunbar Memorial Hospital and opened a small rival hospital in the heart of Black Bottom. In 1930 he made an unsuccessful bid for the presidency of the Detroit branch of the NAACP. Shortly thereafter he ran unsuccessful campaigns for the state senate and for the U.S. Congress. During the 1930s Sweet married again twice. Both marriages were brief and ended in divorce. His brother Otis lived with him in his house on Garland Avenue, as did a sister, a nurse who later died in a car accident. His brother Henry moved in as well, but he died of tuberculosis in 1940.

During the next decade, Sweet bought tracts of land in his hometown of Bartow, Florida, which he rented to local farmers. He also bought a house in Bartow and spent his winters there. He finally paid off the house on Garland Avenue in 1950 but fell behind on his property taxes. He was forced to sell the house in 1958. With nowhere else to go, he moved into his office in Black Bottom. Isolated, depressed, and suffering from chronic pain due to arthritis, Sweet shot himself on 20 March 1960.

In the years following the Sweet trials, racism in the real estate market only intensified, and housing discrimination remained the official policy of many banks and brokers until the late 1960s. Although race relations improved dramatically following the civil rights movement, the neighborhoods of most American cities—perhaps most notably Detroit—remained largely divided along racial lines well into the twenty-first century.

FURTHER READING

Boyle, Kevin. *Arc of Justice: A Saga of Race, Civil Rights, and Murder in the Jazz Age* (2004).

Darrow, Clarence. *The Story of My Life* (1932).

Dray, Philip. *At the Hands of Persons Unknown: The Lynching of Black America* (2002).

Haldeman-Julius, Marcet. *Clarence Darrow's Two Great Trials: Reports of the Scopes Anti-Evolution Case and the Dr. Sweet Negro Trial* (1927).

Vine, Phyllis. *One Man's Castle: Clarence Darrow in Defense of the American Dream* (2004).

Weinberg, Kenneth G. *A Man's Home, a Man's Castle* (1971).

DANIEL WEIN

Switzer, Veryl Allen (6 Aug. 1932–), professional football player, businessman, and historic preservationist, was the youngest of six children born to Fred and Ora Switzer of Nicodemus, an all African American town in northwestern Kansas. He grew up playing football on the dusty dirt streets of Nicodemus. He liked fishing and hunting and especially helping with farm chores. He attended grade school at Nicodemus until the eighth grade and then attended nearby Bogue High School. While in high school he played on the football and basketball teams and ran track. He lettered each year in all three sports.

Upon graduation in 1950, Switzer entered Kansas State University as one of the first African Americans to receive a football scholarship to the university. While at Kansas State he lettered three years in both football and track and was named to the All Big Seven three years in a row. In 1952 Switzer won the Big Seven indoor long jump championship. In football he led the nation with 31.0 yards in punt returns his senior year. Named a co-captain of the West team for the 1954 East–West Shrine Bowl game, he was a runner-up for

Veryl Switzer at his home in Manhattan, Kan., on 27 Feb. 2007. (AP Images.)

the Shrine Bowl's Most Valuable Player Award that year. He graduated in 1954 as an All American and with a bachelor's degree in science and secondary education.

In 1954 Switzer was the first halfback selected and the fourth picked overall in the NFL draft. He played for five years as a halfback for the Green Bay Packers and was the only African American on the team his first year. During his rookie season he topped the NFL record in punt returns with 13.0 yards per return. In 1956 Switzer married Fern Stalnaker in Tulsa, Oklahoma; the couple had three children. His career was interrupted when he joined the U.S. Air Force as a first lieutenant, serving from 1956 to 1958. After leaving the military, Switzer returned to football by playing for the Calgary Stampeders of the Canadian Football League in 1958. His football career came to end after playing for the Montreal Alouettes in 1959–1960.

In 1960 Switzer began work in the Chicago public schools, serving as the system's human relations coordinator from 1966 until 1969, when he accepted a position as the administrative assistant to the athletic director and coordinator of minority and cultural programs at Kansas State University. After receiving a master's degree from KSU in 1974, he became dean of minority affairs in 1978 and three years later became the associate dean of student affairs. From 1988 until his retirement in 2005 he worked as associate director of athletics and as assistant vice president for institutional advancement, during which time he organized the Second Wind Program. The program allows student athletes to return to Kansas State to complete their degrees. During this time he also became the executive director of the Earl Woods National Youth Golf Academy/First Tee. Woods, a Kansas native and KSU baseball star, was the father of TIGER WOODS.

In addition to his athletic career, Switzer stayed close to his Kansas farming roots as the owner of 840 acres of land in Nicodemus. In 2000 he and other African American farmers organized the Kansas Black Farmers Association. Two years later he and other local black farmers became charter members of the Nicodemus Flour Coop, a locally owned cooperative that grows its own wheat and processes it into flour, which it sells along with pancake mix.

Switzer also played a key role in supporting historic preservation efforts in Nicodemus. He collaborated with the community and the Afro-American Institute for Historic Preservation and in 1976 succeeded in getting Nicodemus designated as a National Historic Landmark District. He was inducted into the Big Eight Sportswriters Football Hall of Fame in 1978, and then the Kansas State University Sports Hall of Fame and the Kansas All Sports Hall of Fame in 1990.

FURTHER READING
Program, Kansas State Sports Hall of Fame (5 Oct. 1990).

ANGELA BATES

Swoopes, Sheryl Denise (25 Mar. 1971–), professional basketball player and Olympic gold medalist, was born in Brownfield, Texas, the daughter of Louise Swoopes. The only girl of four children, Sheryl never knew her father, who left when she was a baby. Swoopes became interested in basketball when she was young and played with her brothers and other neighborhood boys, developing an aggressive and physical style. By age seven she played with the Little Dribblers, a youth basketball league. After three years the team made the finals but lost the tournament in Beaumont. Swoopes's long legs earned her the nickname "Legs" at Brownfield High School, where she also ran track and set the school record for the long jump. In 1988, her junior year, the Brownfield High School team won its first state basketball championship. As a senior she won the Texas Player of the Year Award. Following her graduation from high school in 1989, Swoopes accepted a basketball scholarship to the University of Texas at Austin, over four hundred miles from Brownfield. A country girl who had never been far from her small, West Texas hometown, she was homesick and left within days. She then enrolled at nearby South Plains College, where she played for two years. She set fifteen school records and was named junior college player of the year in 1991. She moved on to Texas Tech University in Lubbock, also close to Brownfield, and played for the Lady Red Raiders. Six feet tall, Swoopes played both forward and shooting guard, earning the nickname "Texas Tornado," and was compared to MICHAEL JORDAN. Later she became the first woman to have a Nike shoe named after her, Air Swoopes, much like the successful Air Jordans. In two years Swoopes led the team to a 58–8 record and to its first Southwest Conference title, and she was named to several All-American teams. In 1993 she led the Lady Red Raiders to the National

Sheryl Swoopes during a game at Arco Arena in Sacramento, Calif., on 12 July 2002. (AP Images.)

Collegiate Athletic Association (NCAA) title. She set an NCAA championship record for both men and women by scoring forty-seven points in one game and earning the NCAA Final Four Most Valuable Player Award. That year she also won the celebrated Naismith Player of the Year Award, having scored more than thirty points in five consecutive games. Texas Tech retired her number 22 on 19 February 1994. That same year she received the ESPY Award (created by ESPN in 1993 to recognize excellence in sports) for Best Female College Basketball Player and garnered numerous Southwest Conference honors. Swoopes graduated with a bachelor's degree in sports science, writing a thesis titled "Opportunities for Women in Sports: A Female Athlete's Experience and Perspective."

In 1992 Swoopes tried out for the U.S. Olympic team but twisted her ankle and was unable to compete. In 1993 she played briefly for Basket Bari in Italy, averaging twenty-three points per game. She returned from Italy because of contractual

problems, but there were few options for women basketball players in 1995. Having been on the U.S. team that won the gold medal at the Goodwill Games in Saint Petersburg, Russia, she joined the U.S. Women's National Team to prepare for the Olympics. The team compiled a 52–0 record and won the 1996 Olympic Gold Medal in Atlanta. Swoopes was also on the gold medal teams in 2000 (Sydney, Australia) and 2004 (Athens, Greece).

On 22 January 1997, during the first year of the Women's National Basketball Association (WNBA), Swoopes was recruited by the Houston Comets and signed as a forward. She was pregnant, however, and did not play until 7 August, remarkably only six weeks after giving birth. She was the league's most valuable player (MVP) in 2000, 2002, and 2005, was selected first team All-WNBA in 1998, 1999, 2000, and 2002, and led the all-star voting in 1999, 2000, 2002, and 2003. She sat out the 2001 season with a torn anterior cruciate ligament knee injury. She won another ESPY in 2001 as the best WNBA player. She was the WNBA Player of the Week five times and the top vote getter in all-star balloting five times.

By 2006 Swoopes had played on six WNBA All-Star teams, winning the MVP award in 2005, the year she led the league with an average of 18.6 points per game. In 2002 and 2003 Swoopes was the Defensive Player of the Year, and in 2003 she led the league in steals per game. She was the third WNBA player to record four thousand points (16 June 2006). From 1997 to 2000 the Comets won four league championships with Swoopes. She became only the second player in WNBA history to win both the regular season MVP award and the All-Star Game MVP award in the same season, and she did it twice, in 2000 and 2002. In 1999, she became the first player in WNBA history to record a play-off triple-double, scoring double-digits in the three catergories: 14 points, 15 rebounds, and 10 assists. In June 2006, on the tenth anniversary of the WNBA, Swoopes was selected for the All-Decade Team.

On 26 October 2005 Swoopes announced that she was a lesbian and had lived with her partner Alisa Scott, a former Comets assistant coach, for seven years. She became only the third active player in the WNBA to come out as gay. She said the announcement "set her free" and that "the possibility of me opening up doors, not just for African-American men and women, but for all people, is a great feeling to me." She became a spokeswoman endorsing Olivia Cruises, promoted to lesbians.

Swoopes consistently ranked in the WNBA top ten in points scored, assists, minutes played, steals, and defensive rebounds per game. In the early twenty-first century she was one of only five women who earned NCAA and WNBA championships and Olympic gold medals. She overcame poverty, injury, personal struggles, and a lack of opportunity for women athletes to become a leader and role model.

FURTHER READING

Burgan, Michael. *Sheryl Swoopes*, Women Who Win series (2001).

Johnson, Anne Janette. *Contemporary Black Biography* (1996).

Johnson, Anne Janette. *Great Women in Sports* (1996).

Rappoport, Ken. *Sheryl Swoopes, Star Forward*. Sports report (2002).

Sehnert, Chris W. *Sheryl Swoopes*. Awesome athletes (1998).

Torres, John Albert. *Sheryl Swoopes* (2002).

Wallner, Rosemary. *Sheryl Swoopes* (2001)

Welden, Amelie, and Jerry McCann. *Girls Who Rocked the World: Heroines from Sacagawea to Sheryl Swoopes* (1998).

JANE BRODSKY FITZPATRICK

Sykes, Roosevelt (31 Jan. 1906–11 July 1983), blues pianist, was born in Helena, Arkansas. Little is known about his parents except that they moved to St. Louis with Roosevelt when he was three, later dying within a year of each other before he turned eight. The youngster was returned to Arkansas to live on his grandfather's farm sixteen miles south of Helena. His grandfather, a preacher, had an organ in his home, and Roosevelt began to learn music there. After a neighbor bought a piano, Roosevelt switched instruments, and by age twelve he had learned enough to play blues piano in local drinking establishments, or barrelhouses. He was baptized at age thirteen and remained a believer all his life, seeing no conflict (as did many other blues artists) between his religion and his music.

Around the age of fifteen, he ran away from home. His piano playing helped him gain entrance to juke joints and roadhouses around Helena, where he played for tips to supplement the money he made as a dishwasher and waiter. He also studied such local pianists as Baby Sneed, Joe Crump, and Red-Eye Jesse Bell, his main influence. In the mid-1920s he met another important influence, Leothus "Lee" Green, another local piano player five or six years his senior. As a team, they worked the Mississippi and Louisiana work camp and roadhouse circuit, Green serving as protector and teacher, showing Sykes the technique that would later become the basis for his first recorded hit.

In the late 1920s, by this time a seasoned veteran of southern venues, Sykes returned to St. Louis. He played various clubs and taverns in the city and across the river in East St. Louis, Illinois, and in 1929 was heard by talent scout Jesse Johnson. Impressed, Johnson arranged a trip to New York so that Sykes could record for the Okeh label. Sykes recalled: "I started making records 14th of June 1929. I had been playing eight years or so before I started recording. The first number I made was a hit, '44 Blues,' and every record I made was a star ever since."

While the tune for "44 Blues" was one he had learned from Lee Green, Sykes put lyrics to it and was the first to record this classic piano blues. Sykes was signed to a recording contract for which he said he was paid $1,500, though Johnson reportedly kept the royalty rights.

Back in St. Louis, Sykes invested in an illegal whiskey house where he served fried fish and drinks. Along with the tavern business, which would run on and off at different locations for years, he pursued a prolific recording career. Using pseudonyms—Dobby Bragg, Willie Kelly, Easy Papa Johnson, St. Louis Johnny, the Honeydripper—he managed to record for at least eight different blues labels.

In 1929 he accompanied Edith Johnson at a Paramount session during which she recorded a song she supposedly wrote about him, "Honeydripper Blues," cited by some as the origin of his nickname, although Sykes himself claimed the name went back to childhood: "Girls used to hang around me when I was a young kid. ... So the boys say, 'He must have honey.'"

During the 1930s Sykes used his record industry connections to become a talent scout for Decca and RCA Victor. He also toured the South with one of his finds, pianist St. Louis Jimmy Oden, and made several trips to Chicago, eventually settling there around 1941. In Chicago he continued to record and do club work. In 1942 he put together a band, the Honeydrippers, which included up to a dozen members, and recorded and toured the country in a rented bus with them until 1944 or 1945. In the mid-1940s, he formed a trio with blues legend MEMPHIS MINNIE and her husband, Little Son Joe, and worked Chicago clubs. In the late 1940s and early 1950s he teamed up with another prolific recording artist, guitarist LONNIE JOHNSON.

Then, after touring as a single, Sykes relocated in New Orleans and recorded for one of the post-war rhythm-and-blues labels, Imperial. In the late 1950s he reunited with an old partner and former student, Henry Townsend, playing in Gulfport, Mississippi. He eventually returned to St. Louis, where he became house pianist at the Opera House in Gaslight Square.

In November 1956 Sykes married Mercedes Ducksworth Johnson, a woman he had met about a year earlier in a gulfport market. It was the second marriage for both of them. Although they had no children, each had a daughter by the previous marriage.

As the 1960s began, Sykes became more and more active in the blues revival, traveling to Europe with his old partner MEMPHIS SLIM and touring with subsequent American Folk Blues Festivals. He also remained as active as ever as a recording artist, mostly for documentary labels such as Delmark and Storyville that aimed at the revival audience.

In 1966 he moved to Gulfport, Mississippi. Two years later he became house pianist at the Court of the Two Sisters in New Orleans, where he settled permanently in the French Quarter in 1969, still finding time for more recording sessions.

All told, his recording career spanned some fifty years. As featured artist or sideman, he appeared on several hundred recordings—though the exact number may never be known, given his habit of using aliases and the record companies' practice of not identifying sidemen. He worked with an impressive array of musicians, and many of his songs became classics: "44 Blues," "Highway 61," "Driving Wheel," and "The Night Time Is the Right Time." He was a profound influence wherever he worked, helping shape the styles of Memphis Slim, Eddie Boyd, Willie Mabon, and other pianists in the Mississippi/Memphis/Chicago school; such St. Louis artists as Henry Townsend; and even New Orleans pianists from Smiley Lewis to FATS DOMINO. Blues historian David Evans considered Sykes the leading piano stylist of the 1930s and compared his impact to that of ROBERT JOHNSON on the guitar and SONNY BOY WILLIAMSON No. 1 on harmonica.

Sykes charted a course from country boogie-woogie to a thoroughly urban blues piano style without ever losing touch with his roots. He was a consummate professional, but he played blues in an older way, putting his riffs, fills, and chord changes where he knew they would fit best, even if it meant adding or subtracting a beat here and there, a practice no doubt confusing to later musicians. Nevertheless, Sykes was a sympathetic accompanist, having come from an oral tradition in which musicians listened to each other and followed each other's changes as they went along. As a bandleader, he strove to instill this attentiveness in other musicians, telling them to follow his lead, so that if they were "wrong," they would all be wrong together.

Sykes was a major player through all stages of blues history, working in the barrelhouse circuit in the 1920s, urban blues scenes in Memphis and St. Louis in the 1930s, blues bands in Chicago in the 1940s, rhythm and blues in the 1950s, and the blues revival in the 1960s and 1970s.

Although Sykes professed to be a Muslim years before the advent of the Nation of Islam, he portrayed himself in later interviews as a devout Christian, describing his talent as a divine gift to be used for the public good: "There's a doctor, he has medicine. … [H]e ain't sick, but he makes the stuff for the sick people. So the blues player, he ain't worried and bothered, but he got something for the worried people. … So I works on the soul, and the doctor works on the body" (Barry Lee Pearson, *Sounds so Good to Me* [1984]). Sykes died in New Orleans.

FURTHER READING

Bentley, John. "The Honeydripper: Roosevelt Sykes," *Living Blues* 9 (Summer 1972).

Koester, Bob. "Roosevelt Sykes," *Living Blues* 57 (Autumn 1983).

McKee, Margaret, and Fred Chisenhall. *Beale Black and Blue: Life and Music on Black America's Main Street* (1981).

Oliver, Paul. *Screening the Blues: Aspects of the Blues Tradition* (1968).

Oliver, Paul. *Blues Off the Record* (1984).

Obituary: *New York Times*, 15 July 1983.

DISCOGRAPHY

Robert M. W. Dixon and John Godrich, *Blues and Gospel Records: 1902–1943* (1982).

Mike Leadbitter and Neil Slaven, *Blues Records 1943–1970*, vol. 2 (1994).

Paul Oliver, ed., *The Blackwell Guide to Blues Records* (1989).

This entry is taken from the *American National Biography* and is published here with the permission of the American Council of Learned Societies.

BILL MCCULLOCH AND
BARRY LEE PEARSON

Sykes, Rozzell (25 Dec. 1931–19 Dec. 1994), artist, teacher, and activist, was born in Aberdeen, Mississippi, the son of Cleveland Sykes, a handyman, and Anna Bell Clay. Growing up in Mississippi and in St. Louis, Missouri, Sykes and his eight siblings faced segregation and poverty. In the face of racism and hardship, his parents taught him to treat his home and his neighborhood with care and respect. In 1958 Sykes moved to San Diego, California, where he began painting in his spare time and where he met Erma Thornton. In 1961 he moved again, this time to Los Angeles, where two years later he and Erma were married.

Rozzell and Erma Sykes rented a small bungalow on the 4800 block of St. Elmo Drive in Mid-City Los Angeles. The building was old and dilapidated, but the Sykeses improved it, practicing one of Rozzell's favorite sayings: "If you are given a shoe box, make it the best shoe box in the world" (*Los Angeles Times*, 8 Jan. 1995). In 1964 they were joined by Rozzell's eighteen-year-old nephew Roderick Sykes, the son of Geraldine Bruce, Rozzell's sister. Roderick shared his uncle's love for art, and the two worked together to renovate their new home. Colorful paintings brightened walls, ceilings, and the sidewalks in front of the house. Trees grew metal sculptures, and the once brown lot became green with plants.

In 1965 the sister of Erma Sykes, Norma James Medina, moved into a neighboring bungalow with her five children. Not long after, she passed away from a heart attack, leaving her children in the care of Rozzell and Erma. Sykes supported the family as a painter, and he and Erma housed themselves and all the children in the same one-bedroom house. Sykes shared his passion for art and for life with his family. His adopted son, Benny Medina, remembered, "His life was full, rich and spontaneous, and so was ours" (*Los Angeles Times*, 8 Jan. 1995).

Sykes founded and directed the Studio D'Arte that presented his work and that of other Los Angeles artists. After rent for the studio became too high, Sykes closed it and focused his artistic energy on his home. He and his nephew Roderick began placing their paintings on street corners and on their front lawn, drawing the attention of neighbors and of other artists. Local children visited St. Elmo Village (so called after the Sykeses' nickname for their home and its location on St. Elmo Street) for informal art lessons, and their parents soon became friends and supporters of the family. A local congressman and future mayor of Los Angeles, TOM BRADLEY, was an early and dedicated supporter. The actor Jeff Bridges donated two cacti and helped create a cactus garden. The singer and songwriter WILLIAM EVERETT PRESTON hosted a fund-raising event for the village and included a song called "St. Elmo" on his album *The Kids and Me*, released in 1974.

In 1969 the owner of the bungalows decided to turn them into an apartment complex. Determined to protect what he and his family had built, Sykes organized an art festival and raised a down payment of ten thousand dollars to save the homes from destruction. He bought the property for sixty thousand dollars, and in 1971 St. Elmo Village was incorporated as a nonprofit organization. A vibrant, multicultural haven of art and education, the village grew in an area plagued by joblessness, crime, and physical deterioration. Throughout the 1970s busloads of schoolchildren came to the village almost daily. According to Roderick Sykes, the village did not aim to teach the children art; it aimed to help them discover that they were already artists.

When the boom in crack cocaine brought heightened violence and desperation to Los Angeles in the 1980s, the Sykeses confronted drug dealers and gangs on St. Elmo Drive, telling them to leave the area. The village was a safe zone, where colors thrived beyond the limits of gang association. Visitors continued to flock to the village to learn about art, to share their creativity with others, and to organize ways to spread optimism and cooperation throughout Los Angeles. The village offered workshops not only in painting and sculpture but also in photography, writing, music, and computer skills. Many of these opportunities came free of charge, subsidized by private donations and a steady stream of tourists drawn by the increasing fame of the village.

Sykes's work as a teacher and an activist grew from his passion for art. His paintings have been featured in galleries and museums, such as the California African American Museum and the Ackland Art Museum at the University of North Carolina at Chapel Hill. He also collaborated in the creation of several murals, one of which, *The Children of Mid-City*, involved many of the neighborhood children as painters. Under Sykes's direction they created a three hundred–foot self-portrait of more than one hundred local students and teachers.

Sykes died in Los Angeles in 1994. At his memorial, Mayor Tom Bradley called Sykes "a man of uncommon vision." Bradley stated, "He often said it didn't matter whether you lived in a shoe box or a mansion, you can be all you want to be" (*Los Angeles Times*, 8 Jan. 1995). Although Rozzell and

Erma Sykes had divorced in 1979, they maintained a close friendship throughout the rest of Rozzell's life. After her ex-husband's death Erma continued to work at the village, alongside Roderick Sykes, to ensure that his work in the community endured. Sykes's life and work were the subject of several documentaries, including Sarbon Tamimi's *Right On/Be Free* and an educational video entitled *The Spirit of St. Elmo Village*.

FURTHER READING

Berestein, Leslie. "Hundreds of Mourners Praise Creator of St. Elmo Village," *Los Angeles Times*, 8 Jan. 1995.

Renwick, Lucille. "A Little Slice of Oz in an Area Marred by Gangs and Violence," *Los Angeles Times*, 12 Feb. 1995.

NICO SLATE

Sykes, Thomas A. (1835–c. 1900), public official, prohibitionist, and legislator in two states, was born a slave in Pasquotank County, North Carolina, the mixed-race son of Jane Sykes, a slave, and an unnamed father. His mother's owner was Caleb Sykes, an Elizabeth City, North Carolina, cabinetmaker. Only the year of his birth is recorded. Nothing is known of Sykes's early life, or his education before the Civil War, although he had learned to read and write by the war's end.

Sykes first appears in public records as a delegate to the North Carolina Colored Convention of 1866, and he soon became active in the state's new Republican Party. In 1868, he was selected as a member of the North Carolina Republican Party Executive Committee and was appointed as a magistrate by Governor William W. Holden. The same year, Sykes was also elected as Pasquotank County's first African American member of the North Carolina House of Representatives, joining nearly two dozen other members of his race in the 1868–1869 and 1869–1870 sessions of the general assembly. Following his reelection in 1870, he then served in the House during the sessions of 1870–1871 and 1871–1872, before retiring in 1872.

During his first term in the House, Sykes saw limited service, and was appointed to just one committee, the Committee on Privileges and Elections. During his second term, he remained on that committee and added assignments to the Committee on Enrolled Bills and the Joint House-Senate Committee on Per Diem. He took an active interest in ways of raising state revenue for public education, first proposing a statewide property tax, which failed to pass. Sykes then introduced a successful bill calling for the dedication to education of income from the sale of publicly owned lands. He openly opposed organization of a new state militia, terming it too expensive, although most of his black colleagues favored it for protection from terrorist attacks by the Ku Klux Klan.

Like the majority of legislators of his party and race, Sykes initially opposed Democratic efforts to impeach Governor Holden on a variety of political charges, although he joined two other African American members and the Democratic majority in voting to add a ninth bill of impeachment—for alleged conspiracy to defraud the state in a railroad scandal—which was never considered at trial. Holden was later convicted on other counts and removed from office in 1871, a bitter loss for the freedmen he had once helped.

In 1872, Sykes was a successful merchant and at the height of his political influence in North Carolina, yet the state was increasingly troubled by evidence of racial prejudice and postwar discrimination. In his letter that year to Massachusetts congressman Charles Sumner, published in the *Congressional Globe*, he openly supported passage of a federal civil rights bill. Sykes complained that because of his race he had been denied the right to purchase and use a first-class steamer ticket from a company he had voted to incorporate while in the general assembly. "Sir, if I am a free citizen of this 'grand Republic,'" he asked Sumner, "why am I denied privileges which are given to my white brother, although he might be the basest culprit on earth?" (*Congressional Globe*, 42nd Congress, 2d session, 431).

What had once seemed like a grand environment for self-advancement was losing its luster for Sykes, who shortly thereafter pulled up roots in his native state and moved west to Nashville, Tennessee, and to a new political career. In 1875 Sykes argued at the state's emigration convention that African Americans should leave the state and head farther west, where greater opportunity with fewer legal restrictions awaited them. "Prejudice is stronger than law and may not be destroyed for generations to come," he told his listeners that year (*Union and American*, 20 May 1875).

Appointed a Davidson County magistrate in 1876, he soon became an internal revenue gauger for the U.S. Treasury Department, and in September 1877, he participated in a welcoming reception held by African American citizens for U.S. President

Rutherford B. Hayes, who visited Nashville in September to help lay the cornerstone for the new U.S. Customs House.

Sykes's growing reputation was augmented by his involvement in a reformist alliance, with such formidable local leaders as the city councilman JAMES C. NAPIER and the attorney William H. Young, against the political machine of Republican Mayor Thomas Kercheval. Sykes soon became the state's best-known African American advocate of prohibition and may have studied law privately. Meanwhile this reformist alliance dramatically increased the number of black officeholders and municipal employees. In 1880, Sykes was elected, by a narrow margin over his Democratic opponent, to the Tennessee House of Representatives, one of a dozen African Americans elected to that body between 1872 and 1886.

Sykes's legislative tenure was marked by energetic attempts to remove discriminatory language from state laws and allow African Americans full legal access to jury panels and the University of Tennessee, for example. But with his attempts to redress the situation now thwarted by the majority at almost every turn, Sykes declined to seek reelection in 1882, retiring from public office to run his house furnishings firm, Bosley & Sykes.

When the Tennessee legislature passed laws effectively disenfranchising black voters in 1889, Sykes lost all political power, and by 1890, was reduced to working as an elevator operator at the Customs House where he had once held much higher responsibilities. In the end, Tennessee had provided only a temporary improvement for the ever-restless Sykes, who reportedly left Nashville in 1893 and thereafter effectively vanished from the public record.

Sykes was married at least once. According to the 1870 census, taken while he lived in Elizabeth City, Sykes and his wife Martha (b. 1842–?) were the parents of two daughters, C. J. and E. C. Sykes, but no family members were listed as residing with him in the 1880 census, when he was living in Nashville. No date of death is recorded, but he is believed to have died soon after he left Nashville, before the next 1900 census.

FURTHER READING

Foner, Eric. *Freedom's Lawmakers: A Directory of Black Officeholders during Reconstruction* (1993).

Lauder, Kathy. "A Measure of Success: The Brief Political Career of Thomas A. Sykes," *Nashville Historical Newsletter* (2006).

McBride, Robert M., and Dan M. Robinson. *Biographical Directory of the Tennessee General Assembly*, Vol. II, 1861–1901 (1979).

Tennessee Historical Commission. *This Honorable Body: African American Legislators in 19th Century Tennessee* (2005).

BENJAMIN R. JUSTESEN

Sylvester (6 Sept. 1947–16 Dec. 1988), gay drag performer and musician, was born Sylvester James Jr. in Los Angeles, California, the firstborn son of Sylvester "Sweet" James Sr., whose occupation is unknown, and Letha Weaver James, a domestic and later a dietitian. After having two more sons, John Wesley in 1948 and Larry in 1950, Sylvester's parents divorced. While single, his mother had twin daughters Bernadette and Bernadine in 1956, and another son, Alonzo, in 1959. In 1962 she married aerospace worker Robert "Sonny" Hurd. She later fostered and adopted three children with him: Angelica, Charles, and Tammy. Letha's mother (really her aunt who raised her), the blues singer Julia Morgan, helped to raise Sylvester and his siblings.

Until young adulthood, he was known by his nickname "Dooni." Even as a preschooler, he enjoyed and sometimes wore the flamboyant, elegant clothing his mother and grandmother favored, especially for services at Palm Lane Church of God in Christ. The church's gospel music and expressive Pentecostal style deeply affected him. At six, he was locally acclaimed for singing ARETHA FRANKLIN's "Never Grow Old." From ages eight to twelve, Dooni was sexually abused by an adult male congregation member he never named. The abuser and church members who disapproved of Dooni's "feminine" manner and behavior pressured him out of Palm Lane when he was twelve. Yet he expressed a strong faith in God all his life. From 1963 to 1970 Dooni belonged to the Disquotays, a club of young black working-class drag queens who defied a city law against "female impersonation." In 1969, at age twenty-one, Dooni graduated from David Starr Jordan High School in South Central Los Angeles. In 1970, after moving to San Francisco, he went by his first name alone. Sylvester briefly joined the Cockettes, an experimental, gender-bending, majority-white theatrical troupe. Initially performing as Ruby Blue, a 1930s' blues diva, he then sang soul and rock with the Hot Band. Wearing endlessly creative drag outfits, he preferred, as he did during his whole career, his confident falsetto to his strong baritone voice.

Often along with the Pointer Sisters, Sylvester and the Hot Band appeared in many local clubs. After contributing to the Blue Thumb label's compilation *Lights Out San Francisco*. In 1973 they released two albums on Blue Thumb: *Scratch My Flower*, which sported a "scratch-'n'-sniff" gardenia sticker, and *Bazaar*. Because sales were poor and the Hot Band quit, the label dropped Sylvester.

After further building up his local fan base, Sylvester hired Martha Wash and Izora Rhodes as his backup singers, the Two Tons o' Fun. (They later soloed as the Weather Girls.) Like Sylvester, they were gospel singers from the black church. Sometimes after performances, Sylvester declared, "We had *service*" (quoted in Gamson, 170). Fantasy Records signed Sylvester in 1977. "Over and Over" from his first, self-titled Fantasy album topped the European and Mexican charts and enjoyed minor popularity in the United States. The disco-oriented *Step II* in 1978 went gold and made Sylvester a national and international star, the "Queen of Disco." A genuine fit with Sylvester, disco originated in gay, Latino, and African American dance clubs and ecstatically celebrated androgyny. *Step II* yielded the gold single "You Make Me Feel (Mighty Real)," showcasing Patrick Cowley's keyboard talents, as well as the platinum "Dance (Disco Heat)," featuring the Tons.

Sylvester played a drag queen playing DIANA Ross in the movie *The Rose* starring Bette Midler. In February 1979 the *Billboard* magazine Disco Forum gave Sylvester awards for Top Male Vocalist, Top Light Radio Single, and Top Heavy Twelve-Inch Single. On 11 March 1979 Sylvester premiered his album *Stars* at San Francisco's War Memorial Opera House, becoming the first openly gay performer on its stage. Sylvester's successes heartened San Francisco's lesbian, gay, bisexual, and transgender (LGBT) community, even as it struggled with a growing antigay rights movement and the homophobic assassination of city supervisor Harvey Milk. Sylvester was not only out of the closet; he had decidedly never been *in* the closet.

Almost as soon as Sylvester achieved stardom, there was a national backlash against disco, typified by the Disco Demolition Night at Chicago's Comiskey Park. With the disco market's collapse, Fantasy pressured Sylvester to tone down. He released three more albums on the label, pointedly titling one of them *Sell My Soul*. By 1982 Sylvester had switched to Megatone, an independent label

Patrick Cowley helped run. Sylvester's Megatone debut, *All I Need*, yielded the hit "Do You Wanna Funk." *Call Me* and *M-1015* produced the hit singles "Sex," "Take Me to Heaven," and "Band of Gold." In 1985 Sylvester sang backup on Aretha Franklin's comeback album *Who's Zoomin' Who?*, including the Grammy Award–winning "Freeway of Love." In 1986 Sylvester released *Mutual Attraction* on Warner Brothers.

As the AIDS epidemic hit the United States, Sylvester lost many friends, including Patrick Cowley. Sylvester personally served meals to hospital patients, performed at some of the first AIDS benefit concerts, and found solace at Oakland's Love Center Church, pastored by gospel singer Walter Hawkins, brother of Edwin Hawkins. On 4 September 1987, Sylvester lost Rick Cranmer, his partner of three years, to AIDS, just as he was becoming sick himself. Emaciated and in a wheelchair, Sylvester regally led the People with AIDS contingent of San Francisco's Gay Freedom Day parade on 26 June 1988. He called upon the disproportionately affected black community to face the AIDS crisis. Hoping to give courage to others with the disease, Sylvester declared, "I'll be fine, because my spirit is fine" (*Los Angeles Times*, 10 Sept. 1988).

Just as antiretroviral drugs were becoming available in the United States, Sylvester died in San Francisco at age forty-one. At Sylvester's thronged funeral, Walter Hawkins preached that "AIDS is *not* God's punishment." Sylvester's memorial panel was placed in Block 1172 of the AIDS Quilt. His music continued to influence artists like Bette Midler, PATTI LABELLE, and RUPAUL. His personal dignity and fearlessness inspired more than one generation. The 2002 National Queer Arts Festival in San Francisco featured "Mighty Real," a multimedia celebration of Sylvester's life. As he hoped, Sylvester was most remembered "for being fabulous" (quoted in Gamson, 141).

FURTHER READING
Braunstein, Peter. "Disco," *American Heritage Magazine*, November 1999.
Gamson, Joshua. *The Fabulous Sylvester: The Legend, the Music, The Seventies in San Francisco* (2005).
Johnson, Connie. "Disco Singer Sylvester Confronts AIDS Without Any Regrets," *Los Angeles Times*, 10 Sept. 1988.
Obituaries: *Jet*, 9 Jan. 1989; *New York Times*, 18 Dec. 1988.

MARY KRANE DERR